THE AMERICAN POLITICAL EXPERIENCE

An introduction to government

DAVID V. EDWARDS
The University of Texas at Austin

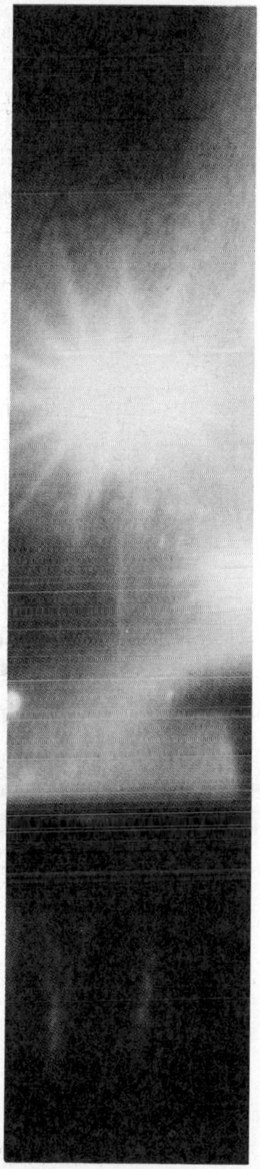

THE AMERICAN POLITICAL EXPERIENCE

An introduction to government

Prentice-Hall, Inc.
Englewood Cliffs, New Jersey 07632

■ **To Earle and Marjorie Edwards,**
my once and future teachers,
with appreciation, admiration, and love.

THE AMERICAN POLITICAL EXPERIENCE
An introduction to government
David V. Edwards

10 9 8 7 6 5 4 3

Printed in the United States of America

■ This book was composed on film in Garamond and Optima, with displayed numerals in Rededication U.S.A. Editing, production supervision, and cover and interior design are by Raymond Mullaney. The production assistant was Mary Helen Fitzgerald, with photo research by Irene Springer. Page layout is by Rita K. Schwartz, and the drawings are by Vantage Art, Inc. The manufacturing buyer was Nancy J. Myers. The cover photograph is by Arthur d'Arazien, New York, courtesy of General Electric. Sources of the part opening photographs are as follows: Part 1, Bettmann Archive; Part 2, Wide World Photos; Part 3, Stan Wakefield; Part 4, *New York Times;* Part 5, American Airlines; Part 6, USDA; Part 7, NASA.

Library of Congress Cataloging in Publication Data

Edwards, David V.
The American political experience.

Includes bibliographies.
1. United States–Politics and government–Handbooks, manuals, etc. I. Title.
JK274.E45 320.9'73'092 78-17034
ISBN 0-13-028373-8

Prentice-Hall International, Inc., London ■ Prentice-Hall of Australia Pty. Limited, Sydney ■ Prentice-Hall of Canada, Ltd., Toronto ■ Prentice-Hall of India Private Limited, New Delhi ■ Prentice-Hall of Japan, Inc., Tokyo ■ Prentice-Hall of Southeast Asia Pte. Ltd., Singapore ■ Whitehall Books Limited, Wellington, New Zealand

OUTLINE

CONTENTS

Chapter 8
The Congress
229

Chapter 9
The Supreme Court and the legal system
270

PART 5

WHAT RIGHTS AND LIBERTIES DOES AMERICAN GOVERNMENT PROVIDE?
395

Perspective 5

Chapter 13

The politics of liberty: civil liberties, civil rights, and human rights
407

Chapter 18
The politics of local relations: urban policy
551

Chapter 19
The politics of global relations: American foreign policy
573

Chapter 20
The politics of the pursuit of happiness: the quality of life
607

Chapter 21
The politics of participation: the quality of democracy
625

LIST OF ACTION UNITS

PREFACE

Everyone experiences reality somewhat differently. This is especially true of the reality of American politics. Some see it largely in terms of the dictates of the Constitution. With these high expectations, the more one learns about what really goes on, the more disillusioned one is likely to become. Others see American politics largely in terms of the actions of self-interested politicians and powerful special interests acting behind the scenes in opposition to the public interest. Those who depend on the mass media for their knowledge and understanding may tend toward this view. They are less likely to become disillusioned – but only because they lost their illusions, and often their hopes as well, long ago.

My own experience of politics, both in school and in the "real world," suggests that neither of these extreme views is very accurate. I have been active in politics from time to time at various levels and in various ways for several decades. And I have taught the introductory course in American government at the University of Texas for more than a dozen years. Over these years, my image of American political reality has changed considerably – as has American politics.

This book reflects my present image of American political reality, of course. It also reflects my present beliefs about how an American government course is best taught – beliefs that have also changed considerably over these years. But I have written this book conscious of the fact that everyone does indeed experience reality somewhat differently. This means that everyone *teaches* American government somewhat differently and that everyone *learns* American government somewhat differently, regardless of what the textbook says. I have therefore designed and written this text in a way that I hope will be interesting and helpful to teachers and students with a wide variety of interests and orientations but with a common humanity and much common experience.

Much of that common experience derives from the fact that we all encounter American government hundreds of ways every day of our lives. We pay taxes. We obey laws. We buy and use products that are regulated by the government for our safety or health. At the same time, in a sense, we all study American government, whether casually or rigorously, most of our lives. Some of that study occurs formally, in high school and college classes. Other study is less formal: watching the news on television or discussing current affairs with friends, for example. Unfortunately, American government and politics are now so complex that all of us need help if we are just to understand what is happening, let alone to act effectively as citizens to affect what happens. In writing this book, I have had the help of the many participants I have talked with and the many scholars I have read. I have tried to write the book so that it in turn will help you to understand politics better and to act effectively in politics if you wish.

To understand American government we must know about the institutions such as the presidency, the bureaucracy, the Congress, and the courts, of course, just as we must know about the political processes such as voting and lobbying. To help you to understand these topics, we shall focus, to a greater extent than most textbooks do, on the activities of the people who are involved. And once we have studied the major institutions and processes, we shall examine specific issues and common concerns, not abstractly, but instead as concrete problems. For example, in the latter part of the book we shall give special attention to minority groups (blacks, Chicanos, Puerto Ricans, and Native American Indians) and to women, the young, and the elderly. In doing so, we shall examine the varying needs and desires of these groups as well as the government's responses to them. And we shall find that even when these needs, desires, and responses are distinctive, they often reflect the kinds of problems that are common to all of us in one way or another or at one time or another. Among the concerns that we shall examine are economic issues such as poverty, taxes, and government regulation of the economy; urban issues such as crime and housing; and policy problems such as human rights, energy, the environment, education, and foreign relations. So in examining both special groups and more general policy problems, we shall really be looking at the American political experience from the human side as well as the institutional side.

□ FEATURES OF THE BOOK

This book has many special features designed to make it as helpful and useful as possible for studying the dynamics of American government.

- □ It emphasizes experience rather than just institutions such as Congress or processes such as policy making. We generally learn best when we can relate what we are studying to our own experience and when we can put ourselves in the places of other people. To make this possible, we shall examine the experience of political actors such as the president, the member of Congress, and the bureaucrat as well as that of citizens such as you and I.
- □ Each of the seven parts opens with a Perspective—a case study or overview that gives a sense of what politics is really like while it introduces the major ideas, questions, and topics that will be discussed in the chapters of that part.
- □ Throughout the book are clear and helpful three-dimensional diagrams, thought-provoking photographs, and informative tables and charts that expand on, and give added meaning to, the text discussion.
- □ Key terms are highlighted in color where they first appear. They are also defined and explained clearly both in the text and in a glossary at the back of the book.
- □ Each chapter ends with suggestions for further reading and study. Here I describe various books, magazines, and other sources that you can use if you wish to learn more about various topics discussed in the chapter.

- The book contains nineteen Action Units. These inserts, which appear at relevant points in the text (see p. xxv), tell you how to do a wide range of political activities, such as effectively lobbying your representative in Congress, finding out what information about you the government has stored in its files, organizing to protect human rights, getting a passport so you can travel abroad, and so on. When such an activity interests you, you'll find that these Action Units enable you to broaden your knowledge and understanding by practical action.

FOR STUDENTS: THE LEARNING GUIDE

In addition, I have developed a companion volume, called a *Learning Guide,* for use by students. It includes the following:

- suggestions on how to study effectively
- outline summaries of each chapter together with definitions of key terms
- questions on the material in each chapter to be used to test your comprehension of the chapter
- questions for you to think about in order to deepen your understanding of topics discussed in each chapter
- the same materials for each Perspective
- a guide to political dictionaries and other research sources
- a guide to political science journals and political opinion magazines
- a discussion of how you might get an "internship" working in Washington, perhaps during summer vacation, so that you may be able to learn about American government by seeing it in day-to-day operation from the inside
- a discussion of jobs you may eventually be able to get if you decide to continue your studies in political science

FOR INSTRUCTORS: THE TEACHING GUIDE AND TEST ITEM FILE

I have also written an accompanying *Teaching Guide,* available on request to teachers from the publisher. It has two basic objectives. First, it is designed to free you, the teacher, from the more routine chores often associated with preparing a course such as this. Second, it is designed to share with you insights I have gained in my dozen years of teaching American government and developing the text and the *Learning Guide.*

The first section

- suggests teaching strategies for the course
- describes various special materials on teaching that I have found helpful
- lists available audiovisual materials and simulations that you might wish to use to supplement the text

The next section presents, for each chapter and perspective,

- ☐ a list of specific learning objectives
- ☐ a comprehensive outline of the major contents of the chapter
- ☐ suggested supplementary lecture topics
- ☐ ways of overcoming student learning obstacles
- ☐ questions for student reflection and for class discussion and topics for student research projects deriving from the chapter

In addition, there is an accompanying *Test Item File.* It contains approximately 1000 true-false, multiple-choice, and short-answer questions.

These materials – however you select and combine them – should enable you to teach your course in American government in a way that suits your own preferences and maximizes the benefits students receive from it.

☐ FOR THOSE WHO HAVE HELPED WITH THE PROJECT

My students at the University of Texas have encouraged me to develop this approach to teaching American government in many ways. They have patiently tested my various experiments. They have made regular critiques of many aspects of the courses. And they have frequently offered helpful suggestions for improvements, many of which I have used in writing this book.

The fellow political scientists who reviewed the manuscript have made challenging and helpful criticisms and suggestions, for which I am very grateful. The task of reviewing the manuscript at one stage or another was taken on by Frans R. Bax, Larry Elowitz, John H. Gilbert, Walter Giles, Don Hall, Allan Hammock, Susan B. Hansen, Nevis H. Herrington, Dennis Ippolito, Howard E. McCurdy, John R. Petrocik, Richard Pious, Tony Rosenbaum, Larry Schwartz, Thomas Scism, Lester Seligman, and Graham Wootton.

Special thanks are due to the excellent professionals of my publisher. Martin Tenney, the Prentice-Hall representative in Austin, first saw promise in the project and recommended it to Prentice-Hall. Stan Wakefield, the political science editor, signed and coordinated the project with enthusiasm and a sympathetic understanding of the problems that inevitably arise between conception and conclusion of such a project. Raymond Mullaney, of Prentice-Hall's Product Development Department, contributed in major and imaginative ways to every aspect of the project. He personally shepherded the project through all its various editorial and production stages and executed the text's design himself as well. It is his vigilance and his unrelenting attention to detail, while maintaining a clear conception of the project as a whole, that give the book the strength and coherence that every author hopes for. It is a particular and rare pleasure to me that this author-publisher collaboration has resulted in friendship as well as the present book. Furthermore, along with these three Prentice-Hall experts, many of their talented colleagues – including especially David Esner, Ed Stanford, John Davis, and Donald Schaefer – have made important contributions. Only an author can know and fully appreciate these professional contributions – but as a reader of this book, you will share the benefits of them.

Finally and especially, thanks are due to Alessandra Lippucci, who believed in the project from the start, who enthusiastically and helpfully discussed much of it with me at its various stages, and who first suggested many of its best features.

In conclusion, let me note that a book like this is never really finished, even when it is published. I hope that you will remember this as you read it and that you will write to me with your comments, criticisms, and suggestions for the next edition.

David V. Edwards
Department of Government
The University of Texas at Austin
Austin, Texas 78712

1

HOW HAS AMERICAN GOVERNMENT DEVELOPED?

☐ Perspective 1: The politics of life and the study of politics

Early in 1975, Dr. Kenneth Edelin was on trial in a state court in Boston for manslaughter – the unlawful killing of a human being without express or implied malice. But this was no ordinary manslaughter case. Instead, the trial had become an important political issue. Attention around the country was focused on the courtroom. Why? What had Dr. Edelin done? He had performed an abortion for a 17-year-old unwed woman. By that time, abortion itself was not illegal. That was not the crime he was accused of. His problem arose out of the fact that the woman had been between 22 and 24 weeks pregnant. The state of medical science was such that about one in every five fetuses of that age could be saved if they were treated as "premature babies" when removed from the womb. Dr. Edelin had not tried to save the fetus. Instead, he let it die of lack of oxygen in the womb before he removed it. Because he did so – because he did not try to save the fetus – he was on trial for murder.

Saving the fetus was, of course, not Dr. Edelin's objective. His intention was to perform an abortion so that the woman would not have to bear a child some 3 months later. For 3 years, Edelin had been performing abortions at Boston City Hospital for poor members of minority groups. The woman for whom he performed this abortion was black and poor. Edelin, himself a black, explained his position at the time of the trial this way: "I believe in quality medical care for *all* people, and this is a small part of it. It is not the ideal method of birth control and should not be used as such. But women have been making a choice about pregnancies they didn't want for as long as they've been on earth. When birth control fails, a woman has a right to have her pregnancy terminated in a safe and professional manner."[1]

Edelin performed the abortion because he believed the woman had a right to terminate her pregnancy. The abortion itself was legal, according to Massachusetts law at the time. But there are various groups that argue that a fetus is a person and so has a "right to life" and that the right of the fetus takes precedence over the woman's right to abort. One of these groups succeeded in getting Massachusetts to try Edelin for violating the right to life of the fetus by not trying to save it when he legally removed it from the woman's womb.

☐ WHAT MAKES A QUESTION POLITICAL?

■ Conflicting claims

There were, then, in the Edelin case, two conflicting claims. The first was the right to abortion, or more generally the right to control of one's own body or reproductive system. The second was the right to life of the fetus. When conflicting claims to rights are made, a way must be found to resolve the conflict. If the conflict is only a verbal disagreement between several people, it may be resolved by more facts or better arguments. But if the conflict involves actual behavior and efforts to control or influence what people do, it is likely, in our system, to end up in court.

This is because in our system courts were es-

[1]Kenneth Edelin, quoted in "Abortion and the Law," *Newsweek,* March 3, 1975, p. 23.

tablished to decide what the law really is and how it should apply to a particular case. In other words, they resolve disputes over what should be done or how people should act. They have the *authority* to resolve such disputes because people expect them to do so.

■ The roles of authority, power, and legitimacy in politics

When we say some institution, such as a court, or some individual, such as a judge or a president, has **authority**, we mean that it or he or she is *recognized* by the people to have the **power**, or capacity, to decide. As long as people accept the decisions of a court as binding on them, that court can be said to have authority. The court has the power to decide for them. If people also believe that the institution or the individual *should* decide for them, or that its, his, or her decisions should be accepted or obeyed, then we also say that the institution or the individual has **legitimacy**. The word "legitimacy" comes from the Latin word *leges,* which means "laws." Something people recognize as legal or right or correct is termed legitimate. Perhaps a few examples will help clarify the meaning of these concepts.

The state traffic police (using roadblocks, fast cars, radar and radio hookups, and guns) have the *power* to get you to stop violating a traffic law. But the state police rarely have to use that power on you because they have *authority* over you – that is, you know or recognize that they have that power. As a result, you slow down of your own accord when you see a state police car by the roadside or pull over when you see a police car with flashing lights in your rearview mirror or hear its siren. The state police usually win court contests because in our system they have *legitimacy* – that is, we, judges who decide cases, and state legislatures that fund the courts all tend to believe that police have a legal right to enforce the law, and most of us are usually glad that they do so.

Another example: The Commonwealth of Massachusetts had the *power* to get Dr. Edelin to stop performing abortions – say, by getting state police to lock him up. But the Commonwealth of Massachusetts didn't have to use that power, because it also had the *authority* to try him in court on the charge of manslaughter – that is, it could announce its intention to do so, and Dr. Edelin would appear for the trial without having to be forced to show up by state police. However, although the local Massachusetts court had the authority to try Dr. Edelin, it did not have enough *legitimacy* to lead him to accept its verdict without appealing. Edelin was not convinced that the local court was entitled to make a final decision on his case, and so he appealed to a higher court, which, in his mind, had more legitimacy. (By calling such a court an "appeals court," the "mind" of the legal system also ranks such a court higher than the local court). Everyone, from Edelin to the Commonwealth of Massachusetts, accepted the decision of the appeals court – the Massachusetts Supreme Judicial Court – as final, or legitimate.

Boston Globe photo

Dr. Kenneth Edelin.

By the 1970s, many people thought the laws prohibiting abortion were wrong. When the United States Supreme Court declared such laws unconstitutional, still other people thought that the Court's decision was wrong. In neither case was the legitimacy of the government directly at issue, because both the laws and the decision had been made in the ways the United States Constitution says they should be made. The government, in other words, remained legitimate even when it produced laws or decisions people thought were wrong.

But if the government were to behave illegally or wrongly – by refusing to leave office when voted out of power, for example – it would then risk being thought illegitimate. It might still have the *power* to remain in office – if it had the support of the military, for example. And it might still have *authority* if the people knew it had that power and if they accepted its rule as unavoidable, even though they thought it was illegal or wrong.

When a government is thought to be illegitimate, or illegal, the people are likely to refuse to obey it and even to try to remove it if they can. When a legitimate government misbehaves in the eyes of its citizens, it runs the risk of losing popular support. This is what happened to Richard Nixon in the Watergate affair, as we'll see in Perspective 4. Nixon was elected president legitimately. But he lied to the people and covered up illegal acts by his deputies – both illegitimate acts. When this became clear, it was decided that he had to be removed from office to protect the legitimacy of the government. If Nixon had not resigned or been removed, the people might have come to associate his own misdeeds with the government, and eventually the government's legitimacy might have come into question.

There is even a risk that this might happen if the government does too many things that are unpopular, even though they are done legally. The government's actions on abortion ran this risk. If enough people believed the government was wrong in its actions on abortion, citizen allegiance and support might erode. In time, the government might find it more difficult to get citizens to obey it.

■ The Edelin case and the politics of life

By the time of Edelin's trial, abortion remained controversial although legal. Because it was finally legal, it had become in most instances just a private matter between a woman and her doctor. Over a million abortions were by then being performed privately and legally every year in the United States. But once Edelin was charged with manslaughter by the Commonwealth of Massachusetts at the urging of antiabortion (right-to-life) groups, this particular abortion decision became a public, political matter rather than just a private, personal matter.

The court had to decide whether or not Edelin was guilty as charged. The judge and jury heard arguments by lawyers for both sides. Then, on February 15, 1975, Judge James P. McGuire sent the jurors off to deliberate on Edelin's guilt or innocence. He cautioned them that they could not find Edelin guilty unless they believed that the fetus at that point – 22 to 24 weeks into pregnancy – was "a person."

There was, in other words, dispute in court over what we would call "a question of fact." No one disputed that Edelin had performed the abortion. No one disputed that the abortion was legal. The dispute was over whether, in performing the abortion, Edelin had killed a person – the fetus. There was no disputing that the fetus was dead. It had even been preserved for medical research, and the jurors had been shown a photo of it, supposedly to help them decide whether it was indeed a person at the point when it was removed from the woman's womb.

Although we call this issue "a question of fact," there may be no "fact" to discover. People disagree on the underlying question of whether a fetus becomes a person at the moment of conception (as the antiabortion forces argue) or at the moment of birth (as supporters of abortion generally claim) or at some time between conception and birth.

Who is to resolve such a dispute? Doctors – experts on medicine and health? Theologians and preachers – experts on religious beliefs about life and death and ethics? Philosophers – experts on the nature of life and on justice? Legislators – who pass laws making abortions legal and making killing illegal? Lawyers – who prosecute and defend those who do abortions?

All of these groups are generally recognized as experts in their fields. But in America there is no consensus on whether the question of when life begins is a medical, religious, or philosophical question. This means that it becomes a political question because the experts disagree, and furthermore because many people disagree as to who the real experts on the question are. Political questions such as this, when they are not resolved by politicians passing laws, tend to be resolved instead by judges and sometimes juries.

The jury in this case debated for 7 hours and finally found Edelin guilty of manslaughter. Jurists said afterward that the photo of the fetus had been a decisive influence in their decision that the fetus was a person. Faced with a possible penalty of 20 years in prison, Edelin was instead given a year's suspended sentence and placed on probation by the state court judge. As we mentioned earlier, he chose to appeal the ruling to a higher court on grounds that the lower court had been mistaken. On December 17, 1976, he got the ruling he sought. The Massachusetts Supreme Judicial Court unanimously overturned the lower court's decision. It ruled that a fetus can be said to be alive only if it is breathing and has a beating heart *outside the mother's womb.* Only then could a doctor be guilty of manslaughter, the court declared, if he or she failed to try to save it.

Dr. Edelin's record was once again clear. The Massachusetts Supreme Judicial Court had the authority to make such a ruling, overturning the decision of the jury in the lower court. Its decision was recognized as legitimate by the Commonwealth of Massachusetts, which then cleared Dr. Edelin's record, and by doctors, who resumed doing such abortions without fear of prosecution. The decision not only resolved Dr. Edelin's fate, but also, in Massachusetts at least, it resolved the legal question of when a fetus can be considered alive. The higher authority and legitimacy of the court enabled it to resolve this political question – at least for Massachusetts and at least for the time being.

Antiabortion demonstration, Washington, D.C.
Wide World Photos

□ ABORTION AS A POLITICAL QUESTION

The Edelin case took place not long after a path-breaking decision by the United States Supreme Court that explicitly legalized abortion in the United States under certain conditions. On January 22, 1973, thirty-one states had laws making performance of an abortion a criminal offense, and fifteen others had laws severely limiting the legality of abortion. But on that day, when the Supreme Court issued its ruling, in the case of *Roe v. Wade,* those laws suddenly became unconstitutional and abortion as suddenly became legal. This happened because the Constitution is the highest law of the land, and the Supreme Court has the authority in our system to resolve disputes over whether laws are consistent with the provisions of the United States Constitution.

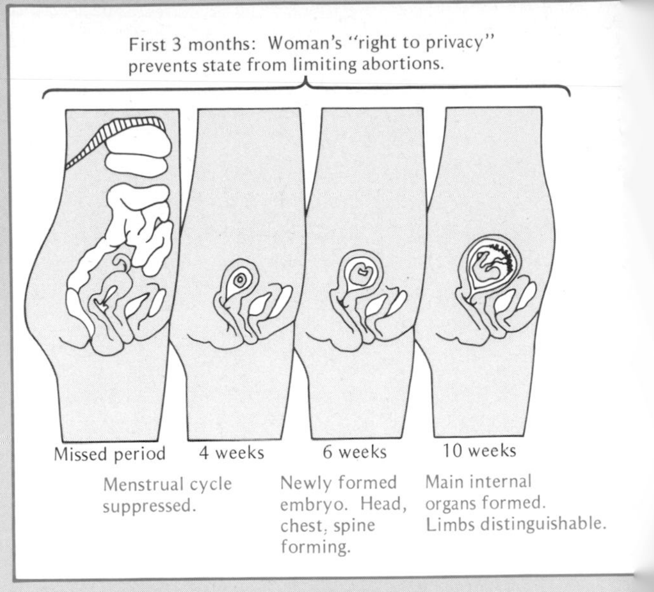

FIGURE P1.1 The Supreme Court's decision on abortion.

■ The "Roe" case in the Supreme Court

The case The case the Supreme Court decided that day was brought by "Jane Roe"–a pseudonym adopted to protect the woman. Jane Roe was a pregnant single Texas woman who challenged a Texas state law that outlawed all abortions except those essential to save the life of the mother. Roe argued that this law violated her rights under the Constitution.

The arguments The Constitution's Fourteenth Amendment asserts that no state can "deprive any person of life, liberty, or property . . . nor deny to any person within its jurisdiction the equal protection of the laws." The state of Texas was arguing that the fetus is a "person" in just these terms and so is entitled to protection by state laws preventing abortion. The Supreme Court studied this argument and concluded that "the use of the word 'person,' as used in the Fourteenth Amendment, does not include the unborn." Thus, the fetus was not automatically protected by the Fourteenth Amendment. But this didn't mean it still might not be protected by some other provision of the Constitution.

Texas also argued that life begins at conception and is present throughout pregnancy, even if the fetus is not yet "a person," and so the fetus–as "life"–is entitled to protection. Lawyers had debated this question vigorously on both sides. In its decision, the Supreme Court noted that experts disagreed strongly about this matter and concluded: "We need not resolve the difficult question of when life begins. When those trained in the respective disciplines of medicine, philosophy, and theology are unable to arrive at any consensus, the judiciary . . . is not in a position to speculate as to the answer."

The decision In the face of such disagreement among nonlegal authorities, the Court avoided deciding the question of when life begins. Instead, it invoked its legal authority to decide the case at issue. Doing so, it upheld Roe's claim that her right to privacy entitled her to an abortion. "The right to privacy," the Court said, "is broad enough to encompass a woman's decision whether or not to terminate her pregnancy."

This right to privacy, to which the Court referred, is not even mentioned in the Constitution, as we'll see in Chapter 13 where we'll discuss it in more detail. It is not, the Court asserted, an ab-

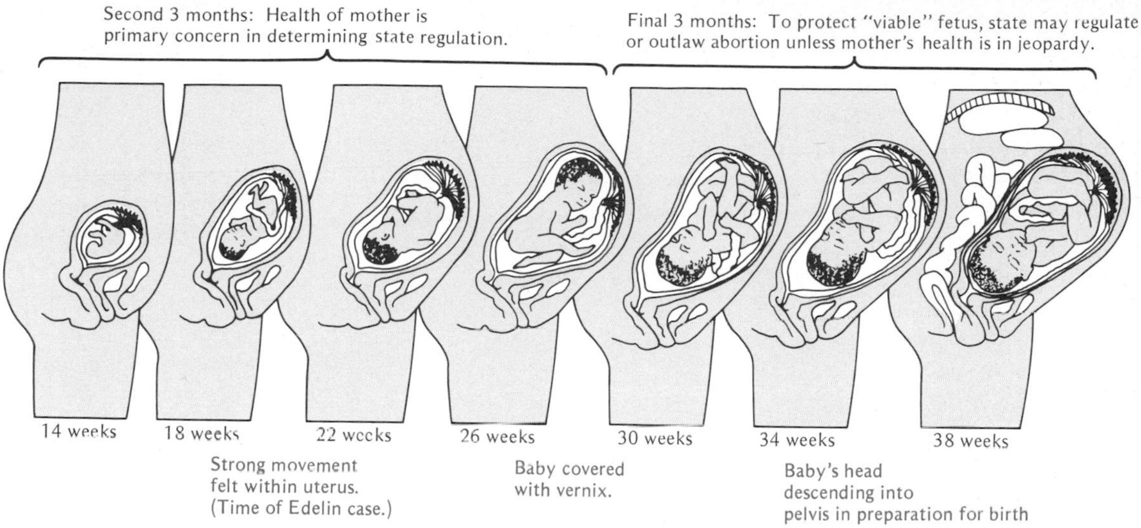

Second 3 months: Health of mother is primary concern in determining state regulation.
Final 3 months: To protect "viable" fetus, state may regulate or outlaw abortion unless mother's health is in jeopardy.
14 weeks
18 weeks
22 weeks
26 weeks
30 weeks
34 weeks
38 weeks
Strong movement felt within uterus. (Time of Edelin case.)
Baby covered with vernix.
Baby's head descending into pelvis in preparation for birth

solute right. Instead, "a State may properly assert important interests in safeguarding health [of the mother], in maintaining medical standards [by regulating how and by whom abortions are performed], and in protecting potential life."

Whatever the unresolved disputes among the various types of experts over when life begins, the Court could not deny that at some stage the fetus reaches "the point of viability"—the point at which, if the fetus were removed from the mother's womb, it could survive as a "premature baby" with intensive hospital care. Nor did the Court deny that the health of the mother was a legitimate matter for the state to be concerned about.

Thus, the Court had to balance the mother's right to have an abortion and the state's right to legislate to protect the mother and the fetus. "In assessing the State's interest," the Court declared, "recognition may be given to the less rigid claim that as long as at least *potential* life is involved, the state may assert interests beyond the protection of the pregnant woman alone."

There were, in other words, three rights at issue: mother's privacy, as protected by the Constitution; mother's health, as protected by state laws; and fetus's life, as protected by state laws.

The Court's decision was an intricate balancing of these three claims, as Figure P1.1 shows. By a seven-to-two vote, it decided that:

- ☐ For the first 3 months after conception, the state cannot limit abortions except to require that they be performed by doctors. This conclusion recognized the woman's "right to privacy."
- ☐ For approximately the second 3 months, the state can specify the conditions under which abortions may be performed, in order to safeguard the health of the mother.
- ☐ For the final 3 months, the state may, if it chooses, regulate, and even outlaw abortion, in order to protect the "viable" fetus, except for cases where the health of the mother is in question.

■ Abortion and the politics of life

Because the Court had refused to answer the question of when the fetus became a person, the case of *Roe v. Wade* did not affect Edelin's fate in the Massachusetts court. Nor did it remove the question of abortion from politics. As we mentioned above, in our system, the Constitution is the highest law of the land. This means that Supreme Court decisions that interpret the Constitution are in effect also a part of the highest law of the land. But the Constitution can be changed by amendment passed by the Congress and approved by the states – a process we'll examine in Chapter 1. If it is, the Court must accept such a change.

Abortion had first become a political question 100 years or so earlier, when states began adopting antiabortion laws. Once these laws were passed and accepted by the people, abortion ceased to be a question for the political system, even though abortions were still performed illegally – and often in ways that were very dangerous to the woman's life. Finally, in the 1960s and early 1970s, some states began to liberalize their antiabortion laws, thus reintroducing the subject into politics. Court cases such as *Roe* and *Edelin* then made abortion even more of a political issue.

In shorthand terms, we might say that any issue that enters the political arena – the arena of government, elections, and public debate – is political. But this doesn't tell us much about what really happens in politics. At one level, what happens is that public disputes get resolved by candidates being elected, by laws being passed, or by court cases being decided. At a deeper level, however, what happens is that people or institutions dispute over who has (or who should have) the authority to make decisions about some aspect of reality – questions of fact or questions of value – for us citizens.

In the case of abortion, Jane Roe disputed with the state of Texas over whether she had the right to get an abortion. Each side claimed that it had the support of the Constitution. Each pointed to particular parts of the Constitution to buttress its argument. Each also disagreed over whether a fetus is a person, or when it becomes one. Each pointed to testimony from doctors, theologians, and philosophers that seemed to lend special authority to its arguments. And each finally appealed to the ultimate legal authority, the court system, to decide the question.

When Jane Roe challenged the Texas law, she was disputing the claim to legal authority made by the law and the courts in Texas. She did so ultimately by going all the way to the United States Supreme Court. Antiabortionists and the Commonwealth of Massachusetts did the same in the Edelin case. They challenged Edelin's authority to do abortions without trying to save the life of the fetus. He then challenged the legal authority of Massachusetts by appealing his conviction to a higher court. And the antiabortionists also challenged the Supreme Court by seeking passage of a Constitutional amendment outlawing abortion that would in effect overturn the Supreme Court ruling.

■ Funding abortions for the poor

On June 20, 1977, the Supreme Court issued yet another ruling on abortion. This one dealt with the question of whether government funds can be used to pay for abortions for the poor who cannot afford them. By 1976 about a quarter of the 1,115,000 abortions per year fell into this category. They were paid for by Medicaid, a government program that helps poor people pay their medical bills. The Court asserted that when an issue involves such sensitive policy choices, "the appropriate forum for their resolution in a democracy is the legislature."

And so the battle over abortion shifted to the Congress. The antiabortion group, the National Right-to-Life Committee, launched a major lobbying effort. Its staff of eight in Washington had a budget of $250,000. Its 1500 local chapters had 11 million members. All were trying to get Congress to prohibit the use of federal funds to pay for abortions for the poor. As the Senate was debating the question that summer, *Washington Post* journalist Haynes Johnson captured the prevailing atmosphere:

> At three p.m. the Senate debate was under way. Outside, as always, were the same kinds of scenes that surround the Capitol day in and out: a man strode back and forth across the steps where Presidents are inaugurated, speaking loudly about repentance, shedding of innocent blood, slaughter of innocent children through a million abortions, waving a placard that read "God Hates Adultery, Covetousness, Ho-

mosexuality, Idolatry, Abortion, Murder . . . " while all around him flowed crowds of citizens, Girl Scouts and high school students, a band, a senior citizens tour, nearly all seemingly oblivious of the demonstrator. Inside, the Senate was considering an amendment to a Health, Education, and Welfare bill.

The debate was about banning public funds for abortions, but really it was about more than that. It was about Rights. The Right to Life. The Right to Choose. The Rights of Women. The Rights of Children. The Rights of the Individual. The Rights of Society. The Rights of Dissent. The Rights of the Majority, the Rights of the Minority. And, perhaps most important of them all, the Right to be Wrong.

Senators don't permit themselves to be photographed while at work. What the public would see, on most occasions, is a cozy chamber, bathed in soft lights, antique in quality, usually more than half empty, the pace leisurely, with a few public servants standing casually around small desks and tiny wastebaskets that look as though they come out of a 19th Century school-room. It's often been called a club, and for good reason; it most resembles a comfortable, fairly stuffy, faintly stilted club—a men's club.

What usually passes for debate is a desultory and tepid exchange couched in such formal language about the honorable and the distinguished senator that it quickly becomes enervating. Only a handful of senators were on the floor on this occasion, but for once there were genuine flashes of emotion, anger, and outrage.

Packwood, of Oregon: ". . . I have been involved this year in politics, active politics, for a quarter century. Abortion is the most divisive basic issue I have run across in my experience. . . . Before we are done with this debate, we will hear stories about killing little children and murder. I am saying that is not the issue . . . to say that we are going to deny abortions to the poor because we disapprove of them is a disdainful, haughty arrogance that should not demean this Congress."

Helms, of North Carolina: ". . . they do not want to confront the inevitable basic question, the only one that really matters. And that, Mr. President, is the deliberate termination of an innocent human life. . . . Let every woman control her body, including the time that she conceives or prior thereto. . . . But after that there is another life, another body, that has some rights too—including the right to live."

The Senate voted to ban the use of federal funds for most abortions.[2]

Dennis Brack/Black Star

Proabortion demonstration, Washington, D.C.

As the Congress moved toward final approval of such a ban, the lobbying grew fiercer. On one side was the National Right-to-Life Committee with its allies, on the other a group called the National Abortion Rights Action League with its allies.

[2]Haynes Johnson, "Rights," *Washington Post,* July 3, 1977.

☐ THE NATURE OF POLITICS

The abortion debate became a governmental question when the Supreme Court and the Congress debated it. But it had been a political question long before it reached the government. As should be clear by now, there are fundamental differences in perspective between the antiabortion (right-to-life) and proabortion groups. Each sees the world, and abortion, differently. Each attempts to get the other side – and even more the uncommitted or undecided – to accept its picture of reality. To do so, each uses arguments and photographs and accounts of personal experiences, for each side wants to convince the other to let *it* decide what should be done about abortion.[3] Each claims the authority to decide, not only for the other, but also for all the rest of us, what will be government policy on abortion. This sort of dispute – in which each party claims the authority to decide the question for others and both sides disagree – is what we always find in politics.

■ A general definition

In general terms, then, we have a political question any time two people or groups or institutions disagree about something, and when each claims the authority to decide the question, to resolve the dispute, as he, she, or it sees fit. Politics, in other words, *is dispute over claims to the authority to decide what some part of reality is or should be.*

We get the term "politics" from the ancient Greeks. It comes from their word *polis,* which referred to "the city," the largest political unit the Greeks had. But the word really referred to the whole people and the ways they lived their lives together. A leading expert on ancient Greece, H. D. F. Kitto, remarks that the polis was

> so much more than a form of political organization. The polis was a living community, based on kinship, real or assumed – a kind of extended family, turning as much as possible of life into family life, and of course having its family quarrels, which were the more bitter because they were family quarrels. . . . In the winning of his livelihood, [the Greek] was essentially individualist; in the filling of his life he was essentially "communist." Religion, art, games, the discussion of things – all these were needs of life that could be fully satisfied only through the polis – not, as with us, through voluntary associations of like-minded people, or through entrepreneurs appealing to individuals. . . . Moreover, he wanted to play his own part in running the affairs of the community.[4]

In later chapters we shall see how politics arises in elections, how it arises in Congress, how it arises in policy making – and even how it arises in our everyday lives. Our greatest interest in this book will be in the government politics that involves citizens as candidates, as voters, as activists, and as leaders.

■ Governmental politics

Most of the time in life there will be disputes over claims to authority. Parties who are disputing will tend to make appeals – to voters, to judges, to the president, to Congress, or whatever. Often, these appeals will be accepted, in which cases the political dispute is over and things can go on without further political struggle. But when such appeals are rejected or contested, we're back to politics as usual. Voters may reject a candidate, or another candidate may appear to contest the election. Judges may reject an argument in court, or a loser in court may contest a judgment and appeal to a higher court. The Congress may reject a bill proposed by the president by refusing to pass it, or the president may reject a bill passed by Congress by vetoing it.

[3]For an interesting diverse collection of readings on the question of abortion, see United States House of Representatives Judiciary Committee, *Hearings before the Subcommittee on Civil and Constitutional Rights: Proposed Constitutional Amendments on Abortion, Appendix* (Washington, D.C.: Government Printing Office, 1976).

[4]H. D. F. Kitto, *The Greeks* (Baltimore: Penguin, 1951), p. 78.

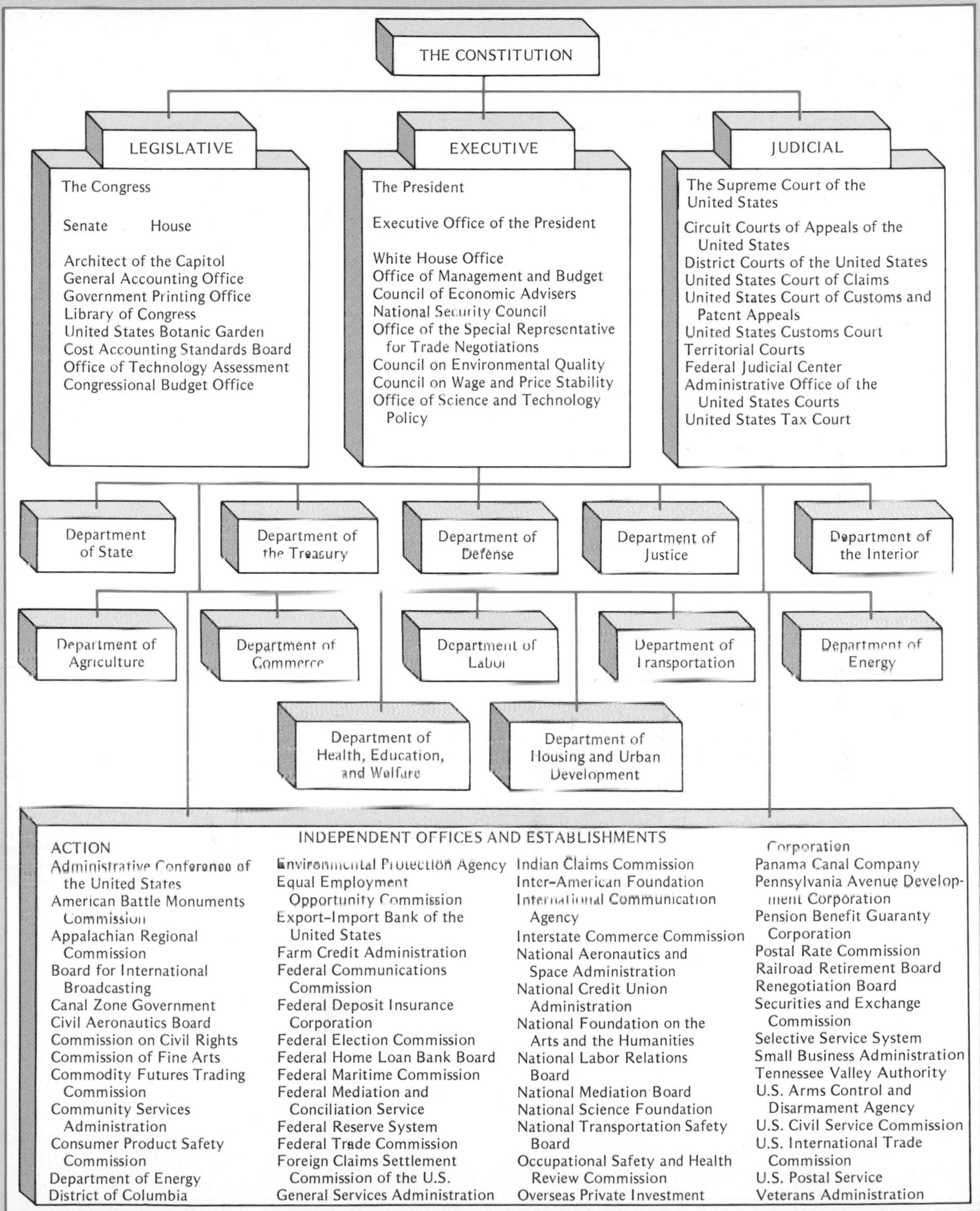

FIGURE P1.2 The government of the United States—the official view.

The sorts of actions just discussed involve disputes over claims to the authority to describe or decide some aspect of reality. They are, in other words, political actions. In this book we shall examine many such political disputes to find out what happens and why it happens as it does. We'll also look often at what could be done to change the politics of American government or to change the policies adopted by American government.

■ The aspects of government

Our word "government" comes from an ancient Greek word meaning "to direct a ship." People still speak sometimes of "the ship of state" that government must captain. When we use the term **government**, we most often mean the public bodies that direct public affairs. The word "public" means "of the people," and public affairs are the concerns of the people—of all the people. In this sense, then, government directs all the people over whom it has power.

In order to understand what does happen and what could happen in politics, we shall have to learn about three different aspects of American government: institutions, processes, and policies.

If we ask the American government to describe itself, it produces the diagram shown in Figure P1.2. This sort of diagram, or organization chart, as it is often called, tells us important things about the government. It shows that there are three branches—legislative, executive, and judicial—and that all three are subordinate to, or ruled by, the United States Constitution. It also shows us the various parts of each branch, such as the president, the Executive Office of the President, the cabinet departments, and the "independent agencies" in the executive branch—all of which we often call "the bureaucracy." And the ways the connecting lines are drawn report "who orders whom around." Thus the president sits on top of everything else in the executive branch, and all the departments and agencies report to him through his Executive Office.

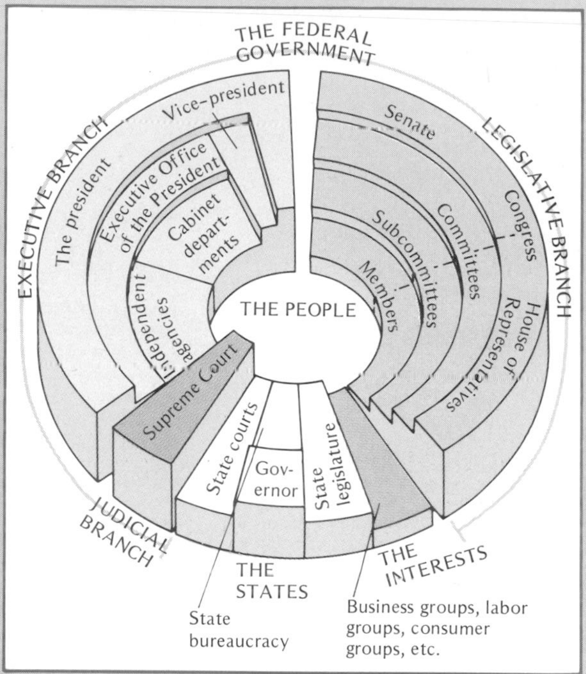

FIGURE P1.3

The government of the United States—another view.

The Constitution and this formal structure of the government are extremely important. They create the *institutions*—such as Congress, the president, the courts, and the bureaucracy—that make up the government. But we also need to know about the processes of government. By *processes* we mean the elections with their campaigning and voting, the lobbying and other forms of influence that citizens and groups in and out of government use to try to affect the outcomes or outputs of the institutions, and the various other types of politicking we find in government as the various parts of the government cooperate and compete with each other.

We can get a better sense of the processes of our government by redrawing the diagram in Figure P1.2 so that it will allow us to emphasize these interrelations among its parts. Take a look at Figure P1.3. It contains the same parts we found in the chart the government itself provided, but they are rearranged a bit into a ring, and to them are added the other major political factors or "actors"; the *states* of the union and the *interests* such as businesses, labor unions, "public interest" lobbyists such as Ralph Nader, antiabortion groups, proabortion groups, and many, many more. Furthermore, all these political actors encircle a core, which is *the people* – each and every one of us.

Figures P1.4 – P1.6, a series of three such circle graphs, shows how abortion entered politics in three different cases; the Supreme Court decision in *Roe v. Wade,* the Edelin case, and the antiabortion movement's effort to get Congress to prohibit the spending of government funds for welfare abortions. You can trace the stages of each case through these somewhat simplified diagrams. We shall trace other political struggles in a similar fashion from time to time in this book.

With this, we have taken special note of both the institutions themselves and the processes by which they relate to one another and to us citizens. This brings us to the third and final major focus of our study: the *policies* that the institutions develop and implement.

In the *Roe* decision, the Supreme Court developed a policy on how to decide cases involving abortion. On the question of using federal funds to pay for abortions of the poor, Congress developed a policy that it passed on to the executive branch – specifically, the Department of Health, Education, and Welfare – to administer. Government is constantly developing policies – decisions about what government will do.

A glance at the evening news or at the morning paper will remind us how controversial many policies are. So will a glance at coming chapters, especially those toward the end of the book, which

FIGURE P1.4

The politics of the *Edelin* case.

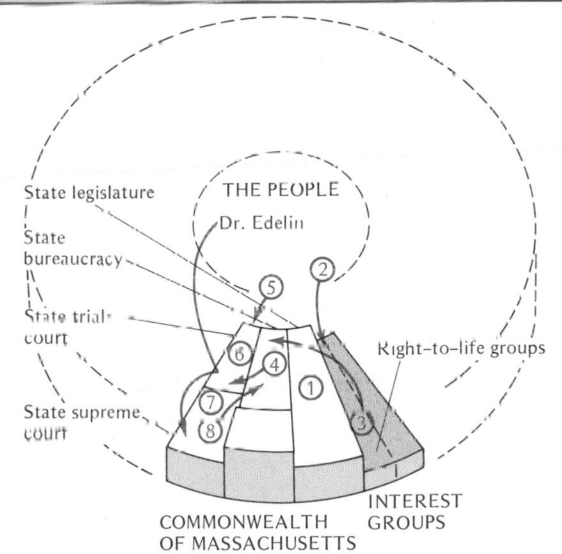

KEY:

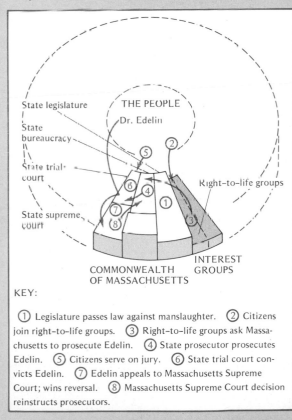

(1) Legislature passes law against manslaughter. (2) Citizens join right-to-life groups. (3) Right-to-life groups ask Massachusetts to prosecute Edelin. (4) State prosecutor prosecutes Edelin. (5) Citizens serve on jury. (6) State trial court convicts Edelin. (7) Edelin appeals to Massachusetts Supreme Court; wins reversal. (8) Massachusetts Supreme Court decision reinstructs prosecutors.

FIGURE P1.5

The politics of the *Roe* case.

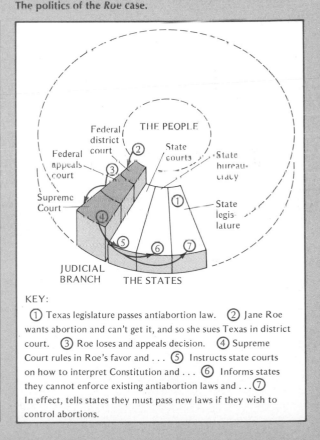

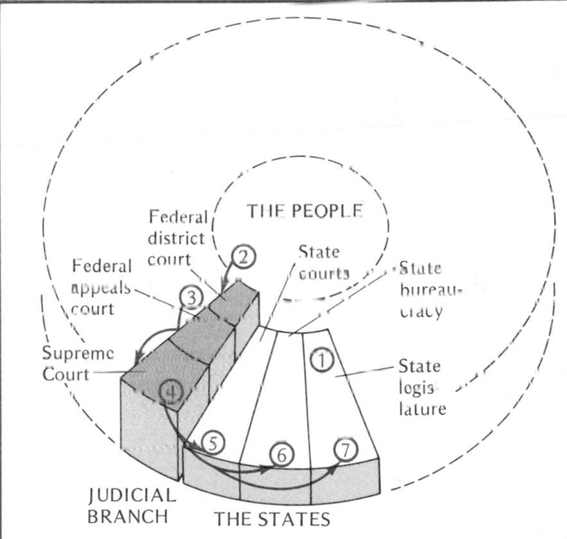

KEY:

(1) Texas legislature passes antiabortion law. (2) Jane Roe wants abortion and can't get it, and so she sues Texas in district court. (3) Roe loses and appeals decision. (4) Supreme Court rules in Roe's favor and . . . (5) Instructs state courts on how to interpret Constitution and . . . (6) Informs states they cannot enforce existing antiabortion laws and . . . (7) In effect, tells states they must pass new laws if they wish to control abortions.

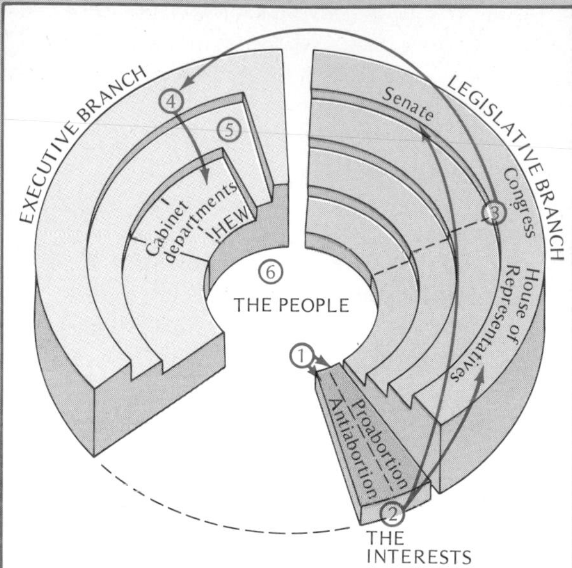

KEY:

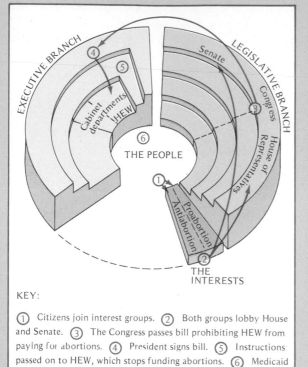

(1) Citizens join interest groups. (2) Both groups lobby House and Senate. (3) The Congress passes bill prohibiting HEW from paying for abortions. (4) President signs bill. (5) Instructions passed on to HEW, which stops funding abortions. (6) Medicaid no longer pays for abortion.

FIGURE P1.6

The politics of the abortion-funding question.

deal with the claims to rights and liberties and special programs made by various groups and with policies adopted to cope with economic, urban, and foreign problems.

As we study institutions, processes, and policies, it is very important to remember that there is always another element involved in the practice of government: we, the people. Abraham Lincoln, in his famous Gettysburg Address in 1863, described ours as "government of the people, by the people, for the people." We must remember – even when the politicians forget and need to be reminded – that our government has us as *subjects* ("government of the people"), as *participants* ("by the people"), and as *objects* or targets ("for the people"). But each aspect of this relationship between us and our government is controversial. And so each raises important questions about government.

■ The major questions concerning government

Although they can be phrased in many different ways, there are three major questions concerning government: (1) How close should government get to the people in ruling them as its subjects? (2) How much should the people be involved in government as participants? (3) In what realms should government rule to serve us best as its objects or targets? The answers our leaders and their followers have given to these questions have changed in important ways over the past 200 years. Let's look at each to see how they arise and why they matter.

How close should government get to the people? The colonists who declared their independence from England in 1776 were fearful of too strong a government. Many of their ancestors had come to this country to escape from European governments that were so close to their people that they were able to dictate even what religion the people were to accept. And at the time of the Revolution, the British government was close enough to the American colonists, even though it was located an ocean away in London, to dictate what taxes the colonists had to pay, without even consulting the colonists.

The colonists feared that a central government might be so powerful that it would curtail the liberties they valued and sought. So when they established a national ruling power, they devised a new type of central government – one prohibited from getting too close to the people. We shall examine what they did and how they did it in Chapter 1. For the moment, we must note three limitations on ruling power that they imposed.

Rights are the first limitation on national ruling power. Some countries have a central government which has total power over every aspect of life. We call them "dictatorships" because they can dictate to the people what can be done. Our central government however, is a *limited government* – limited in two important ways. First, the document that created it, our *Constitution,* says specifically what the government can and cannot do. It declares that we as citizens have certain rights the government cannot infringe or take away. For example, the Consititution prohibits Congress from passing a law declaring something a crime "ex post facto" ("after the fact" or "after the deed"). As a result, citizens cannot be punished for doing something that was not a crime when they did it. This may not seem like much, but only because we take it for granted. And we can only take it for granted because this prohibition is in the Constitution, and the Constitution has legitimacy. Most of the other rights we take for granted are guaranteed to us by the first ten amendments to the Constitution – the Bill of Rights. Among them are freedom of speech and religion and trial by jury. We shall examine these limitations in Chapter 1 as we study how we got our Constitution and what it does for us.

The *federal division of powers* is a second limitation on *national ruling power.* This limitation, also found in the Constitution, is as important as the first. Our government is broken into many different parts, each of which has some power granted to it alone, so that no other part can destroy or dominate it. This limitation works several ways.

One way in which it works is the breaking up of governing power into *levels.* The Constitution *divides* powers among the *national* government and the *state* governments – and then reserves still other powers to the people. We call this division of powers **federalism.** The national government is a federal government – a federation of states that have given up some powers to the central government and kept others for themselves.[5] (The states have also granted some of their powers to their cities, creating yet another level of government – but one wholly dependent on the states for its powers.) We shall describe this division of powers further in Chapter 1; then in Chapter 2 we shall see how American federalism has developed.

The *separation of powers* is a third limitation on *national ruling power.* This breaking up of powers into pieces occurs at each level of government. *Powers are separated* into three "branches," in order to further limit the danger of a too powerful government. As we saw in Figures P1.2 and P1.3, at the national level we have the **executive branch,** headed by the president and including a large bureaucracy; the **legislative branch,** consisting of the Congress; and the **judicial branch,** at the top of which is the United States Supreme Court. The Congress has the power to make laws. The president has the power to enforce these laws. The courts interpret the laws to see whether what the president does is correct and whether the laws Congress makes are consistent with the Constitution, which is the highest law of the land. The states, too, have separated powers in their governments.

And so the Constitution limits the ruling power in our system to guarantee that no one level, and no one branch within any one level, can dominate the others. But all these limits are so compli cated, and all these pieces are so jumbled, that things rarely work in practice exactly as we have outlined them in theory. Thus, the task of governing – or "guiding the ship of state" – is complex, and the way it is done is always controversial.

Such controversy always invites participation, because there is room for great debate as to how things should be done. But complexity tends to discourage participation by all but those with a special interest in what the government does. And so it has generally been: The special interests have been the most active participants in American politics – so much so that we give them their own "slice" of "the political pie" in Figure P1.3. But this large role for special interests has also been controversial, for there was, and is, little agreement on the answer to our second key question.

How much should the people be involved in government? One of the strongest cries of the rebellious colonists was "No taxation without representation." And so the Founding Fathers creating the new government began with the assumption that the people should have representation in the government. But what form was that to take?

To us in these times, the most obvious form would be voting. But, as we shall see in the chap-

[5]For an analysis of the federal division of powers, see David E. Engdahl, *Constitutional Power: Federal and State* (St. Paul: West, 1974).

ters of Part 2, the right to vote belonged only to adult white male property owners in the early years of this country. And it has been a long and difficult struggle to extend that right first to adult white males without property, then to black males, then to women and to Native Americans ("Indians") and finally to 18-to-20-year-olds.

This movement toward democracy (from a Greek word meaning "rule by the people") has also helped to open other types of participation to more people – for example, running for office and serving in appointed government positions. But even this has not resolved the basic questions of who shall rule and who shall have influence. We'll trace the way these questions have been answered in Parts 4 and 5. Answers to them in turn often depend on answers to our third basic question.

In what realms should government rule? Over the past 200 years, commonly accepted notions of what government *could* do, and what it *must* do, for its people have been transformed. One striking instance of this has been the growing and changing involvement of the government with the question of abortion, which we discussed above. But there are many others, from controlling the economy to combatting poverty to protecting consumers, as we shall see throughout Parts 5, 6, and 7.

How such questions are answered

Just how are these three basic questions about government answered in our system? The simple response is: through politics. People preferring different answers to a question meet and compete in politics, and one side wins. At that point, the question is answered – at least until the next election or the next vote in Congress or the next constitutional amendment. But, this view is a bit too simple.

Basic questions are rarely conclusively answered in our system, even when one candidate wins a landslide victory in an election. Here is where the divisions of power between levels and the separations of power between branches become so important. Our questions are not answered by elections so much as they are by legislation. But they are not even answered by legislation until it's implemented or executed. That requires the participation of the president and the millions of bureaucrats who make up the executive branch – and often state and local governments as well. Further, the courts may also intervene and change the answer if someone appeals to them.

Nobody sees things quite the same, and so everybody thinks and acts somewhat differently. These differences, these disputes and their resolutions – however temporary they prove to be – are what make politics interesting and frustrating and important – and a challenge to study. It is on these sorts of disputes and their resolutions that we'll be focusing throughout the rest of this book.

Because we shall focus on disputes among political actors concerning who should decide what is to be done, we shall need to know how these political actors – including, often, citizens like us – see the world. This means we must learn about their *images of reality* – the pictures they have in their minds. It also means we must try to understand their *experiences* in the political world. To learn what it is like to act in politics, we shall examine, for example, a day in the life of President Carter. We shall also cover a day in the life of a member of the House of Representatives and look at the typical experience of other political figures as well. Much of our attention, in other words, will be on the images of reality that shape the behavior of people active in politics. We shall also focus on the experiences of these activists – and the experiences we would likely have should we decide to involve ourselves. These will be our special concerns as we study American political institutions, processes, and policies, in order to understand the nature and prospects of American politics.

To give us the background necessary for such study, we shall first examine briefly, in Chapter 1, how our present government developed from merely a written Constitution and some uncertain hopes of a few million people on an underdeveloped continent two centuries ago. Then, in Chapter 2, we shall see how it grew to be a federal system of some 78,000 different governments ruling some 220 million citizens in a world of over 4 billion people.

1

The politics of the ancestors: the Founding Fathers and the Constitution

On July 4, 1976, there were great celebrations across America. In Philadelphia, the Cradle of Liberty, the Centennial Bell chimed thirteen times at 2:00 P.M. eastern standard time to initiate a nationwide bell ringing in commemoration of America's Bicentennial. It was the culmination of a year-long series of events designed to reaffirm our heritage and to encourage us to rededicate ourselves to the future.

Wagon trains and "freedom trains" crisscrossed the country for a year. A multinational armada of tall sailing ships sailed into New York harbor on July 4. On the same day a group of bicyclists ended a cross-country trip in Philadelphia – as did a man who pushed a watermelon 800 miles on a lawnmower. And Philadelphia, the City of Brotherly Love, geared up for feared radical demonstrations against the official Bicentennial celebration.

In preparation for the occasion, the official governmental Bicentennial Administration had made grants to support particular projects. Included among these grants were $2000 to finance the Truth or Consequences National Shuffleboard Contest and $3500 for a motion picture on the melting of the statue of King George (who had ruled England when the colonies rebelled).[1]

Around America, you could buy Uncle Samwiches, whiskey decanters shaped like the Liberty Bell, red, white, and blue toilet seats, Spirit of '76 burial caskets, and countless other objects whose commercialism led critics to dub the whole affair the "Buy-Centennial." The governmental official in charge, John W. Warner, responded: "The critics are saying, 'You blockheads sitting up there in those bureaucratic castles, get up there and stop this commercialism.' But wow! Just wait until J. Q. Public gets out of his bed one morning to read some bureaucrat in Washington is telling him what he can and can't buy. Then you'll really have a revolution on your hands."[2]

☐ THE ORIGINS OF AMERICAN GOVERNMENT

One view of the American Revolution attributes it in large part to dictation such as that mentioned by Warner. The British Tea Act of 1773, which imposed special duties on tea, provoked the Boston Tea Party in which colonists dressed as Indians

---

[1]Nicholas von Hoffman, "Cashing in on the Bicentennial," *The Daily Texan,* November 19, 1975. Originally published in the *Washington Post.*

[2]Margot Hornblower, "Bicentennial Ripoff Charges Deplored," *Washington Post,* February 8, 1976.

Reprinted by permission of the Chicago Tribune-New York News Syndicate

boarded British ships and dumped tea into the harbor. The British responded with new laws that closed the Port of Boston, curtailed elections and outlawed town meetings in Massachusetts, and forced all colonists to quarter British troops in their homes. Colonists called them the Intolerable Acts.

■ The First Continental Congress

The Massachusetts House of Representatives countered by asking all colonies to select delegates by special conventions to be sent to Philadelphia for what became the First Continental Congress in September–October 1774. That Congress rejected by one vote a conservative proposal for creation of a grand colonial council to share governing power with the British Parliament. Instead, the Congress eventually passed resolutions calling on the colonies to send a petition to King George III, to raise their own troops (the Minutemen), and to boycott all British trade. "On a fateful October day," writes historian Roy Nichols "these delegates agreed upon the first political organization and regulation for what they called 'our country.' "[3] They declared that a committee was to "be chosen in every county, city, and town, by those who are qualified to vote for representatives in the legislature." The duty of these committees would be to "observe the conduct of all persons" and to report in the press any violators of the trade ban. Thus the first act of cooperation among the colonies was based on the democratic principle of election. And that act of cooperation was the first move of the Continental Congress toward becoming, in

[3]Roy F. Nichols, *American Leviathan* (New York: Harper & Row, 1966), p. 47.

a sense, the first national government in America in 1774, nearly 2 years before the Declaration of Independence.

The British, fearful of these early revolutionary developments, took preventive military action against the militiamen at Lexington, near Boston, April 19, 1775. Their attack provoked Paul Revere's famous warning, "The British are coming," and the patriots' response that was to be called "the shot heard around the world."

■ The Second Continental Congress So by the time the Second Continental Congress convened in May 1775, the revolution was in fact underway. Rather than creating a new Continental Army, the Congress simply "adopted" the army then gathering around Boston for "the general defense of the right of America." It designated Virginia Congressman George Washington as its commander-in-chief. Still, the Congress continued to seek peaceful settlement of its grievances with Parliament and on July 6, 1775, declared, "We have not raised armies with ambitious designs of separating from Great Britain, and establishing independent States."

But compromise was not politically attainable, and the military encounters became more and more frequent and serious. Conflict that had been triggered largely by economic grievances became increasingly political in the public debates, with arguments such as the battle cry "No taxation without representation" for the colonies in the British Parliament.

The Resolution of Independence introduced by Richard Henry Lee and passed by the Continental Congress on July 2, 1776.

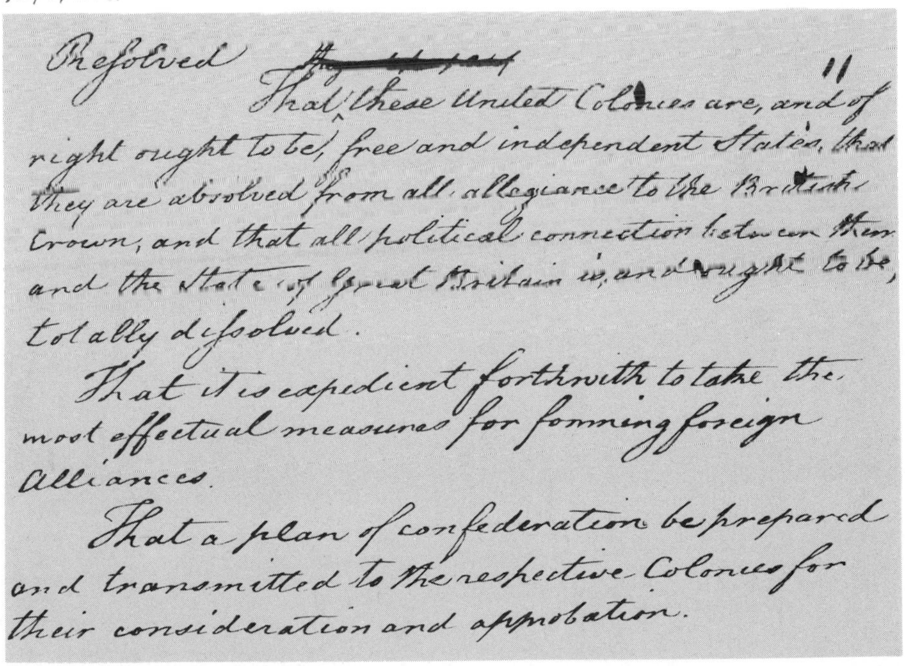
Resolved

That these United Colonies are, and of right ought to be, free and independent States, that they are absolved from all allegiance to the British Crown, and that all political connection between them and the State of Great Britain is, and ought to be, totally dissolved.

That it is expedient forthwith to take the most effectual measures for forming foreign Alliances.

That a plan of confederation be prepared and transmitted to the respective Colonies for their consideration and approbation.

IN CONGRESS, JULY 4, 1776.

A DECLARATION

BY THE REPRESENTATIVES OF THE

UNITED STATES OF AMERICA,

IN GENERAL CONGRESS ASSEMBLED.

WHEN in the Course of human Events, it becomes necessary for one People to dissolve the Political Bands which have connected them with another, and to assume among the Powers of the Earth, the separate and equal Station to which the Laws of Nature and of Nature's God entitle them, a decent Respect to the Opinions of Mankind requires that they should declare the causes which impel them to the Separation.

WE hold these Truths to be self-evident, that all Men are created equal, that they are endowed by their Creator with certain unalienable Rights, that among these are Life, Liberty, and the Pursuit of Happiness—That to secure these Rights, Governments are instituted among Men, deriving their just Powers from the Consent of the Governed, that whenever any Form of Government becomes destructive of these Ends, it is the Right of the People to alter or to abolish it, and to institute new Government, laying its Foundation on such Principles, and organizing its Powers in such Form, as to them shall seem most likely to effect their Safety and Happiness. Prudence, indeed, will dictate that Governments long established should not be changed for light and transient Causes; and accordingly all Experience hath shewn, that Mankind are more disposed to suffer, while Evils are sufferable, than to right themselves by abolishing the Forms to which they are accustomed. But when a long Train of Abuses and Usurpations, pursuing invariably the same Object, evinces a Design to reduce them under absolute Despotism, it is their Right, it is their Duty, to throw off such Government, and to provide new Guards for their future Security. Such has been the patient Sufferance of these Colonies; and such is now the Necessity which constrains them to alter their former Systems of Government. The History of the present King of Great-Britain is a History of repeated Injuries and Usurpations, all having in direct Object the Establishment of an absolute Tyranny over these States. To prove this, let Facts be submitted to a candid World.

HE has refused his Assent to Laws, the most wholesome and necessary for the public Good.

HE has forbidden his Governors to pass Laws of immediate and pressing Importance, unless suspended in their Operation till his Assent should be obtained; and when so suspended, he has utterly neglected to attend to them.

HE has refused to pass other Laws for the Accommodation of large Districts of People, unless those People would relinquish the Right of Representation in the Legislature, a Right inestimable to them, and formidable to Tyrants only.

HE has called together Legislative Bodies at Places unusual, uncomfortable, and distant from the Depository of their public Records, for the sole Purpose of fatiguing them into Compliance with his Measures.

HE has dissolved Representative Houses repeatedly, for opposing with manly Firmness his Invasions on the Rights of the People.

HE has refused for a long Time, after such Dissolutions, to cause others to be elected; whereby the Legislative Powers, incapable of Annihilation, have returned to the People at large for their exercise; the State remaining in the mean time exposed to all the Dangers of Invasion from without, and Convulsions within.

HE has endeavoured to prevent the Population of these States; for that Purpose obstructing the Laws for Naturalization of Foreigners; refusing to pass others to encourage their Migrations hither, and raising the Conditions of new Appropriations of Lands.

HE has obstructed the Administration of Justice, by refusing his Assent to Laws for establishing Judiciary Powers.

HE has made Judges dependent on his Will alone, for the Tenure of their Offices, and the Amount and Payment of their Salaries.

HE has erected a Multitude of new Offices, and sent hither Swarms of Officers to harrass our People, and eat out their Substance.

HE has kept among us, in Times of Peace, Standing Armies, without the consent of our Legislatures.

HE has affected to render the Military independent of and superior to the Civil Power.

HE

FIGURE 1.1

The first printed version of the Declaration of Independence.

In January 1776 a pamphlet appeared in Philadelphia bookstores that galvanized popular sentiment for independence instead of reconciliation. Written by a recent immigrant from England named Tom Paine, the pamphlet, entitled *Common Sense,* rapidly spread throughout the colonies. It sold some 150,000 copies within a year – at a time when the entire colonial population (excluding slaves) was only about 3,700,000. Paine attacked hereditary rule and monarchy and argued for establishment of a Republic: "A government of our own is a natural right," he argued. "There is something very absurd in supposing a continent to be perpetually governed by an island." Instead, Paine's new Republic would become "an asylum for mankind" in a world in which "every spot of the old world is overrun with oppression." The genius of Paine's pamphlet was not its arguments, which were very much "in the air" at the time. Rather, it was his rhetorical style. Instead of following the usual example of arguing with legal precedents and citing

HE has combined with others to subject us to a Jurisdiction foreign to our Constitution, and unacknowledged by our Laws; giving his Assent to their Acts of pretended Legislation:

FOR quartering large Bodies of Armed Troops among us:

FOR protecting them, by a mock Trial, from Punishment for any Murders which they should commit on the Inhabitants of these States:

FOR cutting off our Trade with all Parts of the World:

FOR imposing Taxes on us without our Consent:

FOR depriving us, in many Cases, of the Benefits of Trial by Jury:

FOR transporting us beyond Seas to be tried for pretended Offences:

FOR abolishing the free System of English Laws in a neighbouring Province, establishing therein an arbitrary Government, and enlarging its Boundaries, so as to render it at once an Example and fit Instrument for introducing the same absolute Rule into these Colonies:

FOR taking away our Charters, abolishing our most valuable Laws, and altering fundamentally the Forms of our Governments:

FOR suspending our own Legislatures, and declaring themselves invested with Power to legislate for us in all Cases whatsoever.

HE has abdicated Government here, by declaring us out of his Protection and waging War against us.

HE has plundered our Seas, ravaged our Coasts, burnt our Towns, and destroyed the Lives of our People.

HE is, at this Time, transporting large Armies of foreign Mercenaries to compleat the Works of Death, Desolation, and Tyranny, already begun with circumstances of Cruelty and Perfidy, scarcely paralleled in the most barbarous Ages, and totally unworthy the Head of a civilized Nation.

HE has constrained our fellow Citizens taken Captive on the high Seas to bear Arms against their Country, to become the Executioners of their Friends and Brethren, or to fall themselves by their Hands.

HE has excited domestic Insurrections amongst us, and has endeavoured to bring on the Inhabitants of our Frontiers, the merciless Indian Savages, whose known Rule of Warfare, is an undistinguished Destruction, of all Ages, Sexes and Conditions.

IN every stage of these Oppressions we have Petitioned for Redress in the most humble Terms: Our repeated Petitions have been answered only by repeated Injury. A Prince, whose Character is thus marked by every act which may define a Tyrant, is unfit to be the Ruler of a free People.

NOR

NOR have we been wanting in Attentions to our British Brethren. We have warned them from Time to Time of Attempts by their Legislature to extend an unwarrantable Jurisdiction over us. We have reminded them of the Circumstances of our Emigration and Settlement here. We have appealed to their native Justice and Magnanimity, and we have conjured them by the Ties of our common Kindred to disavow these Usurpations, which, would inevitably interrupt our Connections and Correspondence. They too have been deaf to the Voice of Justice and of Consanguinity. We must, therefore, acquiesce in the Necessity, which denounces our Separation, and hold them, as we hold the rest of Mankind, Enemies in War, in Peace, Friends.

WE, therefore, the Representatives of the UNITED STATES OF AMERICA, in GENERAL CONGRESS, Assembled, appealing to the Supreme Judge of the World for the Rectitude of our Intentions, do, in the Name, and by Authority of the good People of these Colonies, solemnly Publish and Declare, That these United Colonies are, and of Right ought to be, FREE AND INDEPENDENT STATES; that they are absolved from all Allegiance to the British Crown, and that all political Connection between them and the State of Great-Britain, is and ought to be totally dissolved; and that as FREE AND INDEPENDENT STATES, they have full Power to levy War, conclude Peace, contract Alliances, establish Commerce, and to do all other Acts and Things which INDEPENDENT STATES may of right do. And for the support of this Declaration, with a firm Reliance on the Protection of divine Providence, we mutually pledge to each other our Lives, our Fortunes, and our sacred Honor.

Signed by ORDER *and in* BEHALF *of the* CONGRESS,

JOHN HANCOCK, PRESIDENT.

ATTEST.

CHARLES THOMSON, SECRETARY.

PHILADELPHIA: PRINTED BY JOHN DUNLAP.

authorities, he used language "as plain as the alphabet" and offered "nothing more than simple facts, main arguments, and common sense."[4]

That "common sense" captured opinion in the colonies and provoked the Congress to action. On April 6, 1776, it voted to open American ports to commerce with all nations except Britain – an act which itself was in effect a declaration of independence. In May, the Congress advised all colonies to form new state governments unconnected to Britain. And then, on July 2, it adopted a Resolution of Independence: "RESOLVED, That these United Colonies are, and of right ought to be, free and independent States, that they are absolved from allegiance to the British Crown, and that all political connection between them and the State of Great Britain is, and ought to be totally dissolved."

[4]See Eric Foner, "A Volcanic Pamphlet," *New York Times,* January 9, 1976.

■ **The Declaration of Independence** Thomas Jefferson argued that "a decent respect to the opinions of mankind requires that they should declare the causes which impel them to the separation." So, as the leader of a congressional committee, he drafted a Declaration of Independence enumerating the major grievances. It was amended and passed on July 4. To impress and gain support of the rest of the world, Congress sought unanimous approval of the document by the Colonies. This meant that Jefferson's condemnation of slavery would have to be eliminated in order to satisfy South Carolina and Georgia. The draft finally became "The Unanimous Declaration of the Thirteen United States of America" on July 19. It was carefully written by hand on parchment paper by a scribe, and at last, on August 2, was signed by members of the Continental Congress. The first printed version of the Declaration is shown in Figure 1.1 and carries only the printed signatures of John Hancock (president) and Charles Thompson (secretary).

We date the birth of the United States from July 4, 1776, but this account indicates that this is not really accurate. The Resolution of Independence on July 2 and the Declaration on July 4 formally broke the ties with Britain, but the effective break came with the April 6 closing of the ports to Britain and opening of them to others. Congress thus for the first time represented the increasingly united colonies externally. It acted for them in shaping their foreign relations and in effect established a United States able to act in the world of other states. So in one sense, April 6 was the birth date of the United States.

Viewed another way, that birth occurred the previous summer, when the Continental Congress convened and "adopted" the army forming around Boston "for the general defense of the right of America." The Revolutionary War was intended to solidify that independence of what were at first called the "United Colonies" and later the "United States." But the rebels were united, not by a common desire to join together as a unified state, for they did not feel that, but rather by their desire for independence from England. Hostilities ended in 1782, and when a peace treaty was signed in 1783 they were thirteen independent states, instead of thirteen colonies unified by the colonial domination of Britain.

□ THE STRUGGLE TO CREATE NATIONAL RULING POWER BEGINS

With victory and independence, then, began another even more difficult struggle: the struggle for ruling power – the effort to create the power to govern the people in the thirteen independent states. Many hoped that with independence each former colony could go its own way in terms of its internal governance – each developing its own form of government, maintaining or abolishing slavery as it saw fit, and so on. But in terms of external, or "foreign" relations, there were grave doubts. Victory over Britain did not guarantee peaceful relations – either with Britain or with France and Spain, the other states with long-standing interests on the American Continent. Nor did it guarantee peaceful relations with the Indian tribes with whom they shared the continent. The thirteen states depended for their safety on the goodwill of the European powers. For their well-being they depended on commerce, which required protection for the merchant fleet. But they were small and weak. And so a great debate arose over whether they should attempt to unite, and if so on what terms and in what way.

Each state had drafted its own constitution. Eight of these included a "bill of rights" designed to protect citizens against the transgressions of their own independent and sovereign governments. And all of them mandated the separation of the legislative, executive, and judicial powers to protect against tyranny. But in every case the legislature was predominant, even electing the executive or governor in most states. This was done so that there could be no repetition of the experience of domination at the hands of an executive with kingly pretensions.

These state constitutions took care – with varying degrees of success – of the problem of *internal representation* by creating governments to represent the citizens effectively within state borders. But something more was needed to handle problems of *external representation*. Who was to represent the states in their relations with each other on matters of commerce and whenever disputes arose? Who was to handle relations with foreign powers, including, of course, the conduct of the Revolutionary War?

■ The Articles of Confederation

The Second Continental Congress spent $2\frac{1}{2}$ years following its Declaration of Independence developing a proposed form of government for the new states. The document finally developed was called "The Articles of Confederation and Perpetual Union." The term confederation was chosen because it emphasized that the states were joined with (*con-*) each other, or *federated together*, and

FIGURE 1.2

The structure of government under the Articles of Confederation.

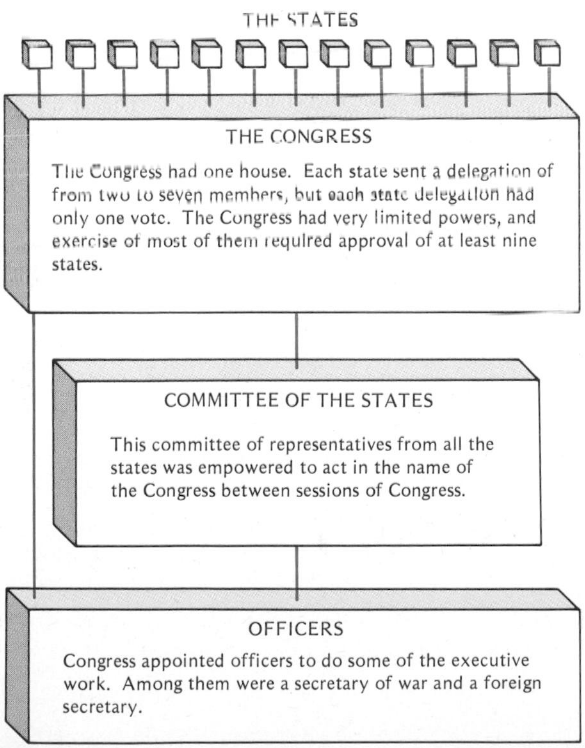

THE STATES
THE CONGRESS
The Congress had one house. Each state sent a delegation of from two to seven members, but each state delegation had only one vote. The Congress had very limited powers, and exercise of most of them required approval of at least nine states.
COMMITTEE OF THE STATES
This committee of representatives from all the states was empowered to act in the name of the Congress between sessions of Congress.
OFFICERS
Congress appointed officers to do some of the executive work. Among them were a secretary of war and a foreign secretary.

continued to act together as the limited government to achieve certain limited common purposes.

Our present system, by contrast, is called a federation, or *federal system,* because it creates a national government that has the power to act *on,* or has power over, the states. When the southern states attempted to withdraw from the United States at the time of the Civil War, they called themselves the Confederacy to emphasize that they wished to reassert "states' rights" against the central government—something of a throwback to the period of the Articles of Confederation.

The government proposed by the Articles was characterized by its drafter as a "firm league of friendship." It established a one-house legislature in which each state would have one vote regardless of size, in which legislation required a two-thirds majority to pass, and in which there would be *no executive,* so that there could be no would-be king. The Congress had virtually no *internal* responsibilities or authority beyond establishing post offices and regulating the coinage of money. It did have *external* powers of war and peace, but, in fact, it could not raise troops because it could not levy taxes. Because it had to depend on voluntary payments from member states and could not regulate commerce, it was still largely at the mercy of the member states. And finally, any amendments to the Articles required the approval of all member states.[5] Figure 1.2 depicts the structure of government under the Articles.

Despite all these constraints designed to protect the member states against domination by the central government, it took until March 1, 1781, for the States to ratify the Articles so that Congress could proclaim the "United States of America." But no sooner had the Articles been ratified and the Revolutionary War won than the confederacy began to disintegrate. Indeed, the Congress could not even get enough states represented in Congress to ratify the peace treaty with Britain within the stipulated 6 months.

As the war came to a close, Tom Paine once again sought to rally opinion to unification. In the last issue of his periodical *The American Crisis* he wrote: "We have no other national sovereignty than as United States. . . . Individuals, or individual states, may call themselves what they please; but the world, and especially the world of enemies, is not to be held in awe by the whistling of a name. Sovereignty must have power to protect all the parts that compose and constitute it; and as UNITED STATES we are equal to the importance of the title, but otherwise we are not."

Abroad, American diplomats found that other powers would not make agreements on trade and other matters because they did not believe that the Congress could compel the states to abide by them. The Congress simply could not represent the confederation adequately in a world of states that were represented by kings and governments with effective ruling power. The Articles had failed at what they were primarily intended to do: represent the states united in the confederation

---

[5] *The* book—the *only* book—on the Articles is Merrill Jensen, *The Articles of Confederation* (Madison: University of Wisconsin Press, 1940).

to the outside world. The primary reason for this failure of external representation was the incapacity of the Congress to do what it in fact was not intended to do: represent the government of the confederation effectively to its own people by legislating, regulating commerce, levying taxes, and raising forces from the states for a national army.

Effective external representation, in other words, required that very sort of effective internal representation that the former colonies resisted because they feared reemergence of the kingship they had rebelled against. The **Federalists**, as those favoring a stronger national government came to be called, were learning from the failures of the Articles of Confederation. They sought to find a way to amend the Articles.

□ THE CONSTITUTIONAL CONVENTION

Because amendment required unanimity, the call to a Constitutional Convention did not come from the Congress, which could not achieve unanimity on anything by that time. Instead, the Virginia legislature called for a meeting of all the states in September 1786. That meeting, attended by only five states, then called for a new Convention to meet in Philadelphia in May 1787. The states appointed seventy-four men to attend that new Convention. The fifty-five who actually attended averaged 42 years of age, were generally college educated (something very rare at the time), and were predominantly lawyers (forty-two of them), businessmen, and farmers, many of whom had served as soldiers in the Revolutionary War. They generally represented wealthy property owners rather than the working class.

This fact has led to sustained debate among historians over the ultimate significance of the Revolution and the Constitution. Historian Charles A. Beard in 1913 wrote a very influential historical study, *An Economic Interpretation of the Constitution,* that emphasized the overriding importance to the framers of achieving economic stability and opportunities for their own financial gain.[6] It is true that wealth was overrepresented, largely because in many states the right to vote was restricted to property owners. At the same time, the expectations of the poor, many of whom had participated enthusiastically in the Revolution, were being disappointed by the failure of the States and the Articles to assist debtors and to foster social reform. By the time the Convention met, as historian Jesse Lemisch has found, there were "waves of bitterness sweeping through the bottom layers of the population," whose members had concluded that the emerging government did not care about them and their concerns. Indeed, on the eve of the Convention, following a long history of unfair taxation, Massachusetts farmers whose land was being seized for failure to pay their mortgage debts had united behind Daniel Shays, a Revolutionary War veteran, in storming an arsenal to seize weapons. They were

[6]Charles Beard, *An Economic Interpretation of the Constitution* (New York: Macmillan, 1913). But see also the critiques of Beard's work: Robert E. Brown, *Charles Beard and the Constitution* (New York: Norton, 1956); Forrest McDonald, *We the People: The Economic Origins of the Constitution* (Chicago: University of Chicago Press, 1958); and Lee Benson, *Turner and Beard* (Glencoe, Ill.: Free Press, 1960).

defeated by the militia, but their daring and desperate act raised fears of popular rebellion in the minds of many in America and Europe. In addition, this action strengthened opposition to popular participation in politics among conservative elements of the population and increased support for a strong central government able to suppress rebellion and preserve the peace. This happened because Shays' Rebellion came at a time when more and more merchants and artisans, like farmers, were becoming increasingly disaffected with political domination by those with economic power.

"The things that were suggested by artisans and shopkeepers," says historian Gary B. Nash, "would make people's hair stand on end – limits on income, redistribution of property, rights of women, abolition of slavery."[7] It was as if the people – or at least a fair fraction of them – had taken seriously the argument of the Declaration "We hold these Truths to be self-evident, that all Men are created equal, that they are endowed by their Creator with certain unalienable Rights, that among these are Life, Liberty, and the Pursuit of Happiness."

The Declaration had continued: "That to secure these Rights, Governments are instituted among Men, deriving their just Powers from the Consent of the Governed, that whenever any Form of Government becomes destructive of these Ends, it is the Right of the People to alter or to abolish it, and to institute new Government, laying its Foundation on such Principles and organizing its Powers in such Form, as to them shall seem most likely to effect their Safety and Happiness." Those men meeting in Philadelphia – eight of whom had signed the Declaration – were in fact once again following the dictates of their consciences. They were appointed to revise the Articles, but they immediately decided instead to start from scratch and draft a new Constitution – something they had to do in secrecy because it was "extralegal" (that is, not within their legal powers).

They sought to establish a new ruling power that was limited enough in its terms that individuals' rights and "states' rights" would survive. Still, it had to be powerful enough to achieve effective internal and external representation for a *United* States of America to succeed the United *States* of America. Using their experience of the weaknesses of the Articles, they quickly reached agreement on a broader set of *powers* for the new national government – *"national supremacy,"* they came to call it.

They then set about determining who would *control* this national government – who would have ruling power. The first specific question was whether the number of representatives in Congress would be determined on the basis of population (as the states with large populations, led by Virginia, favored) or would be equal for each state (as the states with small populations, led by New Jersey, argued). That dispute was settled by the "Connecticut Compromise." This provided for two houses of Congress: the House of Representatives, which represents population, and the Senate, which represents states. The power to elect senators was then given to the state legislatures. (The seventeenth amendment, ratified in 1913, finally gave this power to the citizens of the states.)

[7]These quotations come from Israel Shenker, "Historians Still Debating the Meaning of the American Revolution – If It Was a Revolution," *New York Times,* July 6, 1976, p. 13.

Library of Congress

The committee assigned to draw up the Declaration of Independence. Shown from left to right in this nineteenth-century engraving are Thomas Jefferson, of Virginia, Roger Sherman, of Connecticut, Benjamin Franklin, of Pennsylvania, Robert R. Livingston, of New York, and John Adams, of Massachusetts.

Another major struggle occurred over slavery. Slavery was not outlawed, as delegates from some northern states advocated. Indeed, Article 1, Section 9, specifically prohibited any law ending the importation of slaves before 1808. But slaves, who made up 30 percent of the population in five southern states, were not counted as full persons for congressional representation, as southern states sought. Instead, another compromise provided that slaves were to be counted as "three fifths persons" for both apportionment of congressional seats and apportionment of direct federal taxes among the states.[8] Still another major constitutional compromise resolved the struggle over the question of election of the president. That power went not to the Congress, nor to the people, but to the Electoral College—citizens from each state chosen as the state legislature specified.

All of these major battles reflected the basic underlying issue: Whether this new sovereign government was to be a government of (over) the states (like the Congress set up by the Articles, only stronger) or a government of (over) the

[8]The southern states did not, of course, accept the logical extension of their argument, that if slaves should be counted as persons for representation in Congress, they should also be allowed to vote for those representatives. Indeed, at this time, as we shall see in Chapter 3, only adult white males owning property were generally thought to be suitable voters.

people. Although they were appointed by state legislatures, the framers did not derive their authority from the existing government of the states, which they were flatly (but secretly) contravening. They believed that government *should,* although it rarely did, derive its authority from the people. By providing that their draft Constitution be ratified by special state conventions rather than by the Congress or the state legislatures, they sought to institutionalize this "consent of the governed." At the same time, they would bypass the supporters of the Articles of Confederation in the state legislatures.[9]

■ A republic or a democracy?

Despite beginning the Preamble of the Constitution with the words "We the People of the United States . . . do ordain and establish this Constitution for the United States of America," the framers did not intend that the people play a major role in the day-to-day affairs of the government.

Their support was *not* for a *democracy.* The people scared them. The poor might be stampeded into governmental plunder of the rich; the rich might tend to exploit the rest by seizing control of the governmental machinery and using it for their own benefit. Thus the people—or more exactly those who met voting requirements—would be allowed only to vote for representatives in Congress once they had ratified the Constitution. Should it be necessary, they would also vote on amendments to the Constitution to renew popular consent.

But at the same time, the framers feared as well the chief executive, who might become another despotic king. Thus they sought to avoid a **monarchy**, in which authority resides in a crown, and instead wanted to establish a *republic.* The term republic comes from the Latin words *res* ("thing") and *publica* ("public") and so refers to a "public thing," or "public domain" as contrasted with "royal domain" in a monarchy. A **republic** is a nonmonarchical government whose authority resides ultimately in the people, who delegate it to their elected officials. The republic that the Founders designed became a *democratic* republic in the current sense only very gradually. This occurred as the Bill of Rights was ratified, as the franchise was extended, and as the people achieved the right to elect their senators and, indirectly, their president. As Martin Diamond has written, "for the founding generation it was liberty that was the comprehensive good, the end against which political things had to be measured; and democracy was only a form of government which, like any other form of government had to prove itself adequately instrumental to the securing of liberty."[10]

■ The disposition of power

The task, then, was to design the organs of the republic so that the government was powerful enough to preserve order internally without compromising individual freedom, while preserving the independence and security of

[9]For an account of the origins and development of the notion of popular sovereignty, see Paul K. Conkin, *Self-Evident Truths* (Bloomington: Indiana University Press, 1974), p. 1.

[10]Martin Diamond, "The Declaration and the Constitution: Liberty, Democracy, and the Founders," in *The American Commonwealth 1976,* ed. Nathan Glazer and Irving Kristol (New York: Basic Books, 1976), p. 47.

the country in its external relations. The solution developed was a constitutional system characterized by a unique combination of three qualities:

- *Division of powers* or division of capabilities between the national government, the state governments, and the people. The federal structure made it possible for the framers of the system, in the Tenth Amendment of the Bill of Rights, to *reserve all powers not delegated* to the national government, plus all powers prohibited to it, to the states and the people.
- *Separation of powers* or separation of functions in the national government between three branches: the executive branch, the legislative branch, and the judicial branch.
- *Sharing of powers* or sharing of responsibilities at the national level among the three branches of government through what has come to be called the system of "checks and balances." Sharing of ruling power also developed in practice between the national and state levels in such areas as the power to tax, the power to spend, and the power to regulate business, as we shall see in coming chapters.[11]

These three qualities are what has given our government its distinctive character. Nothing like it had ever before been developed anywhere in the world. Not that each component, each underlying idea, was new. Far from it. The emphasis on liberty can be traced to the writings of the British philosopher John Locke (1632–1704), which most of the framers had read. The finely developed attention to the structure of the government–down to its checks and balances–reflects the influence of the French philosopher Charles de Montesquieu (1689–1755). Others, such as the English legal theorist Blackstone, the French social theorist Rousseau, and the English political theorist Hobbes were also "present in spirit" to influence the framers.[12] Historian Bernard Bailyn, after studying the writings of American authors and activists in the Revolutionary era, concluded: "The theory of politics that emerges from the political literature of the pre-Revolutionary years rests on the belief that what lay behind every political scene, the ultimate explanation of every political controversy, was *the disposition of power.*"[13]

This constant focus on "the disposition of power" led the Founders to combine ideas from philosophers and experience from the Articles of Confederation into "an elaborate and complicated division of newly created power."[14] Figure 1.3 portrays the development of ruling power in the new United States government as the Framers designed it in the Constitution. It lists the major powers that were granted to, or are shared by, the national government and the states.

---

[11]For a discussion of the origin of these ideas, see Conkin, *Self-Evident Truths,* p. 3.

[12]The major relevant works are these: Locke: *Two Treatises of Government;* Montesquieu, *The Spirit of the Laws;* Blackstone, *Commentaries on the Laws of England;* Rousseau, *The Social Contract;* and Hobbes, *Leviathan.*

[13]Bernard Bailyn, *The Ideological Origins of the American Revolution* (Cambridge, Mass.: Harvard University Press, 1973), p. 55. Emphasis added.

[14]Nichols, *American Leviathan,* p. 51.

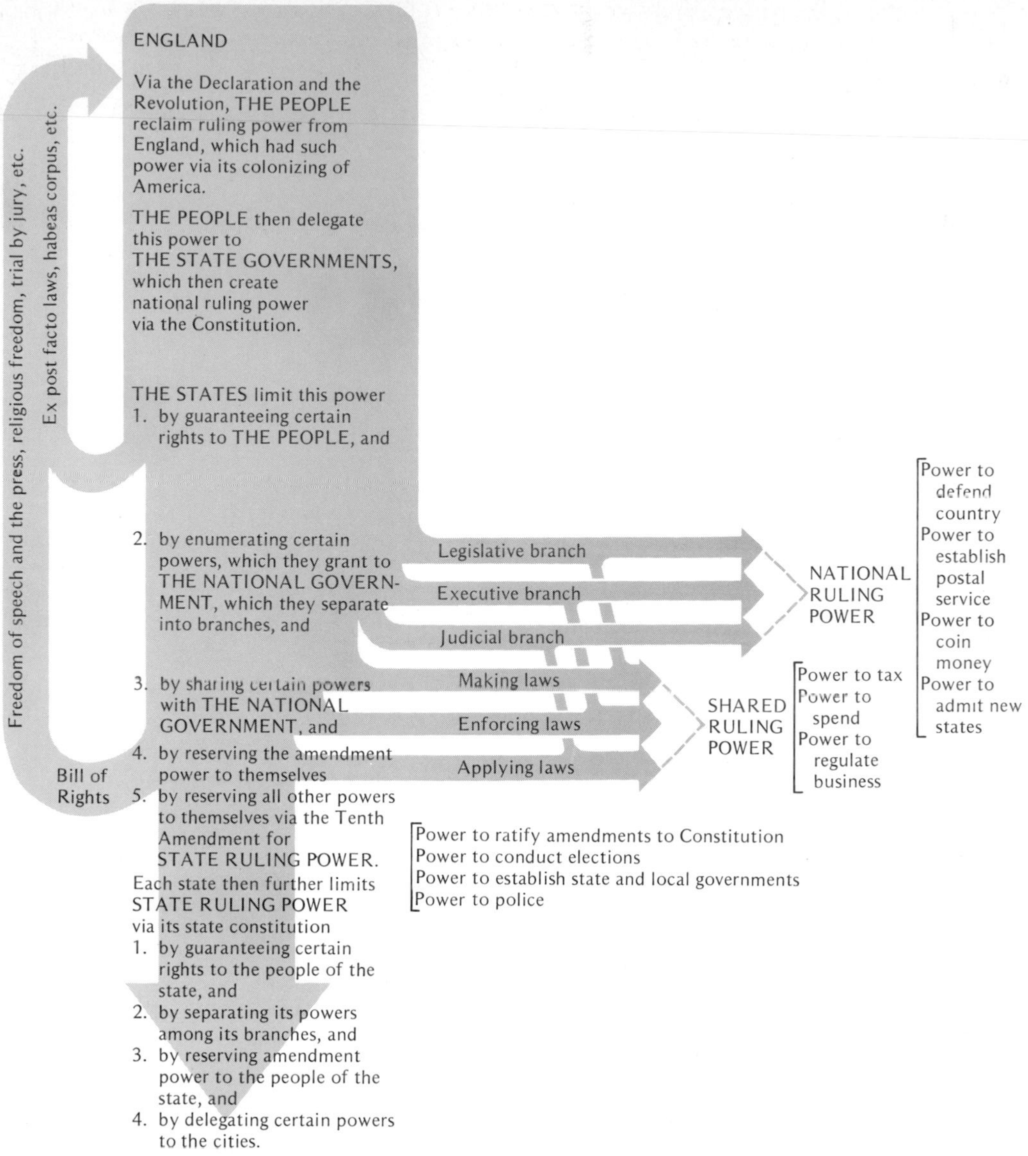

FIGURE 1.3

The development of ruling power in the new U.S. government.

□ THE STRUGGLE OVER RATIFICATION

When the Constitutional Convention completed its work on September 17, 1787, it sent the document to the Continental Congress in New York. Although it was signing its own death warrant, the Congress passed the draft on to the state legislatures. They then passed laws authorizing election of delegates to state conventions that were to vote on it.

Communication and travel were very slow in those days. This meant that the Federalists – the supporters of the new constitution – had a great advantage over the opponents. As framers, they knew what was being done in secret and could prepare for the political battle over ratification, whereas opponents knew nothing of the Convention's deliberations. Furthermore, the Federalists were in large part merchants, bankers, lawyers, planters, and speculators. They lived in urban areas where transport and communication were best. They thus were able to organize and campaign successfully to elect Federalists to the state conventions.

Despite these advantages of the Federalists, a great national debate arose in and around the state conventions. Out of that great debate came a series of essays written by Founding Fathers Alexander Hamilton, James Madison, and John Jay. These essays were published anonymously, under the name "Publius" (Latin for "public man"), in newspapers and later in book form. In form the essays were rather like the pieces by current columnists such as James Reston and Anthony Lewis. But in content they were much more philosophical, carrying to the people the argument for a strong political union – a *federation* (the concept which gave the papers their name) rather than the previous weak *confederation.* They have become known as *The Federalist Papers,* and are to this day the best example of political theorizing ever produced in America.[15]

As the debate developed, ratification became more difficult. Delaware ratified first, and unanimously, on December 7, 1787. Five days later, Pennsylvania agreed, followed 6 days thereafter by New Jersey. Georgia and Connecticut ratified in early January 1788. But then there were bitter struggles in Massachusetts before it agreed. Maryland and South Carolina followed, and on June 21, New Hampshire became the ninth state to ratify. That was enough to put the Constitution into effect formally. But Virginia and New York were such important states that their acceptance was essential. After desperate struggles, both agreed that summer. North Carolina did not ratify for another 15 months, and Rhode Island became the last state to agree, on May 29, 1790.

Meanwhile, Washington had been elected the first president and was inaugurated on April 30, 1789. He had been designated by "electors" chosen by ten state legislatures, rather than by the people. And the Constitution had been ratified by conventions of representatives selected by only 160,000 of the 4 million citizens. So the birth of America was not a very democratic birth – except compared to those of all other countries at that time. Nor was it a very harmonious birth. Almost immediately, strong support arose for limits on the power of the government.

Throughout this period in American history the pendulum swung between strengthening the national government as required by the demands of internal and external representation (or, in the other term we use, by the development of effective ruling power), and preserving and even expanding the rights and liberties of the people. Viewed in this way, the Declaration, the Revolution, and the Articles together can be seen as a movement toward liberty in reaction against a strong

---

[15]There are many editions of *The Federalist Papers.* The most accessible is that of Clinton Rossiter (New York: New American Library, Mentor paperback, 1961). Also helpful is that edited by Benjamin F. Wright (Cambridge: Harvard University Press, 1961).

governmental system that had been tyrannous because it was foreign, unrepresentative, and unresponsive. The Constitution as drafted marked a return swing of the pendulum toward more effective ruling power, which inevitably threatened to curtail the individual liberty protected formally in the Articles. But this development was so novel and so sudden and so troubling to many citizens that it immediately stimulated a backward swing toward individual liberty. This swing was quickly expressed in the first efforts to amend the new Constitution: creation of the Bill of Rights.

□ AMENDING THE CONSTITUTION

The United States Constitution was written to last. It was intended to provide continuity – a sense of national identity – after the Founding Fathers were gone. Still, as Washington wrote just after its drafting, "The warmest friends and the best supporters the Constitution has do not contend that it is free from imperfections; but they found them unavoidable, and are sensible, if evil is likely to arise therefrom, the remedy must come hereafter; . . . and as there is *a constitutional door open for it,* I think the people (for it is with them to judge), can, as they will have the advantage of experience on their side, decide with as much propriety on the alterations and amendments which are necessary, as ourselves."[16]

The "constitutional door open for it" is Article V.[17] In effect, it grants the power to amend to the states, although the process is somewhat more complex, as Table 1.1 reveals.

Amendment was not meant to be easy. On rare occasions, such as the outlawing of slavery by the Thirteenth (1865), the repeal of prohibition of alcoholic beverages by the Twenty-first (1933), and the extension of the vote to 18-to-20-year-olds by the Twenty-sixth (1971), the process has gone quickly. More often, it takes years to get the required three-fourths of state legislatures to ratify an amendment once the Congress proposes it by a two-thirds vote in both Houses. And often, Congress refuses to propose an amendment that is widely supported by public opinion – as on the questions of abortion and school busing. Because of the large majorities required in Congress and among the states, amendments that pass tend to be concerns "whose time has come" after long periods in which public opinion developed.

Thus, the expansion of citizenship rights – especially suffrage, the right to vote – has been the subject of eight amendments:

- □ Thirteenth – abolition of slavery (1865)
- □ Fourteenth – citizenship rights not to be abridged by states (1868)
- □ Fifteenth – black suffrage (1870)
- □ Seventeenth – direct election by the people of their senators (1913)

---

[16]George Washington, letter to Bushrod Washington, November 10, 1787.

[17]For a discussion of constitutional amendment in our and other federal systems, see William S. Livingston, *Federalism and Constitutional Change* (Oxford: Clarendon, 1956), especially chap. 5.

- ☐ Nineteenth – women's suffrage (1920)
- ☐ Twenty-third – suffrage for residents of the District of Columbia (1960)
- ☐ Twenty-fourth – the poll tax outlawed in federal elections (1964)
- ☐ Twenty-sixth – suffrage for all citizens 18 or older (1971)

The growth of the role and power of central government figured especially in the Sixteenth Amendment (income tax, 1913) and the Eighteenth (prohibition of alcoholic beverages, 1919 – repealed by the Twenty-first in 1933). But it also enters into most others in that they generally conclude with the provision that "Congress shall have power to enforce this article by appropriate legislation."

The result of the lengthy and demanding ratification process has been passage of but twenty-six amendments in some 190 years. And if we set aside the ten amendments of the Bill of Rights, the total is only sixteen.

■ The Bill of Rights

The strongest focus of opposition to the Constitution after it was proposed in 1787 was the absence of a Bill of Rights. Bills of rights had originated in 1689 in England with the demands of English lords that the king observe

TABLE 1.1

Amending the Constitution

1. USUAL ROUTE: Congress proposes an amendment by passing it by a two-thirds vote in each house

1a. ALTERNATIVE ROUTE: Congress calls national convention at the request of the legislatures of two-thirds of the states. If convention passes an amendment, it is thereby proposed. (This route has never been used.)

2. Congress stipulates how proposed amendment is to be ratified. This may be either by:

   a. Favorable votes of three-fourths of the state legislatures. Each state can decide whether to ratify by a simple majority vote or by an unusual majority (for example, two-thirds of the votes).[a]

   b. Favorable votes of special conventions called for the purpose in three-fourths of the states. (Used only for Twenty-first Amendment.)

3. After the amendment is ratified in either of the above ways, the amendment is automatically in force—"valid to all intents and purposes, as part of this Constitution" (Article V).

[a]A state cannot legally rescind (or "take back") its ratification, but it can change its mind and vote to ratify after first rejecting an amendment.

certain rights that they claimed. Eight of the new state constitutions had bills of rights designed to guarantee various individual liberties, some of them almost identical to those sought by British citizens a century earlier. The framers of the U.S. Constitution generally believed such a listing of limitations on government power unnecessary because they believed they were creating a government of strictly limited "enumerated" powers. But popular memories of British tyrants were still fresh in some minds. Furthermore, the Constitution did create a government with direct power over the people rather than only over the states (as was the case under the Articles). So state after state demanded a Bill of Rights as a price for ratification of the Constitution.

In 1789, 2 years after the Constitution was drafted, twelve amendments were adopted in the new Congress by the required two-thirds majority in each house of Congress and submitted to the states for ratification. The most important of them asserted prohibitions against laws limiting freedom of speech, the press, religion, assembly, and protest and stated a wide range of rights of the accused. Two years thereafter, in 1791, ratification of the first ten amendments by the required three-fourths of the states was complete, and the new nation had what became known as the "Bill of Rights."[18] We'll discuss its contents in more detail in Chapter 13. (See Table 1.2, chronology of American independence.)

□ ADAPTING THE CONSTITUTION

The Tenth Amendment, the last in the Bill of Rights, declared that "The powers not delegated to the United States by the Constitution, nor prohibited by it to the States, are reserved to the States respectively, or to the people." That was an attempt to limit the growth of national ruling power in favor of state powers. Nonetheless, inevitably, when the first constitutional government came to power in 1789, it began a 12-year process of establishing precedents for strong central government – yet another pendulum swing in the opposite direction from the Bill of Rights.

The "Federalist Era," as these years under George Washington and John Adams came to be called, was characterized by establishment of effective *external* ruling power: treaties were negotiated with Spain, England, and France, and financial credit with European countries was established. Effective *internal* ruling power, as we have noted above, usually increases a state's effectiveness in dealing with other states. In this case, too, America's success abroad was due largely to the fact that the government was exercising its internal ruling power directly over the people with strength and authority.

But this effective internal government was sometimes achieved at the expense of popular expectations about individual liberties and "states' rights." The result was growing opposition from those who wished to limit central

---

[18]The two that were never ratified by a sufficient number of states dealt with apportionment of the House of Representatives and the pay of senators and representatives.

TABLE 1.2

Chronology of American independence

1773	Boston Tea Party and Intolerable Acts
1774	First Continental Congress
1775	Second Continental Congress; organization of Continental Army
1775	Resolution of Independence (July 2) and Declaration (July 4)
1777	Articles of Confederation drafted
1781	Articles of Confederation become effective
1782	End of Revolutionary War; peace talks in Paris
1783	Peace with England; Europe recognizes American independence
1784	Virginia cedes western lands to Congress
1786	Shays' Rebellion in Massachusetts
1787	Constitutional Convention in Philadelphia; Northwest Ordinance
1788	Ninth state (New Hampshire) ratifies Constitution; required two-thirds of states have now ratified Constitution
1789	Government organized under first president George Washington; Congress proposes Bill of Rights
1790	Last state (Rhode Island) ratifies Constitution
1791	Bill of Rights amendments ratified

governmental power and expand the country westward through the admission of new states to the Union. These forces united behind the successful presidential candidacy of Thomas Jefferson in 1800.

Ironically, however, it was Jefferson who presided over what may have been the most important event in the growth of centralized ruling power: the Louisiana Purchase. To understand its impact, we must backtrack a bit. In 1787, while the Convention in Philadelphia was drafting the Constitution, the Continental Congress in New York was drafting the Northwest Ordinance. This law provided that the land on the frontier to the west was to be organized first into territories and then into three to five states. Each of these would be admitted to the Union as equals of the original states once it had 5000 or more residents. In other words, the new nation, instead of getting colonies like the old nations of Europe, would get new member states. Furthermore, these new states were expected to develop their own forms of self-government. This "was to be one of the important instruments that maintained experimentation in developing the capacity for self-government in the midst of the nation's spectacular expansion in wealth and power. It gave elasticity to an organism that might otherwise have become rigid."[19]

In 1803, Jefferson's ministers in France arranged to purchase the whole Louisiana territory—on the French condition that the land would be "incorporated into the Union" and its inhabitants made citizens. The Louisiana Purchase doubled the land mass of the United States and created great economic opportunities on that new frontier. It also offered new ground for struggle between the proslavery and antislavery forces in the Congress, which by Article IV, Section 3, had the power to admit new states into the union.

The spread of self-government experiments into the "territories" where there were no property limits on the right to vote made the greatest

[19]Nichols, *American Leviathan*, p. 58.

contribution to the trend toward greater democracy in America – a trend we'll trace in Chapter 3. The admission of new states into the Union – ten by 1821 and eventually thirty-seven to date – made certain that the territory and the economy of America would grow. It also meant that the government itself would expand in a scale and in directions the Founders could not have foreseen. That expansion would require more national ruling power than the Constitution provided, and more governmental changes than Constitutional amendment requirements would allow.

■ The opportunities for adaptation Jefferson had always preached the strict construction (or literal reading) of the Constitution. He opposed the liberal or loose reading favored by those seeking to strengthen the central government. But when he was confronted with the possibility of purchasing the entire Louisiana territory, he could find nothing in the Constitution that specifically allowed such a transaction. He wrote privately that the purchase was "an act beyond the Constitution," but he overcame his constitutional scruples, and so did the Congress. In Jefferson's words, "as new discoveries are made, new truths disclosed, and manners and opinions changed . . . institutions must advance also, and keep pace with the times."

When constitutional amendment was too difficult or too time-consuming, other forms of adaptation had to be found.[20] The Constitution offered opportunities for adaptation other than by amendment in three major ways. First, *much constitutional language is very general.* This makes it subject to further development and interpretation when circumstances require or merit. For example, its instruction to the president to "take care that the laws be faithfully executed" has allowed for most of the expansion of presidential power from George Washington onward, which we shall discuss in Chapter 6.

Second, *the Constitution is silent on important matters.* For example, it does not specifically grant the Supreme Court the power of "judicial review" – reviewing and even declaring unconstitutional lower court decisions and laws. We shall see in Chapter 9 that this has been an important aspect in American political development, as it was in the case of *Roe v. Wade,* which we examined in Perspective 1. The Constitution is also silent on the role of political parties (our topic in Chapter 4) and of cities (Chapter 18), both of which have gained importance partly because they were not constricted by explicit constitutional limitations.

Third, *words used in the Constitution have changed meanings* with the times. We'll see in Chapter 13, for example, that the language in the Bill of Rights forbidding "unreasonable searches" has been easily redefined to include the use of electronic spying equipment, which was unthinkable in the days of the Framers.

[20]For an interesting discussion of adaptation, see Gerald Garvey, *Constitutional Bricolage* (Princeton, N.J.: Princeton University Press, 1971).

■ Our use and abuse of the ancestors Thus, generalities specified, silences filled in by practice, and words redefined have been important tools in the adaptation of the Constitution to a changing world. Jefferson had declared that "The Constitution belongs to the living and not to the dead," and his actions proved it. Yet all the time there was and still is a countervailing power working against such adaptation. That power is the concept of "the intent of the framers." The "strict constructionists" and the political conservatives try to figure out what the framers really meant by the words they wrote in the document. They do so first by examining the records we have of the debates in the Constitutional Convention.[21] If that is inconclusive, they may ask, "What would the Founding Fathers say and do if they were alive today?"

Our attachment to our ancestors is everywhere obvious. There are monuments to Washington and Jefferson in Washington—and the capital is itself named for the first president. There are statues of various Founding Fathers all around the country. Cities and streets and even citizens are named for them. Their faces appear on our money and our stamps. Why all this obsession with ancestors? Is it a quest for our "roots" as a nation like Alex Haley's quest for his roots as a black Afro-American[22] or our own interest in "climbing our own family tree"?

When the country was founded, George Washington had such stature as a political and military leader that his presidency served to *legitimize* the new country and its government. He had charisma—magnetic appeal—that helped establish a sense of unity among the people. He was also able to unify the leaders of the various factions in the government while allowing them the freedom to develop their followers into what would become the political parties that would help stabilize governance when he retired. In all this he was overseeing the creation of "legal authority" out of "charismatic authority"—legitimacy—so that the government would be able to function well without him.[23]

Washington once remarked that "I do not think we are more inspired, have more wisdom, or possess more virtue, than those who will come after us."[24] But there is always a kind of magic in the founding—and in the founders—that those who come later cannot hope to equal. We may—and do—attempt to have periodic "refoundings" with "new ancestors" such as the

---

[21]If you'd like to try that, the best place to start is the classic work edited by Max Ferrand, *The Records of the Federal Convention of 1787* (New Haven, Conn.: Yale University Press, 1911; rev. ed. 1937), which comes in four volumes. Or you might prefer to start with Ferrand's own summary account, *The Framing of the Constitution of the United States* (New Haven, Conn.: Yale University Press, 1913). An easier route, though one also less reliable, is reading the *Federalist Papers.*

[22]See Alex Haley, *Roots* (Garden City: Doubleday, 1976).

[23]See Marcus Cunliffe, *George Washington: Man & Monument* (New York: New American Library, Mentor paperback, 1960), for a fascinating account of the American hero worship and ancestor worship of Washington.

[24]George Washington, letter to Bushrod Washington, November 10, 1787.

Library of Congress

The veneration accorded to George Washington even in his own lifetime is evident in this 1798 engraving.

popular image of the restoration of the Union under Abraham Lincoln that arose after his assassination during the Civil War or the escape from the Great Depression via the New Deal under Franklin Roosevelt. But in times of trouble, we keep going back to the original Founders for guidance, for relegitimation of our political system.

The underlying reason for this unending appeal to the ancestors seems to be that without them, anything goes—which means there is no compelling answer to the question of how politics should be conducted. The authority of the ancestors appeals to everyone—especially the leaders, who hope some of this authority will rub off on them.

But the danger is that, despite the amendments and adaptations, we will become too tied to old ways of seeing and doing things as we face new problems. Some 70 years after Washington, Abraham Lincoln, in the throes of the Civil War, remarked that "the dogmas of the quiet past are inadequate to the stormy present. The occasion is piled high with difficulty, and we must rise with the occasion. As our case is new, so we must think anew, and act anew. We must disenthrall ourselves, and then we shall save our country."[25] But even Lincoln, one of our "newer ancestors," would be astonished at what passes for everyday life—and for government—today. For he stood and served midway between the old and the new conceptions of what government should be and do.

☐ THE GROWTH OF GOVERNMENT: CHANGING DEMANDS AND EXPECTATIONS

In the years since the new national government was organized in 1789, the government has grown immensely.[26] The First Congress (1789–1791) had sixty-five congressmen, each of whom represented 30,000 constituents; the Ninety-third Congress (1973–1974) had 435, each representing over a half million citizens. The members of the First introduced a total of 144 bills and passed 82 percent; members of the Ninety-third introduced 23,396 but passed only 3 percent.

Even more revealing of the breadth of governmental activity is the size of the federal government's budget—the total sum of money it spends. In the years 1789–1791, that sum was $4,269,000 over 3 years, and it produced a $150,000 surplus of funds received over funds spent. In 1970, the budget was $196,587,786,000, or 50,000 times as much. And by that time the federal debt had increased to $370,918,707,000. That debt amounts to $1811 for each citizen.

---

[25]Quoted in Nichols, *American Leviathan,* pp. 278–279.

[26]On the occasion of the Bicentennial, the United States Census Bureau, which has been counting Americans and their activities ever since 1790, issued a special two-volume report called *Historical Statistics of the United States: Colonial Times to 1970* (Washington D.C.: Government Printing Office, 1976), on which much of the following account relies. For a revealing brief summary, see Robert Reinhold, "Census Statistics Sum Up 200 Years of U.S. Change," *New York Times,* July 6, 1976.

Massive increases like this in the scope and cost of governmental activity do not just happen. They result partly from the sheer growth of the country, from a population of 3,893,635 in 1790 to 215,667,979 on July 4, 1976. Such an increase requires more governmental officials and so costs more money. But even more important as a factor in the expansion of the government has been change in how the population lives. In 1790, only 5 percent of the people lived in cities, and the biggest American city, New York, had only 33,131 residents. But by 1970, the country contained four times as much land, yet 75 percent of the people lived in cities. Over 400 cities were larger than New York was in 1790. Such massive urbanization of the country created many new demands on the government, as we shall see in Chapter 18.

■ Changes in citizen expectations Even this trend toward urbanization does not account for most of the growth in the size and activities of government. We might get a better indication of the causes of that growth from another statistical comparison. In 1790 the average American could expect to live only until the age of 35. Today, the average life expectancy has more than doubled. The causes of this doubling are many, but major credit must go to governmental programs to promote and protect public health. The government conducts vaccination programs, provides health care, and tests the food we eat, the water we drink, and the medicines we take.

Such government programs do not just happen. They result from public demands that the government undertake major new efforts "to promote the general Welfare." Our forefathers, who inscribed those words at the top of the Constitution, would probably envy us our long life expectancy. But they would no doubt be astonished – and probably quite alarmed – at the extent to which we rely on the government for so many services.

Two hundred years ago, government was generally thought of as a necessary evil. It was something people had to have in order "to insure domestic tranquility" (we would say law and order) and "to provide for the common defense" ("national security"). If the government maintained law and order and guaranteed national security, it was believed, the other stated objectives – justice, welfare, and liberty – would follow almost as a matter of course.

But in the late nineteenth century, people began to change their minds about all this. They saw a series of economic depressions that did not simply "cure themselves" and took a terrible human toll. They saw economic interests grow to gain monopoly powers. They saw political "machines" come to dominate life in the growing cities. As a result, people increasingly demanded that the government intervene in the economy to restore prosperity and then preserve some semblance of the economic competition that capitalism required but, nonetheless, tended to destroy. Some also called for the government to take action to restore opportunities for political competition on which democracy depended but that corrupt machines destroyed. The consequence of these new demands was government regulation of the economy and the polity – something the Founders thought unnecessary and even dangerous.

The immediate effects of this growing role of government were more government workers and bigger budgets. The longer-run effects were changes in popular conceptions of the state itself. The old conception of limited government has been called "the negative state" because its responsibility was to protect citizens *against* internal disorder and foreign threats. This view was increasingly replaced by a new conception of a more active government, which has come to be called "the positive state." In this view, the state is expected to guarantee people the economic opportunity, welfare, and equality that they could not expect from the free operation of the economic marketplace and the political arena.

This shift, in other words, was from government providing *freedom from* domestic disorder and foreign threats, to government providing *freedom to* live a better life through measures that would control economic exploitation, expand political opportunities, and increase the health, education, and welfare of all citizens.

■ From expectations to demands on government

Today, we expect the government to provide *education* up to the limit of each citizen's capacity to learn (or, perhaps still, capacity to pay). We expect the government to guarantee *employment* to everyone able and desiring to work, or at least to provide *unemployment insurance* for those unable to find work. We expect government to provide *old age insurance* pensions ("social security," we call it). And increasingly we expect government to guarantee us *health care.*

A hundred years ago, no Americans expected their government to provide these goods and services and opportunities to them simply because they were American citizens. Today, many Americans know they still will not *get* these desires from their government. However, they believe that they *should* get them, and increasingly they demand them, from their government.

Further, they expect government to guarantee that they can *purchase,* if they wish, pure water, electric light and power, heat, and even air conditioning, anywhere they choose to settle. Similarly, they expect the government to see to it that they can receive information and entertainment of their own choice via the mass media. They expect to be able to travel by air or highway (if no longer by sea or rail) anywhere they wish anytime they wish, merely for payment of a fee.[27] How did this change in expectations come about?

When the country was founded, most human needs were met in and by the family unit. According to the Census Bureau, in 1790 half of all households contained six or more people, and only a tenth were one or two people living alone. People generally earned – or won by struggle – their livelihood directly from the land as farmers, hunters, and foresters. Gradually, however, livelihoods shifted toward providing services to other people as life and work became more specialized.

---

[27]For an interesting analysis of this change see Geoffrey Vickers, *Making Institutions Work* (London: Associated Business Programmes, 1973).

And then, inevitably, those services were increasingly provided by *institutions* (supermarkets, dairies, construction companies, factories, and so on) instead of by individuals (merchants, farmers, carpenters, and other artisans). So inevitably people came to gain their livelihood, as well as their goods and services, from those institutions rather than from other people. Through this evolution, the virtually self-sufficient large household unit gave way to the small family. By 1970, only one in ten households had six or more people, and half of all Americans lived alone or with just one other person. More and more responsibilities that once fell naturally on the family unit had gradually become demands on the government.

Indeed, these specific demands increasingly became parts of more general demands. Economically, following the Great Depression in the 1930s, the people and the Congress (in the Full Employment Act of 1946) demanded that the federal government ("with assistance and cooperation of industry, agriculture, labor, and state and local governments") prevent future depressions and seek "to promote maximum employment, production, and purchasing power."

■ From demands on government to demands on citizens

Citizens demand services that require large government. But the people working in big government also develop their own notions about other things that should be done. The result is that big government becomes even bigger. It begins to seem unresponsive and inefficient to the citizens who first made demands for more services. And so citizens demand that there be *less* government—especially when they find that large government makes large demands on its citizens.

Americans have never much liked demands made on them by government. The Constitution is full of prohibitions on government demand making. Indeed, if you read the Constitution and the Bill of Rights you will find in them what one observer has called "45 no's and not's circumscribing governmental power."[28] It was only reluctantly, under the impact of World War I, that Americans, after the ratification of the Sixteenth Amendment in 1913, finally accepted an income tax to pay for strongly desired services.

This ever growing need for money is but one of the demands governments impose today. In wartime (and until recently in peacetime as well) the state drafts its young male citizens to serve it as soldiers. More and more, the government has also demanded that its citizens submit to standardized "identity routines"—from obtaining a Social Security card before beginning to work, to carrying a draft card while eligible for military service, to carrying a passport when traveling outside the country, to presenting a voter registration card at the polls. It also insists that we fill out growing numbers of forms for purposes of taxation and business activity. We also need to have a birth certificate to prove what we claim about our origins. All this led to a "Federal Paperwork Commission" to study ways of curtailing these and other such requirements on citizens and business, and the Congress passed a "Right to Privacy Act" to curtail governmental abuse of the information so obtained.

---

[28]Leonard Read, "The Heritage We Owe Our Children," *Notes from the Foundation for Economic Education*, September 1976, p. 3.

☐ THE CHALLENGE TO THE CONSTITUTION

We shall encounter such happenings – such challenges – time and again in coming chapters. The growing demands of citizens on the government are matched by growing demands of the government on the citizens. Such mutual demands not only cause resentment in many citizens but also place strains on the institutions and processes of government. Looking back on the Bicentennial of the Declaration of Independence in 1976 and forward to the Bicentennial of the Constitution in 1987, historian Richard B. Morris recently remarked:

> I don't think we can afford to take this system for granted. It's obvious that the Constitution was constructed in a different time frame and to meet an entirely different set of problems in an era when the national purpose was conceived of quite differently from the present day. Now—to underscore the differences—our nation is confronted with a serious decline in popular participation in, and a pervasive distrust of, government. We need to find out if the Constitution can continue to function effectively against this background of corrosive distrust in government at almost every level of our society—a distrust perhaps far deeper than in any previous period.[29]

The Constitution has been subject to increasing criticism as outmoded and inadequate. For example, Harvey Wheeler recently concluded an assessment of the Constitution with these harsh words: "Its Gothic territorial federalism no longer conforms to the associational realities and the community needs of our times. Its tripartite provision for governmental powers [legislative, executive, and judicial] is woefully inadequate [in an era when more demands on government require more governmental powers], and its mechanistic paradigm [of checks and balances] has become self-contradictory."[30]

But before we decide whether to accept or reject such a harsh judgment, we must examine both the participation of citizens and the operation of our institutions – both of which are strongly shaped by our Constitution, for better or for worse. And to do that we must first look in more detail at the politics of federalism in our system. For as Roy Nichols has observed, "American democracy had its origin and its experimental grounds in the local units, colonies, territories and states."[31]

☐ SUGGESTIONS FOR FURTHER READING AND STUDY

By now, the literature on early American history is positively massive. Probably the best guide to it is the *Harvard Guide to American History* edited by Frank Freidel (Cambridge, Mass.: Harvard University Press, 1974). Volume 1 of this selective listing of book and periodical writings is arranged by topic,

---

[29]Interview in *U.S. News & World Report,* July 4, 1977, p. 63.

[30]Harvey Wheeler, "Constitutionalism," in *Handbook of Political Science,* vol. 5, ed. Fred I. Greenstein and Nelson Polsby (Reading, Mass.: Addison-Wesley, 1975), p. 78.

[31]Nichols, *American Leviathan,* p. 58.

whereas volume 2 is chronological. A less comprehensive bibliographical guide is Eugene R. Fingerhut, *The Fingerhut Guide* (Santa Barbara, Calif.: ABC–Clio, 1973).

Among the classic works still valuable are Andrew McLaughlin, *The Confederation and the Constitution, 1783–1789,* originally published in 1905 (New York: Collier paperback, 1962); Max Ferrand, *The Framing of the Constitution of the United States* (New Haven, Conn.: Yale University Press, 1913); Merrill Jensen, *The Articles of Confederation* (Madison: University of Wisconsin Press, 1940); Jonathan Elliot, *The Debates in the Several State Conventions on the Adoption of the Federal Constitution* (Philadelphia: Lippincott, 1888).

The more recent works on the Charles Beard thesis of the economic origins of the Constitution are cited in chapter footnotes. Among other more recent works of interest are: Alfred H. Kelley and Winfred A. Harbison, *The American Constitution: Its Origins and Development,* 5th ed. (New York: Norton, 1976); Clinton Rossiter, *Seedtime of the Republic* (New York: Harcourt, Brace, 1953), and his *The Grand Convention* (New York: Macmillan, 1966); Robert A. Rutland, *The Birth of the Bill of Rights, 1776–1791* (Chapel Hill: University of North Carolina Press, 1955); Daniel J. Boorstin, *The Americans: The Colonial Experience* (New York: Random House, 1958); and Broadus Mitchell and Louise Pearson Mitchell, *A Biography of the Constitution* (New York: Oxford University Press, 1961).

The very interesting studies that concentrate on the political and social theories underlying the great American experiment include: Bernard Bailyn, *The Ideological Origins of the American Revolution* (Cambridge, Mass.: Harvard University Press, 1967), which relates American thought to the European liberal tradition; Louis Hartz, *The Liberal Tradition in America* (New York: Harcourt, Brace, 1955); Gordon Wood, *Creation of the American Republic 1776–1787* (New York: Norton, 1972); Roy F. Nichols, *American Leviathan: The Evolution and Process of Self-Government in the United States* (New York: Harper Colophon paperback, 1963), which was originally published under the title *Blueprints for Leviathan: American Style;* William S. Livingston, *Federalism & Constitutional Change* (Oxford: Clarendon Press, 1956), and Gerald Garvey, *Constitutional Bricolage* (Princeton, N.J.: Princeton University Press, 1971), which discuss the process of American Constitutional development; and Seymour Martin Lipset, *The First New Nation* (New York: Basic Books, 1963), an interesting attempt to compare America's development with that of other more recent "new nations."

The politics of federalism: a nation of states or a nation of cities and regions?

Our federal structure was created, as we saw in Chapter 1, as a compromise to ensure strong enough central government while insulating the citizens from full central control. The basis for this structure is *territory.* This means that where you live and where you are strongly affect how you live.

□ THE ROLE OF TERRITORY

Within the broad limits set by the Supreme Court, states have different laws concerning abortion. Some states have laws providing the death penalty for murder, whereas others do not. Some states provide more health and welfare services than do others. Some states do more than others to regulate business and industry to protect our health and safety. And, not surprisingly, in most places the level of taxes reflects the level of services.

The state and local taxes you pay vary considerably from state to state. Nine states – Connecticut, Florida, Nevada, New Hampshire, South Dakota, Tennessee, Texas, Washington, and Wyoming – still have no personal income tax, for example, while an average family of four living in Minnesota may pay $1000 in such taxes each year. Not surprisingly, services provided by state governments also vary considerably. States such as Alaska, Hawaii, and New York (among those with high citizen incomes) and Mississippi, South Carolina, and New Mexico (among those with low citizen incomes) spend more per person, and so usually offer more state services. Such states as Arkansas, Missouri, North Carolina, and Texas, on the other hand, spend much less per person and generally offer fewer goods and services to their citizens.[1]

In a federal system like ours, some governmental functions are reserved to the states; others are delegated to the national government. But the states are defined in terms of territorial areas, rather than in terms of the particular people in them. By crossing a river, or even an invisible line across a highway, you can become a member of a different political system with different laws, different taxes, and different officials. You remain an American, and you must continue to obey the federal law made in Washington and the commands of national officials. But all the rest can change with one small territorial step.

---

[1]See Emil M. Sunley, Jr., "State and Local Governments," in *Priorities: The Next Ten Years,* ed. Henry Owen and Charles C. Schultze (Washington: Brookings Institution, 1976), pp. 371–409, especially p. 387.

□ THE FEDERAL STRUCTURE

The Founding Fathers, as we saw in Chapter 1, concluded that the weak central government with strong states, which had been developed under the Articles of Confederation, was not working well enough. They decided, therefore, to devise a new type of system in which more powers would be granted to the central government. But to protect the liberties of the citizens, they designed the Constitution so that it would delegate only certain specified powers to the central government; all other powers would be reserved to the states and the people.

FIGURE 2.1

Major flows of power in our federal system. (In the figure, labels indicating downward flows read from top to bottom, whereas those indicating upward flows read from bottom to top.)

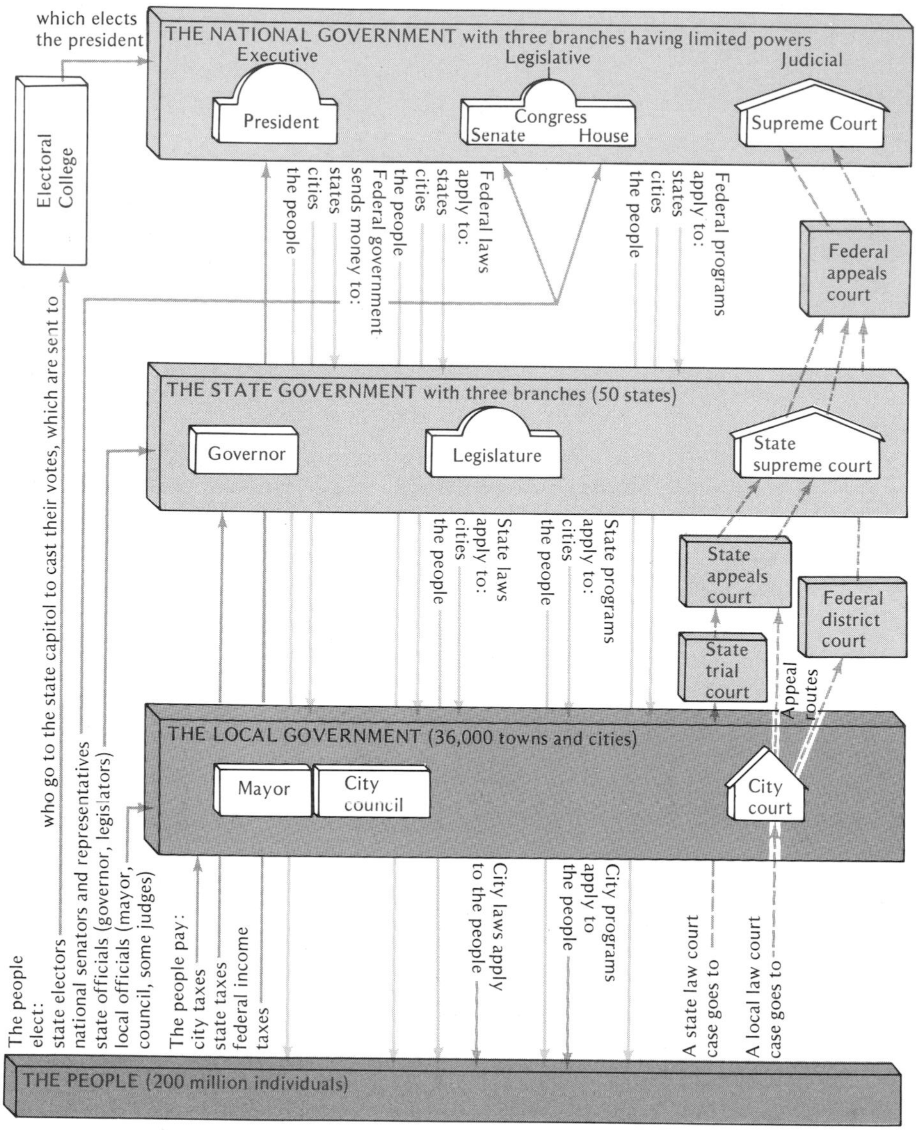

■ **A layer cake or a marble cake?** It is the complex web of power relations (see Figure 2.1) among the national government, the state governments, the local governments, and the people that makes the system *federal.* In Figure 2.1, some of the "power lines" for laws and programs that reach the people come from the national level; others come from the state level and the local level. Thus, each level is a final authority or has some direct ruling power over the people. If all lines came from the national level, ours would be a *unitary* or *centralized* government. If they all came from the states, and the states were loosely linked to a national government, it would be a *confederation,* as under the Articles of Confederation.

For a long time, people describing the federal system used the metaphor of the "layer cake." The top layer was the national, the next layer the state, and then the bottom layer the local. The local layer may include sublayers such as the county, the city, and the school district. As experts studied the federal system more carefully, however, they found that in fact most governmental functions are shared by different levels of government. For example, as we shall see in Perspective 5, public education is financed by a combination of local property taxes, state grants, and programs of federal aid to education. Again, if you are convicted of breaking a local law in a local court, you may decide to appeal the conviction. You would go to a state appeals court on grounds that the law violates the state constitution or to a federal court if you think the law or your court treatment violated your rights as an American citizen. And, by the same token, the federal Constitution says that federal law is supreme in the areas of powers granted to the national government. Thus, Congress can pass laws that are binding on state and local governments.

In addition, and probably most important of all for determining the federal nature of our governmental system in all its levels, each level of government has some power directly over all citizens living within its borders. Thus you must obey laws of your own city, your county, your state, and the nation – and so must state, local, and national officials.

The result, in the words of political scientist Morton Grodzins, is this:

> The federal system is not accurately symbolized by a neat layer cake of three distinct and separate planes. A far more realistic symbol is that of the marble cake. Wherever you slice through it you reveal an inseparable mixture of differently colored ingredients. . . . Vertical and diagonal lines almost obliterate the horizontal ones, and in some places there are unexpected whirls and an imperceptible merging of colors, so that it is difficult to tell where one ends and the other begins. So it is with federal, state, and local responsibilities in the chaotic marble cake of American government.[2]

In other words, in a federal governmental system as it is usually described, there must be several levels or layers of government which rule over the same people, each of which is supreme or sovereign in some spheres. As William Riker, a

---

[2]Morton Grodzins, "Centralization and Decentralization in the American Federal System," in *A Nation of States,* ed. Robert A. Goldwin (Chicago: Rand McNally, 1963), pp. 3–4.

TABLE 2.1

The growth of the United States

State	Year admitted
Delaware	1787
Pennsylvania	1787
New Jersey	1787
Georgia	1788
Connecticut	1788
Massachusetts	1788
Maryland	1788
South Carolina	1788
New Hampshire	1788
Virginia	1788
New York	1788
North Carolina	1789
Rhode Island	1790
Vermont	1791
Kentucky	1792
Tennessee	1796
Ohio	1803
Louisiana	1812
Indiana	1816
Mississippi	1817
Illinois	1818
Alabama	1819
Maine	1820
Missouri	1821
Arkansas	1836
Michigan	1837
Florida	1845
Texas	1845
Iowa	1846
Wisconsin	1848
California	1850
Minnesota	1858
Oregon	1859
Kansas	1861
West Virginia	1863
Nevada	1864
Nebraska	1867
Colorado	1876
North Dakota	1889
South Dakota	1889
Montana	1889
Washington	1889
Idaho	1890
Wyoming	1890
Utah	1896
Oklahoma	1907
New Mexico	1912
Arizona	1912
Alaska	1959
Hawaii	1959

longtime student of the subject, puts it, "Federalism is a political organization in which the activities of government are divided between regional governments and a central government in such a way that each kind of government has some activities on which it makes final decisions."[3]

But as Grodzins reminds us, in today's world most functions are shared between Washington and the states and their cities. Each level has certain special responsibilities and certain superior capabilities. The result of this sharing, or interdependence, is that political relations between the levels often produce conflict and involve efforts by one level to influence the other. Such intergovernmental relations are rarely harmonious, as we shall soon see when we examine highpoints in their evolution through America's 200 years. It is as if no level is fully content with the marble cake structure of intergovernmental relations. Thus, each level struggles to recreate a layer cake – but each level wants to be the top layer. The consequence is that each level seeks more economic resources (through taxes and grants) and more political authority (through lawmaking and policing). The result is that the cake becomes even more marbled.

If our American system is in this sense a marble cake, so, in a sense, is each of us, for our governments operate in and through each of us, making and enforcing laws and providing services. To understand this better, we must sort out the components or ingredients of this marble cake. We must examine how they have developed, why they are important, and what is happening to them in this complex and challenging era. We must study the ways in which we as citizens, not only of America but also of our state and community, may play constructive roles in politics and government at various levels when we so wish.

We shall make our first efforts to examine these ingredients here, where our focus will be on the states in their relations with Washington. In Chapter 18, we shall see many of the same trends from the perspective of local governments.

□ THE DEVELOPMENT OF AMERICAN FEDERALISM

■ Expansion of the Union

The most obvious aspect of the development of American federalism was the expansion of the country by the occasional incorporation of new states. The Constitution (Article IV, Section 3) provides that "New States may be admitted by the Congress into this Union." Beyond the original thirteen "charter members," thirty-seven additional states have been admitted (see Table 2.1). This growth raised problems at each major stage.

The new states were more democratic than the original colonies, as we noted in Chapter 1. They experimented with self-government as territories even before they became states, and they allowed all adult white males to vote whether or not they owned property. This made them generally supporters of the Democratic-Republicans, the anti-Federalist party led by Thomas Jefferson. As we noted in

[3] W. H. Riker, "Federalism," in *Handbook of Political Science,* ed. Fred I. Greenstein et al. (Reading, Mass: Addison-Wesley, 1975), p. 101.

Negotiating the Louisiana Purchase, Paris, 1803.

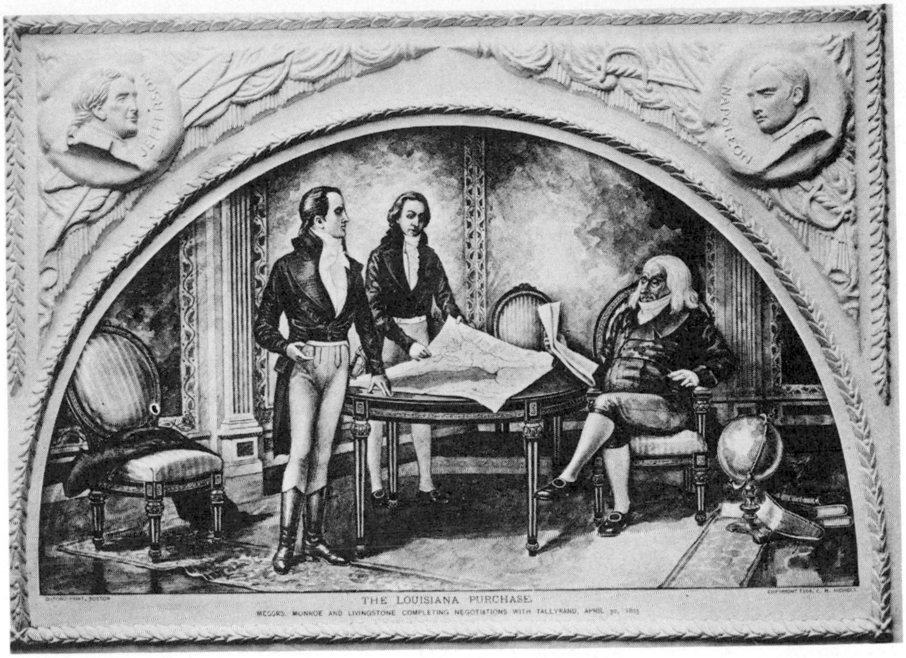

Library of Congress

Chapter 1, the Louisiana Purchase under Jefferson more than doubled the land mass of the United States. It also guaranteed continued political dominance for the Jeffersonians by adding more democratically inclined populations to the American citizenry.

Expansion continued over coming decades. But it became more controversial because the southern states, which maintained the institution of slavery, insisted that slavery be allowed in enough of the new states to prevent the national government from outlawing it. A series of compromises did just that until the Civil War, in the 1860s, finally ended slavery. States continued to be admitted from time to time, as Table 2.1 shows, until the entire forty-eight contiguous (or "touching") states were incorporated with the admission of Arizona and New Mexico in 1912. It was not until 1959 that Alaska and Hawaii, after much political bickering, became the forty-ninth and fiftieth states. Today, there is some discussion concerning statehood for Puerto Rico. This controversial issue will be discussed in Chapter 14.

■ Expansion of the powers of the central government

Physical expansion of the Union was the more obvious development in the early decades of America. But expansion of the powers of the central government, which inevitably came at the expense of the states, was the more important for the future of American federalism. The Constitution *delegated* certain enumerated (or "stated") *powers* to the national government. Among these were the power to make treaties, declare war, coin money, establish post offices, establish national courts, and regulate interstate commerce. It *reserved* all other *powers* to the states and the people. But as soon as the government began to operate, it started acting in ways that served to expand its powers. And almost as soon, that expansion was challenged in the courts.

McCulloch v. Maryland The landmark case that resolved the first attempt to expand government power was *McCulloch v. Maryland* (1819). The national government had established a Bank of the United States and opened a branch in Maryland. It argued that its power to do so was implied by the explicitly stated power to coin money or control the currency. That state of Maryland had imposed a tax on the bank, and James W. McCulloch, the bank cashier, had refused to pay. Before the Supreme Court, Maryland argued that the United States had no right to establish a bank, because the Constitution did not explicitly permit it to do so. In its argument, Maryland also claimed that in any case it had the right to tax such a bank because the power to tax is a power reserved to the states by the Constitution.

The Court unanimously decided against Maryland and for the bank on two grounds that laid the foundation for the continuing growth of the national government at the expense of the states. First, Chief Justice John Marshall wrote in his opinion, "We must never forget that it is a *constitution* we are expounding. . . . [A] constitution intended to endure for ages to come, and consequently, to be adapted to the various crises of human affairs." He then set forth, in defense of Congress's establishing the bank, words that would become known as *the doctrine of* **implied powers:** "Let the end be legitimate, let it be within the scope of the Constitution, and all means which are appropriate, which are plainly adapted to that end, which are not prohibited, but consist with the letter and spirit of the Constitution, are Constitutional."[4]

Marshall then set forth the related *doctrine of national supremacy* in asserting that Maryland could not tax the bank: "The power to tax involves the power to destroy. . . . If the right of the states to tax the means employed by the general government be conceded, the declaration that the Constitution, and the laws made in pursuance thereof, shall be the supreme law of the land, is empty and unmeaning declamation."

Other key court cases The McCulloch case established the principle of implied powers. A related case, *Osborn v. Bank of the U.S.* (1824), allowed a state official who was violating the law to be sued. This case established the principle that the national government could enforce federal law against the states. Together, these two cases clearly asserted the supremacy of the Constitution and national law over state law. Thus, the groundwork was established for national domination in this phase of the struggle for ruling power.

But it was more than a century before the third part of the "triangle of powers" of the national government, to accompany the express and implied powers, was explicitly developed in a Supreme Court opinion in *U.S. v. Curtiss-Wright*

---

[4]The clause under which this doctrine was justified, Article I, Section 8, gives Congress power "To make all laws which shall be necessary and proper for carrying into execution the foregoing powers, and all other powers vested by this constitution in the government of the United States, or in any department or officer thereof." It thus became known as the "elastic clause" because it could be stretched to include so much.

TABLE 2.2

Types of powers in our federal system

Type of power	Origin of power	Examples
Enumerated (national government)	Constitution	Power to make war, to establish post office, to regulate interstate and foreign commerce
Implied (national government)	Constitution, as interpreted in *McCulloch v. Maryland*	Any power that is an appropriate, nonprohibited means to a legitmate end
Inherent (national government)	Supreme Court in *U.S. v. Curtiss-Wright*	Power to acquire territory by exploration, to regulate arms sales
Reserved (state governments)	Constitution	Power to establish state and local governments, to conduct elections, to police
Concurrent (shared by national and state governments)	Traditional practice	Power to tax, to spend, to build roads, to regulate business

Export Corp. (1936). That company had sold arms to Bolivia after Congress had empowered the president to forbid such sales by issuing a proclamation making them a crime. The question was whether Congress could delegate such legislative power to the president in the area of international relations. The Court said yes, ruling that the national government has the powers any nation-state must have, not only to declare war and make treaties (which the Constitution explicitly grants it) but also, for example, to acquire territory by exploration (which the Constitution does not mention). These powers are termed *inherent powers* because they are "necessary concomitants of its nationality." Thus, such powers inhere in the United States as a nation-state, regardless of what the Constitution does or does not say.

The special constitutional powers of the national government, as they have developed, are the express, or enumerated, the implied, and the inherent powers. The special constitutional powers of the state governments are the reserved powers. The most commonly exercised powers, however, are called the *concurrent*, or shared, powers. These are those powers exercised by both levels, national and state, so long as they do not conflict. Among the important concurrent powers are the power to collect taxes, the power to spend, the power to build roads, and the power to regulate commerce within each state. The development of the types of ruling power was shown graphically in Figure 1.3 and is summarized in Table 2.2.

This power to regulate commerce was eventually to become the occasion for more dispute between the national government and the states. But for the first century and a half of America's history, the courts interpreted "the commerce clause"[5] as a license for Congress to subsidize trade and prevent discriminatory treatment of goods by different states – both policies which made major contributions to the economic development of America. As we shall see in Chapter 16, when movements for limitation of child labor and for what we now call consumer protection gained great strength, there were major struggles in the courts over the appropriate extent of national regulation of commerce.

[5]Article I, Section 8: "The Congress shall have power . . . to regulate commerce with foreign nations, and among the several states, and with the Indian tribes."

National Archives
Chief Justice John Marshall.

Over the years, the long-term movement has been toward more extensive national powers and more limited state powers. This struggle, when it involved the question of whether or not to outlaw slavery, led to the Civil War, but only after a conservative-leaning Supreme Court had reaffirmed the constitutionality of slavery in *Dred Scott v. Sandford* (1857). In that case, a slave named Dred Scott, who had been moved by his owner to Illinois where, by state law, slavery was illegal, sued in court for his freedom. But the Supreme Court, dominated by southern judges, made two important rulings. The first was that as a black man Scott could not be a citizen of the United States and so had no right to sue in court at all. The Court reached this conclusion and applied it to Scott in Illinois even though blacks had long been considered citizens in most northern states including Illinois, and so had such a right. The second ruling was that the state law outlawing slavery was unconstitutional because it deprived citizens of their property (slaves) without "due process of law."

The Civil War settled not only the question of slavery but also the question of whether states had the right to secede from the Union, as the South had tried to do. In the Reconstruction era after the war, radical northerners governed southern politics and passed progressive legislation in some Southern states as well as civil rights enforcement laws in the Congress. They also passed and ratified three constitutional amendments: the Thirteenth (1865), which outlawed slavery; the Fourteenth (1868), which guaranteed all persons "equal protection of the laws" against any state's efforts to "deprive any person of life, liberty, or property, without due process of law"; and the Fifteenth (1870), which prohibited denying the right to vote "on account of race, color, or previous condition of servitude."

The pendulum then swung back toward states' rights. But the second decade of the twentieth century, dominated by Woodrow Wilson's presidency, saw major new cooperative programs of national aid to states and localities for agriculture, vocational education, and highway construction. These programs inevitably increased federal control over the states.

And the Depression of the 1930s resulted in a massive increase in national programs under the New Deal. Some of these programs were so controversial in their shift of power from the states to Washington that the Supreme Court ruled many of them unconstitutional.

■ From "dual federalism" to national supremacy

Throughout American history to this point, the Court operated on a principle often called "dual federalism." According to this doctrine, the Court mediated between two power centers, Washington and the states. When it became clear that ending the Depression would require more than mediation and cooperation between the states and Washington, this doctrine was abandoned and national dominance was generally accepted, even by the formerly conservative Supreme Court. In this period major new departures included the Social Security Act of 1935 (which we shall discuss in Chapter 17), which included national grants for state and local unemployment and welfare programs. This period also saw the first national involvement in local public housing via the Housing Act of 1937.

From the New Deal years on, state-national interaction has grown, but always in the general context of national domination.[6] This domination is largely perpetuated by the financial dependence of states on Washington. This in turn derives essentially from the national power to tax incomes – a power granted by the Sixteenth Amendment ratified by the states in 1913.

☐ EFFORTS TO STRENGTHEN THE STATES

Recent presidents have made gestures toward strengthening the powers and increasing the responsibilities of the states. Dwight Eisenhower (1953–1961) applied the term "cooperative federalism" to his efforts. Lyndon Johnson (1963–1969) called his program "creative federalism." Richard Nixon (1969–1974) termed his "the new federalism." The Eisenhower and Kennedy years were notable primarily for the struggle between civil rights and states' rights. The Johnson years of the "Great Society" saw increasing encouragement of state programs. However, all this occurred in the context of centralization of many government programs such as the new federal funding of education, which we shall discuss in Perspective 5. The Nixon administration instituted the one major recent innovation in intergovernmental relations: revenue sharing.

■ Revenue sharing

Programs by which the national government shares revenue it collects with the states and cities by giving monetary grants-in-aid are almost as old as the nation. The first was an 1802 law that provided that revenue from the sale of public lands was to be shared with the states. In 1836 Congress voted to divide a budgetary surplus with the states. But from this point on, programs tended to become more specific, or categorical. They required that funds be spent for particular programs in particular ways.

Such programs were developed because certain important activities, such as education and welfare, were not express or implied powers of the national government according to the Constitution, but were reserved to the States. Thus, if the national government wanted to encourage such activities, all it could do was give money to the other levels of government so that they could do these things themselves. This federal money is raised by taxation, which *is* an express power of the national government by virtue of the Sixteenth Amendment. It is generally given "with strings attached," so that it gives the government in Washington great power over states and localities.

The great enforcement device in intergovernmental relations today is the threat to withhold federal funds. It can be used to force states and cities to take steps to achieve anything from greater racial equality to highway beautification. Until the Depression, the level of federal financial aid to states and localities was low enough

---

[6]For a more detailed description of stages in the evolution of federalism, see Daniel Elazar, "The Shaping of Intergovernmental Relations in the Twentieth Century," in *Annals of the American Academy of Political and Social Science,* May 1965, pp. 11–22.

FIGURE 2.2

The growth of federal aid to state and local governments.

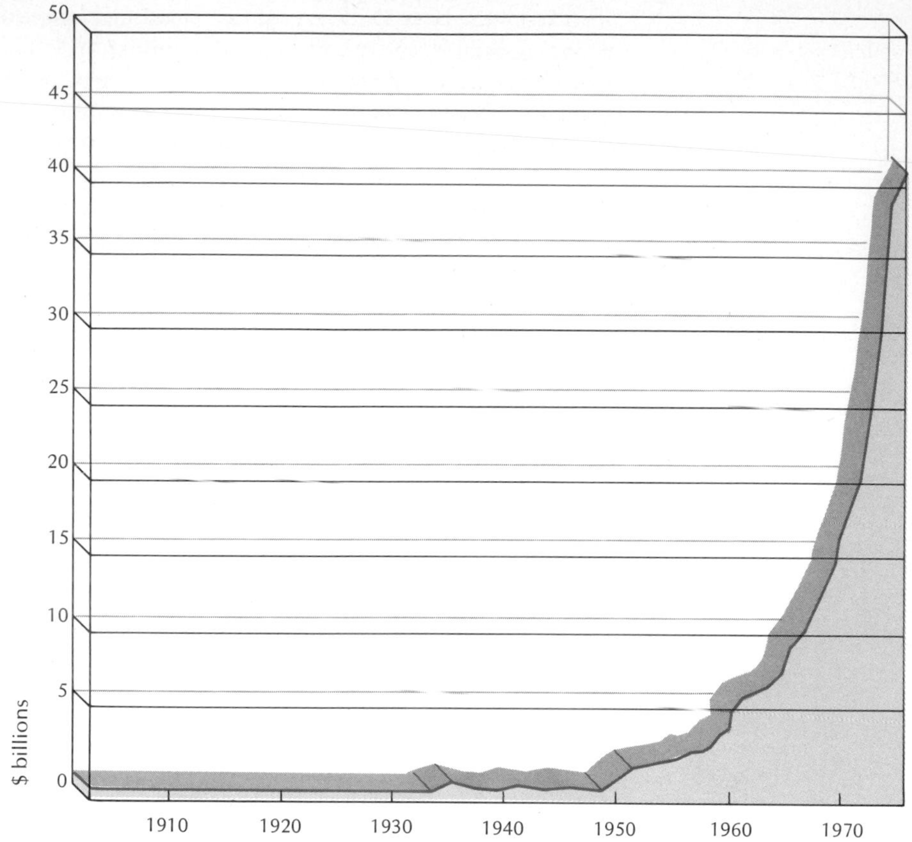

that no real dependency was involved. Figure 2.2 shows the rapid growth of federal aid in recent decades; Table 2.3 shows federal aid as a percentage of total state and local revenue.

In a message to Congress on February 4, 1971, President Nixon noted that most federal assistance takes the form of "highly restricted programs of categorical grants-in-aid. . . . The major difficulty is that States and localities are not free to spend these funds on their own needs as they see them. The money is spent instead for the things Washington wants and in the way Washington orders. . . . State and local governments need Federal . . . money to spend, but they also need greater freedom in spending it."

So Congress passed the State and Local Fiscal Assistance Act of 1972, or **revenue sharing**. Nixon had declared that this program would bring about "a historic and massive reversal of the flow of power in America," because it would provide grants of funds that could be spent in whatever ways states and localities saw fit.

The political struggle that surrounded revenue sharing reveals much about the politics of federalism today. The first proposals of revenue sharing had come 8 years earlier, when it became obvious that states and cities could no longer rely on

TABLE 2.3

Federal aid as a percentage of total state and local revenue

Year	Percent
1950	11.9
1955	10.1
1960	13.8
1965	14.9
1970	16.7
1974	20.1

Source: Statistical Abstract of the United States, 1976 (Washington, D.C.: Government Printing Office, 1976), p. 265.

state and local taxes to finance needed services and programs. Governmental experts expected then that continued economic growth would increase federal revenues year by year and that the war in Vietnam would come to a speedy end, so that the federal government would have surplus funds. Some suggested that these surplus funds should therefore be transferred to the states and cities.

The proposal stimulated a major debate in Congress, where the various interests were well represented, both by congressional supporters and by lobbyists. President Nixon and state governors favored the plan. Governor Nelson Rockefeller of New York formed a National Citizens Committee for Revenue Sharing to lobby Congress in the spring of 1971. Its thirty-three state affiliates, composed of business people, academics, and church groups, did more lobbying. Less enthusiastic were Democratic liberals and members of Congress from large urban areas. They feared that it would end the categorical grants that required spending for the poor and disadvantaged.

Any question that promises to affect strongly all levels of government will bring out strong representation of America's many governments.[7] As of 1972 there were 78,269 governments in America, according to the Census Bureau, in addition to the national and state governments. Included are 3044 counties, 18,517 cities, 16,991 townships, 15,781 school districts, and 23,885 special districts established to provide fire fighting, water, transit, and other services. All of them would be affected in one way or another by the program. So the National Governors Conference lobbied. So did the National League of Cities, the U.S. Conference of Mayors, and the International City Managers Association. And so did the National Association of Counties.

The end result was passage of the bill in 1972. We shall discuss some of the effects of the $30 billion spent over the first 6-year period when we examine urban problems in Chapter 18. The program remained so controversial that when it expired in 1976 it took a great struggle to get it renewed for 4 more years and $36 billion dollars. By that time, it was clear to many that even revenue sharing had not succeeded in overcoming some of the important limitations that our federal system still imposes on our politics. What then are the major effects of our federal structure?

□ THE IMPACTS OF FEDERALISM ON THE AMERICAN POLITICAL SYSTEM

■ Territoriality

The most striking impact of federalism on our politics is the fact that state lines and territoriality, instead of population or special interests, or particular functions like transportation or environmental protection, dominate and shape so much of our politics.

[7]For an account of state and local lobbying, see Donald Haider, *When Governments Come to Washington* (New York: Free Press, 1974).

■ Two sovereignties

A second effect is the creation of a second sovereignty, or source of law, beyond the national government. In fact, because states have delegated some powers to cities and counties, we have three or four sources of law. But only two are sovereign; only two can make laws that the other cannot overturn. This makes life much more complex, especially for business, much of which operates in several states as well as under U.S. jurisdiction.

■ Variety preserved

The federal structure protects variety among the states in many ways. This variety is prominent in matters such as citizen rights. States have different laws on drugs and abortion, for example. It is also present in questions of the proper role of the government. For example, some states but not others control loan sharks who charge outrageous interest rates, taking advantage of people who need to borrow money. More generally, the variety extends to most areas of crime and punishment. The only exceptions are those realms where federal law predominates.

This preserved variety usually benefits some groups at the expense of others. The federal structure was what preserved slavery in the southern states for 75 years after a majority of the country opposed it. Federalism has also sheltered racism in both the South and the North up to the present era. On both slavery and racism, the Supreme Court long ago ruled that state policies and practices are protected from federal meddling. The same has been true of sexism. We shall see more of such preserved variety and its effects on minorities and "outsiders" in Chapters 14 and 15.

■ Limitations on government's economic role

Much the same sort of limitation on federal intervention occurred in the area of economic regulation in the interest of the poor, of small business, and of the consumer. For 150 years, the Supreme Court rather consistently ruled against this, on grounds of the "reserved powers" doctrine discussed earlier. Only when the Great Depression of the 1930s threatened the very survival of capitalism itself did the Court relent. We'll learn more of this in Chapter 16.

■ Creativity and innovation

A fifth effect of federalism is more benign. The fifty states can sometimes serve as fifty laboratories in which policy innovations can be developed and tested. Once lessons are learned at a local level, a national program may be developed. One state innovation is **sunset laws**, which require agencies no longer effective to self-destruct–something we'll discuss in Chapter 7. Another is **zero-based budgeting**, which requires each governmental program or agency to justify itself and each aspect of its budget each year, instead of being automatically assumed to be worth continuing. Sunset laws were tried first in Colorado. Zero-based budgeting was a Georgia innovation of then-governor Jimmy Carter. In a world, and a nation, of growing complexity, bureaucracy, and political stalemate at the national level, such local experiments can prove especially useful.

■ Insulation of the cities from the national government

The final major effect of federalism has been the insulation of the cities – and their problems – from the national government. We shall see in more detail in Chapter 18 how cities derive their powers from the states and how this dependence long kept the federal government out of urban affairs, sometimes for the better and sometimes for the worse.

□ POLITICS AND THE STATES

In recent years, urban problems have grown in prominence. The new attention to the cities has been encouraged by riots, crime, drug problems, bankruptcy, turmoil in the public schools, and other headline-grabbing happenings. One result has been more federal aid and attention – and a consequent lessening of the role of the states in their cities. Another result has been decreasing citizen interest in, and attention to, the states.

Public confidence in state government, like confidence in the federal government, has been declining seriously in recent years. According to a recent nationwide poll, 26 percent of the respondents said that they had less confidence in state government than they had 5 years earlier. In the same survey, 39 percent said they believe state government affects their personal lives a great deal, while 19 percent said "hardly at all." Asked how state government affected them, 46 percent volunteered "taxes," while 15 percent said "highway construction and maintenance"; another 15 percent cited public education. Small percentages mentioned driver's licenses, state police, providing recreation areas, state hospitals, and pollution control as major state activities that affected their lives.

But only 13 percent had ever gone to their state government for any sort of help. In contrast, 24 percent had sought aid from local government. And most of those who sought state help were affluent and from small towns. None were black.[8] Surveys such as this reflect some of the important challenges facing state governments today.

□ FEDERALISM AND REGIONALISM: SUNBELT AND SNOWBELT

In recent decades there has been a large population shift from the older states of the Northeast, the Midwest, and the Northwest (the Snowbelt) to the states of the South and the Southwest (the Sunbelt). A line across the middle of the United States splitting California in two and leaving Virginia in the southern half forms the dividing line between Sunbelt and Snowbelt. From 1950 to 1975 the Snowbelt has grown by 32 percent, while the Sunbelt has grown by 60 percent. Figure 2.3, which shows the changes state by state, also reminds us that the Snowbelt still has almost twice as many people, but the rate of change clearly favors the Sunbelt. And

---

[8]Louis Harris, *Confidence and Concern: Citizens View American Government,* report of a poll taken for the Senate Subcommittee on Intergovernmental Relations, September 1973.

from 1970 to 1975, states such as New York and Pennsylvania actually lost population.

Such population shifts do not simply happen. They are related to other developments. In the last 25 years, many industries in the northern states have either moved to the South or closed down. One reason for this has been high labor costs in the North, where unions are stronger. Another has been outmoded industrial machinery in older northern factories that are expensive to modernize. This shift of industry has meant more jobs in the South and West and fewer jobs in the North. People tend to move to where the jobs are. In turn, this means that per capita (per person) income in each region has changed, too. In 1929, for example, the average income in the Northeast was 150 percent of the national average, while in the Southeast it was only 53 percent. By 1974, the Northeast was down to only 116 percent of the national average, while the Southeast was up to 83 percent. In other words, the people in the Southeast remain poorer on the average than those in the Northeast, but the gap is closing quickly.

This closing of the gap was hastened by the sharp increases in the prices of food and fuel following the energy crisis of 1973–1974 and the strong inflation of the early 1970s. Many states in the Sunbelt have surpluses of energy and food, and so prices are lower there. Furthermore, they need less energy because of the warmer climate. And this is yet another reason why both citizens and industries from the Snowbelt are moving south and west.

Related to these developments has been a shift in federal government spending toward the Sunbelt states. Defense and space program industries, among the newest types in the American economy, have tended to set up plants in the states with lower labor costs and taxes – the Sunbelt. So government dollars have

FIGURE 2.3

U.S. population growth, 1950–1975 – Sunbelt versus Snowbelt.

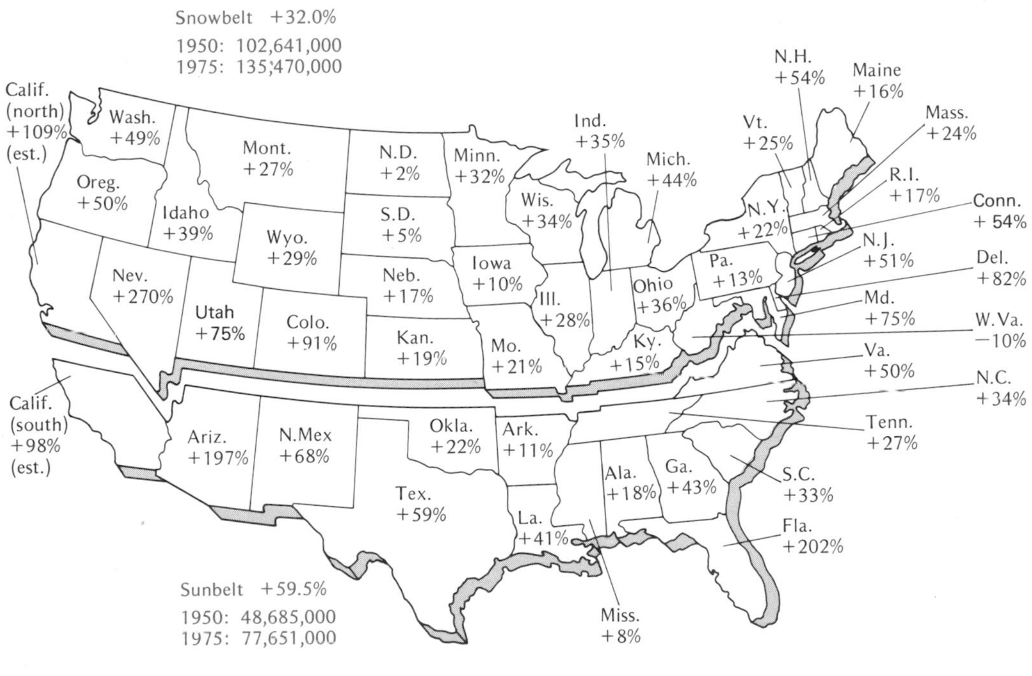

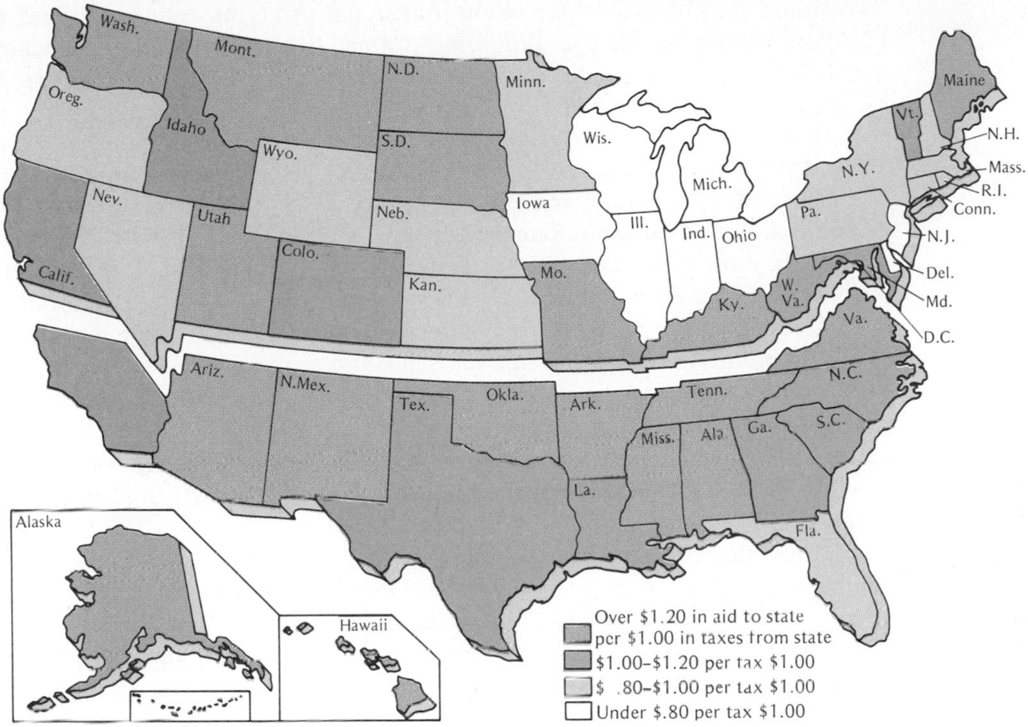

FIGURE 2.4

Federal aid to the states, 1976—Sunbelt versus Snowbelt.

increasingly been spent in these states. Furthermore, special government antipoverty programs have tended to concentrate on the urban poor, and Sunbelt cities such as Houston, Atlanta, and Los Angeles have been major targets.

In 1976, for example, the people and businesses of the fourteen Snowbelt states of the Northeast and Great Lakes areas paid $29.4 billion more in federal taxes than they received from Washington in grants and government spending. The Sunbelt states, by contrast, got $23 billion more back than they paid in taxes. Figure 2.4 shows how much money the federal government spends in each state for each dollar of tax revenue it collects from the state.

Different growth rates have led to a political struggle between the Sunbelt and Snowbelt for jobs, people, and capital.[9] This political struggle was first manifest at the level of governors. In June 1976, the Democratic governors of seven northeastern states formed the Coalition of Northeast Governors (CONEG) to seek "a united front in Congress and before the national Administration on specific economic issues." The following month, the Midwest Governors' Conference called for a reexamination of federal spending priorities. Several months later, representatives of the fourteen states of the two groups met to coordinate their efforts. Meanwhile, House members from sixteen states formed a bipartisan (two-party) Northeast-Midwest Economic Advancement Coalition representing

[9]"The Second War Between the States," *Business Week,* May 17, 1976, pp. 92–114. See also Kirkpatrick Sale, *Power Shift* (New York: Vintage paperback, 1976).

204 House members and 90 million Americans. And the following June a bipartisan Senate Snowbelt coalition was formed. This new solidarity quickly strengthened the efforts of the northeastern states to increase their share of federal aid for economic development.

Battles over how federal funds should be spent have been fought increasingly along regional lines in recent years. The prospect may be for intensification of this regional conflict in coming years. When results of the 1980 census are used to reapportion the 435 House of Representatives seats among the fifty states, the states gaining the most population will gain seats from those falling behind. Projections are that these changes will shift some fifteen seats from the Snowbelt states to the Sunbelt states, giving the South and West a majority for the first time.[10]

The political effects of this shift are difficult to predict. The Sunbelt states are likely to gain voting power in the House. But at the same time, the South will continue to lose power with the retirement, death, or defeat of elderly senators and representatives who have controlled what could be voted on by controlling the committees they chaired. (We shall examine this aspect of power in Congress in Chapter 8.)

It may turn out, then, that growing voting strength will be offset by declining committee domination in the Congress. But in any case it appears likely that the power of cities in Congress – and in state legislatures – will decline. The reason for this is that major cities such as St. Louis, Chicago, Detroit, Pittsburgh, Philadelphia, Jersey City, Newark, and New York are losing people to suburban areas. This is something we shall examine in Chapter 18.

There may also be effects at the presidential level. As we shall discuss in Perspective 2, presidents are actually chosen by "electors" chosen by voters state by state. States with relative gains in population will get more electors and so can have more impact on who wins the presidency. For this reason, Sunbelt states may gain in electoral importance. But because the greatest population concentrations are still in the Northeast and the Midwest, this effect will be less pronounced.

□ THE UNCERTAIN FUTURE OF AMERICAN FEDERALISM

It is difficult to forecast the political impacts and outcomes of shifts in population, capital, and political power for several reasons. First, much depends on future population changes of a sort that have surprised experts in recent years. Second, developments in food, energy, and the economy, both domestic and international, will be very influential. And third, it is still not clear how solidly the states within each region will cooperate or how different regional objectives will become.

An expert with the Advisory Commission on Intergovernmental Relations, a nonpartisan group that studies American federalism, recently concluded that "the move toward regional efforts at problem-solving is widespread and appears to be

[10]See Robert Reinhold, "Population Shift Study Gives 'Sunbelt' House Majority after '80," *New York Times,* January 21, 1976; and "America's 'Sunbelt' Is Growing in People and Power," *U.S. News & World Report,* April 12, 1976, p. 60.

growing. Whether this trend toward competitive sectionalism develops further or shifts toward a more unified effort to encourage expenditure of a larger portion of the Nation's gross national product for economic development purposes remains to be seen."[11]

There are signs of growing cooperation among the states in certain areas, as we have seen above and will see again in coming chapters. In addition, many states are modernizing their governments so that they can operate more effectively, alone or together, in dealing with the federal government and their own cities. Our federal system is intended to facilitate both efforts. As Daniel Elazar writes, "The virtue of the federal system lies in its ability to develop and maintain mechanisms vital to the perpetuation of the unique combination of governmental strength, political flexibility, and individual liberty, which has been the central concern of American politics."[12]

"The future of American federalism," Richard Leach has suggested, "depends first of all on the satisfaction the American people feel about its performance now and in the past."[13] Elazar concludes that "the American people are known to appreciate their political tradition and the Constitution. Most important, they seem to appreciate the partnership, too, in some unreasoned way, and have learned to use all its elements to reasonably satisfy their claims on government."[14]

The discontent and disinterest so apparent in the minds and actions of many Americans in recent years may lead us to wonder whether Elazar is too optimistic. To find out, we shall next examine how the American people use the elements of our federal system in making claims on government.

☐ SUGGESTIONS FOR FURTHER READING AND STUDY

There are several especially helpful studies of the theory of federalism; William Riker, *Federalism: Origin, Operation, Significance* (Boston: Little, Brown, 1964), which is historical, comparative, and critical of American federalism; Kenneth Wheare, *Federal Government,* 4th ed. (New York: Oxford University Press, 1964), which is comparative; and Arthur Maass, *Area and Power: A Theory of Local Government* (Glencoe, Ill.: Free Press, 1950).

The most innovative study of American federalism is Daniel J. Elazar, *American Federalism: A View from the States,* 2nd ed. (New York: Crowell, 1972). For other helpful views, see Morton Grodzins, *The American System* (Chicago: Rand McNally, 1966), which Elazar edited; Richard H. Leach, *American Federalism* (New York: Norton, 1970); Michael Reagan, *The New Federalism* (New York: Oxford University Press, 1972); and two books by William Anderson, who served on the U.S. Commission on Intergovernmental Relations: *The Nation and the States: Rivals or Partners* (Minneapolis: University of Minnesota Press, 1955), and *Intergovernmental Relations in Review* (Minneapolis: University of Minnesota Press, 1960).

A recent study of the governments in our federal system is Michael N. Danielson et al., *One Nation, So Many Governments* (Lexington, Mass.: Lexington Books, 1977). On the allocation of

---

[11]Carol S. Weissert, "Restraint and Reappraisal: Federalism in 1976," *Intergovernmental Perspective* 3, no. 1 (Winter 1977): 22.

[12]Daniel Elazar, *American Federalism. A View from the States,* 2nd ed. (New York: Crowell, 1972), p. 227.

[13]Richard H. Leach, *American Federalism* (New York: Norton, 1970), p. 221.

[14]Elazar, *American Federalism,* p. 227.

powers among states and the federal government, see David E. Engdahl, *Constitutional Power: Federal & State* (St. Paul: West, 1974). The problems of the states are analyzed by a former governor of North Carolina, Terry Sanford, in *Storm Over the States* (New York: McGraw-Hill, 1967). Efforts to solve them politically are the subject of Donald Haider, *When Governments Come to Washington: Governors, Mayors, and Intergovernmental Lobbying* (New York: Free Press, 1974).

Thomas H. Kiefer, *The Political Impact of Federal Aid on State and Local Governments* (Morristown, N.J.: General Learning Press, 1974) is a useful brief survey. For more comprehensive study of revenue sharing, see Paul R. Dommel, *The Politics of Revenue Sharing* (Bloomington: Indiana University Press, 1974); Richard L. Cole and David A. Caputo, *Urban Politics and Decentralization: The Case of General Revenue Sharing* (Lexington, Mass.: Lexington Books, 1974); and Richard P. Nathan et al., *Monitoring Revenue Sharing* (Washington, D.C.: Brookings Institution, 1975).

Intergovernmental relations in general are surveyed in a massive study by W. Brooke Graves, *American Intergovernmental Relations: Their Origins, Historical Development, and Current Status* (New York: Scribner, 1964). See also, for analysis of such experiments as the Tennessee Valley Authority and the Delaware River Basin Commission, Martha Derthick, *Between State and Nation: Regional Organizations of the United States* (Washington, D.C.: Brookings Institution, 1974). And see also the annual reports since 1960 of the U.S. Advisory Commission on Intergovernmental Relations and its quarterly journal, *Intergovernmental Perspective.*

The Council of State Governments publishes a comprehensive manual every 2 years, *The Book of the States* (Lexington, Ken.: The Council), and supplements in alternate years, as well as the monthly *State Government News* and the quarterly *State Government.*

Finally, the quarterly academic journal *Publius* often publishes interesting analyses of aspects of federalism in America and elsewhere.

WHO CARES ABOUT POLITICS?

☐ Perspective 2: The politics of the 1976 presidential election

Over 80 million Americans – 54 percent of those eligible – went to their local polling places on November 2, 1976, to elect someone to be president of the United States for the next 4 years. Or so they thought. Almost all of them thought that they were voting for Gerald Ford, Jimmy Carter, Eugene McCarthy, or one of the less well known candidates. And almost all of them thought, when they heard the vote totals from Walter Cronkite, John Chancellor, or Harry Reasoner on their television sets late that night, that they had collectively elected Jimmy Carter president.

In fact, however, none of these beliefs was true. The real presidential election occurred not on November 2, but on December 13. The votes that were cast by 81,551,659 Americans on November 2 were not for Carter or Ford, but rather for slates of presidential electors whose names often were not on the ballots. The electors were "pledged" to vote for Carter or Ford (or another designated candidate) when the electoral college met on December 13 to elect our president. The votes they cast would be counted on January 6, 1977 – at which time a new president would be declared elected.

All this may seem like unimportant legal technicalities. After all Carter won 40,828,587 votes, some 50.1 percent of those cast on November 2, while Ford won 39,147,613 votes, or 48.0 percent. And Carter, having won a majority of the votes of the people, did immediately begin organizing the new administration, which did indeed eventually take office January 20, 1977.

☐ WHY THE ELECTORAL COLLEGE MATTERS

Before we decide to dismiss the electoral college as insignificant, and look only at the popular vote cast on election day, we should note that instances have arisen in which a candidate got more popular votes than his opponent, but not enough electoral votes to become president. In the 1976 election, Carter had a popular vote plurality (margin) of 1,680,974 votes over Ford, and an electoral vote margin of 297 to 241, as Figure P2.1 shows. Even so, the election was so close that a shift of only about 5000 votes in Ohio and Hawaii would have given Ford the majority of electoral votes and a new term as president. Carter, with some 1,675,000 more votes than Ford, would not have become president.

Furthermore, nothing guarantees that all the electors chosen in November will vote as they are pledged in December. In 1976, only one elector bolted, voting for Ronald Reagan instead of Ford. But if only twenty-nine Democratic electors had for some reason bolted from Carter to Ford, Ford would again have been president.

So the electoral college is important in its potential impact on the outcome of an election after the people vote. But because it can be important afterward, it is also important before the election. It influences the strategies employed by the major parties. This happens because in effect some votes – in large closely contested states – are more important to the outcome than others. This is so even though we usually think that in our system of "one person, one vote," all votes are equal. To understand how the electoral college influences elections today, let us consider how it came to exist at all and how it has been changed through the years.

FIGURE P2.1

The electoral vote, 1960–1976.

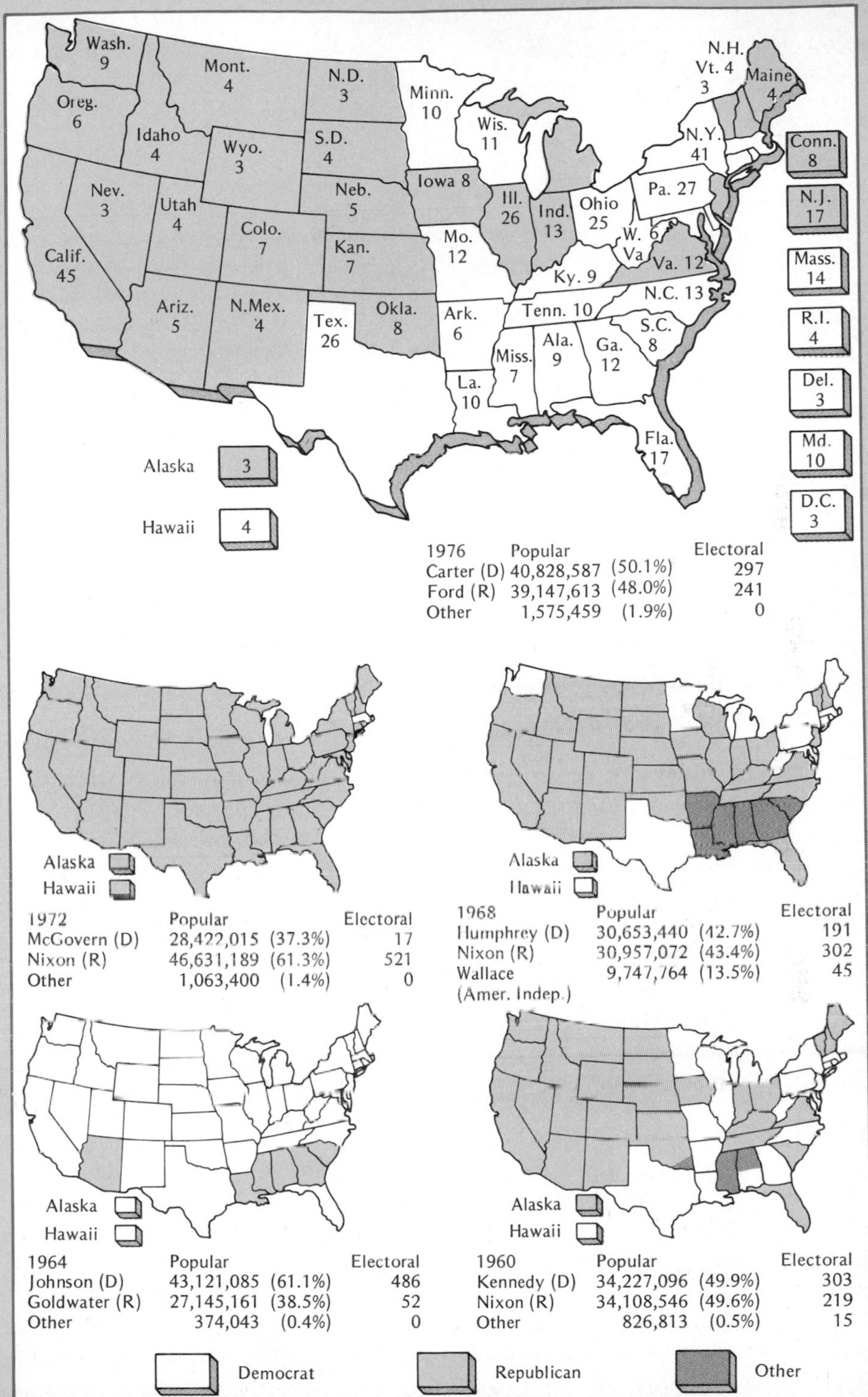

Wash. 9
Oreg. 6
Mont. 4
N.D. 3
Minn. 10
Idaho 4
Wyo. 3
S.D. 4
Wis. 11
Nev. 3
Utah 4
Neb. 5
Iowa 8
Ill. 26
Ind. 13
Ohio 25
Pa. 27
N.Y. 41
N.H. 4
Vt. 3
Maine 4
Calif. 45
Colo. 7
Kan. 7
Mo. 12
W. Va 6
Va. 12
Ky. 9
Ariz. 5
N.Mex. 4
Tex. 26
Okla. 8
Ark. 6
Tenn. 10
N.C. 13
S.C. 8
Miss. 7
Ala. 9
Ga. 12
La. 10
Fla. 17
Conn. 8
N.J. 17
Mass. 14
R.I. 4
Del. 3
Md. 10
D.C. 3
Alaska 3
Hawaii 4
1976 Popular Electoral
Carter (D) 40,828,587 (50.1%) 297
Ford (R) 39,147,613 (48.0%) 241
Other 1,575,459 (1.9%) 0
Alaska
Hawaii
1972 Popular Electoral
McGovern (D) 28,422,015 (37.3%) 17
Nixon (R) 46,631,189 (61.3%) 521
Other 1,063,400 (1.4%) 0
Alaska
Hawaii
1968 Popular Electoral
Humphrey (D) 30,653,440 (42.7%) 191
Nixon (R) 30,957,072 (43.4%) 302
Wallace (Amer. Indep.) 9,747,764 (13.5%) 45
Alaska
Hawaii
1964 Popular Electoral
Johnson (D) 43,121,085 (61.1%) 486
Goldwater (R) 27,145,161 (38.5%) 52
Other 374,043 (0.4%) 0
Alaska
Hawaii
1960 Popular Electoral
Kennedy (D) 34,227,096 (49.9%) 303
Nixon (R) 34,108,546 (49.6%) 219
Other 826,813 (0.5%) 15
Democrat
Republican
Other

Wide World Photos

The Massachusetts electoral college voting to give its fourteen electoral votes to Jimmy Carter on December 13, 1976.

The Founding Fathers did not trust the people to elect their own president. They provided instead that each state would choose distinguished representatives (as many as it had members of Congress) who would gather as the electoral college to elect the best man as president and the runner-up as vice-president. At that time, there still were no political parties as we know them today, and so there was reason to hope that the choice would indeed be a free choice of the best two candidates. Thus was George Washington chosen our first president, in what we call a nonpartisan (nonparty) election. But by 1800, parties had emerged, as we'll see in Chapter 4, and narrowed the field of candidates. As a result, electors in fact increasingly represented parties rather than the states in which they were chosen.

In 1800 there was a tie in the electoral college, between Thomas Jefferson and Aaron Burr. The election had to be decided, as the Constitution provides in such cases, in the House of Representatives, where each state's delegation is allowed only one vote, regardless of how many representatives it has. Jefferson finally won. In 1824, the House, in a similar situation, elected John Quincy Adams president, even though Andrew Jackson had outpolled him. The controversy this caused abated somewhat when, in the next election, Jackson won a landslide victory. But electoral trouble arose once more in 1876 and again in 1888, when presidents who had not won the popular vote were elected by the electoral college. (The situation in 1876 was very complex; the election was eventually decided during February 1877 by an Electoral Commission set up by Congress.)

To this day, every time there is a close election, such as that of 1976, there is fear that a candidate will win the electoral vote but not the popular vote. That fear is compounded by the fact that in most states electors are not legally bound to vote for the candidate they are pledged to. In others, they face little or no legal penalty for bolting.

■ The politics of the electoral college

Why then, if the electoral college creates such fears in so many minds, do we not abolish it in favor of simple popular election? The answer reveals much about political power and strategy in America.

In almost every session of Congress an effort is made to abolish the electoral college by constitutional amendment. President Carter, following his close victory, himself proposed such a change only 2 months after his inauguration. Thus far, all efforts have failed, primarily because many believe that the electoral college specially favors two different interest groups. One is the *small states* like Alaska. Such states get "extra representation" in the electoral college because each state gets two electors for its two senators, regardless of its size. This is in addition to the number of electors the state gets to match its House membership (a number determined by the size of its population). But the more important special interest that many believe is favored by the electoral college is *big urban states* that have the most electoral votes. In these states, the "swing vote" is usually concentrated in the major cities, which therefore get extra attention – and promises – from the candidates. So the small rural states and the large urban states tend, in effect, to unite against the middle to preserve the electoral college.

Whether or not this is an accurate picture of the effects of the electoral college is still being debated by the experts. One complex recent study of the effects in the 1960s and 1970s concluded "that the electoral college has countervailing biases, which result in a net advantage to large states, and a disadvantage to states with 4 to 14 electoral votes. The electoral college also favors inhabitants of the Far West and East, as well as central city and urban citizen-voters. In contrast, it discriminates against inhabitants of the Midwest, South, and Mountain states, as well as blacks and rural residents."[1]

What, then, would be the alternative? Some suggest a simple popular vote election, in which all votes count equally, wherever they are cast. In that case, candidates would probably incline to use even more national television and therefore reduce personal appearances, even in the areas of heavy voter concentration where most such efforts are now focused. "Direct popular election," as this proposal is called, would be much more democratic than our present system, in which all of a state's electoral votes go to the winner, even if he or she receives only one more popular vote than the loser. This means that everyone who votes for the loser in a given state gets no representation in the electoral college, for the whole slate of state electors is supposed to vote unanimously for the person who won the state vote.

The normal effect of this provision is to widen the margin of the winner in the electoral college in comparison to the popular vote margin. Some supporters of the electoral college say this helps lessen the likelihood of a disruptive transition of power in a close election. Others discount this argument, pointing out that few citizens pay any attention to electoral vote totals anyway.[2]

[1]John H. Yunker and Lawrence D. Longley, *The Electoral College: Its Biases Newly Measured for the 1960s and 1970s.* (Beverly Hills, Calif.: Sage, 1976), p. 44.

[2]For a sample of the large literature discussing the electoral college and its effects, see Harvey Zeidenstein, *Direct Election of the President* (Lexington, Mass.: Lexington Books, 1973), and Paul M. Perkins, "What's Good About the Electoral College," *Washington Monthly,* April 1977, pages 40–41.

■ How the electoral college works

Just who are these electors who have again become the focus of such controversy, and what do they actually do? Traditionally, they have been party workers, whose reward for their labors was the honor of being an elector. But recently efforts have been made, especially in the Democratic party, to democratize selection of electors and make them more representative of the state's population, or at least of its party supporters. Thus, for example, the Texas Democratic electors in 1976 were selected in the state convention that also selected delegates to the Democratic National Convention that nominated Carter. They included a man who ran a small-town drive-in grocery, a black woman attorney who taught government at a small black college, a retired auto dealer, a woman who taught high school government, a retired plumber, and an 18-year-old college freshman. Other states had similar contingents.

All the electors gather at the fifty state capitols on the first Monday after the second Wednesday in December of each election year. There they cast their votes, sign the official rolls, and send the certified votes on to the president of the Senate in Washington. He or she then opens these votes in a

Members of Congress applaud following certification of election of Jimmy Carter at a joint session of Congress on January 6, 1977, at which votes of state electoral colleges were tallied.

Wide World Photos

joint session of Congress on January 6 and declares a president elected. This happens just 14 days before the new president is to be inaugurated.

So it was in January 1977, as it had been, with occasional slight modifications, throughout American history. But we still think of the popular election as the real election, and so when we study politics we generally concentrate on the November election.

☐ THE 1976 CAMPAIGN AND THE ELECTION

In 1976 Jimmy Carter, a retired governor of Georgia, came from nowhere to defeat a dozen rivals for the Democratic nomination. He built a massive 33-point lead in the public opinion polls while the Republican Party was still trying to decide who to nominate: the incumbent (a term we apply to one already holding the office) Gerald Ford or the insurgent Ronald Reagan, a retired governor of California and before that a movie star. Once Ford was nominated and the campaign began, Carter's lead in the polls naturally began to shrink as the Republicans united. By election day, most polls showed the rivals neck-and-neck.

Carter's victory in the popular vote on November 2 was not especially close as elections go. He won by more votes than any recent Democratic victor other than Lyndon Johnson.

Jimmy Carter and Walter Mondale before the 1976 Democratic National Convention following Carter's acceptance speech.
Stan Wakefield

TABLE P2.1

How to become president of the United States

1. *Preliminaries*
   a. Make sure you're eligible: at least 35, having lived within the U.S. for 14 years, and a natural-born American citizen.
   b. Decide to run.
   c. Decide which party's nomination you will seek—or whether you will found your own.
   d. Formulate a general campaign strategy.
   e. Register as a candidate with the Federal Election Commission.
   f. Begin your campaign a year or even two before election.
   g. Announce your candidacy.
   h. Make yourself known to party leaders around the country.

2. *Organizing your campaign*
   a. Develop a fund-raising program.
   b. Apply for "federal matching funds" from taxpayers' contributions.
   c. Organize a staff to prepare campaign literature, do research, write speeches, do your campaign scheduling, and handle your relations with the media.
   d. Establish a headquarters.
   e. Develop separate strategies for states that select convention delegates by primaries and states that select them by local, district, and state conventions.
      (1) *For the states with primaries* which you choose to contest (some 30 in 1976, scheduled from February through June):
         (a) Get your name, or a slate of delegates pledged to you, on the ballot by registering with each state's chief election official and submitting petitions signed by supporters, or, in some states, by being a "nationally recognized candidate."
         (b) Campaign in each state until the primary date. Schedule visits in accordance with the importance of the state to you and your likely strength there. Remember that victories in the early primaries will give a psychological boost to your candidacy. Note that some primaries will be to select delegates who may or may not have presidential preferences to the national convention, some will be to instruct delegates about voters' presidential preferences ("advisory presidential-preference primaries"), some will be "winner-take-all-the-delegates" primaries, and some will be "proportional-representation" primaries in which delegates are apportioned to the candidates by the vote percentages.

(2) *For the states with conventions* which you choose to contest (some 20 in 1976, conventions scheduled from January through July):
   (a) Organize supporters by local areas such as voting precincts or townships so they will attend conventions and vote for you or your delegates.
   (b) Campaign in each state, seeking to reach individuals who will attend local conventions.
   (c) Once local conventions select delegates to county or congressional-district conventions, campaign among the delegates personally.
   (d) At the district conventions, get as many delegates to the state convention pledged to you as possible.
   (e) At the state convention, do the same for delegates to the national party convention and get your supporters chosen for state party offices so they will choose, as whatever additional delegates remain to be chosen, people favorable to your candidacy. This will make sure the state party organization works hard for your election once you win the nomination.

3. *The national convention*
   a. Continue your general campaigning nationally.
   b. But concentrate your efforts on wooing uncommitted delegates individually.
   c. Aim to capture more than half of the delegates (the total needed for nomination).
      (1) "Challenge the credentials" of delegates supporting your opponent, on grounds they were wrongly selected and should be replaced by your people.
      (2) Bargain with other weaker candidates, especially over who your vice-presidential selection will be for "running mate" (you might want to offer it to an opponent whose delegates would put you over the top if added to yours).
      (3) In the weeks before the convention, see that your supporters play major roles drafting the party "platform" of pledges on which you will run. Then try to gain delegate strength by agreeing to compromise "planks" in the platform you will be running on.
   d. Have yourself nominated, and your nomination seconded, by various prominent people representing different segments of the party and the population.
   e. When you win, urge your chief opponent to move that your nomination be made unanimous to begin the effort to unify the party behind your candidacy.
   f. Make your choice for vice-president, if you haven't already had to make it to get needed delegate votes, and announce it.
   g. On the last night of the convention, let your running mate make a brief speech, and then make your acceptance speech setting forth the themes of your coming campaign.

4. *The general election campaign*
   a. Plan your final strategy with your best advisors.
   b. Decide whether you want to raise your own funds or accept Federal funds from taxpayers (you can't have both).
   c. Expand your staff to include previous supporters of your opponents to further unify the party.
   d. Get the backing of major interest groups sympathetic to you.
   e. On Labor Day, launch your campaign formally at a big rally in an important city.
   f. Challenge your opponent to debates if you need the publicity and/or believe you will benefit from them.
   g. Concentrate your efforts on the key states critical to your getting a majority of the electoral college—270 of the 538 electoral votes.
   h. Organize special drives to get out the sympathetic voters on election day, again emphasizing the key states.
   i. Don't stop running till the Tuesday immediately after the first Monday in November: Election Day.
   j. Watch the votes come in and the computerized projections by television networks with the rest of us.
   k. Accept your victory, once your opponent concedes, in a spirit of unifying the country behind you.

5. *After the election*
   a. Pick your own White House staff, cabinet officers, and other key officials.
   b. With them begin to develop the programs you will be proposing as well as the changes you will be suggesting to Congress regarding the budget the incumbent has prepared to go into effect the next fall.
   c. Note that the electors meet in their state capitols in mid-December and send their votes to the president of the Senate (who is also the departing vice-president) in Washington—and hope and pray that the electors "pledged" to you actually vote for you.
   d. Note then that the members of the Senate and the House meet in special session in the House chamber at 1 P.M., January 6, to count the electoral votes and declare you elected president.
   e. Attend your own swearing-in ceremony at the Capitol on January 20 around noon, at which you take the oath and deliver your inaugural address.
   f. Begin being president.

Note: These guidelines have been derived from the efforts and successes of recent presidential candidates. Obviously no one could actively follow all of them. Nonetheless, to be successful, a candidate would have to follow most of them as best his or her circumstances allow. For more detail, see the suggestions for further reading at the end of Chapters 3 and 6.

But the 1976 election raised a number of important questions in the minds of analysts and scholars who continue to try to understand the electoral process and the things that determine voting behavior. Carter was the first outsider to win the presidency since Calvin Coolidge, who served from 1923 to 1929. Every one of the eight presidents sincc Coolidge had served in the federal bureaucracy or in the Congress before taking office, and five of them had been vice-president. People wondered how Carter had managed to succeed where all other outsiders in recent decades had failed, first in getting the nomination, and then in defeating an incumbent president. This electoral success was striking because only eight incumbents had been beaten in presidential elections in America's 200 years.

Another question concerned the way in which Ford had cut Carter's early lead so effectively during the campaign but still lost the election despite the momentum that then favored him.

Experts never seem to agree fully on the answers to such questions about American politics. But efforts to answer these questions have uncovered some very important tendencies and trends in American politics that will probably influence future elections. Foremost among these are four factors: (1) the impact of new campaign finance provisions; (2) the growing role of the mass media; (3) the changing strength of the major parties' hold on the population; and (4) the spread of feelings of powerlessness and alienation in the minds of large segments of the American population. These four factors will be important parts of our study of popular participation in politics in the coming three chapters. But before we study participation more generally, let us see what we can learn from a closer look at possible answers to these questions about Jimmy Carter's successful presidential campaign and Ford's failure in the 1976 election.

□ CAMPAIGN FINANCE AND THE ELECTION

Money is often referred to as "the mother's milk of politics." Traditionally, candidates have depended primarily on large contributions from wealthy individuals who sought favors in return for their contributions. They may have sought special legislation or a favorable ruling by a government agency on a commercial venture they were undertaking or even an ambassadorship to a foreign country.

The cost of presidential elections has skyrocketed in recent decades. In 1956, for example, the two candidates together spent over $13 million but in 1960 Richard Nixon alone spent over $10 million in losing, while John Kennedy spent almost as much in winning. In 1966, Nixon spent over $25 million to beat Humphrey's $11 million. And in 1972 Nixon used $61 million against McGovern's $30 million.

■ Campaign finance reform

The 1972 election prompted the Watergate break-in and was the occasion of corrupt activities by Nixon's Committee to Re-Elect the President. As a result, the new Federal Election Campaign Act of 1971, which became effective part way through the campaign, was strengthened by amendment. Among the provisions that finally governed the 1976 election were these:

- □ *public disclosure* of contributions during and after the campaign so the voters could know who was supporting whom
- □ *limits on expenditures* to help equalize the resources available to both major parties—especially important to Democrats, who are almost always outspent by Republicans
- □ *restrictions on contributions,* including a limit of $1,000 from any one individual to a candidate
- □ an offer of *government funding* or subsidization of presidential campaigns from funds contributed in recent years by citizens filing their income tax returns

Both 1976 major party candidates chose to accept the $21.8 million federal subsidy for the presidential contest, and thereby to spend no more than that sum. In addition, they and their opponents had accepted federal matching funds to complement money they raised during their party primaries.

Some of the effects of the acceptance of Federal funding and the spending ceilings it required were obvious to everyone who followed the campaign. Buttons and bumper stickers were too expensive and were much less common. Further, because it reached more people cheaply, there was more use of television advertising.

But the most important effects were less visible. First, experts generally agree that the federal matching funds in the primaries aided Carter. They made it possible for him to expand from his strong base in Georgia (Georgians contributed $1.5 million of the $7.9 million he raised) to win the nomination. In the same way, these funds enabled Reagan to come so close to defeating Ford.

Second, the limit on contributions from individuals and special interest groups curtailed their abilities to "buy a piece" of the candidates. As a result, the Carter administration had come to power much less beholden to anyone than had previous victors.

Third – and most conclusive – the spending limit prevented a last-minute media deluge like that for Nixon in 1968 and 1972. Such a deluge might well have produced victory for Ford. Instead, the limits on funds put a premium on volunteer campaign workers. This area, unlimited by the new law, is the one in which organized labor – the unions – has always been most active, and labor has usually supported the Democratic ticket. In the 1976 campaign, organized labor distributed more than 80 million pieces of literature, made more than 10 million phone calls to voters, and furnished 120,000 volunteers to get out the vote and run car pools to the polls. The payoff, many experts believe, was the Carter victory – attributable in many minds to the combination of effects of the new campaign finance laws.[3]

[3] America's leading expert on campaign finance is Herbert E. Alexander, director of the Citizens' Research Foundation, which has studied campaign finance figures and practices for more than a decade. The best introduction to the subject is his book, *Financing Politics: Money, Elections and Political Reform* (Washington: Congressional Quarterly Press, 1976). On the 1976 campaign, see A. H. Raskin, "The Labor Scene: COPE's Impact on Election Outcome," *New York Times*, December 20, 1976, pp. D1, D7, and Warren Weaver, Jr., "Experts Say New Campaign Law Had Major Impact on '76 Election," *New York Times*, November 12, 1976.

□ THE MASS MEDIA AND THE ELECTION

All told, the national Carter campaign itself spent some $37 million, $21.8 million of that in the general election. Almost $10.5 million was spent on media advertising, predominantly television. Ford's television budget alone was $12 million out of his $21.8 million. Abraham Lincoln's entire campaign in 1860 cost but $100,000. A century later, that sum would buy only a half hour of television time.

No one really knows what impact this transformation of campaigning into media "events" and media advertising has had on voters. But everybody agrees that the media are the most important part of presidential campaigning today. And indeed, immediately after the election, Carter attributed his triumph to the three telecast debates he had with President Ford.

Televised debate between candidate Jimmy Carter and President Gerald Ford.
Wide World Photos

Nonetheless, the media also caused problems for both candidates. Television was always there to capture their occasional mistakes. Journalists were constantly writing critically of both candidates' positions – or lack of positions – on the issues. Many thought the press went overboard in its criticism of the candidates' statements on the issues, and some thought that may have increased citizen disenchantment. We shall examine the mass media in more detail in Chapter 12.

□ CHANGING PARTY IDENTIFICATION

When the election results across the country were finally in, they spelled out a major defeat for the Republican party. Many observers thought the party was closer to extinction than at any previous time in its 122-year history.

The GOP (initials which stand for "Grand Old Party") had not only lost the presidency. Its position in the Senate remained constant (only 38 of 100 seats), and in the House slipped by one (to only 143 of 435 seats). And its control of governorships in the nation dropped by one to 12 – virtually all of them small and politically weak states. In addition, the party suffered serious setbacks at the local level in most parts of the country.

This great electoral failure was matched by – and is perhaps attributable to – a decline in the number of Americans willing to call themselves Republicans. That number had been dropping from year to year, and by 1976 only about one in five persons were registered Republicans.

It is also true that the percentage of people calling themselves Democrats has been declining. But there continue to be almost twice as many Democrats as Republicans. The growth is in those calling themselves Independents – a trend toward what observers call "nonpartisanship."

But the 1976 election seemed to suggest that, at least in terms of presidential preference, many of the traditional supporters of the Democratic Party had come back in the fold, at least temporarily. Surveys by CBS News of voters leaving the polls across the country showed that Carter carried the union vote 62–38 percent, the Catholic vote 55–45 percent, the Jewish vote 68–32 percent, and the black vote, 83–17 percent. These are among the elements of the Democratic victories of the past.

Nonetheless, voting expert Gerald Pomper concluded:

> The Carter coalition, demographically, is a unique alliance. . . . Included are some voters from past Democratic groups and some returning defectors, but also some previous opponents of the party. . . . Southern support for Carter may seem like a return to the region's historical loyalty to the Democratic party. But the past record of the region was built on the votes of whites alone, who supported the one-party system in order to maintain segregation. The vote for Carter, to the contrary, was a biracial vote for a candidate particularly dependent on blacks and with an integrationist record. His regional victory was not a return to the past, but rather the most dramatic evidence of a transformation of southern politics.[4]

In another sense, Carter's victory was fashioned out of a further transformation. Carter got the votes of 27 percent of the people who said they had voted for Nixon in 1972 (including two-thirds of the Democrats who had done so[5]). Ford got the votes of only 17 percent of those who had voted for McGovern. So while the election indicated that the Republican party is in deep trouble, it suggested that the long-term trend away from party identification – as experts call people's saying they belong to (or "identify with") one party or another – may have been somewhat reversed, at least temporarily, by the Democratic party at all levels of government.

---

[4]Gerald Pomper, "The Presidential Election," in *The Election of 1976: Reports and Interpretations*, ed. Pomper et al., (New York: McKay, 1977), p. 64. See also Everett Carll Ladd and Charles Hadley, *Transformations of the American Party System*, 2nd ed. (New York: Norton, 1968).

[5]*Gallup Opinion Index* no. 137, December 1976.

☐ CITIZEN FEELINGS AND VOTING

The turnout on November 2 was the lowest, in percentage terms, since 1948 – even though more people voted than ever before. The 81,552,000 voters were up from 77,700,000 in 1972. But the percentage of those eligible to vote who actually went to the polls declined for the seventh straight election, this time from 55.4 percent in 1972 to 54.4 percent in 1976. Studies have shown that 7 million people who had voted in the 1968 contest between Nixon and Humphrey decided not to vote in 1972; another 8 million who voted in 1972 declined to vote in 1976. That makes 15 million former voters who have decided to stop voting over 8 years (see Figure P2.2).

FIGURE P2.2
Transformation of the electorate, 1968–1976.

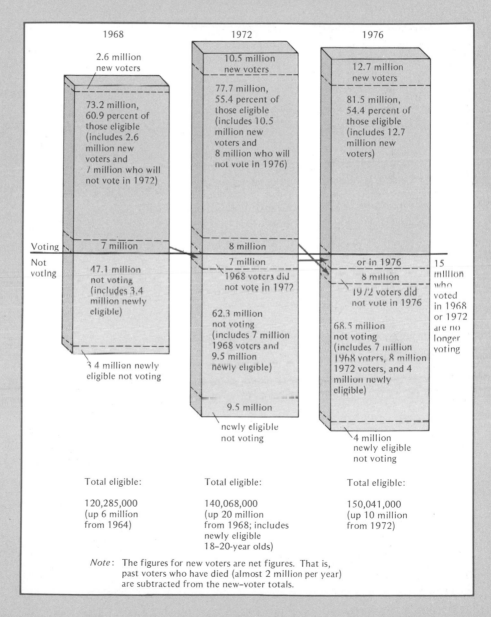

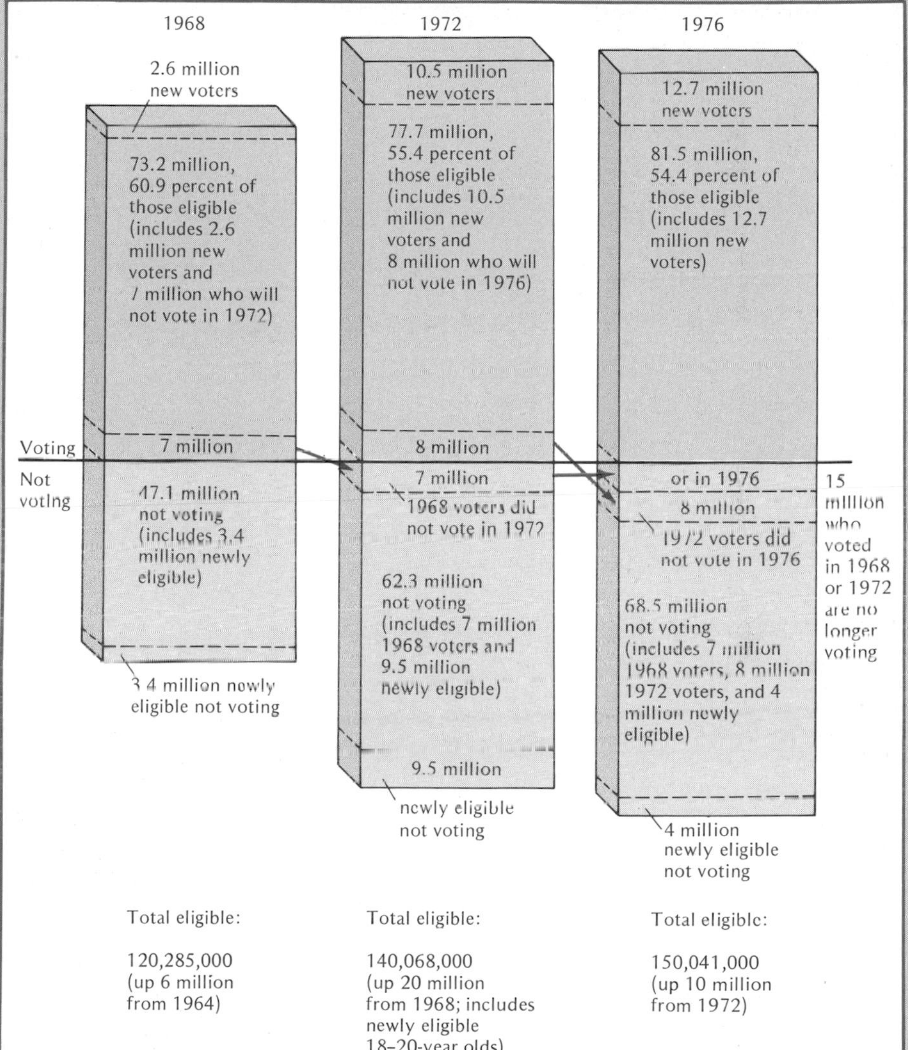

Note: The figures for new voters are net figures. That is, past voters who have died (almost 2 million per year) are subtracted from the new-voter totals.

Michael Abramson/Black Star

Jimmy Carter professing the presidential oath of office before Chief Justice Warren Burger.

Some of this decline might be explained by cynicism aroused by the behavior in office of the man they elected twice, Richard Nixon. But there are three competing general explanations for the continuing decline in voting. One is *apathy.* The term apathy is often used casually by commentators to cover all cases of nonparticipation. However, it should properly be confined to those who truly *do not care* about the election and its outcome, perhaps because they believe it will make no difference to them.

A second offered explanation is *popular disillusionment* with politics in general and with the federal government in particular. People who had high expectations of politics and presidents in the Kennedy and Johnson years may have learned from experience that even good men have great difficulty getting the federal government to solve such problems as poverty, crime, and racial conflicts.

Studies of voters and nonvoters in 1976 suggest, however, that the disillusionment explanation is not accurate. It is true that in a survey conducted by CBS News and *The New York Times,* 55 percent of nonvoters agreed with the statement that "the people running the country don't really care what happens to people like me." But 55 percent of those who *did* vote also agreed with that statement. So voters and nonvoters alike seem equally disillusioned with politics.

There are differences between voters and nonvoters, however, in their feelings of *powerlessness.* Nonvoters are much more likely to say that one person's vote makes no difference. Furthermore, in answer to the question "If people don't like any of the candidates running for an office, should they vote for the one who is the 'lesser evil' or not vote at all?" Voters said "the lesser evil" by 75 to 21 percent, while nonvoters said "not vote" by 50 to 45 percent. This inclination not to vote for "the lesser evil" was especially common among citizens under 30 – a group that now constitutes 31 percent of the electorate. Studies have found that 49 percent of those eligible to vote but not even registered are under 30 years of age. In 1976, about two-thirds of those between 18 and 20, and over half of those 21 to 30, did not vote. Thus much of the nonvoting is by those under 30, great percentages of whom feel more powerless than the older segments of the population.

Yet another indication of the sense of powerlessness in electoral politics felt by nonvoters is their response to the assertion that "the country needs more radical change than is possible through the ballot box." Those who voted in 1976 *disagreed* with that statement by 52 to 41 percent. Those who did not vote *agreed* by 58 to 33 percent.[6]

The ballot box, we must remember, is not the only instrument of political activity. Politics goes on between elections, not only for those elected and appointed to office, but also for those citizens concerned enough to attempt to influence the decisions and actions of officials. And so in Chapters 3, 4, and 5 we shall examine the broad range of these opportunities and efforts, first in elections, then in political parties, and finally in other types of political activity.

---

[6]See Robert Reinhold, "Poll Links Sense of Powerlessness, Not Disillusionment, to Low Vote," *New York Times,* November 16, 1976, pp. 1, 33.

3

Voters and nonvoters

In the presidential election on November 2, 1976, 81 million Americans voted – more people than had ever voted in any election in American history. And yet, this turnout was only 54.4 percent of the people eligible to vote. A low turnout, in percentage terms, was nothing new. The percentage of eligible people actually voting has been dropping rather steadily in recent elections. This was the fifth straight decline, and it reached a level lower than any year since 1948, as Table 3.1 reveals. What was new was the growing percentage of citizens – voters and nonvoters – expressing feelings of disillusionment and powerlessness.

Are these feelings the major factors shaping citizens' decisions about whether to vote and how to vote? Or are other factors more important? To answer these questions, we must begin by considering both obstacles to voting and incentives for voting. To do so, we shall focus on presidential elections, which have the highest turnouts of all types of elections in America.

TABLE 3.1

Voters and nonvoters in presidential elections, 1920–1976

Year	Percent voting for: Democratic candidate	Republican candidate	Other candidates	Percent not voting[a]	Eligible voters (in millions)
1920	15.1	26.6	2.5	55.8	61.6
1924	12.0	24.0	8.0	55.6	65.6
1928	21.3	30.4	0.5	47.7	70.4
1932	30.4	21.0	1.6	47.1	75.0
1936	35.0	21.0	1.5	42.5	79.4
1940	32.7	26.7	0.3	40.4	83.5
1944	28.6	24.6	0.4	46.4	89.5
1948	25.6	23.3	2.8	48.4	94.5
1952	27.6	34.3	0.3	37.8	99.0
1956	25.1	34.4	0.4	40.1	103.6
1960	31.7	31.6	0.2	36.5	108.0
1964	37.9	23.9	0.3	38.0	113.9
1968	26.1	26.5	8.5	39.0	120.0
1972	20.9	33.8	1.0	44.3	139.6
1976	26.7	24.9	1.7	45.6	150.0

[a]Voters and nonvoters do not always total to 100 percent due to rounding.

Source: Adapted from Paul R. Abramson, *Generational Change in American Politics* (Lexington, Mass.: Lexington Books, 1975), p. 5, and updated to include 1976 election data from Census Bureau.

Voter registration, New York City.

Jim Cron/Monkmeyer

☐ WHY SOME PEOPLE DO NOT VOTE

The number of people eligible to vote has been expanding regularly for four main reasons. First, the population has continued to grow. Second, recent civil rights laws have allowed blacks to vote more extensively in the South. Third, the rules and regulations surrounding registration to become eligible to vote have been simplified and reduced in most parts of the country. And fourth, those 18 through 20 years old have recently been given the right to vote.

■ Registration requirements as obstacles to voting

To vote, one still must register first in every state but North Dakota, which has no system of registration. In the past, one could only register at an official building, and there only during normal working hours. In recent years, however, more and more states and cities have developed mobile registrars who open booths in schools, shopping centers, and neighborhoods as elections near. Some states (fourteen in 1976) now allow registration by postcard. Nonetheless, the very fact that one must register to vote – often well in advance of an election, before one is interested – is cited by experts as one reason for the generally low turnout in American elections. This belief leads some to question the necessity of registration.

Why is registration required? There is disagreement over the reasons for requiring registration. Some argue that it was established primarily to control fraud. The system does keep people from voting several times in the same contest. It also helps prevent people from voting in the name of people who are dead or have moved away. Registration requirements, along with the requirement that one be a citizen to be eligible to vote, were introduced toward the end of the nineteenth century. Because of this, some believe their original purpose was to protect business interests against political controls that might be imposed if the emerging industrial working class were to vote in large numbers. Many also feared the new immigrant citizens would simply "vote as they were told" by big city political bosses.[1]

Alternatives to registration Whatever the reasons for their imposition, registration regulations persist to this day and seriously limit the extent of participation, particularly among the poor and less educated. Some have proposed a national registration system, conducted by the federal government, as a way of standardizing procedures and overcoming present discriminatory provisions. One such plan, proposed by Jimmy Carter shortly after he took office, calls for registration on election day, perhaps right at the polling place. Such proposals remain controversial, not least because the Constitution reserves the right to determine voting eligibility to individual states rather than the federal government.[2]

The debate over these proposals continues. On one side are people who fear that the vote will become meaningless if it is made too easy. Some also say that fraud will increase and that a new bureaucracy will be needed to supervise the new process.

Many on the other side favoring greater effort to enroll more voters believe such reforms essential. In the 1976 election, the Census Bureau interviewed voters and nonvoters nationally, and analysis of the results suggested that election-day registration could increase the turnout by perhaps 10 percent. In that election both Minnesota and Wisconsin used the system and got turnouts of 72 and 66 percent, respectively, without evidence of fraud.[3] These findings strengthened the claims of supporters, many of whom agree with former attorney general Ramsey Clark's assessment:

> Those that wield political power today don't want to share it. They don't understand the frustrations of being utterly powerless in America. Politics is a source of power. And if we revitalize democracy in this country and share power with the people, create new constituencies for our representatives, . . . we'll see America flourish. We'll see our people included in this system. We'll see a commitment to the rule of law because they participate in its making.[4]

---

[1]See Walter Dean Burnham, *Critical Elections and the Mainsprings of American Politics* (New York: Norton, 1970), pp. 79–81.

[2]For a comprehensive survey and hostile analysis of proposals for registration reform, see Kevin P. Phillips and Paul H. Blackman, *Electoral Reform and Voter Participation* (Washington, D.C.: American Enterprise Institute, 1975). But see also, for a more favorable view, William J. Crotty, *Political Reform and the American Experiment* (New York: Crowell, 1977), chaps. 2, 3.

[3]Warren Weaver, "Voting Day Registration," *New York Times*, May 25, 1977, p. 18.

[4]Clark made this statement on a public television program called "The Advocates," November 3, 1970.

■ Legal restraints as obstacles to voting

In the past, legal restraints were an important obstacle to voting. Most of the American people were not actually "included in the system" by being allowed to vote until recently. In the early days of the Republic, all women and slaves and those men who did not own property or were not of the proper religion were not allowed to vote. That left perhaps as little as 5 or 10 percent of the adult population as voters. By the middle of the nineteenth century, the growth of democratic sentiment and the expansion of the frontier westward to incorporate new states combined to remove religious and property-owning qualifications generally. Still, many states continued to require that one pay a **poll tax** – a fee, usually several dollars – when one registered. That provisions did not disappear in some parts of the country until the courts outlawed it in 1966.

Once those not owning property were granted the **franchise** (a common term for the right to vote that derives from a French word for freedom or for frankness, and perhaps, therefore, for free expression), the former black male slaves freed as a result of the Civil War were the next intended beneficiaries. The Fifteenth Amendment (1870) affirmed that "the right of citizens of the United States to vote shall not be denied or abridged by the United States or by any State on account of race, color, or previous condition of servitude." But within a half-dozen years the North had abandoned the "freedmen," as they were called, to renewed domination by white southerners. It was not until the Civil Rights Acts of 1957, 1960, and 1964 (which we shall discuss in Chapter 14) and the Voting Rights Act of 1965 that blacks were able to register and vote in much greater numbers across the South.

In the intervening years, blacks and often poor whites as well were kept disfranchised by a series of special southern state laws and regulations. One of these was the so-called **white primary**, in which only whites could vote. Contests were usually decided in these primaries because there were no serious Republican

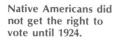

Native Americans did not get the right to vote until 1924.

"MOVE ON!"
HAS THE NATIVE AMERICAN NO RIGHTS THAT THE NATURALIZED AMERICAN IS BOUND TO RESPECT?–[SEE PAGE 363.]

opponents to Democrats then. The votes of blacks in the general election thus had little meaning. Another was the **grandfather clause**, which provided that only those who could demonstrate that their father or grandfather had voted were exempt from strict literacy tests and property requirements that limited the franchise. Special language and literacy laws, often unfairly administered, existed in many states until outlawed by the Voting Rights Act Amendments passed by Congress in 1970.

Women fared somewhat better than southern blacks in their efforts to get the vote. The campaign for women's suffrage was conducted by growing and well-organized groups called "suffragettes." (**Suffrage** is another term for voting, this one deriving from an old church term for intercessionary or petitionary prayer, suggesting that the voter acts to try to change the outcome of something.) The suffragettes lobbied, picketed, paraded, and organized strikes to demand political equality with men, until they finally won the right to vote with the ratification in 1920 of the Nineteenth Amendment. We shall examine the roles of women in politics in Chapter 15.

Native Americans (Indians) finally got the right to vote in 1924. This left young people as the remaining group of disfranchised citizens. Many thought it strange that men could be sent to war at age 18 but could not vote until they were 21 in most states. During World War II, Georgia had lowered its voting age to 18, and by the time the Vietnam War was at its peak, when the argument for the 18-year-old vote was at its strongest, Kentucky and Alaska had lowered theirs. In the 1970 elections, voters in Maine, Massachusetts, Montana, and Nebraska approved the 18-year-old vote. Sentiment grew so strong that in that same year the Congress, which had refused to pass constitutional amendments lowering the voting age for several decades, finally passed a *law* (not a Constitutional Amendment) lowering the age to 18 for *all elections*. But the Supreme Court then ruled (in *Oregon v. Mitchell*) that Congress had the power to legislate the requirement only for federal elections – those for president and Congress. So, at last, the Congress passed a constitutional amendment in March 1971 lowering the age to 18 for all elections. The required three-fourths of the state legislatures had ratified the Twenty-sixth Amendment by July 1971.

Legal restraints on the right to vote are now, therefore, largely a thing of the past for all citizens 18 or over. *Legal limits on the ease of voting* persist. Registration provisions are one type. Residency requirements that demand that someone reside in a given district for a specified period of time, supposedly to become familiar with the district and the candidates, are another. Both continue to limit the turnout in elections.[5]

■ Citizen attitudes as obstacles to voting

There is some evidence, however, that by now the major obstacles to voting are psychological rather than legal. Following the legal progress just recounted, Penn Kimball studied "the disconnected" (his term for nonparticipants) in Newark, New Jersey. "The key difference

---

[5]For a summary of "The Evolution of the Franchise," see Crotty, *Political Reform,* chap. 1.

between voters and nonvoters," Kimball noted, "seemed to be their own opinion of themselves, whether or not they felt they possessed the aptitudes for politics, whether or not they felt that the participation of one individual like themselves would make any difference."[6]

The ominous thing for the future of democratic elections in America is that more and more Americans seem to be concluding that their participation will not make a difference. Table 3.2 shows the reasons nonvoters gave for their failure to vote in the 1968, 1972, and 1976 presidential elections.

In 1976, as in previous elections, the poor, the less well educated, those under 30, and blue collar workers (those with nonprofessional, generally manual jobs) were less likely than others to vote. These are the segments of the population with the least status in contemporary America. Thus, they are the people least likely to feel effective or powerful in politics. Studies consistently reveal that nonvoters tend to feel remote from government and powerless in politics, as our account of attitudes in 1976 in Perspective 2 confirmed.

Of course, it is difficult to conclude that one's own vote matters much in any case. It is a very rare election, at any level of government, that is actually decided by a plurality (or margin) of one vote. Still, twenty-one of our presidential elections have been so close that the results would have been changed if only one in every hundred votes had shifted.[7] And even in those less close, like the 1976 presidential election, the existence of the electoral college makes it possible that a shift of several thousand votes in several states could change the outcome, as we noted earlier.

Voting is "costly" in that it takes time and effort, especially if one attempts to be a well-informed voter. Knowing this, the first question we might well ask of voters is not "whom did you vote for and why?" but rather "why did you vote?" For there are a number of reasons often given for not voting. The most obvious are

[6]Penn Kimball, *The Disconnected* (New York: Columbia University Press, 1972), p. 295. But for a somewhat different perspective, see James D. Wright, *The Dissent of the Governed* (New York: Academic Press, 1976).

[7]Neal R. Peirce, *The People's President* (New York: Simon & Schuster, 1968), pp. 317–321.

TABLE 3.2

Reasons people give for not voting

Reason	Percent citing reason 1976	1972	1968
Not registered	38	28	34
Didn't like candidates	14	10	12
No particular reason	10	13	8
Not interested in politics	10	4	7
Illness	7	11	15
Not an American citizen	4	—[a]	—[a]
New resident	4	8	10
Traveling out of town	3	5	6
Working	2	7	3
No way to get to polls	2	—[a]	—[a]
Didn't get absentee ballot	1	1	2
Miscellaneous other reasons	5	13	3

[a]Less than 1 percent

Source: Gallup Opinion Index no. 9, December 1972, and no. 137, December 1976.

"NOPE, NOT VOTING — I INSIST ON HAVING MORE OF A CHOICE"
TAKE ME, WHOEVER WINS
©1976 HERBLOCK

Copyright 1976 by Herblock in the *Washington Post*

inconvenience and "my vote won't affect the outcome." Beyond these, some argue in particular cases that there is no real, significant choice between the candidates running. This argument was capsulized in the slogan George Wallace used campaigning against Richard Nixon and Hubert Humphrey in 1968: "There's not a dime's worth of difference." The view that the candidates do not offer a real choice is often abandoned—too late—by nonvoters as they see, for example, a Richard Nixon deeply involved in Watergate in a way that would have been unthinkable of Hubert Humphrey.

Even when voters admit that there is a difference between the candidates, they offer still another argument for not voting: They assert that voting for unimpressive candidates "only encourages the bums" and contributes to the public's acceptance of elections and the dominant parties as an adequate way of seeking political change.

☐ WHY SOME PEOPLE DECIDE TO VOTE

So why *do* so many people go ahead and vote? A survey of voters in 1976 found that 53 percent voted because they viewed voting as their "civic duty." Only 10 percent thought their vote would make a difference. About 16 percent gave as their reason strong feelings for their candidate, and 17 percent cited their belief that it was "a very important election."[8]

[8]Robert Reinhold, "Poll Links Sense of Powerlessness, Not Disillusionment, to Low Vote," *New York Times*, November 16, 1976, p. 33.

Yet another factor that may encourage some people to vote is the excitement of the contest plus the opportunity in effect to gamble on the outcome and increase one's involvement by picking sides. This "sporting interest" seems important in explaining other popular activities, especially the widespread attachment to, and rooting for, sports teams. Voters are unlikely to cite it in explaining their behavior, however. Nor are they very likely to cite another possible factor: habit or tradition, which after all govern much of our everyday behavior.[9]

When we consider explaining the act of voting by reference to sporting interest or habit, we are leaving the realm of *conscious reasons* (things someone will have on his or her mind and be able to report if asked) and moving into the realm of *unconscious factors* or causes. When we try to explain why people vote as they do, we shall find ourselves resorting to both reasons and causes.

☐ WHY PEOPLE VOTE AS THEY DO

Every person is unique. Each has his or her own biography, a body and mind shaped by a unique genetic endowment at birth, and a unique set of experiences through life. Still, we have much in common with each other, especially when it comes to political life and action. For everyone's opportunities for experience in politics are shaped by the existing political system and the elections it conducts as well as the decisions it confronts.

This commonality of opportunity for political experience makes it possible for political scientists to study "the American voter" and generalize about the underlying influences on the views and behavior of each segment of the population. There are various common approaches to such voting studies.

■ Conscious reasons

The first and most common approach is simply to *ask the voter for reasons* for his or her voting. These reasons will reflect his or her beliefs about, and perceptions and images of, the parties (partisanship), the issues, and the candidates among which he or she selects.

Partisanship In the 1950s, most Americans were little interested in politics and thought about politics in rather simplistic terms. They seemed basically satisfied with the operation of the political system and generally identified themselves as members of the Democratic or the Republican party. When they voted, they tended to vote for the candidate of their party. The result was a politics that involved little struggle over issues. Americans elected Dwight D. Eisenhower, a popular retired military general, by large margins in 1952 and again in 1956, in elections that were not notable for issue conflicts. Then in 1960 they elected John Kennedy over Eisenhower's vice-president, Richard Nixon, in a very close election characterized

---

[9]For an extended examination of various reasons for and against voting, see William C. Mitchell, *Why Vote?* (Chicago: Markham, 1971).

by little attention to issues and much more concern with the images of the candidates.[10]

After the 1964 Johnson-Goldwater election, partisanship—the tendency of citizens to call themselves members of a party—declined drastically. Figure 3.1 shows a consistent decline in the percentage of people calling themselves members of either major party. There are now almost twice as many Democrats as Republicans, but there are many more independents than Democrats.

The impact of partisanship on voting also shows a long-term decrease. Fewer than half of the people who still call themselves Democrats and Republicans have always voted for their own party's presidential nominee. This percentage was once higher when party loyalty was still encouraged by candidates and felt by voters.

Traditionally, party preference has been transferred from one generation to the next. The children of Democratic parents tended to become Democrats, and to stay Democrats, and the same was true for Republicans. But in the 1960s and 1970s, a majority of new voters have pronounced themselves independents, regardless of their parents' partisanship. And thus party preference, which used to be an important influence—until the 1960s, the major influence—on presidential voting, has lost most of its impact.[11]

Issues In the 1960s, issues increasingly took over the role that party previously played in influencing voters. Studies have shown that citizens in general developed more coherent, consistent views on issues in these years of civil rights and Vietnam. They also seemed to be influenced in their voting by the issue stands taken by candidates—and, occasionally, by the parties. In general, the public has seen Democrats as better able to deal with economic issues and Republicans better equipped to deal with racial issues and foreign policy questions.[12]

---

[10]For a helpful discussion of these elections and those following through 1972, incorporating summaries of most voting studies, see Norman Nie, Sidney Verba, and John Petrocik, *The Changing American Voter* (Cambridge, Mass.: Harvard University Press, 1976).

[11]For studies of this phenomenon, see Burnham, *Critical Elections,* chap. 5; Nie et al., *The Changing American Voter;* and Gerald Pomper, *Voters' Choice* (New York: Dodd, Mead, 1975), chap. 2.

[12]See Nie et al., *The Changing American Voter,* and Pomper, *Voters' Choice,* chap. 7.

FIGURE 3.1

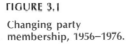

Changing party membership, 1956–1976.

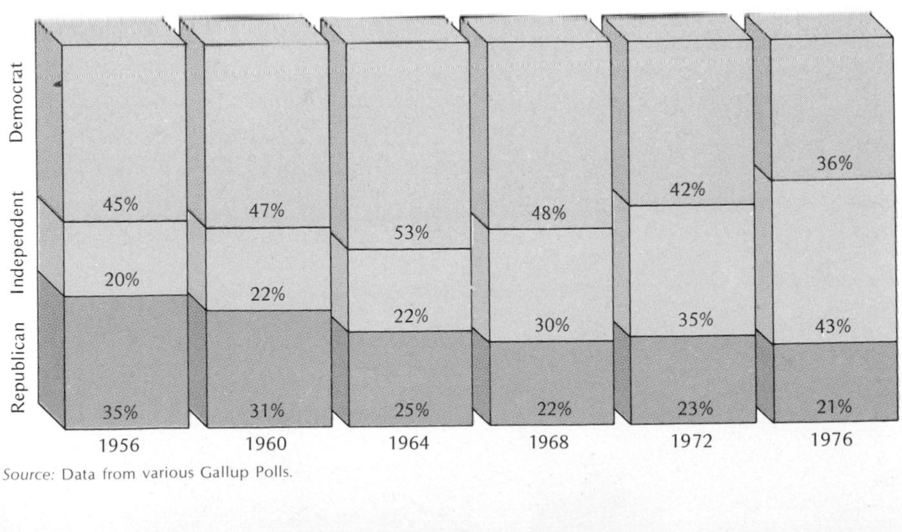

Source: Data from various Gallup Polls.

Candidate images But as the 1970s came along, voter concerns seemed once again to shift, this time away from issues toward the personal characteristics of the candidates. In the 1972 election, for example, voters were very worried about the character of George McGovern, for a variety of reasons related to his apparent indecisiveness and limited leadership qualities.[13]

In general, voters are especially interested in a candidate's perceived strength, integrity, and empathy. Jimmy Carter, in the 1976 election, sought to develop an image in voters' minds of "aggressive leadership." But one survey of voters at the polls suggested that his effort was less than fully successful. When asked why they voted for him, Carter supporters picked "He's my party's candidate" (29 percent) and "He seems more capable" (28 percent) rather than "He has strong qualities of leadership (only 16 percent). Ford voters, by contrast, chose "He seems more capable" twice as often as Carter voters and the leadership response more often too (18 percent).[14]

■ Unconscious or psychological reasons

The importance of these three sets of factors – party, issues, and images of the candidates – is uncovered in voting studies by asking the voters for the reasons for their votes. Although it is rare that a voter will say, "I don't know why I voted for Candidate X," sometimes we may find his or her answer doubtful or too superficial. We may, therefore, decide to move on to the second approach to the study of voter behavior: *looking for deeper, unconscious reasons* for the choice.[15] We might find, for example, that one unconscious reason for a person's voting decision is his or her underlying attitude toward authority – whether he or she tends to defer to strong-willed people, for instance. Alternately, a voter's long-standing experience – such as a family tradition of voting for a particular party, which he or she feels unwilling or unable to break – may be a factor. The big difficulty with such a search for unconscious psychological reasons is that the voter cannot tell us what these reasons are because he or she is not conscious of them. Thus, we must infer them from other things we know about the voter's personality or about the behavior of people like him or her. And when we do so, we cannot test the accuracy of our conclusions by checking with the subject of our study.

Studies of unconscious factors in voting choice can contribute interesting conclusions about what leads citizens to reason as they do when they vote. They also reveal how the basic beliefs underlying voters' attitudes have tended to change over the years, as voting has declined and as party and issue have given way more and

---

[13]For a comprehensive study of such images, with data on views of McGovern and all other candidates through 1972, see Dan Nimmo and Robert L. Savage, *Candidates and Their Images* (Pacific Palisades, Calif.: Goodyear, 1976). But concerning the special attention voters gave to issues in the McGovern campaign, see Warren E. Miller and Teresa E. Levitin, *Leadership and Change: The New Politics and the American Electorate* (Cambridge, Mass.: Winthrop, 1976).

[14]*National Journal,* November 6, 1976, p. 1590.

[15]The pioneering work on various psychological aspects of voting has been carried on since 1948 by a team at the University of Michigan. Their first book was Angus Campbell, Philip E. Converse, Warren E. Miller, and Donald E. Stokes, *The American Voter* (New York: Wiley, 1960). For subsequent works, see the suggested readings at the end of this chapter.

more to personality assessment. One interesting example of such a study will illustrate.

In the presidential election years since 1964, citizens have been asked regularly to assess both their own sense of their competence as citizens and their belief about whose interests are served by the government. Political scientist Gerald Pomper has developed an interesting way of studying the results. Those who disagree with the statement that politics is often too difficult for people like them to understand are characterized as believing themselves *personally competent* in civic terms. Those who feel that the government is run for the "benefit of all the people" rather than to benefit a few "big interests" are classed as having a *benevolent* view of the government. Because each of these two questions can be answered two ways, there are four possible combined answers, each of which forms a category for dividing the population. (1) Those who feel personally competent and view the government as benevolent are termed *supporters*. (2) Those who feel incompetent but believe the government benevolent are called *trustful*. (3) Those who feel competent but believe the government serves big interests are termed *cynics*. (4) Those who feel incompetent and believe the government serves big interests are called *subjectively oppressed*.

In 1964, most Americans were supporters. The cynics, who were the second largest group, were outnumbered three to one. By 1968, that margin of supporters had dropped to two to one. Four years later, in 1972, there were more cynics than any other category. People in general continued to think themselves competent, but they believed their government less and less responsive to public will. As Figure 3.2 shows, these changing attitudes were most pronounced among the young, and especially among the young college-educated population; among new voters in 1972, 40 percent were cynics, 30 percent supporters, 20 percent oppressed, and 10

FIGURE 3.2

Attitudes of college-educated citizens toward the political system.

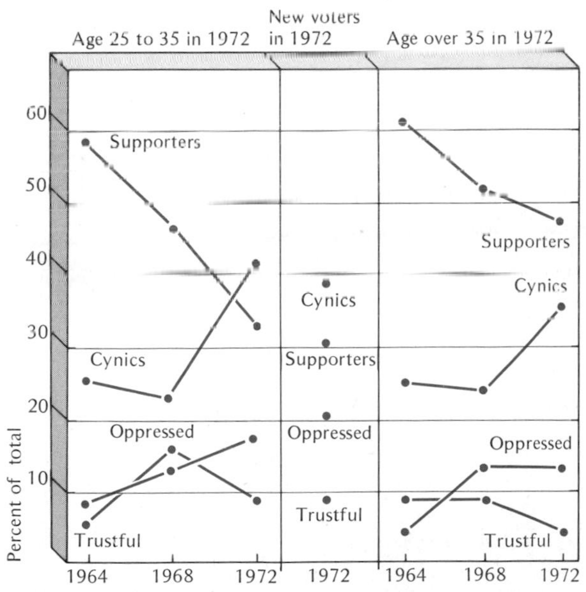

Source: After Figure 5.1 (p. 104) in *Voter's Choice* by Gerald M. Pomper. Copyright © 1975 by Harper & Row, Publishers, Inc. Reprinted by permission of the publisher.

percent trustful. Since that time, public confidence in government has plummeted still further.

When asked why they voted as they did, people wouldn't say, "Because I'm a system supporter" or "Because I'm subjectively oppressed." That is why we class these factors as "unconscious reasons." Experts may turn to such evidence of deeper attitudes of voters toward themselves and toward politicians and government in trying to explain such things as the stunning ascent to the presidency of Jimmy Carter, the outsider campaigning against Washington, or the more general shift toward voting on the basis of personality rather than by issue or by party.

■ Social factors

The third way to study voting behavior is to *look for social factors*. In this approach we find regularities in the combination of basic characteristics of individuals – their age, race, religion, sex, education, and so on – and the way they vote. For example, we might decide that middle-aged white Catholic males tend to vote Democratic. We assume that the fact that there are regularities implies that there is a connection between these characteristics and the voting behavior.

It has tended to be true as a general rule, for example, that poor people vote Democratic and rich people vote Republican. But if we ask each why, neither usually connects his or her economic status with his or her vote. Nonetheless, the combination is such a common phenomenon that we suspect that there is a connection. In the researcher's terms, we hypothesize that wealth tends to cause Republican voting and poverty tends to cause Democratic voting. The more evidence we find of such connections, the more we are inclined to believe we have found a "causal relationship" in this connection, or "correlation," between economic status and party vote.

Such a correlation may turn out to be "spurious." That is, the two factors may not, in fact, be connected to each other as cause and effect; instead, both may be caused by some third factor. For example it is no doubt true that people who wear

Henning Christoph/Black Star

business suits to work tend to vote Republican, whereas people who wear overalls at work tend to vote Democratic. It would be misleading to conclude from this correlation that party preference is caused by one's type of dress at work, however; the truth is that both party choice *and* mode of work dress are traceable to economic status.

So we must be careful about the conclusions we reach on the basis of correlations. We must realize that they are really hypotheses, or "educated guesses," that need continued testing. And we must remember that they become understandable only when we are able to connect them to the conscious reasons people give for their actions. Our observed correlation between economic status and party preference becomes plausible when we consider that Republican policy tends to favor the interests and to respond to the concerns of business and professional people. In contrast, Democratic policy proposals tend to pay special attention to the needs and desires of organized labor. There are exceptions to both of these generalizations, as there are to most generalizations about American politics. But on the whole, over time, they have been true enough that we can establish a *plausible connection* in terms of the beliefs and images of American business executives and workers that give them reasons for their voting behavior.

Once we have discovered such a correlation, we can sometimes predict likely voting from it. We know, for example, that people of high economic status not only tend to vote Republican but also tend to vote more regularly than those of lower economic status, who we also know tend to vote Democratic. We also know that there are many more low-income Americans than high-income Americans. This means that the outcome of a presidential election may depend, in a sense, on the turnout: If it is large, the Democrat is usually more likely to win, if small, the Republican's chances are improved. Turnout, in turn, is affected by everything from the personalities of the candidates, through the get-out-the-vote efforts of organized labor, to the weather on election day. The more we know about such causes of voter activity and voter choice, the better we can be at forecasting election outcomes.

Intensive studies of social factors and voting may be of a particular community that is thought to be representative of the electorate in general or of a "random sample" of the entire population that represents the major types of Americans in accurate proportions.[16] Because such studies have been conducted for several decades, they provide a great range of information about Americans in general and their attitudes and voting behavior in particular. Some of the most revealing conclusions they have reached are discussed in the following sections.

Socioeconomic status Because we spend so much of our waking hours working, it would not be surprising if our occupation correlated with our voting decisions. Furthermore, because our income affects the way we live and what sort of neighborhood we live in as well as our social standing, we would not be surprised to

[16]The latter approach is the basis for the famous Gallup Poll and the Harris Survey, as well as for the foremost political science project, the "American Voter" studies, from which most of the poll data we use are derived. The former approach was pioneered by researchers at Columbia University in the 1940s. See Paul F. Lazarsfeld, Bernard Berelson, and Hazel Gaudet, *The People's Choice* (New York: Columbia University Press, 1944).

find correlations here also. These factors—occupation, income, social class—are often lumped together as "socioeconomic status" (or **SES**) characteristics.

In the years of the Great Depression of the 1930s, voting did correlate very strongly with SES. The poor, the working class, and low-income Americans generally voted Democratic, while the wealthy, professional and white-collar, higher-income Americans voted Republican.

But in subsequent years, America underwent several major transformations. Women entered the work force in larger numbers. They generally performed nonmanual labor and added a second income to their households. This made their families somewhat more middle-class—even if their husbands continued to do manual labor themselves (as 58 percent of nonagricultural working males did as late as 1972).[17] Meanwhile, the family farm was being replaced by large corporate farms. As a result, poor whites from the Midwest and the South and southern blacks increasingly headed for the cities of the North. The resulting racial conflict led to greater Democratic voting by newly enfranchised blacks and less Democratic voting by whites both in and outside the South, so that, on balance, *the class basis of voting declined.*

Age Much of the explanation for the decline of SES as a determinant of voting behavior can be found in the fact that new voters have come along less tied to parties. Each election about 8 percent of the electorate has newly come of age. (In the 1972 election, following the lowering of the voting age to 18, the newly eligible population was about double that.) These new voters have different experiences and memories and less contact with influential elders than used to be the case when people were less mobile and families lived together longer. In 1980, 40 percent of the electorate will not have been old enough to vote in the 1960 election of John Kennedy. Young voters recently have emphasized issues more than their elders, and at the same time have voted less often. This is probably because they generally feel both disillusioned and politically powerless, as we have already noted.

Education As a general rule, people with more formal education are more likely to vote Republican, while those who stopped going to school earlier are more likely to vote Democratic. Table 3.3 clearly shows this tendency. But it also reminds us that even this tendency may be overcome by particularly popular candidates, such as Lyndon Johnson in 1964 and Richard Nixon in 1972, each of whom won a majority of votes among each educational level of voters.

Sex Because sex is an obvious physical and social difference between people, we might expect a significant difference in the way men and women vote. But research shows that there is now very little voting difference between the sexes. Of course, in a close election very small differences could be important. Gallup found in 1976 that women favored Ford over Carter, 51–48 percent. In general, however, rates of

---

[17]These figures can be found annually in the United States Department of Labor's *Manpower Report of the President* (Washington, D.C.: Government Printing Office). My account owes much to Paul R. Abramson, *Generational Change in American Politics* (Lexington, Mass.: Lexington Books, 1975)

TABLE 3.3

Vote by groups in presidential elections since 1952

	1952		1956		1960		1964		1968			1972		1976[a]		
	Steven-son	Eisen-hower	Steven-son	Eisen-hower	Ken-nedy	Nixon	John-son	Gold-water	Hum-phrey	Nixon	Wal-lace	McGov-ern	Nixon	Carter	Ford	McCar-thy
National	44.6%	55.4%	42.2%	57.8%	50.1%	49.9%	61.3%	38.7%	43.0%	43.4%	13.6%	38%	62%	50%	48%	1%
Sex																
Male	47	53	45	55	52	48	60	40	41	43	16	37	63	53	45	1
Female	42	58	39	61	49	51	62	38	45	43	12	38	62	48	51	—[b]
Race																
White	43	57	41	59	49	51	59	41	38	47	15	32	68	46	52	1
Nonwhite	79	21	61	39	68	32	94	6	85	12	3	87	13	85	15	—
Education																
College	34	66	31	69	39	61	52	48	37	54	9	37	63	42	55	2
High school	45	55	42	58	52	48	62	38	42	43	15	34	66	54	46	—
Grade school	52	48	50	50	55	45	66	34	52	33	15	49	51	58	41	1
Occupation																
Prof.-business	36	64	32	68	42	58	54	46	34	56	10	31	69	42	56	1
White collar	40	60	37	63	48	52	57	43	41	47	12	36	64	50	48	2
Manual	55	45	50	50	60	40	71	29	50	35	15	43	57	58	41	1
Age																
Under 30 years	51	49	43	57	54	46	64	36	47	38	15	48	52	53	45	1
30–49 years	47	53	45	55	54	46	63	37	44	41	15	33	67	48	49	2
Over 50 years	39	61	39	61	46	54	59	41	41	47	12	36	64	52	48	—
Religion																
Protestants	37	63	37	63	38	62	55	45	35	49	16	30	70	46	53	—
Catholics	56	44	51	49	78	22	76	24	59	33	8	48	52	57	42	1
Politics																
Republicans	8	92	4	96	5	95	20	80	9	86	5	5	95	9	91	—
Democrats	77	23	85	15	84	16	87	13	74	12	14	67	33	82	18	—
Independents	35	65	30	70	43	57	56	44	31	44	25	31	69	38	57	4
Region																
East	45	55	40	60	53	47	68	32	50	43	7	42	58	51	47	1
Midwest	42	58	41	59	48	52	61	39	44	47	9	40	60	48	50	1
South	51	49	49	51	51	49	52	48	31	36	33	29	71	54	45	—
West	42	58	43	57	49	51	60	40	44	49	7	41	59	46	51	1
Members of labor union families	61	39	57	43	65	35	73	27	56	29	15	46	54	63	36	1

[a]1976 results do not include vote for minor party candidates.
[b]Less than 1 percent.

Source: Gallup Opinion Index no. 137, December 1976, pp. 16–17.

participation for both sexes are comparable, as are attitudes on almost all issues, including even women's rights (as we shall see in more detail in Chapter 15). The only significant difference is in attitudes toward the use of force, which women tend to oppose more than men, both in foreign affairs and in dealing with urban unrest. Apparently as a result of this attitude, in the Vietnam era women tended to vote Democratic more than men.

Religion and ethnic background Traditionally, Catholics and Jews have voted Democratic, while Protestants have tended to be Republicans. In addition, Irish, Italian, Polish, Eastern European, and Slavic voters have generally supported Democrats, while Northern European and Anglo-Saxon voters have voted Republican. These parallels are hardly surprising, because Anglo-Saxons tend to be Protestant and the other ethnic groups tend to be Catholic and Jewish. Recent elections, however, have disrupted some of these patterns. Richard Nixon, for example, got only 33 percent of the Catholic vote in 1968 but 52 percent of it in 1972. And Carter got 57 percent of Catholics in 1976, but only 46 percent of Protestants.

These various tendencies of differing, somewhat overlapping population groups in America can be portrayed graphically by comparing the voting behavior over a series of elections. Gallup Poll data for the presidential elections from 1952 to 1976 do this in Table 3.3.

□ VOTING, ELECTIONS, AND DEMOCRACY

In previous periods, a study of social characteristics was a valuable way to try to understand and explain voting behavior in America. The American voter, then, was thought of as what Gerald Pomper has called "the dependent voter." Voters seemed to pay little attention to political events and issues. Instead, they referred to their social group and their party membership for cues as to how to vote – if they voted at all. Voters, in other words, were dependent on their social and economic situation for cues as to how to vote.[18]

It was not a very flattering picture of the American voter – nor, for that matter, of American democracy as we had always conceived it. One result was a tendency for some people to argue that it is better that such people *not* vote. They should leave the voting to those who are well informed and care enough to take the trouble to learn and to vote. Perhaps democracy should be redefined, some said, to emphasize rule by an expert elite elected by a knowledgeable fragment of the population. Others suggested that perhaps campaigns should be run differently, to emphasize the appearance or image of the candidates, rather than the issues.

One result of these suggestions has been the development of new styles of campaigning and new types of elections – the "merchandising of candidates."[19] Many fear that this new trend is a grave threat to the strength and viability of

---

[18]See Pomper, *Voters' Choice,* p. 7.

[19]See Joe McGinniss, *The Selling of the President 1968* (New York: Trident, 1969).

Polling place on election day.

Sybil Shelton/Monkmeyer

democracy in America, as we shall see in our study of the mass media in Chapter 12. Another, even more important, consequence, which we shall discuss in Chapter 5, has been a growing debate over the nature of democracy and the desirability and justification of various forms of political participation beyond voting.

■ Why so many elections?

The presidential election is but one of about 525,000 races decided by popular vote every fourth year. In addition, many elections for other state and local offices are held in the so-called "off-years." As our governments – national, state, and local – have grown, the number of offices for which citizens can run, and for which they are urged to vote, has ballooned. In some areas of the country, even dogcatchers and public weighers are elected.

Why so many elections? Elections have very important roles or functions in our political system. First, they are the way we select most of our leaders. Second, they are a kind of public referendum on the incumbents and their policies, revealing public approval and disapproval. They may also reveal public desires for change. Third, they are a way of involving the people in the government. They keep people tied to the system without letting them interfere in daily decision making.

But the importance of elections in our system goes deeper. Perhaps the most important answer to the question of why we have so many elections in America is that we define democracy in terms of elections.

When our political units are small enough, all citizens can participate in the actual making of decisions. This is the principle of the town meetings by which much of New England was long governed. Some small cities there are still governed by debates and votes taken by all citizens in regular public meetings. We call this system "pure democracy" because it is direct rule *by* the people.

But most of our cities long ago became too large to be governed this way. So they switched to "representative democracy." In such a system, most decisions are made by officials who are elected at regular intervals by the people and who represent the people when they make decisions for them. What, then, is the specific role of elections in representative democracy? To find out, we must examine the place of power and authority in politics.

■ Power and authority in elections

Any ruler, no matter how he or she becomes ruler, will have power, or else he or she will not last long in office. By **power** we mean the capacity to make people act in accord with one's own wishes when they would rather act differently. Power, thus, is the ability to change people's behavior.[20]

Guns can give you power. So can money. So, sometimes, can a loud voice if it makes it possible for you to be heard and to be convincing in your commands. But power, raw power, is not really very efficient in governing, as rulers in dictatorships quickly find out. The problem with power is that you have to keep using it in order to get your way. This is very costly in terms of energy, bullets and bombs, money, vocal chords, or whatever you are using to make people obey you.

Governments rarely have enough resources – soldiers, police, spies, plus money and goods – to rule by power alone. How long, after all, can one hold an entire population at gunpoint? They must instead rule by *authority.* If we say, "He's an authority on how to play split end," or "She's an authority on the Civil War," we mean that the person knows so much about the subject that we should take his or her word for it. Authorities are people who are known to be able to do something, and accepted as having that ability. In this sense a football authority in sports is like a ruling authority in government. People know his or her power and accept it. They know a football authority has the power to describe the pass patterns a split end runs and to explain why they work or don't work against particular defenses. People also know a ruling or governmental authority has the power to make them do what he or she orders them to do. The authority may perhaps call out the police to jail a lawbreaker or order a bureaucrat to perform some duty. The fact that we know certain people are authorities on certain things means that we do not have to keep testing them, but instead can take their word for it.

In politics, therefore, **authority** is recognized or accepted power. We often speak of "the power of the president." Many people say the president has become too powerful; many say that President Nixon abused his power as president. But most of the time we really mean "authority" rather than just "power" when we speak this way. Most governments, and most officials, operate most of the time with authority rather than with raw, direct power. And this is where elections come in. We can think of our system of elections as a *way of creating and maintaining political,* or ruling, *authority* in our political system.

When we elect someone to office, we grant him or her power, of course. A president, once elected, can use the army and the FBI, just as a mayor can use the

[20] Political scientists and philosophers are still debating about how best to define power. The definition we use here is a clear, simple version of that which is now most widely accepted. For discussions of the problem of definition and examples of many different approaches to the study of power, see Roderick A. Bell, David V. Edwards, and R. Harrison Wagner, eds., *Political Power: A Reader in Theory and Research* (New York: Free Press, 1969).

Reprinted by permission of the Chicago Tribune-New York News Syndicate

local police, to influence or control people's behavior. But even more important, *election grants someone authority* because we all recognize that elections are the way we choose our rulers.

Authority and the 1976 election When Jimmy Carter was elected and then sworn in as president, he did not have to call out the army to march around to show he could issue orders to it that would be followed. Nor did he have to unleash the Washington police to get Gerald Ford to vacate the White House. He did not even have to call on the FBI to get people to pay their taxes. Everyone knew he had been elected president. Everyone knew the office of the president had these powers. The powers go along with the office. So everyone recognized that Carter had the power to do these things. Because everyone recognized his power, he had authority.

Indeed, that is what the election was all about. It was a contest for authority – for presidential authority. Carter and Ford and the other candidates were competing for the authority to run the country – for the authority to decide what should be done by our government.

In a more general sense, each candidate was offering to the voters his or her own image or picture of reality. Each was offering an image of the present state of things at home and abroad, an image of what should be done to improve things, an image of his or her own competence to make those changes and run the country. This situation is well captured in a cartoon by Jeff MacNelly, which appeared during the campaign. In it, the two candidates appear as schoolboys doing their arithmetic exercises on the blackboard. The cartoonist suggests, by implication, that the reality is "2 + 2 = 4." But because Gerald Ford is the incumbent president, responsible for the way things are, he is trying to suggest that things are better than they really are, so he writes "2 + 2 = 5." Carter, as the challenger critical of the job Ford has done, tries to suggest that things are less good than they really are, and so he writes "2 + 2 = 3."

Each candidate offers his own image, or picture, of reality to the voters. The voters have to choose which image to accept as true or better. Ford can list his accomplishments as arguments for his own image, and Carter can list problems that have not been solved by Ford as arguments for his own image. But what the two candidates are really doing is competing for victory in the election. That victory will give one of them the authority to describe reality to the American people for 4 years. Because the president has authority, the chances are most of the people will be influenced by the descriptions of reality that the president offers – at least until the next election, when they have a choice again. In addition, the president has the authority to describe reality – or American beliefs about reality, which he symbolizes and expresses – to the rest of the world. This is so because the rest of the world, too, knows that the president is elected by the people to represent them and their image of reality to the rest of the world.

To get this authority, this ruling authority, a candidate must first convince the voters that they should accept his image of reality. Usually, each starts out by giving arguments for his view. In the 1976 election, Ford was saying, in effect, "I know how to solve our economic problems. Under my administration we've reduced inflation and cut unemployment. Look at my record." Carter, on the other hand, was saying, in effect, "The Republicans don't understand the problems of the ordinary people. Unemployment is still much too high, and inflation is still hurting most Americans. Much remains to be done, and my proposals are the best way to get the improvements we need."

As always happens, the candidates disagree, and voters need to know why they should believe one rather than the other – why they should accept one's image of reality rather than the other's. So almost always the focus of the campaign tends to shift from policy issues and assertions about programs toward statements about personal qualifications. Candidates spend little time arguing about the issues and presenting their proposals. Instead they emphasize their own special qualifications for the office – their talents, their knowledge, their experience.

In the 1976 election, Ford kept pointing out that he had spent most of his life in politics. He implied that we as voters should believe his views about the state of the nation and about the best ways to solve its problems, because he is an authority on politics and an authority on national problems. In other words, he used his career experience as a *claim to authority.* Carter, on the other hand, had very little political experience: one term as governor of Georgia. He emphasized that he had been a good governor. But he also listed the other things he had done: "I've been a farmer, a businessman, a Navy man, a nuclear engineer . . ." he would say. He, too, was using his career experience as a *claim to authority.* At the same time, he was challenging Ford's claim to authority by saying, "I'm not a lawyer, and I'm not from Washington." This implied that Washington lawyers like Ford were isolated from the problems of the people, and so were not as good authorities on the nation's problems as were those people who worked as farmers, businessmen, or nuclear engineers.

Carter also emphasized that he was an honest man who would always tell the truth to the American people. Ford emphasized that the people could trust him. Assertions of honesty and trustworthiness are also claims to authority, for we expect our experts to be honest and trustworthy. We look for those qualities in people to whom we are about to grant great authority.

Each candidate, in other words, was making *claims to authority to describe or interpret the nature of reality* in America for Americans, as any president does. And each was disputing the other's claims to this authority by running against him and debating with him during the campaign. Each wanted to use his personal authority as an impressive candidate to gain the institutional authority of the presidency. Once there, he would use the authority of the presidency to describe or interpret the nature of reality to the American people and to the rest of the world, just as authorities always do.

□ THE ESSENCE OF ELECTIONS AND POLITICS

We can, therefore, conclude that the essence of elections is dispute between candidates concerning their claims to the authority to describe or interpret the nature of reality for the voters.

When we as voters discuss our political preferences, we tend to do the same thing. We may start by describing reality – the candidates and the issues as we see them. But when we disagree among ourselves, we are likely to shift to making claims to authority, such as: "I read in *Newsweek* that . . ." or "I heard him speak at . . ." or "Everyone I know agrees with me that . . ." All these are claims to our own authority as political experts, claims that we are able to make because of our own experiences.

Candidates dispute over claims to authority. Voters do the same. And so do public officials when they disagree among themselves. Two members of Congress may disagree on how to vote on a bill; President Carter and the leader of the Soviet Union may disagree on an arms-limitation proposal or on an issue of human rights.

The important point, as we will see time and again in coming chapters, is that this *dispute over claims to the authority to describe and interpret reality is the essence of all politics.* People often refer to politics as "a struggle for power." In a sense, of course, it is. But we have seen that beneath that obvious competition for power is a dispute over claims to authority.

If we remember this, we shall be better able to understand how politics really works, what politicians are really trying to do, why some people are more successful at it than others, and what we ourselves can do to avoid being fooled by politics and politicians. Such an understanding will help us to be effective in politics ourselves whenever we wish to.

Participating in elections, the subject of this chapter, is only one of many ways to be active in politics. In the next chapter, we shall examine another – political parties. And then in Chapter 5, we shall consider the wide range of other activities that are also political.

☐ SUGGESTIONS FOR FURTHER READING AND STUDY

If you want to know *how* people voted in a particular national election, the official source is *Statistics of the Presidential and Congressional Election,* published regularly by the government. A comparable source is *America Votes,* edited by Richard Scammon and published every 2 years by Congressional Quarterly in Washington.

The question of *why* people voted as they did is more complicated and controversial, as we have seen. The first study of the 1976 election is Gerald Pomper et al., *The Election of 1976* (New York: McKay paperback, 1977). An interesting account of the 1976 campaign is Jules Witcover, *Marathon* (New York: Viking, 1977). On presidential elections generally, see the comprehensive study by Nelson W. Polsby and Aaron Wildavsky, *Presidential Elections,* 4th ed. (New York: Scribner paperback, 1976). For popular accounts of each election from 1960 through 1972, see the series of books written by Theodore H. White and published by Atheneum entitled *The Making of the President.*

Pomper is also the author of an interesting recent study of voting that focuses on the impacts of party, class, sex, youth, and race: *Voters' Choice* (New York: Dodd, Mead paperback, 1975). Another recent effort to reexamine the findings of voting studies over several decades is Norman H. Nie, Sidney Verba, and John R. Petrocik, *The Changing American Voter* (Cambridge: Harvard University Press paperback, 1976). Another recent and useful survey is William H. Flanigan and Nancy Zingale, *Political Behavior of the American Electorate,* 3rd ed. (Boston: Allyn & Bacon, 1975).

There are important classic studies. The first, based on interviews in 1940 in one city, was Paul Lazarsfeld et al., *The People's Choice: How the Voter Makes Up His Mind in a Presidential Campaign* (New York: Duell, Sloan & Pearce, 1944). Then came Bernard Berelson, Paul Lazarsfeld, and William McPhee, *Voting: A Study of Opinion Formation in a Presidential Campaign* (Chicago: University of Chicago Press, 1954). The next, and still dominant, wave, based on "survey research" or polls of a sample of the whole electorate, is studies done at the University of Michigan. See Angus Campbell, Philip Converse, Warren Miller, and Donald Stokes, *The American Voter* (New York: Wiley paperback, 1960), and *Elections and the Political Order* (New York: Wiley, 1966). For a more recent study, see Warren Miller and Teresa E. Levitin, *Leadership and Change: The New Politics and the American Electorate* (Cambridge, Mass.: Winthrop paperback, 1976). See also Paul R. Abramson, *Generational Change in American Politics* (Lexington, Mass.: Lexington Books, 1975), and Philip Converse's answer, *The Dynamics of Party Support: Cohort-Analyzing Party Identification* (Beverly Hills, Calif.: Sage paperback, 1976).

For a different view, see Walter Dean Burnham, *Critical Elections and the Mainsprings of American Politics* (New York: Norton paperback, 1970), and the debate between Burnham, Philip Converse, Jerrold Rusk, and Jesse Marquette on "Political Change in America," in the *American Political Science Review* 68 (1974).

The relation between social science and democratic theory is the subject of Dennis F. Thompson's book *The Democratic Citizen* (Cambridge: Cambridge University Press, 1970). For a now-classic argument that "voters are not fools," see V. O. Key, Jr., *The Responsible Electorate: Rationality in Presidential Voting, 1936–1960* (Cambridge, Mass.: Harvard University Press paperback, 1966). For an examination of the impact of elections on policy, see Gerald Pomper, *Elections in America: Control and Influence in Democratic Politics* (New York: Dodd, Mead, 1968).

4 Political parties

Most elections in America are contested by political parties. A party chooses – or has chosen for it in a primary election – a candidate for an office. The party then works with the candidate to organize the campaign, to raise money to finance it, and even to hold a party election night to celebrate victory or to soften defeat. Many events of political campaigns traditionally have a festive air to them. It might even seem, therefore, that we call our political organizations "parties" because they so frequently hold celebrations.

In recent years, however – years of political assassinations, of Vietnam, of Watergate – this traditional festive quality of our party politics has decreased. As politics has been losing much of its fun, our parties have been losing their members or supporters, as we saw last chapter. By 1971, "party identification" had dropped so much, and party leadership was so weak, that many observers were wondering whether our parties could survive much longer. One of our most astute political observers, the *Washington Post's* David Broder, discussed the situation in a book he called *The Party's Over*. Broder wrote:

> It is called *The Party's Over,* not in prophecy, but in alarm. I am not predicting the demise of the Republicans or the Democrats. Party loyalties have been seriously eroded, the Democratic and Republican organizations weakened by years of neglect. But our parties are not yet dead. What happens to them is up to us to decide. If we allow them to wither, we will pay a high price in the continued frustration of government. But, even if we seek their renewal, the cost of repairing the effects of decades of governmental inaction will be heavy. The process will be painful and expensive. Whatever the fate of our political parties, for America the party *is* over.[1]

Mere months after Broder wrote these words, the Democrats nominated George McGovern and went down to the most smashing presidential election defeat in their history. Some observers wondered whether the Democratic party could recover. Richard Nixon had won reelection in 1972 without even referring to his party or supporting its other candidates. Shortly thereafter, his vice-president, Spiro Agnew, was forced to resign for taking illegal payoffs, Watergate broke wide open, and President Nixon was forced to resign in disgrace. Then his successor, Gerald Ford, lost to Jimmy Carter in the close 1976 election, and the Republicans

[1]David Broder, *The Party's Over: The Failure of Politics in America* (New York: Harper & Row, 1972), p. xvi.

slipped to all-time lows in their totals of congressional, state, and local officeholders. Many observers then wondered whether the Republican party could survive. But by that time few still doubted the vitality of the Democratic party.

Perhaps the party, in the sense of festive political activity, is indeed over. But the dictionary tells us that our term party actually derives from an old Latin term meaning "a division" or "a part"—a body or group of persons on one side of a contest maintaining an opinion or a cause against another such part or group. In this sense, the party will never be over in American politics. Indeed, the more people participate in other ways besides political party membership, the more lively American politics is likely to become. But before we decide to abandon our parties as they are or to reject our present system with two dominant parties in favor of other forms of political participation, we need to know what effects our parties have on our politics.

□ WHAT A PARTY IS

America today has two major parties, the Democratic and the Republican, and a number of smaller parties. These parties nominate candidates for office and campaign to get votes for those candidates. But what or who actually *does* these things? Are the people who actually work for the party the heart of the party? Are the candidates more important? Or the voters who declare themselves Democrats or Republicans? Or "the organization"—the party officials whose role is to keep things going between elections and to see that arrangements are made so that primary elections are held, conventions are convened, funds are raised, and so on?

Why is this important? You can, in a sense, have a party without workers if someone simply announces he or she is running for office on a particular ticket. You can have voters who declare themselves Democrats yet always vote Republican. Many southerners now do this. You can even have parties that do not run candidates. Republican parties in some southern states that remain overwhelmingly Democratic still tend to do this.

This look at the real-world political party has expanded the dictionary definition given earlier, but we still do not know exactly what a party is. Perhaps a look at the *function* of parties—at what parties actually do—will help. Political scientists often define parties as groups that organize to win elections by selecting candidates and running campaigns.

"We may define 'political party' generally," writes one expert, "as the articulate organization of society's active political agents, those who are concerned with the control of governmental power and who compete for popular support with another group or groups holding divergent views."[2]

We can be more specific. In the rather typical words of the Delaware state law that governs parties, " 'Party' or 'Political Party' means any political party, organization or association which elects delegates to a National Convention,

[2]Sigmund Neumann, *Modern Political Parties* (Chicago: University of Chicago Press, 1956), p. 396.

Stan Wakefield

1976 Democratic National Convention.

nominates candidates for electors of President and Vice-President, United States Senator, Representative in Congress, Governor and other offices, and elects a State Committee and officers of a State Committee by a State Convention composed of elected members from each Representative District. . . ."[3]

The keys in such definitions are "organization" and "candidates competing for popular support." It is organization that makes it possible for a party to operate, and it is competing in elections that is the major activity of the organization in the case of major parties.

But parties play other roles or serve other functions in American politics besides (1) recruiting candidates and (2) competing with each other to elect candidates to office. They also (3) attract popular attention to elections by campaigning publicly for votes. They (4) tend to focus that popular attention on the particular issues they emphasize in the campaign to make that choice easier for citizens. These effects often result in yet another function: (5) educating the people about politics and issues generally.

[3]Quoted in Frank Sorauf, *Party Politics in America,* 3rd ed. (Boston: Little, Brown, 1976), p. 8.

In addition, the fact that the parties are seeking to get a majority vote makes them likely to try to (6) integrate various groups (races, classes, and so on) and opinions (liberal, moderate, conservative) in the electorate behind a single candidate. This may tend to unify or stabilize what otherwise could be divisive differences in public opinions.

Finally—once the election is over—the parties (7) serve as links between popular sentiment and interest groups *outside* the government and policy made *within* the government. Ways in which these *linkages* are established and maintained will be a major focus of coming chapters. We'll see, for example, that party unites the president to some members of Congress and divides him from others.

Providing this linkage between people with opinions on the one hand and officials with power on the other is the function of *the party in office*—in the presidency or in the Congress or in a state governorship or state legislature. The other six functions are carried out by *the party organization.* The party organization is made up of party officials and party activists. But although these party organization people make it all happen, they can only do so with the help of the voters. These voters, therefore, form the third element of the party, which is sometimes called *the-party-in-the-electorate.*[4] To understand the roles of parties better, we must know more about both their organization membership and their electorate membership.

□ WHO BELONGS TO OUR PARTIES

In some countries you pay dues to join a party, and it gives you a membership card to carry in exchange. In America, all you have to do is say "I'm a Democrat" or "I'm a Republican" to be one. Neither party even demands "party loyalty"—that members vote for its candidates when elections come along. There are, in other words, no real responsibilities that go with party membership. But there are opportunities—opportunities to participate in the nominating process, to contribute time or money, to help "get out the vote" on election day and to celebrate on election night. Action Unit 4.1 describes such opportunities. Few Americans actually take advantage of these opportunities for active party work—most estimates and surveys suggest something like 5 to 10 percent. This means that most party work is done either by professional, paid employees or by a small group of regular volunteers.

Because this is the case, we might expect to find little difference between the activists of one party and those of the other. And yet there are differences. Tuning your television to both party conventions is enough to demonstrate this difference. Or you could take the word of an expert such as the late conservative political scientist Clinton Rossiter, who observed: "A gathering of Democrats *is* more

---

[4]The term is Frank Sorauf's. See his chapter "Political Parties and Political Analysis" in *The American Party System,* ed. William N. Chambers and Walter Dean Burnham (New York: Oxford University Press, 1967), chap. 2.

☐ ACTION UNIT 4.1: How to work in a political party

Local organization is important within the political party. Active involvement in a party will probably mean that you will have more participation in choosing candidates for local offices and in defining the policies and issues discussed in a campaign.

Your influence can be crucial. Numerous elections have been won or lost by less than one vote per precinct.

Register to vote. List yourself as a member of the political party of your choice (or as an Independent) if you have not already done so. Although party leaders sometimes look askance at members who do not support all the candidates endorsed by the organization, you do not have to support anyone of whom you disapprove.

Secure names and addresses of party leaders in your local area from the election commission, party, or newspapers.

Contact your precinct leader or local political party leader, in person if possible. Volunteer your services. You can accept responsibilities and become involved in party activities right away even though you may have had little previous experience.

Find out when precinct or club meetings and state and local caucuses are held. Ask to be notified about them regularly so that you can plan to attend.

Learn parliamentary procedure. This will enable you to follow what occurs in meetings and to find the best way to bring issues before the group.

Become an expert on one or two issues so that you can express your views in meetings, in debates, and on resolutions committees. Others will soon come to depend on your expertise.

Be willing to knock on doors. Your assignments may include going from door to door in your own area or another neighborhood. This includes canvassing, fund raising, finding voters who will need absentee ballots or assistance in getting to the polls, and getting out the vote.

For further information, contact the various political parties at their local, state, or national headquarters. Addresses are in Action Unit 4.2.

Adapted and reprinted from "How to Work in Politics," a guide prepared by Friends Committee on National Legislation, 245 Second Street N.E., Washington, D.C. 20002

sweaty, disorderly, offhand, and rowdy than a gathering of Republicans; it is also more likely to be more cheerful, imaginative, tolerant of dissent, and skillful at the game of give and take. A gathering of Republicans *is* more respectable, sober, purposeful, and businesslike than a gathering of Democrats; it is also likely to be more self-righteous, pompous, cut-and-dried, and just plain boring."[5]

The 1976 conventions were perhaps somewhat atypical in these respects, because Carter had wrapped up the nomination well before the Democratic convention, whereas Ford and Reagan were still battling down to the convention wire. But this generalization, written in 1960, still seems valid. Our two parties really are different, not only in the policy positions they take and the economic groups that support them (as we shall see shortly), but also in the social backgrounds of those who identify with them. Democrats are much more likely to be city-dwellers, members of labor unions, Catholics or Jews, and members of one or another ethnic minority. Republicans, by contrast, are more likely to be suburbanites, businesspersons or professionals, Protestants, and Anglo-Saxons.

---

[5]Clinton Rossiter, *Parties and Politics in America* (Ithaca, N.Y.: Cornell University Press, 1960), p. 117.

Stan Wakefield

■ Professionals and amateurs

Although the party members differ in these ways, both parties have as part of their activist ranks both professionals and amateurs, or "regulars" and "purists," as they are sometimes called. The professionals tend to place the greatest emphasis on the survival and success of the party as an institution. The amateurs tend to be most concerned with particular candidates and/or special issues, win or lose. The differences in perspective of the two groups are well represented by the following description by Arthur Miller, professional playwright and amateur politician: "The professionals . . . see politics as a sort of game in which you win sometimes and sometimes you lose. Issues are not something you feel, like morality, like good and evil, but something you succeed or fail to make use of. To these men an issue is a segment of public opinion which you either capitalize on or attempt to assuage according to the present interests of the party. To the amateurs . . . an issue is first of all moral, and embodies a vision of the country, even of man, and is not a counter in a game."[6] Austin Ranney, political scientist and Democratic party activist, gives the professional's view:

> The professionals are people who have a substantial commitment to the party itself. They have served it before the nomination contest and expect to serve it after the election. . . . The professionals seek a candidate whose style they think will appeal to the voters they need to win, not necessarily to party leaders. They judge a candidate by how well or badly he runs in the election and by how much he has helped or hurt the rest of the ticket. And they see negotiation, compromise, and accommodation not as hypocrisy or immorality but as the very essence of what keeps parties—and nations—from disintegrating.[7]

[6] Arthur Miller, "The Battle of Chicago: From the Delegates' Side," *N.Y. Times Magazine,* Sept. 15, 1968, p. 29.

[7] Austin Ranney, *Curing the Mischiefs of Faction: Party Reform in America* (Berkeley, Calif.: University of California Press, 1975), pp. 140–141.

If the parties contained no one but professionals, they would rarely stimulate much public interest. If, on the other hand, they were composed primarily of amateur-purists, politics would be fascinating, but parties would come and go with special issues. The fact that the parties contain both elements helps explain their viability. But other factors are even more important.

☐ WHAT SUSTAINS OUR PARTIES

At any given time one or the other of our major parties seems to be in serious disarray. Yet the Democratic party has existed since 1828 and can trace its roots back to around 1800, whereas the Republican party dates from 1854. What explains their long lives and their periodic returns from the shadow of death? Observers cite five major factors: constitutional provisions, historical developments, collusion of the parties, the federal structure of the parties, and party reform.

■ Constitutional provisions

In most cases, survival of political institutions can be traced to constitutional provisions that create and protect them. But the Constitution doesn't even mention political parties. The Founding Fathers, as we have seen in Chapter 1, were generally fearful of parties and hoped to be able to do without them. In his farewell address as our first president, George Washington warned the country against "the baneful effects of the spirit of party." His successor John Adams wrote: "There is nothing I dread so much as the division of the Republic into two great parties, each under its leader."

Despite the wishes of the Founders, and despite the omission of parties from the Constitution, political parties developed quickly and grew stronger – in large part because of certain constitutional provisions. Foremost among these is the requirement that public officials be elected regularly: representatives every 2 years, the president every 4, and senators every 6. Competing in regular elections requires organization. This task in our system is handled by political parties. Such parties might be weak, however, in the absence of two guarantees in the First Amendment of the Bill of Rights: freedom of speech and freedom of assembly. These three constitutional provisions – regular elections and freedom of speech and assembly – taken together, virtually guaranteed that parties would become a standard feature of our political system.

They did not, however, guarantee that our present two parties would survive as long as they have. To understand their long lives we must examine both their development and their operation.

■ Historical developments

Federalists, Democratic-Republicans, and Whigs In the early years, American politics was in flux. The first people to organize a party were called "Federalists." Their Federalist party was established to encourage development of a

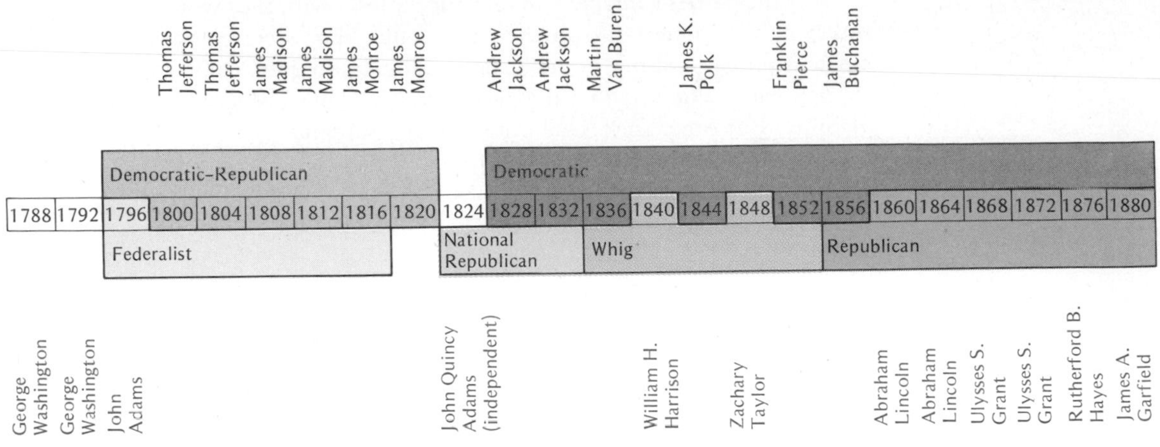

FIGURE 4.1
Presidents and parties, 1792–1976.

strong and effective central government able to protect the new country from foreign enemies and to foster commercial economic development, largely for the benefit of bankers and traders. To oppose this emphasis on commerce and banking, Thomas Jefferson soon organized the Republican party among farmers, frontiersmen, and debtors hostile to banks. This party, which favored weaker central government, dominated politics for a quarter century following Jefferson's election as president in 1800. In those years it came to be known as the Democratic-Republican party. One faction within it supported greater democratization of the political system. When Andrew Jackson, a strong supporter of greater party democracy, became party leader and then, in 1828, was elected president, the faction suspicious of democratization left the party. This faction, known as the National Republicans, favored a stronger legislature rather than a dominant popular president. It eventually joined with fragments of the old Federalists favoring commerce, industry, and finance to form the Whig party in 1832. (The Whigs took their name from a comparable British party of the period; the origins of the name in Britain are unknown.) The faction of the Democratic-Republicans that remained loyal to Jackson eventually became known as the Democratic party.

"Out of the conflict of Democrats and Whigs" in the next quarter century, observed Clinton Rossiter, "emerged the American political system – complete with such features as two major parties, a sprinkle of third parties, national nominating conventions, state and local bosses, patronage, popular campaigning, and the Presidency as the focus of politics."[8]

Democrats and Republicans But the party system we have to this day, dominated by the Democratic and Republican parties, did not emerge until the Whigs were badly beaten in 1852. At that time the issue of extending slavery to new states was shattering both parties. The Democrats, with their strong southern

[8]Rossiter, *Parties and Politics in America,* pp. 73–74.

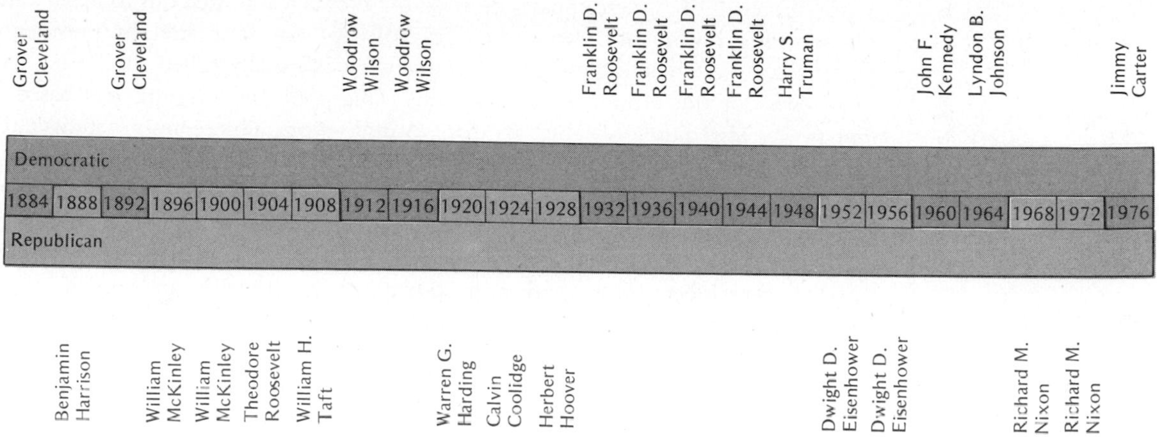

base, were unable to wrestle with the issue. Anti-slavery Whigs left that party in 1854 to form a new Republican party opposing the extension of slavery into the new Western territories then seeking admission to the Union. With Lincoln's election as president in 1860, the Republicans began a period of national dominance that was interrupted only three times until 1932 (see Figure 4.1).

Populism

In the 40 years following the Civil War, there was one major new political movement. **Populism** – a term derived from the Latin word for "the people." A People's Party was formed to protect the interests of farmers against the railroads (which were exploiting the monopoly they had in transporting farm goods to city markets) and the banks (which were seizing farms for nonpayment of mortgage debts). The small populist parties such as the Greenback party (1876–1884) and the People's Party (1892–1908) never won the presidency. However, they did influence the politics of the two major parties, especially the Democratic party, and succeeded in weakening this party by cutting into its voting strength.

Because of this Populist influence, the Democrats remained dependent for support on the more Populist South and West, where the population was relatively constant. They lost strength in the industrial Northeast, where population was growing because of the wave of European immigrants coming to work in the factories. The consequence was that from 1896 on the Democrats lost seven of the next nine presidential elections.

The Democratic New Deal coalition

This losing record did not change until the Great Depression, which created so much economic hardship that it forced a major political realignment. Democrat Franklin Roosevelt replaced Republican Herbert Hoover in 1933, pledging to the American people a "New Deal" – a metaphor that suggests both a new hand of cards in a risky game and a new set of "terms of trade" between government and the people. Both of these implications turned out to be true, as we shall see in Chapter 16.

In terms of American party politics, the New Deal turned out to mean a new Democratic dominance. Roosevelt was able to win four straight presidential elections by establishing and maintaining what is usually called the "New Deal coalition" or the "Democratic coalition." This political grouping was based on what we referred to last chapter as "class voting" – voting by economic status rather than, as previously, along geographical lines.

Roosevelt continued to pay heed to the needs of the many small farmers – the traditional political base of the Democrats. But he began to support legislation to strengthen labor unions and so began to polarize politics along class lines. The poor and workers were more and more Democratic, the rich and much of the professional middle class voted Republican, and the farmers tended to vote according to their most recent harvest.

Recent shifts In the elections since the New Deal years of 1932–1945, the Republicans have fared best when they could break up this class polarization. Dwight Eisenhower won in 1952 by attacking corruption in Democrat Harry Truman's government and pledging to use his experience as a career military man to end America's fighting in the Korean War. Both of these were nonclass issues. Ike, as he was affectionately known to the American people, won reelection by a landslide in 1956 on a platform citing "peace, prosperity, and progress" – achievements that also cut across class lines.

But that prosperity turned into "recession" (an economic decline or slowdown), and Eisenhower's vice-president, Richard Nixon, lost narrowly in 1960 to Democrat John Kennedy, who pledged to "get this country moving again." Kennedy's vice-president, Lyndon Johnson, became president when Kennedy was assassinated on November 22, 1963. Johnson then emphasized economic issues – the problems of the poor in particular – in winning the 1964 election. And it was only by arguing that he had "a secret plan" to achieve peace in Vietnam – another nonclass issue – that Nixon barely defeated Johnson's vice-president, Hubert Humphrey, in 1968. Nixon's reelection in 1972 was built even further upon nonclass issues. In foreign affairs he cited the "winding down" of the war in Vietnam. In domestic affairs, he appealed to what he called "the silent majority." That group was made up of largely middle-class Republicans and traditionally Democratic urban ethnic groups and workers. These voting groups supported his "law and order" campaign against student radicals and against agitation for major new progress on racial integration through school busing and "reverse discrimination" – both of which issues split the traditional New Deal coalition.

As we saw in Perspective 2, the Carter victory in 1976 showed some signs of rebuilding that traditional coalition. One such sign was renewed Democratic success in the South. As a Southerner, Carter was able to achieve this by combining white and black support there. The other major sign was the return to the fold of those concerned about economic issues because America had just been through the worst recession since the 1930s. But whether the major parties should expect or can rely upon a continuance of such class-based voting in a country that has become more and more middle class is something most experts now doubt.

This apparent weakening of class-based strength of our major parties has been reflected in the problems of the Republicans in 1964 (the Goldwater disaster), the Democrats in 1972 (the McGovern disaster), the Republicans in 1976 (unprecedented weakness in Congress and the states). These developments raise anew the question of what sustains our parties, even when they suffer drastic electoral losses. For possible answers we must look beyond electoral history to the relations between the parties over time, and then to the internal organization of the parties.

■ Collusion of the parties

In the years of Populism, we noted above, the Democrats lost seven of nine presidential elections. They won two elections as a minority party only because the Republicans were severely split among themselves. If parties had as their chief objective the winning of elections, we would expect the Democratic party in this period to have changed its policies and its candidates to appeal to a wider range of the population. But the southern Democratic leaders who controlled the party then did not do so. Instead, as one observer has written, "The southern Democrats were content to abandon the presidency as long as the federal government covertly agreed to allow white domination in the South."[9] Following the Civil War, northerners went south and enforced greater political opportunities for blacks. To do so they manipulated elections and passed the constitutional amendments discussed last chapter. As this Reconstruction period came to a close, southern whites restored full-fledged "white supremacy" with the "Jim Crow" segregation laws that were not seriously challenged until 25 years ago.

Some observers think they detect, in this period, a tacit, or unspoken, agreement between the party leaderships to let segregation stand in a South dominated by the Democrats in return for Republican control of the White House. The result of unchallenged Democratic political domination of the South was almost total control of the Congress by southern Democrats. This control, only now beginning to slacken, enabled the South to resist civil rights legislation long after majorities of the American population were opposed to segregation.

This southern domination was made possible by the **seniority system** in Congress. Under this system, a committee is automatically chaired by the majority party committee member who has served longest on the committee. (The system gets its name from the Latin word *senex,* meaning "old man.") Because Republicans rarely challenged Democrats in the South, southern Democrats generally had what are called "safe seats" in Congress. They, therefore, rapidly moved to dominant seniority positions on important committees. Once there they could use complicated congressional rules to keep legislation on civil rights and other liberal matters they opposed "bottled up" in committee. Because of this, the more liberal House or Senate as a whole never had a chance to vote on it. (We shall see in more detail how this seniority system worked, and how it is finally starting to change, in Chapter 8.)

---

[9]Paul R. Abramson, *Generational Change in American Politics* (Lexington, Mass.: Lexington Books, 1975), p. 4. This book presents a very interesting and helpful analysis of changes in the class basis of voting.

This apparent tacit, or unspoken, cooperation between the conservative Republican party and the segregationist southern Democratic party is but one instance of a more general form of what some call collusion between the parties. Such collusion helps to explain how a party that is weak nationally continues to survive. It also helps to explain why each party remains weak locally in some places even when a great Republican or Democrat tide seems to be sweeping the country.

■ **The federal structure of the parties** One way to begin to uncover the roots of this phenomenon of apparent party collusion is to take a look at the structure of the parties. We tend to think of our parties as national parties. It is true that each party runs a single candidate for president across the entire nation. It is also true that each party has a national committee that is supposed to conduct or supervise party affairs from a national perspective. But these national committees are made up largely of representatives selected by the party organizations in each state. And in each state the party organization is dominated by one or more regions (mainly cities or counties) in which the party is traditionally dominant.

Furthermore, within most states, one party is permanently dominant over the other. One expert estimates that in 1904, when the Republican party had achieved the position of ascendancy we described earlier, there were only 6 states where the parties were evenly matched and so actually competed, whereas there were 30 in which there was virtually no party competition.[10] In the 75 years since, there have been relatively few changes.

This party domination is found not so much in the presidential vote, which may vary from election to election, but rather in party strength in state legislatures. The situation there has been such that, in the words of one astute political scientist, "Within a large proportion of the states only by the most generous characterization may it be said that political parties compete for power."[11] This party predominance derives from strength in particular legislative districts, in many of which one party will run no opponent at all, or at most only a token opponent. It extends also to mayoral races in cities and races for U.S. Congress as well. One sign of this is the fact that in 1970, a year of political turmoil and discontent because of Vietnam and campus riots, 375 of 384 members of the House of Representatives who ran for reelection won, in large part because they often had weak opposition regardless of their party.

The point is that political parties at the local and state levels tend to be more than parties. We normally think of a party as a group of candidates, organizers, and voters who combine to support a group of candidates in an election. But at local and state levels, a dominant party is sometimes more like a "political machine" – a well-entrenched organization of leaders and followers who are able in one way or

The late Mayor Richard Daley of Chicago at the 1976 Democratic National Convention.
Stan Wakefield

[10]E. E. Schattschneider, *The Semisovereign People: A Realist's View of Democracy in America* (New York: Holt, Rinehart & Winston, 1960), p. 83.

[11]V. O. Key, quoted in Walter Karp, *Indispensable Enemies* (Baltimore: Penguin, 1974), p. 7. For "the most generous characterization," see Austin Ranney, "Parties in State Politics," in *Politics in the American States,* 3rd ed., ed. Herbert Jacob and Kenneth Vines (Boston: Little, Brown, 1976), who finds 7 "noncompetitive" states, 15 "modified competitive" states, and 28 "competitive" states.

another to control nominations, if not always elections. The late Mayor Richard J. Daley of Chicago, often called "the last of the big city bosses," always referred to "the organization" rather than "my machine," but everyone knew what he meant.

The most important thing to such an "organization" is not winning national elections. Instead, it is maintaining its own position of local control by winning locally and perhaps maintaining a "live and let live" or "we won't challenge you in your backyard if you don't challenge us in ours" relationship with other political organizations of whatever party at whatever level of government.

Machines, as we shall see in Chapter 18, are able to maintain such collusion – and so keep each other in power in separate areas – through a wide variety of devices. One is patronage – jobs given to political supporters, which can be dispensed to members of both parties where the machine wants to keep the other party happy though out of power. Another is reapportionment (redrawing boundaries of legislative districts as populations change), which can be done in a way that strengthens each party in its home base by carving up sections to exclude areas of strong support for an opposing party from districts the machine controls and vice versa. Yet another is *electoral fraud*, made possible by the fact that state law usually gives parties the major responsibility for conducting and policing elections. This allows parties to perpetrate electoral fraud with mutual tolerance. But perhaps the most powerful technique is careful *selection of opposition candidates*.

A striking example of this apparent collusion between "indispensable enemies" is offered by political journalist Walter Karp. "In New York," he writes, "the state Republican organization protects the Democratic bosses of the city [who in turn do not seriously challenge Republican domination of the state government in Albany] by the usual methods of nominating inept condidates, providing no campaign funds, raising no public issues, sabotaging local Republican candidates who show an unseemly desire to win, keeping local Republican clubs in the hands of leaders who want to lose and so on."[12]

Perhaps Karp overstates his case somewhat in applying it to virtually all levels of American politics from the local to the presidential. Experts disagree among themselves. In any case, there is enough insight in it to help us understand how our parties use the federal system to sustain themselves – and each other, as "indispensable enemies."

■ Party reform

Efforts have been made, with increasing success over the years, to overcome some of this organization domination of parties, especially at the presidential level. Chief among them are establishment of the "direct primary" and reform of political conventions.

In the heyday of machine politics, the party bosses controlled candidate selection openly. Local "party clubs" and organizations would nominate local candidates and would select delegates to state and national conventions where other candidates were chosen.

---

[12]Karp, *Indispensable Enemies,* p. 34.

Stan Wakefield

Recent national conventions have had broadened participation by minorities, women, and the young.

The **direct primary** began to be used more frequently around the turn of the century, when efforts were being made to weaken the machines. In it, voters (only party members if it is a "closed" primary; all voters if it is "open") choose a candidate from among those who have signed up or submitted nominating petitions with a specified number of voter signatures. The name "primary" comes from the Latin word *primus,* "the first"; a primary is the first election, to be followed by the **general election** involving candidates from all parties competing.

The direct primary made control of candidate selection more difficult for party bosses. But the bosses were still generally able to control presidential nominations, because they were able to dominate selection of national convention delegates. Increasingly, however, such delegates have themselves been selected by a primary – an **indirect primary** in that it picks delegates who then meet to pick the candidates in a party convention.

But even the selection of national convention delegates by primary was not enough to break control of the bosses. They still ran their candidates and generally "worked the process" better because they knew it better. So in 1968, discontented Democrats achieved passage of a resolution at the national convention to open up the selection of delegates to the 1972 convention. A Commission on Party Structure and Delegate Selection was established. Its cochairmen were Senator George McGovern and Representative Donald Fraser. It issued a report 2 years later proposing four major reforms.

The first proposals were *procedural reforms* ("fair play rules," as they were soon to be called) to ensure that party meetings were open to all members, announced in advance, held in public places, allowed only those actually in attendance to vote, and had written rules (something new to ten states).

Second came a call for *broadened participation* by minorities, women, and youths 18 or older (18-through-20-year-olds had just been granted the vote) "in reasonable relationship to their presence in the state's population" because all had been underrepresented previously.

A third reform proposed *altered delegate-selection procedures* so that delegates would be selected within a year of the election, and at least 75 percent would be selected in state primaries or local conventions. Many delegates were selected even before candidates had announced, and most were picked by the state committee.

A final proposal was to modernize and reinvigorate the party by establishing a "*mini-convention*" to meet in between presidential conventions to modernize rules and update the party platform.

These reform proposals were adopted by the national committee and enforced on the state parties in 1972, when they were used effectively by McGovern himself in his successful drive for the nomination. When McGovern was defeated in the general election, opponents acted to water down the reforms and achieved limited success. But the Democratic party remains a relatively open party – at least, much more open than the Republican.

This survey points to five factors responsible for the sustenance of our parties: (1) their constitutional and legal bases, (2) certain historical developments, (3) the tacit collusion of the party organizations, (4) the federal structure and organization of parties so as to give great power to state and local branches, and (5) the movement to reform party structures and procedures. These factors are all aspects of our American party system, which is characterized most strikingly by two-party dominance. So it is to examination of the nature of the *party system* as such that we now turn.

□ THE NATURE OF OUR PARTY SYSTEM

In national terms, the United States has, since 1800, always had a two-party system. We have seen that smaller parties have come and gone as their special issues – from prohibition of alcohol to socialism – have risen and fallen in public interest. But since the Civil War our politics have been dominated, in somewhat alternating fashion, by the Democratic and Republican parties.

These parties have been loose national confederations of state and local units. Their members have really been more like "supporters" in comparison to party members in other countries, for they do not pay dues and are not compelled, or even often expected, to demonstrate "party loyalty." The result of this decentralized two-party structure has been parties that are, in the late Clinton Rossiter's terms, "creatures of compromise, coalitions of interest in which principle is muted and often even silenced. They are vast, gaudy, friendly umbrellas under which all Americans, whoever and wherever and however minded they may be, are invited to stand for the sake of being counted in the next election."[13]

The major parties have thus lacked consistent strong ideological positions and programs and have often competed with each other for the support of the same groups of voters. Their leaders and candidates have often been virtually indistinguishable.[14] Some experts have suggested that our political figures are more influenced in their attitudes and policy positions by their locations in the political structure than by either their own beliefs or those of the constituents or voters who elected them. This may explain the frequent difficulty a Democratic president has in getting a Democratic Congress to accept and adopt his "legislative program." But not all congressional Democrats agree among themselves.

As a general rule, in recent decades the members of each party in the Senate have tended to be somewhat more liberal than those of each in the House. But in each body there have been conservative and liberal members of each party, sometimes differentiated by their geographical origins

■ How our major parties differ

The differences within each party in Congress may seem to suggest that the parties themselves are not really very different – that each is a collection of liberals, moderates, and conservatives. But this view is wrong in several important ways. First, as we suggested earlier, the parties draw their basic support from different social groups. Republicans tend to be richer and Protestant, for example, whereas

---

[13]Rossiter, *Parties and Politics in America,* p. 11.

[14]For a helpful characterization of our party system, see Everett Carll Ladd, Jr., *American Political Parties: Social Change and Political Response* (New York: Norton, 1970), chap. 2.

TABLE 4.1

Top ten policy priorities of party leaders

Republicans	Democrats
1. Controlling inflation	1. Reducing unemployment
2. Reducing the role of government	2. Controlling inflation
3. Strong military defense	3. Protecting free speech
4. Developing energy sources	4. Developing energy sources
5. Reducing crime	5. Equality for blacks
6. Reducing unemployment	6. Reducing crime
7. Protecting free speech	7. Giving people more say in government decisions
8. Giving people more say in government decisions	8. Equality for women
9. Equality for blacks	9. Strong military defense
10. Equality for women	10. Reducing the role of government

Source: Washington Post, September 27, 1976, p. 1.

Democrats include larger segments of union workers, Catholics and Jews, members of ethnic minority groups, and southerners.

Second, party supporters (voters) do tend to have relatively similar or highly overlapping political philosophies. But candidates, officeholders, and activists do differ significantly by party. In general, studies show that Democratic activists tend to favor government action to cope with problems of poverty, injustice, and inequality. Republican activists, by contrast, tend to rely on the competitive economic system and the personal character of citizens to cope with such problems.[15]

Such differences seem to be increasing, according to a 1976 survey of national, state, and local party leaders. Asked where the blame for poverty lies, Democratic leaders, by a margin of five to one, placed it on "a system which does not give everyone an equal break." By contrast, Republican leaders blamed the poor themselves for their poverty, by four to one. Asked whether the government should guarantee a job to everyone who wants to work, Democratic leaders agreed by a six-to-one ratio, whereas Republican leaders disagreed, ten to one. These same leaders were asked to rank in order of importance ten major national problems. Table 4.1 reveals striking differences in priority, with Democrats emphasizing unemployment, free speech, and racial equality, whereas Republicans emphasized reducing the role of government and strong military defense. Relative agreement occurred only on a high priority for fighting inflation and a moderate priority for developing energy sources and reducing crime.[16]

Members of Congress, too, generally show significant agreement with fellow party members except when there are strong pressures in another direction from their own constituents or from strong interest groups in their districts. Congressional voting studies also reveal significant differences between the ways the majority of Democrats vote and the ways the majority of Republicans vote. These differences are comparable to those found among party activists.

---

[15]The pioneering study of activists' attitudes is reported in Herbert McClosky, Paul J. Hoffmann, and Rosemary O'Hara, "Issue Conflict and Consensus among Party Leaders and Followers," *American Political Science Review,* June 1960, p. 420.

[16]This report is based on a survey of attitudes of American political leaders conducted by the Harvard Center for International Affairs and the *Washington Post,* reported in *The Washington Post,* September 27, 1976, p. 1.

There are, in sum, significant differences between the parties in policy positions. These differences are, however, somewhat reduced by the fact that each of our two major parties contains within its ranks people whose views seem more in harmony with those of the majority of the other party. What accounts for this combination of difference and overlap?

□ WHAT OUR TWO-PARTY SYSTEM DOES TO OUR POLITICS

We have already noted that the two-party structure of our politics makes it easier for the parties and their leaders to collude at local and state levels to protect their strongholds and to avoid competition that might be difficult for both. At the national level, a major effect of the two-party system is to encourage both parties to move toward the center in order to gain enough support to win elections. Some of this support will come from people who usually support the other party but are disenchanted with its current candidate. More of it will come from voters who declare themselves independents and hold moderate or middle-of-the-road views.

■ The spectrum of political positions To explain this point, it may help to use an illustration, even though all such illustrations oversimplify. Imagine that we can categorize likely voters as liberals, moderates, or conservatives. We do not know for sure just how large each group would be, but we would expect to find more moderates than people on either extreme. In Figure 4.2, the so-called bell-shaped curve represents the American electorate. Then we can add curves for normally Democratic and Republican voters, with independents making up the remainder of the electorate. Now we can add a curve representing the views of Democratic politicians and activists, which tends toward the liberal left, and another for Republican activists and politicians, which tends toward the conservative right. But notice that they overlap. We can then note where various presidential candidates might themselves be located by a series of dots, from Barry Goldwater on the extreme Republican right to George McGovern on the left liberal side, with Ronald Reagan, Gerald Ford, Richard Nixon, Jimmy Carter, and Lyndon Johnson in between.

FIGURE 4.2
The spectrum of political positions.

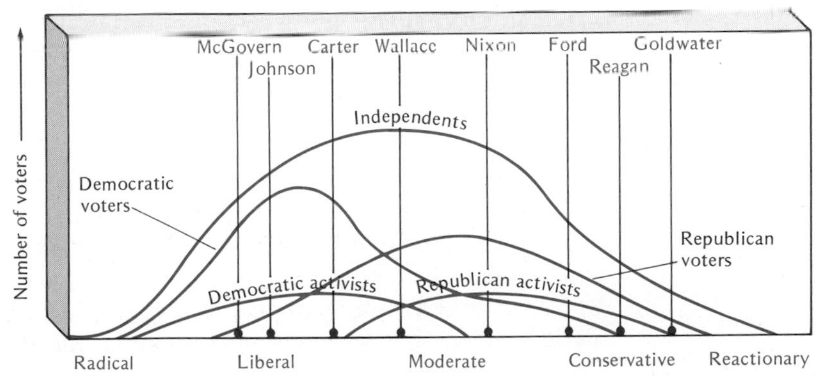

Most of the population is clustered around the middle of the political spectrum. Because there are only two major candidates in most elections after the primaries, presidential candidates will assume they can hold the votes of everyone from their point over in the direction away from the opponent. This usually means that the Democratic candidate gets the liberals and the Republican, the conservatives. Each candidate also expects to get the support of most people who think of themselves as members of or supporters of his or her party – indicated on our diagram as Democratic or Republican voters. This is usually true even though the voters may in fact be more conservative than their Democratic candidate or more liberal than their Republican candidate.

No candidate can win, however, without also getting substantial support from the independents. And each will hope to get defectors from the other party. So in the campaign each party will tend to move toward the center in order to pick up these necessary additional votes. This *competition for the middle* is a consequence of our two-party structure.

If we did not have two-party dominance, there might be a radical party, a liberal party, a conservative party, and a reactionary party, and each might emphasize its distinctiveness in campaigning. Then after the election in such a multiparty (or "many party") system, there would be several possible developments of sorts we find in other democracies. There could be a run-off election between the top two vote getters to determine the winner of a ruling majority. Or there might be bargaining between the parties to form a coalition government made up of several parties in the legislature. Or there might be a "minority government" in which the leading vote getter ruled even without a majority.

Our two-party dominance prevents the uncertainty and instability that may result in a multiparty system. But it also reduces the obvious differences between candidates and parties, for both parties tend to converge on the middle, competing for moderate votes. A two-party system is, therefore, likely to disappoint many voters in any given election who want "a choice, not an echo" (to use Barry Goldwater's characterization of his conservative candidacy in 1968).

□ MAJOR PARTIES AND MINOR PARTIES IN OUR PARTY SYSTEM

If there are many voters unhappy with the two available choices in a given election, they can of course attempt to form a new party that better reflects their views. American history, we have noted, is full of such efforts. But no such "third party" – as it is usually called – has ever won an election, and few have lasted longer than several elections before giving up in discouragement.

What usually happens is that if the new party reflects a major new view of a significant segment of the population, one or the other major party will tend to adopt that position and so woo the unhappy voters to its camp. In the years of Populism, which we discussed above, the Democratic party became more and more Populist and the People's party faded away. In the Depression, the Socialist party campaigned for government intervention in the economy on grounds that capitalism had collapsed. Roosevelt's New Deal eventually adopted major portions of its program, and a party that once won over a million votes in a single election became a very minor party again. Similarly, George Wallace's American Independent party polled well on a law-and-order and anti-school-busing platform until the Republicans under Nixon adopted much of its program. (Wallace's crippling by a would-be assassin in the 1972 campaign was also a factor, of course.)

Eugene McCarthy's independent campaign in the 1976 election was less an issue campaign than one based on his own character and on widespread lack of enthusiasm for either Ford or Carter, particularly among left-wing students. It was, therefore, less likely to have a policy impact on either party. But it does seem to have shifted a handful of key states into the Republican column by taking votes that would otherwise have gone to Carter. McCarthy may thereby have come very close to changing the election's outcome.

There remain, of course, other minor parties. Some of them come and go, while others such as the Prohibition (of alcoholic beverages) party have been running without electoral success for many decades. Action Unit 4.2 lists the major and minor parties still alive in the late 1970s and indicates how you can contact them to learn more about their party positions and candidates.

Poster depicting Republican campaign strategy for the election of 1860.

□ ACTION UNIT 4.2 American political parties and how to contact them

This list includes the major and minor national political parties in America as of the 1976 presidential election. There are in addition many smaller parties with a local or scattered membership. For information on some of them, as well as more information on many of these listed here, see Phyllis Butler and Dorothy Gray, *Everywoman's Guide to Political Awareness* (Millbrae, Calif.: Les Femmes Publishing, 1976).

American Party, also known as the American Independent Party (100 River Road, Box 1098, Pigeon Force, Tenn. 37863). Founded in 1968 with the candidacy of George Wallace, this national organization continues to run candidates for president and certain state offices.

Communist Party of the United States of America (P.O. Box 72116, Watts Station, Los Angeles, Calif. 90002). Founded in 1965, this party has 2500 members who claim to be "Representatives of the American Working Class." It seeks "establishment of the Dictatorship of the Proletariat and the construction of Socialism as a political and economic system in the U.S." and favors détente with the Soviet Union; it publishes a biweekly, *People's Voice,* and a bimonthly, *Red Flag*.

Democratic Party (1625 Massachusetts Ave. NW, Washington D.C. 20036). Founded in its present form in 1848.

Libertarian Party, also known as the National Libertarian Party (P.O. Box 31638, Aurora, Colo. 80011). Founded in 1971, this is an extremely conservative party that has 4000 members and hopes to establish a voluntary society of free markets and free enterprise, in which the role of the government is limited to protecting citizens from the initiation of force against the person and his or her property, and in which there is no draft, no taxes, and no foreign involvements; its presidential candidate in 1976 was Roger MacBride.

National Socialist White People's Party, formerly called the American Nazi Party (2507 North Franklin Road, Arlington, Va. 22201). This extreme right-wing party was founded in 1959 of people who describe themselves as "White Americans of Aryan descent who accept the National Socialist teachings of Adolf Hitler without reservation and are willing to submit themselves to Party discipline." Its program calls for "A White America; White World Solidarity; A New Social Order; An Honest Economy; White Self-Defense; Government by Leaders; A Spiritual Rebirth; An Aryan Culture; A Healthy Environment; A Better Race."

National States' Rights Party (P.O. Box 1211, Marietta, Ga. 30061). Founded in 1948, this party advocates racial segregation and state sovereignty against the federal government; it includes 12,000 "White Gentile Americans of voting age" and publishes the monthly newspaper *Thunderbolt.*

People's Party, formerly called The Coalition (1065 31st Street NW, Washington, D.C. 20005). Founded in 1971, this party is a coalition of various local parties and describes itself as including "People interested in radical political action, including nonviolent direct action, and creation of alternative institutions, as well as electoral politics," seeking to build a political movement that will work at the local level to promote "a more humane approach to social organization" to "help transform America into a nonracist, anti-imperialist country in which all Americans share in the country's wealth."

Progressive Labor Party (GPO Box 808, Brooklyn, N.Y. 11201). Founded in 1962, this party seeks to establish socialism through a revolution to overthrow the governments of the "bosses" and establish the dictatorship of the working class guided by Marxism-Leninism.

Prohibition National Committee (P.O. Box 2635, Denver, CO 80201). Founded in 1869, this is the administrative body of the Prohibition Party, which still runs presidential candidates, and advocates "repeal of all laws which legalize the liquor traffic and the enactment and rigorous enforcement of new laws which prohibit the manufacture, distribution and sale of alcoholic beverages," but criticizes the income tax and federal aid to education.

Raza Unida Party (1410 West Zavala, Crystal City, Tex. 78839). Founded in 1970, this party has 67,000 members, primarily Chicanos, seeking political control of local governments; we shall examine it further in Chapter 14.

Republican Party (310 First Street SE, Washington, D.C. 20003). Founded in 1856.

Socialist Labor Party (914 Industrial Avenue, Palo Alto, Calif. 94303). Founded in 1891, this party seeks "the peaceful abolition of capitalism via the ballot, backed up by an industrial organization," runs various candidates nationally and locally, and publishes the newspaper *Weekly People.*

Socialist Party, U.S.A. (1012 North Third Street, Milwaukee, Wisc. 53212). Founded in 1901, this "right-wing" socialist party was an important political force during the Depression and still runs presidential candidates.

U.S. Labor Party (231 West 29th Street, 15th Floor, New York N.Y. 10001). Founded to compete in the 1976 election, this party ran Lyndon H. LaRouche for president, but he announced his preference for the election of Gerald Ford rather than the election of Jimmy Carter.

Two other groups ran important candidates in the 1976 election: the Committee for a Constitutional Presidency (1223 Connecticut Avenue NW, Washington D.C. 20036), which ran Eugene McCarthy, and the Pro-Life Action Committee (P.O. Box 62, Bellmore, N.Y. 11710), which ran Ellen McCormack.

□ WHAT SUSTAINS OUR TWO-PARTY SYSTEM

Minor parties fail to become major parties. The same two parties remain the major parties. Why? What sustains our two-party system? Political observers offer four major explanations, although there is as yet no consensus.

Some have cited the fact that in the early years there was a *political split* between the northern industrialists, commercialists, and financiers (the Federalists/Whigs/Republicans) and the southern farmers and western frontiersmen (the Jeffersonian Republicans/Jacksonian Democrats). A two party system developed then, and perhaps its persistence has been a combination of habit and inertia based on this early situation.[17]

Another argument notes that there was a general *social homogeneity* in the parties in the early agrarian years of the Republic, perhaps largely because those without property were also without a vote. Perhaps this social consensus has tended to persist even as the franchise has widened. The overlap we found in the attitudes of Republicans and Democrats is cited in support of this view.

A third theory argues that, like our British forefathers, we have always been *"politically mature."* We understand the virtues of stability and the essential role that compromise or accommodation plays in maintaining stability. A two-party system in this view is a sensible conscious selection.

[17]See, for example, the argument of V. O. Key, *Politics, Parties, and Pressure Groups,* 5th ed. (New York: Crowell, 1964), pp. 229ff.

The explanation that convinces most observers is the *institutional.* Our legal system provides for single-member districts: Only one person represents a district in Congress. We also have "winner-take-all" elections: A plurality, or one vote more than the second highest candidate, is all that is required to win. This tends to force parties and candidates to avoid taking more extreme stands in a first election because they cannot then compromise in a runoff. Thus there is little hope for success for extremist parties and positions, and only two parties are likely to survive. In addition, our Constitution provides for a single national executive, the president, and each state has a single governor. This means that a minor party cannot run a minority candidate and then become part of a coalition cabinet government, as often happens in Europe's multiparty systems, because there is only one elected leader.

There is no way of proving that any one of these theories is correct and adequate in explaining why we have a two-party-dominant system. Perhaps all four theories point to important factors in the shaping of American party politics.[18] But do they thereby guarantee that the American system will continue as is in coming years?

---

[18]Frank Sorauf, one of America's leading experts on parties, suggests that this is so following his presentation of all four theories. See Sorauf, *Party Politics in America,* pp. 37–41.

□ WILL OUR TWO-PARTY SYSTEM SURVIVE?

Many political activists and observers have long been unhappy with the way our present party system operates. Some favor greater diversity of the sort that a multiparty system would allow or even foster. Others favor development of a system of "party government" by which parties would be made more "responsible" to the electorate.

■ The "party government" alternative We have seen that our parties are decentralized and heterogeneous. This makes it difficult to know just what each stands for when we vote. It also makes it difficult for a president or even the majority party leaders in Congress to get the Congress to pass promised legislation. The suggestion is made, therefore, that parties should be made to pledge particular programs. The winning party then should compel or "discipline" its members to vote for those programs. It might do this by expelling deviants, denying them committee assignments, and refusing to give them financial help in their next campaign or running another candidate against them.

Such a system of party government would make the parties more ideological and the government more responsible to the electorate. Voters would know what they were getting in advance. If they did not get what they expected, and could collectively vote a ruling party out at the next election by defeating the members of Congress up for reelection, American politics would become more issue-oriented as a result.

But this very ideological, issue-based politics scares some observers, who believe that instability and confrontation would result. They fear that Congress would become less flexible. They also fear that its members, who now are able to be relatively independent and deliberative, would lose this freedom and so could make fewer contributions to the development of constructive legislation. Furthermore, special interests of various sorts, good or bad, would lose the important role they now have.

The debate over the desirability of such party government has been carried on for decades and will no doubt continue.[19] Meanwhile, advocates of change have suggested that a more likely, and perhaps safer, route to the same sort of issue-oriented responsible politics is *"party realignment."*

■ The "party realignment" alternative We have noted that voters are less and less inclined to identify with a particular party. They are also more and more inclined to "split their tickets" when they vote, picking some candidates from one party and some from the other. Furthermore, some join special-interest groups that reflect their policy views and lobby to achieve them. Some observers take these developments as signs that our

[19]For a discussion of the arguments, see Sorauf, *Party Politics in America,* chap. 16. The stimulus for the debate was a report prepared by a group of political scientists: Committee on Political Parties of the American Political Science Association, *Toward a More Responsible Two-Party System* (New York: Rinehart, 1950).

traditional parties do not and cannot any longer express the views and interests of most Americans. If this analysis is correct, one possible outcome is splintering of the two parties into many smaller parties. Another possibility, however, is realignment by which conservatives would be grouped in a new conservative party, and liberals in another party, or perhaps in a revised Democratic party.

When Ronald Reagan lost his struggle for the Republican nomination in 1976, a number of conservative leaders asserted that it was time to form a new national conservative party. They claimed that this could be the new majority party in America if it could break the conservative South away from the Democrats.

Others have suggested that a more likely basis for realignment would be social or economic class. This might produce an upper-class party of wealthy business people and professionals and a working-class party of labor and intellectuals.[20]

Major realignments, changing either the party structure or party postures, have occurred five times in American history: 1800 (the Jeffersonian Republicans); 1828 (the Jacksonian Democrats); 1860 (the Lincoln Republicans); 1896 (the Bryan Populist Democrats); and 1932 (the Roosevelt New Deal). These "critical elections," as they are often called, came at times of political turmoil and had effects that lasted for periods of 30 to 40 years. By such calculation, a realignment may be overdue in America. But experts on the electorate are generally less convinced than are the discontented conservatives that such an upheaval is in the offing.

■ Some trends to watch

There are, nonetheless, trends that bear watching for their still unpredictable implications. Foremost among these is *the decline in party identification* (membership) that we discussed last chapter. Fewer and fewer Americans are "open Democrats" (as distinguished from "closet Democrats" who claim to be independents but still vote Democratic when they get to the polling place) and "open Republicans." This continuing decline in party identification may be a facet of what Walter Dean Burnham has called "the onward march of party decomposition."[21]

On the other hand, it is possible that the parties will find ways of arresting the decline. Or they may compensate for it by attracting new members among the groups long excluded from active party roles, especially ethnic minorities (in all but big-city machines) and the young.

One reason to think that the Democratic party may succeed in doing so is the other, more organizational, trend: *the movement toward greater democratization* of Democratic party rules and activities, which we discussed earlier. It is still too soon to know which of the reforms will survive, let alone what their impact will be. It is also too soon to know whether the Republican party will do likewise. But if the parties take their worsening plight seriously, such moves might help restore their health.

---

[20]For examination of one such suggestion, see Broder, *The Party's Over.*

[21]See Walter Dean Burnham, *Critical Elections and the Mainsprings of American Politics* (New York: Norton, 1970), and his updating article, "American Politics in the 1970s: Beyond Party?" in *The Future of Political Parties,* ed. Louis Maisel and Paul M. Sachs (Beverly Hills, Calif.: Sage, 1975), pp. 238–277.

We may well wonder, however, what would replace parties as organizers of citizen opinion into forms that can shape political outcomes. Interest groups, which we shall examine in Chapter 11, perform some of the same functions of mobilizing opinion and support. But interest groups do not generally select and run candidates for office. Nor indeed do those other leading political organizers, protest groups. So it is not at all clear what would or could step in to fill the void that would be left by the collapse of our parties.

But then, the parties have not yet collapsed, even though fewer and fewer Americans are willing to join them. Lest we think that this refusal to identify with parties means that people have abandoned politics, however, we must examine the various types of political participation, other than party activity, open to citizens.

□ SUGGESTIONS FOR FURTHER READING AND STUDY

Parties have been with us since the beginning, and so, it often seems, have books about American party politics. Our listing here but skims the surface and picks those that are most likely to help you develop your understanding.

Three classic historical treatments are: Wilfred Binkley, *American Political Parties,* 4th ed. (New York: Knopf, 1963), which emphasizes formation of coalitions. V. O. Key, *Politics, Parties, and Pressure Groups,* 5th ed. (New York: Crowell, 1964), which is very comprehensive although dated by now; and Clinton Rossiter, *Parties and Politics in America* (Ithaca, N.Y.: Cornell University Press paperback, 1960), a fascinating brief study. More recent books with strong historical analysis include: James L. Sundquist, *Dynamics of the Party System* (Washington, D.C.: Brookings Institution, 1973); Everett Carll Ladd, Jr., *American Political Parties: Social Change and Political Response* (New York: Norton, 1970); Everett Carll Ladd, Jr., and Charles Hadley, *Transformations of the American Party System,* 2nd ed. (New York: Norton paperback, 1978); the papers edited by William Chambers and Walter Dean Burnham, *The American Party System,* 2nd ed. (New York: Oxford University Press paperback, 1975); and Daniel A. Mazmanian, *Third Parties in Presidential Elections* (Washington, D.C.: Brookings Institution, 1974), which includes an analysis of the George Wallace phenomenon.

There is a large and interesting literature on party reform. It starts with the classic books by E. E. Schattschneider, *Party Government* (New York: Holt, 1942), and *The Struggle for Party Government* (College Park: University of Maryland Press, 1948). Two useful studies of parties and presidential nominations are Judith H. Parris, *The Convention Problem: Issues in Reform of the Presidential Nominating Process* (Washington, D.C.: Brookings Institution, 1972), and William Keech and Donald Matthews, *The Party's Choice* (Washington, D.C.: Brookings Institution, 1976), which examines nominations from 1936 to 1972. Studies focusing on reforms include: David Broder, *The Party's Over: The Failure of Politics in America* (New York: Harper & Row paperback, 1972); John S. Saloma and Frederick H. Sontag, *Parties: The Real Opportunity for Effective Citizen Politics* (New York: Knopf, 1972); Austin Ranney, *Curing the Mischiefs of Faction: Party Reform in America* (Berkeley: University of California Press, 1975); William J. Crotty, *Political Reform and the American Experiment* (New York: Crowell, 1977); and, in a more speculative vein, Walter Karp, *Indispensable Enemies* (Baltimore: Penguin paperback, 1974), and Louis Maisel and Paul M. Sachs, eds., *The Future of Political Parties* (Beverly Hills, Calif.: Sage, 1975).

Parties are, of course, found elsewhere. For comparative perspective, see two classics: Maurice Duverger, *Political Parties: Their Organization and Activity in the Modern State* (New York: Wiley, 1954), and Leon Epstein, *Political Parties in Western Democracies* (New York: Praeger, 1967); and a new comprehensive analysis, Giovanni Sartori, *Parties and Party Systems* (New York: Cambridge University Press paperback, 1976), the first of several projected volumes.

And finally, if there is something else you want to know about parties, try the most comprehensive text, Frank Sorauf, *Party Politics in America,* 3rd ed. (Boston: Little, Brown, 1976).

5 Political activists

How many Americans are political activists? Only about half of all eligible Americans actually vote in presidential elections, and even fewer vote in state and local elections. Only 15 percent of all Americans have ever written a letter to a public official, and two-thirds of all letters written to officials come from only 3 percent of the population.

Facts like these have led many observers to conclude that the American people are not really politically active and that they may not even care much about politics. Some observers lament this conclusion, fearing that it may doom democracy in America. Others, as we shall see, are reassured by it, arguing that too much participation might make our system unworkable. However we may feel about the desirability of mass participation in politics, it is difficult to challenge the conclusion that Americans are apathetic if we accept voting and letter writing as the major types of political participation available to ordinary citizens.

But studies of political behavior increasingly suggest that this conception of political participation is too narrow. There are in fact a great many other types of activity that are political. These range from signing a petition to rioting, from going to court to contest a government ruling to going to Canada to escape the draft. And some would even argue that *not voting* is itself a political act. It signifies a rejection of the system, or of the candidates and their parties. This rejection may have political implications for the future of the country that prove more serious than the actual election results.

To discover what opportunities we may have to take part in politics, and to understand how our system works and the context within which decision makers act, we need to know three things. First: What types of political activity are available to us and to American citizens generally? Second: How widely and how often do citizens engage in such activities? Third: What effects do these activities have – on the people who undertake them as well as on those in authority?

We shall find that citizen action is going on in all parts of our politics, concerning all aspects of policy. We shall refer to it in chapter after chapter to come. Sometimes it will appear as a factor in current policy decisions. Other times it will appear as a possible strategy for political change. Always it will be serving as a *linkage* or connection between the rulers and the ruled. This linkage, in its various forms, is an essential – perhaps *the* essential – aspect of effective and responsive democracy. This is a lesson all citizens must learn. It is also a lesson citizens must, from time to time, teach to wayward politicians who seem to prefer that citizens leave politics to them.

□ THE TYPES OF POLITICAL ACTION CITIZENS CAN TAKE

Political participation, Myron Weiner has written, is "any voluntary action, successful or unsuccessful, organized or unorganized, episodic or continuous, employing legitimate or illegitimate methods, intended to influence the choice of public policies, the administration of public affairs, or the choice of political leaders at any level of government, local or national."[1]

This widely accepted definition, despite its jargon, is helpful because it suggests that political participation *need not be* successful, organized, or legitimate. It also reminds us that the target of the action may be a policy maker, an administrator, or an election. Thus, it is obvious that a wide range of activities would qualify as political participation. Because there are so many, it may be helpful to do some categorizing.

We can divide the types of political action into five groups: (1) working *around* politics; (2) working *in* politics; (3) working *with* politics; (4) working *against* politics; and (5) working *beyond* politics. Having named our categories, let us look in more detail at the types of political activities that can be grouped under each heading.

■ Working around politics

Working around politics includes activities taken by citizens that demonstrate support for the political system. Some of these actions *provide patriotic support or ceremony.* Examples include saluting the flag, singing the "Star-Spangled Banner" before a football game, and saying the "pledge of allegiance." Attending a military parade, cheering the president as he drives by in a motorcade, celebrating national holidays, and flying the American flag would also count. Even putting an "America: Love It or Leave It" sticker on your car's bumper could be considered working around politics. We might even include paying your taxes as a support activity, because without that revenue the government could not function.

Yet another way to "work around politics" is to *keep informed about public issues and governmental activity.* This is, of course, an inward rather than an outward activity, but it becomes an important aspect of outward activism any time we decide to take action. Well-informed activism is, after all, much more likely to be effective than ill-informed activism.

■ Working in politics

Three types of activism fall under our heading of "working in politics." The first two are those we are most familiar with: *voting* and *doing party and campaign work.* We distinguish between these two types of electoral activities because, as we saw in Chapter 3, people generally vote out of feelings of civic duty, while those who do party and campaign work are usually more committed to a cause and expect their actions to be effective.

---

[1]Myron Weiner, "Political Participation: Crisis of the Political Process" in *Crises and Sequences in Political Development,* ed. Leonard Binder et al. (Princeton, N.J.: Princeton University Press, 1971), p. 164.

The other type of "working in politics" is *serving in government as an elected official or an appointed bureaucrat.* Rulers and servers are certainly political activists.

■ Working with politics

Our third category, "working with politics" (or working with politicians), incorporates the various "informational" activities of *lobbying* for legislation or for favorable administrative decisions by government. (We shall examine this in detail in Chapter 11.) It also includes *consulting* – the advising that is done for the government by various companies and individuals specializing in analyzing situations and proposing solutions to problems. And it includes individual citizens informing the government or politicians of their views via *letters, telegrams, telephone calls, and so on, to officials.* In all of these cases, people furnish information to politicians or to the government.

■ Working against politics

The fourth category, "working against politics" – and against politicians – includes a wide range of activities. The first type is *pressure activities* designed to compel desired responses from government. Among the pressure activities are: litigating (going to court to force the government to act as you wish); investigating for exposure, such as journalists do; organizing political support for a movement; making threats to withdraw, or promises to encourage, support for political figures; and appealing to others for support through such acts as writing letters to the editor of a newspaper (see Action Unit 5.2, p. 128).

A second type of "working against politics" is *obstructive activities* designed to make the functioning of the government or another public organization more difficult or even impossible. Unions traditionally organize strikes or slowdowns or boycotts to force companies to give in to their wage and working-condition demands. The same sort of tactics can be used by public employees and citizen groups.

An interesting instance of obstructive activities occurred in the early 1970s. It involved the air controllers who sit in control towers at airports and direct planes on landing and takeoff to help prevent collisions and crashes. They used various disruptive tactics to force their will on their employer, the government. Because, as

Martin Adler Levick/Black Star

□ ACTION UNIT 5.1 How to work in and around politics

The root of political influence lies in political activity organized at the local level—whether within or outside of official party organization. The long-term task of political education is a vital part of the process of political influence in which you can play a major role.

1. Help those around you to become aware of the ways in which decisions made by their representatives affect them. You can encourage others to join or form new discussion and action groups in their own communities, expanding participation and activity wherever possible.
2. Set up a small informal library in your area with information about your representatives, their backgrounds and voting records, as well as with materials on current political issues.
3. Help others to register and vote.
4. Arrange a "telephone tree" for rapid communication among individuals and groups in your area. This can be helpful in informing one another about future activities and meetings, but it is especially useful when urgent messages to your representatives are needed to show support for a particular piece of legislation.
5. Arrange meetings with individual senators and representatives when they are at home. You may want to get local news coverage of some sessions.
6. Several persons can have a session with your representative in his/her legislative office together over the phone by means of a "conference call." (For more information call your local operator.)
7. You may find that no prospective candidate seems to represent your beliefs and interests. If so, consider whether you or someone else in your area might be the potential candidate meeting those requirements.
8. Support the candidate of your choice by organizing appearances for him/her at group meetings and public debates before local citizens. Campaign and make financial contributions.

Adapted from "How to Work in Politics," a guide prepared by Friends Committee on National Legislation.

public employees, they were not allowed to strike, they had "sick-outs" in which large numbers phoned in sick each day. They also used a strategy known as "work-to-rule," which means following every regulation to the letter, regardless of how insignificant the rules are. These tactics delayed plane takeoffs and landings for many hours and created massive dislocation and discontent. Finally, the government was forced by this obstruction to give in to their demands.

In 1977, citizens living near New York City's Kennedy Airport objected to a court decision to allow the British-French Concorde supersonic transport plane to land. Because they lost in the courts, they decided to try to force a reversal of the decision by other means. On certain days, they all piled into their cars and drove to the airport access roads, where they then moved as slowly as possible. The hopeless traffic congestion that resulted stranded some travelers in the airport and blocked others from ever getting to the airport.

In both these instances, the actions undertaken were legal obstructions designed to force government to change its policy or position. Such activities are becoming more and more possible as our society becomes more and more dependent on technology that is easily disrupted. They are also becoming more and more common.

■ Saul Alinsky on direct action

I have emphasized and re-emphasized that tactics means you do what you can with what you've got, and that power in the main has always gravitated towards those who have money and those whom people follow. The resources of the Have-Nots are (1) no money and (2) lots of people. All right, let's start from there. People can show their power by voting. What else? Well, they have physical bodies. How can they use them? Now a melange of ideas begins to appear. Use the power of the law by making the establishment obey its own rules. Go outside the experience of the enemy, stay inside the experience of your people. Emphasize tactics that your people will enjoy. . . .

[One] tactic involving the bodily functions developed in Chicago during the days of the Johnson-Goldwater campaign. Commitments that were made by the authorities to the Woodlawn ghetto organization were not being met by the city. The political threat that had originally compelled these commitments was no longer operative. The community organization had no alternative but to support Johnson, and therefore the Democratic administration felt the political threat had evaporated. It must be remembered here that not only is pressure essential to compel the establishment to make its initial concession, but the pressure must be maintained to make the establishment deliver. The second factor seemed to be lost to the Woodlawn Organization.

Since the organization was blocked in the political arena, new tactics and a new arena had to be devised.

O'Hare Airport became the target. To begin with, O'Hare is the world's busiest airport. Think for a moment of the common experience of jet travelers. Your stewardess brings you your lunch or dinner. After eating, most people want to go to the lavatory. However, this is often inconvenient because your tray and those of your seat partners are loaded down with dishes. So you wait until the stewardess has removed the trays. By that time those who are seated closest to the lavatory have got up and the "occupied" sign is on. So you wait. And in these days of jet travel the seat belt sign is soon flashed, as the airplane starts its landing approach. You decide to wait until after landing and use the facilities in the terminal. . . .

With this in mind, the tactic becomes obvious—we tie up the lavatories. In the restrooms you drop a dime, enter, push the lock on the door—and you can stay there all day. Therefore the occupation of the sit-down toilets presents no problem. It would take just a relatively few people to walk into these cubicles armed with books and newspapers, lock the doors, and tie up all the facilities. What are the police going to do? Break in and demand evidence of legitimate occupancy? Therefore, the ladies restrooms could be occupied completely; the only problem in the men's lavatories would be the stand-up urinals. This, too, could be taken care of, by having groups busy themselves around the airport and then move in on the stand-up urinals to line up four or five deep whenever a flight arrived. An intelligence study was launched to learn how many sit-down toilets for both men and women, as well a stand-up urinals, there were in the entire O'Hare Airport complex and how many men and women would be necessary for the nation's first "shit-in."

The consequences of this kind of action would be catastrophic in many ways. People would be desperate for a place to relieve themselves. One can see children yelling at their parents, "Mommy, I've got to go," and desperate mothers surrendering, "All right—well, do it. Do it right here." O'Hare would soon become a shambles. The whole scene would become unbelievable and the laughter and ridicule would be nationwide. It would probably get a front page story in the London *Times.* It would be a source of great mortification and embarrassment to the city administration. . . .

The threat of this tactic was leaked . . . back to the administration, and within forty-eight hours the Woodlawn Organization found itself in conference with the authorities who said that they were certainly going to live up to their commitments and they could never understand where anyone got the idea that a promise made by Chicago's City Hall would not be observed.

Not all such activities depend on high technology, however. Many are undertaken by the powerless and technology-less. The most imaginative designer of such activities was the late Saul Alinsky, an urban organizer based in Chicago who spent his life helping the powerless gain greater political clout. The box "Saul Alinsky on Direct Action" contains his account of one of his more imaginative—or outrageous—programs for "direct action" of an obstructive sort.

All these programs of obstructive direct action have one thing in common: They are legal. The same cannot be said for the next two categories of "working against politics": civil disobedience and uncivil disobedience.

Civil disobedience has a long history in our country. The most recent frequent instances were parts of the civil rights movement of the 1960s and the antiwar movement during the years of Vietnam. People who commit civil disobedience break a law in order to call attention to the alleged injustice of the law, or to a policy they believe seriously wrong. Being apprehended and punished for the lawbreaking is an essential part of the action. This emphasizes one's commitment to the cause and generates pressure against the system that operates in this allegedly unjust or mistaken way. During the civil rights movement, blacks and whites "sat in" at lunch counters in the South where local or state law prohibited integrated eating. They were generally arrested (and often beaten by police or by outraged local citizens). But their willing submission to the law and acceptance of the punishment called attention to the law and laid the political and legal groundwork for new laws outlawing racial discrimination in public accommodations. Much the same was done by people who resisted the draft, burned their draft cards, or staged sit-ins in Washington during the Vietnam War. Others refused to pay the portion of their income taxes that supported the war or the special "Vietnam War tax" on their telephone bills, for example. Always, in these cases of civil disobedience, the action is nonviolent, and the punishment is accepted as part of the protest.

Other instances of "working against politics" are quite different, and might be termed *"uncivil" disobedience.* Instances of rioting, arson, assassination, terrorist acts, and other forms of violence are one category. Bribery of public officials, ideologically based shoplifting or other theft (assertedly intended to "strike a blow against capitalism"), and other nonviolent deeds constitute another category. They have in common, however, an effort to circumvent the law and to avoid paying the consequences for the act. Their flagrant challenge to the law automatically makes them instances of political activism. The effort to escape punishment makes them all the more dangerous to the existing order in general, and to the rule of law in particular. But it may also make them less likely to get public support.

■ Working beyond politics

Our final category, "working beyond politics," also poses particular challenges to the existing order, but in a somewhat different way. We are all familiar with protest demonstrations, negative bumper stickers (such as "America: Change It Or Lose It," or "Register criminals, not guns"), and popular protest songs. Such actions and statements differ from "working with politics" in that they do not have a particular target that could act as they recommend. These actions and statements are often called *expressive* or *assertive* acts. They express concerns but are intended for

☐ ACTION UNIT 5.2 How to write an effective letter to the editor

Here are some suggestions that can help you to write the kind of letter that is most likely to receive favorable consideration on the editorial desk:

1. If possible, *use a typewriter* and double space the lines. Write only on one side of the paper. If you have no typewriter, write with ink, plainly and neatly.

2. *Express your thought as clearly and concisely as possible.* Editors usually prefer letters of no more than 200 or 250 words, although longer letters may be accepted if they are thought to have sufficient reader interest.

3. *Deal with only one topic in a letter.* It should be timely and newsworthy. Be sure your meaning is clear. Use as simple words as possible. Short words, short sentences, short paragraphs make for easier reading.

4. *Plan carefully your first sentence.* Aim to make it short and interesting. If you begin with a reference to a news item, editorial, or letter in the paper addressed, your letter at once has added interest for the editor.

5. If you write to criticize, *begin with a word of appreciation, agreement, or praise.* Don't be merely critical; end your letter with some constructive suggestion.

6. *Avoid violent language.* A calm, constructive presentation of your thought is more persuasive than ranting.

7. *Help supply the truth* that you feel may be omitted or slanted in reporting the news or editorializing on it.

8. *Don't hesitate to use a relevant personal experience* to illustrate a point. When rightly told, it can be persuasive.

9. *Bring moral judgments to bear* upon the issues confronting the nation and the world. Appeal to the reader's sense of fair play, justice, and mercy.

10. You can also make appropriate changes in your letter and *send it to editors of newspapers in other cities.* When doing so, always send first copies, never carbons. As a rule, do not send exactly the same letter to different papers in the same city.

11. *Always sign your name* and give your address. You can use a pen name or initials for publication, but the editor must know the source of the letter.

12. Don't give up looking for your letter too soon. It may not appear for ten days or even longer. *Don't be discouraged if your letter is not printed.* It reached the editor, and that is worth something.

Adapted from J. Stuart Innerst, "How-to-Write a Letter to the Editor," published by Friends Committee on National Legislation.

consumption not so much—or at least not directly—by politicians as by the public generally.

The other major category of "working beyond politics" that is nonetheless an important type of political activity is *extragovernmental problem solving.* In this century, Americans have tended increasingly to look to the government to solve their major problems. One of the reasons for this tendency has been the growing size and complexity of the problems—from education to space travel, from discrimination to national defense. Another reason has been the power of government, which has grown along with the problems. We have discussed this development in more detail in Chapter 1. But we shall also see here and there throughout this book signs that people are losing confidence that government can solve problems. More and more, people are attempting to regain control over their own lives by doing for themselves what government has previously tried to do.

Examples range from private schools to vigilante groups organized by citizens to police their own neighborhoods. This return to self-help, self-reliance, is itself a form of political activity because it challenges the authority of the government. And more and more Americans are engaging in this "working beyond politics."

□ WHO PARTICIPATES—AND HOW MUCH?

We have just examined briefly a variety of general types of political activity. To some degree, these various activities are open to any American, although few have the opportunity to lobby and relatively few have the occasion to engage in civil or not-so-civil disobedience. But if this wide range of activites is possible for any American, how probable is participation in them. To find out, we can examine the results of some recent surveys that asked representative groups of Americans what types of political activities they engage in from time to time, and what types they have ever engaged in. None of these surveys asked about the whole range of activities we have examined. Nor did they describe those they did ask about in identical ways. For these reasons, the best approach is to examine each study separately.

The most recent comprehensive effort to summarize research on political participation is that of Lester Milbrath and M. L. Goel.[2] They combine results from Milbrath's own survey of the population of Buffalo, New York, with those from a nationwide survey developed by Sidney Verba and Norman Nie. Their findings are summarized in Table 5.1

The survey reported by Milbrath and Goel describes the types of activity of each active segment of the population, but it does not tell us which groups within the population tend to take which actions. To get a better sense of this, we must look more closely at this aspect of Verba and Nie's study.[3]

Verba and Nie divide the population into six groups. The first group, the *inactives* (22 percent of the population) tend to be of lower socioeconomic status (SES). In this group, blacks, the young, the elderly, and women are all overrepresented. Another 21 percent of the population are in the second group; *they vote but do nothing else.* They, too, tend to be of lower SES. The elderly and city dwellers are overrepresented here, whereas those living in rural areas are underrepresented.

The third group is composed of those who *contact officials on particular concerns* but are otherwise inactive; they make up only 4 percent of the population. They tend to live in big cities and are usually Catholics rather than Protestants, whites rather than blacks, and of lower SES. The fourth group (20 percent of the population) are those who *contact officials on broader concerns, cooperate to solve local problems, and usually vote.* They tend to live in rural areas and small towns rather than big cities. They are usually of upper SES, Protestant rather than Catholic, and white rather than black.

---

[2]Lester Milbrath and M. L. Goel, *Political Participation,* 2nd ed. (Chicago: Rand McNally, 1977).

[3]Sidney Verba and Norman Nie, *Participation in America* (New York: Harper & Row, 1972).

TABLE 5.1

Ways citizens relate to the government

Group	Activities of group and percent of group taking part in given activity
Protesters	Join in public street demonstrations (3%) Riot if necessary (2%) Protest vigorously if government does something morally wrong (26%) Attend protest meetings (6%) Refuse to obey unjust laws (16%) (Protesters also take part in activities of other groups)
Community activists	Work with others on local problems (30%) Form a group to work on local problems (14%) Active membership in community organizations (8%) Contact officials on social issues (14%) (Activists also vote fairly regularly)
Party and campaign workers[a]	Actively work for party or candidate (26%) Persuade others how to vote (28%) Attend meetings, rallies (19%) Give money to party or candidate (13%) Join and support political party (35%) Be a candidate for office (3%) (Workers also vote regularly)
Communicators	Keep informed about politics (67%) Engage in political discussions (42%) Write letters to newspaper editors (9%) Send support or protest messages to political leaders (15%) (Communicators also vote fairly regularly.)
Contact specialists	Contact local, state, and national officials on particularized problems (4%) (Specialists are inactive otherwise.)
Voters and patriots	Vote regularly in elections (63%) Love my country (94%) Show patriotism by flying the flag, attending parades, etc. (70%) Pay all taxes (94%)
Nonparticipants	No voting, no other activity (22%) No patriotic inputs (3–5%)

[a]Percentages for the party campaign worker category are based mostly on a national survey of the American public conducted in 1967 and reported by Sidney Verba and Normal Nie, *Participation in America* (New York: Harper & Row, 1972). Percentages for the remaining modes are based on the Buffalo Survey (1968) by Milbrath.

Source: Adapted from Lester Milbrath and M. L. Goel, *Political Participation,* 2nd ed. ©1977 Rand McNally College Publishing Company, pp. 18-19. Reprinted by permission.

The fifth group (about 15 percent of the population) not only *votes* but is heavily *active in campaigns*. This group tends to live in big cities and suburbs, has higher SES, and is little involved in community problem solving. It includes unusual percentages of blacks and Catholics. The final group is those *active in all these ways.* About all that can be said of this 11 percent of the population is that upper SES people are overrepresented, whereas the old and the young are underrepresented.[4]

This study indicates that certain social groups tend to participate more actively than others. It also suggests that there is considerable overlap among types of activity: That is, the same people tend to take different types of political actions. The Verba and Nie survey also examined the extent of this multiple participation.

[4]Seven percent of the population could not be classified in these categories, and so is omitted. See Verba and Nie, *Participation in America*, pp. 118–119.

They found, for example, that 64 percent of the population reported it voted regularly. (We know from Chapter 3 that this is an overstatement; people always tend to overstate their voting rate when asked.) They also found that 25 percent scored high on campaign participation. If these were mutually exclusive activities, that would leave only 11 percent of the population inactive. In fact, however, almost everyone who particpates in a campaign also votes. Only 4 percent do not. This means that 32 percent of the population admits that it neither votes nor works in campaigns.

That finding is really not surprising. But another discovery tells us more. Verba and Nie looked at the six least commonly done conventional political acts: contacting a local official about an issue or problem (which 20 percent report having done); attending a political meeting or rally in the last 3 years (19 percent); contacting a state or national official about an issue or problem (18 percent); forming a group to solve a local problem (14 percent); contributing money to a campaign (13 percent); and being a member of a political organization (8 percent). If no one did more than one of these things, 92 percent of the population would be involved in one way or another. In fact, however, 1 percent of the population do all six, 2 percent do five, 3 percent do four, 6 percent do three, and 13 percent do two. Because only 24 percent do only one, 51 percent do none of the six.[5]

Three major conclusions can be drawn from a survey of participation studies. First, fewer Americans are politically active than we might expect. Second, those who do more than just vote tend to be active in a variety of ways. Many tend to concentrate on campaign activities, some on community activities, and fewer still on protest activities. Third, certain groups in our society are more likely to be active: the college educated and those with higher incomes, especially. Blacks, women, the young, and the old are less likely to be active, but these differences are less pronounced and are declining. We shall have more to say about this in Chapters 14 and 15.

[5]Ibid., pp. 36–37.

Victnam veterans protesting the war in Indochina.
UPI

□ WHY PEOPLE RUN FOR POLITICAL OFFICE

We have already examined, in Chapter 3, the reasons why people do or do not vote. Voting is a relatively easy and common form of political activity. Running for, and serving in, office, on the other hand, is one rarely undertaken – by a maximum of 3 percent of the population according to the Milbrath study. Why, then, do these unusual people run for office?

We could cast this question in various ways. In casual terms, we could ask whether politicians are born, self-made, chosen, or made by upbringing and other circumstance. People sometimes say of someone: "He's a *born politician*," just as they speak of "born athletes." Studies have shown that the firstborn in a family tends to be more assertive and more venturesome – qualities generally valuable to a politician, or course. But we really have no evidence directly relating political activity to one's genetic inheritance. Nor indeed can we link much other behavior to genes.

The model of the *self-made politician* fits better in some cases, as it does in the case of Richard Nixon (whom we shall discuss in more detail in coming chapters). It may also fit other cases it if is understood to focus on the conscious reasons an individual has for choosing a political career.

■ Conscious reasons

One possible reason for a person to enter and remain in politics is his or her having *strong policy interests* that he or she wishes to implement. Politicans indeed tend to give answers in terms of policy interests, as well as service, when they are asked why they are in politics. Observers, however, are often doubtful that such answers constitute the whole truth.

They might be pardoned for being somewhat skeptical. For large egos and politicians seem to inhabit the same always-on-the-run bodies. One result of this skepticism has been development of what is sometimes called *ambition theory* to

Campaign workers.
Mimi Forsyth/Monkmeyer

explain the behavior of politicians in terms of another set of conscious reasons. The case is clearly put by the most active developer of this theory, political scientist Joseph Schlesinger: ". . . Of all those who perform for their fellow man, the politician leaves the clearest tracks between his purpose and his behavior. . . . In politics . . . immediate personal success is so obviously the goal that the social scientist does well to give it primary consideration and surely errs to shun it. This is true even when principle or doctrine are the declared motive of the politician."

But before we have time to lament this "discovery," Schlesinger attempts to put us at ease:

> To slight the role of ambition in politics, then, or to treat it as a human failing to be suppressed, is to miss the central function of ambition in political systems. A political system unable to kindle ambitions for office is as much in danger of breaking down as one unable to restrain ambitions. Representative government, above all, depends on a supply of men so driven; the desire for election and, more important, for reelection becomes the electorate's restraint upon its public officials. No more irresponsible government is imaginable than one of high-minded men unconcerned for their political futures.
>
> The central assumption of ambition theory is that a politician's behavior is a response to his office goals. Or, to put it another way, the politician as officeseeker engages in political acts and makes decisions appropriate to gaining office.[6]

The politician, in other words, often has his eye not on the voters who elected him to his present office, but rather on the voters who could elect him to a higher office should it become available. He lives in a "structure of opportunities," as Schlesinger calls it, which looks rather like a honeycomb or a "jungle gym" or a creation made out of "Tinker Toys" or an "Erector Set." To get a hint as to what this might look like, take an advance look at Figure 6.1 in the chapter on the presidency.

In Schlesinger's analysis, most American politicians start at the local level–often in law enforcement as district attorneys or county attorneys. From there they generally move to the U.S. House of Representatives. Some of them then go on to the U.S. Senate, and occasionally from there they run for president. The other common route upward is the "state route": from the state legislature to the state senate, and from there occasionally to governor. Some governors then transfer to the U.S. Senate. And one, Jimmy Carter, quite atypically went from governor to president.

Schlesinger's study and the ambition theory it is used to bolster are controversial for what they do not explain.[7] If ambition of this sort were truly the

---

[6]Joseph Schlesinger, *Ambition and Politics: Political Careers in the United States* (Chicago: Rand McNally, 1966), pp. 1–2, 6.

[7]For interesting critiques, see Dwaine Marvick, "Continuities in Recruitment Theory and Research," in *Elite Recruitment in Democratic Politics,* ed. Heinz Eulau and Moshe Czudnowski (New York: Sage/Wiley, 1976), pp. 29–44.

major motivating force in elections, it would be difficult to explain why there are so many candidates running for Congress, for example. We noted last chapter that in 1970, 375 of the 384 members of the House of Representatives who ran for reelection were indeed reelected. More generally, there has never been a turnover rate higher than 26 percent in any congressional election year since 1932. Furthermore, it is rare that more than 15 percent of incumbents seeking reelection are defeated. "By almost any standards," one scholar observes, "the opportunity structure of the House of Representatives is restricted; few elective institutions in American political life have achieved the degree of stability which since the depression has characterized membership in the House. Given the limited opportunity structure, why do candidates participate?"[8]

Perhaps the answer is that ambition, or "the power motive" more generally, is less important in political activism that we might suspect. Or perhaps we must look beneath the conscious reasons of candidates and other activists to unconscious reasons or motives.

■ Unconscious reasons

When someone's behavior does not seem rational, we often look to unconscious factors as possible explanations for that behavior. Politics is no exception, as we saw when studying voting in Chapter 3. Some 30 years ago, Harold Lasswell, a leading political scientist, wrote a book called *Power and Personality,* which focused attention on psychological qualities of political figures. "Our key hypothesis about the power seeker is that he pursues power as a means of compensation against deprivation. *Power is expected to overcome low estimates of the self.*"[9] Because certain political people feel personally inadequate, Lasswell argued, they regard power as "compensation against estimates of the self as weak, contemptible, immoral, unloved," and so their "motives are displaced onto public targets and rationalized in the name of public good."[10]

This very negative conception of political participators has not been confirmed by subsequent research. For example, Paul Sniderman studied delegates to the 1956 national party conventions, 60 percent of whom held elective offices. He found that they had *higher self-esteem* than American adults in general, and in particular much higher "feelings of interpersonal competence." They had, in other words, the ability "to feel at ease and self-assured when in the company of others, to be articulate and persuasive, to take the initiative frequently, to be outgoing, active, forceful."[11]

Jeane Kirkpatrick compared male and female American state legislators who were thought by their colleagues to be "effective." She found them to be high in self-esteem, strongly achievement-oriented, and concerned with the welfare of their communities. But there was an interesting difference between the sexes: When asked why they entered politics, women tended to stress the community-welfare

[8]Jeff Fishel, *Party and Opposition: Congressional Challenges in American Politics* (New York: McKay, 1973), p. 31.

[9]H. D. Lasswell, *Power and Personality* (New York: Norton, 1948), p. 39.

[10]Ibid., p. 58.

[11]Paul Sniderman, *Personality and Democratic Politics* (Berkeley, Calif.: University of California Press, 1975).

motive, whereas men emphasized the value of political office in advancing their careers.[12]

"The available evidence suggests," according to Milbrath and Goel, "that persons with great neurotic or psychotic problems are not attracted to normal democratic political action. The chaotic, rough-and-tumble environment of competitive politics carries few rewards for thin-skinned, neurotic personalities."

Milbrath has borrowed the term "gladiators" from the old roman warriors to characterize those who run for office, raise money, or do other party work in campaigns. "The data suggest," he concludes,

> that political gladiators are persons who are particularly well equipped to deal with their environment. They feel personally competent; they know themselves and feel confident of their knowledge and skills; their egos are strong enough to withstand blows; they are not burdened by a load of anxiety and internal conflict; they can control their impulses; they are astute, sociable, self-expressive, and responsible. Although they may desire to dominate and manipulate others, political gladiators do not seem to lean any further in this direction than persons in many other roles.[13]

Sound like pretty nice people, don't they? Probably rather like the rest of us, only perhaps a bit more effective. If this is true, then we may have to conclude that the motivations of political activists are more complex than any of these theories suggest. In this, too, politicians are probably quite like the rest of us. It seems, then, that political activists are neither born, nor self-made, nor chosen. Perhaps the real difference between activists and nonactivists is primarily circumstance—circumstance that limits the opportunities of many of us to participate actively in politics.

☐ WHAT LIMITS POPULAR PARTICIPATION IN POLITICS

The major limitation on participation in politics is *resources*—especially money and time. We noted in Perspective 2 that new campaign finance laws limit the role of "big money" in presidential politics somewhat. But to run for other offices—or to run for nomination for president in the primaries—you still must raise large sums of money. It can cost tens or even hundreds of thousands of dollars just to run for the House, and millions to run for the Senate. Running for other offices is less costly, but still out of reach for most Americans, with or without the help of their friends and supporters.

But the limitations go deeper than just the cost of being elected. Once elected, you must be able to afford to serve. For most people in state or national posts, that immediately requires maintaining two residences—one in the home district and another in the state capital or in Washington, depending on the job.

---

[12]Jeane Kirkpatrick, *Political Woman* (New York: Basic Books, 1974).

[13]Milbrath and Goel, *Political Participation,* p. 85.

Exxon Corp.

Town meeting, Stowe, Vermont.

Furthermore, a politician is expected to be well-dressed and to entertain fashionably if not lavishly. He or she must also support two office staffs (one at home and one in the capital) that generally cost more than his or her "office allotment" of expense funds allows. This means most politicians must either be independently wealthy so they can use their own funds to supplement their salary, or be constantly raising special supplementary funds by public speaking, writing books and articles – or accepting favors from special interests. The upshot is that most of us probably cannot afford to run for office, nor could many of us afford to win.

Furthermore, most of us cannot afford to do much party and campaign work because of our other responsibilities such as school, job, and family. So the roster of political gladiators is further limited this way.

To some extent, energy and imagination may substitute for money and time among political activists, it is true. But even so, few Americans have energy and imagination left over for political work once they meet their normal responsibilities.

If most Americans would find it difficult to be "political gladiators," however, most would not find it difficult to vote. Some 2 percent reported they were unable to vote in the 1976 presidential election because they had to work all day election day, and 7 percent had that problem in 1972. This still leaves them a wide range of other political activities from our list above – from writing to their representatives to demonstrating. However, most Americans seem to believe that writing members of the House and Senate does no good, and only very small percentages of the population have ever joined in protest demonstrations or participated in protest meetings.[14]

■ Overcoming these limitations

What this means is that most of the channels by which ordinary citizens could make known their concerns are actually left to elites – lobbyists and leaders of protest movements, for example. Malcontents are therefore faced with two options:

---

[14] Ibid., pp. 15, 18–19.

infiltrating the elites to get their views represented or developing new channels by which to protest.

There is evidence that various social groups are slowly *infiltrating the elites.* In the years since FDR's New Deal in the 1930s, there has been a gradual broadening of the recruitment base of high officials in government. Most such officials used to be upper-middle-class Protestants from the Northeast and the Midwest. Now more and more come from other classes, other religions, and other regions. A major part of this change has been a shift toward people with specialized technical skills. As an indication, under FDR there were more than six lawyers for every Ph.D. A law degree is a generalized training for government work, but a Ph.D. is a specialized preparation. By the Nixon years, that figure had dropped to less than two lawyers for every Ph.D.[15]

Of course, such changes in the composition of governmental elites are very slow, and it is always possible that by the time these new elements make it into government they will have been so well trained, so well "socialized," that they will think and act rather like everyone else who is already there. Such fears and suspicions, popularly held, encourage the *development of new channels of influence.* In a sense, the George Wallace (1968, 1972) and Eugene McCarthy (1968, 1976) campaigns might be thought of as efforts to redevelop the "protest vote" as a new channel – a channel to "send a message to Washington," in Wallace's memorable phrase.

President Carter's early innovation of national "phone-ins" giving ordinary citizens the opportunity to ask questions of the president could be another one. So was his establishment of a special address for submission of suggestions of how he could remain close to the people as president. But these new channels nonetheless in a sense reflect yet another limitation on political activism by citizens: The government *itself* is a political participant, and it after all has more resources than any one else with which to be a political activist.

□ THE GOVERNMENT AS A POLITICAL ACTIVIST

We usually think of the government as a political responder rather than as a political activist. We hear our political system described as one of "Government of the people, by the people, and for the people." Such a phrase suggests that the government will be responsive to the wishes and actions of the people. The leaders, after all, are *from* the people – representatives *of* the people. They are expected to act *for* the people, in accordance with their needs and wishes.

But we shall see time and again in coming chapters that this is not a fully accurate description of what happens. Our government is indeed a government *of* the people, but it is a government *by only some* of the people and often *for only some.* The government responds more readily to some political activists than to others – as we shall see in Chapter 11 when we discuss the roles of various interests in politics.

---

[15]Kenneth Prewitt and William McAllister, "Changes in the American Executive Elite, 1930–1970," in *Elite Recruitment,* ed. Eulau and Czudnoski, pp. 105–132.

And even when government tries to respond positively, the results may be the opposite of those intended—for reasons that we shall examine in Part 3. This selective responsiveness is itself a form of political action.

Furthermore, the government can make various responses to demands placed upon it. Among the responses it may make when it does not agree with activists seeking to influence policy, five are common: (1) *delay;* (2) *tokenism*—doing only a little of what is asked and thereby seeming to be more responsive than it actually is; (3) *discrediting* the request as being unrepresentative of popular will—as judged by the leaders—or as being impractical, too expensive, or otherwise undesirable; (4) *suppressing* the request by punishing the requesters, jailing them, or keeping them from public attention; and (5) *ignoring,* or pretending not to hear, the request or demand.

Even when it is responding to people, however, the government may be playing even more of a role as a political activist. The government makes most of the news we read and see. Governmental leaders make most of the speeches we hear, and governmental officials take most of the regulating actions that affect our lives. These governmental acts are prominent and convincing because they are *official* acts of a government, and because we still think of that government as representing us, the people, and deriving its authority from us, the people.

What effect does the big role and large influence of government have on the ideas we hold about what government should do? One stark view is offered by political scientist Murray Edelman: "If legislative, administrative, and judicial procedures significantly influence how people see leaders, issues, and themselves and therefore what they will accept, what they want, and what they demand, then those procedures are less likely to express the people's will than to shape it. More precisely, they reflect it only after they shape it, which puts the representation function in a rather different light."[16]

□ WHAT EFFECTS DOES PARTICIPATION HAVE?

What, then, are the consequences of participation on those who participate and on the political system? Edelman concludes that available ways of acting usually help to legitimize the regime and to bring potential dissenters into the system. In some cases, however, they foster discontent and protest. "In either case they significantly influence people's roles, self-concepts, and willingness to accept their own statuses and the official rules. They affect not so much who gets what as who is satisfied or dissatisfied with what he gets and with who orders him around."[17]

There seems to be, then, in other words, a kind of circle. The people elect representatives, and in a sense instruct them from time to time by engaging in political activism. These representatives then turn around and use their authority to help instruct the people on how to see the world, how to define political reality.

[16]Murray Edelman, *Politics as Symbolic Action* (Chicago: Markham, 1971), p. 179.

[17]Ibid., p. 179.

Edelman notes "the remarkable degree of support official governmental acts and policies enjoy even when they bring serious deprivations to their supporters and to others: economic, welfare, civil rights, and regulatory policies that are manifestly tokens or that perpetuate inequalities; virtually continuous wars fought in the name of a peace that appears only intermittently and precariously."[18]

Edelman's assessment may well be too harsh. We shall have to wait until we examine these various policy problems and government efforts to solve them, in Part 6, before we can decide. But even if he exaggerates, his point is an important one. It calls to our attention the extent to which our political participation does generally support the status quo. When we vote, especially when we vote for one of two rather comparable candidates, our action tends to reinforce the status quo. When we decide not to vote, perhaps because we do not like the choice we are offered, we thereby strengthen the existing system by concealing the extent of our discontent. The same seems often to be true for party and campaign work and even for letter writing or demonstrations.

■ Is participation good or bad?

If it *is* true that political participation does generally reinforce the bases of our system, then we would expect to find supporters of the system glad to see more political participation by more people.

But this is not always the case. The strongest advocates of increased participation now are on the political Left, where many call for "participatory democracy." By this they mean a system in which citizens play increased roles in deciding the things that affect their lives. At the other extreme are those – many of them regular advisors of the government in Washington – who now argue that increased participation may make democracies ungovernable. They fear that it will produce further disillusionment, and so disrespect for authority, when the government is unresponsive to the wishes and demands of the activists.[19] We shall be studying the possibilities for, and the effects of, participation throughout this book. Then, in the final chapter, we shall return to the debate over its desirability.

In the meantime, we are left wondering whether the current situation, in which a relatively small segment of the population rules and participates in other ways, necessitates a government responsive to, and controlled by, "some of the people" instead of "all of the people."

□ PARTICIPATION, ELITISM, AND PLURALISM

Political scientists have long disagreed about the answer to the question with which we ended the last section. Two major views have emerged from this debate over how American politics really works and what role popular participation plays in

---

[18]Ibid., pp. 175–176.

[19]For example, compare Daniel C. Kramer, *Participatory Democracy: Developing Ideals of the Political Left* (Cambridge, Mass.: Schenkman, 1972), with Michel Crozier, Samuel P. Huntington, and Joji Watanuki, *The Crisis of Democracy: Report on the Governability of Democraies* (New York: New York University Press, 1975).

FIGURE 5.1

The elitist model of American politics.

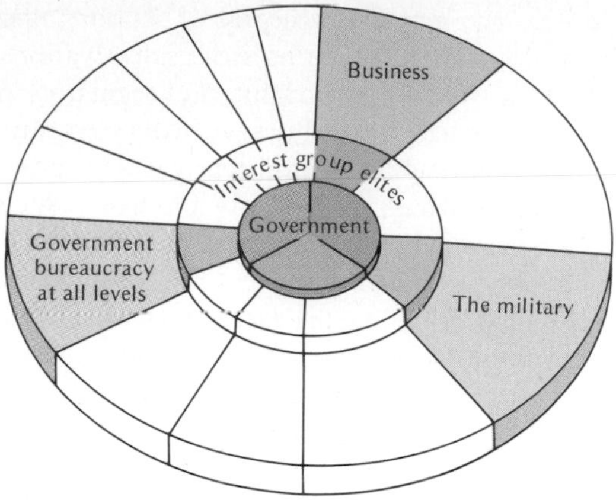

politics. The first view (or "model" or "theory") is generally called the "ruling elite" or "elitist" theory, and the second is most often termed the "pluralist" theory. Let's look briefly at what each argues.

■ The elitist theory

The elitist theory contends that power in America is held and shared by a small group of people who dominate the major institutions–especially the large business corporations, the military, and the governmental bureaucracies. Analysts differ on just which individuals have the most power. They also disagree as to which institutions are the most important. But they tend to agree that there is little room for significant participation is government–or in the economy–by ordinary citizens without power and wealth. Figure 5.1 is one way of representing this elitist structure as it is generally seen by ruling elite theorists.

FIGURE 5.2

The pluralist model of American politics.

■ The pluralist theory

The pluralist theory holds that power in America is shared among a number of different political, economic, and social groups. Each group has enough power to protect its own essential interests with the occasional help of other groups. But no one group has enough power to dominate the others – nor indeed does the military-business-bureaucracy "ruling elite" have enough power to rule by itself. The theory is called "pluralist" because it sees a large number (plural interests instead of the sole interest of the "ruling elite") of groups playing important roles. Just which groups are powerful enough to matter may change from time to time. Business, the military, and the bureaucracy are always important. But so are labor, small business, agriculture, and other interests such as consumer protection and ecology groups. This theory might be represented as in Figure 5.2.

These two theories are extreme formulations. We shall see in coming chapters that political reality in America usually has elements of both. On some issues, the system seems to operate like a ruling-elite system; on other issues the pluralist description seems more appropriate. Neither theory leaves much of a role for popular participation. Yet we shall also see in coming chapters that political activists, too, play important roles in some situations. And they might play much more important roles should they – we – wish to.

■ The continuing question

This diverse picture raises even more sharply the fundamental question: What sorts of activism do we really need? We cannot answer such a question in comprehensive form at this stage of our study. The appropriate forms of activism vary with the issue and with the circumstances. Fundamental questions of whether the resort to violence is ever appropriate, or whether much broader participation is desirable, will be addressed more directly in Chapter 21. We can already see how important it is for political activists to be flexible enough to adjust to changing circumstances and to be open to responses from the government and from other participants.

In the chapters of Part 3 we shall be looking at American government primarily from the perspective of the institutions in Washington: the presidency, the Congress, the bureaucracy, and the courts. Then in Part 4 we shall return to the experience and attitudes of nongovernmental influences: public opinion, interest groups, and the media. In all these chapters, we shall find political activists playing important roles both in and out of government. The first examples will come in Perspective 3, on the politics of the environment.

□ SUGGESTIONS FOR FURTHER READING AND STUDY

There is no end to the literature on activism – nor will there be an end to our discussion of it, until we have finished the final chapter of this book. Among the stimulating general discussions of participation in politics are: E. E. Schattschneider, *Semisovereign People: A Realist's View of Democracy in America* (New York: Holt, Rinehart & Winston, 1960); Robert Lane, *Political Life* (New York: Free Press, 1959), which examines attitudes and other factors affecting political participation; and two books by Murray Edelman: *Symbolic Uses of Politics* (Urbana: University of Illinois Press, 1964) and *Politics as Symbolic Action* (Chicago: Markham paperback, 1971).

The most comprehensive surveys of participation in America are the two books that we rely on in this chapter: Lester Milbrath and M. L. Goel, *Political Participation,* 2nd ed. (Chicago: Rand McNally, 1977); and Sidney Verba and Norman Nie, *Participation in America* (New York: Harper & Row, 1972).

The subject of working *in* politics is discussed from different perspectives in John W. Kingdon, *Candidates for Office: Beliefs and Strategies* (New York: Random House paperback, 1966); Joseph Schlesinger, *Ambition and Politics: Political Careers in the United States* (Chicago: Rand McNally, 1966), which we discuss in this chapter; Kenneth W. Prewitt, *Recruitment of Political Leaders* (Indianapolis: Bobbs-Merrill, 1970); Kenneth W. Prewitt and Alan Stone, *The Ruling Elites* (New York: Harper & Row, 1973); Heinz Eulau and Moshe Czudnowski, eds., *Elite Recruitment in Democratic Politics* (New York: Sage/Wiley, 1976); and John W. Macy, *Public Service: The Human Side of Government* (New York: Harper & Row, 1971).

For discussion of various aspects of working *with* politics, see: Michael Walzer, *Political Action: A Practical Guide to Movement Politics* (New York: Quadrangle, 1971); Dick Simpson and George Beam, *Strategies for Change: How to Make the American Political Dream Work* (Chicago: Swallow, 1976), a book that is actually more comprehensive than this categorization suggests, based as it is on Simpson's experience as a renegade local politician in Chicago as well as a professor of political science; John Gardner, *In Common Cause* (New York: Norton paperback, 1972), by the founder of the "citizen lobby" Common Cause; Donald Ross, *A Public Citizen's Action Manual* (New York: Grossman paperback, 1973), and Center for Study of Responsive Law, *Working on the System: A Comprehensive Manual for Citizen Access to Federal Agencies* (New York: Basic Books, 1974), both products of Ralph Nader's public-interest organizations; and Jeffrey M. Berry, *Lobbying for the People* (Princeton, N.J.: Princeton University Press, 1977), a study of various public-interest lobbies, with special attention to the Fund for Animals and the Women's International League for Peace and Freedom.

Books about working *against* politics can be roughly divided into those dealing with direct action, those analyzing nonviolent action, and those concerned with the use of violence. There are a great many in each category, so we can cite only a few of the most interesting ones here. On direct action, see the two classics by Saul Alinsky: *Reveille for Radicals* (New York: Vintage paperback, 1946), and *Rules for Radicals* (New York: Vintage paperback, 1972); and a handbook by Martin Oppenheimer and George Lakey, *A Manual for Direct Action* (Chicago: Quadrangle paperback, 1964).

On nonviolence, see Joan Bondurant, *Conquest of Violence: The Gandhian Philosophy of Conflict* (Berkeley: University of California Press, 1965); Martin Luther King, *Why We Can't Wait* (New York: Signet, 1963), about the civil rights struggle in Birmingham; Richard B. Gregg's classic, *The Power of Nonviolence* (Nyack, N.Y.: Fellowship paperback, 1959); and Gene Sharp, *The Politics of Nonviolent Action* (Boston: Porter Sargent, 1973), a monumental book that analyzes 198 different methods of nonviolent action.

Among books dealing with working *beyond* politics are John Hunefeld, *The Community Activist's Handbook: A Guide to Organizing, Financing, and Publicizing Community Campaigns* (Boston: Beacon, 1970); the O. M. collective, *The Organizer's Manual* (New York: Bantam paperback, 1971); and George Lakey, *Strategy for a Living Revolution* (San Francisco: Freeman paperback, 1973).

Discussions of elitist and pluralist theories of politics are many. For examples of these types of analysis and a large bibliography, see Roderick A. Bell, David V. Edwards, and R. Harrison Wagner, eds., *Political Power: A Reader in Theory and Research* (New York: Free Press paperback, 1969). Among the classics in the debate are C. Wright Mills, *The Power Elite* (New York: Oxford University Press paperback, 1956); Robert Dahl, *Who Governs?* (New Haven, Conn.: Yale University Press, 1961); G. William Domhoff, *Who Rules America?* (Englewood Cliffs, N.J.: Prentice-Hall paperback, 1967); and Morton Mintz and Jerry S. Cohen, *America, Inc.: Who Owns and Operates the United States* (New York: Dial paperback, 1971). These themes will emerge again in coming chapters – as will the other aspects of participation.

3 WHO DECIDES IN GOVERNMENT?

☐ Perspective 3: The politics of the environment

Until recently, most Americans had fresh safe drinking water available at the turn of a faucet or the cranking of a pump. Many had clear water for swimming as near as the closest stream, lake, or ocean. Fresh air was always around us in all but the biggest cities. In those cities with serious air pollution, most residents were not concerned about what seemed simply a discomfort to be lived with in return for the jobs that factories provided.

☐ RECOGNITION OF THE NEED TO PROTECT THE ENVIRONMENT

In the early 1960s, however, the first alarms began to sound. Rachel Carson published a book called *The Silent Spring* in 1962. It traced the effects of the universally used pesticide DDT on life in the waters and found an ultimate threat to life on earth. Stewart Udall the next year wrote a book called *The Quiet Crisis* that expressed concern about the growing but still unrecognized threats to the environment. With these books, and others which followed, the "conservation" movement in America was transformed into the "environmental" movement.

Conservation had been a popular cause throughout much of the twentieth century.[1] It began with the major initiatives of President Theodore Roosevelt, who set aside lands for national parks and national forests. It received a further boost in the 1930s when President Franklin Roosevelt established the Civilian Conservation Corps – a program to create jobs for the unemployed during the Depression – which put young people to work planting trees and improving recreation lands.

[1]See Norman Wengert, "The Ideological Basis of Conservation and Natural Resources Policies and Programs," *Annals of the American Academy of Political & Social Science,* November 1962, pp. 65–75.

Once the Depression ended and prosperity returned after World War II, the country's focus shifted to economic expansion with an emphasis on industry. However, massive industrial growth brought with it growing pollution of lakes and streams by industrial wastes, raw sewage, and residues of chemical fertilizers and pesticides. At the same time, growing use of automobiles spewed noxious fumes into the city air. Those fumes combined with smoke and chemicals from factory stacks to make city air more and more unpleasant – and, it was later discovered, hazardous to our health.

Because these changes in the environment were gradual, people adjusted to them. Few serious health effects were obvious, for the simple reason that such effects generally take 20 to 30 years to appear – in the form of cancer, heart disease, stroke, and diabetes. Public attention was caught only by major immediate disasters. As the 1960s ebbed, however, such disasters flowed. In 1967, an oil tanker ran aground and dumped 80,000 tons of crude oil on hundreds of miles of beaches in England and France. In 1969, a Union Oil Company well blew out in the Santa Barbara, California, ship channel, coating the beaches and waterbirds with crude oil. In these years, too, the production of chemical wastes had grown so much that other rivers and ship channels became so polluted that they actually caught fire and burned from time to time.

Such events, flashed across television screens, were enough to galvanize public opinion. Surveys showed a new and growing concern for the environment. One poll asked how serious the people thought air and water pollution in their area was compared to other areas. In 1965, 28 percent thought air pollution "very serious" or "somewhat serious," and 35 percent had the same feeling about water pollution. By 1970, the figures had almost tripled, to 69 percent for air and 74 percent for water.[2] In the same year, 1970, the Minnesota Poll, which is usually representative of national sentiment, asked this question: "Some people say life itself is in danger unless something is done about pollution. Others say pollution is not that serious. Do you think life as we know it today will or will not be in serious trouble if nothing is done about pollution?" Fully 87 percent said it will be in serious trouble, and only 10 percent said it will not.[3] Subsequent polls have shown a continuing rise in concern around the nation.[4]

■ The role of government

The obvious ecological disasters set the stage for new governmental attention to what came to be called "environmental quality." Government had been gradually but tentatively getting involved. The first water pollution legislation had been passed by Congress and signed into law by President Truman in 1948; that on air pollution, in 1955. However, the legislation thus far had been based on the assumption that the prevention and control of pollution at its sources was the responsibility of state and local governments. All the federal government could do, according to this view, which was widely held in Congress, was to encourage them to act.

Few states and cities did act, however, for two important reasons. First, local polluting industries and related economic interests were so strong that they could usually prevent adoption of serious pollution-control programs. And second, these special interests were usually able to get their own people appointed to pollution-control boards, and so they had little to fear from "regulation."

Meanwhile, the problem continued to worsen. The chemical industry was developing new plastics and finding more and more uses for them. This caused two new problems. First, the production of

USDA-SCS photo by William R. Bram

Pollution in the Cumberland River north of Nashville, Tennessee.

[2]NORC polls reported in Ben Wattenberg, *The Real America* (New York: Capricorn, 1976), p. 226.

[3]Ibid., p. 227

[4]For a survey, see Cecile Trop and Leslie L. Roos, Jr., "Public Opinion and the Environment," in *The Politics of Ecosuicide,* ed. Roos (New York: Holt, Rinehart & Winston, 1971), pp. 52–63.

plastics pollutes the air and water. Second, there is no way of getting rid of waste plastics without causing more pollution. If you burn them, they give off noxious fumes. If you bury them, they remain in the ground permanently. This is because plastics are not "biodegradable" – they never break down chemically, as paper and metal do. So both making and disposing of plastics became a major source of pollution. We can get some idea of the extent of the disposal problem by realizing that every day on the average each of us Americans generates 3 to 4 pounds of trash, much of it plastic.[5]

□ THE BIRTH OF THE NATIONAL ENVIRONMENTAL POLICY ACT (NEPA)

By 1969, when the Santa Barbara oil spill occurred, public sentiment for environmental protection had created support for legislation. What happened then reveals much about the politics of legislation and administration in American government.[6]

To become a law, a bill must be passed by both the House of Representatives and the Senate and signed by the president. But before either house of Congress will vote on a bill, one of its committees must consider the bill and recommend its adoption. Getting a bill passed is, therefore, likely to involve complex strategy (see Table P3.1 and Figure P3.1 for a summary). Although there were more than 300 committees and subcommittees in Congress, no committee in either house had as its primary responsibility developing environmental legislation. In the House, the Interior Committee, which deals with natural resources, was chaired by Wayne Aspinall (Democrat of Colorado). Aspinall was known as a "friend" of commercial developers of natural resources and an "enemy" of strong environmental protection. He often used his power as committee chairperson to "kill" environmental-protection bills referred to his committee by the House for consideration.

■ A bill is introduced in the House

So a way had to be found to get a bill considered by a committee more sympathetic to environmental protection. The Merchant Marine and Fisheries Committee, because it dealt with fish, was such a committee. Its subcommittee on Fisheries and Wildlife Conservation was controlled by supporters of environmental protection. Its chairperson, John Dingell (Democrat of Michigan), drafted a bill creating a Council on Environmental Quality (CEQ), which was intended to advise the president and report to the public on environmental concerns. But Dingell's committee had jurisdiction only over fish and wildlife. Therefore, his bill had to be attached as an amendment to the Fish and Wildlife Coordination Act which his subcommittee was already considering. Had it been simply submitted to the House as a regular bill, it would have been referred to Aspinall's Interior Committee, the logical place for such a bill. It is likely that Aspinall would have "killed" it – as he had a similar bill Dingell had submitted the previous year.

■ Differing bills are introduced in the Senate

At the same time, in the Senate, two somewhat similar bills were introduced. Senator Henry Jackson (Democrat of Washington) introduced a bill calling for creation of a Council on Environmental Quality – a bill rather like Dingell's House bill. Because Jackson was chairperson of the Senate Interior Committee (the counterpart to Aspinall's House committee), he could simply introduce the bill in the normal fashion knowing it would be referred to his committee for consideration. When it was, he conducted hearings on it during April. In June, his

[5]EPA estimates reported in *U.S. News & World Report,* May 13, 1974, p. 63.

[6]The following account owes much to Richard A. Liroff, *A National Policy for the Environment* (Bloomington: Indiana University Press, 1976); Austin H. Kiplinger, *Washington Now* (New York: Harper & Row, 1975); and Frederick R. Anderson, *NEPA in the Courts* (Baltimore: Johns Hopkins University Press for Resources for the Future, 1973).

committee "reported out" his bill, for consideration by the Senate as a whole. It had two major provisions. First, it established a CEQ. And second, it also required that all government agencies prepare an Environmental Impact Statement (EIS) for each new program or action they undertook. This EIS was supposed to describe the effects the program would be likely to have on the environment.[7]

Senator Edmund Muskie (Democrat of Maine), also a long-standing environmentalist, feared that the Jackson bill would not be effective without an agency to enforce it. So, on June 12, he introduced a bill that would create an Office of Environmental Quality, with enforcement powers. He located it in the Executive Office of the President, which, as we shall see in Chapter 6, contains agencies that assist the president. But Muskie couldn't simply introduce this as a separate bill. As such, it would be referred to Jackson's Interior committee, which was naturally more interested in its chairperson's own bill. So instead Muskie introduced his bill as an amendment to a bill on control of water pollution, which was being considered by the Public Works Committee's Subcommittee on Air and Water Pollution – which he chaired.

The Senate passes a strong compromise bill

The existence of two somewhat comparable bills in different Senate committees created something of a problem. Both Jackson and Muskie wanted to be "father" of the first major environmental protection legislation. Ultimately, despite strong egos, Jackson and Muskie were able to reach a compromise. Jackson's bill, which was numbered S. (for Senate) 1075, became the National Environmental Policy Act (NEPA). Finally passed by the Senate on October 8, 1969, in a form strengthened by Muskie amendments, it created the Council on Environmental Quality in the Executive Office of the President. Muskie's bill, S. 2391, eventually passed by the Senate in April 1970 as the Environmental Quality Improvement Act. It established a new agency, with more staff designed to assist the CEQ. This agency was called the Office of Environmental Quality and was located in the Department of Housing and Urban Development.

The House passes a weak bill

Before these bills could become law, however, there were still more obstacles to be overcome. The House of Representatives also had to approve the bills. In the House, once a bill is passed by a committee, it must be scheduled for consideration by the whole House. That requires getting a "rule" from the powerful House Rules Committee. This committee polices "traffic" of bills going to the House floor by stating how much floor debate will be allowed on each and whether amendments will be allowed. Representative Aspinall, who had been the victim of Dingell's "end run" on the House CEQ bill, was unhappy. But he had friends on the House Rules Committee. Because of this, he was able to force Dingell to accept an amendment that crippled the bill before it could be scheduled for consideration by the House. The amendment stated that the bill would not alter any existing responsibilities of existing agencies. Thus, when the bill passed the House, it passed by an overwhelming majority, but it was only a pale shadow of its former self.

Both Senate and House pass a compromise bill

Dingell was willing to settle for a very weak bill rather than no bill at all because he hoped that something could be worked out in a "conference committee." When the House and Senate pass different bills on the same subject, a conference committee is appointed to try to iron out the differences. This is so that each house can then pass the same, compromise, bill, as is required for a bill to become law. Conference committee members are appointed by the leaders of the House and Senate from among those most involved in preparing and

[7]For a study of the EIS, see Joseph Lee Rodgers, *Environmental Impact Assessment, Growth Management, and the Comprehensive Plan* (Cambridge, Mass.: Ballinger, 1976).

TABLE P3.1

How a bill becomes a law—and what happens then

1. The president proposes a bill to the Congress after it is developed and "drafted" (written in legal language) by an agency in the executive branch. The bill is then "introduced" in the House by a friendly representative, where it is given a number and referred to the committee that has "jurisdiction" over (or responsibility for) that area of legislation. The same thing happens in the Senate.

1a. Or the bill is conceived by a senator or representative, perhaps at the urging of constituents or of an interest group. The bill is drafted by his or her own staff and the legislative counsel and introduced by him or her. The bill is given a number and referred to a committee as above. The same is done by a friendly member of the other house.

2. The committee staff, generally under the guidance of the chairperson, studies the bill, gets the opinion of the Office of Management and Budget in the executive branch on it, and makes a report on its contents and likely impact to the committee chairperson.

3. The committee chairperson refers the bill to a subcommittee, which may "hold a hearing" on it to allow interested parties to comment on it. These parties may include officials from the executive branch with responsibilities in the area the bill involves, interested members of Congress, representatives of interest groups, and even individual citizens.

4. The subcommittee then meets to "mark up" the bill (go over it line by line). It usually tries to rewrite it in a way that will maximize support for it through bargaining with supporters and opponents. At this point, sometimes a subcommittee will adopt as an "amendment" a bill that really should be a separate bill. This is done because the bill would not be reported out of the committee to which it would be referred or would not be passed by the whole House or Senate if it were not a part of a more popular measure.

5. If the subcommittee passes the bill with strong support, the committee as a whole will probably pass it without much debate. The committee staff then prepares a report on the bill explaining it for the record.

6. If the bill is at all controversial, it must be scheduled for debate on the floor of the Senate or the House. In the Senate, scheduling is done by the majority leader (the head of the party with a majority in the Senate), in consultation with the minority leadership and even perhaps with the White House. In the House, for the bill to get any further, the Rules Committee must "grant a rule" for the bill. This is a set of specifications stating whether amendments will be allowed on the floor and how much time will be allowed for debate.

FIGURE P3.1

How a bill becomes law. This is the most typical route; there are other more simple and more complicated routes.

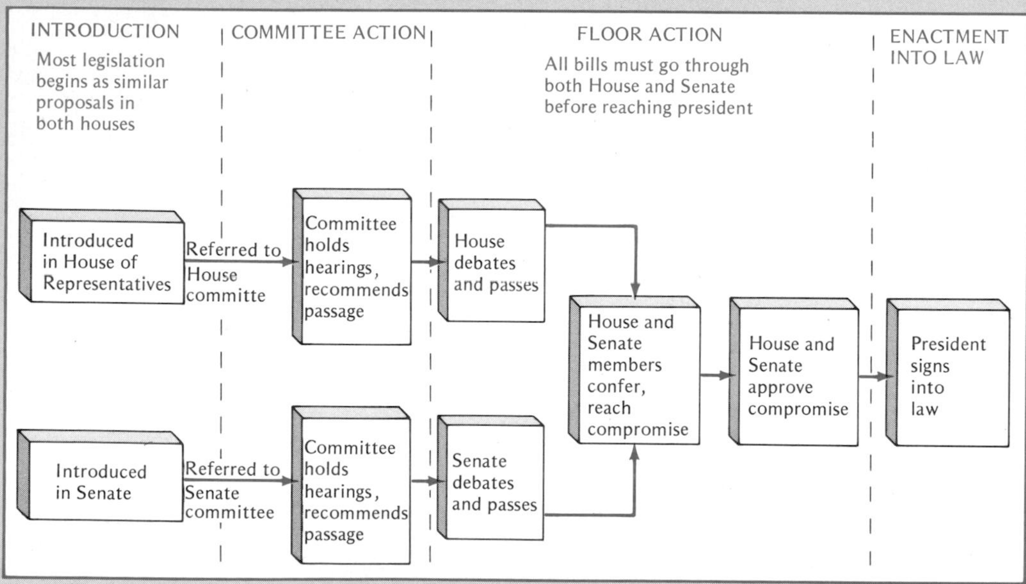

The Speaker of the House and the majority leader then schedule it for debate, usually in consultation.

7. The Senate or the House then debates the bill and votes on it. Amendments are often proposed and sometimes adopted at this stage.
8. A bill passed by one house is then sent to the other house for its consideration, because both houses must pass any bill before it can become law. The other house can either accept the bill as passed by the first house or refer it to the same procedures outlined above before deciding.
9. If each house produces a somewhat different bill on the same subject, a "conference committee" must meet and agree upon a compromise version. The conference committee, appointed by the leadership, usually includes representatives of the committee that originally passed the bill plus other interested members from each house.
10. Once the conference committee agrees on a compromise version, each house must accept the compromise exactly by voting favorably on it.
11. The bill then goes to the president. He may sign it—in which case it becomes law; or veto it. If he vetoes it, the bill does not become law; instead, the president returns it to the Congress with a message giving his reasons for the veto. The bill dies—unless it is then repassed by a two-thirds majority vote in each house; if this happens, the veto is "overridden," and the bill becomes law without the president's signature.
12. Once a bill becomes law, it must be "implemented," or put into effect. This "executing" of the law is the responsibility of the executive branch. Often a department will announce a new policy or issue new regulations to implement the law. It does this by having them printed in full in the *Federal Register,* a daily publication which lists all such official documents. Sometimes the president will issue an executive order to make changes he believes necessary or desirable to implement the bill. From these actions, lower-level bureaucrats get their instructions on how to act.
13. Sometimes, however, a party (a company, an agency, or an individual) affected by the law dislikes either the law or the way it is being applied. This party may go to court to challenge the legality of the government's interpretation of the law, or even the law's constitutionality. If so, the court rules on the case. This ruling may sometimes be appealed by the party who loses in the court to a higher court. The appeal route may lead all the way to the Supreme Court for a final ruling if the Supreme Court gives its permission.

passing the legislation. In this case, the conference committee included Jackson and Dingell, who had introduced the bills being "harmonized." But it also included Aspinall because his committee normally had jurisdiction over environmental questions. In the conference committee, the supporters of a strong bill prevailed and struck the crippling House amendments forced on the bill by Aspinall from the final text. The final version was, therefore, much like the Senate bill developed by Jackson, with one exception: the Jackson bill's language asserting that every citizen has a "right" to a clean environment was dropped as part of the compromise.

■ The president signs the bill

To become law, of course, a bill once passed in identical form by both House and Senate must be signed by the president. During the debate in Congress, President Nixon had been taking action that seems to have been designed to prevent passage of the bill, or at least to make the bill appear unnecessary. On May 29 he announced formation of an Environmental Quality Council (EQC). It consisted of the heads of the cabinet departments concerned with environmental matters. It was supposed to advise the president on matters relating to the quality of the environment. Normally, new bodies such as this are created by congressional laws. But the president also has authority to establish new committees by issuing what are called "executive orders." This time, Nixon used Executive Order 11472 to create his EQC.

But Congress wanted more than advice or policy coordination. And, in any event, the president's move looked more and more like an effort to derail congressional efforts, for the EQC met only three times all year. So the compromise legislation passed Congress with strong support, and Nixon signed this National Environmental Policy Act on January 1, 1970.

Wide World photo

President Nixon passing out pens following his signing of the National Environmental Protection Act on January 1, 1970.

The act established the Council on Environmental Quality (CEQ), which soon replaced Nixon's Environmental Quality Council. The CEQ was intended not only to advise the president, but also to coordinate policy. It was also to report regularly to the American people on the state of the environment. But at this point, no one had yet anticipated the major impact the NEPA was to have. Nor had the campaign actually to protect the environment yet begun.

□ THE CREATION OF THE ENVIRONMENTAL PROTECTION AGENCY (EPA)

At the time the NEPA was passed, responsibility for environmental matters was scattered throughout various existing departments and agencies. Nixon, who generally favored governmental reorganization, soon issued an executive order combining fifteen units into the Environmental Protection Agency (EPA). When the order became effective on December 2, 1970, the EPA incorporated the following program units:

- □ The Federal Water Quality Program – from the Department of the Interior.
- □ The National Air Pollution Control Administration – from the Department of Health, Education, and Welfare (HEW).
- □ Various small pesticide programs from Interior, HEW, and the Department of Agriculture.
- □ Solid Waste – from HEW.
- □ Water Hygiene – from HEW.
- □ Radiology – from HEW.
- □ Radiation standards setting – from the Atomic Energy Commission.
- □ The Federal Radiation Council – from the Executive Office of the President.
- □ The investigative, research, and study activities from the CEQ (which did not have enough staff to handle them). Thus, the EPA became an *independent federal agency* concerned with air, water, solid waste, noise, pesticides, and environmental radiation pollution. Its responsibilities included: establishing and enforcing standards; measuring and monitoring pollution; studying environmental issues; demonstrating environmental improvement possibilities; assisting state and local governments in environmental matters; and providing public information and education.

■ The organization of the EPA

A glance at the EPA's organization chart reveals both its structure and its responsibilities, as well as the fact that it has ten regional offices scattered around the country (see Figure P3.2). The EPA has four major divisions – water and hazardous materials; air and waste management; toxic substances; research and development – each under an "assistant administrator." It also has an "assistant administrator for enforcement," because it must enforce its own orders. And it has an "assistant administrator for planning and management" because it operates on a budget that presently runs about $2 million a day and manages more than 11,000 employees, more than any other regulatory agency.

FIGURE P3.2

Organization chart of the EPA.

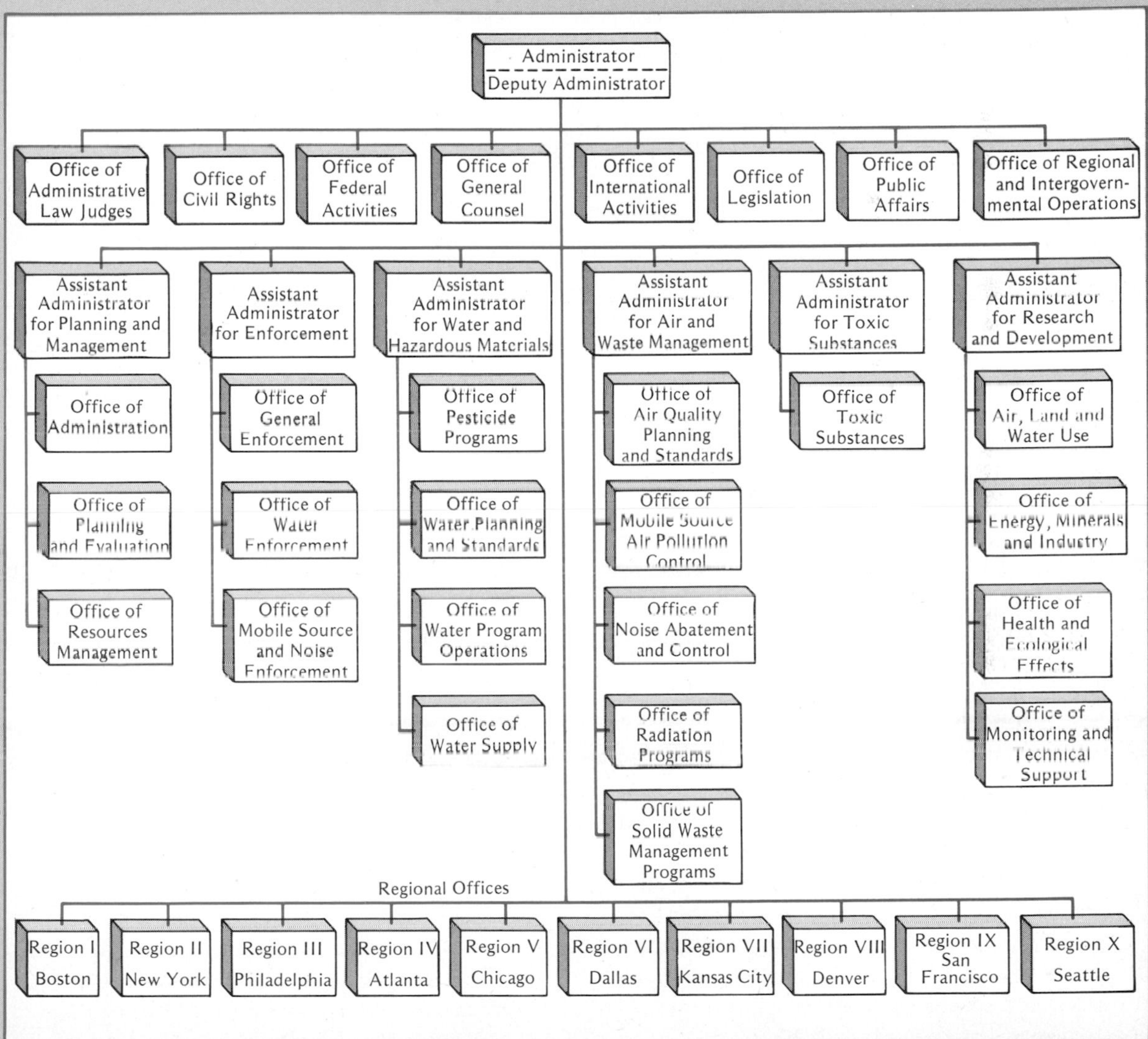

The special "offices" attached to the administrator are typical of those in any independent regulatory agency. For example, it has:

- □ An "office of administrative law judges" because it must hear cases concerning the application of its orders when someone – industry or citizen – complains. These "judges" make "administrative law" (as distinguished from "statute law" – that passed by Congress), which is binding upon those the agency regulates and so is a very important part of government today. We shall discuss "administrative law" further in Chapters 7 and 9.
- □ An "office of civil rights" because all government agencies now must take special care not to discriminate. They must also take "affirmative action" to overcome previous discrimination (something we shall discuss further in Perspective 5).
- □ An "office of international activities" because environmental problems, even more than most governmental concerns today, cross national boundaries. Therefore, activities must be coordinated wherever possible with comparable agencies in other governments.
- □ An "office of legislation" because its powers, like its budget, derive from acts of Congress. Therefore, it must be in constant touch with the committees and subcommittees that have jurisdiction over its activities and its budgetary appropriations.
- □ An "office of public affairs" to inform the public, through publications, films, speakers, and so on, of its activities and concerns.
- □ An "office of regional and intergovernmental operations" because virtually everything it does relates to the state, county, and local governments that still must conduct most environmental protection activities – often with funds from the EPA or other sources.

□ THE POLITICAL LIFE OF THE EPA

Organization charts can tell us about the structure and responsibilities and often even the programs of an agency. But they do not tell us much about the *politics* that inevitably affect and even determine what the agency does and how successful it is. To learn about the politics, we must examine instances in which the agency tries to operate in the field of other agencies, the president, the Congress, the courts, and special interests.

■ The case of the Clean Air Act amendments

Just after the NEPA was passed, and while the EPA was being established, Congress passed the Clean Air Act of 1970. That act was designed to begin the process of establishing uniform federal and state air-quality standards. Eventually, programs under this act were to include controls on motor vehicle emissions and stationary plant emissions (especially power plants that burn oil or coal), as well as controls on proposed uses for land with the goal of reducing auto use and congestion in cities and thereby cutting pollution.

The primary power the EPA had was the power to withhold federal funds for all purposes from states and localities that refuse to develop and implement appropriate environmental regulations. Such a power can be effective. But it is also time-consuming, and subject to political pressures. So it was immediately apparent that other means had to be found to supplement this fundamental federal power.

The Clean Air Act was the first law to include special new powers. It gave the EPA the power to order an emergency halt to discharges which suddenly threatened public health or safety – say, because of stagnant air. The act also was written *to allow individual citizens to sue polluters* in court, or even *to sue the head of the EPA* should he or she fail to perform his or her duty under it. It even allowed the courts to make those being sued pay the legal

EPA agent taking bottom samples in Baltimore Harbor.

United Nations/DOCUMERICA/ J. Pickerell

fees of those who were suing. This provision opened the door to a new breed of activists: public-interest environmental lobbies and law firms.

The momentum of efforts to control pollution was soon interrupted by the energy crisis of 1973. Because of the Arab oil boycott of that fall, there were calls for greater energy self-sufficiency for the United States. This would require more burning of sulfur-laden, highly polluting, coal, which is abundant in the United States, instead of imported oil. The increase in pollution such coal burning causes would not have been permissible without changes in the newly passed Clean Air Act. So the Nixon administration set about drafting amendments to the act and thereby created a major dispute in the executive branch.

The White House – in particular, its chief economic agency, the Office of Management and Budget (OMB) – favored increasing the levels of air pollution allowable from coal-burning plants and auto emissions. It was joined in that position by two other parts of the Executive Office of the President. One was the Federal Energy Office (FEO), a special agency established in the December 1973 oil emergency. And the other was the president's Domestic Council (DC), a group of political advisors and policy makers very close to the president. On the other side, the EPA and the CEQ resisted the massive changes proposed, arguing that smaller changes would suffice. The ensuing struggle to develop an agreed-upon set of proposed amendments to submit to Congress was so virulent that in the end agreement could not be reached. Instead, two sets of proposals were submitted. One consisted of minor proposals agreed to by all segments of the executive branch. The other included the major changes favored by OMB, FEO, and DC, but publicly opposed by the EPA and CEQ.

When the matter reached Congress, the lobbies were arrayed, too. On the side favoring relaxation of regulations were the affected industries, especially the coal industry and the electric power companies. On the other side were the environmentalists. As it developed, the Senate favored only minimal relaxation whereas the House supported greater relaxation. In conference committee, the Senate forces prevailed on major questions. So the final amendments, which became the Energy Supply and Environmental Coordination Act of 1974, were closer to those favored by the EPA and CEQ.

On balance, it was a legislative victory for the environmental forces, including the government's two environmental agencies, despite strong lobbying and a widespread sense of national emergency. But environmental forces are not always victorious, despite the popularity and importance of their cause, as other examples show, for there are often other concerns at odds with environmental goals.

■ The case of clear-cutting limitations

A revealing illustration of how environmental controls can be stymied by vested interests occurred 2 years earlier, in 1972. The CEQ, acting in its role as advisor to the president, had drafted in January a proposed executive order limiting the practice of clear-cutting timber in national forests in areas of "scenic beauty." Clear-cutting is more economical for timber companies, because they move in and cut down all trees in an area at once, instead of cutting only the older ones and thereby thinning the forest so it can continue to grow. Environmentalists fear the consequences of clear-cutting for three reasons. It may increase soil erosion. It disrupts wild animals who live in the forest. And it makes the woodlands ugly. Because of this, they sought to limit clear-cutting on federal lands, where the federal government often sells "timber rights" to private lumber companies.

The White House circulated the proposed executive order limiting clear-cutting to the cabinet departments for comments. The Commerce Department, which has always served as a friend to business interests, sought comments from the National Forest Products Association. (This is but one of the many trade associations in Washington that look out for business interests.) The industry representatives immediately requested an opportunity to meet with high administration officials. They also contacted political figures from the western states, which have large federal land areas with timber. These politicians might fear that restrictions would cut down on the number of jobs available and on business tax revenues. After two sessions between industry representatives and administration officials, plus protests from western governors and members of Congress to the administration, the CEQ decided to withdraw the proposal. Newspaper accounts at the time indicated that officials were concerned about timber company profits, timber supplies, and business support for Republican candidates in an election year.[8]

■ The case of land-use controls

At about the same time, politics scuttled a proposed land-use bill setting up federal guidelines for land-use planning and offering financial assistance to state and local land-use commissions. Land-use planning involves conscious decisions about building, recreational, and other uses of land rather than letting "the forces of the marketplace" determine what happens to land. President Nixon had declared that such legislation was America's "number-one environmental priority." In addition, EPA Administrator Russell Train endorsed it, saying that it would help to "give the citizens of this country a real say in determining the course and quality of our physical growth."

Once the land-use bill reached Congress, coalitions of large interests lobbied furiously on each side. Supporting it were not only environmental groups, but the AFL-CIO, major state, county, and municipal associations, and the National Association of Real Estate Boards. Real estate agents (Realtors) favored it because it would increase property values and therefore increase their sales commissions. Opposing it were the U.S. Chamber of Commerce (the major business lobby), the American Farm Bureau Federation (because farmers now often sell their land for large profits to developers), construction trade unions (who feared it would slow construction of new shopping centers and office buildings, which provide jobs), and the trade association of home builders and cattlemen.

In the face of such opposition, President Nixon suddenly stopped supporting the bill he had recently termed our number-one priority. As a result, the bill lost in the House by a close vote, 211–204. Observers attributed Nixon's change to his desire to solidify conservative support against the Watergate impeachment drive, which was gaining strength. The opposition of the 211 members of the House who voted no, however, was attributable to the powerful coalition of business and some labor interests lobbying hard on the issue.[9]

[8] For an account of this incident, see Liroff, *A National Policy for the Environment,* pp. 60–61.

[9] This tale is told in Kiplinger, *Washington Now,* p. 466.

Presidential leadership

Regulatory bodies like the EPA are called "independent agencies," but their independence, as these examples suggest, is from the cabinet departments rather than from either the president or the Congress. As we shall see in more detail in Chapter 6, strong presidential leadership remains essential to almost all governmental activity. This is especially true of successful regulation. Nixon as president often refused or failed to provide that leadership. The Ford administration was even less supportive of environmental protection than the Nixon administration. President Ford twice vetoed legislation that would have controlled strip-mining (which devastates the surface of the land while unearthing coal, instead of mining it underground). He also supported various bills that would have weakened clean-air regulations. And when the Ford administration left office, at least twenty-one of its top environmental protection officials immediately took jobs with the very industries they had supposedly been policing.[10]

The special interests and the courts

In addition to strong presidential leadership and congressional support, effective regulation also requires an understanding of the problems of those being regulated. But historically American regulatory agencies have been thought to err by going too far in this direction. They have become victims of "clientelism" – overrepresenting, or becoming captives of, the clientele or interests they are supposed to be regulating. We shall discuss this problem again in Chapter 7 on the bureaucracy.

The major innovation that has tended to prevent such clientelism in the EPA is the provision in the NEPA that all federal agencies have to produce an Environmental Impact Statement (EIS) before undertaking any new program or major action. At the time, no one seemed to recognize the potential importance of this provision. Therefore, the legislation passed with little attention from either the special interests in business and industry or the new public-interest organizations especially concerned with environmental protection.

Once the bill was law, this provision rapidly became the key to the success of the new agency. It allowed citizens to sue in court to stop or interrupt programs and actions where such an EIS had not been developed and made public. The courts sustained this report so broadly that within 3 years, over 400 such lawsuits had been filed. We shall see how our courts handle such cases in Chapter 9.

Citizen access

The unusual opportunities for "citizen access," as it is called, coupled with the obvious and growing importance of environmental influences in everyday life, have led to considerable citizen involvement with the EPA. In response, the agency has generally welcomed citizen initiatives and citizen correspondence. Indeed, the agency long followed the practice of volunteering further assistance if desired when it answered citizens' letters. But in April 1976 a Ford administration official sent the following memo to those in the agency in charge of answering letters: "I note on many letters that we graciously offer to be of further assistance to the correspondent. In general, I feel we should omit that offer except for (1) Congressionals and other 'heavies'; (2) other Federal and State agency officials; and (3) other persons we may really want to assist."[11]

The problems of bureaucracy

Developments such as this, which further separate the people from their government and emphasize

[10]See Clayton Fritchey, "A New Deal for the Environment?" *Washington Post,* January 1, 1977.

[11]Leaked to Mike Causey and printed in his *Washington Post* column, April 20, 1976, p. C2.

deference to politicians and bureaucrats instead, are the sort of thing that tends to happen as agencies age. They become more concerned about their survival as institutions than about their service function. These tendencies suggest the importance of continued renewal not only of personnel and program, but even more of bureaucratic procedure, so that the mission does not get lost or submerged in the politics. This is a topic we shall return to in Chapter 8 on bureaucracy.

Environmental problems are here to stay, and so environmental protection efforts and the EPA and its associated agencies are here to stay – in one form or another.[12] There are, however, strong reasons for further consolidation of such agencies. By 1975, besides the EPA, there were an additional fifteen agencies involved somehow in environmental protection activities, plus another eleven devoted to various aspects of studying or predicting changes in our natural surroundings. In addition, six agencies in three departments administered federal recreation areas, four agencies in two departments managed federal lands, and various agencies in three departments managed water resources. The EPA, therefore, has to keep as much of an eye on these various federal agencies as it does on state and local governments and private polluters.

Almost everything the EPA does, like everything we do, affects the quality of the environment, as our emerging ecological consciousness is revealing. And, in turn, our environment affects almost everything we do. In addition, every part of government is involved in environmental protection, as our analysis here reveals. To understand the political decision process in general more fully, we must examine the roles played by these various decision makers – the presidency, the bureaucracy, the Congress, and the courts. This survey will be the focus of the chapters in this part. We shall then return to environmental-protection policy in Chapter 20 as we discuss issues concerning the "quality of life" in the United States.

[12] For an interesting and comprehensive survey of the problems and the politics, see Walter A. Rosenbaum, *The Politics of Environmental Concern,* 2nd ed. (New York: Praeger, 1977).

6 The presidency

Just after noon on January 20, 1977, Jimmy Carter took the oath of office at the Capitol. To the American people, that act made him the thirty-eighth president of the United States. While that ceremony was going on at the front of the platform, toward the rear one man was quietly passing a black box to another man. To the rest of the world, in effect, that act made Carter president of the United States. For that black box was the code box that makes it possible for the person who has it to launch American military might anywhere in the world. It is the portable equivalent of the famous "red telephone," and it follows the president everywhere he goes so he can "push the nuclear button" at a moment's notice.

□ THE PRESIDENCY AND RULING POWER

The public inauguration ceremony transfers internal ruling power from one person to the next, so that the new president can represent the American government to the American people for the next 4 years. That is what we mean when we say, "He's our president." He represents the government to us. The not-so-public passing of "the nuclear button" transfers external ruling power so that the new president can represent the American people to the rest of the world for those next 4 years. That's what other nations mean when they say, "He's their president." He represents us to the other governments.

Internal ruling power – to govern the people in America – and external ruling power – to represent America in the world – are the twin parts of the responsibility of the president in our system, as we saw when examining the founding of the United States in Chapter 1. But while those twin *responsibilities* fall to the president in our system, the *powers* needed to fulfill them do not. Some of those powers, we have already noted, are *divided* between the national level and the states, while others are reserved to the people. Further, the powers allocated to the national level are *separated* between the branches: executive, legislative, and judicial. so the president has the responsibility *to lead the nation at home and abroad.* But to do so effectively he has *to lead the federal government and the people.* Only by leading the government and the people can he mobilize the power to fulfill his responsibilities. So the story of the presidency in our system is always the story of a person trying *to develop the powers of the office of president* and *to mold the organization of the executive branch* so that the whole government will do what he asks it to do. We shall see in this chapter – and again in the coming chapter on the bureaucracy – how the president tries to achieve these twin objectives, so that he can exercise effectively his twin responsibilities of internal and external representation. This has never been an easy task, but it is probably more difficult now than ever before.

When Jimmy Carter was inaugurated that bright and freezing day in January, he put his hand on a family Bible and repeated the same oath of office as the thirty-seven men before him: "I do solemnly swear that I will faithfully execute the office of president of the United States, and will to the best of my ability, preserve, protect and defend the Constitution of the United States." But he concluded his oath by adding "so help me God."

Cynics attributed that change in the language provided in the constitution to his "born again" Baptist religion. Others, more sympathetic, thought that perhaps the new president had learned from his recent predecessors that the job was indeed more than one man could handle well without divine assistance. After all, John F. Kennedy had presided less than 1,000 days – frustrating days, most of them – before being gunned down by an assassin. Lyndon Johnson, his successor, had then tried to combine an activist foreign policy (dominated by the war in Vietnam) with an innovative domestic presidency (epitomized by the "War on Poverty") and had been forced to retire after little more than 5 years with neither objective successfully achieved. Richard Nixon then won two elections, only to see his efforts at reconstruction in foreign policy plagued by the continuing tragedy of Vietnam, and his programs for domestic reform so discredited by Watergate that he was forced to resign in disgrace.

Finally, Gerald Ford, appointed vice-president by Nixon when Spiro Agnew was forced to resign because of corruption, had picked up the pieces and, as Carter said at the beginning of his inaugural address, done much "to heal our land." But his efforts at developing policies and programs had been so unimpressive that, for only the eighth time in the nation's 200 years, the voters had turned an incumbent president seeking reelection out of office and picked instead this man of little experience and less public record from Plains, Georgia.

□ THE LIFE OF THE PRESIDENT

Jimmy Carter's life as president was immediately filled with the same problems that had challenged his predecessor. These years, all presidents face the same basic challenges. They must manage and strengthen the American economy while spreading its benefits to more people at home, and they must strengthen the peace while preserving America's place in the world abroad. The presidential inauguration combines domestic and foreign aspects in the taking of the oath and the passing of the code box. So does most presidential policy making. The strength of our economy and its impact on both rich and poor depend on the price of foreign oil and other vital imports, for example. American jobs and profits at home are affected by those same imports from abroad. At the same time, the world economy is heavily influenced by the economic condition of the world's largest trader, the United States. And so it continues, as we shall see whenever we examine policy questions in coming chapters.

The result of all this is that the life of the president is a constant combination of domestic and foreign activities (see the box titled, "A day in the life of President Carter"). To understand more fully what the president does and why he does it, we must examine the roles of the president, the powers of the office and the resources the occupant uses. Then we shall be able to see the importance of organization as well as presidential skills and personality in the conduct of American politics. We shall also better understand the shaping of policy which results from the interaction of the president with the rest of the government and with the American people.

□ THE ROLES AND POWERS OF THE PRESIDENT

■ According to the Constitution

To find out what the president is supposed to do and how he is supposed to be able to do it, we look first at the Constitution. Article II begins: "The executive power shall be vested in a president of the United States of America." Sections 2 and 3 then list his major constitutional roles and the powers they imply or convey.

- □ "The president shall be commander in chief of the army and navy of the United States . . . ." – and now, of course, of the air force too. In other words, he is *chief officer* in the armed forces of the United States.
- □ ". . . he may require the opinion, in writing, of the principal officer in each of the executive departments . . . and he shall nominate, and by and with the advice and consent of the senate, shall appoint . . . public ministers . . . and all other officers of the United States . . . " and "he shall take care that the laws be faithfully executed. . . ." In other words, he is *chief executive* of the government.[1]

[1] What does it mean to be responsible for the execution of the laws of the United States? Those laws are contained in the *U.S. Code,* which organizes all the laws in force by subject matter and is updated regularly. The index to its 49 "titles" and 1507 "chapters" alone is twenty-six pages long. You will probably find the many-volumed *Code,* published by the government, or a more useful annotated version, published privately, in your college or university library.

■ A day in the life of President Carter

The daily life of the president is full of challenges. The schedule for September 7, 1977, contains many of the "typical" activities in a "typical" day, although of course no two days are alike.

All days begin with an hour or more of "quiet time" during which the president works alone with classical records for background music. Almost always, this is followed by the president's first formal meeting—a foreign affairs briefing by his National Security Affairs Advisor. Almost all days include meetings with other public officials, such as the cabinet or members of Congress. This day, it was those in the Congressional Black Caucus (see Chapter 14) and, later, congressional foreign affairs experts concerned with the Panama Canal Treaty, which Carter was about to sign. Most days also include meetings with private citizens. This day it was "institutional leaders" such as George Meany, head of the AFL-CIO (see Chapter 11), lawyer-lobbyist Clark Clifford (see Perspective 4), and former CIA director William Colby (see Chapter 19), whom he briefed on the treaty, and, later, former president Gerald Ford. Often, the president sees foreign dignitaries as well. This day heads of Latin American countries were in Washington for the signing of the treaty.

The formal schedule printed here does not report the briefer informal meetings with various White House aides. There are often as many as a dozen a day, usually including meetings with the vice-president, the press secretary, and the person in charge of relations with Congress. Nor does this schedule reveal the memos the president reads in his morning "quiet time," after dinner, and between meetings. These memos, often 40 or 50, may total as many as 300 pages a day. This day the president had lunch with his wife, as he does once a week, and an official dinner. Typically he has a "working lunch" with aides or officials and dinner with the family. After dinner, he usually returns to his study to work—often until he retires around 11 P.M. But he also finds time to play tennis on the White House court several times a week with some of his assistants, to swim in the outdoor White House pool with daughter Amy when the weather is nice, and to bowl some evenings in the White House bowling alley, or to see a new film in the White House movie theater.

These special facilities are part of the 132 rooms and 18 acres that make up the White House. They are tended by a staff that numbers over eighty, including six butlers, six maids, four cooks, eleven operating engineers, five electricians, six carpenters, three plumbers, three painters, four floral designers, and a seamstress. The salaries of these and other White House staffers exceed $1.2 million every year, and maintenance costs exceed another $2 million—including a White House electricity bill of more than $180,000 a year.

The president also has a fleet of a dozen limousines and several smaller cars. One limousine has armor-plating to protect the president from assassination when he travels, and it is often flown ahead for his use on trips outside Washington. For these trips the president has what amounts to his own airline: five Boeing 707s, eleven Lockheed Jetstars, five KC-135 tankers, three DC-9s, four Convair jet-props, and a Beechcraft King Air light plane, plus two helicopters—as well as use of any military aircraft he wishes. He flies long distances on a 707, which is called "Air Force One" when he's on board and costs about $2000 an hour to fly with its crew of 17. This plane is actually a small hotel-office, equipped with desks, chairs, and even a bedroom, as well as special communications equipment.

Everywhere he goes, the president is protected by the Secret Service, as are other members of his family. This protection is provided by some 1,650 agents who are assisted from time to time by people borrowed from other law enforcement agencies. The cost of this protection is over $100 million a year.

Such special facilities and protection have led some to conclude that although the president sees many people every day he is really very insulated and lives a life more like that of a king or an emperor than like that of a citizen who happens to be president. And many wonder what effects the insulation and protection and special treatment have on the attitudes and behavior of a president. But even the president himself may not know.

White House photos

8:30 A.M.—meeting with Congressional Black Caucus.

9:30 A.M.—meeting with institutional leaders for Panama Canal Treaty briefing.

The president's schedule

Wednesday, September 7, 1977

7:45	Dr. Zbigniew Brzezinski—National Security Briefing—the Oval Office.
8:30	Meeting with Congressional Black Caucus—the Cabinet Room.
9:30	Panama Canal Briefing for Key Institutional Leaders—the State Dining Room.
11:00	Meeting with Senators John C. Stennis, Sam Nunn, Henry M. Jackson, and Robert B. Morgan—the Cabinet Room.
12:30	Lunch with Mrs. Rosalynn Carter—the Oval Office.
1:30	Meeting with the Honorable Michael Norman Manley, M.P., Prime Minister of Jamaica—the Oval Office and the Cabinet Room.
2:45	Meeting with His Excellency General Kjell Eugenio Laugerud Garcia, President of the Republic of Guatemala—the Oval Office and the Cabinet Room.
4:00	Meeting with His Excellency Carlos Andres Perez, President of the Republic of Venezuela—the Oval Office and the Cabinet Room.
5:15	Former President Gerald R. Ford—the Oval Office.
6:50	Depart via Motorcade en route Pan American Union Building.
	Attend Reception Hosted by OAS Secretary General H. E. Alejandro Orfila and Signing of the Panama Canal Treaty.
8:05	Depart Pan American Union Building en route White House.
8:30	State Dinner following Signing of the Panama Canal Treaty—the State Floor.

11:00 A.M.—meeting with senators.

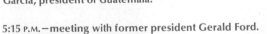

2:45 P.M.—meeting with General Kjell Eugenio Laugerud Garcia, president of Guatemala.

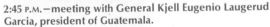

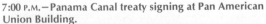

7:00 P.M.—Panama Canal treaty signing at Pan American Union Building.

5:15 P.M.—meeting with former president Gerald Ford.

- "He shall have the power, by and with the advice and consent of the senate, to make treaties, provided two-thirds of the senators present concur. . . ." In other words, he is the *chief of state,* conducting America's foreign relations.
- "He shall from time to time give the Congress information of the state of the union, and recommend to their consideration such measures as he shall judge necessary and expedient. . . ." In other words, he is the *chief legislator,* proposing new laws to the Congress for it to pass or not, and signing or vetoing laws passed by Congress.
- ". . . he . . . shall appoint ambassadors . . . and . . . receive ambassadors and other public ministers" from other countries. In other words, he is *chief diplomat,* conducting formal relations with other countries in order to represent the nation.

There were strong debates among the framers of the Constitution in 1787 over whether to have a president at all. One alternative was a *king*–perhaps an "elective kingship" in which an individual would be elected but then would rule as a king without the limitations that were eventually written into the constitution. Another was what is called "a plural executive"–*a committee*–which would rule collectively, perhaps by majority vote. The framers were attempting to avoid the abuses they had endured while under the rule of the British King George III before the American Revolution. At the same time, they sought to overcome the weakness of the first government that had been established after the Revolution under the Articles of Confederation of 1781, which provided only for a "Committee of the States" to rule when the Congress was not in session.[2] The decision to have a president was a compromise that created considerable debate as the states considered whether or not to ratify, or approve, the new Constitution.

The emphasis in these debates was on "competent" or effective powers. Words in the Constitution describing the powers of the president are just that: words–until they have been made "competent" by the way the president conducts himself in office. Because the Constitution defined presidential roles and powers in broad general statements, there was great uncertainty as to just how the president would perform the roles and exercise the specific powers. Only experience would tell.

■ According to the presidents

From the birth of the Republic in 1787, many presidents have contributed to the strengthening of the executive branch, to make it more "competent." The major contributions to the growth of the roles and of the effective powers of the presidency, most experts would agree, have been those of Presidents George Washington, Thomas Jefferson, Andrew Jackson, Abraham Lincoln, Theodore Roosevelt, Woodrow Wilson, and Franklin Delano Roosevelt. Each of them ruled

[2]A helpful brief account is C. Herman Pritchett, "The President's Constitutional Position," in *The Presidency Reappraised,* 2nd ed., ed. Rexford G. Tugwell and Thomas E. Cronin (New York: Praeger, 1977), pp. 3–23. The classic account of the debate and the decision is Charles C. Thach, Jr., *The Creation of the Presidency: 1775–1789* (Baltimore: Johns Hopkins Press, 1923; reprinted 1969).

Franklin D. Roosevelt Library

President Franklin D. Roosevelt, as commander in chief, in Sicily in 1943 with future president Eisenhower.

in difficult times and acted decisively, so all are known as strong presidents.[3] Indeed, in a 1976 survey of the heads of eighty-five college and university history departments, these seven were rated the most outstanding. The order of ranking was: Lincoln, Washington, FDR, TR, Jefferson, Wilson, and Jackson.[4] The American people as a whole see it somewhat differently. When asked by a Gallup Poll in late 1975 to name the three greatest presidents in history, the results were: Kennedy (mentioned by 52 percent – the historians ranked him thirteenth), Lincoln (49 percent), FDR (45 percent), Truman (37 percent – the historians ranked him eighth), Washington (25 percent), Eisenhower (24 percent – the historians ranked him fifteenth), TR (9 percent), Johnson (9 percent – historians ranked him eleventh), followed by Jefferson, Wilson, and Nixon.[5]

Clearly, the American people in general have a weaker sense of history. Indeed, that same survey found that only 72 percent of the American population could say what important event occurred in 1776 – this at the time of the Bicentennial. History, as it is generally viewed, may not interest the people in general – or even students. But if we are to understand the problems facing our government today, we must know how they have come to be problems. And if we are to understand how the government tries to cope with them – and what it could do but does not – we must know how the powers of government have developed to their present extent. So let us look briefly at what these seven strong presidents did to develop the roles and powers of the presidency.

---

[3]A helpful recent summary of presidential powers and their evolution is William F. Mullen, *Presidential Power and Politics* (New York: St. Martin's, 1976), especially chaps. 1 and 2. For an account with more attention to legal aspects, see Arthur S. Miller, *Presidential Power* (St. Paul: West, 1977).

[4]Poll reported by CBS News, January 22, 1977.

[5]*Gallup Opinion Index* No. 127, February 1976.

George Washington George Washington is called "the Father of His Country" for his service as our military leader during the Revolution and as our first president. He could also be called "the Father of the Presidency," for his presidency was crucial in defining the actual powers of the office. As the first occupant of the office, he set vital **precedents** – actions or statements that established a new approach or pattern and set an example for the future.

The Constitution gives the president the right to appoint officials with senatorial approval, but it says nothing about removal of officials. Knowing that the executive power would mean little if he could not fire those whose work he disapproved of, Washington took control of firing as well as hiring. He also established the practice of meeting regularly with the heads of the three departments created by the first Congress (state, war, and treasury) plus the attorney general. These secretaries of departments formed what we now call the cabinet – something not provided for in the Constitution.

In addition, Washington began the practice of *submitting proposed legislation* to the Congress and, through the efforts of Alexander Hamilton, his secretary of the treasury, getting support for it in the Congress. Many had expected the Congress to take the lead in developing policy via legislation. Washington's strong initiative as chief legislator set a precedent that has lasted to this day. Indeed, it is so strong that when Eisenhower was inaugurated, some 160 years later, and suggested that Congress act on a matter but failed to prepare a proposed bill, a Republican committee chairman in the House of Representatives scolded the president's staff: "Don't expect us to start from scratch on what you people want. That's not the way we do things here – *you* draft the bills and *we* work them over."[6]

Washington also began the practice of vetoing (or negating – a word we derive from the Latin term for "I forbid") legislation he did not approve of or believed unconstitutional. The Constitution made this legal – providing a two-thirds majority of both houses did not vote to override the veto. Washington made it an effective presidential power.

In another blow to congressional dominance, Washington withheld from Congress his own papers and documents on a matter of diplomacy on grounds that the Congress was not constitutionally entitled to them. This precedent became an important protection of presidential power from the prying eyes of political opponents. Some 150 years later, it was labeled **executive privilege**. In the Watergate affair, Nixon claimed that executive privilege entitled him to keep his White House tapes and other materials from the Congress, and even to prevent his officials from testifying before Congress. The controversy that followed was finally resolved against the president by the Supreme Court, as we shall see in Chapter 9. But the principle of limited executive privilege, established by the first president, survives to this day.[7]

---

[6]See Richard Neustadt's two classic articles on "Presidency and Legislation," the first subtitled "The Growth of Central Clearance," *American Political Science Review* 48 (September 1954): and the second, "Planning the President's Program," *American Political Science Review* 49 (December 1955). The Republican Committee Chairman is quoted on p. 1015 of the second article.

[7]See Raoul Berger, *Executive Privilege: A Constitutional Myth* (Cambridge, Mass.: Harvard University Press, 1974).

Washington as *commander in chief* used troops to put down a rebellion in Pennsylvania. As *chief diplomat* and *chief of state* he made foreign policy without consulting the Congress. This precedent surprised the Congress and laid the groundwork for our long history of active foreign policy making by the president, whether for good or ill.

These varied efforts to solidify the powers of the presidency were probably Washington's chief contributions to the establishment of a legitimate government for the former colonies. But at the time many thought his greatest contribution was his *voluntary resignation* after serving two terms of 4 years each. The decision to resign made certain that the office would not become a lifetime possession of someone once he was elected – an "elective kingship," as it was called. Washington's two-term service set a precedent observed by all his successors until Franklin Roosevelt, who was elected, during the Depression and World War II, to four straight terms. Roosevelt's shattering of the precedent was so controversial that it resulted in passage of the Twenty-second Amendment, ratified in 1951, which limits a president to two terms.

This two-term limitation is also important for the power of the presidency, because a president once reelected becomes a lame duck. (This term is commonly used to describe a president who is "lame" in that he can no longer run again.) He loses clout with party members who know they won't have to deal with him much longer and won't have to run on the same ticket with him next election. Even worse, members of his party may begin jockeying for position to succeed him. On the other hand, he may feel freer to attempt innovations in his second term because he need not fear losing potential support for the next campaign. At this time, he may be more concerned about "making his mark" in the history books.

Thomas Jefferson Thomas Jefferson's major contribution to the development of the presidency was to add a sixth role to those the Constitution established: that of *party leader*. As we saw in Chapter 3, by the time of his administration (1801–1809), the Federalists who had written the Constitution and dominated the government had lost power to the opposition, organized into the Republican party by Jefferson. Jefferson then established close ties with his supporters in the Congress and so proved a very effective politician as leader of his party. Since that time, relations between the executive and the legislative branches have always been influenced by party politics, for better or for worse. Presidents have been expected to lead their party – something particularly difficult when a president of one party faces a Congress controlled by the other.

Andrew Jackson The framers had always assumed that the Congress would be more representative of the people than the president. Senators were expected to be attentive to the interests of the states whose legislatures elected them. Representatives were expected to reflect the interests of the people of their congressional districts. The presidency probably was less representative of the people through the time when John Quincy Adams lost the popular vote to Andrew Jackson in 1824 but won the election nonetheless in the electoral college. However, when Jackson

The fates of recent presidents.

Franklin D. Roosevelt. Died in office.

Harry S. Truman. Declined to run for reelection.

Dwight D. Eisenhower. Two inactive terms, health problems while in office.

John F. Kennedy. Assassinated.

beat Adams overwhelmingly in the rematch of 1828, in the first election in which all white males, regardless of property holdings, were allowed to vote, he proclaimed himself the "People's President." His support came largely from small farmers, frontiersmen, and the emerging industrial working class – all of whom believed that the government had been serving the rich and propertied interests. So Jackson sought in his administration to compensate by emphasizing "human rights" over "property rights." Since Jackson, especially in recent decades, the less privileged have often looked to the president to do this when the Congress seemed dominated by special interests.

This transformation of the Presidency into a *representative of the people* added a seventh role and was a major step in the evolution of American democratic politics. At the same time, Jackson brought two innovations to the "administrative politics" of the executive branch. By firing many of the long-serving and mostly unrepresentative bureaucrats and replacing them with men loyal to him (a development we'll examine in more detail in Chapter 7), he sought to make the bureaucracy more responsive to his new policy directions. And by relying for advice less on the Department heads who formed the official cabinet and more on his own informal advisors (often called his **Kitchen Cabinet** because they worked behind the scenes) he received greater loyalty and support. Both these precedents strengthened the political and policy powers of the president and so contributed to the success of Jackson's efforts to democratize the presidency.

Abraham Lincoln Thus far, the expansion of presidential powers had been in the realm of domestic affairs. The contributions of Abraham Lincoln, Theodore Roosevelt, and Woodrow Wilson expanded the presidency's war powers. Lincoln, confronting the prospect of a Civil War, took important actions while Congress was not in session. He suspended certain constitutional liberties, spent funds that had not yet been appropriated by Congress, blockaded southern ports, and banned "treasonable correspondence" from the U.S. mails. All of these acts were of doubtful constitutionality. All were done in the name of his powers as commander in chief and his responsibility to "take care that the laws be faithfully executed" and to "preserve, protect and defend the Constitution." He was, in sum, the father of the war powers that have since been such an important part of presidential powers in the eighth role of the president: *mobilizer of the government* for war. Lincoln's actions preserved the Union in the Civil War. But eventually there was a strong reaction in the Congress – a reaction that reestablished congressional supremacy until the next period of crisis, at the turn of the century.

Theodore Roosevelt In some ways, the modern presidency can trace its ancestry to the contributions of Theodore ("Teddy") Roosevelt (1901 – 1909) and Woodrow Wilson (1913 – 1921). In retrospect, Roosevelt's major contribution to the growth of presidential powers was probably his addition of a ninth role: *mobilizer of the people* to increase the influence of public opinion on government. To do this, he took advantage of the emerging mass-audience newspapers and magazines by inventing the "press conference." He used it effectively to generate popular support for programs he sought to push through the Congress. But he also began to develop the tenth presidential role: that of *world leader* exercising American power in world affairs. Capitalizing on America's newfound enthusiasm for empire and its traditional endorsement of "rugged individualism," he developed the policy of "gunboat diplomacy." Under his leadership, American armed forces were used to police the politics of other (particularly Latin American) countries in order to protect American lives and business interests.

As he later explained his view of the president's role: "My belief was that it was not only his right but his duty to do anything that the needs of the nation demanded, unless such action was forbidden by the Constitution or by the laws. Under this interpretation of executive power I did and caused to be done many things not previously done by the president and the heads of the departments."[8]

Lyndon B. Johnson. Declined to run for reelection.

Woodrow Wilson In a sense, Woodrow Wilson further developed the role of world leader at the same time that he fostered the eleventh and final presidential role: that of *manager of the economy* influencing developments through governmental action. Originally a political science professor, Wilson combined Jefferson's skill at party leadership with TR's activist conception of the office to forge a highly successful legislative record. Among its major achievements were: a lowered tariff for freer international trade; a new antitrust (antimonopoly) law; and establishment of new federal regulation of banking and business. Most important of all, he achieved the introduction of the income tax on wealthy individuals (which first required passage of the Sixteenth Amendment, ratified in 1913) and the passage during World War I of the Overman Act (1918), which gave him virtually dictatorial power over the economy.

Richard M. Nixon. Resigned under threat of impeachment.

These measures and the World War transformed the president into an economic manager while they transformed America into a modern nation-state. World War I was the first war not just between military forces, but also between industrial productive forces. It was, in other words, total war between countries. In the words of Wilson's secretary of war, "Under modern conditions, wars are not made by soldiers only, but by nations. . . . The army is merely the point of the sword."[9]

Gerald R. Ford. Defeated in quest for election.

The United States adopted "universal military conscription" (by which all able-bodied males were to be drafted into the armed forces) and used the massive new revenue from the income tax to finance military mobilization for the world's first "total war." Wilson's new authority over the economy was used to reconstruct industry in the service of the state. It was the end of the period of economic laissez-faire (a French term meaning, roughly, "let it be"), or nonregulation of business and industry. And it was the end of the "limited government" that had been the chief intent of the framers of the Constitution.

Wilson, in contrast to Lincoln, had used his outstanding skills as party leader to get the Congress to give by law to the executive branch the authority to marshal, develop, and coordinate business, industry, and the population at large in the

Jimmy Carter.

[8]*The Autobiography of Theodore Roosevelt,* ed. Mayne Andrews (New York: Scribner, 1958), p. 197.

[9]Quoted in Arthur M. Schlesinger, *Political and Social Growth of the American People, 1865–1940* (New York: Macmillan, 1941), p. 420.

service of the state. As is often the case, these changes, once made by law in time of war, were never to be reversed. They set the stage for the bureaucratization not only of the government but also of the American economy and other institutions. Even the Congress became bureaucratized as it struggled vainly to keep up with the executive branch it had created by legislation and, like the sorcerer's apprentice made famous in Walt Disney's film *Fantasia,* could no longer control effectively.[10]

Wilson laid the groundwork for the large and powerful executive branch we have today, but at the price of the old efficiency and personal mastery that had been the primary attribute of the administrations of active presidents until that time. The combination of the new revenue generated by the income tax and the new demands and opportunities which government assumed because of American involvement in World War I ballooned the federal budget from a normal $800 million a year to over $18 billion in 1919. A president who, before the war, according to the chief usher at the White House, "worked but three or four hours a day and spent much of his time happily and quietly, sitting around with with his family,"[11] found himself increasingly preoccupied with affairs of state both grand and trivial in a way that would soon characterize all presidencies.

The vastly increased scope of government finance following introduction of the income tax and the growth of government activity during the war necessitated a new machinery to manage it. And so the Bureau of the Budget was created in 1921 as a part of the Treasury Department. The subsequent string of conservative administrations under Warren Harding, Calvin Coolidge, and Herbert Hoover can be seen as a reaction against the strong presidency. But that string came to a rapid end with the Great Depression, which brought another remarkable activist president into office in 1932.

Franklin Delano Roosevelt Franklin Delano Roosevelt was an excellent orator and an effective campaigner able fully to exploit the new national radio networks in marshaling public support for his programs. He was also an innovative organizer, and he immediately drew to himself two special groups of assistants: a team of specialists from the universities to develop new policies and legislation (called the "Brain Trust") and an informal set of political advisors and assistants – another "Kitchen Cabinet." His advisors helped to develop the broad range of programs that culminated in the irreversible governmental domination of the economy under the guidance of the president in his eleventh role: economic manager.

□ ROLES REQUIRE POWERS, AND POWERS REQUIRE EXERCISE

We have seen the roles of the president grow from the five specified in the constitution to eleven. Table 6.1 summarizes these roles and their emergence. We have also seen the powers of the presidency grow along with the roles. Such powers as appointment, treaty making, the veto, and the right to pardon were specifically

---

[10]For a more comprehensive account of this transformation, see Roderick A. Bell and David V. Edwards, *American Government: The Facts Reorganized* (Morristown, N.J.: General Learning Press, 1974), especially chaps. 5 and 6.

[11]Irvin H. Hoover, *Forty-two Years in the White House* (Boston: Houghton Mifflin, 1934), p. 266.

TABLE 6.1

The roles of the president

Informal title	Responsibility	Source or prime originator	Occasion for the innovation or experience encouraging it	Where else in this book origins and/or development discussed
1. Commander in chief	Leading our military forces	Constitution, Article II, Section 2	Experience of Revolutionary War	Chapter 1
2. Chief executive	Managing the executive branch and enforcing the law	Constitution, Article I, Article II, Sections 2 and 3	Experience under Articles of Confederation	Chapter 1
3. Chief of state	Representing the American people externally	Constitution, Article II, Section 3	Experience under Articles of Confederation	Chapters 1, 19
4. Chief legislator	Proposing bills to Congress and signing or vetoing bills passed by Congress	Constitution, Article I, Section 7, Article II, Section 3, and Washington	Creating the first administration	Chapter 8
5. Chief diplomat	Making and implementing foreign policy	Constitution, Article II, Section 2, and Washington	Creating the first administration	Chapters 1, 19
6. Party leader	Titular head at least, selecting officials to run the party if he wishes and organizing party support for his program	Jefferson	Rise of political parties	Chapter 4
7. Representative of the people	Voicing the concerns of the people in the government	Jackson	First popular election of a president with universal white adult male suffrage	Chapter 7
8. Mobilizer of the government	Organizing and exercising the governmental powers needed to fight wars	Lincoln and Wilson	Civil War and World War I	Chapters 7, 16, 19
9. Mobilizer of the people	Organizing the power of public opinion to influence government	Theodore Roosevelt	Development of the "press conference" for new mass dailies and use of the presidency as a "bully pulpit"	Chapter 10
10. World leader	Exercising American power in world affairs	Theodore Roosevelt and Wilson	Emergence of America as a world power in Western Hemisphere (following Spanish-American War) and in Europe (following World War I)	Chapter 19
11. Manager of the economy	Influencing economic developments through governmental action	Wilson and Franklin Roosevelt	Passage of the income tax amendment, conduct of World War I, and fighting the Depression	Chapters 16, 17, 20

provided in the Constitution. Other powers have been established by laws passed by Congress. These are called statutory powers because they are found in "statutes" or laws. They include developing the budget (for congressional approval), governing by special powers in times of emergency such as war or economic crisis, and reorganizing the executive branch for greater efficiency or competence.

In a sense, however, the greatest growth in presidential powers has been via what are often called the inherent powers – the powers inherent in any executive branch. The Constitution says that "the executive power shall be vested in a president." Since those words were ratified, presidents have been engaged in *defining through practice* just what those words imply. The president is supposed to "take care that the laws be faithfully executed." This executive responsibility has been the justification for "executive privilege" and for the issuance of perhaps as many as 50,000 executive orders supposedly based on powers derived from the Constitution and statutes. These executive orders are the means by which most things are done by the president. (We saw several examples in Perspective 3 and will discuss this power further later this chapter.)

In the words of constitutional lawyer Arthur S. Miller, "Presidential power . . . is a process, a flow of decisions open-ended and ever-changing, rather than a closed, internally consistent body of rules or principles. Its sources are in the constitution and partially in the statutes; but they transcend both – they may be found in the customs or conventions which have been built up through the years as accepted (and constitutionally acceptable) patterns of behavior."[12]

The powers that derive from customs or conventions can be lost if they are not exercised. President Eisenhower followed two activists in office – Roosevelt and Truman. Because of his temperament and political philosophy he believed that strict limits should be placed on the exercise of presidential power. He was particularly hesitant to use federal power to enforce racial integration in the public schools after the 1954 Supreme Court decision declaring segregation unconstitutional. The result was that it became all the more difficult for those who came afterwards to do so.

The exercise of presidential power can also be overdone, of course, as happened during the Nixon years. President Nixon was accused of "abuse of power" in Article II of the Resolution of Impeachment passed by the House Judiciary Committee just before he resigned. That article began with this charge:

> Using the powers of the office of President of the United States, Richard M. Nixon, in violation of his constitutional oath faithfully to execute the office of President of the United States and, to the best of his ability, preserve, protect, and defend the Constitution of the United States, and in disregard of his constitutional duty to take care that the laws be faithfully executed, has repeatedly engaged in conduct violating the constitutional rights of citizens, impairing the due and proper administration of justice and the conduct of lawful inquiries, or contravening the laws governing agencies of the executive branch and the purposes of these agencies.

---

[12]Miller, *Presidential Power,* p. 9.

This impeachment article then specifically accused Nixon of a number of such "abuses of power." One was meddling with the Internal Revenue Service by trying to get confidential information on citizens' tax returns and then ordering the IRS to investigate certain citizens' returns. Another was ordering illegal wiretapping of certain citizens. It also accused him of maintaining a secret spy unit in the office of the president. And it cited as well his efforts to cover up the Watergate violations.

These abuse-of-power charges were but one of three sets of charges against Nixon when he resigned. The general assertion that Nixon had overstepped the legal limits in using certain powers of the presidency contrasts with the criticism that Eisenhower had made too little use of presidential power. To what can we attribute such utterly different attitudes toward presidential power among two men who worked together in the same administration from 1953 to 1961? The political and economic climates of their presidencies were somewhat different, it is true. But many observers believe the key difference was in the specific personalities of the two men.

□ PRESIDENTIAL PERSONALITY AND EXPERIENCE

■ Prepresidential experience

Presidents are no exception to the rule that people act in accordance with their personality and experience. For most people coming to the presidency, the political experience is relatively typical. (Figure 6.1 portrays the routes taken by all major-party presidential nominees of the past 40 years.) This is not because the Constitution requires a certain type of experience. Quite the contrary, the formal requirements it sets are only three. One must be a native-born citizen of the United States. One must be at least 35 years old. And one must have lived in the United States for at least 14 years. That's all. Political practice or custom has always set other "requirements." These are usually taken seriously until they are successfully broken. For example, until John Kennedy, a Roman Catholic, was victorious, it was widely believed that a Catholic could not be elected president and so should not even be nominated. The same is still believed about Jews and atheists, as well as about blacks and women. In addition, it used to be said as well that "outsiders" – those not experienced in federal governmental service – were not electable. But then "outsider" Carter beat "insider" Ford, at a time when public confidence in government was on the decline and "outsider" status suddenly seemed an advantage.

Normally, whatever differences there may be in upbringing and education, we expect to find the work experience of presidents rather similar. Usually, presidents work their way up through politics – most often, through the Congress. Eisenhower, who was a retired military general serving as a college president when nominated, was an exception. Carter, a farmer and state governor, is another. Interestingly, Johnson and Nixon, with long national political careers, were probably our best prepared recent presidents, according to the conventional wisdom. And yet each overstepped political bounds in ways that terminated his career prematurely. These are conspicuous cases of the failure of previous political experience to prevent disastrous presidential mistakes such as Vietnam and

FIGURE 6.1

Routes to the presidential nomination.

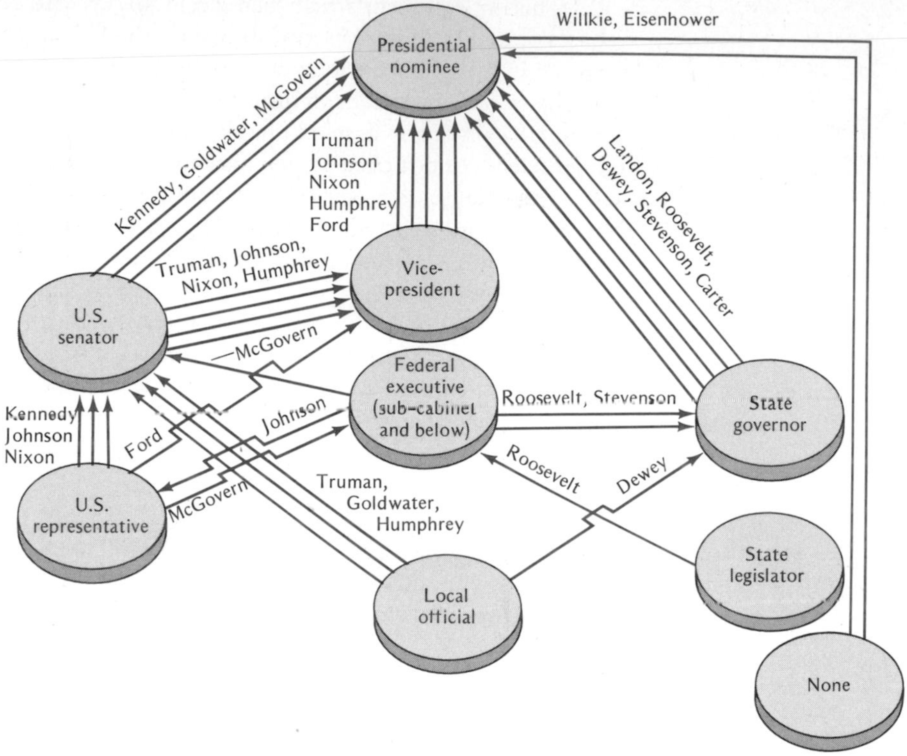

Source: Adapted from Donald R. Matthews, "Presidential Nominations," in *Choosing the President,* ed. James David Barber (Englewood Cliffs, N.J.: Prentice-Hall, 1973), p. 46.

Watergate. They have led observers to wonder whether perhaps personality is more important than it once was thought to be.[13]

By personality we mean psychological predispositions or character and temperament – such features as one's need for privacy, one's sense of self-esteem, and one's need for power or need for achievement. We have no direct way of discovering the nature of a president's personality. We have to examine the way he does a job and how he feels about it. We also refer to psychological theories about personality and try to apply them to the people we study. This approach is now often referred to as study of "presidential character."

■ The presidential character

The leading student of presidential character is political scientist James David Barber. He studies a president's style, character, and world view, as well as his childhood experience, to predict his likely performance under the stress of the office. Barber divides all presidents in two ways. First, he separates those he calls the "actives," who devote a lot of energy to the job, from the "passives," who seldom

[13]One result has been a spate of "psychobiographies" of recent presidents, among them: Garry Wills, *Nixon Agonistes* (Boston: Houghton Mifflin, 1970); Bruce Mazlish, *In Search of Nixon* (New York: Basic, 1972); Doris Kearns, *Lyndon Johnson and the American Dream* (New York: Harper & Row, 1976).

take initiatives. And second, he separates them into the categories of "positives," who seem generally happy and optimistic, and "negatives," who seem sad or irritable.[14] These two distinctions can be combined to yield four categories of presidents, each with a unique character and approach to the office (see Table 6.2).

This pioneering effort to uncover the most important determinants of presidential performance has proved very provocative. Barber has warned that the "active-negative" type may have difficulty controlling his aggressiveness because he is motivated by anxieties and guilt and tends to confuse his own ambitions and psychological needs with national policy. The result may be fixation on a disastrous policy (Vietnam for Johnson, Watergate for Nixon, and the League of Nations for Wilson).

Some have argued that equating these three presidents is indefensible. Alexander George, himself author of a psychobiography of Woodrow Wilson, emphasizes a difference that Barber recognizes: That Wilson's uncompromising behavior was based on strong moral principles, whereas Nixon's was based on personal ambition. Therefore, Barber grants that Nixon may deserve a special subcategory of "active-negative" for those threatened, not by defeat of their moral principles, but rather by attacks on their independence.

But if Nixon deserves a special subcategory for this reason, so would Hoover and Johnson for other reasons, according to George. All of these men differed in their motives and goals, and in their ability to cast their motives in ways that might attain their goals—even though all essentially failed to attain these goals.[15] So some experts believe we may need a different set of primary categories for assessing our presidents' characters and predicting their likely performances. But all seem to have been stimulated by Barber's efforts, and no one else has yet produced an alternative that seems more satisfactory.

---

[14] James David Barber, *The Presidential Character*, 2nd ed. (Englewood Cliffs, N.J.: Prentice-Hall, 1977).

[15] See Alexander George, "Assessing Presidential Character," *World Politics* 26 (January 1974): 234–282.

TABLE 6.2
Presidential character types

Energy level in doing the job	Emotional attitude toward the presidency: Positive	Emotional attitude toward the presidency: Negative
Active	Tends to show confidence, flexibility, a focus on producing results through rational mastery. Examples: Jefferson, Franklin Roosevelt, Truman, Kennedy, Ford, Carter	Tends to emphasize ambitious striving, aggressiveness, a focus on the struggle for power against a hostile environment. Examples: John Adams, Wilson, Hoover, Johnson, Nixon
Passive	Tends to show receptiveness, compliance, other-directedness, plus a superficial hopefulness masking inner doubt Examples: Madison, Taft, Harding	Tends to withdraw from conflict and uncertainty and to think in terms of vague principles of duty and regular procedure Examples: Washington, Coolidge, Eisenhower

Source: Developed from James David Barber, *The Presidential Character*, 2nd ed. (Englewood Cliffs, N.J.: Prentice-Hall 1977).

The ideal presidential personality

The demand for loyalty is the paramount characteristic of every presidential personality. Ideally it will be accompanied by a sufficiently mature sense of security to permit loyal dissent and disagreement. Similarly, the egocentricity that leads men to conclude they can be a better president that anyone else should be tempered by the kind of curiosity and flexibility that instructs changes of view and informs perspective.

Persistence, occasionally to the point of stubborness, is essential to the achievement of most controversial presidential objectives. Unyielding, "I'm-from-Missouri-you've-got-to-show me" skepticism is critical to the intelligent analysis and selection of policy options. So is the sense of security that comes from a well-balanced ego that makes a president personally comfortable in testing policy alternatives on a variety of aides, government officials, outside experts, special-interest representatives, casual office visitors, and opponents. The difficulty in having the relevant facts before a presidential decision is made and the need to take most presidential decisions without all the relevant facts make these particularly desirable personality traits.

All these qualities are likely to be accompanied in most presidential personalities by full measures of shrewd calculation, secretiveness, and pragmatic detachment.

From Joseph A. Califano, *A Presidential Nation* (New York: Norton, 1975), p. 244. Reprinted with permission.

☐ EXERCISE OF POWER REQUIRES RESOURCES

Personality can be an important asset – or a serious liability – to a president. But when trying to be effective, there is still no substitute for resources. The *powers* we have listed *are permissions* in essence. A president is only one person, and there are severe limits to what any one person can do, even when there is no real opposition. In politics, of course, there is almost always opposition, and often much of it. In our system of divided, separated, and shared powers, it is all the more necessary – and difficult – to get others to do what they must do in order for one's own presidential word or deed to have effect. What can a president do to encourage others to support his programs?

The president can use resources, of which he has a great many, primary among them jobs, budgetary monies, access, personal support, and information. It is particularly important to have usable and relevant resources in dealing with the Congress, the bureaucracy, the courts, and the media.

Jobs: presidential appointments

The Constitution gives the president the power to appoint. As we'll see in more detail in Chapter 7 on the bureaucracy, the "civil service" system has gradually whittled down that power, so that when Jimmy Carter took office there were only about 2000 jobs – out of about 2.8 million in the executive branch – that he could fill. Of these jobs, only about a thousand are "policy" jobs (as distinguished from "supporting" jobs such as secretary or chauffeur). Still, those thousand jobs are a source of great power to a new president, for he can appoint not only his own political friends and supporters, but also the friends of people he wants to become his friends and supporters, such as influential members of Congress. In fact, all presidents, during the transition between administrations, find it difficult to select only their own friends and acquaintances, for they don't even know enough reliable people. John Kennedy, faced with the task, is said to have complained that he didn't know any people—all he knew were politicians. Like his predecessors, Carter finally appointed a good many people who were others' candidates. This tactic does, of course, produce "political IOUs" from the supporters, which can be cashed in when the president's program needs support in Congress, for example.

The traditional name for such appointments is patronage—something given by one's patron or boss in exchange for support. But its significance now extends far beyond the traditional usefulness in rewarding political supporters.[17] For example, appointments are the primary way a new president has to influence the Supreme Court indirectly when there are no vacancies on the Court for him to fill.

Here's how that worked in 1977 when Carter came to power. One of his first acts was to appoint the "solicitor general"—the top lawyer in the government, who decides what cases the government will present or "appeal" to the Supreme Court for it to decide and who "argues" the government's position on cases before the Court. As we'll see in Chapter 9, the nine justices make up their own minds. But they tend to pay special attention to the views of the solicitor general—so much so that he (or she—although no woman has yet held the post) is often referred to as "the tenth justice." Carter picked a black, Wade McCree, Jr., who soon became involved in the Bakke case concerning "reverse racial discrimination"—a major case before the Court that we'll examine in Perspective 5.

---

[16]If you're curious about these jobs, which pay up to $66,000 a year and are located around the world as well as in Washington, the official list, which is informally called "The Plum Book" because it lists "political plums" ripe for the picking, is: *Policy and Supporting Positions,* published by the Government Printing Office just after each presidential election.

[17]For a comprehensive study, see Martin Tolchin and Susan Tolchin, *To the Victor . . . : Political Patronage from the Clubhouse to the White House* (New York: Random House, 1971).

A second immediate opportunity Carter had to influence the Court indirectly was the appointment of people to twenty-three vacant lower federal judgeships. These appointments were important because the Supreme Court often delays deciding major issues to see how lower courts handle them, and so the attitudes of new judges can have influence. When Carter took over, there were only nineteen blacks and five women among the 495 federal judges, so he also took this opportunity to increase the representation of these groups on the federal bench.

It is important to remember that, in most major instances, the appointment power is shared with the Congress, which must approve the president's nominations. In the case of federal judgeships, Congress had an even greater role as Carter took power. The courts had long been overcrowded and so there was a need for more judgeships. But the Democratic-dominated Congress delayed creating those new posts during the Nixon and Ford years to prevent them from having the opportunity to appoint Republican judges. Once Carter was in office, Congress could create the judgeships serene in the expectation that Carter would appoint Democrats. Furthermore, individual senators could often have a veto over his choices because of a practice called "senatorial courtesy," which we'll discuss in Chapter 9.

■ Money: budgetary allocations

The Congress is involved in appointments, but it is immersed in the budget. The President's Office of Management and Budget draws up a proposed budget for the whole executive branch and submits it to Congress. What goes into that budget is a matter for bargaining between the president and his close advisors, in one camp, the bureaucracy which will spend the money, in another camp, the Congress, which must appropriate the funds, in a third camp, and the special interests, which will gain or lose by the decisions, in the fourth camp. We'll discuss the politics of the budget at various points in this book, starting in Chapter 8. The president has a special ability to use the decisions on money as political resources because he proposes the budget in the first place, and his fellow employees of the executive branch spend it in the last.

■ Access: the opportunity to get word to the president

Whatever may be the subject, from appointments to budgets, whoever the person, from member of Congress to lobbyist or even bureaucrat, no one gets anything from the president without first having *access* to him. Access is the opportunity to get to see the president, or to phone him and get through to him, or to write him a letter and know it will be passed on to him. This may not seem as if it should be that difficult. But consider just who probably want access to the president: Start with 100 senators and 435 representatives; add fifty state governors; include a good number of those 1000 policy-making officials he appointed when he took office; then don't forget the chief representatives of the special interests, thousands of them, many of whom probably gave money to his campaign hoping to get access to him later for it; and what about his own staff–522 in

White House photo

President Ford with Representative Les Ahrens in the Oval Office. The ability to have access to the president is crucial in the exercise of power.

the White House office alone when Carter took over. And this doesn't even include the heads of 150 or so other countries, let alone the rest of the American people. Viewed in these terms, we shouldn't be surprised that access is very difficult to get, and even hard to keep. So any offer of it which a president makes is very valuable to the recipient, no matter who he or she is, or what he or she wants.

■ Support: the opportunity to get something from the president

Politicians always want to demonstrate their White House access to their constituents. It's a good argument for their reelection: "Keep Jones in Congress; he gets things done for you because he's the president's friend." Such support can be demonstrated by a "Dear Jim" letter, or a "photo opportunity" in which the president lets the press photograph him with Jones, or even a speech by the president in Jones's district, for example. The greatest "gift" from a president, of course, is a program desired by the politician for his or her constituents. But any instance of these sorts of support is appreciated, and this makes support a valuable presidential resource. As Larry O'Brien, whom many term the most successful congressional lobbyist in White House history on the basis of his work for Kennedy, observes:

> A President can't whip members of Congress into line. All he can do is work out a relationship with the members that is comfortable for them and that keeps the lines of communication open. It's a very fragile thing, and it can break apart so easily if you lose touch with each other. The little things are so important—returning their phone calls and setting aside time on the President's schedule for informal, off-the-record meetings with members; getting their constituents on the White House VIP tours; helping them get publicity and speakers in their districts; . . . answering their questions; getting them information that lets them justify their support for something the President wants to do.[18]

[18]Quoted in David Broder, "The Teachings of Larry O'Brien," *Washington Post,* November 24, 1976. See also O'Brien's book, *No Final Victories* (Garden City, N.Y.: Doubleday, 1974).

■ Information: the knowledge for effective action

Perhaps the most important resource of any active individual is information. The more you know about your circumstances and those of your friends and adversaries, the more likely you are to be able to act effectively. The president has access to more information than any other individual. He not only has his own "vantage point," as Lyndon Johnson called it. He also has a personal staff that reads the papers and watches TV and prepares summaries of all that for him. He also has access to the reports on issues and proposals developed by the thousands of members of the executive branch involved in policy making. Further, he gets regular reports from the government's special "intelligence" organizations: the FBI on domestic matters and the CIA and other agencies on foreign affairs. He also has his friends and advisors, always ready to offer information and advice. And he has the American people, who write, wire, and phone him – and reach an assistant – regularly.

The president, it becomes apparent, has access to *too much information* on virtually everything to be able to absorb it, let alone to use it well himself. Yet, "What a President does not know about the activities under way in Defense, State and CIA, to say nothing of the Office of Education and the Bureau of Indian Affairs is incalculable," remarked William D. Carey, Assistant Budget Director, in 1969. "There he sits, overworked and making the best of a bad situation, while all around him his princes and serfs are doing and undoing in thousands of actions the work of his administration without him having a clue."[19] Sometimes, he may be tempted to use his sources to develop damaging or embarrassing information on his political opponents – as Johnson and Nixon were caught doing with FBI, CIA, and IRS files. Always, sitting at the center of a massive flow of information, much of which would be useful if only he could master it, a president is forced to depend on others for sifting and coordinating "paper." To try to convert a great potential resource into a usable resource, they are forced to rely on other people and on organization. To understand what works and what doesn't work here, we must know more about how the personnel and structures of the executive branch have developed.

□ EFFECTIVE USE OF RESOURCES REQUIRES PERSONNEL AND ORGANIZATION

■ The vice-president

We might expect the vice-president to be an assistant president. But that is not what has happened. In the early years, the vice-president was the runner-up in the race for the presidency, and so the two were likely to be political adversaries. The Twelfth Amendment, ratified in 1804, changed that. The Twenty-fifth, in 1967, even allowed the vice-president, in cooperation with the cabinet, of which he is a member, to declare a president disabled and then to replace him – as "acting president" – or to temporarily assume the powers and duties of a president who

[19] Quoted in Richard Rose, *Managing Presidential Objectives* (New York: Free Press, 1976), p. 117.

declares himself unable to perform the duties of office. The same amendment also provided that a vice-president who dies, leaves office (as Spiro Agnew did), or becomes president (as Gerald Ford did) is to be replaced by someone nominated by the president and confirmed by a majority vote of both houses of Congress. If both the president and the vice-president should die at the same time, the Speaker of the House would become president. Next in line is the President Pro Tempore of the Senate, followed by various cabinet officers.

Until recently, the vice-president has been, in Nelson Rockefeller's words, "standby equipment." As president, Gerald Ford began to change that by assigning more responsibility to Rockefeller. But it fell to Carter to make the first major addition to the vice-president's constitutional powers of presiding over the Senate and succeeding a president who dies or quits or is removed from office.

Walter Mondale assumed unprecedented responsibilities once Carter took office. In his own characterization, he was "to be President Carter's general advisor, to be privy to all of the information that he has, to sit in on the crucial meetings, to serve on the central policy-advisory groups, to troubleshoot, and to have foreign assignments as well as domestic. . . ."[20] As a former member of Congress, he also took on special lobbying duties when major bills were in trouble in the Congress. To facilitate his exercising these responsibilities, Mondale received an office very near Carter's – another major change, for previously vice-presidents were exiled to the neighboring Executive Office Building.

Such experiences across a broad range of presidential activities would best prepare a vice-president to succeed to the presidency on short notice, as nine have on the death or resignation of a president, or by later election, as have another four. Performing such broad responsibilities may also help to ease the strain of the presidency or increase the effectiveness of the president. The same is supposed to be true of the cabinet and the White House staff – but has it been?

TABLE 6.3

The evolution of the president's cabinet departments

State	1789
Treasury	1789
War (Army)[a]	1789
Attorney General[b]	1789
Navy[a]	1798
Interior	1849
Justice	1870
Post Office[c]	1872
Agriculture	1889
Commerce and Labor[d]	1903
Commerce	1913
Labor	1913
Defense	1949
Health, Education, and Welfare	1953
Housing and Urban Development	1965
Transportation	1966
Energy	1977

[a]Consolidated with air force into National Military Establishment in 1947. Became Defense Department in 1949.
[b]Became Justice Department in 1870.
[c]Became independent federal agency in 1970.
[d]Split into two separate departments in 1913.

■ The Cabinet

Although the cabinet was not mentioned in the Constitution, it has remained a fixture since Washington's administration. Table 6.3 depicts its departmental evolution since 1789. It usually combines the heads of the various executive departments plus the president and vice-president. The president may designate other officers as having "cabinet rank" and may also invite others to attend cabinet meetings.

In theory, cabinet meetings have two major functions. They allow the president to express his interests and wishes to the people who run the twelve departments that employ 1.5 million people. And they make it possible for these twelve administrative experts and other high presidential aides to discuss policy questions, many of which cross normal departmental lines.

In fact, things rarely work out this way – at least, not once the administration is settled. A major reason is that, as Charles G. Dawes, a vice-president and the first Director of the Budget Bureau, once remarked, "Cabinet

[20]Interview, *U.S. News & World Report,* March 28, 1977. See also Brock Brower, "The Remaking of the Vice President," *New York Times Magazine,* June 5, 1977, pp. 38–48.

WASHINGTON AND HIS CABINET.

Library of Congress

PRESIDENT LINCOLN AND HIS CABINET.

Library of Congress

members are vice presidents in charge of spending, and as such they are the natural enemies of the presidents."[21]

Yet another reason was expressed by President Nixon after a term in office: "It is inevitable when an individual has been in a Cabinet position or, for that matter, holds any position in government, after a certain length of time he becomes an advocate of the status quo; rather than running the bureaucracy, the bureaucracy runs him."[22] Or, as Nixon aide John Ehrlichman remarked, somewhat more picturesquely: After the administration appoints key officials to high offices and they have their pictures taken with the president, "we only see them at the annual White House Christmas party; they go off and marry the natives."[23] The more the cabinet members think in terms of the interests and needs of their departments instead of those of the president, the less likely the president is to rely on cabinet meetings. This then puts more of a policy burden on the White House staff.

---

[21]Quoted in Kermit Gordon, "Reflections on Spending," in *Public Policy,* vol. 15, ed. J. D. Montgomery and Arthur Smithies (Cambridge, Mass.: Harvard University Press, 1966), p. 15.

[22]Quoted in The *New York Times,* November 28, 1972, p. 40C.

[23]Quoted in Richard P. Nathan, *The Plot that Failed: Nixon and the Administrative Presidency* (New York: Wiley, 1975), p. 40.

President Carter at a cabinet meeting.

White House photo/Black Star

■ The White House staff and the Executive Office of the President

The White House office around 1900 consisted of a few presidential assistants, bookkeepers, messengers, secretaries, cooks, and household staff. By 1932, it included only thirty-seven people. But with Franklin Roosevelt it began to grow like a cancer as it tried to develop and then oversee the many new programs designed to overcome the Great Depression.

As such programs multiplied and the government grew, the president's bureaucracy proved unable to keep up. So Roosevelt appointed a special Committee on Administrative Management composed of three experts from business and education. It began its report in 1937 with the words "The President needs help," and proposed a major reorganization of the executive branch. Congress rejected this proposal, but did pass a watered-down version that nonetheless revolutionized the presidency. It created a new Executive Office of the President (EOP) to help Roosevelt oversee and coordinate the bureaucracy. It also moved the Bureau of the Budget out of the Treasury Department and into the EOP where it would be more responsive to Roosevelt's wishes. The old maxim that "he who controls the purse strings controls everything else" began to be confirmed once again.

When the White House office grew so large that much of it was moved across the street–literally as well as figuratively–into the Executive Office Building, in its place, inevitably, grew up a new White House staff. This new staff, which came to be called the White House Office, was formally a part of the EOP. It was intended to coordinate relations between the president and the Congress, and between the president and the rest of the government.

By the Truman years (1945–1953), World War II (1941–1945) had bloated the military establishment, and the Cold War that followed it had reemphasized the continuing importance of foreign affairs. As a result, the National Security Act of 1947 reorganized the Departments of the Army and the Navy into the National Military Establishment (renamed the Department of Defense in 1949) to coordinate the army, the navy, and the new air force. The same act also established a new National Security Council (NSC) in the EOP. There it joined the new Council of Economic Advisors (CEA). The CEA had been created in 1946 to oversee the transition from a wartime economy to a peacetime economy and to advise the president on how to foster economic stability and full employment so that the United States would never suffer another depression.

Truman, like Roosevelt, had a staff organized like a circle with himself at the hub. Eisenhower, a retired general, replaced that system with a pyramid with himself at its tip aided by a powerful chief of staff who had a still-growing bureaucracy beneath him.

Kennedy and Johnson, both activists, returned to a version of the Roosevelt model, with the addition of more special agencies to do things under presidential guidance that were not being done satisfactorily under cabinet supervision. Nixon then took that approach even further. The result was a return to what is generally called "the personalized and centralized presidency."

One expert on executive organization, who eventually helped President Carter organize his own staff, described its operation and its limitations this way:

> The personalized presidency largely depends on the leader's ability to mobilize public opinion to put pressure on the government to perform as he desires and to support what he believes is right. If the President lacks this skill, he cannot compensate in the long run by relying on the inherent strength of the office. The centralized presidency largely depends on the leader's ability to keep lines open to those outside his immediate circle and to resist minutiae. If the President is suspicious of cabinet members and relies too heavily on overworked assistants, he is apt to lose perspective and even his sense of reality.[24]

Many observers attribute the Vietnam disaster and the Watergate catastrophe (both of which we'll examine in Perspective 4) to the failure of the centralized personalized presidencies of Johnson and Nixon, different though they were in significant respects.

Both presidencies were products of the long-term trend toward larger and larger White House staffs, with the resulting weakening of the cabinet. The argument for this centralization has been that most important policy questions transcend the narrow foci of the departments, so the required coordination is best achieved in the less specialized EOP. In such a situation, virtually *all policy* was developed at the White House. Foreign policy was developed by the NSC, with perhaps a hundred employees. Domestic policy was developed by the Domestic Council, established by President Nixon in 1970 and employing about fifty persons. Once policy was made, it then *had to be "sold,"* as the common expression goes. First it had to be "sold" to the president himself by his staff. Then it had to be "sold" to the Congress (as always) and to the segments of the public that might then support it or oppose it in lobbying. But in addition policy now had to be sold to the executive branch bureaucracy itself, which had once developed policy but now no longer did, yet now more than ever was required to carry out policy because it was so complex.

This transformation, in other words, created *a little government* (some 600 or so in the White House Office and over a thousand more in the rest of the Executive Office of the President) *within a government* (about 2.8 million employees in the executive branch bureaucracy). This placed an even greater burden upon the power of the President – not just to move the nation, but also to move the Congress and his own bureaucracy.

■ The Carter compromise

Before he took office, Carter had been warned by his advisors on government organization of the dangers posed by this centralization of policy making in the White House. He and others had also seen the spectacle of an isolated Nixon

[24] Stephen Hess, *Organizing the Presidency* (Washington: Brookings Institution, 1976), p. 8.

White House struggling with the bureaucracy and eventually resorting to the Watergate "dirty tricks" to increase its power – a development we'll detail in Chapter 7 on the bureaucracy. Candidate Carter had pledged various executive branch reorganization measures. So President Carter sought to shrink the numbers and powers of the White House staff, abolishing such EOP agencies as the Domestic Council and the Council on International Economic Policy, in order to increase the policy role of the department secretaries – the cabinet.

FIGURE 6.2

Organization of the executive branch.

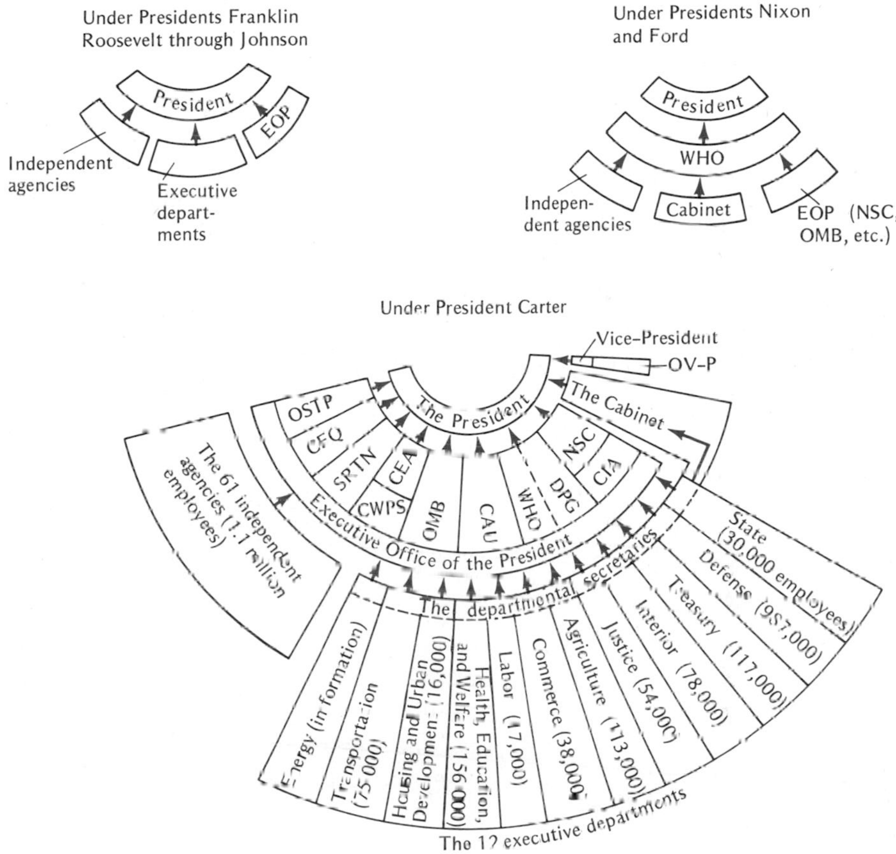

Key

CAU = Central Administrative Unit
CEA = Council of Economic Advisors
CEQ = Council on Environmental Quality
CIA = Central Intelligence Agency
CWPS = Council on Wage and Price Stability
DPG = Domestic Policy Group
EOP = Executive Office of the President
NSC = National Security Council
OMB = Office of Management and Budget
OSTP = Office of Science and Technology Policy
OVP = Office of the Vice-President
SRTN = Special Representative for Trade Negotiations
WHO = White House Office

He developed, therefore, a system he called "cabinet administration of our government." He convened regular weekly cabinet meetings. He also let the cabinet secretaries pick their own subordinates rather than forcing his own political choices on them. And he let them administer their departments, generally without interference from the White House staff. Furthermore, he generally used cabinet officers as his primary policy advisors. But, inevitably, as his administration evolved, it became clearer and clearer that his cabinet members were *recommending* policy, but he was making policy. As he explained it shortly after taking office, "The major decisions will be made ultimately by me as president, which is my constitutional prerogative and responsibility."[25] The cabinet thus had more of a role than in Nixon's terms, but less than in Eisenhower's.

At this point, with all our experience of reorganizations, there is still no way of organizing the executive branch that promises to be especially effective. Figure 6.2 depicts the formal and actual relations between the president and his advisors and assistants – both in the cabinet and in the White House staff, as they have developed from Franklin Roosevelt to Jimmy Carter. We'll return to some of these problems when we analyze "bureaucratic politics" in detail in Chapter 7.[26]

For the moment, we must remember that inevitably the president and his staff must constantly attempt to find ways of motivating those in his executive branch to do his bidding, even when they'd rather not. The power of the president has always depended on his ability to get people to follow orders if they refuse to follow suggestions. But the government has become so big that he cannot possibly even *issue* orders to most bureaucrats, let alone *follow up* to see that they are carried out. Thus, the power of the president more than ever has become the *power of persuasion.*

☐ PRESIDENTIAL POWER AS THE POWER OF PERSUASION

"People talk about the powers of a President, all the powers that a Chief Executive has, and what he can do. Let me tell you something – from experience!" remarked Harry Truman after 3 years on the job. "The President may have a great many powers given to him in the Constitution and may have certain powers under certain laws which are given to him by the Congress of the United States; but the principal power that the President has is to bring people

---

[25]Joel Havemann, "The Cabinet Band – Trying to Follow Carter's Baton," *National Journal,* July 16, 1977, pp. 1104–1112.

[26]By now there is a large literature on government organization and reorganization. The standard source on the present formal structure is the United States *Government Manual,* published each year by the Government Printing Office. For discussion of the present problems of the executive branch, see this account of a conference of experts: Ernest S. Griffith, *The American Presidency: The Dilemmas of Shared Power and Divided Government* (New York: New York University Press, 1976). An earlier, more formal survey is James. W. Davis, Jr., *The National Executive Branch* (New York: Free Press, 1970). On reorganization, see Harvey C. Mansfield, "Federal Executive Reorganization: Thirty Years of Experience," *Public Administration Review,* July–August 1969, pp. 332–345.

in and try to persuade them to do what they ought to do without persuasion. That's what the powers of the President amount to."[27]

Most of the important things a president wants to do require the cooperation of other parts of government. The Congress must pass legislation and appropriate money to establish and fund programs. The various parts of the bureaucracy must follow orders to develop and carry out the programs. The courts, if asked, must rule on whether the programs and the laws are constitutional. And the people must accept the programs and the president who proposes them.

The president, according to the Constitution and tradition, has a wide range of powers as commander in chief, chief legislator, head of state, and so on, as we and Harry Truman noted above. But in fact he shares these powers with other officials and other branches. He depends on others for cooperation. Of course, they too will depend on him from time to time for assistance with various of their projects, and so his power is more than simply that of charm, charisma, or powerful reasoning.

[27]Harry S. Truman, *Public Papers of the President 1948* (Washington, D.C.: Government Printing Office, 1949), p. 247.

The presidential power of persuasion in action

One of the best examples in the Johnson administration involved Treasury Secretary Henry (Joe) Fowler and House Banking Committee Chairman Wright Patman. Fowler was one of Johnson's favorites in the cabinet and Patman had been the president's friend and political ally for a generation, beginning during the New Deal. To stem increases in the prime rate by the major banks in early 1966, Johnson wanted to turn loose the power of his administration and to deposit federal funds in banks that held down interest rates (as well as to remove such funds from banks that increased them). Although generally inclined to use executive power to hold down prices and wages, Fowler opposed the particular jawboning and action program Johnson sought to put into effect. Johnson requested and received an analysis of interest rates for the period Fowler had been Treasury secretary and discovered that, in percentage terms, those rates had risen more during Fowler's brief tenure than during that of any previous secretary in the twentieth century. Johnson immediately called Wright Patman and said, "Wright, there's something you've just got to know. Interest rates have risen faster under Joe Fowler than under any secretary in this century."

Patman was appalled. "Something's got to be done about that, Mr. President," he said.

"That's why I'm telling you," Johnson continued. "If I were you, I'd send him a blistering letter and have him up to testify. You've got to build a fire under him."

"You're absolutely right, Mr. President." By now Patman was getting angry.

"You know, Wright, unless Fowler starts moving on these banks, the New York bankers will just keep hiking the interest rates and rolling in the money. Your committee can't stand for that."

"I'll write him today, Mr. President. We'll call him to testify this week."

By the time Johnson hung up, Patman was sputtering mad. When Fowler received Patman's scathing letter, he called the White House. Johnson passed the word that Fowler had "better tell Patman you'll turn loose some pressure on the banks or else he'll turn your hearing into a Texas barbeque." Fowler agreed and Johnson got a jawboning program with the banks off the ground. Fond as he was of Fowler, Johnson was sufficiently detached to realize that he had to give him a hard shove to get him moving.

From Joseph A. Califano, *A Presidential Nation* (New York: Norton, 1975), pp. 206–207. Reprinted with permission.

But he cannot simply impose his wishes on others, as we noted in our discussion of authority in Chapter 3. He must persuade them to accept his position, his definition of the situation, his policy proposal. "The essence of a President's persuasive task with congressmen and everybody else," as Richard Neustadt once summarized it, "is to induce them to believe that what he wants of them is what their own appraisal of their own responsibilities requires them to do in their interest, not his. Because men may differ in their views on public policy, because differences in outlook stem from differences in duty – duty to one's office, one's constituents, oneself – that task is bound to be more like collective bargaining than like a reasoned argument . . . ."[28]

Even the "collective bargaining" image may sometimes be misleading. A president must often find devious ways of getting information to officials without appearing to be imposing his will on them. Joseph Califano, secretary of health, education, and welfare under Carter, once told an amusing but revealing story of how Lyndon Johnson, whom Califano assisted in the White House, operated in this devious way as president (see the box titled "The presidential power of persuasion in action"). It emphasizes the importance not only of occasional deviousness but also of an understanding of structures and roles and their impact on the effectiveness of persuasion.

□ THE PRESIDENT AND THE PEOPLE

The president's need to persuade does not stop with the government. In order "to move a nation," in former presidential advisor Roger Hilsman's words,[29] the president must move the people, too. Sometimes it is to get them to *support* his program by lobbying their members of Congress, as almost every president since Teddy Roosevelt has occasionally urged. Other times it's to get them to *adopt* his program, such as the energy conservation urged by presidents Nixon, Ford, and Carter. All the time he is trying to satisfy 220 million people making up various interest groups. This task is made especially difficult by the fact that different people want different things, and by the fact that resources are always scarce.

■ The problem of popular confidence

In recent years, both presidents and the executive branch have found such efforts more difficult. One reason seems to be a general decline in public confidence in government. In 1966, 41 percent of the American people were reported by a Harris poll to have "a great deal of confidence" in the executive branch. But 6 years later, as Richard Nixon was winning reelection by a landslide, that figure had dropped 14 points to 27 percent. A year thereafter, as Watergate began to open up, the figure was down 8 more points to 19 percent. and by April 1974, when

[28]Richard Neustadt, *Presidential Power,* 2nd ed. (New York: Wiley, 1976), p. 114. Emphasis deleted.

[29]See Hilsman's memoir of the Kennedy years, *To Move a Nation* (Garden City, N.Y.: Doubleday, 1967).

The president and the people. Town meeting, Yazoo City, Mississippi.

Wide World Photos

Watergate was becoming more of an open floodgate, another survey showed only 13 percent having "a great deal of confidence" in the executive branch and the president. Once Gerald Ford took over from Nixon as president, a Gallup poll found an improvement setting in. By June 1975, after about a year of the Ford administration, 23 percent again had a great deal of confidence in the president and executive branch—although only 14 percent of those under age 30 felt that way. But the figure was still only about half that of a decade earlier, and even further increases under Carter have not restored public confidence to its earlier levels.[30]

These years have been trying for public confidence. One reason was, of course, Watergate. Another was Vietnam and the "credibility gap" of the Johnson years, in which even presidential statements and pledges became suspect. Johnson, after all, had campaigned against Barry Goldwater in 1964 by painting his opponent as a militarist or "war hawk" and pledging that he would not commit American fighting forces in Vietnam—a pledge he broke just months after the inauguration, in what turned out to be but the first of a series of misleading assertions.

The result has been that the American people have come to value "honesty" and "trustworthiness" as the most important characteristics in a presidential candidate. One recent poll of what the public wants in a president produced these ratings: honesty or trustworthiness, 60 percent; concern for people, 37 percent; experience, 20 percent; leadership ability, 19 percent; intelligence and education, 14 percent.[31]

---

[30]For a general discussion of attitudes toward the president, see Fred I. Greenstein, "Popular Images of the President," *American Journal of Psychiatry* 122 (1965): 523–529.

[31]Respondents were asked to list several qualities, so the figures add up to more than 100 percent—which makes the low rating for leadership and intelligence all the more striking. See Mervin D. Field, "Public Opinion and Presidential Response," pp. 59–77 in John C. Hoy & Melvin H. Bernstein, eds., *The Effective President* (Pacific Palisades: Palisades Publishers, 1976).

The president is by far the best-known political figure in America, and the one most watched by the American people. Historically, American attitudes have been positive. As columnist Russell Baker wrote with some whimsy, and before Watergate, "Americans tend to like the President and dislike the people who oppose him. The President is one of those universally revered modern American institutions like Mother, Friday night, the flag, burgers, progress, and plenty of free parking which everybody assumes that all decent, right-thinking citizens approve of and support."[32]

When the president misbehaves seriously, as Nixon did in the Watergate affair, he and the institution suffer loss of respect. But the snap-back under Ford and the relatively high ratings once Carter was sworn in suggest that such setbacks may prove temporary.

■ The roots of popular attitudes

The reasons for the long-standing strong respect for the presidency are important to understand. Political scientist Fred Greenstein, who has watched the public watching the presidents for many years, suggests two major ways in which the people "use" the president psychologically.

First, the president serves as an aid or focus point for thinking about politics and keeping informed, because he is a single, very visible official who seems to dominate politics and serves as head of state.

Second, the president serves as an outlet for citizens' feelings. This function, like that performed by a king or queen in other countries, has several aspects:

- □ Some people may "identify with him," or "live through him" and his interesting life as portrayed in the media, if their own lives are not exciting. As an alternative, if he misbehaves, they may identify with his adversaries – as seemed to happen in the Watergate investigations.
- □ He is a symbol of national unity, drawing together people who may disagree on politics and policies. Or he may divide and polarize the nation, as Nixon did by emphasizing "law and order" themes that alienated blacks and liberals.
- □ He may be a symbol of stability and predictability – someone who tends to the governing of the country even when we pay no attention to that.
- □ He can even serve as a "lightning rod" attracting expressions of opinion – especially outrage – and taking the blame for failures of the government to live up to the high moral standards most Americans are reared to support. Johnson for Vietnam and Nixon for Watergate served this function.[33]

■ The expressions of popular views

Public attitudes are often expressed in communication with the president, by letter, telegram, or phone call to the White House, virtually all of which are

---

[32]Russell Baker, "Nobody Here But Us Presidents," *New York Times,* August 15, 1972.

[33]See Fred I. Greenstein, "What the President Means to Americans," in *Choosing the President,* ed. James David Barber (Englewood Cliffs, N.J.: Prentice-Hall, 1974), chap. 5.

acknowledged in some way. This communication between the people and the president, indirect though it be, happens whether or not the president encourages it – especially when he does something that upsets people. When President Nixon fired the Watergate Special Prosecutor Archibald Cox, who was investigating wrongdoing by the Nixon administration, for example, Western Union reported "the heaviest concentrated volume [of telegrams] on record" to the White House.[34]

Carter, upon taking office, chose to encourage messages from the people. He soon averaged about 75,000 letters a week, many in response to his request for suggestions on how he could stay close to the people as president. In his administration, as in previous ones, such communications rarely if ever reach the president himself directly. But twenty or so White House staff members regularly prepare summaries of opinions expressed and single out typical or unusual messages for the president himself to see, and occasionally to respond to.

☐ WHAT INFLUENCES THE PRESIDENT?

Does public opinion really affect a presidents' behavior? How does the president decide what to do? The president deals with so many different questions, domestic and foreign, that it is difficult even to specify the relative importance of possible influences on his decisions. We know that a president interested in being reelected is likely to be concerned about the general assessment the public gives his work. But is it likely to matter much what position he takes on one particular issue? Perhaps not, although occasionally particular issues – such as President Ford's pardon of Nixon – do make a difference.

Does this mean that the views of his advisors will matter more? Those advisors are more likely to be watching either political implications or technical aspects of a question – but rarely both, as a president must. How about the cabinet and other senior officials? The president knows each has his or her own special interests, and so he is not likely to take a specific cabinet secretary's recommendation without question. And the Congress? He must be concerned about congressional reaction, but he knows that members of Congress represent narrow constituencies and that the Congress expects him to offer national leadership because his constituency is the entire country. What about the vested interests? Or foreign nations if it is a foreign policy question? Or how about the role of intelligence agencies – the FBI domestically and the CIA internationally? Or will his own past experience and personality prove more influential than these momentary suggestions and considerations?

The answer to all these questions is, unfortunately, that no one knows for sure. Presidents themselves may not know, even in retrospect, at least if we can judge by reading the memoirs of former presidents. None of them generalizes about the factors that influenced his decisions. And when Gerald Ford was asked about the

---

[34]Quoted in Greenstein, "What the President Means to Americans," p. 146.

relative influence on his decisions of pressure groups including the Congress and of his own conscience, he responded:

> It is hard to be totally certain whether conscience or some other factor matters most. Some subjective feelings about certain things or certain issues are bound to play a part. In my case, I had a combination of what I thought were good recommendations from people in the administration and my own background and personal convictions. It was a combination of the two—options that came to me and my own experience and convictions—that ended up in whatever decision I made."[35]

If there are no clear and major outside influences on presidential decision, if the president is largely "his own man" in deciding what to do, does this suggest that the office is, or has become, too powerful?

☐ IS THE PRESIDENT TOO POWERFUL?

"The tyranny of the legislature is really the danger most to be feared, and will continue so for many years to come," wrote Thomas Jefferson to James Madison just before George Washington was inaugurated as our first president. "The tyranny of the executive power will come in its turn, but at a more distant period."

■ The use of executive orders

By the Constitution, as we have seen, the president was made commander in chief and given the responsibility to "take care that the laws be faithfully executed." This charge has required presidents to act alone and often quickly, especially in national emergencies. The major instrument developed by presidents for such action has been the executive order, a proclamation requiring agencies or individuals to take certain specific actions without Congress having first passed a law on the subject.

All presidents have found executive orders an essential tool in carrying out their oath to "faithfully execute the office of president," even though the constitution makes no mention of that specific power. From time to time, certain executive orders have been challenged in court on grounds that they overstep the president's authority. But the courts have upheld the president's power to issue executive orders even when they have declared a specific order unconstitutional. tional.

Presidents Johnson and Nixon extended the use of the executive order to new lengths. In doing so, Johnson managed to fight a war in Vietnam without having Congress first "declare it." Nixon managed, with mixed success, to abolish programs and agencies established by Congress without Congress's approval. Both presidents also used their powers less openly to involve bureaus like the FBI and the CIA in domestic spying and violation of the civil liberties of citizens. The peak of

---

[35] *A Discussion with Gerald R. Ford: The American Presidency* (Washington: American Enterprise Institute, 1977), p. 19.

these violations came in and around the Watergate affair, which we shall examine in more detail in Perspective 4.

One major result of Vietnam and Watergate was a widespread conclusion, by politicians, observers, and ordinary citizens alike, that the president had gained too much power. It was time, many argued, to dismantle or at least limit what historian Arthur Schlesinger termed "The Imperial Presidency."[36]

■ The relativity of presidential power Power is a relative thing in any system. If the President has too much power, it may be because the Congress and the courts have too little power to restrain him or to counter his power. In other cases, the Congress or the courts may *choose* not to resist presidential initiatives. This was the case in the Vietnam War, as we shall see in Chapter 9. In the Watergate activities, however, much of what Nixon and his administration did was done in secret. In such cases, neither Congress nor the courts know enough about his actions to be able to resist at the time.

[36]See Arthur Schlesinger, *The Imperial Presidency* (Boston: Houghton Mifflin, 1973).

■ Intelligence agency abuses in "the lawless state"

The clandestine bureaus are the true progeny of the postwar presidency, tracing their legal birthright not to legislation but to presidential assertions of "inherent power." According to bureau spokesmen, the FBI's "authority" to spy on Americans rests upon the "constitutional powers and responsibilities vested in the President." Similarly, the CIA's covert intervention abroad is based not on its legislated charter, but on the president's "inherent foreign policy powers." The National Security Agency and the National Reconnaissance Office, bureaus charged with communications and satellite intelligence respectively, were created entirely by secret executive directive, and annually consume over $4 billion without a statute to define their duties. What is true for programs is also true for techniques: the Justice Department has asserted a presidential power to order warrantless wiretaps, bugs, and "surreptitious entries" (break-ins) against American citizens for intelligence purposes. Even the secrecy that cloaks the intelligence bureaus is based upon a classification system established by executive order, without statutory basis.

The intelligence agencies are assigned the responsibility for routine spying and political policing at home and abroad. Secrecy is necessary, for the primary function of the agencies is to undertake disreputable activities that presidents do not wish to reveal to the public or expose to congressional debate. The agencies also collect secret intelligence information, which helps to justify presidential power by providing it with a claim of special knowledge. The "mysteries of government" do much to still criticism of activities apparently beyond the comprehension of mere citizens or legislators. . . .

Because of the secrecy, the "vicious and unsavory" tactics that are part of the daily routine of the secret agent are hidden from the citizenry, preserving their own sense of decency.

The secret agencies of the president operated for some twenty-five years with few questioning their operations. The national consensus, founded on anti-communism and developed by periodic crises, supported a bipartisan foreign policy and a strong, active presidency. The president's authority to defend the national security was generally accepted, and his instruments went unquestioned.

From *The Lawless State: The Crimes of the U.S. Intelligence Agencies* by Morton H. Halperin, Jerry J. Berman, Robert L. Borosage, and Christine M. Marwick (New York: Penguin Books, 1976), pp. 230–232.

There are, in other words, three different possibilities: (1) inadequate countervailing power; (2) insufficient will to counteract the president; and (3) incomplete knowledge of the president's use (and abuse) of his powers. The problem of presidential power is thus more complex than is sometimes argued. The real excess power, the dangerous power, of the president may be the power to break or evade the law in ways that are kept secret.

One recent study of the abuses of power by the secret intelligence agencies such as the FBI, the CIA, and the supersecret National Security Agency concluded: "The national consensus, secrecy, and the mantle of the presidency enabled the covert bureaus to operate outside the normal checks and balances of the constitutional system, and above the law itself. For over twenty-five years, Congress simply abdicated its legislative and oversight functions."[37]

■ Congressional limitations on presidential power

Vietnam and Watergate appear to have changed all that – or at least some of the most dangerous abuses. Congress in 1973 passed the "War Powers Resolution," which permits the president to use armed forces in an emergency without prior declaration of war by Congress, but requires him to inform Congress immediately and allows Congress to recall the forces after 60 days. President Nixon thought the bill so limiting of his powers that he vetoed it. But Congress then passed it over his veto.

Shortly thereafter, Congress held extensive hearings on abuses by intelligence agencies and established new procedures for its supervision of the agencies. Because the agencies operate in secret, it is difficult to know how effective such "oversight" actually is. But greater investigative efforts by both Congress and the press, as well as nongovernmental groups such as the American Civil Liberties Union and the Center for National Security Studies, seem to be keeping the agencies more honest. This in turn limits the possibilities for abuse of power by the president – or by the agencies acting independently.

■ The impact of Gerald Ford

It may be, however, that the greatest contribution to limitations on presidential abuse of power came from the presidency of Gerald Ford. There were several reasons why Ford exercised less power as president than Johnson or Nixon or Carter.

First, he was an *unelected* president, taking up the office when Nixon was forced to resign. Indeed, he hadn't even been elected vice-president, but instead was appointed to that post when Nixon's original vice-president, Spiro Agnew, was forced to resign by allegations of corrupt behavior. Never having been elected by the American people as a whole, Ford did not have a public mandate to act as a strong President.

Second, as a Republican facing a Congress strongly controlled by the

---

[37]Morton H. Halperin et al., *The Lawless State: The Crimes of the U.S. Intelligence Agencies* (New York: Penguin, 1976), p. 232.

Democrats, his opportunities for strong leadership, like those of Nixon, were limited as well. Third, and perhaps even more important, Ford's philosophy of government emphasized reliance on private enterprise rather than on the federal government, and so on most matters he was not so inclined to be a strong president in the Johnson or Carter mold.

Furthermore, he came into office just when the Congress was trying to recover from its failure to assert itself over Vietnam and Watergate. As a result, it had passed the War Powers Resolution and established a new budgetary system (which we shall discuss in Chapter 8), and had begun to conduct more and stronger investigations of the executive branch. All of these reassertions of congressional power came at the expense of presidential power.

At the same time, in the foreign realm, American influence was declining. The oil-producing states were becoming more powerful, and other raw-materials producers were less docile. Multinational corporations such as International Telephone & Telegraph (ITT) and the oil giants (such as Exxon, Texaco, Mobil, and Gulf) gained power, too, and that meant the American government that Ford was leading had less. (For more on these international developments see Chapter 19.)

All in all, the Ford presidency was a presidency of limited powers. Ford himself, a year and a half into his presidency, was asked about his powers by the *New York Times.* He responded that the president had not lost any of "his basic powers," but that there had been a swing of "the historic pendulum" toward Congress. Ford indicated that he feared that the result might be a "disruptive" erosion of the president's ability to govern, and some presidential advisors and presidentially-oriented observers expressed agreement.[38] Some also saw the difficulties Carter had in dealing with Congress as supporting this conclusion, while others attributed these difficulties to Carter's inexperience as a "Washington outsider"—the first president since Eisenhower to enter office without ever serving in Congress.

□ POSSIBLE REFORMS

■ Demystifying the office and its occupant

By now, widely ranging reforms have been proposed to deal with the various problems of the presidency that we have encountered. In the aftermath of the Nixon years, there was great concern about "demystifying" the office and its occupant—overcoming the attitudes that had created what some were calling "the imperial presidency." Gerald Ford's relaxed and candid conduct seems to have helped considerably toward this objective. Jimmy Carter's behavior—from his use of his diminutive first name and his frequent casual dress to his sending daughter Amy to an integrated public school in Washington, all of these unusual for a president—has continued the trend. More could be done, but perhaps more would overdo it, for the president may need to use his exalted office as a way of involving the people in politics.

---

[38]Philip Shabecoff, "Presidency Is Found Weaker under Ford," *New York Times,* March 28, 1976. For a more detailed study, see Shabecoff's "Appraising Presidential Power: The Ford Presidency," in *The Presidency Reappraised,* 2nd ed., ed. Thomas E. Cronin and Rexford G. Tugwell (New York: Praeger, 1977), chap. 2.

Stan Wakefield

The White House.

Strengthening decision systems

There is always a need to strengthen presidential information and decision-making systems. Many of the occasional reorganizations we've described have been intended to do just this. One major concern is seeing that a wide range of options and viewpoints is presented. Some, therefore, propose what is called a "multiple advocacy" system. As Alexander George describes it, a neutral aide would take steps to see that, whenever an issue comes up, those arguing for different positions get equal chances and resources to present their views.[39]

A plural presidency

Another proposal sometimes made is that of a plural executive – a group of two or more people serving as president. Observers have often asserted that there is little necessary connection between the foreign policy tasks of the president and the domestic tasks, even though, as we noted at the beginning of the chapter, both are entwined in the role of president as it exists. Yet each of these twin roles is large enough that it could be a full-time job. So some propose that we have two presidents, one for each set of responsibilities. Others, such as Senator Mark Hatfield (Republican of Oregon) have proposed splitting the domestic responsibilities into several elected offices – in effect, election of super cabinet officers. But such a move might just increase the political struggles within the executive branch, to the detriment of efficient running of the government. Furthermore, critics point out that this would only increase the difficulty of electing good people by increasing the number of major officers who must be selected and then elected.

Electing better people

In general, most observers seem to think that America has gotten surprisingly good presidents, considering what candidates must go through to get elected.

---

[39]See Alexander George, "The Case for Multiple Advocacy in Making Foreign Policy," *American Political Science Review,* September 1972, pp. 751–785. See also Irving L. Janis, *Victims of Groupthink* (Boston: Houghton Mifflin, 1972), for a study of the problem in such policy cases as Vietnam and a similar set of recommendations.

Experts note that many who would make excellent presidents will not or could not undergo the rigors of the selection process – from long campaigning (Jimmy Carter campaigned nonstop for 21 months, making the staggering sum of 1,495 speeches)[40] through hard political bargaining for convention delegates. This would not be a problem, except that the qualities that make one a good campaigner bear little resemblance to those that make one a good president.

Declining even to be a "favorite son" candidate in his home state of Illinois in the 1976 primary, Senator Adlai Stevenson III explained that "a candidacy today triggers a thousand skirmishes, a welter of endless, draining detail. It plunges the candidate into a morass of unintelligible regulations and dervish-like activity, all largely beyond his control and comprehension."[41]

A year earlier, Senator Walter Mondale had withdrawn from the presidential race, saying:

> I do not have the overwhelming desire to be President which is essential for the kind of campaign that is required. . . . I like to ponder issues, sit down with knowledgeable people and talk about them, chew them over, read a book, let them rest a little, reach a conclusion that I'm comfortable with and go to work. All of that's out the window in a Presidential campaign, and I'd never get a chance to think ideas over. . . . Nationally, it's more theater than the politics I know. I kept getting constant suggestions that I needed to buy different clothes and go to speech instructors and spend two days in Hollywood with a videotape machine. I hated that.[42]

One suggestion to ease the burden is holding but one national primary or several staggered regional primaries to replace the present contests spread across the states from New Hampshire to California and across the months from February through June.

Others emphasize the importance of avoiding the selection of people such as Nixon who will turn out to be unsuited to the job. But no one has developed a way of preventing this. Even greater concern is evidenced over vice-presidential selections, which are usually made on political rather than presidential grounds. Nixon's choice of Agnew put a corrupt politician next in the line of succession. McGovern's choice of Senator Thomas Eagleton (Democrat of Missouri) designated someone with a history of mental illness which had required shock treatment – discovery of which by the press forced him to step down as a candidate. Carter's choice of Mondale seemed based largely on the question of his suitability for the presidency. But it was exceptional – and was possible because Carter already had the nomination sewed up when selection time came, which is infrequent. As a solution to the problem of vice-presidential selection, some suggest that such

---

[40]Charles Mohr, "Carter, With a Long List of Campaign Promises, Now Faces the Problem of Making Good on Them," *New York Times,* November 5, 1977.

[41]"Stevenson Says 'No'", *New York Times* editorial, November 21, 1975.

[42]Quoted in the *New York Times,* December 1, 1974.

choices be made by the presidential nominees well after the convention, after possible candidates have been thoroughly investigated, rather than by the convention the day after the presidential candidate is nominated.

■ Disposing of the mistakes The fact that it took certainty of impeachment and removal before Nixon consented to resign highlights the difficulty of correcting mistakes in the election of presidents. To increase the opportunity, some have suggested the possibility of a *recall* procedure. Some states and many cities require a popular vote on whether or not to remove an official from office if a certain percentage of voters sign a petition demanding it. But there are serious problems with this when applied to the presidency. Our system does not produce new candidates quickly. Furthermore, if a president faces a recall threat he will be tempted to do things that placate the voters but may not be in the interest of the country. And there is no agreement on what percentage of signatures should be required to start recall.

■ Parliamentary government These difficulties have led some in Congress to propose that there be a way for Congress to take a "vote of confidence" on the president, with provision that a two-thirds negative vote would remove him or her from office. A new election would then perhaps be held to pick a successor – and, some urge, to elect a new Congress, so that voters could in effect express their views on the action by the Congress.[43]

Such a move would approach the "parliamentary" system in which the head of government is elected by the legislature, in the same way that he or she is replaced. Some have seen merit in this more radical step, for it would tend to unite the president and the Congress behind a common legislative program.[44]

■ One 6-year term But many others believe that the problem now is that presidents already tend to be *too* sensitive to public opinion and too obsessed with reelection. Some therefore propose that the president be able to have a 6-year term (to give him or her time to develop and implement a program) but only one (so that he or she will have no incentive to worry about reelection). Various public officials, such as Lyndon Johnson and former Senator Mike Mansfield, have advocated this. As Johnson remarked in his memoirs: "The growing burdens of the office exact an enormous physical toll on the man himself and place incredible demands on his time. Under these circumstances the old belief that a President can carry out the responsibilities of the office and at the same time undergo the rigors of campaigning is, in my opinion, no longer valid."[45]

---

[43]See James L. Sundquist, "Needed: A Workable Check on the Presidency," *Brookings Bulletin 10,* no. 4.

[44]Remember in this connection our discussion of "party government" in Chapter 4. For discussion of this and other aspects of increased "accountability," see Charles Hardin, *Presidential Power and Accountability* (Chicago: University of Chicago Press, 1974).

[45]Lyndon B. Johnson, *The Vantage Point* (N.Y.: Holt, Rinehart & Winston, 1971), p. 344.

One 6-year term might indeed ease the physical burden of the office. But there is widespread doubt that it would really reduce the role of politics in the White House. Furthermore, many believe that such an effect – making the president a "lame duck" from the moment of election – would be a big mistake. This case is made strongly by former presidential aide and long-time president-watcher Thomas Cronin: "The presidency must be a highly political office, and the president an expert practitioner of the art of politics. Quite simply, there is no other way for presidents to negotiate favorable coalitions within the country, Congress, and the executive branch and to gather the authority needed to translate ideas into accomplishments. A president who remains aloof from politics, campaigns, and partisan alliances does so at the risk of becoming the prisoner of events, special interests, or his own whims."[46]

■ Looking to the Congress

This survey of proposed reforms[47] has not uncovered proposals with broad support and promise enough to improve the presidency from within. This has led some reformers to shift their attention toward the Congress, as we shall do in Chapter 8. The Congress might help reform the presidency from outside – by increasing its own power. Some think that this reform is already underway. Surveying the situation shortly before he retired as the Democratic leader in the Senate, Mike Mansfield of Montana said, "I believe that Congress will retain momentum. There will be a slow and deliberate effort by Congress to reassert its own power. Of course we have to be sure the pendulum doesn't swing too far in the other direction. But the President will not continue to accumulate more power at the expense of Congress."[48]

Other reformers argue that we should first focus on the federal bureaucracy, for this mass of 2.8 million people must carry out the president's orders for his power to be effective. As we shall see in the next chapter, the bureaucracy does indeed often limit the president. But we shall also see that many believe the bureaucracy at least as much in need of reform as the presidency.

□ SUGGESTIONS FOR FURTHER READING AND STUDY

Among the most helpful general studies of the presidency, all available in paperback editions, are these: Clinton Rossiter, *The American Presidency,* rev. ed. (New York: Harcourt Brace Jovanovich, 1960), which is especially good on the roles of the president; George Reedy, *The Twilight of the Presidency* (New York: World, 1970), a study by a former Johnson press secretary that focuses on the complexities of the job and the isolation of its holder; Arthur Schlesinger, *The Imperial Presidency* (Boston: Houghton Mifflin, 1973), which puts the presidency into historical perspective and focuses

[46]Thomas E. Cronin, *The State of the Presidency* (Boston: Little, Brown, 1975), p. 301.

[47]For discussions of various reforms, see Thomas E. Cronin, *The State of the Presidency* (Boston: Little, Brown, 1975), chaps. 10, 11; Hardin, *Presidential Power and Accountability;* William W. Lammers, *Presidential Politics: Patterns and Prospects* (New York: Harper & Row, 1976), chap. 14; and Norman C. Thomas, "Reforming the Presidency: Problems and Prospects," in *The Presidency Reappraised,* ed. Cronin and Tugwell, Chap. 17, among many other works.

[48]Quoted in Shabecoff, "Presidency Is Found Weaker Under Ford."

on foreign affairs aspects; Emmet John Hughes, *The Living Presidency* (New York: Coward, McCann & Geoghegan, 1973), a thoughtful study by a former Eisenhower aide; Thomas E. Cronin, *The State of the Presidency* (Boston: Little, Brown, 1975), a contemporary study based on many interviews as well as the standard literature; and Louis W. Koenig, *The Chief Executive,* 3rd ed. (New York: Harcourt Brace Jovanovich, 1975).

Several classic studies of the powers of the presidency still merit study. One is Edward S. Corwin, *The President: Office & Powers,* 4th ed. (New York: New York University Press, 1957), which focuses on constitutional and legal aspects, and the other is Richard Neustadt's *Presidential Power,* rev. ed. (New York: Wiley paperback, 1976; first published in 1960). Other helpful studies of presidential powers include: Erwin Hargrove, *The Power of the Modern Presidency* (Philadelphia: Temple University Press, 1974); Robert S. Hirschfield, ed., *The Power of the Presidency: Concepts & Controversy,* 2nd ed. (Chicago: Aldine, 1973); and Theodore Sorensen, *Watchman in the Night: Presidential Accountability and Watergate* (Cambridge, Mass.: MIT Press, 1975), by the former Kennedy and Johnson aide.

For more information on the executive branch and the White House Office, see: Thomas E. Cronin and Sanford Greenberg, eds., *The Presidential Advisory System* (New York: Harper & Row, 1969); Richard Fenno, *The President's Cabinet* (Cambridge, Mass.: Harvard University Press, 1959), which covers Wilson to Eisenhower; James W. Davis, *The National Executive Branch* (New York: Free Press, 1970); and Stephen Hess, *Organizing the Presidency* (Washington, D.C.: Brookings Institution, 1976).

Interaction between the presidency and other parts of the government are examined in: Louis Fisher, *The President and Congress* (New York: Free Press, 1972); Nelson W. Polsby, *Congress and the Presidency,* 3rd ed. (Englewood Cliffs, N.J.: Prentice-Hall, 1976); Robert Scigliano, *The Supreme Court and the Presidency* (New York: Free Press, 1971); Glendon Schubert, *The Presidency in the Courts* (Minneapolis: University of Minnesota Press, 1957); and Elmer E. Cornwell, *Presidential Leadership of Public Opinion* (Bloomington: Indiana University Press, 1965).

Two fascinating paperback studies of White House decision making in relation to the rest of the executive branch are: Richard P. Nathan, *The Plot that Failed: Nixon and the Administrative Presidency* (New York: Wiley, 1975), by someone who was there; and John Kessel, *The Domestic Presidency: Decision-Making in the White House* (North Scituate, Mass.: Duxbury, 1975), by someone who talked to those who were there.

Among interesting treatments of more specialized topics are: Louis Fisher, *Presidential Spending Power* (Princeton, N.J.: Princeton University Press, 1975); James David Barber, *Presidential Character,* 2nd ed. (Englewood Cliffs, N.J.: Prentice-Hall, 1977); and two books by constitutional lawyer Raoul Berger, *Impeachment: The Constitutional Problems* (Cambridge, Mass.: Harvard University Press, 1973), and *Executive Privilege: A Constitutional Myth* (Cambridge, Mass.: Harvard University Press, 1974).

Useful paperback collections of readings covering a wide range of topics are: James David Barber, ed., *Choosing the President* (Englewood Cliffs, N.J.: Prentice-Hall, 1974); Aaron Wildavsky, ed., *The Presidency* (Boston: Little, Brown, 1969); Rexford G. Tugwell and Thomas E. Cronin, eds., *The Presidency Reappraised,* 2nd ed. (New York: Praeger, 1977); Norman C. Thomas and Hans W. Baade, eds., *The Institutionalized Presidency* (Dobbs Ferry, N.Y.: Oceana, 1972); and Charles W. Dunn, ed., *Future of the American Presidency* (Morristown, N.J.: General Learning Press, 1975).

Among the interesting studies of particular presidencies are the following: Robert J. Donovan, *The Inside Story* (Garden City, N.Y.: Doubleday, 1956), a study of the Eisenhower administration based on cabinet notes; Arthur Schlesinger, *A Thousand Days* (Boston: Houghton Mifflin, 1965), and Theodore Sorensen, *Kennedy* (New York: Harper & Row, 1965), both insider accounts of the Kennedy administration; Bruce Miroff, *Pragmatic Illusions: The Presidential Politics of John F. Kennedy* (New York: McKay, 1976); Rowland Evans and Robert Novak, *Lyndon B. Johnson: The Exercise of Power* (New York: New American Library, 1966), and Doris Kearns, *Lyndon Johnson and the American Dream* (New York: Harper & Row, 1976); William Safire, *Before the Fall: An Inside View of the Pre-Watergate White House* (Garden City, N.Y.: Doubleday, 1975), and John Dean, *Blind Ambition* (New York: Simon & Shuster, 1976). All but the first of these are available in paperback editions.

Finally, for regular coverage of the presidency, there is no substitute for two weekly journals: *National Journal* and Congressional Quarterly's *Weekly Report,* available in many academic and reference libraries.

The federal bureaucracy

7

Only 13 percent of the American people have "a great deal of confidence" in the executive branch of government in Washington. Fifty-eight percent believe it is "unresponsive," and 56 percent say they would prefer a "smaller government with fewer services."[1]

These results from national polls taken during the 1976 election campaign and surveys before and since with similar results indicate pervasive popular disillusionment with the federal government. Such feelings are nothing new, but they are deepening and spreading now as never before in this century.

The growth of such attitudes gave strength to George Wallace's campaigns against "pointy-headed bureaucrats" in 1968 and 1972, and to Ronald Reagan's effort to unseat incumbent Gerald Ford in 1976 by campaigning against "the mess in Washington," as well as to Jimmy Carter's emphatic pledge in his 1976 campaigns to reorganize "the bureaucracy" as soon as he was elected president.

His opponent, President Ford, like most of his predecessors since the New Deal years of the 1930s, attacked "big government" and "the bureaucracy" even as he tried to preside over it. In a typical speech, this one delivered to business executives on September 5, 1975, he declared that the bureaucracy's "government rules and regulations" had become a plethora of "red tape, paper shuffling and new heights in counter-productivity." But although Ford pledged, immediately after taking office from Richard Nixon, to cut the size of the bureaucracy, he found himself utterly unable to do so. Within 8 months, it had grown by over 7400 new employees – a pattern of growth that was to continue to characterize his administration, and one that made it easier for Carter to attract support from opponents of "bureaucratic government."

☐ THE BUREAUCRACY AND US

Everybody, it often seems, attacks "the bureaucracy." But one in every six employed Americans works for government – federal, state, or local – and so might be classed as a governmental bureaucrat. If we include the 2 million people on active duty with the armed forces, 5 million Americans work for the federal government. So 5 million of us are, in a sense, part of this "Washington bureaucracy" that is so often

[1]These poll results and others are reported in the *National Journal,* March 3, 1976, p. 38; the *New York Times,* February 24, 1976. pp. 1, 27; and the *Washington Post,* May 16, 1976, pp. 1, 9.

Reprinted by permission of the Chicago Tribune-New York News Syndicate

attacked as bloated, wasteful, and unresponsive to people's needs, even though relatively few actually work in the Washington area.

Most of us encounter the bureaucracy on paper more than in person. We fill out a form to get a Social Security card when we start to work, and we fill out a set of forms to file an income tax return every year. We also fill out a form if we want to get a passport so that we can travel abroad. And we may occasionally write a letter to Washington to request a government publication. The Superintendent of Documents, the bureaucrat who runs the Government Printing Office, the largest publisher in America, currently offers some 27,000 publications, with titles ranging from "The Department of Agriculture Yearbook" to a "Pocket Guide to Babysitting." The government also publishes hundreds of magazines, with titles such as *Postal Life, Plant Disease Reporter,* and *Driver* (this one, complete with pinups, published by the air force, which calls it "the traffic-safety magazine for the military driver.").[2]

The federal bureaucrat we are most likely to encounter delivers our mail – one of 700,000 people the Postal Service employs. That is more than any other agency but the Defense Department, which accounts for over 3 million, or 65 percent of federal bureaucrats, two-thirds of them soldiers and one-third civilians.

But whether or not we personally encounter any federal bureaucrats, our lives are affected by regulations made and enforced by bureaucrats many times every day.

We may think we decide at what time we arise in the morning. But in the summer, whatever the sun may say, it is Daylight Savings Time, which tells us what hour it is. Daylight Savings Time was developed by bureaucrats, standardized by federal legislation, and extended into winter months during the 1973–1974 "energy crisis" by further laws and regulations from Washington. (See the box titled "It's official: winter's here.")

[2]Donald Lambro, "Henry Luce on the Potomac," *Washingtonian,* February 1977.

■ **It's official: winter's here**

Maybe it's presumptuous to fool Mother Nature, but the U.S. government did what it had to do last Monday when, at approximately 6 a.m., it declared winter was here.

According to the calendar, the tilt of the earth and the movements of the sun and all that, winter doesn't get to the East Coast of the United States until 12:36 p.m. EST on Dec. 21.

That's all very well, federal officials declared, but it can and does get cold before winter arrives. So they made a command decision to turn up the heat in most agencies on Monday. The idea of advancing winter a few weeks wasn't taken lightly in government. No hearings were held, but various committees did meet and experts from the weather service, engineering departments and other specialized groups were polled.

It was finally decided—sometime in late October—that all internal apparatus aimed at making air cool would be "terminated" on a Friday, and that heating units would be cranked up to be ready to receive presumably chilled G-persons the following Monday. This is how one Defense Department agency advised workers of the shift from fall to winter:

"Subject: Heating/Air conditioning.

"The General Services Administration has advised this office that the following measures will continue this year with regards to heating/air conditioning in the building.

"1. The air conditioning season will be terminated on 19 November 1976. Chillers, compressors and related equipment will undergo annual inspection and maintenance.

"2. The heating season will commence on 22 November 1976 and temperatures will be maintained as close as possible to 65–68 degress, the range prescribed by the Federal Energy Conservation Program. Automatic data processing centers, communications centers and 24-hour sectors will receive adequate heat and ventilation for their operation.

"3. In addition, window draperies, blinds, etc., should be used to cut down heat losses by setting them to the closed position during the nighttime and on cold cloudy days, setting them to the open position during periods of sunshine.

"4. The operation of heater blowers, threshold heaters and portable heaters in government-owned or leased space is prohibited."

That's all it takes to make winter come sooner. Committees are already being formed to formulate a government policy on spring

From Mike Causey, "Federal Diary," *Washington Post,* November 25, 1976, p. B2. © The *Washington Post.*

Bureaucrats play a big role in our breakfast. Any meat we eat will almost certainly have been inspected – whether carefully or not – by federal agents. Milk's price is influenced by federal "price supports" designed to increase the income of dairy farmers at our expense. The price of the grain that goes into our bread and cereal is influenced by decisions of the Agriculture Department, which makes America's "farm policy," and by the Commerce and State Departments, which determine how much grain can be sold abroad – something that lowers supply at home and so raises prices to us. And all the fine print concerning vitamins and minerals on the cereal box, like that on cans of fruit and vegetables, results from regulations made by the Federal Trade Commission and the Food and Drug Administration. This list could go on and on – as long as our appetites hold out.

Then, as we set off to school, the bureaucrats are involved again. Federal regulations determine safety standards for buses, just as they require seatbelts in cars. In school, just who our teachers are, and what equipment they have to teach with, may be influenced by federal regulations prohibiting discrimination in hiring,

The Bettmann Archive, Inc.

Washington, D.C., in the early 1830s.

Wide World Photos

Washington, D.C., in the early 1970s. Ranged around the Capitol Building (*center*) are the House office buildings (*center left*), the Library of Congress and its annex (*bottom center*), the Supreme Court Building (*to the right of the Library of Congress*),and the Senate office buildings (*center right*). The building under construction at lower left is the Madison Building.

designed to increase the number of minority employees, and by federal grants-in-aid to colleges and universities for certain specified purchases. What we learn, and what teachers teach, are still unregulated by Washington. But if we eventually decide we want to work for the government ourselves, we may have to pass a Civil Service Exam or the Foreign Service Exam developed and administered by the government.

Furthermore, every time we turn on a radio or television, we are getting a message over airwaves that are formally regulated by the Federal Communications Commission. The advertisements that finance commercial TV and radio are sometimes screened by the Federal Trade Commission in an attempt to protect us from lies and misleading statements. On the other hand, if we tune in "public television" what we see may be subject ultimately to approval by – and may also be funded by – the Corporation for Public Broadcasting, which is federally chartered and receives appropriations from Congress as well as private gifts.

And so it goes, from breakfast through school, at work and at play, from shopping through travel, and even in sleep – for mattresses and pillows are regulated (as is revealed by those little tags that list the contents and say "not to be removed") and pajamas must meet federal standards of resistance to fire. Some of these federal regulations reassure us, such as the stamp on meat saying "Inspected by U.S. Dept. of Agriculture." Others may annoy us, such as the requirement that warning buzzers must sound until auto seatbelts on newer cars are fastened. Most of them may pass unnoticed most of the time.

But federal regulation never passes unnoticed by businesses, which must spend considerable time, effort, and money abiding by regulations and reporting to Washington. That fact is reflected not only in greater safety precautions in our jobs and our foods but also in higher prices to cover the costs of the safety measures and of filling out the reports.

As we shall see in Chapter 16, most businesses and many citizens believe there is too much bureaucratic regulation. But few would wish to return to the days when we might well get food poisoning when we ate, be disabled without compensation when we worked, be victimized by false advertising without any recourse, and have no one to complain to when we felt cheated or ill-treated by business or by government.

All these things – the beneficial, the precautionary, the annoying, and the wasteful – are the result of the growth of the government's role in our everyday lives. All these things are done by bureaucrats – whether they are done for us or to us. Many Americans now say they find government – and especially big government in Washington – unresponsive to their needs. But before we can decide whether government really is too big or too unresponsive, we must understand how big it really is. We must learn who the bureaucrats who make it up are, where they work, what they do, and how it all got that way. Then we should be able to understand both the public attitudes toward government and the bureaucrats' actions toward the public. Perhaps then we may also be able to find ways in which "Washington" can be made more efficient and more responsive.

□ WHAT "THE BUREAUCRACY" IS

Today the term "bureaucracy" usually has a negative connotation. Nobody campaigns for office on a platform calling for a bigger bureaucracy, although candidates do make promises that would in fact require more employees. Hardly anybody working for government likes to be called a bureaucrat. Government employees prefer to be termed "civil servants" – people who serve the public. But the term "bureaucracy," which came from the French word meaning first a writing desk and later an office, once meant simply the group of government officials.

■ The nature of bureaucracy

Today the term bureaucracy is used to indicate two important features of larger organizations. First, that the offices or positions in the organization are arranged in a *hierarchy,* so that there are superiors and subordinates, and the superiors give orders to the subordinates. Second, the basis for this giving of orders, the basis for this authority, is *the law* rather than the personal qualities of the superiors and the subordinates or the dictatorial assertions of the chief of government.

In other societies, the authority to give orders may come from the leader's superior strength in battle, or from his or her personal charisma, or from a popular belief that he or she has been chosen by God, or from his or her having been elected by the people. But bureaucrats are not necessarily stronger than those under them, nor are they elected by those they govern. Instead, they are appointed, generally after being assessed for their competence in a competitive exam or screening procedure. Because of this, they are supposed to be experts who could be replaced by other experts who have the same skills, regardless of their other personal qualities. And these experts are supposed to obey and enforce the law, rather than the dictates of a charismatic leader or the expressed wishes of the public.

Bureaucracy and democracy Already we can see the roots of popular discontent with bureaucrats. Bureaucrats are not chosen by the people, nor are they supposed simply to do the will of the people – not, at least, until that will is translated into law by those who make laws in the society.

Thus, bureaucracy is by its nature *nondemocratic.* And in our democratic society it tends to be *antidemocratic* as well, for two important reasons. First, it replaces the traditional arrangement in which the people volunteer their time to decide what should be done and then do it. This system of "pure democracy" is still practiced in some small organizations, but it is impossible where matters are so complex that they require experts who *specialize* in one aspect or another. In other words, in a modern bureaucracy, specialist professionals replace amateurs, and democracy is thereby curtailed.[3]

Second, bureaucracy tends to be antidemocratic because the more efficient it is technically, the more it concentrates expertise, or specialized knowledge, in the higher-level administrators. This makes the people being administered less and less able even to influence decisions. They often cannot even understand the problems, let alone the possible solutions being proposed by the experts on such problems as new forms of energy, auto safety regulations, or pesticide controls.

The chief advantage of bureaucracy – the thing that makes it so efficient where it is effective – is its tendency to *standardize* everything. Even *the bureaucrats themselves are in a sense standardized.* Those who work at the upper level, as professional administrators, receive generalized training so that they are interchangeable. Because their authority derives from their role, that is from their responsibilities, rather than from their personalities, they can always be replaced by others just like them in training. Their replacements in theory should do the job just as well – and even the same way.

Similarly, bureaucrats are supposed to treat every individual they deal with alike, regardless of his or her personality, race, or political views, for example. In other words, *bureaucrats standardize their clients.* We can see how this will tend to alienate citizens, each of whom is likely to believe that his own case is special and requires – and merits – exceptional treatment. But this quality of standardized treatment for all citizens was what made creation of our modern bureaucracy, the civil service, so attractive to reformers who sought to abolish discrimination and preferential treatment in our government.

□ HOW THE BUREAUCRACY DEVELOPED

The early leaders of America after independence were men of aristocratic origin. They were "born to rule" and "bred to rule" as well, and they took their dominant

[3]For an argument that bureaucracy is nonetheless associated with democracy and extended freedom of choice, see Anthony Downs, *Inside Bureaucracy* (Boston: Little, Brown, 1967). And for an account of a nonbureaucratic, pure democratic form of government in action, see Jane Mansbridge, "Conflict in a New England Town Meeting," *Massachusetts Review,* Winter 1976, pp. 631–663.

role in America for granted. What fitted them for ruling was their "fitness of character"—their virtue and public reputation—rather than passing a competitive exam, as is now generally required. These aristocrats readily became professional public servants, and generally continued to serve in office regardless of who was president. But over the years, there grew a new public sentiment favoring broader participation in government.

Library of Congress

Andrew Jackson.

■ Andrew Jackson and the "spoils system"

Finally in the 1828 election Andrew Jackson, a popular general and self-proclaimed "man of the people," was elected president. He chose to abolish much of the pomp of the presidency. Instead of wearing formal dress and riding to his inauguration in a fancy carriage escorted by uniformed troops (as had his predecessor, John Quincy Adams), he chose to wear a plain black suit and walk to the Capital with a group of Revolutionary War veterans and a crowd of citizens.

Historians credit President Jackson with the first major change in the government bureaucracy: firing many of the holdovers from previous administrations and replacing them with men loyal to him. This action was attacked by his adversaries but endorsed by his supporters, who cited the old maxim, "to the victor belong the spoils." Thus was born the spoils system, in which a winner rewards his political workers with jobs. This practice is now more often referred to as "patronage," because it is provided by the boss, or patron, to his workers.

The spoils system was not strictly speaking a Jacksonian invention, for President Thomas Jefferson had practiced the same patronage on a more limited scale. The objective in both instances was less a matter of rewarding supporters than a way of guaranteeing that officials would be loyal to their superiors and would carry out their wishes

But Jackson, like most of his successors, found that changing the personnel alone via the spoils system, was not enough to get the government to act as he wished. So he began the first major effort to reorganize the structure of the government into permanent offices to be filled by rotating employees to make its officials more responsive to his will. In the first 40 years of the government, the organization of the bureaucracy had remained virtually unchanged. Then in Jackson's 8 years, almost every bureau or department was restructured, some a number of times.[4]

Such reorganizations had become possible only because the functions or roles of offices were gradually becoming "separated" from the personal qualities of the individuals who performed them. The role of secretary of the navy, for example, had to be thought of as being independent of whichever person was occupying it, whether he be a former navy officer or a political friend of the president. This separation, developed and implemented by the president usually criticized for originating the spoils system, was the necessary first step toward creation of a

[4]For an interesting account of this, see Matthew A. Crenson, *The Federal Machine: Beginnings of a Bureaucracy in Jacksonian America* (Baltimore: John Hopkins University Press, 1975).

modern bureaucracy in Washington. It made the impersonal, formal, standardized specification of a job's responsibilities possible, so that the job or office would continue regardless of who occupied it, and so that any generally competent individual could perform it.

What actually happens as a bureaucracy is modernized is that "job specifications" are written down, telling just what the individual must do and can do and what resources he or she has to work with. These specifications also indicate which role is superior to his or her role (the person to which he or she therefore reports and from whom he or she receives orders) and which roles are his or her subordinates (the persons who report to him or her and take his or her orders). Once this formal description has been achieved, it becomes possible to draw clearer diagrams of the "chain of command" in an organization. Such diagrams, like that in Figure P3.1 in Perspective 3, represent such relationships graphically without any necessary mention of the actual individuals who may be serving in the various jobs or their personal relationships as friends or confidants.

The Sears Tower, Chicago.

Courtesy of Sears, Roebuck and Co.

■ Buildings, bodies, and budgets

In Jackson's time, the executive branch was located entirely in four drab buildings located at the four corners of the lot on which the White House stood. Today, the Executive Branch is located in 460,000 buildings scattered not only all over Washington but all over the nation and around the world as well. Indeed, the government now owns 356 million square feet of office space (which cost $5 billion to build) and rents another 77 million square feet (for rental fees of $349 million a year). These are staggering figures. But perhaps we can begin to grasp their scale and significance if we compare them to figures for a big office building.

The biggest office building in the world today is the Sears Tower in downtown Chicago. It is 1454 feet tall (about the length of 5 football fields), has 110 stories, and contains 4.5 million square feet of office space. The U.S. government owns the equivalent of 79 of these buildings in office space, and rents the equivalent of 17 more, for a total of 96 super skyscrapers.

But if the physical size of the government has changed so drastically in these 150 years, so has the number of people employed – from about 5000 when James Monroe was elected president in 1816 to the present 2.9 million (see Table. 7.1). The figures in the table include all federal employees, wherever they are located, and whether full-time or intermittent, except for employees of the Central Intelligence Agency. In a typical year now, the federal government hires about 600,000 new people, and a slightly smaller number quit, retire, or die. As a result, the bureaucracy continues to grow at a steady rate.

These numbers have grown as the formal structure of the government has swelled to include more bureaus at lower levels and more cabinet-level departments at the top. Among the most important elements in this burgeoning of the bureaucracy have been the expansion of America's military forces and the development of the "independent regulatory agencies," which we will examine later in this chapter.

TABLE 7.1

The growth of the federal bureaucracy

Year	Number of employees
1816	4,837
1821	6,914
1831	11,491
1841	18,038
1851	26,274
1861	36,672
1871	51,020
1881	100,020
1891	157,442
1901	239,476
1911	395,905
1921	561,142
1931	609,746
1941	1,437,682
1942	2,296,384
1943	3,299,414
1944	3,332,356
1945	3,816,310
1946	2,696,529
1947	2,111,001
1948	2,071,009
1949	2,102,109
1950	1,960,708
1951	2,482,666
1952	2,600,612
1953	2,550,416
1954	2,407,676
1955	2,397,309
1956	2,398,736
1957	2,417,565
1958	2,382,491
1959	2,382,804
1960	2,398,704
1961	2,435,804
1962	2,514,197
1963	2,527,960
1964	2,500,503
1965	2,527,915
1966	2,759,019
1967	3,002,461
1968	3,055,212
1969	3,076,414
1970	2,981,574
1971	2,860,000
1972	2,815,000
1973	2,788,000
1974	2,866,000
1975	2,857,000
1976	2,842,000

Source: 1790–1970, *Historical Statistics, Colonial Times to 1970* (Washington, D.C.: Census Bureau, 1976); 1971 on, *Statistical Abstract of the United States* (Washington D.C.: Census Bureau, 1976), and other Census Bureau data.

One of the primary effects of all this growth has been the expansion of the federal budget – the total sum spent by the federal government. The total budget for the first three years of George Washington's administration was $4,269,000 – an average of $1,423,000 per year. In the first year of Jackson's, it was $15,203,000. By 1977 it was about $410 billion. Current figures work out to about $800,000 *a minute.* Thus, the entire year's budget for Washington's time would finance less than 2 minutes of the government's operation today, and that of Jackson's merely 20 minutes.[5] Figure 7.1 traces the growth of the federal budget from then to the present.

As of 1979, the federal government spends a billion dollars every 18 hours, more or less. How much is that? It is 53 tons of $20 bills – about the weight of fifty Volkswagen Beetles. Or it is one dollar for every minute since the birth of Christ. Or it is the total annual federal income tax payments for a city of about a million people, such as Baltimore, San Diego, or Dallas, or the total annual personal income of the people of a city a fifth that size, such as Macon, Georgia, Poughkeepsie, New York, or Modesto, Calif. Or, put another way, if you started to count a billion dollars in $1 bills at the rate of one bill per second, 8 hours a day, it would take you 95 years.

Despite the enormous costs of upkeep on the government's 460,000 buildings and of purchase and maintenance of military installations, weapons, and ammunition, a surprisingly large proportion of the federal budget goes just to pay the salaries of government employees. The 2.9 million civilian bureaucrats now earn over $42 billion per year.

The "merit system" reform

Efforts to control the size of this federal expenditure, and with it the size of the bureaucracy, are unlikely to make much impact, for most of these bureaucrats have what amounts to guaranteed jobs for life. For despite Jackson's institution of the spoils system, public unhappiness with the quality of government service and indignation over the assassination of President James Garfield by a disgruntled office-seeker in 1881 resulted in the passage of the Pendleton Act – the Civil Service Reform Act of 1883 – which began the movement to replace the spoils system with a permanent career civil service. The bill established a bipartisan Civil Service Commission to supervise competitive exams to fill certain federal jobs – about 10 percent of them at that time.

Since then, the competitive **merit system** has been extended by various congressional acts so that now at least 85 percent of the bureaucracy is under civil service. Furthermore, many of the remaining 450,000 jobs not under civil service are nonetheless competitive because they fall under merit systems operated by such agencies as the foreign service (for diplomats) or the Federal Bureau of Investigation (for FBI agents). The result is that the number of patronage jobs that a new president can fill now totals little more than 2000. This is a smaller number

---

[5]However, these figures are not adjusted for the impact of inflation; in fact, Washington's and Jackson's dollars bought much more then than ours do now. Still, even in "current dollars" there would be a very massive difference.

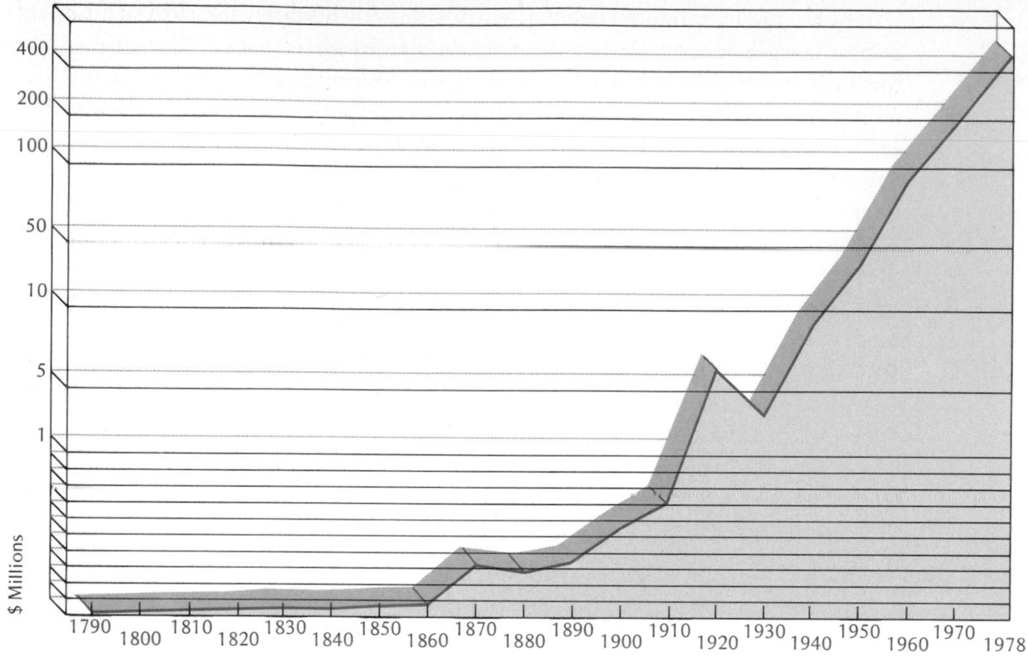

Source: 1790–1970, *Historical Statistics, Colonial Times to 1970* (Washington, D.C.: Census Bureau, 1976); 1971 on, *Statistical Abstract of the United States* (Washington, D.C.: Census Bureau, 1976), and other Census Bureau data.

FIGURE 7.1

The growth of the federal budget. In order to represent the massive increase of the budget on this page, the units in the vertical scale have been compressed toward the top of the figure. If the scale used for the years through 1910 were used for the entire figure, the line for the growth of the budget would be more than 50 feet high by 1978.

than existed at the time of Andrew Jackson, and of these only a half to two-thirds have special importance in policy responsibility and salary. Furthermore, as we noted in Chapter 6, every administration feels compelled to hire various experts who do not have any real loyalty to it for many of these jobs. In the case of the Carter administration, many jobs even went to former Carter opponents, because Carter allowed his cabinet choices to do their own "staffing," and most of those in the cabinet had other political ties.[6]

■ The growing yearning for "spoils" Whatever happens in the "spoils" appointments at the top, the "merit" system, as it actually operates, continues to protect the jobs of the competent and the incompetent, the needed and the unneeded, alike. One particularly negative critic, Charles Peters, recently wrote that "anyone who has had a reasonable amount of contact with the federal government has encountered people who should be fired. There are, of course, some superb civil servants – maybe ten percent of the total – who have every right to become indignant at blanket criticism of government workers. There are another 50 to 60 percent who range from adequate to good. Unfortunately, that leaves 30 or 40 percent in the range downward from marginal to outright incompetent."

Peters recounts the incident of an Internal Revenue Service employee who was fired for repeatedly reporting for work dead drunk. His union got his dismissal overturned. How? By arguing that the IRS was negligent in not establishing

[6]See Robert G. Kaiser, "The 2,000 Carter Jobs: Who Got Them?" *Washington Post,* June 6, 1977.

programs to detect and treat alcoholism among IRS employees. "With that kind of thing the likely product of a series of hearings and appeals that could last for years," Peters concludes, "it is the rare administrator who will attempt to fire anyone."[7]

Firings are rare. In 1976, of the 2,842,000 bureaucrats in the executive branch, 21,710 were "discharged," 56,214 were "laid off," 187,684 were "terminated," and 36,345 were "suspended or put on extended leave without pay."[8] The difficulty in firing incompetents is one reason why many now oppose the merit system on administrative grounds. But there are others. One aide to Lyndon Johnson explained his view to Thomas Cronin this way: "You can't really be an administrator at the White House. You have to get top personnel to carry things out–and that is literally impossible to do with this venal Civil Service system. Frankly, I would abolish it and rather live with a spoils system. You need to be able to make far more appointees than you can now. Civil Service officials can play very tough politics with their senior friends in Congress, and they can resist the White House constantly."[9]

But this problem extends even to political appointees. "It is inevitable when an individual has been in a Cabinet position or, for that matter, holds any position in government," President Nixon remarked as he completed his first term, "after a certain length of time he becomes an advocate of the status quo; rather than running the bureaucracy, the bureaucracy runs him."[10] So curtailing the extent of the merit system in favor of more spoils may not make much difference unless appointees are moved about regularly from one agency to another.

☐ THE BUREAUCRATS AND THEIR EXPERIENCE

■ Where they are and what they do The 2.9 million federal bureaucrats work in some eighty-three major government bureaus, administering 1040 different domestic programs and various foreign programs as well. Their responsibilities range from running the government (which is done generally by the twelve executive departments that constitute the president's cabinet and by the ten bureaus in the Executive Office of the President), to regulating business, industry, and other segments of the "private sector" (which is done primarily by the sixty-one so-called independent agencies).[11]

But just where are all these government employees, these bureaucrats, located? In addition to the 2.1 million members at the armed services, the Pentagon

---

[7]Charles Peters, "A Kind Word for the Spoils System," *Washington Monthly,* September 1976.

[8]Letter from Kenneth Blaylock, national president of the American Federation of Government Employees, *Business Week,* October 31, 1977. The difference between "discharged" and "terminated" is not clear, but the low percentage forced to depart is.

[9]Quoted in Thomas Cronin, *The State of the Presidency* (Boston: Little, Brown, 1975), p. 171.

[10]Quoted in the *New York Times,* November 28, 1972, p. 40C.

[11]These are figures for January 1977. See *The Government Manual 1977/78* (Washington, D.C.: Government Printing Office, 1977), and *Organization of Federal Executive Departments and Agencies* (Washington, D.C.: U.S. Senate Committee on Governmental Affairs, 1977). The figures include 38,441 employees of the legislative branch and 12,050 of the judicial branch.

☐ ACTION UNIT 7.1 How to become a bureaucrat: getting a government job

There are two basic ways to get a job with the federal government. The first involves going to your nearest office of the United States Civil Service Commission (CSC) – check the phone book under "U.S. Government" – and applying. At the office you will talk with a specialist about the sort of jobs you'd be best suited to and then fill out the appropriate application forms. You may also have to take a written test if the job you are seeking is typing, stenography, sales store clerk and checker, or card-punch operator. Whether or not you take an exam, you will be rated by the CSC, and in about 6 weeks you will be notified whether or not it finds you qualified for the job you are seeking. If you are found qualified, you go on the "register" of qualified applicants. You then wait until your name is matched to an opening.

In the old days, this approach usually worked eventually. But in 1976, 5.6 million Americans inquired how to get a job from the CSC, and there were sixty-three applicants for every opening. In 1977, the figure climbed to seventy-six, and experts expect it to keep on rising, while the size of the bureaucracy is actually shrinking slightly. So unless you're in an area of the country where for some special reason the demand is small, this approach is no longer likely to work.

The second approach is to become a "name request." Most hiring above the level of secretaries and clerks takes the form of "name requests." The agency seeking someone sends in a specific name to the CSC along with the job description. It writes the job description in such a way that, most likely, the only person who can fit it is the one it names. If no one else comes up in the CSC computer's "register," the job goes to the person whose name was sent in.

So the secret to getting a government job these years is becoming a "name request." There are two ways to do this. The first is to know someone already working in the agency you want to work in. He or she will be among the first to know about coming job openings and may be able to tailor the description to fit you and only you, and then to propose you as the candidate.

The other way to become a "name request" is to get the help of your member of Congress. If you worked in his or her campaign or contributed money to it, visit him or her and ask for help. He or she can pressure the agency you want to work in to make you a "name request." If he or she does so, your application will be circulated in that agency with "must hire" written on it, and the odds are good that you'll soon be one of our 2.9 million federal bureaucrats.

The alternative is to try state or local government agencies, which are still expanding and so have more openings. The approaches there are likely to be rather similar, as, probably, will the jobs and their rewards.

For more details, see the CSC's book, *Federal Career Directory: A Guide for College Students* (available in libraries, or for $3.45 from the Superintendent of Documents, Government Printing Office, Washington, D.C. 20402). For more on how the system works, write the CSC in Washington and read Ann Pincus, "How to Get a Government Job," in *Washington Monthly*, June 1976.

employs almost a million civilians around the world. Another 220,000 work for the Veterans Administration and are located throughout the country. The Postal Service employs about 202,000 letter carriers among its 700,000 person work force. Smaller numbers are engaged in activities that have long been governmental responsibilities, such as building dams and highways, and managing federal lands. Land management is a surprisingly large task because the federal government owns one-third of all the land in the United States, including 96 percent of Alaska, 87 percent of Nevada, 66 percent of Utah, 64 percent of Idaho, and even 45 percent of California; in these areas the tasks include tending the forests, which requires 14,500 foresters.

Much of the growth in the federal bureaucracy results from new demands on the government: to regulate and manage the economy (there are over 100,000 regulators in the federal government, overseeing everything from the environment to consumer goods); to foster scientific research and technological development (the National Aeronautics and Space Administration, NASA, which flies to the moon and Mars, employs 25,000, for example); and to maintain America's dominant role in world affairs. Indeed, the government employs 132,000 civilians overseas, working in some 3600 buildings that it owns in 136 foreign nations; in addition 480,000 armed services personnel are stationed in 305 American military bases outside the United States.

The budget for all governmental activities totals almost one-quarter of the entire American output. Bureaucrats write an average of 100 checks every second to pay the bills. These same bureaucrats supervise the filling out by American citizens and businesses of 4,500 different federal forms. This produces enough paperwork to fill the Washington Monument eleven times each year.

But such figures don't really tell us much about what the working life is really like for most bureaucrats. In fact, it is usually not much different from life in a large business establishment – paperwork, telephoning, and conferences. The only major difference is that, as we have noted, a governmental official is somewhat less likely to be fired.

■ What they get for what they do But relative job security is not the only attraction of government jobs. There are other important privileges – "perquisites" (or "perks"), as they are called. Bureaucrats get 20 days of paid vacation every year after 3 years on the job, and 26 days after 15 years, as well as 13 days of "sick leave" every year. They also get nine regular holidays a year. They have extensive health insurance, including psychiatric care, on which the government pays half the premium. And they may have large life insurance policies, a third of the cost paid by the government. They may retire at 55 with a pension of up to 56 percent of their highest salary if they worked for 30 years – with a cost-of-living increase that regularly adjusts for the effects of inflation. For this they contribute 7 percent of their salary.

These perquisites, coupled with the relative job security, have made civil service jobs very attractive, both for "white-collar" (professional and managerial positions or desk jobs – so called because traditionally such people wore white shirts and ties to the office) and "blue-collar" workers (labor occupations – so-called after the blue work-shirts traditionally worn in such jobs). Recent figures indicate that among civilian government employees are 211,000 secretaries and clerks, 202,000 letter carriers, 147,000 engineers, 86,000 scientists, 8,000 doctors, 5,000 telephone operators, 3,000 photographers, 2,300 veterinarians, and 461 chaplains. In addition, there are 57,000 manual laborers, 32,000 aircraft workers, 15,000 plumbers, and 11,000 painters and paperhangers.

■ Who they are

But what kinds of people actually have these government jobs? What kinds of people are our bureaucrats? Because the jobs vary so much, the qualities of their holders vary, too. Surveys by the Census Bureau (the same agency that counts you and asks various questions about you and every other citizen every decade) reveal that the "typical bureaucratic executive" came from a middle-class background, is now more than 40 years old, has a college degree, and has worked his way up from the bottom to near the top of his bureau over some 20 years or so. He is also likely to be male rather than female. And he is more likely to be white than black or of Spanish-speaking heritage. Generally speaking, there is less discrimination against women and minorities within the government than outside it, but the many decades of past discrimination have not been overcome at the higher levels because promotion to them requires long service at lower levels.

□ THE FUNCTIONS OF BUREAUCRATS

■ Assuring continuity

The primary function of the bureaucracy is to assure *continuity* in government. Presidents come and go, and the Congress changes somewhat from session to session, but the bureaucracy carries on. This leads some to refer to the bureaucracy as "the permanent government" in contrast to "the presidential government," which is always temporary. Of course, there is some change in the bureaucratic personnel from year to year (about 600,000 new faces per year, as we noted earlier). But, as we have seen, the essence of bureaucracy is the *office* or the *role* rather than personality, so that at least in theory this turnover should not matter, for anyone with the appropriate training can take another's place. The responsibilities are set out by law, and the authority of the individual derives from his or her role in the bureau, rather than from personal qualities.

In practice, however, things do not go quite this smoothly. Inevitably the performance of individuals will be influenced in various ways by the personal relations they have with their superiors and with their subordinates. But, in general, the continuity provided by the persistence of bureaucratic roles in the government does make the government work.

This important contribution of bureaucracy to continuity can be seen most clearly in four critical times. The first is during a sustained major crisis for the system, such as Watergate. The second is at the beginning of a new administration when new political appointees are still "learning the ropes"–generally from the senior bureaucrats in the agency they are to run. The third is at the end of term of a lame duck or retiring president whose power is waning, perhaps along with his interest in governing, and whose chief assistants are often actively job hunting. And the fourth is toward the end of the term of a president seeking reelection, when, except for demanding flashy new developments, a president and his chief assistants are too preoccupid with electoral politics to run things. But because, as we saw in Chapter 6, a president is *always* too preoccupied with various of his other roles to be "a full-time chief executive," the bureaucracy's role is always vital.

■ Implementing decisions

Providing continuity such as this in a political system is only part of the bureaucracy's responsibility. Another vital component is *execution* or *implementation of decisions* made by superiors. In our system, important policy decisions are supposed to be made by the political appointees at the top of the executive branch hierarchy. These decisions may be about what type of federal aid to education to propose to Congress or whether to seek a further strategic arms limitation agreement with the Soviet Union or what position to take on the question of a constitutional amendment to outlaw abortion.

Yet if we trace actual policy decisions from the highest levels, where they emerge as written proposals, through the various stages by which they are converted into governmental actions, we discover that neither the president nor the secretary of health, education, and welfare, nor the secretary of state, actually carries out a policy decision – or even turns it into legislative form for submission to Congress. Nor do they usually publicize it to foster popular support or even see that their subordinates do what they're told. All these various activities, which convert a policy decision into a program of action and then carry it out, are necessarily the responsibilities of the members of the bureaucracy. (We'll see all this in greater detail in the case we examine in Perspective 6).

□ THE POWER OF THE BUREAUCRATS

This absolutely vital and unavoidable bureaucratic responsibility for implementation gives the bureaucracy its greatest political power – as every president ultimately learns.

Harry Truman as president always kept a sign on his desk that read, "The buck stops here." This slogan implied that Truman as president couldn't delegate responsibility any further and couldn't refuse to make difficult decisions. It also implied that his decisions were the ultimate decisions – the ones that determined exactly what would be done. But if Truman thought that would prove to be so, he learned early in his presidency that it was not, when he confronted a bureaucracy already grown to some 2 million people – a scale well beyond the capacity of a president to control effectively. At one point he remarked to NBC Correspondent David Brinkley, "I thought I was the President, but when it comes to these bureaucracies I can't make 'em do a damn thing."[12]

In 1952, as Truman contemplated turning the White House over to General Eisenhower, he mused to his White House assistant Richard Neustadt: "He'll sit here and he'll say, 'Do this! Do that!' *And nothing will happen.* Poor Ike – it won't be a bit like the Army. He'll find it very frustrating."[13]

Truman's hunch – derived from his own 7 years' experience – was prophetic. After six years of Eisenhower's presidency, an aide to the former General remarked: "The President still feels that when he's decided something that *ought* to be the end

---

[12]Quoted by David Brinkley on the public television program, *Thirty Minutes With . . .* , July 13, 1971.

[13]Quoted in Richard Neustadt, *Presidential Power,* 2nd ed. (New York: Wiley, 1976), p. 77.

Harry S. Truman Library

Harry S. Truman.

of it . . . and when it bounces back undone or done wrong, he tends to react with shocked surprise."[14]

Not long after he took office, John Kennedy was asked what he considered to be the most important thing he had learned in his presidency. His reply: the difficulty of getting things done. Subsequently, he was quoted as remarking to someone who made a policy suggestion to him: "Well, I agree with you, but I'm not sure the government will."[15]

Even Lyndon Johnson, a consummate politician with many years of experience in Washington politics when he took office, and operator of the biggest battery of telephones in White House history, had such grave difficulties getting satisfactory results from the bureaucracy as our involvement in Vietnam deepened that he became more and more withdrawn and isolated.

But perhaps the clearest and the most conclusive instance of a recalcitrant bureaucracy was the one that resisted Richard Nixon. Nixon took office in 1969 intending to lead the country in directions very different from those taken by his presidential predecessors. In foreign affairs he sought to improve relations with the Russians, while at the same time opening relations with their neighboring adversaries, the People's Republic of China. As we know, he and Henry Kissinger concluded that they could not trust the State Department bureaucracy to develop these sensitive projects – or even to know of Kissinger's first China visit in advance. Such secrecy characterized foreign affairs in the Nixon-Kissinger years.

But such protective secrecy is impossible in domestic affairs. Here Nixon also sought to turn governmental policy around on a wide range of matters, including the use of busing for school integration and the War on Poverty. He attempted to dismantle the Office of Economic Opportunity (OEO – the bureaucracy created to conduct that war). But everywhere he turned he met opposition, in the very bureaucracy he was attempting to transform, as well as in Congress. Bureaucrats and Senators even went to court in 1973 to block the abolition of OEO.

One day he announced that he was unalterably opposed to "forced busing." The next day his own Justice Department, headed by his longtime business colleague and political crony, Attorney General John Mitchell, filed suit in Austin, Texas, to force busing for school integration. In several speeches in 1971 he announced what he called "a new American Revolution" – a proposed reorganization of much of the bureaucracy into four superagencies. But people barely noticed, and Congress greeted the proposal with total lack of interest, refusing even to hold hearings on it.

Nixon had set up the largest White House staff in history to act as a kind of "counterbureaucracy." But by the end of his first term he was convinced that his "counterbureaucracy," headed by Haldeman and Ehrlichman, had itself become too bureaucratic.[16]

---

[14]Ibid.

[15]Quoted in Roger Hilsman, *The Politics of Policy Making in Defense and Foreign Policy* (New York: Harper & Row, 1971), p. 1.

[16]Garnett D. Horner, "Nixon Looks Ahead: 'A New Feeling of Responsibility. . . . Of Self-Discipline," *Washington Star-News,* September 9, 1972. See also Richard P. Nathan, *The Plot That Failed: Nixon and the Administrative Presidency* (New York: Wiley, 1975).

Meanwhile, programs that he and his aides were developing were continually "leaked" to the press in ways that enabled opposition to unite and vitiate them, often before they were fully developed. The frustration and bitter resentment that these experiences generated in Nixon and in his close aides led eventually to the establishment of the secret task force called "the plumbers" that was assigned to stop "leaks." But gradually the assignments of the "plumbers" expanded to include more and more of the "dirty tricks"–electronic bugging, illegal break-ins into private homes and offices, and so on–that figured so prominently in Watergate.

This drastic reaction to the frustration of his plans by the bureaucracy in alliance with his adversaries outside government led ultimately to Nixon's downfall. But, although many have inclined to attribute his reaction to his character, it is particularly important to recognize and understand its origins, which are more complex. Part of the explanation is the incessant and debilitating bureaucratic resistance to the Nixon White House.

This raises an important question: Why was this resistance so great – so much stronger during the Nixon years then during those of his predecessors? To find the answer, we must go back to the years of the great bursts of hiring in the federal bureaucracy. Apart from the temporary increases during wartime, these large and permanent increases have come during the terms of Democratic presidents Franklin Roosevelt, John Kennedy, and Lyndon Johnson. Republican President Eisenhower sought to restrain, if not actually reverse, that expansion. The result of this pattern of expansion was that by Nixon's time most of the senior civil servants – those who actually run most segments of the bureaucracy under the supervision of political appointees – had joined the government in the FDR years of the New Deal. They were remnants of an era characterized by an activist government dedicated to social reform and government intervention in the economy on the side of labor and consumers. These officials were unlikely to be sympathetic to the Nixon effort to cut or even eliminate many of those social reform programs – especially when their own responsibilities might thereby be curtailed. At the same time, most of the newer and younger bureaucrats had arrived during the Kennedy-Johnson years – again, years of an activist government dedicated to new program innovations.[17] They, too, tended to be unsympathetic to Nixon's efforts at retrenchment.

Thus, when Nixon took office he confronted a gigantic and largely hostile bureaucracy that was led by people with considerable experience in *bureaucratic politics.* They were, in other words, experts at defending the interests of their own agencies, personnel, and programs not only against other bureaucrats but also against political superiors. They did so in order to get their own way on a matter of policy or to get control over a program that would mean more jobs or a bigger budget for the winning agency. The importance of such success is that it makes it possible for them to be responsive to the interest groups, clientele groups, and congressional committees with which they regularly deal, and on which they depend for their budgets and for political support.

---

[17]See Joel D. Aberbach and Bert A. Rockman, "Clashing Beliefs within the Executive Branch," *American Political Science Review* 70 (June 1976); and Allen H. Barton, "Consensus and Conflict among American Leaders," *Public Opinion Quarterly* 38 (Winter 1974–1975).

It is, therefore, hardly surprising that the bureaucracy was able to defy presidential direction so vigorously – and with virtual impunity – when Nixon and his White House staff tried actually to *run* the government like an efficient business rather than the political organization it is. When Gerald Ford, who was even more conservative than his predecessor, took office, he, too, faced the same bureaucratic resistance when he tried to cut back on staff and programs. The likelihood is that any president bent on bureaucratic reform will face the same strong recalcitrance for the foreseeable future, for the bureaucracy is now predominantly activist in disposition.

Bureaucratic maneuvering, like the bureaucratic infighting that occurs over a particular policy decision, may appear insignificant in comparison to the substance of the policy being proposed or implemented. But the fact is that *bureaucratic politicking may be more important* in determining the nature and the success or failure of a program than the *president's decision* or the *congressional legislation*. This is especially true of decisions and legislation on complex matters, which must inevitably leave the "fleshing out" of programs to the bureaucracy. So if we are to understand how American politics really works, we must understand the nature and roots of bureaucratic power.

■ The sources of bureaucratic power Modern bureaucracy has been developed to make administration in a complex society more efficient, just as the assembly line was developed to make production of automobiles more efficient. On an assembly line, each worker puts one part on the auto as it moves down the line. If he should fail or refuse to do so, the car is incomplete and may not even run at all. The same holds true for a bureaucracy. If one bureaucrat withholds his own specialized expert knowledge or provides the wrong "knowledge," the policy developed may prove unworkable or even dangerous. Similarly, if a bureaucrat refuses to pass on orders to his or her subordinate, some part of the required action will not occur, and as a result the entire program may break down or fail.

In a sense, then, we can think of a bureaucracy as an "assembly line of information." Specialized expert information about a situation (which is generally called "expertise") goes up to decision makers, and fragmented information about a decision ("orders") goes back down to the bureaucratic organizations and people who carry out the decision.[18]

This way of viewing a bureaucracy makes it easier to understand how powerful bureaucrats can be. If they fulfill their responsibilities fully, both up and down the assembly line of information, then policies have a chance of working. But if they are either inefficient or uncooperative, they can delay, torpedo, or distort the decision being made or its eventual implementation. Figure 7.2 illustrates briefly and somewhat abstractly the stages of bureaucratic activity, indicating where problems are most likely to arise.The diagram indicates that policy making and implementation depend on bureaucrats for supplying accurate information upward as well as for passing orders downward and executing orders effectively.

---

[18]Karl Deutsch, *The Nerves of Government* (New York: Free Press, 1963), p. 75.

Many instances of distorted information or diversionary orders have been uncovered by journalists and scholars studying bureaucratic politics. These studies and their own experience led two former bureaucrats, Morton H. Halperin and Leslie H. Gelb, to develop "the bureaucrat's ten commandments,"[19] a set of tongue-in-cheek rules assertedly designed to enable the bureaucrat to survive in his or her job and achieve success in shaping policy. Included among them are such rules as:

- "Say what will convince, not what you believe."
- "Veto other options" leaving your own the sole survivor.
- "Predict dire consequences" if your option is not chosen.
- "Argue timing, not substance" to keep others from having a chance to question the basic proposal you are supporting.
- "Leak what you don't like" to enable its various opponents to unite in attacking it.
- "Ignore orders you don't like."

These tongue-in-cheek rules for action in bureaucratic politicking emphasize the importance of information—both expertise offered and orders passed on. They reveal something of the leverage that bureaucrats can exercise against others who must depend on them for information, and they suggest ways in which bureaucrats may struggle among themselves for power to shape policy and practice.

---

[19]Leslie H. Gelb and Morton H. Halperin, "The Bureaucrat's Ten Commandments," *Harper's*, June 1972. See also, for a more serious study, Hugh Heclo, *A Government of Strangers: Executive Politics in Washington* (Washington: Brookings Institution, 1977).

FIGURE 7.2

The stages of bureaucratic activity.

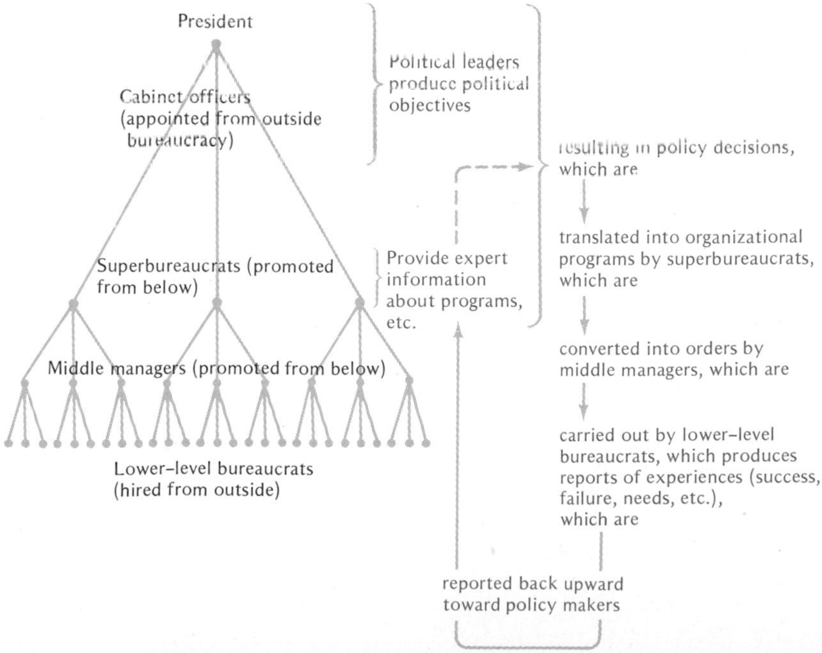

Power struggles among bureaucracies

This sort of struggle is made possible by the fact that most government programs do not fall squarely within the recognized realm of one single bureau. One revealing example of the resultant "bureaucratic infighting" that has become traditional is "interservice rivalry" between the army, the navy, and the air force. When a new type of weapon system is being developed, the various branches of the military often compete in its development and then compete for the responsibility of deploying it. For example, when missiles were first developed, the army claimed that it should have responsibility for them because they were based on land and were, in a sense, merely modified artillery pieces. The air force also claimed them because they would fly through the air when launched against a target. The air force eventually won that struggle with the army, but meanwhile the navy was developing its own missiles to be launched from submarines at sea: the Polaris program, which eventually became the major element of American defenses alongside the air force's land-based Minuteman.

Such competition between the armed servies is often supported or rationalized on the grounds that competition encourages innovation and, therefore, improves the quality of military defense. But competition is also very expensive because it requires so much duplication. In recent years – especially when Robert McNamara was secretary of defense under Kennedy and Johnson – the Defense Department tried to cut down on costly duplication by encouraging more coordination and standardization to limit overlap and bureaucratic quarrels. But this effort to compel standardization caused further problems even while it encouraged the three services to unite and cooperate – against their superior, the secretary of defense.

Problems of competition and coordination can, of course, be found throughout government. In the years following riots in major American cities like Los Angeles, Detroit, and Washington, the federal government intensified its efforts to cope with problems of unemployment, poor housing, law enforcement, public schools, hunger, and so on, in the cities. But because these programs were scattered throughout the Department of Health, Education, and Welfare (HEW), the Justice Department, the Labor Department, and other departments, they could not be well coordinated, nor could duplication be avoided. After his sweeping victory in 1964, President Johnson proposed to bring some of these programs together by centralizing them in a new Department of Housing and Urban Development (HUD), which was done when Congress passed the necessary legislation. Much the same thing happened 2 years later with the establishment of the Department of Transportation.

Such efforts at centralization of responsibility can increase coordination and control but usually result in a bigger bureaucracy. And centralization never succeeds in avoiding the struggles at the lower levels between various agencies, each seeking more programs and a bigger share of the budget. This larger share is necessarily at the expense of others since programs and funds are always more limited than desires.

The unending competition for scarce resources has long engendered bureaucratic strategies designed to get bigger budgets. In theory, a bureau submits

its budget request each year through its department to the central budget bureau in the executive branch (now called the Office of Management and Budget). The OMB modifies it so that it complies with the priorities of the president and the overall size of the budget that the president wants to submit to Congress. But the Congress need not follow the wishes of the president. As a result, bureaus that have long maintained close ties with the congressional committees having jurisdiction over their activities sometimes find themselves getting more money from Congress than the president has requested for them.

Another strategy that may be used by a bureau to increase its budget is to appeal to the special interests its activities benefit. These interests, or "clientele groups," then lobby the Congress to increase the appropriation for the bureau. For example, the agency of HUD responsible for government-guaranteed home mortgages may encourage real estate groups and home builders to ask Congress to increase the funds made available for the program.

Over the years, such strategic moves often become routinized. Bureau chiefs, the lobbyists for concerned special interest groups, and the members of Congress presiding over the concerned committees in some cases meet regularly to decide important questions about programs and budgets – often without even consulting the president or his assistants. These common arrangements, which we shall discuss in Chapter 8 and Chapter 11, are often called "subgovernments" because they are able effectively to decide major questions of policy.[20] Another term for them that reflects their strength is "iron triangles." They provide opportunities for bureaus that are unable to get satisfaction through infighting within the executive branch to achieve their objectives anyway. Subgovernments are facilitated by the fact that certain congressional chairpersons, bureaucratic leaders, and lobbyists tend to hold office for long periods of time – much longer than presidents. Therefore, they are able to establish and maintain such cooperative relationships comfortably. But despite their existence, much bureaucratic politicking continues to occur within the executive branch.

☐ THE IMPACTS OF BUREAUCRATIC POLITICS

■ The effects on the government Experts often criticize bureaucratic politicking. But would we be better off if our government were so highly centralized with instructions from the top down that it never received proposals and objections from the bottom up? Or does our system, which combines proposals from top and bottom, have particular advantages? Both our capitalist economy and our democratic political system are founded on the principle that competition is healthy, both because it provides real alternatives and because it leads to better – usually more efficient – decisions. We might, therefore, be inclined to conclude that bureaucratic competition, too, should be beneficial. But before we settle on that general conclusion, we should

[20]See Douglass Cater, *Power in Washington* (New York: Random House, 1964). See also, for a more detailed study, Randall Ripley and Grace Franklin, *Congress, the Bureaucracy, and Public Policy* (Homewood, Ill.: Dorsey, 1976).

recall the actual costs of this competition, not so much in dollar terms as in terms of its actual effect on particular policies. And we should also assess the effects on the government itself.

We know that the bureaucracy and its politicking are responsible for a larger government with a larger budget than there would be if the structure were more centralized. But centralization would make the government inevitably less attentive and less responsive to the population at large and the interest groups concerned with particular policies and programs.

The plain fact is that if we want our government to develop active programs in such wide-ranging areas as national defense, consumer protection, antitrust activities, insuring our bank accounts, agricultural development, and pollution controls, we cannot escape big bureaucracy. And as long as we have big bureaus dealing with so many different yet often overlapping concerns organized into a governmental structure, no matter what that particular structure is, we will have bureaucratic politicking to accompany bureaucratic administration.

In other words, the bureaucracy – the very same bureaucracy that so often infuriates us with its costs, red tape, and inefficiency – makes government of the sort we demand possible in a large, complex, specialized society like our own.

■ The effects on individuals

But what about bureaucracy's effects on individuals, on the citizens who pay the taxes that pay the salaries, support the offices, and finance the programs of the bureaucracy? What is bureaucracy's actual effect on citizens, and must it stimulate in them such generally negative reactions?

Many people in business, as we shall see in more detail in Chapter 16, have strongly objected to certain aspects of inspection and regulation of business by federal bureaucrats. They have also complained about the large cost in time and money of the filling out of forms they do for those bureaucrats. At the other extreme, the poor who must confront the welfare bureaucracy – which is still largely state and local rather than federal – often voice comparable objections to the bureaucracy. They resent being shunted from place to place, office to office, person to person, and being forced to face frequent interviews with caseworkers who, frequently overloaded and perhaps underpaid, are sometimes inconsiderate to clients.

Encountering the bureaucracy on the unemployment line.

Bill Anderson/Monkmeyer

Most of the rest of us, however, rarely meet federal bureaucrats. Therefore, our reservations about the bureaucracy are more likely concerned with deteriorating mail service and escalating tax rates than with unresponsive small individual cogs in the large bureaucratic machine.

Nevertheless, even experts are still not quite sure about the actual impact of bureaucracy on citizens, for few studies have yet been done of the actual bureaucratic encounters of various individuals. The government has increasingly financed comprehensive studies of the effectiveness of various of its programs, but even these have generally ignored the reactions of the recipients of the various services in programs such as Medicare, welfare, unemployment insurance, and veterans' benefits.

To fill this important gap in our knowledge, the Institute for Social Research at the University of Michigan studied citizens' encounters with bureaucracies at all levels of government. The study discovered that fully one-third of those having relevant problems never even sought bureaucratic assistance despite the fact that most of these individuals said they knew such aid was available.

Of those who did seek bureaucratic help, about two-thirds reported that they were satisfied with the way the office handled their problem, almost half termed themselves very satisfied, and only 14 percent were very dissatisfied. This degree of satisfaction is far from ideal, for we might hope that in a service agency at least 90 percent of clients would be satisfied. But a two-thirds satisfaction level refutes the common assumption that virtually everyone is dissatisfied with the bureaucracy.

Furthermore, the study called into question the common assumption that citizens consider bureaucrats to be disinterested professionals, exploitive politicans, or representatives of an antagonistic race or class. For in answer to the question, "Are the people in the office pretty much people like you?" only 17 percent said "No."

Yet this same random sample of the American population also reaffirmed a number of the conventional negative attitudes toward bureaucracy and bureaucrats. For example, 58 percent agreed with the statement that "the people who gain the most from government offices are the officials who run the agencies." Sixty-two percent believed that "people in the government waste a lot of the money we pay in taxes," while another 31 percent believed they waste "some of it." Forty-five percent believed that "quite a few of the people running the government don't seem to know what they are doing." Finally, 77 percent agreed that "There are too many government offices doing the same thing."

This study seems to reveal a contradiction in the beliefs of this sample of the American population. They have one set of beliefs about the bureaucracy in general – beliefs that are negative and even hostile. But the 57 percent of the survey who have had experience with the bureaucracy have another set of memories and beliefs about their own particular experiences. They are largely positive about their satisfaction and their impressions of the real bureaucrats they met.

It may be that the common popular expressions of unhappiness with bureaucracy in general are really indications of deeper discontent. This extends to such matters as the unfairness of taxation in America or the inability or refusal of the government in Washington to legislate and administer solutions to the serious problems that confront many Americans in everyday life in this country – problems such as health, education, justice, housing, and consumer protection.[21]

Drawing by Dedini.

☐ CAN BUREAUCRACY BE IMPROVED?

We have already seen how the development of our federal bureaucracy has paralleled the development of our society, our economy, and our government. Our bureaucracy was supposed to improve governmental efficiency in such an increasingly complex world because it standardized and rationalized the conduct of governmental operations. But perhaps we have paid too high a price in the alienation of our citizens and in the dehumanization of our bureaucratic employees in order to gain this greater efficiency. Or perhaps the government has become so big and complex that no bureaucracy can function efficiently and humanely.

The historical alternative to bureaucracy – a system of volunteer citizen-administrators – is now dying out even in local politics. Everywhere governments are becoming bureaucratized. They are staffed by professional bureaucrats who tend to specialize in their responsibilities because the matters to be dealt with have become so complex, and because successful management (and hence bureaucratic careers) depends upon the efficient performance of these difficult tasks.

One of the common complaints about bureaucrats is that they are addicted to established practices, even when these practices have become inefficient as the government or the population being governed has grown and changed. In an effort to overcome this inherent conservatism of bureaucracy, some governments have contracted with private business organizations to perform certain services. Cities, for example, have contracted out garbage collection. There is increasing suggestion that mail and parcel delivery nationally should also be turned over to private business. The hope is that the private organizations will be more flexible, because they will have to show good results in order to retain the contract. Such decentralization to private organizations – "reprivatization," as it's often called – may result in an improvement for certain services in the short run. But eventually private organizations too will tend to become bureaucratized if their tasks are large. Some experts, therefore, doubt that this private alternative to bureaucracy is generally very promising.

■ Sunset laws

Disappointment with the results of efforts at bureaucratic reform and decentralization have led more and more governmental units to experiment instead with what are called "sunset laws." A sunset law requires that an existing program or agency be reviewed for its effectiveness regularly. If it passes that review, it is

[21]Daniel Katz, Barbara A. Gutek, Robert L. Kahn, and Eugenia Barton, *Bureaucratic Encounters: A Pilot Study in the Evaluation of Government Services* (Ann Arbor, Mich.: Institute for Social Research, 1975).

extended; if not, the program is terminated or the agency abolished. The sun, in other words, automatically sets on any program or agency that is not purposely extended after a fixed period of time.

This idea is by no means new. A similar policy was suggested when President Franklin Roosevelt was beginning the creation of the many New Deal programs and bureaus to get America out of the Depression. At that time, William O. Douglas, then an assistant to FDR and soon to be appointed Supreme Court Justice, recommended that each agency's charter include a provision for its termination in 10 years. In this way, Douglas hoped to prevent agencies from becoming entrenched captives of the interest groups they were to regulate or serve. The proposal was not then adopted. Indeed, 4 decades passed before it was revived in 1976 by the state of Colorado, which adopted legislation prescribing a 6-year life for state regulatory boards and commissions. Coming at a time of great dissatisfaction with bureaucracy, the Colorado law proved quite contagious, stimulating the proposal of "sunset" legislation at the federal level as well.

Research conducted in 1976 by Common Cause, the "citizen lobby" group in Washington, had revealed that in the previous 15 years, 236 new federal departments, agencies, and bureaus had been created, while only 21 had been abolished.[22] Another study, by Herbert Kaufman, found that 148 of the 175 agencies alive in 1923 were still functioning 50 years later. And this study didn't even count the various agencies in the massive Defense Department and Post Office. Furthermore, Kaufman found another 246 new agencies created to work in the same areas in those 50 years.[23]

Times change, and so do public needs. But because bureaucracies tend to be inflexible and often unresponsive to new demands, the first inclination of both presidents and Congress is to create a new bureau to meet a new problem or need, rather than attempt to remake an old one. At the same time, the established clientele of an old bureau, in league with the bureau's employees, is generally strong enough to prevent the abolition of a bureau whose time has come and gone. And sometimes inactive bureaus just seem to escape people's attention. A few years ago, a bureaucrat named Jubal Hale called the media's attention to the Federal Metal and Non-Metallic Safety Board of Review. It had been created 4 years earlier by the Congress, and Hale had been appointed its director. But it had never been given any cases to review. So Hale simply spent his days reading and listening to Beethoven records in his office, until at his suggestion the agency was finally abolished.[24]

Legal provisions for automatic periodic scrutiny of existing agencies, and for abolition of those not then specifically extended by new legislation, offers some hope of getting greater control over the growth of bureaucracy. It might even help

---

[22] *Sunset: A Common Cause Proposal for Accountable Government* (Washington: Common Cause, 1976).

[23] See Herbert Kaufman, *Are Government Organizations Immortal?* (Washington: Brookings Institution, 1976). The *Government Manual* nonetheless lists, on 12 pages of the 1977/78 edition, about a thousand "abolished and transferred agencies and functions." But when President Carter was trying to cut back the bureaucracy, his Acting Budget Director James McIntyre was heard to remark: "Only two federal programs have ever been flatly abolished – Uncle Sam no longer makes rum in the Virgin Islands and no longer breeds horses for the U.S. cavalry." Quoted in "Washington Whispers," *U.S. News & World Report,* November 7, 1977.

[24] Donald Lambro, "The Five Worst Government Agencies," *Washingtonian,* November 1976, pp. 162–164.

to reduce that growth somewhat, both by putting moribund bureaus to death and by stimulating bureaus that wish to live to a ripe old age to be more responsive to new needs and problems.

Sunset legislation is, of course, intended primarily to cope with the problem of bureaucratic growth and stagnation, rather than that of unresponsiveness. True, a new or renewed agency may be more likely to respond to the needs and wishes of the public at large than an old entrenched agency. But citizens often complain of bureaucratic "red tape" and delay. A different device has been developed to cope with this problem: the *ombudsman.*

■ Ombudsmen or citizen advocates An ombudsman is an individual whose office serves as a channel through which a citizen can express his or her grievances over the operation of a bureau or the action of a bureaucrat and seek whatever redress is appropriate. The term itself is Swedish, because the first such individual was appointed by the Swedish Parliament in 1809 to provide a way for citizens to complain effectively about mistakes, abuses, or neglect in their experience with the king's bureaucracy. The Swedish ombudsman was empowered not only to investigate complaints but also to prosecute a bureaucrat who had broken the law.

In 1962 New Zealand established an ombudsman – the first outside Scandinavia. Thereafter, various Canadian provinces and then a number of American states and cities appointed them. By 1977, seventeen states and thirty-six cities had ombudsmen. Recently some universities and colleges have appointed ombudsmen to help students cope with recalcitrant administrators and faculty. Although federal bureaus have not yet appointed ombudsmen (or "citizen advocates" as they are now often called in America), the trend is probably irresistible and should significantly improve the efforts of individual citizens to seek redress.

Until now, individuals have been dependent for assistance primarily upon their members of Congress. But, although a congressional inquiry to a bureau can be very powerful, members of Congress have virtually no authority to deal with most problems brought to their attention by constituents. In any case, they are both too busy and too removed from the bureaus in question to be able to act effectively on them enough of the time, even though they consider such "casework" a valuable political resource. In any event, should more than the present small percentage of constituents start to depend on their members of Congress for such aid, massive increases in staff would be required.

As a supplement or even an alternative to reliance on members of Congress, Common Cause has proposed establishment of a "White House Office on Citizen Grievances." Such a federal ombudsman would receive complaints, forward them to the appropriate agency (particularly important because the citizen may not know which agency to approach), and monitor the agency's reaction and response to see that the complaint is responded to. Whatever success such a new agency might have, one thing is certain: With the volume of complaints it would likely receive, it would inevitably become a sizable bureaucracy itself. This prospect alone may doom the proposal.

Programs such as these are proving to be important ways of redressing grievances at various levels of government, and their time is certainly coming in the federal government. But if bureaucracy is to survive the erosion of public support, it must not only respond satisfactorily to citizen grievances, but it must also increasingly anticipate and avert difficulties as well. Perhaps the clearest cases of such grievances – and the strongest cases for sustaining an effective bureaucracy – concern the independent agencies, which together with the cabinet departments and the Executive Office of the President make up most of the federal bureaucracy. They affect every citizen's life in important ways every day, just as they affect every business. And the question of bureaucratic responsiveness takes on a special and complex meaning in the case of these agencies.

□ THE CHALLENGE OF THE INDEPENDENT AGENCIES

Few Americans could even name an independent federal government agency, let alone describe its functions and powers. And yet, as we saw at the opening of this chapter, virtually every aspect of our lives is seriously affected by their activities.

The range of activities policed, encouraged, or conducted by specialized federal governmental agencies is staggering, as the agency titles listed at the bottom of Figure P1.2 in Perspective 1 suggest. At last count, the government listed some sixty-one "independent agencies and establishments" along with 120 "boards, committees, commissions" and seven "quasi-official agencies." Included were such groups as the California Debris Commission, the Emission-Law Vehicle Certification Board, and the Commission on Federal Paperwork.

The *quasi-official agencies* foster scientific research and charity operations, run national museums, and supervise most passenger service on railroads. The *boards and commissions* are generally advisory panels that meet occasionally to coordinate governmental programs and advise governmental agencies on the problem each is concerned with. In terms of their importance in the government, it is the *independent agencies* that are most signficant. Included among them are seven major regulatory commissions and about twenty governmental corporations.

■ The independent regulatory commissions

The independent regulatory commissions (IRCs) generally set rates for such things as airfares and rail and truck frieght charges or grant licenses to radio and television stations and banks. Some, such as the Federal Trade Comission and the Interstate Commerce Commission, are primarily concerned with regulation of the economy, and so we shall examine their activities in Chapter 16. The Federal Communications Commission, which regulates television and radio somewhat, we shall consider in Chapter 12 on the media. In a similar fashion, we shall encounter other independent agencies here and there throughout these chapters.

All such agencies regulate a type of commercial activity or a sector of the economy. Often the objective is to protect "free enterprise" from its own abuses as much as to protect the consumer from business abuses. Thus, for example, the

Federal Power Commission, established in 1920, regulates aspects of electic and natural gas utilities, which tend to be "natural monopolies" and so could be abusive if not supervised – abusive of each other, as well as of consumers.

■ The nature of their "independence"

Because the regulation itself could also be abusive, the IRCs were designed to be free from "politics" as we usually thnk of it. For most such IRCs (the EPA, which we encountered in Perspective 3, is an exception), the president appoints five commissioners with Senate approval. But their terms last for 5 to 7 years and are staggered so that at any moment the commission will likely include appointees of various presidents.

These IRCs make rules for the organizations and activities they regulate rather in the way Congress makes laws. These rules are generally referred to as **administrative law** because they are made administratively rather than by congressional legislation, but they still have the force of law because Congress so specified when it established each IRC. Thus the IRCs have what is sometimes called a "quasi-legislative" function.

They also have a "quasi-judicial" function, for they are empowered to hear and resolve disputes among parties that fall under their regulatory power, and their resolutions have the same judicial status as the decisions of the courts.

In these various ways the IRCs are different from cabinet departments, which are directly under the president's control, at least in theory. And because they have legislative and judicial as well as executive powers and functions, they are sometimes referred to as "the fourth branch of government."

These combined responsibilities, although they were supposed to insulate the IRCs from politics, have tended instead to intensify and make more complex the politics in their activities. This has been especially true in recent years, as some of them have become less subject to "clientelism" and more responsive to citizen concerns and citizen involvement.

■ The question of citizen participation

The expanding citizen role is especially important because it has begun to open up the regulatory process to the desires and needs of consumers as never before. This has brought about the involvement of more and more different types of citizens in politics: lawyers, activists, and complainers. Such citizen participation is clearest in the newest (and so most flexible) agency, the EPA. As we saw in Perspective 3, recent environmental politicking has given citizens and environmental lawyers opportunities to act as "citizen lobbies" in Congress. In addition, recent legislation and certain favorable court rulings have encouraged citizen suits against economic interests and against recalcitrant officials of federal, state, and local governments. Another consequence has been actions before the EPA and, experimentally, before other IRCs.

The changing and expanding nature of citizen participation in policy making and governmental action will concern us further in coming chapters. The point at the moment is that the spread and successes of such activism have begun to change the common answer to the most important question about the regulatory commissions – whom or what do they really serve? – by opening them up to greater influence by public-opinion and citizen-action groups, and to greater scrutiny by the media. We may yet see the day when such openness makes the regulatory agencies, which affect so much of our everyday lives, among the more responsive elements of the federal bureaucracy. The question, as we might put it, is "Who will regulate the regulators?" – and, for that matter, the rest of the bureaucracy. That question is of growing concern, not only in the Congress but in the courts as well. It is to an examination of the Congress that we turn next.

☐ SUGGESTIONS FOR FURTHER READING AND STUDY

For a history of the federal bureaucracy that emphasizes the period since reforms, see Paul Van Riper, *History of the U.S. Civil Service* (New York: Harper & Row, 1957). To add an international dimension, see the interesting study by Henry Jacoby, *The Bureaucratization of the World* (Berkeley: University of California Press paperback, 1973). Theoretical discussion may be found in Anthony Downs, *Inside Bureaucracy* (Boston: Little, Brown paperback, 1967), which focuses on incentives, and Bengt Abrahamsson, *Bureaucracy or Participation: The Logic of Organization* (Beverly Hills: Sage paperback, 1977).

Basic questions of the relations between democracy and bureaucracy are raised in: F. C. Mosher, *Democracy and the Public Service* (New York: Oxford University Press paperback, 1968), and Emmette S. Redford, *Democracy in the Administrative State* (New York: Oxford University Press paperback, 1969).

The literature on various aspects of bureaucratic politics is already massive. For an overview of the earlier literature, see Louis C. Gawthrop, *Bureaucratic Behavior in the Executive Branch: An Analysis of Organizaitonal Change* (New York: Free Press paperback: 1969). A classic is Chester Bernard, *Functions of the Executive* (Cambridge, Mass.: Harvard University Press, 1938). Among more recent studies, which tend to focus more on the politics of bureaucracy, see: Peter Blau, *Dynamics of Bureaucracy: A Study of Interpersonal Relationships in Two Government Agencies,* 2nd ed. (Chicago: University of Chicago Press, 1963); Francis E. Rourke, *Bureaucracy, Politics, and Public Policy,* 2nd ed. (Boston: Little, Brown paperback, 1976); Richard Neustadt, *Presidential Power,* 2nd ed. (New York: Wiley paperback, 1976); Hugh Heclo, *A Government of Strangers: Executive Politics in Washington* (Washington, D.C.: Brookings Institution paperback, 1977); Morton H. Halperin, *Bureaucratic Politics and Foreign Policy* (Washington, D.C.: Brookings Institution paperback, 1974); I. M. Destler, *Presidents, Bureaucrats, and Foreign Policy* (Princeton, N.J.: Princeton University Press, 1972); Herbert Kaufman, *Administrative Feedback* (Washington, D.C.: Brookings Institution, 1973) Richard P. Nathan, *The Plot That Failed* (New York: Wiley paperback, 1975); Herbert Kaufman, *Are Government Organizations Immortal?* (Washington, D.C.: Brookings Institution paperback, 1976); and Harold Seidman, *Politics, Position and Power: The Dynamics of Federal Organization,* 2nd ed. (New York: Oxford University Press, 1975), by a high-level bureaucrat.

Among studies concentrating more on the interplay of agencies and public policy implications are: Joseph P. Harris, *Congressional Control of Administration* (Washington, D.C.: Brookings Institution, 1964); Randall Ripley and Grace Franklin, *Congress, the Bureaucracy, and Public Policy* (Homewood, Ill.: Dorsey paperback, 1976); and Jeffrey L. Pressman and Aaron Wildavsky,

Implementation: How Great Expectations in Washington Are Dashed in Oakland . . . (Berkeley: University of California Press paperback, 1973).

On the problem of affirmative action in bureaucracy, see Harry Krantz, *The Participatory Bureaucracy* (Lexington, Mass.: Lexington Books, 1976).

And for continuing coverage of what it calls "the culture of bureaucracy," see the many articles in *Washington Monthly.*

8 The Congress

The Congress was intended to be the first branch of our government. The Founding Fathers drafting the Constitution established it in Article I, before even the presidency. Among the important powers they gave it are making the laws, levying taxes, deciding how money can be spent, and proposing amendments to the Constitution.

And yet, in the words of a retired senator, "Since the foundation of the Republic, Congress has rarely initiated anything, rarely faced up to current problems, even more rarely resolved them." The author of these words, Senator Joseph Clark of Pennsylvania, called his book *Congress: The Sapless Branch.*[1]

The Founding Fathers intended the first branch to be the strongest branch, to represent the people and to protect the rights and liberties of the citizens against the possibility of a tyrannous executive branch. And yet, a Louis Harris survey conducted in 1972 found that only 21 percent of the American people claimed to have "a great deal of confidence" in Congress. That rating was lower than the 27 percent for the executive branch and the 28 percent for the Supreme Court. And in 1975 a Gallup Poll reported only 14 percent as having "a great deal" of confidence and another 26 percent having "quite a lot"—still the lowest ratings in memory and the lowest ratings among all three branches of government.

The rostrum of the House of Representatives has carved in wood above it these words of Daniel Webster (1782–1852), a distinguished early American politician who served there. "Let us develope the resources of our land, call forth its powers, build up its institutions, and promote all its great interests and see whether we also, in our day and generation, may not perform something worthy to be remembered."

Perhaps the Congress has performed "something worthy to be remembered." But if so, this seems to have escaped the attention of the American people. During the 1958 election campaign for the House, 59 percent of the people nationwide said they had neither heard nor read anything about either of the candidates, and less than one in five said they knew something about both candidates. Of those who actually voted that year, 46 percent admitted that they did so without having read or heard anything about either candidate.[2]

---

[1]Joseph S. Clark, *Congress: The Sapless Branch* (N.Y.: Harper & Row, 1964).

[2]These figures are reported in Angus Campbell et al., *Elections and the Political Order* (New York: Wiley, 1966), pp. 204–207.

A more recent Gallup Poll found that 47 percent of the American people did not know the name of their representative in Congress, 75 percent did not know how their representative had voted on *any* issue that year, and 38 percent did not know to which party their representative belonged.[3]

So the American people have little confidence and less knowledge when it comes to the Congress. Are they missing something? Critics of Congress, who are many now, might say no. But others would argue that it was the Congress, with its Watergate investigation and impeachment hearings, that saved our political system from breakdown at the hands of Richard Nixon. They might add that it was growing congressional resistance that finally forced the Nixon and then the Ford administrations to end our roles in the Vietnam War.

To decide between these views – or to decide that there are elements of truth in both – we must learn more about what the Congress is and what it does, who our members of Congress are and what they do, and how the Congress relates to the rest of the government and to us, the people. Only then can we decide what to think – and what to do – about Congress.

□ WHAT IS THE CONGRESS?

The story is often told in Washington of the tourist who approached a U.S. Capitol guide and said: "I've seen the House, and I've seen the Senate, but where do I find Congress?" Such a joke can be told only because, according to one recent survey, 8 percent of the American people believe the Congress is just the Senate, 6 percent believe the Congress is just the House of Representatives, and fully 20 percent believe that the Congress consists of the Senate, the House, and the Supreme Court.[4]

[3]Gallup Opinion Index no. 64, October 1970, pp. 9–14.

[4]Don Radler, *How Congress Works* (New York: Signet, 1976), p. xii.

The Capitol Building, Washington, D.C., the seat of Congress.
Stan Wakefield

■ How we got the Congress we have

Article I, Section 1, of the Constitution says: "All legislative powers herein granted shall be vested in a Congress of the United States, which shall consist of a Senate and House of Representatives."

That decision, for a bicameral (*bi* "two," and *camera*, "chamber") Congress, was agreed upon early in the constitutional debates. Virtually everyone wanted some check upon a popularly elected assembly that might act too hastily and might move against the interests of the well-to-do bankers and businessmen in favor of the interests of the more numerous farmers.

The House was to represent the people as a whole – the majority will – by having its members apportioned by population, district by district. The question of just which people would actually count by being allowed to vote was left essentially to the states. This decision guaranteed that neither blacks nor women – nor even those not owning property – would then be allowed to vote, as we saw in Chapter 3.

The Senate was supposed to protect minority interests against the majority, or House, vote. But which minority? The rich, the bankers, the businessmen? That would be difficult to justify. And it might be difficult to get the people of the states to ratify, or agree to, a Constitution calling for that. So the solution agreed upon was to have the Senate represent the states rather than the people. Each state was to have two senators regardless of its population. This would protect the interests of small states by giving them the same representation as the large ones. Senators would be elected by state legislatures, instead of the people. In this way, they could check the dangers of uncontrolled popular government by the House elected by the people, for each body would have to approve all legislation before it became law. In addition, senators would serve for 6 years, which would exceed both the 2-year House terms and the 4-year presidential term. This was intended to insulate senators from presidential pressures and the need to be reelected frequently.

The Congress shares power with the executive. For a bill to become law, Congress must pass it and the president must sign it, as we saw in Perspective 3. Each branch of government also has checks upon the other. The President can *veto* a bill. But if both houses of Congress then pass the bill once again, this time by a two-thirds majority, it becomes law anyway. Furthermore, as we saw in Chapter 6, another check is the requirement that presidential apppointments and treaties must be approved by the Senate.

But these checks and balances are only part of the story. The actual operation and effectiveness of Congress depends especially on two further features: the powers of Congress and the rules by which Congress operates. The Constitution enumerates the powers. It also provides that "Each house may determine the rules of its proceedings," and we shall see below how important this "self-government" of each house has been.

■ The powers of the Congress

The Constitution specifies rather precisely the powers of Congress in Article I, Section 8. Some of them are specific to the time of the founding: the power "to define and punish piracies and felonies committed on the high seas," for example. But most remain important to this day.

"The Congress shall have Power," begins Section 8, "To lay and collect taxes [and] duties [on imported goods], . . . To borrow money, . . . To regulate commerce with foreign nations, and among the several states . . ." The same section gives Congress the power to establish uniform rules of naturalization (by which foreigners may become American citizens) and uniform bankruptcy laws, to coin money and regulate its value, to provide for the punishment of counterfeiting, to establish post offices, to enact patent and copyright laws, and to create lower federal courts under the Supreme Court. Then come the major foreign-affairs powers: to declare war and to provide for armed forces. Finally, Congress is granted the power to govern the federal city, which we call the District of Columbia, or Washington, D.C.

Among these enumerated powers, the American experience has shown the most important to be the power to tax, the power to regulate commerce, and the power to ratify treaties. Elsewhere in the Constitution, Congress is given the power to impeach and remove from office officials guilty of "treason, bribery, or other high crimes and misdemeanors." Congress also receives the power to admit new states to the Union and to initiate constitutional amendments that must then be ratified in the states. But in a sense the most important power is that contained in the last clause of Article I, Section 8: the power "to make all Laws which shall be necessary and proper for carrying into execution the foregoing powers, and all other powers vested by this constitution in the government of the United States, or in any department or officer thereof."

This "necessary and proper" clause, as it is often called, is a kind of "blank check" for congressional legislating on any capability "vested by this constitution in the Government." It has been used as such time and time again by the Congress, and in the process it has been stretched so much that it is also called "the elastic clause."[5]

Powers, of course, become significant when they are exercised. We saw in Chapter 6 that the powers of the presidency have been enhanced beyond what the Constitution provided by presidential actions and by law. Congress, on the other hand, has often chosen not to exercise all the powers granted to it. It often delegates some powers to the executive branch. The exercise of power by the Congress depends in part on the procedures that the Congress adopts to govern itself. But even more the exercise of power by Congress depends on the members of Congress: who they are and what they actually want to do.

☐ WHO ARE OUR MEMBERS OF CONGRESS?

If you were a member of Congress, you'd have an annual salary of $57,500. You'd have a free office in Washington and at least one free office in your home state or district. You'd get cut rates at the Capitol barbershop or beauty parlor and at a

[5]For a useful discussion of congressional powers and their development, see Congressional Quarterly, *Origins and Development of Congress* (Washington, D.C.: Congressional Quarterly, 1976), especially chap. 5, and the same organization's *Powers of Congress* (Washington, D.C. Congressional Quarterly, 1976).

private congressional restaurant. Parking at the Capitol, which is almost impossible for ordinary citizens, would be free, and if you nonetheless parked illegally you would not get a ticket. You would be entitled to forty or more free trips a year back to your home to see your constituents. You'd get up to $6500 a year to buy stationery, and the privilege of mailing newsletters and other official letters and documents free of charge. You'd have a budget ranging from $200,000 to $800,000 to hire office staff, depending on the size of your district or state. If you got sick you'd have free care in the Capitol medical clinic, and if you wanted exercise, the Capitol gym and swimming pool would be yours to use. When vacation time came around and Congress was not in session, you could take a free "fact-finding" trip abroad to study something relevant, or not quite so relevant, to your congressional work, such as the Paris Air Show or the NATO meetings in Brussels.

Sounds like a pretty good life, doesn't it? And yet, most members of Congress can't live on their salaries and benefits and have to dip into savings or rely on outside income to make ends meet. Fortunately, most of them have savings – at last count in 1976 there were twenty-two representatives and sixteen senators who admitted to being millionaires. In addition, many more own stocks and bonds that provide substantial extra income. Those who do not, and so are more like typical Americans, have to make special adjustments to maintain two homes, pay high taxes, entertain constituents, and often pay off leftover campaign debts.

But even those members of Congress having trouble making ends meet are not much like the population in very many other ways. For while the Congress represents the people in political terms, it is not very representative in economic, racial, sexual, educational, or religious terms.

A study of the Ninety-fifth Congress, which served from 1977 to 1978, revealed that House members averaged 49 years old, whereas Senators averaged 54 – and four were born last century. The average American is just under 29. In terms of sex and race, members of Congress were even less typical of the population at large. In 1978 there were no elected women in the Senate,[6] and only seventeen in the House. Racial and ethnic minorities totaled only 5 percent of the House (sixteen blacks, four Spanish-speaking, and two of Oriental descent) and 4 percent of the Senate (one black and three of Oriental descent). Such minorities make up about 20 percent of the population. Only 3 percent of the Senate and 9 percent of the House lack a college degree, and 79 percent of senators and 64 percent of representatives have advanced graduate degrees. In terms of religious preference, Catholics are but 27 percent of the House and 12 percent of the Senate; 72 percent of the Senate and 64 percent of the House are Protestants, although Protestants are about half of the population.

These statistics indicate that the members of Congress are not very typical of the American population. The underrepresentation of women and minorities may make it difficult for the Congress fully to understand and respond to the problems of these groups. But, in general, these statistics tell us relatively little about how the Congress is likely to act.

---

[6]Muriel Humphrey was appointed to serve as senator from Minnesota in her late husband's stead until a special election was held.

■ A day in the life of Representative Andrew Maguire

A member of Congress spends relatively little time on the House floor, as the schedule of Andy Maguire's activities on October 5, 1977 reveals (see p. 236). On that day, the House as a whole went into session at 10 o'clock, but Andy Maguire's workday began 2 hours earlier with a working breakfast with fellow Representatives to discuss economic issues with expert Gar Alperovitz. Maguire then met with members of the staff in his office to discuss his schedule and the bills and issues he would be dealing with. After checking in at the House to establish that a quorum was present and that he would be listed as present himself, he went off to attend a committee meeting.

He had his choice of several meetings, for both of the committees he is on—Interstate and Foreign Commerce, and Government Operations—were meeting at the same time. Such conflicts are common, as a glance at the schedule of all committee meetings that day, which is reprinted as Figure 8.1 elsewhere in this chapter, will confirm. Maguire is a member of three subcommittees of Interstate and Foreign Commerce: Energy and Power, Oversight and Investigations, and Health and Environment. He is a member of two Government Operations subcommittees: Manpower and Housing, and Government Activities and Transportation. These wide-ranging responsibilities involve him in many different policy questions. Among those arising this day were: regulations to require air bags in new cars, controls on genetic research, regulation of medical laboratory testing, supervision of government museums, and national energy policy.

But he also had various public activities. The first was the dedication of a new school established by a bill which one of his committees had passed. He sent a staff assistant to represent him there, as he also did late in the day in the case of a meeting of a medical interest group. He also taped several television and radio interviews in breaks between meet-

Photos by Stan Wakefield

8:00 A.M.—breakfast with economic expert Gar Alperovitz.

Members of Interstate and Foreign Commerce Committee chatting before hearing.

9:00 A.M.—meeting with staff.

10:00 A.M.—at session of Interstate and Foreign Commerce Committee.

ings. And he met at various times with a student intern, officials from the executive branch, and even a visiting member of Great Britain's Parliament.

All day long, however, he was interrupted by ringing bells. These bells are installed in offices, meeting rooms, and even some nearby restaurants. They ring to inform members of quorum calls, adjournment, or roll-call votes about to take place on the House floor. That day, there were a half-dozen important votes on labor law reform. Whenever the bell rang, Maguire and other members would leave their meetings, and hurry to the floor, either by the city sidewalks or by the special subway car underground, whichever is quicker from where they happened to be.

At the entrance to the House floor there is a lobby—which is usually filled with lobbyists waiting to talk with members of the House before or after they are on the House floor. Lobbyists also occasionally "buttonhole" a member while he is lunching in the House dining room—as do other representatives. But as we shall see in detail in Chapter 11, lobbyists more often use other approaches that reach members when they are not so hurried.

Periodically during the day, Maguire would return to his office, to read mail and messages, to sign letters, to return phone calls, and to see visitors. And while he was working on the House floor or in meetings, his staff of over a dozen assistants would continue working to prepare him for coming sessions and to handle casework problems for constituents. The staff was also making plans for Maguire to return to his district in northern New Jersey—as he does every weekend, while the House is not in session. On such trips he makes speeches, sees constituents, holds "town meetings" to get citizens' views and complaints, and meets with political leaders to discuss possibilities and plans for the next election. For, facing another election every 2 years, a representative is never able to stop campaigning.

Lunch with Representative Jack Brooks (Democrat of Texas).

Returning a phone call to a constituent.

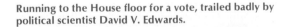

Running to the House floor for a vote, trailed badly by political scientist David V. Edwards.

With labor lobbyists in lobby just off House floor.

Strategy session with Joan Claybrook, head of National Highway Traffic Safety Administration, concerning vehicle air bag requirements.

3:00 P.M.—meeting with a group of representatives first elected to the 94th Congress to discuss mutual concerns and problems.

5:00 P.M.—meeting to discuss strategy on the foreign aid bill.

Representative Maguire's schedule

Wednesday, October 5, 1977

8:00	Breakfast with Representatives Moffett, Carr, and Miller and analyst Gar Alperovitz in the Members' Dining Room.
9:00	Meeting with staff on labor reform legislation which is being debated on the House floor today.
9:30	Democratic National Congressional Committee meeting in Room 2154 RHOB (Rayburn House Office Building).
10:00	HOUSE IN SESSION
10:00	Full Commerce Committee "mark-up" in Room 2123 of House Resolution 7897 on DNA research, and House Concurrent Resolution 273, to disapprove Federal motor vehicle safety standard 208 requiring air bags in cars.
10:00	Government Operations full committee meeting in Room 2154 RHOB to approve reports.
10:00	Dedication of Gallaudet College's Model Secondary School for the Deaf. Gladys Herschel to represent Maguire.
12:30	Taping of a television interview with Mr. Dean Norland, WAVE-TV in Louisville. Room B-364 RHOB.
1:00	Meeting in 1314 with officials from HEW to discuss legislation on medical laboratories inspection.
1:30	Meeting in 1314 with Greg Jackson from Ridgewood, N.J., a student intern attending Princeton who is interested in talking about the possibility of working for Maguire.
2:00	Health Subcommittee mark-up of bill on hospital cost containment in Room 2218 RHOB.
2:00	Government Activities and Transportation Subcommittee in Room 2358 RHOB. Joint hearings with the Subcommittee on Libraries and Memorials re Smithsonian Institution.
3:00	Energy and Power Subcommittee in Room 2123 RHOB.
3:00	94th Members Caucus Executive Committee meeting in Room H-122, the Speaker's Dining Room.
4:00	Meeting in 1314 with Mr. Rathbone, Member of Parliament in Great Britain.
5:00	Meeting to discuss strategy on foreign aid bill with Representative Long (Maryland) in Room 2304 RHOB.
5:00	American College of Obstetricians and Gynecologists, 444 North Capitol Street, Suite 408. Connie Schmidt to attend representing Maguire.
5:00	Fundraiser at the National Democratic Club. For Representative Bob Drinan.
6:00—8:00	Association for Work and Learning Reception. Gold Room in the Rayburn Building.

One other statistic, however, may be somewhat more revealing. Forty-nine percent of the House and 65 percent of the Senate are lawyers by profession. Some observers believe that this domination of Congress by lawyers inclines members of Congress to write and pass laws that only lawyers can understand, although there is no way of proving this conclusively. Citizens rarely if ever actually even *see* a law – it's probably just as well.

☐ WHAT DO MEMBERS OF CONGRESS DO?

Images of laws and lawyers may conjure up the wrong notions of what a member of Congress does, just as the long list of privileges may suggest more comfort than is usual. The best way – perhaps the only way – to understand what the life of a member of Congress is like is to follow one through a typical day. So that's what we do in the box titled "A day in the life of Representative Andrew Maguire."

■ "Casework" for constituents

Most members of Congress report that a very large part of their time goes to personalized work for constituents – "casework," as it is called. Studies find that about a quarter of a member's time and half to two-thirds of his or her staff's time is so committed.[7] We still call members of Congress "legislators," a term derived from the Latin word *leges,* or "laws." But Representative Jim Wright, now majority leader of the House Democrats, complained in his book *You and Your Congressman,* "I came here to write laws and what do I do? I send out baby books to young mothers, listen to every maladjusted kid who wants out of the service . . . and give tours of the Capitol to visitors who are just as worn out as I am."[8] One former senator kept a tally and once reported that his office received an average of 275 phone calls a day, had 6000 visitors a year, and got 45,938 letters (which it responded to with 50,678 letters!) in 1 year. Indeed, in 1976, members of Congress mailed 401 million letters to the American people marked "official business" – an average of five to each household in the country.

Individual members of Congress relate in varying ways to large numbers of the people. Casework such as we have just described is one way. But despite Representative Wright's remark, it is only a part – and a relatively small part – of the life of most. Congress does serve as the major route for citizen complaints about government. But it also makes laws – lots of them. When it does this – as it does most days of the week – its members are also relating to their constituuents, but in very different – and controversial – ways.

■ Legislating for constituents

Legislators disagree about the proper way to relate to the views of their constituents. The most common conception of the role of a legislator is that of

---

[7]See, for example, John S. Saloma, *Congress and the New Politics* (Boston: Little, Brown, 1969), and Roger Davidson, *The Role of the Congressman* (New York: Pegasus, 1969).

[8]Quoted in the Ralph Nader Congress Project's study by Mark Green et al., *Who Runs Congress?* (New York: Bantam, 1972), pp. 203–204.

Library of Congress

Henry Clay addressing the Senate in 1850.

trustee. This concept is generally traced to the British writer and politician Edmund Burke, who told his constituents after they elected him to the House of Commons (the British equivalent of our House of Representatives) in 1774:

> Certainly, gentlemen, it ought to be the happiness and the glory of a representative, to live in the strictest union, the closest correspondence, and the most unreserved communication with his constituents. Their wishes ought to have great weight with him, their opinions high respect, their business unremitted attention. . . . But his unbiased opinion, his mature judgement, his enlightened conscience, he ought not to sacrifice to you, to any man, or to any set of men living. . . . Your representative owes you, not his industry only, but his judgement, and he betrays, instead of serving you, if he sacrifices it to your opinion.

The representative, in other words, is a free agent according to this view. Studies have shown that in most legislative bodies a majority of representatives view their role in these terms.[9] But there is another role concept, less commonly held by legislators but more commonly held by constituents: that of the representative as a delegate or an agent of the voters who elected him or her. This view is common in the House, but less so in the Senate.[10] As one representative told Lewis Dexter, "I'm here to represent my district. . . . This is part of my actual belief as to the function of a congressman. . . . What is good for the majority of districts is good for the country. What snarls up the system is these so-called

[9]See John C. Wahlke, Heinz Eulau, William Buchanan, and Leroy C. Ferguson, *The Legislative System* (New York: Wiley, 1962).

[10]For results of a study, see Roger H. Davidson, *The Role of the Congressman* (New York: Pegasus, 1969), p. 117. Davidson found that in a group of eighty-seven representatives, 46 percent were "politicos," 28 percent were "trustees," and 23 percent were "delegates."

statesmen – congressmen who vote for what they think is the country's interest. . . . Let the senators do that. . . . They're paid to be statesmen; we aren't."[11]

Scholars who have studied the behavior – not just the public statements – of members of Congress have developed a third category: politico. The politico is someone concerned primarily with reelection or personal advancement. He or she will vary his or her views depending on the circumstances and rewards. Many think that most members of Congress act in fact as politicos.

But there is more to serving in Congress than casework and representation of one's constituents. The Congress was designed *to represent "the people"* as a whole in the government. Just what do we mean when we say that the Congress does or should represent the people? Different people mean quite different things.

■ Representing the people in theory

One view, often called the *authorization* concept, emphasizes elections. The people authorize certain individuals – members of Congress – to represent them by *electing* them to serve.

Others argue that the essence of representation is *accountability* – the fact that representatives must stand trial for their behavior in elections by which they can be supported or validated by reelection or rejected by defeat.

Still others suggest that the essence of representation is *similarity* – the similarity, sameness, likeness, or resemblance of the representative and those he or she is representing. This is what we mean when we speak of a photograph or a painting as being "a good representation" of its subject. In a political representative, this similarity may be in background, attitudes, or behavior.

There is another, more difficult view. It holds that representation is *symbolization* – that the representative is a symbol standing for what he or she represents. We know this best in our flag, which represents or symbolizes our nation. Indeed, we even "pledge allegiance *to the flag* of the United States of America, and to the Republic *for which it stands*. . . ." Notice, we do not simply say "I pledge allegiance to the Republic for which the flag stands." We may view the president in the same way, as a symbol of the people as well as of the country, not only when he goes abroad to represent us externally to other nations and peoples, but also when he speaks to us at home as our government.

But something is missing from all four of these concepts of representation – something that most Americans seem to feel is important in a representative. That something is *responsiveness* – a tendency to solicit, understand, and take account of the views of his or her constituents. As Hanna Pitkin remarks, after surveying these other concepts of representation,

> It seems to me that we show a government to be representative not by demonstrating its control over its subjects but just the reverse, by demonstrating that its subjects have control over what it does. Every government's

[11]Lewis A. Dexter, "The Representative and His District," in *New Perspectives on the House of Representatives,* ed. Robert L. Peabody and Nelson W. Polsby (Chicago: Rand McNally, 1963), p. 6.

actions are attributed to its subjects formally, legally. But in a representative government this attribution has substantive content: the people really do act through their government, and are not merely passive recipients of its actions. . . . For in a representative government the governed must be capable of action and judgment, capable of initiating government activity, so that the government may be conceived as responding to them."[12]

■ Representing the people in practice Which of these concepts of representation is relevant to the way our Congress represents us, the people? The concept of *representation as authorization by election* seems of limited relevance in our system where barely a majority of those eligible vote for president, and even fewer vote in Congressional elections.

The concept of *representation as accountability by reelection* suffers, too, for study after study shows that voters are largely ignorant of the positions taken by incumbents. In addition, there seem to be significant built-in advantages to incumbency in elections – ranging from free mailing privileges to greater visibility in the media – that limit the power of the discontented to oust the occupant.

The concept of *representation as similarity between elected and electors* seems not to apply well because, as we saw above, our members of Congress are very unlike the electorate in such terms as age, sex, race, religion, wealth, and previous occupation.

What of the concept of *representation as symbolization?* Our legislators may fare better as symbols. It is significant that studies report that people look negatively upon the Congress and yet have generally positive assessments of their own individual senators and representatives. The question does arise, as Richard Fenno put it in the title of a recent article: "If, as Ralph Nader Says, Congress Is 'The Broken Branch,' How come We Love Our Congressman So Much?" Fenno concludes: "Our standards of judgment for individual performance are more easily met; the individual member works harder winning approval for himself than for his institution; and Congress is a complex institution, difficult for us to understand."[13] But it may be more simple than that: The member of Congress may be able to symbolize the government as a whole in much the same way that the president, or even the flag, does.

We are left nonetheless with our fifth concept of *representation as responsiveness.* On this we have much more information. Studies we shall examine below conclude that representatives do often seem to vote in accordance with their images of what their constituents want. But there is ample evidence that these images are often inaccurate and generally somewhat foggy. As one pioneering study concluded, "Busyness blocked effective communication of constituents' views to their congressmen. A congressman can seldom readily inform himself as to how his constituents feel about any issue. A sense of acting in the dark about public opinion plagued many of the legislators we interviewed."[14] These researchers concluded, "A

---

[12]Hanna Pitkin, *The Concept of Representation* (Berkeley: University of California Press, 1967), p. 235.

[13]In Norman J. Ornstein, ed., *Congress in Change: Evolution and Reform* (New York: Praeger, 1975), p. 286.

[14]Raymond Bauer, Ithiel Pool, and Lewis Dexter, *American Business and Public Policy* (New York: Atherton, 1963), p. 413.

congressman very largely gets back what he puts out. . . . He controls what he hears both by his attention and by his attitudes. He makes the world to which he thinks he is responding."[15] To the extent that this is true, the representative plays much the same role as the president and other political figures in shaping political images in the minds of the public – a role we examined in our discussion of participation in Chapter 5.

It may be, then, that as our present system operates, the representative actually functions less as someone who responds to constituency input or The Will of the People and more as someone who generates support for the existing system in the minds of the public by serving as a "symbol of responsiveness."[16]

But even if this is largely true, our representatives still must face their constituents and stand for reelection from time to time. And in between they must legislate. Large, almost philosophical questions of how to "represent the people" may rarely arise in daily legislation. But critical questions of how to vote certainly do. We've already seen something of what a day in the life of a member of Congress is like in practical terms. Now let's approach the subject from the other direction to see what a day in the life of the Congress is like. Only then will we have the knowledge necessary to examine the legislative behavior of the members in the institutional context where it occurs, so that we can understand it.

☐ WHAT DOES THE CONGRESS DO?

If we wish to know what Congress actually does, a sensible place to look would be the *Congressional Record.* This official daily publication describes itself as containing "proceedings and debates of the Congress" and has been published every day Congress is in session since 1872. A glance at it suggests that it prints every word every member says on the floor of either house, for it averages perhaps 250 pages of small print a day.

On October 18, 1972, the *Congressional Record* reports, Representative Hale Boggs (Democrat of Louisiana) addressed the House. "In the next few minutes," he is quoted as saying, "I would like to note for members the great amount of significant legislation enacted during the session." After doing so, according to the report, he wished every representative a Merry Christmas and a Happy New Year.

Observers might disagree about the impressiveness of the record of that session of Congress. But no one could fault the sentiments, coming as they did as the Congress was about to adjourn. However, any follower of Congress, or any reader of the daily paper, would question the report that Hale Boggs had addressed the House that day. For Hale Boggs had been killed in an airplane crash in Alaska 2 days earlier.

---

[15]Ibid., pp. 420–421.

[16]John Wahlke, a close observer of legislative politics, has suggested something like this. See his article "Policy Demands and System Support: The Role of the Represented," in *Modern Parliaments: Change or Decline?* ed. Gerhard Loewenberg (Chicago: Aldine-Atherton, 1971), pp. 141–171. My tracing of these arguments owes much to an unpublished manuscript on the concept of representation in American politics by Jack D. Jacobs.

■ The activities of Congress

The reason for this and occasional similar bizarre reports is that the Congress has developed a way of allowing members to record not what they actually said, but what they would have said had they been present and had there been time. Members are so busy with other important tasks that they cannot always – or often – be present. Indeed, at any given time, unless an important vote is actually being taken, there are unlikely to be more than a handful of members "on the floor." Nor is there often time enough. If each of the 435 representatives spoke only once for only 1 minute, on a bill being debated, the debate alone would take more than 7 hours! In the session Representative Boggs was "addressing," 17,230 bills were introduced in the House, 954 were reported out of committee for floor debate, and 858 were passed. (In the Senate, 4133 bills were introduced, 930 were reported out of committee, and 927 were passed.) If the House were in continuous round-the-clock session 7 days a week for 2 years, there would only barely be enough time for each representative to speak for 1 minute on each bill. Table 8.1 shows the number of bills and laws dealt with by the Ninety-fourth Congress.

The work load of Congress – and therefore of every member – is staggering, even if we omit the constituency services and consider only the legislation. It should be clear that it is virtually impossible to have actual *debate* on a proposed bill on the floor – debate that might change someone's mind, or even just inform him or her of what the bill *says* (bills are almost always too long to read), let alone what it will really *do.*

This means that members of Congress are generally dependent on their staffs for assistance – and often for instruction – on how to vote. But even more, it means that the Congress itself is dependent upon its committees for the real work. And in turn the committees are dependent on their staffs of professionals

TABLE 8.1

Congressional workload, Ninety-fourth Congress, 1975–1976

	Senate	House	Total
Days in session	320	311	–
Time in session	2210 hours, 12 minutes	1788 hours, 7 minutes	
Number of pages in *Congressional Record*	41,358	25,654	67,012
Measures introduced and referred to committee	4912	19,371	24,283
Measures reported out of committee for action	1376	1495	–[a]
Measures passed	1552	1624	–[a]
Public laws passed[b]	208	380	588
Private laws passed[c]	42	99	141
Conference reports	61	172	
Bills vetoed	12	27	39
Vetoes overridden	3	4	7

[a]For the most part, the same measures are included in House and Senate totals.
[b]Public laws are what we normally think of as laws and deal with general legislative concerns.
[c]Private laws deal only with a specific matter or a specific individual, often concerning permission to immigrate or become a citizen, or giving a citizen permission to sue the government in court to correct an alleged wrong.

Senate

Meets at 9 a.m.

Committees:

Agriculture, Nutrition & Forestry—9 a.m. Open. Comte Bus. 322 Russell Office Bldg.

Banking Subcmte on Consumer Affairs—10 a.m. Open. Consumer protection aspects of electronic funds transfer system; Roy Green-US League of Savings Assn, Eugene Tangney-ABA, Maurice Gregg-Natl Retail Merchants Assn, others. 5302 Dirksen Office Bldg.

Banking Subcmte on Rural Housing — 10 a.m. Open. Housing in rural America; Vondal Gravlee-Natl Assn of Home Builders, Walter Benning-Manufactured Housing Inst, Gerald Sinclair-Salem Natl Bank, Salem, Ill. 6226 DOB.

Commerce, Science & Transportation—10 a.m. Open. S 61- Transportation Security Act of 1977; Rep. Paul McCloskey (R-Cal.), Harry Havens-GAO, Jack Carlson-U.S. Chamber of Commerce, Alan Ferguson-Public Interest Economic Center, others. 5110 DOB.

Environment & Public Works Subcmte on Transportation—9:30 a.m. Open. Fed aid highway program; Alice Rivlin-Dir, CBO, William Stokes-American Public Transit Assn. 4200 DOB.

Finance—10 a.m. Open. Mark up Energy Tax Act. 2221 DOB.

Energy & Natural Resources Subcmte on Parks & Recreation—10 a.m. Open. Natl Redwood Forest expansion; T. C. Nelson-USDA, Robert Herbst-Interior Dept, Beatrice Burgoon-Labor Dept, others. 3110 DOB.

Foreign Relations—9:30 a.m. Open. Panama Canal Treaty; Sens. Mike Gravel, Paul Laxalt, Bob Dole, William Scott, Jesse Helms, Reps. John Murphy, Larry McDonald. 4221 DOB.

Judiciary Subcmte on Penitentiaries & Corrections—10 a.m. Open. Function of prisons today; Robert Martinson, Judith Wilkes-Center for Criminal Justice, Norman Carlson-Fed Bur of Prisons. 1114 DOB.

Judiciary—10 a.m. Open. Comte Bus. S126 Capital.

Judiciary Subcmte on Criminal Laws—9:30 a.m. Open. Erosion of law enforcement intelligence gathering capabilities; Robert Chasen-U.S. Customs. 1318 DOB.

House

Meets at 10 a.m. on labor reform bill.

Committees:

Aging—10 a.m. Open. Retire., Income & Employ. Subc. oversight hrngs. on Older Americans Act. Dept., pub. wit. 2200 Rayburn House Office Building.

Appropriations—9:30 a.m. Open. On HR 9090—disaster payments exemption. H-140 Capitol.

Armed Services—10 a.m. Open. Invest. Subc. (non-approp. fund panel). On military club systems. Dept. wit. 2337 RHOB.

Armed Services—10 a.m. Open. Mil. Personnel Subc. On service academies' honor code Superintendents of various military academies. 2212 RHOB.

Armed Services—8:30 a.m. Open. Mil. comp. subc. Cont. briefings on mil. retire. system. Pub. wit. 2216 RHOB.

Banking, Finance & Urban Affairs—9 a.m. Open. Financial Instit. Super., Reg. & Insur. Subc. Mark up HR 7325—Intl. Banking Act. 2128 RHOB.

Banking, Finance & Urban Affairs—10 a.m. Open. Econ. Stabil. Subc. Cont. on HR 8652—national domestic develop., pub. wit. 2220 RHOB.

Budget—10 a.m. Open. Budget process task force. Hrngs. on progress & problems of budget process. MC. 210 Cannon House Office Building.

Budget—10 a.m. Open. Natl. security task force. Cont. hrngs. on Navy shipbuilding programs & problems. Dept. wit. 1302 Longworth House Office Building.

District of Columbia—9 a.m. Open. Fiscal & Govt. Aff. Subc. Cont. hrngs. on health services in D.C. 1310 LHOB.

Education & Labor—9:30 a.m. Open. Elem., Secondary & Voc. Edu. Subc. Cont. on HR 15—Elem. Secondary Edu. Act. Dept., pub wit. 2175 RHOB.

Education & Labor—9:30 a.m. Open. Econ. Opportunity Subc. Oversight hrngs. on head start prog. Dept. wit. 2257 RHOB.

Government Operations—10 a.m. Open. Pending business. 2154 RHOB.

Government Operations—9:30 a.m. Open. Intergov'l. Rel. & Human Res. Subc. Cont. hrngs. on AFDC program. 2247 RHOB.

House Administration—3 p.m. Open. Contracts Subc. Pending business. H-328 Cap.

Interior & Insular Affairs—9:45 a.m. Open. On HR 1609—Coal Pipeline Act. HR 3350—deep seabed mining. 1324 LHOB.

International Relations — 2 p.m. Open. Africa Subc. On aid policy for Africa. Dept. wit. 2255 RHOB.

International Relations—1 p.m. Open. Asian & Pacific Aff. Subc. On H. Con. Res. 331—U.N. Comm. on MIA's in SE Asia. MC, pub. wit. 2172 RHOB.

Interstate & Foreign Commerce—10 a.m. Open. On H. Con. Res. 273—disapprove fed. motor vehicle safety stnd. 208, HR 7897—recombinant DNA. 2123 RHOB.

Interstate & Foreign Commerce—1:30 p.m. Open. Commun. Subc. Panel discussion on intl. commun. 2123 RHOB.

Interstate & Foreign Commerce—2 p.m. Open. Health & Environ. Subc. Cont. mark up Hospital Cost Containment Act. 2218 RHOB.

Judiciary— 9 a.m. Open. Full comte. Cont. mark up HR 1—financial disclosure. 2141 RHOB.

Merchant Marine & Fisheries—10 a.m. Open. Coast Guard & Navigation Subc. Oversight hrngs. on marine safety program. Dept. wit. 1334 LHOB.

Post Office & Civil Service—9:30 a.m. Open. Civ. Service Subc. Cont. hrngs. on veterans' preference. Pub. wit. 311 CHOB.

Post Office & Civil Service—9:30 a.m. Open. Comp. & Employee Benefits Subc. on HR 4320—relating to judges' annuities. Dept. wit. 304 CHOB.

Public Works & Transportation—9 a.m. Open. Aviation Subc. Cont. hrngs. on airline deregulation. Pub. wit. 2167 RHOB.

Science & Technology—1 p.m. Open. Transport., Aviation & Weather Subc. on FAA program review. 2325 RHOB.

Science & Technology—9:30 a.m. Open. Space Sci. & Applications Subc. Cont. hrngs. on NASA program review. Dept. wit. 2318 RHOB.

Small Business—9 a.m. Open. Capital, Invest. & Bus. Opportunity Subc. Hrngs. on govt. monitoring of product liability insurance reserves. Dept., pub. wit. 2359 RHOB.

Ways & Means—9:30 a.m. Open. On issues relating to the Tech. Corrections Act. Comte. room, LHOB.

Select Committee on Assassinations—9:30 a.m. Closed. Kennedy Subc. pending business. 2118 RHOB.

Source: Washington Post, October 5, 1977, p. A18.

FIGURE 8.1

Congressional calendar, October 5, 1977.

for most of the work that prepares legislation for committee consideration, arranges committee hearings, and does background research. By 1976, there were almost 20,000 people working as congressional staff.

The best account of "a day in the life of Congress," in other words, would not be the "transcripts" of "debates" and "speeches" in the *Congressional Record,* but rather its "Daily Digest," which lists the day's schedule of floor action and committee meetings (see Figure 8.1 for a simplified version of the "Digest").

Given how many things members of Congress have to do, we could be excused for wondering how legislation ever gets passed. In a sense, the obstacles are doubled by the fact that both houses of Congress must pass each bill in identical form before it can become law. And if they don't agree, they have to appoint members to serve on a conference committee to iron out the differences or construct a mutually acceptable compromise.

■ The functions of Congress

If we look deeper, we find that the challenge is even greater. For Congress has three basic functions on most topics: making policy, providing funds, and oversight (checking how programs are carried out).

Policy making

The first function is to *develop and approve* policy on a question or topic. Congress generally does this on a long-term basis by passing a bill establishing a government agency or instructing an existing agency to take on a new task or program. Once such an agency or program is set up this way, it may carry on for many years without further long-term congressional policy making.

Funding Then, second, Congress must provide the funds necessary to carry out its policy instructions. This is done in three stages.

First, Congress passes a "budget resolution" early each year that sets targets for spending in all areas of government activity. We'll discuss this stage in more detail shortly.

Second, Congress *authorizes* expenditure of a certain specified sum for a program or agency over the coming year. This decision of how much to authorize for what is made in a committee specializing on the subject. The House International Relations Committee and the Senate Foreign Relations Committee, for example, prepare and recommend an authorization bill for our foreign aid program, for our contributions to the United Nations, and for the running of our diplomatic embassies around the world and the State Department here at home. The whole House and the whole Senate then must approve the authorization bill. But the "authorization," despite its name, doesn't really authorize or allow the agency to actually spend the money. Instead, it sets a kind of limit or ceiling as to how much may eventually be appropriated and establishes short-run policy principles and guidelines for bureaucracy to follow.

Then comes the third stage of funding, the *appropriations* phase. Each house of Congress has an Appropriations Committee. Its job is to gather together all the authorizations and, taking a broader view of the financial state of things, to decide how much of what has been authorized can actually be spent. The constitution requires that all revenue bills originate in the House, and precedent makes all appropriations bills originate there, too. The reason for this is that the House is closer to the people because its members are elected every 2 years from smaller districts. The hope of the founders was that the House would be less willing to spend money than the Senate, because the House would recognize that the people would dislike the higher taxes that higher spending would require. So appropriations bills originate in the House and then go to the Senate for approval or modification. Of course, if the Senate makes changes—as it always does—another conference committee must develop a compromise, which then must be passed in identical form by both houses.

The House Judiciary Committee just prior to the start of debate on the articles of impeachment of President Nixon on July 26, 1974.

Wide World Photos

TABLE 8.2

Senate and House committees, Ninety-fifth Congress

Senate	House
Agriculture, Nutrition, and Forestry	Agriculture
Appropriations	Appropriations
Armed Services	Armed Services
Banking, Housing, and Urban Affairs	Banking, Finance, and Urban Affairs
Budget	Budget
Commerce, Science, and Transportation	District of Columbia
Energy and Natural Resources	Education and Labor
Environment and Public Works	Government Operations
Ethics	House Administration
Finance	Interior and Insular Affairs
Foreign Relations	International Relations
Governmental Affairs	Interstate and Foreign Commerce
Human Resources	Judiciary
Judiciary	Merchant Marine and Fisheries
Rules and Administration	Post Office and Civil Service
Select Indian Affairs	Public Works and Transportation
Select Intelligence	Rules
Select Nutrition and Human Needs	Science and Technology
Select Small Business	Small Business
Special Aging	Standards of Official Conduct
Veterans' Affairs	Veterans' Affairs
	Ways and Means

Oversight Once money has been both authorized and appropriated, and the president has signed both bills, the agency or program in the executive branch may spend the money. But that doesn't end the role of Congress. The third major legislative responsibility of Congress is to keep an eye on how well the various parts of the executive branch are fulfilling their responsibilities to carry out the laws, and how effectively they are spending their appropriations. This function is generally called congressional oversight, and we shall examine it later in this chapter.

Policy making, funding, and oversight are very large responsibilities, even on any one matter. They must be done by the Congress on each of hundreds of problems, from national energy policy to day care, from foreign affairs and military policy to relations with cities, from space exploration to urban housing. With so many concerns on which they must act and vote, members of Congress inevitably tend to specialize on one or two problems. But even if they settle for one field of concentration matters are so complex that they need massive help. The result is that the major responsibility falls to the committees.

■ The committee and subcommittee system

A century ago, a young political scientist named Woodrow Wilson wrote a book on Congress. As president he would later be accused of failing to understand the powers and privileges of Congress. But when he wrote *Congressional Government* he understood perfectly.

"The House sits," he wrote, "not for serious discussion, but to sanction the conclusions of its committees as rapidly as possible. It legislates in its committee rooms, not by the determination of majorities, but by the resolutions of specially commissioned minorities; so it is not far from the truth to say that Congress in session is Congress on public exhibition, whilst Congress in its committee rooms is Congress at work."[17]

It hadn't always been that way. Both houses got along fine without standing (permanent) committees in the early years of the Republic. The House began slowly to establish them from 1795 on, and the Senate began to follow suit in 1816. By the time Wilson wrote, in 1885, there were some sixty in the House and seventy in the Senate. And it was not until the Legislative Reorganization Act of 1946 that numbers went from over a hundred in each house to nineteen in the House and fifteen in the Senate. But the result of the pruning of committees has been a multiplication of subcommittees (there are 145 in the House and 111 in the Senate). And it is probably fair to say that what Wilson saw happening in committees now happens instead in subcommittees. Table 8.2 lists House and Senate committees. The abundance of subcommittees to these committees reveals the extent of the multiplication, even after the further Senate reorganization and pruning done in 1977.

[17]Quoted in Warren Weaver, *Both Your Houses* (New York: Praeger, 1972), p. 60.

Drawing by Stan Hunt. ©1977 The New Yorker Magazine, Inc.

"There are days, Hank, when I don't know who's President, what state I'm from, or even if I'm a Democrat or a Republican, but, by God, I still know how to bottle up a piece of legislation in committee."

There is evidence that subcommittees are now sometimes more powerful than committees themselves. In 1977, for example, two veteran House members passed up the opportunity to head a standing committee (Merchant Marine and Fisheries) in order to keep their places as chairpersons of subcommittees of another more important committee (Interstate and Foreign Commerce).[18]

Members of Congress are so busy, and the congressional agendas are so long, that committees and subcommittees gain more and more responsibility – and more and more power. One study of the Senate revealed that if 60 to 80 percent of a committee voted for a provision, that provision would be passed on the floor of the whole Senate 90 percent of the time. If more than 80 percent of committee members supported it, its passage by the Senate was a certainty.[19] This suggests the extent to which members depend on the judgment of their committees and thus reveals something of the power of committees in general.

But some committees are more powerful than others. As we have already seen, the appropriations committees "control the purse strings" and, therefore, have greater power than other committees. And because money bills originate in the House, the House Appropriations Committee is more important than the corresponding committee in the Senate. Each house also has a committee that has jurisdiction over tax and other revenue bills: the House Ways and Means Committee and the Senate Finance Committee. Every American knows the importance of taxes, so the importance of the tax committees is not surprising.

What has surprised observers has been the sudden importance of two new committees: the Budget Committees. As we saw in Chapter 6, the executive branch long had a Bureau of the Budget, which was replaced by the even stronger Office of Management and Budget in 1970. This large agency has charge of preparing the budget that the President submits to Congress. In the past, when Congress took issue with specific presidential recommendations, the president could claim that he had a comprehensive budget plan but Congress did not. So in 1974 Congress finally established Budget Committees to develop a budget independent of the White House to be approved by both houses of Congress before they start to work examining the president's budget. This makes it possible for Congress to compare the president's budget each year with its own guidelines established for that year. No longer can the Congress be accused of simply reacting on an item-by-item basis to presidential proposals.

This new budgetary process was developed to give the Democratic controlled Congress more clout in dealing with the Republican-held White House under President Nixon. Nixon had developed a greater tendency than his predecessors to use a practice called **impoundment** – prohibiting agencies from spending funds appropriated by the Congress by "seizing" and holding them. Congress and other observers claimed that impoundment was illegal. The president, they argued, was obliged by law to spend whatever funds Congress appropriated

[18]Michael J. Malbin, "Subcommittee Musical Chairs," *National Journal,* March 5, 1977, p. 360.

[19]Donald Matthews, *U.S. Senators and Their World* (New York: Vintage, 1964).

as Congress directed. The courts generally agreed when specific cases were brought before them. But Congress concluded that constant resort to the courts was no solution. So as a part of the act establishing its own budgetary process, it formally outlawed impoundment.

Innovations in Congress are relatively infrequent, and assessment of their success must always await lengthy trial. The Budget Committees are no exception. The fact that the new system continued to function in the Carter years, when the same party controlled both houses of Congress and the White House, suggests that it may prove successful. Meanwhile, Congress has a new and stronger role and two new committees that show signs of becoming especially important.[20]

■ The House and the Senate

Certain differences in committee power derive from differences in the ways the two houses operate. Because the House has 435 members, the time allowed for debate must be limited. In practice this is done by the House Rules Committee. The Rules Committee is extremely powerful, because it has charge of deciding which of the bills "reported out" (approved) by committees will be scheduled for consideration by the House as a whole, whether amendments will be allowed on the floor, and how much debate will be permitted. This decision by the committee is called **granting a rule**. The "rule" is the statement of terms on which the bill may be considered by the House. The Rules Committee has usually acted as an arm of the leadership – one reason why it has long been powerful. For many years its members were mostly Republicans and southern Democrats, and its influence was very conservative. In recent years, its ability to "kill" bills has been limited somewhat by changes in its membership and in House procedures. But is continues to be a very powerful committee.

The Senate, with only 100 members and a tradition of unlimited debate, operates quite differently in these matters. The majority leader – the elected head of the party which has a majority in the Senate – determines the scheduling of bills. And Rule 22 of the Senate allows unlimited debate unless **cloture** is voted. Cloture, or closing of debate on a given bill, can be forced only if (1) sixteen senators sign a petition requesting it, (2) 2 days pass, and then (3) three-fifths of the senators present vote for cloture. If all this occurs, then no senator may speak for more than one additional hour on the bill before a vote must be taken.

The importance of the cloture rule is that is is the only way of preventing a small group of senators from "killing" a bill by "talking it to death." Even a single senator can **filibuster**[21] a bill by talking nonstop for several days. With the help of a few colleagues he or she can delay proceedings so long that others give up and agree

---

[20]For a discussion of impoundment and related questions, see Louis Fisher, *Presidential Spending Power* (Princeton, N.J.: Princeton University Press, 1975), especially chap. 7.

[21]No one knows how this term, which originally meant a "pirate," came to be applied to a political speech. Perhaps it is because the speaker hijacks or seizes the debate, or commandeers the body, by his intrusion. For a less venturesome discussion of the term, see William Safire, *The New Language of Politics* (New York: Random House, 1968), p. 143.

TABLE 8.3

Major differences between the House and the Senate

House	**Senate**
Larger (435 members)	Smaller (100 members)
More formal	Less formal
More hierarchically organized	Less hierarchically organized
Acts more quickly	Acts more slowly
Rules more rigid	Rules more flexible
Power less evenly distributed	Power more evenly distributed
Longer apprentice period	Shorter apprentice period
More impersonal	More personal
Less "important" constituencies	More "important" constituencies
Less prestige	More prestige
More "conservative"	More "liberal"

Source: Lewis A. Froman, *The Congressional Process: Strategies, Rules, and Procedures* (Boston: Little, Brown, 1967), p. 7. Copyright © 1967 by Little, Brown and Company, Inc. Reprinted with permission.

to let the bill die so the Senate can get on with bills the senators are more interested in. This is how southern senators long prevented passage of civil rights legislation, until the cloture rule was eased in the 1960s.

This variation in limits on debate is but one of the important differences between the Senate and the House. Generally, it is from the Senate rather than the House that presidential candidates come. And Representatives often try to "advance" to the Senate when an opportunity arises, while there is no known case of a Senator seeking to switch to the House. Table 8.3, developed by Lewis Froman, a longtime student of both houses, capsulizes important differences between them.

■ Rivalry between the House and the Senate

Not surprisingly, there tends to be strong rivalry between the two houses. This rivalry may well be an outgrowth of the different functions each house has. The Senate, as we have seen, has more foreign policy responsibilities, because it must ratify treaties and confirm or reject presidential appointments. These responsibilities tend to make it more sysmpathetic to the presidential perspective. The House, on the other hand, with special revenue responsibilities and smaller districts in which members face elections every 2 years, is bound to identify more closely with the taxpayers. This situation is likely to be reflected in more conservatism in the House as a whole. On the other hand, Senators, freer from electoral pressures generally because of their 6-year terms, are more likely to find strong liberal voting blocs like blacks, Jews, and organized labor able to help their reelection. Thus, there are special incentives for the Senate to be more liberal than the House.[22]

The policy impact of these differences must contantly be reconciled in the conference committees that compromise serious differences in perhaps 10 percent of all congressional bills.[23] They may also be moderated somewhat by the effects of party membership on legislative behavior.

□ HOW BOTH HOUSES OPERATE

■ The role of party

The Democrats have had majorities in the House and the Senate continuously since 1955. Indeed, as Figure 8.2 shows, in the last half century the Republicans have controlled the House and the Senate together only in 1947–1948 and 1953–1954. We might expect the fact that the same party usually controls both houses to foster greater cooperation between them. After all, on the face of it, the most important organization and division of Congress is not into committees but into parties. Seating on the floor of each house is arranged by party, with Democrats on one side, Republicans on the other, and the occasional independent located in between.

[22]This argument is developed in Neil MacNeil's study of the House, *Forge of Democracy* (New York: McKay, 1964).

[23]The figure is Warren Weaver's, in his book *Both Your Houses*, p. 131.

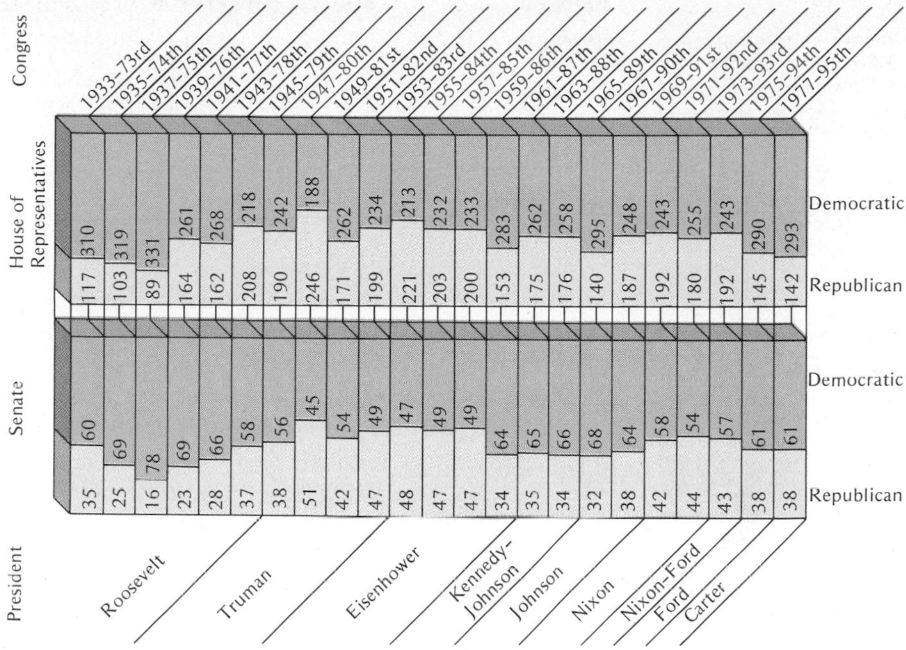

FIGURE 8.2

Party strength in Congress. In the years printed in color, Congress was controlled by the party in opposition to the president.

The party caucus Party is especially important in determining *leadership* of each house. Each party has its own **caucus** in each house. The caucus is a meeting of all party members. (The name comes from an old American Indian term for "elder" or "counselor.") The caucus meets and decides on candidates or policy positions, and these decisions are then "counsel" or advice to members on how to vote in the body as a whole. This caucus is extremely important at the beginning of each 2-year "session" of Congress, when newly elected members arrive and nominations for officers are made and voted upon.

The party leadership Each party caucus in the Senate chooses candidates for *party leader,* and for *whip* (the person who, with deputy whips, is responsibile for rounding up, or whipping into line, party members when a vote is coming). It also elects a Policy Committee to discuss party positions on legislation, and a committee (the Steering Committee for the Democrats, the Committee on Committees for the Republicans) that then appoints party members to the various standing committees of the Senate.

In the Senate, the party leader of the majority party (almost always the Democrats in the past 50 years) becomes the effective leader of the Senate. The Constitution provides that the vice-president of the United States will serve as the president of the Senate, but in fact he is rarely there to preside unless he anticipates a close vote on an important bill on which he could cast the deciding vote in the event of a tie. The Constitution also creates the office of president pro tempore (Latin for "for the time being") to preside in the vice-president's absence. In practice, though, that post has generally gone as an honor to the longest serving senator, who usually is not interested in the unexciting job of presiding. As a result, the task of presiding is passed around among senators—particularly "junior" senators (those who have served least long).

The situation in the House is somewhat different. The Constitution says "The House of Representative shall chuse their Speaker and other officers." The Speaker of the House is necessarily powerful, for he or she presides over sessions, decides who will be "recognized" to speak, and appoints member of "select" (as distinct from "standing") committees to conduct special investigations. The Speaker is elected by the House as a whole, but invariably is in fact the candidate chosen by the majority party in its caucus. Nonetheless, the majority party also has a "majority leader" and a "majority whip," just as the minority has a "minority leader" and a "minority whip." Through history the actual power of the Speaker has varied. At present, that power is somewhat limited by recent Democratic reforms, which we shall discuss shortly. Nonetheless, the House Speaker in the Ninety-fifth Congress, Thomas P. O'Neill, rapidly gained power in Congress and influence with the Democratic president.

Wide World Photos

Senator Lyndon B. Johnson greets House Speaker Sam Rayburn at the Johnson house in Washington on the occasion of Rayburn's sixty-ninth birthday, January 6, 1951.

■ The role of leadership

Speaker O'Neill often refers to "little things you can do for people." But the effectiveness of a Speaker depends on much more. A senior Democratic representative who several times tried and failed to win a leadership role, Richard Bolling (Democrat of Missouri), long watched the techniques of Sam Rayburn (Democrat of Texas), Speaker from 1940 to 1961, and generally conceded to be the most effective speaker in modern history. Bolling later wrote, in a book lamenting the requisites of leadership: "To maintain personal influence the Speaker is forced to engage in a savage political scramble involving sectional interests, local claims and personal advancements, all of which are more fondly regarded by the inner circle of the House [of which the Speaker has long been a member] than party loyalties or vital national issues. All too often, wise and just legislation becomes a subordinate issue and frequently a total casualty."[24]

Rayburn developed and practiced his varied leadership skills with a group of trusted colleagues. One of them was Lyndon Johnson, who moved on to the Senate where he became known for his own brand of leadership, often called "The Treatment." Historian Arthur Schlesinger, for a time an LBJ aide, later conveyed Johnson's own description of his technique as Senate majority leader:

> The Treatment began immediately: a brilliant, capsule characterization of every Democratic Senator, his strengths and failings, where he fit into the political spectrum; how far he could be pushed, how far pulled; his hates, his loves. And who must oversee all these prima donnas, put them to work, knit them together, know when to tickle this one's vanity, inquire of that one's health, remember this one's five o'clock nip of Scotch, that one's

[24]Richard Bolling, *House Out of Order,* quoted in Weaver, *Both Your Houses,* p. 156.

nagging wife? Who must find the hidden legislative path between the South and the North, the public power men and the private power men, the farmers' men and the unions' men, the bomber-boys and the peace-lovers, the eggheads and the fatheads?"[25]

Such roles fall generally to the leadership. Some leaders welcome the opportunities, while others resist them. Johnson's successor until 1977 was Senator Mike Mansfield (Democrat of Montana). He was often criticized for being a weak leader – a criticism to which he once replied: "I am neither a circus ringmaster, the master of ceremonies of a Senate nightclub, a tamer of Senate lions, or a wheeler and dealer."[26]

The place of personality in legislative leadership should be clear from these brief portraits. But before we conclude that leadership is everything, we should examine the role of the rules.

■ The seniority system

The rules of any body are subject to change, as they are to interpretation. For an organization – or two organizations – run personally, the Congress is remarkably influenced by its rules. We have already examined the rules concerning selection of leadership and the rules regarding floor debate. But the rule that observers believe most important is the seniority system.

The term "seniority" comes from the same Latin root, meaning "old," as do "senior," "senile," and even "Senate." The seniority system provides that whoever has served longest gets first choice of whatever is to be chosen. Its important consequences in Congress are for selection of chairpersons of committees and for choice of committee assignments or memberships. According to the seniority rule, the chairperson of a committee is always whichever committee member from the majority party has served longest on that committee. And when a committee slot opens up through death, retirement, or defeat, the member of Congress with the longest consecutive service in the Congress gets first choice as to whether he or she wishes to trade a present committee post (perhaps on a less important committee) for the newly available slot.

Because southern members of Congress came from "safe districts" and were reelected usually without opposition, they rapidly gained seniority. The result was that as long as the Democrats controlled Congress, southern conservative Democrats controlled committee leadership. In recent years, two things have happened to change this situation, which so frustrated liberals. First, some northern liberal Democratic members of Congress have developed safe seats and gained seniority while Republicans have begun to contest some seats in the South previously safely Democratic. And second, both parties have begun to move away from an automatic seniority rule.

---

[25]Quoted in Rowland Evans and Robert Novak, *Lyndon B. Johnson: The Exercise of Power* (New York: New American Library, 1966), pp. 104–105.

[26]*Congressional Record,* November 27, 1963, p. 22862.

In 1971 House Republicans decided to vote by secret ballot for "ranking" minority committee members (the people who would become chairpersons if the Republicans should gain control of the House). Then in January 1973 House Democrats, too, decided to vote. The results were identical to the seniority lists that year. But in 1975, with the influx of new, generally liberal, Democratic members, the caucus voted to replace three old senior southern chairpersons. The Senate Democratic members also changed their rules to allow voting for chairpersons. Thus far, the changes have been minor. But the rule has been broken, and further change seems very likely.

The proof of the rules changes, of course, will be in the legislating. We have already discussed key stages in the process by which a bill becomes a law. In Perspective 3, we traced the NEPA through its legislative life into law. In this chapter, we repeated certain key features of the lawmaking process, which was summarized in Table P3.1 and Figure P3.1 in Perspective 3. But these legislative outcomes – and those that do not result in successful legislation – are based on the decisions of 435 representatives and 100 senators. What can we learn about influences on the behavior of these 535 members of Congress?

□ INFLUENCES ON CONGRESSIONAL CAREER BEHAVIOR

Four basic features are likely to have a general influence on the behavior of members of Congress as their congressional careers develop. First, we have already discussed differing conceptions of the proper role of a legislator – trustee, delegate, and politico – and the more general question of how Congress should represent the people. One's image of how one should behave as a representative is bound to have a general influence on one's conduct. Second, the conduct of members of Congress will be influenced by their own personal objectives. A third important factor will be the member's image or understanding of the rules by which a member of the Senate or the House is expected to operate. And fourth will be his or her beliefs about effective strategies for success in Congress. We have already examined the first of these. Now we must look briefly at the other three. Then we can examine more specific influences that may operate when a member decides how to vote on particular legislation.

■ Objectives of members of Congress

The common good If we thought about it in the abstract, or listened only to the rhetoric of our representatives, we might conclude that the objective of a member of Congress is to discover *the common good* of the country, the state, or the legislative district and then act so as to achieve it. This action would presumably include developing, supporting, and voting for good legislation. Some politicians may indeed believe that this is their major objective and may act accordingly. But, these days anyway, few observers would.

Personal gain A possible alternative to this selfless pursuit of the common good is seeking *personal gain* or special benefits for oneself. Members of Congress have long been subject to criticism for "conflict of interest." This term refers to a situation in which someone acts in his or her role as an official in a way that benefits himself or herself as an individual. In other words, one's own personal interest is in conflict with the public interest. In other bodies, such as the courts, an official will usually remove himself or herself from a case if it involves, for example, a company in which he or she owns stock and so could benefit from his or her own decision. Members of Congress, however, have never been known to disqualify themselves from voting on legislation in which they have personal financial interests. Nor have they been known to sell their stocks before serving to prevent such situations from arising. In fact, quite the opposite has often been true. Drew Pearson and Jack Anderson about a decade ago wrote a massive book called *The Case Against Congress* that documented case after case of apparent conflict of interest.[27] On most issues, however, most representatives have no personal material interest. What influences their votes then?

Reelection Perhaps it is the third factor often cited – what political scientist David Mayhew calls "the electoral connection." Mayhew argues that members of Congress act as "single-minded seekers of reelection." Virtually everything they do, he argues, can be understood best as motivated by the wish to guarantee their own victory in the next election. According to him there are really only two things a political figure in Congress can do that can be converted into votes: credit claiming and position taking. *Credit claiming* involves doing something that can be cited as a personal accomplishment in office. *Position taking* is stating popular views on issues of public concern. According to Mayhew, the daily chores of the Congress, especially legislating, are done *despite* the fact that voters rarely pay attention to them. Voters rarely hold members of congress responsible for their votes. Indeed, as we noted earlier, voters rarely know how their representatives voted on particular issues.[28]

[27] Drew Pearson and Jack Anderson, *The Case Against Congress* (New York: Simon & Schuster, 1968).

[28] See David R. Mayhew, *Congress: The Electoral Connection* (New Haven, Conn.: Yale University Press, 1974).

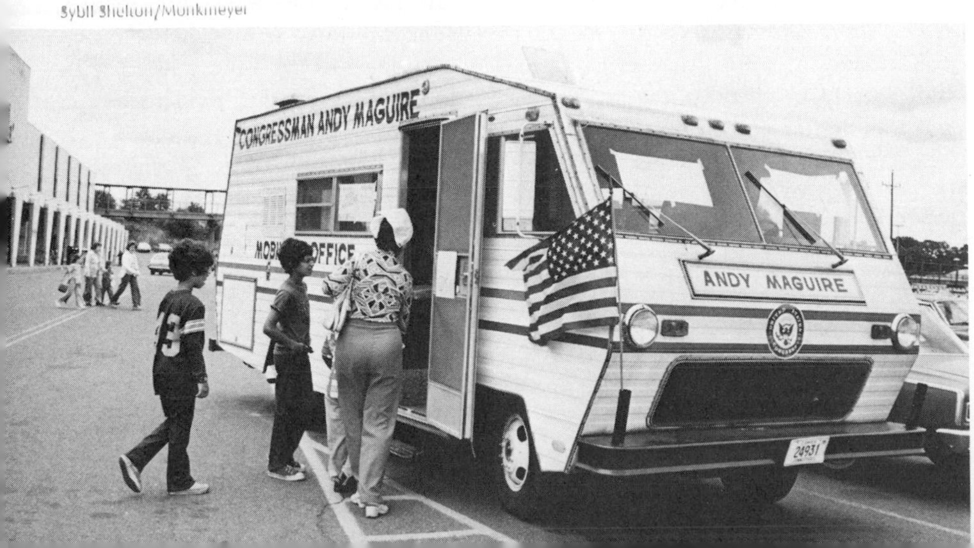

Representative Andrew Maguire, whom we met earlier, uses a mobile office to keep in contact with his constituents.

Sybil Shelton/Monkmeyer

Higher office There is, however, another theory that takes issue with, or at least qualifies, this "reelection theory." We met it in Chapter 5 when we considered participation. It is "ambition theory," and it argues that some politicians are not so much interested in being reelected to their present positions as they are in laying the groundwork for election to higher office. This objective is not necessarily a bad one, according to the developer of "ambition theory," Joseph Schlesinger. "If ambition is the motive force in politics," he writes, "then the leader with progressive ambitions is the hero, the man who brings others together and provides unity and cohesion. If anyone is going to search for solutions, it is the man whose career depends on finding solutions. The politician with static ambitions is far more likely to be driven by immediate pressures, whether it be the pressure of opinion, party, or special interest groups. . . ."[29]

Constituency service Doing favors for your constituents is often a good way to advance your career prospects, especially if you pick constituents with political influence. But both ambitious and stodgy members of Congress are likely to get satisfaction in helping those who live in their states or districts. So constituent interests may also be a factor in influencing decision—especially those of members of the House, who are closer to their populations than are senators.

Power in Congress—and in Washington A final factor in shaping the decisions of some members of Congress is the desire for personal power in Congress—and perhaps in government generally. Some members appear from the outside to be without ambition, but in fact have considerable power within the Congress. They spend their time and energy not in seeking national publicity, as the more outwardly or upwardly ambitious do, but rather in studying and using the rules and procedures of the House or Senate to make their influence *felt, not seen,* in the outcomes.

■ Images of "the rules of the legislative game"

"There are unwritten rules of behavior, which we have called folkways, in the Senate," wrote Donald Matthews in a pioneering study in 1960. "These rules are normative, that is, they define how a senator ought to behave. Nonconformity is met with moral condemnation, while senators who conform to the folkways are rewarded with high esteem by their colleagues. Partly because of this fact, they tend to be the most influential and effective members of the Senate."[30]

"Should the new legislator wish to be heard," wrote George Washington in 1787, "the way to command the attention of the House is to speak seldom, but to important subjects. . . ."[31] Almost 200 years later, newly elected Senator

---

[29]Joseph Schlesinger, *Ambition and Politics* (Chicago: Rand McNally, 1966), p. 209.

[30]Matthews, *U.S. Senators and Their World,* p. 116.

[31]J. A. Carroll and M. W. Ashworth, *George Washington,* vol. 7 (New York: Scribner, 1957), p. 591. (Volumes 1–6 by Douglas S. Freeman.)

Joseph Clark, while having lunch with Senator Hubert Humphrey, asked Humphrey to tell him how he should behave when he got to the Senate. "He did – for an hour and a half. . . . In essence he said, 'Keep your mouth shut and your eyes open. It's a friendly, courteous place. You will have no trouble getting along. . . . Don't let your ideology embitter your personal relationships. It won't if you behave with maturity. . . . And above all keep your mouth shut for awhile."[32]

In recent years, such "rules" have been relaxed, and junior members of Congress now take more active roles than they used to. But there persists a general set of "rules of the game" by which legislators often find it convenient to operate. One survey of almost 500 members of state legislatures in California, New Jersey, Ohio, and Tennessee found forty-two such rules mentioned by various individuals. The following are those most commonly cited, listed in declining order of frequency of mention: (1) keep your word and abide by your commitments; (2) respect other members' legislative rights; (3) be impersonal in your dealings and, in general, do unto others as you would have them do unto you; (4) practice self-restraint during debate; (5) observe common courtesies; (6) be frank, honest, and open in explaining bills; (7) don't be a prima donna or a publicity hound; (8) be known as a person of integrity; (9) preserve you independence from outside control.[33] Perhaps the best general summary of these rules is former Speaker Sam Rayburn's axiom, "If you want to *get* along, *go* along."[34]

■ Beliefs about effective strategies Some of these "rules of the game" involve primarily courtesy, whereas others contain valuable information for the person who wishes to be an effective legislative strategist. A member of Congress is most likely to be effective if he or she *specializes in a given area of legislation* and becomes known as an expert on it. It also helps to be willing and able to "make deals" or *exchange votes* with colleagues on matters of no great personal concern – the "log rolling" behavior for which Congress is famous. Controlling information important to others, as any specialist does, is a great instrument of power in a complex world, as we shall see time and again in this book. So, in a different sense, is a vote that can be given to, or held back from, a colleague who is strongly interested in getting a given bill passed.

But beyond such rather obvious instruments of power are others. One is *having an important position* such as committee or subcommittee chairperson. Another is *knowing and using the rules.* These instruments of power are well revealed by a study of Graham Barden, Democrat and chairman of the House Committee on Education and Labor until his retirement in 1960. Barden claimed to favor federal aid to education, but he continually used his power and his knowledge of the rules to prevent bills supporting such aid from passing.

---

[32]Clark, *Congress: The Sapless Branch,* p. 2.

[33]See John C. Wahlke et al., *The Legislative System* (New York: Wiley, 1962), pp. 146–147.

[34]Quoted in Davidson, *The Role of the Congressman,* p. 180, but widely heard on Capitol Hill as elsewhere in America.

Among other things he: adjourned a committee meeting on grounds that a quorum (the minimum number of members necessary) was not present, when in fact a quorum was present; refused to call upon committee members with whom he disagreed, so they couldn't speak; and called a "quickie" vote of the committee to kill legislation when it happened that a majority of members present opposed the program.[35] Committee chairpersons are less likely to get away with such high-handed behavior nowadays because of reforms that we shall discuss shortly. But the rules and positions of power can still be used effectively by those who know how and have the opportunity.

□ INFLUENCES ON CONGRESSIONAL VOTING BEHAVIOR

Many factors may influence how a member of Congress votes on a given bill. The general factors we have just examined sometimes play a role. Also important may be his or her perception of the wishes of the president, of the congressional leadership, or of influential individuals such as campaign fund contributors. But we should not conclude from this that a legislator ignores the merits of the bill in question.

The point, rather, is that patterns often do emerge in voting behavior. These patterns make it possible for us as outside observers to generalize about factors that influence voting, although members of Congress may not be conscious of the influences we uncover. Research in this area is still in its early stages, and so our conclusions must be tentative. But let's see what several scholars have found.

■ Cue taking

A study of senatorial voting in 1962–1963 by John Jackson found the influence of constituencies – the *delegate* conception which we earlier discussed – to be by far the most important.[36] A study of House voting in 1969 by John Kingdon attempted to determine the influences on members' votes not only of constituency but also of House colleagues, of interest groups, of his or her party leaders, of the Nixon administration, and of his or her own staff. The research found that no one factor was dominant enough to be called *the* major influence. So instead Kingdon concluded that members of the House use a kind of "consensus model of decision" in which they *"take their cues,"* as some would say, *from various individuals and groups.*[37]

---

[35]The devices Barden used are reported in Saloma, *Congress and the New Politics,* p. 120.

[36]John E. Jackson, *Constituencies and Leaders in Congress: Their Effects on Senate Voting Behavior* (Cambridge, Mass.: Harvard University Press, 1974).

[37]The term "cue taking" is not Kingdon's, but rather comes from a study by Donald R. Matthews and James A. Stimson, *Yeas and Nays: Normal Decision-Making in the U. S. House of Representatives* (New York: Wiley, 1975). Their 1969 study found considerable support for the following hypothesis: "When a member is confronted with the necessity of casting a roll-call vote on a complex issue about which he knows very little, he searches for cues provided by trusted colleagues who – because of their formal position in the legislature or policy specialization – have more information than he does and with whom he would probably agree if he had the time and information to make an independent decision. Cue-givers need not be individuals. When overwhelming majorities of groups that the member respects and trusts – the whole House, the members of his party or state delegation, for example – vote the same way, the member is likely to accept their collective judgment as his own" (p. 45).

When House members begin to consider how to vote on a bill or amendment, Kingdon found, their first question is, "Is it controversial?" If there is no disagreement among fellow representatives, interest groups, party leaders, the administration, and his or her staff, the representative "votes with the herd." But if there is some conflict in his or her total environment, the representative then must decide whether the source of the conflict is important for him or her. A Republican, for example, might worry about the Nixon administration's views, while a Democrat wouldn't. A Democrat, on the other hand, might well worry about organized labor, while a Republican wouldn't. In other words, at this second step the question is whether there is conflict in what Kingdon calls the "field of forces" that would likely affect the representative's own decision. Usually, there isn't, and if that's the case, he or she votes with that field. If there is conflict among those important forces, the member then proceeds to the third step, which is to see how many actors in the "field of forces" are disagreeing with the rest. If it's only one, he or she is highly likely to vote against that one actor. If there are two, he or she is quite likely to vote against that pair. But if there are more than two forces out of line, the representative faces a major difficult choice where such informal, perhaps nonconscious "cue-taking" decision rules are not helpful, and the decision must be made on other grounds. However, this is rare: It happened in only 14 of the 222 controversial voting decisions Kingdon studied. What Kingdon has developed is called by scholars a "model of Congressional voting decision." This model and the results it produced when applied to the 222 actual cases Kingdon studied are summarized in Figure 8.3.[38]

[38]John W. Kingdon, *Congressmen's Voting Decisions* (N.Y.: Harper & Row, 1973), esp. chap. 10.

Source. Adapted from John W. Kingdon, *Congressmen's Voting Decisions* (New York: Harper & Row, 1973), chap. 10.

FIGURE 8.3

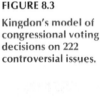

Kingdon's model of congressional voting decisions on 222 controversial issues.

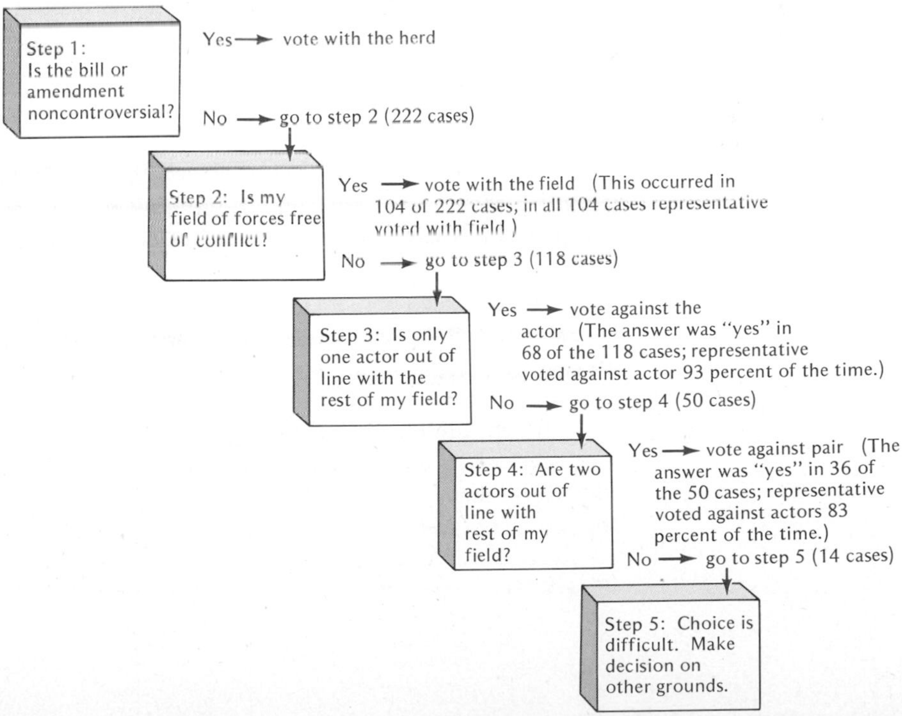

■ Policy areas

Others take different approaches to determining how members of Congress make up their minds. One of the most interesting is Aage Clausen's study of Senate and House voting decisions from 1953 to 1964. Clausen focused on the policy issues involved, instead of on the decision process itself. He divided votes into five policy areas: civil liberties; international involvement (such as foreign aid and trade); agricultural assistance (such as farm subsidies); social welfare; and government management (including government regulation of the economy, conservation, balancing the budget, and so on).

Clausen then examined the policy positions taken by individual members of Congress in this 12-year period and looked for patterns of influence upon them by three major factors: party, constituency, and the president. This is what he found. *Government management issues* are most influenced by *party.* Democrats tend to favor government intervention in economic affairs, while Republicans tend to oppose it. The voters – the constituents – have no real role, according to Clausen, because policy alternatives are complex and often unpredictable. Indeed, the voter can't even have an opinion on alternatives being considered. All he or she can do is complain when economic conditions worsen. *Agricultural assistance and social welfare issues* are influenced by both *party* and *constituency. Civil liberties issues* are exclusively influenced by *constituency,* with northerners supporting and southerners opposing civil rights laws. *International involvement issues* are dominated by the *president,* but constituency is also an important consideration.

One of Clausen's general conclusions was that "the differences in the policy positions of congressmen elected from the same state and party are minimal on the four domestic policy dimensions, while remaining substantial on the international involvement dimension."[39]

But this conclusion may be less true today, according to a more recent but less extensive study. Taking a different approach, this examination of voting by all senators and representatives in 1975 found what appeared to be a "generation gap" in Congress. Those first elected after Vietnam, the environmental movement, and "good government" public-interest lobbying voted quite differently from more senior members.

Junior northern Democrats are more liberal than senior ones on environmental policy, defense spending, and congressional and campaign reform questions, the study concluded, but all northern Democrats vote about the same on economic and public-welfare issues. Junior southern Democrats and northern Republicans, on the other hand, are more liberal than their more senior colleagues on economic, public-welfare, and defense-spending issues, but both groups tend to vote with their seniors when there is a conflict between energy development and the environment. Seniority is not a significant factor in the way southern Republicans vote.

These results appear to suggest that geography and age are the major determinants. But the study reached a somewhat different conclusion: "The differences that show up . . . are less a product of age or tenure than a reflection of the issues that were important when a Member first was elected. Thus new Members

[39]Aage R. Clausen, *How Congressmen Decide: A Policy Focus* (New York: St. Martin's, 1973), p. 231.

tend to reflect new issues, while veterans echo the issues that predominated when they first came to Congress. Voting by seniority, therefore, is less a cause of differences than the result of existing differences."[40]

Where do these varying studies leave us? With certain disagreements needing further study, but nonetheless a better sense of the likely relevance of such influences on voting behavior as legislative practices, party, constituents, presidential leadership, and individual judgment. We should recognize that these studies are all based on roll-call voting. And we must be careful not to jump to conclusions about the significance of results based on studies of voting records alone, for voting records may be misleading accounts of what our representatives actually do and really support (see Action Unit 8.1).

[40]Michael Malbin, "Times Change, But Congressmen Still Vote the Way They Used To," *National Journal,* March 20, 1976, pp. 370–374.

□ ACTION UNIT 8.1 How to find and interpret congressional voting records

All "record" or "roll call" votes on the floor of either house on bills and amendments are printed in the *Congressional Record.* You can find the *Congressional Record* in most large libraries. You can also purchase individual copies for particular days at 25 cents each, or subscribe for $3.75 per month or $45 per year, from the Superintendent of Documents, Government Printing Office, Washington D.C. 20401. Congressional Quarterly's *Weekly Report* (which we discuss in the bibliography at the end of the chapter) is available in many libraries and prints records of all important votes. Some newspapers such as the *New York Times* and the *Washington Post* print the breakdown of votes on major topics. And many local papers will print weekly summaries of how local representatives and senators voted on key issues. But unless you've been following a certain issue and know just what was being voted on, this is not likely to tell you very much. A member of Congress may vote with public opinion in his or her constituency on final passage of a bill but may have voted against this public opinion in committee or during the amending process. A member may also change his or her vote once voting is completed. For example, if a member voted with the party and against the interests of his or her district and then discovers that his or her vote was not crucial, the member may have his or her vote changed. The representative gets credit in public for voting with his or her constituency, when in fact he or she voted against the constituency the first time around.

To examine key votes – usually on amendments before final passage – you really need studies prepared by interest groups. By a recent count, twenty-one organizations prepare such lists after each session of Congress, rating the members by whether they vote as the groups believe they should. Among the major rating groups, to which you can write for their latest set of ratings, are the following, each identified by its special interest or political preference: AFL-CIO Committee on Political Education (COPE), 815 16th St. NW, Washington, D.C. 20006 (*organized labor*); American Conservative Union, 422 1st St. SE, Washington, D.C. 20003 (*conservative*); American Farm Bureau Federation, 425 13th St. NW, Washington, D.C. 20004 (*farmers*); Americans for Democratic Action, 1424 16th St. NW, Washington, D.C. 20036 (*liberal*); Consumer Federation of America, 1012 14th St., NW, Washington, D.C. 20005 (*consumer*); Environmental Action, 1346 Connecticut Ave. NW, Washington, D.C. 20036 (*environmentalist*); League of Women Voters, 1730 M St. NW, Washington, D.C. 20036 (*nonpartisan*); National Associated Businessmen, Inc., 1000 Connecticut Ave. NW, Washington, D.C. 20036 (*business*); National Council of Senior Citizens, 1511 K St. NW, Washington, D.C. 20005 (*elderly*); Women's Lobby, Inc., 1345 G St. SE, Washington, D.C. 20003 (*women*).

TABLE 8.4

State representation in the House of Representatives

Alabama	7
Alaska	1
Arizona	4
Arkansas	4
California	43
Colorado	5
Connecticut	6
Delaware	1
Florida	15
Georgia	10
Hawaii	2
Idaho	2
Illinois	24
Indiana	11
Iowa	6
Kansas	5
Kentucky	7
Louisiana	8
Maine	2
Maryland	8
Massachusetts	12
Michigan	19
Minnesota	8
Mississippi	5
Missouri	10
Montana	2
Nebraska	3
Nevada	1
New Hampshire	2
New Jersey	15
New Mexico	2
New York	39
North Carolina	11
North Dakota	1
Ohio	23
Oklahoma	6
Oregon	4
Pennsylvania	25
Rhode Island	2
South Carolina	6
South Dakota	2
Tennessee	8
Texas	24
Utah	2
Vermont	1
Virginia	10
Washington	7
West Virginia	4
Wisconsin	9
Wyoming	1
Total	435

Nonetheless, these findings do advance our understanding of how and why members of Congress act as they do – especially if we bear in mind a conclusion Clausen urges upon us:

> the individual members of Congress, when seen behind the trappings of office, are persons of few extraordinary endowments. The congressman is not a political virtuoso constantly performing political maneuvers of great complexity with an unerringly delicate sense of political balance. Members of Congress are best understood as typical participants in the politically activist segment of our citizenry, with no special calling to the ministry of policymaking. Their decisions result from a blend of prejudice, reason, and practicality. These decisions are sometimes based upon much information and at other times upon little; they are sometimes the product of political necessity and at other times the result of unencumbered judgment.[41]

☐ HOW CONGRESS HAS CHANGED

In the early years some distinguished participants in the founding of the Republic served in the Congress. By the 1820s, some observers found the Senate full of statesmen and the House peopled by ordinary citizens. Over the years, as more states were admitted to the Union, the number of Senators grew from the original 22 to the present 100, reached when Alaska and Hawaii were admitted. The House, too, grew with the population, from an original 59, until in 1929 the Reapportionment Act made the total number permanently 435 and required that these seats be reapportioned among the states every time there is a new census. (The House membership by state based on the 1970 census is shown in Table 8.4.)

Actual *apportionment* has been left to the states, which decide where district lines are drawn, or which voters will vote together to pick a representative. Over the years, districts were often malapportioned, in ways that protected incumbents or dominant parties by creating districts that were unequal in numbers of voters or strangely shaped in terms of territory. This is often called gerrymandering, in "honor" of Elbridge Gerry, who was Governor of Massachusetts in 1812 when the state legislature carved up Essex County in a way that favored his party, making a district that looked like a salamander. Finally, in 1964, the Supreme Court ruled in *Westberry v. Sanders* that districts must have equal populations. The long-standing tendency of state legislatures to apportion in ways which overrepresented rural voters and underrepresented city voters began to be corrected.

Other changes in Congress have been more striking. In his journal, Senator William Maclay recorded the events of one day, April 3, 1790, of the First Congress with these words: "We went to the Hall. The Minutes were read. A message was received from the President of the United States. A report was handed to the chair. We looked and laughed at each other today for half an hour, then adjourned." A

[41] Clausen, *How Congressmen Decide*, p. viii.

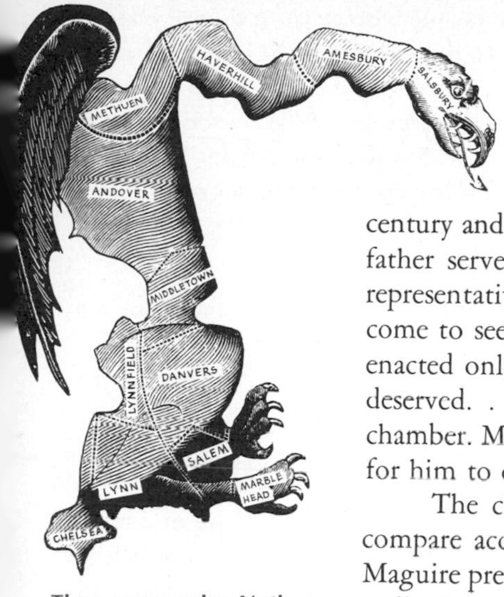

The gerrymander. Voting districts in Essex County, Massachusetts, in 1812.

century and a half later, in 1954, Representative Martin Dies of Texas wrote: "My father served in Congress from 1909 to 1919 from the state of Texas. . . . A representative got about 15 letters a week. Only at rare intervals would a constituent come to see him. He had no pressure groups to contend with. Because Congress enacted only a few bills each session, legislation got the deliberative attention it deserved. . . . A good debater had no trouble getting a large audience in the chamber. Most of the member's time was spent on legislation. There was little else for him to do."[42]

The changes in the life of a member of Congress are obvious when we compare accounts like these with the day in the life of Representative Andrew Maguire presented earlier this chapter. The institution itself continues to change as well. As we have seen, the seniority system has been modified. Further, the committee system in the Senate was restructured in 1977, and new regulations have opened most committee meetings to the public where previously some 40 percent were held behind closed doors. Other reforms, too, are in the works, including even live television coverage of floor debates for the first time in history, and efforts to ease the administrative burdens on members, committees, and staffs. Some of these changes are intended primarily to make the lives of members less hectic. Some are intended to improve citizen access to Congress. But others being attempted are designed to increase the impact of Congress on government and policy.

☐ CONGRESS AND PUBLIC POLICY

Despite the changes recently made, many observers believe that Congress is too weak to make a major contribution to the formulation of public policy. The president proposes and the Congress disposes, they often say. Or, in the words Jimmy Carter often used during the 1976 campaign, "I have great respect for the Congress, but the Congress is not capable of leadership. Our Founding Fathers never felt the Congress would lead this country."

Some have argued that the problem is the rules and procedures – and that reforms of the sort we've mentioned, which Congress has recently made, could bring about a great improvement. Time will tell.[43]

Others argue that the basic problem is the people in Congress. A few years ago, during the late phase of Vietnam and the early phase of Watergate, Washington journalist Elizabeth Drew was led to write:

---

[42]Both quotations are from Green et al., *Who Runs Congress?* p. 196.

[43]For a variety of studies, and some speculation, see Lawrence C. Dodd and Bruce I. Oppenheimer, eds., *Congress Reconsidered* (New York: Praeger, 1977), and Ornstein, *Congress in Change.*

Congress does not do more because the people who are in it do not choose to do more. A great many members of Congress, it must be remembered, do not think that there is very much to do. Moreover, many of them are weary, and old, and only infrequently capable of energetic legislative action. This is the sort of thing would-be reformers know, but dare not say out loud; the pretense that the Congress is an institution capable of doing a great deal more is critical to getting it to do any more.

Drew was not entirely pessimistic, however. She concluded that "there are some vital, even remarkable, members of Congress whose spirit does not get beaten."[44] And in the years since she wrote this, additional spirited members have been elected and then reelected.

There is also a third position on the assessment of the policy impact of Congress. "Congress is powerful," one of its advocates, Gary Orfield, recently wrote, "and it has regularly exercised considerable power in the shaping of domestic policy." Orfield dismisses "the perception of Congress as an obstacle to progressive social policy proposed by the President." He cites the constructive and innovative role of Congress on voting rights, on federal aid to education, and on school desegregation, and its initiation of public jobs legislation.[45] Another observer argues that the Senate has played a major innovative role in such recent programs as Medicare, pension reform, the 18-year-old vote, political campaign reform, pollution control, reducing America's role in Vietnam, and minimum wage increases.[46]

"It is vital to realize," Orfield concludes,

that the making of national domestic policy takes place in a context of genuinely divided power, and that the Congress as well as the President possesses both the ability to initiate and the power to veto major policy changes. The system works well when there is a clear consensus in the country, or clear control of both branches by the dominant wing of either party. Usually these conditions are not present and the system is biased either toward compromise and incremental change, or toward confrontation and inaction.[47]

It is essential to remember that Congress is but one of three coequal branches of our government. This suggests that its record should be compared to those achieved by the president and the bureaucracy, on the one hand, and the courts on the other. But it also suggests that to get an accurate picture of the record of Congress, we must look also at the relations Congress has with these other branches – especially the president and the bureaucracy.

---

[44] Elizabeth Drew, "Members of Congress Are People," *New York Times,* January 29, 1973.

[45] Gary Orfield, *Congressional Power: Congress and Social Change* (N.Y.: Harcourt Brace Jovanovich, 1975), p. iv.

[46] S. Rich, "Congress Has Lead in Major Programs," *Washington Post,* February 1975.

[47] Orfield, *Congressional Power,* p. 325.

Dennis Brack/Black Star

President Carter's energy speech to Congress, April 20, 1977.

■ The Congress and the president

Over the years, the Congress has generally sought to convert the separation of powers into more of a sharing of powers. It has asked for more consultation in advance of treaty making abroad and policy making at home. In recent years, it has also begun inserting in bills something called the legislative veto. This provides that once an agency develops a program, it must submit the program to the Congress ("the two-house veto") or to a congressional committee ("the committee veto"), or to the entire House or Senate ("the one-house veto") for possible rejection. By 1976, Congress had built one or another type of legislative veto into thirty-seven major laws. The War Powers Act, for example (which we'll discuss in Perspective 4), has a two-house veto provision. The Trade Act of 1974 (which we'll encounter in Perspective 6) has a one-house veto. And the amendments to the National Traffic and Motor Vehicle Safety Act of 1966 (which Representative Maguire's committee was debating the day we followed him) has a committee-veto provision. Such provisions have not yet been fully tested in court for their constitutionality. It is clear, however, that they far exceed the intentions of the Founders.[48]

[48]For an account, see Robert G. Dixon, Jr., "Congress, Shared Administration, and Executive Privilege," in *Congress against the President,* ed. Harvey C. Mansfield, Sr. (New York: Praeger, 1975), pp. 125–140.

This quest for "shared administration" can be seen as a response to the growth of executive initiation of legislation. Some 80 percent of bills passed by Congress now originate, in some form, in the executive branch, which after all has primary responsibility for national concerns just as the Congress has a more regional and local focus.[49] And if most bills originate in the executive branch, *all comprehensive policies* do so, too, necessarily. Congressional committees have jurisdictions so limited and so jealously guarded that the Congress cannot coordinate military and foreign policy programs, or fiscal and monetary policy into a total economic policy, for example. Except in the area of the budget, remarks James Sundquist, a sympathetic critic, "there remains no regular institutional structure in either house to deal effectively with matters that cut across the jurisdictions of two or more committees. . . . Congress still has no way of setting an agenda, or priorities, for its own activities, no way of ensuring consistency and completeness in its consideration of the country's problems."[50]

■ Congress and the bureaucracy Relations between the Congress and the president may change when the presidency changes hands, but relations between the Congress and the bureaucracy tend to be much more stable. Contact between the two occurs formally over budgets, appointment of high-level officials, decisions about where geographically to locate projects, and occasional decisions to establish, reorganize, or abolish programs or agencies. Contact also occurs much more frequently and less formally between bureaucrats and congressional staffers who are doing casework to cope with the needs of constituents. But there are two other major contacts between Congress and the bureaucracy. The first is exercise of the formal congressional responsibility of oversight. The second is the less formal phenomenon often referred to as "subgovernments," which consist of members of Congress, bureaucrats, and lobbyists who confer to develop policy in a given area. We have dealt with this practice in Chapter 7.

Congressional oversight is extremely important because it is the only regular way for the Congress – and so the people – to get information on how well the bureaucracy is doing its job. As we saw in Chapter 7, there are many forces that operate against good bureaucratic performance. Congress has long realized this, and so when it reorganized itself in 1946 it directed each committee to "exercise continuous watchfulness of the execution by the administrative agencies concerned of any laws, the subject matter of which is within the jurisdiction of such committee."[51]

The chief instrument of congressional oversight is the investigation – research and often "hearings" in which bureaucrats testify about their past activities and future plans. Some regular oversight is performed by the General Accounting

---

[49]The figure is from Ira Katznelson and Mark Kesselman, *The Politics of Power* (New York: Harcourt Brace Jovanovich, 1975), p. 288. It refers only to public bills.

[50]James L. Sundquist, "Congress and the President: Enemies or Partners?" in *Congress Reconsidered,* ed. Dodd and Oppenheimer, p. 240.

[51]Legislative Reorganization Act of 1946.

Office (GAO), an instrument of Congress that audits expenditures and increasingly evaluates operations of agencies.[52] But Congress itself has shown little evidence of interest in expanded oversight responsibilities. Nor do most observers believe it handles its present efforts particularly well, with occasional exceptions such as Watergate.[53] "Congress fails to conduct oversight of the bureaucracy," Lawrence Dodd has argued,

> not because there are no incentives to it (there are, power and publicity for those who conduct it) nor because it fails to help reelection (being a member of a powerful oversight committee would be a sure-fire method of ensuring widespread publicity). Congress fails to conduct oversight because most members of Congress *fear* its impact on the authority of their existing committee assignments and *fear* the power that a strong oversight committee would have in Congress and in national policy making.[54]

■ Reform and renewal

Many efforts at congressional reform and renewal in recent years seem to have foundered on, or been crippled by, this same desire of individual members to protect personal power. What has been done to make Congress more democratic and open (such as less power for committees and more open meetings) has often come at the expense of efficiency. Congress now spends more time than ever in committee meetings, not just because the issues are more complex, but also partly because chairpersons are less able to run things dictatorially, and partly because so many meetings are open to the press – which encourages more vocal participation.

It is already clear that reform does not necessarily conduce to efficiency. Nor may it conduce to a more responsive Congress. Many reformers have argued for abolition, rather than just moderation, of the seniority system for selecting committee leadership. But no one has come up with an alternative principle that would not cost much more time and energy in battles for leadership – time and energy that would be diverted from the efforts to improve public policy. Others have argued for longer terms for representatives, who now have to begin worrying about reelection the moment they win a 2-year term and so have less time to ponder policy problems. But it is this very obsession with reelection that makes representatives as responsive to the public – and to public problems – as they are.

There have recently been renewed efforts to publicize, if not to control, the influence of special interests on Congress. Interest groups exist in large part to operate upon or influence indirectly the legislative process. The ways and means they use to do so will be the subject of Chapter 11. Those ways and means at the federal level have been somewhat limited by the 1946 "regulation of lobbying" act.

---

[52]See Joseph Pois, "Trends in General Accounting Office Audits," in *The New Political Economy: The Public Use of the Private Sector,* ed. Bruce L. R. Smith (London: Macmillan, 1975), pp. 245–277.

[53]The most comprehensive recent study of oversight is Morris S. Ogul, *Congress Oversees the Bureaucracy* (Pittsburgh: Univ. of Pittsburgh Press, 1976).

[54]Lawrence C. Dodd, "Congress and the Quest for Power," in *Congress Reconsidered,* ed. Dodd and Oppenheimer, p. 295.

But because that act requires the registration only of organizations and individuals whose "principal purpose" is lobbying, few have registered. Some of the corruption surrounding Watergate involved lobbyists making illegal campaign contributions or other gifts to members of Congress. That embarrassment stimulated efforts to further regulate lobbying. But little real progress has yet been made, despite the fact that between 1969 and 1977 some fifteen members of Congress were charged with violations, and twelve pleaded guilty or were convicted.[55] The major reason seems to be that, as we'll see in Chapter 11, lobbyists play very important roles in the legislative process, above and beyond such questionable activities.

□ CONGRESS AND US

Limitations on lobbying will affect not only the business and labor interest groups, but also the so-called "public-interest" groups such as those Ralph Nader has organized (which we'll discuss in Chapter 11). That's why Nader joined the stronger special interests in opposing stricter lobby-control laws. The result of these efforts – and failures – at reform is a Congress that continues to be, as we saw early in this chapter, not very representative of the people at large who are neither organized nor powerful – including, probably, most of us.

But need it be this way? Must our representatives be so unrepresentative? According to Warren Weaver:

> More and more, as Congress continues to demonstrate its incapacity to adapt a great but imperfectly realized concept to the times it must serve, the people have less and less choice. If Congress can make the arduous and humbling decision to face reality and find effectiveness, there can be great hope, stability, and even inspiration in the institution. If it cannot, there is nothing but trouble ahead, like it or not.
>
> There is less time left to avert disaster than almost anyone in Congress suspects, although there can be opportunity, money, and knowledge enough to do the job if the people recognize that today's Congress is basically inadequate and unresponsive—and demand change. Only this realization, broadly held and keenly pursued, can provoke the laggard members into reshaping an institution worthy of the Capitol and the people it was built to serve.[56]

Still, it may well be true, as Gary Orfield has argued, that "recent Congresses have rather accurately reflected the values and the confusion of the public in dealing with the major issues of social change. . . . Most of the time, we have the Congress we really want and the Congress we deserve. We send the same members back to Washington time after time. Congress is inherently neither liberal nor

---

[55] "Public Officials for Sale: Now a Crackdown," *U.S. News & World Report,* February 28, 1977, pp. 36–38.

[56] Weaver, *Both Your Houses,* pp. 292–293.

☐ ACTION UNIT 8.2 How to communicate with your members of Congress

Most members of Congress are so busy, as we've seen in this chapter, that they can't possibly read all their mail – incoming or outgoing. However, you can take certain steps to make it more likely that the member of Congress to whom you write will see your letter. If your letter asks a question that cannot be answered by a form letter, someone will have to answer your letter personally. If you are an expert on the matter your letter discusses or have otherwise written a particularly analytical letter with well-thought-out arguments, it is likely that the staff member who opens the letter will set it aside for the member of Congress to read personally. But the best way to assure that the member will read your letter is to refer to any personal contact you might have had with him or her or with his or her family, friends, or staff.

The following are some helpful hints prepared by Representative Morris K. Udall (Democrat of Arizona) for the League of Women Voters: (1) Be sure your letter is addressed properly: to Senator ______________ or Representative ______________, at the U.S. Senate or the U.S. House of Representatives, Washington, D.C. 20515 (House) or 20510 (Senate). (2) If the subject of your letter is a bill or issue, mention it in the first paragraph. (3) Write as soon as possible; don't wait until a bill has been passed. (4) Keep your letter as brief as possible. (5) Give your reasons for taking a stand. Be specific and constructive. (6) Don't make threats or berate your representatives. (7) Say "well done" when it's deserved.

You can also contact your member of Congress by phone, telegram, or personal visit.

Phone calls can be made simply by dialing (202) 224–3121, the number for both the House and Senate, and then asking for the member's office. When the receptionist answers, give your name and ask for the legislator by name. If he or she is not in or is busy, ask to speak with the "legislative assistant" who handles the subject you're concerned about. He or she talks almost every day with the legislator and helps develop his or her positions on issues, and so your views are quite likely to be noted.

Communicating by *telegram* is more expensive than by letter but also possibly more impressive. You can send a "Personal Opinion Message" of fifteen words or less to a member of Congress or the president for only $2.00; it will be delivered within 24 hours. Or you can send a Mailgram of up to 100 words, which looks like a telegram but is delivered with the next day's mail, for $2.75. Call Western Union at the number listed in your phone book for more information or to send your message.

If you can get to Washington, you may be able to *visit* your legislator personally there. Write or phone for an appointment before you go. A better bet, however, is to visit your legislator when he or she is in the district – most weekends, most holidays, and during congressional recesses. You'll find a listing in the phone book under "U.S. Government" for your legislator's local or district office. This office is always staffed by one or more assistants who will be happy to hear your views as well as to arrange appointments in the home district.

The most likely way to get to see your legislator, however, is to invite him or her to speak to a group, even one you set up just for the occasion. Most legislators are especially interested in speaking to student groups. At such a meeting, you will usually get to express your views, too. Representative Udall's guidelines for letter writing apply here also: be brief; give you arguments for taking a stand; be specific and constructive; don't make threats; and give the legislator a pat on the back if deserved. After the visit, write a letter of thanks and restate your views. If the legislator does what you urged, write again to say "well done."

Positive contacts with your legislator – whether by mail, phone, or personal visit – will make it easier for you to have access the next time an issue that concerns you arises. And if you find yourself in general agreement with your legislator, volunteering to help in the local office or in the next campaign can be an excellent way to strengthen your access and even your influence. It is also a fascinating way to learn more about politics from the inside.

conservative. Its political tendencies change with the times, with political circumstances, with the delayed responses of the seniority system, and with tides of public opinion."[57]

Those "tides of public opinion," after all, are – or at least could be – generated by waves of letters, telegrams, phone calls, and visits to members of Congress by concerned and informed citizens. As Action Unit 7.2 suggests, there *are* ways of making sure your messages and your visits have maximal impact upon your legislators. Only if you and your friends and neighbors – and many others like and unlike you – do so, are your "representatives" likely to become *your representatives.* And only if they do will it be possible for the Congress to become, as the Founders intended, the representative branch – the first branch – of our government, rather than "the sapless branch" that some critical legislators claim it is or "the broken branch" that some unhappy observers see it to be.

☐ SUGGESTIONS FOR FURTHER READING AND STUDY

If you want to know who's in Congress, or who your representative and senators are, you can consult the *Congressional Directory,* published each year by the government and available either in most libraries or from the Government Printing Office, Washington, D.C. 20402 for $6.50 in paperback. It includes biographies of all members, maps of their districts, lists of committees, their members and staffs, as well as lists of government departments, agencies, and courts. To learn more about your members' views and the politics of their districts, take a look at the *Almanac of American Politics,* edited by Michael Barone et al., and published every several years as a paperback distributed by Dutton.

You could follow what happens in Congress by subscribing to the official *Congressional Record.* But you'll understand more if you read instead the *Weekly Report* published by a private Washington research organization called Congressional Quarterly (CQ). This covers all important happenings in Congress, as well as many developments in the executive and judicial branches. Most academic libraries subscribe to the CQ *Weekly Report.* You can, too, as a student, for $36 per year, from CQ, 1414 22nd Street NW, Washington, D.C. 20037.

For accounts of how Congress works, its powers and politics, see the second edition of CQ's *Guide to Congress,* over a thousand pages of facts and analysis published in 1976. CQ also publishes a wide range of other books on Congress, including an annual *Almanac,* along with a weekly newsletter.

Several members of Congress have written interesting books using their own experience to analyze the institution and in some cases suggest reforms. These six are well worth reading: Joseph Clark, *Congress: The Sapless Branch* (New York: Harper & Row, 1964); Richard Bolling, *House Out of Order* (New York: Dutton, 1965); Paul H. Douglas, *In the Fullness of Time* (New York: Harcourt Brace Jovanovich, 1971); Donald Riegel, *O Congress* (Garden City, New York: Doubleday, 1972); Clem Miller, *Member of the House* (New York: Scribner, 1962), a collection of very thoughtful and revealing letters to constituents; and Donald G. Tacheron and Morris K. Udall, *The Job of the Congressman* (Indianapolis: Bobbs-Merrill, 1966).

Among helpful outsider accounts by academics based on interviews with members are these: C. L. Clapp, *The Congressman: His Work as He Sees It* (Washington, D.C.: Brookings Institution, 1963); Roger H. Davidson, *The Role of the Congressman* (New York: Pegasus paperback, 1969); and Donald Matthews, *U.S. Senators and Their World* (New York: Vintage paperback, 1964).

---

[57]Orfield, *Congressional Power,* pp. 9–10.

The scholarly literature on Congress by now is immense. Much of it appears in academic journals that we cannot detail here. We must limit ourselves to some of the most helpful book-length studies, organized here by general topic.

Interesting analyses of influences on voting, besides those by Kingdon and Clausen discussed in the text, include: Donald R. Matthews and Joseph A. Stimson, *Yeas & Nays: Normal Decision-Making in the U.S. House of Representatives* (New York: Wiley, 1975); Morris P. Fiorina, *Representatives and Their Constituencies* (Lexington, Mass.: Heath, 1974); and David R. Mayhew, *Congress: The Electoral Connection* (New Haven, Conn.: Yale University Press paperback, 1974).

For revealing case studies of the passage of particular bills, see: Stephen K. Bailey, *Congress Makes a Law* (New York: Columbia University Press, 1950), a study of the Employment Act of 1946; Eugene Eidenberg and Roy Morey, *An Act of Congress* (New York: Norton paperback, 1969), the Elementary and Secondary Education Act of 1965; Robert L. Peabody et al., *To Enact a Law* (New York: Praeger paperback, 1972); and Eric Redman, *The Dance of Legislation* (New York: Simon & Schuster, 1973).

Among the most helpful studies of various aspects of congressional committees are these: William Morrow, *Congressional Committees* (New York: Scribner, 1969); Richard Fenno, *The Power of the Purse: Appropriations Politics in Congress* (Boston: Little, Brown, 1966), and *Congressmen in Committees* (Boston: Little, Brown, 1973), which compares six House committees with six Senate committees; Lewis A. Froman, *The Congressional Process: Strategies, Rules & Procedures* (Boston: Little, Brown paperback 1967); George Goodwin, *The Little Legislatures* (Amherst: University of Massachusetts Press, 1970); David J. Vogler, *The Third House* (Evanston, Ill.: Northwestern University Press, 1971), on conference committees; Barbara Hinckley, *The Seniority System in Congress* (Bloomington: Indiana University Press, 1971); and a whole series of studies by the Ralph Nader Congress Project, most of which focus on particular committees, but one of which, while somewhat outrageous, is general and interesting: Mark Green et al., *Who Runs Congress?* (New York: Bantam paperback, 1972).

On party leadership, see Randall Ripley's two books, *Party Leaders in the House of Representatives* (Washington, D.C.: Brookings Institution paperback 1967), and *Power in the Senate* (New York: St. Martin's, 1969).

Books with a broader focus on Congress and its relations with other parts of government or its policy role include: Ralph K. Huitt and Robert L. Peabody, *Congress: Two Decades of Analysis* (New York: Harper & Row paperback, 1957); Robert L. Peabody and Nelson Polsby, *New Perspectives on the House of Representatives,* 2nd ed. (Chicago: Rand McNally paperback, 1969); James Sundquist, *Politics and Policy: the Eisenhower, Kennedy, and Johnson Years* (Washington, D.C.: Brookings Institution, 1968), David Price, *Who Makes the Laws* (New York: Schenkman, 1972); Nelson Polsby, *Congress and the Presidency,* 3rd ed. (Englewood Cliffs, N.J.: Prentice-Hall paperback, 1976); Randall Ripley and Grace Franklin, *Congress, The Bureaucracy, and Public Policy* (Homewood, Ill.: Dorsey paperback, 1976); Gary Orfield, *Congressional Power: Congress and Social Change* (New York: Harcourt Brace Jovanovich paperback, 1975); Leroy N. Rieselbach, *Congressional Reform in the Seventies* (Morristown, N.J.: General Learning paperback, 1977); and Morris P. Fiorina, *Congress—Keystone of the Washington Establishment* (New Haven, Conn.: Yale University Press paperback, 1977).

9

The Supreme Court and the legal system

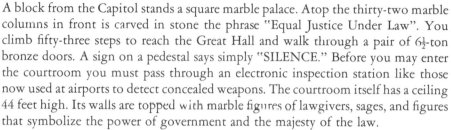

A block from the Capitol stands a square marble palace. Atop the thirty-two marble columns in front is carved in stone the phrase "Equal Justice Under Law". You climb fifty-three steps to reach the Great Hall and walk through a pair of $6\frac{1}{2}$-ton bronze doors. A sign on a pedestal says simply "SILENCE." Before you may enter the courtroom you must pass through an electronic inspection station like those now used at airports to detect concealed weapons. The courtroom itself has a ceiling 44 feet high. Its walls are topped with marble figures of lawgivers, sages, and figures that symbolize the power of government and the majesty of the law.

At the front of the courtroom is a long bench with nine high-backed, padded chairs, each of different design. As a visitor, you sit in benches like church pews facing them. The marshal raps his gavel, commands "All rise!" and pronounces the traditional cry, "Oyez! Oyez! Oyez!" ("Hear ye! Hear ye! Hear ye!"), announcing the appearance of "The honorable, the chief justice and the associate justices of the Supreme Court of the United States."

On a typical day, the nine justices in flowing black robes enter quickly and silently in groups of three through each of three dark-red-curtained doorways and take their seats at the bench. The marshal continues: "All persons having business before the honorable, the Supreme Court of the United States are admonished to draw near and give their attention, for the Court is now sitting. God save the United States and this Honorable Court." On a typical day, Mondays through Wednesdays for 9 months a year, within seconds come the words "Counsel, you may proceed whenever you are ready," and the Court begins "oral argument" sessions of an hour per case on four of the 200 or so cases it is considering that term.

Early in October, the Court begins a new year or "term." On opening day, instead of hearing oral argument by lawyers on cases, the Court announces decisions it has made over its summer recess on some 700 of the 4000–5000 petitions it gets each year asking that it consider a case. The Court is now entitled to decide which cases it will consider. We shall learn shortly how the Court makes such decisions.

October 12 was opening day of the 1971 term, and so it was not a typical day of oral argument. But that autumn day in 1971 was not typical in yet another important way. Only seven justices entered the courtroom through those curtained doorways. There were two vacancies on the court that fall. For those whose cases come before the Court, a vacancy or two can spell the difference between victory or defeat. For others, it can spell the difference between having one's case heard by the Court and having to accept the decision of a lower court as final, as we shall soon see.

☐ THE SUPREME COURT, THE CONSTITUTION, AND THE JUSTICES

The Constitution provides, in Article III, that "the judicial power of the United States, shall be vested in one supreme Court, and in such inferior courts as the Congress may from time to time ordain and establish. The judges, both of the supreme and inferior courts, shall hold their offices during good behaviour. . . ." Their terms, therefore, are for life, or until they retire, resign, or are impeached and removed for bad conduct. According to the Constitution, the president "shall nominate, and by and with the advice and consent of the Senate, shall appoint . . . judges of the supreme court. . . ."

In 1968, Earl Warren announced his retirement after serving 15 years as chief justice. Before leaving office, President Johnson nominated Associate Justice Abe Fortas to succeed Warren as chief justice. But the Senate refused its "advice and consent," and when further investigation raised questions about Fortas's financial dealings, Fortas resigned from the Court altogether. This left two vacancies for the new president, Richard Nixon, to fill: Warren's place as chief justice and Fortas's as associate justice. Those two would bring the Court once again up to its full membership of nine – the size set by Congress in a law passed in 1869.[1]

In his successful campaign for the presidency, Richard Nixon had criticized the Court for being too liberal, especially in expanding the legal rights of accused criminals. He had pledged to appoint judges who were more conservative – ideally, judges from the South, a region whose votes Nixon was courting. Nixon's first act as president was to nominate conservative Federal Appeals Court Judge Warren Burger for chief justice. The Senate concurred. He then nominated Judge Clement

[1]Originally, in 1789, Congress had provided for a chief justice and five associate justices. In 1807, it increased the size by one, in 1837 by two more, and in 1863 by one more, bringing the total to ten. In 1869 it was changed to nine, where it has stayed since despite occasional efforts to change it. The most famous of these was President Franklin D. Roosevelt's effort to expand it to fifteen in the 1930s to stop it from ruling his New Deal legislation unconstitutional. Roosevelt failed in his effort to get the Congress to change the size of the Court. But shortly after the threat was made, the Court began to find the legislation constitutional for a change – a change that it often referred to as "the switch in time that saved nine."

The chambers of the Supreme Court.
Fred Ward/Black Star

Haynesworth of South Carolina to succeed Fortas. But civil rights and labor leaders objected that Haynesworth was unsympathetic to their concerns, and at the same time conflict-of-interest charges about his financial dealings grew. Finally, the Senate voted not to confirm him as associate justice. Nixon then nominated Florida District Judge Harrold Carswell for the post. Carswell earlier in his career had publicly proclaimed himself a segregationist. That fostered opposition by the same liberal groups. But this time opposition included claims by lawyers that Carswell was not competent to serve on the Supreme Court. Finally, he, too, was defeated in the Senate, in an unprecedented show of congressional scrutiny of Supreme court nominees.[2] Nixon's next choice, Appeals Court Judge Harry A. Blackmun of Minnesota, also a conservative, was confirmed.

But just before the Court opened its new term in the fall of 1971 Justices Hugo Black, a liberal, and John Marshall Harlan, a conservative, left the court for reasons of health. So there were two vacancies still unfilled as the Court began its new term on October 12, 1971. That very day in a press conference Nixon announced that he would have two new nominations ready the following week. But in the meantime, the Court would continue its deliberations and decisions with only seven justices.

□ THE SUPREME COURT IN ACTION

Rather than enter here into an abstract discussion of the courts, law, and the legal system, we shall look at the Supreme Court in action in three major political crises of the recent past: the Vietnam War, the "Pentagon Papers," and Watergate. This will reveal what the Supreme Court is, what its justices do, and how it interacts with other institutions of the legislative, executive, and judicial branches. Then with this practical knowledge, later in the chapter we'll discuss the law, the courts, and justice in America in greater detail.

■ The Supreme Court, the Constitution, and the Vietnam War

The news from the Supreme Court on October 12, 1971, included a decision to uphold a law prohibiting federal employees from striking and another to reject a challenge to a program to encourage racial integration of unions. But buried in the announcement of its refusal to hear some 600 cases on appeal were the words: "No. 71–9T. *Orlando et al. v. Laird, Sec. of Defense, et al.* L.A. 2d Cir. Certiorari[3] denied. Mr. Justice Douglas and Mr. Justice Brennan are of the opinion that certiorari should be granted."

Orlando v. Laird By these words, the Supreme Court was in effect ruling that the Vietnam War was constitutional, even though the Constitution specifically

---

[2]The fascinating story of the Carswell battle is told in Richard Harris, *Decision* (New York: Dutton, 1971).
[3]An order to a lower court to send up the records of a case for review.

says that "the Congress shall have power . . . to declare war" (Article I, Section 8), and *Congress had never declared war on Vietnam.* How and why did the Court reach such a conclusion? To figure this out we must examine both the facts of the case and the practices of the Court.

This case, and several others like it (notably *Berk v. Laird*), involved young soldiers assigned to fight in Vietnam.[4] Salvatore Orlando, of Rockville Center, New York, had originally enlisted in the Army in 1965 and then reenlisted in 1968 as an aviation repairman and requested assignment to Vietnam. Gradually, he became disillusioned with the war. When he was assigned to Vietnam, he wrote to General William Westmoreland, commander of American forces, asking to be allowed to withdraw his original request for assignment to Vietnam. His request was refused. Orlando fought this decision in district court in New York.

His lawyers argued that he could not be sent to Vietnam because the state of New York has a civil rights law that includes the following words: "No citizen of this state can be constrained to arm himself, or to go out of this state . . . without the grant and assent of the people of this state, by their representatives in [the New York State] senate and assembly, except in the cases specially provided for by the Constitution of the United States." For Vietnam to qualify under the final phrase of this law, according to Orlando's lawyers, the Congress would have to specifically declare war.

There had been previous cases challenging the constitutionality of the Vietnam War. But the courts had refused to hear them on grounds that the war was "a political question" and so was not "justiciable" – that is, was not something that could be decided by the courts, by the judicial branch of government.[5]

The doctrine of "political questions" The courts have used the doctrine of "political questions" to refuse to rule on various cases involving international law. They have also used it to avoid ruling on the validity of ratifications of constitutional amendments – a question that threatened to reach the courts again when some state legislatures tried to rescind, or withdraw, their previous ratifications of the ERA in the late 1970s. They also refused to rule on the constitutionality of laws concerning legislative apportionment, on grounds that apportionment, too, was a "political question," until the famous *Baker v. Carr* decision in 1962. In this case the Supreme Court ruled that federal courts must consider suits alleging that malapportionment of state legislatures violates the "equal protection" clause of the Fourteenth Amendment. In 1964, in *Reynolds v. Sims,* the Court ruled that both houses of state legislatures must be apportioned on the basis of equal protection, the "one man, one vote" principle.

---

[4]For an account of this case and the *Berk* case, including transcrips of testimony and texts of lawyers' briefs to the court and judges' decisions, see Leon Friedman and Burt Neuborne, *Unquestioning Obedience to the President* (New York: Norton, 1972).

[5]The Supreme Court terms cases "nonjusticiable" if the person bringing the suit has no direct interest in it, if other remedies have not been exhausted, or if it does not have jurisdiction to handle the case. In this instance it used the term to assert that the power to make the kind of decision involved has been constitutionally delegated to one of the two "political" (as distinguished from the "judicial") branches of the government: the executive or the legislative. This made it a "political question."

Legal experts who have tried to find or develop a consistent definition of "political question" as used by the courts have failed. In the words of one, "The term 'political questions' is a magical formula which has the practical result of relieving a court of the necessity of thinking further about a particular problem. It is a device for transferring the responsibility for decision of questions to another branch of the government; and it may sometimes operate to leave a problem in mid-air so that no branch decides it."[6]

The Supreme Court's earlier refusals to rule on the constitutionality of the Vietnam War in a sense did just this. They left it up to the Congress to take responsibility. But the Congress, instead of confronting the issue directly, chose simply to continue to vote appropriations for conduct of the war. The result was that lower courts frequently interpreted these continuing appropriations as evidence of a congressional recognition of a state of war, which was, in effect, a congressional declaration of war.

Massachusetts v. Laird In the most prominent case, the Massachusetts state legislature passed a resolution in April 1970 instructing its attorney general to bring suit against U.S. Secretary of Defense Melvin Laird. It asked the Supreme Court to declare U.S. participation in the war "unconstitutional in that it was not initially authorized or subsequently ratified by congressional declaration." And, if Congress did not declare war within 90 days, it asked the Court to prohibit Defense Secretary Laird "from carrying out, issuing, or causing to be issued any further order directing any inhabitant of the Commonwealth of Massachusetts to Indochina for the purpose of participating in combat or supporting combat troops in the Vietnam war."[7]

The Supreme Court refused to hear the case. We may presume that the reason was that it was a "political question," but we cannot know because the Court does not give reasons in such cases. Sometimes, when the Supreme Court refuses to hear a case, one can still get satisfaction in a lower court. So Massachusetts then brought suit in a lower court, the federal district court. But that court dismissed the case on two grounds. First, it argued that the case was "not justiciable"–in other words, that it was a "political question" rather than a judicial one. Second, it asserted that the fact that Congress continued to appropriate funds for the war implied congressional authorization even without a declaration of war. The next higher court, the court of appeals, agreed, and the case was lost.

The same general argument was made by the lower courts in the *Orlando* case and in the comparable case of *Berk v. Laird.* The Supreme Court, as we saw earlier, on October 12, 1971, simply refused to consider the *Orlando* case and thereby ended efforts to use the courts get a ruling on the question of the constitutionality of the Vietnam War.

Why did the Court refuse to hear *Orlando?* Because the Court gave no reasons, we cannot know for sure. But experts have tried to figure out what the Court's

---

[6]John P. Frank, cited in Edmond Cahr, ed., *Sureme Court and Supreme Law* (Bloomington: Indiana University Press, 1954).

[7]*Commonwealth of Massachusetts v. Laird,* 400 U.S. 886.

reasoning must have been. "That it did not simply declare the problem to be a political question," writes Philippa Strum, "probably indicates its unwillingness to establish the rule that a President could not be stopped from involving the country in a war" by congressional refusal to go along. Strum suggests that if the Court had declared the question "nonjusticiable," presidents could expect members of Congress concerned about reelection to be unwilling to risk the accusation of having denied weapons to American soldiers. Therefore, presidents could simply commit troops unilaterally and then demand the necessary appropriations from Congress. In other words, what President Johnson did on Vietnam would become a legal precedent if the Court declared the question simply political. On the other hand, Strum argues, the Court could have followed the example of lower courts in citing congressional appropriations for the war as equivalent to a declaration of war. The fact that the Court did not do this, she writes, suggests that it wanted to preserve the constitutional requirement of a specific declaration of war, even when it was not observed, in hopes that it would be more powerful in another case. "The remaining possible decree – that the war was unconstitutional – would have resulted in a confrontation between the judiciary and the legislative which the judiciary might well have felt it could only lose."[8]

Another expert on the court, the late Alexander Bickel, concluding a strong argument that the war was in fact unconstitutional, wrote:

> . . . The Court cannot declare the war unconstitutional and then do nothing about it. That would deny its nature as a court of law, sitting to decide cases and see controversies to their resolution. And it is on its nature as such an institution of law that the Court's whole claim to authority rests. The Court cannot well forbid – as it has been asked to do – the sending of some soldiers or sailors to Vietnam, while allowing those already there to remain indefinitely. It cannot well declare the war unconstitutional and then fail to respond to a further suit asking it to direct the President's agents to stop the war. The Court, rather, would inevitably be drawn into directing and supervising the conclusion of the war, just as it has directed and supervised the desegregation of the public schools in the South, and the reapportionment of state legislatures and of the federal House of Representatives. We would thus match the wrong way of getting out of a war to the wrong way of having got into it."[9]

Enforcing Supreme Court decisions The judiciary in general, and the Supreme court in particular, operate in dangerous areas of conflict. There is conflict between levels of government: federal, state, and local. There is conflict between government action and the Constitution. And there is conflict between the branches of the federal government over the requirements of the Constitution. The Supreme Court is supposed to resolve such conflicts. But once a ruling is made resolving a conflict,

---

[8]Philippa Strum, *The Supreme Court and "Political Questions": A Study in Judicial Evasion* (University: University of Alabama Press, 1974), pp. 144, 145.

[9]Alexander M. Bickel, "The Constitution and the War," *Commentary,* July 1972, pp. 54–55.

something must be done to enforce the resolution on the parties to the conflict. The Supreme Court consists of nine justices and a staff of some 300 – including law clerks assisting the justices, policemen protecting them, and other aides from cooks to a cabinetmaker. Thus the court itself cannot possibly attempt to enforce – or even to oversee the enforcement of – its decisions. So the task of enforcement must fall primarily to the executive branch, and the task of oversight, to the lower courts. Because of this, the Court tends to be very cautious about what and how much it decides. But it still accepts and decides cases of great import regularly.

■ The Supreme Court, the Constitution, and the "Pentagon Papers"

The same Court that opened its session on October 12, 1971, by declining to hear *Orlando* and more than 600 other petitions, had closed its previous year's session just 3 months earlier with a momentous decision. The cases combined for decision were *U.S. v. New York Times Company* and *U.S. v. Washington Post Company.* But they were generally known as the "Pentagon Papers" case, and they obviously raised grave questions of freedom of the press. Further, like the Vietnam War cases we have been examining, these cases also raised questions of the democratic control of foreign policy.[10]

On Sunday morning, June 13, 1971, readers of the *New York Times* found themselves reading parts of a "top secret" government report. On the front page was an article summarizing a highly confidential, or "classified," study of the origins and conduct of the Vietnam War. The study, 3000 pages long, had been written in secret by thirty-six authors for Secretary of Defense Robert McNamara in 1967. This article in the *Times,* the first of a promised series, revealed that the United States had been actively involved in Vietnam hostilities long before the undeclared war began publicly with American air strikes on North Vietnam in February 1965. The story was full of secret information on decision making and reprinted many "top secret" documents from the study. It fascinated citizen readers. But it alarmed officials.

The next day a second article appeared. Attorney General John Mitchell telegraphed the *Times* threatening court action if the series were not stopped because it would cause "irreparable injury to the defense interests of the United States." The *Times* went ahead the next day and published a third article on the decision in April 1965 to commit American ground forces to the war. A federal district court judge in New York City then issued an order prohibiting further articles. The Justice Department announced an FBI investigation of the "leaking" of this confidential document to the *Times.* The newspaper obeyed the court order and stopped publishing.

But on Friday, the *Washington Post* began to publish other aspects of the study. When on Monday a federal district judge in Washington refused a government request to issue an order stopping the *Post* from publishing articles, the court superior to the district court, the court of appeals of the District of Columbia,

---

[10]For a brief account of the case and copies of relevant documents, see Martin Shapiro, ed., *The Pentagon Papers and the Courts* (San Francisco: Chandler, 1972).

overruled him and granted the government's request. Then the next day, the *Boston Globe* began a series on the study, and when the government went to court again, the *Globe* was immediately ordered to stop by a district court in Boston.

The Supreme Court enters the case Meanwhile, both the *Times* and the *Post* appealed the bans on their publishing such articles to the Supreme Court. On Friday, July 25, five members of the Court, a majority, voted to hear the appeal. But this did not mean that the other four justices were opposed to the position of the newspapers. On the contrary, they voted against hearing the appeal because they believed the papers should have been immediately allowed to resume publication of the study, so strong was their claim to freedom of the press. So the other four justices were voting "no" because they believed the hearing wasn't necessary. And this meant that the newspapers were virtually assured of their four votes when the case was heard in a special Saturday session. The papers needed only one more vote to win the case.

The Court then debated the matter, behind closed doors as always, for several days. Then suddenly, at midday Wednesday, June 30, it announced a special session for 2:30 that afternoon. Lawyers, journalists, and tourists flocked to the Supreme Court building for the momentous occasion. The decision, a six-to-three vote allowing the papers to resume publication, was announced by the brief statement in Figure 9.1. (The annotations explain some typical aspects of Supreme Court decisions.) But, in an unusual outpouring of commentary by the Court, each justice issued his own written opinion explaining his vote.

FIGURE 9.1

The per curiam decision in the Pentagon Papers case.

714 OCTOBER TERM, 1970

Per Curiam 403 U.S.

PER CURIAM.

We granted certiorari in these cases in which the United States seeks to enjoin the New York Times and the Washington Post from publishing the contents of a classified study entitled "History of U. S. Decision-Making Process on Viet Nam Policy." Post, pp. 942, 943.

"Any system of prior restraints of expression comes to this Court bearing a heavy presumption against its constitutional validity." *Bantam Books, Inc.* v. *Sullivan*, 372 U. S. 58, 70 (1963); see also *Near* v. *Minnesota*, 283 U. S. 697 (1931). The Government "thus carries a heavy burden of showing justification for the imposition of such a restraint." *Organization for a Better Austin* v. *Keefe*, 402 U. S. 415, 419 (1971). The District Court for the Southern District of New York in the *New York Times* case and the District Court for the District of Columbia and the Court of Appeals for the District of Columbia Circuit in the *Washington Post* case held that the Government had not met that burden. We agree.

The judgment of the Court of Appeals for the District of Columbia Circuit is therefore affirmed. The order of the Court of Appeals for the Second Circuit is reversed and the case is remanded with directions to enter a judgment affirming the judgment of the District Court for the Southern District of New York. The stays entered June 25, 1971, by the Court are vacated. The judgments shall issue forthwith.

So ordered.

Annotations:

- "Per curiam" means "for the court" in Latin; indicates that this is the decision the Court reached by voting on the case.
- Volume number of *U.S. Reports*, the official series in which all decisions and opinions are printed.
- "Certiorari" means "to be informed of" in Latin; indicates that the Court sent a message to the lower court informing it to send up the materials on the case because the Supreme Court has decided to review it "on appeal."
- Indicates that the *Post* case was combined with the *Times* case for argument. Page numbers indicate location in this volume of *U.S. Reports* on which case appears.
- Volume number of *U.S. Reports* in which cited case appears.
- The Court quotes language of opinions in previous cases that it finds relevant to this case also (precedents) and cites additional relevant cases so that readers can refer to them.
- Page number in *U.S. Reports* on which text of decision appears.
- The Court summarizes what the lower courts found and indicates that it agrees with the lower courts' decisions.
- The Court agrees with (affirms) the decision of the lower court.
- The Court disagrees with (reverses) the decision of another lower court, which had "overturned" the first decision.
- The Court sends the case back to the court with which it disagreed, instructing it on what to conclude.
- The Court announces that specific instructions will be immediately forthcoming.
- The Court ends ("vacates") the "stays" (orders prohibiting further publication of the Pentagon Papers).
- The Court announces that it is issuing the orders, thereby disposing of the case.

This case raised serious issues of freedom of the press and of the public's right to know important information about foreign policy decision making involving war. But on the other side were issues concerning the government's right to secrecy on sensitive matters of foreign relations and policy making. These considerations, or alleged constitutional rights, conflicted. The split vote of the Court revealed that conflict and may even have intensified it by giving minority recognition to the losing side.

The actual outcome was the same with the six-to-three vote as it would have been had the Court been unanimous, for all it takes to decide a case is a majority vote. The newspapers resumed publication of their articles, and soon most of the American public was well aware of the Pentagon Papers.

On major issues the Court is often split. But occasionally, on issues of the gravest national concern, the Court makes a special effort to achieve unanimity so that its decision will have special impact. One such case was the decision in 1954 known generally by its short title, *Brown v. Board of Education.*[11] This was the decision that declared that "separate but equal" schools for blacks and whites were inherently unequal and so unconstitutional. In the summer of 1974, another case arose in which unanimity, if it could be obtained, would be very valuable in reinforcing the Court's difficult role.

■ The Supreme Court, the Constitution, and Watergate

The investigation of the Watergate affair had broken wide open. The Special Senate Watergate Committee had held hearings the previous summer. It had subpoenaed certain presidential records and tapes of White House conversations. A **subpoena** action is serious because it can involve legal punishment of refusal to comply. The term itself comes from Latin words *sub* ("under") *poena* ("punishment"). In this case, the president was being asked to provide these materials, with the threat of (unspecified) punishment if he refused.

President Nixon had indeed refused to comply with the request, on grounds of "executive privilege." As we note in Chapter 6, the term "executive privilege' refers to the asserted privilege of the executive, the president, to refuse to testify before Congress, and to refuse to allow his assistants to testify, in cases in which be believes that the independence of the executive branch would be eroded or compromised. The principle is recognized as an important protection for the separation of powers between the branches.

What has *not* been recognized or accepted is *how far* executive privilege extends, and *who* decides whether a claim to it is too great. These two questions became the heart of the legal dispute that reached the Supreme Court in the summer of 1974.

---

[11]Court cases get their titles from the names of the parties to them. In this case, it was Oliver Brown, a railroad welder and part-time minister, whose daughter Linda was then a black student in a black elementary school in Topeka, Kansas, versus the Board of Education of Topeka. Each case also gets assigned to it a special reference number which guides the researcher to the decision and the texts of opinions in the official Supreme Court records published as *United States Reports.* In this case, that number is 347 U.S. 483 (1954), which tells us that the decision is printed in volume 347 beginning on page 483, and that it was decided during the 1954 term.

The question of the separation of powers After refusing to let the Senate committee have the tapes, the president then refused them to the Special Watergate Prosecutor, Harvard law professor Archibald Cox, whom he had appointed to investigate criminal wrongdoing on the matter. Defending this decision, the president, through his lawyers, argued in court that:

> In the exercise of his discretion to claim executive privilege the President is answerable to the nation but not to the courts. The courts, a co-equal but not a superior branch of government, are not free to probe the mental processes and the private confidences of the President and his advisors. To do so would be a clear violation of the constitutional separation of powers. Under that doctrine the judicial branch lacks power to compel the President to produce information that he has determined it is not in the public interest to disclose.

Special Prosecutor Cox responded that "the grand jury is seeking evidence of criminal conduct that the [president] happens to have in his custody. . . . All the Court is asked to do is hold that the president is bound by legal duties in appropriate cases just as other citizens – in this case, by the duty to supply documentary evidence of crime."

For his trouble – or his refusal to accept Nixon's claim that only the president could decide what information to release – Cox was fired. Gone with him were Attorney General Elliott Richardson, who resigned rather than fire Cox, and Deputy Attorney General William Ruckelshaus, who was fired for the same refusal. But the event, on November 2, 1973, which became known as the "Saturday Night Massacre," backfired on Nixon. It created such public outcry that Nixon was forced to release the subpoenaed tapes and appoint a new, truly independent Special Watergate Prosecutor, Houston lawyer Leon Jaworski, who carried on the investigation just as Cox had done. The tapes released included one with a crucial and mysterious 18-minute gap, which generated more suspicion of the president's own role in the Watergate affair and its "cover-up."

The Watergate grand jury Jaworski then presented evidence to a special Watergate grand jury. A grand jury is a group of citizens asked to decide whether there is enough evidence to merit a trial in a given case.[12] This grand jury on March 1, 1974, found that indeed there was. It indicted ("charged") seven of Nixon's high-ranking aides for conspiracy to defraud the United States and for "obstruction of justice." And, we later learned, it named Nixon himself secretly as an "unindicted co-conspirator." This meant that there was already enough evidence to prosecute Nixon in the minds of the grand jury members. But the fact that he was president meant, the grand jury believed, that he could not be subjected to criminal prosecution while in office, and so would have to be impeached in Congress rather than tried in court.

---

[12] A "grand jury" is distinguished from what we normally call a "jury." The latter is historically called a "petit jury," or "small jury," and is selected to hear only one case. The grand jury, which may sit for several months, evaluates the evidence to decide whether it is sufficient to hold trials in a number of cases.

The "Watergate tapes" case reaches the Supreme Court From there, Jaworski and his staff moved fast. On April 16 he asked the district court to subpoena sixty-four more tapes. Nixon then, on April 30, released edited transcripts of forty-three conversations to the House Impeachment Committee, which was then investigating Nixon on its own. But Nixon's lawyers went to court to get the tape subpoena "quashed" or nullified. And the Supreme Court agreed to hear the case, with extraordinary rapidity, on July 8.

In his "brief," or written argument, to the Court, Nixon's new lawyer, Boston attorney James D. St. Clair, argued that "At its core, this is a case that turns on the separation of powers. All other considerations are secondary, because preserving the integrity of the separation of powers is vital to the preservation of our Constitution as a living body of fundamental law. If the arguments of the Special Prosecutor were to prevail, the constitutional balance would be altered in ways that no one alive today could predict or measure."

The Court was packed at 10 A.M. on Monday, July 8, for the oral argument of this extraordinary case. For a highly unusual 3 hours, the opposing lawyers made arguments to the justices and answered questions from them.

"Now" Jaworski summarized,

> the President may be right in how he reads the Constitution, but he may also be wrong. And if he is wrong, who is there to tell him so? And if there is no one, then the President, of course, is free to pursue his course of erroneous interpretations. What then becomes of our constitutional form of government? . . . in our view, this nation's constitutional form of government is in serious jeopardy if the President, any President, is to say that the Constitution means what he says it does, and that there is no one, not even the Supreme Court, to tell him otherwise.

"The President is not above the law," concluded St. Clair. "Nor does he contend that he is. What he does contend is that as President the law can be applied to him in only one way, and that is by impeachment, not by naming him as a co-conspirator in a grand jury indictment, not by indictment or any other way."

The Watergate decision Fifteen days later, long lines began to form on those fifty-three steps at the front of the Supreme Court building. People were coming a whole day and a night early, equipped with food and even sleeping bags, to guarantee they'd get first-come-first-served places in the "public pews" the following day for the next announced session of the Court. The subject, as usual, had not been announced in advance. But everyone assumed that it would be the historic resolution of the Watergate case. Shortly after 11 A.M. on Wednesday, July 24, 1974, Chief Justice Warren Burger, Nixon's own choice for chief justice, delivered the opinion of the Court. The lengthy, careful examination of the various aspects of the case included two especially important assertions. One explained the conclusion that the subpoena must be observed, and the tapes surrendered: "We conclude that when the ground for asserting privilege as to subpoenaed materials

Thomas Carew/Monkmeyer

The Supreme Court building.

sought for use in a criminal trial is based only on the generalized interest in confidentiality it cannot prevail over the fundamental demands of due process of law in the fair administration of criminal justice. The generalized assertion of privilege must yield to the demonstrated, specific need for evidence in a pending criminal trial."

Earlier in the opinion, however, the Court answered Nixon's assertion in more general, almost philosophical terms:

> In the performance of assigned constitutional duties each branch of the Government must initially interpret the Constitution, and the interpretation of its powers by any branch is due great respect from the others. The President's counsel, as we have noted, reads the Constitution as providing an absolute privilege of confidentiality for all Presidential communications. Many decisions of this Court, however, have unequivocally reaffirmed the holding of *Marbury v. Madison* (1803), that "it is emphatically the province and duty of the judicial department to say what the law is." . . .
>
> Our system of government "requires that federal courts on occasion interpret the Constitution in a manner at variance with the construction given the document by another branch." *Powell v. McCormack.* And in *Baker v. Carr* . . . the Court stated: "Deciding whether a matter has in any measure been committed by the Constitution to another branch of government, or whether the action of that branch exceeds whatever authority has been committed, is itself a delicate exercise in constitutional interpretation, and is a responsibility of this Court as ultimate interpreter of the Constitution." Notwithstanding the deference each branch must accord the others, the

"judicial power of the United States" vested in the federal courts by Art. III sect. 1 of the Constitution can no more be shared with the Executive Branch than the Chief Executive, for example, can share with the Judiciary the veto power, or the Congress share with the Judiciary the power to override a presidential veto. Any other conclusion would be contrary to the basic concept of separation of powers and the checks and balances that flow from the scheme of a tripartite government.

The decision, as read, was unanimous.[13] Because Supreme Court deliberations are always held in utmost secrecy with none but the justices present, "Only the justices and their clerks knew how total the agreement was." Extensive research by Bob Woodward and Carl Bernstein of the *Washington Post,* who earlier had done so much to break Watergate wide open, as we shall recount in Perspective 4, pieced together parts of this story:

> On July 9, just a day after the oral arguments, the justices had unanimously decided against the President. Burger had assigned himself to draft the opinion. He shared some of the President's sentiments about executive privilege and wanted to establish a constitutional standard for the doctrine. The other justices, however, found his opinion inadequate and suggested major revisions. Burger worked hard to stitch the suggestions into a consistent whole, but he still did not produce a satisfactory opinion. . . . Finally, Justice Potter Stewart undertook to coauthor the opinion. Gradually, the other justices returned the working drafts with fewer changes. The day before the decision was to be announced, the justices accepted a final version which acknowledged a constitutional basis for executive privilege but rejected the President's particular claim as "generalized" and "undifferentiated." In careful but clear language, the Court ordered the President to turn over the tapes of sixty-four subpoenaed conversations to Judge Sirica.[14]

Those tapes revealed that Nixon's claim of executive privilege was itself a part of the very "cover-up" Nixon had denied even knowing about. The evidence was so damaging that the last vestiges of political support for Nixon evaporated, and 16 days later he became the first American president to resign.

The Courts were not solely responsible for removing Nixon from office. Far from it, as we shall see in Perspective 4. But they played an essential role. And that role was *the* role that the courts *are* to serve in the realm of Constitutional law: that of interpreting and applying the law. In the case of *United States v. Nixon* (418 U.S. 683, 94 S. Ct. 3090, 1974) – or, as it might in effect have been called, *The Nation v. Its Leader* – the Nation was the ultimate victor, but the American legal system was, in a sense, the immediate victor. To understand *this* significance of the case, we must know more about both the law and our legal system.

---

[13]The vote was only eight to zero. One justice, William Rehnquist, did not participate in the case because he had worked under John Mitchell in the Department of Justice during the Nixon Administration.

[14]Bob Woodward and Carl Bernstein, *The Final Days* (New York: Simon & Schuster, 1976), p. 262.

□ WHERE THE COURTS GET THE LAW TO INTERPRET

The courts, it is always said, interpret the law. But where do they find the law they interpret? The major source – or at least the most basic source – is the Constitution, which is the highest law of the land. But the Constitution is a very brief document. Its 7500 words couldn't possibly cover adequately most of the cases that come before the courts. The people who wrote it only intended it to provide general guidelines for government. The specific rules were to come primarily from four other sources: statutory law, common law, equity, and administrative law.

■ Constitutional law

The Supreme Court is primarily concerned with **constitutional law**. The cases we've just looked at reveal that this term refers to much more than just the words in the Constitution. The "opinions" we have quoted from above deal with terms such as "executive privilege" that do not appear anywhere in the Constitution. And the Court's deliberations make constant reference to previous decisions and the language used in those opinions. All of this is included in what we mean by constitutional law. It is law invoking the interpretation and application of the Constitution. It is concerned primarily with describing the extent and limits of governmental power and the rights of individuals.

■ Statutory law

Most court cases are not concerned with constitutional law. Rather, they involve what we call **statutory law** – law made by statutes, or, in other words, legislation. Such statutory law covers a wide range of subjects, because governments make laws on a wide range of topics. At the federal level, it is law made by Congress. At the state level, it is law made by state legislatures. At the local level, it is law made by county governing bodies, city councils, and other such groups.

■ Common law

But even though it often seems that there are laws concerning virtually everything, in fact much of the time judges are still applying what we call **common law**. Common law is customary law or precedent – the ways things have traditionally been done. It is based on the totality of decisions made by judges in past cases decided in past years. In fact, common law can be traced back to twelfth-century England, where judges began to travel around the country deciding cases in terms of local customs – the practices of the common people. These decisions were generally intended to repair damages once they were done, rather than to prevent damages from occurring. When the English came to America, they brought their common law with them. When America gained its independence, it kept its common law heritage, so that there was law to be applied on all sorts of subjects even before there was a Congress to begin passing statutes.

Stare decisis The fundamental principle of common law is the continuity of precedent, or previous court decisions. This principle is reflected in the maxim *stare decisis,* a Latin term meaning "let the decision stand." But of course each region has its own unique experience, its own history of judges' decisions, and so the common law differs from state to state. (The exception is Louisiana, which, because of its French heritage, has a legal system based on a "civil code" of statutory law instead.) Thus in the United States we have forty-nine somewhat different state common law systems.

■ Equity

There is another component of our legal system: **equity**. Equity, in everyday usage another term for fairness, provides guidance to judges where the common law does not apply. Common law, as we said above, usually applies after the fact, to correct matters once damage is done. So equity law was developed to allow judges to order that something not be done, in order to prevent damage, or to order that something be done, in order to avert damage. Equity is applied where waiting until the law is broken would make it too late.

■ Administrative law

So far we have been examining forms of law developed by legislation and judicial decisions. We have not yet mentioned the fastest-growing type of law: **administrative law**. We noted in Chapter 7 that bureaucratic agencies have developed their own ways of making regulations that are as binding on us as if they were laws passed by Congress. Indeed, in an indirect sense they are laws passed by Congress, because Congress often grants such agencies the power to issue binding regulations, as we saw when we examined the Environmental Protection Agency and the Council on Environmental Quality. Congress also allows or instructs these agencies to establish their own internal court systems to review compliance with their regulations and to hear complaints about them. If a citizen or a business is unhappy with an administrative ruling, he, she, or it has the right to appeal the decision to the regular federal court system, where the courts will generally compare the ruling with the terms of the original statute establishing the agency.[15]

These, then, are the major types of law that are likely to affect us as citizens.[16] Some of these laws are **criminal laws**. They define crimes against the public order, and have "criminal penalties" prescribed for their violation. Others are **civil laws**, in that they apply to relations between individuals, involving such things as contracts.

□ WHAT THE LAW IS

But what makes all these things law? Philosophers have been debating this question for thousands of years, offering abstract definitions of law. Dictionaries tend to do the same. Generally, they define law as "a uniform system of rules to

---

[15]See Martin Shapiro, *The Supreme Court and Administrative Agencies* (N.Y.: Free Press, 1968).

[16]We have not considered several others. *Admiralty and maritime law* is federal law concerning shipping on rivers and on the high seas. *International law* is the law of custom, treaty, and agreement among nation-states.

govern or prescribe certain behavior for everyone living within a given area or legal jurisdiction."[17] But an abstract definition like this doesn't help us much in understanding what law really is. For that, we need to put some historical flesh on these eternal bones.

Any society, to be and remain a society, requires predictable, common behavior by its members. In "traditional" societies – those we often call "primitive" or "underdeveloped" because they have not been transformed by industrialization – this "social control" is generally maintained by custom. People grow up living as their parents did, expectations don't change much, and so behavior is quite consistent. If someone deviates, it doesn't take a judge to see this and "convict" the deviant. Everyone recognizes it. "Punishment" for deviance often takes the form of more intense efforts to integrate the deviant into the society, rather than exiling or imprisoning him or her. We sometimes refer to these accepted rules of conduct as **customary law**, but they don't look much like what we usually think of as law, especially because they aren't written down.

Customary law works well as long as society is stable, and as long as outside influences such as colonization or even trade are limited. But in a world of rapid social change, with growing commerce and industry, social stability tends to break down. As it does, customary law becomes less effective. However, no society can long survive without law. It is impossible, in a complex and changing world, to depend on actual police power for social control. There are never enough police around to observe and channel every person's every action. It is essential for society to move toward "voluntary compliance." But in order to comply voluntarily, you must know the rules and believe them somehow deserving of your acceptance. There must, in other words, be law.

We might think of law as "paper power," replacing the "gun power" and "police power" that keep whatever order there is where law does not exist or has broken down. But we shouldn't be fooled into thinking that "paper power" is weaker than "gun power" or "police power." Quite the contrary. We refer to this type of social control as "paper power" because it is based on law printed on paper just as money is printed on paper. In the cases of both law and money, mere pieces of paper affect people's behavior because people believe that the paper *means* something in the society. The society stands behind the paper as being law and as being money. The people accept the society, and so they accept the printed paper as real money and real law. In other words, the existence of "paper power" is an indication of the strength and stability of the society, whereas reliance on "gun power" is a sign of weakness.

This law and the legal system that develops and interprets it operate in a context of change.[18] The legal system must therefore develop ways of maintaining the law while changing it, so that people will continue to accept it. Every society

---

[17]For philosophical discussions of the nature of law, see M. P. Golding, ed., *The Nature of Law* (New York: Random House, 1966). And for a particularly stimulating study, see H. L. A. Hart, *The Concept of Law* (New York: Oxford University Press, 1961).

[18]For a fascinating account of American law up to 1900, see Lawrence M. Friedman, *A History of American Law* (New York: Simon & Schuster, 1973).

thus faces a dual problem: first, to maintain law and order; and second, to remain flexible enough to alter that law and order in the face of new challenges to the society. The legal dimension of the problem has two aspects. The first is to find ways to change the law enough so that people will continue to accept it as fair, appropriate, binding, or legitimate in changing circumstances. But the second is to avoid changing it so much that people begin to see the law as nothing more than the momentary whims of the people, or of the ruling power, in which case they may lose respect for the law as an institution. Laws that change too quickly may threaten the legal system every bit as much as laws that do not change quickly enough.

One reason for this is the fact that even when the old bases for customary law and equity have disappeared, beliefs still linger in the minds of the people perpetuating aspects of the old legal principles as to what is right and wrong, good and bad, natural or evil. Today, for example, "gay (homosexual) rights" activists and proabortion groups are vehemently opposed by many who continue to believe these activists are violating "the laws of God" or "the laws of nature," even where "the laws of man" as our legislatures have passed them and our courts interpreted them no longer say they are. And these opponents attack the law that deviates from these traditional standards and attempt to restore it to its previous condition.

There is another way in which rapid change in the law may threaten the legal system. As society becomes more complex, the law becomes more complex and more extensive. It thus becomes *harder* for citizens – and even for enforcement officials and lawyers – *to know what the law actually is* on a given subject. If you don't know what the law is, you may well have trouble obeying it, of course. But your responsibility to do so remains just the same. And so you and I and the other 220 million Americans determine the state of law and order and justice in America.

□ LAW, DISORDER, AND JUSTICE IN AMERICA

■ Law and order and us

If you were born in a large American city, the odds are almost one in fifty that you will be murdered some day. If you were born in a city like Detroit or Cleveland or Atlanta, those odds may be more like one in twenty. If you're a male, the odds of being murdered at some point during your life are even greater, and if you're black they're greater still.[19] A murder is committed somewhere in America every 26 minutes, day and night, on the average. There is a violent crime (murder, forcible rape, robbery, or assault with intent to kill) every 31 seconds. Forcible rape occurs once every 9 minutes, robbery once every 68 seconds, and auto theft once every 32 seconds.[20]

But you don't have to be out on the streets to experience violence or even to

[19]These figures, calculated for babies born in the early 1970s, and so slightly less for those born earlier, come from research by a team at Massachusetts Institute of Technology headed by Arnold Barnett. See Alan L. Otten, "The Shortening Odds on Murder," *Skeptic,* special issue no. 4 (December 1974), p. 10.

[20]Federal Bureau of Investigation, *Crime in the U.S. – Uniform Crime Reports, 1975* (Washington, D.C.: Government Printing Office, 1975), p. 9.

be murdered. Two places we all frequent are even more dangerous than the streets: the home and the school.

A quarter of all murders occur within the family – half of these, husband or wife killings. Estimates are that over half of all married women suffer physical abuse at the hands – or weapons – of their husbands. That means 28 million wives. And in many states, the wife still has no legal recourse in such cases other than filing a criminal complaint against her husband. Only 2 percent of the men who beat up their female living partners are ever prosecuted. Sex crimes are also commonly committed in the home and rarely prosecuted in the courts. In most states, a man cannot be charged with rape of a woman if she is his wife, no matter what the circumstances.

Even more stunning, estimates are that there are 7 or 8 million cases of children physically abused by their parents every year. And some experts believe that as many as a million of these are cases of *incest* – sexual relations between a parent and child. Indeed, some claim that one in every four women in America has been involved in incest or otherwise sexually molested. There are, of course, no exact figures, because few such acts are reported to police or other authorities. But there is growing agreement among experts that figures such as these express the scale of family violence today.[21]

School, too, seems just as bad. A congressional subcommittee investigating violence in the public schools in the 1970s found that about 10,000 rapes occur every year in schools – many of them rapes of female teachers. In addition, "More children were killed in the schools, often in gun fights with other pupils, between 1970 and 1973, than soldiers in combat in Vietnam."[22]

The highest proportion of arrests for murder, forcible rape, robbery, and aggravated assault in recent years has been of 18-year-olds. For burglary and auto theft, 16-year-olds have the highest arrest percentage. Most of them are males: 90 percent of those arrested for violent crimes and 80 percent of those for property crimes. Female crime is increasing but seems unlikely ever to equal male crime.

Serious crime has been steadily on the increase in America since 1960, jumping from 3.4 million offenses in that year to 11.3 million in 1976 – a rise of 232 percent. This meant that by 1975 your odds of being a victim of a serious crime in a given year were better than one in twenty, rather than the one in fifty of 1960. This steady growth in crime produced support for harsher anticrime measures and for "law and order" political campaigns.

■ Law and order and white-collar America

"Today it is comparatively safe to break the law," proclaimed Richard Nixon in his victorious 1968 presidential campaign. "Today all across the land guilty men walk free from hundreds of

[21]See, for example, Edward Schumacher, "Home Called More Violent than Street," *Washington Post,* February 25, 1976; "Family Violence," *Parade,* October 23, 1977; Gay Pauley, "Of Cries, Whispers, and Incest," *Philadelphia Bulletin,* October 3, 1977; Elsa Goss, "Wife Abuse Is a National Problem," *Philadelphia Inquirer,* September 18, 1977.

[22]Harriet Van Horne, "The Plague of Our Day: Youth Violence," *New York Post,* October 14, 1977.

"Warrington Trently, this court has found you guilty of price-fixing, bribing a government official, and conspiring to act in restraint of trade. I sentence you to six months in jail, suspended. You will now step forward for the ceremonial tapping of the wrist."

courtrooms. Something has gone terribly wrong in America." Nixon's remark took on a certain ironic cast 5 years later, when his own selection as vice-president, Spiro Agnew, famous for his own "law and order" rhetoric, walked free from a federal courtroom after pleading no defense against serious corruption charges. Only a year later, Nixon himself was revealed by his own "White House tapes" to be guilty of covering up criminal deeds by his closest aides – which is itself a crime – and had to resign in disgrace. But Nixon was saved even having to enter a courtroom by a presidential pardon from his hand-picked successor, Gerald Ford. Many Nixon aides, however, including his Attorney General John Mitchell and his assistants Bob Haldeman and John Ehrlichman, did go to prison – if only briefly – for their own lawbreaking. But a number of others, including Attorney General Richard Kleindienst, who in effect lied under oath to a congressional committee, and many business leaders who admitted giving funds illegally to the Nixon campaign, "walked free from courtrooms" with only a rebuke or a small fine.

Watergate crimes and political corruption such as this are classed as "white-collar crime" – or "crime in the suites," instead of "crime in the streets" and the homes and the schools that we have been surveying. White-collar crime, too, has been on the rise. More than 11,000 cases a year of bank embezzlement and consumer-related fraud are now recorded by the government, for example. And at least 1000 federal, state, and local officials were convicted on federal corruption charges in the years from 1970 to 1975.[23]

But few of these white-collar criminals went to jail for their corruption. Few white-collar criminals ever do, even though their crimes are estimated to cost the nation between $40 billion a year (the Chamber of Commerce estimate) and $200 billion a year (the late Senator Philip Hart's estimate). Included in the Chamber figure are: $21.7 billion in robbery, shoplifting, employee theft, arson, and so on; $7 billion in bribery, "kickbacks," and "payoffs"; $6 billion in fraud; and $5 billion in the cost of anticrime measures taken to try to prevent these losses. Hart's estimate includes the fraud, extortion, bribery, and theft that rob the government and so the taxpayers, of many millions more. Whatever the accurate figure, it is clearly far higher than the cost of "blue-collar" or "T-shirt" crime.[24]

---

[23]Marianne Means, "A Basic Right to Know," *Austin American-Statesman,* August 19, 1976.

[24]See "A $40 Billion Crime Wave Swamps American Business," *U.S. News & World Report,* February 21, 1977, pp. 47–48; and "How People Cheat Uncle Sam Out of Billions," *U.S. News & World Report,* July 11, 1977, pp. 16–19.

■ Law enforcement in America

Nonetheless, the jails and prisons are full – a quarter of a million people in 1975, with the number rising at about a 10 percent per year clip. And although only 23 percent of our population is between the ages of 17 and 29, over half of the prison population is that age.

There is ample evidence that the jails would be even fuller were our law enforcement system more efficient. It is not much a matter of lenient judges, as Nixon, Agnew, and others have argued, although it is true that many offenses are committed by repeaters. Instead, the major enforcement problem is the fact that most crimes are never even solved.

In one study of criminal behavior by adults, people were asked which of forty-nine offenses other than traffic violations they had committed without being caught. Ninety-nine percent of the people admitted they had committed one or more offenses for which they might have received jail or prison sentences had they been caught. Among the males, 26 percent admitted auto theft, 17 percent burglary, and 13 percent grand larceny. Some 64 percent of the males and 29 percent of the females admitted to committing at least one felony for which they had not been caught.[25]

The fact is that only about half of all serious crimes (murder, forcible rape, robbery, aggravated assault, burglary, larceny over $50, and auto theft) are ever even reported to the police by the victims. Of all serious crimes reported, in only 19 percent of the cases is a suspect ever arrested, although the figure can go as high as 78 percent for murder. Only about half of all suspects arrested are ever convicted. And only about a quarter of those convicted actually ever "do time" for their crime.

The odds are, then, that you, like most Americans, have done something criminal but were most likely not even apprehended, let alone jailed. Yet you probably do not think of yourself as a criminal. One reason for this may be that you were not apprehended. Another may be that you do not believe that what you did was really criminal, even though it was against the law – whether it was taking drugs, dodging the draft during the Vietnam War, gambling, taking a payoff in a business venture, or cheating on your income tax. If you fall into this category, you have lots of company, and you probably know it. And this very fact tends effectively to change the definition of crime in our society.

■ The social construction of crime and the criminal

The concept of crime is socially constructed in our – or any – society. So is the role of criminal. Many Americans do not believe that Richard Nixon is a criminal. This view can be defended. He was, after all, never convicted of a crime in a court of law – and in our system, everyone is presumed innocent until proved guilty. True, he was pardoned by President Ford – but only for any offenses he might have committed, not for something he had actually done. Many Americans also believe that the things Nixon did were not really criminal acts. One rationale for this view is the belief that everyone in

[25]Reported in *The Challenge of Crime in a Free Society: A Report by the President's Commission on Law Enforcement and Administration of Justice* (Washington, D.C.: Government Printing Office, 1968).

positions of power acts in a similar manner, and this legitimizes the actions, whatever the law may say formally. Another view is that Nixon didn't intend to break the law, and so it should not be held against him.

Whatever the specific views and arguments, these facts about public opinion on Nixon and his deeds are important because they remind us that law is socially created and socially sustained. When influential figures declare the innocence of a president, they are especially powerful in shaping legal reality, whatever the written law may say.

As sociologist Richard Quinney has written:

> The reality of crime that is constructed for all of us by those in a position of power is the reality we tend to accept as our own. By doing so, we grant those in power the authority to carry out the actions that best promote their interests. This is the *politics of reality.* The social reality of crime in politically organized society is constructed as a political act. Both private and governmental groups have a vested interest in constructing particular criminal conceptions that instruct official policy.[26]

■ The social objective of the system Underlying this "politics of crime" is the deeper political question of what our basic social objective is. For some, the basic objective is *order.* They tend to define crime broadly, with emphasis on protecting property.

For others, the primary objective is *justice.* For thousands of years, philosophers have debated the meaning of "justice," and they continue to debate today.[27] The preamble to our Constitution asserts that our government is created to "establish justice"—but it nowhere says what "justice" is. Most of us have a general sense that the concept as a goal refers to some sort of fairness or equality of treatment, as is implied by the words "Equal Justice Under Law" inscribed over the entrance to the Supreme Court. But beyond that it is hard to find much agreement. Still, we can say that in general those who emphasize justice as the objective of society tend to favor protection of life over protection of property.[28]

Still others would emphasize as the prime objective of the social order the *legitimacy of the system.* For them, what is important is public acceptance of the existing order and its institutions as being worthy or correct.[29] So obedience to the law tends to become more important to them than exactly what the law is. If the law is generally obeyed, the system will tend to appear legitimate. It will thus be more likely to survive, and so will its rulers, who tend to be the strongest supporters of this concept.

---

[26]Richard Quinney, *The Social Reality of Crime* (Boston: Little, Brown, 1970), pp. 303–304. See also his subsequent book, *Critique of Law and Order* (Boston: Little, Brown, 1975).

[27]See, for example, the essays in Carl J. Friedrich and John W. Chapman, eds., *Justice,* which is vol. 6 of *Nomos* (New York: Atherton, 1963). And see Otto A. Bird, *The Idea of Justice* (New York: Praeger, 1967).

[28]For a prominent discussion of concepts of justice and rcommendation of a concept of "justice as fairness," see John Rawls, *A Theory of Justice* (Cambridge, Mass.: Harvard University Press, 1971).

[29]See the discussion of legitimacy in Perspective 1.

■ Concepts of punishment and their problems

Along with differing concepts of social objectives go differing concepts of proper punishment. In general, those seeking order think of punishment in terms of *deterrence.* Those emphasizing justice usually see punishment as *treatment* of the criminal to restore him or her to a proper social role. Those emphasizing legitimation of the system as the goal tend to think in terms of *retribution,* to pay back an offender and thereby demonstrate to all that the law was both right and effective.

The biggest blow to the seekers of legitimacy is governmental crime – something, as we've noted, that we've had plenty of in recent years. For when the government itself or one of its officials breaks the law, it tends to call its legitimacy into question in the minds of citizens.[30] And because the offending officials are rarely punished severely, the public's sense of satisfaction with the justice system is threatened.

The biggest problem to seekers of order through deterrence is what experts call "recidivism" – the tendency of offenders to become repeaters. By doing so, they demonstrate the failure of the deterrence model of punishment. We might expect that anyone knowing that only 1.5 percent of all committers of crimes ever do time would be unlikely to be deterred by our justice system. It appears that even those who are caught and punished often become repeaters. FBI statistics report that 67 percent of those who serve time or are pardoned for a serious offense are arrested again for a serious offense within 3 years. And of those paroled (released early under the supervision of a law officer), 64 percent are again arrested within 3 years.[31]

---

[30]See Jethro Lieberman, *How the Government Breaks the Law* (Baltimore: Penguin, 1973), for an appalling survey. And for a more recent study of abuses by intelligence agencies, see David Wise, *The American Police State* (New York: Random House, 1976).

[31]*Crime in the U.S. – Uniform Crime Reports.* For an account of another study, which found a recidivism rate of only 23 percent in the 1970s (versus 33 percent in the 1960s), see Selwyn Rabb, "U.S. Study Finds Recidivism Rate of Convicts Lower Than Expected," *New York Times,* November 7, 1976.

Late-nineteenth-century photograph of city court tent in Guthrie City, Oklahoma.

Western History Collections, University of Oklahoma Library

Experience thus suggests that punishment neither deters, as advocates of order as a social objective would hope, nor rehabilitates, as seekers after justice would hope. A prison term is rare even for serious offenders, and the average criminal in prison spends only 17 months behind bars before being released.[32] Furthermore, many convicted offenders are released early or are never even sentenced to prison because our prisons are grossly overcrowded. And white-collar criminals, if they go to prison at all, which is rare, go usually to "gentlemen's prison farms" that are unlikely to deter or rehabilitate – or to offer the retribution that might increase public confidence in the legitimacy of our "justice" system.

Soft treatment seems common also when occasionally a kingpin of organized crime is convicted of tax evasion or racketeering. Such crimes usually draw sentences of no more than 2 years – sentences that are often suspended. Yet these are people who preside over an empire that plays a major role in corrupting public officials and nets perhaps $25 billion in illegal, untaxed profits each year on gambling, drugs, prostitution, pornography, and loansharking.[33]

■ Proposals and prospects

These paragraphs but skim the surface of the problems of our justice system today. Some of the problems will probably decline with the birthrate, for most violent crimes are committed by the young, and the country's teenage population started to shrink in 1977. If we make progress controlling the drug problem, that too will cut crime, because much burglary is committed to finance drug habits.[34] Further, if times are good economically, the crime rate should drop, for much crime is committed by people without jobs or economic prospects.

If judges do indeed deal more harshly with criminals, that may postpone their return to the streets at the least. If we have *more* judges, as Chief Justice Warren Burger and others have sought, so we can have faster trials, that too may help. So would any ways of making punishment more certain.

Some argue that more severe sentences, including even widespread use of the death penalty, will increase the deterrence of crime. Most research evidence does *not* confirm this argument. In the words of several experts, "those studies which do attempt to separate the effects of severity and certainty . . . indicate that certainty rather than severity of legal sanctions is the primary deterrent factor."[35]

But all these measures still leave untouched the problem of reforming our prisons so that they rehabilitate prisoners. Ninety-five percent of those in prison will

---

[32]This figure is from the National Council on Crime and Delinquency. See Patrick Oster, "U.S. Criminal Justice is Story of Attrition," *Chicago Sun-Times,* April 24, 1977.

[33]Jack Anderson, "The Shadow of the Mafia over Our Government," *Parade,* August 7, 1977. For a recent survey of this problem with recommendations, see *Organized Crime,* the Report of the Task Force on Organized Crime to the National Advisory Committee on Criminal Justice Standards and Goals (Washington, D.C.: Government Printing Office, 1976).

[34]Jackson Toby, "A Prospect of Less Crime in the 1980's," *New York Times,* October 26, 1977.

[35]Richard Salem and William Bowers, "Severity of Formal Sanctions as a Deterrent to Deviant Behavior," *Law and Society Review* 5 (August 1970): 21. The most comprehensive study of the alleged deterrent effect of capital punishment has concluded that there is none. See Hans Zeisel, "The Deterrent Effect of the Death Penalty: Facts v. Faiths," in *Supreme Court Review 1976,* ed. Philip B. Kurland (Chicago: University of Chicago Press, 1977), pp. 317–343.

sooner or later be released back into society. Today they are rarely well prepared for that return. As one group of critics has pointed out:

> While we cannot predict those who will be dangerous to society, we can predict some of the responses by those who are subjected to the brutalizing environment of prisons. Resentment, rage and hostility on the part of both keeper and kept, are the punitive dividends society reaps as a result of caging. . . . the punishment of prison damages persons, and consequently, creates *more* danger to society. . . . The negative effects of caging reach beyond prison walls, allowing citizens a false sense of safety. Prisons, by their very existence, exonerate communities from the responsibilities of providing the necessary human services which might effectively reduce 'crime.'[36]

So some argue for more prisons, some for better prisons, some for no prisons at all. Some argue for more judges, some for harsher judges. Some argue for retribution, others for rehabilitation, and others for restitution (by which a convict repays his or her victim for the damage done, rather than just "doing time"). Experts disagree as widely as ordinary citizens on the question of how to improve what everyone recognizes as an inadequate and dangerous system.

But, as Jerome Skolnick, a Berkeley professor of criminology, reminds us:

> There are no easy prescriptions for crime in America. It has become an intrinsic part of life in this country as a result of fundamental contradictions of American society. We maintain an egalitarian ideology amidst a history of slavery and contemporary unemployment. We say we are against organized crime, but millions of us enjoy and consume its goods and services—drugs, gambling, prostitution, pornography. We demand heavier punishment—longer prison terms—yet fail to appreciate the social and economic costs of prisons. We support the Constitution and its protection of individual liberties—yet criticize judges who insist the police conduct themselves in accord with [it].[37]

☐ THE COURTS WE HAVE

Constitutional protection—of the accused, of the police themselves, and of us as ordinary citizens—comes to us, if at all, through our courts. We normally think of the Supreme Court as our chief protector, followed by the "lower" federal courts. But of the 10 million court cases annually, less than 2 percent are in federal courts.

---

[36]Fay Honey Knopp et al., *Instead of Prisons: A Handbook for Abolitionists* (Syracuse, N.Y.: Prison Research Education Project, 1976), p. 41. For a less drastic view, see American Friends Service Committee, *Struggle for Justice: A Report on Crime and Punishment in America* (New York: Hill & Wang, 1971).

[37]Jerome H. Skolnick, "The Frustrations of Having No Easy Solutions for the Complicated Problems of Crime in America," *Washington Post*, September 15, 1977.

The rest are in state and local courts. The reason for this is that the Constitution reserves general police powers to the states. This means that such crimes as murder, robbery, assault, and rape are normally state offenses, rather than federal crimes. The Congress determines what "federal offenses" are by passing bills outlawing certain things. The list of federal offenses now includes:

- offenses against the U.S. government or its property
- offenses against U.S. government employees while they are on duty
- offenses by U.S. government employees while they are on duty
- offenses that involve crossing state lines (and so would involve two different state legal systems)
- offenses that involve interference with interstate commerce
- offenses occurring in federal territories or reservations
- offenses occurring on the high seas

Cases that concern constitutional questions such as freedom of speech or assembly are also tried by federal courts.

■ The federal courts

Federal cases originate in federal district courts (see Figure 9.2). There were nine-four such districts in 1977: one or more for each state, and one each for the District of Columbia, Puerto Rico, the Virgin Islands, the Canal Zone, and Guam. Each district has a group of federal Judges, the number related to the number of cases it generally gets. There are some 400 district judges in all.

A party that loses a case in a district court may attempt to appeal that decision to a higher court. There are eleven such U.S. courts of appeals, each of which is

FIGURE 9.2

The court system of the United States.

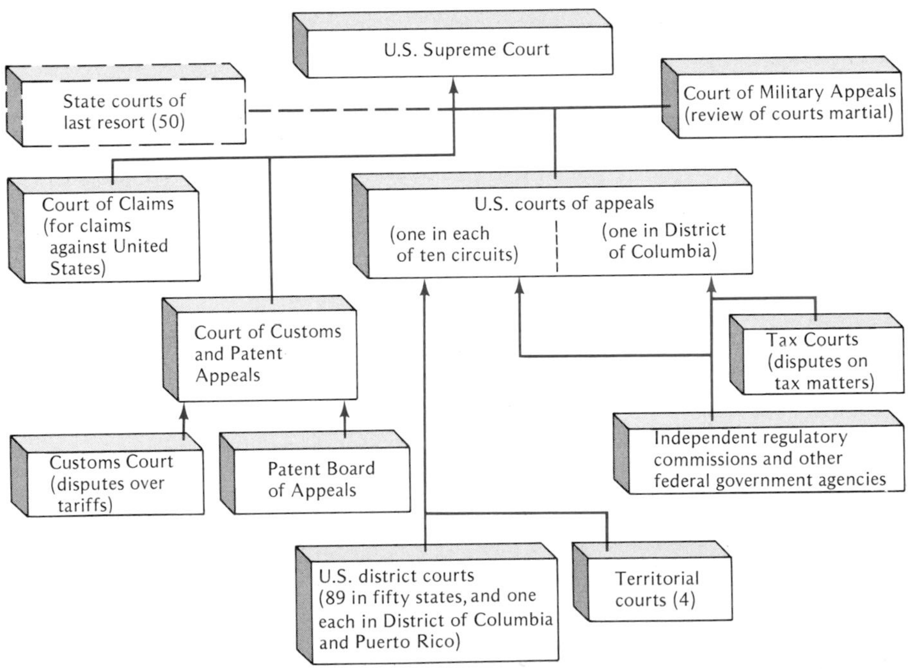

called a "circuit." The appeals courts hear perhaps 5000 cases a year. A loser in an appeals court may then ask the Supreme Court to hear the case and many do so. These appeals from lower courts are the bulk of the 5000 cases submitted to the Supreme Court each year. Appeals are supposed to be made in cases that involve questions of law and constitutionality, rather than simply to examine new evidence. If an appellate court agrees to hear a case on appeal, it issues a **writ of certiorari**, which is an order to the lower court to send up the records of the case for review. By the unwritten "rule of four" observed for some 50 years now by the Supreme Court, any four Supreme Court justices can agree to "grant cert," as it is called, and the Court will then review the case, either hearing oral argument on it or deciding it without oral argument.

There are, in general, four types of cases which may finally reach the Supreme Court on appeal:

- A case involving a private individual or a corporation and a government agency disputing the meaning of a federal law being applied by the agency to the private party.
- Two private parties disputing the meaning of a federal law and a federal agency's enforcement of it.
- A federal *or state* criminal prosecution in which the defendant being prosecuted claims that the law being enforced violates the U.S. Constitution, or that the way he or she was arrested, investigated, tried, or sentenced was a violation of his or her federal constitutional rights.
- A suit asking the court to order a public official either to stop doing something prohibited by the Constitution (called an **injunction**) or to do something required by the Constitution. However, the only individual with "standing to sue" (that is, with a position entitling him or her to go to court) in these instances is one who can show that he or she has been personally harmed by the administration of the law in question. One generally shows this by violating the law and being punished for the violation.

The Supreme Court also gets some cases on "original jurisdiction"—as the first and only court to hear them. These are cases involving disputes between two states, and disputes between a state and the federal government. Figure 9.3 indicates the routes cases may take to the Supreme Court.

■ The state and local courts

The individual state court systems vary greatly. Their general structure is relatively common, however. At the bottom are local "courts of limited jurisdiction" such as justices of the peace, police courts, traffic courts, family courts, small claims courts, juvenile courts, and so on. These courts handle minor cases. Next come the general trial courts, which handle major offenses against state laws. These courts have various names in various states: district, circuit, "common pleas," or superior courts. Some states then have an intermediate or appellate court to hear appeals based on points of law after the facts have been determined and the case first tried and decided by the lower court. At the top in all states comes the state court of last

FIGURE 9.3

How cases get to the Supreme Court.

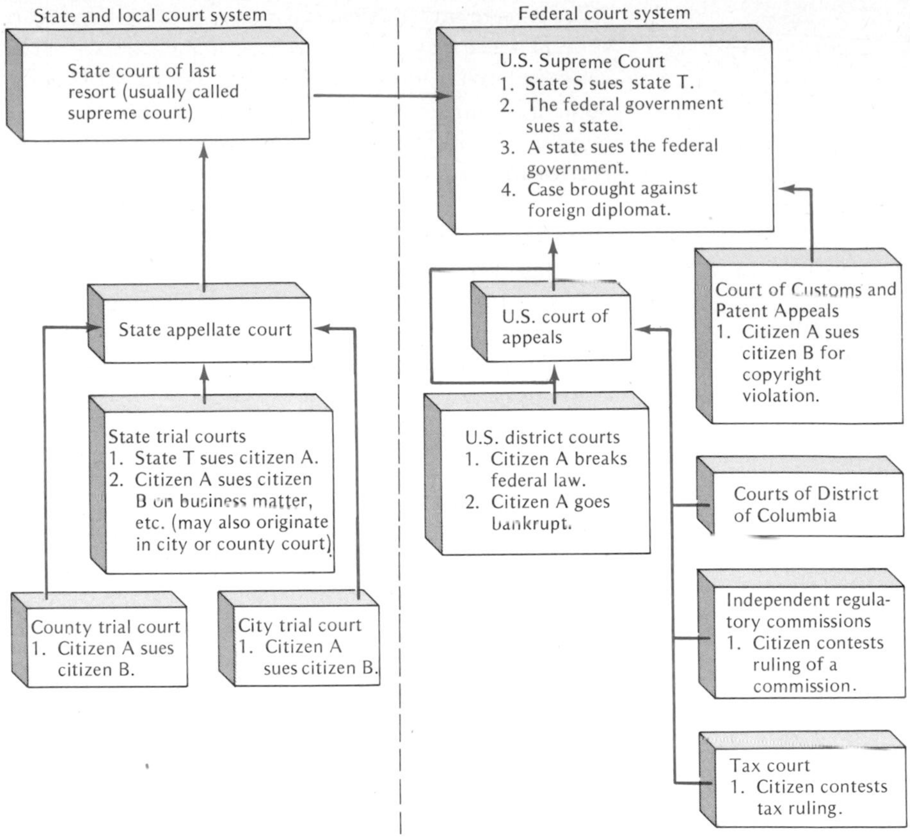

Note: Case descriptions within boxes indicate original jurisdiction (the power to accept a case directly rather than on appeal from a lower court); colored arrows indicate appellate route.

resort, usually called the supreme court, which is the final interpreter of the state constitution and laws and hears appeals of decisions from lower courts. Cases can go from the state court of last resort to the U.S. Supreme Court if a federal question is involved and if the Supreme Court agrees to review the case.

□ WHO ARE OUR COURTS?

■ Supreme Court justices

Throughout the entire 190-year history of the Supreme Court, only 101 men have served as justices. Because tenure is for life or until retirement, or, in rare cases, resignation, justices generally serve long times. Because all federal judges selected are lawyers by profession, justices are inevitably an elite group. But they are much less representative of the population than lawyers as a whole are. Through 1977, all 101 justices have been men, and all but one (Thurgood Marshall) have been white. Indeed, about 90 percent have been of British ethnic origin, and over 85 percent have been Protestant. In recent times it has been customary to have a Catholic and a Jew on the Court. But President Nixon declined to refill "the Jewish seat" with a Jew, and so that token variety disappeared. The result is that the "typical" justice has been a white, male, Protestant, Anglo-Saxon, from an upper-class or an upper-middle-class urban family, with a law degree and a career including previous public service and often political activity as well.[38]

■ Other federal judges—and senatorial courtesy

Federal judges in lower courts have generally been slightly less atypical of the population—although they are still usually WASP males—and *much* less distinguished. The primary reason for this is the custom called senatorial courtesy. According to this practice, the president is expected to consult with the senators from the state to which a district judge is to be appointed. If a senator and the president are of the same political party, the senator is allowed to have an absolute veto over the choice. The result, not surprisingly, is a tendency to appoint political friends of senators, appointees who may have better political than legal qualifications.

Legal qualifications of possible and actual nominees are usually assessed by a special Committee on the Federal Judiciary of the American Bar Association (the major professional association of lawyers in America). Some critics believe the ABA's standards of adequacy are too lax. But they have at least made it more difficult for a president to appoint political hacks who are officially rated incompetent by the lawyers who would be practicing law before them.[39]

---

[38]For details on "judicial recruitment," as the selection of justices is called, see John R. Schmidhauser, *The Supreme Court: Its Politics, Personalities, and Procedures* (New York: Holt, Rinehart & Winston, 1960), and Henry J. Abraham, *Justices and Presidents* (New York: Oxford University Press, 1974).

[39]See Harold W. Chase, *Federal Judges: The Appointing Process* (Minneapolis: University of Minnesota Press, 1972), and Joel B. Grossman, *Lawyers and Judges: The ABA and the Politics of Judicial Selection* (New York: Wiley, 1965).

The justices of the Supreme Court: in the front row (*left to right*) are Associate Justices Byron White and William Brennan, Chief Justice Warren Burger, and Associate Justices Potter Stewart and Thurgood Marshall; in the back row (*left to right*) are Associate Justices William Rehnquist, Harry Blackmun, Lewis Powell, and John Paul Stevens.

Wide World Photos

□ THE LIFE OF A SUPREME COURT JUSTICE

Once selected and confirmed by the Senate, the life of a judge is one of prestige but rarely one of leisure. Lower court judges are, by common observation, seriously overworked. Supreme Court justices now work in "the great marble palace," as it is often called, are paid $72,000 a year, and have assistants to help with everything from looking up the laws to keeping in good physical shape. But they too are extremely busy, considering some 4000 cases a year. The facilities haven't always been so comfortable, but then until recently the Court was not so busy. The Court began life in 1789 in a commercial building in New York City, eventually moved to the Old City Hall in Philadelphia, and finally spent 75 years in spare rooms of the U.S. Senate. Only in 1935 did it move to its present palatial quarters.

Each justice has his "chambers" – four private offices, for himself, his three or four law clerks (recent graduates of top law schools), and two secretaries – clustered near the courtroom. Justices are very secretive about their activities, but we have recently learned something of what their working lives are like. They generally spend 4 hours each of 3 days every two weeks (a total of 24 hours a month) hearing oral argument on a total of twenty-four cases per month in Court. They have secret conferences on Wednesday afternoon and all day Friday of the weeks they hear oral argument. At these meetings they vote, debate, and decide who will write opinions. Some of the justices occasionally eat lunch together in their private dining room. But "for the most part," as Justice Lewis F. Powell, Jr., told an American Bar Association convention in 1976, "perhaps 90 percent of the time, we function as nine small, independent law firms," meeting as a group only for the oral argument sessions and the conferences. The justices, he reported, communicate with each other mostly in writing. "Indeed, a Justice may go through an entire term without being once in the chambers of all the other eight members of the court." The Court, he concluded, is not at all the collegial body he expected to find it, despite the homogeneity of background of its members. Rather, it is "one of the last citadels of jealously preserved individualism."[40]

□ WHAT JUDGES AND COURTS DO

■ Judicial powers

Such an account of the way Supreme Court judges work says little about what roles they play in our legal system or about what functions the legal system has in our society. The brief passage on the judicial power in the Constitution says only that "the judicial power shall extend to all cases, in law and equity, arising under this Constitution, the laws of the United States, and Treaties made, or which shall

---

[40]John P. MacKenzie, "Powell Calls Court Criticism 'Alarmist,'" *Washington Post,* August 12, 1976, p. A28. See also two articles by Richard L. Williams: "Supreme Court of the United States: The Staff That Keeps It Operating" and "Justices Run 'Nine Little Law Firms' at Supreme Court," *Smithsonian,* January and February 1977. And on Court decision making, see Nina Totenberg, "Conflict at the Court," *Washingtonian,* February 1974.

be made, under their authority. . . ." This language tells us which cases the federal courts can handle. But it says nothing of how "the judicial power" will conduct itself.

Judicial decision Our system is called an "adversary" system of justice because in most cases each party to a dispute is represented by a lawyer who argues that side as strongly as he or she can. The judge and/or jury then decides which party has the better case given the existing law and decides the case in favor of that party.[41]

Judicial "lawmaking" The judge is supposed to be a neutral observer applying the law to the case. But in fact, inevitably, he or she has to interpret the law – figure out what it really means or what it really implies about the particular case. And this role of interpretation – of applying general laws to specific cases – inevitably requires that judges *make law.* The laws and the Constitution are full of general terms such as "reasonable care," "due process," "adequate notice," and "unreasonable search and seizure." In deciding what these terms mean, judges are extending them to cover cases that they did not previously cover – perhaps because the situations did not exist when the words were first written. This is what is meant by the term "judge-made law."

The role of the Supreme Court here is special because it is the highest court in the land. In the famous words of the late Justice Robert H. Jackson, "We are not final because we are infallible, but we are infallible only because we are final."[42] The Supreme Court, as the "court of last resort," can overrule a decision by a lower court. But the only thing that can overrule a Supreme Court decision is another Supreme Court decision. In the words of Justice Byron R. White, "This Court has overruled itself more than 150 times since 1789: Justices will change their minds, and new Justices do come along; they renew the Court."[43]

Judicial review and the case of *Marbury v. Madison* Not surprisingly, justices are more apt to overrule others than they are to overrule themselves. When judges examine behavior they will sometimes find that the behavior conflicts with the stipulations of the Constitution. In the case of *U.S. v. Nixon,* for example, the president's claim to executive privilege was found inconsistent with the constitutional provision of separation of powers. Similarly, in the Pentagon Papers case, the government's efforts to suppress the publication of news articles was found inconsistent with the right to press freedom. Particular actions such as these are from time to time found unconstitutional.

More significant, perhaps, but less common are the instances in which the judges interpreting a law conclude that the law itself conflicts with the terms of the

---

[41]Other systems work quite differently. In much of Europe, for example, the judge acts as the inquiring lawyer as well as the decider. And in China courts may in a sense decide that both parties are somewhat right and hand down two decisions, one for each party, so that there need not be a winner and a loser as in our system.

[42]Quoted in Jethro Lieberman, *Milestones* (New York: Oxford University Press, 1976), p. 67.

[43]Quoted in Williams, "Justices Run 'Nine Little Law Firms' at Supreme Court," p. 90.

Constitution, which is "the highest law of the land." In its 190-year history, the Supreme Court has declared just over 100 federal laws – or parts thereof – unconstitutional. The Court also declares state and local legislation unconstitutional. This happens more frequently, in large part because there are 50 different states, 3000 counties, and 35,000 cities passing laws that may conflict with the federal Constitution. No one has counted the number of such cases.

The Constitution does not explicitly give the Supreme Court the power to decide that a law or an act is unconstitutional. That power was "read into" the Constitution by the Court when it decided the landmark case of *Marbury v. Madison* in 1803. The case arose because Federalist President John Adams appointed some political friends to be judges on the day before he left office after being defeated by Thomas Jefferson in 1800. One of them, William Marbury, was given a 5-year appointment as a justice of the peace for Washington, D.C. But Adams' secretary of state, John Marshall, forgot to deliver to Marbury the certificate (or "commission," as it was called) declaring him a judge. When Jefferson took office the next day, his secretary of state, James Madison, refused to deliver the commission to Marbury. Congress had stated in the Judiciary Act of 1789 that one could ask the Supreme Court directly for a writ of mandamus (Latin for "we command"). Such a writ orders a government official or court to perform duties required of it by law. Marbury therefore asked the Supreme Court for a writ requiring Madison to give him his commission so he could serve as a justice of the peace.

John Marshall, who had forgotten to deliver the commission to Marbury, had by then taken up his appointment as Chief Justice. He and the rest of the Court agreed that Marbury had a legal right to his commission. But it refused to issue the writ of mandamus. It ruled instead that it had no power to do so because the Constitution says that the Court only has "original jurisdiction" (the power to accept a case directly rather than on appeal from a lower court) in cases involving ambassadors and cases in which a state is a party. The Judiciary Act of 1789 was thus, it said, an unconstitutional attempt to enlarge the power of the Court. The Court defended this decision with the statement that "The particular phraseology of the Constitution of the United States confirms and strengthens the principle, supposed to be essential to all written constitutions, that a law repugnant to the constitution is void, and that courts, as well as other departments, are bound by that instrument."[44]

This was the first time the Court declared a law unconstitutional – and the last time it did so for another 50 years. Judicial review, as it came to be called, remained a controversial doctrine. Jefferson and many others continued to argue that all three branches of government were coequal, and so each had to be the final judge of the constitutionality of its own acts. If differences arose, they argued, those disputes should be resolved through the political process – by such clearly

---

[44]For an account of this interesting case, including its political context, which we cannot summarize here, see Donald O. Dewey, *Marshall versus Jefferson: The Political Background of Marbury v. Madison* (New York: Knopf, 1970), or Charles Warren, *The Supreme Court in U.S. History,* vol. 2 (Boston: Little, Brown, 1926), pp. 169–316.

constitutional devices as impeachment or elections. This was basically the same argument that President Nixon and his lawyers made 170 years later concerning the Watergate tapes, as we saw earlier in this chapter. But others have pointed to various statements made during the drafting of the Constitution and again during the debates over its ratification by the states in which the power of judicial review was ascribed to the judicial branch.[45]

"The doctrine of judicial review," as it has come to be called, has survived the objections of Jefferson and Nixon and many in between. It remains the basis for an important part of the power of the courts. This power to "review" the actions of individuals and agencies or the laws of Congress, of states, or of localities may be exercised by a judge or a court at any level of the federal system. But it is most effective when done by the Supreme Court, from whose decision there is no further legal appeal.

Still, the Court, with good reason, employs the power with great restraint. For as James Bradley Thayer remarked, in a book on John Marshall written at the turn of the century, the exercise of the power of judicial review, "even when unavoidable, is always attended with a serious evil, namely that the correction of legislative mistakes comes from the outside, and the people thus lose the political experience, and the moral education and stimulus, that comes from fighting the question out in the ordinary way, and correcting their own errors."[46]

Judicial opinions All it takes to get a Supreme Court *decision* is a majority of the justices voting the same way on the question of whether to "affirm" (sustain) or to "reverse" (overturn) a decision by a lower court. But voting is not all the justices do. And often in the longer run the actual vote proves to be less important than the "opinions" the judges write to explain their reasoning in voting as they do.

If a case is clear to the justices or if it seems relatively insignificant as they decide it, there may be no opinions, only a vote. If the Court's decision is unanimous, there may be but one opinion—as in *U.S. v. Nixon.* In a case of considerable difference, such as that of the Pentagon Papers, there may even be nine different opinions. When opinions are written, there is a majority opinion expressing the views of the majority of the Court and usually one or more dissenting opinions by those voting the other way. In addition, if someone voting with the majority disagrees on the *grounds* for the decision or on the *route* to the conclusion, he may write a concurring opinion instead of signing the majority opinion

Writing these opinions—some 150 in a typical year term—is hard work. Writing them so that a number of independent-minded justices can agree on them and will sign them is particularly demanding. So why do they do it so often? The majority opinion is the primary means by which the Court makes and communicates policy.

---

[45]See, for example, Raoul Berger, *Congress v. the Supreme Court* (Cambridge, Mass.: Harvard University Press, 1969), pp. 8–285.

[46]James Bradley Thayer, *John Marshall* (Boston: Houghton Mifflin, 1901), p. 106.

To whom? There are various audiences. The first, obviously, is *the two parties to the case.* The opinion explains and justifies the decision to them. Second is *the lower courts* in which the case orginated, and whose decision the Court has either affirmed or reversed. The opinion further instructs these lower courts as to how the Supreme Court viewed the case and why it decided as it did.

But the opinion is also directed to *other citizens, administrators, and lawyers with similar cases, and to other lower courts.* To all of these, it offers guidelines on how to interpret the law so as to avoid having a case end up in the Supreme Court, or to know when to appeal it to the Court.

In addition, the opinion may be directed at *other citizens, public officials, lawyers, and even Congress.* Sometimes it invites submission of further cases, as when it says, "Nothing in this opinion should be taken to apply to a case in which. . . ." Other times it may suggest legislation by saying, "In the absence of action by the Congress, we. . . ."

Opinions are also sometimes directed to lower-level *officials whose behavior the Court wishes to change.* The most common instance of this are decisions on criminal procedure designed to change the behavior of police. The Court in the years under Chief Justice Earl Warren (1953–1969) issued a number of decisions reversing traditional police behavior. For example, *Mapp v. Ohio* held that evidence improperly seized (for example, without a search warrant) could not be admitted at state trials. And *Miranda v. Arizona* held that no confession would be admissible unless the person arrested had been informed of his or her rights before he or she confessed and had been warned that whatever he or she said could be used against him or her.

But how does the message from the Court, expressed in the majority opinion, get to the police officer? Certainly no officers read Court opinions as a matter of course. In large police forces, special instruction is often given by superiors. But for most officers, television and newspapers – which rarely give literal quotations from opinions – tend to be the major sources. Clearly, much improvement in communication is needed here.[47]

There is another major audience for Supreme Court opinions that should not be overlooked: *the Court and its justices* themselves. Many assertions in dissenting opinions are pointed directly at assertions by fellow justices. "I disagree with Brother So-and-so on . . ." they may say. But it often goes deeper or further than that. Justice Felix Frankfurter once wrote to Justice Frank Murphy about a dissenting opinion: "This is a protest opinion – a protest at the Bar of the future – but also an effort to make the brethren realize what is at stake. Moreover, a powerful dissent . . . is bound to have an effect on the lower courts as well as on the officers of the law. . . . And so in order to impress our own brethren, the lower courts, and enforcement officers, it seems to me vital to make the dissent an impressive document."[48]

---

[47]See Stephen L. Wasby, *Small Town Police and the Supreme Court: Hearing the Word* (Lexington, Mass.: Lexington Books, 1976), especially chaps. 2, 8.

[48]Quoted in Daniel M. Berman, *It Is So Ordered: The Supreme Court Rules on School Segregation* (New York: Norton, 1966), pp. 60–61.

And Charles Evans Hughes (who had been a justice from 1910 to 1916, and was later chief justice from 1930 to 1941) in 1928 commented that "a dissent in a court of last resort is an appeal to the brooding spirit of the law, to the intelligence of a future day when a later decision may possibly correct the error into which that dissenting judge believes the court to have been betrayed."[49]

■ Principles of judicial restraint

Such situations of dissenting opinions arise relatively rarely, for several important reasons. The first stage in judicial behavior is the decision of whether even to take up a case, and, as we have seen, the Court in most cases decides not to decide at all. But once a case is chosen as being important enough to merit the sustained attention of a very busy Court, there are other guiding principles which tend to restrain the Court and its justices.

Archibald Cox, whom we met earlier as Special Watergate Prosecutor, once wrote of the principles of restraint that seemed to guide the Court under the leadership of Chief Justice Warren:

> First, the courts should avoid constitutional issues wherever possible. Such issues should be decided only when raised in ordinary litigation by one who could show that his own constitutional rights were violated and who could not prevail without a constitutional decision.
>
> Second, the courts should not invalidate laws unless they were inconsistent with some specific constitutional prohibition.
>
> Third, wherever there was room for rational difference of opinion upon a question of fact or upon the relative importance of different facts or conflicting interest . . . the doctrines of federalism and separation of powers would require the Court to uphold the legislation.[50]

□ THE WARREN COURT AND THE BURGER COURT

The Supreme Court, then, tends always to be conservative in intervening. Still, there are differences from one period to another. The Warren Court was known as an "activist" court. Chief Justice Earl Warren was appointed by President Eisenhower and presided for some 16 years. He regarded the Court's legislative reapportionment decisions (which we discussed earlier), effectively opening the political process to many more people, as the most important decisions of his tenure. But he also singled out decisions on public school integration and on the right of an accused to have a lawyer as being important.[51] These two areas represent the major controversial emphases of the Warren Court. Warren and the "liberal" majority on the court in most of those years were, in the words of Archibald Cox,

---

[49]Quoted in Henry J. Abraham, *The Judicial Process,* 2nd ed. (New York: Oxford University Press, 1968), p. 182.

[50]Archibald Cox, *The Warren Court* (Cambridge, Mass.: Harvard University Press, 1968), pp. 3–4.

[51]See Congressional Quarterly, *CQ Almanac 1968* (Washington, D.C.: Congressional Quarterly, 1968), p. 539.

"influenced by an extremely self-conscious sense of judicial responsibility for minorities, for the oppressed, for the open and egalitarian operation of the political system, and for a variety of 'rights' not adequately represented in the political process."[52] As a result, they made decisions and issued opinions that greatly expanded civil rights and civil liberties.

One set of decisions extended civil rights of blacks by outlawing segregation in public schools (*Brown v. Board of Education,* 1954, followed by numerous other cases), racial gerrymandering (*Gomillion v. Lightfoot,* 1960), poll taxes (*Harper v. Virginia,* 1966), and laws prohibiting racially "mixed" marriages (*Loving v. Virginia,* 1967).

Another set of decisions increased the civil liberties of the accused in state and local criminal proceedings under the Fourth Amendment (against illegal searches and seizures – *Mapp v. Ohio,* 1961); the Fifth Amendment (against self-incrimination – *Malloy v. Hogan,* 1964); the Sixth Amendment (the right to counsel – *Gideon v. Wainright,* 1963 – to speedy trial, and to trial by jury, among others); and the Eighth Amendment (the prohibition against cruel and unusual punishment – *Robinson v. California,* 1962).

Some of these new or strengthened limitations on government power have since been redefined or limited by what has come to be called the Burger Court. In the years since Burger replaced Warren in 1969, he and other Nixon and Ford appointees have changed the Court's political complexion. The Warren Court was increasingly criticized for being too protective of the rights of alleged criminals at the expense of the rights of the victims. It was also criticized for being too sensitive to the needs of the poor and powerless. Perhaps in reaction to these criticisms, recent decisions of the Burger Court have made it more difficult for the

[52]Archibald Cox, *The Role of the Supreme Court in American Government* (New York: Oxford University Press, 1976), p. 36. For other views of the Warren Court, see Philip Kurland, *Politics, the Constitution, and the Warren Court* (Chicago: University of Chicago Press, 1970), and Alexander Bickel, *The Supreme Court and the Idea of Progress* (New York: Harper & Row, 1970), among a great many other books.

Retiring Chief Justice Earl Warren (*left*) and incoming Chief Justice Warren E. Burger pose with President Richard M. Nixon following the formal swearing in of Burger on June 23, 1969.
Wide World Photos

underprivileged to get relief in Court. The actions of the Burger Court have inspired every bit as much controversy as those of the Warren Court, although on different grounds by different people. Laughlin McDonald, an official of the American Civil Liberties Union, an organization established to defend civil liberties, concludes that "Burger Court decisions have fallen most cruelly upon those least able to protect themselves."[53] He and other civil libertarian critics point to a variety of decisions to support this view. In one, the Burger Court denied Social Security benefits to children who are termed "illegitimate" because they are born of parents who are not legally married – children who would have received the benefits automatically had they been "legitimate." In another, the court refused to allow poor people in Kentucky to sue over the curtailment of services to indigents by local hospitals. The Court also, in another case, in effect told city employees that when they are fired and the reasons given for the firing are false, they cannot seek help in the federal courts because the Constitution doesn't protect against such "mistakes."

Still, we should recognize that the record of the Burger Court is mixed on such questions. Further, it is still being shaped by sitting justices. The court did at first rule state death penalty laws to be "cruel and unusual punishment" that deprived the accused of "due process of law" (*Furman v. Georgia,* 1972). But then, in 1976, it recognized as constitutional new death penalty laws that had been passed by Georgia, Florida, and Texas.

There have been other decisions by the Burger Court modifying or even in effect reversing some of the civil liberties decisions of the Warren Court. Some decisions gave cities greater leeway to declare certain printed materials obscene. Others allowed police more latitude while interrogating suspects than the *Miranda* case suggested was proper. And one milestone 1976 term case declared that Congress could not set minimum wages and maximum hours for state and local public employees, thus overruling a 1968 Warren Court decision.

The Burger Court has in general been more supportive of the legal position of women, however. We discussed its abortion ruling, *Roe v. Wade,* in Perspective 1. But, important as this was, it is just a part of the broad expansion of constitutional protection for women, much of it relating to employment. In recent years, the Burger Court has rejected the traditional argument that sex discrimination is tolerable as long as it is "reasonable." Instead, the Burger Court has held that distinctions based on gender can be constitutional only if they establish "important" government objectives and if they further those objectives in "substantial," not merely "reasonable," ways. In addition, the Burger Court has ruled that laws that grant women special compensatory treatment for past economic discrimination are constitutional. But it has also ruled that a woman on pregnancy leave is not eligible for temporary disability or sick-pay benefits – a ruling opposed by women's groups. Many of the women's rights decisions of the Court are applauded by most of those who in general lament the passage of Court leadership

---

[53]Laughlin McDonald, "Has the Supreme Court Abandoned the Constitution?" *Saturday Review,* May 28, 1977 p. 14.

Reprinted by permission

from Warren to Burger. But even these popular decisions sometimes serve to highlight the change. As McDonald remarks, "Other minorities – those that do not cut across racial, social, and economic lines – remain locked in a continuing, often bitter legal struggle for rightful treatment. Their marginal position in American society is underscored by the quick successes of the women's movement and demonstrates their abiding need for the constitutional protection increasingly being denied them by the Burger Court."[54]

Those more sympathetic with Burger's views would note, with attorney Nathan Lewin, that "since he believes that the courts are overworked, he is unwilling to expand their jurisdiction into new areas or to enlarge, beyond what is absolutely necessary, the number of groups that may demand the aid of a court."[55]

□ HOW JUDGES DECIDE

This disagreement reminds us that the courts are organizations like other segments of government. As such, they have responsibilities and capabilities that change somewhat with their personnel. Because Court deliberations are always secret, it is virtually impossible to know how such changes come about. Similarly, it is very difficult to generalize about how individual justices make up their minds.

Many years ago, a decade before he was appointed to the Supreme Court, Appeals Court Judge Benjamin Cardozo gave what is probably still as good a characterization of judicial decision making as we have:

[54]Ibid., p. 14.

[55]Nathan Lewin, "A Peculiar Sense of Justice," *Saturday Review,* May 28, 1977, p. 16.

My analysis of the judicial process comes then to this, and little more: logic, and history, and custom, and utility, and the accepted standards of right conduct, are the forces which singly or in combination shape the progress of the law. Which of these forces shall dominate in any case must depend largely upon the comparative importance or value of the social interest that will thereby be promoted or impaired. . . . If you ask how [the judge] is to know when one interest outweighs another, I can only answer that he must get his knowledge just as the legislator gets it; from experience and study and reflection; in brief, from life itself."[56]

From the perspective of a Supreme Court watcher rather than that of a jurist, Mary Walker warns that "It is difficult, and perhaps dangerous, to generalize about the Supreme Court," but offers this "tentative comment":

> Judicial decision-making is an inexact art. Although they are the beneficiaries of a certain mystique, the Supreme Court judges do not arrive at conclusions by engaging in transcendental meditation or listening for ethereal voices. Their verdicts are the product of hard work and imperfect—though generally superior—human intelligence. The judges' opinions are obviously and inevitably influenced by their past experiences and ideas. . . . Their opinions are usually the result of sincere effort tempered by inevitable biases. Thus, within its own sphere and style, the Court is a discretionary policy-making body. Inasmuch as Court decisions influence public policy, they become a part of public policy.[57]

□ THE SUPREME COURT AS A POLITICAL INSTITUTION

The Court *is* a political institution, one of the three branches of the federal government and, with the presidency, the bureaucracy, and the Congress, one of the four major decision makers. When the court refuses to rule on a question such as the constitutionality of the Vietnam War on grounds that it is a "political question" that should be left to the "political branches," it is even then making a political decision.

The notion that the executive and the legislative are the "political branches," Philippa Strum has written,

> is an interesting one, primarily because it reflects a desire on the part of both rulers and ruled to ignore the actual function of the judiciary under a system of separation of powers and judicial review. The interpretative power of the

[56]Benjamin N. Cardozo, *The Nature of the Judicial Process* (New Haven, Conn.: Yale University Press, 1921), pp. 112–113.

[57]Mary M. Walker, *The Evolution of the United States Supreme Court* (Morristown, N.J.: General Learning Press, 1974), pp. 61–62.

courts serves as a methodology by which a supposedly neutral third force can arbitrate between the government and its citizens when a difference of purpose or of understanding arises between them. . . . Popular belief in an independent judiciary enables the courts to place a final stamp of legitimacy upon all governmental acts, including those which might otherwise come under direct attack in the form of disobedience.[58]

In other words, the Supreme Court is also *more* than a political institution on a par with the other two branches. It is, perhaps, in the words of the late Alexander Bickel, "the least dangerous branch,"[59] for it has no enforcement powers of its own and a stronger respect for tradition and hence a greater tendency toward conserving existing arrangements and practices as political tradition. But the power of the Court should not be understated – least of all when it has that very tradition and almost 200 years of recognition behind it.

That tradition serves to legitimate not only the Court's decisions but also the actions by the other federal branches and by the states that the Court chooses *not* to challenge.[60] The existence – and the activism – of the Court helps preserve respect for law and for government. But, in Strum's words, it also "absolves the citizen from what might otherwise be the uncomfortable necessity of participating in an unending re-examination of political actions and assumptions."[61]

But if the Court goes too far in adapting the law and the institutions, it runs the grave risk of sacrificing its own legitimacy in the minds of the people. In the same way, it may also, as Archibald Cox has warned, encourage "excessive reliance upon courts instead of self-government through democratic processes," which "may deaden a people's sense of moral and political responsibility for their own future, especially in matters of liberty, and may stunt the growth of political capacity that results from the exercise of the ultimate power of decision."[62]

Thus far, this double fear seems unwarranted. The Court is held in higher esteem than its partner branches, largely, it appears, because of its greater activism. At the same time, our legal system, including the Supreme Court, leaves much to the people and to the more obviously "political" branches.

Oftentimes the courts are too slow; other times their decisions are too unresponsive; and still other times the interests concerned are too strong. In such instances, citizens, interest groups, and other elements in the political society actively attempt to influence decisions in one or even all three branches of government. In Part 4 we shall examine such influences, beginning with two issues so great that they could not be contained by the politicians: Vietnam and Watergate.

---

[58]Strum, *The Supreme Court and "Political Questions,"* p. 2.

[59]Alexander Bickel, *The Least Dangerous Branch* (Indianapolis: Bobbs-Merrill, 1962).

[60]This argument is made by Philip Kurland. See his book *Politics, the Constitution, and the Warren Court,* for example.

[61]Strum, *The Supreme Court and "Political Questions,"* p. 3.

[62]Cox, *The Role of the Supreme Court in American Government,* p. 103.

☐ SUGGESTIONS FOR FURTHER READING AND STUDY

There is no substitute for seeing the Supreme Court in action. If you have a chance to get to Washington, try to attend a Court session, morning or afternoon, Monday through Wednesday, October through June. Arrive an hour before the beginning, and once at the Court building, join the line for those wishing to see the entire session rather than that allowing a mere 5-minute tourist visit. To find out what is being discussed, look in the morning's *Washington Post* for a schedule, or call the Clerk of Court at 393–1640. You can also visit other federal and state courts nearer your home or school, as well as local courts.

There are various ways to follow the Supreme Court from afar. All Court decisions and opinions are published in volumes of *U.S. Reports,* published by the government, and in two more elaborate, annotated versions published privately: *United States Supreme Court Reports, Lawyers' Edition,* and *Supreme Court Reporter.* Any academic library will have *U.S. Reports,* and probably the preliminary pamphlets containing decisions and opinions that are produced between volumes. Some will also have one of the more elaborate weekly services, *United States Law Week* and *U.S. Supreme Court Bulletin.*

For more general and comprehensive summaries, see the annual reviews prepared by Paul C. Bartholomew and published in the December issues of the *Western Political Quarterly* and, since 1974, in the *Journal of Public Law.* Bartholomew also regularly updates his *Summaries of Leading Cases on the Constitution* (Totowa, N.J.: Littlefield, Adams paperback, usually every second year).

There are by now many "casebooks" that reprint important cases for use by political scientists. Among them are Martin Shapiro and Rocco J. Tresolini, eds., *American Constitutional Law,* 4th ed. (New York: Macmillan, 1975); and Alpheus T. Mason and William B. Beaney, eds., *American Constitutional Law,* 6th ed. (Englewood Cliffs, N.J.: Prentice-Hall, 1978).

For accounts of individual cases in great detail, which offer a more comprehensive understanding of how the courts work, see Richard Kluger, *Simple Justice* (New York: Vintage paperback, 1976), on *Brown v. Board;* Alan F. Westin, *Anatomy of a Constitutional Law Case* (New York: Macmillan paperback, 1956), on the "steel seizure case" more formally known as *Youngstown Sheet & Tube Co. v. Sawyer;* and Anthony Lewis, *Gideon's Trumpet* (New York: Vintage paperback, 1964), on *Gideon v. Wainwright.*

For more general historical background, the following books will be interesting and helpful: Charles Warren, *The Supreme Court in U.S. History,* rev. ed., 2 vols. (Boston: Little, Brown, 1926); William F. Swindler, *Court and Constitution in the Twentieth Century,* 2 vols. (Indianapolis: Bobbs-Merrill, 1970); Alfred Kelley and Winfred Harbison, *American Constitution,* 4th ed. (New York: Norton, 1970); C. Herman Pritchett, *American Constitutional System* (New York: McGraw-Hill, 1971); and two books by Robert McCloskey: *The American Supreme Court* (Chicago: University of Chicago Press paperback, 1960), and *The Modern Supreme Court* (Cambridge, Mass.: Harvard University Press, 1972).

There are several good books by judges: Benjamin N. Cardozo, *The Nature of the Judicial Process* (New Haven, Conn.: Yale University Press, 1921); and Robert H. Jackson, *The Supreme Court in the American System of Government* (Cambridge, Mass.: Harvard University Press, 1955).

Among the helpful studies by outsiders are these: Charles G. Haines, *American Doctrine of Judicial Supremacy,* 2nd ed. (Berkeley: University of Calif. Press, 1959); Paul A. Freund, *The Supreme Court of the U.S.* (New York: Meridian paperback, 1961); John R. Schmidhauser, *The Supreme Court* (New York: Holt, Rinehart & Winston, 1960); Alpheus T. Mason, *The Supreme Court: Palladium of Freedom* (Ann Arbor: University of Michigan Press, 1962); Charles L. Black, *The People and the Court: Judicial Review in a Democracy* (Englewood Cliffs, N.J.: Prentice-Hall, 1960); Herbert Jacob, *Justice in America: Courts, Lawyers, and the Judicial Process* (Boston: Little, Brown, 1965); Henry J. Abraham, *The Judicial Process,* 3rd ed. (New York: Oxford University Press, 1975), which includes helpful material on federal and state systems as well as those of other countries; Stuart Nagel, *The Legal Process from a Behavioral Perspective* (Homewood, Ill.: Dorsey, 1969), and Glendon Schubert, *The Judicial Mind: Attitudes and Ideologies of Supreme Court Justices, 1946–1965* (Evanston, Ill.: Northwestern University Press, 1965), both of which pioneer in presenting new approaches to the study of judicial behavior that are still extremely controversial; and Walter F. Murphy, *Elements of Judicial Strategy*

(Chicago: University of Chicago Press paperback, 1964), which examines judicial decision making in the context of American politics.

The great debate over judicial activism in general and the Warren Court in particular has produced a great many books and articles. Among the leading ones are: Wallace Mendelson, *Justices Black and Frankfurter: Conflict in the Court* (Chicago: University of Chicago Press, 1961); Alexander M. Bickel, *The Least Dangerous Branch: The Supreme Court at the Bar of Politics* (Indianapolis: Bobbs-Merrill paperback, 1962); Bickel's subsequent volume, *The Supreme Court and the Idea of Progress* (New York: Harper & Row, 1970); Philip Kurland, *Politics, the Constitution, and the Warren Court* (Chicago: University of Chicago Press, 1970); two books by Archibald Cox: *The Warren Court* (Cambridge, Mass.: Harvard University Press, 1968), and *The Role of the Supreme Court in American Government* (New York: Oxford University Press, 1976); and Fred Graham, *The Self-Inflicted Wound* (New York: Macmillan, 1970), on the Supreme Court's effort to police the police.

There are also helpful books on relations between the Court and the rest of government. For the presidency and the executive branch: Robert Scigliano, *The Supreme Court and the Presidency* (New York: Free Press, 1971); Martin Shapiro, *The Supreme Court and Administrative Agencies* (New York: Free Press, 1968); and Sanford J. Ungar, *FBI* (Boston: Little, Brown, 1975). For the Congress: Walter F. Murphy, *Congress and the Court* (Chicago: University of Chicago Press, 1962); Raoul Berger, *Congress v. the Supreme Court* (Cambridge, Mass.: Harvard University Press, 1969); and John R. Schmidhauser and Larry L. Berg, *The Supreme Court and Congress: Conflict and Interaction 1945–1968* (New York: Free Press, 1972). On general topics: Richard Claude, *The Supreme Court and the Electoral Process* (Baltimore: Johns Hopkins Press, 1970), on the Court and voting; and Clement Vose, *Constitutional Change* (Lexington, Mass.: Heath, 1962), on the courts and social and political change.

Finally, on organized crime, see Donald R. Cressey, *Theft of a Nation* (New York: Harper & Row paperback, 1969); and on crime more generally, see former attorney general Ramsey Clark's book, *Crime in America* (New York: Simon & Schuster paperback, 1970).

WHAT INFLUENCES GOVERNMENTAL DECISIONS?

Perspective 4: Winding down Vietnam and closing Watergate

LYNDON JOHNSON AND VIETNAM

On the evening of March 31, 1968, President Lyndon Johnson spoke to the nation on television. Our war in Vietnam was 3 years old. Half a million American military personnel were there. American planes were bombing North Vietnam day and night. Two months earlier, the enemy had launched the Tet (New Year's) offensive, occupying for a time the cities of South Vietnam that we had believed safely under our control. Our efforts to force North Vietnam and Vietcong guerrillas to negotiate peace on our terms had been scorned. And now the military was asking for another 206,000 troops.[1]

Johnson announced that night that we were stopping the bombing of most of North Vietnam, and he expressed the hope that North Vietnam would respond in a way that would bring about peace talks. This decision to start "winding down" America's role in the war, at a time when our military position seemed weaker than ever and the Pentagon wanted more troops sent, surprised most listeners and viewers. Then, after a brief pause, Johnson added words that were to shock the audience even more: "With America's sons in the fields far away, with America's future under challenge right here at home, with our hopes and the world's hopes for peace in the balance every day, I do not believe that I should devote an hour or a day of my time to personal partisan causes or to any duties other than the awesome duties of this office – the Presidency of your country. Accordingly, I shall not seek, and I will not accept, the nomination of my party for another term as your President."

These words stunned everyone – friends and political enemies alike, political observers and ordinary citizens. All had assumed that Johnson, a "born politician" in most minds and a stubborn man as well, would seek a second term, if only to vindicate his Vietnam policy. Why, then, had he decided to wind down the war? And why had he decided not to run again?

The decision not to run again: Johnson's own account

Johnson's speech implied that these two decisions were really only one: a decision to take whatever steps were necessary to achieve peace in Vietnam. He asserted that he was withdrawing to strengthen his efforts to achieve peace in Vietnam and stability in an America torn by dissent over the war and by racial discord.

Personal health In his memoirs, written once he left office, he elaborated on his reasons for not running. His health had not been good: A heart attack in 1955 and already two operations while in the White House made him wonder whether his body could stand the strain of another 4 years.

Domestic policy Domestic issues weighed heavily on Johnson's mind. He wrote: "On that

[1]For the story behind this request, and the political maneuvering that underlay it, see Herbert Y. Schandler, *The Unmaking of a President: Lyndon Johnson and Vietnam* (Princeton, N.J.: Princeton University Press, 1977).

last morning in March, as I moved toward one of the most significant hours of my life, several factors relating to the state of the nation fed into the decisions I was preparing to announce. First, we faced the absolute necessity of an increase in taxes," to finance the war and control inflation, and it would be difficult to get a tax increase through Congress in an election year if he were a candidate, he thought. "Second, we faced the possibility of new riots and turmoil in the cities in the summer of 1968. We had experienced widespread disturbances the previous summer, many of them exploited, I believe, by men who took advantage of distressed people to advance their own political causes. . . .[2]

Wide World Photos

President Johnson announcing his decision not to seek reelection.

Foreign policy Finally, there was Vietnam and the need to unite the people. Johnson had received informal word that North Vietnam would be willing to negotiate if the United States stopped the bombing of North Vietnam.

> I wanted to announce our new initiative for peace. If we were going to take the risk of a bombing pause, I felt I should make it clear that my decision had been made without political considerations. I wanted that decision to be understood by the enemy and by everyone everywhere as a serious and sincere effort to find a road to peace. The most persuasive way to get this across, I believed, would be to couple my announcement of a bombing halt with the statement that I would not be a candidate for reelection.
>
> I also hoped that the combined announcement would accomplish something else. The issue of Vietnam had created divisions and hostilities among Americans, as I had feared. I wanted to heal some of these wounds and restore unity to the nation. This speech might help to do that. I deeply hoped so.[3]

Domestic politics Further on, in the midst of another discussion, Johnson raises what many observers have thought was the real reason for his decision not to run again: domestic politics.

> March was a month of profound political frustrations. I was delaying announcement of my decision not to be a presidential candidate in 1968. That delay resulted in several misunderstandings and disappointments, the most obvious of which was the New Hampshire primary of March 12. I would have preferred to announce my intentions not to run before that primary, since this would have resulted in a clean break and would have been much simpler for me and, I think, much better for the Democratic party. But all things considered—and these things included the Tet offensive, the bombing halt, and my legislative program—I had concluded that the end of March was the earliest moment I could make my move.

"I must admit that the results of the New Hampshire primary surprised me," Johnson continues.

---

[2]Lyndon B. Johnson, *The Vantage Point* (New York: Holt, Rinehart & Winston, 1971), page 426.

[3]Ibid., p. 427.

I was not expecting a landslide. I had not spent a single day campaigning in New Hampshire, and my name was not even on the ballot. And the fact that I received more votes, as a write-in candidate, then Senator [Eugene] McCarthy—49.5 per cent as against 42.4 per cent—seems to have been overlooked or forgotten. Still, I think most people were surprised that Senator McCarthy rolled up the vote he did. I was much less surprised when Bobby Kennedy announced his candidacy four days later. I had been expecting it."[4]

By Johnson's own account, then, these key decisions to de-escalate the war and withdraw from the race for Democratic nomination were shaped primarily by his commitment to peace by negotiation. They were reinforced by his fears for his health, his concern for his legislative program, and his desire to reunite a country torn by racial strife and dissent over the war.

■ The decision not to run again: other accounts

Foreign policy Others, from the outside, saw it differently. Journalist David Halberstam, who interviewed many of the participants, cites the impact of the Tet offensive.

For the first time the patience, durability and resilience of the enemy became clear to millions of Americans. In the past, the Vietcong and NVA [North Vietnamese Army] had always fought in distant jungle or paddy areas, striking quickly and slipping into the night, their toughness rarely brought home to the American people. In the Tet offensive they deliberately changed that. For the first time they fought in the cities, which means that day after day American newspapermen, and more important, television cameramen, could reflect their ability, above all their failure to collapse according to American timetables. . . . The Tet offensive had stripped Johnson naked on the war, his credibility and that of his Administration were destroyed. . . . Hanoi had managed to make the White House look particularly foolish; now the President faced an election year suddenly more vulnerable than ever. . . ."[5]

Domestic politics After New Hampshire came Wisconsin, the second primary. Johnson was on the ballot there, but he was getting little support and less enthusiasm. Halberstam reports that Johnson's leader there, long-time party activist Larry O'Brien, warned him that he might get only 30 percent of the vote there once Bobby Kennedy had joined Eugene McCarthy in the race. "Lyndon Johnson knew then that he was beaten. He knew that he was locked in; he could not do what he wanted on Vietnam and run for reelection. Rather than absorb one more defeat, he withdrew from the race on the eve of the Wisconsin primary and announced that he was pulling back on the bombing. The war was finally turning around; it was time for de-escalation. For Lyndon Johnson it was all over."[6]

Advisors and elite opinion Halberstam emphasizes Johnson's personal political situation as a factor. He also points out that certain of Johnson's advisors – especially corporate Washington lawyer Clark Clifford – were turning against the war. "The Wise Men, as they were called, were telling him what the polls and the newspapers had told him: that the country had turned on the war."[7]

Doris Kearns, a Johnson assistant in those years and after, puts this latter point more starkly in her "psychobiography" of Johnson. Clark Clifford, she writes, was "an emissary from the corporate world, a world of men apart from the personal and

[4]Ibid., pp. 437–438.

[5]David Halberstam, *The Best and the Brightest* (New York: Random House, 1972), pp. 653–654.

[6]Ibid., p. 654

[7]Ibid. For a detailed account of the shift in opinions of some advisors, see Townsend Hoopes, *The Limits of Intervention* (New York: McKay, 1969), and Schandler, *The Unmaking of a President.*

political motives which Johnson believed characterized most of the dissent, where the only standards of judgment were interest, utility, and power."[8] And Johnson aide Harry McPherson quotes Clifford, in a March 28 meeting with other advisors at work on the upcoming speech, as saying:

> Now, I make it a practice to keep in touch with friends in business and the law across the land. I ask them their views about various matters. Until a few months ago, they were generally supportive of the war. . . .
>
> Now all that has changed. There has been a *tre*–mendous *e*–rosion of support for the war among these men. . . . [They] now feel that we are in a hopeless bog. The idea of going deeper into the bog strikes them as mad. They want to see us get out of it.
>
> These are leaders of opinion in their communities. What they believe is sooner or later believed by many other people. It would be very difficult—I believe it would be impossible—for the President to maintain public support for the war without the support of these men.[9]

[8]Doris Kearns, *Lyndon Johnson and the American Dream* (New York: Harper & Row, 1976), p. 345.

[9]Quoted in Harry McPherson, *A Political Education* (Boston: Atlantic-Little, Brown, 1972), pp. 433–434.

Popular opinion Clifford's reported account of the changing opinions of the elite is important, especially because it is commonly believed that business supported the war because business profited from it, receiving much of the $150 billion the war cost. Evidence does not seem to support this view of general war profiteering.[10] In this instance, although Clifford seems not to have realized it, it appears that popular opinion in general may have been ahead of elite opinion. From our first direct military involvement in 1965, Gallup polls had been asking: "In view of the developments since we entered the fighting in Vietnam, do you think the U.S. made a mistake sending troops to fight in Vietnam?" Figure P4.1 indicated that May 1967 was the last time that a majority (50 percent) thought it was *not* a mistake.[11] By the time John-

[10]See, for example, Seymour Melman, *The Permanent War Economy* (New York: Simon & Schuster, 1974), especially chap. 10; and see also Robert W. Stevens, *Vain Hopes, Grim Realities: The Economic Consequences of the Vietnam War* (New York: Watts, 1976).

[11]For a discussion of arguments about the roles of public opinion in our Vietnam policy, see Bruce Andrews, *Public Constraint and American Policy in Vietnam* (Beverly Hills, Calif.: Sage, 1976). For accounts of the actual development of public opinion on the war, see Alan D. Monroe, *Public Opinion in America* (New York: Dodd, Mead, 1975), chap. 11, and Robert Weissberg, *Public Opinion and Popular Government* (Englewood Cliffs, N.J.: Prentice-Hall, 1976), chap. 7. For a skeptical assessment of opinion polls on Vietnam, see Michael Wheeler, *Lies, Damn Lies, and Statistics: The Manipulation of Public Opinion in America* (New York: Liveright, 1976), chap. 7.

FIGURE P4.1

Responses of the American people to the question, "Do you think the U.S. made a mistake in sending troops to Vietnam?"

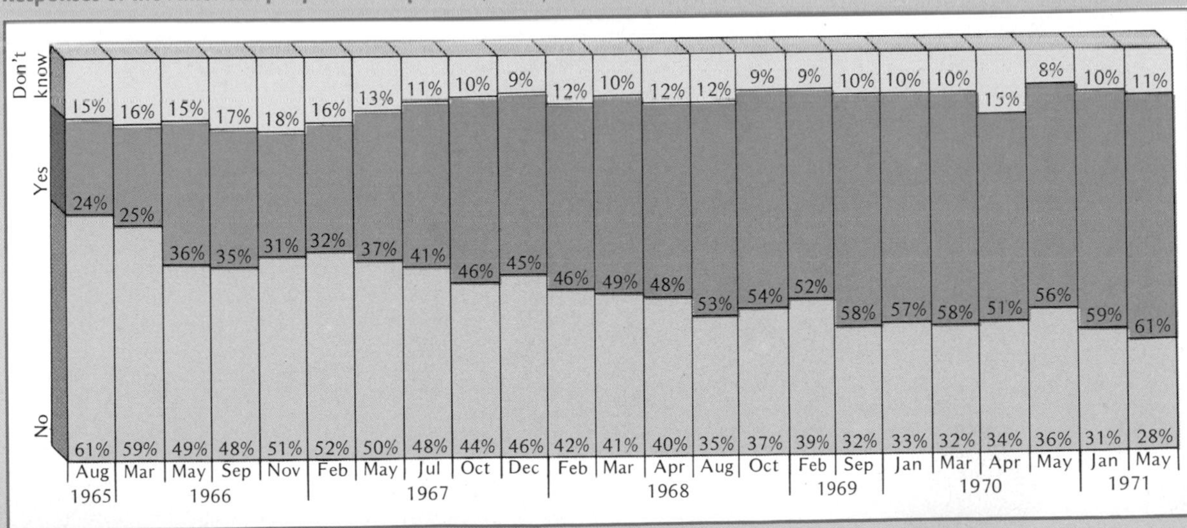

Source: Data from various Gallup Opinion Indexes.

son made his de-escalation and political withdrawal decision, only 41 percent supported the military involvement, while 49 percent thought it a mistake. And from that summer on, a clear majority considered it a mistake.

Kearns reports a conversation with Johnson once he had left office that, when combined with Clifford's representation of the interests and concerns of business leaders, probably sums up as well as any the outside influences on Johnson's decision to withdraw. She quotes Johnson as saying:

> I felt that I was being chased on all sides by a giant stampede coming at me from all directions. On one side, the American people were stampeding me to do something about Vietnam. On the other side, the inflationary economy was booming out of control. Up ahead were dozens of danger signs pointing to another summer of riots in the cities. I was being forced over the edge by rioting blacks, demonstrating students, marching welfare mothers, squawking professors, and hysterical reporters. And then the final straw. The thing I feared from the first day of my Presidency was actually coming true. Robert Kennedy had openly announced his intention to reclaim the throne in the memory of his brother. And the American people, swayed by the magic of the name, were dancing in the streets. The whole situation was unbearable for me. After thirty-seven years of public service, I deserved something more than being left alone in the middle of the plain, chased by stampedes on every side.[12]

Those stampedes, then, were among the various influences which we normally expect to find at work: advisors, mass public opinion, and opinion leaders – in this case, business, the political Left, antiwar activists, and black civil rights activists.

The mass media Many observers believe that the mass media played a role, too. Television, it is said, made the Vietnam War America's first "living-room war." But whether this "bringing the war home" actually lessened support for it is debatable. John Mueller studied poll results and found that "whatever impact television had, it was not enough to reduce support for the war below the levels attained by the Korean War [1950–1953], when television was in its infancy, until casualty levels had far surpassed those of the earlier war."[13]

It does seem clear, in retrospect, that the press and television reporting of the Tet offensive as a major military disaster for American forces was not accurate. The attack did embarrass American and South Vietnamese forces by its unforeseen scale and temporary success. But the casualties taken, especially by the Vietcong guerrillas, who did most of the fighting and dying in the offensive, seriously weakened their forces. This probably actually improved the military picture for South Vietnam – in the short run, at least. Journalist Peter Braestrup has studied press coverage of the Tet offensive and concludes that the coverage was "a distortion of reality" that was great enough to help spur major repercussions in domestic American politics.

One of the those domestic repercussions was, of course, Johnson's decision to step down. But as we have seen, the groundwork for that decision had been long since laid by opposition to the war in the general public, opposition to Johnson in the Democratic party, and disbelief of administration rhetoric on the war in both quarters. Thus the reporting of Tet by the media was "only one of several factors in the turnabout."[14]

■ Some conclusions on the politics of influence

We could do a comparable study of other turning points in our involvement in Vietnam, such as the

[12]Kearns, *Lyndon Johnson and the American Dream,* p. 348

[13]John E. Mueller, *War, Presidents and Public Opinion* (New York: Wiley, 1973), p. 167. One possible reason for this was the policy of "news manipulation" pursued by all administrations involved in Vietnam.

[14]See Peter Braestrup, *Big Story: How the American Press and Television Reported and Interpreted the Crisis of Tet 1968 in Vietnam and Washington* (Boulder, Colo.: Westview Press, 1977).

Paris "peace accords" of early 1973, which ended America's fighting there, or the refusal of Congress to vote more aid for South Vietnam in the spring of 1975, which culminated in the final collapse of South Vietnam. We would find relatively similar patterns of influence: public opinion turning more and more against American policy, presidential advisors and opinion leaders doing likewise, and eventually even the Congress beginning to resist further involvement recommended by the president.

Public opinion, interest groups, and mass media operate from outside the government. Advisors, the bureaucracy, the Congress, and the courts work on the inside. Which of these influences is most important varies with the issue, as we shall see in the case of Watergate and the Nixon resignation.

Johnson's "concerns for the present and the future, for national unity and posterity, for the war and the economy, joined together," writes Kearns. "He decided to retreat with honor."[15] Six and a half years later, another president decided to retreat from politics. But Richard Nixon's was a retreat in disgrace.

□ RICHARD NIXON AND WATERGATE

■ The decision to resign: Nixon's own account

On the evening of August 8, 1974, President Richard Nixon addressed the nation. It was, he pointed out, the thirty-seventh time he had done so. It was also to be the last. "All the decisions I have made in my public life I have always tried to do what was best for the nation," he began.

> Throughout the long and difficult period of Watergate, I have felt it was my duty to persevere to make every possible effort to complete the term of office to which you elected me.
>
> In the past few days, however, it has become evident to me that I no longer have a strong enough political base in the Congress to justify continuing that effort. . . .
>
> From the discussions I have had with Congressional and other leaders I have concluded that because of the Watergate matter I might not have the support of the Congress that I would consider necessary to back the very difficult decisions and carry out the duties of this office in the way the interests of the nation will require.
>
> To continue to fight through the months ahead for my personal vindication would almost totally absorb the time and attention of both the President and the Congress in a period when our entire focus should be on the great issues of peace abroad and prosperity without inflation at home.
>
> Therefore, I shall resign the Presidency effective at noon tomorrow. Vice President Ford will be sworn in as President at that hour in this office. . . . By taking this action, I hope that I will have hastened the start of that process of healing which is so desperately needed in America.

[15] Kearns, *Lyndon Johnson and the American Dream*, p. 348.

President Nixon announcing his decision to resign the presidency.
Wide World Photos

■ The "Watergate" crimes

With these words, and the letter he submitted the next day, Richard Nixon became the first president ever to resign in the history of the country. His had been a presidency in which people in and around the White House had been guilty of:

- □ "breaking and entering" the offices of the Democratic Party National Committee in the "Watergate office building" on June 17, 1972
- □ wiretapping (listening to and recording) other people's conversations without either their permission or a court order approving it
- □ stealing documents from a private citizen's office (the office of the psychiatrist treating Daniel Ellsberg, who had released the Pentagon Papers)
- □ lying to a grand jury
- □ falsifying records presented to a grand jury
- □ withholding information requested by a federal court
- □ distributing a forged, inaccurate letter concerning a Democratic presidential candidate
- □ soliciting and accepting political contributions from large corporation
- □ "laundering" campaign contributions (sending them to Mexican banks and then exchanging them for new cash which was supposed to be more difficult to trace)
- □ taking money for political favors

Bob Woodward (*right*) and Carl Bernstein (*left*) in the offices of the *Washington Post*.
Lebeck/Black Star/Copyright Stern

All these and many other acts during the Nixon administration were illegal. A study by Ralph Nader's Corporate Accountability Research Group found that appeals courts had ruled 897 acts by federal agencies illegal in the period from January 1971 to August 1974. These acts ranged from Nixon's illegal impoundment of sewer funds to illegal tax charges by the Internal Revenue Service but included none of the Watergate misdeeds. Thus the "tone" of the Nixon administration was not one to foster concern for legality among its own employees.[16] And Nixon himself escaped trial and punishment for his own role in Watergate and its coverup because he was soon pardoned by Gerald Ford, the very man whom he had chosen to be his vice-president when Spiro Agnew was forced to resign for corruption.

Uncovering the cover-up It all began, in terms of the law, when five men were arrested in the Democratic Party Offices in the Watergate office building on June 17, 1972. But because few paid any attention to what Nixon's Press Secretary Ronald Ziegler called "a third-rate burglary attempt," the Watergate issue almost died right there.

A presidential election was in the offing: Nixon up for reelection against Democrat George McGovern. But try as he did, McGovern couldn't get people interested in the break-in during the campaign. He went down to a crushing defeat in November.

The following January, the seven men eventually indicted for the break-in were tried. Five confessed and the other two were found guilty by the jury. Federal Judge John Sirica gave long sentences to the group. This earned him the nickname "Maximum John." It also led one of the men, James McCord, to write Sirica a letter saying that the men were under political pressure to plead guilty, that some had lied during the trial, and that the break-in had been approved by higher-ups. Sirica read the

---

[16]William Chapman, "Nader Unit Reports 897 Illegal Acts by U.S. in Nixon Years," *Washington Post,* December 12, 1976. For a more detailed study, see Jethro Lieberman, *How the Government Breaks the Law* (Baltimore: Penguin, 1973).

letter aloud in Court, and that in effect reopened the case.

One result of this was the beginning of hearings on the affair by the Senate Select Committee on Watergate, which began May 17, 1973, and ended several months later. Another result was Nixon's appointment of Archibald Cox as Special Watergate Prosecutor. Cox took over the Justice Department's investigation on May 18, 1973, and served until he was fired in the "Saturday Night Massacre" of October 20. Yet another result was greater investigation by the media.

The role of the media The conventional account of Watergate implies that it was the diligence of the press – especially Bob Woodward and Carl Bernstein of the *Washington Post* – that broke Watergate wide open. In fact, this conventional account overstates the role of the media, especially in the critical first few months after the break-in.

Press critic Ben Bagdikian found that only about 15 of the 433 Washington-based reporters were assigned to cover Watergate – some of these only for a short time. *Washington Post* columnist Robert C. Maynard found that of the 500 or so pieces written by national columnists such as William F. Buckley and James Reston from June to the election in November, fewer than two dozen concerned Watergate. Edwin Diamond and the News Study Group examined all TV network newscasts during the period and found that viewers got "a straight, unquestioning serving of 'news' that – it is clear, in hindsight – advanced the cover-up."[17]

CBS-TV spent almost twice as much time on Watergate in those months as the other two networks. However, as its White House correspondent Dan Rather wrote a year later, "CBS News was putting some stories about Watergate on the air, more than our broadcast competitors, but pitifully few. . . ." Rather places responsibility for this on "the deadly daily diet of deceit sent us from the White House. . . . They lied, schemed, threatened, and cajoled to prevent network correspondents from getting a handle on the story. And they succeeded."[18]

As the scandal unfolded despite the cover-up, Nixon aides increasingly claimed that the president was being "hounded from office" by the press. Nixon himself, after he left office, asserted that it was the news media who "built this into a federal case."[19] But Diamond concludes from his study that "The record of the Watergate coverage discloses no hounding of the President. Quite the contrary. The press did not speak as a chorus with one voice. The president had his own defenders; equally important, his [campaign] in 1972 initially came across louder than the message of Watergate."[20]

The conventional account of Watergate as primarily a media achievement, then, is at best only partially true. Indeed, readers of Woodward and Bernstein's memoir, *All the President's Men,*[21] are well aware of the importance not only of Judge Sirica's role, but also – especially – of the contribution of "Deep Throat." "Deep Throat" was the source of major leaks to "Woodstein," as the pair came to be known. His identity is still not publicly known. The common supposition is that he was a government bureaucrat close enough to the parties involved to be very well informed, but far enough away to escape suspicion.

Other members of the executive branch were also important. Clearly, Special Prosecutor Cox and his successor Leon Jaworski played vital roles in pursuing the case in the face of White House resistance and obstruction. John Dean, once the President's counsel and then a leading witness against his White House colleagues before the Senate Watergate Committee, was also important, as his memoir, *Blind Ambition,* recounts.[22] Another important

[17]Edwin Diamond, *The Tin Kazoo* (Cambridge, Mass.: MIT Press, 1975), p. 217.

[18]Dan Rather, "Watergate on TV," *Newsday,* December 16, 1973. This quote and the information preceding it on press coverage come from Diamond, *The Tin Kazoo,* chap. 11, "Myths of Watergate."

[19]"Nixon Admits 'Stupid Mistake,'" *Austin American,* October 23, 1975.

[20]Diamond, *The Tin Kazoo,* p. 218.

[21]Carl Bernstein and Bob Woodward, *All The President's Men* (New York: Simon & Schuster, 1974).

[22]John Dean, *Blind Ambition* (New York: Simon & Schuster, 1976).

figure was Alexander Butterfield, previously a Nixon aide, who revealed in his Senate testimony that Nixon had installed a system to tape all his conversations. Many still believe that without this knowledge and the texts of tapes that were eventually obtained, Nixon would have been able to serve his full term as president.

But those tapes would never have reached the Special Prosecutor or the Congress and the public were it not for the federal courts. As we saw in Chapter 9, they ruled that Nixon had to turn the tapes over once they were subpoenaed.

The decision to resign: other accounts

But even after the court rulings, after the media revelations, after the bureaucratic leaks, Nixon was still president, with 2½ years left to serve. So why did he then resign? While all this was going on, Nixon's popularity in the polls was taking a severe beating, as Figure P4-2, which indicates major developments, too, reveals.

By the November 1972 elections, only 52 percent of the people had heard of Watergate. But by the start of the Senate hearings in the summer of 1973, 97 percent had.[23] Americans that summer had their eyes and ears glued to their TV sets and radios. What the people were seeing and hearing was fascinating and troubling – the more so once the tapes were released. By the time Nixon resigned, only one in four Americans approved of his conduct of the presidency.

Public opinion and the Congress Some have therefore concluded that it was the pressure of public opinion on Congress that forced the issue that summer. Public opinion, it is said, forced the House to decide that it had to impeach Nixon. And the same opinion forced senators to line up in favor of removal from office in such numbers that in the final days Nixon could count on only several dozen likely votes there against conviction.

[23]*Gallup Opinion Index*, June 1973, p. 2.

But does a drastic decline in popularity explain Nixon's fall? Lyndon Johnson had slipped to a 35 percent favorable rating in 1968 and managed at least to survive the rest of his term. And Harry Truman in 1951 and 1952 had plummeted to a 25 percent rating comparable to Nixon's but even more sustained through time.

The impeachment hearings Why, then, did Nixon have to go? Was it his Watergate crimes? The articles of impeachment that the House Judiciary Committee voted on through those final days were an appalling indictment. Article I cited the "cover-up," an illegal obstruction of justice on a grand scale. It was passed by a twenty-seven-to-eleven vote on July 27, 1974. Article II covered "abuse of power," with emphasis on a wide range of violations of citizens' constitutional rights. It passed by a twenty-eight-to-ten vote on July 29. Article III cited Nixon's defiance of congressional subpoenas commanding him to turn over tapes and documents. It passed the next day. The committee then rejected a proposed article concerning the illegal concealment of the bombing of Cambodia during the Vietnam War and another alleging income tax fraud by the president by identical twelve-to-twenty-six votes.

This is a stunning bill of particulars, of "high crimes and misdemeanors" (as the Constitution defines impeachable offenses). But offenses rather similar to these had been committed at one time or another by other presidents. Indeed, Nixon's record in this regard may not be much different as a whole from those of Truman and Johnson and is probably better than those of Wilson and FDR – let alone Lincoln.[24]

The Kiplinger thesis It can be argued, with longtime Washington observer Austin Kiplinger among many others, that "never before. . . . had so many of these practices been perpetrated at the same time by the same administration at such high levels. Watergate was new in its scale and complexity. It was

[24]See Victor Laski, *It Didn't Start with Watergate* (New York: Dial, 1977).

FIGURE P4.2

Percent of Americans giving President Nixon a positive rating.

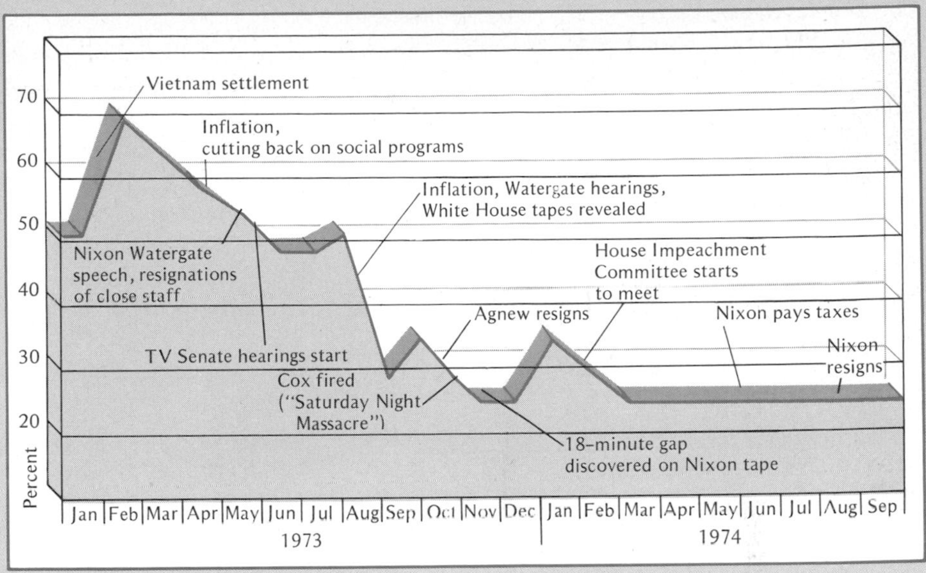

Source: Data from various Gallup Opinion Indexes.

unique in its combination of bugging, spying, and covering up. And it was new in the spectacle of a President being caught in the middle of it all."[25]

The Von Hoffman thesis Perhaps this is an adequate discription of the conditions. But does it really explain "the fall?" Columnist Nicholas Von Hoffman of the *Washington Post,* over the next year and a half, developed a new analysis of the how and why of Nixon's fall – one that may prove more accurate and is at least more intriguing. Von Hoffman first examines Nixon's position about the time of his second inauguration from the points of view of major power groups in America.

- The Congress, he argues, resented Nixon because he refused to pretend publicly that it was an equal branch of government and instead generally ignored it.
- The Pentagon, the CIA, and the State Department, according to Von Hoffman, "had come to think him a dangerous man, not only because they had been cut out of the decision making, but also because they thought he was moving toward military disaster for us in his negotiations with the Russians."
- The bureaucracy was fearful because, shortly after his reelection, Nixon had demanded the resignations of the 2,000 top Washington bureaucrats, "At one stroke," Von Hoffman argues, "he threatened every structure in the government and invited large-scale disloyalty to him. Historians will want to test the hypothesis that a frightened bureaucracy defended itself by passing huge amounts of compromising information to the media and Congress."
- The cabinet departments and the interest groups, too, were upset, for Nixon had decided to create a kind of "super Cabinet" that would be able to run the government directly out of the White House. "The vast and elaborate departmental and regulatory system is the indispensable prop to every important interest group in the country from oil refining to social work," writes Von Hoffman. Nixon's reorganization plans threatened the structures we have analyzed in earlier chapters as "subgovernments."

[25] Austin H. Kiplinger, *Washington Now* (New York: Harper & Row, 1975), pp. 65–66.

Wide World Photos

Richard Nixon waves goodbye from his helicopter as he leaves Washington for California following his resignation.

Von Hoffman writes: "What Richard Nixon contemplated doing was actually running the government, something no President in seven decades had attempted. To do it he'd not only alienated the government he proposed to run but he was also planning to do it in such a way as to cause every interest group to worry that its long held privileges and influence were in danger, thanks to this new centralization of power."[26]

In an article published a year later,[27] Von Hoffman adds the Left (alienated by Vietnam) and the Right (alienated by Nixon's "wage and price controls" and his support of liberal welfare reform) to the list of malcontents. And he argues that business, too, had turned on Nixon because he couldn't manage the economy effectively and supported environmental and consumer protection. In addition, he says, important business leaders resented the pressure they had been put under to contribute corporate funds illegally to the Nixon campaign–something many of them were eventually fined for doing.[28]

Furthermore, because Nixon had run his own campaign in 1972 and even in effect supported some Democrats, he had lost the support of the Republican party. And there was no one outside the government to organize popular support for him either, except a retired rabbi named Baruch Korff.[29]

"Nixon couldn't bring it off," Von Hoffman writes. "He didn't have enough trustworthy people to put in pivotal positions, nor did he have a large personal following, a la George Wallace, that he might have used to intimidate opponents. As the smarter observers said at the time of his landslide reelection, his support was a thousand miles wide and five inches deep."[30]

"Nixon's downfall was a political, not a conspiratorial act," Von Hoffman concludes,

> The representatives and leaders of all the various powers and groupings that Nixon had alienated never had to meet in a room to plan. . . . After his second inaugural the lead-

[26]Nicholas Von Hoffman, "Who or What Caused the Downfall of Nixon?" *Washington Post,* March 5, 1976. He credits author Marcus Raskin as a source of many of these ideas. This analysis was later corroborated in large part by Nixon's closest aide, H. R. Haldeman, who wrote in his memoir *The Ends of Power* (New York: Quadrangle, 1978): "Mr. Nixon, as president, felt unable to take control of the federal bureaucracy. Pitted against him were four great power blocs of Washington–the press, the bureaucrats, the Congress, and the intelligence community." Haldeman called these blocs "the wolves." See Haynes Johnson, "Haldeman Places Blame on Nixon for Watergate Burglary, Tape Gap," *International Herald Tribune,* February 17, 1978. For Nixon's own account, which most observers found to contain little important new information, see *RN: The Memoirs of Richard Nixon* (New York: Grosset & Dunlap, 1978).

[27]Nicholas Von Hoffman, "The Breaking of a President," *Penthouse,* March 1977.

[28]For additional evidence of Nixon's alienation of business, see Terry Robards, "Watergate Causes Nixon to Lose Large Share of Business Support," *New York Times,* August 6, 1973.

[29]Korff's National Committee for Fairness to the Presidency collected $600,000 to run ads supporting Nixon in the press. Another support group, Americans for the Presidency, which had been organized by some business executives, also ran ads. These groups were matched by campaigns of a number of proimpeachment groups, including the AFL-CIO, the Americans for Democratic Action, the League of Friends of Thomas Jefferson, and the Committee for the Resignation of the President. For details on these "impeachment interest groups," see Carol S. Greenwald, *Group Power: Lobbying and Public Policy* (New York: Praeger, 1977), pp. 103–105.

[30]Von Hoffman, "Who or What Caused the Downfall of Nixon?"

> ing members of the factions that were opposed to him could see that their counterparts felt the same way merely by picking up a paper. . . . Six months after his second inaugural, he had become a president in name only. A year later he'd even lost the name. The domestic reforms or changes that he'd attempted had vanished. Everything he did is viewed today as sowing the seeds of American dictatorship. . . . But . . . the crimes of the Nixon administration merely provided the means with which his political enemies were able to destroy him.[31]

Or in other words, as Nixon himself said in his farewell address, "I no longer have a strong enough political base in the Congress." He might have added "or anywhere else." For by then, whatever the causes, whether Von Hoffman or Kiplinger is closer to the full picture, Nixon was finished as president.

[31]Von Hoffman, "The Breaking of a President," p. 153.

■ Some conclusions on the politics of influence

Nixon's decision to resign (thereby saving his pension and perhaps "earning" a pardon) had been brought about by actions of various elements of the government: the courts, the bureaucracy, and the Congress. But it had been influenced as well – as was Johnson's decision not to run again – by the elements so often important in American politics from the outside: public opinion, interest groups, and the mass media. To better understand how these outside influences operate, we turn now to a more detailed examination of each in turn.

10 Public opinion

Each of us has what could be termed a small piece of "public opinion." It's that collection of views we have on public questions, such as how well the president is doing his job, whether our political system is really democratic, whether or not marijuana should be legalized, and indeed anything else that concerns government or politics. More specifically, public opinion is generally taken to include preferences about candidates, policies, and party, and political knowledge and ideology (or set of general beliefs and values with which to interpret things). To be public opinion rather than private opinion, in the way these terms are generally used, a view must concern a public question and must be held by more than one person. These public views are sometimes studied by politicians as guidance on how they should act or indications of the risks to them if they act unpopularly. Public opinion is also studied by observers such as pollsters, who sometimes report to politicians, business leaders, and other interested groups on what the public believes and wants. At other times, various polling organizations report their findings to the people themselves so that the people can determine what they as a whole are thinking.

People who study public opinion, whether they are politicians or political scientists, usually break the population down into various categories. By doing so, they can study and compare the opinions held by the elites (business executives, for example, or professors, or members of Congress) and those held by the masses or by segments of them (workers, for example, or the poor, or the young). In this way, they can talk about the opinions of various "special publics," as well as the general public.[1] And they can act, if they are politicians, in ways designed to affect the views of a certain segment.

As a result of studies of what people actually believe, experts have come to question whether there really is any such group as "the public." Studies show that it is very difficult to find any topic on which everyone has an opinion of any sort, let alone the same opinion. Nonetheless, politicians still talk about what "the public" wants, what public opinion on a given question is, and what "the people" will or won't stand for. And so, particularly in a democracy, it is important to know not just what public opinion is, but how it is shaped, how it is uncovered and measured, and what role it plays in politics. These are the major questions we will examine in this chapter.

---

[1]See V. O. Key, *Public Opinion and American Democracy* (New York: Knopf, 1961), p. 10.

☐ HOW WE GET OUR OPINIONS

Everything we believe, every little component of our image of reality, or our world view, can be thought of as an opinion – an opinion more or less accurate, more or less developed, more or less strongly held. Where do we get these opinions or beliefs? The easy answer is that we get them from our experience in the world. We experience our environment, which generally consists first of family, then of friends, then of schools, and eventually of a work situation. All of these aspects act or operate to shape our views of things in certain geographical locations and circumstances. Among the factors that may influence us are mass media, religion, and other groups of people. We've seen, in our discussion of voting in Chapter 3, ways in which these factors matter. In terms of our own lives, the first influential factor is "socialization." So let's look at how it shapes and reshapes our political attitudes and thereby tends to determine our public opinions.

■ Socialization

We often hear it said that a human being is by nature a social animal. When a child is born, the animal part seems dominant. The child has bodily needs for food and affection and demonstrates them immediately. The social part develops as the child gets a sense of other people and of his or her relations with them and feelings toward them. Social scientists refer to this process of learning as "socialization."

During this process, children learn ways of relating to other people. They may learn to be friendly or aggressive, for example. They may learn to be trusting or suspicious. They learn to obey authority – at least under certain conditions. They learn how best to get their own way when that is important to them, and how to help and hurt, to love and hate, both other children and adults. When they have learned these sorts of things, we say they have been "socialized." The attitudes and behaviors they have learned may be good for society or bad in our judgment.

Schools are an important influence on a person's values, attitudes, and opinions.

Museum of the City of New York

Library of Congress

Children, then, begin to learn about politics as a part of this socialization. They seem to learn attitudes toward our leaders as well as attitudes toward the country. And they also begin to learn to "play politics"—to campaign for a leadership role, as we would say of an adult, or to lead other people, for example. Learning these things helps to prepare children to participate in politics later on. But *just what they learn* may be very important in determining whether they become obedient citizens who fulfill their responsibilities (voting, obeying the law) regularly, or whether they become discontented dropouts or even revolutionaries.

To find out how important childhood experiences are in later political behavior, we study *political socialization*—the process by which we learn about politics, and by which we then teach our friends, children, and students about politics.

We would like to know what factors are most important in shaping the political opinions and behavior of adults. How important is the family? Schools and teachers? Peer groups (friends and others of the same age or group)? What roles do government itself and the mass media play? And how does this political socialization happen?

Unfortunately, studies are still at an early stage, and there is little certainty about how to answer these questions.[2] Perhaps the basic problem is that we still can't answer with certainty the basic question of *how socialization happens.* There are four major theories which try to answer it.

Theories of socialization The first, and the most obvious, theory is called the *accumulation* theory. It says that we learn about politics bit by bit, fact by fact, belief by belief. These bits accumulate into the image of political reality that we hold when we act politically. There are two major problems with this theory. First, it doesn't tell us why we learn some of the political facts we come upon but not others. Nor, second, does it tell us how we come to have feelings and make judgments about various political figures such as the president. To explain this, experts may turn to a second view, called the *interpersonal transfer* theory. This theory says, for example, that a child learns how to relate to his father as an authority figure in the family and then transfers that attitude or feeling to the president once he learns that the president is an authority figure for the nation.

A third theory is called the *identification* theory. It holds that the learner identifies with, or tends to feel himself or herself identical with, some person he or she admires. The learner therefore imitates that person, adopting the views that person holds. A child may identify with a parent, or a student with a teacher, for instance.

So far, all of these theories seem to assume that anyone can learn anything anytime, so long as the conditions are right. But many experts on the ways children learn now believe that there are limits to what one can learn at a given stage. The fourth view is a theory of the way our thought capabilities develop. Experts call it

---

[2]For a current summary of research findings, see Stanley A. Renshon, ed., *Handbook of Political Socialization* (New York: Free Press, 1977).

the *cognitive development* theory. It holds that what you can learn depends on how much you already know plus how well developed your capacity to think abstractly is. The more you know about politics, the better you can learn about the differences in candidates' positions, for example. And the better you are at abstract thinking, the more you can learn about the differences in political ideologies such as liberalism and conservatism, which are quite abstract.[3]

Each of these theories seems helpful in examining and explaining a part of the political socialization we undergo. Studies have found that the child's initial attachment is to his or her political community or nation. The child's first emotional reaction to the system is favorable, and his or her attitude toward its leaders tends to be trusting. Between age 12 and 15, a young person's image of political reality usually becomes deeper, clearer, and more precise. He or she tends to connect issues with political parties, to think of the nation as more than the president, and to assess politics and the government more realistically.[4]

We might then assume that the major authority figures (parents and teachers) and institutions (family, school, and the mass media) in the lives of children in these years are important influences. But there is reason to believe that the wider social and political environment – the government, social groups such as labor unions and private organizations, and even the general "atmosphere" in a given period – may also be quite important. The general notion of what forms of political participation are possible, or of what a citizen's political obligation is, may be influential, even though these notions are not taught by parents and schools.[5] Also, parents may be less influential than we might suppose. In these times of rapid change they may themselves be "going through changes" in the stages of their lives at the very time they are supposed to be setting clear authoritative examples for their children. These factors may help explain why children do not simply turn out to believe the things their parents do – or the things the schools teach – about politics.[6]

We are not born with our opinions. Nor do we think them up from scratch – otherwise there would be some 220 million different images of political reality held by the American people. Figure 10.1 summarizes briefly the influences on opinions that we have been discussing here and in Chapter 3. As it reminds us, our knowledge and opinions do not simply come from our parents, our schools, or other early influences. Our adult experiences of peers and work are also important. But what makes us susceptible to these various influences? And why are we more susceptible to some influences than to others? The important underlying factor is our experience of ignorance and authority.

---

[3]These theories are summarized by two experts on political socialization, Robert D. Hess and Judith V. Torney, *The Development of Political Attitudes in Children* (Chicago: Aldine, 1967). For a comprehensive survey, see Richard E. Dawson, Kenneth Prewitt, and Karen S. Dawson, *Political Socialization,* 2nd ed. (Boston: Little, Brown, 1977).

[4]For a summary, see Judith V. Torney, A. N. Oppenheim, and Russell F. Farnen, *Civic Education in Ten Countries* (New York: Wiley, 1975), especially pp. 24–32.

[5]See, for suggestion of this, Ronald Inglehart, "The Silent Revolution in Europe: Intergenerational Change in Post-Industrial Societies," *American Political Science Review* 65 (1971): 991–1017.

[6]See Neal E. Cutler, "Toward a Generational Conception of Political Socialization," in *New Directions in Political Socialization,* ed. David C. Schwartz and Sandra Kenyon Schwartz (New York: Free Press, 1975).

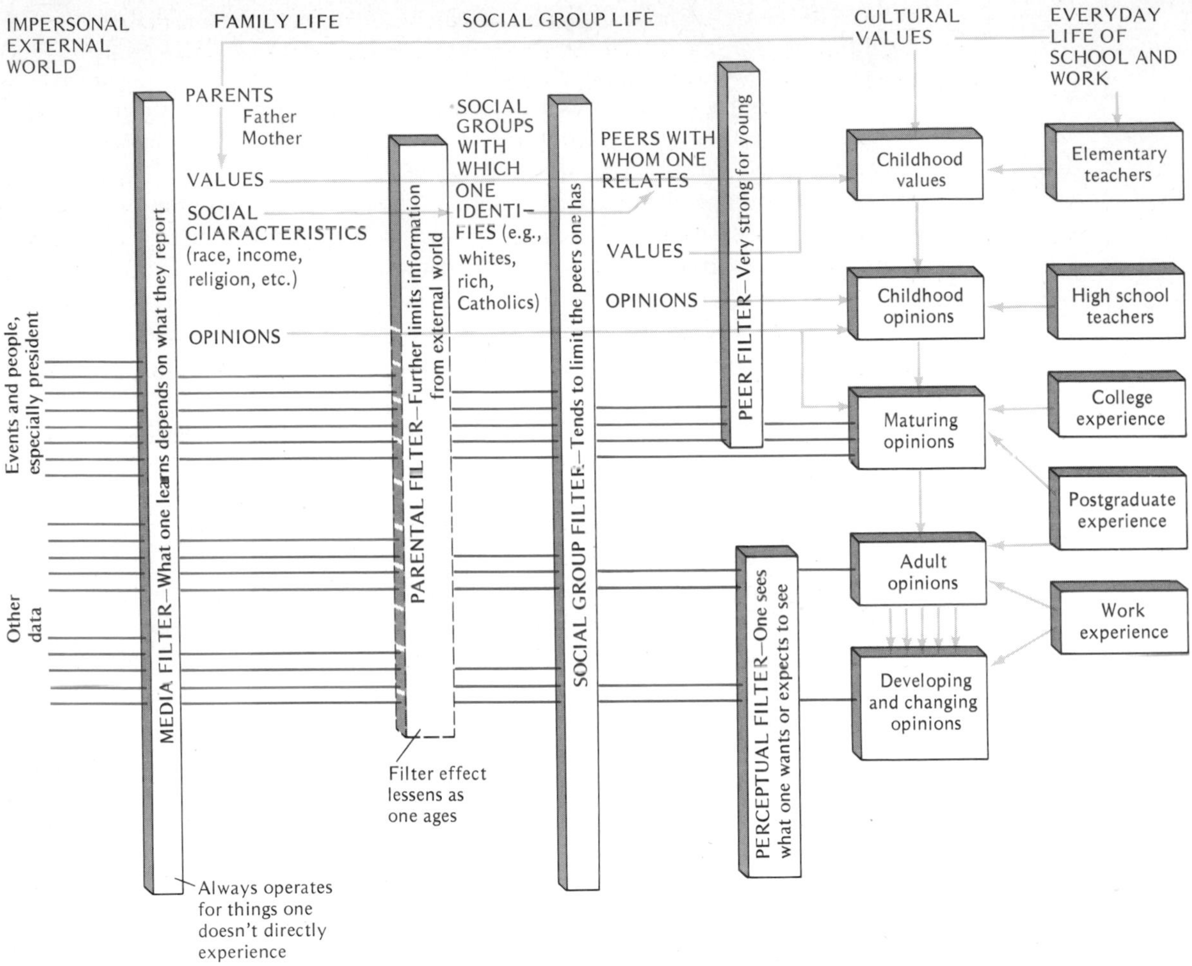

FIGURE 10.1

A model of influences on a person's attitudes and values.

■ Reliance on authority

Ignorance varies tremendously from one individual to the next. Studies show that there is at one extreme in the United States an "attentive public," as it has been termed by political scientists. This is the group of people who pay attention to public affairs and know much more about them than the average citizen. This segment includes perhaps somewhere between 15 and 30 percent of the population at any given time, on any given issue. At the other extreme are the large numbers of people who answer "don't know" to pollsters' questions about everything from whom they favor for president to what the First Amendment says, and even to the question, "Who is your Congressman?"

Given such ignorance, *authority* is especially important in shaping attitudes and opinions. In a complex world, everyone depends on experts for decisions and opinions about many difficult questions in which the experts specialize. If people take the views of these experts seriously, we say that for them the experts have authority. Authority, as we've noted in earlier chapters, is a recognized or believed capacity to describe something accurately, to reach a judgment about something that is sensible or compelling, or to give good reasons for one's views if asked. Because people grant such authority to other people, or believe that those experts have earned such authority, experts play a major role in shaping public opinion.

Each of us has a unique set of *genes* and a unique biography of *life experiences,* as well as a different *perspective* on the world from the exact point at which we stand. So we might expect there to be no such thing as public opinion, but rather 220 million private, individual, opinions on each and every topic. The thing that prevents this from happening is the fact that we all grant authority to others to describe, interpret, and explain large areas of reality to us and for us. Public opinion is shaped by teachers who teach about politics, by authors who write about politics, and also by movie stars and sports heroes who endorse candidates – as well as by politicians themselves, as we noted in Chapter 3.

Indeed, as we have already seen, one way of understanding what happens in politics is to think of *politics* as *disputes over claims to the authority to describe, interpret, explain, or influence the nature of reality.* Because people see reality differently, they are constantly disagreeing about what reality is, as well as about what should be done. People are always, in other words, disputing about the nature of reality. Because of this, and because real agreement is so hard to achieve on important questions, people must select individuals to decide and act for them. This is the function politics plays in a democracy: It provides opportunities for people to select authorities to resolve their differences by reinterpreting reality or influencing reality for them. Thought of in this way, the essence of everyday life is dispute over various aspects of the nature of reality. *The essence of politics,* however, in these terms, is *dispute over claims to authority* to interpret and influence reality. In our politics, as we saw in Chapter 3, candidates dispute before the voters about which one deserves the authority to act for the people by running the government. As the basis of his or her claim to authority, a candidate may cite or emphasize personal character, experience, education, party membership, physical appearance, or almost any other quality. If the people prefer one candidate's claims to authority to those of a rival, they designate him or her as their authority, to serve in office deciding for them what should be done and thereby interpreting, explaining, and influencing reality for them.

The same sort of politics, as we already know, occurs in the government as well. Members of Congress dispute with each other for the votes of their fellow legislators in the same way, and the president may dispute with the Congress or the bureaucracy over who should have the authority to interpret and change reality. And so on, throughout the government.[7]

[7]And, indeed, throughout the rest of life as well. This general definition of politics enables us to see and better understand the politics in, for example, relations between a parent and children, where politics may arise over the question of what rules children should obey, or whether a child should go to college and if so to which one. Politics also arise between a teacher and students, or between two students disagreeing over a point, or two books that dispute each other's arguments.

Thinking of politics in this way—as dispute over claims to the authority to describe, interpret, explain, and influence the nature of reality—can be especially helpful in studying the role of public opinion in politics. For public opinion gets shaped by authorities who define reality for others, whether those who are the shaping authorities are politicians or not. In authoritarian or dictatorial systems, authority comes only from the top down, from the leader to the people. In democracies, some authority goes from the bottom up, from the people to the leader, as in elections, lobbying, and other expressions of public opinion that are strongest in a functioning democracy.

☐ STUDYING PUBLIC OPINION

■ Who has an opinion?

Those who study public opinion generally begin by distinguishing between the *elites* (those people who dominate major institutions such as politics, business, labor, and the professions) and the *masses* (everyone else). For the purpose of studying public opinion, this distinction is too general, and so scholars usually follow Gabriel Almond in making two further distinctions: dividing the "elites" category into leaders and elites; and dividing the "masses" category into the "attentive public" and the "general public." The result is a division of the population that can be graphically represented as in Figure 10.2.

Here we are primarily concerned not with power but with attention to politics. Power, we have seen, is held largely by leaders and elites, but it is shared somewhat with members of the public who vote or otherwise participate in the ways and to the degrees we outlined in Chapter 5.

One study measured attention to politics by signs of: interest in politics generally, interest in national election campaigns, talking about politics, self-exposure to political information, engaging in political activities, and caring about elections and politics.

This study concluded that the people most likely to be attentive to politics are those with high-status occupations, higher incomes, and more education, although one-fifth of those who didn't finish high school qualify as attentive and half of the high school graduates are attentive. Attentiveness did not vary greatly with sex, race, or age. Newspapers were found most important in generating attentiveness: about 40 percent of the population was attentive to them most of the time. Political campaigns themselves were second, hovering around 35 percent. Then came personal conversations and general political attention, followed by magazines.[8] It is worth noting that as of 1964, when this study was done, television was not significant. There was no real difference between those otherwise attentive and those not attentive in their following of politics on TV. There is reason to believe that this has changed considerably since then, as we shall see when we examine the mass media in Chapter 12.

---

[8]Donald J. Devine, *The Attentive Public* (Chicago: Rand McNally, 1970).

FIGURE 10.2
Degrees of citizen attentiveness.

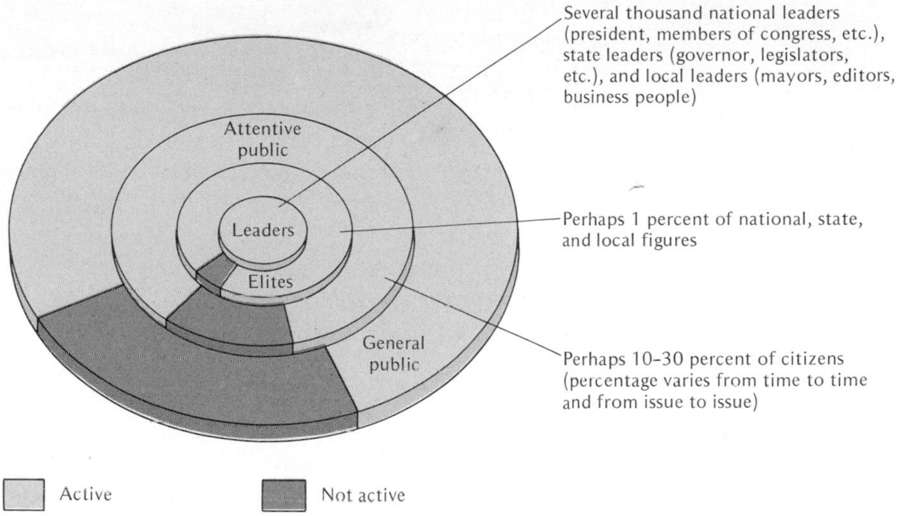

■ Opinion polls

You've probably taken a public opinion poll—or at least a semipublic one—some time in your life. Just asking some of your friends whom they plan to vote for or how they feel about abortion or who they think will win the Superbowl could count as an opinion poll. But the results of such a poll probably wouldn't be very interesting to anyone besides those interviewed, because no one would expect your friends to be representative of the public at large, or of any other group except perhaps the group "your friends."

Candidates often say, "The only poll that counts is on election day," and they are right in a sense. But candidates and the media are full of polls throughout any major campaign just the same, and both candidates and voters seem to be influenced by reports of their results. Many people even believe that voting is affected by poll reports in that they may create a "sympathy vote" for the underdog or a "bandwagon" effect for the leader. Research on this is inconclusive.

A **poll** is a survey of a few people that is supposed to represent with considerable accuracy how everyone involved thinks. No one can afford to poll everyone, and so pollsters have developed ways to pick small numbers of people whose views should be somehow typical of the ones who aren't asked. This process of *sampling* the population is the reason why you almost certainly have never been interviewed, say, by the Gallup Poll, and probably never will be in your entire life, even though the Gallup organization is always polling all year round on all sorts of subjects. For it only interviews about 350,000 people each decade.

If they never ask you, me, or most other Americans, how can the major pollsters be so accurate in predicting election outcomes? There are two important secrets to it. First, they generally use *random samples.* And second, they pick a sample size large enough to give *a low probability of error.* What do these "secrets" mean in practice?

Wide World Photos

Conducting an opinion poll.

Random sample **A random sample** is a group – in polls, a group of people – in which each individual within the whole population being surveyed has an equal chance of being selected. Most major national polls interview about 1500 people to represent the American adult population of about 140 million people. The way the sample is "drawn" is too complex to be described in detail here. The suggested readings at the end of this chapter will lead you to sources that will guide you if you wish to understand more about sampling. Briefly, a polling organization picks people by where they live. It may start with counties or election precincts and break them down to neighborhoods, streets, and buildings and then down to, say, the person living there who has the longest first name. The point is to get people scattered all over the country in all sorts of living conditions, so that in fact their views will represent the views of the population because they themselves as a group are generally like the population. In the old days, polls of samples drawn from telephone directories were often used. They were also often wrong, because then rich people were much more likely to have phones, so their opinions were overrepresented in the sample. That is why census tracts – which show who lives in every house and apartment in the nation and are updated every 10 years – are now commonly used.

Margin of error Once the pollster has a sample, he or she knows the probability of error because the "laws of statistical probability" tell how likely a certain size sample is to be typical. The 1500 person sample of the population gives a range of accuracy of plus or minus 3 percentage points 95 percent of the time. What does this actually mean? Let's take an actual example.

In the 1976 campaign, the final Gallup Poll, taken the week before the election, reported Ford with 47 percent of the votes, and Carter with 46 percent, with 4 percent undecided, so Gallup said the race was too close to call. The reason was that its sampling error of plus or minus 3 percent means that "Ford 47–Carter 46" could also be "Ford 50–Carter 43" or "Carter 49–Ford 44," and the Gallup Poll would still be "right" within its stated "margin of error." And 5 out of every 100 polls, it could be even farther off. Nonetheless, since a major disaster in 1948 when all the polls were wrong, the major polls have on average predicted the presidential vote within less than 2 percent of the actual totals, which is an impressive performance.

Drawing by Weber. © 1975 The New Yorker Magazine, Inc.

"That's the worst set of opinions I've heard in my entire life."

Still, the matter of the allowable margin of error points out why it is important to read poll results carefully, if at all. They rarely actually mean what they appear to say, although we rarely are reminded of this fact except when a poll gets it wrong, as Gallup seemed to in 1976.

In fact, that final total announced also includes a number of important judgment calls as well as the probability error. A pollster has to try to determine how likely each respondent is to vote on election day and then somehow build that into his or her final total. Also a pollster may allocate to the various candidates those "undecideds" who seem likely to vote in the election. This may be done on the basis of how the trend seems to be going – as it seemed to be going to Ford in 1976, for example.

In addition, polls on issues may be affected by the way questions are asked. A loaded question with emotional language or a complex question with only yes-or-no answers allowed may produce a result that doesn't really reflect the opinions of the people being interviewed.

Polls often do not find out the *direction* of an opinion. Often a person's opinion on a given issue is not a simple yes-or-no matter but can range from "strongly in favor" through "indifferent" to "strongly opposed." They also may not reflect the *strength or intensity* with which an opinion is held. Nor will they reflect an opinion's *stability or fluidity* unless they are repeated over a period of time. Furthermore, they rarely reveal the *relevance or salience* of an opinion to the people – how important it is to them.

So there is much to be learned about public opinion beyond what the pollsters usually tell us – even when what they tell us proves to be accurate despite their necessary use of their own judgment in processing their raw data. Some of what is missing can be learned from in-depth interviews of the sort we relied on in our study of voting in Chapter 3.

Thus most experts on polls and polling urge caution in reading and interpreting polls. Here are some questions to ask about a poll which are suggested by the experts:

- ☐ *Who was interviewed?* Was it a national sample or a special population group? Was it a random sample (generally the most reliable kind), or some other type?
- ☐ *How big was the sample?* For any large population group, reliability declines markedly as the sample size drops below 1500.
- ☐ *What questions were asked, and in what order?* Could you have answered them confident that your answers would accurately reflect your views?
- ☐ *How were the interviews conducted?* Those done in people's homes are usually most reliable. Telephone comes next, with mail and street-corner polls not reliable.
- ☐ *When were the interviews conducted* in relation to opinion-influencing events or elections?
- ☐ *Who did the polling?* A reliable firm such as Gallup, Harris, Roper, the National Opinion Research Center? Or an unknown (or, worse, an unmentioned) firm?
- ☐ *Who sponsored it – and why?* Was it sponsored by a political candidate to show his or her strength? Or by newspapers without any particular vested interest in the outcome? Or by an academic research organization such as the University of Michigan's Survey Research Center?

Bearing in mind questions like these, and aware of the inescapable limitations we discussed above, you can judge a poll in ways that can make its information useful.

■ What the polls show: the ignorance of citizens

One thing polls show quite conclusively is that many Americans are quite ignorant of important fundamental facts about our political system. One survey, for example, asked "What do you know of the Bill of Rights?" Some 21 percent had a reasonably accurate idea of its contents, 12 percent had an incorrect notion, 36 percent claimed they'd heard of it but couldn't identify it, and 31 percent said they'd never heard of it.[9]

During the Bicentennial, various surveys were made of the political knowledge of the American people. A Gallup Poll found that 28 percent of the American people could not identify the important event that occurred in this country in 1776. The same survey found that 92 percent could correctly identify Columbus, but only 41 percent could identify Karl Marx.[10]

If we hope that younger Americans, who are getting more education and have greater access to the media, will do better, we seem likely to be disappointed. A major national survey of 13- and 17-year-olds sponsored by the government found the following:

- ☐ Forty-seven percent of 17-year-olds do not know that each state has two U.S. senators.
- ☐ One of every eight 17-year-olds believes the president can appoint members of Congress.
- ☐ Half of the 13- and 17-year-olds believe the president can appoint members of Congress.
- ☐ Half of the 13-year-olds believe it is against the law to start a new political party.
- ☐ Twenty-nine percent of 17-year-olds do not know that local governments operate the public schools they are in.

These figures must certainly trouble both those who believe that public opinion is important in American politics and those who believe that it should be. We do not have fully comparable results testing the American people as a whole. But on learning of these results, Evron Kirkpatrick, executive director of the American Political Science Association, remarked: "We do know that there is a

---

[9]A 1946 NORC poll reported in *Public Opinion Quarterly,* Winter 1946-47, page 604. Quoted by Devine, *Political Culture,* p. 37.

[10]Gallup Poll reported in the *New York Times,* Nov. 30, 1975.

Political polls are sometimes wrong.
Wide World Photos

considerable lack of knowledge about government on the part of the general population, and that it is not confined to high school students. I suspect that if the same questions were given to a sample of the students' parents, the results would be just about the same."[11]

Perhaps the closest equivalent survey conducted rather regularly is that by Gallup and other pollsters asking whether citizens know the name of their member of Congress. The results have been rather consistent over time. For example, in 1966 some 46 percent said they did, while in 1970 it was 53 percent. But even more interesting is the breakdown that shows the *distribution* of that knowledge among different groups in the population. The surveys find that males are more likely to know than females, that whites are more likely to know than blacks, and that those with higher levels of education, income, and occupation are more likely to know. None of these results is surprising. But two other findings may be.

First, young adults, although they are better educated and should have more at stake because they'll live longer, are less likely to know the name of their member of Congress. The explanation for this may be, Norval Glenn suggests, that young adults tend to get distracted by such things as getting a degree, getting married, and starting a career. Furthermore, young adults tend to move more frequently and so may pay less attention to local politics.

Second, the size of one's city seems to be important. Residents of small towns are less well informed than others – perhaps because they have less education. But those who live in large cities are also less likely to know the name of their member of Congress, although their education and race do not differ enough to account for this. Perhaps they too, like the young, are distracted by the stresses of daily life.[12]

□ THE OPINIONS AMERICANS HOLD

■ American political culture

Ignorance of current political happenings and personalities is widespread in America, as study after study documents. But does this mean that the American people don't really believe anything? Or does it mean that they have no basic attitudes in common?

Donald Devine has examined opinion poll data to see whether there are beliefs held in common by most Americans. He refers to these beliefs as being the "American political culture" – the values held by most citizens that influence their political and social attitudes and behavior.[13] Devine found a group of eleven key

[11]Gene L. Maeroff, "Many Teen-Agers Are Ignorant About Government, Survey Finds," *New York Times*, January 2, 1977.

[12]For further results and analysis, see Norval Glenn, "The Distribution of Political Knowledge in the U.S.," in *Political Attitudes and Public Opinion*, ed. Dan Nimmo and Charles Bonjean (New York: MacKay, 1972), pp. 272–283.

[13]The concept was developed by Gabriel Almond and employed by Almond and Sidney Verba in their influential book *The Civic Culture* (Boston: Little, Brown, 1963), where it is defined as "attitudes toward the political system and its various parts, and attitudes toward the role of the self in the system."

TABLE 10.1

Popular support for the values of the liberal tradition over time

Value	Average percentage of the people supporting each value in each period		
	1936–1945	1946–1955	1956–1970
1. Popular rule and elections	—	86	79
2. Legislative predominance	71	62	78
3. Federalism	65	—	65
4. Decentralized parties	62	69	73
5. Liberty	72	72	68
6. Equality	98	—	85
7. Property	60	66	66
8. Achievement	74	—	86
9. Belief inGod	96	95	98
10. Religion	70	72	73
11. Altrusim	—	—	73
Average support for the political culture as a whole (all eleven values) in each period	74	75	77

Source: Adapted from Donald Devine, *The Political Culture of the United States* (Boston: Little, Brown, 1972), p. 230.

values in the American political culture.[14] They include *liberty, equality,* and *property* – the three central values in the philosophy of the British philosopher John Locke, who influenced Jefferson, Madison, and other Founding Fathers. Two other values Devine found are *belief in God* and *support for religion.* There was also strong support for *altruistic* ("do-gooder") *community service.* An *emphasis on achievement* was a seventh widely held value. And in addition there were four qualities of politics supported in surveys: *popular rule* including elections; *predominance of the legislative branch; a federal structure of government* – national, state, and local; and *decentralized political parties* responsive to local needs and desires. The average percentage support for these values in the various polls Devine examined in each of three periods is given in Table 10.1.

The American people consistently say they believe in these values. More detailed studies, however, reveal that on specific questions they may not stick to these beliefs. A 1970 CBS news survey took a list of ten rights, from free speech to trial by jury, and asked a random sample of 1136 American people questions to find out whether they supported or opposed them. Take a look at Table 10.2 and compare those results with the guarantees in the First, Fourth, Fifth, Sixth, and Seventh Amendments to the Constitution. Five of those ten rights guaranteed to us by our Bill of Rights are not supported by a majority of our fellow citizens.

■ Political subcultures

Studies find strong differences in the attitudes and political knowledge of different parts of the population. This argues for further study of the political

[14]Donald Devine, *The Political Culture of the United States* (Boston: Little, Brown, 1972).

culture of America – study that breaks the culture down into what social scientists call *subcultures* or parts of the culture. This can be done in various ways. In earlier chapters we indicated that geographical region, religion, nationality or ethnic groupings, social class, and rural-versus-urban location can affect what people believe and how they vote. We cannot examine all of these subcultures again here, but several studies will indicate what we may find.[15]

Sectional differences Throughout American history the North-South sectional or regional conflict has been dominant. Some 30 years ago, V. O. Key wrote: "In its grand outlines the politics of the South revolves around the position of the Negro. It is at times interpreted as a politics of cotton, as a politics of free trade, as a politics of agrarian poverty, or as a politics of planter and plutocrat [rich ruler]. Although

[15]Alan D. Monroe, *Public Opinion in America* (New York: Dodd, Mead, 1975), chap. 6.

[16]V. O. Key, *Southern Politics in State and Nation* (New York: Knopf, 1949), p. 5

TABLE 10.2

Support for, and opposition to, guarantees in the *Bill of Rights*.

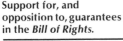

1. *Peaceful Assembly:* "As long as there appears to be no clear danger of violence, do you think that any group, no matter how extreme, should be allowed to organize protests against the government?"

   Yes–21% *No*–76% *Sometimes*–0% *No response*–3%

2. *Free Press:* "Except in time of war, do you think newspapers, radio, and television should have the right to report any story, even if the government feels it's harmful to our national interest?"

   Yes–42% *No*–55% *Sometimes*–1% *No response*–2%

3. *Free Speech:* "Do you think everyone should have the right to criticize the government, even if the criticism is damaging to our national interest?"

   Yes–42% *No*–54% *Sometimes*–1% *No response*–3%

4. *Double Jeopardy:* "If a man is found innocent of a serious crime, but new evidence is uncovered later, do you think that he should be tried again for the same crime?"

   Yes–58% *No*–38% *Sometimes*–1% *No response*–3%

5. *Preventive Detention:* "If a person is suspected of a serious crime, do you think the police should be allowed to hold him in jail, until they can get enough evidence to officially charge him?"

   Yes–58% *No*–38% *Sometimes*–1% *No response*–2%

6. *Trial by Jury:* "In most criminal cases, the judge conducts the trial and a jury decides guilt or innocence. Instead of the jury, would it be better if the judge alone decides guilt or innocence?

   Yes–14% *No*–82% *Sometimes*–1% *No response*–3%

7. *Search and Seizure:* "If the police suspect that drugs, guns, or other criminal evidence is hidden in someone's house, should they be allowed to enter the house without first obtainng a search warrant?"

   Yes–32% *No*–66% *Sometimes*–1% *No response*–1%

8. *Self-Incrimination:* "At their trials, do you think suspected criminals should have the right to refuse to answer questions if they feel their answers may be used against them?"

   Yes–54% *No*–42% *Sometimes*–1% *No response*–3%

9. *Public Trial:* "In criminal cases, do you think the government should ever have the right to hold a secret trial?"

   Yes–20% *No*–75% *Sometimes*–1% *No response*–4%

10. *Confronting Witnesses:* "During court trials, do you think the government should ever be allowed to keep the identity of witnesses secret from the defendant?"

    Yes–40% *No*–54% *Sometimes*–2% *No response*–4%

Source: Reprinted from *Public Opinion* (R. R. Bowker, New York, 1972. Copyright © 1972 by Columbia Broadcasting System, Inc.) by permission of CBS, Inc.

such interpretations have a superficial validity, in the last analysis the major peculiarities of southern politics go back to the Negro."[16]

In the last 30 years the South has come a long way, as we shall see more clearly in Chapter 14. So have southerners, who have moved north and west in large numbers. As one student of public opinion notes:

> While the South has obviously been on the antiliberal side of racial questions for two centuries, its reputation as a bastion of conservative opinion on all political issues is not justified by the facts. On issues that are nonracial and noneconomic in nature [such as legalizing abortion, controlling pornography, and permitting prayer in public schools] there is a tendency for the South to be less liberal than the other regions, but the difference is relatively slight. In part this tendency toward social conservatism may be traced to the fact that the South is more rural and less affluent than the other regions; it may also represent some spillover effect from opinions on race. On economic issues, however, there is no such deviation.[17]

Elazar's "cultural streams" One interesting effort to account for this difference in the South as well as other differences in the American political culture has been made by Daniel Elazar.[18] He argues that America was settled by three streams of migrants. The first was the Yankees from New England, who spread out across the northern United States. They took with them their strong Calvinist Protestantism, their middle-class values, their business orientation, and their loyalty to the Republican party. The second was the middle stream from New York, New Jersey, and Pennsylvania, which spread out through the central United States with its Catholic (or hierarchical Protestant), individualist views. This group came from many classes and had mixed party loyalties. The third was the southern stream, which moved west with its traditionalism, its ethnic differences, and its Democratic party loyalties.

The Yankee stream was then reinforced by more immigrants from the British Isles. The middle stream was joined by English, Irish, French, German, and other northern European immigrants. And the southern stream, which had originated in Eastern Europe and the Mediterranean area, took with it blacks and encountered Mexicans, both of whom became dominated peoples in that region. Figure 10.3, developed by Alan Monroe, portrays the movements of these streams across America.

These distinctions are indeed only tendencies. No region of America contains but a single type of political subculture, even though one or another type may be dominant there. But if the experts are right, "the political culture into which an individual is socialized seems to exercise a significant, if unnoticed, influence over his political behavior. We must beware of assuming direct correlations between

---

[17]Monroe, *Public Opinion in America,* pp. 106–107.

[18]Daniel J. Elazar, *Cities of the Prairie: The Metropolitan Frontier and American Politics* (New York: Basic Books, 1970).

FIGURE 10.3

Generalized pattern of cultural settlement in the United States.

Source: Figure 6.2, "Generalized Pattern of Cultural Settlement in the United States," from *Public Opinion in America,* by Alan D. Monroe. Copyright © 1975 by Harper & Row, Publishers, Inc. Used by permission of Harper & Row, Publishers, Inc.

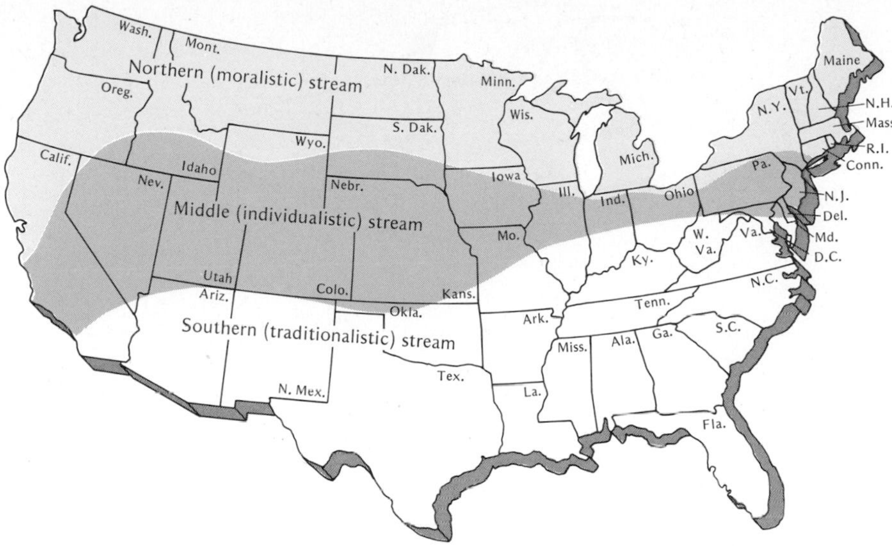

culture and opinion, however," warns Monroe. "At the present time, it would appear that the moralistic culture is on the liberal side of most issues, but this has not always been so, and one can certainly find evidences of persons embodying moralistic orientations who would advance an extremely conservative ideology. The cultural differences lie more in the broad expectations people have about the role of the political system rather than in their specific preferences, more in the style of the political action they desire than in its substance."[19]

■ How political culture influences public opinion

The impact of political culture on public opinion is somewhat indirect. One observer, Walter A. Rosenbaum, suggests that political culture may influence opinion in three basic ways.[20]

Defining the context First, it may define the general context within which opinions are developed and expressed. It does this by teaching a person how to form his or her political opinions, how to express them, and to which offices or institutions he or she should address them. Our political culture emphasizes the importance of the presidency, for example. This encourages citizens to look to the president for guidance in forming their views and to express them to the president where they seem to be desired or needed by him.

Screening information Second, the political culture helps the citizen screen political information so he or she need only pay attention to what is real and

[19]Monroe, *Public Opinion in America,* p. 115.

[20]Walter A. Rosenbaum, *Political Culture* (New York: Praeger, 1975), pp. 121–128.

Drawing by W. Miller.
© 1975 The New Yorker
Magazine, Inc.

meaningful. What is real or believable is usually determined for most citizens by leaders and other members of the political elite whose roles are given importance by the political culture – from the president to the person who anchors TV network news programs.

Shaping expectations Third, the political culture shapes expectations about government "inputs" (demands on government from people and interests) and "outputs" (policies and actions adopted by government). The major way the political culture does this is by defining what is an appropriate matter for government to act upon and what is not. We now believe that governments should create and run public schools, for example, where once we did not. On the other hand, we do not believe the government should dictate what types of art and music are "American" and what are "un-American" – although we seem somewhat undecided about the question of pornography. All these views are attitudes shaped by values that are part of our dominant political culture.

□ POLITICS, OPINIONS, AND POLICY

■ How politics influences opinions It is clear that our politics influences our political culture. As long as things are going well, we tend to accept the values underlying our system (our political culture) without very much questioning. Our political culture then, as we have just noted, helps to shape – or at least to limit – the opinions we hold on public questions. On the other hand, when we are disappointed and disillusioned by our politics, our political culture may undergo changes.

But politics influences our opinions more directly as well. When we discussed political participation in Chapter 5, we described the role of the government as a political participant that often actively shapes people's political thoughts. In Chapter 12, when we discuss the mass media, we shall cite instances of government efforts to manipulate public opinion by using and abusing the media.

Influences of politics on opinions are so common they do not surprise us. Some of them simply fall in the category of "leadership" – opinion leadership by those better informed than we citizens. But many of the government's influences on opinion are less necessary. They are also not necessarily what we would expect to find in a democracy if we read democratic theorists, who tend to emphasize the role of public opinion in influencing politics.

■ Do opinions influence politics?

Our system, we well know, is not a "pure democracy." The people don't themselves together make the decision. There are too many of us to do that, and too many decisions as well, as we have noted in previous chapters. Instead, we have a "representative democracy." The people choose individuals who make decisions for them. We assume that these officials make decisions that "represent" the people in some way. As we noted in Chapter 8 on Congress, people have different notions of what this means. Not all agree that officials should be "delegates" who do the bidding of the citizens. So decisions may not represent the opinions of the citizens, even though officials may represent the people nonetheless in their own minds.

Our system does tend to assume that the people will vote, and vote intelligently. In the abstract, "The political theory of democracy," wrote the late Paul Lazarsfeld, "requires that the electorate possess appropriate personality structures, that it be interested and participate in public affairs, that it be informed, that it be principled, that it correctly perceive political realities, that it engage in discussion, that it judge rationally, and that it consider the community interest."[21]

We know already, from previous chapters, that this is a set of conditions rarely met in practice. James Madison argued in *Federalist* no. 10 that "It may well happen that the public voice, pronounced by the representatives of the people, will be more consonant to the public good than if pronounced by the people themselves, convened for the purpose."

But do public officials really take public opinion seriously? How do they even know what it is? Elections may reveal something – but only half or fewer of the citizens vote. Letters, telegrams, and other messages may also help – but very few Americans ever send such messages.

This leaves our politicians with opinion polls as their major source of information on public opinion over and above their own hunches. We are told that politicians are always examining polls – but these are usually polls about their own popularity rather than polls about popular opinion on public issues. When they do examine polls on public issues, what do they learn?

"The term 'public opinion' as used in polling is quite distinct from the historical concept of public opinion as a state of mind, diffuse, shapeless, and shifting as a cloud," writes opinion expert Leo Bogart. "For many years, philosophers and poltical scientists dealt with public opinion as though it represented . . . one force among many in the complex flux of politics. These forces were like currents of the air or ocean, constantly changing in their contours and directions. The public opinion survey method requires that these elusive currents be treated as though they were static, that we define and measure what was formerly undefinable and unmeasurable. Once this is done, and done over and over

---

[21]Paul Lazarsfeld, "Democratic Theory and Public Opinion," *Public Opinion Quarterly* 16 (1952).

again," Bogart warns, "it is easy to succumb to the illusion that the measurements represent reality rather than a distorted, dim, approximate reflection of a reality that alters its shape when seen from different angles."[22]

■ Do opinions influence policy?

Still, experts study the extent to which these public opinions are related to – "congruent with" is the term they use – government policy. Robert Weissberg made an extensive study of opinion-policy congruence on domestic issues (defense spending, health care, income tax rates, integration, religion in the schools, gun control, and the death penalty) and foreign policy questions (Vietnam, foreign aid, and admission of China to the United Nations) over the past 40 years. He concluded that opinion-policy congruence does occur, but it varies with the topic and the time period, and there are frequent instances of incongruity. For example, the majority agreed with government action on the question of Communist China's admission to the United Nations for a period of 20 years. Yet public opinion has disagreed totally with court rulings and government actions prohibiting prayer in the public school. Other cases vary from year to year – capital punishment for murder, for example.[23] Other experts would generally agree with Weissberg that there is no clear pattern of congruence between opinion and policy.

So policy clearly is not simply based upon, or a reflection of, public opinion. Why then do we do so much polling? Bogart suggests that "Opinion surveys have become a mechanism through which the public becomes sensitized to its own needs and self-conscious about its own collective stance. . . . An entire generation of Americans now has grown up accepting polling as a commonplace institution and poll findings as part of the normal daily flow of expected information."[24] By this reasoning, polls may be more important to us, the people, than to them, the politicians.

Opinion surveys, Bogart reminds us, "are often dubious indicators of actual behavior because they do not, and perhaps cannot, measure the seething, changing character of the public temper. They generally fail to embody the rich context of motivation and cross-communication out of which opinions arise and activate people in the mass.[25]

The motivations that "activate people in the mass" – that is, in large groups – create interest groups out of "special publics." The cross-communication that makes possible this organizing of opinion now depends heavily on the media. Opinions without communication can have little influence on people. Opinions without action can have little influence on politics. So to get to a fuller understanding of the ultimate impact of public opinion on our politics, we must also examine interest groups and the media. These will be our topics in the next two chapters.

---

[22]Leo Bogart, *Silent Politics: Polls and the Awareness of Public Opinion* (New York: Wiley, 1972), p. 15.

[23]Robert Weissberg, *Public Opinion and Popular Government* (Englewood Cliffs, N.J.: Prentice-Hall, 1976), chaps. 8–11, esp. p. 244.

[24]Bogart, *Silent Politics,* p. 15

[25]Ibid., pp. 17–18.

☐ SUGGESTIONS FOR FURTHER READING AND STUDY

For a good general orientation to the study of public opinion, three already classic pieces can be recommended: V. O. Key, *Public Opinion and American Democracy* (New York: Knopf, 1961); Gabriel Almond, *The American People and Foreign Policy* (New York: Praeger, 1960); and Philip Converse, "The Nature of Belief Systems in Mass Publics," in *Ideology and Discontent,* ed. David Apter (New York: Free Press, 1964), pp. 206–261. Among the more recent and comprehensive texts are Bernard Hennessey, *Public Opinion,* 2nd ed. (Belmont, Calif.: Wadsworth, 1970); Norman R. Luttbeg, *American Public Opinion* (New York: Wiley, 1973); and Alan D. Monroe, *Public Opinion in America* (New York: Dodd, Mead paperback, 1975).

On socialization, a good overview is Richard E. Dawson, Kenneth Prewitt, and Karen S. Dawson, *Political Socialization,* 2nd ed. (Boston: Little, Brown paperback, 1977). For more specialized pieces summarizing recent research, see Stanley Allen Renshon, ed. *Handbook of Political Socialization* (New York: Free Press, 1977).

The concept of political culture is developed in Gabriel Almond and Sidney Verba, *The Civic Culture: Political Attitudes in Five Nations* (Princeton, N.J.: Princeton University Press, 1963; Boston: Little, Brown paperback, 1965). The concept is analyzed in Walter A. Rosenbaum, *Political Culture* (New York: Praeger paperback, 1975). For an application to America, see Donald Devine, *The Political Culture of the United States* (Boston: Little, Brown, 1972). And for an intriguing and different approach, see Daniel Elazar, *Cities of the Prairie: The Metropolitan Frontier and American Politics* (New York: Basic, 1970).

The best general introduction to polling is Charles W. Roll and Albert H. Cantril, *Polls: Their Use and Misuse in Politics* (New York: Basic Books, 1972). For guidance on how to conduct polls, see Frederick F. Stephan and Philip J. McCarthy, *Sampling Opinions: An Analysis of Survey Procedures* (New York: Wiley, 1958) and Leslie Kish, *Survey Sampling* (New York: Wiley, 1965). For a very critical view of the way polling is carried out, see Michael Wheeler, *Lies, Damned Lies, and Statistics: The Manipulation of Public Opinion in America* (New York: Liveright, 1976).

For reports of actual opinion surveys, see Lloyd A. Free and Hadley Cantril, *The Political Beliefs of Americans: A Study of Public Opinion* (New York: Simon & Schuster, 1968); Richard Scammon and Ben Wattenberg, *The Real Majority* (New York: Coward, McCann paperback, 1970); and a series of books sponsored by the Potomac Institute, including Albert H. Cantril and Charles W. Roll, *The Hopes and Fears of the American People* (New York: Universe paperback, 1971); and William Watts and Lloyd Free, *The State of the Nation* (New York: Universe paperback, 1973), and subsequent editions.

Finally, to keep up to date on current surveys, you may consult the *Gallup Opinion Index,* a monthly journal that reprints the Gallup polls. Even more helpful, because it summarizes polls from most pollsters, including international polls, is the monthly *Current Opinion* published by the Roper Center. For occasional surveys on specific topics and discussions of questions concerning polling and public opinion, see the scholarly journal *Public Opinion Quarterly.*

11 The interests: public, special, and vested

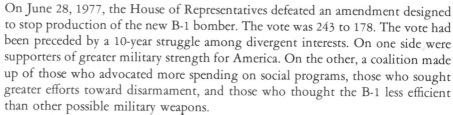

On June 28, 1977, the House of Representatives defeated an amendment designed to stop production of the new B-1 bomber. The vote was 243 to 178. The vote had been preceded by a 10-year struggle among divergent interests. On one side were supporters of greater military strength for America. On the other, a coalition made up of those who advocated more spending on social programs, those who sought greater efforts toward disarmament, and those who thought the B-1 less efficient than other possible military weapons.

When the House voted to reject the amendment offered by Representative Joseph P. Addabbo (Democrat of New York), the long struggle was over at last, and supporters of the B-1 had won. Or so it seemed to participants and observers.

President Carter had said during the 1976 campaign that the B-1 was "an exotic weapons system that serves no real function." Asserting that it would be "wasteful of taxpayers' dollars" he concluded that it "should not be funded." But once he took office he indicated that he would reexamine the question carefully, studying "classified analyses and information about weapons systems which I did not have before."

He had announced his intention to make a final decision by June 30, the time when the new military appropriations bill would be nearing completion and a decision would be necessary. Supporters and opponents alike spoke with him about it from time to time during the spring months, attempting to influence his decision. Most came away from the meetings sensing that Carter was leaning more and more strongly toward approving the B-1.

Many thought his secretary of defense, Harold Brown, would urge him in that direction. Brown, after all, had been involved in the original decision to design the new supersonic bomber when he worked in the Pentagon under President Kennedy. This role had even given him the nickname "Father of the B-1."

Carter was to announce his final decision at a press conference June 30. But the House was so confident of his decision and sure of its own that it went ahead and voted funds to build the plane 2 days before that. The Senate was expected to follow suit shortly thereafter.

"This has been one of the most difficult decisions that I've made since I've been in office," Carter said, opening his June 30 press conference. "In the past few months, I've done my best to possess all the factors involving production of the B-1 bomber. My decision is that we should not continue with deployment of the B-1s. And I am directing that we discontinue plans for production of this weapons system."

Mike Peters, *Dayton Daily News*

The decision astonished virtually everyone. Air force officials were dismayed. One air force colonel wisecracked that without the B-1 the United States might have to "charter an air force from Pan Am [the commercial airline]." An official at Rockwell International, the industrial giant that had the contract to build the plane, said, "This was the best-kept secret since the atom bomb. And that's the way it hits us." The Rockwell official in charge of the program, Bastian ("Buz") Hello, called the decision "a great surprise and deep shock."

In the House, reactions were even stronger. Representative Robert Dornan, who represented the district where Rockwell's main B-1 work was being done, said, "They're breaking out the vodka and caviar in Moscow," implying that the Soviets were the real beneficiaries. (The Russians, however, were silent on the matter.) And Republican leader John Rhodes called it "a rather gratuitous slap in the face" to the House. The House then went ahead that afternoon and passed the Defense Appropriations bill with the B-1 money still in it, leaving it up to the Senate to strike the item when it took up the matter.[1]

□ INTERESTS AND INTEREST GROUPS IN POLITICS

President Carter, explaining how he made the B-1 decision, told that press conference: "I always try to keep an open mind and make my decision based on what I think is best for our country." He might as well have said he decided it in terms of "the public interest." Presidents and most all politicians claim to be deciding questions in terms of the public interest, whether in candor or to avoid seeming to defer to special interests.[2] Yet companies such as Rockwell International

---

[1]These reactions were reported by *Time,* July 11, 1977, pp. 8–12.

[2]For a negative view of the use of the term as rhetoric designed to make the population quiescent, see Murray Edelman, *The Symbolic Uses of Politics* (Urbana: University of Illinois Press, 1967).

claim that projects such as the B-1 are "in the public interest" or "in the national interest," while opponents such as the National Campaign to Stop the B-1 Bomber say that their position represents "the public interest."

What are we to make of these disputes over just what is in "the public interest"? If people and groups disagree so much on specific cases, can we look to a general definition to find out who's right? Unfortunately, political scientists and philosophers also disagree on what the public interest is, and even on whether or not it exists.[3]

■ Private interests and special interests

Everyone grants that there are **private interests** – the interests of individuals. When a number of people – as individuals or perhaps as a firm like Rockwell – have the same private interest, we may refer to this as a **special interest** – an interest "shared by only a few people or a fraction of the community." Special interests are those that "*exclude* others and may be *adverse* to them."[4]

In politics, two things can make a special interest especially important. One is that those sharing the same special interest can *organize into a special-interest group* in order to increase their chances of getting what they want. When we speak of "special interests" in politics, often we refer to organized special interest groups or "pressure groups," such as the National Association of Manufacturers (NAM), the AFL-CIO, or the Campaign to Stop the B-1 Bomber. Political scientists generally define an **interest group** as an organized group whose members have common views about certain policies or actions and so undertake activities to influence government officials and policies.[5]

■ Vested interests

The other thing that can make a special interest especially important in politics is being *vested.* The term "vested" comes from the French word for a cloak or garment in which one is wrapped for protection, and we still use it to refer to the vest of a suit of clothes. In politics, it refers to an interest "wrapped in," or protected by, the status quo – the distribution of wealth or privilege, for example – or benefiting from a particular program. The defense industries and some labor unions benefit from a large defense budget, and so we may refer to them as vested interests when the subject of defense spending is being debated. **Vested interests,** in other words, are special interests that are already getting their way, already benefiting specially from the way things are, and seek to keep it like that.

---

[3]For a discussion of concepts of the common good and the public interest, see Glendon Schubert, *The Public Interest* (Glencoe, Ill.: The Free Press, 1960); Richard Flathman, *The Public Interest* (New York: Wiley, 1966); the symposium on interests in the journal *Political Theory* 3, no. 3 (August 1975); J. D. B. Miller, *The Nature of Politics* (London: Duckworth, 1962), chap. 4; and Barry M. Mitnick, "A Typology of Conceptions of the Public Interest," *Administration and Society* 8, no. 1 (May 1976): 5–28.

[4]These words belong to the late E. E. Schattschneider, but the concept is found in political writings since the ancient Greeks. See Schattschneider, *The Semi-Sovereign People* (New York: Holt, Rinehart & Winston, 1960), pp. 23–24.

[5]For a discussion emphasizing the role of groups in politics – one that has been very influential in political science – see David B. Truman, *The Governmental Process,* 2nd ed. (New York: Knopf, 1971), chap. 2.

■ The public interest

What, then, about the "common interest," the "general interest," or, as it's most often called, the "public interest"? Here, there is no agreement. Before the term "public interest" became widely used, it was generally believed that there were truths about human beings, their needs, and their values that existed beyond time and place, beyond specific individuals. The common good, as it was then usually called, was the body of basic truths or principles by which politics and policy could be judged to see whether they were right. But as the growth of science and the spread of revolution shattered belief in this shared world view, it became more difficult to believe the notion that there was a single, eternal common good.

Politics therefore became more individualistic, more conflictual, less stable. As this occurred, people began to think of politics not as a way of achieving an ideal order but rather as a way of expressing and reconciling or compromising individual differences without resorting to violence. So the focus shifted from the common good to individual interests. A second notion of the public interest, as some cumulation or compromising of a wide range of private interests, gradually began to spread.

Since then we have had several centuries of pragmatic, individualistic politics. But with rare exceptions they have failed to show that the concept of the public interest as a cumulation of private interests can unite a fragmented society behind constructive programs. The old belief was that if every person pursued his or her own private interests, the general good or the public interest would be served in the longer run. This view, which we'll encounter again in coming chapters, argued that there was "an invisible hand" that would make it turn out that way. It followed that government should intervene as little as possible in the economy and in society. But time has shown "the invisible hand" to be quite arthritic or crippled. So the search is on for new notions of the public interest. These notions, most agree, must include the interests of the weak as well as the strong, of the poor as well as the rich, of the women as well as the men, and of the yet unborn as well as the living.

It is a big order – a big challenge to our thinkers and an even bigger one to our politicians. Our thinkers can try to develop a notion without worrying about immediate problems and decisions. But our politicians must develop and use such a notion in the day-to-day struggles we call politics, while being buffeted by special interests on all sides.

When President Carter spoke of making the B-1 decision "based on what I think is best for our country," he was echoing a conception of the public interest similar to that of the late E. E. Schattschneider, who wrote. "Presumably no community exists unless there is some kind of community of interests, just as there is no nation without some notion of national interests. . . . The reality of the common interest is suggested by demonstrated capacity of the community to survive. There must be something that holds people together. . . . Perfect agreement within a community is not always possible, but an interest may be said to have become public when it is shared so widely as to be substantially universal."[6]

---

[6]Schattschneider, *The Semi-Sovereign People,* p. 24.

But even if we believe, as Carter clearly was assuming, that national security and economic efficiency are twin elements of the public interest as most Americans would conceive of it, this does not solve the problem of the political leader. For, as J. D. B. Miller has written, in practice the common interest "is something which manifests itself from time to time, but is neither constant nor reliable. It is more applicable to ends than to means; it may dissolve under the pressure of arguments about how it is to be served."[7]

The problems for political leadership caused by interests, public, special, and vested, are clearly manifest in the case of the B-1 bomber. So are the roles of interest groups in the political process. So let's look in more detail at the interests and interest groups in this case.

□ THE INTERESTS AND THE B-1

■ The vested interests

In the case of the B-1, one major vested interest was the United States Air Force, which had developed a new bomber and wanted to keep it and build hundreds of "copies" of it (at a cost of about $100 million per plane).

Another vested interest was Rockwell International. The B-1 was contributing only about 5 percent of Rockwell's $5-billion-dollar-a-year income. But if production of 150 to 244 B-1s had been decided upon, the profits to Rockwell over the years of large-scale production would have been massive.

Those profits would also have been shared with other companies around the country. The standard practice of a company getting a big contract like this is to "subcontract" much of the work out to other firms, in many different congressional districts. This increases political support for a project, because most members' districts would lose jobs if the project were cut back or canceled. In the case of the B-1, dozens of companies located throughout the United States had major subcontracting roles.

Companies with their profits or losses are not the only ones with vested economic interests, however. Workers employed by those companies also have a stake in the decision. Nationally, the B-1 program employed some 40,000 persons designing and building the five trial models of the plane. Most would soon be out of work.

[7]J. D. B. Miller, *The Nature of Politics* (London: Duckworth, 1962), p. 83.

The B-1 bomber on a test flight at Edwards Air Force Base, California.
Rockwell International

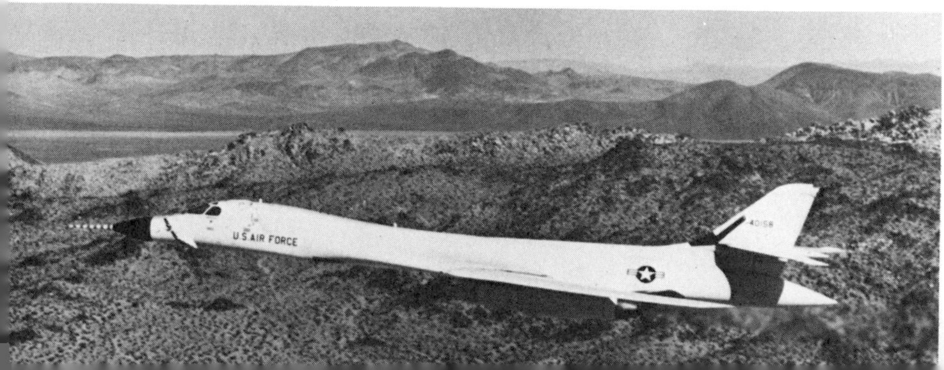

"I thought they'd go ahead with some production, but instead they ruin lives and cause unemployment," complained Jerry Whipple, a regional director for the major labor union in Southern California's aerospace industry. "We have environmental impact reports on trees and rivers and air, but why doesn't the Government do a study of the impact of its decisions on people – what it does to families and communities."[8]

Other people were affected, too. Those who owned shares of stock in the companies involved had a vested interest. The day Carter's decision was announced, Rockwell shares fell 4¼ points in value on the New York Stock Exchange.

■ The other special interests

So the major vested interests – the air force, the industrial producers, and their workers and stockholders – suffered a setback with Carter's decision. At the same time various other special interests were affected in other ways. Among them were the so-called "defense intellectuals" – experts on military strategy and defense policy. Some of them favored producing the B-1, and they were unhappy. But most seemed to believe the new bomber less efficient for the money than the cruise missiles (small, computer-guided missiles) that Carter decided to develop to replace it, and they were pleased.

Also affected were the various parts of the Campaign to Stop the B-1 – peace activists, disarmament supporters, and those favoring greater spending for social needs. These groups had banded together to lobby against the B-1, and on June 28, when the House voted down the Addabbo amendment, they thought they'd finally lost. They were pleasantly surprised and delighted by Carter's decision.

Other special interests affected were outside the United States. One was the Soviet Union, America's major military adversary. The Soviets were silent on the decision, as they always had been on the B-1. This led some to believe that the Soviets agreed with Carter's ultimate assessment, that it would be wasteful, and therefore hoped we'd decide to build it. If so, they were disappointed by Carter's decision. Other special interests were America's allies in Europe and Asia. They were split. Some argued we should develop every new weapon system we could. Others, more conscious of costs, agreed that the B-1 was an inefficient way to spend precious dollars needed elsewhere for defense.

■ The public interest

In the case of the B-1, it was particularly difficult to say what the public interest was. In a sense, it was, of course, to have "an adequate defense." But what makes a defense adequate? The experts have never agreed on that.[9] In addition, defense decisions have very important economic implications. Experts were certain

[8]Quoted in Robert Lindsey, "Carter's Decision on Bomber Jars Rockwell and Its Workers," *New York Times*, July 1, 1977.

[9]For some accounts of examples of the debate, see Alain Enthoven et al., *How Much Is Enough?* (New York: Harper & Row, 1971); Daniel Lang, *An Inquiry into Enoughness* (New York: McGraw-Hill, 1965); Bruce M. Russett, *What Price Vigilance?* (New Haven, Conn.: Yale University Press, 1970); and Jerome H. Kahan, *Security in the Nuclear Age* (Washington, D.C.: Brookings Institution, 1975).

the B-1 program would cost some $25 billion in its first 8 years and thought it might eventually cost up to $100 billion for the full program. Such costs would produce budget deficits that might cause imbalance in the economy to the detriment of the public interest.

Perhaps progress on arms control and disarmament should be included as an aspect of the public interest. The B-1 would have been yet another weapon system out of control. But the cruise missile chosen by Carter to replace the B-1 was also beyond the limits of the strategic arms control agreements that the United States had entered into with the Soviet Union.

Finally, important social programs, such as major welfare reform and national health insurance, were then commonly seen as in the public interest. The cost of the B-1 program would tend to preclude them. But military weakness leading to war would render such programs irrelevant. So how they fit into the calculation of the public interest on the question of the B-1 remains uncertain.

Indeed, unless and until Carter writes his memoirs, we may never know just how he conceived of the public interest in this decision, beyond the question of military efficiency. Nor are we likely to know whether he thought any of the special interests that had argued for the decision he made also expressed the public interest. We may assume that the special interest expressed by the air force, and that of Rockwell and the other military contractors, did not seem to express the public interest in his mind. But beyond that we cannot go far. The public interest thus remains as difficult to find and specify as it is important to consider.

The various special interests, on the other hand, are clearer in a particular case like B-1 as they are more generally in American politics. So let's look in more detail at the ways special interests operate in American politics in general, before examining their roles in the case of the B-1.

☐ HOW SPECIAL INTERESTS OPERATE

■ The Washington lobbyists

No one knows just how many representatives of special interests there now are in Washington. One recent directory suggests about 5000. We usually call all Washington representatives of special interests lobbyists because they originally hung around the lobbies of the House and Senate waiting for chances to talk to the legislators about their concerns. Lobbyists still "work the lobbies," of course, but in fact usually spend more of their time in other activities designed to protect the special interests of their employers.

■ Lobbyists and Congress

In dealing with Congress, lobbyists use a variety of tactics. First, they *provide information* to legislators and their assistants on how the special interest views the matter in question, and often even on what is in question. Senator John F. Kennedy described this role of lobbyists clearly some 5 years before he became president:

> Lobbyists are in many cases expert technicians and capable of explaining complex and difficult subjects in a clear, understandable fashion. They engage in personal discussions with Members of Congress in which they can explain in detail the reason for positions they advocate. Lobbyists prepare briefs, memorandums, legislative analysis, and draft legislation for use by committees and Members of Congress; they are necessarily masters of their subject and, in fact, they frequently can provide useful statistics and information not otherwise available.[10]

But, as Senator Kennedy added, a legislator must be on guard to see that the information is accurate, if not necessarily balanced and fair.

Kennedy's emphasis on the *authority* of lobbyists as experts on their subject describing their image of reality to politicians highlights the political nature of their activity. It also reminds us of how necessary lobbyists are. As the late Senator Lee Metcalf (Democrat of Montana) remarked during a congressional debate on revision of the lobbying law, "We would have to multiply our staffs fourfold or fivefold if it were not for the information that the lobbyists give us, supply us, and the reliable information . . . upon which we can act."[11] In other words, information is power. And the lobbyists who can provide the most comprehensive and seemingly accurate information are likely to be powerful and effective. There is nothing secret about the basic technique. Charles E. Walker, once a high-level official in the Treasury Department and now a leading lobbyist, describes it succinctly: "We translate legislative proposals into jobs, payrolls, or economic growth for the Congressman's district or the Senator's state. We leave a briefing paper behind and then mail out a follow-up letter a few days later."[12]

But the lobbyists' actions in Congress are not all of such a purely informational nature. Another category of action involves *support*. Lobbyists will often *promise support* (in the form of campaign contributions, for example), or may threaten to *withdraw support* when necessary. Furthermore, they may also *offer enticements*—from fancy dinners and tickets to Washington Redskins football games to sexual favors from available call girls where information and campaign support are inadequate.

On occasion, lobbyists may *"go partisan,"* openly supporting an opponent of someone who votes against their interests. This step is unusual. The common practice is to contribute to both candidates in a race, on the theory that whoever wins, you win, because you helped fund his or her campaign

According to the law as of 1978, the following limits apply to campaign contributions:

- ☐ Individuals may contribute up to $1,000 in the primary and $1,000 in the general election to any candidate for Congress.

[10]John F. Kennedy, quoted in Congressional Quarterly, *The Washington Lobby,* 2nd ed. (Washington: CQ, 1974), p. 6.

[11]*Congressional Record,* 94th Cong., 2d sess. p. S-9269.

[12]Quoted in "The Hidden Army of Washington Lobbyists," *U.S. News & World Report,* July 25, 1977, p. 30.

- □ Individuals may give no more than a total of $25,000 to all federal candidates in any calendar year.
- □ Organizations or groups (political action committees, as they are called) may contribute up to $5,000 in the primary and $5,000 in the general election to any candidate for Congress. Groups are not limited as to the total number of candidates they may give to.
- □ An individual may contribute up to $5,000 to a multicandidate committee – a committee formed to give money to a number of political candidates.
- □ An individual can contribute up to $20,000 to political committees maintained by a national political party.

Lobby contributions to congressional campaigns have recently risen sharply. In 1975, according to Common Cause, the "citizen lobby," they totaled $12,525,586. In 1976, the figure was up to $22,571,912, including some $8 million from labor interests, $7 million from business interests, $2.7 million from health interests (doctors, drug firms, insurance companies, hospitals, and so on), and $1.5 million from agricultural interests. Many of these contributions are "targeted" to reach members – usually from both parties – of Senate and House committees that

TABLE 11.1

Committee targeting of 1976 campaign contributions by special interests

Special interest	Contributed to campaigns of members of	Amount contributed
Maritime related unions	*House Committee on Merchant Marine and Fisheries.* This committee would be considering "cargo preference" legislation that could force shippers to use more expensive American vessels to import oil—thereby raising the cost of oil to consumers while providing more jobs to members of maritime unions.	$ 98,438 to 24 of 27 Democrats 5,900 to 6 of 13 Republicans $104,338
Dairy interests	*Housing Agriculture Committee.* This committee would be considering bills to increase price supports for dairy farmers—thereby raising the cost of milk to consumers while increasing dairy farmers' incomes.	$181,225 to 17 of 31 Democrats 24,761 to 6 of 15 Republicans $205,986
American Medical Association	*House Ways and Means Committee.* This committee would be considering plans for national health insurance—which would be likely to limit doctors' income while lowering the cost of health care for Americans.	$ 37,250 to 19 of 25 Democrats 37,253 to 10 of 12 Republicans $ 74,503
National Education Association	*House Education and Labor Committee.* This committee considers all legislation involving federal aid to education.	$ 47,700 to 20 of 25 Democrats 6,380 to 5 of 12 Republicans $ 54,080

Source: Developed from statistics supplied by Common Cause.

handle bills of special interest to the special interest. Table 11.1 shows some examples uncovered by common cause in campaign contributions for the 1976 elections.[13]

■ Lobbyists and the public

Lobbyists also often *"go public,"* engaging in advertising campaigns and other public relations activities for their cause. The purpose of this is to develop public support that will be conveyed to Washington by citizens and other interests. Such "going public" may also help to control what is often called the public agenda – the list of topics considered appropriate for government action. Interests may attempt to keep something *off* the public agenda – as the American Medical Association has tried to keep government-funded medical care off the public agenda since 1935.[14] Or they may attempt to get something *on* the public agenda by making it of interest to public opinion – as environmentalists did in the 1960s.

In addition, once an issue is on the public agenda, interests will attempt to build the record or set the context within which the issue is defined and debated. They can do this by testifying publicly before Congress and becoming recognized as leading authorities on the issue itself, not just on their own special interest conception or definition of it.[15]

■ Lobbyists and the bureaucracy

Lobbyists do not confine their efforts to the Congress and the public, of course. They also "go to the bureaucracy" to influence the development and implementation of programs. Prime examples of this are the subgovernment relations we discussed in Chapters 7 and 8 – in which lobbyists combine with bureaucrats and congressional leaders to make decisions outside channels. Special interests maintain access to government in part by hiring former politicians and bureaucrats as their lobbyists or as their officials, as we have noted in previous chapters, or by getting the government to hire their own officials as policy makers.

■ Lobbyists and the courts

The special interests may also "go to court" to seek favorable judicial rulings when they can't get satisfaction elsewhere. One of the clearest instances of this approach was when the National Association for the Advancement of Colored People went to court to challenge segregation in public schools. This move was finally successful in the case of *Brown v. Board of Education* in 1954, as we saw in Chapter 9.

---

[13]See *Report to the American People on the Financing of Congressional Election Campaigns* (Washington: Common Cause, 1977).

[14]See, for example, Richard Harris, *A Sacred Trust* (Baltimore: Penguin paperback, 1969); Theodore R. Marmor, *The Politics of Medicare* (Chicago: Aldine, 1970).

[15]See Roger W. Cobb and Charles D. Elder, *Participation in American Politics: The Dynamics of Agenda Building* (Boston: Allyn & Bacon, 1972).

Stan Wakefield

Lobbyists do not contact government leaders only in the lobbies of the Capitol. Here a lobbyist stops by to chat with Representative Andrew Maguire during lunch.

■ Seeking direct popular legislation Sometimes, finally, interest groups may bypass lobbying to achieve direct legislation by the voters. Some states and localities have constitutional provisions for the **initiative.** If a percentage of the voters signs petitions requesting it, a proposed law is put on the ballot for a vote by the general public. If it passes, it becomes law even though the legislature or city council has refused to pass it. Related to the initiative is the **referendum,** whereby action by the legislature or council is put to a popular vote for ratification (approval). The legislature may decide on its own to call for a referendum or may be prompted to do so by citizen petition. If an interest group finds the legislature dominated by hostile interests, it may choose to go the initiative route – as environmentalists often do these years on bills to abolish or tax throwaway bottles and cans for drinks, for example.

Over the years, both initiative and referendum have been used in most states and many cities by labor unions, farm groups, education organizations, groups supporting the aged, and religious and civic groups. Business groups have been especially fond of referenda as ways of canceling legislation of which they disapprove. One major appeal of this approach is that there can be no amendment of the proposal. A legislative body can amend a bill to satisfy enough interest groups to get it passed, but the voters must say either yes or no to a referendum, and so it is usually easier to unite opponents to a measure.[16]

We have seen, then, that lobbyists for interest groups may "go to the lobby" of the legislature, "go partisan," "go public," "go to the bureaucracy," or go to court to attempt to get their way. But just who are these interest groups?

□ WHO ARE THE SPECIAL INTERESTS?

■ Trade and professional associations Washington columnist George Will once offered his readers "Will's Rule of informed citizenship." "If you want to understand your government," it goes, "don't begin by reading the Constitution. . . . Instead read selected portions of

---

[16]For a discussion of such "direct legislation," see Abraham Holtzman, *Interest Groups and Lobbying* (New York: Macmillan, 1966), chap. 6.

■ Will's Rule of informed citizenship

Consider Will's Rule of informed citizenship. If you want to understand your government, don't begin by reading the Constitution. It conveys precious little of the flavor of today's statecraft. Instead, read selected portions of the Washington Telephone Directory, such as pages 354–58, which contain listings for all the organizations with titles beginning with the word "National."

There are, of course, the big ones, like the National Association of Manufacturers, and the National Association of Broadcasters. But the pages teem with others.

National Cigar Leaf Tobacco Association. National Association of Mirror Manufacturers. National Association of Miscellaneous Ornamental & Architectural Products Contractors. National Association of Margarine Manufacturers.

National Candy Wholesalers Association. National Barrel & Drum Association. National Clay Pipe Institute. National Fibre Can & Tube Association. National Fishmeal & Oil Association. National Limestone Institute. National Liquor Stores Association. National Wooden Pallet & Container Association. Etc.

Some of these organizations are here for the kind of lobbying that is offensive in several senses. They want to bend public power to their private purposes, which always include enrichment. But most of these organizations spend most of their time in self-defense, trying to temper the government's ravenous appetite for regulating.

When government decrees new brake standards for trucks, truck stop operators may need expensive new equipment. And they are affected by whatever the Environmental Protection Agency thinks about control of fuel vapors. The Operators Association exists, in part, to warn operators when the government is about to strike.

The National Ice Association? The government in its wisdom considers ice a "food product." This means that Antarctica is one of the world's foremost food producers. It also means that while the Occupational Safety and Health Administration is worrying about the use of ammonia in ice manufacturing, the Food and Drug Administration can worry about the purity of the product.

The Crushed Stone people worry about (among other things) depletion allowances for various kinds of stones. The Ready Mixed Concrete people worry about Federal Highway Administration quality control standards. The National Limestone Institute has one eye on the Mining Enforcement and Safety Administration (What? You've never heard of it? What did you study in high school civics class?) It has another eye on the federal highway program, which is a joy to people who sell limestone.

The Barrel & Drum Association represents the businesses that recondition the 60 million 55-gallon drums currently in circulation. The Association is busy deciphering the desires of the Department of Transportation's Office of Hazardous Materials, which is worried about leakage in the transportation of things like pesticides. And the association also is encouraging Congress to restrain or even ban the use of lightweight throwaway drums which are, the association believes, an ecological outrage, not to mention a menace to drum reconditioning businesses.

The National Wooden Pallet & Container Association (a pallet is a portable platform for storing and moving freight) is fretting about the growing restrictions on lumbering in national forests.

I could go on—there are more than a thousand such organizations here—but you get the picture. It is a picture of government and the economy inextricably intertwined. Pages 354–58 of the Washington telephone book comprise an X-ray of today's political economy, and of the solar system of organizations that orbit around the vast star, the government.

Source: George F. Will, "Government by Association," *Washington Post,* April 8, 1976, p. A19.

the Washington Telephone Directory . . . which contain listings for all the organizations with titles beginning with the word 'National.'" He then explained that these special interest groups portray "a picture of the government and the economy inextricably intertwined." (See the box titled "Will's Rule of informed citizenship.")

Lest we think that these organizations do not represent *us,* there are such groups as the National Student Association and the National Student Lobby. And when we add Washington telephone listings beginning with the word "American," we include the American Association of University Professors and the American Political Science Association, as well as the American Association of University Women.[17]

It once was thought that virtually all Americans belonged to at least one such organization, and that most belonged to several. We now know that this is not true. Indeed, a recent study by Robert Salisbury found that, including churches, only about 75 percent of Americans belong to any organization, and just under half belong to more than one. Table 11.2 reports the results broken down by percentages belonging to the various types organizations. Perhaps a third of them could be considered political interest groups. Among these, the professional, veterans, and farm groups are usually active.[18]

---

[17]Another way to find such groups is to look in the Washington Yellow Pages under "associations," where you'll find thirty columns – eight pages – of societies, councils, institutes, alliances, leagues, federations, committees, and so on – some 1600 in all.

[18]See Carol S. Greenwald, *Group Power: Lobbying and Public Policy* (New York: Praeger, 1977), pp. 38–39.

TABLE 11.2

The organization memberships of Americans

Type of organization	Percent of Americans belonging to organization
Church	41.8
Sports	17.5
School service	17.5
Fraternal	13.7
Professional	13.0
Youth	10.3
Literary, art, study	9.2
Hobby	9.6
Veterans	8.9
Service	8.9
Political	4.4
Farm	4.2
Nationality	3.5
Percent of Americans belonging to an organization	74.5
Percent belonging to two organizations	18.9
Percent belonging to three or more organizations	29.9
Percent of Americans belonging to two or more organizations	48.8

Source: Robert Salisbury, "Overlapping Memberships, Organizational Interactions, and Interest Group Theory" (unpublished American Political Science Association paper, Chicago, Ill. 1976), p. 4. These figures are for 1974.

Trade associations top the list in terms of political activity. The oldest trade association still in business is the New York Chamber of Commerce, formed by twenty merchants in 1768. The next oldest is the New York Stock Exchange, established in 1792. In the century following, only a dozen or so national groups were formed. Today, a century later, however, the Commerce Department reports 20,000 national and international, 25,000 regional and state, and perhaps 400,000 local associations. There are so many such groups that there is even a group made up only of officers of such groups – the American Society of Association Executives, established in 1920.

Trade organizations exist to provide services to their members. Many of those services are things that would fall under the various lobbying activities we discussed above. That's why more than a quarter of the 4700 largest national trade groups have headquarters in Washington, where they spend perhaps a billion dollars a year and employ some 40,000 persons, many of whom might qualify as lobbyists by our broad definition. The Washington location is becoming essential. As William Utz of the National Shrimp Congress explains it, "The reaction time to new rules and regulations is faster if the headquarters is based in Washington. If you have an ear here, you can translate things as they happen."[19]

In fact, it is not only an ear, but a mouth, or a mouthpiece, which special interests want in Washington. A pocketbook is also helpful. The most effective lobbies tend to combine all three elements: gathering information, dispensing information, and dispersing resources where they'll do the most good.

Among the most effective lobbies through the years are: the AFL-CIO, representing most labor unions; the United States Chamber of Commerce, the National Association of Manufacturers, and the Business Roundtable, representing business; and Common Cause and Ralph Nader's Public Citizen groups, representing what they assert is "the public interest." But some observers would claim that the most powerful lobbyists in Washington are the individuals and firms known collectively as the "superlawyers" – lawyers who "know the ropes" in Washington and are available for hire by anyone who can afford their help. Let's look in more detail at the major lobby groups.

■ Labor lobbies

The American Federation of Labor-Congress of Industrial Organizations (created by a merger of the AFL and the CIO in 1955) consists of some 110 unions with about 14 million members. Of course it lobbies for special labor concerns. It also lobbies for social programs, such as national health insurance and tax reform, in cooperation with other liberal lobbies. And it lobbies for high defense spending and new technological projects such as the supersonic transport (SST) and the Alaska oil pipeline, in cooperation with business lobbies, partly because these programs promise more jobs, and partly because AFL-CIO leadership is generally conservative in its attitudes toward foreign affairs.

Many of the larger unions also maintain their own lobbyists in Washington.

---

[19]Quoted in Greenwald, *Group Power,* p. 65.

These usually work in tandem with the AFL-CIO lobbyists but occasionally take independent action when their positions differ. Among the large independent unions that lobby actively are the United Mine Workers and the Teamsters.

■ Business lobbies

The business lobby includes thousands of trade organizations but is dominated by three powerful coalitions. The first is the United States Chamber of Commerce, which represents about 65,000 businesses, including 3,500 local chambers of commerce and trade associations. The leading segments include manufacturers (26 percent), retail trade (14 percent), construction (13 percent), finance, insurance, and real estate (11 percent). Dues produce a budget of over $14 million a year. The "National Chamber," as it is called, uses this money to lobby on Capitol Hill, where it has been a prominent opponent of a consumer protection agency, of stronger antitrust legislation, and of national health insurance. Its effectiveness is partly a product of its Congressional Action System, a network of 100,000 business people who contact members of Congress directly. It has also established a new organization called Citizen's Choice, designed to mobilize "Americans who resent high taxes, inflation, and increasing government interference in their lives," so that they too will lobby for Chamber objectives. And the Chamber in 1977 established the National Chamber Litigation Center (NCLC), which it calls a "public-interest law firm." Citizen's Choice seems to be an alternative to Common Cause, while the NCLC is a counter to the Nader operation – both of which we shall discuss shortly.[20]

In June 1976 the Chamber announced plans to merge with the National Association of Manufacturers, which represents some 13,000 corporations and collects about $7 million a year in dues. The new organization, primarily an effort to pool strength in combatting the influence of organized labor, was to be called the Association of Commerce and Industry. But the merger was opposed by many members who thought the stronger voice would represent primarily the bigger corporate members. So it did not occur.

Meanwhile, the real growth in business lobbying strength was being shown by the Business Roundtable. This group of the chief executives of 160 of the largest corporations in America is based in New York but operates actively in Washington by using personal contacts with the president as well as members of Congress. It has taken a special interest in opposing creation of a consumer protection agency and obstructing passage of laws designed to curb monopolies and break up large corporations.

Small-business lobbies

The "big three" tend to focus their efforts on concerns of big business. Smaller businesses are represented by several major groups. The biggest is the National Federation of Independent Business. It employs 600 people nationwide and represents 507,000 small business owners. It regularly polls its

---

[20]For the Chamber's own account of its activities, see "The Voice of Business Grows Stronger in Washington," *Nation's Business,* March 1977, pp. 20–36.

members and reports results of its surveys to Congress. It also rates members of Congress on their voting on issues of interest to small businesses. The other leading advocate for small business is the National Small Business Association, which represents 50,000 members but acts through an executive committee rather than by polling its members.

■ Public-interest lobbies

What is sometimes thought of as "the other side"–the interests of consumers and ordinary citizens–is represented primarily by Common Cause and various public-interest law and lobbying organizations, many of them under the guidance of Ralph Nader.[21]

Public-interest organizations representing the concerns of those without great economic power or influential political position are nothing new in America. The movements to expand the right to vote, which we discussed in Chapter 3, were such. So were the various civil rights movements, designed to improve the lot of the blacks, and so was the union movement in its earlier phases. The Anti-Saloon League and the more general prohibition movement to outlaw alcoholic beverages would qualify, as would Planned Parenthood, the American Civil Liberties Union, and, more recently, the environmental groups we cited in Perspective 3.

These organizations have sought to change the dominant conception of the public interest–and have sometimes succeeded. They have operated on the principle that government should protect citizens from unjust practices of all sorts. And they have used the First Amendment guarantee of "the right of the people . . . to petition the government for a redress of grievances."

Some of these groups have emphasized lobbying, while others have relied primarily upon appeals to the courts. Still others have used research and distribution of their findings to generate public interest in their crusades. "Many of these organizations," writes observer John Guinther, "can point to successes, some legislative, some judicial. In many instances, however, the significant contribution has been a [philosophical] one. By its propagandizing, over the years the organization implants in the public consciousness a general perception of right and wrong which the people come to believe in and sometimes act upon."[22]

Common Cause is a national citizens' lobby with a membership of about a quarter of a million people. It has focused its attention on Congress, lobbying for campaign finance reform and laws requiring that lobbies disclose their gifts to politicians and the sources of their funds. It has also drafted and supported "sunset" laws providing that government agencies self-destruct after a given period of time if they cannot demonstrate their continued usefulness. It has favored creation of ombudsmen to help make bureaucracy more responsive. And it has supported various congressional reforms such as altering the seniority system. It was founded in 1970 by John Gardner, who had been a foundation executive and secretary of

---

[21]For an interesting study, see Jeffrey M. Berry, *Lobbying for the People: The Political Behavior of Public Interest Groups* (Princeton, N.J.: Princeton University Press, 1977).

[22]John Guinther, *Moralists and Managers: Public Interest Movements in America* (New York: Anchor paperback, 1976), p. xv.

HEW under Lyndon Johnson. It has since grown not only in membership but also in branches in various states that have turned their attention to reforming state government as well.

Ralph Nader, then a young lawyer, got his start in the early 1960s pursuing General Motors for making unsafe cars. When GM in turn pursued him, hiring a "private eye" to snoop on his private life, he won a court judgment against GM. He used that money to establish what has become a kind of conglomerate of public-interest research, lobbying, and litigating groups. His Public Citizen raises money for the projects. His Center for the Study of Responsive Law produces research on how to make the law and the legal system more responsive to public concerns. Other research on special topics is done by the Health Reseach Group, the Tax Reform Research Group, and Public Interest Research Groups (PIRGs) in many states and universities. In addition, Congress Watch studies congressional activity on issues of consumer, environmental, and other public-interest concerns. Other subsidiaries come and go with the issues and activities they focus upon.

Nader and his colleagues have been very influential on a wide variety of issues, from auto safety to antismoking regulations, and from opposing nuclear power plants as unsafe to supporting congressional reform. Many business officials have resented and opposed his activities. But some observers have pointed out that he is far from being the revolutionary troublemaker business people tend to see him as. For he seems devoted to making our existing capitalist economic system and our present political system more responsive to public concerns in order to save them from their own faults and weaknesses.

Of course much the same claim might be made by most, if not all, of the special-interest groups we have been examining. It would also be made by the American Medical Association, which opposed Medicare and national health insurance, or by the National Rifle Association, which opposes all gun-control legislation.

This fact again raises the problem of the concept of "the public interest." Perhaps the best solution to deciding what groups qualify as public-interest groups is that used by Jeffrey Berry. He insists on two criteria. First, *the group must seek a "collective good."* The term "collective good" refers to any public policy whose benefits may be *shared equally by all people,* whether or not they join or support the group. One example would be clean air, which we all benefit from whether or not we have joined the antipollution groups that struggle to get it. Another example is national defense, which we all get equally whether or not we're in the armed forces or paying the taxes that finance them. The second criterion is that the *achievement of the good must not selectively and materially benefit the group's members or activists.* These criteria would rule out the AMA, whose opposition to national health insurance specially benefits its member doctors, and the NRA, whose opposition to gun controls specially benefits its gun-using members.[23]

Now that we have learned something about who the interests are and the specific ways in which they operate, we can examine the roles of special interests in the B-1 case with which we began this chapter.

---

[23]Berry, *Lobbying for the People,* pp. 6–11.

☐ HOW SPECIAL INTERESTS OPERATE: THE CASE OF THE B-1

■ The air force

The idea for a new weapons system usually originates in the Pentagon, in the branch of the armed services that seeks it. Since the 1950s, the air force has relied on the B-52 for its long-distance, or strategic, bombing capability. This constitutes one leg of our three-legged nuclear capability, along with land-based missiles and submarine-carried missiles. The last B-52 was produced in 1962. Since the 1950s, the air force has regularly modernized its B-52s while looking for a new generation of bombers better able to penetrate Soviet defenses.

Eventually, air force experts decided they wanted a plane able to fly long distances at rapid speed, one that could come in low – 200 feet off the ground – to sneak in under Soviet radars without being detected. That plane became the B-1. The Pentagon selected Rockwell International as prime contractor in charge of developing the airplane and building some test models. Its competition had been Boeing (which built the B-52 and is the world's leading maker of civilian aircraft as well) and General Dynamics (which built the other recent American bomber, the F-111).

■ Rockwell International

Rockwell International was created by the merger of Rockwell Standard and North American Aviation. North American built many American warplanes and space vehicles over several decades before it hit hard times. Rockwell Standard made power tools, auto parts, plumbing equipment, and other consumer goods. The merger diversified the new company, but the B-1 rapidly became a major part of Rockwell's defense business. For this reason, Rockwell lobbied hard and long to build support for the B-1. (See the box titled "The lobbying for the B-1 bomber.")

■ The military-industrial complex

The term "military-industrial complex" was coined by President Eisenhower, himself a retired general, in his "farewell address." He warned, in 1961, that "this conjunction of an immense military establishment and a large arms industry is new in American experience. The total influence – economic, political, even spiritual – is felt in every city, every statehouse, every office of the Federal government. . . . We must guard against the acquisition of unwarranted influence, whether sought or unsought, by the military-industrial complex."

The Department of Defense (DOD) is the "primary employer, contractor, purchaser, owner, and spender in the nation."[24] The payroll costs for civilians employed in defense work was over $8.5 billion in 1968. DOD signs contracts with some 22,000 prime contractors and 100,000 subcontractors every year. It owned over $200 billion worth of assets within America during the 1960s (the most recent figures available), plus 429 large bases and another 2,972 smaller bases overseas. And its budget is about $100 billion a year.[25]

[24]James Clotfelter, *The Military in American Politics* (New York: Harper & Row, 1973), p. 51. See also Richard E. Kaufman, *The War Profiteers* (Indianapolis: Bobbs-Merrill, 1970).

[25]These figures come from Greenwald, *Group Power*, pp. 298–299.

News from

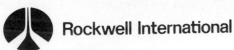

Rockwell International

B-1 Division
International Airport
Los Angeles, California 90009
(213) 670-9151

B-1 FACT SHEET

PRIMARY FUNCTION:	Strategic heavy bomber replacement for aging B-52
POWER PLANT:	Four General Electric F-101 turbofan engines (30,000 pounds thrust class)
MAXIMUM SPEED:	Over Mach 2 at high altitude; high subsonic on the deck
RANGE (UNREFUELED):	Intercontinental
TANKER SUPPORT	Compatible with existing KC-135
CREW:	Four: pilot, copilot, and two systems operators (with provisions for two instructors)
MAXIMUM GROSS TAKEOFF WEIGHT:	350,000 - 400,000 pounds
WEAPONS PAYLOAD:	Approximately twice as great as B-52
DIMENSIONS:	(Approximately 2/3 the size of B-52)
WING SPAN: WINGS FORWARD:	137 ft.
WINGS SWEPT:	78 ft.
LENGTH:	151 ft.
HEIGHT:	34 ft.
RUNWAY REQUIREMENTS:	Significantly shorter than B-52
ROLLOUT:	Summer 1974
FIRST FLIGHT:	Fall 1974
PRIME CONTRACTOR:	Rockwell International, B-1 Division Los Angeles, California
DATE OF CONTRACT AWARD:	June 5, 1970

#####

032174

Your Choice: B-1 Bomber or $50 Billion for You and Me!

What is it? A manned strategic bomber to replace the B-52 for nuclear war and future Vietnams.

How much? $50 billion or more.

Whose is it? Ours, unless we stop it.

Why stop it? In order to build a more peaceful world, we must call a halt to investing our resources in war machinery. We need to use our resources for housing, employment, education, public transportation and the general welfare of all people. Money for these areas of human need has been drastically cut from the federal budget while millions of dollars are spent on war planes. The U.S. is the world's leading military power but we are 18th in doctor-patient ratio, 15th in literacy, 15th in infant mortality and 26th in life expectancy.

With its noise, atmospheric pollution and sonic boom, the B-1 bomber would be harmful to the environment. In addition, the tremendous fuel consumption of a fleet of 241 B-1 bombers would use up fuel that is essential for civilian needs.

The effectiveness of the B-1 as a deterrent to war is both unproven and unlikely. The U.S. already has 360 more long-range bombers than has the U.S.S.R. Where military confrontations have occurred, as in the Cuban missile crisis and the Berlin crisis, compromise—the work of diplomacy—saved us from military threat. The more we rely on weapons, the less we rely on diplomacy.

When you get right down to it, who really needs the B-1 bomber? Senator William Proxmire says: "The fact is, among intelligent defense experts, the B-1 is a joke. It is a public works project for the aerospace industry rather than a needed weapon for the defense of the U.S."

Who Wants it? To answer that, we must ask other questions. Who would profit most from its construction? Three U.S. corporations—General Electric, Rockwell International and Boeing—have major contracts to build B-1 prototypes. Rockwell has a $1.37 billion contract to build the airframes; G.E. has a $458 million contract to construct the jet engines; Boeing is under contract for $77.4 million to provide the electronic equipment. If a final decision to go ahead on the bomber is made, it will mean billions of dollars in contracts for these three corporations. An estimated 4,100 subcontractors will share in the profits.

Why does the Air Force push for it? If the Air Force gets the B-1 bomber, it will enhance its prestige among the other branches of the military and hold on to its share of the military budget. The U.S. Air Force has continually waged a campaign for a new strategic bomber. After the Secretary of Defense rejected its B-70 bomber in 1962, the Air Force started again by promoting the B-1.

A Rockwell fact sheet on the B-1 (*left*) and anti-B-1 literature from the American Friends Service Committee (*above*).

Such economic activity would make the Pentagon powerful in any case. The connections between the military and industry increase that power. In 1969, the top 100 military contractors employed 2,124 former high-ranking military officers. In the next 4 years, industry hired another 1,101 while the Pentagon was hiring 232 corporation executives to make defense policy.[26] And in 1976 alone another 1,044 high-ranking officers retired and took jobs in industry, accompanied by 264 Pentagon civilians. That year, the Pentagon hired another 374 corporation executives. The "revolving door," as it is called, is spinning faster and faster.[27]

■ Organized labor

But labor got into the act as well. Military spending creates jobs, and so labor unions have tended to support it. The United Auto Workers (UAW), which

---

[26]Ibid., p. 301.

[27]"Tomorrow," *U.S. News & World Report,* April 25, 1977, p. 18.

■ The lobbying for the B-1 bomber

The rallying of the arms lobby around the cause of the B-1 bomber is a stirring demonstration that the military-industrial complex has survived the embarrassments of the past and has lost none of its prehensile vitality. . . .

Backers of the B-1 say it will assure U.S. supremacy in the air in the foreseeable future; opponents say it is already obsolete in a strategic world dominated by intercontinental missiles. But where vast expenditures are involved, arguments on the merits tend to get drowned out by the self-interests.

Each great weapons system develops by natural law an aggressive lobby to clear its path. The process by which pursuasion and pressure are brought to bear on the government process has been honed to an art form; success depends as much on political influence as professional competence.

In the executive suites of almost all the top defense contractors are retired generals and admirals who are on first-name basis with the Pentagon's big brass. They help to sell the weapons system to their former comrades in the armed forces. At the critical stage, the campaign becomes focused on Capitol Hill. Then the pressure people take over—affable lobbyists who know the right people in the backrooms of Congress.

Whether the B-1 program should be adopted or not, based on the merits, has been lost in the lobbying effort. This effort is directed by the prime contractor, Rockwell International, on mostly extraneous, pork-barreling, log-rolling arguments, thus demonstrating once again that the vulnerability to well-financed lobbies is the Achilles heel of American democracy. From our own investigation, consider these findings:

—Rockwell carefully listed the members of the key Senate and House committees in a document stamped "Not to be disclosed to unauthorized persons." Next to each member's name is a list of the companies in his district that have received subcontracts from the B-1 project. Sen. Clifford Case (R-N.J.), for example, has a $400,000 Bendi[illegible] tract in his state, and Rep. Louis Stokes, (D[illegible] has $227,000 going to the Cleveland Pneum[illegible] Company in his district.

—When Rep. Jonathan Bingham (D-N.Y.), asked for the basic economic facts about the B-1, Rockwell rushed him some charts that ignored his question but showed how the program would generate 45,000 jobs and $2.3 billion in business for New York and New Jersey.

—Rockwell President Robert Anderson has urged all the firm's 119,000 employees to write their congressmen in behalf of the B-1, complete with stationery, stamps and envelopes.

—Rockwell has produced a film touting the B-1 and has distributed it to various Chambers of Commerce. Nowhere in the film is it mentioned that Rockwell was the producer.

—Key Pentagon officials in charge of the B-1 project have been wined and dined by Rockwell at its Maryland hunting lodge. The Pentagon's former research chief, Malcolm Currie, was fined one month's pay after accepting a trip to Rockwell's Bimini resort as the guest of Rockwell's Robert Anderson.

—The company has funneled campaign contributions to 18 key members of the House Armed Services and Appropriations committees. It also conducted a newspaper advertising blitz for the B-1 last year.

—Holding out the promise of 70,000 new jobs, the B-1 proponents have also enlisted the support of AFL-CIO President George Meany and the United Auto Workers. Not mentioned is the fact that the jobs would be only temporary. For that matter, twice as many jobs would be created by spending the same money on housing construction, say, or on education.

Source: Jack Anderson, "The Lobbying for the B-1 Bomber," *Washington Post,* April 3, 1977. ©1977, United Feature Syndicate, Inc.

represents aerospace workers, supported the B-1. And the AFL-CIO executive council in February 1977 passed a resolution endorsing the program. There was, however, less than unanimity. The Communications Workers of America (CWA) and the American Federation of State, County, and Municipal Employees (AFSCME) opposed it. However, the AFL-CIO council gave the majority view. "Building the B-1 would provide many jobs in the aerospace and associated industries," the council said in a statement. "But we do not argue for the B-1 as a job-creating measure. . . . without a strong national defense, which must include strategic bombers, America is not safe and therefore no job is safe."

Reasoning like this had led some observers to refer to the "military-industrial-labor complex." But the unanimity previously found in labor is decreasing. A major reason is that studies have shown that money spent on defense projects might have created more jobs if spent in other ways. Representative Les Aspin (Democrat of Wisconsin), himself a former Pentagon employee, pointed out in an article in the *Washington Post* that although $1 billion spent on the B-1 would create 51,952 jobs, the same expenditure would create 57,656 jobs in private home construction, 60,126 jobs in public housing construction, 88,955 jobs in veterans' health care, and 136,464 jobs in manpower training."[28]

The trouble with this argument was that workers already had jobs working on the B-1, and discontinuing the project would put them out of work. Therefore, opponents of the B-1 developed a program to pay up to 90 percent of the wages of unemployed B-1 workers while they got free retraining to do other jobs; even the workers' moving expenses would be paid. This "peace conversion" legislation did not pass the Congress. But the possibility of such programs was used as an argument by opponents of the bomber against arguments for the plane put forth by Rockwell and the labor unions.

TABLE 11.3

Members of the "National Campaign to Stop the B-1 Bomber"

- American Baptist Churches
- American Friends Service Committee
- Americans for Democratic Action
- Business Executives Move for New National Priorities
- Campaign for a Democratic Foreign Policy
- Catholic Peace Fellowship
- Church of the Brethren
- Clergy and Laity Concerned
- Common Cause
- Congress Watch—Public Citizen
- Environmental Action
- Episcopal Peace Fellowship
- Federation of American Scientists
- Fellowship of Reconciliation
- Friends Committee on National Legislation
- Friends of the Earth
- Gray Panthers
- International Longshoremen's and Warehousemen's Union
- Jesuit Conference/Office of Social Ministries
- National Association of Social Workers
- National Coalition to Fight Inflation and Unemployment
- National Organization for Women—Labor Caucus
- National Student Association
- National Taxpayers Union
- NETWORK
- Oil, Chemical, and Atomic Workers Union (AFL-CIO)

■ The National Campaign to Stop the B-1 Bomber

The campaign became much more active on both sides over the almost 5 years of debate on the plane. Opponents were organized into what became the Washington-based National Campaign to Stop the B-1 Bomber. Leading the way in establishing the National Campaign were two groups. One was the American Friends Service Committee, a Quaker organization long active in peace, education, race relations, and other humanitarian causes. The other, Clergy and Laity Concerned, was a primarily religious group formed to oppose the Vietnam War, which broadened its concerns once the war was over. Over the years many other organizations joined the coalition. The final list (Table 11.3) reveals the scope of peace and antimilitarist lobbying in the 1970s.

A staff that sometimes got as large as half a dozen plus volunteers ran the Washington office. Its goals were three. First, to stop production of the B-1. Second, to expose and challenge the power relationships among the corporations,

[28]Les Aspin, "The B-1 Bomber as Flying Pork Barrel," *Washington Post,* December 22, 1974, Outlook section. Another reason why military spending has limited economic benefits is that it does not result in goods which can ordinarily be consumed and need to be replaced and so keep the economy producing.

TABLE 11.3 (*cont.*)

SANE
Southern Christian Leadership Conference
Textile Workers Union of America
Unitarian Universalist Association
United Church of Christ
War Resisters League
Women's International League for Peace and Freedom
Women Strike for Peace

the military, and the government. And third, to create more interest in, and support for, "peace conversion" – the redistribution of power and resources so that human needs increasingly replace military spending.

To achieve these ends, the coalition lobbied in Congress when key appropriations votes on B-1 were coming up. It also organized talks, discussions, and letter-writing campaigns on the issue among citizens and groups across the country. And it prepared pamphlets, spot radio ads, and even suggested sample letters for people to write to their representatives in Washington or to local newspapers.

Among its most effective actions, however, were the demonstrations it organized across the country on key dates such as income tax day, when everyone pays for the B-1, and the day the B-1 flew its first test run. One of the most striking demonstrations, this organized by the American Friends Service Committee, was a silent vigil of about 40 people from across the street from Carter's home in Plains, Georgia, around Christmas time just before Carter took office. The vigil was primarily to oppose the B-1 and support reconciliation with Vietnam. Carter himself came out to greet and speak with the demonstrators. And when night fell and candles were lit, Carter's mother, Miss Lillian, came, told the people she was glad they were there, and took a candle and joined the vigil.[29]

Demonstrators at other times and places were less solemn. In March 1976 protestors from Buffalo, N.Y., gave their representative, former pro quarterback Jack Kemp, a certificate marked "Bomb of the Year" for "his outrageous voting record." Kemp responded: "If this award is for my wanting a defense second to none, I accept with great pleasure."

And several days after Carter took office, a picket line outside the White House braved 28-degree cold and high winds to carry placards saying "Ban the Bomber – Stop the B-1," "Bombers do nobody any good," and "Make the world safe for Rockwell."

In a more serious vein, the coalition visited stockholders' annual meetings of Rockwell and General Electric, asking questions about management's plans for peace conversion if the B-1 were terminated and proposing resolutions calling for an end to the program. At one such Rockwell meeting, board chairman Willard Rockwell, Jr., was interrupted by protesters several times from the floor as he defended the B-1. "You can be sure the enemies of the B-1 will be shooting off their

[29] Paula Herbut, "Carter, Miss Lillian Greet Quakers at Vigil in Plains," *Philadelphia Bulletin*, December 21, 1976.

Lillian Carter joins group protesting the B-1 at Plains, Georgia, Christmas 1976.
American Friends Service Committee

firecrackers, blowing their horns, and beating their drums as you have already seen this morning," he responded. "Now, I believe most sincerely that people have every right to express their opinion. In fact, the very reason we need the B-1 and a strong defense is to insure that all of us in America retain our basic freedoms, including the right of free speech."[30]

■ The final efforts

But Rockwell officials weren't so calm in the face of the anti-B-1 campaign once Carter, after announcing his early opposition to the plane, had been elected president. In December 1976 Crosby M. Kelly, Rockwell's vice-president for communications, charged in an interview with Associated Press that the Soviet Union was secretly funding opponents of the bomber.[31] Members of the anti-B-1 campaign knew that their average contribution was a check for $15 in response to a mail appeal for funds and said so in terming Kelly's charge "laughable." When the National Campaign was in full swing in the summer of 1976 it consisted of two young men being paid $100 a week working in a $70-a-month office. But they were effective enough to trigger full-page ads in newspapers by the American Security Council, a conservative, promilitary foundation, complaining of "a massive, highly organized and well-financed campaign of the anti-defense lobby." The campaign's budget for the year was less than $20,000. The American Security Council spends $2 million a year, much of it contributed by corporations such as Rockwell.[32]

Rockwell itself responded with full-page ads telling why the B-1 is essential to American security. And when key congressional votes were coming up, Rockwell's president distributed a pamphlet asking all of the firm's 119,000 employees who supported its B-1 to contact their members of Congress supporting it. It told how to write, phone, or wire representatives and contained a list of "facts to use in your letters." Rockwell also distributed stationery, envelopes and stamps. Union officials said people were given "company time" to write, although a Rockwell spokesman denied this.[33] In addition, according to Pacific News Service, Rockwell International asked the help of conservative religious and political groups in the last-minute lobbying effort.[34] The Christian Anti-Communist Crusade, led by radio evangelist Dr. Billy James Hargis, sent a mailing to 150,000 American households in May stating: "Our 30-year fight for the work of the Christian Crusade against communism and for a strong America has never had a more important issue than the B-1 bomber. If the B-1 is scrapped, every town and city in the United States will soon be defenseless."

In addition, the United States Industrial Council, of which Rockwell is a corporate member, distributed "guest editorials" in favor of the B-1 to more than 300 newspapers across the country to increase public support.

---

[30]"Fireworks Over Rockwell's B-1," *San Francisco Chronicle,* February 15, 1976.

[31]"Official Says Soviets Financing B-1 Foes," *Wilmington* (Del.) *Morning News,* December 21, 1976.

[32]Mary McGrory, "The B-1 Bomber and the Slingshot," *Washington Star,* Aug. 27, 1976.

[33]"Rockwell Asks Employees to Lobby for B-1 Production," *Los Angeles Times,* August 23, 1976.

[34]John Markoff, "Heavy Lobbying Conducted for B-1," *Daily Texan,* June 21, 1977.

Wide World Photos

A model of the B-1 bomber provided by Rockwell International attracts little attention at the California Business and Industry Show in Los Angeles, June 30, 1977. A few hours earlier President Carter had announced his decision to halt B-1 production

Lobbying was thus taking place not only in the government but also among the public and among the experts on security policy. The public opinion lobbying effort produced interesting figures from time to time. For example, Environmental Action, noting that there was much concern with energy efficiency, calculated that the B-1 uses 2000 gallons of fuel an hour and gets only about 440 *yards* to the gallon. It also figures out that the 300 million gallons the full fleet would use each year equal half the annual total used by all urban mass transit systems combined.

Others got city councils and the National Council of Mayors to express their opposition publicly. The Boston City Council, for example, on April 5, 1976, passed a resolution noting the B-1's threat to the environment and high cost and "opposing any further government expenditures on the B-1."

Then on January 11, 1977, seven national organizations took a new tack. They filed suit in federal court to stop further funding of the B-1 on grounds that the air force's 1971 "environmental impact statement" on the bomber did not consider alternatives to it and gave only superficial attention to the plane's impact on air quality, noise levels, and the ozone layer. The seven organizations were the Environmental Action Foundation, the Federation of American Scientists, Americans for Democratic Action, the Oil, Chemical, and Atomic Workers International Union, Friends of the Earth, the Council on Economic Priorities, and Environmental Action – all but two members of the National Campaign.

Meanwhile, the public opinion campaign was having an impact. By January 1977 a Harris Poll reported that Americans opposed the B-1 by 42 to 33 percent, with 25 percent undecided. Harris also found that 62 percent think there is "a lot of waste in U.S. defense spending."

Each year, the number of House members voting against the bomber had grown: 94 in 1973, 96 in 1974, 164 in 1975, 186 in 1976. Following that 1976 vote, Senator William Proxmire wrote to the campaign: "Your tremendous effort the last few weeks has been highly successful in exposing the B-1 as a useless boondoggle. Thanks to your efforts the bomber is extremely controversial, and you have created a climate in which the next President can terminate the B-1 program. You've made remarkable progress and I hope you'll keep up the good work."

So it did, and so Carter did. But in the end it was not clear just how much impact the National Campaign and public opinion had. At the least, it created a political climate in which the value of the B-1 could be questioned.[35] But Carter's explanation of his decision emphasized considerations of military effectiveness. The major factor seemed to be a study published by the Brookings Institution in February 1976. Brookings is a large, public-policy research group in Washington. The study, written by two former Pentagon analysts, Alton H. Quanback and Archie L. Wood, concluded that the B-1 would be a costly mistake. Instead it argued for equipping B-52s or modified Boeing-747 civilian aircraft with cruise missiles. Cruise missiles are small, cheap, computer-guided missiles that can be carried by planes or ships and fired from great distances to attack enemy targets, flying low and evasive paths so they're very hard to defend against. Great progress had recently been made in their development, and the Soviets lagged far behind in both making them and defending against them.[36]

Ultimately, Carter's decision was very close to that recommended in the Brookings study. How influential that study was is hard to know. Other studies by Carter's National Security Council reached similar conclusions, as did Defense Secretary Brown. In other words, the authorities on defense policy tended to agree with those opposing the plane, while the authorities on the political aspects in the Congress were split, largely as a result of the National Campaign's continuing lobbying. The military-industrial complex, then, became somewhat fragmented on the issue. That fact seemed to make it easier for the president to take a position against the wishes of the air force and powerful industrial and labor interests.

□ INTEREST GROUPS IN AMERICAN POLITICS

■ The life of the lobbyist

It should be clear from this case study of the B-1 decision that interest groups vary immensely in membership, in clout, and in lobbying activities, within and outside the government. The most comprehensive study of Washington lobbyists, by Lester Milbrath, found that lobbyists spend most of their time receiving and sending communications – mostly in their own offices. Personal conversation with members of Congress or other governmental officials are important, but not very time-consuming, Milbrath found. Even less useful, and less frequent, is the stereotypical lobbying activity, entertainment. Much more important, the lobbyists said, is time spent traveling around visiting local groups in order to improve communication with the people and groups who support them and "to stimulate a flow of communications from the grass roots to governmental decision-makers."[37] Thus we could not describe a typical day in the life of a typical lobbyist. But it is clear that we couldn't imagine a day in American politics without lobbies or lobbyists.

---

[35]See Nicholas Wade, "Death of the B-1: The Events Behind Carter's Decision," *Science,* August 5, 1977, pp. 536–539.

[36]Alton H. Quanback and Archie L. Wood, *Modernizing the Strategic Bomber Force* (Washington, D.C.: Brookings Institution, 1976).

☐ ACTION UNIT 11.1 How to be a lobbyist

You may already have been a lobbyist – a one-person lobby – if you have written or visited your members of Congress.

If you're interested in getting further into lobbying, you might benefit from the following rules for being a successful lobbyist. They derive from what Lester Milbrath learned in his study of 114 Washington lobbyists and their targets in government. (*The Washington Lobbyist,* Chicago, Rand McNally, 1963, pp. 220–226.)

- ☐ Be pleasant and nonoffensive.
- ☐ Convince the official that it is important for him or her to listen – ideally by pointing out the relevance for his or her constituents of your concern.
- ☐ Be well-prepared and well-informed, so that your presentation is helpful to the target.
- ☐ Be personally convinced, but show that you understand the various sides of the question.
- ☐ Be succinct, well-organized, and direct.
- ☐ Use the "soft sell," being careful not to push too hard and recognizing that compromise is the usual outcome in legislating.
- ☐ Leave a *short* written summary of the case you are presenting.

Lewis Dexter (*How Organizations Are Represented in Washington,* Indianapolis, Bobbs-Merrill, 1969, p. 89) considered another rule:

- ☐ Present your position, if possible, as a request for a favor.

"I suspect one reason for the unpopularity of some serious-minded lobbyists who stress the public interest," he reports, "is that they do not ask for favors; they come to *tell* congressmen what the latter *ought* to be thinking. Many congressmen, that is, do not concede that anybody else knows more than they do about the public interest: but they are willing and eager to do favors."

Of course, as a lobbyist you are most likely to be effective if you too can do favors for those you seek to influence. As Dexter remarks, "The best thing of all for a Washington representative is to be able to approach a congressman or senator with something that will somehow enable the latter to increase his ability to get campaign contributions or speaking dates, his respect from his colleagues, his influence downtown in the bureaus or back home."

The biggest favor usually is the campaign contribution, which we discuss elsewhere in this chapter. But there are other ways in which a lobbyist with imagination can favor those of whom he or she is asking favors, as some of the books listed in the chapter's bibliography report.

The best guide to the thousands of organizations already active in lobbying, for which you might work, is the *Washington Information Directory* published annually by Congressional Quarterly, Inc., in Washington; it is available in most libraries.

■ The basic function of interest groups

The real function of the interest group is to offer its own view or image of reality – how the world is and how it ought to be – in an effort to convince citizens and policy makers that they should accept it themselves. To encourage them to do so, lobbyists who represent special interests may use everything from information through arguments to threats, promises, and favors, as we have seen. Ultimately, they are making *claims to authority* – authority to interpret the public interest, to express special interests, to predict the political future of those they seek to influence. Special interests, then, are politicians in our sense just as elected officials are.

In American politics, these interests often clash. The pluralist theorists, whose views we summarized in Chapter 5, believe that the interests diverge, conflict, and compete in ways that countervail each other and generally make it possible for the public interest to emerge through competition and compromise.

The elitist theorists, as we noted in Chapter 5, believe this a mirage. The major special interests in our system are *vested* interests, with special benefits in the status quo that they seek to protect and expand, according to elitists. They get their way more often because they have more money and occupy more positions of authority and power. The public interest is therefore a victim more often than not, according to this view.

■ The regulation of interest groups

As a result, elitist theorists often emphasize the importance of regulating the lobbies. But so far such efforts have had limited success. Congress passed the Federal Regulation of Lobbying Act in 1946. But the act was carelessly drafted and hurriedly passed; as a result, it has never been effective in controlling lobbying. It applies only to individuals and groups who are paid for the principal purpose of influencing legislation by direct contact with individuals in Congress. They are required to register with the House and Senate and file quarterly reports of their own spending. But in fact few register, and those who do rarely file full spending totals. Supreme Court decisions have upheld this limited interpretation of the requirements of the law. So all agree that the law is inadequate.[38]

After Watergate, a new bill with stricter registration and reporting provisions supported by Common Cause almost passed Congress in 1976. It died in the closing hours of the session under attack from business, labor, and Ralph Nader. *National Journal* explained this rare split among the public interest lobbying groups this way: "Common Cause is more interested in issues of governmental and political procedures than it is in the substance of policy, while the Nader groups are more concerned with the policy questions. As a result, Common Cause is anxious that an improved lobbying law be adopted, while the Nader organization worries that such a law might limit its influence on policy issues that are important to it."[39]

Others worry that strict regulation may violate the "right to petition for redress of grievances," which is an important part of the First Amendment to the Constitution. The fear of some civil libertarians is that laws requiring even small groups of citizens advocating a particular policy to register with the government will deter many individuals and groups from even entering the lobbying process. The spreading opposition led one observer to conclude that for lobbying reform to succeed, its advocates must develop a plan that "is as comprehensible to the interested citizen as it is to the lawyer. Failure to do so will ensure that the capital's league of lobbyists remain essentially anonymous to most Americans – except those who vote in Congress."[40]

---

[37]Lester Milbrath, *The Washington Lobbyists* (Chicago: Rand McNally, 1963), p. 121.

[38]See Congressional Quarterly, *The Washington Lobby,* for background.

[39]*National Journal,* July 31, 1976, p. 1076.

[40]Richard E. Cohen, "The Short Life of Lobbying Reform," *National Journal,* November 12, 1977, p. 1775.

The situation now is that some interests are more vested than others in American politics. Some advocates of democracy argue that this is undemocratic because it weights the political process in favor of the status quo. Others, as we have seen, believe that the system allows those who really care enough, or have the most to lose, to express their concerns effectively. In this sense, ours is indeed a politics of special interests. It is doubtful that a large, diversified country's politics could be any other way.

But could we indeed have a politics in which the public interest received greater attention and got stronger support from the people? For that to be true, the people would at the very least have to be both more active and better informed than we have found them to be today. Much of the responsibility would have to fall to our major sources of information, the mass media. Are they up to the task of informing the citizenry? That is a key question that we shall examine in the next chapter.

☐ SUGGESTIONS FOR FURTHER READING AND STUDY

The footnotes to this chapter will lead you to some interesting and helpful case studies of lobbies in action. For more general studies, see: V. O. Key, *Politics, Parties, and Pressure Groups,* 5th ed. (New York: Crowell, 1964), E. E. Schattschneider, *The Semi-Sovereign People* (New York: Holt, Rinehart & Winston paperback, 1960), and David B. Truman, *The Governmental Process,* 2nd ed. (New York: Knopf, 1971)—all classics. For a different theory of interest groups, see Robert Salisbury, "An Exchange Theory of Interest Groups," *Midwest Journal of Political Science* 13 (February 1969): 1–32; and Mancur Olson, Jr., *The Logic of Collective Action: Public Goods and the Theory of Groups,* rev. ed. (Cambridge, Mass.: Harvard University Press, 1971), which uses economic analysis of individual self-interest and analyzes the size of coalitions. See also Robert Alford, *Health Care Politics* (Chicago: University of Chicago Press, 1975). For a survey and classification, see Graham Wootton, *Interest Groups* (Englewood Cliffs, N.J.: Prentice-Hall, 1970), and for a more general survey, see Harmon Zeigler and G. Wayne Peak, *Interest Groups in American Society,* 2nd ed. (Englewood Cliffs, N.J.: Prentice-Hall, 1972). For an attack on the pluralist theory of interest groups, see Grant McConnell, *Private Power and American Democracy* (New York: Knopf, 1966). And for a recent survey emphasizing public policy effects, see Carol S. Greenwald, *Group Power: Lobbying and Public Policy* (New York: Praeger paperback, 1977).

Public-interest lobbies are examined in Jeffrey Berry, *Lobbying for the People* (Princeton, N.J.: Princeton University Press paperback, 1977). For consideration of the concept of the public interest, see the sources cited in the chapter footnotes.

Finally, for further information on how interest groups operate, see: Lester Milbrath, *The Washington Lobbyists* (Chicago: Rand McNally, 1963); James Deakin, *The Lobbyists* (Washington, D.C.: Public Affairs Press, 1966), which is anecdotal; Lewis A. Dexter, *How Organizations Are Represented in Washington* (Indianapolis: Bobbs-Merrill paperback, 1969), which is practical; and Andrew M. Scott and Margaret A. Hunt, *Congress and Lobbies* (Chapel Hill: University of North Carolina Press, 1966), which is academic.

12 The mass media

If you are an average American, by your late teens you have seen some 350,000 commercials on television. By the time you reached age 15 you had seen 13,000 killings on television – for there are an average of seven killings in every hour of television programming. According to Professor Joyce Sullivan, whose research produced these findings, television teaches the child that life is simple. "The message is, you don't have to work out problems – simply destroy the enemy," she concludes. A survey by ABC-TV found that 22 out of 100 confessed juvenile offenders had copied criminal techniques seen on television, she reports.

If television does indeed have such power of suggestion – something experts still disagree about – then it seems to be a real school for crime, as well as for consumption. And by age 17 most children have spent more hours before the television screen than they have in the classroom.[1]

To most Americans, this viewing is entertainment. To most, this entertainment is what comes to mind when the "mass media" are mentioned – entertainment with occasional interruptions for the evening news reported by Walter Cronkite or David Brinkley. Many of us also listen to the radio regularly – but mostly for background music rather than news. Many of us read a daily newspaper, or parts of one – where we may occasionally encounter investigative writing by Bob Woodward and Carl Bernstein or their counterparts. And many – particularly the young – are regular consumers of long-playing records and the stereos to play them on.

All of these are experiences of the mass media. Most of them may not seem to have any political relevance. But in its ultimate effects, crime is political, and so is our economic activity. This makes the media potentially politically important, not just when they are reporting the news, but also when they are presenting programs designed to entertain the viewing public.

Our everyday life is riddled by media. But most of the media that deal with public affairs and offer entertainment programs are owned outside our communities and programmed largely from New York and Washington via giant networks and news wire services. We are remarkably unaware of the impact that *national* media such as CBS-TV or the Associated Press or *Time* magazine have, not just on our image of politics, but on our image of reality in general. And our image of reality to a great extent shapes our lives.

---

[1]Kathy Goforth, "Studies Cite Dangers of Television," *Austin American-Statesman,* July 24, 1977.

Polls from time to time have shown that Walter Cronkite is "the most trusted person in America."[2] Few Americans seem to realize that his reports are only as trustworthy as his reporters and script writers. With occasional exceptions, Cronkite ceased being a reporter working in the field and actually "covering" news stories many years ago.

Every day some 65,000,000 Americans watch the news on one of three major television networks: CBS, NBC, and ABC. When asked "Where do you usually get most of your news about what's going on in the world today," 64 percent mention television; 50 percent say newspapers; 21 percent, radio; 6 percent, magazines; and 4 percent, other people. When asked which sources they most believe, 48 percent say television; 21 percent, newspapers; 10, magazines; and 8, radio.[3]

A recent survey of the confidence Americans have in the people running various institutions found 57 percent of the citizens confident of the people in medicine, 52 percent confident of those doing local trash collection, 44 percent positive toward those in higher education and toward the local police. Then at 41 percent came the people doing television news, ahead of the military (40), organized religion (36), the United States Supreme Court (33), the Senate (30), the press (30), the House of Representatives (29), local government (28), the executive branch, or bureaucracy (19), and the White House (18).

Those results were from a survey of the American people as a whole. A survey of leaders taken at the same time produced quite different results. Leaders had more confidence in local police and in the Supreme Court. But while 41 percent of the people had confidence in television news, only 17 percent of the leaders (whose activities were being reported by television news, we may presume) did. And while 30 percent of the people had confidence in the press, only 19 percent of leaders did.[4]

The average report of a major event by a correspondent on the nightly television news lasts 60 to 90 seconds. On radio, spot reports are often even briefer.

---

[2]For example, in a 1973 Minnesota Poll, 25 percent said they trusted Cronkite "wholeheartedly"—versus 23 percent for Senator Walter Mondale, 19 percent for Senator Hubert Humphrey, 18 percent for newscaster Harry Reasoner, 16 percent for then-Vice-President Ford, 14 percent for John Chancellor, 11 percent for then-President Nixon, and 9 percent for George McGovern. See *Current Opinion,* March 1974, p. 28.

[3]The Roper Organization, "What People Think of Television and Other Mass Media, 1959–1972," (New York: Television Information Office, 1973).

[4]*Confidence and Concern: Citizens View American Government,* a Louis Harris survey for the Senate Government Operations Committee, 1974.

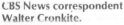

CBS News correspondent Walter Cronkite.

Courtesy of CBS News

TABLE 12.1

The average student's daily exposure to communications media

Media channel	Exposure (minutes)
Television	63
Newspapers	53
Radio	78
Magazines	30
Books	149
Records	15
Movies	3
Posters, etc.	19
Conversations lasting under 5 minutes	144
Conversations lasting over 5 minutes	125
Lectures	140
Other	13

Source: W. Phillips Davison, James Boylan, and Frederick Yu, *Mass Media* (New York: Praeger, 1976), p. 105.

Do we really believe such brief accounts can tell us what actually happened? And could they possibly tell us why? When, where, and how do we – or could we – get the background that makes such reports meaningful?

We often say that democracy is based upon, depends upon, an informed citizenry. But in fact democracy is based upon, or depends upon, only a voting electorate – and it doesn't even take a majority vote to sustain the process, as we have noted. The political system goes on whether or not the citizenry is well-informed. In the same way, the news shows go on, and the newspapers are published, whether or not they are accurate and informative – and whether or not the people are paying attention.

The mass media in America have become so important they are often referred to as "the fourth branch of government" – or, in terms borrowed from the French Revolution, the Fourth Estate. Some are suggesting that the media are even more important than that. Editor Edward Hunter argues that "the press is now the Third Estate and the Congress is the Fourth Estate. Our legislators – and the Administration first determine what the press will or will not use and set policy accordingly."[5]

Perhaps this view overstates the case. Certainly the media's status as a part of government is not official. But in this chapter we shall see how the media have grown, what has made them "mass" media, and how the media and the government are intertwined. This will prepare us to ask what responsibilities the media should have, not only to the government but to us as citizens.

□ WHY WE CALL THEM "MEDIA"

A "medium" (plural, "media") is a means of transmission. The term basically means "middle." The same word is used for a newspaper and for a mystic who claims to be able to put people in touch with the spirits of their departed loved ones. In each case, and many others, the medium makes communication possible. This communication requires four things: a *source,* a *message,* a *medium* to transmit the message from the source, and a *receiver* to which the message comes. For television, communication involves a station and its employees, which together are the source; a broadcast signal (we call the information it carries a "program"), which is the message; the airwaves, which are the medium; and a set and viewer, which together are the receiver.

It is easy to see how television, newspapers, books, the telephone, and radio are communications media. Included are person-to-person conversation, letter writing, junk mail, records, movies, and so on. But our communications experiences are much broader than just these. Recently a Columbia University professor asked his students to keep a log of the communications media to which they were exposed in a 24-hour period. The results, shown in Table 12.1, though probably not typical of the American people as a whole, help us realize how much of the time we are engaged in communication.

[5]Quoted by Kevin Phillips, "Busting the Media Trusts," *Harper's,* July 1977, pp. 23–34.

Today we depend on the media for information vital to most aspects of our lives. We depend specially upon the media for the information we need to act as responsible citizens – and to get the government to act responsibly. The media are able to provide more information to more people than ever before because they have indeed become "mass" media.

☐ WHY WE CALL THEM "MASS"

Communication, we noted above, rquires a source, a message, a medium, and a receiver. Such contact can be on a small scale, as when I write a message to you through the medium of a letter. But it can also be on a very large scale, as when Prentice-Hall sends this message to you and your fellow readers by editing, printing, and distributing this book. Book publishing has become a mass medium, just as television, radio, newspapers, and magazines have.

Why do we call them "mass" media? First, because they now *reach large masses* of people. Second, because all aspects of this communication have been *standardized* to reach the mass audiences. And third, because the ownership and control of these media have become increasingly *concentrated* or massed.

■ Mass audiences

There are now more television sets in America than there are telephones or toilets. Over 97 percent of American homes have at least one set (a third have two or more, and a tenth have three or more). The average set is on some 6 hours a day, with the average viewer watching for almost 3 hours, and the average child 6 to 17 watching more than 4. In winter and spring, some 75 million Americans on the average are watching TV any given night. In addition, spot checks show that about 85 percent of our population over the age of 12 listens to radio at some point any given day.[6] And some 62 million newspapers are bought every day, many of them read by several people.[7] The audiences, or recipients, of the messages sent by the media in America today are clearly of enormous size.

■ Standardized communication

To reach these mass publics, the media attempt to standardize as many aspects of communication as possible. They use *standardized production equipment,* such as printing presses and radio and television tape and film systems. They use *standardized content:* Reports from national news services such as Associated Press (AP), United Press International (UPI), the New York Times News Service, and radio and television network programs are "fed" to local stations from New York. They use *standardized transmission* via telegraph, telephone, satellite, and other electronic hookups. And they use *standardized reception* by our radios, televisions, and even our ears, eyes, and brains – all of which are "built" to receive the same messages in about the same ways.

---

[6]These statistics on mass audiences come from Edwin Diamond, *The Tin Kazoo* (Cambridge, Mass.: MIT Press, 1975), pp. 13, 14, 16.

[7]*Statistical Abstract of the United States, 1975* (Washington, D.C.: Government Printing Office, 1975), p. 521.

Dennis Brack/Black Star

Newsroom at the *Washington Post.*

TABLE 12.2

CBS, a typical media conglomerate, in 1976

CBS
1976 total sales:
$2.23 billion

PRINCIPAL OPERATIONS:

Broadcasting:
Owns five TV stations (New York, Los Angeles, Philadelphia, Chicago, St. Louis); seven AM radio stations and seven FM radio stations

Records:
Columbia, Epic, Portrait

Columbia Group:
Record and tapes club
Musical instruments (e.g., Steinway pianos, Leslie speakers, Rogers drums, organs)
67 Pacific Stereo retail stores
Creative Playthings (toys)

■ Concentrated ownership and control

There are a great many message senders in this country: 6700 commercial radio stations; 700 commercial television stations; and about 1750 daily newspapers.[8] But this variety of message senders or media is more apparent than real. The news the media distribute comes primarily from two major news or wire services: AP and UPI. Many of those 6700 commercial radio stations are linked into four large radio networks: CBS, NBC, ABC, and Mutual, while the noncommercial stations form National Public Radio. The 700 commercial television stations belong for the most part to the three large networks: CBS, NBC, and ABC, while almost 300 noncommercial stations form the Public Broadcasting Service. And the 1500 or so daily papers have more and more been bought by "chains" such as: Gannett, which owns papers in fifty-five different cities across the country; Thomson, with fifty-seven; Knight-Ridder, which owns forty-four different papers; and Newhouse, which owns thirty. In recent years, chains have even been merging with each other to create even bigger chains.

Another aspect of this concentration is the disappearance of competition. Take newspapers. In 1910, there were 100 million Americans and 2400 daily newspapers. Today, there are 220 million Americans, but only about 1750 papers. Yet even these figures tell only part of the story. In 98 percent of the cities with daily papers today, there is only one newspaper publisher, even though sometimes it owns and publishes several seemingly competing papers. In 1920, there were 700 cities with competing papers, but today there are fewer than 50.

In 1930, chains owned 43 percent of the circulation of daily papers in the United States. In 1960, it was 46 percent. Today, it is over 70 percent. The prospect, many fear, is the end of the independent daily paper. "The approaching disappearance of even small independent newspapers is not only economically but

[8]See Herbert I. Schiller, *The Mind Managers* (Boston: Beacon, 1973), p. 19.

TABLE 12.2 (*cont.*)

Publishing:
Holt, Rinehart and Winston and subsidiaries
Popular Library
W. B. Saunders
NEISA—Latin American and Spanish books

Magazines:
Field and Stream
Road and Track
Cycle World
World Tennis
PV4
Popular Gardening Indoors
Astrology Your Daily Horoscope
Astrology Today
Your Prophecy
Psychic World
Popular Crosswords
Popular Word Games
Special Crossword Book of the Month
New Crosswords
Giant Word Games
The National Observer Book of Crosswords
Popular Sports: Baseball
Popular Sports: Grand Slam
Popular Sports: Kick-Off
Popular Sports: Touchdown
Popular Sports: Basketball
Mechanix Illustrated
Woman's Day
Rudder

Source: Kevin Phillips, "Busting the Media Trusts," *Harper's*, July 1977, pp. 26–27.

politically important," remarks journalist Ben Bagdikian, "because almost all dailies are local monopolies, exerting substantial influence in their congressional or state legislative districts."[9] Such changes are ominous because they will limit the media that are independent-minded and that reflect the needs and interests of the local regions they operate in.

Competition between media is also becoming limited. A Federal Communications Commission study found that there are 72 cities and towns in which the only local newspaper owns the only local radio station. It also found that in another 180 cities, a daily paper owned one of the broadcasting stations. Perhaps even more ominous is the recent growth in media conglomerates—companies that own newspapers, TV stations, radio stations, magazines, and even book publishers. Sometimes they even own quite different businesses as well; for example, RCA, the electronics corporation, owns a carpet factory, a food company, and a car rental company—as well as NBC and a large book publisher. Table 12.2 lists the media owned by CBS, another major "media conglomerate," as they are called.

The result of this "massification" of ownership and control, some observers believe, is that we as consumers get *choice without diversity.* The giant corporations tend to aim for the "middle" just as our giant political parties do, and so picking between NBC and CBS, or *Time* and *Newsweek,* may be much like picking between Carter and Ford. Furthermore, this tendency toward appealing to the middle is intensified by the fact that all these mass media depend for their profits on advertising revenue. Except in the case of cable television, which we'll discuss shortly, we listeners and viewers don't pay for our radio and TV programs at all, the way people in Britain, for example, do. And, to take another example, the cost of printing and mailing a news magazine—let alone the cost of paying the staff to write for it—is more than we pay per copy for it. Advertising makes up the difference and adds the profit as well.

Recently, however, there have been attempts to make at least some of the media less controlled from above and more responsive to local needs. Included are: *"Underground" papers* created, written, and published to meet the needs of some people for specialized information and assistance; *"city magazines"* such as *New York* and *Los Angeles* published in and for the people of a city rather than a national audience; *citizen organizations to improve broadcasting* that monitor the media and lobby for better coverage; *local journalism reviews* in a dozen or more cities that criticize the performance of the press and other media in regular magazines; *"truth-in-advertising" groups* that have achieved important checks on media advertising; *"feedback" columns in newspapers* that have opened the pages of some newspapers to citizens;[10] and the *National News Council,* which was established in 1973 "to examine and to report on complaints concerning the accuracy and fairness of news reporting in the United States, as well as to initiate studies and report on issues involving the freedom of the press." Periodic reports of the *National News Council* are now published in the *Columbia Journalism Review.*

[9]Ben H. Bagdikian, "Newspaper Mergers—the Final Phase," *Columbia Journalism Review,* March–April, 1977, p. 19.

[10]See, for an early survey, Alfred Balk, *A Free and Responsive Press* (New York: Twentieth Century Fund, 1973).

□ ACTION UNIT 12.1 How to talk back to your TV set

There are now many citizen action organizations seeking to improve broadcasting as they see it. You can form your own local organization to influence local programming – or even to threaten to challenge a local station's license when it comes up for renewal every third year – if you believe it is not living up to its public service obligations as a free user of the public airwaves.

Such license challenges are sometimes based on programming (percentage of time given to news and public affairs) and sometimes on hiring practices and the station's failure to use women and minorities on the air. To find out specifically what a local station does do, and how other citizens react to it, go to the station's headquarters and ask to see its "public file," which by law must be available free to the public during regular business hours.

For more detailed instructions on how to appeal to the Federal Communications Commission, see Chapter 7 of James R. Michael, ed., *Working on the System* (New York: Basic Books, 1974), and for encouragement and guidance see the book by Nicholas Johnson, a former renegade FCC Commissioner, entitled *How to Talk Back to Your Television Set* (New York: Bantam paperback, 1970). Johnson is now the chairman of the National Citizens Committee for Broadcasting, one of the six organizations described below. These groups represent various perspectives, and one or more might be helpful to you in your lobbying.

Accuracy in Media, AIM (425 13th St. N.W., Washington, D.C. 20004), was founded as a nonprofit educational organization to combat what it considers inaccuracies and distorted reporting by the major media. It publishes *AIM Report.*

Action for Children's Television, ACT (46 Austin St., Newtonville, Mass. 02160), was founded in 1968 to make networks more responsive to the desires of parents and teachers concerning television programming for children.

The National Citizens Committee for Broadcasting, NCCB (1028 Connecticut Ave. N.W., Washington, D.C. 20036), was founded in 1974 as a national, nonprofit group to represent the public in broadcasting. It published a newsletter, *Media Watch,* for members, who pay dues of $15 a year.

National Black Media Coalition (244 Plymouth Ave. South, Rochester, N.Y. 14608) is made up of over forty local black organizations, each dedicated to eliminating racism from radio and television.

National Latino Media Coalition (1028 Connecticut Ave. N.W., Suite 1007, Washington, D.C. 20036) was founded in 1973 to enhance the opportunities for Spanish-surnamed people to participate in the media.

National Organization for Women, NOW (1107 National Press Building, Washington, D.C. 20004), has a *Task Force on Broadcast Media and the FCC* that gives technical assistance and advice to those working to promote both the employment and the image of women in broadcasting.

□ THE POLITICS OF COMMUNICATION

Information is essential to all aspects of living. But it is especially vital to political action because politics usually takes place beyond our own direct experience. In other words, we depend upon authorities for political information more regularly than we do for economic information about the cost of living, for example, because we experience the cost of living personally whenever we shop.

"Beyond our limited daily experience," writes media expert Robert Stein, "it is television, radio, newspapers, magazines and books – the media – that furnish our consciousnesses with the people, places, and events that we agree to call reality. But reality, in a literal sense, is what happens to three and a half billion people all over the world twenty-four hours a day. Out of that teeming experience, the media can only give us, in words and pictures, a representation of tiny fragments that are deemed significant or suggestive."[11]

We have, now, new authorities (those in the media) able to compete with our traditional authorities (those in the government), as Stein argues in the box titled "Media power." They may also compete with each other, as Cronkite and Brinkley do, or as television and the newspapers do. But the most important competition is the dispute over claims to the authority to represent reality for us that the media and the government sometimes wage. So we must now examine the "politics of communication" as it arises at each stage of communication: source, message, medium, receiver. Then we can consider the basic question of the impacts of, and controls upon, our media and our politics.

TABLE 12.3

Channels of information for 2850 front-page stories in the *New York Times* and the *Washington Post*

Routine (58.2%)	
Official proceedings (12.0%)	
Press conferences (24.2%)	
Nonspontaneous events (4.5%)	
Informal (15.7%)	
Background briefings (7.9%)	
Leaks (2.3%)	
Nongovernmental proceedings (1.5%)	
News reports, editorials (4.0%)	
Enterprise (25.8%)	
Interviews (23.7%)	
Spontaneous events (1.2%)	
Reporter's own analysis (0.9%)	
Not ascertainable (0.3%)	

Source: Leon V. Sigal, *Reporters and Officials: The Organization and Politics of Newsmaking* (Lexington, Mass.: Heath 1973), p. 121.

■ The politics of the source and the message

The major original sources of media messages are still governments, in large part because what governments and their officers do is what is considered news. More specifically, studies show that networks get most of their material from the national wire services, which in turn get most of their material from officials. Local stations get half or more of their stories from press releases by public figures and public relations handouts by businesses, while the rest comes from police and fire department radio monitors.[12]

A study of the nation's leading papers, the *New York Times* and the *Washington Post,* found that of their front-page stories, about half came from U.S. government officials, a quarter from foreign or international officials, and 15 percent from other U.S. citizens. Leon Sigal examined all stories in both papers for their origins and divided them into "routine" (for public statements and official events), "informal" (for briefings, leaks, and so on), and "enterprise" (for cases where reporters used their own initiative to get the story). Table 12.3 shows the breakdown.

The foremost official source, of course, is the president. As former presidential press secretary George Reedy has written:

> Presidents have considerable leverage with which to manipulate part of the press and all try to do so with varying degrees of success. The principal source of the leverage is the unusual position of the President as one of the very few figures in public life who has in his exclusive possession a type of news virtually indispensable to the social and economic security of any reporter assigned to cover the White House full time. This category of newsworthy material consists of the President himself—his thoughts, his relationship with his friends and employees, his routine habits, his personal likes and dislikes, his intimate moments with his family and his associates.

[11]Robert Stein, *Media Power: Who Is Shaping Your Picture of the World?* (Boston: Houghton Mifflin, 1972), p. xi.

[12]David Altheide, *Creating Reality: How TV News Distorts Events* (Beverly Hills, Calif.: Sage, 1976), p. 16.

The fact that these things constitute "news" of a front page variety gives the President a trading power with individual newsmen of such magnitude that it must be seen at close quarters to be credited.[13]

Many of the things a president – or another official – says and does may be what historian Daniel Boorstin has called "pseudo-events."[14] Pseudo-events, according to Boorstin, are not spontaneous, but rather happen because someone planned, planted, staged, or incited them. The major reason for their being planned or planted is so that they can be reported, and they are therefore arranged to occur for the convenience of the media. Such events as press conferences, news leaks, campaign debates, the public signing of proclamations or of newly passed bills – all are pseudo-events in Boorstin's terms.

In recent years, antigovernment activists have learned this approach from politicians. The result has been a flood of pseudo-events – now more often called "media events" – such as demonstrations, marches, and civil disobedience. These pseudo-events or media events are designed primarily to "make news" and thereby advance the cause. In the era of media events, you don't have to be a political figure, nor do you even have to have any sort of usable political power, to "make news" – to be a source and, in a sense, to create or even almost become a message in the media.

---

[13] George Reedy, *The Twilight of the Presidency* (New York: World, 1970), pp. 100–101.

[14] Daniel J. Boorstin, *The Image: A Guide to Pseudo-Events in America* (New York: Harper, 1961).

■ Media power

In the past, our picture of the world was largely shaped by the established institutions of the society. Most vital information was, at least for a time, the exclusive property of government officials, military men and business leaders. News, with rare exceptions, was what they wanted us to know. Throughout most of its history, journalism was limited to mediating between the public and those who held power. Like education, journalism was concerned with describing and cataloguing our condition rather than questioning and changing it, and like education, journalism operated largely within the received values of the society.

Now, in little more than a generation, technology has changed this situation. In making it possible for the media to give us more words and pictures than ever before and to give them to us instantaneously, television and transistors have, at the same time, loosened the grip of authority on our consciousness. In an era of instant and almost universal communication, such control is hardly possible. . . .

. . . If knowledge is power, it is no longer concentrated in the hands of the powerful. From thousands of sources every day, information bypasses those in authority and flows directly to the media, and, in the case of television, not just information but experience: the raw sights and sounds of conflict and pain. As substantial control over what we know has passed from established institutions, a new force has emerged in American life: Media Power. By shaping our picture of the world on an almost minute-to-minute basis, the media now largely determine what we think, how we feel and what we do about our social and political environment.

Courtesy of NBC News

NBC News correspondents John Chancellor (*left*) and David Brinkley (*right*).

■ The politics of the medium

We use the term "medium" in two main ways when speaking of the news media. One medium is the reporter; the other is the newspaper or radio station or television equipment that delivers the report to us over the airwaves. Each of these has political aspects, because each involves conflicts or disputes over claims to authority – to the authority to present reality to us.

We might assume that a journalist would conceive of his role as that of *neutral or objective observer and reporter.* Edward R. Murrow, one of the great broadcast journalists of all time, once remarked that "the communication system . . . is totally neutral. It has no conscience, no principle, no morality. . . . It will broadcast filth or inspiration with equal facility. . . . It is, in sum, no more or no less than the men and women who use it."[15] An NBC News pamphlet asserts that a reporter has an obligation "to put news into perspective, to interpret and to analyze" because "the bare statement of a development may confuse and mislead when it is divorced from essential background and context."[16] Many observers believe that the less a reporter interprets the news in this sense, the more likely he or she is to be used by public officials in ways that distort the news. When an official says something, it's news whether it's true or not. But an interpretative journalist would also claim that the fact that an official's statement is false is also news and should be reported.

However, this view tends to shift the reporter from a position of neutral reporter to one of *participant reporter.* As such, he or she may be *the representative of the people,* seeking the truth and providing information to the public, and guarding the public interest. Alternately, the reporter may be a *critic of the government.* But the reporter as critic may tend toward a third participant role – that of *policy maker* or actor in the policy process, something few reporters would claim that they intend to

---

[15]Quoted in I. E. Fang, *Television News* (New York: Hastings House, 1968), p. 218.

[16]Quoted by Robert M. Batscha, *Foreign Affairs News and the Broadcast Journalist* (New York: Praeger, 1975), pp. 30–1.

be. Some, however, will take a fourth role: that of *advocate of policy* via editorial or commentary. Such figures as Eric Sevareid, David Brinkley, and Roderick MacLeish have done this on the networks in recent years.[17]

Newspeople differ not only in their concepts of the role they should play, but also in their notion of just what is news. But they do tend to agree that people in authority make news. Edward R. Murrow once referred critically to this: "The bias I refer to is in the direction of authority, and in this case authority means anything which is organized, which has a name, and which gives speeches. . . . In covering the news . . . the press tends . . . to take its cues from established authority."[18] This happens in the White House press room,[19] and it happens in any city.

We may be influenced by the authority we grant to correspondents just as they may be by the authority they grant to established individuals and organizations. These are effects of the personal media. But what of the mechanical media? Do the peculiar features of the mass media, and especially television, have impacts upon us as well? Many believe they do.

Television as a medium tends to *fragment* information. The news on television consists of a rapid-fire series of unrelated items lasting only seconds apiece. Furthermore, the news is interrupted by commercials regularly. Finding meaning in all this may be difficult indeed.

Information on television is also *immediate.* Instant reporting is an essential feature of television news as we have come to view it. This too limits the meaning in the news by limiting its pattern or structure in the minds of its recipients.

Furthermore, television tends to make the viewer passive. Like parades, spectator sports, movies, and radio, once you're there you tend to take what comes. The most you are likely to do with television is switch channels. To prevent such switching, even the news may be tailored to suit viewers' tastes. For instance, ABC news producer Av Westin wrote a memo to his news staff during the Vietnam War: "I have asked our Vietnam staff to alter the focus of their coverage from combat pieces to interpretive ones, pegged to the eventual pull-out of the American forces." He wrote the Saigon Bureau: "I think the time has come to shift some of our focus from the battlefield, or more specifically American military involvement with the enemy, to themes and stories which can be grouped under the general heading: We Are On Our Way Out of Vietnam." The only trouble with these instructions was, the war was still raging, and it was to be more than four years before American troops did indeed stop fighting and leave Vietnam.[20]

All in all, the combination of fragmentation, immediacy of information, and passivity of viewers may have important effects on what we learn from

---

[17]For a description of the major columnists and commentators—and their biases—see Carl Kalvelage and Morley Segal, *Research Guide in Political Science,* 2nd ed. (Morristown, N.J.: General Learning Press, 1976), chap. 6.

[18]Quoted in Louis M. Lyons, ed. *Reporting Television News* (Cambridge, Mass.: Harvard University Press, 1965), p. 154.

For a comprehensive study of concepts of news and objectivity by a widely experienced newsperson, see Bernard Roshco, *Newsmaking* (Chicago: University of Chicago Press, 1975).

[19]See Michael B. Grossman and Martha J. Kumar, "White House Press Operations and the News Media" (paper delivered at the American Political Science Association annual meeting, Washington, D.C., 1977).

[20]This story is told in Edward Jay Epstein, "The Selection of Reality," *The New Yorker,* March 3, 1973, pp. 41–77. The practice more generally is discussed by Diamond in *The Tin Kazoo* pp. 23–25.

television. One strong critic, Professor Herbert I. Schiller, argues that "the lethal combination of intentionally devitalized programming and physically inactivating communications technology is the machinery of contemporary American mind management."[21]

Others argue that television tends to destroy or prevent the development of the experience and skills that are essential to the effective functioning of our democratic politics. Jarol Manheim argues that "as the reliance on television as a teaching/learning device (in the largest sense) increases, many interpretive and interactive skills may fall into disuse and decay. And since human interaction is the very heart and soul of the political process, a general decline in the analytical and expressive skills which characterize that interaction in the society as a whole cannot help but be reflected in the polity as well."[22]

Others are more optimistic. For example, critic Edwin Diamond, noting Nixon's inability to use the medium well in Watergate and the failures of many recent "media" election campaigns, concludes that "it just may be that television is no longer as potent a political tool as the textbook wisdom holds. Or, to put the same heretical thought in another way, it may be that the audience – the political consumer – of the 1970s has changed in some critical ways. . . . Perhaps viewers are simply smarter, more sophisticated, or more skeptical."[23]

■ The politics of the receiver

One Washington correspondent wrote that "the year 1976 deserves to go down in history as the campaign year in which 'junk news' came into its own. Never was so much that meant so little presented in such technologically perfect fashion to such a widely yawning public."[24] What messages do get through depends not only on the source (candidates) and the medium (the media), but also on the receiver (the electorate).

If the electorate, the audience, was yawning widely, was that by choice or was it an effect of the coverage? Veteran journalist Henry Fairlie criticized the print media after the election for trying to find and speak to "a general readership," as the term goes. "There is no great sea of readers – each drop of water indistinguishable from the other – out there to be captured by marketing methods. If one knows anything about the habit of reading – as distinct from watching television – it is that it is an individual occupation, which separates people into individual selves."[25] So the receiver may matter more for the print media than for the electronic media.

Increasingly, however, the electronic media seem to be homogenizing us, the receivers, by standardizing us in giving us but one message that we must take or leave. And if we choose to "leave" it by changing channels, we are quite likely to find something approximating the same awaiting us elsewhere around the dial. The media may also be doing the same to our politics.

---

[21] Herbert I. Schiller, *The Mind Managers,* p. 31.

[22] Jarol B. Manheim, "Can Democracy Survive Television?" *Journal of Communication,* Spring 1976, p. 85.

[23] Diamond, *The Tin Kazoo,* p. 8.

[24] James McCartney, "The Triumph of Junk News," *MORE,* January–February, 1977, p. 17.

[25] Henry Fairlie, "The Harlot's Prerogative," *The New Republic,* April 30, 1977, p. 25.

□ IMPACTS OF THE MEDIA ON POLITICS

The media, especially television, have had wide-ranging effects on politics in general and elections and political campaigns in particular. In the 1960s, television news programs publicized the civil rights and antiwar movements. In the 1970s, the media have focused on, and helped to generate, in the views of some, a widespread disenchantment with politics.[26] However, the most immediate impact of the media has been on elections and political campaigns.

The first political commercials appeared in the 1952 presidential campaign, along with the first televising of the party conventions. There were then only about 15 million sets in American homes – a total that climbed to about 54 million in 1960, 93 million in 1970, and well over 100 million since then. The impact of television on elections has, understandably, grown with the spread of sets through the population. (See the box titled "Television and political campaigns.")

Research indicates that in general roughly a third of the voters decide whom to vote for before the conventions, another third during the conventions, and a final third during the fall campaign. Television is the major information source on both conventions and campaigns, and so it probably plays an important role in these voting decisions, even though voters rarely attribute influence to television itself.[27]

---

[26]See Michael J. Robinson, "Television and American Politics: 1956–1976," *The Public Interest* 48 (Summer 1977): 3–39.

[27]See research reports summarized in Sidney Kraus and Dennis Davis, *The Effects of Mass Communication on Political Behavior* (University Park: Pennsylvania State University Press, 1976), chap. 3.

Media coverage at the 1976 Democratic National Convention.
Dennis Brack/Black Star

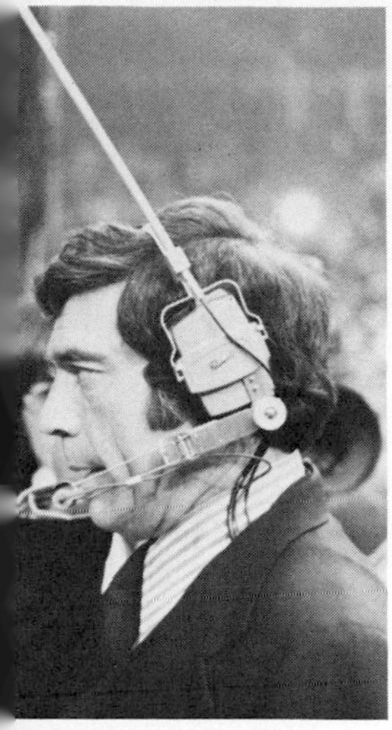

Stan Wakefield

CBS News correspondent Dan Rather at the 1976 Democratic National Convention.

Two political scientists, Thomas Patterson and Robert McClure, studied the influence of television on voters in the 1972 presidential election. They reported their study in a book whose title gives away their conclusion: *The Unseeing Eye: The Myth of Television Power in National Elections.*[28] "The only noticeable effect of network campaign news," they found, "is an increased tendency among voters to view politics in the same trivial terms that the newscasters depict it. Regular viewers of network news are likely to describe an election campaign as a lot of nonsense rather than a choice between fundamental issues."[29] What does reach viewers, they found, is political advertising, which actually has more issue content than network newscasts. But their research discovered that advertising is almost as likely to benefit one's opponent as it is to benefit the one who is paying for it, because viewers tend to see in it what they want to see.

Patterson then did a follow-up study of the 1976 campaign. This time he concentrated on media coverage and voters' experiences of it. He found that the media coverage tended to focus on the "horse-race" aspects of the campaign instead of the important substantive questions of the issues, the candidates' policy positions, the candidates' characters and abilities, their public records, and their personal backgrounds. Table 12.4 shows the percentages of coverage of different subjects given by various media.

"An emphasis on the horse race affects a campaign's opinion climate, heightening somewhat the feeling some voters have that campaigns really are not very important and that candidates really are not very noble fellows," says Patterson. "At the least, by cluttering people's minds with other things, and dominating the

[28]New York: Putnam, 1976.

[29]Ibid., p. 22. Patterson and McClure studied every newscast of all three networks in the 1972 campaign and interviewed 2000 viewers as well. For another view of the same campaign, see C. Richard Hofstetter, *Bias in the News: Network Television Coverage of the 1972 Election Campaign* (Columbus: Ohio State University Press, 1976).

TABLE 12.4

Press coverage of the 1976 presidential campaign[a]

	Network evening news	Los Angeles *Times*	Erie, Pa., *Times*	*Time/ Newsweek*
The Horse Race:	62%	51%	57%	55%
Winning and losing	16	17	25	19
Strategy logistics and support	22	19	18	28
Appearance and crowds	24	15	14	8
The Substance:	24	30	24	31
Candidates' issue positions	10	13	6	9
Candidates' characteristics and backgrounds	6	7	7	13
Issue-related (e.g., party platforms)	8	10	11	9
The Rest:	14	19	19	14
Campaign events calendar	2	4	6	3
Miscellaneous (e.g., election procedures)	12	15	13	11

[a]Figures based on a random selection of at least 20 percent of the coverage by each news source. Figures include opinion and analysis as well as regular news reports.

Source: Thomas E. Patterson, "The Media Muffed the Message." *Washington Post,* December 5, 1976. © The *Washington Post.*

■ Television and political campaigns

With the advent of television, campaign itineraries and speeches were timed for prime-time viewing hours to get maximum audiences. National nominating conventions are scheduled with a view to providing maximum exposure to the American people while putting the party in the best possible light. Presidential candidates now seem to be chosen in the open—rather than in smoke-filled rooms. Television makes it possible for candidates to reach the farthest corners of a constituency, and it makes candidates more familiar to the electorate. Candidates are sometimes chosen because they have appealing personalities, smiling families, and good television presence. Sometimes issues are left undefined and positions unclarified as candidates project their personalities and toss irrelevancies into campaigns to attract attention. When candidates are nominated and campaign on personal factors, the parties tend to be downgraded and become less important. The candidate is not necessarily a party personage, but a popular personality in his own right. Some believe that a leader with access to radio and television facilities and a forum like the White House or a governor's mansion has little need for the party organization and machinery to achieve his electoral success.

From Herbert Alexander, "Broadcasting and Politics," in *The Electoral Process,* ed. Kent Jennings and Harmon Zeigler (Englewood Cliffs, N.J.: Prentice-Hall, 1966), p. 81.

headlines, the horse-race emphasis diffused the messages that Ford and Carter were trying to get across to voters. The press can never give the voters what many of them really want," he concludes, "which is the 'truth' about the candidates. . . . But the press could give the voters more facts, so that their opinions will be informed. If they chose to do so, reporters could place more emphasis on what the candidates are saying on the issues, on their public records, on their qualifications, and so on. The horse race does not have to occupy 50 percent or more of the news space."[30]

□ IMPACTS OF THE MEDIA ON THE GOVERNMENT

So the media tend to standardize their reports. We noted earlier that they also tend to standardize their audiences. It is important to remember that one of the media's important audiences is the government itself. The government too seems more and more to find the media stereotyping it—and perhaps thereby homogenizing it as well. Researchers who combed the literature on media effects concluded that "the audience is not so malleable as merely to follow in the ways advocated on the editorial pages of the newspapers or in the commentaries of the networks. But its members do take their cues about the nature of the world about them from the media. And these cues influence what they do."[31] The media, in other words, may "set the agenda" for the public. Much the same might be said about the government as an audience. After Watergate, no politician can long afford to ignore the media. Indeed, few did so before Watergate.

[30]Thomas E. Patterson, "The Media Muffed the Message," *The Washington Post,* December 5, 1976, pp. 1, 4.

[31]Lee B. Becker, Maxwell E. McCombs, and Jack M. McLeod, "The Development of Political Cognitions," in *Political Communication,* ed. Steven H. Chaffee (Beverly Hills, Calif.: Sage, 1975), p. 58. See Kraus and Davis, *Effects of Mass Communication on Political Behavior,* chap. 6.

■ The Nixon-Agnew charges

In 1969, Vice-President Spiro Agnew made a speech that got instant attention in the media. In it Agnew attacked television news for being unrepresentative: "A small group of men, numbering perhaps no more than a dozen," he charged, "decide what 40 to 50 million Americans will learn of the day's events in the nation and the world. . . . To a man these commentators and producers live and work in the geographical and intellectual confines of Washington, D.C., or New York City. . . . They draw their political and social views from the same sources. Worse, they talk constantly to one another, thereby providing artificial reinforcement to their shared viewpoints."[32]

Nixon and his colleagues believed the media were out to get him. Agnew was attacked in the press for this and similar speeches, and Nixon eventually remarked, in an interview with David Frost in 1977: "As far as Spiro Agnew is concerned, I would say that because he was conservative, because he was one who took on the press, he got a lot rougher treatment than would have been the case had he been one of the liberals' favorite pin-up boys." In the same interview, Nixon remarked about the press: "I don't want them repressed, but believe me, when they take me on, or when they take any public figure on . . . I think the public figure ought to come back and crack 'em right in the puss."[33]

Some argued there was something to his charge. Bruce Herschensohn, who was a Nixon assistant in 1973–1974, wrote a book called *The Gods of Antenna* in which he listed with examples some twenty-six "techniques that can discredit ideas and people and can also be used to advance other ideas and other people" and were used against Nixon, he believes. Among them: selectivity of interviewees (choosing an unbalanced, unrepresentative group of people to interview); the inclusion or omission of crowd reaction (depending on how warm or hostile it is); catch phrases – such as "antiwar movement" (implying that opponents of the

[32]Quoted by Richard Reeves, "President Carter vs. the Press," *New York,* December 20, 1976, p. 112.

[33]Interview of Richard Nixon by David Frost telecast May 25, 1977, quoted in *Columbia Journalism Review,* July–August, 1977, p. 6.

President Carter at a press conference.
Dennis Brack/Black Star

movement, including the President, are "prowar"), or "Saturday Night Massacre"; and story placement (what comes first is thought by the audience to be the most important).[34]

The experts still disagree on whether or not television news has much of an effect at all on people. There hasn't yet been enough study of the question for us to be able to decide the matter. But it is a very important question. If our examination thus far has not convinced you of this, consider the results of three other studies. In one, W. P. Davison found that even diplomats get most of their information about world developments from the media, despite the fact that they have access to diplomatic and intelligence channels. In another, Bernard Cohen found that the press often plays a major part in "setting the agenda" of problems for public officials. And in the third C. H. Weiss studied opinion leaders and found that the media actually serve to link leaders in various sectors of government and society better than do, for example, private meetings.[35] So everyone seems to depend on the media, and so everyone is subject to whatever influence the media have.

□ IMPACTS OF GOVERNMENT ON THE MEDIA

The influence process works the other way, too, of course. The government regulates the media, to varying degrees, through laws and regulatory agencies. And it may also attempt to influence or control the media politically in various ways.

■ Regulation of the media: the First Amendment and the FCC

The First Amendment protects freedom of the press, and so government's efforts to control the print media often fail, as we saw happen in the Pentagon Papers case in Chapter 9. Laws concerning publication or distribution of pornography have fared better, and so have prohibitions on libel or slander of someone's character in print.[36]

The First Amendment says nothing about radio and television, of course, for radio was invented in 1896 and television came into public use some five decades later. When radio began operating, the secretary of commerce laid down certain restrictions on broadcast frequencies. (Frequencies are the levels of broadcast signals that determine where on your dial you get a station. Regulations control them so that each signal is clear and not mixed with another, so that you can hear it.) In 1926, a court ruled that the secretary of commerce had no such power, and competitors then began to use signals that overlapped and interfered with each other. When the broadcast industry protested, Congress passed the Radio Act of 1927. That bill created the Federal Radio Commission (FRC) and gave it power to regulate frequencies. In 1934 the FRC was combined into the new Federal

---

[34]Bruce Herschensohn, *The Gods of Antenna* (New Rochelle, N.Y.: Arlington House, 1976).

[35]These and other studies are summarized in William L. Rivers, Susan Miller, and Oscar Gandy, "Government and the Media," in *Political Communication*, ed. Chaffee, pp. 217–236.

[36]For a survey of the present state of a rapidly changing legal field, see Harvey L. Zuckman and Martin J. Gaynes, *Mass Communications Law* (St. Paul: West, 1977).

Communications Commission (FCC). The new agency was given broader powers to regulate in order to achieve "a fair, efficient, and equitable" broadcasting system responsive to the "public interest, convenience, or necessity."

Over the years, the FCC developed three primary guidelines. First, that the basic purpose of broadcasting is "the development of an informed public opinion through the public dissemination of news and ideas concerning the vital public issues of the day." Second, that the news and information should come from "diverse and antagonistic sources." And third, that radio and television should be basically local institutions, reflecting local needs and desires.

The FCC can issue licenses to stations to use the "public airwaves" – but there are few frequencies still available. It can also revoke or refuse to renew licenses when they come due every 3 years – but it only very rarely does so, in cases of extreme violations of its guidelines. And it can make regulations on how stations should serve the public interest – without censoring what is broadcast. The FCC has developed the "fairness doctrine," which requires a station to broadcast a range of public-affairs opinions to avoid monopolistic control of content. It has also limited ownership of multiple broadcast stations in an area by a single company and ownership of television stations by newspapers in the same city.

As an independent regulatory agency, the FCC is supposed to be removed from politics. But the president, with the approval of the Senate, appoints a new member whenever a term expires. This means that interest groups can play a role – both industry and citizen groups. And FCC decisions can be appealed to the courts – which adds yet another political dimension.[37]

■ Control of the media

Politics entered governmental broadcasting policy more directly when Nixon established an Office of Telecommunications Policy (OTP) in his Executive Office of the President in 1970. Its first director, Clay Whitehead, made a speech in 1972 attacking the networks for "ideological plugola," or bias in the news, which kept the OTP a controversial agency until it was finally abolished by President Carter in 1977.

Attacks by Agnew and Whitehead were only parts of the Nixon administration's efforts to influence the media. Through budgetary controls, it sought to change programming on the largely government-funded Public Broadcasting Service, which provides certain programs to the nation's almost 300 noncommercial stations and which Nixon believed too liberal in its programming content. It also used the courts to try to force reporters to reveal the confidential sources of their exposés, with some success.[38]

Even when political pressure is not applied, there are factors at work that tend to inhibit the media – especially those representatives who cover the White House.

---

[37]For accounts of regulation, see Erwin G. Krasnow and Lawrence D. Longley, *The Politics of Broadcast Regulation* (New York: St. Martin's, 1973) and Edward Jay Epstein, "The Selection of Reality," *The New Yorker,* March 3, 1973, pp. 41–77.

[38]For an account of these and other efforts, see William E. Porter, *Assault on the Media: The Nixon Years* (Ann Arbor: University of Michigan Press, 1976).

The White House press corps covers the president from comfortable quarters paid for by the taxpayers and travels with him as well. One member of that group recently wrote of the strong temptation to become part of the president's "court"—"to depict the president as larger than life, to assume an air of self-importance and to view the White House as the center of the universe."[39] But the White House in Washington is far from the only source of news for the media. Increasingly, we may be getting news from "white houses" everywhere across America through the growth of what is called "media access."

□ MEDIA ACCESS FOR THE PUBLIC

■ Rules governing access

Journalist A. J. Liebling used to say that "freedom of the press belongs to the man who owns one." We have already discussed evidence of broader access to the print media. Increasingly, the courts and the FCC in the past decade have been agreeing that citizens should have more access to the broadcast media as well. Action Unit 12.2 describes the developing right of media access and how citizens can take advantage of it. There are by now four key rules concerning access that apply to broadcasters.

- □ *The fairness doctrine* requires that a broadcaster give air time to opposing spokespersons to present their views on controversial issues.
- □ *The personal-attack rule* gives individuals or groups a right to reply if they are maligned on the air.
- □ *The political-editorial rule* gives candidates whose election is opposed by a station editorial the right to reply.

---

[39]John Herbers, *No Thank You, Mr. President* (New York: Norton, 1976). For further pictures of this tendency and the cynicism it can also breed, see Timothy Crouse's book on the press corps in the 1972 election, *The Boys on the Bus* (New York: Random House, 1973).

"Attention out there! We now bring you an opposing viewpoint to a CBS editorial!"

Former FCC Commissioner Nicholas Johnson, now head of the National Citizens' Committee for Broadcasting.

- *The equal-time rule* gives a candidate the right to the same air time that his or her opponent gets.

Practices concerning access

Not all access is forced by rules, of course. Sometimes it is invited by editors and directors seeking out varying views. Other times it comes about through the "newsworthiness" of citizens or groups and their activities. However, Edie Goldenberg points out that "resource-rich" news sources, such as established business and social groups, are in a much stronger position to bargain with reporters and to manage the news than are "resource-poor" groups. Resource-rich groups are usually thought to be more newsworthy, they are more often a part of a reporter's regular "beat" or specialization, and they can more easily help the reporter in collecting the news. "Resource-poor sources are at a disadvantage both in initiating contacts with the press and in regularizing them," she concludes. Yet, as Goldenberg points out, such contacts can carry the message of resource-poor groups to policy makers and can strengthen a group's position in the political arena.[40]

Cable television

Former FCC Commissioner Nicholas Johnson, now head of the National Citizens' Committee for Broadcasting, which tries to facilitate access, says: "People are used to being programmed by their TV sets. They aren't used to thinking that they might do some television programming themselves."[41]

One way in which this possibility is becoming a reality is the growth of cable television. Cable television is brought to the home by a wire from a tall antenna able to pick up distant signals and amplify them. Cable thus allows a set to receive broadcasts from other cities, as well as local ones. The first cable system was developed in 1948, and the system spread first in rural and mountain areas where local television was weak or absent. Today there are about 3500 cable systems serving 8000 cities. About 11 million of our nation's 90 million television households subscribe to cable services, for which they pay a monthly fee.[42]

In the early 1960s the FCC began to regulate cable television, largely to protect the business interests of the regular stations, which feared they would lose advertisers to cable. The first regulations limited the number of distant signals or programs a cable company could transmit. But in the early 1970s the FCC began to require cable companies to originate some programs on their own, thereby becoming miniature television stations.[43] This rule set the stage for development of Public Access Cable Television (PACT). PACT rules require that a cable company make available free certain cable channels to the public on a first-come-first-served

---

[40]Edie Goldenberg, *Making the Papers: The Access of Resource-Poor Groups to the Metropolitan Press* (Lexington, Mass.: Lexington Books, 1975), p. 145. See also Roshco, *Newsmaking,* especially chap. 6, "Being a News Source vs. Becoming a News Source."

[41]Nicholas Johnson, speech at the University of Texas, March 5, 1977.

[42]Paul W. MacAvoy, ed., *Deregulation of Cable Television* (Washington, D.C.: American Enterprise Institute, 1977), chap. 1.

[43]See Leonard Ross, *Economic and Legal Foundations of Cable Television* (Beverly Hills, Calif.: Sage, 1974).

□ ACTION UNIT 12.2 How to talk on your TV station

Commercial television stations are private businesses using the public airwaves for profit – and, sometimes, for news coverage and editorial statements that affect citizens' interests. Because they do so, the FCC and the courts are in the process of developing regulations and procedures for giving citizens access to the media. This is creating a new field within the law. For summaries of its development as it concerns television and other media, see Benno C. Schmidt, Jr., *Freedom of the Press vs. Public Access* (New York: Praeger, 1976). See also Fred A. Friendly, *The Good Guys, the Bad Guys, and the First Amendment* (New York: Random House, 1976). And for a handbook that will be valuable should you wish to secure access rights, see Andrew O. Shapiro, *Media Access: Your Rights to Express Your Views on Radio and Television* (Boston: Little, Brown, 1976). You may also get further guidance on media access from the NCCB, which is described in Action Unit 12.1.

basis. Such a system was first instituted in Dale City, Virginia, south of Washington, D.C., in 1968, and since has spread to other cities at the urging of the FCC. Cities have the power to grant franchise rights to cable companies to let them operate. Some cities have begun requiring that cable channels be provided to the local government or the school system for public use. At this point, regulations are still developing and the outcome is not yet clear. But because cable systems can offer up to thirty or forty channels to any given city, there may be room for much public access to free or inexpensive media communication.[44]

■ Other possibilities for greater public roles

Various proposals are being developed to broaden electronic or cable communication. The late Peter Goldmark, inventor of the long-playing record, proposed a system designed to telecast everything from cultural events to the daily newspaper from large cities to rural areas. Others have argued that such systems should be two-way, allowing the recipients of such programming to use the facilities to react to it or even to present their views on, say, public issues to a central source. Such a two-way system could increase the prospects for participatory democracy by allowing two-way discussions and referenda. It could also facilitate education by allowing viewers to direct inquiries and requests for information to central data banks. Whether such instant two-way interaction would be desirable is a question few have yet considered – but one that must be examined quickly, for the technology required is by now imminent.[45]

What role the government should play in regulating such developments is still not agreed upon.[46] Indeed, there is growing question about whether

---

[44]See Gilbert Gillespie, *Public Access Cable Television in the U.S. and Canada* (New York: Praeger, 1975).

[45]See Noah Lemelshtrich, *Two-Way Communication: Political and Design Analysis of a Home Terminal* (Beverly Hills, Calif.: Sage, 1974). And see Ithiel de Sola Pool, ed., *Talking Back: Citizen Feedback and Cable Technology* (Cambridge, Mass.: MIT Press, 1973).

[46]See MacAvoy, *Deregulation of Cable Television,* for the argument for cable deregulation.

government regulation of broadcasting is in the public interest as it is done.[47] Questions of regulation and indications of the possible benefits of public access reach much of the public most clearly now in the phenomenon of citizen-band radio. CB has done for radio what the copying machine has done for the press: given every person the opportunity to be his or her own broadcaster and publisher.

☐ THE QUESTION OF MEDIA RESPONSIBILITY IN DEMOCRATIC POLITICS

With these opportunities have come new questions of responsibilities of the media, of the government, and increasingly of the public – the audience that seems more and more to be turning into sources of messages, with growing opportunities for influencing the development of new media or channels.

What is the responsibility of the media in democratic politics. Is it to be objective reporters or interpreters or critics? Is it to inform or entertain or both? Is it to give the public what it needs or what it wants? Should the media be run as businesses? One television magnate, Lord Thomson, characterized a television station's license as "a license to print money," and broadcasters often refer to the business as "failure-proof" because it is so profitable even for stations poorly run. In 1976, the three networks alone had incomes of over $2.5 billion dollars, and the local stations took in almost $3.5 billion, with profit margins often running a staggering 30 percent.[48]

The press also is highly profitable. "Both its power and its role come from one source: the Constitution's protection of press freedom," writes journalist-critic Charles Seib. "That's the only constitutional protection given a private business. It carries with it awesome responsibilities. . . ."[49] These responsibilities – uncertain and under debate as they still are – extend to the government, which regulates the media, too.

And what of the citizens? Experts increasingly refer to the prospect of "the wired city." But the same technology that makes information from around the world and around the corner available in one's own home may separate people from each other even further. Critic Erik Barnouw warns: "What disturbs me is that the writer, the teacher, or the communicator is getting further away from the audience. . . . The viewer, meanwhile, is becoming more and more isolated. Tomorrow, he won't have to go to the polling place any more. He'll be able to vote by pushing buttons. He doesn't have to attend class; he can take the course from home. . . . The result is that people are getting out of touch with humanity. Everything is pretended participation."[50]

---

[47]See, for example, the argument for broadcast deregulation by L. A. Powe, Jr., "Of the [Broadcast] Press," *Texas Law Review,* December 1976.

[48]Les Brown, "Television Becomes the 'Failure-Proof Business,'" *New York Times,* March 15, 1976.

[49]Charles B. Seib, "Journalistic Conflicts," *Washington Post,* November 26, 1976, p. A23.

[50]Interview in *U.S. News and World Report,* March 1, 1976, pp. 27–29.

Furthermore, the same technology that brings messages to us can be used – by the government or by private interests – to eavesdrop on our daily lives and even perhaps to dictate our behavior to us. So there are important questions of civil liberties raised by the very advances that can also promise to increase our civil rights. The mass media have thus become much more than an influence on governmental decision. They have become as well a promise of greater liberty and at the same time a challenge to our liberty. We shall next examine the politics of liberty.

☐ SUGGESTIONS FOR FURTHER READING AND STUDY

A helpful guide to the whole media field is the *Aspen Handbook on the Media,* edited by William Rivers (Palo Alto, Calif.: Aspen Institute Project on Communications and Society paperback, 1975), which includes a guide to bibliographies. For a guide to much of that literature, see Ithiel de Sola Pool et al., eds., *Handbook of Communication* (Chicago: Rand McNally, 1973), which covers the period up to 1970. A survey of research on political aspects with helpful annotated bibliographies attached to each chapter is Sidney Kraus and Dennis Davis, *The Effects of Mass Communication on Political Behavior* (University Park: Pennsylvania State University Press, 1976). For a discussion of the Washington media, see Austin Kiplinger, *Washington Now* (New York: Harper & Row, 1975), chap. 20, and Timothy Crouse's often riotous yet troubling account of reporters in the 1972 campaign, *The Boys on the Bus* (New York: Bantam paperback, 1973). For the political aspects of television with special attention to that campaign, see the studies cited in chapter footnotes by Patterson and McClure, Hofstetter, and Diamond. And on television's development see Erik Barnouw's interesting account, *Tube of Plenty: The Evolution of American Television* (New York: Oxford University Press, 1975).

To keep up with current developments in the communications industry, the trade journal *Broadcasting* is helpful. In addition, interesting articles on a wide variety of media topics appear in the *Journal of Communication,* the *Columbia Journalism Review,* and *MORE.*

5 WHAT RIGHTS AND LIBERTIES DOES AMERICAN GOVERNMENT PROVIDE?

☐ Perspective 5: The politics of education

Allan Bakke was a Vietnam veteran and an engineer with a promising career in Northern California when he decided that he really wanted to be a doctor. He took the required premed courses in off hours from his job and worked as a hospital volunteer. Then, at age 32, he applied for admission to medical school. He was turned down in 1973 and again in 1974 by eleven different med schools, including his alma mater, the University of Minnesota, and the nearby state school, the University of California at Davis.

Bakke had a good record: a 3.5 grade-point average (GPA) and a good score on the Medical College Aptitude Test (MCAT) – a standardized test taken by med school candidates throughout the country. He learned that his academic record was better than that of some of those whom U.C. Davis admitted. The only explanation, it seemed to him, was that they were black, Chicano, Asian-American, or Native American Indian, while he was white.

So Bakke sued U.C. Davis, alleging that it had discriminated against him solely on grounds of race – because he was white. Davis med school had a policy at that time of admitting 100 students a year. But it held 16 places of the 100 for "disadvantaged students," which in practice meant members of minority groups. Some of the minority students who were admitted had GPAs of 2.1 or 2.2; all whites under 2.5 were automatically rejected; Bakke's score was 3.5. There were, however, thirty-five applicants in 1973 and thirty-two in 1974 who ranked higher than Bakke yet were not admitted. And the dean of the med school was allowed to select 5 of the 100 admittees using his own judgment – which some said was used for the benefit of children with political or financial connections.[1]

Davis admitted using race as one criterion for admission, arguing that the people of California would benefit if there were more minority students becoming doctors. Many of these new doctors would practice in ghettos, improving the health care of minorities and the poor generally, it said. In addition, minority doctors would serve as "role models" for minority college students, encouraging the latter to go into medicine. Thus the policy of holding places for minority students was part of **affirmative action** – the policy of making active efforts to recruit more minority and female students and employees that the federal government requires schools and businesses to follow.

Was Bakke therefore a victim of racial discrimination just like that experienced by blacks and other minorities but outlawed by the Fourteenth Amendment? Or was he merely the unfortunate victim of a policy adopted at government urging by a state medical school to try to overcome centuries of discrimination against minority groups in the United States?

The debate was left to the courts to decide. But it was a much more important case than decision of the fate of a single applicant to medical

---

[1]Basic Sources for this account of the Bakke case include James W Singer, "Reverse Discrimination – Will *Bakke* Decide the Issue?" *National Journal,* September 17, 1977, pp. 1436–1441; "The Furor over Reverse Discrimination," *Newsweek,* September 26, 1977, pp. 52–58; George A. Silver, "Beyond the Bakke Case," *Washington Post,* September 18, 1977; Ralph R. Smith, "The Truth about the Bakke Case," *Focus,* July 1977, pp. 3, 8; and Lou Cannon, "Bakke Also Vied with the Well-To-Do," *Washington Post,* October 2, 1977.

school suggested. It appeared likely to become the first major court test of the policy of affirmative action and the limits of what many called **reverse discrimination** – discrimination in favor of minorities, and therefore against whites, intended to overcome the legacy of previous discrimination.

The rationale for affirmative action had been stated by President Johnson in 1965: "You do not take a person who, for years, has been hobbled by chains and liberate him, bring him up to the starting line of a race and then say, 'You are free to compete with all the others,' and still justly believe you have been completely fair." Affirmative action, as a guide to how to make decisions on education, was a novel principle in 1965, when it was initiated by Executive Order 11246. But even the principle of "merit" – that the brightest students should get the opportunities for further education, as Bakke argued – was a drastic departure from the ways education had been developed in America.

Wide World Photos
Allan Bakke.

☐ THE DEVELOPMENT OF AMERICAN EDUCATION

The first laws concerning education in America were the Massachusetts Bay Colony Act of 1642 and the Old Deluder Satan Act of 1647. These laws, passed by the ancestor of the state of Massachusetts, required that local communities establish schools. Those schools were to teach the Bible so that the "Old Deluder," Satan, would not be able to fool and corrupt the children of the colony.[2] Under the Articles of Confederation, the Continental Congress in 1787 declared that "religion, morality, and knowledge, being necessary to good government and the happiness of mankind, schools and the means of education shall be forever encouraged." To do so, it set aside some money from the sale of public lands in the Northwest to create local schools.

Since that time, however, education has been primarily the responsibility of the states. They, in turn, have delegated control over schools and the responsibility for financing them to localities. In the early years, the schools generally charged the parents for their children's education. In other words, the principle of *ability to pay* determined who got formal education.

Gradually, a movement for statewide systems of free (because tax-supported), non-church-run schools spread. The principle of "ability to pay" was giving way to the principle of *democracy*, or opportunity for all – except in most cases minorities and in some cases women. Public colleges and universities too were being established in these years. They received their biggest impetus with Congressional passage of the Morrill Act in 1862. That Act was formally called the Land Grant College Act because it gave federal land to states for creating colleges specializing in agriculture and home economics.

More and more states, in the early twentieth century, also passed laws making attendance at school compulsory up to a certain age. But they allowed parents to send their children to private

[2]See Norman C. Thomas, *Education in National Politics* (New York: McKay, 1975, p. 19.

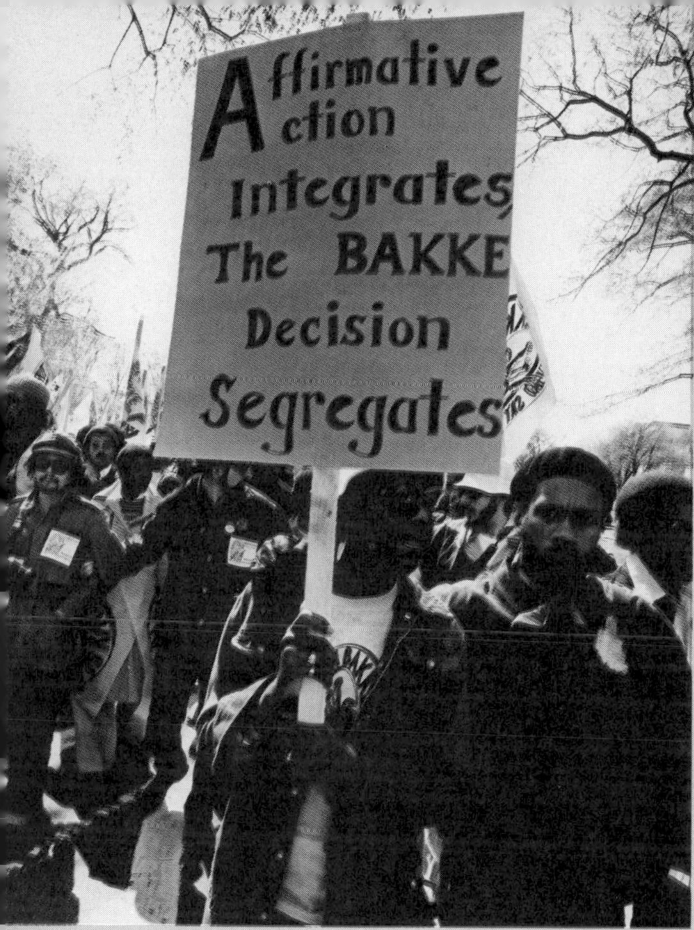

Martin A. Levick/Black Star

schools (almost all of them church-related, many of them Catholic) if they preferred. Thus the principle of *freedom of choice* was applied within the broader principle of *compulsory education.*

But the old principle of "ability to pay" had not disappeared from American education. It had only moved into private schools and higher education. However, American business and American education needed more well-trained people than the "ability to pay" criterion allowed into our better schools. And so scholarships to bright but needy students became more common. The principle here was *merit.* And until community colleges spread in the 1950s and 1960s, merit seemed to be replacing not only wealth but also democracy or equality of opportunity as the major criterion determining who could and would get higher education.

The growth of federal scholarships, from the "GI Bill of Rights" (passed in 1944, later renewed for the Korean and Vietnam War veterans) through the "Basic Educational Opportunity Grants" (BOGs) passed in 1972, offered the chance at higher education to others than the brightest able to earn scholarships on merit.

■ Affirmative action

At the same time, however, the application of the principle of merit was itself being qualified or limited in higher education by the principle of *affirmative action.* Court decisions in the 1950s began to open up equal educational opportunities, in a legal sense, to blacks. But where the Court called for "all deliberate speed" in desegregation, school officials took even more time. The Civil Rights Act of 1964 not only called for desegregation of public higher education, but also prohibited discrimination wherever federal funds were involved (which was by then all of higher education).

In 1965, as the concept of affirmative action was being developed, the Higher Education Act—the first major commitment to federal aid—provided for compensatory services to those deprived of adequate preparation. Further moves in that direction were made in the Education Amendments of 1972. But more and more it became clear that simply providing equal opportunity and compensatory services would not bring about desired increases in minority enrollments. The consequence at the lower levels of public schools was busing for integration. At the higher levels it was programs of affirmative action designed to guarantee special treatment for minority—and female—youths interested in further education.

One approach was opening more places in schools that had been especially restrictive, such as schools of law and medicine. This brings us back to the Bakke case. In the years he applied to med school, about 43,000 other Americans did too. About 3000 of them were members of minority groups, and of them, 1400 were admitted. But that total was still less than 9 percent of all admissions, and by 1976 that percentage was actually declining once again. In addition, less than 3 percent of all practicing doctors are members of minority groups, even though minorities make up almost 20 percent of the population, as we'll see in Chapter 14. As a response to the civil rights movement of the 1960s, medical schools attempted to improve the plight of minority students seeking to be doctors. They opened 4900 more places for new students from 1968 to 1974. But 77 percent of those new admittees turned out to be whites. This fact, too, argued for allocating a certain number of places to minorities, if no other way could be found to guarantee that more minorities are admitted.

□ EDUCATION IN POLITICS

The importance of medical training is clear, both for doctors (who make a very good living) and society (which needs and wants more medical care). In the case of most other types of education, the values are somewhat less obvious – but strongly believed nonetheless.

■ Education for what?

Thomas Jefferson favored mass public education to create wise citizens and widen their opportunities to develop their talents. Andrew Jackson opposed the elitism then characteristic of education and society by arguing for "common schools." Education may serve to select and train elite leaders, of course, but its main function is to socialize people into being good workers in the economy and good citizens in the polity.

However, economist Samuel Bowles points out that "the history of United States education provides little support for the view that schools have been vehicles for the equalization of economic status or opportunity. Nor are they today. The proliferation of special programs for the equalization of educational opportunity has had precious little impact on the structure of education, and even less on the structure of income and opportunity in the economy."[3]

By this reckoning, our schools have been largely successful in economic socialization, although at the expense of equal economic opportunity. The notion that the schools should contribute to economic reform is not commonly held by educators, any more than is the notion that schools should contribute toward political reform. Instead, the common view is that schools exist, and should function, to train people to understand and appreciate their economic and political system.

■ Education for whom?

The influence, whatever its strength, has reached different population groups differently. In the past decade, according to the Census Bureau, 40 percent of the population – some 80 million people – have experienced a year or more of elementary or secondary school. Yet the educational achievement of various population groups is still very different.

Schooling Women, for example, are now more likely to finish high school than men are, but they are less likely to go to college. In 1974, half of all males age 25–34 had finished at least one year of college (50.6 percent of white males, 36.9 percent of black males), while 46 percent of females had (46 percent of whites, 43 percent of blacks).

But college attendance is still very much affected by the economic level of the family, regardless of race or ability. About 54 percent of those with family incomes of $15,000 and over go to college, while only about 13 percent of those under $3000 do so.[4]

[3]Samuel Bowles, "Educational Reforms under Fire," *New York Times*, July 26, 1976. Bowles believes that educational reform is impossible without economic reform: participatory workers' control and democratic socialism. The argument is developed in Bowles and Herbert Gintis, *Schooling in Capitalist America* (New York: Basic Books, 1976).

[4]Census Bureau, *Social and Economic Characteristics of Students: October 1973*, Series P-20, no. 272 (Washington, D.C.: Government Printing Office, 1974), pp. 43–44.

Another governmental study found that not only family income but also the father's education has a marked effect on a child's likelihood of attending college, again regardless of race or ability. For example, in the same income bracket, a child of a college graduate is much more likely to attend college than the child of a nongraduate.[5] Thus, high income may overcome lack of family educational background, but low income usually means no college even for the child of a college graduate.

As the cost of higher education skyrockets, the impact will most likely increase. However you are managing your own college education you're likely to find paying for that of your children a real challenge. In the late 1970s the average total cost of a year at a private college was over $7000, and that at a state school over $4000. These costs have been increasing at a rate of about 6 percent a year. This means that if you have a child in the next few years, putting him or her through college is likely to cost almost $50,000 at a state school or almost $90,000 at a private school. And that doesn't even include any graduate education. To provide for 4 years of state school education for a child born today, you'd have to start immediately putting $1500 in a savings account every year for 18 years. How many Americans will be able to do anything like this? The likely result, unless drastic steps are taken, will be that opportunities for higher education will again be governed by the ability to pay.

[5]Census Bureau, *School Enrollment of Young Adults and Their Fathers: October 1960*, Series P-20, no. 110 (Washington, D.C.: Government Printing Office, 1961), p. 15.

Illiteracy It might help also to look at the opposite extreme. In 1969 the U.S. Census found that 1 percent of all Americans 14 or older – 1,400,000 people – were totally unable to read and write in any language. HEW finds too that nearly 5 percent of all youths 12–17 – a total of a million – have less than a fourth-grade-level reading ability. And a 1970 Harris Poll of Americans 16 or older found that 8 percent couldn't do well enough to fill out a driver's license application, and 11 percent were unable to complete a simple bank account application, while 34 percent were stumped by an application for medical aid. The U.S. Office of Education, looking for basic abilities such as reading a newspaper grocery ad, or addressing an envelope, concludes that one in every five American adults may in this sense be "functionally illiterate."[6]

Bilingual education In addition, some 2,500,000 American children have difficulty with English because Spanish, Eskimo, or one of forty other languages is their native tongue. They need "bilingual education" – teaching in two languages. But until 1967 when Congress passed the Bilingual Education Act, no concerted efforts were being made to help them. And until 1974, when the Supreme Court ruled San Francisco schools were violating the civil rights of Chinese-speaking students by not offering bilingual teaching, little energy was shown. By 1975, some 200,000 students were receiving bilingual education – but 10 times as many needed it.

[6]"Why 1.4 Million Americans Can't Read and Write," *U.S. News & World Report,* August 19, 1974, pp. 37–40. Herman Wong, "Illiteracy: Fear and Shame: 1 Out of 5 Adults May Not Be Able to Read This," *Austin American-Statesman,* November 15, 1976.

□ POLITICS IN EDUCATION

The classifying of bilingual education as a civil right of non-English-speaking Americans marks yet another expansion of our rights. So does the adoption by the federal government of "right to read" programs to overcome illiteracy. But, as we have seen again and again, getting something declared a right and getting that right actively and successfully provided to citizens can be very different things. And very political things.

■ The politics of school control

The politics in education operate at every level, as different forces, different groups, and different individuals seek to control or influence educational policy and practice. There are 16,000 local school systems in America today. Each one has its political conflicts among parents, teachers, administrators, and the school board – and occasionally, where they're given a role, students too.

Parents have often complained, sometimes with success, about the content of courses (especially on sex and evolution) and of textbooks and the school library.[7] But generally their powers are limited.[8]

However, this may be changing. Some years ago, in a protest against the Vietnam War, five Des Moines children wore black arm bands to school. They were suspended for doing so. The parents of three of them sued. The Supreme Court, in *Tinker v. Des Moines School District* (1969) held that the suspension violated their First Amendment right to freedom of speech, saying that the wearing of an armband is an act of "symbolic" speech, and holding that students do not "shed their constitutional rights to freedom of speech or expression at the schoolhouse gate."

Court decisions such as this have opened up the field of parent and student rights. Because it is a new realm of rights, it is still growing and being shaped by court decisions and by federal and state laws. As of 1978, among the major rights were these:[9]

- □ the right to appeal a school policy or decision which prevents a student from expressing controversial views, so long as they are not obscene, slanderous, or libelous, and so long as they do not cause serious disruption – recognized by all states
- □ the right to take action against a school official if a student is disciplined with "excessive or unreasonable" physical force – recognized by all states
- □ the right to appeal suspension from school – recognized by all states
- □ the right to appeal an administrator's decision prohibiting a female student from trying out for and playing in male-dominated sports – recognized by all states *except* Louisiana, Iowa, Illinois, Indiana, Kansas, Kentucky, Minnesota, Nebraska, North Dakota, New Mexico, and Wyoming
- □ the right to be educated at home instead of in school, providing the education meets conditions and standards set by your state – recognized by Alabama, Alaska, Arizona, California, Colorado, Connecticut, Florida, Georgia, Hawaii, Illinois, Iowa, Maine, Maryland, Massachusetts, Minnesota, Mississippi, Nevada, New Hampshire, New York, North Carolina, Ohio,

[7]For an interesting study, See Dorothy Nelkin, *Science Textbook Controversies and the Politics of Equal Time* (Cambridge, Mass: MIT Press, 1977).

[8]See Tyll van Geel, *Authority to Control the School Program* Lexington, Mass: Lexington Books, 1976).

[9]These and other rights of parents and students are summarized in several publications by the National Committee for Citizens in Education, founded in 1973, at 410 Wilde Lake Village Green, Columbia, Maryland 21004. It has a 24-hour toll-free phone "hotline," (800) NETWORK, which you can call to report problems, get advice on school-related problems, or get a free copy of its "Parent Rights Card." It also publishes a newsletter, *Network*, for members, and a book by David Schimmel and Louis Fisher, *The Rights of Parents in the Education of Their Children* (1977). And it has some 300 local affiliate organizations across the country.

Pennsylvania, Vermont, West Virginia, and Wisconsin

- □ the right to be excused from studying subjects the parents object to on religious, moral, or other *reasonable* grounds – recognized by Alaska, Arizona, Colorado, Delaware, Florida, Idaho, Illinois, Indiana, Iowa, Louisiana, Maryland, Michigan, Nevada, New Hampshire, New York, North Carolina, Ohio, Pennsylvania, Vermont, West Virginia, and Wisconsin

At the level above the parents, teachers' unions have recently become very strong in many large cities, especially in the North. They are now playing bigger roles not only in curriculum and salaries, but in school budgets as a whole. In long-time observer Fred Hechinger's view, the new teacher militance derives from "the unconscionable past exploitation of teachers as underpaid servants and second-class citizens – a system in which teachers and children were equally the victims." But since unionization, "the harsh fact," he argues, is "that the children's interests occupy a low place on the scale of the establishment's priorities and self-interest."[10] How true this is of individual districts is beside the point. What is important to recognize is that old concerns about curriculum and method now are often decided in larger arenas where political power predominates. And teachers, like administrators, are becoming more organized and more powerful. The National Education Association, with some 1,800,000 teacher members, and the American Federation of Teachers, a growing union affiliated with the AFL-CIO, together represent all but about 100,000 of the nation's 2,200,000 elementary and secondary school teachers. When they cooperate, they are a very powerful lobby at all levels from the school district to the national.

■ The politics of school finance

Increasingly, educationists are meeting resistance from another growing group: taxpayers opposing increased school taxes on their property. At the same time, school property taxes are under attack from another direction: citizens claiming that equality of educational opportunity is denied to many because rich school districts get more tax revenue to spend on their schools than do poor districts.

In one case, Demetrio Rodriguez, a Mexican-American laborer, was concerned about the quality of education which his three children who live in a poor part of San Antonio were able to get. Their school district couldn't raise as much money by taxing its less valuable homes and other property as other districts with more valuable property could raise. Rodriguez sued in 1968 to get the property tax declared unconstitutional as a means of financing schools. He argued that it violated the constitutional right to "equal protection." His lawyers contended that even though education is not mentioned in the Constitution, it is so fundamental to other guaranteed rights such as voting that it should be protected.

In 1973, the Nixon-appointed Burger Court majority disagreed. By a five-to-four vote the Court decided *San Antonio Independent School District v. Rodriguez* by rejecting Rodriguez's claim that education is a right guaranteed by the Constitution. That left the question once again to the states. The states, which provide about 40 percent of all funds for schools (compared to 50 percent local funds and 10 percent federal) have constitutional responsibility for education. But state legislatures are rarely sensitive to the needs of the poor and minorities. And so, as Rodriguez himself commented, "The poor people have lost again."

Since the *Rodriguez* decision little progress has been made toward equalizing the quality of public education among the rich and the poor at any level. But more has been learned about who really pays for public higher education. State colleges and universities get 17 percent of their revenue from tuition and almost all the rest from state taxes. The Carnegie Corporation made a comprehensive study of higher education finance. It concluded, in the words of chairman Clark Kerr: "You could say that low-tuition for the middle class, that can afford to

---

[10]Fred M. Hechinger, "An Exploded Myth," *New York Times*, February 17, 1976.

pay more, is a subsidy of the middle class, at the expense of the high-income groups who pay much more in taxes, and particularly at the expense of the low-income groups whose kids can't afford to go to college."[11]

The politics of federal aid

Of course, as the federal government's role in education grows, the federal politics of education increase. In the Johnson years, sixty education-related bills became law and government spending on schools shot up from $2.3 billion in 1963 to almost $11 billion in 1968 – by 1976 the annual total was about $22 billion.[12] Johnson was responsible for many major innovations, such as new Department of Health, Education, and Welfare (HEW) desegregation guidelines, extension of integration requirements to northern schools, and large federal aid to disadvantaged areas. Included also were education "laboratories" to test innovations, college student loans, work-study programs, and Head Start and Follow Through programs to give special preschool training to the disadvantaged to prepare them for public school.[13]

But some idea of the underlying political struggles is given by Francis Keppel, then Commissioner of Education, in reminiscences in the Johnson Library. Keppel reports that Johnson very much wanted all school boards – northern as well as southern – to agree to desegregation programs. So HEW put the pressure on, threatening to withhold federal funds for noncompliance. One such threat went out to Chicago, well-known for its segregated schools, after complaints had been made to Washington of its policies. But Mayor Richard Daley complained directly to Johnson. So LBJ called in Wilbur Cohen, assistant secretary of HEW, "and said, 'Fix it.' He didn't say it quite as bluntly as that, but pretty nearly. He said, 'Look, this is a ridiculous situation,' and [later] . . . he said, 'Lady Bird [Johnson's wife] has got her beautification bill up there [on Capitol Hill]. Now, we can't mess up the beautification bill in Congress, just on account of this little mess, so fix it.'" Cohen, Keppel reports, worked out an agreement with the Chicago school board for some small steps toward desegregation, and federal funds flowed again. Shortly thereafter, Keppel was replaced.[14]

It should be clear, then, that political struggles over education occur at every level of our political system. And often they involve various levels at once. This is particularly true when the principle of affirmative action is at stake, as we can see by returning to the Bakke case.

THE POLITICS OF THE BAKKE CASE

The case goes through the courts

Allan Bakke filed his suit seeking admission to the U.C. Davis Medical School in California trial court in 1974, alleging that his exclusion violated his rights under the Fourteenth Amendment, which says that "no state shall . . . deny to any person within its jurisdiction the equal protection of the laws." The court agreed, even though it found that because of his ranking he would not in fact have been admitted were there no affirmative action admissions program at U.C. Davis. The university then appealed to the California Supreme Court. It, too, supported Bakke. In its decision of September

[11]Quoted in Iver Peterson, "Carnegie Panel Bids Middle Class Pay Bigger Share of College Cost," *New York Times*, July 13, 1973. The Carnegie study is entitled *Higher Education: Who Pays? Who Benefits? Who Should Pay?* (New York: McGraw-Hill, 1973).

[12]These figures are from the National Center for Education Statistics. HEW counts rather differently and arrives at significantly lower totals.

[13]For interesting studies of many of these and other programs, see Joel Spring, *The Sorting Machine* (New York: McKay, 1976); Norman C. Thomas, *Education in National Politics* (New York: McKay, 1975); and Thomas Wolanin and Lawrence Gladieux, "The Political Culture of a Policy Arena: Higher Education," in *What Government Does*, ed. Matthew Holden and Dennis Dresang.

[14]This reminiscence is from an oral history transcript made by Keppel for the Lyndon B. Johnson Library and available there. It was reported by Lawrence Feinberg, "The Johnson Papers and the Politics of Education," *Washington Post*, February 15, 1972.

16, 1976, it suggested as alternative practices enlarging the med school, doing more minority recruiting, and not considering GPAs and MCAT scores. The state court also pointed out that recent United States Supreme Court rulings required that a particular institution have a history of discrimination before such drastic measures as quotas could be justified. U.C. Davis had only been open since 1968, and so it had no such history. The university decided to appeal to the Supreme Court. In late 1976, the Court agreed to hear 2 hours of oral argument on the case during its next term. That argument, in the case of *Regents of the University of California v. Allan Bakke,* was scheduled for October 12, 1977.

Some of the briefs filed in the Bakke case, with the Supreme Court building in the background.
Wide World Photos

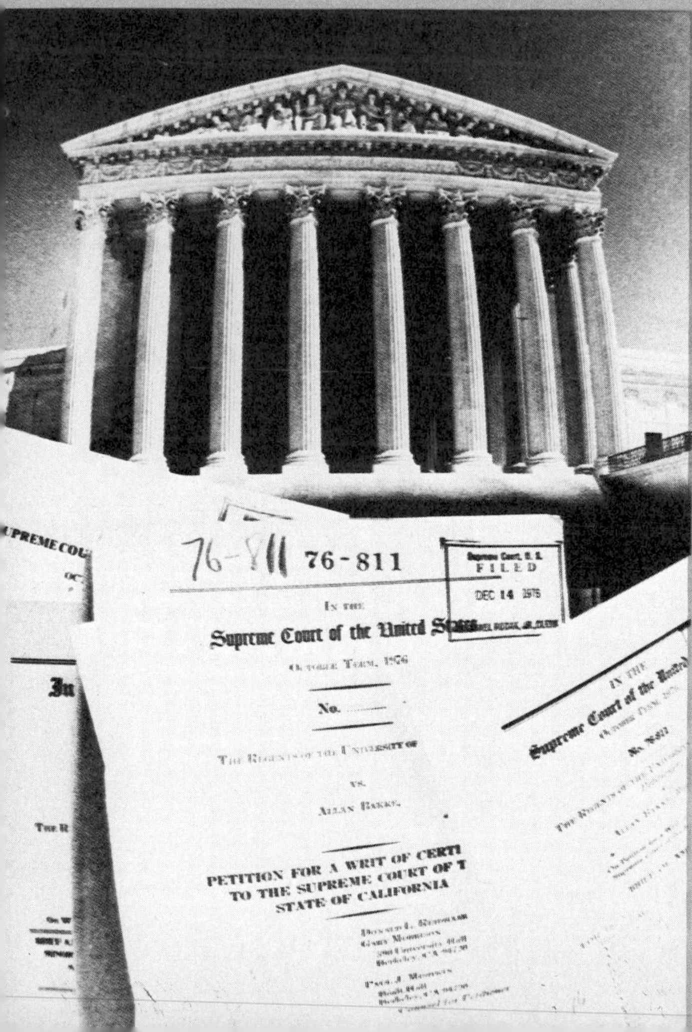

■ Interest groups intervene

Knowing the case would be coming up for argument, various other organizations with interests in the general principles involved decided to file *amicus curiae* ("friend of the court") **briefs** on it. Such briefs are really arguments to the Court recommending a particular decision or way of reasoning about it. As the months passed, more and more organizations filed such briefs. By hearing time, the number was close to sixty – an all time record for a single case, according to Court observers.

The lineup was interesting. Among the briefs supporting the university were those from other colleges and universities, minority students, some unions, and civil rights groups. Supporting Bakke were the American Federation of Teachers, the Chamber of Commerce, Jewish groups, and some other ethnic groups. The ethnic groups believed their members often were victims of such quotas.

■ The U.S. government intervenes

But the *amicus curiae* brief everyone was waiting for was that from the U.S. government. For months, the Justice Department worked on a draft. In charge were Solicitor General (chief lawyer) Wade H. McCree, Jr., and Assistant Attorney General Drew S. Days, 3d, both black lawyers. After months of debate and drafting, they came up with a statement that endorsed affirmative action but questioned the Davis plan because it involved quotas. The draft urged the court to support Bakke.

The brief was circulated for comments to government officials concerned with affirmative action and to White House staffers attentive to political impact. It was also leaked to the press. The result was an almost unanimous outcry. Among the opponents were HEW Secretary Joseph Califano, Equal Employment Opportunity Commission chairperson Eleanor Holmes Norton, HUD Secretary Patricia Roberts Harris, UN Ambassador Andrew Young, and the Congressional Black Caucus.

The Caucus wrote Carter saying that "this position is not only contrary to the relevant civil rights law, but will also have the effect of irretrievably undermining the affirmative action programs of public and private entities. . . . A government brief opposing affirmative action programs would be a statement to the black community indicating the government's reversal of its commitment to civil rights in this country."

As a result of this concerted opposition, Carter and the Justice Department decided to redraft the brief. In its final form it strongly supported affirmative action and avoided the question of quotas, recommending that the Court return the case to the California court for further consideration, rejecting Bakke's claim to be admitted.

In the summer of 1978 the Court announced its decision, one that Alan Dershowitz of Harvard Law School termed "an act of judicial statesmanship."

■ The Supreme Court decides the case

On June 28, 1978, the Supreme Court handed down its long-awaited decision. It was a two-sided one that tried to placate both sides on the Bakke issue. First, the Court affirmed the constitutionality of college admissions programs that give special consideration to members of minority groups in an effort to remedy past discrimination. Second, it ruled that Bakke must be admitted to the U.C. Davis Medical School because its admissions policy used race as the sole criterion for the sixteen positions it held open for minority applicants. The Court's position was that race could be one of many criteria for admission, but not the only one. In doing so it upheld the constitutionality of affirmative action programs.

□ EDUCATIONAL RIGHTS AND POLITICAL STRUGGLES

The Bakke case brought the criteria of merit and affirmative action head-to-head, as previous struggles and previous governmental actions had confronted the principle of ability to pay with the principle of democracy. Questions such as these, at the heart of our politics, are also, inevitably and continually, at the heart of our educational system. In education, as in politics, there are no final answers to the basic questions of "for whom?" and "for what?" Even the question "by whom?" gets only temporary answers.

■ The role of the government

At this point, many parents call for community control of education, objecting to the growing federal involvement in education. But as one observer has written:

> **There is no conspiracy; indeed almost no one believes in federal control abstractly. Federal control is created instead by the actions of scores of agencies and hundreds of bureaucrats each tailoring alternatives to fit their idiosyncratic view of education. The bureaucracy is so decentralized and its regulations often of such low visibility that it is hard to imagine federal or congressional action consistently restraining it. Without some constitutional standard, the federal tailors will continue to design the future of American education."[15]**

The efforts of the "federal tailors" these years are often efforts to grant or extend rights and liberties to people who have not yet had the benefit of them, as we shall see in coming chapters in this part. Always, they are bureaucratic, and sometimes they defeat the very objectives they seek, as we shall see not only in the coming chapters on rights but also in the following section on policies.

■ The attitudes of the people

The attitudes of the public as revealed by a Gallup Poll at the time of the Bakke case reflect a striking agreement that ability (merit) rather than affirmative action should determine college admissions and

---

[15]George LaNoue, "Is the Federal Government Controlling Education?" *Education & Urban Society* 9, no. 2 (February 1977): p. 213.

TABLE P5.1

Attitudes toward ability vs. affirmative action as criteria for college and jobs

Question: Some people say that to make up for past discrimination, women and members of minority groups should be given preferential treatment in getting jobs and places in college. Others say that ability, as determined by test scores, should be the main consideration. Which point comes closest to how you feel on this matter?

	Give preferential treatment	Ability main consid-eration	No opinion
The "National Sample" representing the entire American population	10%	83%	7%
Sex			
Male	10	84	6
Female	11	82	7
Race			
White	8	86	6
Nonwhite	27	64	9
Education completed			
College	10	84	6
High school only	8	87	5
Grade school only	18	70	12

Source: Gallup Opinion Index, June 1977, p. 23.

job opportunities. As Table P5.1 reveals, 83 percent of the national sample favored ability and only 10 percent called for preferential treatment of women and minorities. Even more striking, only 11 percent of women and only 27 percent of nonwhites – the groups that would benefit directly – favored preferential treatment. "Rarely is public opinion, particularly on such a controversial issue, as united as it is over this question," said Gallup's summary of the results. "Not a single population group supports affirmative action. Attitudes are fairly uniform from region to region and among all age groups."[16]

Fifty-three percent of all the public did indicate support for preferential treatment limited to a government program offering free educational or vocational courses to help minority groups do better on such exams, in a poll taken several months later.[17] But, over all, the poll results lend support to the accuracy of a conclusion of a study of black attitudes published about the same time. "Most black Americans believe there is a changing mood in this nation, compared to the late '50s and early '60s," wrote Faustine Jones, "and that this mood has shifted from institutional intervention on behalf of black progress. Black Americans feel that a significant proportion of the white population has shifted priorities from eliminating the vestiges of racial discrimination as the major goal in this society to reviving a feeling that blacks have had as much help as they need and deserve."[18]

When public opinion shifts away from support of claims to rights, the burden falls more strongly on both the government and the claimants. We'll see the growth of those claims and the varied nature of government's responses in Chapters 13, 14, and 15. As we do, we might remember the words with which Meyer Weinberg concluded his recent study of race and education in America:

> Race was admitted into the select circle of scientific problems only when the impingement of minority peoples in practical affairs stirred new political discontents. Only a century after the Civil War were racial and ethnic concerns finally permitted to assume the status of 'problems.' The political element was still dominant, but it was a new politics. For the first time in American history, through a more democratic politics than ever before, American education was forced to contemplate the requirements of a system to educate all the children of all the people. . . . In the perspective of several centuries, the future cannot but be influenced by a novel feature: millions of minority parents and children are self-aware of their rights and increasingly skilled in contending for those rights. The schools cannot long resist such a momentous fact.[19]

[16]*Gallup Opinion Index,* June 1977, p. 22.

[17]Gallup Poll, reported in *Philadelphia Inquirer,* November 20, 1977.

[18]Quoted in Haynes Johnson, "On Progress," *Washington Post,* September 14, 1977.

[19]Meyer Weinberg, *A Chance to Learn: A History of Race and Education in the United States* (New York: Cambridge University Press, 1977), p. 363.

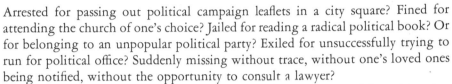

13 The politics of liberty: civil liberties, civil rights, and human rights

Arrested for passing out political campaign leaflets in a city square? Fined for attending the church of one's choice? Jailed for reading a radical political book? Or for belonging to an unpopular political party? Exiled for unsuccessfully trying to run for political office? Suddenly missing without trace, without one's loved ones being notified, without the opportunity to consult a lawyer?

The chances are you don't even know anyone to whom any of these things has happened, unless you know a Jewish refugee from Nazi Germany or an exile from a Communist country or an escapee from a dictatorship in Latin America, Africa, or Asia.

Political persecution such as this is rare in the countries of the Western World that we call "democratic." But it wasn't always that way. And there are still groups, even in our own country, that sometimes experience treatment somewhat resembling this. For example, in the years of black militance, in the late 1960s, groups such as the Black Panthers regularly reported or alleged instances of police provocation, harassment, and brutality. Over the years, to take another example, various socialist parties and organizations too have claimed such mistreatment. And for many years American citizens lost jobs and even served jail terms for belonging to the Communist party.

Infringements of such civil liberties as freedom of religion and freedom of speech were major factors in the decisions of Europeans to colonize America hundreds of years ago. They continue to be reasons for some immigrants to come to America from countries with repressive regimes today.

Yet Americans have not always enjoyed full exercise of these **civil liberties**. Even today there are continuing revelations of wiretapping and break-ins by the FBI and the CIA, especially during the Kennedy, Johnson, and Nixon administrations. These violations of the right to privacy remind us that our civil liberties are always potentially in jeopardy. Despite constitutional guarantees, such civil liberties are best preserved by being regularly exercised. For in the words of Wendell Phillips, the nineteenth-century advocate of the rights of slaves and women, which are carved in stone at the entrance to the National Archives, "Eternal vigilance is the price of liberty."

Much the same might be said of our **civil rights** – especially the right to vote. American history has been a record of the extension of this right to more and more groups: males not owning property, blacks, women, Native American Indians, and most recently 18-to-20-year-olds. In more recent years, to these civil rights – rights to participate in civil or governmental affairs – have been added "human rights."

The concept of **human rights** can be traced back to the beliefs of the Founding Fathers that "all men are endowed by their Creator with certain unalienable rights [to] life, liberty, and the pursuit of happiness." In our era, in the United States, human rights take the form primarily of economic and social rights: the rights to a job, to earn a livelihood; the right to an education; the right to medical care; the right to a sufficient retirement income. Around the world these rights are increasingly sought by citizens of various countries appealing to the Universal Declaration of Human Rights passed by the United Nations in 1948.

Support of the movement for human rights around the world recently became a major foreign policy objective of the American government under the leadership of President Carter. This occurred at the same time as the struggle for ratification of the Equal Rights Amendment for women and the growing demands for civil rights made by and on behalf of Native American Indians, Chicanos, and other ethnic minority groups. And all along there has been another intense debate over the rights of all Americans. This debate has raged between those advocating "the right of women to control their own bodies" by having abortions and those who call themselves the "right-to-life" advocates. Right-to-life activists oppose both abortions and what others call the right to "death with dignity" – the right to choose to die rather than live on when one's mind has gone or when one has a terminal illness.

Thomas Jefferson (1743-1826). Jefferson wrote to Madison in 1787: " . . . a bill of rights is what the people are entitled to against every government on earth."

White House Collection

☐ WHAT DO WE MEAN BY "LIBERTIES" AND "RIGHTS"?

People making claims to new opportunities or new forms of treatment tend to call these objectives "liberties" or "rights." Those opposing them are as likely to refer to the claims as "special privileges" or "reverse discrimination."

The terms "liberties" and "rights" tend to carry with them a claim to legitimacy in our way of thinking. When we can find the claims upheld by the language of the Declaration of Independence or the Constitution – freedom of speech or freedom of religion, for example – we may well agree at once. But when someone claims a right nowhere mentioned in the Constitution, nor even in legislation – such as "the right to abort" an unborn fetus – we need to know how to tell whether to agree that this is a right or not. To try to answer that question, we must be certain just what we mean by rights and liberties, and we must know where they come from and to whom they apply.

■ Civil liberties as freedom from the state

"Of all the loose terms in the world, liberty is the most indefinite," wrote the British philosopher and politician Edmund Burke in 1789. He was contemplating the American and French revolutions, which were grounded in appeals to liberty as a "natural right of man." The American Constitution of 1787 guaranteed the right to personal liberty in absence of demonstrated cause for imprisonment, as it assured the right to a jury trial. But Jefferson wrote to Madison the same year that ". . . a bill of rights is what the people are entitled to against every government on earth." And it was the Bill of Rights – the first ten amendments to the Constitution, adopted in 1791 – that provided the basis for the civil liberties we now perhaps take for granted.

The very notion of civil liberties makes sense only in a society governed by law. Man may have a "natural right" to freedom, but as the French philosopher Jean-Jacques Rousseau observed in a famous passage written in 1762, "Man is born free, but everywhere he is in chains." Government is established, in the view generally held by the Founding Fathers, to preserve people's rights to life, liberty, and property from the chaos, violence, and theft characteristic of a condition of anarchy – the absence of government. But government uncontrolled may become a tyranny. And a tyranny may prevent individuals from enjoying these rights every bit as much as does a state of anarchy. For this reason, government's power to interfere with individual liberty must be restricted, the Founding Fathers believed.

Government, in other words, does not provide liberty. It only provides or fosters the conditions of legal order in which liberty can be exercised by individuals doing as they wish so long as they do not interfere with the liberty of others. But if the government gets too strong, it becomes the chief threat to the achievement and exercise of liberty. So government's powers must be limited. This is why we have a Bill of Rights that sets limits to government powers and actions. It protects citizens' liberties against arbitrary governmental demands, unfair legal processes, and especially political interference with the individual exercise of the rights to speak freely, to assemble, to worship, or to publish. In the form in which they appear in the Bill of Rights, these legal guarantees that establish our civil liberties assert *negative governmental duties* or prohibitions. In doing so, they also *imply positive individual* liberties. But these civil liberties take on significance only as they are actually exercised by individuals, and then only if the government abides by the Constitutional limitations and does not interfere.

This concept of civil liberties holds that they provide and guarantee *freedom from the state.* It was adopted in an era of optimism about the individual's ability to fulfill himself or herself if only he or she is left alone. Slavery and its aftermath of discrimination made it clear that such "negative" civil liberties were not enough to guarantee equal citizen participation in political and economic life. So Americans became less optimistic about a human being's ability to be free individually and at the same time more optimistic about government's ability to help achieve or restore equality among all people. The emphasis in politics gradually shifted from civil liberties (prohibitions against state interference in public life) to civil rights (regulations permitting state interference to guarantee rights of full political participation to groups that had been excluded by law or custom or conditions of poverty).

■ Civil rights as freedom to take part in the state

Civil liberties thus grant *freedom from the state.* Civil rights by contrast grant state assistance in interfering to remove obstacles to citizenship activities such as voting. In other words, civil rights allow the individual *freedom to take part in the state.* The trend toward democratization that arose in the last century and continues to the present is thus usually referred to as a "civil rights movement." These rights are won in the struggle to get new laws that guarantee them not just to individuals, as is generally the case with civil liberties, but to members of a group previously excluded from these rights and privileges. The civil rights laws, for example, gave the federal government power to supervise elections in the South so it could guarantee to blacks the right to vote.

The expansion of liberties and rights has not stopped there, however. Instead, there has been a growing movement to grant or guarantee what are often called "positive rights." These are rights to basic human needs that are not otherwise attainable in a society with large-scale inequality. Among the positive rights increasingly sought is the right to a job, or to economic opportunity and security. Other positive rights include the right to health and medical care, the right to retire in old age with a pension, and the right to an education. In earlier eras characterized by greater individualism and self-sufficiency, and less industrialization and urbanization, these rights were generally thought to be the individual's – and his or her family's – own responsibility. Increasingly, in recent times, they have come to be seen as beyond most individuals' ability to attain without *positive governmental assistance.*[1]

The argument that these are rights or entitlements is based on what may be a return to the old concept of "the rights of man." But today, in an interdependent world linked by mass communications, these rights are more and more conceived of as "human rights." They are, in other words, rights to which all individuals, wherever they live and under whatever sort of government they live, should be entitled, simply by virtue of being human beings. We shall understand them better, even in their global context, if we first examine them more specifically in their American context, where they continue to pose policy questions for American politics.

□ WHAT ARE YOUR RIGHTS AS AN AMERICAN CITIZEN?

■ From natural rights to civil liberties The Declaration of Independence asserted that all men had "unalienable rights" – rights they could not lose, renounce, or have taken from them. Among these, it said, are "life, liberty, and the pursuit of happiness." This formulation, this assertion of natural rights, is too general to guide the government. For more specific guidance we turn to the Constitution. The Constitution includes guarantees of seven "civil liberties," as we generally call them.

---

[1]For a helpful discussion of these types of rights and their development, see Richard P. Claude, "The Classical Model of Human Rights Development," *Comparative Human Rights,* ed. Claude (Baltimore: John Hopkins University Press, 1976), chap. 1.

- □ Habeas corpus (Article I, Section 9, Clause 2). This Latin term means "you may have the body." It guarantees that someone who has been imprisoned can ask a Federal court for a **writ of habeas corpus.** If the court finds that the imprisonment violates the Constitution or the laws of the United States, it issues such a writ and the prisoner must be released.
- □ Bill of attainder (Article I, Section 9, Clause 3, and Section 10, Clause 1). A **bill of attainder** is a special law passed to declare that some person or group has committed a crime and to impose punishment. The Constitution prohibits such bills because under our system of separation of powers only a court can try a person or impose punishment.
- □ Ex post facto laws (Article I, Section 9, Clause 3, and Section 10, Clause 1). *Ex post facto* is Latin for "after the fact" or "after the deed." An **ex post facto law** declares something a crime only after it has been done. The Constitution prohibits such laws.
- □ Trial by jury (Article III, Section 2, Clause 3). The Constitution provides that all federal crimes must have trial by jury – by a group of fellow citizens, instead of just a judge – except for impeachment of an official, which involves a trial by the United States Senate. The courts have held that the provision need not hold for petty offenses ("small crimes"), nor when a defendent says he or she doesn't want a jury.
- □ Trial location (Article III, Section 2, Clause 3). Trials must be held in the state where the crime has been committed.
- □ Treason (Article III, Section 3). Treason is the only crime defined by the Constitution. "Treason against the United States," it says, "shall consist only in levying war against them [the United States], or in adhering to their enemies, giving them aid and comfort." But the Constitution thereby protects people who express unpopular views from being prosecuted as traitors, and goes on to require "the testimony of two witnesses to the same overt Act" or "confession in open court" for conviction of treason.
- □ Religious tests (Article 6, Clause 3). The prohibition of "religious tests" or vows about one's religious beliefs for those who want to serve their country protects citizens from religious discrimination in federal jobs.

These seven civil liberties offer important protection to citizens. But, as we saw in Chapter 1, when the Constitution was being debated, many feared that they were not sufficient. As a result, a "bill of rights" was drawn up and submitted to the states for ratification. The ten articles, which were then quickly ratified, became the first ten amendments to the Constitution.

■ The Bill of Rights

The First Amendment provides for freedom of religion, freedom of speech, freedom of the press, and freedom to assemble peaceably and protest to the government. This amendment over two centuries has been the cornerstone of the liberty of ordinary Americans in everyday life.

The Second and Third Amendments protect the right "to keep and bear arms" and prohibit forced quartering of soldiers in private homes. These arose out of special colonial era concerns and have had little practical significance in American constitutional history since that time. But the right "to keep and bear arms" is still cited by opponents of gun control in support of their position.

The next five amendments provide special protection for those involved in the justice system and have been subject to considerable interpretation by the courts over the years. Among their major provisions are these:

- The government may not search a person or his or her home, or seize his or her personal possessions, unless it has good reason to believe a crime has been committed and it obtains a "search warrant" – Fourth Amendment.
- A person cannot be tried a second time for the same crime if he or she has once been acquitted ("double jeopardy") – Fifth Amendment.
- The government cannot compel someone to testify against himself or herself ("self-incrimination") – Fifth Amendment.
- "Nor shall any person . . . be deprived of life, liberty, or property, without due process of law" – Fifth Amendment. This clause protects us against arbitrary or unfair procedures in judicial or administrative proceedings and against laws that could affect our personal or property rights.
- An owner must be justly compensated by the government if his or her private property is taken for public use – Fifth Amendment.
- Someone being criminally prosecuted is entitled to a fair trial – one that is speedy, public, and with a jury; one in which he or she is informed of the charges against him or her; is allowed to cross-examine any witnesses against him or her; has the power to force favorable witnesses to testify for him or her; and has the right to be represented by a lawyer – Sixth Amendment.
- The government may not require excessive bail (money the accused puts up to obtain his or her release while awaiting trial) or impose excessive fines or "cruel and unusual punishment" – Eighth Amendment.

The Ninth Amendment provides that the fact that certain rights are specifically listed in the Constitution does not mean that other rights are not also "retained by the people." And the Tenth asserts that "the powers not delegated to the United States by the Constitution, nor prohibited by it to the States, are reserved to the States respectively, or to the people."

Japanese Americans at an internment camp during World War II.
Wide World Photos

□ ACTION UNIT 13.1 How to get—and how to lose—American citizenship

The chances are you're an American citizen. If you were born in the United States, regardless of who your parents were, or of whether they were American citizens, you are an American citizen. (There are a few unlikely exceptions: If you were born of a foreign king, queen, or diplomat, or on a foreign public ship while it was in American waters, or of an enemy occupying the United States, you would not be an American citizen.) Indeed, if you were born on an airplane while it was flying over the United States, you're a citizen. You're also a citizen if you were born abroad of an American parent.

You don't have to remain an American citizen. You may renounce your citizenship, simply by declaring that you no longer wish to be a citizen. The official term for this is "voluntary expatriation" (from *ex,* "out of," and *patria,* the "fatherland" or "country"—you put yourself "out of the country").

If you were born in the United States or had an American parent, you are called a "natural-born citizen." If you weren't born in the United States and didn't have an American parent, you are called an "alien" (a term derived from the Latin word for "other"). As an alien, you may still be able to become a "naturalized" citizen. Sometimes Congress "blankets in" a whole group—it did so for Native American Indians in 1924, for example. More often, an individual applies for citizenship.

To become a naturalized citizen, you must meet certain qualifications. You must show that you entered the country legally. You must have "good moral character." You must be able to read, write, speak, and understand English. You must pass a test showing that you know the history, principles, and form of American government, and you must pledge allegiance. You must renounce any titles of nobility, such as lord or prince, which you may hold in your previous country of citizenship. You will not be granted citizenship if you are a polygamist, a draft evader, or a deserter from the armed forces, an anarchist, or a member of a Communist party.

To become a citizen, you normally must file a petition with the government. To be allowed to do so, you must be 18 or older and must have lived in the United States for 5 straight years. The Immigration and Naturalization Service then investigates you and holds a preliminary hearing on your application. If you get that far—and most applicants do—a federal or state court judge holds a final hearing (which is usually perfunctory) and then administers an oath and issues a certificate of naturalization.

A naturalized citizen has all the rights of a natural-born citizen except that he or she is not eligible to be president or vice-president. In addition, naturalized citizenship can be cancelled or revoked if it is found that someone lied when applying for it.

Until the 1960s, the federal government could revoke your citizenship if you deserted from the armed forces in wartime or voted in an election of another country. In a landmark case, *Afroyim v. Rusk* (1967), the Supreme Court finally forbade revocation of citizenship altogether, on grounds that such action violated the Fourteenth Amendment.

■ The "nationalization" of the Bill of Rights

Later amendments have further extended and strengthened our rights as American citizens. The Thirteenth outlawed slavery. The Fourteenth extended citizenship rights automatically to "all persons born or naturalized in the United States," but its most important effect is to extend to the states the limitations imposed on the federal government by the Bill of Rights: "No State shall make or enforce any law which shall abridge the privileges or immunities of citizens of the United States; nor shall any state deprive any person of life, liberty, or property, without due process of law; nor deny to any person within its jurisdiction the equal protection of the laws."

Ratified in 1868, the Fourteenth Amendment has been more and more actively and extensively interpreted by the Supreme Court since 1925. This process is sometimes referred to as "the nationalization of the Bill of Rights." As Kenneth Karst has written, "The Fourteenth Amendment began as an act of positive law. Its framers surely thought that their most important task was to extend to the South a system of liberties and equality under the law that already existed elsewhere in the Nation. Today, the Fourteenth Amendment embodies much of what has become our natural-law constitution. After a century, the amendment stands as a symbol of national unity and a practical guarantee of nationally established rights."[2] Major aspects of the process of "nationalization" have included the outlawing of private acts of discrimination when these are enforced by a state, and the outlawing of unequal apportionment of state legislatures as contrary to the "equal protection" clause.

The Fifteenth, Nineteenth, Twenty-fourth, and Twenty-sixth Amendments extended the right to vote, as we saw in earlier chapters. The Twenty seventh or "Equal Rights Amendment," which was submitted to the states for ratification in 1972, was designed to abolish unfair and unreasonable discrimination against women by the laws of the federal and state governments. These extensions of rights to particular groups of citizens such as blacks or women are generally termed "civil rights" or "special rights" to distinguish them from the "general rights" or "civil liberties" we have been discussing.

■ What determines which rights we have?

Lists of our rights such as the one we have been developing here may seem to imply that rights are made by constitutions and amendments. But, in the words of one expert, Jay Sigler, "No one can say with finality just which rights Americans do possess. The Constitution and several important amendments to that document provide the best guide, but ambiguity shrouds the significance of almost every important phrase. Courts, legislators, presidents and governors must define our rights for us, and even though they often refer to constitutional language, the terms almost always require interpretation."[3]

Scholars have found that the most important precondition for the development of rights and liberties is the existence of a secure legal system that has basically solved the problem of social organization. Without this *stable social order and legal code,* people are too much concerned with strengthening the political regime's authority to concern themselves with the freedoms of the individual.

Once such political order exists, the key factor seems to be *communication.* The government must communicate its expectations to the people to influence their behavior. The people may also communicate their needs and desires to the government – especially if the political order is democratic or responsive. This is the

---

[2]Kenneth L. Karst, "Not One Law at Rome and Another at Athens: The Fourteenth Amendment in Nationwide Application," *Washington University Law Quarterly* 1972, no. 3 (Summer 1972): 383.

[3]Jay A. Sigler, *American Rights Policies* (Homewood, Ill.: Dorsey, 1975), p. 1.

[4]See the chapters in Claude, *Comparative Human Rights.*

origin of a right "to petition the government," and also of the right to free speech when citizens communicate with each other.[4]

Because these conditions have generally existed in America, both the courts and the legislatures have continued to interpret and expand the dominant conceptions of rights and liberties. In the era of the so-called Warren Court in the 1960s, both civil rights (for blacks) and civil liberties (especially for accused criminals) were expanded. In subsequent years, the Burger Court has seemed to react against these expansions, emphasizing "society's rights" instead of "criminals' rights." This apparent shift, which we discussed in Chapter 9, reflects the constant tension between order and liberty that is present at the founding of any new state and that reemerges frequently thereafter. On balance, though, the history of America has been one of expanding liberties.

■ The right to know

In the past few years, one important area of dispute and change has been the realm of individual privacy on the one hand and an alleged "right to know" on the other. Over the years, as we have noted in previous chapters, the government has refused to disclose information in its files on grounds of "executive privilege." Citizens and businesses objected often that the government was unnecessarily secretive. Finally, in 1966 Congress passed the Freedom of Information Act. Its purpose was to make "information maintained by the executive branch more available to the public." It provides that "access and disclosure" be the policy, rather than secrecy, unless disclosure would constitute "a clearly unwarranted invasion of personal privacy." The act also requires that the government tell citizens how to get access to information it holds, and gives citizens the right to appeal to the courts if agencies refuse to open their records.

The government collects data on us and on the country for two basic purposes. One is to conduct its specific responsibilities: The Internal Revenue Service, for example, collects information on you and everyone else as a part of its task of collecting taxes. The second is to have general-purpose statistics for use by the government and the public in analyzing social and economic factors affecting the nation. General-purpose information is gathered by four agencies: the Census Bureau, the Bureau of Labor Statistics, the Statistical Reporting Service of the Agriculture Department, and the National Center for Health Statistics in the Department of HEW.

As a result of all this data collection, the government knows a lot about you – and about virtually everyone else, including most businessess and organizations in the country, as Action Unit 13.2 reports. At this point, much of this information is decentralized – some held in one agency's files, other in other agencies' files. But because this is inefficient, there are strong pressures to pool it all in a giant "data bank" where it would all be computerized for instant access. If that happens, any government agency might be able to learn everything about you at the push of a few buttons.[5]

---

[5]For a discussion of these issues, see Stanton Wheeler, ed., *On Record: Files and Dossiers in American Life* (New Brunswick, N.J.: Transaction, 1976), especially chaps. 1, 14.

☐ ACTION UNIT 13.2 What the government knows about you—and how to get access to it

"The government has a dossier someplace . . . on just about everyone," said former Supreme Court Justice William O. Douglas in 1966. At that time, most of the files were for income tax returns, social security payments, veterans' military service or draft classification status, passport applications, and civil service job applications. Since then, the number of government agencies keeping files on Americans has increased greatly, and many files have been computerized for instant access and for transmission anywhere in the country.

If you have a gun collection, the Bureau of Alcohol, Tobacco, and Firearms has a file on you. If you have a registered boat, the Coast Guard knows you. For a pilot's or plane license, it's the Federal Aviation Agency. If you're a ham radio operator or a CB owner, you're on file with the FCC. If you've had any encounters with the law, the Justice department knows about it. If you've ever had a student loan, the Department of Health, Education, and Welfare knows a lot about you and your parents. If you've ever lost your driver's license, or failed to get one, the Department of Transportation knows why, and reports it regularly to state and local authorities. Nine of every ten jobholders is on file with the Social Security Administration, and that probably includes you. Over 15 million veterans and their dependents are listed in Veterans Administration files.

You can hope you're not on the secret Service's list of "about 150,000 persons" who are cranks, criminals, forgers, counterfeiters, or potential presidential assassins. And you can hope you haven't made the Passport Office's "Lookout File" of 250,000 persons who are defectors or expatriates wanted on criminal charges, are involved in child custody or desertion cases, or are in debt to the government, or are subversives, or are AWOL military personnel. You can also hope you've avoided the Customs Bureau's list of "suspects," which is updated around the clock to all ports of entry into the United States.

You can *hope* you're not in these, or any of the other 800 or so federal data-collection systems, including those kept by the FBI and the CIA. Or at least you can hope that, if you are included, at least the files are *accurate.* But the only way to be sure is to file a request under the Privacy Act of 1974. This law gives you as a citizen the right to get copies of personal records collected by federal agencies and to correct any inaccuracies in those records.

If you want to find out what personal records the federal government maintains on you, here's what you need to do:

1. Select the agency whose files you wish to examine, such as the FBI (for criminal activity or political activity—9th and Pennsylvania Ave. N.W., Washington, D.C. 20535); the Veterans Administration (Vermont Ave. N.W., Washington, D.C. 20420); the State Department (for activities abroad—Department of State, Washington, D.C. 20520); the Department of Health, Education, and Welfare (for student loans—200 Independence Ave. S.W., Washington, D.C. 20201); or the CIA (for who-knows-what—Central Intelligence Agency, Washington, D.C. 20505). You'll find other agencies and their addresses in the *United States Government Manual* in your library.

■ The right to privacy

One question this raises is, who will protect our privacy? Do we actually have "a right to be let alone" or a "right to privacy"? Until recently, the courts have not thought so. In 1927, in *Olmstead v. U.S.,* the Supreme Court upheld the tapping of telephones as a legal source of information on bootleggers during Prohibition. But in a dissent in that case, Justice Louis Brandeis argued that the Founding

2. Write a letter to the "Privacy Act Officer" of that agency in Washington (or elsewhere, if it is a local office you wish to ask). Your letter should read something like this:

Dear Privacy Act Officer:

In accordance with the Privacy Act of 1974, 5 U.S. Code 522a, I hereby request a copy of [describe as accurately and specifically as possible the records you want, and provide all the relevant information you have concerning them].

If there are any fees for copying the records I am requesting, please inform me before you fill the request. [Or: – please supply the records without informing me if the fees do not exceed $_____.]

If all or any part of this request is denied, please cite the specific exemptions(s) that you think justifies your refusal to release the information. Also, please inform me of your agency's appeal procedure.

In order to expedite consideration of my request, I am enclosing a copy of [some document of identification].

Thank you for your prompt attention to this matter.

Sincerely,
[Your name, address, city, state, zip, and social security number]

3. Include proof of your identity, such as a copy of an official document containing your name, address, and signature, or a copy of your signature notarized by a notary public, and your social security number.

4. Be prepared to pay a fee of about 10 cents per page of the file; the agencies can charge this copying fee, but cannot charge for their time in searching.

5. Expect a response within 10 working days of receipt of the request, and the files within 30 working days, as the law provides. If you do not receive an answer, write again inquiring why.

6. If your request is denied, you may appeal the denial to the head of the agency, or even to the courts, where, if you win, the government must pay your reasonable attorney's fees.

7. If you find erroneous information in a file, you may write requesting that your records be amended.

For further guidance on special exceptions to the law, on appeal procedures, and on going to court, as well as information on using the Freedom of Information Act as amended in 1974 to get other types of government documents, write your member of Congress for a free copy of the Government Operations Committee's report, *A Citizen's Guide on How to Use the Freedom of Information Act and the Privacy Act in Requesting Government Documents.* You can also get help from the American Civil Liberties Union, 22 East 40th St., New York, N.Y. 10016, or from any of its regional offices. And if you wish further information on the FOIA, write for a free booklet to the Center for National Security Studies, 122 Maryland Ave. N.W., Washington, D.C. 20002. Finally, for the most comprehensive guide see James T. O'Reilly, *Federal Information Disclosure* (New York: Shepard's Inc./McGraw-Hill, 1977), available in law libraries.

Fathers had granted citizens "the right to be left alone – the most comprehensive of rights and the right most valued by civilized men."

But it was not until 1965, in *Griswold v. Connecticut,* that the Court found privacy a right peripherally protected by the First Amendment. This decision overthrew a Connecticut law prohibiting the sale or distribution of contraceptives, and so has become known as "the birth-control case." In his majority opinion,

Justice William O. Douglas found the right to privacy a constitutional right formulated by the specific guarantees of the First, Third, Fourth, Fifth, and Ninth Amendments, which, the Court said, "have penumbras, formed by emanations from those guarantees that help give them life and substance." The Court concluded that "various guarantees create zones for privacy." The citing of the Ninth Amendment was especially significant, for it suggested, in the words of a concurring opinion, that the framers intended it "as a declaration, should the need for it arise, that the people had other rights than those enumerated in the first eight amendments."

Soon thereafter, the Burger Court extended the doctrine of the right to privacy even further, using it as the basis for overturning a Texas law prohibiting abortion. In this case, *Roe v. Wade* (1973), which we examined in Perspective 1, the Court declared privacy a "fundamental right" – but one subject to limitation when it conflicted with a "compelling state interest."

But specifying the extent of the right to privacy has been left to the Congress. The Privacy Act of 1974 was the first law to regulate the use of personal information records by the federal government. It gives citizens the right to see and copy most records about them stored by federal agencies. It also gives citizens the right to challenge and correct any inaccurate information in federal files, in the way described in Action Unit 13.2.

That act also established a permanent Privacy Protection Study Commission. It has found a wide range of abuses: Medical records are gotten by employers and insurance investigators, to be used against people. Tax returns have been used by various government agencies with such ease that the IRS is termed "a national lending library." Private investigators dredge up malicious gossip and put it in company files without checking it.[6]

[6]For an account of the development of privacy rights in the United States, see E. Jeremy Hutton et al., "The Right of Privacy in the U.S., Great Britain, and India," *Comparative Human Rights,* ed. Claude, chap. 5.

A gun-type electronic eavesdropping device. The right to privacy is but the latest in a long line of civil liberties that American citizens have sought for themselves.

Wide World Photos

David Linowes, a professor and head of the commission, points out that credit-reporting companies, which tell stores about you every time you ask for credit, have detailed files on many millions of Americans, and some of these companies are being bought by foreign investors. This raises in his mind the possibility of foreign political forces eventually controlling such secret information about American citizens. "We have a credit-card society," he points out, raising another invasion of privacy. "Everything you buy, every magazine you subscribe to, every book you purchase, every place you travel, organizations you belong to, the charities you contribute to, all are in that data bank. They can profile a pretty exact picture of you. . . . One mailing-list compiler has a catalogue that's about an inch and a half thick that just lists the names of lists you can rent from them. They include such titles as 'Inquisitive Kids,' 'Republican Fat Cats,' 'Affluent Catholic Professionals.' "[7]

The right to privacy is but the latest in a long line of civil liberties that American citizens have sought for themselves and that the American political system has, gradually, moved to protect or guarantee. Like all civil liberties, its nature and extent are far from clear—as its value to society is often far from clear to citizens at large and officials.

Public opinion has been uneven and governmental leadership has been sporadic on the extension of such civil liberties. But when the government has recognized free speech or privacy as a right, it has generally extended the right, as it defined it, to all citizens. This is why such civil liberties are often referred to as "general rights." The situation is very different, however, in the cases of other rights that we may think at least as important, such as the right to vote. The uneven extension of such civil rights makes them better understood as "special rights," or rights belonging to or granted to particular groups.

☐ WHAT ARE YOUR RIGHTS AS A MEMBER OF A GROUP?

■ From civil liberties to civil rights The United States, as we have seen, was created to be a republic but not necessarily a democracy. The government was supposed to be responsive to the needs of the citizens but not necessarily directly responsible to them. The political history of America since those early years has been the history of the extension of the opportunity to participate in politics to more and different groups of people. These rights to participate in politics are the heart of what we usually refer to as "civil rights." They are "special" rather than "general" rights because historically they have been extended to some groups—and at the same time, by implication, denied to other groups.

There are five major components or stages to civil rights as they have developed in America.

[7]Interview with David F. Linowes, *U.S. News & World Report,* May 2, 1977, p. 36.

The most fundamental is the act of *voting* itself. We traced the extension of the right to vote in Chapter 3.

The second is the protection of the right to vote through development of the *secret ballot* and of laws against vote buying, electoral tampering, and fraud in general.

Third comes the effort to *equalize* the weight of *each person's vote* in terms of its impact on an election, by abolishing malapportionment and geographical discrimination.

Next comes efforts to establish and protect all groups' rights or opportunities to *nominate* candidates. This can be done by lowering economic barriers such as fees that must be paid by candidates when they file for office. It can also be aided by rules opening party conventions to various minorities, such as those recently adopted by the Democratic party.

The fifth and present stage in democratization is *increasing the public's control over public policy* between elections. This is generally attempted through regulations on lobbying and political contributions, designed to equalize public influence.[8]

Still another stage, to which we have not yet progressed, is *expanding government service* to include the whole population. Should we eventually decide to attempt this, the logical way would be by drawing lots for political offices, each of which would have a short term, so that roles rotated among any and all members of society rather in the way that jury service now does.

We still think first of blacks when the topic of civil rights is raised. Government action toward equal rights for blacks has moved through three major phases. The first, which lasted from the Civil War through the end of World War II, can be called the laissez-faire approach of *inaction.* The second, or *conciliation,* period emphasized creating situations where the races were brought together informally, by laws against discrimination and mechanisms for receiving complaints for violation of those laws, but without government enforcement or litigation power.[9]

The third and present phase can be termed that of *affirmative action.* It involves, as we saw in Perspective 5, both empowering this existing machinery to take action to compel compliance, and requiring past offenders to demonstrate that they are in fact remedying failures before the government does any further business with them. Recent civil rights laws are summarized in Table 13.1.

□ The "popularization" of the Bill of Rights

The three phases that characterized efforts to overcome racial discrimination, can now be seen, in a briefer period, in efforts to combat sex discrimination. We may also soon see them in the struggle against discrimination based on age – the very young and the elderly – or on handicap or even on status as previous mental patients. In the next two chapters

[8]For a discussion of these five stages, see Stein Rokkan, *Citizens, Elections, Parties* (New York: McKay, 1970), pp. 147–68.

[9]Ved P. Nanda, "Racial Discrimination and the Law," in *Comparative Human Rights,* ed. Claude, chap. 8.

TABLE 13.1
Major provisions of recent civil rights laws

Civil Rights Act of 1957	Made attempting to prevent someone from voting a federal crime; established the Civil Rights Commission
Civil Rights Act of 1960	Strengthened prohibitions against obstructing voting; empowered the federal government to appoint special registrars to black voters in southern states
Civil Rights Act of 1964	Forbade discrimination in employment on grounds of race, color, religion, sex, or national origin (later extended to include age and handicapped status) and created the Equal Employment Opportunity Commission to enforce these prohibitions; barred discrimination in public accommodations such as motels, service stations, restaurants, theaters, buses, and trains; empowered the federal government to sue to integrate public schools and authorized the withholding of federal aid from segregated schools; made a sixth-grade education in the English language a presumption of literacy
Voting Rights Act of 1965	Strengthened the powers of federal voting registrars or examiners in the South; permitted the outlawing of discriminatory literacy tests
Civil Rights Act of 1968	Outlawed racial and religious discrimination in selling and renting housing; prohibited interfering with the legal activities of civil rights activists
Voting Rights Act Amendments of 1970	Extended the provisions of the 1965 act for another 5 years and expanded them to cover areas of the North as well as the South
Voting Rights Act Amendments of 1975	Extended the provisions of the 1965 act until 1982 and broadened the provisions to cover language minorities such as the Spanish speaking and Native Americans

we shall examine these various groups to discover their conditions and the governmental policies designed to improve their conditions. In each case, their civil rights, or opportunity to participate in politics specifically and in social life more generally, are at issue.

We saw the "nationalization" of the Bill of Rights in the movement to increase civil liberties so that they covered state actions as well as federal actions. In a similar sense we see the "popularization" of the Bill of Rights in the movements to extend participation, or civil rights, to the various segments of the population whatever their social and economic status. Now, as we move to a consideration of human rights, we shall see what might be called the "internationalization" of the Bill of Rights.

□ WHAT ARE YOUR RIGHTS AS A HUMAN BEING?

■ Human rights in the American political system

In earlier eras citizens were expected to be self-sufficient, depending on themselves or their families for their own welfare. As industrialization spread and mobility increased, families separated and people in need had to depend on private charity in time of unemployment, sickness, and old age. As labor unions grew in strength and political parties appealed to broader segments of the population for support, government became the focus of more and broader demands for aid. The result was the emergence of new ideas about rights—*positive rights* to health, education, welfare, jobs, pensions, and so on. Leadership in this belief that the government should provide such rights came from the socialist and communist countries of the world. Capitalist countries like the United States followed with reluctance. They hesitated to abandon the belief in self-reliance and the economic incentive to hard work which that belief supposedly fostered.

■ Human rights in the international political system

In 1947, shortly after it was created, the United Nations established a Commission on Human Rights. Its head was Eleanor Roosevelt, the widow of the late American President Franklin D. Roosevelt. That body of international representatives drafted a Universal Declaration of Human Rights. This was the first effort to set common standards of achievement in human rights for all peoples of all nations. It was passed unanimously by the United Nations on December 10, 1948.

In later years, the United Nations also drafted an International Convention on the Elimination of All Forms of Racial Discrimination (1965), an International Covenant on Economic, Social, and Cultural Rights (1966), and an International Covenant on Civil and Political Rights (1966). These last three documents are efforts to specify and implement the general rights outlined in the Declaration. The United States still had not ratified these three documents, nor signed the latter two, when President Jimmy Carter took office. One of his first pledges made in a speech at the United Nations was to endorse the latter two and seek congressional ratification of all three. On October 5, 1977, he signed the latter two in a ceremony at the United Nations, but he delayed submitting them to Congress for fear they would not be ratified.

Immediately upon taking office, Carter made human rights an issue in world affairs and an objective of American foreign policy. He spoke out in defense of political prisoners in other countries, appointed an Assistant Secretary of State for Human Rights and Humanitarian Affairs, and pledged to use American influence—and American foreign aid—to attempt to strengthen human rights around the world.

It is difficult to find people who say they support torture and imprisoning of political critics. But it is easy to find people who oppose emphasis on human rights in American foreign policy. Some critics say that we must support dictators because they are the strongest opponents of communism. Others on the opposite side say we should seek Détente with the USSR and so should not upset the Russians by criticizing their handling of Jews and dissidents. Still others say we should improve the human rights of our own citizens before trying to improve those of foreigners. Yet others claim we should mind our own business instead of meddling in the internal affairs of other countries whatever their politics. And some human rights

Wide World Photos

Demonstrators alleging violations of civil liberties in Iran protest the Shah of Iran's visit to Washington, D.C., in November 1977.

activists fear that *governmental* pressure for global human rights will "politicize" what they try to keep a "humanitarian" rather than a political issue, and so will set back progress in the long run.

All these views are well represented among experts on American foreign policy, and this has made the Carter emphasis on human rights very controversial. Much of the conflict seems traceable to varying concepts of human rights. As Denis Goulet, an expert on political and economic development, has written, "Different approaches to human rights are observable across ideological borders. Socialist regimes, the older as well as the more experimental recent ones, emphasize economic and social rights, at least of oppressed masses, while often downplaying political and civil rights. Conversely, liberal democracies tend to err in the opposite direction, placing great weight on politico-civil rights while relegating economic rights to a secondary position."[10]

The dispute over which rights people do have and should have – over which rights are indeed "human rights" – continues to this day inside the United States as it does within the world community. Because mass communications are now worldwide, the different conceptions of human rights penetrate the borders of the Soviet Union, of Uganda, of Chile – and of the United States.

■ The "internationalization" of the Bill of Rights

The result is, in a sense, the "internationalization" of the Bill of Rights in a double sense. Other countries come to take more seriously the political liberties that were the original emphasis in our Bill of Rights, as well as the civil rights that have been the more recent focus of Supreme Court interpretations of the Bill of Rights. In this way, the Bill of Rights is in a

[10]Denis Goulet, "Thinking About Human Rights," *Christianity and Crisis,* May 16, 1977, p. 100.

sense "internationalized" to other countries. At the same time other countries' emphases on social and economic rights become more contagious or influential in the United States, leading to a greater acceptance of such needs as health, housing, and welfare as legitimate human rights of the American people. Our courts have not yet found a basis for these human rights in the Bill of Rights. But some observers believe it will only be a matter of time before they do, and if that occurs it will be at least in part an instance of attitudes from abroad influencing or "internationalizing" our own concepts underlying our Bill of Rights.

☐ RIGHTS, DUTIES, AND OPPORTUNITIES

The American government, we sometimes say, expects its citizens to obey the law. We mean by this that our leaders expect us to follow. Indeed, they believe we have a *duty* to obey the law as it is passed by Congress, implemented by the executive, and interpreted and assessed by the courts.

Philosophers for thousands of years have debated the nature and extent of *political obligation* – the duties of citizens. They still do not agree.[11] There is a major dispute over whether citizens are obliged to obey an unjust law, which turns into the problem of "civil disobedience." Some argue that if we have rights, the government cannot or should not order us to do something that violates these rights. And if it does, we should refuse, they say. Others say that rights only make sense, only have value, if the state exists and functions well. This means, they say, that we must obey the state and support the laws even if it means sacrificing some of our rights. This is an argument often made to defend the claim that citizens should risk their lives to defend the state. Without the state, it goes, there would be no actual or effective rights.

If philosophers have been unable to resolve these disputes in thousands of years of debating, we certainly won't be able to solve them in several paragraphs. What we can do is note that in practice our courts do tend to uphold obedience to the law as our duty as citizens. "Rights imply duties," as the saying goes. The courts also tend to set limits on our exercise of our rights. One way the limits are expressed is the saying that "your right to swing your fist stops in front of another person's nose." Another famous statement of limits was Justice Oliver Wendell Holmes's assertion that the right of free speech does not extend to falsely yelling "fire!" in a crowded theater and causing a panic. The point is that courts and societies are always engaged in settling limits to rights to preserve social order.

If society and government are usually engaged in setting limits to rights in order to preseve themselves, this means that the burden of defending, preserving, and extending rights often falls to individual citizens, lawyers, and activist groups. In America there are plenty of all three. And these years they pay growing attention

[11]For interesting recent examples and analyses of the debate, see Eugene V. Rostow, ed., *Is Law Dead?* (New York: Simon & Schuster, 1971), and Burton Zwiebach, *Civility and Disobedience* (New York: Cambridge University Press, 1975).

to such new spheres of "rights" or claims to rights as the right to travel, rights of animals, and the rights of the earth or the ecosystem. We'll certainly be hearing more about such claims to emerging rights in coming years.[12]

Stuart Scheingold has studied the underlying attitudes toward the law and rights held by citizens and by lawyers. He calls the faith that we tend to have in the law "the myth of rights." His analysis leads him to conclude that "the myth of rights . . . encourages us to associate rights with social justice. The myth also suggests that rights are timeless and can thus serve as guides to change. Finally, according to the myth of rights, the legal processes of governance offer effective protection to the rights of Americans. We are, in sum, led to believe that legal processes deserve to play and do in fact play an important *independent* role in American politics."[13]

Lawyers encourage us to believe this. So do politicians. And so, often, do many human rights interest groups. Some of these groups are international: Amnesty International, the International Commission of Jurists, the International League for the Rights of Man, and the International Committee of the Red Cross, for example. Others are national. Among the American human rights organizations are the American Civil Liberties Union, the National Association for the Advancement of Colored People, and the National Welfare Rights Organization.

Many believe that the law and our legal institutions do indeed provide opportunities for extending and strengthening human rights. But Scheingold warns against too much confidence: "At all points, law and politics are inextricably intertwined and in this combination politics is the senior partner. Laws are delivered to us by the dominant political coalition as are the judges and other officials responsible for interpretation and implementation. As a consequence our rights are always at risk in the political arena and therefore provide very little independent leverage."

Because of this, Scheingold argues, "Rights are no more than a political resource which can be deployed, primarily through litigation, to spark hopes and indignation." Nonetheless, "Rights can contribute to political activation and mobilization, thus planting and nurturing the seeds of mobilization," and "there is evidence to indicate that legal tactics can be useful. The civil rights experience provides the clearest demonstration that legal tactics – even with reluctant legal leaders – can release energies capable of initiating and nurturing a political movement."[14]

It is to an examination of the civil rights movement for minorities in America – its successes, its failures, and its prospects – that we turn in the next chapter. What we learn there should make us better able to assess the views of optimists and pessimists alike on the question of rights and liberties. And it should give us a firmer basis for considering, in Chapter 15, the claims of others still largely excluded from American politics: women, the young, and the elderly.

---

[12]For a discussion of some, see Sigler, *American Rights Policies,* chap. 15.

[13]Stuart A. Scheingold, *The Politics of Rights: Lawyers, Public Policy, and Political Change* (New Haven, Conn.: Yale University Press, 1974), p. 203.

[14]Ibid., pp. 203–204, 211.

☐ ACTION UNIT 13.3: How to organize to support human rights

If you wish to learn more about struggles for human rights at home and around the world, a good way to start is by writing to one or more of the organizations active in the field for information on their programs.

The foremost organization in the field is *Amnesty International* (U.S. branch, 2112 Broadway, New York, N.Y. 10023). It was founded in 1961 by British lawyer Peter Benenson to fight to obtain release of political prisoners around the world. By 1977 it had 168,000 members in 107 countries. It concentrates on the cases of prisoners who have neither committed nor advocated violence but have been jailed for their political, racial, or religious beliefs. It estimates that there are over 250,000 such "prisoners of conscience" in 90 countires around the world, and it attempts to win their freedom – and to oppose torture and the death penalty – by publicity, lobbying, legal aid, and letterwriting focused on the cases of specific individuals.

Operating in the American political sphere is the *Coalition for a New Foreign and Military Policy* (120 Maryland Ave. N.W., Washington, D.C. 20002), which unites three dozen national religious, peace, labor, professional, and social action organizations. It seeks to develop support for a noninterventionist, humanitarian U.S. policy. Its Human Rights Working Group monitors human rights legislation in Congress and lobbies on Capitol Hill. It will put you on its mailing list to receive background information on human rights and notice of relevant legislation in Congress.

Other organizations engaged in human rights activities include the *International League for the Rights of Man,* which concentrates its efforts at the United Nations; the *National Council of Churches,* which has a special Office on Human Rights; and the *International Commission of Jurists,* a group of thirty-eight eminent international lawyers that regularly reports on the human rights situation in various countries.

With the help of such organizations, you can organize special meetings devoted to human rights of various local organizations and develop a group to lobby your representative and senators on relevant legislation by mail and visits. The Coalition for a New Foreign and Military Policy can provide you with needed materials, from leaflets to films. Or you can organize a local chapter of Amnesty International U.S.A. and take on the cause of specific "prisoners of conscience" in various Eastern and Western countries.

☐ SUGGESTIONS FOR FURTHER READING AND STUDY

As a general introduction to civil liberties and civil rights in their judicial context, Henry J. Abraham, *Freedom and the Court: Civil Rights and Liberties in the United States* (New York: Oxford University Press Paperback, 1977), provides a useful discussion of the development of the Bill of Rights. See also Jonathan Casper, *The Politics of Civil Liberties* (New York: Harper & Row, 1972). For a comprehensive discussion of rights, see Norman Dorsen, ed., *The Rights of Americans: What They Are – What They Should Be* (New York: Random House, 1971). And for a more recent survey, see Jay A. Sigler, *American Rights Policies* (Homewood, Ill.: Dorsey, 1975).

Two books by Alan F. Westin on the right to privacy are helpful: *Privacy and Freedom* (New York: Atheneum, 1967), and *Data Banks and a Free Society* (New York: Quadrangle, 1976).

The field of human rights is still developing. But see Vernon Van Dyke's pioneering book, *Human Rights, the United States and World Community* (New York: Oxford University Press, 1970), and the collection of studies edited by Richard P. Claude, *Comparative Human Rights* (Baltimore: John Hopkins University Press, 1976).

14 Minorities in majority politics: blacks, Chicanos, Puerto Ricans, and Native Americans

The chances are you're a white Protestant. But the chances are only slightly better than even, for by now only 55 percent of the American population is white Protestant. Two hundred years ago about half the population was of English origin. In the 1800s heavy immigration from Europe, come to work in American factories, changed that. But enough of those Europeans were Protestants – and all of them were white – so that white Protestants are still holding on to a bare majority. Another 25 percent of the population is Catholic, 10 percent black Protestant, and about 10 percent Jewish or atheist or "other." Thus we could speak of Catholics, Jews, and black Protestants as minorities in America today and be correct. But we rarely do so. Instead, we tend to reserve the term "minority" for what we now usually call "racial" or "ethnic" minorities.

☐ THE MAKING OF MINORITIES IN AMERICA

In American history, Protestants from England were the first majority. They imported people with black skins from Africa as slaves to do the hard labor. They also encountered people with reddish-brown skins who were already living here when they arrived and when they later moved west. Further west and south, they ran into tan-skinned Mexicans, and on islands due south they found other tan-skinned peoples whose leaders, at least, spoke Spanish. The reddish-brown peoples were generally obstacles to the move westward and to economic development because they thought they had a claim on the use of the land. The tans also were obstacles in many cases, but they were workers too, as were the Europeans who came in large numbers in the nineteenth century.

All these other groups became "minorities" because there was a "majority" with the will and the power to dominate. The black slaves, who were kidnapped or bought from many different tribes throughout west Africa with many different cultures, and who spoke many different languages, were lumped together by the white, Anglo-Saxon Protestants (WASPS) as "Africans" or "slaves" or "Negroes" or "blacks" – all terms applied collectively to people who didn't think of themselves as having anything in common but their "involuntary servitude" (the legal term the dominant have often used instead of the word "slavery").

The reddish-brown natives, who came from many hundreds of different tribes, again with vastly different languages and cultures, the colonizers chose to bunch together as "Indians" (because the early explorers thought they'd landed in India) or as "redmen" or, as we now say, as "Native Americans."

The tan or brown people of southern origins, already colonized by Spaniards and so somewhat homogenized linguistically, we have come to call Mexican Americans, or Chicanos, and Puerto Ricans. When we lump them together further and add Cuban Americans, we generally say "Hispanics" or "Spanish-speaking" or "Spanish-surname" for obvious reasons.

Even the whites from Central Europe, Protestants though some of them are, we have long referred to as Germans, Czechs, Slavs, Croatians, Poles, Italians, and so on.

The major point of all this is that the peoples who live in the United States have vastly varying national, cultural, linguistic, and religious origins. But they often find themselves lumped together rather indiscriminately by WASPS, by the federal government, by real estate agents selling houses, by politicians, by professors, by authors, and by ordinary citizens.

In discovering – or, more accurately, making – a minority group, we generally look first for identifiable qualities such as skin color, eye shape and color, specific language, or accent. We also generally find, whether we look for them or not, less power and worse treatment than is the case with the majority. And finally, these days at least, we shall probably find awareness on the part of the members that they belong to a minority group.

□ THE HUMAN CONSEQUENCES OF MINORITY STATUS

There are various ways of studying and describing the impacts of minority status (or, for that matter, majority status) on people. Three are particularly important for our purposes.

Class in American history at the Hampton Institute, Hampton, Virginia, 1899.

Collection, the Museum of Modern Art, New York/gift of Lincoln Kirstein

The first is usually called "distributive." It focuses largely on material effects of the way in which group members are arrayed in the social structure. The major aspects are income, occupation, education, political power, and life chance (or one's opportunity to advance or improve one's standing throughout one's life).

The second may be referred to as "organizational." It focuses on the organizational effects and responses that follow from minority status. What sorts of associations or relations – especially political – do members form as a result of their distributive position in society? What religious, educational, or voluntary associations, for example? What are the goals and strategies of these organizations? How do they interact with dominant organizations?

The third important aspect, "consciousness," refers to the individual's awareness of reality – especially regarding the psychological effects that the social structure and organizations (points one and two above) have on the way the individual thinks, acts, and interacts. Members of minority groups often suffer from what we might call "dominated consciousness" – a situation in which their images of reality, including their images of themselves and of their possibilities, are imposed on them by the dominant culture or majority.

To get a better sense of the present situation and the prospects for each large minority group, we need to look more closely at each of these aspects and at the roles and responses of the political system. First, we'll compare the distributive status of all the groups, then we'll examine each group's organizational status and the system's response to it. Finally we'll consider consciousness more generally.

□ THE DISTRIBUTIVE STATUS OF MINORITIES

■ The sizes of our major minority groups

Blacks are now about 12 percent of the population. Chicanos, or Mexican Americans, are about 4 percent, and Puerto Ricans about 1 percent. Native Americans, or Indians, total about half a percent. That is the breakdown according to official Census Bureau figures. But those figures do not include illegal aliens. Some observers believe there as many as 8 million Mexican citizens illegally in the country doing farm and domestic work – again as many as the Mexican Americans who are legally here. Excluding illegal aliens, then, just under 20 percent, or one in five Americans, is a member of one or another of these large minority groups.

■ Economic status

But these same minorities who make up 20 percent of the population are about 35 percent of the poor and 40 percent of those on welfare. Table 14.1 shows more specifically the economic status of each group, comparing it to the status of whites. It reveals that about 35 percent of blacks are below the poverty line. But even worse off are Native Americans, 38 percent of whom are poor. When whites are compared to the minorities, we learn that the poverty rate among whites is only about one-third of what it is among minorities. And the per capita income of the minorities is less than 54 percent that of whites.

TABLE 14.1

Economic status of minority groups

	Blacks	Chicanos	Puerto Ricans	Native Americans	Whites
Per capita income	$1818	$1716	$1794	$1573	$3314
Percent of persons in poverty	34.8	27.7	29.5	38.3	10.9
Percent of families getting public assistance	17.6	11.9	24.3	18.9	4.0

Source: Data from 1970 census. The figures for whites actually include Chicanos and Puerto Ricans, and so they understate the differences slightly. Partial figures for 1976, also from the Census Bureau, show 9.7 percent of whites, 31.3 percent of blacks, and 26.9 percent of those of Spanish origin below the poverty line.

Other figures show that in the years 1960–1973 black family income doubled. This gave blacks a better income ratio in relation to whites: In 1960, blacks made an average of only 52 percent of what whites made, but by 1973 the figure was 58 percent. However, the actual dollar gap between the races widened: In 1960, black families averaged an income of $2,846 less than white families, but by 1973 the average gap was up to $3,326.[1] These figures change slightly from year to year. In hard times, for example, minorities get significantly worse off in absolute terms as well as relative to whites. But the general pattern as outlined here persists over the years.

■ Employment status

Figures on the sorts of jobs minorities tend to have help account for their relatively lower incomes. As Table 14.2 shows, unemployment is higher, laborer jobs are more common, and the percent of males working full time is lower for minorities. In general, blacks have the worst-paying jobs of any minority, but Native Americans have the highest unemployment rates. In times of increased economic difficulties during the 1970s, the employment situation worsened for all groups, but for minorities more than for whites, and most of all for black teenagers. By late 1977, for example, the unemployment rate for all Americans was 7 percent, but for whites it was only 6.1 percent, while for blacks it was 15 percent; for white teenagers it was 14.8 percent, but for black teenagers it was 40 percent.

[1] Sar Levitan et al., *Minorities in the U.S.* (Washington, D.C.: Public Affairs Press, 1975), p. 12

TABLE 14.2

Employment status of minorities

	Blacks	Chicanos	Puerto Ricans	Native Americans	Whites
Percent of workers in service and laborer occupations					
Males	36	33	27	29	15
Females	44	32	16	36	19
Percent unemployed					
Males	6.3	6.1	5.6	11.6	3.6
Females	7.7	8.9	8.7	10.2	6.8
Percent of males working	70	74	76	63	77
Percent of males working the full year	58	59	62	50	68

Source: Data from 1970 census.

TABLE 14.3

Educational status of minorities for persons 25 and older

	Blacks	Chicanos	Puerto Ricans	Native Americans	Whites
Percent with a high school diploma	31	24	23	33	58
Percent with less than 8 years of school	44	59	54	44	27

Source: Data from 1970 census.

■ Educational status

In measuring education, the Census Bureau looks only at those 25 and older, because they are likely to have finished their schooling. Table 14.3 shows percentages who have gotten a high school diploma and percentages who never even finished eighth grade. Here, presumably largely because of the special difficulties of schooling for people whose native language is likely to be Spanish, blacks and Native Americans fare better in comparison to Hispanics – but again far worse than whites.

■ Geographical concentration

One indicator of the degree of integration of minorities into the dominant society is their geographical concentration. Almost 90 percent of all Chicanos live in five states: California, Texas, Arizona, Colorado, and New Mexico. Fully 75 percent of all Puerto Ricans live in New York and New Jersey – indeed 60 percent live in New York City. Some 60 percent of all Native Americans live on or near official reservations.

The situation of blacks is a bit more complex. Fifty-three percent still live in the South, although only 28 percent of whites live there. Twenty-eight percent live in the ten largest cities of the nation – versus only 9 percent of whites. Location becomes even more interesting when we focus on the dominant white Protestant majority. About 65 percent of this group live in localities of less than 100,000 people, and only 25 percent reside in areas of 250,000 or more.

We can see, then, that in broad terms *America is still largely a nation of ethnic concentrations,* if not actually "ethnic purity." And when we look at neighborhoods, we find high degrees of residential segregation by ethnicity.

Figures such as these on distributive status can reveal the broad contours of the social structures within which our minority groups find themselves and the economic conditions with which they must struggle. But they tell us very little about the struggles. To understand the life circumstances and prospects of minorities more fully, we must also examine their organizational status and its relations to the dominant – especially political – structures.

□ THE ORGANIZATIONAL STATUS OF BLACKS

■ Black challenges to the American political system

The first Africans to arrive in the colonies were twenty slaves sold to Virginia settlers in 1619, a year before the landing of the *Mayflower.* By the time of the American Revolution, blacks were about 20 percent of the population – all but 60,000 of them slaves. The arrival of waves of European immigrants once the slave trade was ended slowly halved their percentage in the population, but did little to improve their status. From time to time there were slave uprisings, and there also developed a strong antislavery movement in the North, much of it led by women. Finally, by 1860, when the Civil War broke out, there were about half a million Negroes in America who were free in legal terms. But they were rarely free in practical political and economic terms.

The Civil War and the Thirteenth Amendment abolished slavery in America. But when the war ended, whites in the southern states passed a series of harsh laws to keep Negroes in virtual slavery. These "Black Codes," as they were called, led Congress to impose the Reconstruction on the southern states, in an effort to relieve the misery of blacks, and perhaps to further punish southern whites for their revolt. But as the North and the Congress ceased trying to control the South, whites took control again and passed harsh segregation laws. Blacks had been granted the right to vote under the Fifteenth Amendment (1870), but terrorist activities by the Ku Klux Klan and other white groups plus the restrictive laws we discussed in Chapter 3 prevented most from ever exercising it.

Legal challenges to segregation were pressed from time to time. But in 1896, in *Plessy v. Ferguson,* the Supreme Court ruled that laws providing separate public facilities for blacks were constitutional so long as the facilities were equal. Not until *Brown v. Board of Education,* more than half a century later, which we discussed in Chapter 9, did the legal move toward integration resume.

The past twenty years have seen important efforts to expand the political and economic rights of blacks in education, in access to public accommodations such as restaurants and hotels, in employment, and in voting, as well as other aspects of political participation.

Participation In 1964 only 41 percent of adult blacks in the South reported ever having voted.[2] In 1960 the black registration in the South was only 29 percent. By 1972 it was up to 64 percent, primarily because the 1965 Voting Rights Act brought federal intervention to protect and encourage black southern voters. In recent years, as we saw in Chapter 3, voting has fallen off among blacks and whites alike. Still, blacks now tend to vote at about 90 percent the rate of whites nationwide.

Representation The increase in black voters in the past 15 years or so has brought with it an increase in black elected officials, as Table 14.4 shows. But it is important to note, in the 1974 figures, that the 16 black representatives are but 3 percent, and the 239 state legislators but 3 percent, of the total elected. And although the total number of black elected officials rose to 3979 in the 1976 election, that total was still less than 3 percent of America's elective offices. Thus blacks are still far from being proportionally represented in electoral politics. Furthermore, with few exceptions,

[2]Donald R. Matthews and James Prothro, *Negroes and the New Southern Politics* (New York: Harcourt Brace Jovanovich, 1966), p. 44.

TABLE 14.4
Black elected officials

	1964	1968	1970	1972	1974
U.S. total	103	1125	1860	2625	2991
House of Representatives					
United States	5	9	13	15	16
From South	0	0	2	4	4
Senate					
United States	0	1	1	1	1
From South	0	0	0	0	0
State legislatures					
United States	94	172	198	238	239
In South	16	53	70	90	90
Mayors					
United States	–	29	81	83	108
In South	–	17	47	49	63
Local					
United States	–	914	1567	2288	2627
In South	–	468	763	1242	1452

Source: The Social and Economic Status of the Black Population in the U.S., 1974 (Washington, D.C.: Census Bureau, 1974).

most blacks elected have come from largely black districts. And by now most of the largely black districts already have black representatives. This means that the opportunities for further gains will be quite limited unless and until largely white districts start electing blacks.

Administration Another important sign is the percentage of blacks in high-level government posts. Looking at the top six slots of each section of the federal bureaucracy we find that in the decade from 1962 to 1972 the number of blacks increased by 8000, or 600 percent. But remembering our discoveries in Chapter 7 about how many bureaucrats there are, we'll not be surprised that these gains only brought the total percentage of blacks in high posts up to 3 percent. The total of blacks in all federal jobs is now about 15 percent–but that only reveals how concentrated they are toward the lower end of the salary and skill spectrum.

The situation of blacks in the private sector is generally even worse. In business, blacks now hold but 2 percent of high-level posts. Elsewhere, in local police, it's up to 7 percent; state police, 2.3 percent; lawyers, 1.3 percent, state and local judges, 2.3 percent; local union officials, 5.7 percent; military officers, 2.2 percent.[3]

Organizations Much of what progress there has been can be attributed to a series of black organizations. Throughout this century, these groups have attempted both to mobilize blacks so as to increase their power and to pressure public and private organizations to make concessions to blacks. But their ancestry reaches much further back in American political history.

As early as the 1790s, small groups of free blacks petitioned state legislatures to grant them the right to vote. Later, similar groups asked the Congress to grant

[3]These figures, the latest available, are for 1972. See Levitan, *Minorities in the U.S.*, p. 32.

that right and to abolish slavery. During Reconstruction, blacks participated actively in the elective political process. But when that opportunity was foreclosed, they returned to group activity.[4]

The first major organization with the power to last was the National Association for the Advancement of Colored People (NAACP). It was founded in New York in 1909 by a group of white and black activists. To this day it has sought equality for blacks, largely through the use of the law and through legal reform. Perhaps its greatest success was the Supreme Court ruling against "separate but equal" schools in *Brown v. Board of Education.*

In 1911, whites concerned about the plight of blacks migrating to the cities organized the National League on Urban Conditions Among Negroes. The Urban League, as it came to be called, sought housing and jobs for urban blacks. It remained conservative but often effective until 1961, in the midst of the civil rights movement, when Whitney Young's leadership made it more activist.

The first of the modern protest organizations was the Congress of Racial Equality (CORE). It was organized in 1942 to conduct nonviolent protests against segregation in Chicago. It became prominent nationally only in 1961 when, under James Farmer's leadership, it organized "freedom rides" in which blacks and whites rode buses South to protest segregation in bus travel. As a result of these freedom rides, the Interstate Commerce Commission finally issued regulations banning segregation on buses and in terminals.

On December 1, 1955, a black seamstress named Rosa Parks took a seat in the "Whites Only" front section of a public bus in Montgomery Alabama. When ordered to leave it so a white man could sit there, she refused. The police arrested her and in response the black community organized a bus boycott, walking everywhere instead of riding in "the back of the bus." The boycott, under the nonviolent leadership of Rev. Martin Luther King, Jr., and a coalition of church groups called the Southern Christian Leadership Conference (SCLC), lasted over a year until, in December 1956, the Supreme Court outlawed segregation on public buses.[5]

The following years brought court orders requiring integration of various colleges and public schools in the South. Time and again, students, parents, and outside agitators demonstrated and rioted against those blacks who sought to enter all-white schools. Federal troops had to be called in to protect students in Little Rock, at the University of Alabama, and elsewhere. State legislatures adopted a policy called "massive resistance" to integration, passing law after law to shore up segregation. A hundred southern members of Congress signed the "Southern Manifesto" opposing the Court decision on school integration as unconstitutional and vowing to use all lawful means to reverse it.

These were difficult times in America. Ugly attitudes surfaced and vicious behavior flared up. But through it all more and more courageous blacks in the south

---

[4]See Hanes Walton, Jr., *Black Political Parties: An Historical and Political Analysis* (New York: Free Press, 1972).

[5]For the story of the boycott and the philosophy underlying it, see M. L. King, *Stride Toward Freedom* (New York: Harper, 1958).

Wide World Photos

Voter registration drive in Atlanta, Georgia.

and some courageous southern whites demonstrated both personal strength and deep commitment to the values of racial brotherhood, nonviolent direct action for social change, and democracy.

These courageous southerners were joined by more and more concerned northerners. Out of this, in 1960, grew the Student Nonviolent Coordinating Committee (SNCC), the most radical of the civil rights protest groups. Led by Stokely Carmichael, it organized "sit-in" demonstrations, in which black and white students would sit at lunch counters in dime stores and other public places waiting to be served. Stores would refuse to serve them, local whites would beat them, and local police would arrest them. But SNCC would organize national boycotts of chains that refused to serve lunch to blacks in the South. And eventually the campaign succeeded.

The civil rights movement From buses and lunch counters the civil rights movement, as it came to be called, spread to public libraries, swimming pools, public parks, and voting booths. Finally, after President John Kennedy was assassinated, under southerner Lyndon Johnson's leadership Congress passed the Civil Rights Act of 1964, which outlawed segregation in public accommodations and facilities, in federally funded projects, and in unions. It also strengthened the federal government's hand in protecting the right to vote and in integrating public schools. (See Table 13.1 for a summary of recent civil rights laws.)

With the passage of the Voting Rights Act of 1965, the civil rights movement began to dissipate. *Legal* barriers to blacks had been largely removed. *Economic* barriers, however, were as strong as ever, for most blacks remained poor. And *mental* barriers – attitudes which obstructed progress – in both blacks and whites were still present. The result was a shift among activist blacks toward what came to be called "black nationalism."

The Black Power movement Black Muslims led by Malcolm X had begun arguing that blacks should seek to improve their own situations without depending on whites. Malcolm X was assassinated, but the black nationalist movement continued to grow. Finally, in 1965, Stokely Carmichael coined the term "Black Power" as a goal for the movement. At this point, the movement split and diversified. Black Panthers and others emphasized armed self-defense and threatened to resort to violence if necessary to gain full equality. Martin Luther King increasingly emphasized the problems of poverty and the connections between American racism, black poverty, and the war in Vietnam. While leading a "Poor Peoples March" to Washington in April 1968, King was assassinated in Memphis. One of his followers, Rev. Jesse Jackson, then organized "Operation Bread Basket" in Chicago, and turned more and more toward emphasizing economic self-help for blacks. Still others placed their emphasis on Black Power – on building cultural and political strength in cities such as Newark, Gary, Cleveland, and Detroit, all of which soon had black mayors.

The years since the early days of Black Power have been difficult ones for blacks and whites alike. The Vietnam War distracted attention of activists and government alike from race and poverty at home to foreign affairs. The worst recession since the 1930s then hit blacks a much harder blow than whites and set back their economic progress more than all the resistance efforts of racists had managed. Urban riots in the mid-1960s have left black ghettoes charred and scared down to this day in some cities. A spreading hard-drug problem that has at last hurt the children of the white middle class has devastated sections of black ghettos. The urban crime that whites now fear so much is much more than a fear to most urban blacks.

These facts indicate the depth of the continuing problem. But they do not reveal the breadth of the progress that has been made, through governmental programs and self-help actions alike.

■ Responses of the American political system to blacks

The black quest for equality has been fought first and foremost in the courts. The Supreme Court eventually did rule segregation unconstitutional in schools, buses, and elsewhere. But, as Milton Morris suggests, "What the Court has been doing on behalf of blacks – or more precisely its greater willingness in recent years to extend basic constitutional protection to blacks – is merely an undoing of the formidable obstacles to black advancement which it helped to erect."[6] Or, in the words of another critic, Lewis Steel, on racial issues the Court "has waltzed in time to the music of the white majority – one step forward, one step backward and sidestep, sidestep."[7]

In recent years blacks have tended to look toward the presidency and its bureaucracy for progress, first in proposing and backing legislation, and then in its implementation. In their pronouncements, presidents have been increasingly sympathetic to black concerns, with the notable exceptions of Nixon and Ford. Cynics attribute this to the growing strength of black bloc voting in the northern

---

[6]Milton Morris, *The Politics of Black America* (New York: Harper & Row, 1975), p. 249.

[7]Lewis M. Steel, "Nine Men in Black Who Think White," in *White Racism,* ed. Barry Schwartz and Robert Disch, (New York: Dell, 1970), pp. 362–372.

cities as well as in the south. But whatever the reasons for their vocal support, no president has yet developed a prominent and effective mechanism in the White House policy machinery with the clear responsibility for civil rights.

In Congress, the thirteen black representatives organized into the Congressional Black Caucus in 1971 to attempt to develop and present in Congress and to the president unified sets of policy proposals. It has provided a focus for black citizens around the country as well as for the media. But it has not yet been able to develop the leadership role once hoped for. One reason for this weakness is the small number of black representatives who must share the work. Another is the relatively quiescent role of the Congress on racial matters in all but times of the strongest popular and presidential pressure. And yet another has been the presence in the White House of unresponsive presidents themselves facing serious and distracting economic and foreign policy challenges.[8]

One expert, Milton Morris, surveying the American political system's response to blacks, reached four important general conclusions: (1) Federalism has allowed the states to sustain black subordination for many decades, and the separation of powers has complicated efforts at change that require action by all three branches. (2) Efforts by blacks and whites to achieve change have worked best when there have been regional or partisan divisions among whites. Northerners favored civil rights and especially school integration when they were being imposed in the South, for example, but became opponents of "forced busing" when efforts were made to integrate northern city schools. (3) Most governmental responses

[8]See Marguerite Ross Barnett, "A Historical Look at the CBC," *Focus*, August–September 1977, pp. 3–4.

Michael Abramson/Black Star

he Great Society has been shot down on the battlefield of Vietnam."
— DR. MARTIN LUTHER KING, Jr.
HELP THE POOR IN THE SOUTH

have been incremental rather than comprehensive, even though both the problems and the needed measures had long been clear. For example, it took five separate major civil rights laws from 1957 on to achieve a barely adequate program. (4) "Finally, governmental responses to demands by blacks for change in the pattern of race relations have not been systematic and carefully planned, so that change is often hampered by administrative inefficiency, disorganization, and even deliberate bungling."[9]

Blacks have always been a special problem in American politics and for American government. But the more they have become urbanized, the more many of their needs and desires have become similar to those of other urbanized minorities such as Puerto Ricans. Similarly, as other ethnic minorities such as Chicanos have become larger and their poverty more pressing, blacks and Chicanos have come to have more problems in common. The growth and isolation of urban ethnic ghettos walled off by suburbs may also have created some commonality between blacks and Native Americans on reservations.

☐ THE ORGANIZATIONAL STATUS OF CHICANOS

■ Chicano challenges to the American political system

Whereas blacks were brought to this country by slave traders, the ancestors of the people of mixed Native-American and Spanish ancestry whom we now call Mexican Americans or Chicanos were here, in small numbers, before the early colonists, or "Anglos" (as whites are called in the Southwest).

Early last century, Mexico formally possessed much of the Southwest and California. But by 1853, the United States had added the present states of Texas and New Mexico, along with parts of Colorado, Arizona, Utah, Nevada, and California, by a combination of war, treaty, and purchase. In the century since, Mexican citizens have continued to immigrate to the United States, sometimes fleeing Mexican politics, other times seeking better jobs. Some of those already here have also moved northward to such places as Chicago, Indiana, Ohio, and Pennsylvania. Only in the Southwest, however, have they been large enough in number to play significant political roles as a distinct minority group. But even there, except in New Mexico, their role has been limited.

Participation Nationally, as of 1972, 73 percent of whites and 68 percent of blacks otherwise eligible to vote were registered, while only 44 percent of the Spanish-surnamed were registered. Differences in actual voting are even greater. In that same year, 65 percent of registered whites and 54 percent of the blacks voted, but only 38 percent of the Spanish-surnamed. Historically, Chicanos have faced many of the same barriers to voting that blacks have – with the added problem that English often is not their native language.

---

[9]Milton Morris, *The Politics of Black America,* p. 245.

Representation and administration Chicanos are very weakly represented in national politics. When in December 1976 a Hispanic Caucas was formed in the House, it had only five members: a Puerto Rican from New York City, the resident Commissioner from Puerto Rico, two Texas Chicanos, and a California Chicano. Because of their regional concentration, Chicanos do somewhat better in state legislatures, where they had elected seventy-four members in five states by 1976. But their percentage representation never equals their population percentage. For example, they are 19 percent of the Texas population but only 6 percent of the legislature; in California they are 16 percent of the population but only 4 percent of the legislature. They are equally underrepresented in bureaucratic positions, at both state and national levels.[10]

Organizations Historically, Mexican Americans relied on their Catholic churches and on local community organizations called *mutualistas* for assistance. Once large-scale migration to the United States began after World War I and the Mexican Revolution, other organizations were formed. The Orden Hijos de America (Sons of America) was established in San Antonio in 1921. The League of United Latin American Citizens (LULAC) was born in Corpus Christi, Texas, in 1929, and spread throughout the Southwest. LULAC began as an organization to facilitate assimilation of Mexican Americans into the Anglo culture. Its official language is English. With the experience of segregation and discrimination in World War II, it took to the courts like its black counterpart, the NAACP, in often successful efforts at the state level to remove discriminatory barriers in education, employment, and public facilities. In these efforts it was often joined by the G.I. Forum, a Mexican-American veterans' group especially active in the 1950s and 1960s. The G.I. Forum was founded after private cemeteries and mortuaries in Texas refused to handle the body of a Mexican American soldier – discrimination rather typical of what Mexican Americans have faced.

In these postwar years, another group, the Community Service Organization (CSO) created in Los Angeles in 1947, emphasized voter registration and political action in the style of Saul Alinsky, whom we discussed in Chapter 5. Many current Mexican-American leaders such as Representative Edward Roybal and migrant farmworker organizer Cesar Chavez were active in CSO.

The movement toward greater political action gained strength in the 1960s. The Mexican American Political Association (MAPA) in California and the Political Association of Spanish-Speaking Organizations (PASO) in Texas worked in local politics with some success. The American Coordinating Council on Political Education (ACCPE) was a comparable group active in Arizona.

These organizations all focused on legal and political equality, leaving aside the social and economic inequalities that were then believed to be "nonpolitical." But the growth and successes of the black civil rights movement suggested a broader perspective. So did the Black Power movement's emphasis on separatism instead of assimilation. And finally so did the pledges of aid that blacks received

---

[10] *Current Population Reports,* no. 253, 1972, p. 20.

Wide World Photos
Cesar Chavez with his cousin, Manuel Chavez.

after the big city riots – more aid than Mexican Americans had ever gotten in all their years of peaceful protest and efforts at assimilation.

The result was a new militancy among Mexican Americans. Cesar Chavez began organizing farm workers in Delano, California, in 1962. Reis Tijerina began a movement in New Mexico to regain lands lost in the Anglo conquest, even appealing to the Mexican government for support and then occupying certain forests until expelled by troops. Rodolfo "Corky" Gonzalez in Denver founded La Crusada Para La Justicia ("Crusade for Justice"), which protested police brutality and opposed the Vietnam War. In 1967 new militant youth groups were formed: The Mexican American Youth Organization (MAYO), the United Mexican American Students (UMAS), and the Brown Berets. It was at this point that the outlines of a new ideology were emerging. The militants generally preferred to be called Chicanos – a term whose origins are not certain but that once referred to lower-class Mexican Americans.[11] More and more, the emphasis was on self-determination with preservation of the native culture – *chicanismo* – rather than assimilation.

The major vehicle for this movement soon became La Raza Unida party. A Chicano political party, it was founded in Crystal City, Texas, in 1969 by Jose Angel Gutierrez, a MAYO organizer. Chicanos often refer to themselves as *la raza* ("the race"), so the party's name translates as "the united race." Gutierrez's group had organized a school boycott to make the schools more reflective of the Mexican-American majority in Crystal City. The struggle that followed unified the Chicano population and the outcome was election of a Chicano majority on the school board, followed by victories in other city and county elections after hard voter registration work.[12] From Crystal City the party spread elsewhere, even running candidates for governor of Texas in subsequent elections and establishing itself in California, Colorado, New Mexico, and Arizona. When it held its first national convention in El Paso in 1972, over 3000 delegates from seventeen states and the District of Columbia attended.

Chicano political organizing – labor, community, and political party – is still in its early stages. Already it has made major progress in the agricultural fields of California, in the barrios (or neighborhoods) of San Antonio, and in the elections of south Texas. Its prospects are potentially as great as the large Mexican-American populations of the five southwestern states – but so too are the difficulties.[13]

---

[11]The most commonly accepted view is that it derives from the way rural Native Americans of Mexico pronounced "Mexicano": "Meh-chee-cano."

[12]For an account of the takeover, see John Shockley, *Chicano Revolt in a Texas Town* (Notre Dame, Ind.: University of Notre Dame Press, 1974). For a study of popular attitudes and their formation in Crystal City, see Herbert Hirsch and Armando Gutierrez, *Learning to Be Militant: Ethnic Identity and the Development of Political Militance in a Chicano Community* (San Francisco: R & E Research Associates, 1977).

[13]For helpful accounts of various Mexican-American organizations, see Maurilio Vigil, *Chicano Politics* (Washington, D.C.: University Press of America, 1977). Among other useful books on Chicano politics, beyond those already cited, are F. Chris Garcia and Rudolph O. de la Garza, *The Chicano Political Experience* (North Scituate, Mass.: Duxbury, 1977); Joan W. Moore, *Mexican Americans,* 2nd ed. (Englewood Cliffs, N.J.: Prentice-Hall, 1976); Armando Rendon, *Chicano Manifesto* (New York: Macmillan, 1971); F. Chris Garcia, *La Causa Politica* (Notre Dame, Ind.: University of Notre Dame Press, 1974); and Leo Grebler, Joan W. Moore, and Ralph C. Guzman, *The Mexican-American People* (New York: Free Press, 1970).

■ Responses of the American political system to Chicanos

Meanwhile, the federal government's responses continue to be limited and mostly symbolic at best. President Johnson established a Cabinet Committee for Spanish-Speaking People, which his successors continued. President Nixon presented a "sixteen-point program" for greater job opportunities and created an office in the Civil Service Commission to enforce it. As a result, by 1973 about 3 percent of federal employees were Spanish-surnamed – but of course these groups are about twice that proportion of the population. Meanwhile, however, the National Economic Development Association, a nonprofit group created to help businesses owned by Spanish-speaking people, was established in 1970 by government agencies. In its first 6 years, it lent half a billion dollars to some 9000 Hispanic small businesses. Still, this is a small sum in comparative terms. For thus far federal responses have been limited and largely symbolic. In this they reflect the continuing limits to the degree of political clout in Washington thus far achieved by Spanish-surnamed Americans. But even this seems to be changing. Chicanos are now represented in Washington by the National Council of La Raza, and Hispanics by the National Congress of Hispanic American Citizens. Both groups believe that large-scale immigration plus a high birth rate will make the Spanish-speaking the largest minority group in America by 1985. That should change American politics nationally as well as regionally. But how much impact it has will depend on the degree of cooperation between Chicanos and Cubans and Puerto Ricans – something that has yet to develop very far.

□ THE ORGANIZATIONAL STATUS OF PUERTO RICANS

The United States took control of Puerto Rico after the U.S. victory in the Spanish-American War in 1898. The Spanish had ruled the island southeast of the American mainland for 400 years after "discovering" it early in the sixteenth century. At that time the island was inhabited by "Indians" who were relatively peaceful and so tended to assimilate the Spanish culture. The result was a population of widely mixed Spanish and "Indian" origins, with the addition of some black slaves brought in to work on sugar plantations. But everyone spoke Spanish.

The United States controlled Puerto Rico as a colony for 50 years. The population was granted American citizenship by the Jones Act in 1917 and was allowed to elect its own governor starting in 1947. But not until 1950 was it allowed to draft its own constitution and create a new government. On July 25, 1952, Puerto Rico became an American "commonwealth," having besides common citizenship and common military defense, a common market (free trade between the island and the mainland) and a common currency (the American dollar). Since then Puerto Ricans have disputed whether to retain commonwealth status, to seek full independence, or to seek to become the fifty-first state.

Puerto Rican Community Development Project, Inc.

As in the case of blacks in the South, Puerto Ricans in northern cities have sought to increase their political clout through voter-registration drives.

Independence would give Puerto Rico greater control over its economy, especially newly discovered oil, now largely owned by Americans from the mainland, and its politics. But it would also put an end to the large sums of economic aid, welfare payments, and so on, that now flow from Washington to the people of Puerto Rico. Statehood too would limit the control Puerto Ricans would have over their own affairs. So the issue of the island's future is clouded by disagreement and uncertainty.

At the same time, the question of the prospects of the island's 3,162,000 citizens is clouded by the large migration flows to and from the mainland. Because Puerto Ricans are American citizens, immigration is easy, and there are now 1,800,000 Puerto Ricans on the mainland. Because they are Spanish speaking and generally have less formal training than mainland Americans, adjustment and economic success are hard. The result is that many Puerto Ricans come to the mainland for a time and then return to the island. This makes it all the more difficult for Puerto Ricans to develop and maintain an effective political organization, even in New York City, where some 60 percent of them live.

Because most Puerto Rican families in America are first or second generation arrivals (immigrants themselves or children of island-born parents), their progress in education, occupation, and income has been limited thus far. Politically, much the same is true. Because they are American citizens by birth, they can vote in American elections as soon as they establish residence on the mainland, while other immigrants must first achieve citizenship. But Puerto Ricans are still small minorities in most communities where they have settled, and so they tend to lack political clout. And even in New York city, where they are concentrated in several barrios and constitute at least 10 percent of the city's population, fewer than 35 percent are registered to vote, and so they have little representation in city government and but one member of Congress in Washington.

Most Puerto Rican organizing thus far has been of a nonpolitical, community-service sort. In big cities, political machines try to control political organizations, of course, and so maintaining a nonpolitical posture probably helps the organizations to aid "mainland islanders" (as they are often called). But at the same time it limits the extent to which the Puerto Ricans can develop the only kind of political strength that will force a city to take note of them politically: effective organization that can turn out votes. Even sporadic terrorist bombing, mostly in New York City, for which credit has been claimed by the Puerto Rican Liberation Front seeking independence for the island, has had little impact.

■ Responses of the American political system to Puerto Ricans

The American political system's response to the needs and desires of Puerto Rican Americans thus far has been limited. Antipoverty and job-opportunity programs have been made available to "mainland islanders" in the same way they are to other impoverished groups, but there have been few special federal programs directed to them. Perhaps the most striking—but also least relevant—response was President Ford's call for statehood for the island just before he left office. Both Puerto Ricans and Americans agreed that the proposal was at best premature. So, in a sense, are other system responses likely to be, until Puerto Ricans in America develop more political muscle.[14]

☐ THE ORGANIZATIONAL STATUS OF NATIVE AMERICANS

■ Native Americans challenges to the American political system

Native Americans' cars and pickup trucks often carry a bumper sticker saying "America: Love It . . . Or Give It Back To Us." That slogan capsulizes half the story of our relations with the peoples who inhabited the continent, from the North Slope in Alaska to the southern tip of South America, for perhaps 30,000 years. When Europeans "discovered" America, there were already somewhere between 9 and 100 million natives living there, with about one-ninth of them in what we call the United States. By 1900 the number left in the United States had shrunk to a mere 245,000, thanks to diseases brought from Europe by the white man, starvation resulting from seizure of Native Americans' farm lands, and extermination by American settlers and cavalry in the "Indian Wars."

Today, the number is rising again, for their birthrate is about double that of Americans as a whole. The Census Bureau in 1970 counted 793,000 who identify themselves as "Indians" when asked. The U.S. Bureau of Indian Affairs, which requires proof of at least a quarter Indian ancestry, found 450,000 living on or near

---

[14]For recent discussions of the status and prospects of Puerto Rican Americans, see Levitan, *Minorities in the U.S.*, chap. 4, and Ineke Cunningham and Anibal Molina, "Puerto Rican Americans: A Study in Diversity," in *The Minority Report*, ed. Anthony G. Dworkin et al. (New York: Praeger, 1976), pp. 190–220. For a more general study, see Joseph P. Fitzpatrick, *Puerto Rican Americans* (Englewood Cliffs, N.J.: Prentice-Hall, 1971).

reservations in 1970. Native American activists who look for people active in Indian affairs put the number at about a million. They are most heavily concentrated in Arizona, Oklahoma, New Mexico, and California.

On November 19, 1969, a party of 250 Indians landed on Alcatraz Island. They claimed the island in San Francisco Bay with an abandoned federal prison as Indian land. Recalling that colonists had "bought" Manhattan Island (now New York City) from Indians for about $24 worth of glass beads and red cloth 300 years earlier, they offered to buy Alcatraz for the same sum. In a "Proclamation: to the Great White Father and All His People" mocking the traditional treatment of the Indians they continued:

> We will give to the inhabitants of this island a portion of that land for their own, to be held in trust by the American Indian Bureau of Caucasian Affairs, to hold in perpetuity—for as long as the sun shall rise and the rivers go down to the sea. We will further guide the inhabitants in the proper way of living. We will offer them our religion, our education, our life-ways, in order to help them achieve our level of civilization and thus raise them and all their white brothers up from their savage and unhappy state. We offer this treaty in good faith and wish to be fair and honorable in our dealings with all white men.[15]

The federal government chose to outwait the occupation force. Finally, in the summer of 1971 federal marshals surprised the twenty remaining occupants and escorted them back to shore. The occupation was over, but the point had been made by the occupiers, who had chosen to call themselves "Indians of All Tribes."

Even today there remain 481 different Indian tribal groups, which at one time spoke some 300 different languages—50 of which are still in use. Of these tribal groups, 267 have special reservations—pieces of land "reserved" for use by the tribes, held "in trust" for them and supervised by the Bureau of Indian Affairs in Washington. These reservations total about 53 million acres, or just about 2 percent of the total land area of the United States. Most of the reservations are in the West, and 77 percent of all Native Americans live west of the Mississippi. Furthermore, about half now belong to nine basic tribes: Navajo (97,000), Cherokee (66,000), Sioux (48,000), Chippewa (42,000), Pueblo (31,000), Lumbee (28,000), Choctaw (24,000), Apache (23,000), and Iroquois (22,000).

■ Responses of the American political system to Native Americans

The situation was very different in the time of the Revolutionary War. Then, in 1778, the United States, still without a Constitution, signed a treaty with the Delaware Indians that envisaged the formation of an Indian "state whereof the Delaware Nation shall be the head and have a representative in Congress."[16]

---

[15] "Proclamation," reprinted in T. C. McLuhan, *Touch the Earth* (New York: Dutton, 1971), pp. 164–165

[16] Angie Debo, *A History of the Indians of the U.S.* (Norman: University of Oklahoma Press, 1970), p. 71.

Had such a possibility come to pass, the fate of the Indians in America might have been very different. In wartime, Indian strength was valued. But once peace was achieved, Indian lands were coveted.

In 1787, as we saw in Chapter 1, the Continental Congress passed the Northwest Ordinance concerning the development of the Northwest Territory, then possessed by Indians. It contained this pledge: "The utmost good faith shall always be observed toward the Indians; their lands and property shall never be taken from them without their consent; and in their property, rights, and liberty, they shall never be invaded or disturbed, unless in just and lawful wars authorized by Congress."[17]

The succeeding 200 years have been a record of the violation of these promises. In these two centuries, federal policy has vacillated between the conflicting aims of separation and assimilation. But until very recently Indian self-determination has never been a course acceptable to Washington.

The 100 years of war The Constitution (1789) gave the federal government power to negotiate treaties with "the Indian nations." Indians were then viewed as foreign nations, and so in 1824 when a Bureau of Indian Affairs (BIA) was first established it was located within the Department of War.

White settlers then wanted more land, and the new state of Georgia claimed jurisdiction over Cherokee Indian lands within its borders that had been recognized by federal treaty. The Supreme Court, in *Worcester v. Georgia,* ruled that "The Cherokee nation, then, is a distinct community occupying its own territory, with boundaries accurately described, in which the laws of Georgia can have no force, and which the citizens of Georgia have no right to enter, but with the consent of the Cherokees themselves, or in conformity with treaties, and with the acts of Congress." Court decisions are supposed to be enforced by the president. But the president then was Andrew Jackson, the famous Indian fighter. He is reported to have remarked: "That's Marshall's decision; let him enforce it."

Meanwhile the Congress in 1830 had passed the Indian Removal Act, instructing the BIA to relocate all Indians west of the Mississippi River – but only with their consent. Those Indians who refused consent were forced to move by the military. Subsequent legislation in 1849 transferred the BIA to the Interior Department the very agency trying to free Indian lands for white settlers. The result, not surprisingly, was continued military defeats and removals of Indians farther and farther westward away from their ancestral homelands to virtually worthless, often unfarmable land – the reservations Indians still occupy today.

In 1871 Congress decided that Indians were no longer to be viewed as nations, or sovereign political units. Instead, they were to be assimilated into the mainstream of the United States by becoming farmers. Each family was allocated 40 to 160 acres within the reservation by the General Allotment Act (or Dawes Act) of 1887. All leftover land was then sold by the federal government to white settlers. Thus were the reservations further whittled down – from 138 million acres to only 47 million

[17]Quoted in D'Arcy McNickle, *The Indian Tribes of the U.S.* (London: Oxford University Press, 1961), p. 30.

by 1934. Tribes that resisted "allotment" were "terminated" immediately: Their reservations were abolished and they had to fend for themselves in American society.[18]

The 50 years of accommodation The last military battle with Indians was fought in 1890 – the famed Wounded Knee Massacre.[19] When thousands of Indians volunteered to serve in the army in World War I, Congress responded by granting Indians citizenship – and so the right to vote – in 1924. But this right in law did not become fully a right in practice until 1948, when the Supreme Court struck down clauses in the constitutions of Arizona and New Mexico forbidding Indians from voting.

By the Indian Reorganization Act of 1934, Congress granted Indian tribes the rights to develop their own constitutions, administer justice (subject to Congress's limitation), and determine tribal membership. And that same year the Johnson-O'Malley Act laid the groundwork for what we might call "foreign aid" to Indian tribes: educational, medical, and other services to be paid for by Washington but provided by states and later private groups. This marked the high point of Indian-federal relations.

The growth of Indian organizations In the twentieth century Indians made new efforts to organize to make their views felt. In 1911 the Society of American Indians (SAI) was formed with the twin objectives of "pan-Indianism" (uniting all Indians) and "assimilation" (adopting the culture and lifestyle of the non-Indian majority). But pan-Indianism did not gain real strength until the founding of the National Congress of American Indians (NCAI), in 1944, by returning veterans no longer willing to accept discrimination and inequality. The NCAI was active in lobbying the government and litigating in the courts.

When the Eisenhower administration sought to "terminate" federal aid to tribes, the NCAI led opposition. Still, the BIA continued to try to relocate Indians from the economically depressed reservations to urban areas where jobs and training opportunities were greater. This policy of encouraging assimilation met with growing resistance. Leaders of that resistance were militant young Indians who formed the National Indian Youth Council (NIYC) in the early 1960s.

This new militance resulted in a series of direct action projects. One was the Alcatraz occupation in 1969. Another was the occupation of Wounded Knee, South Dakota, in 1973, by 200 members of another activist group, the American Indian Movement (AIM), which had been founded in 1968 and now has chapters throughout the Midwest.

Another action, which like Wounded Knee received major media attention, was a march on Washington in the fall of 1972, conducted by AIM, NAIC, NIYC and other national Indian organizations. Earlier, President Nixon had declared a

---

[18]For a discussion of this and other important aspects of Indian history, see Curtis E. Jackson and Marcia J. Galli, *A History of the Bureau of Indian Affairs and Its Activities Among Indians* (San Francisco: R & E Research Associates, 1977).

[19]See Dee Brown, *Bury My Heart at Wounded Knee* (New York: Holt, Rinehart & Winston, 1970).

Courtesy of the New-York Historical Society

General George A. Custer attacking a Cheyenne Indian Camp, 1868. The last military battle with Indians was the famed Wounded Knee Massacre in 1890.

Wide World Photos

Assistant U.S. Attorney General Harlington Wood (in white shirt) is escorted into Wounded Knee, South Dakota, by armed members of AIM upon his arrival for negotiations.

"New Trail" for the American Indian. In a message to Congress on July 8, 1970, he asserted that "American Indians have been oppressed and brutalized, deprived of their ancestral lands, and denied the opportunity to control their own destiny." He declared that "it is long past time that the Indian policies of the federal government began to recognize and build upon the capacities and insights of the Indian people." Shortly thereafter certain ancestral lands were restored to their tribal owners, and the BIA was reorganized to give Indians more of a role in it. But Congress resisted most of Nixon's proposals, and the BIA did not become more responsive. And so the Indian groups called their 1972 march on Washington "The Trail of Broken Promises." When their 4-mile-long caravan arrived, it met with some resistance in the BIA. The outcome of what seems to have been a series of confusions was a 6-day occupation of the BIA by the Indians. During the occupation they destroyed some property and seized some records. They and columnist Jack Anderson, to whom they showed some of the records, found a history of mishandling of Indian affairs by the BIA.[20]

As one important outcome of the reports about these documents, Congress established an American Indian Policy Review Commission. It concluded in 1977 that the BIA had mishandled Indian money, neglected Indian safety, and failed to protect Indian property rights. The report also called for abolition of the BIA and its replacement by a Department of Indian Affairs independent of the Interior Department.[21]

---

[20]The story is told briefly in Joseph Stauss, Bruce A. Chadwick, and Howard M. Bahr, "Indian Americans: The First Is Last," in *The Minority Report,* ed. Dworkin, pp. 221–253.

[21]See the *Final Report* to the American Indian Policy Review Commission (Washington D.C.: Government Printing Office, 1976).

The Carter administration, when it came to power, faced a changed situation. Tribes in many states were making new claims on land taken from them illegally by white settlers over 100 years ago, and the government was recognizing the legal validity of some claims. At the same time, twenty-two tribes whose lands contain oil and coal reserves were setting up a Council of Energy Resource Tribes patterned on the Organization of Petroleum Exporting Countries (OPEC) to gain more advantages in the leasing of their lands to oil and coal companies.

Attempting to increase the role of Native Americans in government, the Carter administration decided to ask 200 tribes for nominations for the new post of assistant secretary of the interior for Indian affairs, intended to supervise the BIA. Two names emerged as tribal favorites, and Carter then picked Blackfoot Indian Forrest J. Gerard for the post. Gerard immediately ordered a sweeping audit of the BIA's affairs. He also pledged to make major new efforts in strengthening the role of the Indians themselves in shaping their own programs.

But there are serious conflicts among Indians over how best to do this. On one side are the militants, on the other are the traditionalists, or nationalists, as they are sometimes called. Vine Deloria, Jr., has remarked that "most Indians are nationalists. That is, they are primarily concerned with the development and continuance of the tribe. As nationalists, Indians could not, for the most part, care less what the rest of the Society does. . . . Militants, on the other hand, are reactionists. They understand the white society and they progress by reacting against it."[22]

This highlights an important distinction made by Frances Svensson, herself an Indian, that helps explain the differences between Indians and other minorities, and so the difficulties of coalition building.

> In general, Indians have found relatively little in the activities of other minority groups attempting to assert similar claims to land (for example, the Chicanos in the Southwest or the Black Muslims in the Deep South) or for a special legal relationship with the American government and American society. . . . Where the Black goal has seemed to be equal participation in the benefits and privileges of American society, the fundamental Indian objective is best summed up as the right not to have to participate and still maintain an autonomous Indian identity, legally rooted in the historic treaty relationship and the traditional land base."[23]

"Indian tribes need greater political power to act," asserts Indian leader Mel Thom. "This country respects power and is based on the power system. If Indian communities and Indian tribes do not have political power we will never be able to hang on to what we have now."[24]

---

[22]Vine Deloria, ed., *Custer Died for Your Sins* (New York: Macmillan, 1969), p. 237.

[23]Frances Svensson, *The Ethnics in American Politics: American Indians* (Minneapolis: Burgess, 1973), p. 39. This short book contains an excellent introduction to American Indians in politics. For a more general study, see Murray L. Wax, *Indian Americans: Unity and Diversity* (Englewood Cliffs, N.J.: Prentice-Hall, 1971).

[24]Mel Thom, quoted in Alvin M. Josephy, Jr., *Red Power* (New York: American Heritage Press, 1971), p. 68.

But an older Indian responds to that view: "As Indians we will never have the efficient organization that gains great concessions from society in the marketplace. We will never have a powerful lobby or be a smashing political force. But we will have the intangible unity which has carried us through four centuries of persecution. We are a people unified by our humanity – not a pressure group unified for conquest. And from our greater strength we shall wear down the white man and finally outlast him. . . . We shall endure."[25]

☐ MINORITY-MAJORITY RELATIONS

■ Governmental approaches to solving the problems of minorities

Both dominant elements and the subordinate peoples in society view the problem posed by minorities differently at different times. This means that beliefs about what the appropriate remedies are will also vary through time. We could usefully examine the development of society's beliefs about the problem posed by any minority through time. For example, let's take blacks.

Emancipation When the problem was seen as *slavery,* the solution was **emancipation** by destroying slavery or the society that sustained it. The Civil War did that, but of course race relations did not really improve very much as a result.

Abolishing legal segregation People then concluded that the problem was **discrimination** – a set of *residual practices* based on race, left over from slavery. The way to solve that problem, it appeared, was to change those practices. The legal practices were declared unconstitutional by the Supreme Court or changed by new laws. At that point, it was believed that *abolishing legal segregation* would result in desegregation.

Education But that approach was not sufficient either, although it certainly improved the conditions of many blacks in the South. Perhaps, then, the problem was not so much residual practices of discrimination, but rather *residual attitudes* of discrimination – or **prejudice**. This suggested that what was needed was *more education about race and about prejudice,* with two important goals. The first was to show people that their beliefs about the inferiority of blacks were unfounded: that there was no factual basis for discrimination because blackness was only "skin-deep," or perhaps only "culture-deep." Coupled with this was emphasis on the desirability of an unprejudiced, integrated society, in which brotherhood replaced hostility.

Integration Experience showed that even this was not enough, however. The next stage in the struggle to solve our racial problems involved efforts to increase

[25]Quoted in Virginia Armstrong, *I Have Spoken* (Chicago: Swallow, 1971), pp. 162–163.

Wide World Photos

Arkansas National Guard troops turn back blacks attempting to enter all-white Central High School, Little Rock, September 1957.

what is sometimes called *"equal status contact"* – actual contact between whites and blacks of the same social status, occupations, incomes, or whatever. The theory behind this approach relied on the fact that forced contact in the military between the races engaged in common tasks with the same rank had usually overcome prejudice. But the question was how to bring about such contact among people so prejudiced that they resisted it. The answer was *a shift in emphasis from* **desegregation** (removing barriers to contact) *to* **integration** (bringing people together).

Compulsion There are two basic approaches to achieving integration: compulsion and incentives. Both have been tried, for example, in public schools. The *compulsion approach* simply decrees that the races will be joined in the same school, perhaps by consolidation of white and black schools, or perhaps by busing of students. This approach, widely used, has achieved some success but much turmoil and apparent hardening of attitudes, especially in big cities such as Boston, has accompanied it.

Incentives The *incentive approach* has generally worked better where it has been tried. One way it is used is simply letting students transfer to a better school. This usually involves blacks transferring to a predominantly white school because white schools have usually been better than black schools. In such cases, the incentive of a better school draws blacks to the white school and also keeps whites there. In recent years, however, a more active effort has been tried: development of "magnet schools." Magnet schools are special schools developed with special strength such as emphases on science or the performing arts. They attract students of all races from a whole region by their special programs. Magnet schools seem to be more successful at fostering integration than other efforts. The drawback is that they are expensive to run and only work to integrate students who are especially interested in good education – something many students of all races no longer seem to be.

Affirmative action To cope with situations where such incentives to participants were not available, other approaches had to be found. This led to the next stage: *a movement from providing equal opportunity to requiring affirmative action* to achieve integration. We discussed this approach in detail in Perspective 5.

■ Racism

Racism is the belief that a person's race should be used as a criterion to determine how he or she is treated, implying that some races are or should be treated better than other races. Racism has been a characteristic of the views of many citizens throughout American history. We call this attitude personal racism.

Personal racism In a sense, the civil rights movement of the early 1960s was based on the assumption that racial problems were problems of individual attitudes. Racially prejudiced people – people who feared strangeness, difference, or foreignness – were generally thought of as misinformed and even mentally sick. Efforts were made to correct that misinformation or treat that sickness by achieving education and contact.

Institutional racism But the civil rights movement died in part because even when there was more contact and less prejudice, the problems of minorities were not solved. This led more and more observers and activists to conclude that the problem was deeper than attitudes – that it was more than just personal. Instead, many came to believe, the United States suffered not just from personal racism but also from institutional racism. According to this view, whatever people's views may be, our institutions set contexts within which some people are kept poor and powerless by being denied real opportunities for education, good jobs, good housing, and political roles.

Our economic system, for example, is based on capitalist competition. Those with money have economic power. Those with good educations and good connections do best at earning money. People who are born into well-off families have an easier time getting these advantages. So the system, through its institutions, tends to perpetuate the same economic classes in power.

Furthermore, political power tends to depend on economic power. If you are poor you can't take time off from your work to run for office, nor can you contribute money to someone's campaign to get him or her to do you favors. In addition, the system tends to set *economic prerequisites* to participation such as poll taxes for voting (now outlawed) or high costs for good housing, or the ability to take time off from work to serve on juries. Patterns such as this tend to perpetuate unequal opportunity *regardless of people's attitudes* about race. This suggests that changing the status and prospects of minorities will require *changing the economic and political system.* Simply changing peoples' attitudes won't be enough.[26]

---

[26]For a presentation of various aspects of institutional racism, see Charles Bullock and Harrell Rodgers, *Racial Equality in America* (Santa Monica, Calif.: Goodyear, 1975). See also Joe R. Feagin, "Indirect Institutional Discrimination," *American Politics Quarterly,* April 1977, pp. 177–199.

■ Problems of consciousness

The attitudes and deeper beliefs of people are still important, however, and may even hold the key to the next stage of progress for minorities. But the attitudes that are most important may be those, not of the prejudiced dominant people, but rather of the dominated minorites.

Discrimination and domination tend to make the victims feel inadequate, unequal, and incompetent. The victims tend to grow up believing they are less valuable and less able to act effectively in society. Until recently, the major resistance to domination has been occasional revolts and riots, strikes and boycotts, and traditions of ethnic humor and culture. In recent years, however, groups dominated economically, socially, and politically have been working to combat their situation at the level of consciousness as well.

Leaders have been much more actively emphasizing the *strengths* of the minority cultures, their *values,* and the *prospect of power:* black power, brown power, and red power. These efforts seem to have developed greater ethnic pride in many members of the minority groups we have examined. This pride has contributed to a greater sense of efficacy, or ability to operate effectively in society, even while the society remains racist in many ways. One result of this is higher hopes in many young people – hopes that motivate greater efforts.

"Peoplehood" is the name historian Page Smith gives to this new sense of self and of possibilities. "Peoplehood," he writes, "is a particular kind of self-definition whereby masses or wards of the public seek to achieve an identity and a power of their own. . . . the definition always comes out of the mass; it can never come from outside, from well-intentioned liberals, benefactors, reformers, philosophers, psychologists, sociologists." Smith goes on to point out that "the dependent group in the process of defining itself, of creating itself, of speaking itself into life, draws on remarkable new sources of energy and releases these into the world. . . . They become electrified, plugged in, almost literally, to history. They sense that they, too, can make history."[27]

This new sense of power and the new hopes that go with it give strength to activists. But they also create hopes that increase the risk of disillusionment should the dominant society be unresponsive or inflexible. This uncertainty about the prospects makes it all the more important for the ethnic groups to be as clear as possible about their choice among various possible objectives.

■ American goals and minority groups

Paternalism Historically, American society seems to have had paternalism as its goal in handling minority groups. This term, derived from *pater,* the Latin word for "father," refers to maintaining dominance over another while deciding what is best for the one dominated.

Recently, some observers have argued that America has used a special variant of paternalism called "domestic colonialism" or *"internal colonialism,"* treating

[27]Page Smith, "From Masses to Peoplehood," *Historical Reflections* 1, no. 1 (June 1974): 134–135.

blacks, Chicanos, Puerto Ricans, and Native Americans as if they were a colony. There are four major characteristics of internal colonialism as it is usually described.

- □ Forced entry of subordinates into the world of the dominant – by slavery for blacks and conquest for Chicanos and Native Americans.
- □ Forced transformation of the culture of the minority group – by requiring the use of English and prohibiting the use of native languages, for example.
- □ Management and manipulation of economic and political affairs of the dominated by the dominant – such as white ownership of stores in the black ghettos or white officials running the Bureau of Indian Affairs.
- □ Racist attitudes held by the dominant and imposed where possible on the minorities so that they believe they are basically inferior.[28]

Divide and conquer A second strategy that has seemed to be operating in recent decades is *divide and conquer* – setting one minority group against another to prevent them from uniting to achieve greater power. This strategy has been especially common where the government has been distributing resources such as aid money or business contracts. When blacks struggle with Chicanos for antipoverty funds, for example, the government gains power. It has, understandably, been very difficult for minority groups who have little in common besides their subordinate status to form coalitions thus far.

Anglo conformity The longer-term goal of U.S. society in its handling of minorities has usually seemed to be *Anglo conformity*. This term refers to desires and requirements that minorities adopt the attitudes, life-styles, and culture of the dominant Anglo society. In ethnic terms, this is often called *acculturation* and *assimilation*.

The melting pot At the same time, there has long been an American ideology of the *melting pot*. This view holds that America is a mixture of many different nationalities and that the people's strengths come from a combination of the special qualities of different minorities, all "melted down" into a new "American" culture.

This view sounds appealing, and for decades it was widely accepted. But then leaders of various minorities began to argue that it was not happening in fact. In the angry words of one Chicano militant, "The United States has been anything but a melting pot, because the gringo has purposely segregated, separated, and relegated the non-Anglo to an inferior and degraded status. Melting pot has meant surrender of one's past and culture to something euphemistically called American society or culture. The melting pot worked only for immigrants with a white skin who came to America."[29]

---

[28]For one of many recent discussions of internal colonialism, see Harry H. F. Kitano, *Race Relations* (Englewood Cliffs, N.J.: Prentice-Hall, 1974).

[29]Rendon, *Chicano Manifesto,* p. 107.

Wall at Resurrection City, Washington, D.C., during Poor People's Campaign, Summer 1968.

By now, it is hard to find a supporter of the melting-pot approach. Even the immigrants with a white skin – the Italians, the Irish, the Germans, the Greeks, the Poles – are reemphasizing their ethnic roots and cultures. But the strongest opposition to the melting-pot image comes from the most "unmeltable" ethnics, the "people of color." As Earl Shorris has written of the Native American, "Conquered and loved, butchered and smothered, the Indian staggers into the battle for a pluralistic society; he has seen death in the melting pot."[30]

Cultural pluralism   And so most ethnic groups have "staggered" – or charged – into the battle for a pluralistic American society. But **cultural pluralism** – in which each individual culture survives and flourishes within a broader framework – can take various forms. (1) One image now much in favor is that of the symphony orchestra. In such a society, every group plays a different instrument, but all are playing their own part in a larger piece. This image raises two unanswered questions: Who will conduct the orchestra? And who will compose the symphony? Many of the more militant and younger ethnic leaders fear the answer in both cases will be Anglos. And they also suspect that if they don't play it the way the Anglos write it and conduct it, they'll be thrown out of the orchestra. (2) So some favor a second image or objective, which might be that of a jazz combo. There would still be a piece to be played, and the performers would have to cooperate and support each other. But each would also be able to improvise from time to time, and the piece would be somewhat different every time it's played. (3) The more extreme image, just short of total separatism (which few now favor) could be termed "separate but equal recitals," taking place, to stretch the metaphor, in the same recital hall.

[30]Earl Shorris, *The Death of the Great Spirit* (New York: New American Library, 1972), p. 61

Perhaps no one is now certain which of these ultimate objectives is the most desirable. Perhaps few sense just what would be required to achieve any of them. But several important points are clear even now. First, each of us must be more open to other cultures and more supportive of their efforts at self-determination. Second, our government must be supportive—especially with funds for development—without insisting on shaping and dominating the activities of our various cultures. And third, the members of each subgroup must continue to explore and experiment and try to develop greater agreement among themselves. Ultimately, each group would then be likely to develop its own variation of the principle of self-determination as it has been advocated for Native Americans, for example.

"The process of building Indian 'nations' will inevitably take many years, especially since it must be fundamentally guided and motivated by tribal initiatives," says one observer.

> As earnestly as federal officials may want to solve the problems with appropriations, or as much as a compassionate or guilt-ridden public may want to lend a hand, non-Indians can only be limited "nonvoting" partners in the process of Indian development and self-determination. Ultimately, Indians must decide the future course of their culture. Federal policy, a chain of mistakes and tragedies extending almost to the present, must at last leave the resolution of "the Indian question" to Indians.[31]

□ SUGGESTIONS FOR FURTHER READING AND STUDY

The footnotes scattered throughout the chapter will lead you to helpful books on each of the minority groups discussed. For an analysis of WASPs, see Charles H. Anderson, *White Protestant Americans* (Englewood Cliffs, N.J.: Prentice-Hall, 1970). A book that combines a biographical study of a leading unconventional black activist with a survey of the development of the civil rights movement is Nick Kotz and Mary Lynn Kotz, *A Passion for Equality: George Wiley and the Movement* (New York: Norton, 1977). A helpful treatment of race relations generally is Michael Banton, *Race Relations* (New York: Basic Books, 1967). For a skeptical view of affirmative action as a solution to race problems, see Nathan Glazer, *Affirmative Discrimination* (New York: Basic Books, 1976). But consider again the discussion in Perspective 5.

---

[31]Sar Levitan and William B. Johnston, *Indian Giving: Federal Programs for Native Americans* (Baltimore: Johns Hopkins University Press, 1975), p. 80.

15 Outsiders in insider politics: women, the young, the elderly, and others

The largest "minority group" in America is the majority: the 51.3 percent of the population that is female. Women in our country are the most *underrepresented* group in our political system and in our economic system. But women are not the *least active* group in American politics. That distinction goes instead to the young, who are barred not only from serving in national office until they are 25, but also from voting for candidates for any office until they are 18. The distinction of being the *least visible* element in our population, on the other hand, falls to the 11 percent of the American people who are over the age of 65.

Women, the young, and the elderly – along, we should remember, with the handicapped, the mentally ill, and the homosexual – are the outsiders in American politics. The members of racial and ethnic minorities, so long excluded from most of the benefits of American life, and from most of the rights to shape those benefits, are at last being inducted into politics, whatever the reasons, whatever the methods, whatever the degrees, as we saw last chapter. But most of those being so inducted are male, middle-aged, and of sound mind and body. For American politics in general is still off limits to women, to the young, to the elderly, and to those of unusual physical, mental, or sexual characteristics. By examining each of these groups to determine its size, its interests, its activities, and the way our political system responds to it, we should be able to better understand what seem likely to become the next great waves of unrest and activism in America: the campaigns of the outsiders against the insiders to tear down the walls that bar them from full, active and profitable roles in American politics.

□ OUTSIDERS AND POLITICS

Politics, as we have seen time and again, is made up of actions by individuals who run for office, work in campaigns, vote, lobby, make policy, and execute policy. But most of this political activity is undertaken by individuals organized into groups in order to have more influence or make better policy or govern more effectively.

Most groups in politics are organized around a candidate, as is a political party in a campaign, or around an issue, as is the anti-gun-control lobby. But when one segment of the population is particularly unrepresented in politics, or generally not listened to, the time will come when it will tend to organize simply to gain a fairer share of political power. The prospect that a group such as blacks, who are about 13 percent of the population, might begin to vote actively as a bloc and to lobby for the same general goals almost regardless of their wealth or social position was enough to bring about major new legislation. The same may increasingly occur with groups such as the elderly or the handicapped, for example, each of which is a sizable distinct minority.

The prospect of the same sort of political solidarity among women, or even just among a substantial percentage of women, should be enough to bring massive changes in American politics. Why, then, did so fundamental a quest as ratification of the Equal Rights Amendment (ERA) run into such staunch resistance? To explain this, and more generally to understand why "outsider groups" continue to have such difficulty in American politics, we must look at two key features of what we might call "the politics of advocacy."

■ The politics of advocacy

The first, most striking, point is that the outsiders must advocate their positions to the insiders – to those who control politics. In the case of ERA, the activist women and their male supporters had to convince the male-dominated Congress to pass, and thereby propose, the amendment, and then had to convince two-thirds of the state legislatures, also dominated by males, to ratify it.

Second, and probably more significant ultimately, the active outsiders who want "in" must convince the other members of their social group to support their cause. In the instance of ERA, supporters had to advocate their case for adoption to unconvinced and even fearful women. With relative unity, they would be a political force difficult to resist even for the most male-chauvinist state legislators. But without it, their case became much weaker.

Dino Pellegrino/Black Star

■ The politics of policy

Even if an outsider group wins these battles in the politics of advocacy, however, there remains the serious battles of "the politics of policy" – the struggle over what sort of action the political system should, will, and eventually does take in response to the outsider group. We can get a better idea of the importance and actual operation of the politics of advocacy and the politics of policy by examining the recent experiences of the women, the young, and the elderly in American politics.

□ WOMEN IN AMERICA TODAY

■ The status of women

The earnings gap between men and women is greater today than it was back in 1965, when the contemporary women's movement began with publication of Betty Friedan's book *The Feminine Mystique.* Back then, men averaged 68 percent more income than women, but by the mid-1970s men were making 75 percent more than women. Table 15.1 shows the breakdown. When it released these figures, the Labor Department attempted to explain things this way:

TABLE 15.1

Earnings of women and men for full-time work

Annual earnings[a]	Women (%)	Men (%)
Less than $3000	9.4	4.6
$3000–$4999	26.2	6.6
$5000–$6999	29.2	12.6
$7000–$9999	23.8	24.9
$10,000–$14,999	9.7	31.2
$15,000 and over	1.7	20.0

[a]These figures are for persons 14 years of age and older working full time year round. The year is 1972, the most recent for which such figures are available.

Source: Adapted from Department of Labor, *Women and Work,* Employment and Training Administration R & D monograph 46 (Washington, D.C.: Government Printing Office, 1977), p. 3.

> **Historical patterns concerning "men's jobs" and "women's jobs" still persist . . . Such sex stereotyping still seems to restrict or discourage women from entering many higher paying, traditionally male occupations . . . although women are as well educated as their male counterparts in terms of median years of schooling, there are differences in the kinds of education, training, and counseling they receive, which directs them into traditional and low-paying jobs."[1]**

This brief analysis reflects much of the general situation of women in America today. Women are now almost men's equals in education, but they are held back in the societal roles they play by a combination of their own attitudes and men's attitudes. Neither women nor men, on the average, yet believe that women can and should do every job men do, and neither yet believe that women should be paid what men are paid when they do so. More women are working than ever before – twice as many as in 1950 – but they are being paid less and less, relative to men, than before. All this despite some 15 years of an active and growing "women's movement."

This is not to say there's been no real improvement over these years. In 1950 only 66 women for every 100 men received four-year college degrees. By 1975 that total had risen to 77 women per 100 men. Similarly, in 1950 only 10 percent of all Ph.D.s were women, while by 1974 it was 16 percent. But if we look at men and women with similar educations and similar careers aged 30 to 44, women make an average of $3000 a year less than men. Table 15.2 shows these differences for various occupations in 1972 (the figures are for those 14 years old and older working the year round).

These figures can be elaborated almost without limit,[2] but several basic points will suffice. First, women are still paid less than men. But, second, this fact is all the more important because so many more women are working now than previously.

[1]Department of Labor, "The Earnings Gap Between Men and Women," (Washington, D.C.: Department of Labor, 1976).

[2]Indeed, the Census Bureau now publishes regularly a large booklet entitled *A Statistical Portrait of Women in the U.S.,* first issued in April 1976, which does just that.

TABLE 15.2

Earnings of women and men for full-time work, by occupation

Occupational group	Median[a] annual wage or salary income: Women	Median[a] annual wage or salary income: Men	Women's median annual income as percent of men's	Percent of all employees who are women
Professional and technical workers	$8796	$13,029	67.5	42
Managers and administrators	7306	13,741	53.2	21
Sales workers	4575	11,356	40.3	43
Clerical workers	6039	9656	62.5	79
Crafts workers	5731	10,429	55.0	5
Machine operators (including transport)	5021	8702	57.7	31
Service workers (except private household)	4606	7762	59.3	58
Private household workers	2365	—[b]	—	97
Nonfarm laborers	4755	7535	63.1	9

[a]Median income is the middle income; half of all workers in this occupation earn more than this and half earn less.
[b]There are less than 75,000 men employed here, so the figures are not calculated.

Source: Adapted from Department of Labor, *Women and Work*, Employment and Training Administration R & D monograph 46 (Washington, D.C.: Government Printing Office, 1977), p. 3.

Of every 100 jobs in the U.S. economy, forty-one are held by women. And that percentage is rising, because women are now getting about 55 percent of the 3,300,000 new jobs the economy is creating each year. As of 1977, there were about 40 million women in the workforce – 48 percent of all women 16 or older. Over 13 million of them were single, widowed, or divorced, and so could not depend on a man for support. Nonetheless, 58 percent of the female work force is married. And indeed some 53 percent of all women 18 and over are in the work force. But lest we think that these problems affect only adults 18 or over, we might note that as of 1970, according to the Census Bureau, there were 289 women who had been both widowed and divorced and were still only 14 years old or younger. And lest we think that the problems affect only women, by 1972 the Census Bureau found in the category of "homemaker" (someone with no job beyond that of "keeping house") 25,300,000 women and 96,000 men.

■ Attitudes toward women

The United States, like the rest of the world, is still beset by *sexism,* "the range of attitudes, beliefs, practices, policies, laws, and behaviors discriminating against women (or against men) on the basis of their gender."[3] These attitudes are nothing new. Indeed, they have lessened somewhat over the years. When abolitionist Abby Kelly requested permission to speak at a meeting of the Connecticut Anti-Slavery Society in 1840, the members voted to grant her

[3]Constantina Safilios-Rothchild, *Women and Social Policy* (Englewood Cliffs, N.J.: Prentice-Hall, 1974), p. 1.

permission. This may not seem a notable event to us today, but in its time it was quite unusual, for women were supposed to be "seen, not heard." Indeed, it was so unusual that the chair*man* of the meeting immediately resigned his post with the declaration that he would not sit in a chair where women were allowed to speak. "I vacate this chair," he declaimed. "No women shall speak or vote where I am moderator. I will not countenance such an outrage on decency. I will not consent to have women lord it over men in public assemblies. It is enough for women to rule at home."[4]

Yet 135 years later, Pope Paul VI reminded the faithful and the world that woman's essential role is motherhood and her "prime importance" is to be caretaker of the family. He did grant that men and women are "equal before God" and that they should be equal in professional and social life. But he warned that the movement for equality was being "blindly pushed forward by our materialistic society and thereby runs the risk of either virilizing [making manly] women or of depersonalizing them. In both cases," he concluded, "it does violence to women's deepest qualities."[5]

Whatever may be "women's deepest qualities," many women and growing numbers of men would agree with Dr. Joyce Brothers' assertion that "no one should be denied equal rights because of the shape of her skin."[6]

☐ WOMEN AND THE POLITICS OF ADVOCACY

■ Wants and beliefs

It is impossible to speak of "what women want" or "what women believe" as such, because the more than 100 million women hold quite varying views. Despite the wide variations in women's views, certain important trends in opinion can be discerned. For example, popular support for the Equal Rights Amendment has increased considerably, to the point where at the time of the 1976 election some three-quarters of all women supported it. Incidentally – and of equal significance – so did three-quarters of all men. But three-quarters of the state legislatures – the number required to ratify a constitutional amendment – did not.[7] But the ERA asserts simply that "Equality of rights under the law shall not be denied or abridged by the United States or by any state on account of sex." In fact, the concerns of activist women – and the males who agree extend far beyond an end to such denial of equal rights.

One expert, Carol Whitehurst, suggests the breadth and depth of concerns motivating the women's movement and the differences among women over them.

---

[4]Quoted by Lillian O'Connor, *Pioneer Women Orators* (New York: Columbia University Press, 1954), p. 36.

[5]"Pope Paul Assails Feminists Who Risk 'Virilizing' Women," *New York Times,* February 1, 1975.

[6]*Washington Post,* March 6, 1971.

[7]These figures are from the 1976 edition of the famous University of Michigan Election Study. They are reported in Virginia Sapiro, "News from the Front: Inter-Sex and Inter-Generational Conflict over the Status of Women" (paper delivered at the annual meeting of the American Political Science Association, Washington, D.C., 1977).

Suffragette parade, Washington, D.C., 1913.
Library of Congress

One group sees the root cause of oppression in economic exploitation, and suggests that women's liberation is part of a worldwide struggle of all exploited people against more powerful classes. . . . Another group within the movement is less interested in the economic basis of oppression than in the power struggle between men and women; it sees the oppressor not as the capitalist system but as men. . . .

Depending on which branch of the movement she identifies with, a women may feel that other women are selling out or being bought off with token changes, or dividing women by rejecting those who are happy in traditional roles. Some feel the women's movement is only a fad which takes attention away from the more pressing problems of black liberation.

Whitehurst nonetheless finds a common core to the movement: belief in the existence of sexism and in the necessity of changes to free people from oppression and create new alternative opportunities.

"In more specific terms," she writes,

"there is a certain amount of agreement on particular issues including equalizing legal rights; eliminating economic and employment discrimination; granting women rights to and control over their own bodies; and increasing political power. There is also some agreement on certain broader and more amorphous goals: to reduce and eliminate stereotyping, particularly in the

Pro-ERA rally, Washington, D.C., 1977.
Martin Adler Levick/Black Star

mass media; to reduce the need for artifice and increase the value of naturalness; to be able to pursue alternatives without stigma; to be willing to accept greater responsibility along with greater rights and freedoms; and to develop a sense of history, solidarity, and sisterhood. Feminist women hope to improve their own self-images, and they hope to increase women's opinions of women as a group. Once a feeling of self-regard and sisterhood is attained, women are more able to consider the meaning of liberation for all people. Most women need to develop their own selves to the point where they do not have to defer to males, for only then can they begin to see their brothers as oppressed as well."[8]

■ What women do in politics

Voting The voting *turnout* of women has increased to the point where it is now about equal to that of white men, except in the South, where more traditional attitudes keep some women from voting. But even on issues of women's

[8]Carol A. Whitehurst, *Women in America: The Oppressed Majority* (Santa Monica, Calif: Goodyear, 1977), pp. 145–147.

□ ACTION UNIT 15.1: How to contact women's political organizations

Black Women's Community Development Foundation (1028 Connecticut Ave. N.W., Washington, D.C. 20036) develops educational programs of interest to black women.

Center for the American Woman and Politics, Eagleton Institute of Politics (Rutgers University, New Brunswick, N.J. 08901), a nonpartisan research and educational center, sponsors programs to increase knowledge about American women's participation in government and politics.

Eagle Forum (Box 618, Alton, Ill. 62002), founded by Phyllis Schlafly, a leader in the campaign against the ERA.

Human Rights for Women (National Press Building, 529 14th St. N.W., Washington, D.C. 20045) conducts and sponsors research on equal rights for women, provides legal services, and issues reports.

League of Women Voters (1730 M Street N.W., Washington, D.C. 20036) consists of women and men interested in nonpartisan political action and study and works to increase participation and to provide information on candidates, platforms, registration, and balloting; also has state and local branches throughout the country, listed in the telephone book, which publish booklets on how state and local government work and how women can be politically effective.

National Congress of Neighborhood Women (4408 8th St. N.W., Washington, D.C., 20017) seeks to organize a network of neighborhood working-class women active in community affairs.

National Council of Negro Women (1346 Connecticut Ave. N.W., Washington, D.C. 20036) is a coalition of national organizations and individuals that encourages the development and use of black women in society.

National Organization for Women (425 13th St. N.W., Suite 101, Washington, D.C. 20004), which consists of women and men interested in civil rights for women, acts through political, educational, and legal means to improve the condition of women.

National Woman's Party (Sewall-Belmont House, 144 Constitution Ave. N.E., Washington, rights, as on almost all political issues, there is no significant difference between men's and women's votes, as we saw in Chapter 3. But how well has the voting research of the last several decades understood women and their activity? Recently, some social scientists have challenged the facility of many interpretations.

Two scholars, Murray Groot and Elizabeth Reid, have studied the way women's behavior has been described and explained by political scientists. They find that there is "sexist scientism" in many of the conclusions reached. They examine and challenge what they find to be conventional assumptions or conclusions of voting studies: that children adopt the party preference of their father; that wives follow their husbands; that women are more conservative than men; that women are traditionalists; that women are fickle; and that women personalize politics. They assert that "the accepted view is that they [women] do not engage or interpret for themselves that which does get through to them; they merely accept it. The images of women we have encountered, from uncomplaining followers of their husband on one side to fickle or arbitrary decision-makers on the other, all take this for granted."[9]

---

[9]Murray Groot and Elizabeth Reid, *Women and Voting Studies: Mindless Matrons or Sexist Scientism?* (Beverly Hills, Calif.: Sage, 1975), pp. 33–34.

D.C. 20002) is composed of women seeking equal rights; it supports the ERA and has done educational work since 1913.

National Women's Educational Fund (1532 16th St. N.W., Washington, D.C. 20036) offers technical training to prepare women for party and political office.

National Women's Political Caucus (1921 Pennsylvania Ave. N.W., Washington, D.C. 20006) is composed of persons interested in greater involvement of women in politics, runs workshops on practical politics for potential candidates, and publishes educational materials as well as a newsletter.

Washington Institute for Women in Politics (Mount Vernon College, 2100 Foxhall Rd., Washington, D.C. 20007) develops work-study programs for students, provides on-the-job training for women interested in public service, and runs conferences and workshops.

Women's Campaign Fund (Box 24145, Washington, D.C. 20024) is a nonprofit campaign fund-raising group that seeks to raise money for outstanding women candidates for elective office at the federal or state level.

Women's International League for Peace and Freedom (1213 Race St., Philadelphia, Pa. 19107) since 1915 has campaigned for peace, freedom, justice, education, and international action, using the slogan "A woman's place is in the world."

Women's Legal Defense Fund (1424 16th St. N.W., Washington, D.C. 20036) is composed of lawyers and interested citizens, provides free legal assistance in sex discrimination cases, and publishes educational materials on employment discrimination, credit problems of women, and married women retaining their maiden names.

Women's Lobby Inc. (1345 G. St. S.E., Washington, D.C. 20003) informs on the status of legislation related to equal rights, minimum wage, credit, abortion, tax reform, and other issues and testifies on bills of concern to feminists.

Sources: Literature provided by various organizations, Congressional Quarterly's *Washington Information Directory,* and Phyllis Butler and Dorothy Gray, *Everywomem's Guide to Political Awareness* (Millbrae, Calif.: Les Femmes Publishers, 1976).

In conclusion, they argue that

> much of the work we have reviewed simply assumes the dominant values of the dominant groups of society. The values taken for granted here are the values of the (male) researchers operating in a male dominated society in which they too are numbered among the beneficiaries. The electorate is passive, but some are more passive than others. Insofar as anyone constructs a world of politics or work the builders are men. This is the ultimate insult accorded the woman voter. But it is not, as we have endeavored to show, the only one.[10]

It is important to recognize and understand such analyses, for they are now being done by feminists and male sympathizers for all aspects of life. They often reveal unquestioned biases in attitudes still held by most Americans – and by most institutions. They also reflect many of the concerns and objectives of the women's movement today, in politics and in the rest of life.

Representing The American Congress is still effectively a male club. Never in history have there been more than two women senators – and since 1973 there had been none until Muriel Humphrey assumed her late husband's seat in 1978. In the House there were nineteen women in 1975–1976 – an all-time record, but still a mere 4 percent of the total. The numbers haven't changed much over the past several decades: there were sixteen congress*women* and one woman senator in 1955. But there has been one important change in the House. Until recently, most women there (like almost all in the Senate) were first elected by what is called "the right of widow's succession" – being elected to the seat previously held by one's husband on his death. Now women are more likely to win congressional seats on their own. But no woman has yet held any important leadership post in either house. Would the presence of more women in Congress affect policy outcomes? No one can say for sure. But a study of the voting records of the nineteen women in the House in 1975 reached several interesting conclusions. All nineteen voted against U.S. involvement in the Angola civil war – including the five Republicans, who were voting against President Ford's wishes. Large majorities also voted against funding the B-1 bomber, against military aid to the Chile dictatorship, and against using government funds to plan assassinations of foreign leaders, among other issues on which they opposed the Ford administration. A majority of women in both parties had voting records that were more liberal than their party leaders.[11]

There is good evidence that the American people are ready to support more women in politics. Gallup Polls show that 70 percent believe the nation would be governed as well or better if more women held political office. And 73 percent in

---

[10]Ibid., p. 35. For an earlier, somewhat similar study, see Jean Grossholtz and Susan C. Bourque, "Politics as an Unnatural Practice: Political Science Looks at Female Participation" (paper delivered at the 1973 annual meeting of the American Political Science Association).

[11]Clayton Fritchey, "The Women's Caucus," *Washington Post,* April 24, 1976.

1976 said they'd vote for a women for president – up from 66 percent 4 years earlier and only 31 percent in 1937. But the first complete count ever of all women elected to public office in the United States, taken in 1975, found that women occupy only 5 percent of all elective offices. In state legislatures, only 4 percent of senators and 9 percent of representatives are women. This underrepresentation extends even to local school boards, which have only 13 percent women.[12]

Administering These years, women tend to get favorable mention as job candidates from politicians – but little else. The percentage of women in high posts in the government bureaucracy in 1972 was still only 2.3 percent – up from 2 percent 5 years earlier. In 1969, President Nixon declared that "a woman can and should be able to do any political job that a man can do." But he never appointed a woman to the cabinet or the Supreme Court. His successor, Gerald Ford, did appoint a woman to his cabinet. But when he was urged by many, including his wife, to appoint a woman to the Court, he found it impossible to find a "qualified" woman.

That decision reminded some of Abigail Adams' plea to her husband, John Adams, to "Remember the Ladies" while drafting the Constitution. John Adams's response was, "I cannot but laugh. . . . We know better than to repeal our Masculine systems." And when Betty Ford stated her support for abortion, President Ford criticized the Supreme Court decision making it constitutional. So Letty Cottin Pogrebin, a feminist activist, wrote: "Thanks to Abigail Adams and Betty Ford, we have learned that we cannot marry power; we must have it ourselves. . . . Asking men to Remember the Ladies just won't do. We must speak for ourselves, fight for ourselves, invent our own futures. In the nation's third century, let us celebrate the Bicentennial in the only way that makes sense. By using our vote, our voice and our rage to plot the next and deepest American Revolution – the one that frees the real silent majority: womankind."[13]

Women's challenges to the American political system

Movement origins Women were active in the antislavery movement early last century, and in a sense the origins of the women's rights movement might be traced to their experience there. In 1840 there was a World Antislavery Convention in London. The American women delegates were refused admission to it because of their sex. When the American men then refused to participate, a compromise was reached: the women were allowed to sit in the balcony – but only with a curtain drawn in front of them so they wouldn't distract the men by their presence.[14]

The outrage of women at this treatment by supposedly enlightened men led eventually to the calling of a Women's Rights Convention at Seneca Falls, N.Y., in 1848. It issued a "Women's Declaration of Independence," modeled on the

[12]The survey was conducted by the Center for the American Woman and Politics at Rutgers University. Eileen Shanahan, "Women Occupy 5% of Elected Offices, First Count Shown," *New York Times,* January 26, 1976.

[13]Letty Cottin Pogrebin, "Sexism Rampant," *New York Times,* March 19, 1976.

[14]Page Smith, "From Masses to Peoplehood," *Historical Reflections* 1, no. 1 (1974): 118.

Burt Glinn/Magnum

American Declaration and drafted by activist Elizabeth Cady Stanton. The Declaration said in part: "We hold these truths to be self-evident: that all men and women are created equal. . . . The history of mankind is a history of repeated injuries and usurpation on the part of man toward woman, having in direct object the establishment of absolute tyranny over her. . . . He has endeavored in every way that he could, to destroy woman's confidence in her own powers, to lessen her self-respect and to make her willing to live a dependent and abject life."

Stanton and some others advocated then that women have "a sacred right to the elective franchise." But this question of the right to vote split the movement then. For some time thereafter, most active efforts were directed at self-help through trade union organization and negotiation with employers. But at this time, as we shall see in more detail in Chapter 16, even men had difficulty organizing unions, and little was gained by women using this approach.

The turn toward legal protection As a result, women turned to governments for protection. Constitutional interpretation at that time reserved to the states the power to police business and private property in the interest of health, welfare, and safety. So appeals were made to the states. The leading organization then was the Women's Christian Temperance Union (WCTU). Its name, however, is misleading, for it campaigned not only against alcoholic beverages, but also for city sanitation, child labor laws, abolition of prostitution, improved working conditions, and many other progressive causes. The WCTU was very well organized. It has some forty departments and perhaps 10,000 local "unions" or branches. It succeeded in getting passed a variety of laws protecting women, particularly in the workplace. But because the laws did not apply to men also, men were able to get and keep the riskier, more demanding jobs. So to women were left the jobs with lowest pay and least prospects of advancement.[15]

The turn toward legal equality When it became clear that such protective legislation was not enough, women shifted to seeking laws designed to achieve equality. This has been the focus of what is now usually called the women's liberation movement (WLM) in its political manifestations. The WLM could trace its origins back at least as far as the early years of this century, as the description of presently active women's political groups in Action Unit 15.1 reveals. Two organizations have been particularly prominent in recent efforts to achieve equality through law: the National Organization for Women (NOW) and the National Women's Political Caucus (NWPC).

Women's organizations The National Organization for Women (NOW) was founded in 1966 and has headquarters in Chicago. Within a decade it had about 60,000 members, mostly white and middle-class. Its concerns have been such issues as passage of the ERA and improvement in the job opportunities and pay of

[15]The WCTU continues active to this day, claiming some 250,000 members and 4500 local unions and fighting the abuse of alcohol while opposing the ERA.

working women. In recent years, in an effort to broaden its base and meet criticism, it has also taken up concerns of housewives, such as obtaining job training for divorced or widowed homemakers and establishing a "homemakers' bill of rights" giving each partner in a household legal right to equal portions of household income.

But because NOW has not met the needs of certain groups of women, other groups have sprung up. One such is the National Congress of Neighborhood Women, which tries to serve the needs of working women in poor neighborhoods. Using federal funds, it develops special courses and services to train working women, and deals with problems of housing, health care, day care, and employment.

Aimed at the housewife is another, newer group, the Martha Movement (Suite 2610, 1022 Wilson Blvd., Arlington Va. 22209), which takes its name from the Biblical figure who was Mary's sister and spent her time working in the kitchen. Its local chapters attempt to offer support to women who wish to remain housewives but don't like the criticism and hostility they get. The focus is on establishing "women's centers" where women can compare experiences and "child-care entertainments" at shopping centers to free the mother to shop. Thus far, the Martha Movement has not moved into political action.

Such lobbying is done by NOW and by other groups such as the Women's Lobby in Washington. But the practical, political arm of the women's movement is the National Women's Political Caucus, founded in 1971 by such activists as Representative Bella Abzug, black organizer Fannie Lou Hamer, author Betty Friedan, and journalist Gloria Steinem. At the founding meeting, Steinem declared: "We don't want to elect female Uncle Toms who are themselves imitating men, and who, once in power, only serve to keep their sisters down. But we do want to take our rightful position as 50 percent of every elected and appointed body in this country. No one gives political power. It must be taken. And we will take it."[16]

Since then, NWPC has run technical workshops on electoral politics at its biennial conventions, proposed women as nominees for governmental jobs, lobbied political parties for greater female representation, and lobbied candidates for more support of women's issues and passage of ERA.

□ WOMEN AND THE POLITICS OF POLICY

■ Responses of the American political system to women

The women's movement has already achieved passage of important legislation. In 1963 Congress passed the Equal Pay Act, which extended protection to some—but far from all—women workers. In 1964 opponents of the Civil Rights Act inserted women in it as another group to be protected. They did so in order to increase opposition to the bill, which was intended to help blacks. But favorable public reaction to the inclusion of women instead helped the bill pass.

---

[16]Quoted by Tim O'Brien, "Women Organize—For More Power," *Washington Post,* July 11, 1971.

An amendment to the Equal Pay Act passed in 1972 extended its coverage to the professions. Subsequent executive orders by presidents have banned job discrimination against women and minorities in the federal government and by federal contractors. Nonetheless, studies of government salaries still show considerable inequality. As one observer concluded after studying government pay scales, "When women – black, white, red, or Spanish-speaking – yell about pay discrimination, they have something to yell about."[17]

Most of the progress being made in women's rights is being made in the courts. It hasn't always been that way. In 1948 the Court upheld a law that prohibited a woman from being a bartender unless she was the wife or daughter of a male bar owner. This ruling meant that a woman could be a bartender if her father owned the bar but not if he died and her mother became the owner. It meant that a woman could tend bar in a tavern owned by her husband, but not in one owned by her brother – or by herself. It meant that a woman could be a waitress in a bar but not a bartender.

None of this bothered the Court in 1948. But in 1976, just 28 years to the day after the original decision, the Court changed its mind. It held unconstitutional an Oklahoma law which prohibited the sale of 3.2 percent beer to men under the age of 21 and to women under the age of 18. It held that this discrimination – against young men – was unconstitutional because it was not "substantially related to important governmental objectives." In other words, sex discrimination is only legal if it involves a matter of important governmental objectives.

This decision was the first sign that there might be a Court majority opposed to most sex discrimination. But 1977 decisions against "sick-leave" pay for pregnancy and against Medicaid abortions for the poor raised new doubts. Meanwhile, the laws, both federal and state, are full of sex discrimination. And without the ERA every such law must be struck down by the courts, one by one.[18] Progress *has* been made. Until recently court cases on sex discrimination averaged but 5 a year – 500 total in 100 years. But in a 10-month period in 1974–1975 there was a burst of over 300, and the number has been increasing rapidly ever since.

Meanwhile, Congress has passed more laws guaranteeing to women the right to get credit, the right to participate equally in school sports, and the right to

---

[17]Mike Causey, "Men Top U.S. Pay Scales," *Washington Post,* December 29, 1976.

[18]For an account of this case, see the editorial "Equal Rights: Still a Way to Go," *Washington Post,* December 27, 1976.

Anti-ERA rally, Washington, D.C., 1977.
Wide World Photos

pensions and to tax deductions for childcare expenses, as well as the right to attend the military academies. But, in the words of Margaret Gates of the Center for Women's Policy Studies, "In effect, Congress wins votes by saying 'Thou Shalt Not Discriminate' – but when it comes right down to it, they back off on putting teeth into it. That's where we have to go next – to Congress and the agencies" to get stronger enforcement provisions.[19]

The breadth of women's policy issues can be seen in the list of priorities specified as a "bill of rights" for women by the first NOW national conference in 1966:

- □ passage and ratification of the ERA
- □ enforcement of laws banning sex discrimination in employment
- □ gaining maternity leave rights in employment and in social security benefits
- □ granting of tax deductions for home and child-care expenses for working parents
- □ availability of child day-care centers for all
- □ achievement of equal and nonsegregated education
- □ provision of equal job training opportunities and special allowances for women in poverty
- □ recognition of the right of women to control their reproductive lives through access to contraception and abortion[20]

It is a mark of the successes of the movement thus far that progress has been made on all of these objectives. But it is an indication of the extent of the needs and problems that, at its tenth anniversary conference in 1977, new concerns were added to the agenda (especially those dealing with needs of housewives), but none could yet be removed as having been fully achieved.

□ THE RIGHTS OF THE YOUNG

■ The right to vote

Eighty million American citizens are still legally denied the right to vote – because they are "children." They constitute the largest group in the country – larger than that of adult men, and larger than that of adult women.

Why are all people (with the exception of a few in several states) under the age of 18 denied that right? Is it because they are not competent to vote? No adults are checked for competence. Is it ignorance? We've seen in earlier chapters the extent of ignorance of many adult voters, yet they are not therefore denied the right to vote. Presumably, we deny the young that right because they are in some sense immature or incapable of voting – or perhaps of voting wisely. But why 18? Why not 16? or 14? or 10?

A supporter of the present voting age of 18 might counter by saying that there's no real reason why they should be allowed to vote. He or she might point

---

[19]Quoted in *U.S. News & World Report,* July 21, 1975, p. 22.

[20]See Jo Freeman, *The Politics of Women's Liberation* (New York: McKay, 1975).

out that 18-year-olds were granted the right when they were being required to fight in Vietnam and so had a special interest in public policy. But children too have a large and growing interest in public policy – not just on issues of war and peace, but also on education, health, welfare, and discrimination. Just when is a child mature enough to vote and to influence public policy? Does a child have rights?

■ The rights of children

As recently as 1967, children had no rights at all. Until that time, the Bill of Rights was thought to apply only to adults. In that year, the Supreme Court decided a case called *In re Gault,* brought by the father of one Gerald Gault, seeking his release from an industrial school. Gault had been sentenced in juvenile court to 6 years in the school for making an obscene phone call. In his hearing he did not have a lawyer, his parents were not allowed to see the complaint against him, he was not allowed to cross-examine the person who complained, and he was prohibited from appealing by Arizona law. Had he been over 18, the maximum Arizona sentence for making an obscene phone call would have been a fine of $5 to $50 or 2 months in jail, and he would have been entitled to the above rights and the others in the Arizona and U.S. Constitutions.

The Supreme Court considered the case and decided, for the first time in history, that "it would be extraordinary if our Constitution did not require the procedural regularity and the exercise of care implied in the phrase 'due process.' Under our Constitution, the condition of being a boy does not justify a kangaroo court," one which pays no attention to fair rules of procedures. This decision granted children new rights – some, but not all, of the rights guaranteed by the Bill of Rights. The Bill of Rights uses language such as "no person" and "the accused" that might seem to be universal. But according to the courts, children still don't have rights to bail or trial by jury, for example.

■ The political system's treatment of children

As one expert, Gilbert Steiner, has written, "When politicians consider legislation affecting children generally, they do so hesitantly and reluctantly, knowing that the American social system presumes that barring economic disaster or health crisis, a family should and will care for its children without public intervention."[21] But many of them need, and a large number get, governmental help, as Steiner indicates:

- □ About 8 million get "aid to families with dependent children," one type of welfare, every month – but more than 9 million live in poverty and need.
- □ Some 25 million get federally subsidized school lunches.
- □ About 285,000 preschool youngsters from poor families are in Head Start programs.
- □ Some 3 million children get state or local welfare aid.
- □ And another 140,000 get private aid of one sort or another.

---

[21]Gilbert Y. Steiner, *The Children's Cause* (Washington, D.C.: Brookings Institution, 1976), p. 1.

The federal government has a long but slowly growing history of involvement. The first White House conference on children occurred in 1909. Three years later, a Children's Bureau was set up to study and report on the welfare of children. When Congress passed several bills outlawing child labor, in the 1920s the Supreme Court declared them unconstitutional overextensions of federal power. Congress then passed a proposed constitutional amendment granting it the "power to limit, regulate, and prohibit the labor of persons under eighteen years of age" in 1924, but only twenty-eight of the thirty-eight required states ratified it. Eventually, the Court sustained child labor laws passed in 1937. But private Catholic charities in big cities, which got public money for their child welfare programs, were sufficiently strong to force the government to limit other federal programs to rural children until 1958. And it was only in the Johnson and Nixon years that federal programs for children grew by leaps and bounds, with programs such as limited day care and Head Start, and a new Office of Child Development in the Department of Health, Education, and Welfare.

The lobbyists for children In the development of such programs, the interests of children are lobbied for by various groups. The oldest of them is the Child Welfare League of America (CWLA), founded in 1920 as a league of voluntary organizations and today the most conservative child lobby. At the other end of the action spectrum is the Children's Defense Fund (CDF), a nonprofit organization of lawyers, researchers, and lobbyists, supported by foundations. CDF is dedicated to long-range advocacy for children, with six priority areas of concern:

- the right to education for children excluded from school
- elimination of classification and labeling of children (as retarded, for example)
- the right to treatment and education for children in special institutions
- the proper care and treatment of children by juvenile justice systems
- the right to adequate medical care and the delivery of health services for children.
- the use and abuse of children as subjects for medical and drug research.[22]

The coming questions of children's needs and rights

If anything, the needs of children seem to be growing. Two million children ran away from home in 1976. Suicide is the third leading cause of death for those between the ages of 15 and 24. The juvenile crime rate is higher than that of any other age group and is growing faster than the juvenile population. The rate of childbirth out of wedlock has doubled in the last 30 years. These signs indicate there will be plenty of issues to be studied and programs to be supported by organizations like the CDF.

Many issues raise questions of children's rights directly. There is still a major dispute over whether children should have the right to medical care including

[22]For an account of children's lobbies and the politics of government programs, see Steiner, *The Children's Cause.*

contraception and abortion without their parents' consent. Similarly, it is unclear whether children have a right to decide which parent gets custody of them when the parents divorce. Does a child have a right to keep whatever money he or she earns working? Should children be able to sue their parents for neglect?

The questions of the rights of young people seem almost endless. Few of them have yet found their way into legislation or adjudication in court.[23] The states or the federal government already try to protect children from such abuses as child labor, exploitation, incest, physical brutatility from parents, drugs and alcohol, pornography, rape, and other problems. But what about hitchhiking, for example? And what about the questions involving the rights of students in school?

By the same token, the welfare-oriented actions that the governments undertake for children are now being questioned by some while others term them grossly inadequate. Steiner's conclusion is that "the children's policy most feasible – and most desirable – is one targeted on poor children, handicapped children, and children whose parents cannot provide them a start equal to that provided most children.[24] But others note Reginald Lourie's warning that "there is serious thinking among some of the future-oriented child development research people that maybe we can't trust the family alone to prepare young children for this new kind of world which is emerging."[25] So children and politics seem certain to be linked more and more in coming years.

□ THE ELDERLY IN AMERICA

Today, one in every ten Americans is 65 or older. But by the time you're that old, if you're a typical college student, one in every five Americans will also be old. In large measure, the elderly are supported by governmental services paid for by taxes that are paid by those still working. In 1955, there were seven people working and paying taxes for every retired person whom those taxes in part supported. In 1969 there was one retiree for every four workers. In 1974 there were three workers for every retiree. Now, every day in America 4000 people celebrate their sixty-fifth birthday, while 3000 people over age 64 die. This means that, because the death rate in America is at an all-time low, there are 1000 more elderly Americans every day. So by next century, a mere 20 years off, there will be but two workers for each person retired. In 1900 those over 65 made up only 4 percent of the U.S. population. By 1920 the figure had risen to 4.6 percent; by 1940, to 6.8 percent; by 1960, to 9.2 percent; and by 1975, to 10.4 percent. According to some projections, those over 65 will make up over 20 percent of the U.S. population by the year 2000. Figure 15.1 projects the growth of the U.S. population age 65 and older.

The aged are indeed "our future selves," for each of us who lives long enough will sooner or later become aged. But they are in another sense parts of our present

---

[23]For a status report, see the paperback volume edited by Alan Sussman for the American Civil Liberties Union, *The Rights of Young People* (New York: Avon, 1977).

[24]Steiner, *The Children's Cause,* p. 255.

[25]Quoted from 1971 congressional testimony by Steiner, *The Children's Cause,* p. 255.

selves, for we live in society with them, help to support them, and feel the impact of their actions quite regularly in economics, society, and politics.

Many of these elderly are poor. Some 16 percent are below the poverty line now—compared to 30 percent in 1961, before Medicare and increased social security. But the median (or middle) income of the elderly is $4,888 a year, compared to $12,400 for those aged 18 to 64. The poor especially depend on us for help, but today not all of them get it, although polls show that 80 to 90 percent of the American people believe that society should support the aged because they have earned such support by working all their lives.

■ The problems of the aged

The biggest problem of our aged today is *economic security.* They have to live on relatively fixed incomes in an era of large inflation, so their limited dollars buy less and less. A Harris Survey in 1975 found that 15 percent of the aged cited "not enough money to live on" as a serious problem. The White House Conference on Aging in a 1971 poll found that over half of the elderly didn't have enough money to cover marginal living expenses. One reason for this is the rapidly rising cost of health care. Even with Medicare, the average older American had to pay $392 out of pocket for health in 1975.

A second growing problem for the elderly living in big cities is *physical security.* The rapid rise of crime takes its highest toll against the elderly, who are least able to escape or to defend themselves against hoodlums and deceivers.

Finding ways to live *a meaningful life* after retirement is a third major problem. In 1900, some 68 percent of all men over 65 were still working. By 1960 that figure had dropped to 30 percent. Since then, with the spread of "mandatory retirement" rules, it is down to 25 percent. In fact, the average retirement age continues to drop and is now approaching 60. By 1970 only 75 percent of all men 60 to 64 were still working. Early and mandatory retirement are problems in our society, not only because they often increase the ranks of the poor, but also because we tend to view retirement, not as an achievement, but rather as withdrawing from something. As a result, many people miss their work once it is behind them.

FIGURE 15.1

U.S. Census Bureau's projection of growth of the U.S. population age 65 and over, 1980-2040.

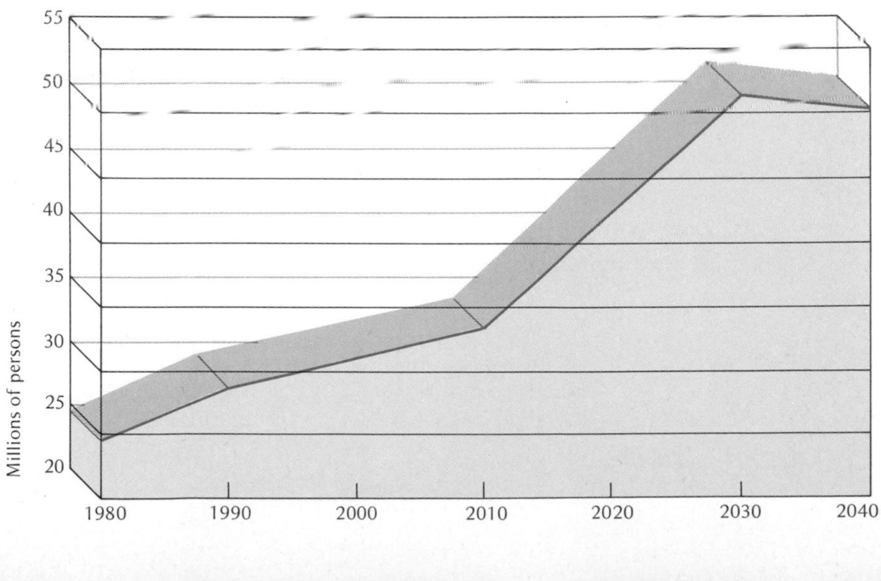

In June 1976 the Supreme Court, by an eight-to-one vote, upheld a Massachusetts law requiring policemen to retire at age 50, regardless of their health. It argued that states are justified in assuming that the ability to perform official duties decreases with age, and so in forcing early retirement. In the Court's view, drawing a line at age 50, unlike using race or religion as a criterion, "cannot be said to discriminate only against the elderly. . . . Instead, it marks a stage that each of us will reach if we live out our life span." In fact, all the judges on the Court had already reached and passed that stage – and were still working. The youngest justice was then 51 and the average age of the justices was 63. But all of them were protected by the Constitution against forced retirement at any age except for bad behavior.

The following year, however, Congress passed a law extending the Age Discrimination in Employment Act so that it prohibits mandatory retirement until 70 for federal workers and private industry workers alike. This action followed similar laws passed by a number of states from Maine to California. An end to mandatory retirement before 70 will please the many active employees who don't want to quit working as they approach 65. But it also makes it more difficult for the young and minorities to get jobs, because fewer new jobs are being opened up by retirement. So this is a case where ending discrimination against one group automatically brings increased discrimination, practically speaking, against others.

Of course, continued work is not the only way for the elderly to maintain or increase their feelings that life is meaningful. Continuing or adult education is another – and one increasingly being tailored to the needs and interests of the aged.

For those who no longer like their jobs, early retirement may open up new possibilities – if they have adequate pensions. But fewer than half of all retirees now have pensions, and so the rest must live on Social Security alone – if they have that. Thus early retirement may not be an option for most, unless and until the benefits available to the elderly are improved.

■ **What the elderly believe politically** Studies show that the elderly tend to be more conservative than the rest of the population on such issues as school busing, abortion, legalization of marijuana, women's rights, and protest politics generally.[26] These findings led many to conclude that as you get older you get more conservative. This phenomenon is called a "maturational effect" because maturing seems to cause the change. However, more careful analysis of the studies has disproved this conclusion. What actually happens is that the attitudes of people aging generally stay the same, but the views of new, younger generations become more liberal. So when we compare the actual views held by the elderly (which are basically the same views they've held all their adult lives) with the views of others younger than they, we are really noticing a "generational fact" rather than a "maturational fact."[27]

---

[26]See Neal E. Cutler and John R. Schmidhauser, "Age and Political Behavior," in *Aging,* ed. Diana Woodruf and James Birren (New York: Van Nostrand Reinhold, 1976), chap. 18.

[27]See Norval Glenn, "Aging and Conservatism," *Annals of the American Academy of Political and Social Science* 415 (1974): 176–186.

TABLE 15.3

The elderly in Congress, 1976

	In the Senate	In the House
Percent over 65[a]	24	12
Number 65–74	18	43
Number 75–84	8	7
Median age[b]	56	50

[a]In the U.S. population, 10 percent are over 65.
[b]Median age is the age which divides the group into two equal sections, half older than it and half younger. The median age of the U.S. population is 28 years.

There are only two major exceptions to this general rule. As they get older, people tend to get more liberal on two questions: support for Medicare and for government guarantees of full employment. Beyond these, the elderly usually do not forsake their lifetime attitudes and voting patterns.

■ What the elderly do politically

Voting One in every six voters now is over the age of 65. But it is commonly believed that as people age they lose their interest in politics and vote less. It is true that those who are old now as a whole vote less than those who are middle aged. But we find generally that the better educated people are the more they vote. We also find that historically women have voted less than men. The majority of the present elderly are less well educated, and the majority are women. So experts now believe that the fact that those presently aged vote less is a reflection of these long-standing tendencies. In other words, those elderly who don't vote now didn't vote when they were younger either. Indeed, research shows that in fact the interest in politics actually grows as people get older. The aging seem to engage in all but the most strenuous types of political activity, such as canvassing.[28]

Serving We still know relatively little about officeholding among the elderly except those at the national level, where it's easy to count. Table 15.3 shows the overrepresentation of the elderly in the Senate and House in comparison to their percentage in the population. This overrepresentation might suggest that the elderly would be well taken care of. But experience suggests, to the contrary, that the elderly in Congress rarely show special concern for the elderly in the population.

Administering Federal law until 1977 prohibited people over the age of 70 from continuing to serve in the bureaucracy – but not in appointive posts, such as justices of the Supreme Court or ambassadors, nor in elective posts. In 1977, as we noted earlier, Congress removed the provision for mandatory retirement at 70, but this new law's effect has not yet been widely felt.

■ The elderly's challenges to the American political system

Groups supporting the elderly first became prominent during the Depression of the 1930s. A major reason for this, besides the troubled economic times, was the fact that the Social Security Act of 1935 provided for government payments to citizens who reached old age. This made it possible for the aged to live alone even after retirement, where previously they generally had to live with their children when they could no longer support themselves. Further, the precedent of Social Security drew more attention to pensions generally, which were in most cases still inadequate to support the few elderly lucky enough to have them.

[28]See Norval Glenn and M. Grimes, "Aging, Voting, and Political Interest," *American Sociological Review* 33 (1968): 563–575.

Wide World Photos

Senior citizens rallying at the New York state capitol in Albany to protest cuts in health-care programs for the elderly.

Interest groups Today, there are three major groups representing the interests of the elderly. The oldest, dating from 1921, is the 200,000 member National Association of Retired Federal Employees (NARFE). The largest is the combination of the National Retired Teachers Association (NRTA), established in 1947, and the American Association of Retired Persons (AARP), founded in 1958. The first, more specialized group includes half a million retired teachers. The second, AARP, is made up of 9.5 million people 55 or older. The two groups have the same staff and devote most of their attention to providing services to members such as insurance, travel programs, and tax assistance.

The most politically active of the three groups is the National Council of Senior Citizens (NCSC). This group grew out of the 1960 "Senior Citizens for Kennedy" groups and was established to fight for passage of Medicare. It consists of about 3500 local clubs and twenty-three state affiliates, many of whose members come from organized labor. It keeps its members informed of important votes coming up in Congress so that they can lobby effectively.

The liberal and labor-oriented political stance of the NCSC encouraged the 1975 founding of the more conservative National Alliance of Senior Citizens (NASC), with some 20,000 members, free from labor influence, but still without much political clout.

Other somewhat specialized groups have also been founded recently. In 1970 came the National Caucus on the Black Aged, established to represent its 2 million aged black members. And then in 1975 the Asociacion Nacional Pro Personas Mayores was founded in Los Angeles to do the same for Spanish-speaking elderly.

But perhaps the most interesting of the special groups is the Gray Panthers, founded in Philadelphia in 1970 to combat "ageism" abuses through direct action inspired by Saul Alinsky. The Gray Panthers were founded with the motto "age and youth in action," and the group includes young as well as older members in its fifteen chapters in various cities.

Other interest groups represent professional gerontologists – those who study and work with the aged. The Gerontological Society, for example, established in 1945, has 2500 members. And the National Council on the Aging (NCOA), founded in 1950, has 2200 involved organizations as affiliates. Both serve as information sources for professionals.

Because some 4 percent of the elderly are in nursing homes, there are interest groups concerned with them too. On one hand is the American Association of Homes for the Aging, which has as members 1400 nonprofit homes and 200 professionals involved with them. On the other hand is the American Nursing Home Association, which is "reputed to be extremely powerful in gaining immunity from public accountability and from enforcement of regulations"[29] for the owners of profit-making nursing homes.

Lobbying How important these organizations are in influencing legislation is far from clear. So far, the evidence is that there is not an "aging vote" as such, and politicians are aware of that. Nonetheless, there are occasional instances where aging interest groups play important roles.

In 1974 the administration stopped spending funds for housing for the elderly. The NCOA and the AAHA then formed a coalition to seek funds in Congress for its continuation. They worked in cooperation with the Republican Task Force on Aging in the House and with the Senate Select Committee on Aging staff. The House authorized funds following a flood of letters from senior citizens across the country. And in the conference the Senate agreed to a compromise sum. But the Housing and Urban Development Department (HUD) tried to prevent the program nonetheless by refusing to issue regulations and release funds for it. So the "gray lobby" organized a group of elderly picketers, who paraded around HUD headquarters. HUD gave in.

In another instance, large flows of letters from the aging asking regulation of the funeral industry prompted action by the Federal Trade Commission.

Such examples suggest that the aged can have an influence when they are mobilized. But up to now, the organizations tend to represent only the middle-class aged and those with trade union connections. The large numbers of elderly who are poor still lack adequate representation. Nonetheless, many government programs on the aged have been intended to help them.

■ Responses of the American political system to the elderly

Social Security was the first major federal program directly addressing the needs of the aging. Since 1935, the United States has moved closer and closer to becoming a welfare state in which the government meets the various human needs of the citizens. More and more it appears that the "welfare state is fundamentally focused on the aged."[30]

Today, some government programs are "*direct income maintenance*" programs. Social Security and related programs are the strongest examples. Others involve "*indirect income maintenance*" through food stamps, for example, which free up some income for other uses by providing food free or at a discount. Others involve *health*

---

[29]See Robert B. Hudson and Robert H. Binstock, "Political Systems and Aging," in *Handbook of Aging and the Social Sciences*, ed. Binstock and Ethel Shanas (New York: Van Nostrand Reinhold, 1976), p. 386. This piece discusses organization of the aging. So, in more detail, does Henry J. Pratt, *The Gray Lobby* (Chicago: University of Chicago Press, 1976). For guidance on action, see Linda Horn and Elma Griesel, *Nursing Homes: A Citizens' Action Guide* (Boston: Beacon, 1977), and Robert Butler, *Why Survive? Growing Old in America* (New York: Harper & Row, 1975), especially pp. 343–349.

[30]Harold Wilensky, *The Welfare State and Equality* (Berkeley: Univ. of California Press, 1975), p. 27.

care: Medicare and Medicaid. Still others provide *social services* such as nutrition and legal services programs. And still others are *regulatory actions* such as controls over nursing homes.

The proliferation of federal programs has several important causes. It is, of course, true that the proportion of old people in the population is growing. But as we have seen the aged themselves have had a rather limited role in the passage of new laws. Organized labor has been a major factor. But also important is the fact that the Social Security program legitimized aid to the aged and created large bureaucracies with vested interests in more such programs. At the same time, it encouraged organization of professionals dealing with the aged outside the government into strong groups, such as the American Public Welfare Association (of state and local welfare officials), the National Association of Social Workers, and the National Conference of Social Workers.

These programs make important contributions. But where they are confined to the elderly, they miss much of the problem, for many of these needs – housing, income, health care – arise long before one turns 65. Nonetheless, there are signs that the elderly themselves may be taking a more active role helping themselves and each other to meet their special needs.[31] It remains for us as a society to decide what rights the elderly do have and should have, above and beyond those owing to all citizens. In doing so, we would be wise to listen more closely than before to the beliefs of the elderly themselves. As time passes, our elderly will inevitably become better educated, more socially skilled, more affluent, and in better physical health. Because they also, as elderly, will have high levels of political activity, they may become a powerful force for social change.[32]

But how will political action by the elderly, should it come in greater force, relate to the needs of other groups in society? Will the elderly be fighting for scarce resources against minorities, women, the young, and the handicapped? Or will the fact that so many of the elderly are also members of others of these groups lead them to take a broader view of the continuing, developing needs and desires of Americans? To a large extent, these decisions may well come to lie in our hands – not because we will make them for the elderly, but rather because we will be the elderly.

□ THE OTHER OUTSIDERS

The outsiders we've been studying – women, the young, and the elderly – are the most prominent groups commonly excluded from or limited in participation in politics. But they are hardly the only ones.

■ Homosexuals

Perhaps the other group most actively coming to our attention now is *homosexuals.* There are such social – and political – stigmas attached to homosexuality

[31]See Beth B. Hess, "Self-Help Among the Aged," *Social Policy,* November–December 1976, pp. 55–62.

[32]This argument is developed in B. Neugarten, "Age Groups in American Society and the Rise of the Young-Old," *Annals of the American Academy of Political and Social Science* 415 (1974): 187–198.

that relatively few males ("homosexuals") or females ("lesbians") now "come out," or admit publicly their sexual preferences. Most experts seem in agreement, however, that probably 10 percent of the U.S. population is homosexual, or "gay"—the term most commonly preferred by homosexuals today. There are raging disputes among psychologists, clergy, and other professionals as to the causes of homosexuality and its "naturalness." As a result, there is a patchwork of laws concerning gays around the country—and the Supreme Court has thus far refused to hold that laws discriminating against homosexuals are unconstitutional. Thus the subject of gay rights remains controversial as the gays in society increasingly "come out" and demand an end to discrimination against them.

■ The mentally handicapped

Another large group facing discrimination and exclusion is present and former mental patients, or the *"mentally handicapped"* (as they are increasingly called). No one really knows how many mentally handicapped there are in America. But we do know that one in every ten Americans spends time in a mental institution at some time in his or her life. And according to a recent estimate by the President's Commission on Mental Health, almost 15 percent of the American people are in need of mental health services for problems ranging from serious mental disturbances to alcohol and drug problems, juvenile delinquency, and anxiety.[33] And this figure does not include the 6,400,000 mentally retarded people in America today—1,057,000 of them children.

The problems of the mentally handicapped vary considerably, and so therefore do their needs. So, unfortunately, does the public's willingness to accept former mental patients who can live outside institutions. The result has been government regulations requiring any company having government contracts in excess of $2500 to take affirmative action to employ the mentally and physically handicapped. The government also has new programs to hire the handicapped itself. It also funds special programs to train the retarded. By 1977, twenty-two states and some cities had passed laws recognizing the rights of the handicapped. In addition, private organizations such as the Mental Health Law Project file suits to expand the recognized rights of these people. There are also "mental patient liberation" groups scattered about the country, devoted to giving mutual support to former patients and to defending their rights.

■ The physically handicapped

The physically handicapped have special problems too. Barriers such as curbs, stairways, counters, and so on, make mobility difficult. But most of the handicapped would argue that the most difficult barriers to overcome are social: the unwillingness of most nonhandicapped people to relate openly and comfortably with those who, for example, have lost limbs, cannot speak, or are deaf or blind. Gradually, progress is being made in these areas too. For example, in 1976 the Federal Communications Commission finally approved the use of an electronic system that allows television stations to broadcast printed captions to programs that

---

[33]"Estimated Mental Illness Increases," National Association of Social Workers *News,* October 1977, p. 7.

TABLE 15.4

Number of handicapped American children and teenagers

Handicap	Number affected
Speech impaired	2,293,000
Mentally retarded	1,507,000
Learning disabilities	1,966,000
Emotionally disturbed	1,310,000
Crippled and other health impaired	328,000
Deaf	49,000
Hard of hearing	328,000
Visually handicapped	66,000
Deaf-blind and other multihandicapped	40,000

Source: National Advisory Committee on the Handicapped, *Annual Report,* 1976.

can be received and decoded by special equipment but are otherwise invisible on a normal television set. They would be carried on "line 21," which is the black band that flutters up when you twist the vertical-hold knob on your set. If the networks agree, these "closed" captions would supplement or eventually replace the "open" or visible captions now being telecast by the Public Broadcasting Service on some of its programs to serve the needs of our 13,400,000 Americans with hearing loss. This decision is symptomatic of the gradual progress being made, with private and governmental help, toward equal opportunity for the handicapped. Such progress builds on Public Law 94–142, the Education for All Handicapped Children Act passed by Congress in 1975 and often referred to as the "Bill of Rights for the Handicapped." This law guarantees for all handicapped children an appropriate education – something until then available to only half of such children. (Table 15.4 shows the number of handicapped children and teenagers according to types of handicap in 1976).

The list of "outsiders" can be extended further – even to dwarfs[34] and fat people. Like those whose problems we have been examining here – women, the young, and the elderly – such outsiders confront a world and a political system designed and run by people who may neither know nor care about their special needs and desires. But as our account has shown, outsiders, like minorities, are increasingly challenging our political system. Sometimes they do so by opposing the insiders who run it. Other times they do so by posing policy problems for the system to resolve. In Part 6 we shall examine how the government and the interests interact to produce public policy. And we shall consider major current policy problems involving the economy, poverty and property, the cities, and foreign affairs.

☐ SUGGESTIONS FOR FURTHER READING AND STUDY

The chapter footnotes in each section have already pointed to many useful works, but several others should be mentioned. On women, for history see Eleanor Flexner, *Century of Struggle: The Women's Rights Movement in the United States* (Cambridge, Mass.: Harvard University Press, 1959), and Jo Freeman, *The Politics of Women's Liberation* (New York: McKay, 1975). For policy, see Jessie Bernard, *Women and the Public Interest: An Essay on Policy and Protest* (Chicago: Aldine-Atherton, 1971); Constantina Safilios-Rothschild, *Women and Social Policy* (Englewood Cliffs, N.J.: Prentice-Hall, 1974); and Dorothy Jongeword and Dru Scott, *Affirmative Action for Women: A Practical Guide* (Reading, Mass.: Addison-Wesley, 1973). And for further guidance to the movement or the literature, see Phyllis Butler and Dorothy Gray, *Everywomen's Guide to Political Awareness* (Millbrae, Calif.: Les Femmes Publishers, 1976). On children, see Richard Farson, *Birthrights* (New York: Macmillan, 1974).

The most accessible comprehensive introduction to the aging is Robert N. Butler, *Why Survive? Being Old in America* (New York: Harper & Row paperback, 1975). But for comprehensive treatment in depth of a wide range of more specialized topics, there is no substitute for Robert H. Binstock and Ethel Shanas, eds., *Handbook of Aging and the Social Sciences* (New York: Van Nostrand Reinhold, 1976).

[34]Joseph O. Whitaker, "Dwarfs Measure Up to Huge Problems," *Washington Post,* June 20, 1976.

6 WHAT POLICIES AND PROGRAMS DOES GOVERNMENT PRODUCE?

☐ Perspective 6: The politics of policy making: the case of shoe imports

Take a look at the shoes you're wearing. Where were they made? More likely than not, they were made in a foreign country. If they were either very cheap or very expensive, the odds are overwhelming that they were foreign made. By buying them, you became a part of – part of the cause of – a major policy problem for the United States government.

☐ THE POLITICS OF SHOES

America's policy on shoe imports affected the choice of shoes you had and the price you finally paid, whether or not the shoes you bought were imported. It also continues to affect the cost of living for all of us, the jobs of thousands of Americans, the profits (or losses) of many businesses, and our nation's relations with other countries. Examining the politics behind the development of that policy will tell us much about the process of policy making in America.

On January 6, 1977, just 2 weeks before President Carter took office, the United States International Trade Commission recommended a *tariff-rate quota* on shoes. By doing so, it presented Carter with one of his first difficult policy decisions. To understand what was at issue, and what was at stake, we must first look more broadly at the place of the shoe industry in America's economy, and in the world economy as well.

■ The shoe industry in America

Like all countries, the United States has long had its own shoe industry. Until recently, the factories, concentrated in Massachusetts, Ohio, Wisconsin, Maryland, and Pennsylvania, made most of the shoes Americans wore. In the early 1960s, they employed almost 250,000 people making over 600 million pair of shoes a year, more than three pair for every American each year.

Shoemaking is what is called a labor-intensive, low-skill business. This means the major ingredient is labor, with a low level of skills, rather than capital (money, to buy expensive modern equipment). Because of this, shoemaking is an easy business for a less developed country to enter, for such a country has plenty of unskilled labor but little capital to invest in machinery.

In the 1960s, this is just what happened. In the United States, the cost of making shoes was increasing, for several reasons. American factories did not modernize by developing and buying new, more efficient equipment. Labor costs, at the same time, were increasing three ways. First, wages were rising. Second, employers had to contribute more and more to Social Security and pension plans for many workers. And third, they also were required by our government to improve the working conditions in their factories.

The result was that shoes could be made much more cheaply in a country like Italy. So American businesses began importing more and more shoes from Italy and other countries to sell here to Americans. To import them, they had to pay "duty" – a tax that is a percentage of a product's value – to the government. This duty, or tariff, as it is also called, is imposed in part to raise revenue. Indeed, before the income tax was imposed, such tariffs were the chief source of income for the federal government. But duties have another function: to *protect* domestic industry from foreign competition by raising the price of imported goods.

In earlier years, America had high tariff barriers – a policy often referred to as **protectionism**. In recent decades, efforts have been made by many countries to lower tariffs on most goods and move toward "free trade." Ninety-eight countries do this by getting together and negotiating under what is called the General Agreement on Tariffs and Trade (GATT).

By the 1970s, the American tariff on shoes was only 10 percent of their value. This meant that it would pay a business to import shoes if their cost abroad was low enough that they could still be sold more cheaply once the 10 percent tariff and the cost of shipping were added.

As American wages rose, this became more and more true. By 1976, wages for shoemakers averaged $3.25 an hour in America but only $1.79 in Italy, for example. In 1963, we imported only 14 percent of our shoes. By 1975, it was 45 percent, and in 1977 it was more than 50 percent. In 1963, 604 million pair were "made in U.S.A.," but by 1975 that had dropped to only 413 million. In 1976, some 380 million pair were imported. As a result, some 70,000 U.S. shoe workers had lost their jobs over the years since 1968. And over 15 years the number of American shoe factories had dropped from 1000 to 350. Furthermore, the outlook was for even worse drops. Other countries, with even lower shoe-worker wages, were now exporting to the United States: Spain, 98 cents an hour; Taiwan, 52 cents; and South Korea, 47 cents. Indeed, Taiwan and Korea alone sent 200 million pairs to the United States in 1976, almost all sold for less than $10. Italy shipped 47 million pairs, Spain 39 million, and Brazil 27 million.

Ellis Herwig/Stock, Boston

Workers in New England shoe factory.

The interests and the imports Among those who benefited from this increase in imported shoes were the *consumers*, who were spending a smaller percentage of their incomes on shoes (and other clothing) in the 1970s than they had in previous decades. Other major beneficiaries were the *shoe importers*, of course, and the *retail merchants* who could sell more shoes because prices were lower. In addition, *shipping companies* benefited somewhat, as did the *foreign workers* employed to make shoes for the American market.

But others were badly hurt. Many American *shoe manufacturing companies* – especially the smaller ones – were going out of business because they couldn't compete. And as a result, more and more American *shoe workers* were losing their jobs – permanently.

The result was that the shoe industry and labor both appealed for help from the government. Industry was represented by the American Footwear Industries Association (one of those Washington lobbies we examined in Chapter 11). The workers were represented by such AFL-CIO unions as the United Shoe Workers of America (which represents 40,000 workers) and the Boot and Shoe Workers' Union (35,000).

Industries and unions that want protection from foreign competition go to the United States International Trade Commission (ITC). The ITC was originally created as an independent agency by Congress in 1916, when it was called the Tariff

Commission. In 1970, the shoe interests had asked it for aid. At that time, according to law, such protection could only be granted if imports were the "major" cause of an industry's distress and if there had recently been a tariff reduction. The six commissioners split three to three on the request, and so no aid was granted.

Both industry and labor were unhappy with the difficulty of getting protection from the old commission. At the same time, supporters of freer trade were unhappy with existing limits on how far the president could go in negotiating away existing tariffs. They also opposed the way Congress could delay approving such tariff cuts.

So finally the protectionists and the free-traders reached a compromise agreement on the Trade Act of 1974. That act gave the president the power to negotiate with other countries to reduce or eliminate many tariff barriers. It also provided that Congress had only 60 days to reject the president's proposals before they automatically took effect. Both of these provisions improved the prospects for freer trade. But in return for these concessions, the protectionists got a loosening of the criteria for protection against imports. All that need be shown now is that imports are "a substantial cause" of injury to a domestic industry. The old Tariff Commission was renamed the International Trade Commission and empowered to decide these cases by the Trade Act.

In the Trade Act, the shoe interests were powerful enough to get shoes mentioned specifically as deserving protection. So of course the industry immediately appealed for aid. In 1976, the ITC recommended protection, but President Ford vetoed the suggestion for two main reasons. First, he considered it inflationary, for it would raise the cost of shoes to American consumers. Second, he feared it would cause unrest in Italy among leftist workers who would lose *their* jobs making shoes for America and might then threaten the conservative Italian government, which was an American ally.

Then in 1977, as mentioned at the beginning of this chapter, the ITC once again recommended protection: a "tariff-rate quota." This meant that there would be a new, 40 percent (instead of 10 percent) "tariff rate" on all shoes from a given country above the number imported from that country in 1974 – the "quota." The ITC estimated that this protection would increase production of shoes in America by 15 million pairs a year, increase jobs in the shoe industry by 5000, and cost consumers $190 million a year in higher shoe prices.

■ The interests and the policy makers

According to the law, Carter had 60 days to accept or reject the ITC proposal once it was formally submitted. Immediately, he became subject to intense lobbying from various sides. The shoe industry and labor believed that the recommended protection was insufficient. Instead, they wanted an absolute quota that prohibited any country from shipping any more shoes than it did in 1974. Such a policy would of course result in more domestic shoe production, more jobs, and even higher prices to consumers. Industry and labor argued that if the United States did not protect its domestic shoe industry, soon the whole industry would go out of business. At that point, some suggested, the foreign producers and the importers would be able to raise prices as high as they wished and the United States would have no alternative but to pay. Some even suggested that we might face an "organization of shoe exporting countries" like the oil cartel (Organization of Petroleum Exporting Countries). And still others raised the ominous prospect that, were a war to break out and so interrupt trade, the United States might find itself virtually shoeless.

But there were powerful forces on the other side too, resisting protection and favoring free trade. *Consumers*, who would have to foot the bill, were represented by the Consumer Federation of America (a citizen-interest-group federation of national, regional, state, and local consumer groups). They pointed out that protection would cut the supply of cheap shoes, which are purchased primarily by low-income Americans. They estimated it would raise the price of shoes anywhere from $2 to $10 or more a pair. *Shoe retailers*, who wanted cheaper shoes to sell, joined the opposition too.

They were led by the Volume Footwear Retailers of America, another trade association, which commissioned a study that concluded that the quotas would cost American consumers a total of $500 million a year in higher shoe prices.

Also joining the opposition were those who believe in the principle of free trade, including *exporters*, whose business depends on freer trade. They feared other countries would respond to American shoe protection by other types of protection directed at goods America, the largest exporter of manufactured goods in the world, was then selling abroad.

This lobbying outside the government was matched by comparable debates within it.[1] As part of his introduction to the presidency, President Carter, immediately after his inauguration, was given a series of "Presidential Review Memoranda." PRM 7, given to Carter the day after he took office, concerned a wide range of international trade issues, one of which was shoe imports. Prepared by the National Security Council, which advises the president on foreign policy matters, PRM 7 spelled out the implications of the shoe-import decision Carter would soon have to make.

Meanwhile, other parts of the executive branch were at work on the matter too. The Trade Act of 1974 had established the post of *Special Representative for Trade Negotiations*, in the Executive Office of the President. The Special Representative was made responsible for supervising and coordinating the trade-agreement program. He or she was also to direct American participation in trade negotiations with other countries. The Special Representative is thus a very powerful individual, able to do favors for many important people in the business world as he or she negotiates. He or she also gets a salary of $66,000 a year plus offices in Washington and in Geneva (where most negotiations occur).

Because the Special Representative is so involved in trade questions, it was natural for the occupant of the office to be involved in deciding the American policy on shoe imports. There was only one problem: there was no Special Representative, no occupant of the office. The previous occupant, a Republican, had left with the Ford administration. The post was so important that the various special interests outside the government were lobbying hard to influence Carter's choice of a new appointee. So were other interests within the government, including especially the Departments of Labor, State, and Treasury. The lobbying was so intense that Carter did not make up his mind on a candidate for the post until a month after he took office.

But the lack of a head for this office did not stop its permanent staff, the career, or civil service, officials, who continue to serve under any presidential appointee. Indeed, lack of a head official rarely if ever stops a bureaucracy from functioning, as we noted in Chapter 7. These career bureaucrats sent a memo on the case to the *Economic Policy Group* (EPG) on February 4. It listed five major options

Labor rally, Washington, D.C., April 1975.
Martin Adler Levick/Black Star

[1] We know an unusual amount about how the Carter administration made its decision on shoe imports. As part of his effort to reorganize the White House staff, Carter commissioned studies of how eight important decisions were made, emphasizing good and bad features of the decision process as it actually worked. One of them was the shoe import case. Journalist David Broder of the *Washington Post* was given access to the report on this decision by the White House. He wrote about its contents in "The Case of the Missing Shoe-Import Option," *Washington Post*, July 23, 1977. Many of the details of the following account rely on this article, which, as Broder wrote, gives one "a rare look at the way in which bureaucratic conflicts and sometimes sheer accidents can shape a major decision by the American government."

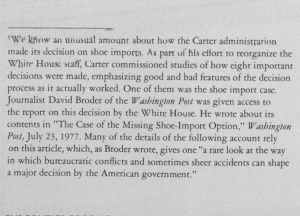

for consideration as United States policy on shoe imports.

The EPG, as its name indicates, is a group of officials formed to advise Carter on questions of economic policy such as shoe import restrictions. The EPG is co-chaired by the secretary of the treasury and the head of the president's Council of Economic Advisors. It includes the vice-president, the secretaries of commerce, labor, and state, the president's National Security Affairs advisor, the Assistant to the President for Domestic Affairs, the director of the Office of Management and Budget, and the Special Representative for Trade Negotiations. All these officials are busy with other responsibilities, but all are involved in economic policy making, and so all bring important perspectives to such a question. The EPG scheduled a meeting for March 25 to discuss the issue.

Lobbying on the issue, inside the government as well as outside, continued through February and March. *The Department of Labor*, not surprisingly, supported the position of labor. Its new deputy under secretary for international affairs, Howard Samuel, had just come to the government from the Amalgamated Clothing Workers Union – a union particularly concerned about large imports of textiles and apparel. The Department of Labor argued that workers needed protection – especially because those most likely to lose their jobs were generally women, minorities, old people, and young people. Also supporting the ITC's recommendation for tariff-rate quotas were the *Departments of Commerce* and

FIGURE P6.1 Conflicting interests in the shoe-import case

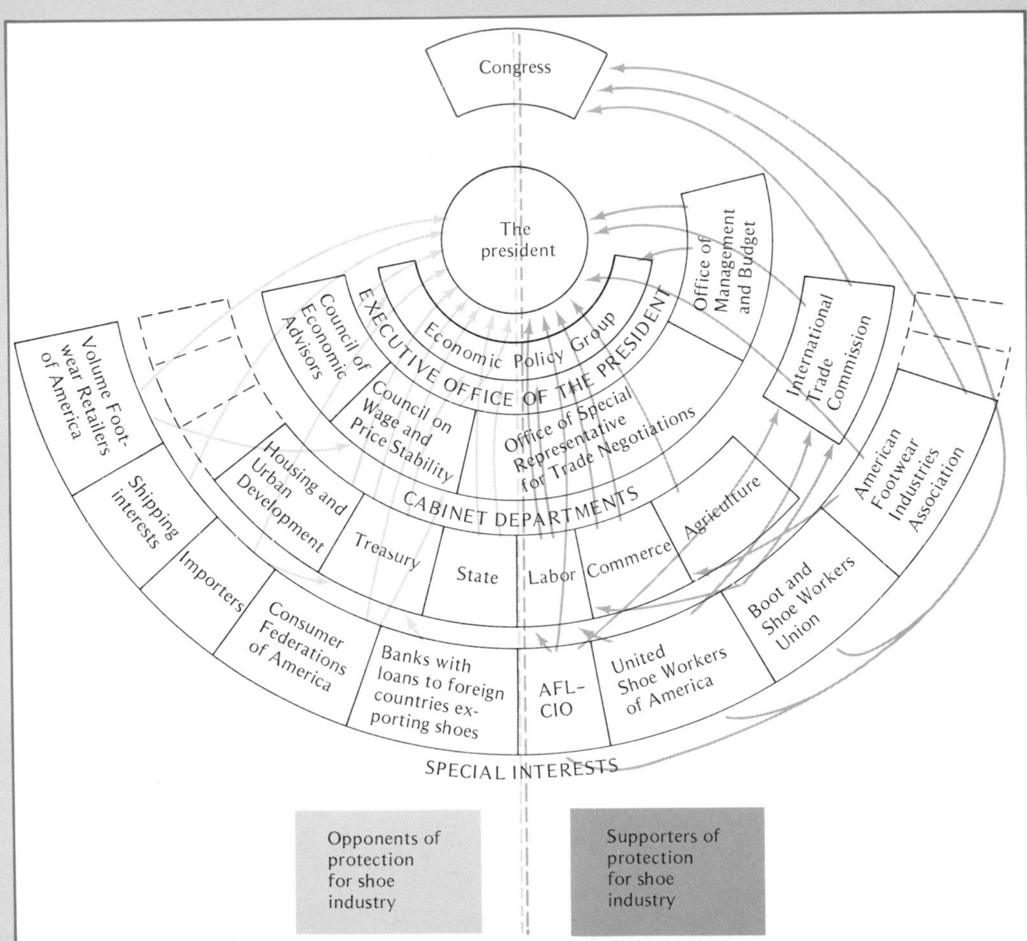

Agriculture, the *Office of the Special Representative for Trade Negotiations,* and the *Office of Management and Budget.*

On the other side, opposing protection, were five agencies. The White House *Council on Wage and Price Stability* opposed the proposal because it would be inflationary. So did the *Council of Economic Advisors,* a group of economists who advise the President on such questions. The *Department of State* opposed it because it prefers having flexibility to offer trade concessions (such as lower tariffs) to other countries in return for their support on political and military questions. The *Treasury Department* also opposed the plan. It supports freer trade as a way of creating greater international economic harmony and stability. It also argues that in the long run American business is hurt by protection, which coddles inefficiency at home and triggers responses of protection abroad, both resulting in economic slowdown. The *Department of Housing and Urban Development* also joined in the opposition, concerned as it is with the interests of consumers and particularly the urban poor.

■ The policy options

Carter faced these conflicting interests arrayed as portrayed in Figure P6.1. He had five major options, as they had been spelled out in the February 4 memo from the Office of the Special Representative to the Economic Policy Group.

1. At the protectionist extreme, he could grant labor and the shoe industry's request to set outright *quotas* limiting the number of shoes that each country could export to the United States in any year. There seemed to be considerable support for such a position in Congress, too, where these interests had lobbied hard.

2. He could accept the recommendation of the ITC for tariff-rate quotas – something that would at least please, if not fully satisfy, labor and the shoe industry, and perhaps the Congress as well.

3. He could reject the ITC recommendation and opt for the status quo: relatively free trade in shoes – a low 10 percent tariff with no quotas at all. This approach would please not only the Departments of Treasury and State, but also the shoe exporting countries and the American consumers and shoe retailers. However, it would infuriate labor, which would then pull out all the stops to get Congress to reverse the decision – a right that Congress had reserved for itself under the Trade Act. Other industries seeking comparable protection – among them steel, electronics, textiles, apparel, and sugar – would also lobby for reversal. They would, however, most likely be opposed by agricultural interests, who fear foreign reprisals against their food exports if America goes protectionist.

4. He could attempt to lessen the impact of shoe imports by increasing "trade adjustment assistance" to workers. This program provides special payments – 70 percent of earnings up to $190 a week for a year – to workers losing their jobs, as well as job retraining. But this program would never satisfy labor, which often refers to adjustment payments as "burial payments" or "flowers on the grave." Labor points out that the program makes no provision for job creation once people are retrained, so that they may well remain unemployed, especially if their closed factory is in a small town with few other job opportunities. Further, such adjustment assistance makes no provision for older workers who can no longer reenter the job market. In the words of an AFL-CIO lobbyist, "It sounds great if you're an economist, but it's pretty pitiful if you're a person. It's roughly an extra year of unemployment compensation for losing a job for the rest of your life."[2]

5. Carter could opt for an OMA – an "orderly marketing agreement." An OMA is a "voluntary" agreement between the United States and an exporting country to limit the number of goods the country ships to the U.S. It is voluntary in the sense that it is not imposed directly by the United States. But it would only be accepted by an exporting country – if at all – under the threat that higher tariffs or quotas would be the only alternative. And it might not satisfy any of the special interests.

[2]Quoted in Robert J. Samuelson, "Will the U.S. Trade Protectionism for Harmony Abroad?" *National Journal,* February 14, 1977, p. 278.

■ Carter's considerations

No one knew just what decision President Carter would make, but most observers expected that he would accept the ITC recommendation. During the campaign he had said, in an address to the Foreign Policy Association, "There are many ways democracies can unite to help shape a more stable world order. We can work to lower trade barriers. . . ." But at the same time he was sending a message to the Amalgamated Clothing and Textile Workers Union saying, "You may be assured as president I would always keep a watchful eye out for your industry to insure that it was not unreasonably prejudiced by unrestrained foreign competition." The shoe manufacturers had raised $100,000 to lobby the Carter administration. They also had contributed small amounts, legally, to his campaign, after being rebuffed by Ford in 1976, and claimed that their support in Ohio, Wisconsin, Maryland, and Pennsylvania had helped elect Carter.

Carter's decision on shoes was complicated by the fact that at the same time the ITC was recommending similar relief for manufacturers of television sets and sugar producers. And the case of textiles and apparel would come to a head shortly, for the existing OMA in that area would expire at the end of 1977, and both labor and industry wanted more relief from foreign competition.

One problem Carter faced was that any move to limit imports would stir fears in other countries that the United States was turning protectionist. These countries might retaliate by cutting their imports of U.S. goods, which would hurt other U.S. businesses. It would also hurt labor, because one of every six American jobs in manufacturing now produces for the export market. Or the countries might simply default on repayment of loans they have from the U.S. government or from U.S. private banks. By 1977, developing countries had outstanding debts of about $250 billion – some $40 billion of it owed to American banks. If these countries cannot sell goods to the United States, they cannot earn the money required to pay off these debts as they come due. If they did default, this would disrupt – and might bankrupt – the major U.S. banks. The consequence of that would be the collapse of the U.S. economy. So even American businesses and banks have a strong interest in allowing other countries to sell their shoes, textiles, and television sets in America.

This means that decisions on protectionist measures are basically "no-win" situations for an American president, in both domestic and international terms. Regardless of his decision, President Carter would have to carry on careful political negotiations with American interests at home and foreign interests abroad in order to carry it out.

The major figure in the diplomatic negotiating abroad is the Special Representative for Trade Negotiations. The threatened business and labor interests wanted a sympathetic supporter of protection appointed to this post. The State and Treasury Departments wanted a free-trade advocate. Neither group got what it wanted. Instead, Carter picked a politician of sorts: Robert Strauss, who had just served as the Democratic Party's national chairman and chief fund raiser. Strauss was known as a good negotiator, able to bring business and labor together. President Carter obviously hoped he would be able to negotiate not only with domestic interests but with foreign interests as well. Perhaps Carter's choice as Special Trade Representative should have foreshadowed his decision on the shoe question. But few read it that way.[3]

The actual process by which the final policy decision was reached was more complex than a simple compromise. It involved bureaucratic politicking of the sort we discussed in Chapter 7. But it also involved bureaucratic mistakes of the sort that no president likes but that a new-to-office president must expect to occur occasionally.

■ The final policy-making process

Round one: the EPG When the Economic Policy Group met as scheduled on Friday, March 25, it

[3]For an account of the politics of Strauss's selection that reveals many of the same political interests as were at work in the shoe-import case, see Robert G. Kaiser, "Politics of Trade Post," *Washington Post*, March 13, 1977.

considered the five available options. Every agency represented favored "adjustment assistance" for the industries, communities, and workers affected by rising shoe imports. But as we noted above, Labor, Commerce, Agriculture, OMB, and the Special Representative for Trade Negotiations favored the ITC recommendation of tariff-rate quotas, while State, Treasury, HUD, and the Council of Economic Advisors opposed any further import relief.

After the meeting, Carter's new appointee as Special Representative, Robert Strauss, sent a memo to Carter summarizing the views of the EPG. In it he developed arguments for and against the major options that had been supported by one faction or the other: adjustment assistance, tariff-rate quotas, and no import relief at all. He did not even mention the orderly marketing agreement (OMA) option, because it had not received support from either the protectionists or the free-traders in the EPG, in that it was something of a compromise.

United Nations/B. Wolff

Shoe factory in Liberia, 1977.

Round two: the EPG and Carter   President Carter was scheduled to meet with the EPG 3 days later, on Monday, March 28, to decide what policy to adopt. Normally such a meeting would decide among the options that had been "staffed out" (studied by the staff of the EPG) and presented in Strauss's memo. But in such a meeting the advice of the Assistant to the President for Domestic Affairs, Stuart Eizenstat, is also asked.

In this case, the White House "paper flow" had been fouled up, and Eizenstat had not gotten a copy of Strauss's memo. So he was unable to comment on the several options as they had been presented there. However, on his own he had previously studied the question in terms of its domestic consequences and the attitudes of Congress and had been leaning toward the OMA option as a compromise. So he raised that option anew, to the surprise of Carter, who had not been prepared for it by Strauss's memo.

Vice-President Mondale, a member of the EPG, had been unable to attend the Friday meeting, but one of Strauss's deputies had, by chance, sent him a different report on the session. In his memo, he raised again the OMA option, pointing out that it might be a good compromise, especially in view of congressional support for protection. As a former senator, Mondale saw the attraction of the OMA option. So when Eizenstat raised it in the Monday meeting, he chimed in with his support.

The result was that discussion shifted away from the two extremes of no protection and tariff-rate quotas toward the OMA option. Carter then instructed Strauss to prepare a new memo on the OMA option.

Round three: memos to Carter   Before Strauss could do so, Eizenstat gave Carter a new memo endorsing OMA. Carter returned it on Wednesday, March 30, with a pencilled note saying he wished he had been given such advice prior to the Monday meeting. Later that afternoon, Strauss's memo arrived. It, too, supported the OMA option

On the same afternoon, Carter was hit by a blizzard of memos on the subject. State sent one opposing OMAs as too protectionist and favoring voluntary self-restraint by Korea and Taiwan. Labor sent one attacking voluntary restraints as inadequate and terming OMAs only slightly better. And in addition an official in London making preparations for the upcoming international economic summit meeting sent in a memo. It favored voluntary restraints as the best policy for the United States to adopt in preparation for Carter's first major international economic conference.

Round four: Carter decides Later that afternoon, Carter finally decided on the OMA option, with an expanded program of "trade adjustment assistance" to total $56 million over 3 years. Two days later, on April 1, he announced the decision as the new American policy on shoe imports. He declared: "I am very reluctant to restrict international trade in any way. For 40 years, the United States has worked for the reduction of trade barriers around the world, and we are continuing to pursue this goal because this is the surest long-range way to create jobs here and abroad." He knew that of the annual world trade of about a trillion dollars in value, almost one-tenth was in exports by the United States. So the general American interest in freer trade was clear. But the policy he announced was without doubt one restricting international trade nonetheless.

It fit into a patchwork of special U.S. controls, constraints, and subsidies that made the profession of a belief in free trade somewhat difficult to believe. Not only the shoes, but also the ships in which they and other goods including oil are sometimes transported, benefit from protection. To Carter, the choice in the case of shoe imports was a compromise between the free trade position he advocated in the abstract, and intense special interest pressures he felt in the concrete.

Round five: Strauss implements Even the compromises were gambles unlikely to satisfy any of the interests most involved. In the case of the shoe imports, Carter charged Strauss with obtaining a voluntary curtailment in shoe imports to the United States from Taiwan and South Korea, which were chiefly responsible for the recent increases in imports. Taiwan agreed to cut its shipments to 122 million pair in the first year, from 156 million in 1976. Korea agreed to reduce its shipments from 44 million to 33 million. The agreements were reached in less than 2 months. As a result, although none of the interests involved was wholly satisfied, Carter and Strauss had managed to achieve a compromise program on the shoe import question.

Round six: Congress considers and agrees But announcement of a policy decision and negotiation of an OMA are not enough to make a policy final. As we noted earlier, Congress has 90 days after the president announces his decision in which to overturn the decision if it wishes to. This means that the politicking shifts to the Congress, where special interests of many sorts often have more access. In this case, by March 18, Carter had received letters from Congress signed by 47 senators and 149 representatives urging him to adopt the ITC's recommendations. So he could anticipate unhappiness with his weaker, compromise position.

He had attempted to soften up the congressional opposition by sending Strauss, who was popular "on the Hill," to brief congressional leaders the morning of April 1 as he was about to announce his decision. Strauss later described the session:

> When I walked into [House Speaker Thomas P.] Tip O'Neill's office, after I had called him and asked him to assemble the 30–40 Congressmen and 15–20 Senators who were primarily interested in the shoe case, they all knew, of course, I was coming to say that we were going to reject the ITC decision and I said, 'I want to tell you what the President is going to do today,' and Tip said, 'I know what he has done; he's sent the only fellow in town up here that could bring the message you are going to deliver and get out without getting lynched.' Everybody laughed . . . but after everyone had had a chance to tell me how terrible the decision was, and what an operator he [Carter] was, how the Senate and House weren't going to stand for it—it took somebody to say, 'Now wait a minute, all Bob's asking for is 60–90 days to work something out and he'll solve this thing if you give him 60–90 days. He's solved it before and that's the least we can do. There is plenty of time to kick him in the ass or override the President." And we did solve it.[4]

[4]Interview, *National Journal*, July 9, 1977, p. 1077.

Whether or not Congress would finally go along with the OMA on shoes, or instead override the president, depended in large part on how the special interest groups reacted. After deliberation, and after analyzing the agreements, the American Footwear Industries Association announced that "it's a good start." The Volume Footwear Retailers of America, the stores, were unhappy. They commissioned yet another study – this one of the impact of the OMA on shoe prices. The study concluded that the OMA would raise the average price of shoes by almost 10 percent in the first 12 months. This meant it would cost American consumers $1 billion in the first year in higher prices. Furthermore, it would result in a "reduced range of choices" of shoes for low-income consumers, according to the study.[5]

Indeed, the Volume Footwear Retailers were so unhappy with the decision that in June they filed suit in a federal court in Brooklyn, New York, seeking to block the OMAs with Taiwan and Korea. Such suits are usually dismissed. But even when they are, they make actions by the government more difficult, and often suits are pressed by both sides. For the Trade Act of 1974 gives industries the right to appeal to the courts, as well as to the Congress, if their requests for government assistance are denied.

In this same period, the administration also reached a similar OMA with Japan limiting its export of television sets to the United States. These OMAs were *programs to deal with specific problems.* But as they increased in number they contributed toward the construction of a *general policy* to deal with the problems caused by increased imports by voluntary agreements rather than by import quota imposed by the United States.

On June 2, Treasury Secretary Michael Blumenthal, in his first press conference since he took office, made the emerging policy clearer. He defended the OMAs on television sets and shoes as necessary to avoid more drastic protectionist measures. He asserted that the Carter administration would continue to resist the extension of import quota restrictions to other industries as the ITC was recommending. He admitted that "any restriction [on imports] is a deviation from open trade principles" to which the United States still subscribes. But he announced that "we would like to see the spread [of OMAs] to other industries."[6]

Thus was the Carter administration's policy on trade and trade restrictions finally clarified. It had begun as responses to particular situations such as shoes and television sets and eventually had become formalized in an announced intention to rely on OMAs. It was finally ratified or legitimated when Congress took no action to overturn the OMAs that Strauss had negotiated.[7] Only time would tell how successfully Carter, Strauss, and other officials could resist the political and economic arguments for stronger protection from the more powerful interests such as steel and the textile-apparel industrial-labor complex.

There are always challenges to policy as it is implemented, just as there are efforts to influence its making. These are but several of the aspects of shoe-import policy making that are typical of policy in many areas. Growing demands of citizens and interest groups tend to focus on the government. These demands, and their outcomes, will vary somewhat from one group of citizens to another, from one agency of government to another, and from one policy area to another. But some sort of compromise or reconciliation is eventually reached in almost every case, through the political process that we call policy making. So let's look more generally at policy making and the policy process. Then we'll compare what we found happening in the case of shoe imports with what usually happens to see how typical the case of shoes is.

---

[5]Richard Lawrence, "Footwear Import Curbs Seen Costing Consumers $1 Billion," *Journal of Commerce,* May 25, 1977.

[6]Hobart Rowen, "U.S. to Resist Spread of Import Quota Curbs," *The Washington Post,* June 3, 1977, p. D10.

[7]Sources for this account of the politics of shoe imports, besides those cited above, include Nick Thimmesch, "The Shoe Tariff Controversy Is Giving Carter Tight Fits," *Chicago Tribune,* April 20, 1977; Philip Shabecoff, "Washington & Business: A Pragmatic Stance on Free Trade," *The New York Times,* June 2, 1977; "Carter's Plan to Stem Imports," *U.S. News & World Report,* April 11, 1977, p. 94.

□ THE NATURE AND TYPES OF POLICY

■ The nature of policy

All of us are policy makers in our everyday lives. We constantly face decisions about what to do – whether to spend the afternoon going to classes or relaxing, whether to spend our limited funds on books or beer, whether to study one subject or another. Often we make these decisions on a momentary, individual case, or ad hoc basis, especially if we think they aren't all that important. When something important is at stake – say, our future opportunity to qualify for a trade or to go to law school – we tend instead to adopt a *policy,* such as "study hardest in the courses that matter most for one's job prospects."

FIGURE P6.2

Common patterns of involvement in policy making

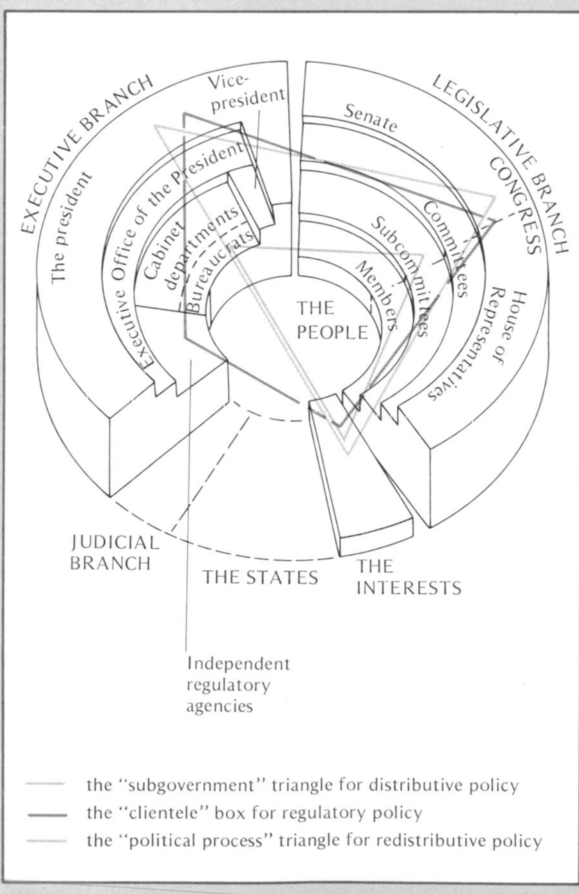

A policy, then, is *a general principle concerning the pattern of activity,* or a general commitment to the pattern of activity, developed or *adopted for use in making particular decisions.*

We often speak of U.S. foreign policy. By this we mean the principle – or really a collection of principles – concerning how our country will relate to other countries: who our allies are, and how we treat them; who our enemies are, and how we relate to them; what economic aid we give to other countries; how we respond to military threats, and so forth. The government uses its foreign policy in deciding how to act in particular cases or how to resolve specific dilemmas. We'll examine American foreign policy in Chapter 19.

The *domestic policy* of the United States is really a large collection of policies on a wide range of subjects. Urban policy includes principles about federal aid for housing and job programs, for example – topics we shall examine in Chapter 18. Policies on minorities are designed to achieve equal opportunities for blacks, browns, and others – our focus in the chapters of Part 5. Economic policy includes principles about how to deal with inflation, unemployment, monopolies, taxes, and other topics we'll study in Chapter 16. Human resources policy covers health, education, and welfare. Natural resources policy includes principles for dealing with pollution of various sorts and energy. And agricultural policy obviously consists of principles about how to guarantee supplies of food to consumers while seeing that farmers get good incomes. Different observers would organize these various policies under different headings, of course. And this list covers only the major topics that arise often in this book, leaving out such other subjects as space policy, medical research policy, and postal service policy.

■ The types of policy

Distributive policy Because there are so many different domestic policy areas of importance, it may be useful to divide the major ones into three categories, as Theodore Lowi has suggested.[8] The first category is *distributive* policies: those by which government tries to stimulate private activity that citizens or groups would not otherwise undertake. The major tool here is a subsidy—a grant of money or special privilege to, say, farmers to grow wheat or a shipping company to maintain its fleet or a railroad to keep up unprofitable service.

Regulatory policy The second type is *regulatory* policies: those by which government sets conditions under which private activities operate. The regulatory agencies such as the Environmental Protection Agency (which we studied in Perspective 3) and the Federal Communications Commission (Chapter 12) make rules or issue licenses to regulate some business and industry.

Redistributive policy The third category is *redistributive* policies: those in which the government acts in ways that benefit one group of people at the expense of another group. A policy of taxing the rich to pay welfare benefits to the poor is an example.

Just which policy makers are important in shaping policies tends to depend on the type of policy being made. For example, distributive policy is most often made by "subgovernments," as we discussed in Part 3 – bureau officials, congressional subcommittee representatives, and lobbyists for the interests involved. Regulatory policy is often made by the process we discussed in Part 4 as "clientele" influence – the regulator-bureaucrats and the congressional figures responding to the needs and desires of those in the private sector who are supposed to be regulated. Redistributive policy, on the other hand, is generally made by the conventional political process as we normally think of it – the president and Congress responding to the influential groups or associations representing private-sector groups.[9]

We may list a wide range of actors who are often or sometimes involved in the policy-making process. Our discussions of the politics of the environment, or of Vietnam, Watergate, and other policy problems elsewhere in this book, have demonstrated how each can be involved. But we shall always find that some actors are more important than others, depending on the issues and the circumstances. Figure P6.2 portrays some common patterns of involvement in policy making in the United States.

☐ THE TYPICAL STAGES IN THE POLICY PROCESS

How do these actors get involved in policy making, and what happens when they do? It is possible to develop a model or outline of the stages of the policy process, and many scholars have done so.[10] These models have much in common, just as does policy making from one topic to the next. To get a clearer idea of what the typical stages in the policy process are, let's examine them in terms of the case of shoe-import policy making.

■ Getting on the agenda

The first stage in policy development is *getting on the agenda* in order to get a problem to government. As we saw, both shoe manufacturers and labor unions got the problem of shoe imports on the agenda by submitting it to the International Trade Commission. The ITC is obliged by law to consider cases brought to it, just as the president is obliged by the same law to consider the ITC's recommendations.

---

[8]Theodore Lowi, "Distribution, Regulation, Redistribution: The Functions of Government," in *Public Policies and Their Politics*, ed. Randall B. Ripley (New York: Norton, 1966).

[9]These are the findings that Randall B. Ripley and Grace A. Franklin reported in their book *Congress, The Bureaucracy, and Public Policy* (Homewood, Ill.: Dorsey, 1976), especially pp. 167–168.

[10]For a survey of the field and the literature, see Charles O. Jones, *An Introduction to the Study of Public Policy,* 2nd ed. (North Scituate, Mass.: Duxbury, 1977).

■ Formulation of a policy proposal

Once a problem is "on the agenda," a *policy proposal* must be *formulated.* This second stage typically involves (1) collecting information, (2) passing it to relevant actors, (3) developing alternative policies for consideration, (4) advocacy by supporters of various alternative policies before those who will decide, and (5) the decision or selection. In the case of shoe imports, the industry and unions (1) gathered information about the scale of imports, the closing of factories, and the loss of jobs and then (2) submitted it to the ITC, which did further research and gathering of data. The ITC then (3) developed various possibilities such as higher tariffs, quotas, tariff-rate quotas, and doing nothing. It then (4) heard arguments by various interested parties, and (5) decided to recommend tariff-rate quotas to the president.

■ Legislation or pronouncement

The ITC's recommendation is only that: a recommendation. But that's as close as an advisory body can get to actually making policy. The law in this case requires that the president pronounce his own policy decision, and then that Congress decide whether to accept that policy pronouncement or legislate a different one. *Legislation or pronouncement* is the third stage of the policy process.

Often, before this third stage can occur, the actor responsible for it – the president in the case of imports – must go back and repeat the stages of policy formulation. The reason for this is that the president must consider all interests, domestic and foreign, while the ITC is responsible only for the interests of hurt industries and workers. So Carter and his assistants had to develop and consider a broader group of alternatives, based on a broader range of information. He also heard more and different advocacy of various possibilities.

Carter finally weighed all the arguments and made his decision – his pronouncement in favor of an OMA to be negotiated with foreign countries that exported shoes.

■ Legitimation

But this decision was not enough to produce a final policy. Carter's pronouncement first needed *legitimation* – it needed to be made legitimate, or lawful, by congressional action. Policy must go through some sort of legitimation stage to become effective. Most policies cost money to implement: a subsidy to farmers, for example, or foreign aid to a developing country or job training grants to the unemployed. In such cases, Congress provides the legitimation by appropriating money for the program or activity – usually after a budgetary request by the executive branch.

In the case of Carter's decision to seek an OMA on shoes, no money was required. Instead, what was needed was congressional acquiescence. Congress had to decide not to pass a law adopting the ITC recommendation. For the law, as we noted, gives Congress the power to override the president if he rejects an ITC recommendation.

■ Implementation

Congress did accept the Carter policy, at least as a temporary effort worth trying. This moved the matter on to the fifth stage in the policy process: *implementation.* In this case, implementation required actually achieving an OMA with Taiwan and South Korea. And of course once such an agreement was reached, the shoe-exporting countries themselves had to implement that agreement, which was a new policy for them: restraining their own shoe exports to the United States.

■ Intergovernmental cooperation

Most policy then requires a sixth stage: *intergovernmental cooperation.* In domestic affairs, this usually means coordinating efforts of the federal government, state governments, and local governments – as in crime control. In foreign affairs, the federal government has full responsibility. But it must sometimes coordinate activities with foreign countries.

■ Policy adjudication

Once a policy has been implemented, another, seventh, stage may become necessary: *policy adjudication,* or settling of disputes as to what the policy is, what it requires, or who is to conduct it. In the case of the shoes, disputes might arise as to whether the term "shoes" includes slippers or rubbers or boots. The affected parties may try to negotiate a settlement, but if they fail to agree they may have to turn to an outside arbiter.

■ Monitoring

Even then, the policy process is not complete. For the policy must be *monitored* to see what effects it is having. Monitors look especially for undesirable unintended effects. In the case of shoe imports, the questions to be monitored included whether industry production increased, whether more jobs developed, and how much prices to consumers rose – as well as how the policy affected our foreign relations and our other trade.

■ Evaluation

Once the policy effects are monitored, the policy can be *evaluated* to see whether it has succeeded or failed. But that determination can be made only in terms of particular objectives. There may be dispute over which objectives should be used to test its effects and over who should do the evaluating.

■ Policy modification

Finally, the tenth and last stage in the policy process is *policy modification.* If the policy fails, or better ideas emerge, there is likely to be pressure or desire to change the policy. In that event, the whole policy process may start over again.

From this survey and our references to the case of shoe imports we have a better sense of the ten typical stages in the policy process. Not all policies go through all stages, we must remember. But policy making is complicated enough, especially in a country with a politics of active interest groups, and the world is complex enough, that most of the time we will find these stages in the process by which most policies are born, live, and eventually die.

Policies once developed may be effective or ineffective, and they may be consistent among themselves or contradictory with each other. They may be adopted or developed after careful study, or they may be selected haphazardly or without much thought. We can assess policies in all these ways. We shall do so from time to time in coming chapters, as we examine governmental policies, actual and proposed, for wrestling with major challenges confronting the country today and tomorrow.

□ COMMON TENDENCIES IN POLICY MAKING

Experts who have studied the making of public (that is, governmental) policy in America have uncovered certain common tendencies in policy making, almost regardless of its subject. These tendencies have impacts on how well or how poorly policy works, or indeed on whether it can be made and implemented effectively at all. So let's survey some of these common (if not necessarily typical) features of policy making.

1. *The interaction of special interests at every stage of policy making tends to produce compromise policies.* Different values produce conflicting demands made upon the government. This makes it especially difficult to develop a strong, single-minded policy on almost anything important. In the case of shoe imports, the conflict among domestic interests (shoe manufacturers and workers versus traders, retail sellers, and consumers) and that between domestic interests (the ITC and the Department of Labor) and foreign interests (developing countries and their bank creditors) forced President Carter to settle upon a policy of some protection – a policy

President Lyndon B. Johnson (*back to camera*) discussing pending legislation with congressional leaders. Such dialogue among actors is important in the policy process.

Courtesy of the Lyndon B. Johnson Library

that was a compromise among these interests. In general, the watchword – the ultimate favorable comment about a policy – tends to be that it is "balanced."

2. *The policy compromise tends to result in "differential dissatisfaction" for almost everyone.* This simply means that all the interests will be dissatisfied to some extent, but some will likely be more unhappy than others, with the policy compromise. The shoe import OMA displeased free-traders somewhat, but it displeased the hurt industries and workers even more.

3. *Policy once established tends to be maintained by bureaucratic inertia.* Once the government or a bureau starts doing something, it tends to keep doing it unless and until events force it to stop. The ITC started recommending aid for the shoe industry years earlier and kept doing so yearly. President Nixon, on the advice of his bureaucracy, rejected the suggestion; so then did President Ford; and so eventually did President Carter. In each case, Treasury and State continued to recommend rejection.

4. *Policy tends to be vitiated* (weakened, crippled, or terminated) *by a changing world.* The do-nothing policy on shoe imports was finally made inadequate by the massive new exports – 200 million pair of shoes a year – by Taiwan and South Korea, who weren't in the business a few years earlier.

5. This suggests that changing policy consciously, in the absence of drastic new developments recognized by all, is very difficult. Instead, *policy is usually changed consciously by "incrementalism"* – by a series of small increments or "pieces" or "steps" that together constitute a larger change. America's policy of freer trade rather than more tariffs and quotas became a policy of OMAs, not by a sudden decision so much as by a series of compromise programs to aid the shoe industry, the television set industry, and others by negotiating OMAs. These compromise changes were sought by those in government who were especially sympathetic to hurt industries – or fearful of their political power.

6. Policy change by incrementalism may be conscious or unconscious, sought or not. But *the most common sort of policy change sometimes seems to be unconscious policy change by program change.* Small changes in programs dealing with the needs of hurt industries tended to cumulate into a policy of seeking OMAs, perhaps to the surprise of some governmental officials, who were not consciously seeking to change America's previous policy.

7. *Many different issues are substantively interdependent.* The content of one policy on one issue will often affect the effectiveness of other policies. A policy of limiting shoe imports will limit the income of developing countries; they will therefore have trouble maintaining their economic growth; they will also have trouble repaying their loans from American banks. Thus America's policy of limited protection will tend to interfere both with America's foreign policy of encouraging economic growth in poorer countries and with America's domestic policy of maintaining the soundness of its

banking industry. But if, on the other hand, the United States denied protection, that policy would produce economic distress in some industries and put more people on welfare – both developments contradicting America's policy of economic stability at home. This interdependence is true of most policies.

8. Just as *many issues and policies* are substantively interdependent, so they *are also inevitably fiscally interdependent.* Resources are always scarce in government. Most policies cost money. This means that different policies and programs struggle for money. That struggle occurs in what is called the budgetary process – the making of the federal budget by the executive branch and the passage of appropriations bills by the Congress.

The politics of the budgetary process can be harsh indeed.[11] They concern the distribution of scarce resources. But they also concern questions of income – taxation – and the decision of how much of a budgetary deficit, if any, there should be. Thus struggles that seem to be about "fiscal responsibility" (balanced budgets) or "economic stimulation" (greater government spending) also involve questions of how big a budgetary "pie" there will be to slice up for the competing interests. So policy decisions on the budget and taxes, and on programs, are interdependent fiscally as well as substantively.

9. The result of all these tendencies is that *policy makers usually have less real control over policy making than we would expect* from looking at their apparent powers.

□ POWER IN POLICY MAKING

But we should not be fooled by this conclusion into thinking that people and bureaus do not and cannot have power in policymaking. There are two important sources of power in policy: political resources and information. Political resources involve the ability to deliver *votes* – in an election, in Congress, or sometimes in bureaucratic politicking. The importance of this is obvious.

The power role of *information* is less obvious, perhaps. But after our study thus far we should have a fair sense of how it works. The only way an official can operate effectively in a large organization like the government is by having accurate and useful information about what is happening, what is to be decided, who stands where on it, what is possible, and so on. Just as citizens must depend on experts for information about politics, so politicians must depend on experts for information about policy. The president would be lost without the "assembly-lines of information" we discussed in earlier chapters. But so would his underlings. People with good information have power in government – often power enough to shape the policy alternatives that are considered, and sometimes power enough to decide the outcome of those considerations by the ways they share information with others.

Once again we can see that *government is a matter of authority.* Those who will take your information seriously, or take you for granted, give you authority to influence policy decisions. Increasingly, as policy questions become more complex, the role of authority moves outside the normal channels of bureaucrats. Instead, authority concerning political resources is held by political advisors. And authority on technical questions is gained and held by nongovernmental experts, who act as advisors or consultants.[12]

[11]For a historical analysis, see Arthur Smithies, *The Budgetary Process in the United States* (New York: McGraw-Hill, 1955). For a study of political aspects of the process at all levels of government, see Ira Sharkansky, *The Politics of Taxing and Spending* (Indianapolis: Bobbs-Merrill, 1969). For a strategic analysis of federal budget making see Aaron Wildavsky, *The Politics of the Budgetary Process,* 2nd ed. (Boston: Little, Brown, 1974). But see also, for more recent developments in the Congressional aspects, the frequent reports in *National Journal* and *Congressional Quarterly Weekly Report.*

[12]For an interesting analysis with case studies, see Howard Margolis, *Technical Advice on Policy Issues* (Beverly Hills, Calif.: Sage, 1973). For a more hostile analysis, see Daniel Guttman and Barry Willner, *The Shadow Government: The Government's Multi-Billion-Dollar Giveaway of Its Decision-Making Powers to Private Management Consultants, "Experts," and Think Tanks* (New York: Pantheon, 1976).

"Knowledge will forever govern ignorance," wrote Founding Father James Madison. "And a people who mean to be their own governors, must arm themselves with the power knowledge gives. A popular government without popular information or the means of acquiring it, is but a prologue to a farce or a tragedy or perhaps both."

The constitutional model

Madison's conception of the ideal form of government was, as we have seen, a republic, or representative government. In the *constitutional model,* which the founders developed, policy was to be primarily a legislative responsibility. The legislature was to represent the interests and opinions of the people. But the separation of powers and the checks and balances in the federal government were supposed to limit the national role in policy making by requiring consensus among different political interests before action could be taken.

The interest-group, or pluralist, model

But it wasn't long, in American politics, before the very thing the Founders feared came to pass. Political parties emerged and were soon captured by special interests. As the world grew more complex, government became more bureaucratized. The specialization of bureaucracy within the government strengthened the specialization of interests outside it. The result was a new model of policy making: the *interest-group model,* which eventually became known as "pluralism."

According to pluralism, as we noted in Chapter 5, policy is the outcome of the interaction of groups, or special interests, none of which is powerful enough to prevail except in a coalition with others. Of course, the only groups able to participate are those that are organized and are allowed to enter the political arena. Until recently, this requirement excluded minority groups and women outright.

The ruling-elite model

It also excluded the poor and the inarticulate – immigrants, for example, who could not use the English language effectively. In general, these uninvolved and unorganized groups have been those most in need of governmental policies to improve their education, health, and welfare. But is their fate much different from that of the common person in terms of ability to influence policy? Many have thought not. They have seen policy as the product of small groups of skilled and informed individuals able to manipulate the instruments of power to their own advantage. Those seeing things this way use the *ruling-elite model* of policy making, which we also discussed in Chapter 5. According to this view, elites have more in common with each other than they do with the groups from which they come or which they supposedly represent. Policy making thus becomes more a product of bargaining or trading and compromising among the privileged and the powerful.

The participatory model

There has been growing dissatisfaction with both the pluralist and elitist possibilities, coupled with widespread realization that the constitutional model did not apply for long if indeed it ever did. One consequence of this has been disillusion and despair – reflected in the falling rates of electoral participation. But another product has been a new or renewed concept of *participatory democracy,* grounded in the belief that people should gain greater control over the institutions that affect their lives. One implication of this is that the people should be actively involved in policy making. In coming chapters we shall see just how far popular participation in policy making now extends.[13]

[13]For a discussion of the expansion of the role of citizens in bureaucracy, see Harry Krantz, *The Participatory Bureaucracy* (Lexington, Mass.: Lexington Books, 1975). For more general discussion of participatory democracy, see Chapter 21 below.

16 The politics of production: capitalism and democracy

"To promote the general welfare," the framers stated in the Preamble to the Constitution almost 200 years ago, was to be a major objective of the new national government they were creating. Since then, this objective has served to justify the growing governmental role in our economy in good times and in bad. But despite government's active involvement, poverty has persisted, and there have been occasional upsurges in unemployment, recession, and inflation, even in eras of economic growth. As a result, many have been led to wonder, from one era to the next, just what the proper economic role for the government should be.

□ THE GENERAL WELFARE

The "general welfare" does not mean a government welfare program for every citizen. Nonetheless, it is true, as we noted in Chapter 7, that almost half the nation's people get a significant portion of their income from government – perhaps 30 million of them under some sort of welfare program. It is also true that the total of government subsidies to individuals and businesses is well over $100 billion per year. But if earned income, welfare grants, and subsidies were not what the Founders had in mind, what were they seeking?

We will get a better sense of the meaning of the Founding Fathers attached to that phrase, "to promote the general welfare," if we return to the Declaration of Independence. "We hold these Truths to be self evident," that document asserted, "that all Men are created equal, that they are endowed by their Creator with certain unalienable Rights, that among these are Life, Liberty, and the Pursuit of Happiness." This assertion was grounded in the views of the British philosopher John Locke, whom the framers had read and accepted as a guide to establishing a new republic.

Locke argued that all men, by virtue simply of being men, had a "natural right" to *life, liberty,* and *property.* But Locke's concept of property was quite different from ours. He believed that a person should own only as much land as he could farm: "As much land as a Man Tills, Plants, Improves, Cultivates, and can use the Product of, so much is his Property."[1]

Like Locke, Thomas Jefferson, who drafted the Declaration, and indeed most Americans of the eighteenth century, believed that true happiness – contentment

[1]John Locke, *Second Treatise,* sect. 32.

and a sense of fulfillment – was to be found in working one's own land. *The function of government,* and its primary justification, in this view, *was to protect one's natural right to the land one needed* to farm in order to live. The early Americans, 95 percent of whom lived in rural areas, did not foresee that cities would develop so fast and so widely that people would leave the land for the city. They never imagined that eventually even rural land would become scarce, as it now is near most cities.

Thus in America's early years the asserted natural right to happiness presumed a natural right to property – to sufficient land to farm oneself. But even then artisans in the cities and slaves in the countryside were deprived of this natural right to property. Further, as the population grew and immigration from Europe continued, new Americans were not granted equal access to the land. Instead, they became urban laborers and worked in the new factories that made America an industrial power and made some citizens, owners of the factories or of the land on which they were built, very rich. The result was an effective end to the right to happiness through self-sufficient farming. Instead, "happiness" and the "general welfare" came more and more to be associated with material possessions – consumer goods and investments, as we call them. As historian Paul Conkin has asserted:

> Today only a small minority of Americans have property in the eighteenth century sense of an exclusive claim to a part of nature joined with work, management, and consumption. Practically, most people do not have the remotest possibility of owning such property. . . . Through time, the commitment to life, liberty, and property shifted to life (procedural guarantees), unhampered religious and verbal expression, the right to vote, and broad educational opportunities. If the old idea of property has any contemporary currency, it takes a strangely inverted form—the right to work, and not the right to own and manage the means of production. In a sense, we now proclaim the right of servility, for *work* usually denotes employment, a job, taking orders, and finding satisfaction in wages and not in the work experience. In a highly collectivized America, the image of a fulfilling life has shifted from the proximate ownership and artful management of property to a college education, high-status employment, investment success, and a high level of consumption.[2]

☐ THE ECONOMIC TRANSFORMATION OF AMERICA

This transformation of the typical American from a small, relatively self-sufficient rural farmer working his own land in 1780 to a wholly dependent urban factory worker selling his or her labor for a wage has continued to this day. In 1780, about 80 percent of the nonslave population (slaves constituted about one-fifth of the population) was self-employed and 20 percent worked for hourly wages or salaries.

---

[2]Paul K. Conkin, *Self-Evident Truths* (Bloomington: Indiana University Press, 1975), pp. 189, 191–192. On Locke's views, see Conkin, pp. 95–99 and C. B. MacPherson, *The Political Theory of Possessive Individualism* (Oxford: Clarendon Press, 1962), pt. V.

One hundred years later, only 37 percent were self-employed, and 62 percent were employed by others as workers. Today, another 100 years later, the self-employed are down to less than 10 percent, the wage and salary workers are 84 percent, and some 7 percent serve as managers or other supervisory officials.[3]

■ Laissez-faire capitalism

When the nation was founded, its economy was moving toward what we now call "free-enterprise capitalism" or "laissez-faire capitalism." The term **capitalism** indicates that the means of production (factories and machines and land) are owned by individuals and operated by them and their assistants for a profit, employing the rest of the work force as laborers. The term "free enterprise" means that anyone can get involved, setting up a busines if he or she can get the necessary capital (money) somewhere, or selling his or her own labor if he or she can find an available job. The French term "laissez-faire" is loosely translated "leave things alone." It implies that there are no legal regulations which would prohibit even disadvantageous types of activity, such as development of a monopoly (in which one company drives out all competition) or selling dangerous goods to an unsuspecting public.

The leading theorist and proponent of laissez-faire capitalism was a Scot named Adam Smith, whose great book *The Wealth of Nations* was published in 1776, the year of the Declaration of Independence. Smith argued in favor of free, unregulated enterprise in which every individual looked out only for his or her own selfish interests. He claimed that this would inevitably result in the most efficient production and distribution of goods and services, as if, in his words, there were an "invisible hand" at work constantly adjusting things for the better.

The United States developed as essentially a laissez-faire capitalist country during its first 100 years or so. The national government then had three major roles in the economy. The first was to develop a common currency for all states and citizens to use. The second was to institute a tariff (a fee charged on each item that is imported into the country from abroad) to produce revenue to run the government because there was then no income tax. The third was to sell public lands, especially in frontier areas, to land speculators – who wouldn't use the land themselves, as Jefferson had intended, but instead would sell it to anyone who could pay for it as a homestead.

By the time this free-enterprise capitalist era ended in the 1880s, America was an industrializing and an urbanizing nation. The country was also dominated by powerful capitalist landowners, railroad owners, and industrialists who were behaving in ways that conclusively disproved Adam Smith's theory that an "invisible hand" would cause unregulated selfish behavior by all to be of benefit to everyone. On the contrary, there was grinding poverty in the cities, and child labor (young children working long hours in dangerous factories) was common everywhere. Furthermore, efforts to control these abuses failed because the vested interests were too strong politically as well as economically.

---

[3]See Michael Reich, "The Evolution of the U.S. Labor Force," in *The Capitalist System,* ed. Richard Edwards et al. (Englewood Cliffs, N.J.: Prentice-Hall, 1972), p. 175, for more detailed statistics.

■ The government and business

The result was that Americans began to abandon free-enterprise capitalism in favor of government-regulated capitalism. The Congress began to pass laws establishing regulatory agencies to control railroads, industrial monopolies, food and drugs, and banks. The Interstate Commerce Act of 1887 set up an Interstate Commerce Commission (ICC) to regulate railroad rates and stabilize railroad revenues, to the benefit often of both businesses using the railroads for shipping and businesses running the railroads for profit.

The Sherman Antitrust Act of 1890 was the first in a series of acts designed to limit the ability of companies to merge into monopolies or to engage in unfair "restraint of trade or commerce" to cut down competition.[4] Then in 1914 came the Clayton Act, which extended antitrust controls. In the same year came the Federal Trade Commission Act, intended to oversee the business trading practices of corporations.

None of these regulatory agencies worked well in this period. They all tended to be dominated by representatives of the businesses they were supposed to regulate. And the courts often ruled on cases in ways that limited the agencies' effective power. But they nevertheless set the stage for further movement in recent years, as we shall soon see.

The Progressive Era is the name often given to the period 1900-1916 dominated by Teddy Roosevelt, who was President from 1901 to 1908. In it, the reformist focus was broadened to seek regulation of the exploitation of natural resources, as well as controls on trusts, and passage of the first legislation to improve the conditions of labor.

■ The government and labor

Working conditions for urban labor—primarily impoverished immigrants and their children—were poor throughout these decades: 10- or 12-hour workdays were typical, wages were too low to meet minimal human needs, factories were unsafe, and on-the-job accidents were commonplace.[5] Furthermore, there were no disability payments for those hurt on the job, and no retirement benefits for those too old to work. Sporadic efforts by workers to organize into local unions and to strike were always resisted by owners—frequently with violence, and sometimes with the cooperation of local police. In 1894, the resistance even included federal troops in the famed Pullman strike in Chicago.

In the late nineteenth century, labor groups made efforts to gain strength through affiliation with other local unions in confederations like the National Labor Union and the Knights of Labor. Others joined socialist and anarchist

---

[4]The term "antitrust," still generally used today to refer to antimonopoly programs, came from the practice of many companies combining to designate a group of men as "trustees" with control over the stock. The resulting arrangement, which gave these men complete control over all member companies, was called a trust. The most famous was the Standard Oil Trust that in 1879 controlled forty different oil companies and thereby eliminated competition among them.

[5]See Stephen B. Wood, *Constitutional Politics in the Progressive Era: Child Labor and the Law* (Chicago: University of Chicago Press, 1968).

Jacob A. Riis Collection, Museum of the City of New York

Working conditions—especially for immigrants and children—were poor in the late nineteenth century.

organizations. The culmination of this effort at labor organizations was the expansion of the Federation of Organized Trades and Labor Unions, established in 1881, into the American Federation of Labor (AFL) in 1886.

At this point, the right of workers to organize into unions was still not widely recognized, and the struggle to win that right was far from over. Courts had generally held that both labor organization and business combinations were illegal, until businessmen were given the right to organize early in the nineteenth century. The Sherman Antitrust Act of 1890, designed to combat business monopolies, was then applied by the courts to unions, treating them as illegal monopolies of workers. The Clayton Act of 1914 declared that human labor was not to be considered a commodity or article of commerce subject to such restrictions, but the courts continued to apply antitrust regulations to unions until 1942.

Meanwhile, in the 1930's, laws were passed protecting the right of labor to organize. The most important was the National Labor Relations Act (or Wagner Act) of 1935. Finally, in 1938, the Fair Labor Standards Act was passed. It set a minimum wage of 25 cents an hour and a maximum workweek of 44 hours, and it outlawed child labor. Subsequently, the Labor Management Act of 1947 (or Taft-Hartley Act) placed new regulations on union activities, and the Landrum-Griffin Act of 1959 curtailed the powers of union leaders over their members. Both of these laws represented efforts to adjust the balance between business and labor once again. Some then believed that the Wagner Act, intended to make unions able to compete effectively with big business, had gone too far, although labor vehemently disagreed.

■ The government and the economy In a sense, the most significant aspect of this collection of labor legislation was its further expansion of the powers of the federal government to intervene in and police the economy. At the same time, that power was growing on its other two dimensions, the regulation of business and the development of the federal government's own, direct economic activities.

Government regulation The major regulatory steps in this period were creation of the Federal Trade Commission (FTC, described above) in 1914, and Federal Power Commission (FPC) in 1920 to regulate interstate electrtic power and natural gas, and the Federal Communications Commission (FCC) in 1934 to regulate radio, telephone, and (once it was developed) television. In addition, following the collapse of the stock market in the 1929 Depression, the Securities and Exchange Commission (SEC) was established in 1934 to regulate the issuance of securities (stocks) and the conduct of stock exchanges such as Wall Street's New York Stock Exchange, in order to protect investors from deceit and manipulation by companies or stock sellers.

Government spending In the same period, the government was itself becoming more and more of a business in several important ways. First, the growth of the federal budget continued to increase. We can of course measure this growth in dollar terms – by the total cost of all government expenditures – as we did in Figure 7.1. But it is more revealing to examine the total value of all goods and services produced and provided in the entire country (the gross national product, or GNP, as it's called), and see what percentage of that total is purchased by the government. In 1930, the federal budget was only 3.6 percent of the GNP; in 1950 this had risen to 14 percent; in 1970, to 20 percent; and in 1975, to 22.5 percent. This growth, by World War II, made the U.S. government by far the biggest customer for U.S. business and industry. Indeed, more than one out of every five dollars spent for goods or services in the United States today is spent by the U.S. government.

Government production In addition, the federal government has itself gone further and further into such production of goods and services for sale to the people. Its premier venture was the national postal system. Subsequently, the government has developed waterways and rivers and even gone into the electric power business, most extensively with the Tennessee Valley Authority (TVA) established in 1933. TVA not only provides power but also controls floods, manufactures minerals for fertilizers and explosives, and develops conservation and recreation programs for the states of Tennessee, North Carolina, Kentucky, Virginia, Mississippi, Georgia, and Alabama.

Fiscal and monetary policy These regulatory, purchasing, and production powers of the federal government further increased its influence over the economic and social health of American business and labor. But the major contribution to government's capacity to influence if not control the economic situation in America came with the development of new ways of intervening in the economy generally.

There are two basic ways government can do this. The first is through what is called monetary policy. Basically, monetary policy involves decisions about "how much money to print" or how much credit to create for banks to use in making loans to businesses and individuals. The second is fiscal policy – essentially, decisions about what taxes to impose on whom, and how much money to spend on what.

The origins of these capabilities lie in the Federal Reserve Act of 1913 and in the New Deal laws of the 1930s. The Federal Reserve Act established a national central bank to influence the behavior of other banks. The New Deal legislation during the Depression was designed to create new jobs and train workers, to raise farm prices to benefit farmers, and to establish the Social Security system to provide income for the elderly and the disabled.

■ The crises of capitalism

The new government regulatory programs established from 1887 on were clear indication that even the governmental subsidies (protective tariffs, land grants to railroads, cheap land sales to developers, and so on) in the mid-nineteenth century were not enough to achieve and maintain economic stability and growth. The Great Depression then convinced even the diehards that what was left of the free-enterprise capitalist system wouldn't work well enough, even with governmental regulation. But even the pioneering federal programs of the New Deal were insufficient to end the Depression. Only World War II managed to do that – and then only with massive military spending, extensive governmental planning, price controls, and direct governmental production. As a result, most economic experts had little faith in the conventional capitalist system. Instead, they generally believed we must rely upon an activist government to develop and sustain economic growth. But with economic growth came governmental growth, and with governmental growth came governmental influence extending to more and more spheres of human life. With the government possessing so much influence, economists and politicians came to believe that the economy could always be controlled by the use of monetary and fiscal policy – "fine-tuning," as this regular manipulation of the money supply, taxation, and government spending is often called

Then came the severe and long-lasting recession of the early 1970s. Coming in a time of growing felt needs for more regulation to protect the environment and the consumer, it raised new doubts about the knowledge of economic experts, the effectiveness of governmental controls, and even the viability of American capitalism itself.

□ CAPITALISM

■ The principles of capitalism

Through it all, through boom and bust, most Americans have clung to beliefs about economics that qualify them as capitalists – or at least capitalist sympathizers. The central tenets of capitalism are five:

- □ *Capital* – wealth and any goods that can be converted into wealth – should be *owned by individuals* and disposed of as they wish.
- □ *Accumulation of capital* in private hands results in investment that *produces economic development* that benefits everyone.

- ☐ *Corporations* (groups of investors or owners) are the *most efficient* agents of capital accumulation (also called "capital formation") and investment.
- ☐ *Profit* is the motive that makes investment possible and so *is essential and desirable.*
- ☐ *The "free market" where individuals and corporations compete is* the most *efficient* way to have economic decisions made through the operation of "supply and demand."

These beliefs together constitute what might be called the "culture" of capitalism. It emphasizes private ownership, competition and profit, arguing that these will result in two beneficial effects. First, people will get what they deserve, on the basis of their work. And second, people will be able to exercise "consumer sovereignty" – they will decide what goods and services they are willing to pay for, and the "market system" will offer them to the people so the companies can make profits. In a sense, people vote for goods with their dollars.

■ Challenges to capitalism

In recent decades, the principles of this basic capitalism have been challenged by socialists and communists, who reject it entirely, and by today's liberals who believe capitalism will only work with stronger governmental intervention. Socialists and communists generally argue that the state, rather than individuals, should own the "means of production," so that inequality is avoided and so that wasteful competition is replaced by planning and efficiency. Today's liberals, less willing to junk capitalism, argue instead for reforms. Government must regulate the economy, provide goods and services that private firms will not or cannot offer (everything from national defense to clean air), and develop long-term plans to see that human and social needs are met, according to liberal reformists.

■ The types of capitalism

The growth of both the radical alternative and the liberal reformist critique has led everyone to a renewed appreciation of the connections between the economy and politics. One result of this new appreciation has been uncertainty as to how best to characterize our present economic system. Everyone recognizes that we no longer have the "pure capitalism" of which Adam Smith wrote 200 years ago. But experts disagree on what to call what we have. There are essentially four possibilities:

- ☐ *controlled capitalism,* in which the government exerts enough control to limit capitalist abuses somewhat but at the same time protects capitalist firms by laws and subsidies
- ☐ *welfare capitalism,* in which the government protects the interests of the poor unable to work or to earn enough to live and provides major benefits for ordinary citizens as well
- ☐ *corporate capitalism,* in which corporations are so large and so powerful economically and politically that they are able to dominate public policy where their interests are involved – even at the expense of the interests of the people

- ☐ *state capitalism,* in which government's role, through extensive regulation and massive defense spending, for example, has virtually eliminated conventional capitalist firms and competition and made everyone and everything dependent upon the government

Which of these characterizations seems most accurate to you depends on where you look and what you're looking for. The controls on business and labor are obvious to all by now. So in some sense we certainly have a controlled capitalism. But whether the controls benefit the citizens generally (welfare capitalism) or primarily businesses (corporate capitalism) is less clear, even after careful study.

It is clear that the standard of living of most Americans has improved in recent decades. But so has the condition of business and industry. The United States is basically a very rich country. A recent survey by the Conference Board, a business research group, found that the total value of all the physical assets in America (homes, cars, factories, machinery, and so on) is about $6.2 trillion.[6] That works out to about $28,600 for every American. Yet we shall find in the next chapter that most Americans don't own anything like that much, nor have they the savings that would allow them to buy such goods. Instead, some of this wealth is owned by the government, and much of it, we shall find, is owned by a very small percentage of the people – as we shall also see in the next chapter. Further, American businesses do generally make substantial profits as a whole. For example, in the second quarter (April through June) of 1977, corporate profits totaled about $105 billion – or $780 per person and an annual rate of $3120 per working person. That figure is over half the average total annual income of $6002 per working person in 1976.

It is clear, then, that corporations do indeed benefit, and often at scales that dwarf gains for individuals. But there are big differences among corporations too, not only in profitability but in size. There are more than 1,800,000 corporations in the United States, but few of them are very big either in annual sales income or in number of employees, as Table 16.1 reveals. Nonetheless, there has been a recent growth in the tendency of big companies to swallow up smaller companies. All these are reasons to term our system "corporate capitalism."

But as we pointed out earlier, the government itself has continued to grow more and more important in the economy. The federal government alone, to take just one example, spends some $3.5 billion just to buy food to serve to its military and civilian employees. This makes it obviously a major factor in American

[6]"Tomorrow," *U. S. News & World Report,* March 7, 1977, p. 11.

TABLE 16.1

The small world of big business (1,800,000 U.S. corporations)

Number of corporations	Annual sales	Number of corporations	Number of employees
184	$1 billion	31	Over 100,000
198	$500 million to $1 billion	46	75,000–99,999
2513	$50 million to $500 million	96	50,000–74,999
28,882	$5 million to $50 million	238	25,000–49,999
144,824	$1 million to $5 million	498	10,000–24,999

Source: Adapted from *Dun's Review,* July 1976, p. 42.

TABLE 16.2

Consumer prices, 1965–1975

Year	Percent increase in consumer prices
1965	1.7
1966	2.9
1967	2.9
1968	4.2
1969	5.4
1970	5.9
1971	4.3
1972	3.3
1973	6.2
1974	11.0
1975	9.1

TABLE 16.3

Unemployment rates, 1966–1976

Year	Percent of civilian labor force unemployed
1966	3.8
1967	3.8
1968	3.6
1969	3.5
1970	4.9
1971	5.9
1972	5.6
1973	4.9
1974	5.6
1975	8.5
1976	7.7

agriculture and food processing.[7] In this sense, then, perhaps we do indeed have a system of "state capitalism."

Because a case can be made that our system is indeed each of these four types, some observers choose simply to call it "mixed capitalism." But how long the present mix – of welfare for citizens and benefits for business, in a context of great government controls and large government roles – can survive without shifting predominantly one way or another is anybody's guess.

■ Contemporary capitalism's policy problems

Most Americans are well aware of major economic problems facing our system, because these problems affect them or their acquaintances. These problems include inflation, unemployment, economic stagnation, pollution, and consumer protection.

Inflation Inflation continues at a high rate, with both prices and incomes rising regularly but unevenly. Table 16.2 indicates how consumer prices have increased in recent years.

Unemployment Unemployment continues at a high rate, well above what seems "acceptable" to policy makers, let alone to the individuals looking for work but unable to find it. It strikes members of minority groups, particualrly the young ones, especially hard, as we indicated in Chapter 14. Furthermore, unemployment tends to persist at high levels even when the economy recovers from recession, as recent experience and Table 16.3 remind us.

Stagnation *Stagnation* in the rate of growth of the economy now recurs quite often. The term "stagnation" means that the economy is not producing more *goods* to meet the demands or needs of people (and so prices of the goods that are produced tend to rise). It also means that the economy is not producing new *jobs* for those seeking work. This is especially important because the growth of our population is such that just to reach an unemployment rate of 4 percent our economy must produce 72,000 new jobs every week from now till 1985.[8] That is double the rate of job creation in the decade from 1965 to 1975, and no one knows how it will be managed – especially because new technology keeps reducing the number of jobs available. We will return to this problem in Chapter 20.

Pollution Waste and pollution continue to plague us, as we'll see in more detail in Chapter 20. Coping with them will require new and stronger government intervention in business and industry in coming years, which will further complicate economic activity.

Consumer problems Consumer problems have always been with us. But people have only recently come to believe the government should protect consumers. This,

---

[7]"U.S. Taking Steps to Reduce $3.5 Billion Annual Bill for Food," *New York Times,* July 31, 1977, p. 31.

[8]"Challenge to U.S.: 72,000 New Jobs Needed Every Week," *U.S. News & World Report,* June 28, 1976, pp. 20–24.

as we'll see in Chapter 20, demands still more and deeper government involvement in the economy.

The way government attempts to cope with such problems is by involving itself more actively in the economy. It may impose wage and price controls to attempt to control inflation, as President Nixon did in 1971 without much success. It may spend more money, stimulating the economy, to create more jobs and lower the unemployment rate – but this risks new inflation. It may attempt to regulate pollution – but at the risk of raising prices and of driving some firms out of business and so increasing unemployment and slowing economic growth. It may impose new regulations to protect consumers – but at the cost of higher prices for goods and less efficiency in production. And so on.

We can already see at work here one of the tendencies of policy making that we discussed in Perspective 6: the interconnectedness of everything and the consequent interdependence of various policies intended to solve different problems. Economists are paid to try to develop policies to solve such problems, just as politicians are picked and paid to adopt the right ones. So far, neither the politicians nor their economists have been any too successful. Thus it will come as no surprise that we cannot here propose policies that will promise such successes.

What we can do is survey the scope of government intervention and then raise briefly the issues that arise when the government intervenes. We can then look to the future to try to envisage possible new approaches that may emerge as political issues.

□ THE SCOPE OF GOVERNMENT INTERVENTION

Perhaps the best way to survey the scope and extent of government intervention is to examine Table 16.4. This table reveals something of the growth in both economic regulatory agencies (from eight to ten) and social regulatory agencies (from twelve to seventeen) in the early 1970s. This was the period in which government began to respond actively to new demands for equal oportunities for minorities and women, for environmental protection, for consumer protection, and for job safety. As a result, the spending by the economic regulatory agencies went

The littered and polluted Rock Creek in Washington, D.C. Waste and pollution are key policy problems of capitalism today.

Environmental Protection Agency

from $166 million in 1970 to $428 million in 1975. That of the social agencies grew from $1.4 billion in 1970 to $4.3 billion in 1975.

Sometimes regulation is welcomed by those being regulated because it serves their interests. Broadcast stations welcome and demand federal regulation of channels, for example, as we saw in Chapter 12. On the other hand, some aspects of the growing regulation have long caused resentment and stimulated opposition among those being regulated. One is the *paperwork* required by federal agencies. It is massive. A report by the Commission on Federal Paperwork in 1977 estimated the cost at from $25 billion to $32 billion per year. General Motors, for example, has calculated that to certify its cars for sale it has to file documents every year that, if piled one on top of another, would make a stack some fifteen stories high. By 1975

TABLE 16.4 The extent of government intervention in the economy

Agency and date created	Number of employees	Budget ($ millions)	Function
Antitrust Division of the Justice Department (1890)	900	27	Regulates all activity that could affect interstate commerce.
Civil Aeronautics Board (1938)	800	102	Regulates airline fares and routes.
Commodity Futures Trading Commission (1974)	400	14	Regulates futures trading on commodity exchanges.
Comptroller of the Currency (1863)	2800	89	Charters and regulates national banks.
Consumer Product Safety Commission (1972)	890	39	Prepares regulations to reduce product-related injuries to consumers by mandating better design, labeling, and instruction sheets.
Corps of Engineers of the Defense Department (1824)	700	35	Concerned with construction along waterways and marshlands and dredging operations and mine dumping.
Environmental Protection Agency (1970)			Develops and enforces standards for clean air and water. Controls pollution from pesticides, toxic substances, and noise. Approves state pollution abatement plans and rules on environmental impact statements.
Equal Employment Opportunity Commission (1964)	2500	70	Investigates complaints of employment discrimination based on race, religion, and sex.
Federal Aviation Administration of the Department of Transportation (1958)	5000	228	Regulates aircraft manufacturing through certification of airplane airworthiness. Also licenses pilots.
Federal Communications Commission (1934)	2100	60	Regulates broadcasting and other communications and interstate telephone and telegraph service.
Federal Deposit Insurance Corp. (1933)	3500	83	Shares regulatory powers with the states over state-chartered banks not in the Federal Reserve System, and over mutual savings banks.
Federal Energy Administration (1973)	4000	996	Controls the price of most domestic crude oil and some refined products, principally gasoline. Charged with developing a national energy policy.
Federal Energy Regulatory Commission of the Department of Energy (1930)	1450	42	Regulates interstate transmission and wholesale price of electric power, rates and routes of natural gas pipelines, and the wellhead price of gas for interstate shipment.
Federal Home Loan Bank Board (1932)	2900	105	Charters and regulates federal savings and loan institutions, and insures deposits through a subsidiary.

the *Code of Federal Regulations,* which includes all the regulations developed by the federal government and currently in force, had grown to be 72,200 pages in length.[9]

■ Why regulation?

Regulation may be supported for a variety of reasons. Many of them concern efficiency. Sometimes an activity is a **natural monopoly** such as a telephone system. If there were two phone companies in town competing, you'd have to have two phones if you wanted to be able to talk to people who had signed up with each one. To prevent this inefficiency, the town government picks one

[9]"Government Intervention," *Business Week,* April 4, 1977, p. 47.

TABLE 16.4 (*cont.*)

Agency and date created	Number of employees	Budget ($ millions)	Function
Federal Maritime Commission (1936)	300	9	Regulates foreign and domestic ocean commerce.
Federal Reserve Board (1913)	26,000	700	Regulates state-chartered banks that are members of the Federal Reserve System and has jurisdiction over bank holding companies. Also sets money and credit policy.
Federal Trade Commission (1914)	1700	55	Has broad powers to curb unfair trade practices, protect consumers, and maintain competition.
Food & Drug Administration of the Department of Health, Education and Welfare (1931)	7000	240	Responsible for the safety and efficacy of drugs and medical devices and the safety and purity of food. It also regulates labeling.
Interstate Commerce Commission (1887)	2100	57	Regulates rates and routes of railroads, most truckers, and some waterway carriers.
Mining Enforcement & Safety Administration (1973)	2000	95	Enforces all mine safety regulations, including air quality and equipment standards.
National Highway Traffic Safety Administration of the Department of Transportation (1970)	800	100	Regulates manufacturers of autos, trucks, buses, motorcycles, trailers, and tires.
National Labor Relations Board (1935)	2700	83	Regulates labor practices of unions and companies and conducts representation elections.
Nuclear Regulatory Commission (1973)	2500	256	Regulates civilian nuclear safety, which basically involves licensing atomic power plants.
Occupational Safety & Health Administration of the Labor Department (1971)	2400	128	Responsible for regulating safety and health conditions in all workplaces—except those run by governments.
Office of Federal Contract Compliance Programs (1962)	107	15	Administers prohibitions against discrimination by race or sex on the part of employers holding federal contracts.
Pension Benefit Guarantee Corporation (1974)	521	21	Oversees pension plans under the Employee Retirement Income Security Act.
Securities & Exchange Commission (1934)	2000	56	Regulates all publicly traded securities and the markets on which they are traded. Administers public disclosure laws and polices securities fraud.

Source: Adapted and updated from the *U.S. Government Manual,* 1978, and *Business Week,* April 4, 1977, pp. 52, 53, 56.

Wide World Photos

Unemployment lines in Detroit. Providing jobs and a decent income for all is a prime goal of government economic policy.

phone company and gives it monopoly power. But the government then regulates it because there is no competition to otherwise protect consumers or the public interest.

Some commodities, termed **public goods,** must be supplied to everyone if they are supplied to anyone, so it is difficult to get consumers to pay for them voluntarily. Because of this government produces them and taxes people for providing them. Examples of such public goods include national defense, police, and public health programs.

Another reason for some government regulation is what are called *third-party effects.* An example is education, which is thought to benefit others, third parties, besides the teacher and the one taught, and so is often provided and regulated by government.

The *absence of competition* is a rationale for some regulation – particularly antitrust moves against monopolies, which are not otherwise checked in the marketplace.

Inability to obtain information is a situation which sometimes calls forth regulation. Consumers can't test the purity of drugs or meat, for example, so the government does this and then requires accurate labeling of them. (See the box titled "Government regulation of the hot dog.")

Some regulation is clearly intended to *change the distribution of income.* Special farm price supports or crop-size limitations, which guarantee a certain income to farmers, would fall in this category.

Other regulation comes about because an *interest with political power demands it.* The Interstate Commerce Commission, which we discussed earlier, falls in this category. So do tariff and quota provisions of the sort we discussed in Perspective 6. And so does the recent consumer protection regulation that we shall discuss in Chapter 20.[10]

□ THE TOOLS OF GOVERNMENT INTERVENTION

The government has a wide range of powers to intervene and many instruments to succeed at it. The most important are these:

Imposing wage and price controls When given the authority by the Congress, the president can set limits to the possible increases in wages and prices. Nixon was given this authority in 1970 and used it in 1971.[11]

Rationing Given the authority, the president can also take the more drastic step of rationing, or apportioning, goods which may be in short supply – as he has done in wartime.

Regulating prices Government agencies set prices in certain activities such as airfares (set by the Civil Aeronautics Board) and rail rates (by the ICC), and the rate of interest on your savings in banks (by the Federal Reserve).

Licensing, franchising, and issuing permits Government permission to operate, which automatically excludes those not given it, is used by the FCC for broadcasters, the CAB for airline routes, and the Federal Reserve for bank charters, for example.

Setting standards Various agencies set minimum health standards, grades for meat, eggs, and grain, allowable levels of auto emissions, for instance – something that involves the regulators deeply in the day-to-day affairs of the businesses.

Granting cash subsidies Bureaus may grant gifts of money or free services to businesses, farmers, or others to encourage them to do certain things. The CAB has long granted subsidies to small local and regional airlines, for example. The Department of Agriculture pays a wide range of subsidies to farmers.

Granting tax subsidies The government grants various special tax breaks to businesses and individuals in efforts to affect their behavior. Business has various "tax loopholes" to encourage it to invest in expansion, for example. People buying their own homes are allowed to deduct the interest they pay on their mortgages from their taxable income to encourage home ownership and help the housing industry. In fact, the total of tax subsidies is now well over $125 billion a year, spread among many American citizens and businesses. This means the governent loses $125 billion dollars it would otherwise collect in taxes each year. Table 16.5 lists the tax subsidies that benefit ordinary citizens like you and me. You might ask yourself how many of these tax subsidies you are personally benefiting from. In addition to these individual subsidies, $23 billion in taxes is lost due to tax subsidies

---

[10] For a discussion of rationales, see George Daly and David W. Brady, "Federal Regulation of Economic Activity," in *Economic Regulatory Policies*, ed. James E. Anderson, (Lexington, Mass.: Heath, 1976), chap. 14.

[11] For a historical account of wage controls, see Daniel Quinn Mills, *Government, Labor, and Inflation: Wage Stabilization in the U.S.* (Chicago: University of Chicago Press, 1975). For a study of the 1971 freeze, see Arnold R. Weber, *In Pursuit of Price Stability* (Washington, D.C.: Brookings Institution, 1973).

for investors, businesses, and farmers (dividend exclusion, special treatment of capital gains, deferral of interest on U.S. savings bonds, and so on), and $32 billion is lost due to special tax subsidies for corporations (investment tax credit, depreciation deductions, research and development expenses, exploration and development costs, and so on).

Allocating resources directly Agencies sometimes may decide which people or which regions will get certain goods and services. For example, during periods of energy shortages the federal government decides how much gasoline and fuel oil must be provided to different parts of the country by the oil companies.

Promoting competition The FTC uses its powers to issue orders and decrees, and the Justice Department goes to court to sue, to break up monopolies or stop monopolistic practices that restrain free trade.

Taxing to regulate The government may impose special taxes to influence behavior. High excise, or "luxury" taxes on liquor and tobacco are examples. So would be high taxes imposed on gasoline to encourage conservation.

Expropriating The government has the right of **eminent domain**, or superior power, to seize private property for public use. The Constitution's Fifth Amendment requires that the owner of such seized property be given "just compensation."

TABLE 16.5

Tax subsidies for individual citizens

Income not taxed	Estimated annual tax loss ($ millions)
Pension plans—company contributions plus annual earnings of plan investments	9,940
Company-paid insurance, other nonwage benefits	7,100
Social Security benefits	4,685
Unemployment-insurance benefits	2,445
Interest on life-insurance savings	1,995
Pension contributions of self-employed, others	1,535
Military benefits and allowances	1,260
Veterans' benefits	1,080
Deferral of capital gains on home sales	935
Maximum tax on personal-service income	855
Workers'-compensation benefits	810
Scholarships, fellowships	285
Railroad retirement-system benefits	205
Income earned abroad by U.S. citizens	135
Public-assistance benefits	105
Capital gain on home sale for persons 65 and over	70
Sick pay	55
Others	70
Total	33,565

Personal deductions and credits	Estimated annual tax loss ($ millions)
State, local income and sales taxes	9,870
Charitable contributions	6,040
Mortgage interest on owner-occupied homes	6,030
Property tax on owner-occupied homes	4,995
Medical expenses	2,870
Interest on consumer debt	2,565
Earned-income credit	1,350
Exemption for people over age 65	1,280
Credit for child and dependent-care expenses	870
Parent's exemption for students 19 or over	770
Tax credit for the elderly	440
Casualty losses	380
Credit and deductions for political contributions	35
Exemption for the blind	20
Total	37,515

Source: These figures, for 1978, were supplied by the Treasury Department and the Joint Committee on Taxation of the Congress. They were printed in *U.S. News & World Report,* August 1, 1977, pp. 64–65.

Government regulation of the hot dog

You may not worry about the hot dogs you eat, but the government certainly does. Among the federal regulations that now govern the manufacture and sale of hot dogs are these:

1. The hot dog must meet "pure food" standards—which means that there's a definite limit to how much extraneous matter (such as rodent fecal matter) may be included.

2. The hot dog cannot be more than 30 percent fat.

3. The hot dog cannot be more than 10 percent water.

4. If "extenders" (such as soy flour or cereal) are added, they cannot be more than 3½ percent of the hot dog's weight, and their presence must be indicated in the name of the hot dog.

5. The meat cannot be artificially colored—only the "casing," or skin, may be colored, and the dyes used to color it must be shown not to be injurious to health.

6. The preservatives added so the hot dogs can sit in warehouses, stores, and your refrigerator for a long time cannot be more than 1 part in 5000 parts of hot dog ingredients.

7. The label must list all ingredients in descending order of amount included, must tell you the net weight and manufacturer's name and address, must have a federal inspection stamp, and must be approved in advance by the government.

8. If the hot dog is shipped from one state to another ("interstate commerce") the plant must be inspected by federal agents.

If you're like most of us, you probably have two varying reactions to viewing your hot dogs this way. First, you may be surprised that the federal government should be so deeply involved in such a small matter. But second, you may wonder what sorts of conditions stimulated this government involvement. The answer to that is that research revealed that many hot dogs were not made out of pork or beef, as we'd all assumed; indeed, some were not made out of meat at all; and few were all meat. Most of the government rules you just read were imposed to protect you from poison, disease, and deception when you ate hot dogs. As a consequence, hot dogs are now mostly meat.

Adapted from *U.S. News & World Report*, June 30, 1975, p. 27.

Contracting The government can also influence behavior of businesses and individuals through its large-scale purchasing. It presently refuses to do business with firms that discriminate, for example.

THE COSTS AND BENEFITS OF GOVERNMENT INTERVENTION

The costs to businesses and citizens

There can be no doubt that government regulation is costly. The budgetary cost for government's role in it is usually put at about $3 billion a year. This covers the costs of issuing some 25,000 or more federal regulations every year and following up by inspection to see that they are observed. It also covers the distribution of over 5000 different federal reporting forms to business and the processing of responses by some 74,000 bureaucrats. And these figures do not include tax reports.

Once government issues regulations, business must abide by them. Filling out government forms is said to cost business some 130 million work-hours a year. And no one knows for certain how much it then costs business actually to do what the regulations require. General Motors estimates its "compliance cost" as $1.3 billion each year – costs passed on to consumers, of course, in the form of higher prices. And a recent study estimated the total cost of federal regulation in 1976 as $65.6 billion, or $307 for each American.[12]

■ The benefits to citizens

This may suggest that regulation isn't worth the cost. But remember that it is regulation that has protected citizens from poisoned food, deadly "medicines," unsafe working conditions, and other serious threats. There can be no doubt that some regulation is inefficient, for safety rather than economic efficiency underlies some rules. Certainly some regulation results in special benefits such as subsidies for businesses, but other rules benefit consumers at business's expense. Regulation may limit technological innovation and diversity of products – but to increase safety.[13]

■ The benefits to business

Conservatives and businesses tend to be very critical of regulation. Former Assistant Secretary of the Treasury Murray L. Weidenbaum writes that "no realistic evaluation of the overall practice of government regulation comfortably fits the notion of benign and wise officials making altogether sensible decisions in the society's greater interests. Instead we find waste, bias, stupidity, concentration on trivia, conflicts among the regulators and, worst of all, arbitrary and uncontrolled power."[14]

And yet when deregulation – freeing business from government regulation – is proposed, the affected industries often protest wildly. When President Ford proposed deregulating the airlines and the trucking industry, those special interests were fearful and outraged. The reason was that both benefited from regulation that protected them from the free-enterprise competition they would otherwise have faced.

■ The problem of "captured" regulators

Some regulation limits competition automatically and purposely. Other regulation becomes limiting because the industry being regulated "captures" the regulating body. One reason for this development stems from the fact that each individual has but a small interest in regulatory policy, whereas the industry or business being regulated has a very large interest. The special interest therefore works harder to influence regulation favorably. Further, regulation of complex businesses requires special knowledge that is best – and perhaps often only – had by people who have worked in the industry. One study by a House Commerce Subcommittee found that half of the 120 commissioners recently appointed to nine regulatory agencies came from the

---

[12]Robert DeFina, *Public and Private Expenditures for Federal Regulation of Business* (St. Louis: Washington University Center for the Study of American Business, 1978).

[13]For a transcript of a debate on the subject, see W. S. Moore, ed., *Regulatory Reform* (Washington, D.C.: American Enterprise Institute, 1976).

[14]Murray L. Weidenbaum, "An Army of Regulators," *Houston Chronicle,* October 12, 1975.

industries they were supposed to regulate. Where are their sympathies likely to lie?[15] Some observers, furthermore, assert that there is a kind of "life cycle" for regulatory agencies. They begin by regulating because they have been established as a result of political pressures for regulation. But over the years, for the reasons noted here, they are "captured" by the industries they are supposed to regulate.[16]

☐ PROPOSED REFORMS

■ Deregulation

This perceived pattern has created more interest in various reforms of the regulatory agencies. One such reform is general *deregulation.* It seems most likely to occur in transportation and energy, where there are growing political pressures for it – to make transportation cheaper, and energy more expensive.

■ Sunset and sunshine laws

Another reform gaining increased favor is **sunset laws.** As we saw in Chapter 7, these laws provide that an agency is automatically abolished, or self-destructs, after a period of years (perhaps 7 or 10) unless Congress passes a law extending it. The theory is that this abolition would occur before the agency had been captured, and that it could then be replaced by a new, fresher, more public-interest-oriented agency if regulation were still deemed desirable.

Other proposed reforms are designed to make regulators more responsive. One is to make their deliberations less legalistic and more social and economic in their content, so that citizens could participate in and better understand their activities. Another calls for including consumer representatives on commissions or helping consumers to testify before them. And another, now partially in effect, called **sunshine laws,** requires that meetings be held in the open – in the sunshine – so that all can see what is happening.

■ Government ownership

Some have even proposed government ownership of industries that need regulation. Such is virtually the case with railroads now. But some railroads were near financial collapse when most of their passenger operations were largely taken over by Amtrak, a federal agency. And when later control over certain freight operations was taken over by Conrail, another governmental body, it was also because of economic troubles. Healthy regulated industries seem unlikely to face strong pressures for government takeover because of popular opposition to "socialism."

Some observers see developments such as these, coupled with capture of regulatory agencies by those regulated, as evidence of the further "blurring" of the

---

[15]In addition, as we noted in Perspective 3, until President Carter prohibited the practice for his employees, many regulators took jobs in the industries they regulated when they left government. This practice is often called the "revolving door" between business and government.

[16]See Marver Bernstein, *Regulating Business by Independent Commission* (Princeton, N.J.: Princeton University Press, 1955).

original line between the public and the private. In Mark Nadel's view, "through their considerable financial and organizational resources, corporations have attained superior access and leverage in the political system. Through a combination of inadequate legislation and their own efforts, giant corporations have been able to influence heavily and even, at times, to control the regulatory agencies that were supposed to hold the reins in the name of the wider public interest. Even more troublesome, . . . corporations themselves have been the promulgators of *public* policy – either in concert with government agencies or unilaterally."[17]

Thus, in a sense, government regulation of business is sometimes matched by what might be called business regulation of government. Some would say the same is true of labor because of its large-scale influence on campaigns (as we saw in Perspective 2) and in Congress. And, as will become clearer in Chapter 20, the role our government plays in influencing other governments is more and more matched by influence on the United States from other governments such as those of oil-exporting states. In addition, of course, business and labor influence each other, just as large American multinational corporations influence other governments which are trying to regulate them.

☐ THE QUESTION OF PLANNING

Relations among major segments of the economic and political world are thus very complex. So, we have learned, are the problems that must be dealt with by the public policy that is developed. As a result, there is growing belief that the existing approach of government intervention is inadequate.

■ Back toward a free-market economy?

". . . we face general economic problems with a bag of tools for government interference with economic processes that were fashioned piecemeal, over a long period of time, to cope only with specific problems," writes economist Jonathan R. T. Hughes. "The mechanisms of control are not coordinated where they are effective; their effects spill over into areas of economic life which are not subjected to the same controls, and the consequences are generally disruptive." The problems, Hughes argues, "have brought into focus the unhappy fact that the federal nonmarket control structure is a halfway house, without the virtues of either economic planning or free-market economy. This," he says, "is the greatest economic problem of our time."[18]

If so, it is also thereby a great political problem. For economics and politics can no more be separated today than the economy and the government. The question is, what should be done to cope with the problems? "The private sector is the productive sector for the most part," Hughes argues. "Significant reform must

---

[17]Mark Nadel, *Corporations and Political Accountability* (Lexington, Mass.: Heath, 1976), p. 199. See especially chap. 5.

[18]Jonathan R. T. Hughes, *The Governmental Habit: Economic Controls from Colonial Times to the Present* (New York: Basic Books, 1977), pp. 6, 12.

therefore create greater scope for the private economy – fewer controls, lower taxes, reduced (at least proportionately) public expenditures – so long as inflation persists."[19]

But while Hughes and some colleagues argue for a return toward a free-market economy, others believe the movement toward planning has gone too far to be reversed. They point out that even conservative President Richard Nixon attempted to move the nation farther in this direction, so widespread was the agreement that planning was becoming necessary and so pervasive was existing government intervention.

■ On toward national planning?

"Once the state has accepted the obligation to intervene intermittently, in order to secure some desirable condition for society, it soon discovers that its actions exert a powerful influence," writes British economist Andrew Shonfield. There is then no turning back to pure market capitalism.

> A responsible government cannot opt out of the duty of assessing the long-term consequences of these intermittent interventions. Once it begins to make such an assessment, there is a strong inducement to examine the nature of the more fundamental objectives that it would in any case pursue, in default of these short-term pressures. The next stage is an attempt to organize these objectives into a coherent design, in which the various parts are consistent with one another, and then to put them inside the framework of a timetable. Introduce a periodic check on how far events are keeping pace with the timetable—and the main instruments of modern economic planning are in position."[20]

And so, if this analysis is correct, one thing leads to the next. The original interventions for regulation produce certain effects, not all anticipated. These effects are evaluated and then compared with general economic and social objectives. Efforts are then made to be more consistent in developing objectives. This encourages the government to set up schedules for achieving those objectives. And finally systems are devised to check on the progress toward achieving them.

■ What kind of planning and for whose benefit?

"At a certain point," says historian Otis Graham, "people see that planning is almost here, and they had better decide whether they want it or not. That is where Americans have arrived . . ."[21] But there are still questions: What kind of planning? For whose benefit? Any planning government, liberal Democratic or conservative Republican,

---

[19]Ibid., p. 242.

[20]Andrew Shonfield, *Modern Capitalism: The Changing Balance of Public and Private Power* (New York: Oxford University Press, 1965), p. 122.

[21]Otis L. Graham, Jr., *Toward a Planned Economy: From Roosevelt to Nixon* (New York: Oxford University Press, 1976), pp. xii.

■ Building a democratic economy

If planning is to work for a majority of Americans . . . we must directly confront the need for public control over major economic decisions now in the hands of the private sector. . . . we must develop a practical, sensible alternative that uses the power of Government to construct an economy that serves human priorities first. At the same time, we must take seriously the development of new democratic arrangements to avoid the dangers of centralized bureaucratic power. . . .

Over the next decade and beyond, Americans will be asked to make major adjustments and sacrifices. Only when there is a sense of community and a sense of participation will such plans have the confidence and trust of the population. One important step on the path to restoring a sense of community in America will be the encouragement of employee ownership and participation in management. . . .

Second, as we move deeper into a planned economy, it is imperative that we begin to widen participation in the planning process itself. Fortunately, we do not have to start from scratch. We have behind us some ten years of experience with various attempts at citizen participation and community planning—from urban renewal to transportation to anti-poverty programs. . . . Many critical skills needed to build the capacity for democratic planning have been learned.

. . . Ultimately, *community* plans for population growth, job development, housing, and transportation could and should be the basis upon which national resources are allocated. . . .

Because we are Americans our vision must be practical. It must show how jobs can be provided for all, how prices of necessities can be stabilized, how new values can be encouraged. These are the true needs of the vast majority of citizens, so our vision must demonstrate how the majority can, in fact, achieve its goals. It must also have an overriding premise: The major decisions in our economy are now or will soon become explicitly political; democracy, therefore, cannot stand still. If it is to survive, it must be extended to the economy.

From Gar Alperovitz and Jeff Faux, "Building a Democratic Economy," *The Progressive,* July, 1977, pp. 15-19.

would have to create the institutions that make planning possible: forecasting groups, policy coordination bodies, organizations to assess the impact of technology, and so forth. Any planning-oriented government would also have to try to control the bureaucracy, improve the budgetary process, and rein in the independent agencies. And any administration would have to seek to coordinate all important aspects of policy: economic policy, raw materials, energy, land-use, population size and distribution.

But there would be differences depending on whether the first American administration to embrace national planning is liberal or conservative. As Graham suggests, "Liberal planning may be expected to make income redistribution one of its goals; to turn more readily to nationalization; to tilt toward consumers rather than producers. Conservative planning would leave redistribution to the workings of natural selection (or the market), prefer competition to nationalization, tilt toward producers rather than consumers."[22] Further, there is the possibility that such planning will involve greater public participation, as Gar Alperovitz and Jeff Faux advocate in the box titled "Building a democratic economy."

---

[22]Ibid., p. 308.

The selection of national priorities is always a crucial and difficult decision in governmental long-range planning.

Martin Adler Levick/Black Star

There are, in other words, major issues of economic and social policy still far from decided, far from agreed upon, within government and among the people. The politics of production, with which we have been concerned in this chapter, leaves much to be decided by the politics of scarcity. There is growing concern that many resources vital to our growth may be running out, and that there may therefore be limits to production with which our system has not yet come to terms. Some even argue that our assumption that growth itself if necessary and desirable should be questioned. We'll return to these vital questions in our discussion of the Politics of Energy in Perspective 7. In any case, the politics of production also leaves much to be decided by the politics of consumption. And consumption depends upon property – the distribution of income and wealth. So it is to the politics of property that we next turn our attention.

□ SUGGESTIONS FOR FURTHER READING AND STUDY

For background on the evolution of Western capitalist economies, see Barrington Moore, *The Social Origins of Democracy and Dictatorship* (Boston: Beacon paperback, 1966) and Karl Polanyi, *The Great Transformation* (Boston: Beacon paperback, 1957). A helpful survey of modern developments is Emmette S. Redford, *American Government and the Economy* (New York: Macmillan, 1965). For a controversial analysis, see John Kenneth Galbraith, *The New Industrial State* (Boston: Houghton Mifflin paperback, 1967). And for an argument that the only way to control business effectively is for the federal government to charter corporations (a responsibility now left to the states), see Ralph Nader, Mark Green, and Joel Seligman, *Taming the Giant Corporation* (New York: Norton paperback, 1976). Finally, for an argument that the problem is capitalism itself, see Paul A. Baran and Paul M. Sweezy, *Monopoly Capital: An Essay on the American Economy and Social Order* (Baltimore: Penguin paperback, 1975). To keep up with current developments in the economy and government's role, the best sources are the major business periodicals: *Business Week, Fortune,* and *Forbes.*

17 The politics of property: the rich and the poor

One in every 900 Americans is now a millionaire – there were 240,000 of them at the last count.[1] But one in every eight Americans lives in poverty[2], and studies suggest that many of these are malnourished or go to bed hungry every night.[3] We cannot really understand the challenges confronting the American political system without taking note of the great distance between the rich and the poor in America – and the relatively large numbers of citizens who live at these extremes.

America is by far the richest large nation in the world, if we consider the total wealth of the country divided among the number of citizens. As we saw last chapter, that wealth is now estimated at $6.2 trillion, or $28,600 for every American. But of course that wealth is not really divided among the citizens with anything approaching equality. Indeed, roughly 25 percent of all wealth in America is held by 1 percent of American adults – a figure that has remained remarkably constant over the 150 years for which figures are available. And the richest 20 percent of the population holds 75 percent of the wealth, while the poorest 20 percent holds but 0.2 percent. So it is clear that the disparities between the extremes are massive.

We may have occasional contact with either the very rich or the very poor – in charity drives, for example, in volunteer work, or in political campaigns. But most of us rarely encounter those at either extreme in *their* daily lives, any more than they see us when they enter into *our* daily lives.

Our imaginations may be good enough to conceive of what it would be like to be rich. But they are rarely good enough to imagine the hunger and cold and illness and hopelessness of being poor in the richest large nation on earth. Yet if we are to understand the successes and failures of our government in wrestling with the problems of the poor, we must make such an imaginative leap. So let us try to imagine, with the help of some experts, what life is like for perhaps the most invisible American poor of all, the migrant agricultural workers.

---

[1] "Boom in Millionaires," *U.S. News & World Report,* July 26, 1976, p. 40.

[2] Census bureau, *Money Income and Poverty Status of Families and Persons in the U.S.: 1976* (Washington, D.C.: Government Printing Office, 1977). Publication Series P-60, no. 107.

[3] In 1972, for example, the Citizens' Board of Inquiry into Hunger and Malnutrition in the United States issued a report that concluded that "47 percent of the total poor receive enough only to purchase a diet at the bare survival level; and that 12 percent receive less than three-fourths of the recommended dietary allowances. For 43 percent of the nation's poor there is no federal help at all." See its report, *Hunger U.S.A.* (Washington, D.C.: The Board, 1972). See also Nick Kotz, *Let Them Eat Promises: The Politics of Hunger in America* (Garden City, N.Y.: Anchor paperback, 1971).

☐ THE EXPERIENCE OF MIGRANT WORKERS

On May 18, 1971, a ranch hand came across a body in a shallow grave in a peach orchard along the Feather River near Yuba City, California. A week later, another ranch hand stumbled upon another shallow grave nearby. Sheriff's deputies called to the scene found several more such graves. On one body was a receipt naming a farm labor contractor who lived nearby. Armed with a search warrant, deputies found in his home a crude map with a number of strange marks, several of which seemed to correspond to the sites of the graves that had been discovered. They resumed their digging in a drizzling rain by searchlight, and by 4:30 in the morning they had found six more bodies. All had the same deep lacerations about the head and puncture wounds in the chest. Only two had any identification on them. All appeared to be transient white farm workers. They had been dead, according to coroner's estimates, from 48 hours to 6 or 7 weeks. The farm labor contractor was arrested, protesting his innocence. With the aid of the map found in his house, the search continued. Three more bodies were found that morning, bringing the total to twelve. Another three were unearthed the next day, and six more the following day. Four more bodies found during the following week brought the final total to twenty-five.

Twenty-five men had been killed and buried over a period of several months. What had suddenly become the largest mass murder in American history was shocking enough. But even more stunning was the fact that *none of these men had been missed* once they had disappeared over this period of several months. All were migrant farm workers. What is it, some Americans suddenly wondered, about the situation of farm labor that could make such a mass murder so possible and so unnoticeable?

■ What migrant workers do

We eat the fruits – and vegetables – of the labor of our farm workers at almost every meal. We continue to enjoy the cheapest and most diversified produce of any developed country. Yet we rarely wonder how that produce gets from the trees and furrows to our supermarkets and restaurants. We might suspect that by now machines handle the planting, weeding, and picking. It is true that more and more of our produce is "weeded" with chemical poisons and picked by steel fingers. Nevertheless, the labor of men, women and children remains essential in the harvesting of tomatoes, potatoes, cucumbers, onions, lettuce, oranges, apples, pears, cherries, peaches, and many other items. Most of that work is "stoop labor" – bending at the waist for 8, 10, or 12 hours at a time – or "ladder labor" – reaching into trees from the top of a ladder and moving the ladder through the orchard from tree to tree as the sun moves through the sky.

■ Who the migrant workers are

Who does this backbreaking and dangerous labor? No one really knows very precisely, because farm workers tend to be anonymous and often invisible, like those twenty-five who met their deaths at early ages, flat broke, at the hands of a farm labor contractor who hired them. The family farm has been steadily disappearing since the Depression, and now most farms are gigantic establishments owned by large corporations called "agribusinesses," operated by managers and plowed and planted by machines. Nonetheless, the crops are still largely picked by human labor, and that human labor is migrant labor, because there are no family members on hand to do the harvesting, and the local residents no longer want to do the backbreaking work – least of all for the going wage, which generally ranges from $1 to $2 an hour.

And so at harvest time the migrants are trucked in or bused in – some 200,000 of them from winter quarters in Florida, southern Texas, and southern California, and some 600,000 or more from Mexico. The latter enter the country illegally to pick, dodge the law throughout the harvest season, and then return home in winter.

There are three typical "migrant streams" as they are called. One, consisting primarily of blacks and Puerto Ricans, moves up the east coast from the Florida citrus groves to the Long Island potato fields and the New England apple orchards. A second, consisting largely of Mexican Americans and Mexicans, starts in southern California picking citrus and moves north to pick celery, grapes, and lettuce on the way to the Pacific Northwest cherry, peach and apple harvest. The third and biggest stream, which consists largely of whites and Mexican Americans, begins in southern Texas. These American citizens are forced to fan out into most states of the Union at harvest time because of competition from the many Mexican citizens who cross the border, legally or illegally, and work in the fields of Texas for wages so low that Americans could not subsist on them. These American citizens hit the road, in their jalopies or in buses or trucks provided by the "crew boss" – a business man who rounds them up, transports them for a fee, sells them food en route (usually at outrageously high prices, which he can demand and get because the workers have no way of getting to stores), and takes a commission from every wage the workers earn. At the end of the harvest in the northern states, they retrace their route back south.

Migrants work when and where they can, usually remaining in one place for several weeks and then moving on when the crop is picked. If it rains, the harvest may be delayed a week, and if so they get no wages and have to borrow from the crew boss. If they get sick, they have no health insurance, and so must borrow from the crew boss – if they can find a doctor who will treat them, or a hospital that will admit them, transient and impoverished as they are.

The work is backbreaking. The sun is often overpowering. There are rarely any toilet facilities near the fields. The day lasts as long as the workers can hold out, because the crop must be picked quickly before it spoils, and because they must earn as much as they can while there is still picking to be done.

■ **How the migrant workers make out** For this work, migrant farm workers have always earned well below the federal minimum wage that protects most other workers. At last, in 1966, despite continued strong opposition from agricultural interests, the Congress passed a special minimum wage for agricultural workers. But the law established that wage at 30¢ an hour lower than the minimum wage for industrial and service workers and

Michael Heron/Monkmeyer

Migrant workers in Texas.

made it applicable only to those working on very large farms. Smaller farms are covered only by state minimum-wage laws, and few states have included farm workers under these laws. This is why wages in fact tend to range from $1 to $2 an hour. But even this pittance is earned only when one is actually working.

Migrant farm workers who are 20 years old or more average $12.05 a day, according to a recent Department of Agriculture study. If they are 14 to 19, their daily earnings average only $9.10.[4] Yet these figures are misleading, because on the average migrants are only able to work 74 days a year – the number of days when the harvest is ready and when they can get to the fields that need harvesting. Consequently the average income of a migrant farm worker is only $1654 a year. Out of this he or she must pay not only expenses on the road but also living costs when he or she is without work back at "home base" in the off-season, perhaps in Florida or in South Texas. But these homes, more often than not, are migrant camps or housing projects with inadequate heat, light, and ventilation. In 1970 a group of doctors inspected conditions in migrant camps in southern Florida and southwest Texas. They found crowded living conditions that fostered the spread of contagious disease and an almost total lack of minimal medical care and health services. They reported:

> We saw people with most of the dreadful disorders that weaken, disable, and torture, particularly the poor. High blood pressure, diabetes, urinary tract infections, anemia, tuberculosis, gallbladder and intestinal disorders, eye and skin diseases were frequent among the adults. Almost without exception, intestinal parasites were found in the stool specimens examined.

---

[4]Tony Dunbar and Linda Kravitz, *Hard Traveling: Migrant Farm Workers in America* (Cambridge, Mass.: Ballinger, 1976), p. 95.

■ The plight of migrant children

". . . if my child looks right up at me and says he thinks we live a bad life, and he thinks just about every other child in the country is doing better than he is—I mean, has a better life—then I don't know what to say, except that we're hard-working, and we do what we can, and it's true we're not doing too well, that I admit. Then my girl, she's very smart and she'll tell me that sometimes she'll be riding along with us, there in the back seat, and she'll see those houses we pass, and the kids playing, and she'll feel like crying, because we don't have a house to stay in, and we're always going from one place to another and we don't live so good, compared to others. But I try to tell her that God isn't going to let everything be like it is, and someday the real poor people, they'll be a lot better off, and anyway, there's no point to feeling sorry for yourself, because you can't change things, no you can't, and all you can do is say to yourself that it's true, that we've got a long, hard row to hoe, and the Lord sometimes seems to have other, more important things to do, than look after us, but you have to keep going, or else you want to go and die by the side of the road, and someday that will happen, too, but there's no point in making it happen sooner rather than later—that's what I think, and that's what I tell my girls and my boys, yes sir, I do.

"Now, they'll come back at me, oh, do they, with first one question and then another, until I don't know what to say, and I tell them to stop. Sometimes I have to hit them, yes sir, I'll admit it. They'll be asking about why, why, why, and I don't have the answers and I'm tired out, and I figure sooner or later they'll have to stop asking and just be glad they're alive. Once I told my girl that, and then she said we *wasn't* alive and we was dead, and I thought she was trying to be funny, but she wasn't, and she started crying. Then I told her she was being foolish, and of course we're alive, and she said that all we do is move and move, and most of the time she's not sure where we're going to be, and if there'll be enough to eat. That's true, but you're still alive, I said to her, and so am I, and I'm older than you by a long time, and why don't you have faith in God, and maybe do good in your learning, in those schools, and then maybe you could get yourself a home someday, and stay in it, and you'd be a lot better off, I know it, and I wish we all of us could—I mean, could have a home."

> Most of the children had chronic skin infections. Chronically infected draining ears with resulting partial deafness occurred in an amazing number of the smaller children. We saw rickets, a disorder thought to be nearly abolished in this country, and every form of vitamin deficiency known to us that could be identified by clinical examination was reported. . . . There was one case of leprosy.[5]

The doctors cited statistics that bear out the findings: the life span of migrants is about 20 years less than the national average; infant and maternal mortality is 125 percent above the national average; and the death rate from pneumonia, influenza, and tuberculosis is over 200 percent above the national average.

---

[5]Raymond M. Wheeler, M.D., testifying before the Senate Subcommittee on Migratory Labor, July 20, 1970. Printed in "Migrant and Seasonal Farmworker Powerlessness," Part 8-A (Washington, D.C.: Government Printing Office, 1970).

Migrant life has perhaps its greatest effect on the children. In order to make ends meet in even the most minimal way, migrant laborers must take their entire families with them as they move from harvest to harvest. Even the children, once they are 5 or 6, do piece-work picking in the fields alongside their parents to supplement the meager family income.

Because of this, and because migrants on the road are not subject to compulsory school attendance laws, and special schools for migrants are few and far between, the estimated 1 to 2 million migrant children are rarely able to get an education that might prepare them for a life outside the stream. So migrant children generally grow up to be migrant adults, and then usually in turn perpetuate the chain by having itinerant children who manage if they are lucky just enough schooling to be able to read and write. The words of migrants themselves often tell more about the migrant experience than our statistics. See the box titled "The plight of migrant children" for one migrant mother's story, explained to psychiatrist Robert Coles, of how she coped with the attitudes of her children.

□ THE OTHER POOR

Migrants are not the only poor in America. They may be the poorest, and they are certainly the poorest of those who do work when they can. However, the millions of members of migrant farm labor families who hit the road every year are but a small fraction of the poor in America today.[6]

In 1977 there were 24,975,000 Americans living below the official "poverty line" of $5815 in income per year for a family of four, or $2884 for a nonfarm single person living alone, according to the Census Bureau. This amounted to about 12 percent of the entire American population. Who are they? Table 17.1 shows the breakdown and percentages.

The Census Bureau began keeping such statistics in 1959, determining the poverty line by calculating the cost of a basic nutritionally adequate diet for a family of four and then multiplying it by three because it found that families spend a third of their income on food. Any family whose income falls below that poverty line will likely be unable to live at minimal levels of nutrition, shelter, and health.

This poverty line of $5815 can be contrasted with the annual median (or middle) family income of $14,960. Clearly the average family lives much better than the family at the margin. But a recent study of this "average wage earner" (a 38-year-old father of two who lives with his wife in a relatively comfortable home and drives a fairly new car) discovered that even he has trouble making ends meet on his income. He tends to spend about $500 more per year than he makes, and he hasn't enough savings in the bank to pay for his own funeral if he dies.[7] If this

[6]Migrants and their families are hard to find and track, so there are no reliable figures on their numbers. Government estimates range from a low of 255,400 workers alone to a high of 2.7 million workers and dependents combined. But a public-interest group called Rural America offers as "conservative" an estimate of 1.6 million migrant and seasonal farm workers with 3.2 million dependents—a total of 4.8 million. *New York Times* October 8, 1977.

[7]Harry Atkins, "Typical Wage Earner in the Red," *Boston Globe*, September 13, 1976.

Wide World Photos

The elderly, especially those living in cities, make up a large proportion of the poor in the United States today.

Eric Kroll/Taurus Photos

Only a small proportion of the elderly are able to enjoy a comfortable existence in the years following their retirement.

middle-level wage earner finds making ends meet so difficult, how much worse must it be for the really poor? That will depend to some extent on who and where they are.

The poor are found in every part of America today. Government studies show that poverty is greatest among two groups, as Table 17.1 indicates. One is the elderly, who generally have no jobs and poor health and live on inadequate Social Security or welfare payments that are fixed – that is, payments do not automatically rise when inflation raises the cost of living. The other poor group is families that are black, Mexican American, or Native American Indian – especially those headed by women. Greater *percentages* of these groups – the old and the rural minorities – are poor. But because these groups are small percentages of the total American population, the largest *numbers* of the poor are white people and live in cities. In fact, about two-thirds of all poor people are white, and about 40 percent of all poor people live in central cities.

Consequently, if we were to try to locate a "typical" poor American, we would look among whites living in the central cities of America, and we would most likely settle upon an individual who moved his family into the city (perhaps Los Angeles, Chicago, or Detroit) from Oklahoma, for example, or the rural Deep South. But the poor are found in every area of the country. As of 1975, the South Central states led the nation in terms of the percentage of total population below the poverty line with 19 percent; the figure for New England was 8 percent; the Mid-Atlantic states, 10 percent; the Great Lakes states, 8 percent; the Great Plains states, 10 percent; the South Atlantic states, 13 percent; the Mountain states, 12 percent; and the Pacific states, 11 percent.

Another important point about the poor revealed by government statistics is the fact that about four out of every ten poor Americans are *children* under the age

TABLE 17.1

Who are the poor?

Category	Number of people in category who are poor	Percentage of people in category who are poor
All persons	24,975,000	11.8
Race or minority group		
White	16,713,000	9.1
Black	7,595,000	31.1
"Spanish origin"	2,783,000	24.7
Age		
Under 14	7,982,000	16.9
14 to 21	4,350,000	13.2
22 to 44	5,738,000	8.6
45 to 54	1,688,000	7.2
55 to 59	932,000	8.6
60 to 64	972,000	10.5
65 and over	3,313,000	15.0
Residence		
Central cities	9,482,000	15.8
Suburban	5,747,000	6.9
Rural	9,746,000	14.0
Families		
All families, total	5,311,000	9.4
All families, father present	2,768,000	5.6
All families, father absent	2,543,000	33.0
White families, total	3,560,000	7.1
White families, father present	2,182,000	4.9
White families, father absent	1,379,000	25.2
Black families, total	1,617,000	27.9
Black families, father present	495,000	13.5
Black families, father absent	1,122,000	52.2
Individuals outside families	5,344,000	24.9
Male	1,787,000	19.7
Female	3,557,000	28.7

Source: Census Bureau, *Money Income and Poverty Status of Families and Persons in the U.S.: 1976*, Series P-60 #107 (Washington, D.C.: Government Printing Office: 1977).

of 16, many of them living in families headed by a woman because the father is dead or gone. Emerging from poverty is difficult enough for a child in a typical household. It is much harder if the household is headed by a woman, because women still face major job and wage discrimination and have a more difficult time working while raising children. Moreover, that discrimination is compounded when the woman is black or Puerto Rican or Mexican American, as many poor mothers are. More than half of the children living in families headed by women are poor – eight times the percentage of poor children in families headed by men. Their prospects for escaping poverty are bleak.

Although there are more poor whites than poor blacks, the *percentage* of blacks who are poor is almost four times as great as the percentage of whites who are poor. Almost one in every three blacks is below the poverty line, while only one in every eleven whites is. Blacks are one-third of the poor, but because they are only one-eighth of the population, blacks who are *not poor* are only one-twelfth of all those who are not poor. In other words, the common belief that most poor people are black is false; two-thirds of the poor are white. But it is true that a much higher percentage of black people than white people is poor.

Another common misconception is the belief that the poor are poor because they do not, or will not, work. In 1975 over 40 percent of the heads of poor families worked the entire year or were unemployed less than 15 weeks or were in the military or at school. Almost a quarter of these heads of poor families work full time all year long – as do many poor single individuals. Only 4 percent of the heads of poor families did not work at all in 1975 – this because they could not find a job. In addition, one in every five poor families has two or more income earners and still remains below the poverty line.[8]

The point is that just working – even full time all year long – does not necessarily prevent poverty. If wages are not high enough, a family cannot escape poverty through work. Indeed, if a person worked full-time for all 52 weeks of the year with no holidays at the 1977 federal minimum wage of $2.30 an hour, he or she would earn only $4784 before paying Social Security and any taxes or other deductions. That would still be over $1000 less than the poverty-line income for a family of four! So even full-time work at the minimum wage is not enough for a family provider to enable the family to escape poverty.

☐ WHO ARE TODAY'S RICH?

The percentage of poor in America has remained relatively constant in recent years, but the number of rich has skyrocketed, even in years of economic slowdown. In 1948 there were only 13,000 Americans who owned real estate, goods, stocks, and bonds worth a million dollars or more. However, by 1953 that number had more than doubled, and by 1969 it had increased almost ten times to 121,000. During the next seven years it doubled again, so that by 1976 estimates were that 240,000 Americans were millionaires – one in every 900 people. What is more, these individuals together own a total of $417 billion worth of property, or 12 percent of all individually held property in America.[9]

Who are these American millionaires? Not much is known about their personal lives, for both scholars and the government tend to study the poor rather than the rich.[10] We do know that about one-third are 65 and older, while another one-third are under 50. And about half are women. However, although millionaires account for only about 0.1 percent of all Americans, those Americans with net worths of $100,000 or more total 5 million people, or more than 2 percent of the population.

---

[8]Charles E. Starnes, "Contemporary and Historical Aspects of Officially Defined Poverty in the U.S.," in *Understanding Social Problems,* ed. Don H. Zimmerman et al. (New York: Praeger, 1976), p. 44.

[9]"Boom in Millionaires," *U.S. News & World Report,* July 26, 1976, p. 40.

[10]One exception is Ferdinand Lundberg, whose book *The Rich and the Super Rich* (New York: Lyle Stuart, 1968) was widely criticized for inaccuracies. Another exception (and a critic of Lundberg) is former Census Bureau official Herman P. Miller, whose book *Rich Man, Poor Man* (New York: Crowell, 1971) has a chapter devoted to the rich. Unfortunately, its data are so old now as to be virtually meaningless, given the "boom in millionaires."

□ WHO OWNS AMERICA?

Although 2 percent of the people own property worth $100,000 or more, 10 percent still own nothing, or owe more than they own and so have a net indebtedness. *Ownership of property* (real estate, goods, stocks, bonds, and cash) is the most important measure of poverty and wealth in America. If we split the population in two, the bottom half owns only 3 percent of the privately held property, while the top half holds the other 97 percent—and 56 percent of that is owned by the richest 10 percent. Figure 17.1 gives more details.

A second important indicator of poverty and wealth is *annual income*. The top half receives 77 percent of all income, compared to 23 percent for the bottom half. The top 10 percent receives 29 percent while the bottom 10 percent receives only 1 percent. Figure 17.2 shows income distribution by fifths of the population for various years since 1929, revealing how little income distribution has changed.

The importance of these figures on annual income is two-fold. First, they reveal that many Americans have such small incomes that they have difficulty making ends meet, and so few can save enough to accumulate property or wealth. Second, the distribution of income is so unbalanced that in general the rich do indeed get richer while the poor tend to get poorer. Furthermore, what redistribution has occurred in recent years has favored whites over blacks, and suburbanites over city-dwellers. As a result, the problems of the center cities, where blacks and other poor people tend to be concentrated in urban ghettoes, continue to worsen year by year—a problem we'll return to next chapter.

FIGURE 17.1

Distribution of wealth in the U.S. population.

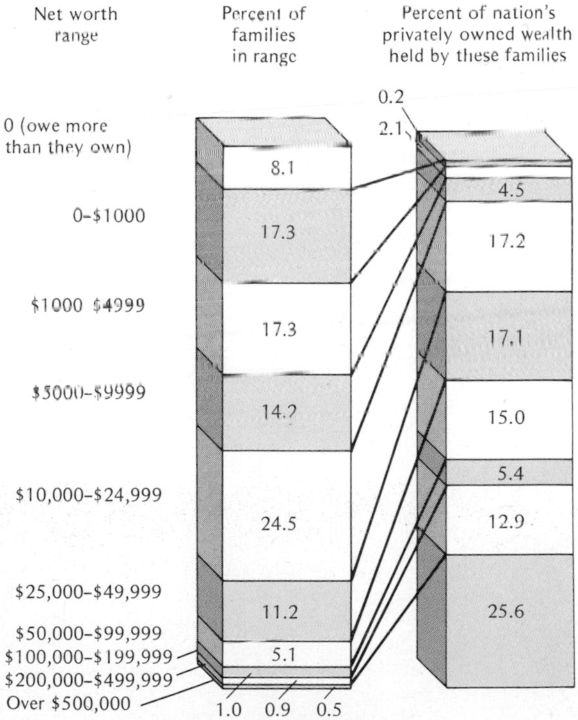

Source: Data from "Survey of Financial Characteristics," *Federal Reserve Bulletin,* March 1964, p. 291.

□ THE PLIGHT OF THE WORKING MIDDLE CLASS

■ Where the typical American's money goes

These years, the average American taxpayer pays about 35 percent of his or her earnings in taxes – federal, state, and local. That means $1 of every $3 you earn is likely to go to the tax collectors. Viewed another way, if you work, you work for the tax collectors from January until early May, and after that your earnings are yours to spend on housing, food, clothing, and other items. Or, viewed yet another way, in a typical 8-hour day, your first 2 hours and 42 minutes are spent working for the tax collectors. Then, if you're a typical American, you work another hour and 30 minutes to pay for your housing and an hour and 8 minutes to pay for food. After this comes 40 minutes for transportation, 26 minutes for medical care, 25 minutes for clothing, and 20 minutes for recreation. The last 49 minutes of the work day go for such things as personal items, educations, savings, and so on. It doesn't take much calculating, given figures like these, to see why the average American doesn't improve his or her financial situation much.

■ How the working American's income has changed

Most Americans call themselves "middle class." Still, we can separate out those who are not "professionals" (such as doctors and lawyers and teachers) and not managers (salaried business executives). Those left are the group usually called the lower middle class. Income for this group now ranges from $5000 to $15,000 per year. Forty percent of all American families now have incomes in this range. In the decade from 1946 to 1956, the take-home pay of this group rose by about 2 percent per year after allowing for inflation. In the next decade, 1956–1966, this real take-home pay rose by only 1.4 percent per year. But in the decade 1966–1976, it rose by only 0.3 percent per year. This works out to an average gain of $5.66 in weekly income over 10 years – of which almost $4.00 went to higher state and local taxes.[11] So the only

[11]See "The New Two-Tier Market for Consumer Goods," *Business Week,* April 11, 1977, pp. 80–83.

FIGURE 17.2
Distribution of income in the U.S. population.

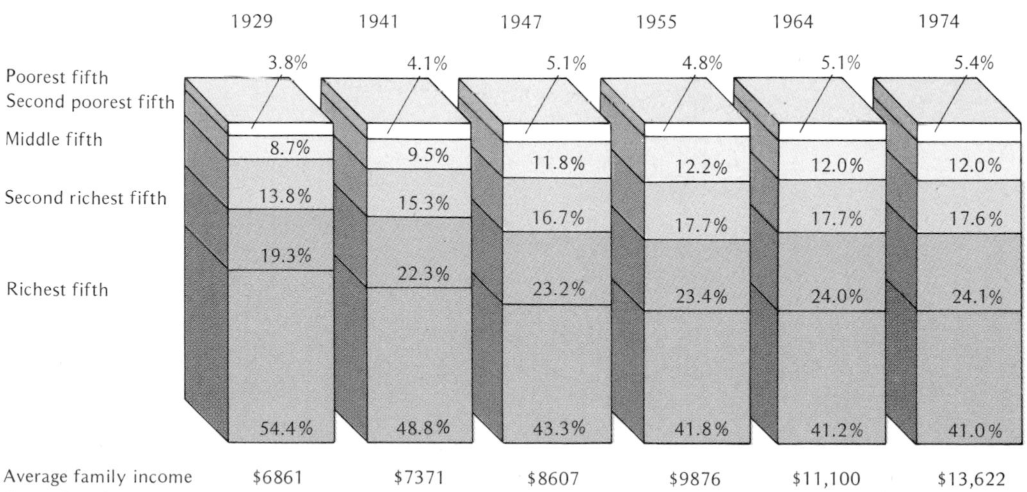

Source: Data from *New York Times Magazine,* July 4, 1976, p. 102.

way for such a worker's family to increase its income significantly has been for the spouse to go to work. We saw in Chapter 15 that this has been happening increasingly. But the limits to job opportunities for largely untrained women are such, as we saw, that the impact of the second income is quite limited.

The next group up, which is often called the upper middle class, with incomes ranging from the median (about $15,000) to $30,000, is having troubles too. In 1967 an urban family of four needed $13,050 to sustain a comfortable standard of living, according to government estimates. A decade later, in 1977, that figure had almost doubled, to $24,850, according to the Labor Department.[12] The result is growing resentment. Much of it focuses on taxes, which have been increasing rapidly at the state and local levels. In particular, local property taxes to support local government have grown greatly in recent years. As a result, many homeowners have found it difficult if not impossible to pay these taxes, and some have even been forced to sell their homes. The result has been a growing "tax revolt" among homeowners. An early example of this revolt was the passage by California voters of Proposition 13 in the spring of 1978. This new law set strict limits to property tax increases and reduced the tax bills of some homeowners by as much as 60 percent. In doing so, it also cut the revenues of local governments and forced cutbacks in many services. Such tax revolts seem likely to spread in coming years. But beneath such revolts is antagonism toward government, which sets tax levels and often seems to pay more attention to the needs and desires of the rich and the poor than it does to those of the middle class. To understand the bases for these feelings, we must look further at the causes of wealth and poverty in our system and at programs supposed to change them. This means looking at taxes and welfare, as well as at government programs designed to increase jobs.

□ THE CAUSES OF POVERTY

It is easy to describe the causes of poverty in economic terms. As two economists summarize, the poor

> have small quantities and low qualities of resources. The market places a low value on the services they provide in the market [that is, the jobs they can do well]. The low productivity and, therefore, the low pay of the poor are due to low levels of training and education, misfortune, relatively small inheritances, and discrimination. The poor are in a vicious circle which is difficult to escape. What they need in order to move out of poverty they do not have and cannot afford to acquire [such as better education and training]. So they remain poor.[13]

We have already discussed discrimination against minorities, women, and the elderly in Chapters 14 and 15. We examined unemployment last chapter and

---

[12] "Squeeze on the Middle Class," *U.S. News & World Report,* May 2, 1977, pp. 50–51.

[13] Richard H. Leftwich and Ansel M. Sharp, *Economics of Social Issues,* rev. ed. (Dallas: Business Publications, 1976), p. 221.

education in Perspective 5. The case of migrant workers highlights the importance of – and obstacles to – education. It also emphasizes the role of underemployment, the inability to work regularly, in causing and prolonging poverty. But the problems and obstacles go deeper than this.

In recent years, some sociologists have argued that the poor are poor and remain poor because they live in a "culture of poverty" that traps them in attitudes and experiences that are difficult to overcome. This assertion has stimulated much debate.[14] But whether or not the poor are trapped by attitudes and experiences, they are hurt by what some now call "information poverty."[15] The lack of skills such as reading ability among the poor is exacerbated not only by poor education, but also by the frequent fact that English is not their native language. In addition, the poor have health problems that they cannot afford to have corrected, some of which affect their hearing and eyesight and therefore make learning more difficult. Furthermore, their backgrounds tend to make them inexperienced in such skills as budgeting and bargaining in purchasing, and so their economic plight may worsen.

The poor, in this sense, tend to live in an "information ghetto." They do receive information from outside via the media – especially from radio, television, and movies. But the media available to them tend to emphasize entertainment and fantasy rather than information useful for coping with real problems. Furthermore, the impact of their own social group's images, ideas, myths, and folklore will tend to be reinforced by limitations on personal contacts with people outside their ghetto, and so these images and myths will shape their understanding of how to relate to the outside world.

Because the surrounding outside world is governed by a different culture of information – the set of images, ideas, myths, and folklore that are dominant and therefore determine the chances for success – people in the information ghetto are at a disadvantage mentally as well as physically. This mental domination and insulation help to explain why the poor may not know how to get help for such immediate physical problems as a shortage of food or an illness or rat bites – even though social service programs may exist in their neighborhood or their city.

Perhaps even more devastating to the life chances of the poor are the attitudes toward themselves and toward their future prospects that the poor tend to hold. Because our culture tends to emphasize that people get what they deserve, whether in the capitalist marketplace or in the religious afterlife, the poor tend to believe that they are poor because in some way they deserve to be poor, or at least because they do not deserve to be better off. Furthermore, they tend to believe that the future holds little opportunity for improvement, and so they sometimes resign themselves to their impoverished existence and try to make the most of a bad situation. Thus they suffer from what experts often term "a negative self-image" and "a low feeling of efficacy" coupled with "a fatalistic, pessimistic attitude toward the future." In other words, they tend to believe themselves undeserving and unable to succeed, and they believe the future unpromising. Having such attitudes, they tend to participate less in politics than any other group, as we noted in Chapter 3.

---

[14]For examples, see Eleanor B. Leacock, ed., *The Culture of Poverty: A Critique* (New York: Simon & Schuster, 1971).

[15]Thomas Childers, *The Information-Poor in America* (Metuchen, N.J.: The Scarecrow Press, 1975).

TABLE 17.2

Effective federal tax rates on income

Income range	Tax rate (%)
0–$3000	0.5
$3000–$4999	1.7
$5000–$9999	5.1
$10,000–$14,999	8.6
$15,000–$19,999	10.5
$20,000–$24,999	11.8
$25,000–$49,999	13.9
$50,000–$99,999	22.2
$100,000–$499,999	31.0
$500,000–$999,999	32.8
Over $1,000,000	34.2
Average for all ranges	11.0

Source: Charles L. Schultze et al., *Setting National Priorities: The 1973 Budget* (Washington, D.C.: Brookings, 1973), p. 434.

□ THE CAUSES OF WEALTH

It may seem strange to speak of the causes of wealth as we do of the causes of poverty. Yet no one believes that wealth is somehow a natural state of man. Many people are, of course, born wealthy, as children of the rich. Research has shown that "one cause of the inequality of property and skills is the degree of privilege conferred by one's socioeconomic background and other parental influences."[16] One such influence is *educational advantage.* Another is parental "pull" or *connections* (friends and acquaintances) that are helpful in getting jobs and making money. Also important is *financial inheritance* itself, although one study has found that actual estates are on average inherited when the heir is 38 years old, and further that "the children of the rich in America tend to regress toward mean (average) incomes—and thereby prevent the increasing concentration of wealth."[17]

The other major factor in determining wealth that cannot be overlooked is *taxation.* The federal income tax is supposed to be "progressive"—to tax those with larger incomes at higher rates. But there are so many loopholes of the sort we discussed as tax subsidies last chapter that much of the progressive effect is lost. Table 17.2 reports the "effective" rate of federal income taxes (the actual rate after allowed deductions) for each income group. It reveals that those with incomes under $10,000 do indeed pay smaller percentages. But there is surprisingly little difference in the rate someone making $10,000 pays compared to that of someone making up to five times that much. Further, an income of $100,000 and an income of many millions are taxed at almost the identical rate in practice. So the federal tax rate is really more "tiered" than progressive.

State and local taxes, especially those on consumption, which we call "sales taxes," tend to be "regressive"—to tax the poorest the most, because everyone has to buy food, clothing, medical supplies, and so forth, but those taxed purchases are a bigger percentage of the income of the poor. When we add in all state and local taxes—on income and property as well as on consumption—the net effect is virtually to equalize almost everyone's burden at around 35 percent.[18]

These tax provisions—special subsidies and relatively constant tax rates—make it easier for the rich to become richer, for they leave the rich with more after-tax income to use in making still more income. Our inheritance laws do the same.[19] The inheritance tax rate can go as high as 77 percent (on estates of over $10 million). But there are so many loopholes so well used that the actual rate was about 0.2 percent even before some rates were lowered in 1977. And this means that most family fortunes are passed on from one generation to the next largely intact.

[16]John A. Brittain, *The Inheritance of Economic Status* (Washington, D.C.: Brookings Institution, 1977), p. 1. For a survey of studies on this subject, see C. Russell Hill and Frank P. Stafford, "Family Background and Lifetime Earnings," in National Bureau of Economic Research, forthcoming volume of the Conference on Research in Income and Wealth, and Brittain, p. 78.

[17]Stanley Lebergott, *The American Economy: Income, Wealth and Want* (Princeton, N.J.: Princeton University Press, 1976), pp. 176, 211.

[18]These matters are now widely discussed in the literature. See, for example, Miller, *Rich Man, Poor Man,* chap. 2, and Joseph Pechman and Benjamin Okner, *Who Bears the Tax Burden?* (Washington, D.C.: Brookings Institution, 1974).

[19]See Lester Thurow, *Generating Inequality* (New York: Basic, 1975).

Library of Congress

The number of the very rich has skyrocketed in recent years. In 1884, the millionaires of the United States were pictured on a single lithograph; today the United States has over 240,000 millionaires.

☐ POLICIES AND PROGRAMS TO COMBAT POVERTY

■ The origins of governmental antipoverty programs

Until recently, the federal government paid little attention to the poor. Aid to the poor was mostly the province of private charity and big-city "machines." The legislation and government programs affecting the poor that did exist often did more to control the poor (for example, restrictions on unionizing) than to help them meet their day to day needs, let alone to help them escape poverty. Politicians, of course, had long talked of such improvements. In 1928, President Herbert Hoover had declared: "We shall soon, with the help of God, be in sight of a day when poverty will be banished in the nation." But Hoover instead found himself presiding over the coming of the Great Depression. Four years later there were 13 million unemployed, more than a quarter of the workforce. It took Franklin Roosevelt's New Deal and World War II just to return America, almost 20 years later, to approximately the working conditions of 1928.

The keystone of the New Deal was legislation providing greater economic security for all Americans, rich as well as poor. The Social Security Act of 1935 established the system of contributions by workers into a *social security* fund called "Old Age, Survivors, and Disability Insurance" (OASDI) that paid pensions to the unemployed elderly. Similarly, a program of contributory *unemployment insurance* was established, which for the first time granted some of those losing jobs support payments for a period while they looked for new jobs. Both of these programs, with certain modifications, persist to this day as the heart of the federal government's approach to the problems of the poor – but these programs are available to everyone, rich and poor alike.

■ The extent of federal income-support programs

By 1977, about one-third of all Americans, some poor but many far from poor, received assistance of some sort from federal programs. These programs together cost almost $250 billion per year by 1977. Included was $82.4 billion for Social Security, $20.8 billion for Medicare, $13.9 billion for unemployment insurance, $9.9 billion for Medicaid, $6.4 billion for Aid to Families with Dependent Children, $5.4 billion for Food Stamps, as well as funds for retirement programs, veterans' benefits, and other direct-payment and tax-benefit programs. The $250 billion total works out to 17 percent of all personal income in America and averages $1150 per American, although the benefits are not spread at all evenly. Some of this aid is in Social Security payments and public assistance for the 32 million people who are blind, disabled, or elderly and for poor families with dependent children. But most Social Security, unemployment insurance, and veterans' benefits payments go to those who are not poor. And many other individuals, some far from poor, receive special government benefits. For example, the federal government spent $124 million subsidizing by 6¢ each many of the 2.2 billion half-pints of milk drunk by 60 million school children in 1975. In the same year, 3 million veterans received an average of $270 per month in educational benefits. In addition, cut-rate loans subsidized by the federal government went to 800,000 college students. And 82,000 cotton farmers received up to $20,000 apiece in subsidies. These are only a few instances of the general pattern of government subsidies, some of which we itemized last chapter, and many of which go to those wealthy Americans who often criticize "handouts" to the poor.[20]

■ The extent of the welfare system

Our concern at this point is with the part of this colossal spending that is intended to help the poor – the welfare system, as it is called. It is by now a massive system. By 1977 it provided aid to 23.4 million people at a cost of over $38 billion. Doing so required 346,000 employees, 4000 of whom were federal and the rest state and local officials. Table 17.3 shows the major programs of the welfare system and how they have grown. Most of these programs are administered by state and local governments but largely financed and controlled – by Washington. The sole exception is what is called "general assistance," which is organized and financed by states and localities. One result of this decentralization of some programs is that welfare spending per poor individual varies considerably from state to state, as Table 17.4 reveals.

A more general result of this overlapping of responsibilities and funding is the complexity of the welfare system. Jimmy Carter, like most politicians, campaigned on a pledge to reform welfare. His secretary of health, education, and

[20]"Government Payouts: Something for Almost Everyone," *Austin American-Statesman,* August 22, 1976.

TABLE 17.3

Growth of the welfare system

	Recipients (millions)			Payments ($ billions)		
	1965	1976	Percent increase 1965–1976	1965	1976	Percent increase 1965–1976
Aid to Families with Dependent Children	4.4	11.2	154	1.7	9.9	480
Aid to aged, blind, and disabled	2.8	4.2	50	2.1	6.0	185
Medicaid	13[a]	24.4	87	3.3[a]	15	354
Food Stamps	0.8	17.3	2060	0.03	5.3	17,566
General assistance	0.7	0.9	28	0.38	1.6	321

[a]These figures are for 1968, the first year of Medicaid figures.

welfare, Joseph A. Califano, put the problem well: "Given the vast resources this nation spends on income assistance, it is appalling that our programs are so poorly coordinated . . . , unfairly exclude millions from adequate aid, contain absurd incentives to break up families or discourage work . . . and are an administrative jungle, incomprehensible to legislators, administrators and the American people alike." Califano should know, for his department, HEW, shares with the Labor Department the primary responsibility for what we call our welfare system.

What should be done about welfare? One observer has characterized the present situation as one "in which there is no political will to retreat on existing commitments and no social vision to move forward. . . . If there is to be any productive advance in the social-policy debate, it will depend," he asserts, "on finding some kind of new amalgam of ideas and self-interests that the ordinary citizen can understand and accept. This would imply a situation where the values involved are so widely shared that there is a sense that the policy costs involved are not irrelevant, but 'worth it,' in terms of what is being achieved."[21]

Obviously, we cannot in this chapter solve a problem that is massive and complex enough to stymie our government. But we can clarify the objectives of the welfare program and the politics of the debate over welfare reform. With that

[21]Hugh Heclo, "A Question of Priorities," *The Humanist*, March-April 1977, p. 24.

TABLE 17.4

Total welfare spending per poor individual by state, 1976

$1850–$3033
California
Connecticut
Hawaii
Illinois
Massachusetts
Michigan
New Jersey
New York
Pennsylvania
Rhode Island
Vermont
Wisconsin

$1389–$1850
Colorado
District of Columbia
Maine
Maryland
Minnesota
Ohio

$950–$1389
Alaska
Delaware
Georgia
Indiana
Iowa
Kansas
Nevada
New Hampshire
Oregon
Washington

$370–$950
Alabama
Arizona
Arkansas
Florida
Idaho
Kentucky
Louisiana
Mississippi
Missouri
Montana
Nebraska
New Mexico
North Carolina
North Dakota
Oklahoma
South Carolina
South Dakota
Tennessee
Texas
Utah
Virginia
West Virginia
Wyoming

accomplished, we should be able to examine the various programs, both those already attempted and those proposed, to see which seem most promising in terms of the objectives and most possible in terms of the politics.

■ The objectives of the welfare system

The fact of the matter is that there is no agreement on just what the objectives of the welfare system are or should be. When the American people are asked whether they favor the welfare system, they say no. In 1977, for example, a national survey found that 58 percent disapproved of "most government-sponsored welfare programs."[22] Included in that majority of disapprovers was even a majority of those who had received welfare! On the other hand, these same people favored food stamps for the poor by 81 to 13 percent, favored aid to poor families with dependent children, 81 to 13 percent, and favored health care for the poor, 82 to 13 percent. So the same people who oppose "welfare" favor the three major welfare programs.

Perhaps these attitudes reflect the common uncertainty about just what objectives welfare programs should seek to achieve. There seems general acceptance of the objective of improving the living conditions of the poor to a decent level. But what is a decent level? Even most of the poor in America are better off now than most citizens were in 1900, at least in certain respects. For example, in 1900 only 15 percent of all living quarters had flush toilets, but by 1975 it was 86 percent. In 1900 only 3 percent had electricity, but by 1975, 99 percent did. In 1900 only 1 percent of all Americans had central heating, while by 1975, 62 percent of the poor had it.[23] The important point is that the poor are better off in *absolute* terms but remain worse off in *relative* terms. They suffer from what sociologists call *relative deprivation*—being deprived of something relative to what other people have.

Does this mean, then, that the American people, who favor overcoming various types of relative deprivation, support *equality* as a social goal? There have always been some liberals who advocate extensive equality—*an equal start* and *equal treatment under law,* of the sort we discussed in Chapters 14 and 15. Some go further to advocate virtual *equality of income and even of possessions.* These are the socialists. Conservatives, at the other extreme, tend to support only so much equality as is necessary to preserve societal stability. If there were too much inequality, the result might be revolution in which the privileged would lose everything. This fear can be a powerful reason to support welfare programs. Indeed, some argue that a major function of such programs—and other government activities—has been to keep the working class quiet.[24]

Conservatives have also generally believed that *inequality* is functional for capitalism, because it creates incentives for the poor to work harder, and it allows the system to give greater rewards to those who take risks or contribute specially.[25]

[22]A *New York Times*-CBS News Poll, July 1977, reported in *New York Times* August 3, 1977.

[23]See Lebergott, *The American Economy,* pp. 326–375, for these and other comparisons.

[24]For interesting discussions of some of these points, see Frances Fox Piven and Richard Cloward, *Regulating the Poor* (New York: Pantheon, 1971), and Murray Edelman, *Politics as Symbolic Action* (Chicago: Markham, 1971).

[25]For a discussion of this "functionalist theory of inequality" see Michael Best and William Conolly, *The Politicized Economy* (Lexington, Mass.: Heath, 1976), chap. 3.

Conservatives thus tend to prefer efficiency and liberty to equality, while liberals prefer the reverse.[26] But public policy on the question of the welfare system rarely comes down to such basic attitudes, because both poverty and welfare programs already exist and continue to grow. Thus the question policy makers and would-be reforms have to confront is how serious the present situation is.

■ The definition of the welfare problem

There are basic differences in beliefs about the nature, causes, and cures of poverty that have important implications for the design of welfare programs. We shall review some of these different beliefs here.

Is poverty basically caused by individual factors such as effort, motivation, genetic inheritance, being old, and so forth? Or is it primarily caused by situational factors such as growing up in a poor family, getting a bad education, seeking work in a time of high unemployment, facing racial or sexual discrimination, and so forth?

Those who consider poverty primarily a product of individual factors tend to hold the poor person responsible for his or her poverty. They also tend to be pessimistic about the likely success of antipoverty programs. So they generally favor only as much welfare as is required to keep the population quiet.

Those who see poverty as primarily situational are more likely to support welfare programs. They may hope that such programs will change the situational factors such as poor job training or widespread unemployment. Or they may see welfare programs as "tiding over" the victim until the economy improves or discrimination lessens, for example.

The situational view of poverty assumes that poverty can be temporary, if only conditions can be changed. The individual view, on the other hand, must expect poverty to be lasting in the absence of character change or "lesson-learning" by the poor. Which is closer to the truth? Until very recently, statistics seemed to show that most people who were poor stayed poor. From 1962 to 1963, for example, according to one study of Census Bureau figures, 6.9 million families remained in poverty while 1.8 million moved out of poverty only to be replaced by another 1.7 million moving in.[27] Most observers thought that many of those 1.8 million who moved out of poverty in 1963 would be back whenever economic conditions in the country worsened.

But a large-scale study of a representative sample of 5000 families from across the United States in the 1970s found that there are relatively few such "hard-core poor" who stay in poverty year after year. This study, carried out at the University of Michigan, found that poverty is a temporary situation for most people. People may move into poverty when they get divorced or first leave the home of their parents. But they may also leave poverty by getting married, changing jobs, or getting more

---

[26]For a discussion of this, see Arthur M. Okun, *Equality and Efficiency: The Big Tradeoff* (Washington, D.C.: Brookings Institution, 1975).

[27]Robert J. Lampman, *Ends and Means of Reducing Income Poverty* (Madison: Institute for Research on Poverty of the University of Wisconsin, 1971), p. 62.

schooling. The fact is that while one of every eleven American families is in poverty at any given time, *only about a quarter of these families is likely to stay in poverty for 5 years in a row.* Those which do are most likely to be families headed by uneducated blacks, but some have elderly, female, or disabled heads. On the other hand, the study found that *nearly one-third of all people fell below the poverty line for at least one of the 9 years over which the study has been conducted.*[28]

So fewer people are "persistently poor" than we had thought, if this study does indeed represent the American population. But, as William Ryan concludes from this study, "The economic fate of most of us is not within our own control, but is, rather, intertwined with that of countless others. This means that at least seven out of ten families are economically vulnerable, with at least an even chance of spending some years of their lives in financial distress. It is not merely some vague minority called 'the poor' who stand in economic peril; it is the majority of Americans.[29]" But though each of us may thus someday be affected by how the welfare system operates, few of us are involved in welfare reform. Nor are the interests of the majority of Americans of direct concern to those engaged in reshaping the program.

■ The politics of welfare reform

Nobody admits to liking the welfare system the way it is, so everyone's for welfare reform. But different groups mean different things by "welfare reform." To the public, most of whom say they oppose welfare as it is, reform means lower costs and less fraud. To welfare recipients, many of whom dislike it, reform means better benefits. These two positions are already in conflict – but neither group plays much role in shaping welfare programs. That responsibility is shared by the Departments of HEW and Labor, which oversee the programs, by the Congress, which passes the laws creating and funding them, and by the huge "welfare bureaucracy" that has developed in state and local governments. State and local governments face the prospect of bankruptcy as welfare costs soar, and so they favor having Washington pay the shares they now pay. Many in Washington agree. Jimmy Carter campaigned for the presidency terming the welfare system "an insult to those who pay the bill and those who honestly need help" and pledged to "federalize" or "nationalize" it – to have the federal government pay the state and local shares. Timothy Connor, director of Income Security Planning in HEW, says, "We must set up a system so that each level of government does what it does best. The thing the federal government does best is raise money and write checks. It is at its worst in dealing with individual problems."[30]

But what the government raises money and writes checks for, it also tries to control. State and local government welfare bureaucrats fear such federal control. They have become a big part of the payroll in state and local government. The

[28]The Panel Study on Income Dynamics, directed by James N. Morgan at the University of Michigan. See Robert Reinhold, "Poverty Is Found Less Persistent But Wider Spread Than Thought," *New York Times,* July 17, 1977; and "A Surprising Profile of America's Poor," *U.S. News & World Report,* November 8, 1976, pp. 57–58.

[29]William Ryan, "Most of Us Are Kept on a Short Leash," *New York Times,* July 10, 1977.

[30]Quoted in *Business Week,* January 17, 1977, p. 55.

welfare bureaucracy now offers many places for politicians to put their friends and supporters in comfortable jobs. So they – employees and politicians – are generally opposed to federal control.

So the task of reformers in the White House and the cabinet departments involved is very difficult politically – as Presidents Johnson, Nixon, and Carter all found out. They were always dealing with all these vested – and competing – interests while trying to bring order to, and make more effective and efficient, a wide range of programs costing some $40 billion a year by 1977.

■ The range of welfare programs

Many different welfare programs have been attempted or proposed over the years. In general, these fall into five major categories:

1. The *direct income* programs attempt to increase the consumption of recipients by increasing their income directly. Foremost among these are the *social insurance* programs such as Social Security, unemployment insurance, and workers' compensation (which pays benefits to those injured on the job); and *public assistance* programs such as Aid to Families with Dependent Children. This group also includes proposals for a guaranteed family income or a negative income tax that would pay money directly to those poor who earn less than a minimum income.

2. The *direct services* programs provide needed services directly to those who can't afford them. The *food stamps* program, which grants coupons spendable only for food to the poor, at 20 to 30 percent of their face value, is one such program. *Housing assistance,* which we'll discuss next chapter, is another. *Medicaid,* which provides federal funds to states to pay for medical care for certain poor people, is yet another. Other such programs furnish day care, family planning assistance, community legal services, and social casework services.

3. The *indirect services* programs provide services such as *education* or *manpower training* in job skills so that the poor can get better jobs.

4. The *indirect income* programs foster *economic development* of depressed areas to create jobs for the poor and *minimum wages* and *unionization* to improve the labor market for the poor.

5. The *community organizing* programs attempt to strengthen the political power of poor neighborhoods so that they can demand better treatment from local government and businesses.[31]

■ The War on Poverty and the Great Society

Many of these programs were established in the years of President Lyndon Johnson's Great Society. In his first State of the Union message, shortly after the assassination of President Kennedy, Johnson asserted: "This Administration today, here and now, declares unconditional war on poverty in America." Later that year, on June 26, 1964, in a speech outlining his Great Society program, Johnson declared: "We stand at the edge of

---

[31]For a summary of programs in these various categories, see Sar A. Levitan, *Programs in Aid of the Poor,* 2nd ed. (Baltimore: Johns Hopkins University Press, 1976).

the greatest era in the life of any nation. For the first time in world history, we have the abundance and the ability to free every person to find fulfillment in the works of his mind or the labor of his hands."

■ Effects of the War on Poverty

In the Johnson years, federal aid to the poor almost doubled, from $7.7 billion in 1964 to $14.6 billion in 1968. Indeed, it kept rising in the Nixon-Ford years as well, to $17.9 billion in 1970, $27 billion in 1974, and about $40 billion in 1977. But public sentiment for these programs of cash support, employment and training, community and economic development, education, health, housing, food, and child care, was eroding year by year.

The major reasons for this slackening of public support are not hard to find. President Johnson had decided to wage undeclared war on Vietnam (at an eventual cost of some $150 billion) at the same time that he waged declared war on poverty. The resulting stresses and distortions in the American economy culminated in the unprecedented combination of inflation and recession under Richard Nixon. Americans became more conscious of their own economic problems and less willing to help the even more impoverished poor. The attitude underlying the opposition was clearly expressed in Nixon's presidential campaign of 1968, in which he declared: "For the past five years we have been deluged by government programs for the unemployed, programs for cities, programs for the poor, and we have reaped from these programs an ugly harvest of frustration, violence, and failure across the land."

This was an assessment growing numbers of Americans seemed to share. It was not shared by the poor, who had experienced real, if limited, improvement in their actual, if not their relative, economic position. The Congressional Budget Office, a nonpartisan research group, in 1976 studied the impact of the various governmental programs, from Social Security to the War on Poverty, on the economic situation of the poor. It estimated that without any government benefits including Social Security about 20.2 million American families—more than a quarter of all Americans—would be living below the poverty level. When it estimated the size of various government money payments and added the cost of such nonmoney (or "in-kind") benefits as Medicaid and food stamps, it concluded that the number actually living in poverty in 1976 was only 5.4 million, or 6.9 percent of all American families. This study seemed therefore to indicate that the Great Society programs have been more effective in fighting poverty than is generally recognized.[32] But many experts were skeptical of the study's reliability.

But if experts disagreed about just how many people remained poor, they also disagreed in their assessment of the Great Society programs intended to lower the numbers of the poor. Some increasingly looked back with favor on the

---

[32]The Congressional Budget Office study is *Poverty Status of Families under Alternative Definitions of Income,* background paper no. 17, 1977. Its conclusions differ substantially from those of the Census Bureau, which we reported earlier this chapter. The Census Bureau is skeptical of the validity of the study on a number of grounds, which are discussed briefly in its *Characteristics of the Population Below the Poverty Level: 1975,* Series P-60, no. 107 (Washington, D.C.: Government Printing Office, 1977). Further criticisms may be found in works referred to there.

achievements of the Great Society programs. Others believed the whole package was so inadequately conceived and administered, so riddled with difficulties, and so lacking in sound evaluation that it had been doomed to failure.

One of the leading experts on poverty in America and programs to combat it, Sar Levitan, assessed the Great Society programs in a book published in 1976 and entitled *The Promise of Greatness.* He found the goals realistic and the programs "reasonably efficient." They "moved the nation toward a more just and equitable society, mitigating the problems of the disadvantaged and disenfranchised," he concluded. But "by the mid-1970s, however, a plateau had been reached and new initiatives were required if the previous momentum were to be renewed."[33]

But other experts argue that the War on Poverty, like the war on Vietnam, must ultimately be assessed as a defeat, for in each instance the United States government tried mightily and failed and finally decided to withdraw from the struggle. In the words of one strong critic, "Like the Vietnam War, the War on Poverty made the world's most powerful government look ignorant, foolish, and helpless. And in both cases, the cause of misfortune was the same – the heavy investment of resources, lives, and the government's faith and credit in projects that did not even pretend to respect the requirements of social technology and seldom considered the relationship of means and ends in any serious way."[34]

This perspective suggests a more careful examination of *the conduct* of the War on Poverty, rather than just its actual effects on the lives of the poor. For it implies that the War on Poverty may epitomize mistakes previously made, and still being made, in the design and implementation of governmental efforts to legislate away poverty.

■ The politics of the War on Poverty The War on Poverty was intended to be a comprehensive attack on various components, causes, and consequences of poverty, including tax burdens of the poor, civil rights violations, regional economic imbalances, problems of youth, need for vocational training, and hospital care insurance. But this very broadness of the campaign was a major cause of its limited success in the minds of many critics, for several important reasons. First, it created tremendous conflicts within the government, for it established an Office of Economic Opportunity (OEO) to develop and administer programs that often overlapped and sometimes conflicted with existing programs in such departments as HEW, Labor, and Agriculture. The result was endless bureaucratic politicking of the sorts we discussed in Chapter 7 that only hindered efforts to help the poor.

This proliferation of overlapping programs also inevitably created confusion in the mind of an individual who wanted help. For example, a high school dropout in need of assistance might not know whether to go to the local branch of the Office of Education of HEW, the Office of Juvenile Delinquency of the Labor

---

[33]Sar A. Levitan and Robert Taggart, *The Promise of Greatness* (Cambridge, Mass.: Harvard University Press, 1976), pp. 7–11.

[34]Theodore Caplow, *Toward Social Hope* (New York: Basic Books, 1975), p. 167.

Department, the OEO's Neighborhood Youth Corps or Job Corps – or the local welfare bureaucracy.[35]

But the problems and limitations of the War on Poverty went even deeper. For one thing, as contrasted with the various foreign wars the United States has waged, including the contemporaneous one in Vietnam, the War on Poverty was underconceived and underfinanced in terms of the scale of the problem. Take, for example, its efforts to eliminate unemployment. Unemployment in the cities was greater among blacks than among other groups, and greatest among black teenagers. The Job Corps was intended to rectify this situation by training young blacks for new jobs. But the new jobs did not always exist once people had been trained, and they were rarely created by the program. Further, the largest scale the program ever achieved was in 1967, when it was training but 41,000 people out of the millions in need of work. And finally, it concentrated on black teenagers at the expense of those individuals with the gravest needs: the older workers with large families to support and no jobs.

There were other problems of the War on Poverty that, whatever the good reasons for them, in fact crippled its effectiveness. Because local political and welfare bureaucracies were so often either corrupt or incompetent, officials in Washington decided to bypass them in designing and implementing the federal programs. The unfortunate but unsurprising result was that state and local officials often united to prevent such programs from succeeding, or even to keep them out all together.

Furthermore, the commendable provision that poverty programs should be developed with "maximum feasible participation" locally by those to be helped was so vague and unmanageable that local governments and vested interests often gained control and kept the poor out, resulting in what Daniel Patrick Moynihan later termed "maximum feasible misunderstanding."[36]

Probably because they were more visible and easier to reach, the program increasingly concentrated on urban blacks, even though, as we have seen, this group constitutes a minority of the poor. The result was that other possible support for the

---

[35] For a discussion of this and other problems, see Ben Seligman, *Permanent Poverty: An American Syndrome* (Chicago: Quadrangle, 1970).

[36] Daniel P. Moynihan, *Maximum Feasible Misunderstanding* (New York: Free Press, 1969).

VISTA

A VISTA volunteer working with children in Spanish Harlem in New York City. VISTA (Volunteers in Service to America) is a U.S. government program established in 1964 to provide volunteers to work at improving the living conditions of persons living in impoverished areas of the United States, its possessions, and Puerto Rico.

program was missed, and when urban blacks became more militant and seemed ungrateful, public and congressional support for the programs virtually evaporated.

Perhaps the root of the problem was disagreement over the fundamental objective of the War on Poverty, based on different analyses of American social problems and their dynamics. This created serious divergence over the proper course for the government to take. One view, developed by Moynihan in a special and very controversial report to the president in 1964, was that the root of the problem of the cities, and so of much poverty more generally, was *instability of the black family structure,* which led to households headed by women, to demoralized absent black males, and to underprivileged and underdisciplined children. The corresponding program designed to stabilize the black family emphasized raising the occupational status and income of black males, improving the education of blacks, and providing community services to overcome material disadvantages.

But an alternative view argued that the problem was *white racism,* which resulted in continuing segregation of, and discrimination against, blacks. This view led to an emphasis on integration of schools, communities, and employment.

Yet a third view asserted that the underlying problem was *class exploitation* rather than racism. This analysis used the colonial analogy borrowed from international relations but substituted urban blacks and other groups of poor people for the native peoples of colonized lands as the class being exploited. The recommendation therefore was for liberation that would result in each community's economic autonomy and control of its own politics, policy, schools, banks, stores, and so forth, to be achieved by "community action programs" that mobilized the people against outside interests, institutions, and controls.[37]

The War on Poverty as it developed combined aspects of all three approaches – a political compromise as understandable as it was self-defeating to the cause of elimination of abject poverty in the world's richest nation. The result was that the War on Poverty did not really attack the underlying problem: the grossly unequal distribution of income in America, which perpetuates poverty even when people can work because so many jobs pay so poorly and those at the low end of the pay scale are the first to be cut when the economy falters – as it soon began to under the strains of Vietnam. The United States in the mid-1970s entered the worst, most prolonged, least understood, and worst-coped-with recession since the Great Depression of the 1930s. Most of the gains that the War on Poverty had achieved for the poor were soon devalued and many were eventually wiped out.

□ THE CONTINUING QUESTIONS OF POVERTY AND WELFARE

■ Tax reform

Any major welfare reform is bound to cost more money. "Federalization" of the costs would add another $25 billion, experts believe, and addition of childless couples now not eligible would add another $10 billion. Where would this money

[37] These three approaches are summarized in Caplow, *Toward Social Hope.*

TABLE 17.5

What the American people own and what they owe

On the plus side	$ billions
Savings accounts	881.0
Corporate stocks	734.8
Pension-fund reserves	435.5
Life-insurance reserves	174.6
Cash and checking accounts	171.9
State and bonds	80.4
Mortgages	80.0
U.S. savings bonds	72.0
Other U.S. Government securities	49.6
Corporate bonds	71.8
Other financial assets	56.8
Total assets	2,808.4
On the minus side	
Mortgages outstanding	566.9
Consumer credit	217.8
Other debts	84.2
Total debts	868.9
Net financial assets	1,939.5

Source: These figures, as of January 1, 1977, were provided by the Federal Reserve Board and published in *U.S. News & World Report,* April 1, 1977, p. 21.

come from? Liberals argue it will require steeper, more progressive income tax rates. If income taxes are raised for the wealthy and a "negative income tax" is adopted to transfer money to the poor, the income tax might yet become an instrument for income redistribution. But that prospect raises objections not only from the upper middle class, but from those who hope someday to join that group.

For inevitably it is the upper middle class that must bear most of the burdens of welfare spending – as of defense spending and indeed any government programs. People seeing the uneven distribution of income that we described earlier this chapter sometimes conclude that we could "soak the rich" to spread the wealth. But as of 1974 there were only 783,000 families with incomes of more than $50,000. If all their income were taxed at 100 percent and spread around, it would mean only about $1000 per family nationwide.[38] The really rich, in other words, as we also noted above, are *rich in wealth,* rather than in income. As of 1977 the American people as a whole had assets of $2808.4 billion and debts of $868.9 billion – net assets were thus $1939.5 billion, as Table 17.5 details. Yet, as we noted above, about 75 percent of this wealth is owned by the top 20 percent of the population, while the lowest 20 percent own only 0.2 percent of it. If we imposed a wealth tax to tax away all this wealth and redistribute it among all American families, each family would receive over $30,000. So there *is* a tax reform that could abolish poverty. Of course, it would also abolish capitalism. And that's something the American people – even the poor – show little sign of desiring.[39]

■ The poorest of the poor: migrant workers

There are marginal improvements in the situation of migrant workers from time to time. Perhaps the most encouraging is the progress in education for migrant children. HEW has a special migrant education program that provides funds to special programs in twelve states that have special migrant education centers and to other states with special programs. As a result of such programs, in 1977, 4792 migrant youths graduated from high schools in the United States – up from 1460 the year before. In addition, HEW reports it is supporting educational programs for some 503,985 migrant students now. But that total is still perhaps only a quarter of those who would be in school if they were not migrants. And unfortunately there is still no national school credit transfer system, so the studying that children do in a school while "up the road" in one state usually does not transfer to their school in their home base.

This problem typifies the difficulties faced by migrants. Neither the laws nor the antipoverty programs are developed with migrants in mind, and so migrants never benefit fully even when laws and programs are applied to them. Two experts, Tony Dunbar and Linda Kravitz, discuss what they feel is the most important way of improving what might be done to improve the plight of the migrants in the box

[38]"Tomorrow," *U.S. News & World Report,* October 4, 1976, p. 8. For a comparable calculation for 1970, see Lebergott, *The American Economy,* pp. 21–32, "On Confiscation."

[39]For a discussion of some of these issues, see Lester Thurow, "Tax wealth, not income," *N.Y. Times Magazine,* April 11, 1976, pp. 32–33, 102–107. For a comprehensive study of tax reform in its various forms, see Robert M. Brandon et al., *Tax Politics: How They Make You Pay and What You Can Do About It* (New York: Pantheon paperback, 1976).

■ Healing the wounds inflicted by migration

A final healing will occur only when wages on the farm go up. Nothing would do more to improve wages and working conditions in agriculture, and to eliminate the abominable labor contractor system, than the widespread development of a farm workers' union. At present, the federal government blocks the development of such a union by denying agricultural workers the right to organize under the National Labor Relations Act. Extending this act to include farm workers would be a mixed blessing, however, because workers protected by the NLRA are subject to the provisions of the Taft-Hartley Act: their right to boycott is severely limited, and the president may send strikers back to work for a "cooling-off" period if he believes this to be in the national interest. What little power farm workers' unions have gained has been through boycotts and by exploiting the short-lived vulnerability of the farm owner who must harvest his crops quickly when they are ripe. A "cooling off" period would remove this main weapon from the farm workers' arsenal.

It would be better to establish a separate federal agency to oversee collective bargaining in agriculture. The workers' right to elect a union and to bargain collectively must be recognized. At the present time, the farm workers' right to strike is not worth very much because so many illegal aliens are standing in line to take the jobs, and this situation will not change until the federal government is directly involved with labor relations in agriculture. . . .

From Tony Dunbar and Linda Kravitz, *Hard Traveling: Migrant Farm Workers in America* (Cambridge, Mass.: Ballinger, 1976), pp. 144–145.

titled "Healing the wounds inflicted by migration." But they also point out that "government, from the county food stamp office to the U.S. Congress, is unresponsive to migrants because migrants, in most cases, are nobody's constituents. They only work and pay taxes."[40]

■ Programs for the rest of the poor

In this, at least, we have found migrant workers are not so different from a surprising number of the poor. Only about 10 percent of those on welfare are able-bodied males who could work if jobs were available. Thus, ending poverty, or even curtailing it, will require much more than continued or expanded welfare payments. Among the programs that Sar Levitan and other experts argue are essential if poverty in America is to be significantly lessened are:

- progress on birth control
- programs of care for the special needs of children, including health, special education, and day care
- remedial education at the elementary and secondary levels
- further employment and training programs for employable poor
- greater progress in equal employment opportunities for blacks, Chicanos, Native Americans, women, and the elderly
- increases in the level and coverage of the minimum wage
- progress toward an adequate guaranteed annual income for all Americans.[41]

---

[40]Dunbar and Kravitz, *Hard Traveling,* p. 99.

[41]For further discussion of such proposals, see Levitan, *Programs in Aid of the Poor,* especially chaps. 4, 5.

Assessing antipoverty programs

Evaluation of government programs, both before they are adopted and after they have been tried, has long been inadequate. One reason for this is the difficulty of measuring impacts. Another is the lack of clarity about objectives. And a third is the varying political motivations that go into the shaping of programs by bureaucrats and politicians.

Antipoverty programs are no exception. Still, certain criteria must be used to assess proposals and programs. One group of experts has developed such a set of criteria for assessing antipoverty programs.[42] These experts found that the "negative income tax" proposal rated higher on balance than forty-seven existing programs and fifteen other proposals. Rating almost as highly were the proposal that the government serve as an "employer of last resort" (offering a job to anyone who cannot find one in the private sector) and the program of unionizing farm workers. But as we know, each of these has serious limitations: the first two because of their very high cost and the third because it only reaches a small percentage of the poor.

New approaches, attitudes, and behaviors

This only serves to emphasize once again the magnitude of the problem of poverty in America – and the inadequacy of the efforts undertaken thus far. "Although the issue of social welfare continues to attract well-intentioned concern," writes Thomas C. W. Joe of the University of Chicago's Center for the Study of Welfare Policy, "this concern is not being effectively translated into the monetary, technical, and managerial capacity. . . . It is here that the challenge to the concerned humanitarian becomes manifest: to gather up and develop all the tools and opportunities available – fiscal, political, constitutional, legal, bureaucratic, organizational – and apply them to poverty, misery, and alienation."[43]

Hugh Heclo suggests that "beyond this there will be a need for gradually building a sense of social solidarity – a sense that there are some things that we all owe to each other for our own good. . . . The democratic welfare state of the future . . . should help improve chances for individuals to make themselves happy, to find their own meaning, and to care whether others have a similar chance to do the same."[44]

After noting that it is not just the poor but the majority of Americans who

---

[42]These criteria assess: (1) the impact of a program on the individual who is poor (the program's impact on the person's self-concept, on his or her incentive to work, and on the stability of his or her family, and its encouragement of economic self-sufficiency); (2) the impact of a program on the poor as a group (its effect on the distribution of income and of basic goods and services, which segments and what percentages of the poor it reaches, and the percentage of the benefits going to those who are not poor); (3) the impact of a program on society as a whole (its effects on racial integration, social class divisions, and the distribution of political influence between the poor and other groups in society); and (4) the overall feasibility of a program (its popularity with the population generally, its political vulnerability to cutbacks with changes in administration and noncooperation from state and local governments and officials, its economic vulnerability to recessions or other problems, and its administrative vulnerability to snafus or attempted sabotage. See John B. Williamson et al., *Strategies Against Poverty in America* (New York: Schenkman/Wiley, 1975), chap. 6.

[43]Tom Joe, "Sweeping the Poor under the Rug," *The Humanist,* March-April 1977, p. 30.

[44]Heclo, "A Question of Priorities," p. 24.

are in economic peril, William Ryan contends that "security and progress, then, cannot be gained by individual action, but only by simultaneous action of all who are intertwined together. . . . The somewhat paradoxical moral," he concludes, "is that tens of millions of individuals will remain vulnerable until they learn to function collectively – to act, together, to get, for each other, a bigger piece of the pie."[45]

Political sociologist Morris Janowitz draws a further lesson from the growing economic plight of the middle class: "People have to take a more realistic view of how society operates. . . . if we're to have an effective government, we need a wide variety of grass-roots activity. That means that people must participate voluntarily in their community affairs – donate their time to serve on local boards and commissions, get involved in self-help activities. One big thing the middle class must learn is that life does not limit itself to the family. People have to be more involved in the community."[46] It's to such local relations and their politics that we turn next.

□ SUGGESTIONS FOR FURTHER READING AND STUDY

For further information about migrant workers, see Tony Dunbar and Linda Kravitz, *Hard Traveling: Migrant Farm Workers in America* (Cambridge, Mass.: Ballinger, 1976); William Friedland and Dorothy Nelkin, *Migrant: Agricultural Workers in America's Northeast* (New York: Holt, Rinehart & Winston, 1971); Robert Coles, *Uprooted Children* (New York: Harper & Row paperback, 1970); and William A. Rushing, *Class, Culture, and Alienation* (Lexington, Mass.: Lexington, 1972). See also Nick Kotz, *Let Them Eat Promises: The Politics of Hunger in America* (Garden City, N.Y.: Anchor paperback, 1971).

On poverty and equality, see Herbert Miller, *Rich Man, Poor Man* (New York: Crowell paperback, 1971); Herbert Gans, *More Equality* (New York: Pantheon paperback, 1968); Christopher Jencks et al., *Inequality: A Reassessment of the Effect of Family and Schooling in America* (New York: Basic Books paperback, 1972); and the many publications of the Census Bureau.

On welfare, see Michael Harrington, *The Other America* (New York: Macmillan paperback, 1963), the book largely responsible for stimulating interest in the problems of the poor; Gilbert Y. Steiner's two books, *Social Insecurity: The Politics of Welfare* (Chicago: Rand McNally, 1966), and *The State of Welfare* (Washington, D.C.: Brookings Institution, 1971); Daniel P. Moynihan's two books, *Maximum Feasible Misunderstanding: Community Action in the War on Poverty* (New York: Free Press paperback, 1969), and *The Politics of a Guaranteed Income* (New York: Random House paperback, 1973); William Ryan, *Blaming the Poor* (New York: Pantheon paperback, 1971); and Frances Fox Piven and Richard Cloward, *Regulating the Poor* (New York: Pantheon paperback, 1971).

On taxes, see Louis Eisenstein, *Ideologies of Taxation* (New York: Ronald, 1961), which discusses the theories underlying various types of tax systems; Joseph A. Pechman, *Federal Tax Policy*, 3rd ed. (Washington, D.C.: Brookings Institution paperback, 1977), a basic analysis of our tax system, and, with Benjamin Okner, *Who Bears the Tax Burden?* (Washington, D.C.: Brookings Institution paperback, 1974); for strong criticisms of the system, see Philip M. Stern, *The Rape of the Taxpayer* (New York: Random House, 1973), and Robert M. Brandon et al., *Tax Politics: How They Make You Pay and What You Can Do About It* (New York: Pantheon paperback, 1976). And for updating, check the regular publications of the Tax Foundation, 50 Rockefeller Plaza, New York, N.Y. 10020, and Ralph Nader's Tax Reform Research Group, P.O. Box 14198, Washington, D.C. 20044, which publishes a monthly bulletin called *People & Taxes*.

---

[45]Ryan, "Most of Us Are Kept on a Short Leash."

[46]Interview, *U.S. News & World Report*, May 2, 1977, p. 57.

18 The politics of local relations: urban policy

Only one in ten Americans lives in a rural area, but one in four wishes he or she could. One in every three Americans lives in a large central city, but only one in eight would live in a city of over 100,000 if given the choice. Three-quarters of big city residents wish they lived in a smaller city – over half wanting a village, town, or rural setting as home. But 69 percent of those who *do* live in a rural area would choose to live in a rural area if given free choice. Figure 18.1 shows what people say about where they would like to live. But changes in America's population patterns show what Americans actually *do* about where they live.

An examination of how people "vote with their feet" – or more often with their cars – shows that through history Americans, like others, have continued to move toward large urban areas. There are signs that in the United States this trend toward urbanization is now leveling off, but it has been there throughout our history,[1] from the earliest days, when only 5 percent lived in cities, to the present, when most Americans are city dwellers.

□ CITY LIFE TODAY AND YESTERDAY: BETTER OR WORSE?

Why do most Americans say they'd rather live in the country, but still remain in the city? Historically, the city has offered more and better-paying jobs than rural areas. And even today, city dwellers on the average have higher standards of living than rural citizens.[2] But the biggest opportunities, and the most positive views of the state of things, now belong to suburbanites. When Americans are asked: 'All things considered, is life in the U.S. getting better or worse?" 17 percent say "better," 47 percent say "staying the same," and 36 percent say "worse." By contrast, 51 percent of central city dwellers say "worse." (The complete results of this survey are shown in Table 20.2 in Chapter 20.)

Why do urbanites more than others say things are getting worse? News reports and novels, presidents and poets – all recount to us the city's problems today. City services such as fire fighting and trash collecting are declining. Slums and poverty are found in many parts of most cities. Crime in the streets is becoming more common. Well-to-do whites are leaving the cities for the suburbs, and their

[1]See Claude S. Fischer, *The Urban Experience* (New York: Harcourt Brace Jovanovich, 1976), pp. 23, 258.

[2]See, for example, W. Alsonso and M. Fajans, "Cost of Living and Income by Urban Size," working paper no. 128 (Berkeley, Calif.: Institute of Urban and Regional Development, 1970).

place is being taken by blacks from rural areas and new immigrants, not from the countryside, as in days of old, but rather from other countries, such as Cuba, Puerto Rico, and recently Vietnam. As a result of these changes, cities are losing their "tax base" (well-off residents and companies able to pay large sums in local taxes) and facing bankruptcy.

More than a third of our sixty-seven largest cities are in serious financial trouble, according to a recent congressional study. More and more, they suffer from high unemployment, declining population, and shrinking city budgets. Included among them are: Washington, D.C., Boston, Long Beach, Atlanta, Seattle, New York, Los Angeles, Philadelphia, Detroit, Baltimore, Milwaukee, San Francisco, New Orleans, St. Louis, Denver, Pittsburgh, Cincinnati, Toledo, Oakland, Akron, Jersey City, Yonkers, Syracuse, Cleveland, and Portland.[3]

Things are bad today in many cities, in other words. Before we jump to conclusions, however, we need a bit of historical perspective. Political scientist Charles Adrian has studied city life not only today but also in the nineteenth century. He reminds us that most of the problems our cities face today were faced by our cities in the last century too. Today's pollution comes from cars and factories. Then, it was horses and slaughterhouses. Disease then was rampant – smallpox, yellow fever, malaria, cholera, and typhoid – and it was often spread by unsanitary drinking water. Crime too was common: less mugging, but more pickpocketing, and much murder. There were riots too. The first race riot flared up in Philadelphia in 1828, and ethnic battles were quite common. In short, according to Adrian, the problems of our nation's cities, bad as they are today, were generally worse a century ago.[4]

There were, however, important differences. To understand them, we must know more about the evolution of American cities and their present problems.

[3]"U.S. Cities in Trouble," *Washington Post,* July 30, 1977.

[4]"Studies Find U.S. Cities Even Worse in the Past," *New York Times,* December 5, 1976.

FIGURE 18.1
Where people want to live.

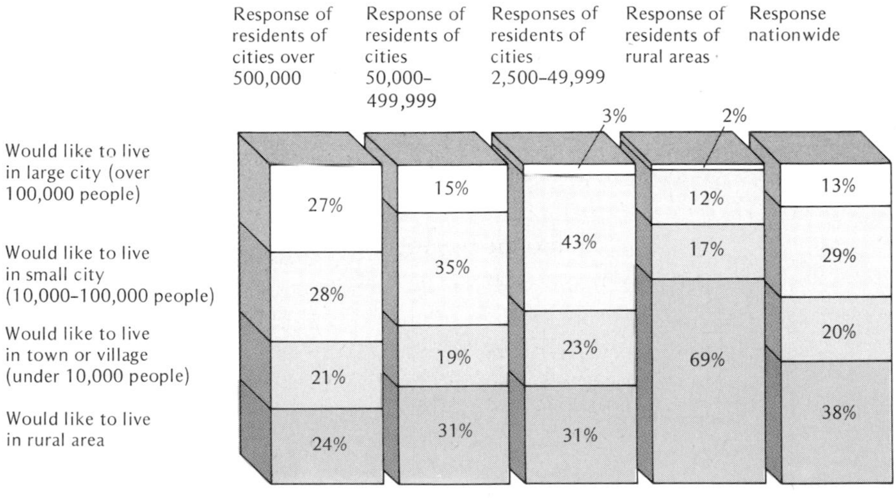

Source: Data reported in "Global Survey Finds Rush to Cities Likely to Go On," *Washington Post,* November 26, 1976, p. A3.

Library of Congress

The first great boost to the development of U.S. cities came with the construction of railroads. Michigan Avenue, Chicago, 1860.

THE EVOLUTION OF AMERICAN CITIES

Frontier development

The earliest American cities were, of course, seaports on the Atlantic Ocean. They conducted trade with Europe and between the colonies as well. As America developed, the frontier moved westward. In its wake it left new towns of traders, where goods were brought on their way to and from the coastal cities and Europe. The towns often grew to be cities as manufacturing developed locally.

The first great boost to the development of our cities came with the construction of railroads. By 1860, they extended from the east to Milwaukee, St. Louis, Memphis, and New Orleans, and soon they crisscrossed the country. Cities then grew up at railroad junctions. With the arrival of railroads, an area no longer needed to be self-sufficient in farming and manufacture, for trade with other specializing areas was much easier.

Immigration

Perhaps the greatest change in our cities is traceable to the arrival of new waves of immigrants from Europe. The first big waves reached America's eastern shores in the middle of the last century, before the Civil War. The immigrants came looking for work in the new factories that were springing up, or in the service trades such as shoemaking and baking. New waves then followed after the Civil War and on into the twentieth century. By 1920, a majority of the American people lived in urban areas – a figure that would jump to 75 percent by 1970.

These waves of immigrants had two major effects. One was to create ethnic neighborhoods or ghettoes, each populated by new arrivals from a given country. The other was the consequent flight of the natives to new neighborhoods as far removed from the city centers as local transportation – trains, buses, and eventually private cars – allowed.[5]

[5]See Anselm L. Strauss, *Images of the American City* (New Brunswick, N.J.: Transaction Books, 1976), especially chap. 6.

■ **Migration**

This same pattern of "invasion" and "flight" was then repeated in the mid-twentieth century when rural blacks and whites headed from the South to the Northeast and the Midwest. The slum poverty that has resulted from these latest waves of migration into our cities is different from the slum poverty of previous decades. In earlier eras, most of this poverty was in a sense temporary – suffered by the first generation as it struggled to improve the fate of its children. Eventually, the family moved out of the slum neighborhood, and even out of the often menial work it started out doing.

■ **Discrimination and poverty**

Today, most of the migrants to the cities are black or Puerto Rican or Chicano. All of these – but especially the blacks – suffer from discrimination that limits both their job opportunities and their housing possibilities. As a result, today's urban poverty tends to be passed on from one generation to the next.

We have discussed these problems of prejudice and poverty in previous chapters. For our present purpose – understanding the problems of our cities – we must take note of a second major difference between today's urban poverty and yesteryear's. Until recently, the city's poor were largely left to fend for themselves, with the help of local political machines (about which, more shortly) and charitable organizations such as churches. Thus slum populations were not serious economic burdens for cities, nor did they demand much attention or many services from the city. Today, however, as the poverty passes from one generation to the next, despair and resentment – and militance – increase, threatening law and order and commanding more and more city resources in the form of welfare payments, police and fire protection, and special programs. The result is a growing threat of bankruptcy for cities that are losing much of their tax base as business and the upper and middle classes desert the city for the suburbs.

■ **Suburbanization**

This pattern can be seen in Figure 18.2 which shows the population shifts in percentage terms between central city, suburban, and "nonmetropolitan" (rural and small town) areas. Between 1950 and 1970 the suburbs' share increased by 12

FIGURE 18.2
Percent of U.S. population in suburban areas, central cities, and nonmetropolitan areas, 1950–1970.

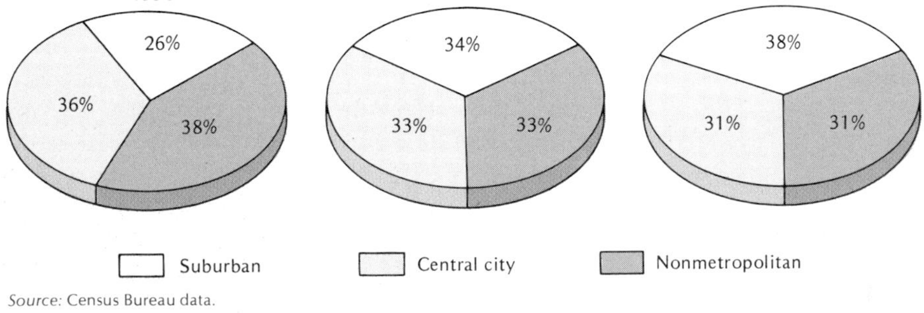

Source: Census Bureau data.

percent, whereas the cities lost 5 percent and the nonmetropolitan areas, 7 percent. The suburbs now are growing at the expense of both the cities and the rural areas. The 12 percent increase in the suburbs from 1950 to 1970 is made up of 35 million new suburbanites.

This suburban shift may be one reason why relatively few Americans say that local government affects their lives personally. Even though people pay local taxes and get local services such as police and fire protection, a Harris Poll in 1973 found that only 38 percent thought local government affected their lives "a great deal." Another 33 percent said "only somewhat." The 26 percent who said "hardly at all" may be mostly the rural people who tend to be rather removed from both local taxes and local services. The same survey found that only 24 percent of the people had ever gone to their local government for help with some problem or had any direct contact with local officials other than paying taxes and filling out forms.[6]

□ OUR DESIRES AND DEMANDS: THE PROBLEMS OF URBAN LIFE

So most of us have not directly encountered our local government. Nonetheless, "We are not strangers to an urban world," as President Lyndon Johnson pointed out in a 1966 message to Congress. "We know that cities can stimulate the best in man, and aggravate the worst. We know the convenience of city life, and its paralysis. We know its promise, and its dark foreboding. What we may only dimly perceive is the gravity of the choice before us. Shall we make our cities livable for ourselves and our posterity? Or shall we by timidity and neglect damn them to fester and decay?"

Convenience or paralysis, promise or foreboding, livable or festering and decaying. Is this the range of options for our cities in our third century as a nation? The problems facing the city and its residents are real enough, and human enough, and numerous enough. Among them seven stand out as most critical in human terms: education, housing, economic opportunity (especially jobs and antipoverty programs), law and security, transportation, health, and pollution. Many of these problems are discussed elsewhere in this book. Here, we shall look in more detail at the problems of housing and economic opportunity.

■ Housing

The average price of a new single-family home in America by 1977 was close to $45,000, and some experts expected it to soar toward $75,000 to $80,000 by the early 1980s. Even the 1977 price is one that only about 15 percent of all Americans can afford with a large mortgage loan. About 65 percent of all Americans presently own or are buying their own homes—a figure lower than those for at least nine other countries.[7] But these recent increases in prices mean that, unless something

[6] *Confidence and Concern: Citizens View American Government,* a Louis Harris survey for the Senate Government Operations Committee, 1974.

[7] Those countries with higher rates of home ownership, according to United Nations figures, are India, Israel, Australia, Mexico, Tunisia, South Korea, the Philippines, Pakistan, and Mongolia. See David M. Kinchen, "At Least 9 Countries Top U.S. in Percentage of Homeowners." *Washington Post,* October 8, 1977.

drastic happens to lower the cost of building houses, 85 percent of Americans who are now young will never be able to buy a new home of their own. One effect of this is already being felt. By 1976, 80 percent of all new homes sold for $25,000 were so-called mobile homes – homes that are small, often poorly built, and frequently unsafe in high winds. Another effect of the unbearably high price of new homes is more demand for older homes. But more demand means higher prices there too, and the average price of second-hand homes is not far behind that for new ones. Furthermore, many existing old "housing units" (homes and apartments) are substandard according to city safety codes. Five and a half percent of all inner city homes have been found substandard, as have 3 percent of all the units in the nation. These units need replacing – but people who now live in them couldn't afford to buy or rent any replacements that were built. Indeed, many urban units are in such bad shape that they have been simply abandoned by their occupants and owners. In 1970, for example, there were only 62.9 million households (families and single individuals) to occupy 68.6 million units, so 5.7 million were unoccupied, most of them substandard.

The earliest housing problems were quite different. In a sense, America always had a housing shortage. People therefore lived in crowded conditions – often averaging more than one person per room.

The Housing Act of 1949, which authorized the building of "public housing," began with a declaration "that the general welfare and the security of the Nation and the health and living standards of its people require . . . the realization as soon as feasible of the goal of a decent home and a suitable environment for every American family." Almost two decades later, the 1968 Housing and Urban Development Act restated the principle. Apparently it had not yet been "feasible" to achieve "the goal of a decent home . . . for every American family." The general quality of housing was improving. The percent that was substandard dropped from 37 percent in 1950 to 7 percent in 1970. Overcrowding (more than one person per room) fell from 16 percent in 1950 to 8 percent in 1970. Further, more new housing units were built than new households were formed by children going off on their own and marriages breaking up.

In this period, federal housing programs demolished much substandard housing through "urban renewal" programs and created new units through "public housing" construction. Under urban renewal, first established by the 1949 Housing Act, local government could buy run-down land and buildings, clear the land, and resell it to new users. The goals and means of the program were also then expanded. The Kennedy administration required that cities develop broader "Community Renewal Plans" as a part of urban renewal, for slum creation seemed to be outpacing slum removal.

In the Johnson years, the focus expanded to renewing the cities themselves and improving the economic situation of the citizens who lived in them via the "Model Cities Program." "It amounts to 'total therapy' for selected cities, with massive attention to both physical decline and poverty," wrote urbanist Scott Greer; "it envisions physical and social planning, public and private cooperation, local and regional and national cooperation. It assumes great fiscal capacity, great political agreement on goals and cooperation, great intellectual capacity to analyze, prescribe, and execute, and great cultural capacity to absorb such radical innovations."[8]

To direct this new departure, a new cabinet department was established by the Housing and Urban Development (HUD) Act of 1965. HUD took over programs concerned with housing and with other urban problems. It continued programs developing *low-rent housing.* In addition to the poor generally, such programs have focused on the special needs of the elderly, veterans, and families displaced by urban renewal. Further, it developed a *rent subsidy program,* by which the government pays part of the rent for poor families directly to the private landlord. Then in 1968 a new *home ownership program* was developed with subsidized mortgage payments to enable lower-income families to buy their own homes.

There are, then, two basic ways of coping with inadequate housing. First, producing more units; and second, providing financial assistance to those unable to afford good housing. "Unfortunately," writes former HUD official Irving Welfeld, "the distinction between housing production and financial assistance has been blurred in the framing of American housing subsidy programs. The basic programs have attempted to solve the 'housing problem' by constructing dwelling units for those who cannot afford them."[9] Yet the programs of financial assistance have reached only about 10 percent of those otherwise unable to afford decent housing. The problem is not public support. A Harris Poll found in the mid-1970s that 68 percent favored governmental help for housing the poor, while only 12 percent objected. The difficulty is compounded by the racial segregation that persists in urban areas. Whites leave the cities for the suburbs as blacks move in, and thus they form white suburban rings around black urban cores.

There have been recent signs of improvement. Both whites and blacks are now engaged in renovating center-city houses. In most cases middle-income families purchase run-down old homes and redo them. Unfortunately, in many instances these new owners displace poor tenants who then have even more trouble finding other housing.

Some cities now also have "urban homesteading" programs. A hundred years ago, farmers went out to the prairies to "homestead"; they were given land on

---

[8]Scott Greer, *The Urbane View: Life and Politics in Metropolitan America* (New York: Oxford University Press, 1972), p. 270.

[9]Irving Welfeld, *America's Housing Problem* (Washington, D.C.: American Enterprise Institute, 1973), p. 5.

Burt Owen

condition that they built their own houses and tilled the soil. Today, families are given an old but structurally sound home in the city on condition that they repair it and live in it. To aid them, the federal or city government often provides special loans. Urban homesteading programs are working well now in such cities as Wilmington, Delaware, and Baltimore, Maryland, and are underway in several dozen other cities too. Baltimore also initiated a comparable "shopsteading" program in 1977 to enable small merchants to restore abandoned storefront buildings as shops.

At the same time, some cities have tried to overcome segregation in housing by passing "open housing" laws that prohibit discrimination in the sale of homes. Such laws can increase housing opportunities for minorities who can afford available homes. But they cannot prevent people from moving when their neighborhood becomes integrated, whatever their reasons. So these laws have not – at least not yet – had a major impact upon residential segregation.[10]

This reminds us of the broader housing-related problem of neighborhoods. "Housing is more than shelter," write William Gorham and Nathan Glazer. "It is fixed in a place in a neighborhood. The place and the neighborhood supplement the shelter of the house by meeting other needs and desires: personal security, information, access to jobs, credit, friends, as well as standard public services. It is infinitely more difficult to improve neighborhoods than it is to improve shelter."[11]

■ Economic opportunity and access to jobs

If a neighborhood lacks jobs, residents must commute to work by public transportation or private car. If a city lacks jobs, residents are unemployed. Increasingly, that is what's happening. In the years 1970 to 1974, for example, the total number of jobs in the United States increased by 9.3 percent. But in those same years, Detroit lost 18.5 percent of its jobs, St. Louis, 18.3 percent, Baltimore, 12.7 percent, Philadelphia, 12.1 percent, Washington, 10.2 percent, Chicago, 8.4 percent, and New york 6.4 percent.

Eventually, loss of jobs results in loss of population once people decide the loss is permanent and find a way to move. In those same years, Detroit lost 11.8 percent of its population. St. Louis lost 15.6 percent, Baltimore, 6.0 percent,. Philadelphia, 6.9 percent, Washington, 6.0 percent, Chicago, 8.0 percent, and New York, 5.2 percent. All together, ten industrial cities of the Northeast and Midwest lost more than 11 percent of their people, while nine cities in the Sunbelt, which stretches across the South, gained from 29 percent to 15 percent. The only northern city in the top ten gainers was Anchorage – in Alaska, where business was booming because of the Alaskan oil pipeline. The problems of the cities – whether jobs or housing or crime or health – become political problems when the government tries to deal with them, just as they do when the government tries to avoid them. And when citizens are unhappy with a given situation or an existing policy, their first inclination these days may well be to try to get the government to change things.

---

[10]See William Gorham and Nathan Glazer, eds., *The Urban Predicament* (Washington, D.C.: Urban Institute, 1976).

[11]Ibid, p. 5.

☐ THE POLITICS OF URBAN GOVERNMENT: WHO HAS THE POWER TO DECIDE?

We normally look first to the chief executive officer of a political unit when we want something done. In most cities, this is the mayor, who is usually elected "at large" by the whole city's population. Most large cities also have a city council made up of representatives elected from districts within the city. In theory, or in appearance, mayors and city council members have governing authority, presiding over the city bureaucrats who run city affairs. In practice, things are often quite different.

In the early days of the country, cities were run by a small elite elected by the mere 5 to 10 percent of the population (adult white male property owners) allowed to vote. This elite was referred to as "the city fathers" – a term that survives to this day despite the growing percentage of women active in local electoral politics.

Two things happened to break the hold of this elite. First, cities kept growing on their fringes, and this small elite did little to maintain its political control over the new neighborhoods. Much the same thing is happening again today with the growth of suburbs outside the city limits. The second development – the rise of machine politics – was even more important.

■ Machine politics

After about 1840, the waves of European immigrants arriving to work in urban factories began. These new arrivals needed help coping with poverty, jobs, language problems, city services, and other matters. The existing elite was neither able nor willing to offer this help. The result was the development of what we call the political "machine" – a new organization in which each city block had its organizer, each neighborhood had its "political club," each district or ward had its leader, and the whole machine had its "boss." The machine served the people by offering its own "welfare" programs such as free turkeys for the poor for the holidays, city jobs for the unemployed (or an "introduction" to a local businessman anxious for machine-granted city contracts), a way to complain about poor city services, and so on. Politically, the machine served as a way of linking together the fragmented neighborhoods and ethnic groups into a strong political power able to elect and reelect the mayor – or the boss.

The years of the great machines, such as those in New York City, Jersey City, Kansas City, and Philadelphia, are over now. And when Mayor Richard Daley of Chicago died in December 1976, he was widely called "the last of the big city bosses." Daley's success had been built on the uniting of the major ethnic groups in Chicago: the Irish, the Poles, and later the blacks. When he died, the remnants of the machine – or "the organization," as Daley was always careful to call it – struggled over the succession. The deputy mayor was a black – a concession made by Daley to help sustain his coalition. One might assume that the deputy mayor would naturally succeed the mayor. But not so in Daley's Chicago, where the blacks were by then always important, but never that important. Instead, the machine settled on a compromise candidate, Michael Bilandic, who is of Croatian ancestry. The reformers, hoping to beat the Daley machine at last, picked a black. But it was black votes that gave Bilandic the victory over the black candidate and a renegade Pole in the next Democratic primary. So the machine lurched on, weakened but still organized, and still able to defeat the reformers.

■ Reform politics

Elsewhere things were not so favorable to machine politics. The civil rights movement of the early 1960s and the anti-Vietnam War movement of the late 1960s had nurtured a new breed of "community power" activists and reformers who combined with older liberals to modernize politics in other cities. The cry of the reform movement was usually the claim that local government should be *administration rather than politics.* (Chicago's new Mayor Bilandic also campaigned on the slogan, "I'm not a politician, I'm an administrator.") The argument was that human services (police, fire, public health, and so forth) should be provided in efficient and honest fashion, without the payoffs, "kickbacks," and graft that had long characterized machine politics. To achieve this shift from "politics" to "administration," the reformers sought both to break up the system of centralized "machine" power and to establish strong administrative control over city government. Unfortunately, there was a serious conflict between these two objectives in practical terms. To prevent a machine monopoly of political power, they deliberately fragmented power by parceling it out to independent boards and commissions. But once this was done there was not enough power left to achieve coherent administrative control over the city government and its service delivery. As Douglas Yates remarks, "having divided power in the hope of taming it, there was no way to simultaneously achieve stronger and more coordinated public control of urban bureaucracies and service delivery. Rather the political order of reform added new political fragmentation to the existing administrative fragmentation in the city."[12]

Furthermore, some reformers began to point out that new reformist forms of government could not deny or overcome the fact that service delivery systems are essentially political agencies, disputing over how human needs should be seen and what should be done to meet them.[13] The disputes over service delivery were, in other words, political disputes. By this analysis, the best – perhaps the only – way to improve the government is to improve the politics.

□ THE POLITICS OF URBAN POLICY: WHO HAS INFLUENCE AND WHO GETS RESOURCES?

■ Politicians and interests

Public officials such as mayors and council members make policy decisions in urban politics. But how much power do they have to make those decisions as they see fit? Political scientists still debate this question. Some, as we have seen in

---

[12]Douglas Yates, "Service Delivery and the Urban Political Order," in *Improving Urban Management,* ed. Willis A. Hawley and David Rogers (Beverly Hills, Calif.: Sage, 1976), p. 160.

[13]See, for example, Richard Cloward and Frances Fox Piven, *The Politics of Turmoil* (New York: Pantheon, 1971).

earlier chapters, argue that public policy is the outcome of influences by organized groups (such as business, labor, or citizen activists) on politicians seeking to ensure their own reelection. In this view, politicians try to balance off special interests and tend to act as the final balance recommends.[14]

Others claim that political figures are most influenced not by such organizational interests, but instead by their own ideologies – their beliefs about such things as race (black-white relationships), class (employer-employee relationships), and authority (citizen-official relationships). In urban politics, these ideological beliefs concern especially the role of citizen participation and the importance of rational, efficient administration.

David Greenstone and Paul Peterson studied the behavior of urban politicians in various cities. They found that *machine politicians* act according to the principle of balancing special interests even when that tendency results in less popular participation or less efficient administration. *Conservative reformers,* like those we described above, act to achieve greater efficiency rather than to play off the special interests against each other. *Liberal reformers,* by contrast, tend to act to extend democratic participation.

They found that both types of reformers are active in American city politics today. The importance of their findings should not be overlooked. The traditional argument, that politicians act according to the balance of interests and its implications for their reelection, suggests that actual citizen participation or sharing of power is not important, because politicians will take their interests into account. But the fact that this research found politicians willing to act *counter* to the balance of forces, and hence to their own electoral interests, emphasizes that it is not enough for unrepresented groups such as blacks and the poor simply to vote. If they are to influence policy outcomes in cities, they must be deciders of policy themselves. They cannot rely on their potential electoral power to bring about politics and policies they support.[15]

■ "Street-fighting pluralism"

This tendency may be one reason why urban policy so often fails to meet or even recognize the needs and interests of urban citizens. And another factor may be the frequency of what Yates calls "street fighting pluralism." He suggests that often "the new urban policy or 'solution' is injected into a political and administrative system that is fragmented to the point of chaos. Further, there is no coherent administrative order to implement and control new policies. What exists instead is an extreme pluralism of political, administrative, and community interests . . . and in this context, the likely fate of the new policy initiative is that it will be ripped apart in the street fight between rival political interests."[16]

---

[14]For applications of this view to urban politics, see Edward Banfield, *Political Influence* (New York: Free Press, 1961), a study of Chicago; and Robert Dahl, *Who Governs?* (New Haven, Conn.: Yale University Press, 1961), a study of New Haven.

[15]J. David Greenstone and Paul E. Peterson, *Race and Authority in Urban Politics* (New York: Russell Sage Foundation, 1973).

[16]Yates, "Service Delivery, and Urban Political Order," p. 149.

This situation is particularly characteristic of urban politics, according to Yates, for three important reasons. First, in most large cities, the politicians such as council members are underpaid and overworked and so pay little attention to citizen interests. Second, there are so many overlapping political jurisdictions (council member, state representative, state senator, national representative and senator, among others) that it is rarely clear who should represent whom on what issues. Third, citizens disagree with each other as to what services should be sought and provided, and so they are often unable to unite to make demands.

The failure or inability of the various ethnic minorities among the urban poor to unite is a particularly potent example of the last point. One recent report found that despite antipoverty programs, inner city neighborhoods had less success than other metropolitan areas in reducing poverty and maintaining stable families. Only a new willingness to cooperate on the part of racial and ethnic groups that now see themselves in competition for scarce resources could begin to change this, the report concluded.[17]

■ The poverty of urban politics But beneath this political weakness of urban peoples is the poverty of urban politics and government. This poverty has both political and economic aspects. The first is the generally *low quality of local politics,* which is often characterized by corruption, incompetence, administrative disorder, a lack of party competition, and "street-fighting pluralism."

A *weak fiscal base* is a second flaw in urban government. Cities depend for their spendable revenue primarily on taxes. Most income comes from property taxes. Yet much property is not taxable, either because it is owned by some government or by nonprofit groups such as churches, colleges, or hospitals, or because its holders get special tax breaks. In recent years New York City has been hovering on the verge of bankruptcy. One reason is that the city loses out on $923,191,000 in property tax revenue each year because of such special exemptions.[18]

The third major factor that weakens city government is its *inability to exercise power beyond the city's rim.* Cities are surrounded by suburbs, counties, states, and the United States. Each of these units has powers over aspects of the city's life. All are largely beyond the city's control. Thus increasingly those dissatisfied with city politics are urged or driven to move outside or beyond the city for remedies.

□ OUTSIDE THE CITY

■ The dependence of cities on states Cities are not mentioned in the Constitution. They therefore derive their authority from the states in which they are located. The classic formulation of this authority was made by a state judge named John F. Dillon in 1872 in words that have become known as **Dillon's Rule**. This rule states that a city's powers are

[17]National Center for Urban Affairs, *Who's Left in the Neighborhood* (Washington: NCUA, 1976).

[18]Gerald Benjamin, "New York City's Costly Tax Exemptions," *New York Times,* March 28, 1976.

strictly limited to those expressly granted by the state, those necessarily implied by that grant of powers, and "those essential to the accomplishment of the declared objects and purposes" of the city.[19] This legal dependence has made cities subject to domination by their states and often unable to protect themselves against exploitation by their political environment. In recent years, the greatest threat has come from suburbs.

■ Suburbanization

By 1970, more people lived in the suburbs that ring America's large cities than lived in either the rural areas or the cities themselves. The movement to the suburbs seems to have been partly a *pushing* away of people by cities with racial problems, congestion, pollution, high housing costs, and so on. But it was also partly a *pulling* or an attraction of people to areas that offer more space for raising a family, more social homogeneity, more privacy, and so forth. What made it all possible, of course, was the development first of public transportation (especially commuter trains) and then the spread of the private automobile.[20]

This fact helps explain how and why the suburbs came to challenge and threaten the cities they ringed. Most suburbanites continued to work in the big cities and often shopped and found entertainment there as well. This meant that they benefited from a wide range of city services, from garbage collection to public concerts. But because they lived in suburbia, they paid their property taxes to their suburban communities instead of to the cities. So city services began to decline with city revenues. And when city services declined, businesses located in the cities, and so paying city taxes, began to follow their employees to the suburbs. So cities went further into debt and decay. But because they depended on the states for their political authority, there was often little they could do to defend themselves. More and more, some argue, America's great cities have come to resemble the reservations on which Native Americans have been isolated and kept from enjoying the full benefits of life in America.

This "suburbanization" of America has complicated politics too. For each local unit must have its own local government, but in addition there must be new political units cutting across the city and suburb units to plan and coordinate such transurban services as education, transportation, water supply, pollution control,

---

[19]John F. Dillon, *Commentaries on the Law of Municipal Corporations*, 5th ed. (Boston: Little, Brown, 1911), I. 448.

[20]For an account of various theories, see William M. Dobriner, *Class in Suburbia* (Englewood Cliffs, N.J.: Prentice-Hall, 1963).

H. Armstrong Roberts

sewage, and police and fire protection. The result has been a proliferation of independent or semi-independent governing bodies with different but overlapping borders. The New York metropolitan area, for example, had by one count 1467 different governing bodies by the early 1960s (see Figure 18.3).[21]

■ Consolidation

In recent years there have been growing efforts to consolidate at least the major planning functions of regions. The primary approach has been establishment of councils of governments (COGs) to integrate urban and suburban planning with financial inducements from the federal government. These COGs are supposed to review requests for federal grants from various local units, develop area priorities, and coordinate related activities among different units. But because they are voluntary they lack the power to impose their will on member units. So some observers believe that on balance they only complicate matters.

[21]See Robert C. Wood, *1400 Governments* (Cambridge, Mass.: Harvard University Press, 1961); see also Wallace S. Sayre and Herbert Kaufman, *Governing New York City* (New York: Russell Sage foundation, 1960).

FIGURE 18.3
Overlapping governments in the New York metropolitan area.

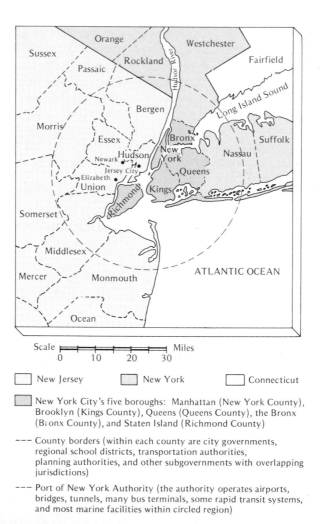

New Jersey

New York

Connecticut

New York City's five boroughs: Manhattan (New York County), Brooklyn (Kings County), Queens (Queens County), the Bronx (Bronx County), and Staten Island (Richmond County)

--- County borders (within each county are city governments, regional school districts, transportation authorities, planning authorities, and other subgovernments with overlapping jurisdictions)

--- Port of New York Authority (the authority operates airports, bridges, tunnels, many bus terminals, some rapid transit systems, and most marine facilities within circled region)

At the same time that these efforts at consolidation or centralization are underway, other programs are fostering greater decentralization. Among these are (1) movements for greater *home rule,* (2) federal *general revenue sharing,* and (3) development of *neighborhood councils* for direct citizen participation.

■ Political decentralization by "home rule"

Because cities derive their authority from the states, state legislatures must approve their system of government. Normally the state offers a *city charter* to a city. A city charter is the city's constitution, in effect. But because it is granted by the state it can be changed by the state. The exception to this is the home-rule charter, which is drafted by the city and cannot be changed by the state legislature. More than three-quarters of our large cities now have home-rule charters. But even they cannot take action that exceeds the general grant of powers the particular state has made to its cities. Thus matters like taxation and even education generally remain subject to state control.

The most interesting recent experiment in this direction took place in Montana in 1976. The new state constitution of 1972 provided that each community debate and decide on its own form of local government in 1975–1976 and every 10 years thereafter. Any city wanting home rule may have it under a system of shared powers with the state government. This provision allows localities to make laws in any area not prohibited by the state constitution or the legislature. This Montana system has been adopted by Illinois, Florida, Texas, Alaska, Pennsylvania, Massachusetts, Iowa, and South Dakota.[22] It is likely to become more and more common as states recognize their inability to solve many local problems and cities rebel against the state strictures that shackle them in trying to solve problems themselves.

■ Fiscal decentralization by revenue sharing

We usually think of the federal government as dealing with national problems and local government as dealing with local problems. The major tool for such coping, apart from the laws themselves, is money—money spent to solve problems. But if we expect local governments to dominate local governmental spending, we shall find ourselves mistaken.

The city of Dayton, Ohio, is often thought to be as representative of the country as any city can be. A recent study of government spending in the Dayton area highlighted important facts about politics and finance. In 1973, governmental agencies at all levels spent $1.4 billion in Montgomery County, where Dayton is located. Of this sum, $643 million was spent on Wright-Patterson Air Force Base. Of the remaining millions, the federal and state governments spent $571 million in the county, while the local governments altogether raised and spent only $270 million. In other words, once federal and state tax dollars trickle down to the people again, they far outnumber—by more than two to one—the money spent by local government on "community problems."

[22]See Neal R. Peirce, "A Model of Self-Government at Last Chance Gulch," *Washington Post,* July 24, 1976.

Direct spending in Montgomery County, Ohio, is done by twenty-seven federal agencies, the county government, ten cities, seven villages, thirteen townships, nineteen school districts, and sixteen special districts. And as if that weren't complexity enough, consider spending for problems of crime and delinquency. This totals but 5 percent of all government spending, but it is done by forty-nine different local departments and forty-seven separate federal grants.

Furthermore, of all government spending, 17 cents out of every dollar went for the cost of administering the programs, rather than for direct benefits to people such as Social Security payments, veterans' benefits, and welfare. It's no wonder government is complex and programs are inefficient when so many different agencies are involved. And it shouldn't surprise us if some programs are not effectively responsive to local needs when so much of the spending is done by Washington rather than by local governments.[23]

Washington has long played a major role in local finance. Much of this role came about because local politics was dominated by conservative vested interests unwilling to undertake programs to help the poor and the disadvantaged. Over the years, federal programs grew and grew. Washington made some payments directly to the people, such as Social Security and veterans' benefits, and others to the states and cities. But the grants to the states and cities had strings attached. The funds, called *categorical grants,* had to be spent for certain specified categories of activities, as we discussed in Chapter 2.

Finally, in 1971, President Nixon proposed a fundamental change. In a message to Congress he noted that "states and localities are not free to spend these funds on their own needs as they see them. The money is spent instead for the things Washington wants and in the way Washington orders. Because the categories for which the money is given are often extremely narrow, it is difficult to adjust spending to local requirements. And because these categories are extremely resistant to change, large sums are often spent on outdated projects. Pressing needs often go unmet, therefore, while countless dollars are wasted on low priority expenditures. . . . State and local governments need Federal . . . money to spend, but they also need greater freedom in spending it."[24]

The result, once Congress passed the State and Local Assistance Act of 1972, was general revenue sharing. The act provided that Washington would give states and localities from $5 to $6 billion a year for 5 years. The money would be allocated, one-third to states and two-thirds to local governments, by a formula considering population, per capita income, and the degree of state and local taxation. The money was unrestricted – it could be spent on police, fire protection, streets, mass transit, libraries, health, or other needs. Recipients included all fifty states plus the District of Columbia, 3046 counties, 18,778 cities, 16,986 townships, and 346 Native American tribes and Alaskan native villages. The city of Dayton, for

---

[23]This study was conducted by Community Research Associates and the Miami Valley Regional Planning Association. It is reported in Jonathan Wolman, "Dayton-Area Study Weighs U.S., State, Local Expenditures," *Washington Post,* November 26, 1976.

[24]Nixon's program was a variant of a proposal by Walter Heller, a liberal Democratic economist. Its appeal to Nixon was in large part the opportunity to curtail spending on minorities and increase spending on the "Middle Americans" who were his strongest supporters.

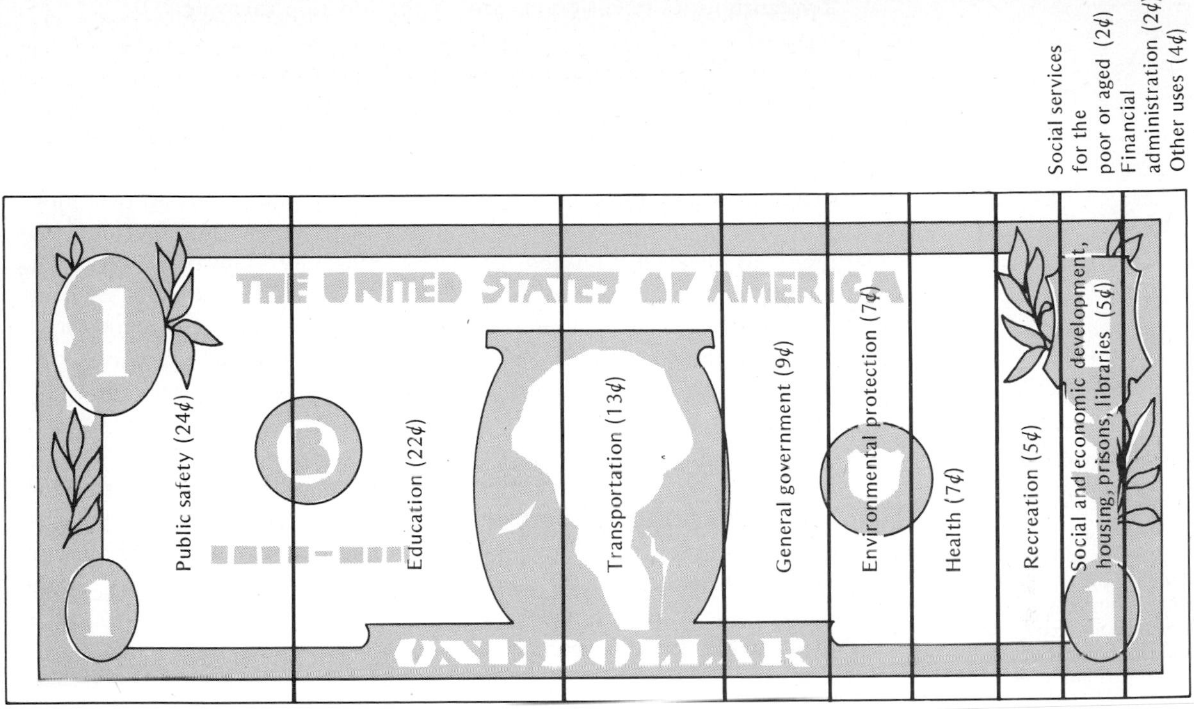

Source: Adapted from U.S. Treasury Department, Office of Revenue Sharing, *Reported Uses of General Revenue Sharing Funds, 1974–1975* (Washington, D.C.: Government Printing Office,1976), p. 7

FIGURE 10.4

Uses of the revenue-sharing dollar.

example, in 1974 used its revenue-sharing funds to provide free ambulance service, clean streets on a monthly schedule, hire twenty-five new police officers, install 600 street lights in residential areas, tear down 100 substandard buildings, start a public-service careers program, improve the downtown area, and improve parks and streets. Figure 18.4 shows the average uses of revenue sharing funds.

Categorical, or "tied," grants continued, although at lower spending levels than before. Eventually some of these were replaced by *special revenue-sharing funds* given for six key needs: urban community development, rural community development, elementary and secondary education, manpower training, law enforcement, and transportation. Under this special revenue sharing, governments could spend funds freely within each of these categories for which they were allocated.

Revenue sharing has generally been welcomed by both states and cities, which were finding it more and more difficult to raise taxes for services. Others have criticized it, most often on grounds that it led to less actual aid to the poor and the disadvantaged who had little local political power to bargain for new programs. Evidence supports this claim. Aid that once went to ghetto areas and decaying sections of the inner cities now goes increasingly to well-to-do neighborhoods and suburbs by choice of local governments.[25]

---

[25]See, for example, Paul Delaney, "St. Louis Epitomizes Shift of Federal Urban Funds," *New York Times,* April 19, 1976.

Two authorities recently summarized the situation this way:

> . . . 20 years ago federal direct intervention in cities was minimal; it reached its height in the late 1960s and has been on the decline since then. Although there are mixed views about the justification and merit of spending more money, practically no voices at the moment are arguing for more substantive federal intervention in city problems. The arguments over block grants are about providing assurances that a fair share will go to this or that group, to this or that purpose, or to this or that city—they deal with target groups and formulas, not with program philosophy. This is not to say that there is widespread satisfacion with the state of our cities, only that a smaller percent of the population care about the cities, while even fewer have confidence that the federal government (or any other level of government for that matter) knows how to make things better.[26]

On the morning that the mayor of Pittsburgh was to open an antilitter, cleanup campaign, officials decided that the streets were a bit too clean. Here city workers are strewing litter that will later be picked up by the mayor and council members.
Wide World Photos

But if few believe any governments—including city governments—know how to make things better, does that mean that things, and people, are hopeless? Not at all. For if going to the local government for help has failed, and improving local politics has proved difficult, and if going beyond or outside the city to other governments has proved largely ineffective, that still leaves one important possibility: citizen participation.

□ CITIZEN PARTICIPATION

■ Community organization

When we examined political participation in Chapter 5 we found that it was low in most types of activity, including voting in local elections and lobbying in local politics. We also noted Saul Alinsky's efforts to organize the poor and excluded urban citizens into effective political action groups. It is citizen action groups that are now the most important opportunity for effective participation in urban affairs.[27] Many of those that are now active owe their inspiration to Alinsky.

One of them, not surprisingly, operates in Alinsky's home town of Chicago: the Citizens Action Program (CAP), founded in 1970 to organize citizens so they have power to force city government to respond to their needs. CAP is affiliated with the Midwest Academy, a school to train activists in the skills and strategies that make an effective organization. Similar organizations exist many other places now, at the neighborhood as well as the city level. And many are growing, like ACORN, a loose confederation of groups that originated in Arkansas and spread to Texas and then to other states. In addition, a large group of elected public officials and activists now gathers twice a year to compare notes on new approaches to solving city and state problems under the banner of the Conference on Alternative State and Local Policies.

[26]Gorham and Glazer, *The Urban Predicament,* p. 14.

[27]See John H. Hutcheson, Jr., and Jann Shevin, eds., *Citizen Groups in Local Politics: A Bibliographic Review* (Santa Barbara, Calif.: Clio Books, 1976).

This group is closer to conventional political action than organizations like CAP and ACORN, because many of its members are elected officials. Other groups are closer still. For example, under President Johnson's War on Poverty the *Community Action Program* called for maximum feasible participation by the poor in developing and overseeing antipoverty programs in cities. These efforts, as we noted last chapter, were far from successful in many cases. In addition, they have been criticized for "coopting" radical community leaders – or integrating them into the system in a way that makes them more conservative.[28] But they did organize many members of ethnic ghettoes into political groups and give them experience which could later prove useful in further urban activism.

■ Local self-reliance movements

Not every urban activist pays such attention to politics, however. Some concentrate on finding ways to solve local problems in the neighborhood without even depending on the broader economic system. For example, the Institute for Local Self-Reliance (ILSR) in Washington has developed ways of growing vegetables on rooftop gardens and raising fish in basements in the downtown areas of big cities so that residents needn't depend on others outside the community for good food.[29] Others have undertaken the urban homesteading that we described above.

■ Citizen advisory groups

But there are still other types of urban citizen action besides neighborhood organization and local self-reliance. Increasingly, city charters are establishing Neighborhood Advisory Commissions (as they are called in Washington, D.C.) or Community Boards (as they are called in New York City), elected from neighborhoods to advise city government.

■ National associations of neighborhood groups

Furthermore, locally established citizen action groups like Chicago's CAP have united into a National Association of Neighborhoods (NAN), established in 1975, which meets twice a year around the country to develop ways of mutual support. The NAN office offers help in organizing, fund raising, publicity, and even lobbying in Washington. Similar lobbying is done by other groups such as National People's Action, formed in 1972 by neighborhood groups from across the country, and the National Center for Urban Ethnic Affairs, established in Washington in 1970. These two groups were instrumental in getting a law passed to protect people obtaining home mortgages in 1975, and since then they have worked to support other urban-oriented legislation.[30] They help keep urban issues in the forefront of attention in Washington. (See Action Unit 18.1 for a list of urban groups.)

---

[28]See Cloward and Piven, *The Politics of Turmoil.*

[29]For more detail, see Karl Hess and David Morris, *Neighborhood Power* (Boston: Beacon, 1975). Or see the interview with Hess in *Mother Earth News,* no. 37.

[30]Rochelle L. Stanfield, "Are Brighter Days Ahead for the Nation's Decaying Cities?" *National Journal,* October 30, 1976, pp. 1551–1557.

□ ACTION UNIT 18.1 How to contact urban groups and lobbies

There are a great many organizations with special interests in urban affairs and community development. Listed here are some that represent differing perspectives and activities.

The Center for Community Change (1000 Wisconsin Ave. N.W., Washington, D.C. 20007) works with minority community organizations and community development corporations, especially on federal funding.

The Federation for Economic Democracy (Suite 607, 2100 M St. N.W., Washington, D.C. 20063) is a national network of persons working to organize, finance, educate, and give technical assistance to employee self-managed enterprises; it publishes a monthly newsletter.

The National Association for Community Development (1424 16th St. N.W., Washington, D.C. 20036) consists of individuals, public agencies, and community action organizations concerned with community development.

The National Association of Neighborhoods (1901 Q St. N.W., Washington, D.C. 20009) is described in this chapter.

The National Center for Urban Ethnic Affairs (4408 8th St. N.E., Washington, D.C. 20017) promotes ethnic awareness and preserves and revitalizes urban neighborhoods through community organization and development.

The National Home Buyers & Home Owners Association (1225 19th St. N.W., Washington, D.C. 20036) promotes consumer interests in housing.

The National Urban Coalition (1201 Connecticut Ave. N.W., Washington, D.C. 20036) is a coalition of minority groups, business people, and civic leaders that conducts local model urban programs through its coalition affiliates.

The Urban Alternatives Group (P.O. Box 303, Worthington, Ohio 43085) publishes *Doing It! Humanizing City Life,* a bimonthly journal.

□ THE URBAN PROSPECT

Everyday life for most of us keeps many of those same urban issues in the forefront of our own minds. That the problems in our cities are as difficult to solve as they are serious is beyond dispute. But what the future holds is still very much in question.

Cities "are physically obsolete, financially unworkable, crime-ridden, garbage-strewn, polluted, torn by racial conflicts [and] wallowing in welfare, unemployment, despair and corruption," wrote Columbia University professor Eugene Raskin in the early 1970s. He concluded that they were "unsalvageable" and "deserved extinction."[31]

"If nothing is done to help the cities recover, if present trends continue," said James E. Peterson of the National Council for Urban Economic Development in 1976, "the cities will be reservations for dependent people. They won't die; they won't just go away. The federal programs already in place will see to that. They will just fester."[32]

Agriculture Department economist Don Paarlberg predicts that Americans will soon reverse the historic trend of migration to the cities. "The attractions of the country, with its warmer personal relationships, cleaner air and water, greater

---

[31]Quoted by Neal R. Peirce, "Cities Make a Comeback," *Washington Post,* July 7, 1977.

[32]Quoted in Stanfield, "Are Brighter Days Ahead?" p. 1555.

privacy, and greater social stability, will look better and better as the years pass. We will be able to provide most of the social services and utilities that formerly were to be found only in the cities."[33]

But urban historian Sam Bass Warner takes yet another view.

> Although some neighborhoods are ravaged by heroin, many are afflicted by poverty, and all suffer the disease of white racism, there is no reliable historical evidence which suggests that local government, local institutions, or local life are decaying. The behavior of local government and the studies of social science show that a broad consensus on what constitutes a decent American life runs throughout the city. A decent job, a good education for one's children, a comfortable home, and adequate health care are on everyone's list of priorities, and the cultural variations which give specific meaning to these priorities are not very wide. Wide enough to tip the balance in a local election, to be sure, but narrow enough to support a common set of public and private institutions in all but the impoverished sections of the city. . . .
>
> American urban neighborhoods are not nor have they ever been peasant villages; nor are they nor have they ever been model republics. Yet to an extraordinary degree, considering the rapid movement of millions of American families, they have been able to muster men and women who pass petitions, sit patiently for hours on local boards, and help out their friends and neighbors in emergencies. To the extent that the American city is now rotten, it is rotten at the top, not the bottom. What the neighborhoods need at the present moment, and what they have been needing ever since our cities became the creatures of large interconnecting economic forces and institutions, is the assistance of democratic national and regional planning.[34]

But even without that planning, some observers see signs of a turnabout. Urban expert Neal Peirce concluded, after studying developments across the country in 1977 and talking with many mayors, that

> the inner cities of America are poised for a stunning comeback, a turnabout in their fortunes that could be one of the most significant developments in our national history. The recovery from decades of middle-class desertion, housing abandonment and intolerable levels of poverty and crime will not be a smooth or tidy process. The cities' renewal may trigger social discord as the affluent and the poor fight for their share of the urban turf. And there surely will be backwaters of urban desperation for years to come.
> But . . . [there is] evidence that the critical mass needed for city recovery has finally fallen into place. The chief ingredients accelerating middle-class

[33]"Economist Predicts American Return to Rural Areas," *Austin American-Statesman,* January 2, 1977.

[34]Sam Bass Warner, *The Urban Wilderness* (New York: Harper & Row, 1972), pp. 275–276.

return to the cities are the energy crisis, the explosion of the post-World War II baby boom into the new household market, changing lifestyles and mounting dissatisfaction with suburban life—especially among young people.[35]

So once again the experts disagree. Once again the roles of the citizens, and how they may change in coming years, promise to play an important part in shaping the future of America and of our politics. That this is true of our cities may, upon reflection, not be so surprising. Our cities have always been so interdependent that our citizens are important factors in shaping them and their prospects. By now, however, interdependence extends far beyond the city to the world of nation-states, as we shall see in the next chapter.

□ SUGGESTIONS FOR FURTHER READING AND STUDY

Among the many interesting surveys of urban politics are Edward Banfield and James Q. Wilson, *City Politics* (Cambridge, Mass.: Harvard University Press paperback, 1963); Charles E. Gilbert, *Governing the Suburbs* (Bloomington: Indiana University Press, 1967); Robert C. Wood, *1400 Governments* (Garden City, N.Y.: Anchor paperback, 1964). See also Banfield's controversial *The Unheavenly City Revisited,* 2nd ed. (Boston: Little, Brown paperback, 1974), and Alan A. Altshuler, *Community Control: The Black Demand for Participation in Large American Cities* (New York: Pegasus paperback, 1970).

For a helpful survey of the major problems now facing the cities, including finance, transportation, schooling, housing, and crime, see William Gorham and Nathan Glazer, eds., *The Urban Predicament* (Washington, D.C.: Urban Institute paperback, 1976). For special attention to problems of finance and urban development, see Bernard J. Frieden and Marshall Kaplan, *The Politics of Neglect: Urban Aid from Model Cities to Revenue Sharing* (Cambridge, Mass.: MIT Press paperback, 1975).

If you're interested in looking at the politics of a major American city in more detail, there's no better place to look than Chicago, my hometown. You could start with Banfield's classic book, *Political Influence* (New York: Free Press paperback, 1961). But perhaps the best thing to do is to focus on the life and works of the late Mayor Daley, on which there are two interesting books: Mike Royko, *Boss: Richard J. Daley of Chicago* (New York: Dutton paperback, 1971); and Milton Rakove, *"Don't Make No Waves, Don't Back No Losers"* (Bloomington: Indiana University Press paperback, 1976).

---

[35]Peirce, "Cities Make a Comeback."

19 The politics of global relations: American foreign policy

Our everyday lives are entangled with the lives of other peoples around the world in many ways. For a long time we have been living with products made in other countries: Japanese clock radios to wake us up; Swiss watches to tell us the time through the day; morning coffee from Brazil or Angola, or tea from Ceylon or China; bicycles made in England or France, motorcycles made in England or Germany or Japan, and cars made in Europe or Japan; music recorded in England or elsewhere and played on stereos made in Japan or Germany; alcoholic beverages brewed in Scotland or France or Spain or Italy or Mexico. . . . The list is endless.

□ OUR EXPERIENCE OF THE WORLD

We have long known that we bought these goods from other countries, but few of us have realized the effect of our purchases on those other countries. When we import foreign goods, that creates more jobs for workers in industries abroad that export goods to us and unemployment in countries whose goods we no longer buy – or, as we saw for the case of shoes in Perspective 6, in our own. But our impact on other peoples extends way beyond our purchase of foreign goods. When we buy auto insurance or make a deposit in a local bank, for example, those funds may end up invested in a new factory in Brazil or an apartment complex in Iran. Our contributions to charitable organizations that work abroad also affect the lives of many people. Money we give to CARE feeds the hungry around the world. Medical supplies or clothing or funds we give to the American Friends Service Committee provide assistance to refugees and medical care to the world's poor.

There are a great many *connections* between peoples of various countries around the world. Those that are *political* are generally conducted by governments and their representatives. Nonetheless, citizens of one country now often sign petitions and write letters to foreign governments protesting violations of human rights or opposing explosion of nuclear weapons that cause dangerous radioactive fallout to spread quickly across boundaries around the world. Those connections that are *economic* are usually undertaken by business corporations and their employees. Still, citizens can and do boycott goods from countries whose policies they disapprove. Those relations that are *cultural* (the exchange of orchestras or rock bands or dance groups, for example), *sporting* (the Olympics, tennis's Davis Cup, track meets, and so on), or *educational* (foreign student exchange, importing of books and magazines, and so on), involve governments, businesses, and citizens.

■ Our own foreign policies

As individuals we decide whether or not to buy foreign goods, meet foreign individuals, applaud or protest acts of foreign countries, or encounter foreign ideas. In making these decisions, *each of us has his or her own foreign policy* – his or her own set of ideas about what foreign contacts are valuable, what international activities to undertake, such as study or business abroad, what developments in other countries to hope for or to fear, and what to do to perpetuate or change experiences involving peoples and organizations in other countries.[1]

■ Interdependence

The point is that by now the average American's life is *interdependent* with the lives of others. Each, in other words, is affected by and affects not only what his or her nation and other nations do, but also what organizations and individuals in other nations do. It is still true that the foreign policies of countries are usually very remote from individuals. Wars, trade disputes, international boycotts, and so forth, occur often and without consultation with the people they affect. Because of this, it often seems that we as individuals and citizen groups are powerless to affect the lives of people in other states, for good or for ill, because we cannot control our own country's foreign policy. But, in fact, the more interaction between peoples increases, and the more it spreads to new parts of the world, the more we may be able to affect the foreign policies of our country – and of other countries too.

Growing interdependence, and what we might call growing "penetration" of one culture by another, of individuals' lives by other individuals, are facts in today's world. Today, you can fly from Washington, D.C. or New York City to London or Paris in 3½ hours if you take the Concorde supersonic airliner. Each year some 8 million Americans travel overseas, and almost 5 million foreigners travel to the United States. We send about a billion pieces of mail abroad, and make over 50 million overseas telephone calls each year. The rest of the world sends about 50,000 students to America to study each year – and almost 200,000 of us go abroad to study. Others have invested some $27 billions in America, while Americans have invested about $135 billion in other countries.

All these connections, all these contacts, make it all the more important that we as individuals know what the situations of other peoples are, and what impacts we have upon them, just as we must continue to know about the relations of our government with other governments.

To get a better understanding of America's role in the world, we must take note of what America has been doing and how American foreign policy has been and is being made. We must also discover how the rest of the world is changing, and the way these changes are transforming not only the American nation's prospects, but also our own opportunities and challenges, as private American citizens, and even perhaps as "citizens of the world."

---

[1]See Chadwick F. Alger, "Increasing Opportunities for Effective and Responsible Transnational Participation," *Mershon Center Quarterly Report*, Summer 1976, pp. 1–8.

☐ ACTION UNIT 19.1 How to get and use a passport

If you want to travel anywhere outside the country besides Mexico, Canada, and the Caribbean isles, you need a passport. Other countries require that you show it to enter them, and the U.S. Immigration and Naturalization Service, which guards the ports of entry to the United States, requires that you have one to get back in – and fines you $25 when you return if you lose it while traveling.

Getting a passport used to be difficult, and applicants had to have specific plans for a trip to qualify. Now, all that's changed. Any citizen can get one – about 700,000 do every year – by following these simple steps:

1. Bring a piece of identification that proves your American citizenship, such as a birth certificate or a certificate of naturalization.

2. Bring identification that connects you to your certificate by signature, such as a driver's license or a school ID, or else bring along a friend who will identify you.

3. Bring two identical, wallet-size front-view photos of yourself taken within the past 6 months, either black-and-white or color. You must sign the photos on the front along the left-hand side.

4. Bring a check or money order for $13.

5. Take all of these items to the Passport Agency (offices in Boston, Honolulu, Los Angeles, Miami, New Orleans, New York, Philadelphia, San Francisco, Seattle, Washington, D.C.), or to the clerk of the federal or state or probate court in your "county seat" (where county government is located), or to a certified postal clerk if your post office has one.

6. Fill out the application form there and submit it with all these items.

7. Your passport will be mailed to you within a week or two if it's "off season," or a month or two during the summer.

If you already have an old passport, all you have to do to get a replacement is get the special pink renewal form #DSP-82 from the post office or the government, fill it out, and send it in as indicated with your old passport and a $10 renewal fee. Your new passport will be sent to you by mail.

To use your passport to travel to Western Europe all you need do is hop a plane. To use it in most other countries, you must first get a *visa* from the embassy or a consulate the country maintains in the United States or elsewhere. The visa will indicate that you are to be admitted to the country for a certain purpose (such as tourism or research) for a given period of time.

Should you have any trouble with the law while traveling, you should contact the nearest American embassy's "consular affairs" officer, or call the State Department's Office of Special Consular Services at 202-632-8089 or 202-632-7823. But don't assume that this office will be able to help you if you're picked up on a drug offense. About 80 percent of the American citizens in jails around the world are there for drug offenses, and most are serving long sentences.

When you return from abroad, you must pass through "customs," where you declare what you have purchased abroad and its value, and may have to pay "duty" on some goods.

For more information on passports and visas, and copies of the pamphlets *You and Your Passport* and *Your Trip Abroad,* write to PA/MS/PCD, Public Correspondence Division, Bureau of Public Affairs, The State Department, Washington, D.C. 20520. And for more information on customs and a copy of the pamphlet *Know Before You Go,* visit your nearest customs office or write U.S. Customs Service, P.O. Box 7118, Washington, D.C. 20044.

□ THE AMERICAN NATION AND THE WORLD

■ The nineteenth century

The Founding Fathers and our early presidents had a foreign policy of avoiding "entangling alliances" with the traditional – and, in American eyes, corrupt – states of Europe. The reason for this policy was not that America was not interested in the fate of Europe. Rather, it was that the former colonies were not strong enough militarily to influence European developments directly. So they decided instead to increase their new nation's power while setting an example for their corrupt former colonizers. The example they chose to set, they said, was that of a new order so attractive it would lead Europe to reform itself politically, in accordance with the dictates of our Declaration of Independence and our Constitution.[2]

■ The United States becomes a world power

This desire to abide by moral standards and set a moral example for others in foreign affairs has persisted in America to this day, although the actual moral standards have changed considerably. The United States generally stayed aloof from conflicts in Europe until the end of the nineteenth century. Then, in the Spanish-American War (1898), it defeated Spain and took away Spain's colonies of Puerto Rico, Cuba, Guam, and the Philippines. Following that brief, successful war, the United States returned to isolation until German provocations during World War I (1914–1918) enticed the country to enter that war in Europe. Victorious in World War I, President Woodrow Wilson sought to reform Europe in the Treaty of Versailles. Wilson advocated freedom – "self-determination," he called it – for the various East European nationalities that had been dominated by Germany and the Austro-Hungarian Empire. He also took the lead in supporting the creation of a *League of Nations* which, together with a World Court, under American leadership, was supposed to resolve international conflicts peacefully so there would never be another world war.[3]

---

[2]For an interesting account of American foreign policy in this era, see Selig Adler, *The Isolationist Impulse* (New York: Abelard Schuman, 1957).

[3]See Norman Levin, *Woodrow Wilson and World Politics* (New York: Oxford University Press, 1968).

The United States abandons isolation and enters World War I. U.S. troops arriving in London, August 1917.
National Archives

Return to isolationism

But at that time, following the experience of the war, the American people's isolationist impulses were so strong that President Wilson could not convince the United States Senate to ratify our membership in the League of Nations. This ratification was required by the Constitution, as we have noted in earlier chapters. So America withdrew again from European world politics. Nonetheless, we continued to use our military forces and political power to dominate much of Latin America in these decades. This policy derived from our proclamation of the Monroe Doctrine in 1823, which attempted to keep European powers from intervening there. But we did not return to the world arena until World War II (1939–1945) was well underway in Europe and the Japanese bombed the American naval fleet in Pearl Harbor, Hawaii, in December 1941.

The United Nations and the Cold War

Victory over Japan, Germany, and Italy in that war left the United States an industrial and military giant – the only major country in the world whose homeland had not been severely damaged by the war. But this time the American government, with strong popular support, decided to participate actively in the postwar settlement. The United States took the lead in organizing the United Nations, which was composed of the "nations united" against Germany and Japan. Soon thereafter, the United States developed the *Marshall Plan*, a massive program of economic recovery aid to the war-torn countries of Europe, named for the American secretary of state who proposed it, General George Marshall.

During the war the Soviet Union had been invaded by Hitler's Germany. This brought it into the war as an ally of the Western countries. But after the war, relations between the Soviets and the Western countries deteriorated quickly. Diplomats and historians still disagree about why this happened, and about which country was most reponsible for it. But everyone agrees that what came to be called the "Cold War" (to distinguish it from the "hot war," World War II) drastically transformed world politics.[4]

The Soviets sought protection against the possibility of yet another attack from Germany – something that had happened several times previously. They therefore insisted that Germany be split up among the allies. They then gradually imposed Communist governments in the smaller countries of Eastern Europe, seeking to create a buffer between them and the Germans. In the words of the British leader Winston Churchill, an "Iron Curtain" descended, separating Europe into West and East. Hostility and provocation increased along that border, and the nations on each side rearmed and eventually established alliances to coordinate defenses. Much of the world increasingly became divided into two great blocs confronting each other in Central Europe. This situation is generally called a "bipolar world" – a world of nations organized around two "poles" – the United States and the Soviet Union.

---

[4]The literature on the Cold War is by now unmanageably large. For one helpful analysis, see John Lewis Gaddis, *The United States and the Origins of the Cold War* (New York: Columbia University Press, 1972).

United Nations/M. Tzovaras

The UN General Assembly opens its thirty-second session, September 20, 1977. The admission of Djibouti and Vietnam as members at this session brought UN membership to 149 nations.

■ Global alliances

First, the United States joined other Western European countries in the North Atlantic Treaty Organization (NATO) in 1949.[5] Then, when the Western countries decided to rearm West Germany, in 1954 the Soviets gathered their Eastern European allies into the *Warsaw Pact.* Relations in Europe between the two blocs (see Figure 19.1) then remained conflictual and militaristic until tensions were finally relaxed in the period called Détente (a French diplomatic term for relaxation of tensions) some 15 years later.

■ Limited wars

Meanwhile, in Asia lines were also being drawn. China, which had been corruptly ruled as an American ally by Chiang Kai-shek, was finally taken in a peasant revolution under the Communist leader Mao Tse-tung in 1949. This led to fears in the West that the Soviet Union and China, united as Communist powers, might come to dominate the rest of the world. And so, when military conflict broke out on the Korean Peninsula in 1950, the United States, with United Nations approval, came to the aid of South Korea. The Korean War was fought to a virtual standstill in 1953. In American eyes, the Korean War was fought to teach other states—and particularly the Chinese, who had sent in "volunteers" when American troops approached the Chinese border—that we would refuse to allow military movements that would change the political and military status quo.

If American resistance in Korea had achieved this effect, presumably there never would have been a Vietnam War. But the French, who had previously colonized Indochina, engaged in a losing struggle to hold on to it in the early 1950s

---

[5]On the origins and development of NATO, see Robert E. Osgood, *NATO: The Entangling Alliance* (Chicago: University of Chicago Press, 1962). For a somewhat different perspective, see David Calleo, *The Atlantic Fantasy: The U.S., NATO, and Europe* (Baltimore: Johns Hopkins University Press, 1970). And for a recent analysis of the alliance, see Elliot R. Goodman, *The Fate of the Atlantic Community* (New York: Praeger, 1975).

and finally partitioned the region into Cambodia, Laos, North Vietnam, and South Vietnam. The region had been composed of various tribal groupings that rarely got along harmoniously. The political boundaries the French left behind rarely coincided with traditional divisions. And so over the next decade turmoil grew and instability increased. The United States chose to take the place of the departed French, supporting the forces in control of Cambodia, southern Laos, and South Vietnam. Finally, in the early 1960s, the American-supported forces found themselves under growing pressure from civil uprisings within their territories. The rebels were aided by Communists to the north, and indirectly by the Chinese and the Soviets.

■ The war in Vietnam

This set the stage for the longest war in American history – and the only war the United States effectively lost. The United States began long-term bombing of North Vietnam and Laos in 1965. We then sent in American combat troops, whose numbers grew regularly from 1965 until they totaled over half a million by 1968. The eventual cost of our presence was some $150 billion and 56,717 American lives.

FIGURE 19.1
U.S. military alliances and the Warsaw Pact.

- NATO (Belgium, Canada, Denmark, France, Great Britain, Greece, Iceland, Italy, Luxembourg, Netherlands, Norway, Portugal, Turkey, United States, West Germany
- SEATO (Australia, France, Great Britain, New Zealand, Philippines, Thailand, United States
- Inter-American Treaty (Argentina, Barbados, Bolivia, Brazil, Chile, Colombia, Costa Rica, Dominican Republic, Ecuador, El Salvador, Guatemala, Haiti, Honduras, Mexico, Nicaragua, Panama, Paraguay, Peru, Trinidad-Tobago, United States, Uruguay, Venezuela
- Bilateral treaties with United States (Japan, Nationalist China, Philippines, South Korea)
- ANZUS Alliance (Australia, New Zealand, United States)
- Warsaw Pact (Albania, Bulgaria, Czechoslovakia, East Germany, Hungary, Poland, Rumania, USSR)

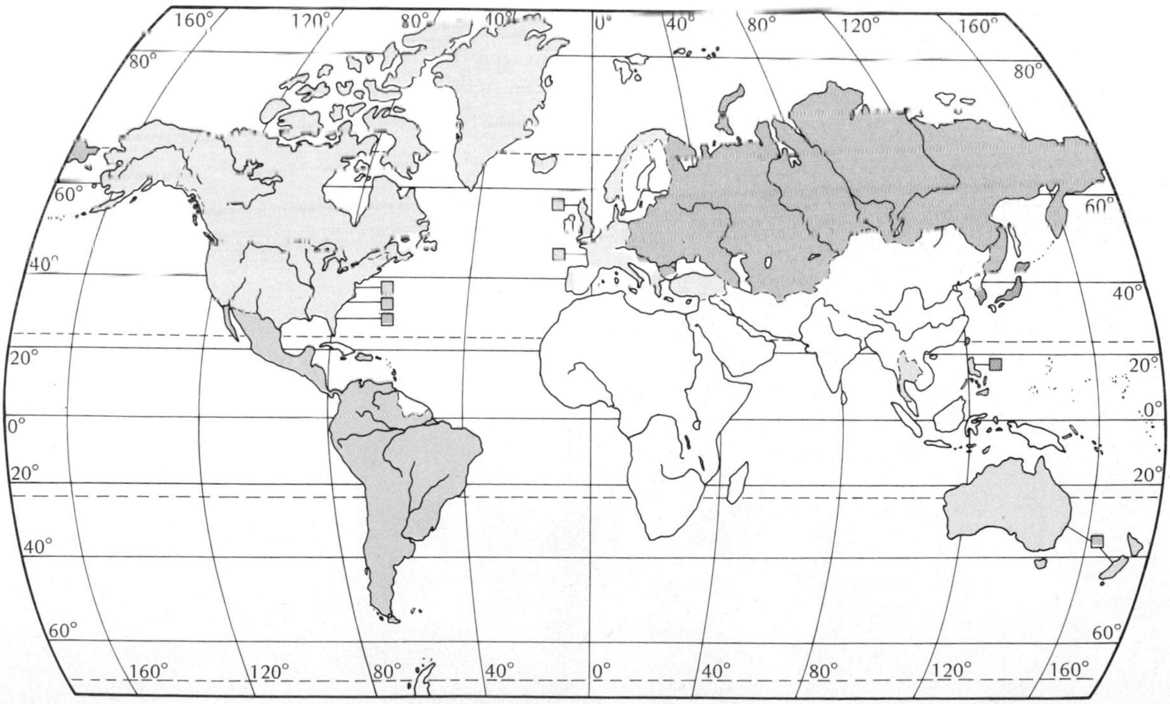

Despite all this, the best the United States could finally engineer, when domestic opposition forced it to withdraw in 1973, was a ceasefire. That truce deteriorated almost immediately. Finally, in April 1975, America's allies in Cambodia, Laos, and South Vietnam collapsed totally, and the Communists took over.

What had started out as an effort to shape the future of the world in accordance with our interests and what we perceived to be the interests of the people of Indochina had ended in disaster. The disaster led many to a new questioning of the roots of American foreign policy. American policy had come full circle from the years of active, even enthusiastic intervention around the world to the years of the Nixon Doctrine, which proclaimed that other countries would have to bear the military burden of their defense themselves. The world too had changed, from "bipolarity" to "multipolarity" – organization of states around many poles or into many smaller alliances, such as NATO, the Warsaw Pact, the Arab bloc, and the Organization of African Unity. The disaster also led to a reexamination of the way American foreign policy is made.

□ THE MAKING OF AMERICAN FOREIGN POLICY

■ The cabinet departments

The process by which the United States decides what efforts to make to protect its own interests short of resorting to war is an old one, but a changing one too. It dates back to the establishment of the Departments of State and War in 1789 as two of the first executive departments. Through the centuries the military component has proliferated: the Department of the Navy was created in 1798, and when an idependent air force was created in 1947 the three services were united into the National Military Establishment (renamed the Department of Defense in 1949).

There has always been some question as to the actual roles of the military and the diplomatic components in the making of American foreign policy. The only certainty has been that as both military commander in chief and diplomatic

President Carter and the National Security Council meet to discuss U.S.-Soviet Strategic Arms Limitation Talks (SALT).

White House photo

chief of state the president has ultimate responsibility for developing a unified policy. But as America's role in the world increased, and as economic factors became much more important in policy, that task became much more demanding, regularly involving such other departments as Treasury, Commerce, Agriculture, and even Labor.

■ The National Security Council

To assist the president, a new organization was established in the Executive Office of the President in 1947: The National Security Council. Its function, according to its official description, is "to advise the President with respect to the integration of domestic, foreign, and military policies relating to the national security." Formally, it consists of the president, the vice-president, the secretary of state, and the secretary of defense. In fact its meetings are attended by representatives of many other departments plus the intelligence services and are under the supervision of the assistant to the president for national security affairs.

Henry Kissinger It was that position which Henry Kissinger, then a professor of government at Harvard University, assumed when Richard Nixon became president in 1969. In the next 8 years, under Nixon and Ford, Kissinger played a major – most observers would say *the* major – role in formulating American foreign policy. It was a period that saw 4 more years of fighting in Vietnam, ending several years further on with the eventual collapse of our allied forces there. Before that collapse, Kissinger and his counterpart in North Vietnam had received a controversial Nobel Peace Prize for the interim agreement they had reached. Diplomatic relations with China were resumed for the first time since 1949. In addition, considerable progress was made in arms negotiations with the Soviet Union to stabilize the political situation in Central Europe and to limit the nuclear missiles built by each side ("arms control," as this is called). There was also continuing American mediation in the Middle East conflict between Israel and the Arab States.[6] All of these policies were later carried on by the Carter administration as well.

■ The bureaucratic "policy machinery"

Kissinger's tenure, first as a presidential advisor (1969–1974) and then as secretary of state (1973–1977), rekindled an old debate over whether individuals make foreign policy, or whether it is the bureaucracy that actually matters most.[7] The foreign policy bureaucracy includes not only the departments of State and Defense, but also the Treasury (because international economic affairs are now so important) and such other

---

[6]There are by now many books on Kissinger. On his world view, see Stephen Graubard, *Kissinger: Portrait of a Mind* (New York: Norton, 1974). For a favorable "insider" biography, see Marvin Kalb and Bernard Kalb, *Kissinger* (Boston: Little, Brown, 1974). For a somewhat more critical view, see Roger Morris, *Uncertain Greatness: Henry Kissinger and American Foreign Policy* (New York: Harper & Row, 1977).

[7]Kissinger held both posts for several years. For the foreign policy debate, see Morton Halperin, *Bureaucratic Politics and Foreign Policy* (Washington, D.C.: Brookings Institution, 1974).

Dennis Brack/Black Star

Henry Kissinger.

segments as the Central Intelligence Agency and often the departments of Commerce and Agriculture. But the "policy machinery," as it is often called, should also be thought of as including the Congress, which must pass the budget each year, approve major presidential appointments, and ratify treaties (the latter the responsibilities of the Senate).[8] And it should include as well the various vested interests (business groups, labor unions, professional groups, and active citizens) which lobby Congress and the executive on foreign policy concerns. Thus the foreign policy machinery is a complex organization, itself consisting of a collection of complex organizations. As we have seen time and time again in previous chapters, in such policy machinery, conflicts often develop. Some of the conflicts arise openly and are resolved by the machinery – questions about whether to give military aid to a particular country, for example, or about whether or not to sell wheat to the Soviet Union. But other conflicts emerge only after a policy has been made and implemented by one cog in the machinery and then turns out to conflict with something another cog is doing or attempting.

■ The Central Intelligence Agency

Many of the recent examples of such conflicts that have surfaced have involved the CIA. The CIA has tended to operate both autonomously and secretly. The problems such activities have created for those attempting to coordinate American policy could fill a book – and in fact have filled two massive congressional reports and numerous books by investigative journalists.[9] The challenge of these problems has led to renewed efforts to get greater control over such "covert" CIA operations. The success of these efforts, however, is not easy to determine or estimate from the outside. The failures become known only when they are leaked by disgruntled officials or uncovered in infrequent congressional investigations. The successes are even less likely to be publicized.

■ Foreign policy successes and failures

But neither, for that matter, is the success of other, more public, American policies and actions easy to determine. There are several important reasons for this difficulty. First, there is no clear and public statement of America's long-term objectives in the world – beyond the common platitudes of national security, peace, prosperity, democracy, progress, and the like. Were there such a generally recognized statement, it could be used as a criterion for some evaluation of short-term achievements. Second, things now change so rapidly that what may appear to be success at one moment (a victory in Vietnam, say, or a truce in the Middle East or a trade agreement with the Soviet Union) may soon seem outdated or inadequate.

And if it is difficult to assess the success or failure of particular policies, it is all

[8]See John Lehman, *The Executive, Congress, and Foreign Policy* (New York: Praeger, 1974).

[9]See Allen Dulles, *The Craft of Intelligence* (New York: Harper & Row, 1963), by the agency's first director; Victor Marchetti and John D. Marks, *The CIA and the Cult of Intelligence* (New York: Knopf, 1974), and Philip Agee, *Inside the Company: CIA Diary* (New York: Stonehill, 1975), both by dissident former agents; and David Wise, *The American Police State* (New York: Random House, 1976), about the agency's domestic transgressions.

the more difficult to assess the roles and contributions of the parties participating. One reason for this is that deliberations take place in secret, and the full story is hard to discover in public statements by officials, even when they are supplemented by "leaks" to the press. Furthermore, the various bodies may have different interests in a given situation. For example, State may want to institute a conservative democratic civilian regime. Defense may want to strengthen the reliable military. Treasury may want to protect private American investment, and CIA may want to engineer a coup. These various, conflicting objectives were approximately those held during the brief rule in Chile of Marxist President Salvador Allende. Allende was overthrown by the Chilean military with the encouragement from both the CIA and agents of American multinational corporations. In such situations of different interests, agencies may act at cross-purposes, and praise or blame may be difficult to apportion.

The war in Vietnam may be the clearest case of this. There the civilian officials tended to blame the military for not succeeding despite massive technological superiority and virtually unlimited spending. The military blamed the civilians for requiring that it fight "with one hand tied behind its back" by prohibiting obliteration bombing, and even invasion, of North Vietnam. Some observers blamed the Congress for "abdicating its responsibilities in wartime" by allowing the executive to wage an undeclared war despite the constitutional provision that wars must be declared by Congress. Other observers blamed the advisors to Presidents Kennedy and Johnson for misunderstanding the impossible political situation in Vietnam, and so being unjustifiably optimistic throughout the war. And many government officials blamed the intelligence agencies for not reporting accurately, while the intelligence agencies blamed the policy makers for not taking their reports and interpretations correctly and seriously.

Vietnam was such a deep and prolonged catastrophe for America that there is probably sufficient blame to go around. But for our efforts to improve upon the past, to learn the lessons of our mistakes as well as of our successes, we would like to know more about who did what, and why it produced the outcomes it did, than we are ever likely to learn. Consequently, neither the policy machinery and policy-making process, nor the policies themselves, are likely to change fast enough to keep pace with the rapid changes in the world.

□ POWER IN QUESTION: THE WORLD IN TRANSFORMATION

It is never certain just which new developments in the world will prove to be the most important and the longest-lasting. Some people refer to the period since 1945 as the years of Cold War and Détente. They tend to emphasize the importance of the contest between the United States and the Soviet Union. Others call the period the "nuclear age," focusing on the invention, use, and spread of nuclear weapons as the major feature of these years. Still others refer to it as the "age of decolonization," emphasizing the emergence from colonial domination by Britain, France, and several lesser colonial powers of a majority of the world's population.

Those who focus on the Cold War and Détente emphasize "international politics as usual" – struggles for power and dominance by great nations that often seem just like those of earlier centuries. Those who refer to the "nuclear age" tend to see the period as one of unusual politics – politics dominated by previously unknown destructive military machines. Those who concentrate on decolonization emphasize the spread of the long-standing desire of peoples to be free to choose their own governments and their own ways of life.

■ The Cold War

If the Cold War, which we described earlier, was in a sense "international politics as usual," it was at the same time politics with new and different means or instruments. The United States ushered in the nuclear age by developing atomic bombs and dropping them on the civilian populations of the Japanese cities of Hiroshima and Nagasaki in August 1945. We claimed that we used the A-bombs to hasten the end of World War II in Asia, although some experts argue that their use was unnecessary because Japan was already ready to surrender. They were weapons of previously inconceivable destructive power.

Once the Soviets developed nuclear weapons it became difficult for either country to conceive of fighting a nuclear war with the other, because both would likely be largely destroyed in the process. But the nuclear stalemate in a sense once again made smaller-scale wars more possible, and the years since 1945 have seen hundreds of violent conflicts resulting in insurrections, civil wars, armed border conflicts, and even occasional "conventional wars" between various countries.[10]

■ Nuclear spread

Since then, two other important developments have further transformed relations among states. The first is the continuing *spread of nuclear weapons capability.* Britain, France, China, and India had all demonstrated this capability by the 1970s, and such states as Israel and South Africa developed the capability shortly thereafter. Many others can be expected to join the "nuclear club" in coming years, thereby making the world an even more dangerous place.

■ Limits on the utility of force

The second transforming development is a growing sense of the *practical limitations on the effective use of military force* in world affairs. Americans, as the military leaders of the world, have been slow to recognize these growing limitations. The American success in World War II only confirmed a long-held belief that overwhelming force would prevail. The stalemate in Korea led to a new belief in the necessity and promise of military technology – airpower plus counterinsurgency electronic gear and weaponry – as the salvation of those resisting aggression. A recent study by the Brookings Institution found that the United

---

[10]For one account of such conflicts, which takes a different perspective from the one I adopt in this chapter, see Klaus Knorr, "On the International Uses of Military Force in the Contemporary World," *Orbis,* Spring 1977, pp. 5–27. See also Adda B. Bozeman, "War and the Clash of Ideas," *Orbis,* Spring 1976, pp. 61–102, for a fascinating account of different cultures' conceptions of conflict and violence.

States deployed its military forces, usually in ways short of war, at least 215 times from 1945 to 1975. The Soviet Union did the same at least 115 times.[11]

In Vietnam, the most flagrant and long-lasting American military action, the United States used the most advanced nonnuclear military technology without ultimate success. But we were opposing forces expert in unconventional, generally guerrilla-style war. The Viet Cong and their North Vietnamese allies were so deeply committed to their struggle that they would not give up in the face of our massive technological superiority, and instead consistently found ingenious ways to get around and through our efforts.

Ultimately, the reliance upon military force to compel an unattractive political solution in Vietnam failed utterly there. In addition, it had further bad consequences at home: inflation coupled with recession, student rebellion, disillusionment, and a general popular distrust of political authorities.

■ Mimicry

In addition, however, America's actions in Vietnam and elsewhere have set bad examples for other states, friends and foes alike. Any such action by the strongest and most prominent actor inevitably tends to set an example for others. World affairs in our era are often characterized by the phenomenon of *mimicry*—imitation for the sake of imitation, almost regardless of its likely promise. Mimicry is, of course, a common human trait. We see it in fashion, in the arts, and in political campaigns, for example. In these instances it is usually harmless, but in world politics it can be very dangerous. Any nation that fears another is likely to imitate the other. The reason it does this is to avert the possibility that its adversary will be able to make a significant breakthrough before it can understand what is happening and take countermeasures. If only one side has a space program, for example, it may discover a surprising military use of space, such as spy satellites or orbiting bombs, which could then be a serious threat to the other if it hasn't developed its own space capability.[12]

[11]Barry M. Blechman and Steven S. Kaplan, *The Use of the Armed Forces as a Political Instrument* (Washington, D.C.: Brookings Institution, 1976).

[12]For a discussion of this phenomenon, see David V. Edwards, *Creating a New World Politics* (New York: McKay, 1973).

Top U.S. military commanders and Defense Department officials meet in the National Military Command Center at the Pentagon to discuss plans, policies, and procedures.
Wide World Photos

We can see this phenomenon of mimicry at work in American-Soviet relations throughout the Cold War years of competition. It occurred not just over military development and space exloration, but also over the training of specialized engineers and scientists, foreign aid, cultural exchange programs, athletics, and so on. Now, as other states become stronger, they too are tempted to imitate the large states in developing their military forces as well as constructing their other foreign activities.

One widespread result of all this is temptations for many states to "go nuclear" for military uses and for the generation of electrical power. Another result is efforts to develop massive military establishments that far exceed local defense needs (such as, for example, those developed by Iran, Saudi Arabia, and Libya, with their oil revenues). In these ventures, the countries have the assistance of the world's leading arms merchants, the United States and the Soviet Union. Ultimately, this resort to developing large military forces destabilizes political situations, distorts economies that are in desperate need of capital for economic development projects, and results in greater political turmoil and repression within many of these countries. This set of effects is not very promising for the future of the world.

■ New developments

But there may be grounds for hope nonetheless in several other developments. One is the spreading recognition that resources such as oil and gas are rapidly diminishing as development increases and population grows. Population growth in addition puts greater strain on agriculture and makes hunger and occasional famine a growing reality for more and more of the people of the world, as we shall see in more detail in Perspective 7.

Such fears of shortages of energy–fuel for machines and food for people–seem increasingly likely to compel diversion of more resources toward agriculture and development of domestic energy resources. This in turn will necessarily mean fewer resources for further increases in military establishments. But the danger now is that before these trends can take effect, states will be encouraged to use the weapons they already have as a consequence of the bad examples set by the big powers coupled with the provocations from cartels (like the Organization of Petroleum Exporting Countries, OPEC), multinational corporations (such as Coca-Cola, General Motors, or Kennecott Copper), or revolutionaries inside or outside their borders.

□ STATES IN QUESTION: NEW ACTORS IN WORLD AFFAIRS

The notion that the states of the world, which had dominated world politics for centuries, would have to "share" world politics with such "nonstate actors" as cartels and multinational corporations would have shocked most foreign policy makers in the years of the Cold War conflict between the United States and the Soviet Union. International relations have traditionally been just that: relations among nations – nations that have territorial boundaries. Even in the Cold War years international relations were being opened up to new "actors" – the countries which had been colonies of Britain and France but were insisting on and winning independence.

■ New states

At the close of World War II there were less than fifty independent states in the world. Thirty years later, there were three times that number. Many of the new states remain under the strong influence of a former colonial master such as Britain or France. Others are effectively the clients of one or the other superpower. Nonetheless, most are active members of major international organizations. The United Nations, for example, had 149 members by 1977.

■ New economic actors and issues

Both the World Bank (which makes loans to developing countries) and the International Monetary Fund (which coordinates national currencies in international economic relations) have gained new members. These new states have made international affairs much more complex and much more difficult for the major powers to control. And all the signs suggest that this difficulty will grow as the newer states get more experience in operating effectively in world affairs, and as our needs for their raw materials and cheap labor increase.

TABLE 19.1

Selected national living standards

Country	Life expectancy at birth (years)	Food (calories per day and percent from animal sources)	Education (teachers per 1000 population)	GNP per capita (1970 dollars)	Electric power (kilowatt hours per capita per year)
Australia	70	3160/45%	4.8	2900	4300
Bolivia	50	1760/14	1.7	200	160
Brazil	61	2620/15	3.8	390	490
Canada	72	3200/46	14.0	3700	9500
Chad	32	2240/8	0.1	70	10
China (Communist, including Tibet)	50	2050/9	–	90	–
Czechoslovakia	71	3030/27	3.1	1500	3100
Egypt	53	2900/7	2.0	210	230
West Germany	70	3150/42	5.0	3000	4000
Guinea	27	2060/3	0.7	82	110
India	41	1950/5	2.0	1000	110
Ireland	71	3460/41	3.5	1300	2000
Ivory Coast	41	2430/6	0.7	300	130
Jamaica	64	2280/17	1.0	600	840
Japan	72	2450/14	6.1	1800	3400
Malawi	39	2400/5	0.2	70	30
Nepal	41	2030/6	0.6	85	7
Nigeria	37	2300/5	0.3	99	30
Peru	54	2270/14	3.0	360	440
Saudi Arabia	42	2080/8	0.9	360	100
South Africa	49	2800/20	–	700	2500
Sri Lanka (Ceylon)	62	2200/4	–	170	65
United States	71	3250/40	8.5	4700	8000
USSR	70	3180/21	–	1150	3100

Source: Adapted from George L. Tuve, *Energy, Environment, Populations, and Food: Our Four Interdependent Crises* (New York: Wiley, 1976), pp. 210–215.

■ Living on less than $200 a year

To begin to understand economic development we must have a picture of the problem with which it contends. We must conjure up in our mind's eye what underdevelopment means for the two billion human beings for whom it is not a statistic but a living experience of daily life. Unless we can see the Great Ascent from the vantage point of those who must make the climb, we cannot hope to understand the difficulties of the march.

It is not easy to make this mental jump. But let us attempt it by imagining how a typical American family, living in a small suburban house on an income of six or seven thousand dollars, could be transformed into an equally typical family of the underdeveloped world.

We begin by invading the house of our imaginary American family to strip it of its furniture. Everything goes: beds, chairs, television set, lamps. We will leave the family with a few old blankets, a kitchen table, a wooden chair. Along with the bureaus go the clothes. Each member of the family may keep in his "wardrobe" his oldest suit or dress, a shirt or blouse. We will permit a pair of shoes to the head of the family, but none for the wife or children.

We move into the kitchen. The appliances have already been taken out, so we turn to the cupboards and larder. The box of matches may stay, a small bag of flour, some sugar and salt. A few moldy potatoes, already in the garbage can, must be hastily rescued, for they will provide much of tonight's meal. We will leave a handful of onions, and a dish of dried beans. All the rest we take away, the fresh vegetables, the canned goods, the crackers, the candy.

Now we have stripped the house: the bathroom has been dismantled, the running water shut off, the electric wires taken out. Next we take away the house. The family can move to the toolshed. It is crowded, but much better than the situation in Hong Kong, where (a United Nations report tells us) "it is not uncommon for a family of four or more to live in a bedspace, that is, on a bunk bed and the space it occupies—sometimes in two or three tiers—their only privacy provided by curtains."

But we have only begun. All the other houses in the neighborhood have also been removed; our suburb has become a shantytown. Still, our family is fortunate to have a shelter; 250,000 people in Calcutta have none at all and simply live in the streets. Our family is now about on a par with the city of Cali in Colombia, where, an official of the World Bank writes, "on one hillside alone, the slum population is estimated at 40,000—without water, sanitation, or electric light. And not all the poor of Cali are as fortunate as that. Others have built their shacks near the city on land which lies beneath the flood mark. To these people the immediate environment is the open sewer of the city, a sewer which flows through their huts when the river rises."

And still we have not reduced our American family to the level at which life is lived in the greatest part of the globe. Communication must go next. No more newspapers, magazines, books—not that they are missed, since we must take away our family's literacy as well. Instead, in our shantytown, we will allow one radio. In India, the national average of radio ownership is one per 250 people, but since the majority of radios is owned by city dwellers, our allowance is fairly generous.

Now government services must go. No more postman, no more fireman. There is a school, but it is three miles away and consists of two classrooms. They are not too overcrowded since only half the children in the neighborhood go to school. There are, of course, no hospitals or doctors nearby. The nearest clinic is ten miles away and is tended by a midwife. It can be reached by bicycle, provided that the family has a bicycle, which is unlikely. Or one can go by bus—not always inside, but there is usually room on top.

Finally, money. We will allow our family a cash hoard of five dollars. This will prevent our breadwinner from experiencing the tragedy of an Iranian peasant who went blind because he could not raise the $3.94 which he mistakenly thought he needed to secure admission to a hospital where he could have been cured.

Meanwhile the head of our family must earn his keep. As a peasant cultivator with three acres to tend, he may raise the equivalent of $100 to $300 worth of crops a year. If he is a tenant farmer, which is more than likely, a third or so of his crop will go to his landlord, and probably another 10 percent to the local moneylender. But there will be enough to eat. Or almost enough. The human body requires an input of at least 2,000 calories to replenish the energy consumed by its living cells. If our displaced American fares no better than an Indian peasant, he will average a replenishment of no more than 1,700–1,900 calories. His body, like any insufficiently fueled machine, will run down. That is one reason why life expectancy at birth in India today averages less than forty years.

But the children may help. If they are fortunate, they may find work and thus earn some cash to supplement the family's income. For example, they may be employed as are children in Hyderabad, Pakistan, sealing the ends of bangles over a small kerosene flame, a simple task which can be done at home. To be sure, the pay is small: eight annas—about ten cents—for sealing bangles. That is eight annas per gross bangles. And if they cannot find work? Well, they can scavenge, as do the children in Iran who in times of hunger search for the undigested oats in the droppings of horses.

And so we have brought our typical American family down to the very bottom of the human scale. It is, however, a bottom in which we can find, give or take a hundred million souls, at least a billion people. Of the remaining billion in the backward areas, most are slightly better off, but not much so; a few are comfortable; a handful rich.

Of course, this is only an impression of life in the underdeveloped lands. It is not life itself. There is still lacking things that underdevelopment gives as well as those it takes away: the urinous smell of poverty, the display of disease, the flies, the open sewers. And there is lacking, too, a softening sense of familiarity. Even in a charnel house life has its passions and pleasures. A tableau, shocking to American eyes, is less shocking to eyes that have never known any other. But it gives one a general idea. It begins to add pictures of reality to the statistics by which underdevelopment is ordinarily measured. When we are told that half the world's population enjoys a standard of living "less than $200 a year," this is what the figures mean. . . .

This difficulty will be increased by the fact that the world today is characterized by growing disparities in economic development, as economist Robert Heilbroner portrays graphically in the box titled "Living on less than $200 a year," and as Table 19.1 reveals statistically. The newer states are becoming less willing to settle for the status of permanent paupers in world affairs and are demanding in the United Nations and other international organizations major steps toward creating what a 1974 UN declaration called a "New International Economic Order." This declaration begins with the following words:

> *We, the Members of the United Nations,*
>
> *Having convened* a special session of the General Assembly to study for the first time the problems of raw materials and development, devoted to the consideration of the most important economic problems facing the world community,
>
> *Bearing in mind* the spirit, purposes and principles of the Charter of the United Nations to promote the economic advancement and social progress of all peoples,

Solemnly proclaim our united determination to work urgently for THE ESTABLISHMENT OF A NEW INTERNATIONAL ECONOMIC ORDER based on equity, sovereign equality, interdependence, common interest and cooperation among all States, irrespective of their economic and social systems which shall correct inequalities and redress existing injustices, make it possible to eliminate the widening gap between the developed and the developing countries and ensure steadily accelerating economic and social development and peace and justice for present and future generations, . . .[13]

■ Economic unions

Older states too are combining to coordinate their economic activities. The most advanced instance of this is the European Community, which joins nine countries (Belgium, the Netherlands, Luxemburg, France, West Germany, Italy, Denmark, Great Britain, and Ireland) in a "common market" with free trade among members and identical tariff barriers to the rest of the world. The Communist countries of Europe have also combined into a Council of Economic Mutual Assistance (which we usually call COMECON – for *com*munist and *econ*omic). Other regions too are attempting similar collaboration, particularly in Latin America and Scandinavia.[14]

■ Multinational corporations

Another major complicating factor is the increase in nonstate actors in world affairs.[15] The most familiar of these nonstate actors today are multinational corporations (MNCs) – major companies like General Motors or the largest oil companies (Exxon, Royal Dutch Shell, British Petroleum, and the others) that have plants scattered around the world and engage in mining, manufacturing, trading, and/or selling wide varieties of products in a great many countries. These MNCs are often so big and so important economically that they can influence the politics as well as the economies of many countries in which they operate. The alleged efforts of International Telephone and Telegraph (ITT) to topple the elected Marxist government in Chile in the early 1970s, or the payments made by Lockheed Aircraft to politicians in various countries in order to get these countries to purchase Lockheed planes, may be typical of the illegal activities of some MNCs. Most of what MNCs do in order to get favorable trade arrangements is quite legal in the countries where they operate. Much of it is welcomed by the "host" countries as contributing to their economic development. But the most important point for our understanding of international relations is that MNCs often act in the world almost as if they themselves were states.

---

[13] United Nations, "Declaration on the Establishment of a New International Economic Order," May 1974.

[14] See Werner J. Feld, *The European Community in World Affairs: Economic Power and Political Influence* (Port Washington, N.Y.: Alfred, 1976), and on public attitudes see Feld and John K. Wildgen, *Domestic Political Realities and European Unification* (Boulder, Colo.: Westview, 1976), and Ronald Inglehart, *The Silent Revolution: Changing Values & Political Styles among Western Publics* (Princeton N.J.: Princeton University Press, 1977).

[15] See Richard W. Mansbach, Yale H. Ferguson, and Donald E. Lampert, *The Web of World Politics: Nonstate Actors in the Global System* (Englewood Cliffs, N.J.: Prentice-Hall, 1976).

These MNCs have (in the terms we used earlier when speaking of individual citizens) foreign policies of their own. Often these corporate foreign policies do not relate to, and may even contradict, the policies of the countries in which their headquarters are located. A revealing example of this occurred in the fall of 1975 when the United States was supporting a conservative faction in the Angola civil war. Gulf Oil, headquartered in Pittsburgh, which had major oil-drilling rights in Angola, was at the same time paying millions of dollars in oil royalty fees to the Marxist faction in Angola, which controlled the capital city and government, but which the American government was opposing. Gulf suspended these payments only when public outrage at this "unpatriotic" behavior of an American-based multinational, coupled with the State Department's requests, became too difficult to resist. And as soon as the Marxist faction triumphed, Gulf resumed its payments. In this case and generally, MNCs have little or nothing to gain from war. They thus tend to become important forces for peace in many places of political conflict. But they can also be very destabilizing influences on nations' foreign policies.

■ Cartels

Political and economic activity of even the largest states can also be heavily influenced by other new nonstate actors. Everyone now knows about OPEC – the Organization of Petroleum Exporting Countries – because of the increases in oil prices and the oil boycott of 1973 by the Arab members of OPEC, which created long lines at American gas stations. The continuing series of oil price increases decreed by OPEC have made almost everything in our daily lives more expensive. OPEC too is a nonstate actor – a *cartel* of producer nations – which acts almost as if it were a state and influences the policies of its members and of virtually all oil-consuming states. There is a somewhat similar cartel in industrial and gem diamonds. And there are growing efforts to create other cartels involving such products as bauxite (the ore of aluminum), natural rubber, copper, and coffee.[16]

■ Terrorists

Terrorist organizations are yet another type of nonstate actor. There have always been terrorists and assassins, but until recently they tended to confine their occasional activities to civil war situations. Now they may claim to represent a group of people without a territory (as the Palestine Liberation Organization and its various allied organizations in the Middle East do) or an international revolutionary conspiracy. Examples of their activities include the hijacking of airplanes on international flights, the attacks on Israeli Olympic athletes in Munich in 1972, and the kidnapping of the OPEC oil ministers as they met in their Vienna headquarters in 1974. They are now active in most parts of the globe, from Northern Ireland to Argentina, from Yugoslavia to the Philippines, from the Soviet Union to the United States. One survey found that in the years 1968 to 1974, there were 507 incidents of international terrorism, resulting in the death of 520 persons, the wounding of 830, destruction estimated at $163 million and the loss of

[16]See "Creeping Cartelization," *Business Week,* May 9, 1977, pp. 64–83.

SIPA Press/Black Star

In late 1973, pro-Palestinian hijackers blew up a Japanese airliner in Benghazi, Libya, after releasing hostages. The plane had been hijacked in Amsterdam.

$32 million in ransom money.[17] Terrorists commonly take hostages and demand that imprisoned fellow terrorists be freed in exchange for the hostages. But whatever their actions, they too make international relations more dangerous and more difficult for states to control, just as they further increase the interdependence of peoples across state boundaries. And should terrorists develop or steal nuclear weapons, their leverage – and the destruction they cause – may become greater.

□ ALLEGIANCE IN QUESTION: CHANGING ATTITUDES OF CITIZENS

Many terrorists, international bureaucrats working for organizations such as the United Nations, and officers of MNCs have developed allegiances to organizations other than the states in which they were born. In doing so, they become examples of another important new development in the world. It may turn out that the greatest check on the inclination of states to wage war against each other in coming years will be the growth of new attitudes in the citizens of states large and small.

■ Antimilitarism and separatism

There are already signs of a growing "antimilitarism" (opposition to military adventures and even to military spending) in economically advanced states such as Japan, Great Britain, and France. Recent years have seen new growth of localism and "separatist" attitudes in minorities within major states who seek independence or lessened external control over their lives. Examples include the Quebecois in Canada, the Scots and Welsh in Britain, the Bretons in France, and the Basques and Catalans in Spain. The spread of these attitudes to minorities in more and more countries may make it more difficult for states to support and conduct military adventures as usual.

The populations of many developed countries seem to be becoming more interested in local autonomy and preserving their cultural distinctiveness, and less interested in continung an imperial policy of dominating other states. In other words, the trend toward antimilitarism seems often to be coupled with the emergence of political attitudes that combine a transnational concern for the

[17]Cherif Bassiouni, ed., *International Terrorism and Political Crime* (Springfield, Ill.: Charles C. Thomas, 1975), p. 537. See also Yonah Alexander, ed., *International Terrorism* (New York: Praeger, 1976).

welfare of other peoples with a growing interest in subnational or local ethnic, cultural, religious, and linguistic practices. The citizens of French Alsace and German Baden, for example, have joined to organize resistance to the building of nuclear power plants that they consider dangerous. Their feeling of unity across national boundaries is strengthened by the common dialect they speak, as well as by their regular trips across the Rhine River – the French to work in Baden factories, the Germans to shop in French markets.

The big question, to many observers, is whether these new attitudes that we find in the Western countries will also emerge in the Eastern, Communist countries. Both the Soviets and the Chinese have a history of serious "nationality problems," as they are called. These difficulties for the Soviet Union are traceable to the fact that the "Great Russians" conquered many smaller Asian and East European nationalities to make the "Union of Soviet Socialist Republics" out of Beylorussians, Ukrainians, Georgians, Uzbeks, and others. And similarly the Chinese Han conquered Mongolians and Tibetans among others on their fringes to create the Chinese state. So the major Communist powers, like many Western powers, may increasingly find themselves facing growing popular attitudes that weaken the state's ability to mobilize its peoples and resources for wars outside its boundaries.[18]

■ Interdependence among nations

Meanwhile, the growing pressure on the world's shrinking supply of vital food, energy, and mineral resources will tend to increase *interdependence.*[19] The same effect will also be strengthened by the growing threat to the earth's ecosystem from industrial and other types of pollution.[20] And the growing tastes for material goods not locally available plus the spread of technology will further intertwine economies. Recognizing these new developments, one citizen interest group asked historian Henry Steele Commager to develop a Declaration of *Inter*dependence as part of its observance of the Bicentennial. This declaration reads in part:

> When in the course of history the threat of extinction confronts mankind, it is necessary for the people of The United States to declare their interdependence with the people of all nations and to embrace those principles and build those institutions which will enable mankind to survive and civilization to flourish. . . .
>
> To establish a new world order of compassion, peace, justice and security, it is essential that mankind free itself from the limitations of national prejudice, and acknowledge that the forces that unite it are incompar-

---

[18]See Nathan Glazer and Daniel P. Moynihan, eds., *Ethnicity* (Cambridge, Mass.: Harvard University Press, 1975).

[19]See, among recent studies, Gerhard Mally, *Interdependence: The European-American Connection in the Global Context* (Lexington, Mass.: Lexington Books, 1976), and Robert S. Keohane and Joseph S. Nye, *Power and Interdependence: World Politics in Transition* (Boston: Little, Brown, 1977).

[20]For a drastically different, highly optimistic view, see Herman Kahn et al., *The Next 200 Years: A Scenario for America and the World* (New York: Morrow, 1976). Kahn concludes that "200 years ago almost everywhere human beings were comparatively few, poor and at the mercy of the forces of nature, and 200 years from now, we expect, almost everywhere they will be numerous, rich and in control of the forces of nature" (p. 1).

□ ACTION UNIT 19.2 How to influence American foreign policy

You can, of course, attempt to influence foreign policy by writing public officials, demonstrating, lobbying, and so forth, just as you might on other issues. But you may wish to join with others having similar interests in organizations devoted to study and action on foreign affairs questions. Among the more prominent such organizations are the following, most of which publish newsletters, pamphlets, and other educational materials;

The Air Force Association (1750 Pennsylvania Ave. N.W., Washington, D.C. 20006) informs the public of aerospace developments.

The American Friends Service Committee, Peace Education Division (1501 Cherry St., Philadelphia PA. 19102) opposes militarism and advocates nonviolent action for change.

The Arms Control Association (11 Dupont Circle N.W., Washington, D.C. 20026) seeks to broaden public interest in arms control, disarmament, and national security policy.

The Association of the United States Army (1529 11th Street N.W., Washington, D.C. 20036) informs the public of army-related developments.

The Center for Defense Information (122 Maryland Ave. N.E., Washington, D.C. 20002) studies the defense budget, weapons systems, and troop levels to educate the public.

The Coalition on National Priorities and Military Policy (110 Maryland Ave. N.E., Washington, D.C. 20002) publishes materials on arms control and reducing military spending.

The Coalition for a New Foreign and Military Policy (120 Maryland Ave. N.E., Washington D.C. 20002) publishes background materials and legislative updates on foreign policy issues.

The Council for a Livable World (100 Maryland Ave. N.E., Washington, D.C. 20002) supports political candidates favoring arms control and reduced military spending.

The Council on Economic Priorities (84 Fifth Ave., New York, N.Y. 10011) analyzes the impact of American corporations on society and foreign policy.

The Council on National Priorities and Resources (1620 I St. N.W., Washington, D.C. 20002) is an association of national labor, religious, and political organizations working to reorder government spending.

The Defense Orientation Conference Association (1330 New Hampshire Ave. N.W., Washington, D.C. 20036) promotes continuing education through tours of defense installations.

The Federal Union (1736 Columbia Rd. N.W., Washington, D.C. 20009) promotes a supranational federation of the United States, Canada, and Western European democracies.

The Federation of American Scientists (307 Massachusetts Ave. N.E., Washington, D.C. 20002) lobbies on questions of the use of science in society, especially for weaponry, and in favor of disarmament.

The Fellowship of Reconciliation (Box 271, Nyack, N.Y. 10960) is a pacifist organization supporting nonviolent methods for social and political change.

The Friends Committee on National Legislation (245 Second St. N.E., Washington, D.C. 20002) lobbies Congress and the president on foreign policy questions from a Quaker perspective.

The Institute for Policy Studies (1901 Q St. N.W., Washington, D.C. 20009) does research and public education on public issues.

The Institute for World Order (1140 Avenue of the Americas, New York, N.Y. 10036) works to transform the international system around four values: redistribution of wealth, redistribution of power, war prevention, and ecological stability.

The Navy League of the United States (818 18th St. N.W., Washington, D.C. 20006) supports strengthening American naval power.

New Directions (1692 K St. N.W., Washington, D.C. 20036) was founded as a foreign affairs counterpart to Common Cause and lobbies and educates the public on nuclear proliferation, arms sales abroad, foreign aid, and other policy questions.

SANE (318 Massachusetts Ave. N.E., Washington, D.C. 20002) organizes to mobilize support for American initiatives for peace, arms control and disarmament, reduced military spending, and so on.

The United Nations Association/USA (300 E. 42nd St., New York, N.Y. 10017) educates the public on the United Nations and its activities and supports American initiatives in the United Nations.

The Women's International League for Peace and Freedom (120 Maryland Ave. N.E., Washington, D.C. 20002) is the Washington lobbying office of the national organization that supports human rights, arms control, and reduced military spending.

The World Federalists Association (1424 16th St. N.W., Washington, D.C. 20036) supports world peace through world law with justice.

ably deeper than those that divide it—that all people are part of one global community, dependent on one body of resources, bound together by the ties of a common humanity and associated in a common adventure on the planet Earth.[21]

There remain major political threats to peace around the world. There are still risks of major nuclear war or of new imperialist ventures such as an effort by Western industrial powers to seize Middle Eastern oilfields by force—something once hinted at as a possible last resort by Henry Kissinger. But the longer the world survives these risks, the less able major states are likely to be to wage traditional wars, and the less willing populations are likely to be to sustain the sacrifices such wars would entail.

In the interim, the effort to avoid major war and renewed imperialism will make major demands upon states and nonstate actors alike. Many observers believe it will require a general balance among a great many states. This is what is usually meant by the "balance of power." It will also require, most agree, delicate efforts to sustain restraint in the relations between the superpowers. This is what is meant by Détente.[22] Given these basic conditions, for stability and progress to be achieved, all states will have to cooperate more than they ever have thus far in a basic restructuring of economic relations between the rich and the poor that will give all states an interest in refraining from the resort to military force. This is what is meant by a "new international economic order."

The major states show every sign of appreciating the importance of the balance of power and of Détente. But both of these are *conservative* concepts and *conservative* approaches. The "new international economic order," however, is not. It is, or calls for, a drastic change in world relations—a change that will challenge our democratic political attitudes and our capitalist political interests as they have never before been challenged. Many observers wonder whether American policy makers and the interests that influence them will be able to overcome the

[21]Henry Steele Commager, "A Declaration of INTERdependence," prepared for the World Affairs Council of Philadelphia, October 24, 1975.

[22]Many basic documents on, and analyses of, Détente are collected in Robert J. Pranger, ed., *Détente and Defense* (Washington, D.C.: American Enterprise Institute, 1976).

conservative tendencies of our foreign policy bureaucracy and our foreign policy process to develop the needed new departures. Only time will tell.

Meanwhile, the almost inevitable conservatism of the foreign policy process puts a greater burden on those most removed from it: the American people. The American people have a tradition of concern for the welfare of peoples in need elsewhere in the world. With memories of Vietnam still in their minds, they are also weary of the sacrifices compelled by mistaken military adventures. Because they hold these attitudes, the American people may have to play a growing role in reminding their leaders of the need to work with diligence and imagination to adjust constructively and humanely to a world changing more rapidly than policy makers in Washington, immmersed in day-to-day responsibilities, may realize.

This citizen responsibility for influencing policy makers is what energizes the organizations described in Action Unit 19.2, which lobby to influence American foreign policy. At this point, no one really knows what adjustments will be required in our own life-styles by the growing needs, demands, and requests of the less developed two-thirds of the world's peoples. In Perspective 7 we'll examine the problems of food and fuel in their global context. As we do so, we might also consider the questions posed by those who are already advocating what they call "right sharing" of the world's resources – questions that involve conservation of scarce resources by the rich and sharing of them with the poor. These questions, at one extreme, and the public statements of our leaders, at the other, all serve to remind us that in our own small ways we too have foreign policies that will need considerable and regular adjustment in this unstable world of growing interdependence. Time and our efforts will tell whether here, as in race relations and urban affairs, for example, our leaders might learn from, and be inspired by, our own private efforts.

□ SUGGESTIONS FOR FURTHER READING AND STUDY

A good general survey of contemporary world politics is Harold Sprout and Margaret Sprout, *Toward a Politics of the Planet Earth* (New York: Van Nostrand-Reinhold, 1971). This book includes a very interesting chapter (11) on different types of maps and how they shape the ways we see the world.

Among books that examine the newer developments in world affairs are: Lester Brown, *World without Borders* (New York: Vintage paperback 1972), still valuable although dated; Seyom Brown, *New Forces in World Politics* (Washington, D.C.: Brookings Institution paperback, 1974); Robert Keohane and Joseph Nye, *Power and Interdependence: World Politics in Transition* (Boston: Little, Brown paperback, 1977); Saul Mendlovitz, ed., *On the Creation of a Just World Order* (New York: Free Press, 1975); and Herman Kahn et al., *The Next 200 Years* (New York: Morrow paperback, 1976), which offers a drastically different perspective of optimism.

To learn more about the making of American foreign policy, you may find these books helpful: Graham Allison, *The Essence of Decision* (Boston: Little, Brown paperback, 1971); Roger Hilsman, *The Politics of Policy Making in Defense and Foreign Affairs* (New York: Harper & Row paperback, 1971); John F. Campbell, *The Foreign Affairs Fudge Factory* (New York: Basic Books, 1971), which examines the State Department; Morton Halperin, *Bureaucratic Politics and Foreign Policy* (Washington, D.C.: Brookings Institution paperback, 1974); Richard Barnet, *The Roots of War* (New York: Penguin paperback, 1972); and John H. Esterline and Robert B. Black, *Inside Foreign Policy* (Palo Alto, Calif.: Mayfield paperback, 1975).

WHAT ARE THE PROSPECTS FOR AMERICAN POLITICS?

□ Perspective 7: The politics of energy: food, fuel, and America's future in a global community

□ THE PROBLEM OF UNDERSTANDING THE PROBLEMS

When governments and experts talk about food and fuel, they usually use terms and measures that mean very little to us. We as citizens are increasingly told that the future of life on earth depends on improvements in "the world food situation." And we're warned that continuation of our standard of living depends on overcoming "the energy crisis." But when it comes to public policy, we're confronted with "barrels of oil" and "bushels of wheat." How are we to understand what's at issue?

Let's start with the two levels that often disappear in discussions of American food policy and American energy policy. One of these levels is *the individual's level*– our own food and fuel situations and those of others like us. If we can't relate personally to these things, we're not very likely to be able to understand, let alone decide what we believe should be done, and what we ourselves might do.

The second level often neglected is *the global level.* We hear increasing talk about "interdependence." Every country is now dependent on many others, for raw materials, manufactured goods, and so forth, and so there is a "web of dependences" connecting most states. Many people now refer to the planet as "spaceship Earth," pointing out that we're all passengers, traveling on it through space, regardless of our nationality or our wealth. But even though politicians, journalists, teachers, and ordinary citizens use these terms, how many of us know the nature of interdependence today? What is the United States dependent on others for, and what do others depend on us for?

In this chapter, we'll trace briefly the important basic points about the individual and the global levels of food and fuel. Then we'll use that understanding as a basis for examining the broad possibilities of national policy and international cooperation on these global problems of energy.

□ FOOD AND US

We generally hear of food policy in terms of bushels of wheat and head of cattle, although of course we don't eat either one as such. Nonetheless, both are important for an understanding of what we do eat and how that affects the world food supply.

■ The politics of diet in America

Experts in nutrition tell us we need to eat carbohydrates (starch and sugar), fats, and protein to get the energy to live. We also need protein, minerals, vitamins, and water to enable our bodies to maintain and rebuild themselves. We call the energy "calories"; the same calories that most Americans are often trying not to eat in order to lose weight are the things that make continued life possible. The trick is to get enough calories to be able to breathe, to work, and to play without getting the extra calories that make us fat. Just how many calories we need to be active depends on our size, our activity, and our sex. On the average an adult male needs about 3000 calories a day while an adult female needs 2200. But just getting adequate calories isn't enough. We also need protein to keep our bodies healthy. In general, adults need 35 grams of protein a day – twice what children need.

What does all this have to do with politics? In the old days, when people lived on farms and grew their own animals – very little. But today few of us live on farms. And even those who do, tend to specialize in wheat or corn or soybeans or cattle. The result is that to get adequate nutrition we depend on buying many of the things we need to eat. And that's where the government comes in.

We noted in previous chapters that the government inspects and regulates much of the food we eat. It also acts to control – usually to raise – the prices we pay for milk and other farm products in order to protect farmers, a powerful special interest group. In recent decades, however, the government has come to influence the prices of wheat and cattle by its trade policies. When the government limits the importing of beef produced abroad, it cuts the total supply available to us and so we pay more for our steaks and for the 50 billion hamburgers we eat each year. When the government arranges sales of our wheat to the Soviet Union or China, it lowers the supply for us and again prices go up. In recent years there have been poor crops of wheat and other grains (for example, rice, corn, and oats) in many countries. The results have been threats of widespread starvation in large areas of Africa and some of Asia. The U.S. government has provided foreign aid in the form of grain for many of the countries harshly affected, under a program we call "food for peace." It has also helped American grain companies sell wheat to the Soviets by giving credit to the Soviet Union and negotiating deals for the companies. The results for us were higher food prices in all these instances.

This is not necessarily bad on balance, because higher food prices usually mean higher profits for farmers. They then produce more so the world has more food available. Surveys show that the American people are willing to pay higher food prices to help feed the hungry around the world.

Shelly Katz/Black Star

■ The politics of global hunger

But there are growing questions of whether there will – or even can – be enough food in the world to meet the needs of the rapidly growing population.[1] In April 1976, according to expert calculations, the world population passed 4 billion people. It is growing at the rate of 2 percent a year – which doesn't sound like much until you realize that at that rate it will double in about 35 years. This means that the food supply too must double in 35 years simply to keep pace. Experts say that 400 to 500 million people are malnourished today, and millions still die of starvation every year. If we want to improve the diets of the hungry as well as keep pace with population growth, we must make much more food available.

Here is where things become a bit more complicated. It appears that even today the world simply doesn't produce enough food. But that is not necessarily true. Distribution is a major problem. Much food that is produced does not get to the people who are hungry. There are always surpluses in some countries. And there is always food that perishes when it isn't eaten where it is produced. In addition, rats and other critters eat a lot of food

[1]For provocative discussions of the problems of global hunger, see Frances Moore Lappé and Joseph Collins, *Food First: Beyond the Myth of Scarcity* (Boston: Houghton Mifflin, 1977), and Susan George, *How the Other Half Dies: The Real Reasons for World Hunger* (Montclair, N.J.: Allanhead, Osmun, 1977)

Wide World Photos

Millions of people die of starvation throughout the world each year. Nigeria, 1968.

which could feed the hungry here at home and abroad.

But there is even more to the problem. The easiest way to get a good diet in terms of calories is to eat grains such as wheat. If you eat meat, the animal these days is usually first fattened on grain. It takes about 10 calories of food energy in grain eaten by a cow, for example, to make 1 calorie of food energy in meat. Nearly four-fifths of all the grain American farmers produce is fed to animals, most of which we later eat. This means that the average American eats about 2000 pounds of grain a year, or more than 5 pounds a day – but most of it indirectly, by eating meat. The average citizen of a developing country, by contrast, eats very little meat, and eats only about 400 pounds of grain a year. (You can compare percent of caloric intake from animal sources in various countries in Table 19.1.) He or she could live for a week on the grain that has gone into 1 pound of beef. But of course he or she never gets the chance in many cases, because we've already fed the grain to our cattle.

These figures, and many more like them, have led some to argue that we Americans – and the Western Europeans, who are more and more like us in meat eating – should change our diets. Enough grain is grown in the world today to feed about 6 billion people on a nonmeat diet – and there are only 4 billion people in the world. If all we in the United States did was to switch back to grass-fed beef from grain-fed beef, we'd free up enough grain to feed another 225 million people – the equivalent of the entire American population. Chickens eat less calories in grain per calorie in meat produced compared to cattle. If we Americans substituted chicken for a third of the beef we eat, we'd free up enough more grain to feed 100 million people a year.

However, it is important to note that a diet of mostly grain is not likely to be a very good diet. That's a reason why the health of people in the poorer countries is generally worse than ours. Meat is the easiest way to get the vital *amino acids* that help our bodies make efficient use of the food we eat. If we were to give up meat, we would have to be careful to eat diets that include what are called "complementary" foods, such as wheat combined with beans.[2]

But we wouldn't even have to give up beef to improve the world food situation. Instead, we could simply be less wasteful. A recent study of the garbage thrown away by Tucson, Arizona, households found that the average family threw 10 percent of its food into the trash. Among middle-class households, it was 25 percent. And none of this includes what is put down disposal units in sinks – only what is thrown into the trash and picked up by the city.[3]

[2]For a fascinating account of the possibilities, replete with recipes, see Frances Lappé, *Diet For a Small Planet* (New York: Ballantine paperback, 1971.

[3]This study was done by Professor William L. Rathje and his students. For a report on it, see Jack Thomas, "The Hungry and the Wasteful," *Boston Globe,* September 27, 1976.

There are other things we *could* give up but surely won't. For example, the liquor and beer industry in the United states consumes over 50 million bushels of corn, 85 million bushels of barley, 12 million bushels of rice, and 3 million bushels of rye in making liquor and beer each year. That totals enough grain to feed up to 20 million people, at the rate of 400 pounds of grain a year. The Distillers Feed Research Council, one of those trade associations we discussed in Chapter 11, responds that 90 percent of this grain is later recycled for animal feed. But it is still lost to direct, efficient human consumption.[4]

Another thing we could give up is pets. Americans have some 60 to 80 million dogs and cats as pets. They now eat almost 4 million tons of food a year, including 1 million tons of meat and fish by-products and 2 million tons of grain – at a cost of $1.6 billion. Many of these resources too could be diverted to human consumption should we choose to do so.[5]

Americans as a whole are not going to give up either liquor or pets, any more than they are going to become vegetarians. I myself enjoy beer and have several cats as pets, and I eat meat as well. The chances are, you do too. But all of us must recognize that the growing pressure of our expanding population on the earth's limited resources will force some rather drastic changes in certain aspects of our life-styles.

We are already feeling some of that pressure, as a result of the "energy crisis." By the mid-1970s, the United States was importing about half its oil supply. Most of these imports come from the Middle East – an area where political developments may result in a shutoff of oil at any time – as they did during the oil embargo of 1973. We generally think of the energy problem as separate from the food problem, because we think of energy as important for factories, homes, and cars. But this is misleading.

☐ ENERGY AND US

■ The energy in food

The main reason why American agriculture is so productive is that we use massive quantities of energy in farming. We use immense amounts of fertilizer, some of which is made from oil and gas. The same for pesticides. We use machinery at every stage of farming, and it runs on gas. We use energy to pump water to irrigate, and energy to dry grain when it's harvested, and energy to transport the food to factories, and energy to pack it and ship it and store it and sell it. And you and I then use energy driving to the store, energy refrigerating the food we buy, and energy disposing of our wastes.

"If we look at farming from the standpoint of calories of food crop delivered to the American table compared to calories of energy expended in the form of fuel, electricity, chemicals (including pesticides as well as fertilizer), energy tied up in the manufacture of farm tools, transportation devices, supermarket refrigerators, etc., etc.," writes energy expert Donald Carr, "we come to the appalling conclusion that the American food system devours over 9 times as many calories as it produces. Instead of being the most efficient system, it is energetically by far the least efficient system of agriculture that has ever existed or that we can imagine."[6]

■ The sources of energy

How can we be that inefficient? The simple answer is that the sun continues to bless us with new energy, and meanwhile we are living largely off old, unused solar energy stored in the ground as coal,

[4]Florence Mouckley, "Liquor, Beer Grain: Food for Millions," *Christian Science Monitor,* November 20, 1974.

[5]"The Pet Population Problem," *Washington Post,* September 15, 1974.

[6]Donald E. Carr, *Energy and the Earth Machine* (New York: Norton, 1976), p. 178

oil, and gas. Of course, as we are now constantly reminded, these are "nonrenewable resources"—there won't be any more of them when these are gone. Most experts now think we'll run out of natural gas in about 25 years, oil in 30 to 80 years, and coal in 100 to 300 years—all depending on how fast demand grows. Many hope that nuclear power will fill in once these "fossil fuels" are gone. At the moment, almost 80 percent of the world's energy comes from fossil fuels, about 20 percent from burning trash and dung, and a very small amount from nuclear plants. The growing public fears about the safety of nuclear reactors, plus the skyrocketing costs of nuclear plants and fuels, makes many doubt how much of a contribution nuclear power will be able to make, at least at the present level of technology. What then does that leave as an energy source?

■ Solar energy

The sun sends down at the earth 400,000 times as much energy as the entire capacity of all the electric companies of America. You'd think that would be enough to take care of our needs. In fact, it would be enough virtually to vaporize us. But here the earth comes to our rescue, reflecting 30 percent of that energy back into space. Another 47 percent is absorbed by the atmosphere, water, and land. That's what makes life livable on earth. Most of the 23 percent of solar energy that remains makes the water and air on earth move, which gives us tides and winds and rain and tornadoes.

That leaves two one-hundredths of 1 percent (0.0225 percent) of the incoming solar energy to be absorbed by trees, vegetable plants, grain, grass, and other greenery. These greens then provide the energy for animals and us by producing the food we eat. Much of the rest of the solar energy could be used for heating. More and more people are now using solar energy to heat their homes and water. In theory, we could also gather solar energy and convert it into electricity. But that would require technology we don't yet have because the sun's rays are so diffuse.[7]

■ Other energy sources

There are other likely sources of energy besides solar. *Tides and waves* are very powerful and may be harnessed to drive motors, rather in the way that waterfalls now produce "hydroelectric" power. *Hydroelectric* power too is still largely undeveloped, especially in Western countries. *Wind* may soon make a comeback as cheaper windmills are developed. *Geothermal* ("earth heat") sources such as geysers and steam vents can be used to produce power when they spout steam. And there is room for more progress in one of the oldest types of energy production: *processed waste* such as garbage and dung, burned to release energy. Finally, some believe that solar collectors in space could orbit the earth, gather solar energy, and transmit it to the earth in concentrated rays.[8]

In a sense, then, in energy as in food, the

[7]A splendid survey, on which this account relies heavily, is Earl Cook, *Man, Energy, Society* (San Francisco: Freeman, 1976).

[8]See Gerard O'Neill, *The High Frontier:Human Colonies in Space* (New York: Morrow, 1977).

Courtesy of Owens-Illinois

Solar energy collectors atop a federal office building in Saginaw, Michigan.

point is not that there is not, or could not be, much more than we now have. The point is that all this production of food and fuel takes time and technology – and, of course, still more energy and more money. You can't make energy without spending energy to produce, store, and transport it, just as you can't make food without spending energy to grow, process, and ship it. The costs of all this are climbing very rapidly, for a number of reasons. One is that high technology is expensive. Another is that oil-producing countries are insisting on more revenue, anticipating the day when the oil is gone. Yet another is that energy is produced by large companies that can influence prices in their favor. And coupled with these is the fact that everywhere governments are levying special taxes on energy partly to get revenue but also to try to limit consumption and so preserve resources. These are the places where politics and energy become inextricably linked.

□ GLOBAL ENERGY POLITICS

■ Global consumption

Most of the energy resources (especially coal, oil, and gas) are found in the northern countries. Both the United States and the Soviet Union are large producers of all three, while China in coal and the Middle East in oil are also major producers. A recent UN study found that global production of energy has tripled over a 25-year period. Most of the demand for energy is still in northern countries, too. That demand now far outruns supply in the United States, Western Europe, and Japan. Only the Communist countries have a relative balance between their own resources and their demand. The same UN study found that the per capita consumption of energy in the industrialized countries is sixteen times greater than in the developing countries.[9]

■ American consumption

The United States has little more than one-twentieth of the world's population, yet it consumes one-third of the world's annual fuel supply for energy. By the early 1970s, we were pumping 150 billion gallons of petroleum a year from American wells, which works out to more than 3 gallons a day per motor vehicle. But even that wasn't enough, and so we were importing about a quarter again as much. And even that couldn't keep pace with the growing demand. By the late 1970s we were importing about half of the oil we used. Much of it was coming from the Middle East, where we were embroiled in the politics of the dispute between the Arabs and the Israelis.

■ Global interdependence

This dependence on foreign oil gives other countries important leverage over us. The same situation holds with many other raw materials that we have to import in large quantities, such as natural rubber (of which we import 100 percent), manganese (93), cobalt (92), chromium (91), aluminum (81), platinum (76), tin (75), nickel (71), mercury (57), zinc (51), and so on.[10] On the other hand, the countries that supply us with these raw materials are also dependent on us for manufactured goods (from tractors to mining equipment to computers) and sometimes for food. This is the real meaning of interdependence in the world today. The fact that everybody now recognizes this interdependence makes it more and more possible to talk about the world as a "global community." But this global interdependence doesn't prevent political and economic struggles between countries, as we saw in Chapter 19. Nor, of course, does it prevent political struggles inside countries.

---

[9]Kathleen Teltsch, "Energy Output Tripled in 25 Years, U.N. Says," *New York Times*, July 30, 1975.

[10]These figures, from the Interior Department, are from 1972, the last year for which full figures are available.

☐ NATIONAL ENERGY POLITICS

The federal government has been involved in energy since the 1920s. For decades, its role was to limit the supply of plentiful oil and gas to protect the producers. And when shortages recently became a problem, the government stepped in to allocate energy among businesses and private homes and among parts of the country.

Actually, the government has a double involvement. It continues to influence imports, prices, and allocations by its "national energy policy." In addition, it owns most of the remaining energy resources in the country: oil lands under the ocean floor of the Atlantic, Pacific, and Gulf coasts, coal deposits in the western states, and even uranium. What sort of policy has emerged from this?

The Nixon administration was faced suddenly with the Arab oil boycott of 1973 in the midst of the Watergate investigation. It opted for "energy independence" by 1980, hoping that somehow by then we would no longer need to import oil. When Gerald Ford took over as president, he revised the date to 1985 but retained the objective of independence. Little progress was made in efforts to control consumption, and imports continued to increase. As a result, Carter's efforts have been aimed at cutting oil imports and limiting the growth of domestic consumption through more use of coal and incentives for home insulation and use of solar heating, along with restrictions on inefficient, "gas guzzling" cars.

■ Energy conservation

The emphasis, in other words, has been shifting toward conservation. The reason for this is that America's use of energy is remarkably inefficient. Figure P7.1 shows that *about half the energy that we use is wasted,* in the sense that it doesn't contribute to the end result desired, such as heating or powering transportation. Some of this waste is inevitable because of the limits of efficiency. But many believe that about half the waste – or a quarter of the energy we consume – could be saved by conservation measures. Savings could be achieved in many different ways. For example, if all homes had 6 inches of insulation, the equivalent of 600,000 barrels of oil per day could be saved; if clothing were washed in warm or cold water, 100,000 barrels; if the average load of a commuter car were increased by one person, 700,000 barrels; and if all electric motors were made only 1 percent more efficient, 1 million barrels.[11]

These figures, in "barrels of oil equivalent per day," don't mean very much by themselves. That's one of the problems in conveying the facts about our energy situation to the people, and one of the reasons why the people rarely understand how serious the problem is. A Gallup Poll taken in May 1977, in the midst of great national debate about energy policy, found that only 52 percent of the people knew the United States had to import oil, and 33 percent thought we were self-sufficient in oil – at a time when the United States was importing almost 8 million barrels a day.[12]

The term "barrels of oil equivalent per day" means "the amount of energy that would be produced by this number of barrels of oil if they were used to produce energy." But what, then, is a barrel of oil? Oil doesn't come in barrels – at least not any more. It comes in pipelines from wells and in tanker ships from overseas. But it's still measured that way. A barrel is 42 gallons, which weigh 300 pounds. When we *refine* crude oil, we heat and treat it to make it into gasoline, propane gas, butane gas, petrochemicals used for fertilizers, fabrics, drugs, and so on, and fuel for jets, diesels, and furnaces, as well as lubricants and the asphalt that is used to pave most of our roads. The proportions we get in this refining can be varied, but usually we get about 45 barrels of gasoline and 55 barrels of the other products from every 100 barrels of oil we refine.

[11] "Where Savings Could Be Made," *Newsweek* April 18, 1977, p. 73.
[12] "Only About Half of Public Knows U.S. Has to Import Oil, Gallup Survey Shows," *New York Times*, June 2, 1977.

FIGURE P7.1

Percent of available energy used and wasted.

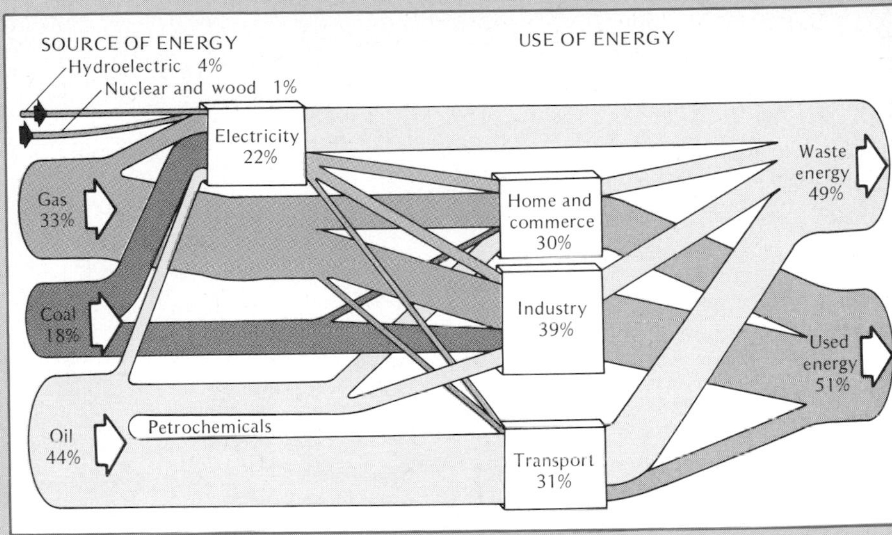

Source: Redrawn from Brian J. Skinner, *Earth Resources*, 2nd ed. (Englewood Cliffs, N.J.: Prentice-Hall, 1976), p. 24. Data for 1972.

This list of products we get from oil suggests how important it is to our standard of living. One recent study found that Western Europe, Japan, and America achieve similar standards of living—but with very different uses of energy. In every case, the United States uses much more energy. The reasons for this include our sprawling geography, our preference for the single family home instead of the apartment, and our love of the automobile.[13]

There are, of course, specific things individuals can do to conserve energy. For example, radial auto tires decrease rolling resistance and so can cut fuel costs by about $65 a year on the average. Storm windows and doors can save 15 percent on fuel bills. Driving at 55 miles per hour instead of 70 cuts gasoline use by 20 percent. Turning down home thermostats in the winter 6 degrees will save 15 to 20 percent in heating bills. In the summer, 78 degrees instead of 72 in air-conditioned houses will cut cooling costs almost in half. The list could go on and on.

□ ENERGY AND ENVIRONMENT

So, too, could the questions. There are, as we have seen, close connections between food and fuel as forms of energy. There are also close connections between energy and environment. Measures to protect the environment by requiring industrial plants to remove chemicals and wastes from the air and water they discharge use energy. Shifting from natural gas and oil to coal in power plants creates more pollution that must be cleaned up. Antipollution devices on cars lower gas mileage. Bans on the strip-mining of coal make coal more costly to mine. There is, in sum, a "trade-off" between energy and the environment. This trade-off requires a national policy on the relative emphasis to be set between the two. If our decision ultimately is to sacrifice environmental protection for energy production, we will pay a high price in health and comfort in

[13]Resources for the Future, *How Industrial Societies Use Energy*, reported in *National Journal*, April 30, 1977 p. 664.

There are close connections between food and fuel as forms of energy and between energy and environment. Oil well in wheat field in northern Texas.

Texas Highway Department

coming years. But if we suffer severe energy shortages, we may pay different but still uncomfortable prices in health and comfort now. There are, in other words, important questions concerning *the quality of life* that we must confront. We'll look further at them in Chapter 20.

The same sort of dilemma faces us in our relations as a nation with other countries. There is a growing foreign dependence on our food and manufactured goods by countries seeking to develop economically. But there is also a growing resentment of our position as almost a monopolizer of the world's energy supplies and many of its natural resources. If we choose to continue to consume so much more than "our share" of the world's resources, we'll foster more and more resentment among others – some of whom are our suppliers. There are both practical political questions and historic ethical questions here that we must face. We must decide what position we hold on the question of *equity* in the distribution of the world's resources, and then we must try to relate our energy policy and actions to that decision.[14]

But these are not just questions for the nation, they are also questions for us as citizens. The way we eat and the way we use fuel will in large measure determine America's chances for maintaining its quality of life. They also will contribute to the life chances of peoples elsewhere in the world. We have found in previous chapters that the prospects for American politics are highly dependent on the actions of the American people. Now, as we broaden our focus, we discover that our own prospects and those of our fellow citizens are also bound up with those of our fellow passengers on spaceship earth. In the last two chapters, we shall look further at the prospects for the quality of life and the quality of democracy in an America increasingly a part of a global community.

[14]For several interesting studies, see L. S. Stavrianos, *The Promise of the Coming Dark Age,* (San Francisco: Freeman, 1976), and William Ophuls, *Ecology and the Politics of Scarcity* (San Francisco: Freeman, 1977).

20 The politics of the pursuit of happiness: the quality of life

The Declaration of Independence asserted everyone's "unalienable rights [to] life, liberty and the pursuit of happiness." In the difficult early years of the Republic, the right to life was thought of primarily in terms of survival, the right to liberty in terms of freedom from British domination, and the right to pursue happiness in terms of owning and working one's land. In years of trial, when none of these rights is guaranteed to anyone, all of them tend to be thought of in such minimal terms. But when things get better, hopes rise – and with them, beliefs about what people are entitled to, by virtue of being human beings. In this chapter, we'll look at what's happened to people's concerns about work and play, consumption and the environment, and what the political system does to affect them.

□ THE QUALITY OF LIFE

The concept of the quality of life, once life itself seemed assured, changed with the times. In times of economic difficulty such as the Great Depression of the 1930s, *material sufficiency* was the keystone. But in the 1960s there seemed to develop a general sense that material prosperity – food, clothing, shelter, and transportation – was not enough. True, people would still tell pollsters they were "very happy" or "fairly happy," as the poll results in Table 20.1 reveal. But over the 25

TABLE 20.1

The happiness of the American people, 1946–1970

Date	Very happy	Fairly happy	Not very happy[a]	Other response
April 1946	39%	50%	10%	1%
December 1947	42	47	10	1
August 1948	43	43	11	2
November 1952	47	43	9	1
September 1956	53	41	5	1
September 1956	52	42	5	1
March 1957	53	43	3	1
July 1963	47	48	5	1
October 1966	49	46	4	2
December 1970	43	48	6	3

[a]In the 1963, 1966, and 1970 polls, the final column read "not happy" rather than "not very happy."

Source: Data gathered by the American Institute of Public Opinion.

years covered by these polls, per capita income rose by 62 percent while the percentages of people saying they were happy hardly changed at all.[1]

But more and more emphasis was put on having opportunities for leisure pursuits, feeling a sense of personal fulfillment, developing an ability to appreciate and enjoy nature and the arts. But just as the concept of "the good life" was shifting toward these less tangible pursuits, many Americans started to notice with growing alarm rapid increases in smog, traffic congestion, air and water pollution, urban decay, and the destruction of forests and the countryside. A sense emerged that while life was relatively secure in terms of personal material needs, the *quality* of that life was threatened—apparently by the very industrial production that offered more and more goods and services, coupled with the more widespread enjoyment of these goods and services. A national survey in 1971 found 17 percent of the people believing that life in the United States was getting better and 36

[1]See Tibor Scitovsky, *The Joyless Economy* (New York: Oxford University Press, 1976), pp. 133–137.

TABLE 20.2

"Is life in the United States getting better, staying the same, or getting worse?"

	Getting better	Staying same	Getting worse	Total	Number responding	Ratio: worse/better
All	17%	47%	36%	100%	2126	2.1
Sex						
Males	20	44	36	100	897	1.8
Females	14	51	35	100	1229	2.6
Age						
18–24	24	45	31	100	330	1.3
25–34	15	44	41	100	438	2.7
35–44	16	50	34	100	366	2.1
45–54	14	54	32	100	351	2.3
55–64	20	42	38	100	283	1.9
65 or older	13	52	35	100	357	2.8
Educational attainment						
Eighth grade or less	12	55	33	100	463	2.9
Some high school, no diploma	11	52	37	100	392	3.3
High school diploma	17	47	36	100	698	2.1
Some college, no degree	22	42	36	100	328	1.6
College degree(s)	27	38	35	100	234	1.3
Race						
White	17	47	36	100	1845	2.2
Black	17	50	33	100	221	1.9
Income						
Less than $3,000	12	52	36	100	290	3.0
$3,000–4,999	13	49	38	100	280	2.9
$5,000–6,999	15	50	35	100	265	2.3
$7,000–9,999	17	47	36	100	362	2.1
$10,000–11,999	16	47	37	100	264	2.4
$12,000–16,999	20	48	32	100	319	1.6
$17,000 or more	24	41	35	100	261	1.4
Size of community						
Central cities	13	36	51	100	224	4.0
Large cities	20	42	38	100	238	1.9
Suburbs	21	44	35	100	451	1.7
Small cities and towns	16	51	33	100	670	2.0
Rural areas	15	53	32	100	543	2.2

Source: Table 8.1 from "The Country as a Domain of Experience," in *The Quality of American Life: Perceptions, Evaluations, and Satisfactions,* by Angus Campbell, Philip E. Converse, and Willard Rodgers. © 1976 by Russell Sage Foundation, New York. Data for 1971.

TABLE 20.3

Ways in which Americans say life in the United States is getting better

Category	Percentage mentioning category
Behaviors and attitudes of individuals in social situations	11[a]
Living conditions	11
Economic conditions	19
Health: medical care	10
Racial situation	4
Education: quality and availability	13
Science, technology	18
Home conveniences	8
No way in which life in the United States is getting better	38

[a]Percentages add to more than 100 because some respondents gave more than one answer to the question. Some respondents gave two or more answers that were coded into the same major category, and other answers were coded into miscellaneous categories not listed in this table.

Source: Table 8.2 from "The Country as a Domain of Experience," in *The Quality of American Life: Perceptions, Evaluations, and Satisfactions,* by Angus Campbell, Philip E. Converse, and Willard Rodgers. ©1976 by Russell Sage Foundation, New York. Data for 1971.

percent believing it was getting worse, as Table 20.2 reports. Those things that people singled out as getting better and worse are reported in Tables 20.3 and 20.4.

Five years later, a 1976 Harris Survey reported that while 33 percent of the American people believe that the quality of life has improved in the past decade, 19 percent think it hasn't changed and 44 percent believe it has gotten worse.[2]

People have come to talk more and more about the *quality* of life, placing emphasis not only upon opportunities for meaningful work, better education, and pleasureful leisure experiences, but also upon environmental protection and quality goods and services. Our society is so complex and our economy so highly developed that it is almost impossible for individuals themselves to satisfy their desires for better work experiences, more constructive play opportunities, consumer protection, and so forth. Indeed, even organizations – such as labor unions, consumer groups, and environmental activists – have difficulty meeting citizen needs and desires. So in these as in other spheres citizens and groups increasingly turn to the government – local, state, and national – for assistance.

In the early years of the Republic, government's chief roles in influencing the quality of life were providing a national postal service and giving state sanction to marriage. In the next century and a half, the government came to play a greater and greater role in shaping the standard of living by increasing its regulation of the economy, as we saw in Chapter 16.

In recent years, this *economic regulation* of markets and rates has been supplemented by what is sometimes called *social regulation.*[3] Such regulation concerns the characteristics of goods and services produced as well as the working conditions under which they are produced and even the conditions under which they are consumed.

---

[2]"The Harris Survey," *Washington Post,* November 8, 1976.

[3]See William Lilley III and James C. Miller III, "The New 'Social Regulation,'" *The Public Interest,* no. 47 (Spring 1977), pp. 49–61.

TABLE 20.4

Ways in which Americans say life in the United States is getting worse

Category	Percentage mentioning category
Behavior and attitudes of individuals in social situations	52[a]
Use of drugs	17
Values and morals	17
Individuals' reactions to modern life and to each other: e.g., interpersonal differences, powerlessness, other indications of alienation	21
Young people—students; hippies	14
Sociological problems: institutions, economy, general living conditions	48
Inflation, high cost of living	17
Taxes	10
Ecological concerns	12
Crime and law enforcement system	24
Crime	17
Protests and protest movements	19
Protests concerning race; racial problems, race riots, backlash on racial protests	9
Government, governmental policies, and practices	14
War or the military	7
Science, technology, or education	4
No way in which United States is getting worse	13

[a]Percentages add to more than 100 because most respondents gave more than one answer to the question. Many respondents gave more than one answer that was coded in a particular major code category listed on this table, others gave miscellaneous answers not fitting the listed categories.

Source: Table 8.1 from "The Country as a Domain of Experience," in *The Quality of American Life: Perceptions, Evaluations, and Satisfactions,* by Angus Campbell, Philip E. Converse, and Willard Rodgers. © 1976 by Russell Sage Foundation, New York. Data for 1971.

We saw in Perspective 3 how the Environmental Protection Agency controls pollution, and in Chapter 16 how the National Labor Relations Board regulates unions and management. In this chapter we shall look at the activities of others of the several dozen *social regulatory agencies* that govern work, consumption, and play in America today. We shall seek to learn what contributions they attempt to make to the quality of life in America, what political disputes arise in and around them, and what important policy questions in these areas remain to be answered.

The unemployment problem has been aggravated by advances in technology; today machines are capable of performing many tasks once performed by many men and women.

Ford Motor Company

General Motors Corporation

□ THE QUALITY OF WORK

In the colonial years, there was a shortage of labor in America, despite the fact that slaves constituted perhaps 20 percent of the population. It was with the great influx of immigrants seeking a better life in America some 100 years later that unemployment first became a sustained problem. By the mid-1970s, the problem was so great that, as we saw in Chapter 16, some 7 or 8 million Americans were consistently unable to find work. This unemployment costs some $20 billion a year in various unemployment benefit programs, over and above its human costs. Simply bringing it down to 4 percent and absorbing workers displaced by new machines and people seeking their first jobs will require creation of an average of 72,000 new jobs every week for a decade.[4]

So America continues to have a problem of the *quantity* of work. But at the same time the movement for improved quality of work is gaining momentum. Workers still respond to questions of whether "you are satisfied or dissatisfied with the work you do" by saying "satisfied" in general. But when asked if they would work if money were not needed, 31 percent say no, as Figure 20.1 shows. Further, studies show that productivity (the amount of goods or services produced by a worker) is falling. Furthermore, alcoholism, absenteeism, sabotage, and turnover – all marks of dissatisfaction – are increasing among American workers generally, as the box titled "The quality of work" indicates.

■ The safety of work

So some have no jobs while others have jobs they find unsatisfying. But in addition, many workers have jobs that are unsafe, not only because of the risk of accident, but also as a consequence of exposure to chemicals, heat, gases, radiation, noise, and so forth. Government reports estimate that some 14,500 workers die each year from on-the-job injuries. But another 100,000 die each year as a result of long-term exposure on the job to conditions or materials that cause various cancers, emphysema, and other fatal disorders. And a comprehensive study by the government's National Institute of Occupational Safety and Health in 1977 found that one out of every four Americans is exposed on the job to some substance thought to be capable of causing death or disease.[5]

The Occupational Safety and Health Act was passed by Congress in 1970. The law requires employers to see that the place of employment is "free from recognized hazards that are causing, or are likely to cause, death or serious physical harm to his employees" and gives employees the right to file complaints if they think there is a violation. Under the law, the Occupational Safety and Health Administration (OSHA for short) sets standards and inspects America's 5 million workplaces to see that the standards are observed. But thus far enforcement has been difficult for several reasons. First, OSHA has been given far too few inspectors – only about one

---

[4]"Challenge to U.S.: 72,000 New Jobs Every Week," *U.S. News & World Report,* June 28, 1976, pp. 20–24.

[5]See David Burnham, "1 in 4 Americans Exposed to Hazards on Job, Study Says," *New York Times,* October 3, 1977. See also James R. Michael, ed., *Working on the System* (New York: Basic Books, 1974), chap. 16.

FIGURE 20-1
How many would work if they didn't have to?

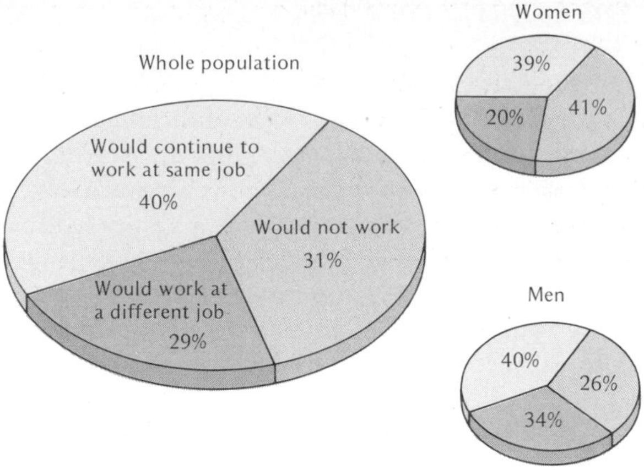

Source: Data reported in Angus Campbell, Philip E. Converse, and Willard Rodgers, *The Quality of American Life: Perceptions, Evaluations, and Satisfactions* (New York: Russell Sage Foundation, 1976), p. 291.

for every 10,000 factories, or one for every 120,000 employees. Second, many of its inspectors still lack adequate training to detect health problems. Third, penalties for violations are so low that it can be preferable for factories to continue to violate the law and pay occasional fines rather than pay to correct the violation. And fourth, in December 1976 a federal court in Idaho declared unconstitutional the part of the law that provides that inspections are to be unannounced so that violators do not have warning enough to correct violations. While such rulings prevail, the agency has no authority to inspect looking for violations.[6] The operations, and indeed the very existence, of OSHA have been controversial among industrialists from the first, despite these limitations. Under the Carter administration, OSHA has shifted its emphasis from safety to health. But the struggle over what role the government should play in protecting workers is far from over.

■ Worker democracy

Meanwhile, the government may soon become further involved in questions of working conditions. Here the issue is not simply safety, but also what is usually termed the "movement for worker democracy." In some European countries, worker representatives now must be allowed to serve with management representatives on the "board of directors" of an industrial firm. This has not yet happened in the United States, but unions are beginning to propose such "co-determination," as it is called in Europe, and many observers believe that it is inevitable.

Such a step, once it comes, may be only the first in a move toward further economic reform. Jeremy Rifkin, of the Peoples Business Commission (PBC), calls

---

[6] "Job Safety Inspection Held Illegal without a Warrant," *Washington Post,* January 4, 1977.

■ The quality of work

Significant numbers of American workers are dissatisfied with the quality of their working lives. Dull, repetitive, seemingly meaningless tasks, offering little challenge or autonomy, are causing discontent among workers at all occupational levels. This is not so much because work itself has greatly changed; indeed, one of the main problems is that work has not changed fast enough to keep up with the rapid and widescale changes in worker attitudes, aspirations, and values. A general increase in their educational and economic status has placed many American workers in a position where having an interesting job is now as important as having a job that pays well. Pay is still important: it must support an "adequate" standard of living and be perceived as equitable—but high pay alone will not lead to job (or life) satisfaction.

There have been some responses to the changes in the workforce, but they have been small and slow. As a result, the productivity of the worker is low—as measured by absenteeism, turnover-rates, wildcat strikes, sabotage, poor-quality products, and a reluctance by workers to commit themselves to their work tasks. Moreover, a growing body of research indicates that, as work problems increase, there may be a consequent decline in physical and mental health, family stability, community participation and cohesiveness, and "balanced" sociopolitical attitudes, while there is an increase in drug and alcohol addiction, aggression, and delinquency.

From *Work in America,* Report of a Special Task Force to the Secretary of Health, Education, and Welfare (Cambridge, Mass.: MIT Press, 1973), Summary.

for a second American revolution to "extend democratic principles to the economic institutions of our country. . . . A democratic economy is composed of firms controlled and managed by the people who work in them. Employees determine broad company policy and elect management on the principle of one person, one vote. In a self-managed firm all participants share in the net income of the enterprise. The members jointly determine the income levels for different job tasks in the firm."[7]

A national poll taken in 1975 by Peter D. Hart Research Associates for the PBC in which those surveyed were given a choice of which type of economic system they would prefer to work in reported the following results:

- □ A system of companies "in which the stock is owned by outside investors who appoint their own management to run the company's operations" (our present capitalist system) was preferred by 20 percent of the population.
- □ A system of companies "in which the government owns the stock and appoints the management" (a form of *state socialism* or Communism) was supported by only 8 percent.
- □ A system made up of companies "in which the stock is owned by the employees who appoint their own management to run the company's operations" was preferred by 66 percent.

---

[7]Jeremy Rifkin, *Own Your Own Job: Economic Democracy for Working Americans* (New York: Bantam, 1977), pp. 28, 30. Subsequent references to the PBC survey come from this book (pp. 51–52). The PBC can be reached at 1346 Connecticut Ave. N.W., Washington, D.C. 20036.

Despite these preferences, 49 percent said there is little chance that such employee control of U.S. companies will come about within a decade. They are almost certainly right, especially given what we have learned about the distribution of wealth in America (Chapter 17) and about the political power such wealth gives to vested interests (Chapter 11). But the 44 percent who believe there is "some" or "great" possibility of such "economic democracy" may well represent future political possibilities. In the meantime we are likely to find growing movements for "job enrichment" to make work more meaningful, and for "profit-sharing" with workers.

Furthermore, we are likely to see more and more companies owned in large part or entirely by their employees – as are United Parcel Service (the chief alternative to the U.S. Post Office, which delivers packages everywhere in the country in those dark brown boxy trucks), the Chicago and North Western Railway, and *U.S. News & World Report* magazine. Experience shows that workers tend to be more efficient and more committed when they become owners, and this fact alone may make employee stock ownership more common in years to come.

□ THE QUALITY OF CONSUMPTION

■ Consumer discontent

Fully 74 percent of the American people told the Hart survey for PBC that they favored "a plan whereby consumers in local communities are represented on the boards of companies that operate in their local region." Why?

- □ Each year 20 million Americans are injured by products commonly found in the home, and more than 30,000 are killed, according to the United States Consumer Product Safety Commission.[8] The dollar cost of these accidents in medical care, disability payments, and lost productivity is estimated at over $5.5 billion a year.[9]
- □ On a typical day, the Consumer Product Safety Commission will receive some 300 calls about hazardous products on its toll-free hot line (the telephone number is 800-638-8326), with calls escalating to over 1000 a day when a "crisis" news story appears.
- □ Some 100 calls a day came in to a comparable hot line for auto defects established on a trial basis by the Department of Transportation in 1976. And the Center for Auto Safety in Washington, a Ralph Nader organization, receives some 12,000 such complaints a year. The center estimates that for every person who writes there are another thousand with a similar problem.[10]

---

[8] "More Muscle in the Fight against Unsafe Products," *U.S. News & World Report,* March 11, 1974, p. 49.

[9] "A Flood of Shoddy Products – What's Being Done to Stem It," *U.S. News & World Report*, February 24, 1975, p. 39.

[10] William H. Jones, "Detroit: Repairing Consumer Confidence," *Washington Post,* August 18, 1976.

These represent the *dangerous* consumer problems. But there is much more to consumer unhappiness. A study of 2400 urban households by Ralph Nader's Center for the Study of Responsive Law in 1976 found that one of every four purchases by American consumers results in some problem. In addition, 10 to 17 percent of all purchases of expensive items such as TVs or cars are actually received broken. Also, consumers find the first repair job inadequate and have to get another in 26 percent of auto repairs, 19 percent of home repairs, and 13 percent of appliance repairs.[11]

■ Consumer sovereignty?

Why are things so bad? In theory, our capitalist system is supposed to be self-correcting. If consumers don't like what they buy, they stop buying it, and the company can't sell its defective product. Furthermore, the system is supposed to operate on the principle of **consumer sovereignty**: The consumer has the power to decide what he or she wants, and the business then produces it to sell. In fact, however, it doesn't work that way. Consumers may have "free choice" among whatever is produced. But no consumer can get a business to produce something he or she wants unless he or she can find a lot of others who want it too. And even then they must somehow get word to business about what they want. There is no regular way for consumers to pass that word, because producers and suppliers control advertising, the usual information channel. All consumers can usually do is refuse to buy whatever is available – a sort of "consumer veto."

■ Consumer protection

The growth of consumer discontent has led the government to intervene to protect the interests of the consumer. The earliest stages of this intervention were the creation of the major regulatory agencies such as the Federal Trade Commission (1915) and the Food and Drug Commission (1931). In Chapter 16 we learned that historically they have tended to be more sympathetic to, and even under the dominance of, the businesses they are supposed to regulate. So recent years have seen the emergence of new legislation and new agencies intended to help the consumer. The Fair Packaging and Labeling Act was passed in 1966, followed by the Truth-in-Lending Act (designed to tell borrowers what credit really costs them in interest rates) in 1968. These were followed by the Public Health Smoking Act, which required warnings of health hazards on cigarette packages.

[11]Center for the Study of Responsive Law, *Talking Back to Business: Voiced and Unvoiced Consumer Complaints* (Washington: CSRL, 1976).

American Cancer Society

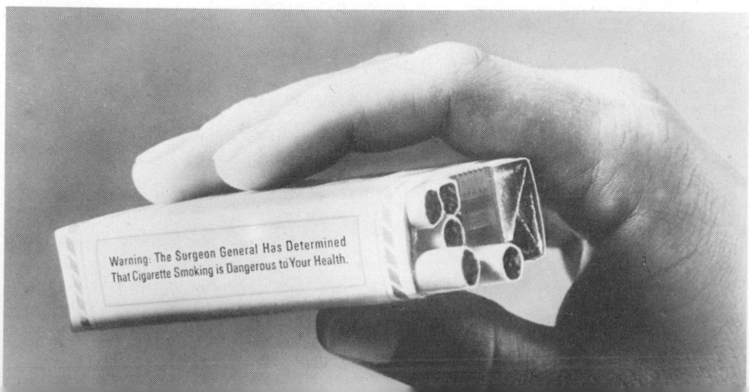

Recent years have seen the emergence of new legislation and new agencies intended to help the consumer. One example is the Public Health Smoking Act, which required warnings of health hazards on cigarette packages.

□ ACTION UNIT 20.1 How to get consumer advice or make a consumer complaint

There are two primary sources of consumer advice: the federal government and "public interest" consumer organizations. The government can help in several ways. First, it tests many products before buying them, and you can now get copies of the results of its tests, as well as of other consumer-oriented government publications, by ordering them from *Consumer Information Catalog.* This free periodical is issued every 3 months by the General Services Administration's Consumer Information Center. You can get your copy at federal offices (such as Social Security offices or agricultural extension offices), at many libraries, or by writing to Consumer Information, Public Documents Distribution Center, Pueblo, Colo. 81009. Many of the 250 pamphlets each issue lists are free, and most others cost a dollar or less.

You can also get a free copy of the government's *Guide to Federal Consumer Services,* which tells which offices offer which services and gives names and phone numbers. This guide is published by the Office of Consumer Affairs of the Department of Health, Education, and Welfare, and is also available from the above address.

In addition, the government publishes *Consumer News,* a twice-a-month newsletter to report on government programs for consumers. It can be ordered for $4 a year from the same address.

There are also many private groups that offer consumer advice. Probably the best known is **Consumers Union** (256 Washington St., Mt. Vernon, N.Y. 10550), which publishes the monthly *Consumer Reports* (available on newsstands and in libraries) rating product quality and economy. It also publishes a *Guide to Consumer Services* that deals with financial matters such as insurance and professional services such as doctors and dentists. Another prominent consumer organization is the Ralph Nader public interest conglomerate **Public Citizen** (P.O. Box 19404, Washington, D.C. 20036). It includes the Health Research Group, the Tax Reform Research Group, and various other projects. These groups regularly publish new consumer guides on various topics.

Other important sources of information for consumers are the following:

The **Center for Science in the Public Interest** (1779 Church St. N.W., Washington, D.C. 20036) researches such issues as energy, environment, food and nutrition.

The **Chamber of Commerce of the United States, Consumer Affairs Section** (1615 H St. N.W., Washington, D.C. 20006) publishes general information about consumer issues and promotes consumer redress programs among businesses.

The **Conference of Consumer Organizations** (3201 Landover St., Alexandria, Va. 22305) is made up of volunteer consumer organizations and individuals from corporate and government consumer affairs offices. It assists in the development of state and local volunteer consumer organizations and promotes the improvement of consumers' relations with government and industry.

The **Consumer Federation of America** (1012 14th St. N.W., Washington, D.C. 20005) is a federation of national, regional, state, and local consumer groups and other interested groups. It promotes consumer programs in such areas as product pricing, quality, servicing and warranties, regulatory agencies, credit and insurance, housing, food, drugs, and medical care, safety, energy, and natural resources development.

The **National Association of Manufacturers** (1776 F St. N.W., Washington, D.C. 20006) represents industry's views on national and international matters and provides information on many consumer issues, including consumer agency legislation and regulation.

The **National Consumer Information Center** (3005 Georgia Ave. N.W., Washington, D.C. 20001) initiates programs to protect consumer interests and promote better consumer-merchant relations.

The **National Consumers Congress** (1346 Connecticut Ave. N.W., Washington, D.C. 20036) is a citizens' interest group that provides local consumer groups with information on such issues as government policies on food and energy

If you wish to create your own consumer group, you can get a free booklet entitled *Forming Consumer Organizations* from the Office of Consumer Affairs, Department of Health, Education, and Welfare, Washington, D.C. 20201.

All the information in the world may not avert misfortune. A useful general guide to where to complain in business and industry and in state and federal government is Joseph Rosenbloom's *Consumer Complaint Guide* (New York: Macmillan paperback, published annually). Generally the best complaint route is: first, the merchant who sold you the product or performed the service; second, the manufacturer of the product; and third, government consumer agencies – either a state consumer agency in the state attorney general's office, or the Federal Trade Commission, Consumer Product Safety Commission, or other agency in Washington as appropriate.

The following are some rules for complaining effectively:

- □ Address your complaint to a specific individual, such as a company director or head of an agency (names you can find in your public library or by calling the company or agency).
- □ Put your complaint in writing, rather than telephoning, so that you can keep a copy for future use if necessary.
- □ Be brief, clear, and unemotional, and type or write legibly.
- □ State what you have already done to try to solve the problem. Include copies of documentation such as a sales slip or warranty if you can, but always keep the originals.
- □ State just what you want the recipient to do.
- □ Identify yourself fully and state how and when you can be reached by a response.
- □ Follow up with an inquiry if you haven't received a response after several weeks.
- □ Write to government agencies and/or your representatives in the state capital or Washington if you are not satisfied with responses by a store, manufacturer, or other target.

To find out which federal government agency may be able to help you, either write to Public Citizen at the address above or call your regional Federal Information Center (FIC) at the toll-free number listed under "U.S. Government" in your local phone book.

The Consumer Product Safety Act created the Consumer Product Safety Commission (CPSC) in 1972. The CPSC can set safety standards for many thousands of consumer products and can fine violating producers up to half a million dollars. Nonetheless, until the Carter administration came to power, it was known as a "do-nothing" agency. In its first 5 years, it was able to develop design standards only for architectural glass used in doors, windows and walls, for matchbook covers, and for swimming-pool slides. Consumer advocates found the latter two of the three inadequate. Since then, the CPSC has developed priorities so that it can concentrate its attention on the most urgent matters. Among these are power lawn mowers (160,000 injuries a year), gas space heaters (8,700), children's playground equipment (229,000), and toys with sharp points and edges (179,000). The CPSC is also actively concerned with improving the safety of bicycles, aluminum electrical wire, cooking ranges and ovens, television sets, ladders, bathtubs and showers, power tools, and skiing equipment.

The slow pace of the CPSC and the wide-ranging concerns of consumers and consumer groups have increased the pressure for creating an Agency for Consumer Advocacy, or a Consumer Protection Agency. Such an agency would have the legal power to intervene in government activities – by suing the agencies if necessary – in order to represent the interests of consumers. The Nixon and Ford administrations consistently opposed creation of such an agency, fearing that it would virtually paralyze the government by intervening everywhere. President Carter has strongly supported it against intense lobbying by the business interest groups we described in Chapter 11. Supporters have included organized labor, Ralph Nader, and the Consumer Federation of America (CFA). The CFA is an organization of consumer-oriented groups founded in 1967. It includes 215 nonprofit groups, among them forty-five state and local consumer bodies, sixty-six rural electric cooperatives, seventeen credit union leagues, sixteen national labor unions, and such special interests as the National Education Association and Consumers Union (which publishes *Consumer Reports*).[12]

Where the federal government's role in influencing and protecting consumers will expand to next is anybody's guess. But because consumers are only now beginning to organize – and because, after all, all of us are consumers – the outlook is for more and more "politics of consumption" at every level. (See Action Unit 20.1 for guidelines on how to get consumer advice.)

□ THE QUALITY OF THE ENVIRONMENT

Traditionally, Americans have welcomed increased production as bringing an improved "standard of living." In recent decades Americans have found that manufactured goods are less reliable, less long-lived, than they used to be, or at least than they seem to have been. Furthermore, growth, development, and production have produced crowding and pollution and brought threats that vital resources such as gas and oil will be exhausted in our lifetimes. The result of all this has been major new interest in the environment or the ecosystem. Some experts have suggested that there are distinct "limits to growth."[13] And many have argued that if we want to preserve – let alone improve – the quality of life, we must set limits to our ravaging of the environment before even those absolute limits to growth set in.

This challenge to the government has been made in large part by citizen environmental action groups such as those described in Action Unit 20.2. The primary governmental responsibility lies with the Council on Environmental Quality (CEQ), which makes policy, and the Environmental Protection Agency (EPA), which sets and enforces standards. We examined the politics of the establishment of the EPA in Perspective 3. Since its establishment, the agency has been under political fire from environmentalists for being too soft and from industry for being too demanding. Such politics of environmental protection will be with us as long as environmental problems remain a concern of government. The continued growth of American industry and the growing discovery of the wide range of environmental threats that poses suggest that they can only increase.

---

[12]Frances Cerra, "A Lobbyist for Consumers," *New York Times,* October 31, 1976. See also "Consumers' Cast of Characters," *National Journal,* Dec. 4, 1976, p. 1740.

[13]See Dennis Meadows et al., *The Limits to Growth* (Washington: Universe Books, 1972).

□ ACTION UNIT 20.2 How to contact environmental action organizations

Among the environmental lobbyists now active in Washington and elsewhere are such old naturalist organizations as the **Sierra Club** (530 Bush St., San Francisco, Calif. 94108), founded in 1892 by mountaineers; the **National Audubon Society** (1130 5th Ave., New York, N.Y. 10038), founded in 1905 by birdlovers; the **National Parks and Conservation Association** (1701 18th St. N.W., Washington D.C. 20009), founded in 1919; the **Izaak Walton League of America** (1800 N. Kent St., Arlington, Va. 22209), founded in 1922 by fishermen; the **Wilderness Society** (1901 Pennsylvania Ave. N.W., Washington, D.C. 20006), founded in 1935; and the **National Wildlife Fed-** (1412 16th St. N.W., Washington, D.C. 20036), founded in 1936. These older organizations have become more generalist in their concerns and more militant in their actions as well since the first environmental lobbying commenced in the 1950s.

They have also been joined by several dozen newer and even more activist groups. Both the **Environmental Defense Fund** (1525 18th St. N.W., Washington, D.C. 20036) and the **Natural Resources Defense Council** (917 15th St. N.W., Washington, D.C. 20005) wage legal battles. **Environmental Action** (1346 Connecticut Ave. N.W., Washington, D.C. 20036) and **Friends of the Earth** (620 C St. S.E., Washington, D.C. 20003) lobby and conduct public education programs. The **League of Conservation Voters** (324 C St. S.E., Washington, D.C. 20003) rates members of Congress on their environmental votes and each election draws up a list of the twelve leading "enemies of the environment," which it calls the "Dirty Dozen." Its campaigns to defeat these members of Congress have had a number of successes–most prominent among them the 1974 defeat of Wayne Aspinall, the representative who led opposition to NEPA in the House.

These citizen environmental lobbies have had occasional successes in Congress, such as stopping production of the supersonic transport because it would damage the environment and getting highway funds shifted to mass transit to cut auto pollution. But their major successes have come in the courts, where they have used NEPA to support and encourage EPA efforts to ban DDT and other dangerous pesticides, and to stop construction of new dams and nuclear power plants.

They–and still more with similar interests, listed annually in Congressional Quarterly's *Washington Information Directory*–would welcome your support. Many offer memberships and provide information on environmental policy to citizens.

Take, for example, the case of the chemical industry, which develops about 1000 new chemicals every year. Until recently such new chemicals were not even registered publicly, let alone tested for safety. The Toxic Substances Control Act of 1976 finally provided for registration, and surveillance is improving efforts to protect us from poisons. By 1976, some 12,000 chemical compounds were on the government's list of poisons, some 1500 of which were suspected of causing tumors and 30 of which were known to cause cancer and yet were still in use in industry. Others, such as components of decaffeinated coffee and plastic seat covers, had already been subject to control. But there is no sign that the development of new chemical compounds will end, any more than will other forms of pollution. And so even greater efforts to control their dangerous environmental effects will be required.

Much the same is true of pollution caused by the production of energy. In the present time of short supplies and high prices of energy, there is special pressure

Eric Kroll/Taurus Photos

■ What air pollution does to life in New York City

These economic benefits of clean fuel regulations derive mainly from the damage dirty air does to metals, buildings, cloth, vegetation, and other materials. Most metals corrode faster, some of them (like nickel) nearly 100 times faster, in New York City air than in still-pristine regions. On a large scale, this means that bridges and elevated subways and highways age faster or must be repaired more often, or else the danger of collapse increases. On a small but just as economically harmful scale, air pollution damages low-voltage electrical contacts, relays, and switches. It may incapacitate semiconductors and miniaturized equipment. It requires large expenditures for cleaning or for using precious non-corroding metals like gold for the sensitive electronic equipment which is so abundant in Manhattan, the communications center of the nation.

More than $100 million in repainting alone is required in New York City every year because of the onslaught of air pollution. Cloth disintegrates sooner and dyes fade faster in our sulfurous air, and curtains and clothing must be washed more frequently, adding a considerable expense to hotels and other businesses.

Pollution creeps through the windows and doors of our city's museums and erodes the varnish from paintings, blackens bronze objects, and tarnishes ancient jewelry. It damages paper and thereby destroys valuable records, necessitating expensive microfilming.

Airborne poisons destroy many of the city's remaining trees. Sulfur oxides deposited in the atmosphere by smokestacks travel hundreds of miles and are often then washed back to earth, causing an "acid rain" that has already damaged crops over wide areas of the Northeast and increased the acid levels in streams and lakes, killing many fish.

From Michael Gerrard, "The Economic Benefits of a Clean Environment." *Washington Post,* July 20, 1976.

against limits to the use of high-sulfur fuel, whether oil or coal. The need for limits is not so obvious, but still very impressive, even when put only in economic terms. Michael Gerrard, a consultant to the New York City Council on the Environment, describes the pollution problem in the box titled "What air pollution does to life in New York City."

In 1977 the CEQ projected that pollution-control costs in America over the following 10 years would total the staggering sum of $271 billion. Included are $116 billion to fight water pollution, $137 billion to fight air pollution, $4 billion to fight noise pollution, $8 billion to fight pollution from solid waste and radiation, and $6 billion to fight pollution from public buildings and facilities.[14]

At the time of the energy crisis of 1973 and the subsequent recession, many industries argued that the nation could not afford environmental protection because it would cause a diversion of spending that would reduce the number of jobs in America and cause depression. But this fear now seems misplaced. Subsequent studies have shown a net gain in employment due to environmental efforts of at least 400,000 jobs by 1976, when environmental spending alone accounted for over 1 million new jobs.[15]

□ THE POLITICS OF PLAY

The government's role in environmental matters will no doubt remain as controversial as it is comprehensive. But even greater controversy attends its efforts to regulate aspects of private life and leisure such as sex, pornography, alcohol, mind-altering drugs, professional sports, gambling, and the arts.

These are all instances of the *positive state,* an activist government intervening in the private lives of some people in the name of protecting the interests of society as a whole. The specific laws in force change from time to time. Some laws are ruled unconstitutional – the laws forbidding contraception and abortion, for example, or regulations banning certain books from libraries or bookstores because they are "obscene." Others are rather rarely enforced – laws against homosexuality, prostitution, or "unnatural" sexual practices. Others are sometimes changed by referenda – laws prohibiting the sale of alcoholic beverages, laws prohibiting gambling. Still others persist – laws requiring motorcyclists to wear helmets, laws banning the possession or use of marijuana and other drugs, laws protecting the "ownership" of players by particular sport teams. The list could go on.

Each of these government efforts to control or influence an aspect of play, leisure, or private life is controversial. On each, a case can be made for protecting society (or the young, or the innocent, or those who "don't know any better") from possible corruption. On the other side are arguments in favor of individual liberty, freedom of choice, or the right to do with oneself whatever one wishes – only limited, perhaps, by any infringement on the rights of others.

---

[14]See "A Clean America: Will People Pay the Price?", *U.S. News & World Report,* February 7, 1977.

[15]John Oakes, "The Battle for the Environment," *New York Times,* December 2, 1976.

Mimi Forsyth/Monkmeyer

Governments have long sought to intervene in our private lives and leisure in these ways. No doubt they will continue to do so in coming years. The general trend in the past several decades seems to be away from restraint toward greater liberty. But there are plenty of exceptions, in which cases certain individuals pay dearly, losing their liberty for a time.

■ The arts

Not all such government intervention is opposed as restricting liberty. Perhaps the most welcome instance is the federal government's growing role in the arts. The National Endowment for the Humanities spends close to $100 million a year, part of it to sponsor special cultural exhibits (such as the exhibit of the artifacts from the tomb of Egyptian King Tut that toured the country in 1977 and 1978). The National Endowment for the Arts spends even more giving grants to museums, orchestras, theater groups, dance groups, and artists. In all, there are forty commissions, agencies, and departments that run some 250 programs involving the federal government with the arts.

Perhaps the most controversial is the "Art-in-Architecture" Program (AIA). In 1962, a federal commission recommended that fine arts be incorporated into every new federal building, anywhere around the nation. From 1962 to 1966 the government spent $1,176,500 commissioning artists to do sculptures, mosaics, murals, stained glass panels, and so on, for new buildings. Then the Vietnam War intervened and budgets got tight. Since 1972, however, AIA has commissioned another seventy-four projects for another $2,864,000. When Jack Beal's four giant oil-on-canvas murals tracing the history of labor in America were unveiled at the Labor Department in Washington, President Carter remarked: "The arts are a cherished part of the American experience and an important medium of communication. In public buildings such as this they can be effectively used to depict the vitality of our cultural heritage as well as the continuing ability, resourcefulness and imagination of our people coping with problems of everyday life."[16]

■ Drugs

The government may, of course, act to encourage one form of leisure pursuit—as in the case of the arts. It may also act to discourage another. So it is with marijuana and other drugs. Federal customs agents in 1976 seized $631 million worth of drugs and arrested 21,000 persons on drug charges. It was an all-time record. In a message to Congress that year, President Ford declared that "the cost of drug abuse to this nation is staggering. More than 5000 Americans die each year from the improper use of drugs. Law-enforcement officials estimate that as much as one half of all 'street crime'—robberies, muggings and burglaries—are committed by drug addicts to support their expensive and debilitating habits. In simple dollar terms, drug abuse costs us up to 17 billion dollars a year."

The federal government itself spends close to a billion dollars a year to fight

---

[16]Judd Tully, "Behind the Bat: How the Government's Art in Architecture Program Really Works," *The New Art Examiner,* April 1977, p. 11.

the drug problem. But much of its efforts—and even more of the efforts of local police—are focused on marijuana, which everyone agrees is the least dangerous drug. Many question this priority, especially because the government grants that drug abuse as a whole is more costly to society than alcoholism, but less costly than tobacco smoking. And yet the government does little to discourage tobacco smoking.

Recent studies have found that more than half of the 1976 high school graduating seniors had used marijuana, 22 percent of youths then 12 to 17 years old had done so, 55 percent of all college students had used it, and 53 percent of those 18 to 25. Another study found that 59 percent of all military recruits used marijuana, and nearly half were regular users of one or more drugs. The drug problem, in other words, has certainly not abated along with the counterculture of the 1960s. Instead, the young people who once were hippie or radical "heads" (as drug users are often called) have kept their marijuana habit even after they have returned to straight society and become professionals.

"We're all getting older now," said Keith Stroup, executive director of the National Organization for the Reform of Marijuana Laws (NORML), at its 1976 convention in Washington. "Most of the people here are young professionals—maybe the average age is 35. We're the ones who turned on in the 60s and simply kept smoking. The only difference is that we were on the streets then and now we've worked our way up to places where we have a lot of impact."[17]

NORML and its 15,000 members have been instrumental in getting about a dozen state legislatures to reduce the penalty for possession to a small fine. But many states retain a stiff penalty, despite an endorsement of "decriminalization," as the change is called, by President Carter himself within a few months after he took office. NORML continues to press its campaign with an annual budget of around $300,000—which qualifies it as a significant special interest lobby.

■ Gambling

Another, much stronger, special interest lobby supports efforts to legalize gambling. A University of Michigan survey found that 61 percent of the adult population—about 88 million people—participated in some form of gambling in 1974. Since that time, many states have opened new legal gambling institutions, from race tracks to lotteries. Experts believe that there may be as many as 9 million compulsive gamblers in America. And some estimate the total sum gambled at more than $100 billion every year.

Many think of gambling as a "victimless" crime that therefore should not, or need not, be punished. Others see it as harmful to society because of its connections with organized crime and its impacts on the poor. The poor cannot really afford to gamble and yet do so anyway—often, now, at the urging of states that run lotteries or other programs to raise revenue. What is play for some people is business for others, in sum. The government's varied involvements with gambling must indeed influence the quality of life for a great many citizens. But whether the influence is positive or negative is a judgment subject to much disagreement.

---

[17]Laurence Feinberg, "Pro-Pot Group Holds Posh Parley," *Washington Post,* December 12, 1976.

□ THE PROSPECTS FOR THE QUALITY OF LIFE

We have seen in this chapter disagreements over what contributes to an improved quality of life and bitter struggles over how that is to be achieved. But we have also seen both a continuing involvement of our governments in the struggle to improve the quality of our lives and, perhaps even more important, a growing popular involvement in various parts of this struggle. Whether these small-scale, single-issue campaigns will contribute to improvement of the quality of life in America depends somewhat on popular values, beliefs about what is good, about what the government should do, and about what we as citizens should do. We should not be surprised that there is little agreement on these questions at this time. Whether, despite all this discord, these signs of growing citizen involvement are promises of improvement in the quality of democracy is a question we'll ask in our final chapter.

□ SUGGESTIONS FOR FURTHER READING AND STUDY

There is a large literature on the problems and possibilities of work. For accounts of what it's really like, see Studs Terkel, *Working* (New York: Random House paperback, 1975), and Barbara Garson, *All the Livelong Day: The Meaning and Demeaning of Routine Work* (New York: Penguin paperback, 1977). For a study of the relation between technological development and work organization, see Harry Braverman, *Labor and Monopoly Capital* (New York: Monthly Review Press, 1975). And on experiments with worker participation, see David Jenkins, *Job Power: Blue and White Collar Democracy* (New York: Penguin paperback, 1974), and the collection of readings edited by Jaroslav Vanek, *Self-Management: Economic Liberation of Man* (New York: Penguin paperback, 1975). For further information on worker democracy, write the Federation for Economic Democracy, Suite 607, 2100 M St. N.W., Washington, D.C. 20063.

For a psychological analysis of the problems of consumption, see Tibor Scitovsky, *The Joyless Economy: An Inquiry into Human Satisfaction and Consumer Dissatisfaction* (New York: Oxford University Press paperback, 1976). On the development of the consumer movement and its limitations, see Lucy Black Creighton, *Pretenders to the Throne: The Consumer Movement in the United States* (Lexington, Mass.: Lexington Books, 1976). For a hostile view, see Ralph K. Winter, *The Consumer Advocate versus the Consumers* (Washington, D.C.: American Enterprise Institute, 1972). And for the legal and political aspects, see Mark Nadel, *The Politics of Consumer Protection* (Indianapolis: Bobbs-Merrill paperback, 1971), and Robert N. Katz, ed., *Protecting the Consumer Interest: Private Initiative and Public Response* (Cambridge, Mass.: Ballinger, 1976).

For a survey of environmental problems, see Barry Commoner, *The Closing Circle* (New York: Bantam paperback, 1971). On the politics and the legal aspects of environmental protection, see J. Clarence Davies, *The Politics of Pollution* (New York: Pegasus paperback, 1970), and Lettie McSpadden Wenner, *One Environment Under Law: A Public Policy Dilemma* (Pacific Palisades, Calif.: Goodyear paperback, 1976). Interesting articles on various aspects of the environment appear regularly in the magazine *Environment*.

21 The politics of participation: the quality of democracy

"Politics as usual" in America is "nonparticipatory." As we have seen, barely a majority of those eligible to vote actually does vote in our presidential elections, and a smaller percentage votes in most state and local elections. And while perhaps one in five will occasionally attend a political meeting or rally, only one in seven ever contacts a political official, and but one in thirty-three ever runs for any political office.

Of course, the country was established two centuries ago, not as a democracy, but rather as a Republic—a government intended to represent the interests of its citizens. But we have seen in previous chapters what many have long argued: That governmental officials in their actions more often represent the interests, not of the public as a whole (the "common good"), but rather of collections of special interests. In this sense, American politics continues to be not only nonparticipatory, but also nonrepresentational, in terms of the average citizen.

□ POWER *FROM* THE PEOPLE—AND POWER *AGAINST* THE PEOPLE

Our Republic was based, as we have seen, on the principle of popular sovereignty. The Declaration of Independence asserted that "governments are instituted among men, deriving their just powers from the consent of the governed," and the Constitution began with the words "We the People of the United States . . . do ordain and establish this Constitution. . . ."

■ Concepts of democracy

As decades passed, formal or legal obstacles to participation—to voting, and then to campaigning for office—decreased. America was, we have said, becoming more democratic. Such a conclusion presumes, of course, a concept of democracy grounded in the right of the citizens to vote for their leaders. But if the right to vote in free elections is a common definition of democracy, it is far from the only one.[1]

Some people define democracy in terms of *majority rule*—rule by 50 percent plus one of the voters. But in our system one can generally win an election with less than that—as Nixon did in 1968 with 43.4 percent, for example. So perhaps we

[1]See Carole Pateman, *Participation and Democratic Theory* (Cambridge: Cambridge University Press, 1970).

Can we discern a trend toward greater democracy in an America of declining participation in electoral politics?

should think of democracy as *plurality rule* – rule by whoever gets more votes than any other candidate. Either of these criteria would allow the Soviet Union to qualify as a democracy, even though in that country there is only one candidate for any office. Perhaps then the important point is to have a meaningful *electoral choice among candidates,* whether or not the victor then pays attention to the interests of the voters. Or perhaps, as some say, democracy should be thought of in terms of citizens having a high degree of *access* to, and *influence* upon, their elected officials, whether or not they choose to exercise it.

The concepts of democracy are, as we can see, many and varied. Indeed, one observer suggests that there are perhaps 200 different definitions in use.[2] By virtually any of the most common definitions, we could say that American government is more democratic now than it was when Americans had slaves and when women and those without property were not allowed to vote.

■ Democracy in America

But is America continuing to become more democratic? Or is the "power from the people" still frequently "power against the people"? Everyone will answer this question somewhat differently, depending not only on his or her concept of democracy, but also on his or her image of contemporary political reality in America. In the same way, we may disagree over just how democratic America actually is today, when compared to our own ideal concept.

One of the most demanding, and most thought-provoking, sets of criteria for assessing how democratic America is has been offered by historian Howard Zinn. These criteria are listed in the box titled "How democratic is America?"

Previous chapters have portrayed progress toward greater democracy on many of these dimensions, while they have suggested serious limitations to the actual

---

[2]Massimo Salvadori, *Liberal Democracy* (Garden City, N.Y.: Doubleday, 1957).

"democraticness" of America in terms of these criteria. But can we conclude that America is still on the way toward becoming more democratic when the government remains seriously unrepresentative – both in the types of people who serve in it and in the policies it adopts? And even more, can we discern a trend toward greater democracy in an America of declining popular participation in electoral politics?

■ The debate over political participation

In the 1960s, as electoral participation declined seriously, less conventional forms of political participation – protest meetings, marches, street demonstrations, and even riots – increased dramatically. With the proliferation of these new (or, more accurately, revived) forms of participation there emerged a vigorous public debate over the import and value of participation.

The battle cry of "power to the people" mobilized the Left – and especially students – in their movement to gain full civil rights for blacks and then in their opposition to the Vietnam War. The general argument was that too much power had been transferred from the people to the government – or taken from the people

■ How democratic is America?

I propose a set of criteria for the description "democratic" which goes beyond formal political institutions, to the quality of life in the society (economic, social, psychological), beyond majority rule to concern for minorities, and beyond national boundaries to a global view of what is meant by "the people," in that rough, but essentially correct view of democracy as "government of, by, and for the people."

Let me list the criteria . . .

1. To what extent can various people in the society participate in those decisions which affect their lives: decisions in the political process and decisions in the economic structure?

2. As a corollary of the above: do people have equal access to the information which they need to make important decisions?

3. Are the members of the society equally protected on matters of life and death – in the most literal sense of that phrase?

4. Is there equality before the law: police, courts, the judicial process—as well as equality *with* the law-enforcing institutions, so as to safeguard equally everyone's persona and his freedom from interference by others, and by the government?

5. Is there equality in the distribution of available resources: those economic goods necessary for health, life, recreation, leisure, growth?

6. Is there equal access to education, to knowledge and training, so as to enable persons in the society to live their lives as fully as possible, to enlarge their range of possibilities?

7. Is there freedom of expression on all matters, and equally for all, to communicate with other members of the society?

8. Is there freedom for individuality in private life, in sexual relations, family relations, the right of privacy?

9. To minimize regulation: do education and the culture in general foster a spirit of cooperation and amity to sustain the above conditions?

10. As a final safety feature: is there opportunity to protest, to disobey the laws, when the foregoing objectives are being lost – as a way of restoring them?

From Howard Zinn, "How Democratic Is America?" in *How Democratic is America?* ed. Robert A. Goldwin (Chicago: Rand McNally, 1969, 1971).

by the government. It was time instead to decentralize political decision making, shifting power back to the people so that they could make on their own the important decisions that affected their lives. This movement became known as the "New Left" because it sought the same objectives of equality, justice, and liberty as the traditional political Left had sought, but it had lost the faith that leftists traditionally had that big, centralized government could achieve these objectives. Instead, it emphasized "participatory democracy," focused on the local level and extending beyond politics into the economic sphere as well, where it sought greater economic equality and worker democracy.

As this New Left developed, it was joined in its concern for less reliance on big government to solve problems and for more emphasis on individual liberty by what came to be called the "New Right." The members of this amorphous group of radical conservatives often termed themselves "libertarians" because of the emphasis on the need for more individual liberty, almost regardless of its cost in decreased governmental power at home and abroad.

The New Left and the New Right parted company on the extent to which equality was to be valued, as well as on the extent to which government at the local level was to be relied upon. But they were in agreement on the call for returning "power to the people."

In this, they were at odds with traditional Marxists, who sought state socialism, and with anarchists, who sought to abolish all government. They also found themselves at odds with a new grouping of old liberals and conservatives who were united in the belief that greater popular political participation, both conventional (voting, campaigning, and so on) and unconventional (such as protests and riots), posed a grave threat to the survival of the state. Their thesis is well-expressed in the phrase "the ungovernability of democracies" which is often used by the bankers, businesspeople, and academics who have come to share this view. The boxes titled "Participatory democracy" and "The ungovernability of democracies" contain the basic views of both groups.

□ CHANGING CONCEPTS OF CITIZENSHIP

These arguments will rage at least as long as the American political system is unable to solve the difficult problems and resolve the fundamental conflicts that continue to challenge it from Right and Left, domestically and internationally. The eventual outcome may be decentralization emphasizing "power *to* the people," whether or not it confirms "the ungovernability of democracies" thesis. Another possibility is restoration of a conventional political status quo of "power *from* the people," whether or not it turns out to be largely "power *against* the people."

Whatever the ultimate outcome, however, the arguments, the theorizing, and the experimentation have brought about significant changes. Some of these changes have been in the way we, the American people, think about politics. Others have been in the types of actions we take, or believe it appropriate for others to take, in attempting to perform the responsibilities of citizenship in a democracy.

■ Participatory democracy

We regard men as infinitely precious and possessed of unfulfilled capacities for reason, freedom, and love. In affirming these principles we are aware of countering perhaps the dominant conceptions of man in the twentieth century: that he is a thing to be manipulated, and that he is inherently incapable of directing his own affairs. We oppose the depersonalization that reduces human beings to the status of things—if anything, the brutalities of the twentieth century teach that means and ends are intimately related, that vague appeals to "posterity" cannot justify the mutilations of the present. We oppose, too, the doctrine of human incompetence because it rests essentially on the modern fact that men have been "competently" manipulated into incompetence—we see little reason why men cannot meet with increasing skill the complexities and responsibilities of their situation, if society is organized not for minority, but for majority, participation in decision-making.

Men have unrealized potential for self-cultivation, self-direction, self-understanding, and creativity. It is this potential that we regard as crucial and to which we appeal, not to the human potentiality for violence, unreason, and submission to authority. . . .

We would replace power rooted in possession, privilege, or circumstance by power and uniqueness rooted in love, reflectiveness, reason, and creativity. As a social system we seek the establishment of a democracy of individual participation, governed by two central aims: that the individual share in those social decisions determining the quality and direction of his life; that society be organized to encourage independence in men and provide the media for their common participation.

In a participatory democracy, the political life would be based in several root principles:

- ☐ that decision-making of basic social consequence be carried on by public groupings;
- ☐ that politics be seen positively, as the art of collectively creating an acceptable pattern of social relations;
- ☐ that politics has the function of bringing people out of isolation and into community, thus being a necessary, though not sufficient, means of finding meaning in personal life;
- ☐ that the political order should serve to clarify problems in a way instrumental to their solution; it should provide outlets for the expression of personal grievance and aspiration; opposing views should be organized so as to illuminate choices and facilitate the attainment of goals; channels should be commonly available to relate men to knowledge and to power so that private problems—from bad recreation facilities to personal alienation—are formulated as general issues. . . .

From *The Port Huron Statement* drawn up by a group of young New Left members of the Students for a Democratic Society in 1962.

■ In politics, around politics and beyond politics

Traditionally, most everyone seeking change has focused his or her attention on politics. There has always been, therefore, a *reformist* movement in politics. In recent years that movement captured – and 4 years later lost – the leadership of the Democratic party. Reformists were able in 1972 to secure the nomination of George McGovern by a convention whose delegates were more representative of the diversity of the American people than were those of any other political convention before or since.

Other elements in this political reformist movement active in recent years include the citizen lobby Common Cause, the Ralph Nader Public Citizen conglomerate of researchers, lawyers, and lobbyists, both of which we examined in Chapter 11, along with numerous other special interest groups trying to influence elections or legislation.

But while such reformist political activity has continued and even grown in recent years, those same years have seen growing disillusionment with, and rejection of, political approaches and political solutions to human problems. The result has been two other types of approach. One is a general movement *around politics.* This is an effort to circumvent politics carried out by such activist groups as feminists, ecologists, and pacifists, who believe the political system to be too unresponsive and politics too superficial to solve major human problems.

■ The ungovernability of democracies

American society is characterized by a broad consensus favoring democratic, liberal, and egalitarian values. For much of the time, the commitment to these values is neither passionate nor intense. During periods of rapid social change, however, these democratic and egalitarian values of the American creed are reaffirmed. The intensity of belief during such creedal passion periods leads to the challenging of established authority and to major efforts to change governmental structure to accord more fully with those values. . . . The slogans, goals, values, and targets of all these movements are strikingly similar. Consequently, the implication of this analysis is that in due course the democratic surge and the resulting dual distemper in government will moderate.

Al Smith once remarked, "The only cure for the evils of democracy is more democracy." Our analysis suggests that applying that cure at the present time could well be adding fuel to the flames. Instead, some of the problems of governance in the United States today stem from an "excess of democracy." . . . Needed, instead, is a greater degree of moderation in democracy.

In practice, this moderation has two major areas of application. First, democracy is only one way of constituting authority, and it is not necessarily a universally applicable one. In many situations, the claims of expertise, seniority, experience, and special talents may override the claims of democracy as a way of constituting authority. . . . The arenas where democratic procedures are appropriate are, in short, limited.

Second, the effective operation of a democratic political system usually requires some measure of apathy and noninvolvement on the part of some individuals and groups. In the past, every democratic society has had a marginal population, of greater or lesser size, which has not actively participated in politics. In itself, this marginality on the part of some groups is inherently undemocratic, but it also has been one of the factors which has enabled democracy to function effectively. Marginal social groups, as in the case of the blacks, are now becoming full participants in the political system. Yet the danger of "overloading" the political system with demands which extend its functions and undermine its authority still remains. Less marginality on the part of some groups thus needs to be replaced by more self-restraint on the part of all groups. . . .

Over the years . . . the American political system has emerged as a distinctive case of extraordinarily democratic institutions joined to an exclusively democratic value system. Democracy is more of a threat to itself in the United States than it is in either Europe or Japan. . . . Political authority is never strong in the U.S., and it is peculiarly weak during a creedal passion period of intense commitment to democratic and egalitarian ideals. In the United States, the strength of the democratic ideal poses a problem for the governability of democracy in a way which is not the case elsewhere.

. . . A value which is normally good in itself is not necessarily optimized when it is maximized. We have come to recognize that there are potentially desirable limits to economic growth. There are also potentially desirable limits to the extension of political democracy. Democracy will have a longer life if it has a more balanced existence.

From *The Crisis of Democracy: Report on the Governability of Democracies to the Trilateral Commission* (New York: New York University Press, 1975), pp. 112–115.

The Korean Rev. Sun Myung Moon and his followers represent an attempt to move *beyond* politics. Such groups generally emphasize faith and spiritual practices rather than politics as the best way to solve the problems facing humankind.

Stan Wakefield

The second alternative approach gaining favor in recent years has been a movement *beyond politics.* This is an effort to transcend politics by reasserting spiritual attitudes and emphasizing spiritual activities. In this category fall such groups as Scientology, the "Moonies" (followers of Korean Rev. Sun Myung Moon), the Hare Krishna groups often found chanting near college campuses, and the long-lived Campus Crusade for Christ.

The spiritualists often see the same worldly problems as the circumventers and the reformers, but generally emphasize faith and spiritual practices as the best way to resolve problems – by transcending them. The circumventers on the other hand tend to emphasize the importance of heightening people's consciousness. They point to the need for greater understanding of the roots of current problems, not in politics or economics, but rather in deeper attitudes. The feminists, for example, tend to find the roots of sexism, and perhaps of war and racism as well, in male chauvinist presuppositions of male superiority and of patriarchy – the view that men were made to rule women. Ecologists often trace similar evils to humankind's common desire to dominate nature rather than live in harmony with nature. And pacifists sometimes trace these problems to the corruption of ethical standards of conduct by resurgent animalistic tendencies, discredited religious doctrines, and a culture of competition rather than of brotherhood and sisterhood.

Distinctive as each of these views is in important ways, they have in common a rejection of the traditional analysis that politics is both the root of the problem and the route to its solution. In the aftermath of the activism of the civil rights movement and the antiwar movement, important lessons have been learned about the range of effective actions open to "change agents" and about the most appropriate strategies and tactics to maximize the effectiveness of political action.

■ New – and renewed – types of action

The underlying sense that seems to be emerging among the advocates of change in America today is that, contrary to appearances, *the people have the power.* That is, they have it if they really want to exercise it and are prepared to do the hard work of developing effective strategies and organizing those who seek or would benefit from political change.

Conventional political action In a sense, of course, this has always been true since the right to vote was extended to the vast majority of the American people, most of whom were benefiting little from the way politics was conducted. But it is difficult to get the poor and pessimistic to take seriously resort to the ballot box to change their condition. This is especially so when the candidates in most elections have been selected by "party regulars" who tend to be conservative. The conventional act of *voting* therefore seems less promising today, at least at the federal level. At the local level, election of change-oriented mayors, city councils, and others, more and more of them members of previously excluded groups such as women, blacks, Chicanos, and Puerto Ricans, has recently begun to change this pessimism in some places.

The conventional political act of *lobbying,* which used to be engaged in primarily by representatives of vested interests, has in recent years been undertaken by those formerly excluded. The pioneering public venture was the Poor People's Campaign of 1968 organized by the late Rev. Martin Luther King, Jr., and his Southern Christian Leadership Conference, which we discussed in Chapter 14. It set a public precedent of poor ordinary people going to Washington to lobby. This example has since inspired others, including especially advocates of welfare rights and Native Americans, to use lobbying methods previously left to the vested interests.

Yet another recent expansion of use of conventional political devices has been the movement to institute and use the old Progressive era devices of *initiative, referendum,* and *recall,* which we discussed in Chapters 7 and 11. But perhaps the most significant recent reinvigoration of conventional political participation has been the growth of *efforts by nonelites to serve* in government. As we saw in Chapter 14, more and more blacks are running for and winning political office, especially at local levels. The same, we saw in Chapter 15, is true of women. Such participation by the previously uninvolved and still underrepresented is especially important because its public, visible nature may stimulate others to follow suit. In terms of actual influence on policy, however, more important may be the movement toward what is now being called "participatory bureaucracy." This is a bureaucracy staffed with more, and more representative, minority and female government employees.[3]

Unconventional: violent action The failure of conventional political activities in the 1960s to bring quick success led some on both the Left and the Right to resort to violence. Violence has a long history in America. Early Americans used it against the Native Americans, as well as to control their slaves. Business, often with the assistance of the government, sometimes dealt violently with militant labor. The Ku Klux Klan and other racist and anti-Catholic groups often handled those they opposed with violence. And through it all some police have handled activists and members of minority groups violently. Violence is, in the memorable words of black power activist H. Rap Brown, "as American as cherry pie." Furthermore, our

[3]Harry Krantz, *The Participatory Bureaucracy* (Lexington, Mass.: Lexington Books, 1976). See also Willis O. Hawley, "The Possibilities of Nonbureaucratic Organizations," in *Improving Urban Management,* ed. Hawley and David Rogers (Beverly Hills, Calif.: Sage, 1976), pp. 209–263.

foreign policy, like those of other countries, has always relied ultimately on violence, and in the meantime on the threat of violence, to preserve and protect its interests around the world.

Small wonder, then, that it should occur to the downtrodden, the dispossessed, and the angry that violence is the established and effective way to achieve their ends. There are certain arguments often made for the resort to violence. Some say it strengthens one's sense of power, self-confidence, and pride to use violence on one's enemy. Others say it instills fear in one's adversary, which makes the adversary more likely to give in, and even more likely to treat one with respect.

One major problem with using violence is that it tends to elicit violence in response. Some advocates then argue that this effect is good, because it shows the weak willed and tenderhearted whose side the authorities are on and thereby forces them to rally to the cause.

These are all controversial assertions, and no single analysis will ever resolve differences on the question. But there are several other important points that need to be made when the desirability of resorting to violence is considered.

One is the response to the common citation by leftists of Mao Tse-tung's dictum that "all power comes from the barrel of a gun." The point was well put by Saul Alinsky, the organizer we met in Chapter 5 and will meet again shortly. Alinsky was fond of pointing out the absurdity of making and accepting such an assertion when the other side the police, the armed forces, and the vigilante citizens – has all the guns. In modern times, so dependent on high technology, the state will always have a virtual monopoly on usable military force. The only exception to this is terrorist activities such as assassinations and bombings. Terrorist activities can cause serious disruption, especially in highly technological societies such as ours. But disruption rarely translates into construction, and so the prospects of achieving positive ends by resorting to violence are slight.

The other important negative effect of the resort to violence is the impact of means on ends. The movements for social change in this country are based on a belief in humanized relations among people. But using violence against others is the most dehumanizing act one can commit. Part of the point is that it is difficult for those you use violence against to relate humanly to you afterwards. A more important part, however, is how difficult it is for one to retain his or her commitment to human ends when using dehumanizing means. We often see evidence of this in the effects of war on soldiers once they return home in peacetime. We can see the same tendency at work perverting revolutions after they succeed. Most violent revolutions, after all, are carried out in the name of humanity. But few if any manage to salvage those ends, once they succeed, from the rubble of the death and destruction that quick, violent success seemed at the time to demand.[4]

Unconventional: "direct action" This pessimistic conclusion about the efficacy of the resort to violence has led to greater interest in the strategies of "direct

[4]For a thoughtful analysis, see Gordon Zahn, "The Bondage of Liberation," *Worldview,* March 1977.

UPI

Nonviolent protest and demonstration has become an increasingly popular form of political participation.

action." Saul Alinsky pioneered development of many such techniques, as we saw in Chapter 5. Alinsky and those who work in similar ways are not necessarily opposed to violence on principle. Rather, they find that obstruction, embarrassment, and other techniques of "direct action" work more effectively in achieving social change. Many community action groups across the country now train activists in these methods and practice them as well.[5]

Unconventional: nonviolent action Some activists are on principle opposed to the use of violence because they believe it is immoral. These people are "pacifists" – a term meaning "peaceful ones" derived from the Latin word *pax* ("peace"), which also gave its name to the Pacific Ocean. Many leaders of the civil rights movement, which we discussed in Chapter 14, such as Rev. Martin Luther King, were pacifists, as were some leaders of the movement against the Vietnam War. Pacifists often serve as the "conscience" of movements for social change, although they are rarely able or willing to take power themselves. This is because political power today still seems to demand of those who exercise it a willingness to use force and violence against other peoples – and even against the peoples of one's own country – from time to time.

---

[5]For an interesting survey, see Judy MacLean, "Training Organizers for the Future," *In These Times,* August 3–9, 1977, pp. 11–14.

☐ LESSONS FOR STRATEGY AND TACTICS

We live in an era of "multiple manipulation." There are always people trying to manipulate us – our leaders, advertisers, our enemies, and even our friends. At the same time, we try to manipulate others – our leaders, our adversaries, and even our friends. The world is full of books on how to manipulate others, many of them bestsellers. This too has been a book about manipulation, focusing on both how politics and politicians tend to manipulate us and how we might manipulate politics and politicians. There is no escaping manipulation in the kind of world we live in. But we may be better able to see it coming and avoid it if we know how to recognize it. And we may also become better able to turn it to the ends we seek – if we have enough confidence in the rightness of those ends. There are important things to be learned from our experience of politics, and from the experience of others too. Everyone, as we well know, sees the world somewhat differently, so everyone will learn somewhat different lessons from the study of American politics. But three lessons stand out in my mind: (1) the importance of experience; (2) the role of information – and its control; and (3) the different roles people may play.

■ The importance of experience

Each of us sees the reality somewhat differently, as we have noted time and again in earlier chapters. Another way to say this is, each of us has a different experience of the world. We act in accordance with our own experience of the world – we have to, because it's all we know.

Realizing this has very important implications for social change, or even for political success of any sort. You can make someone do what you want if you have the *power* to force him or her to do it. But the most effective way to affect someone's behavior is to get him or her to see the world the way you do. This is what we mean by having *authority:* being able to describe, interpret, or explain reality to others in a way that they will accept.

Ronald Laing, a British psychologist, has put the point well in a little book he calls *The Politics of Experience:* "All those people who seek to control the behavior of large numbers of other people work on the *experiences* of those other people. Once people can be induced to experience a situation in a similar way, they can be expected to behave in similar ways. Induce people all to want the same thing, hate the same things, feel the same threat, then their behavior is already captive – you have acquired your consumers or your cannon fodder."[6]

Laing speaks of this as a dangerous thing. And well it can be, as we see in the history of white American attitudes toward blacks, or male attitudes toward females, or the attitudes of the rich toward the poor. But the insight can be put to better ends too. As Alinsky reminds us, "When you are trying to communicate and can't find the point in the experience of the other party at which he can receive or understand, then you must create the experience for him."[7]

---

[6]R. D. Laing, *The Politics of Experience* (New York: Ballantine paperback, 1968), p. 95.

[7]Saul Alinsky, *Rules for Radicals* (New York: Vintage paperback, 1972), p. 85.

That's also what I have been trying to do in this book: to create for you as the reader the experience that will make it possible for us to communicate. My understanding of American politics is built upon what I know about how our leaders live and think and act, and about how that affects the lives of others. So as part of our study of the presidency, we looked at a day in the life of President Carter. And elsewhere we've used quotes from presidents to explain how they saw things. The more you know of what it's like to be president, the more likely you'll be able to understand why presidents act as they do. If that's *all* you know, it probably won't occur to you to question what presidents do. So, to help you get a broader perspective we look at the experiences and views of other political figures and ordinary citizens. Having a number of different outlooks to examine, you will be better able to develop your own views further.

So as author of this book I have relied on the same insight that allowed Alinsky to organize the poor in Chicago and Buffalo. But it's also the same insight that allowed Nixon to fool most of the American people for a long time about his actual involvement in Watergate. So it's a powerful and potentially dangerous insight—but one that can make the difference between success and failure in a leader or in an activist for political change.

■ The role of information—and its control

The most compelling kind of experience is, of course, actually living through something. No one who's never fought in a war will ever know fully what it's like, no matter how many movies and books and conversations about it he or she experiences. But the actual direct, lived experiences each of us—including presidents—can have is limited. So most of us depend most of the time on other people's accounts of their own experience. Another way of putting this is to say that most of our experience consists of getting information from other people.

We may choose to accept or reject the information we get from others. If we accept a certain piece of information, we are recognizing the person who gives (or sells) it to us as an authority. If we find people telling us conflicting things and each is trying to get us to agree with him or her, we are in the midst of a political dispute. That's why we have defined politics in earlier chapters as *dispute over claims to the authority to describe, interpret, or explain reality.* The person who can convince us to accept his or her view, his or her information, has authority for us. He or she therefore has effective, recognized political power—at least until he or she is challenged. E. E. Schattschneider puts this point another way, asserting that "the definition of the alternatives is the supreme instrument of power."

> In the competition of conflicts . . . *all depends on what we want most.* The outcome is not determined merely by what people want but by their priorities. What they want more becomes the enemy of what they want less. Politics is therefore something like choosing a wife, rather than shopping in a five-and-ten-cent store.
>
> The conflict of conflicts explains some things about politics that have long puzzled scholars. Political conflict is not like an intercollegiate

> debate in which the opponents agree in advance on a definition of the issues. As a matter of fact, *the definition of the alternatives is the supreme instrument of power;* the antagonists can rarely agree on what the issues are because power is involved in the definition. He who determines what politics is about runs the country, because the definition of the alternatives is the choice of conflicts, and the choice of conflicts allocates power. It follows that all conflict is confusing.[8]

This indicates the important role information plays in politics – and how vital it is to control information, so you can affect other peoples' experience and thereby influence their behavior. That's why presidents make speeches to the nation and hold press conferences while they're in office – and write their memoirs when they leave office. But it's also why activists for political change hold demonstrations, lobby, or even resort to violence. The object is to control the information other people – from presidents to plumbers, from senators to sanitation workers – get and thereby to shape their experience and so their behavior. But different people use information differently, and that brings us to the third and final lesson.

■ The different roles people have You can talk about people's roles in many different ways. For politics, the major roles are these five: organizer, leader, participant, follower, and subject.

The organizer usually works behind the scenes while the leader works in public. Alinsky, himself an organizer, once wrote that "The ego of the organizer is stronger and more monumental than the ego of the leader. The leader is driven by the desire for power, while the organizer is driven by the desire to create. The

[8] E. E. Schattschneider, *The Semisovereign People* (New York: Holt, Rinehart & Winston, 1961), p. 68.

The president has a unique ability to organize the government because he alone sits at the information center. President Carter delivering his State of the Union message to Congress, January 1978.

organizer is in a true sense reaching for the highest level for which man can reach – to create, to be a 'great creator,' to play God."[9] Alinsky asserted that the organizer must have curiosity, irreverence, imagination, a sense of humor, "a bit of a blurred vision of a better world" (so he or she knows where to try to go), "an organized personality" (so that he or she can function in the midst of disorganization and irrationality), ego, and a free and open mind. "Change comes from power," he reminded us, "and power comes from organization. In order to act, people must get together."[10]

We normally expect our presidents to be leaders and organizers both. They must lead the people and at the same time organize the government so that it responds to their will. We have seen in our discussion of the president and the bureaucracy that a president has a unique ability to organize the government because he or she alone sits at the information center. But we also noted how difficult it is in practice to act effectively because even the president has no monopoly on information in our system.

Members of Congress, bureaucrats, experts, journalists, and ordinary citizens all have information that the government may want or need. Also, each of these groups or individual members may influence the experience of others, including the president, by the ways they act. So, potentially, everyone in our system has power. Everyone can be a politician.

☐ A NEW TYPE OF DEMOCRACY IN AMERICA?

The realization that everyone can be a politician in America is not necessarily good news. By now most Americans have become rather skeptical of politicians, for one thing, and some may feel we already have enough. For another, the disappointing rate of participation in politics shown by so many Americans fosters skepticism about the likelihood that people actually will become politicians.

If popular action is to improve our politics and make our system more democratic, this will require development of three things: a democratic consciousness, a democratic conscience, and democratic practice. Let's look at each in turn.

■ A democratic consciousness

Everyone has an understanding of political reality. We refer to this understanding as one's "political consciousness," or awareness. Some of these understandings are better than others in terms of their contributions to the strength of democracy. A society in which everyone takes the authority of the leaders for granted, no matter how reliable that authority may be, is not very conducive to strong democracy. The strength of democracy depends on the people's abilities to see how dependent they are upon authorities and then develop ways to find multiple authorities. If there are multiple authorities, there will be political

[9]Alinsky, *Rules for Radicals,* p. 61.

[10]Ibid., p. 113.

competition. There will also be more opportunities for people to participate in, and to matter in, politics. So by a democratic consciousness we mean a widespread understanding of the necessity not only for authority but also for competing authorities – for active politics.

■ A democratic conscience

In our culture we are usually raised by being told that our conscience will bother us if we don't behave properly. Conscience refers to our sense of responsibility and the values we have learned, or "internalized." For a democracy to flourish, its citizens must internalize beliefs that emphasize the value of other people and of their views and the usefulness of democratic competition.

A major weakness of American democracy until now has been the pervasiveness of the belief that "everybody gets what he or she deserves" – or, put another way, that we are not responsible for our fellow citizens. The government may try to meet the needs of the minorities and the outsiders in the society. But unless the people themselves share a concern for the welfare of the members of these groups, the government will find it has neither the money nor the personnel to implement such a policy. So a widespread democratic conscience is also essential.

■ Democratic practice

Consciousness and conscience are still insufficient. No democracy in our present world can long survive without what we might call "democratic practice." By this we mean a way of acting by citizens that contributes to the transformation of society. It is not enough to understand what needs to be done. One must also be able to figure out how it can be undertaken successfully. This is what we mean by "democratic practice" – experience in acting effectively to further democratize society and improve the fate of those less fortunate.

■ Reality construction and reality creation

The social sciences recently have helped us to understand two important fundamental social processes. The first of these is often called *reality construction.* This is the technical term for the notion that each of us has his or her own image of reality. Each of us "constructs reality" in our mind, and then acts on the basis of this construction. Much of that construction of reality is a product of the influence of authorities, and much of it is simply learned from our families, friends, and schools.[11]

But we also know that people act in accord with their beliefs and expectations about the nature of reality. And we have research showing that people tend to respond to the expectations others have of them.[12] What this means in practical

---

[11]See Peter Berger and Thomas Luckmann, *The Social Construction of Reality* (Garden City, N.Y.: Doubleday Anchor paperback, 1966), and Burkhart Holzner, *Reality Construction in Society,* rev. ed. (Cambridge, Mass.: Schenkman, 1972).

[12]See, for example, Robert Rosenthal and Lenore Jacobson, *Pygmalion in the Classroom* (New York: Holt, Rinehart & Winston, 1968). And for a more comprehensive application of this insight to politics, see David V. Edwards, *Creating a New World Politics* (New York: McKay, 1973).

terms is that neither the world nor other people's behavior is fixed and unchanging. With carefully designed strategies one can change others' behaviors by changing their experiences. What this then means to us is that the range of choices open to us is greater than we are usually led to expect. To put it another way, there is a wider range of *choices openable to us* to reconstruct politics democratically – to create a new political reality. *Reality creation* is the second social process it is important to understand.

☐ GUIDELINES FOR CREATING THE FUTURE

Everyone must decide for himself or herself how he or she wishes things to change and what he or she believes it important to do. No hard and fast projects can yet be recommended in a book such as this. Still, there are certain guidelines for thinking and acting which emerge from the analysis thus far. Here are some of the more important ones. You can develop more.

- ☐ Regenerate the ethical sense that gives us objectives and responsibilities.
- ☐ Improve sources of information so that they report the needs, desires, possibilities, and projects of ordinary people and leaders everywhere, not just of government figures.
- ☐ Foster creative analysis of problems and opportunities, especially by those most involved.
- ☐ Regain the optimism about what we can do that until recently has always been part of the American character.
- ☐ Work where it will work in politics – especially locally – in order to achieve successes, however limited, that protect against disenchantment.
- ☐ Remember the relevance of the extragovernmental sphere – especially the economic possibilities and the informational opportunities available through the use of the media and education.
- ☐ Devise new imaginative strategies and tactics that confront the powers that be where they are vulnerable, but in constructive ways, as suggested by Alinsky and other creative activists.[13]

☐ OPPORTUNITIES FOR GUIDING POLITICS

Where can we put these and other guidelines to work? The opportunities are many, once we are willing and able to look beyond conventional politics. The leading opportunity now is in community organization, which we have discussed in previous chapters. But even the young have special opportunities as well in

---

[13]See also, for example, Paulo Freire, *Pedagogy of the Oppressed* (New York: Seabury paperback, 1972); Edgar S. Cahn and Barry A. Passett, eds., *Citizen Participation: Effecting Community Change* (New York: Praeger, 1971); and, for a guide to other readings, Michael Marien, *Societal Directions and Alternatives* (LaFayette, N.Y.: Information for Policy Design, 1976).

learning, leading, and teaching politics. If you have found this book encouraging – or if you've found it infuriating – then a career in politics may be for you. Most people who work in politics start at the local level, and some then go on to state and even national politics. Most work either in campaigns or in community organizing, but some, of course, become candidates.

But there are also more strictly pedagogical opportunities for you if you are interested in politics. You might become a teacher of political science in a high school or a college.[14]

Much of what is to be done now, according to the argument of this chapter, is rather pedagogical: working to heighten people's consciousness so that they can learn more about politics as it actually works and then act more effectively in politics. In a sense, then, politics itself is becoming more pedagogical. This also means that we never know enough about politics to stop learning. Or to stop helping others to learn.

---

[14]For a history of the discipline, see Albert Somit and Joseph Tanenhaus, *American Political Science* (New York: Atherton, 1964). Ask your political science or government department for a copy of a booklet by Mary H. Curzan, *Careers and the Study of Political Science: A Guide for Undergraduates,* also available from the American Political Science Association, 1527 New Hampshire Ave. N.W., Washington, D.C. 20036.

We the People

of the United States, in order to form a more perfect Union, establish Justice, insure domestic Tranquility, provide for the common defence, promote the general Welfare, and secure the Blessings of Liberty to ourselves and our Posterity, do ordain and establish this Constitution for the United States of America.

Article I

[illegible]

Article II

[illegible]

Article III

[illegible]

Article IV

[illegible]

Article V

[illegible]

Article VI

[illegible]

Article VII

[illegible]

The Word "the," being interlined between the seventh and eighth Lines of the first Page, The Word "Thirty" being partly written on an Erazure in the fifteenth Line of the first Page. The Words "is tried" being interlined between the thirty second and thirty third Lines of the first Page and the Word "the" being interlined between the forty third and forty fourth Lines of the second Page.

done in Convention by the Unanimous Consent of the States present the Seventeenth Day of September in the Year of our Lord one thousand seven hundred and Eighty seven and of the Independance of the United States of America the Twelfth In witness whereof We have hereunto subscribed our Names,

attest William Jackson Secretary

G° Washington — Presidt and deputy from Virginia

New Hampshire: John Langdon, Nicholas Gilman

Massachusetts: Nathaniel Gorham, Rufus King

Connecticut: Wm Saml Johnson, Roger Sherman

New York: Alexander Hamilton

New Jersey: Wil: Livingston, David Brearley, Wm Paterson, Jona: Dayton

Pennsylvania: B Franklin, Thomas Mifflin, Robt Morris, Geo. Clymer, Thos FitzSimons, Jared Ingersoll, James Wilson, Gouv Morris

Delaware: Geo: Read, Gunning Bedford jun, John Dickinson, Richard Bassett, Jaco: Broom

Maryland: James McHenry, Dan of St Thos Jenifer, Danl Carroll

Virginia: John Blair —, James Madison Jr.

North Carolina: Wm Blount, Richd Dobbs Spaight, Hu Williamson

South Carolina: J. Rutledge, Charles Cotesworth Pinckney, Charles Pinckney, Pierce Butler

Georgia: William Few, Abr Baldwin

☐ The Constitution of the United States of America*

(Preamble)

We the People of the United States in Order to form a more perfect Union, establish Justice, insure domestic Tranquility, provide for the common defence, promote the general Welfare, and secure the Blessings of Liberty to ourselves and our Posterity, do ordain and establish this Constitution for the United States of America.

■ Article I

(Legislative powers)

Section 1 All legislative Powers herein granted shall be vested in a Congress of the United States, which shall consist of a Senate and House of Representatives.

(The House of Representatives, how constituted, apportionment, impeachment power)

Section 2 The House of Representatives shall be composed of Members chosen every second Year by the People of the several States and the Electors in each State shall have the Qualifications requisite for Electors of the most numerous Branch of the State Legislature.

No Person shall be a Representative who shall not have attained to the Age of twenty five Years, and been seven Years a Citizen of the United States, and who shall not, when elected, be an Inhabitant of that State in which he shall be chosen.

Representatives and direct [Taxes][1] shall be apportioned among the several States which may be included within this Union, according to their respective Numbers, [which shall be determined by adding to the whole Number of free Persons, including those bound to Service for a Term of Years, and excluding Indians not taxed, three fifths of all other Persons.][2] The actual Enumeration shall be made within three Years after the first Meeting of the Congress of the United States, and within every subsequent Term of ten Years, in such Manner as they shall by Law direct. The Number of Representatives shall not exceed one for every thirty Thousand, but each State shall have at Least one Representative; and until such enumeration shall be made, the State of New Hampshire shall be entitled to chuse three; Massachusetts eight; Rhode-Island and Providence Plantations one; Connecticut five; New-York six; New Jersey four; Pennsylvania eight; Delaware one; Maryland six; Virginia ten; North Carolina five; South Carolina five; and Georgia three.

When vacancies happen in the Representation from any State, the Executive Authority thereof shall issue Writs of Election to fill such Vacancies.

The House of Representatives shall chuse their Speaker and other Officers; and shall have the sole Power of Impeachment.

(The Senate, how constituted, impeachment trials)

Section 3 The Senate of the United States shall be composed of two Senators from each State, [chosen by the Legislature thereof,][3] for six Years; and each Senator shall have one Vote.

Immediately after they shall be assembled in Consequence of the first Election, they shall be divided as equally as may be into three Classes. The Seats of the Senators of the first Class shall be vacated at the Expiration of the second Year, of the second Class at the Expiration of the fourth Year, and of the third Class at the Expiration of the sixth Year, so that one third may be chosen every second Year; [and if Vacancies happen by Resignation, or otherwise, during the Recess of the Legislature of any

*This text of the Constitution follows the engrossed (formally handwritten) copy signed by General Washington and the deputies from twelve states (see facing page). Original spelling, capitalization, and punctuation have been retained. Brackets within the text indicate passages altered by subsequent amendments.

[1]Modified by the Sixteenth Amendment.

[2]Replaced by Section 2 of the Fourteenth Amendment.

[3]Superseded by clause 1 of the Seventeenth Amendment.

State, the Executive thereof may make temporary Appointments until the next Meeting of the Legislature, which shall then fill such Vacancies.][4]

No Person shall be a Senator who shall not have attained to the Age of thirty Years, and been nine Years a Citizen of the United States, and who shall not, when elected, be an Inhabitant of that State for which he shall be chosen.

The Vice President of the United States shall be President of the Senate, but shall have no Vote, unless they be equally divided.

The Senate shall chuse their other Officers, and also a President pro tempore, in the Absence of the Vice President, or when he shall exercise the Office of President of the United States.

The Senate shall have the sole Power to try all Impeachments. When sitting for that Purpose, they shall be on Oath or Affirmation. When the President of the United States is tried, the Chief Justice shall preside: And no Person shall be convicted without the Concurrence of two thirds of the Members present.

Judgment in Cases of Impeachment shall not extend further than to removal from Office, and disqualification to hold and enjoy an Office of honor, Trust or Profit under the United States: but the Party convicted shall nevertheless be liable and subject to Indictment, Trial, Judgment and Punishment, according to Law.

(*Election of senators and representatives*)

Section 4 The Times, Places and Manner of holding Elections for Senators and Representatives, shall be prescribed in each State by the Legislature thereof, but the Congress may at any time by Law make or alter such Regulation, except as to the Places of chusing Senators.

The Congress shall assemble at least once in every Year, and such Meeting shall [be on the first Monday in December,][5] unless they shall by Law appoint a different Day.

(*Powers and duties of the houses of Congress: quorum, rules of proceedings, journals, adjournment*)

Section 5 Each House shall be the Judge of the Elections, Returns and Qualifications of its own Members, and a Majority of each shall consitute a Quorum to do Business; but a smaller Number may adjourn from day to day, and may be authorized to compel the Attendance of absent Members, in such Manner, and under such Penalties as each House may provide.

Each House may determine the Rules of its Proceedings, punish its Members for disorderly Behaviour, and, with the Concurrence of two thirds, expel a Member.

Each House shall keep a Journal of its Proceedings, and from time to time publish the same, excepting such Parts as may in their Judgment require Secrecy; and the Yeas and Nays of the Members of either House on any question shall, at the Desire of one fifth of those Present, be entered on the Journal.

Neither House, during the Session of Congress, shall, without the Consent of the other, adjourn for more than three days, nor to any other Place than that in which the two Houses shall be sitting.

(*Compensation and privileges of senators and representatives*)

Section 6 The Senators and Representatives shall receive a Compensation for their Services, to be ascertained by Law, and paid out of the Treasury of the United States. They shall in all Cases, except Treason, Felony and Breach of the Peace, be privileged from Arrest during their attendance at the Session of their respective Houses, and in going to and returning from the same; and for any Speech or Debate in either House, they shall not be questioned in any other Place.

No Senator or Representative shall, during the Time for which he was elected, be appointed to any civil Office under the Authority of the United States, which shall have been created, or the Emoluments whereof shall have been encreased during such time; and no Person holding any Office under the United States, shall be a Member of either House during his Continuance in Office.

(*Legislative procedures: bills and resolutions*)

Section 7 All Bills for raising Revenue shall originate in the House of Representatives; but the Senate may propose or concur with Amendments as on other Bills.

Every Bill which shall have passed the House of Representatives and the Senate shall, before it become a Law, be presented to the President of the United States; If he approve he shall sign it, but if not he shall return it, with his Objections to that House in which it shall have originated, who shall enter the Objections at large on their Journal, and proceed to reconsider it. If after such Reconsideration two thirds of that House shall agree to pass the Bill, it shall be sent, together

[4] Modified by clause 2 of the Seventeenth Amendment.

[5] Superseded by Section 2 of the Twentieth Amendment.

with the Objections, to the other House, by which it shall likewise be reconsidered, and if approved by two thirds of that House, it shall become a Law. But in all such Cases the Votes of both Houses shall be determined by yeas and Nays, and the Names of the Persons voting for and against the Bill shall be entered on the Journal of each House respectively. If any Bill shall not be returned by the President within ten Days (Sundays excepted) after it shall have been presented to him, the Same shall be a Law, in like Manner as if he had signed it, unless the Congress by their Adjournment prevent its Return, in which Case it shall not be a Law.

Every Order, Resolution, or Vote to which the Concurrence of the Senate and House of Representatives may be necessary (except on a question of Adjournment) shall be presented to the President of the United States; and before the Same shall take Effect, shall be approved by him, or being disapproved by him shall be repassed by two thirds of the Senate and House of Representatives, according to the Rules and Limitations prescribed in the Case of a Bill.

(Powers of Congress)

Section 8 The Congress shall have Power To lay and collect Taxes, Duties, Imposts and Excises, to pay the Debts and provide for the common Defence and general Welfare of the United States; but all Duties, Imposts and Excises shall be uniform throughout the United States;

To borrow Money on the credit of the United States;

To regulate Commerce with foreign Nations, and among the several States, and with the Indian Tribes;

To establish an uniform Rule of Naturalization, and uniform Laws on the subject of Bankruptcies throughout the United States;

To coin Money, regulate the Value thereof, and of foreign Coin, and fix the Standard of Weights and Measures;

To provide for the Punishment of counterfeiting the Securities and current Coin of the United States;

To establish Post Offices and post Roads;

To promote the Progress of Science and useful Arts, by securing for limited Times to Authors and Inventors the exclusive Right to their respective Writings and Discoveries;

To constitute Tribunals, inferior to the supreme Court;

To define and punish Piracies and Felonies committed on the high Seas, and Offences against the law of Nations;

To declare War, grant Letters of Marque and Reprisal, and make Rules concerning Captures on Land and Water;

To raise and support Armies, but no Appropriation of Money to that Use shall be for a longer Term than two Years;

To provide and maintain a Navy;

To make Rules for the Government and Regulation of the land and naval Forces;

To provide for calling forth the Militia to execute the Laws of the Union, suppress Insurrections and repel Invasions;

To provide for organizing, arming, and disciplining, the Militia, and for governing such Part of them as may be employed in the Service of the United States, reserving to the States respectively, the Appointment of the Officers, and the Authority of training the Militia according to the discipline prescribed by Congress;

To exercise exclusive Legislation in all Cases whatsoever, over such District (not exceeding ten Miles square) as may, by Cession of particular States, and the Acceptance of Congress, become the Seat of the Government of the United States, and to exercise like Authority over all Places purchased by the Consent of the Legislature of the State in which the Same shall be, for the Erection of Forts, Magazines, Arsenals, dock-Yards, and other needful Buildings; – And

To make all Laws which shall be necessary and proper for carrying into Execution the foregoing Powers, and all other Powers vested by this Constitution in the Government of the United States, or in any Department or Officer thereof.

(Restrictions on powers of Congress)

Section 9 The Migration or Importation of such Persons as any of the States now existing shall think proper to admit, shall not be prohibited by the Congress prior to the Year one thousand eight hundred and eight, but a Tax or duty may be imposed on such Importation, not exceeding ten dollars for each Person.

The Privilege of the Writ of Habeas Corpus shall not be suspended, unless when in Cases of Rebellion or Invasion the public Safety may require it.

No Bill of Attainder or ex post facto Law shall be passed.

No Capitation, or other direct, Tax shall be laid, unless in Proportion to the Census or Enumeration herein before directed to be taken.

No Tax or Duty shall be laid on Articles exported from any State.

No Preference shall be given by any Regulation of Commerce or Revenue to the Ports of one State over those of another: nor shall Vessels bound to, or from, one State, be obliged to enter, clear, or pay Duties in another.

No Money shall be drawn from the Treasury, but in Consequence of Appropriations made by Law, and a regular Statement and Account of the Receipts and Expenditures of all public Money shall be published from time to time.

No Title of Nobility shall be granted by the United States: And no Person holding any Office of Profit or Trust under them, shall, without the Consent of the Congress, accept of any present, Emolument, Office, or Title, of any kind whatever, from any King, Prince, or foreign State.

(Restrictions on powers of states)

Section 10 No State shall enter into any Treaty, Alliance, or Confederation; grant Letters of Marque and Reprisal; coin Money, emit Bills of Credit; make any Thing but gold and silver Coin a Tender in Payment of Debts; pass any Bill of Attainder, ex post facto Law, or Law impairing the Obligation of Contracts, or grant any Title of Nobility.

No State shall, without the Consent of the Congress, lay any Imposts or Duties on Imports or Exports, except what may be absolutely necessary for executing its inspection Laws: and the net Produce of all Duties and Imposts, laid by any State on Imports or Exports, shall be for the Use of the Treasury of the United States; and all such Laws shall be subject to the Revision and Controul of the Congress.

No State shall, without the Consent of Congress, lay any Duty of Tonnage, keep Troops, or Ships of War in time of Peace, enter into any Agreement or Compact with another State, or with a foreign Power, or engage in War, unless actually invaded, or in such imminent Danger as will not admit of delay.

Article II

(Executive power, election and qualifications of the president)

Section 1 The executive Power shall be vested in a President of the United States of America. He shall hold his Office during the Term of four Years, and, together with the Vice President, chosen for the same Term, be elected, as follows:

Each State shall appoint, in such Manner as the Legislature thereof may direct, a Number of Electors, equal to the whole Number of Senators and Representatives to which the State may be entitled in the Congress: but no Senator or Representative, or Person holding an Office of Trust or Profit under the United States, shall be appointed an Elector.

[The Electors shall meet in their respective States, and vote by Ballot for two Persons, of whom one at least shall not be an Inhabitant of the same State with themselves. And they shall make a List of all the Persons voted for, and of the Number of Votes for each; which List they shall sign and certify, and transmit sealed to the Seat of the Government of the United States, directed to the President of the Senate. The President of the Senate shall, in the Presence of the Senate and House of Representatives, open all the Certificates, and the Votes shall then be counted. The Person having the greatest number of Votes shall be the President, if such Number be a Majority of the whole Number of Electors appointed; and if there be more than one who have such Majority, and have an equal Number of Votes, then the House of Representatives shall immediately chuse by Ballot one of them for President; and if no Person have a Majority, then from the five highest on the List the said House shall in like Manner chuse the President. But in chusing the President, the Votes shall be taken by States, the Representation from each State having one Vote; A quorum for this Purpose shall consist of a Member or Members from two thirds of the States, and a Majority of all the States shall be necessary to a Choice. In every Case, after the Choice of the President, the Person having the greatest Number of Votes of the Electors shall be the Vice President. But if there should remain two or more who have equal Votes, the Senate shall chuse from them by Ballot the Vice President.][6]

The Congress may determine the Time of chusing the Electors, and the Day on which they shall give their Votes; which Day shall be the same throughout the United States.

No Person except a natural born Citizen, or a Citizen of the United States, at the time of the Adoption of this Constitution, shall be eligible to the Office of President, neither shall any Person be eligible to that Office who shall not have attained to the Age of thirty five Years, and been fourteen Years a Resident within the United States.

---

[6]Superseded by the Twelfth Amendment.

[In Case of the Removal of the President from Office, or of his Death, Resignation, or Inability to discharge the Powers and Duties of the said Office, the Same shall devolve on the Vice President, and the Congress may by Law provide for the Case of Removal, Death, Resignation or Inability, both of the President and Vice President, declaring what Officer shall then act as President, and such Officer shall act accordingly, until the Disability be removed, or a President shall be elected.][7]

The President shall, at stated Times, receive for his Services, a Compensation, which shall neither be encreased nor diminished during the Period for which he shall have been elected, and he shall not receive within that Period any other Emolument from the United States, or any of them.

Before he enter on the Execution of his Office, he shall take the following Oath or Affirmation: – "I do solemnly swear (or affirm) that I will faithfully execute the Office of the President of the United States, and will to the best of my Ability, preserve, protect and defend the Constitution of the United States."

(Powers of the president)

Section 2 The President shall be Commander in Chief of the Army and Navy of the United States, and of the Militia of the several States, when called into the actual Service of the United States; he may require the Opinion, in writing, of the principal Officer in each of the executive Departments, upon any Subject relating to the Duties of their respective Offices, and he shall have Power to grant Reprieves and Pardons for Offences against the United States, except in Cases of Impeachment.

He shall have Power, by and with the Advice and Consent of the Senate, to make Treaties, provided two thirds of the Senators present concur; and he shall nominate, and by and with the Advice and Consent of the Senate, shall appoint Ambassadors, other public Ministers and Consuls, Judges of the supreme Court, and all other Officers of the United States, whose appointments are not herein otherwise provided for, and which shall be established by Law; but the Congress may by Law vest the Appointment of such inferior Officers, as they think proper, in the President alone, in the Courts of Law, or in the Heads of Departments.

The President shall have Power to fill up all Vacancies that may happen during the Recess of the Senate, by granting Commissions which shall expire at the End of their next Session.

(Powers and duties of the president)

Section 3 He shall from time to time give to the Congress Information of the State of the Union, and recommend to their Consideration such Measures as he shall judge necessary and expedient; he may, on extraordinary Occasions, convene both Houses, or either of them, and in Case of Disagreement between them, with Respect to the Time of Adjournment, he may adjourn them to such Time as he shall think proper; he shall receive Ambassadors and other public Ministers; he shall take Care that the Laws be faithfully executed, and shall Commission all the Officers of the United States.

(Impeachment)

Section 4 The President, Vice President and all civil Officers of the United States, shall be removed from Office on Impeachment for, and Conviction of, Treason, Bribery, or other high Crimes and Misdemeanors.

■ Article III

(Judicial power, courts, and judges)

Section 1 The judicial Power of the United States, shall be vested in one supreme Court, and in such inferior Courts as the Congress may from time to time ordain and establish. The Judges, both of the supreme and inferior Courts, shall hold their Offices during good Behaviour, and shall, at stated Times, receive for their Services, a Compensation, which shall not be diminished during their Continuance in Office.

(Jurisdiction)

Section 2 The judicial Power shall extend to all Cases, in Law and Equity, arising under this Constitution, the Laws of the United States, and Treaties made, or which shall be made, under their Authority; – to all Cases affecting Ambassadors, other public Ministers and Consuls; – to all Cases of admiralty and maritime Jurisdiction; – to Controversies to which the United States shall be a Party; – to Controversies between two or more States; – [between a State and Citizens of another State;][8] – between Citizens of different States, – between Citizens of the same State claiming Lands under Grants of different States, [and between a State, or the Citizens thereof, and foreign States, Citizens or Subjects.][9]

[7]Modified by the Twenty-fifth Amendment.

[8]Modified by the Eleventh Amendment.

[9]See the Eleventh Amendment

In all Cases affecting Ambassadors, other public Ministers and Consuls, and those in which a State shall be Party, the supreme Court shall have original Jurisdiction. In all the other Cases before mentioned, the supreme Court shall have appellate Jurisdiction, both as to Law and Fact, with such Exceptions, and under such Regulations as the Congress shall make.

The Trial of all Crimes, except in Cases of Impeachment, shall be by Jury; and such Trial shall be held in the State where the said Crimes shall have been committed; but when not committed within any State, the Trial shall be at such Place or Places as the Congress may by Law have directed.

(*Treason*)

Section 3 Treason against the United States, shall consist only in levying War against them, or in adhering to their Enemies, giving them Aid and Comfort. No Person shall be convicted of Treason unless on the Testimony of two Witnesses to the same overt Act, or on Confession in open Court.

The Congress shall have Power to declare the Punishment of Treason, but no Attainder of Treason shall work Corruption of Blood, or Forfeiture except during the Life of the Person attainted.

Article IV

(*Full faith and credit clause*)

Section 1 Full Faith and Credit shall be given in each State to the public Acts, Records, and judicial Proceedings of every other State. And the Congress may by general Laws prescribe the Manner in which such Acts, Records and Proceedings shall be proved, and the Effect thereof.

(*Privileges and immunities of citizens, fugitives*)

Section 2 The Citizens of each State shall be entitled to all Privileges and Immunities of Citizens in the several States.

A Person charged in any State with Treason, Felony, or other Crime, who shall flee from Justice, and be found in another State, shall on Demand of the executive Authority of the State from which he fled, be delivered up, to be removed to the State having Jurisdiction of the Crime.

[No Person held to Service or Labour in one State, under the Laws thereof, escaping into another, shall, in Consequence of any Law or Regulation therein, be discharged from such Service or Labour, but shall be delivered up on Claim of the Party to whom such Service or Labour may be due.][10]

(*Admission of new states*)

Section 3 New States may be admitted by the Congress into this Union; but no new State shall be formed or erected within the Jurisdiction of any other State, nor any State be formed by the Junction of two or more States, or Parts of States, without the Consent of the Legislatures of the States concerned as well as of the Congress.

The Congress shall have Power to dispose of and make all needful Rules and Regulations respecting the Territory or other Property belonging to the United States; and nothing in this Constitution shall be so construed as to Prejudice any Claims of the United States, or of any particular State.

(*Guarantee of republican form of government*)

Section 4 The United States shall guarantee to every State in this Union a Republican Form of Government, and shall protect each of them against Invasion; and on Application of the Legislature, or of the Executive (when the Legislature cannot be convened) against domestic Violence.

Article V

(*Amending the Constitution*)

The Congress, whenever two thirds of both Houses shall deem it necessary, shall propose Amendments to this Constitution, or, on the Application of the Legislatures of two thirds of the several States, shall call a Convention for proposing Amendments, which, in either Case, shall be valid to all Intents and Purposes, as Part of this Constitution, when ratified by the Legislatures of three fourths of the several States, or by Conventions in three fourths thereof, as the one or the other Mode of Ratification may be proposed by the Congress; Provided that no Amendment which may be made prior to the Year One thousand eight hundred and eight shall in any Manner affect the first and fourth Clauses in the Ninth Section of the first Article; and that no State, without its Consent, shall be deprived of its equal Suffrage in the Senate.

---

[10]Superseded by the Thirteenth Amendment.

■ Article VI

(*Debts, supremacy, oaths*)

All Debts contracted and Engagements entered into, before the Adoption of this Constitution, shall be as valid against the United States under this Constitution, as under the Confederation.

This Constitution, and the Laws of the United States which shall be made in Pursuance thereof; and all Treaties made, or which shall be made, under the Authority of the United States, shall be the supreme Law of the Land; and the Judges in every State shall be bound thereby, any Thing in the Constitution or Laws of any State to the Contrary notwithstanding.

The Senators and Representatives before mentioned, and the Members of the several State Legislatures, and all executive and judicial Officers, both of the United States and of the several States, shall be bound by Oath or Affirmation, to support this Constitution; but no religious Test shall ever be required as a Qualification to any Office or public Trust under the United States.

■ Article VII

(*Ratification*)

The Ratification of the Conventions of nine States, shall be sufficient for the Establishment of this Constitution between the States so ratifying the Same.

Done in Convention by the Unanimous Consent of the States present the Seventeenth Day of September in the Year of our Lord one thousand seven hundred and Eighty seven and of the Independence of the United States of America the Twelfth. *In witness* whereof We have hereunto subscribed our Names.

The amendments

ARTICLES IN ADDITION TO, AND AMENDMENT OF, THE CONSTITUTION OF THE UNITED STATES OF AMERICA, PROPOSED BY CONGRESS, AND RATIFIED BY THE LEGISLATURES OF THE SEVERAL STATES PURSUANT TO THE FIFTH ARTICLE OF THE ORIGINAL CONSTITUTION.

(*The first ten amendments – known as the Bill of Rights – were passed by Congress on September 25, 1789. They were ratified by three-fourths of the states by December 15, 1791.*)

■ Amendment I

(*Freedom of religion, the press, and assembly, and right of petition*)

Congress shall make no law respecting an establishment of religion, or prohibiting the free exercise thereof; or abridging the freedom of speech, or of the press; or the right of the people peaceably to assemble, and to petition the Government for a redress of grievances.

■ Amendment II

(*Militia and the right to keep and bear arms*)

A well regulated Militia, being necessary to the security of a free State, the right of the people to keep and bear Arms shall not be infringed.

■ Amendment III

(*Quartering of soldiers*)

No Soldier shall, in time of peace, be quartered in any house, without the consent of the Owner, nor in time of war, but in a manner to be prescribed by law.

■ Amendment IV

(*Protection against unreasonable search and seizure*)

The right of the people to be secure in their persons, houses, papers, and effects, against unreasonable searches and seizures, shall not be violated, and no Warrants shall issue, but upon probable cause, supported by Oath or affirmation, and particularly describing the place to be searched, and the persons or things to be seized.

■ Amendment V

(*Grand juries, double jeopardy, self-incrimination, due process, and eminent domain*)

No person shall be held to answer for a capital or otherwise infamous crime, unless on a presentment or indictment of a Grand Jury, except in cases arising in the land or naval forces, or in the Militia, when in actual service in time of War or public danger; nor shall any person be subject for the same offence to be twice put in jeopardy of life or limb; nor shall be compelled in any criminal case to be a witness against himself, nor be deprived of life, liberty, or property, without due process of law; nor shall private property be taken for public use, without just compensation.

Amendment VI

(Criminal court procedures)

In all criminal prosecutions, the accused shall enjoy the right to a speedy and public trial, by an impartial jury of the State and distict wherein the crime shall have been committed, which district shall have been previously ascertained by law, and to be informed of the nature and cause of the accusation; to be confronted with the witnesses against him; to have compulsory process for obtaining witnesses in his favor, and to have the Assistance of Counsel for his defence.

Amendment VII

(Trial by jury in common-law cases)

In suits at common law, where the value in controversy shall exceed twenty dollars, the right of trial by jury shall be preserved, and no fact tried by a jury, shall be otherwise reexamined in any Court of the United States, than according to the rules of the common law.

Amendment VIII

(Bail, fines, and cruel and unusual punishments)

Excessive bail shall not be required, nor excessive fines imposed, nor cruel and unusual punishments inflicted.

Amendment IX

(Retention of rights by the people)

The enumeration in the Constitution, of certain rights, shall not be construed to deny or disparage others retained by the people.

Amendment X

(Reserved powers of the states)

The powers not delegated to the United States by the Constitution; nor prohibited by it to the States, are reserved to the States respectively, or to the people.

Amendment XI

(Proposed on March 4, 1794, ratification completed on February 7, 1795; suits against the states)

The Judicial power of the United States shall not be construed to extend to any suit in law or equity, commenced or prosecuted against one of the United States by Citizens of another State, or by Citizens or Subjects of any Foreign State.

Amendment XII

(Proposed on December 9, 1803, ratification completed on June 15, 1804; election of the president and vice-president)

The Electors shall meet in their respective States and vote by ballot for President and Vice-President, one of whom, at least, shall not be an inhabitant of the same State with themselves; they shall name in their ballots the person voted for as President, and in distinct ballots the person voted for as Vice-President, and they shall make distinct lists of all persons voted for as President, and of all persons voted for as Vice-President, and of the number of votes for each, which lists they shall sign and certify, and transmit sealed to the seat of the government of the United States, directed to the President of the Senate; – The President of the Senate shall, in the presence of the Senate and House of Representatives, open all the certificates and the votes shall then be counted; – The person having the greatest number of votes for President, shall be the President, if such number be a majority of the whole number of Electors appointed; and if no person have such majority, then from the persons having the highest numbers not exceeding three on the list of those voted for as President, the House of Representatives shall choose immediately, by ballot, the President. But in choosing the President, the votes shall be taken by states, the representation from each state having one vote; a quorum for this purpose shall consist of a member or members from two-thirds of the states, and a majority of all the states shall be necessary to a choice. [And if the House of Representatives shall not choose a President whenever the right of choice shall devolve upon them, before the fourth day of March next following, then the Vice-President shall act as President, as in the case of the death or other constitutional disability of the President.][11] The person having the greatest number of votes as Vice-President, shall be the Vice-President, if such number be a majority of the whole number of Electors appointed, and if no person have a majority, then from the two highest numbers on the list, the Senate shall choose the Vice-President; a quorum for the purpose shall consist of two-thirds of the whole number of Senators, and a majority of the whole number shall be necessary to a choice. But no person constitutionally ineligible to the office of President shall be eligible to that of Vice-President of the United States.

Amendment XIII

(Proposed on January 31, 1865, ratification completed on December 6, 1865)

(Abolition of slavery)

Section 1 Neither slavery nor involuntary servitude, except as a punishment for crime whereof the party shall have been duly convicted, shall exist within the United States, or any place subject to their jurisdiction.

(Power to enforce this article)

Section 2 Congress shall have power to enforce this article by appropriate legislation.

Amendment XIV

(Proposed on June 13, 1866, ratification completed on July 9, 1868)

(Citizenship rights, due process, equal protection of the laws)

Section 1 All persons born or naturalized in the United States, and subject to the jurisdiction thereof, are citizens of the United States and of the State wherein they reside. No State shall make or enforce any law which shall abridge the privileges or immunities of citizens of the United States; nor shall any State deprive any person of life, liberty, or property, without due process of law; nor deny to any person within its jurisdiction the equal protection of the laws.

(Apportionment of representatives)

Section 2 Representatives shall be apportioned among the several States according to their respective numbers, counting the whole number of persons in each State, excluding Indians not taxed. But when the right to vote at any election for the choice of electors for President and Vice-President of the United States, Representatives in Congress, the Executive and Judicial officers of a State, or the members of the Legislature thereof, is denied to any of the male inhabitants of such State, being twenty-one years of age, and citizens of the United States, or in any way abridged, except for participation in rebellion, or other crime, the basis of representation therein shall be reduced in the proportion which the number of such male citizens shall bear to the whole number of male citizens twenty-one years of age in such State.

(Persons prohibited from holding office)

Section 3 No person shall be a Senator or Representative in Congress, or elector of President and Vice-President, or hold any office, civil or military, under the United States, or under any State, who, having previously taken an oath, as a member of Congress, or as an officer of the United States, or as a member of any State legislature, or as an executive or judicial officer of any State, to support the Constitution of the United States, shall have engaged in insurrection or rebellion against the same, or given aid or comfort to the enemies thereof. But Congress may by a vote of two-thirds of each House, remove such disability.

(Validity of public debts)

Section 4 The validity of the public debt of the United States, authorized by law, including debts incurred for payment of pensions and bounties for services in suppressing insurrection or rebellion, shall not be questioned. But neither the United States nor any State shall assume or pay any debt or obligation incurred in aid of insurrection or rebellion against the United States, or claim for the loss or emancipation of any slave; but all such debts, obligations, and claims shall be held illegal and void.

[11]Superseded by Section 3 of the Twentieth Amendment.

(*Power to enforce this article*)

Section 5 The Congress shall have the power to enforce, by appropriate legislation, the provisions of this article.

Amendment XV

(*Proposed on February 26, 1869, ratification completed on February 3, 1870*)

(*The right to vote*)

Section 1 The right of citizens of the United States to vote shall not be denied or abridged by the United States or by any State on account of race, color, or previous condition of servitude–

(*Power to enforce this article*)

Section 2 The Congress shall have power to enforce this article by appropriate legislation.

Amendment XVI

(*Proposed on July 12, 1909, ratification completed on February 3, 1913; income taxes*)

The Congress shall have power to lay and collect taxes on incomes, from whatever source derived, without apportionment among the several States, and without regard to any census or enumeration.

Amendment XVII

(*Proposed on May 13, 1912, ratification completed on April 8, 1913; direct election of senators*)

The Senate of the United States shall be composed of two Senators from each State, elected by the people thereof, for six years; and each Senator shall have one vote. The electors in each State shall have the qualifications requisite for electors of the most numerous branch of the State legislatures.

When vacancies happen in the representation of any State in the Senate, the executive authority of such State shall issue writs of election to fill such vacancies: *Provided,* That the legislature of any State may empower the executive thereof to make temporary appointments until the people fill the vacancies by election as the legislature may direct.

This amendment shall not be so construed as to affect the election or term of any Senator chosen before it becomes valid as part of the Constitution.

Amendment XVIII

(*Proposed on December 18, 1917, ratification completed on January 16, 1919*)

(*National prohibition of liquor*)

[Section 1 After one year from the ratification of this article the manufacture, sale, or transportation of intoxicating liquors within, the importation thereof into, or the exportation thereof from the United States and all territory subject to the jurisdiction thereof for beverage purposes is hereby prohibited.

(*Power to enforce this article*)

[Section 2 The Congress and the several States shall have concurrent power to enforce this article by appropriate legislation.

(*Seven-year limit for ratification*)

[Section 3 This article shall be inoperative unless it shall have been ratified as an amendment to the Constitution by the legislatures of the several States, as provided in the Constitution, within seven years from the date of the submission hereof to the States by the Congress.][12]

Amendment XIX

(*Proposed on June 4, 1919, ratification completed on August 18, 1920; women's suffrage*)

The right of citizens of the United States to vote shall not be denied or abridged by the United States or by any State on account of sex.

Congress shall have power to enforce this article by appropriate legislation.

Amendment XX

(*Proposed on March 2, 1932, ratification completed on January 23, 1933*)

(*Terms of office*)

Section 1 The terms of the President and Vice-President shall end at noon on the 20th day of January, and the

[12]Repealed by the Twenty-first Amendment.

terms of Senators and Representatives at noon on the 3d day of January, of the year in which such terms would have ended if this article had not been ratified; and the terms of their successors shall then begin.

(*Time of convening Congress*)

Section 2 The Congress shall assemble at least once in every year, and such meeting shall begin at noon on the 3d day of January, unless they shall by law appoint a different day.

(*Death of president-elect, failure of president-elect or vice-president-elect to qualify for office*)

Section 3 If, at the time fixed for the beginning of the term of the President, the President elect shall have died, the Vice-President elect shall become President. If a President shall not have been chosen before the time fixed for the beginning of this term, or if the President elect shall have failed to qualify, then the Vice-President elect shall act as President until a President shall have qualified; and the Congress may by law provide for the case wherein neither a President elect nor a Vice-President elect shall have qualified, declaring who shall then act as President, or the manner in which one who is to act shall be selected, and such person shall act accordingly until a President or Vice-President shall have qualified.

(*Congress and the election of president or vice-president*)

Section 4 The Congress may by law provide for the case of the death of any of the persons from whom the House of Representatives may choose a President whenever the right of choice shall have devolved upon them, and for the case of the death of any of the persons from whom the Senate may choose a Vice-President whenever the right of choice shall have devolved upon them.

(*Effective date of sections 1 and 2*)

Section 5 Sections 1 and 2 shall take effect on the 15th day of October following the ratification of this article.

(*Seven-year limit for ratification*)

Section 6 This article shall be inoperative unless it shall have been ratified as an amendment to the Constitution by the legislatures of three-fourths of the several States within seven years from the date of its submission.

Amendment XXI

(*Proposed on February 20, 1933, ratification completed on December 5, 1933*)

(*Repeal of national prohibition of liquor*)

Section 1 The eighteenth article of amendment to the Constitution of the United States is hereby repealed.

(*Transportation of liquor into "dry" states prohibited*)

Section 2 Transportation or importation into any State, Territory, or possession of the United States for delivery or use therein of intoxicating liquors, in violation of the law thereof, is hereby prohibited.

(*Seven-year limit for ratification*)

Section 3 This article shall be inoperative unless it shall have been ratified as an amendment to the Constitution by conventions in the several States, as provided in the Constitution, within seven years from the date of the submission hereof to the States by the Congress.

Amendment XXII

(*Proposed on March 21, 1947, ratification completed on February 27, 1951; number of presidential terms*)

No person shall be elected to the office of the President more than twice, and no person who has held the office of President, or acted as President, for more than two years of a term to which some other person was elected President shall be elected to the office of the President more than once.

But this Article shall not apply to any person holding the office of President when this Article was proposed by the Congress, and shall not prevent any person who may be holding the office of President, or acting as President, during the term within which this Article becomes operative from holding the office of President or acting as President during the remainder of such term.

Amendment XXIII

(*Proposed on June 17, 1960, ratification completed on March 29, 1961*)

(*Presidential electors for the District of Columbia*)

Section 1 The District constituting the seat of Government of the United States shall appoint in such manner as the Congress may direct:

A number of electors of President and Vice President equal to the whole number of Senators and Representatives in Congress to which the District would be entitled if it were a State, but in no event more than the least populous State; they shall be in addition to those appointed by the States, but they shall be considered, for the purposes of the election of President and Vice President, to be electors appointed by the State; and they shall meet in the District and perform such duties as provided by the twelfth article of amendment.

(*Power to enforce this article*)

Section 2 The Congress shall have power to enforce this article by appropriate legislation.

Amendment XXIV

(*Proposed on August 27, 1962, ratification completed on January 23, 1964*)

(*Bars poll tax in federal elections*)

Section 1 The right of citizens of the United States to vote in any primary or other election for President or Vice President, or for Senator or Representative in Congress, shall not be denied or abridged by the United States or any State by reason of failure to pay any poll tax or other tax.

(*Power to enforce this article*)

Section 2 The Congress shall have power to enforce this article by appropriate legislation.

Amendment XXV

(*Proposed on July 6, 1965, ratification completed on February 10, 1967*)

(*Vice-president to succeed president*)

Section 1 In case of the removal of the President from office or of his death or resignation, the Vice President shall become President.

(*Choosing a new vice-president*)

Section 2 Whenever there is a vacancy in the office of the Vice President, the President shall nominate a Vice President who shall take office upon confirmation by a majority vote of both Houses of Congress.

(*Presidential disability*)

Section 3 Whenever the President transmits to the President pro tempore of the Senate and the Speaker of the House of Representatives his written declaration that he is unable to discharge the powers and duties of his office, and until he transmits to them a written declaration to the contrary, such powers and duties shall be discharged by the Vice President as Acting President.

(*Presidential disability*)

Section 4 Whenever the Vice President and a majority of either the principal officers of the executive department of such other body as Congress may by law provide, transmit to the President pro tempore of the Senate and the Speaker of the House of Representatives their written declaration that the President is unable to discharge the powers and duties of his office, the Vice President shall immediately assume the powers and duties of the office of Acting President.

Thereafter, when the President transmits to the President pro tempore of the Senate and the Speaker of the House of Representatives his written declaration that no inability exists, he shall resume the powers and duties of his office unless the Vice President and a majority of either the principal officers of the executive department or of such other body as Congress may by law provide, transmit within four days to the President pro tempore of the Senate and the Speaker of the House of Representatives their written declaration that the President is unable to discharge the powers and duties of his office. Thereupon Congress shall decide the issue, assembling within forty-eight hours for that purpose if not in session. If the Congress, within twenty-one days after receipt of the latter written declaration, or, if Congress is not in session, within twenty-one days after Congress is required to assemble, determines by two-thirds vote of both Houses that the President is unable to discharge the powers and duties of his office, the Vice President shall continue to discharge the same as Acting President; otherwise the President shall resume the powers and duties of his office.

Amendment XXVI

(Proposed on March 23, 1971, ratification completed on July 1, 1971)

(Lowers voting age to 18 years)

Section 1 The right of citizens of the United States, who are eighteen years of age or older, to vote shall not be denied or abridged by the United States or by any State on account of age.

(Power to enforce this article)

Section 2 The Congress shall have the power to enforce this article by appropriate legislation.

Proposed Amendment XXVII

(The amendment relative to equal rights for men and women was proposed by the Ninety-second Congress. It passed the House on October 12, 1971 and the Senate on March 22, 1972.)

JOINT RESOLUTION PROPOSING AN AMENDMENT TO THE CONSTITUTION OF THE UNITED STATES RELATIVE TO EQUAL RIGHTS FOR MEN AND WOMEN

Resolved by the Senate and House of Representatives of the United States of America in Congress assembled (two-thirds of each House concurring therein), That the following article is proposed as an amendment to the Constitution of the United States, which shall be valid to all intents and purposes as part of the Constitution when ratified by the legislatures of three-fourths of the several States within seven years[13] from the date of its submission by the Congress:

ARTICLE

Section 1 Equality of rights under the law shall not be denied or abridged by the United States or by any State on account of sex.

Section 2 The Congress shall have the power to enforce, by appropriate legislation, the provisions of this article.

[13]Ratification deadline extended until June 30, 1982.

Section 3 This amendment shall take effect two years after the date of ratification.

Proposed Amendment XXVIII[14]

(The amendment proposing that the District of Columbia be treated as a state for purposes of congressional representation and election of president and vice-president was proposed by the Ninety-fifth Congress. It passed the House on March 2, 1978, and the Senate on August 22, 1978).

Resolved by the Senate and House of Representatives of the United States of America in Congress assembled (two-thirds of each House concurring therein), That the following article is proposed as an amendment to the Constitution of the United States, which shall be valid to all intents and purposes as part of the Constitution when ratified by the legislatures of three-fourths of the several States within seven years from the date of its submission by the Congress:

ARTICLE

Section 1 For purposes of representation in the Congress, election of the President and Vice President, and article V of this Constitution, the District constituting the seat of government of the United States shall be treated as though it were a State.

Section 2 The exercise of the rights and powers conferred under this article shall be by the people of the District constituting the seat of government, and as shall be provided by the Congress.

Section 3 The twenty-third article of amendment to the Constitution of the United States is hereby repealed.

Section 4 This article shall be inoperative, unless it shall have been ratified as an amendment to the Constitution by the legislatures of three-fourths of the several States within seven years from the date of its submission.

[14]For our purposes we have labeled this the proposed Twenty-eighth amendment. If it is ratified before the ERA amendment, it will officially become the Twenty-seventh Amendment.

Glossary

administrative law Regulations made by bureaucratic agencies that have the binding power of laws passed by Congress.
adversary system Our system of law in which each side argues its case as strongly as possible and opposes the other, with the judge or jury deciding between them.
advice and consent The power of the Senate, granted in Article II, Section 2, of the Constitution, to approve treaties made by the president and certain presidential appointments (for example, Supreme Court justices and ambassadors).
affirmative action The policy of making active efforts to recruit more minority and female students or employees to overcome the effects of previous discrimination.
alien A foreign-born resident who has not been naturalized and is still a subject or citizen of a foreign country.
amendment An alteration or addition to a motion, bill, or constitution.
***amicus curiae* brief** Literally, a "friend of the court" brief or argument filed in court by an outside observer to recommend a particular analysis of, or decision on, a case.
antitrust laws Laws designed to prevent or reverse the merging of businesses into monopolies or the engaging in unfair activities to cut down competition.
appeal A legal proceeding by which a case is brought from a lower court to a higher court for rehearing.
apportionment The allocation of seats in a legislative body to certain delineated population groups.
appropriation A bill actually granting an agency permission to spend funds in specified amounts for specified purposes, the funds having been first authorized.
Articles of Confederation The document that, when ratified on March 1, 1781, formed the first constitution of the United States of America.
assimilation The process by which a minority group is integrated by adopting the life-style of the majority.
attentive public The portion of the masses that tends to pay attention to, and become involved in, political issues and affairs and to take a somewhat more active role in society.
authority Recognized power.
authorization A bill establishing a ceiling for spending by an agency.

bail Money put up as security by the accused to obtain release from jail while he or she is awaiting trial.
bandwagon effect The tendency of people to vote for the candidate who is ahead in the polls so as to be on the winning side.
bicameral A legislature consisting of two houses or chambers.
bilateral treaty A treaty between two nations.
bill of attainder A law that declares a person or group to have committed a crime and inflicts punishment for it.
Bill of Rights The first ten amendments to the Constitution.
bipartisan Characterized by accord and cooperation between two major political parties.
Black Codes A series of harsh laws passed by whites in southern states following the Civil War, which were designed to keep blacks in virtual slavery.
brief A written argument presented to a court.
budget, federal The total appropriation of money to be spent by the federal government annually.
bureaucracy An organization of offices or positions arranged hierarchically and operating according to rules rather than personal relations.
bureaucrat Someone who works for a bureaucratic organization.

cabinet The body made up of the heads of government departments.
capitalism An economic system in which the means of production are owned by individuals and operated by them and their assistants for a profit, employing the rest of the work force as laborers.
cartel A voluntary union of independent enterprises or nations that supply like commodities in a way that limits competition and presents a common front.
casework Personalized work that members of Congress do for their constituents.
categorical grant Financial aid from the federal government to the states that must be spent for specific categories of activities.
caucus Meeting of a group such as members of a party in one house of Congress to decide a position on electing leadership, voting on a bill, etc.
certiorari, writ of An order from an appeals court to a lower court to send up the records of a case so that it can be studied on appeal.
charisma The magnetic appeal of a leader to the people.

checks and balances, system of The system by which government institutions or branches exercise checks on, and balance the activities of, other government institutions and branches.

Chicanos Mexican Americans.

citizen A native or naturalized person who owes allegiance to a state and is entitled to protection by the state.

city charter A city's "constitution," granted to it by the state.

civil disobedience The act of breaking a law in order to call attention to the alleged injustice of the law or of a policy and then accepting punishment for the act.

civil law Law that applies to relationships between individuals or groups involving contracts, etc.

civil liberties Prohibitions against state interference in the lives of its citizens.

civil rights Regulations permitting state interference to guarantee the rights of full political participation to groups previously excluded.

civil servant A person who works for the government as a member of the civil service.

civil service The administrative service of the government, exclusive of the armed forces.

clientele group The special interest or interests served by a particular agency.

clientelism The tendency of a regulatory agency to overrepresent, or become captive of, the clientele it is supposed to regulate.

closed primary A primary in which only party members are allowed to vote for a candidate for their party's nomination.

cloture Provision by which the Senate cuts off debate if three-fifths of senators present vote to do so at least 2 days after at least sixteen senators sign a petition requesting it; once cloture is voted, each member may speak only for 1 more hour on the measure.

Cold War Post-World War II conflict between Communist countries and Western countries, not involving the use of arms.

collective bargaining Negotiations between an employer and representatives of a union.

collective good Any public policy whose benefits may be shared equally by all people, whether or not they join or support the group seeking to pressure the government to adopt the policy.

commerce clause Clause in the Constitution (Article I, Section 8) giving Congress power "to regulate commerce . . . among the several states."

Committee of the States Under the Articles of Confederation, a committee of representatives of the states that acted in the name of Congress when Congress was not in session.

committee veto See legislative veto.

common law Customary law or precedent applied to redress harm.

concurrent powers Those powers exercised by both national and state governments.

concurring opinion Written explanation of the views of one or more justices voting with the majority but disagreeing on the grounds for, or route to, the decision.

confederation An organization of states that retain most powers for themselves.

conference committee A committee composed of members of both houses of Congress whose task it is to agree on a compromise version of a bill when each house has produced a different version of the bill.

conflict of interest A situation in which someone acts in his or her role as an official in a way that benefits, or might be thought to benefit, himself or herself as an individual.

Connecticut Compromise The decision reached at the Constitutional Convention whereby membership of the House would be determined by population, whereas each state would have equal representation in the senate.

constituency A body of citizens entitled to elect a representative to a legislative or other public body.

constitution A written document embodying the rules of a political or social organization.

constitutional law Law derived from a constitution.

consumer sovereignty The principle, supposed to operate in capitalism, that the consumer can determine what is produced by his or her purchasing decisions.

council-manager charter A form of city charter that empowers the city council to hire a professional city manager.

criminal law Law that defines crime against the public order.

cultural pluralism The view that each individual culture does or should survive and flourish within a broader common cultural framework.

customary law Unwritten practice accepted as binding.

democracy Rule by the people.

deregulation The act or process of removing regulations or restrictions to free an industry from government regulation.

desegregation Removing barriers to contact among the races or other segregated groups.

Détente The relaxation of strained relations between nations.

Dillon's Rule The principle of the city's legal dependence on the state for its authority, first stated by Judge John F. Dillon in 1872.

direct action A type of political participation generally involving obstruction within the limits of the law directed at the vulnerability of political power.

direct popular election Election by simple popular vote.

direct primary A preliminary election in which voters nominate a candidate to run in a general election.

discrimination Prejudicial treatment based on race or some other characteristic.

disenfranchise (disfranchise) To deprive of the right to vote.

dissenting opinion Written explanation of the views of one or more justices voting in the minority on a case.

distributive policy Policy intended to stimulate private activity that citizens or groups would not otherwise undertake, as by granting of a subsidy.

division of powers The division of ruling power between state and national governments and the people in the American federal structure of government.

double jeopardy Being tried a second time for the same crime if previously acquitted.
dual federalism Doctrine that the Supreme Court mediates between two power centers, the national government and the states.
due process A course of legal proceedings carried out in accordance with established principles and rules.
duty A tax on an imported good that is a percentage of the good's value.

elastic clause Clause in the Constitution (Article I, Section 8) giving Congress power "to make all laws which shall be necessary and proper" for executing its enumerated powers.
elector A member of the electoral college.
electoral college The group of presidential electors from all states who meet state by state in December after a presidential election to cast the official votes for president.
electoral votes Votes cast by presidential electors in the December electoral college meetings.
electorate All those entitled to vote.
elites Those people who dominate major institutions such as politics, business, labor, and the professions.
elitist theory The theory that power is held and shared by a small group of people, a ruling elite, who dominate the major institutions.
emancipation The act of freeing a person from servitude.
eminent domain The right of the government to seize private property for public use.
enumerated powers Those powers explicitly stated in the Constitution.
Environmental Impact Statement A document that must be prepared by any government agency initiating a new project or program in order to assess the impact of such a program on the environment.
Equal Rights Amendment The proposed Twenty-seventh Amendment to the Constitution, which provides that "Equality of rights under the law shall not be denied or abridged by the United States or any State on account of sex."
equity law Law developed by judges to be applied to prevent harm where common law does not apply.
ethnic group An unorganized group of related people with a distinctive identity in a national population.
executive branch The branch of government headed by the president and including the bureaucracy.
executive order A presidential proclamation requiring agencies or individuals to take specific actions without Congress first having passed a law on the subject.
executive privilege The principle by which the president can withhold sensitive papers from Congress.
expatriation The act of renouncing one's citizenship.
ex post facto law A law that declares something to be a crime only after it has been done.
express power A power specifically granted to one of the branches of government by the Constitution.
external representation The way government represents the people and the state outside its borders.
external ruling power Power to represent the United States and the U.S. people to the rest of the world.

favorite son A person favored by the delegates of his or her state at a presidential nominating convention.
federalism A system of government in which governing power is divided into levels and shared between a central government and state or regional governments.
Federalists Those who, in the early years of the Republic, favored a strong central government.
Federalist Papers A series of essays by Alexander Hamilton, James Madison, and John Jay in 1787–1788 stressing the need for a strong government and conformity of the Constitution with the principles of republican government.
federal system A system of government in which power is shared by a central government with its constituent member states.
federation An organization of states under a government with power over its member states.
filibuster A term for the process by which a small group of senators can "talk a bill to death," eventually forcing the bill's withdrawal so that other business can be dealt with.
fiscal policy Policy relating to taxation, public revenues, and public debt.
floor leader A member of a legislative body chosen by his or her party to have charge of its organization and strategy on the floor.
franchise The right to vote; suffrage.
free trade The policy of setting few or no tariff barriers.
full faith and credit The requirement in the Constitution (Article IV, Section 1) that each state recognize the public acts, records, and judicial proceedings of every other state.

general election An election in which candidates are elected in most constituencies of a nation or state.
general public The people of any society taken as a whole.
gerrymander To divide a territorial unit into election districts to give one political party an electoral majority in a larger number of districts while concentrating the voting strength of the opposition in as few districts as possible.
GOP Initials for "Grand Old Party," a traditional term for the Republican party.
government The public bodies that direct public affairs.
grandfather clause A provision that only those who could demonstrate that their father or grandfather had voted were exempt from strict literacy tests and property requirements that limited the franchise.
grand jury A group of citizens convened to decide whether or not there is enough evidence in a given case to merit a trial.
granting a rule Process by which House Rules Committee decides that a bill passed by committee will be allowed to be voted on by the entire House and specifies under what terms such consideration can occur.

grants-in-aid Financial aid from the federal government to the states, usually for specific purposes.
gross national product (GNP) The total value of goods and services produced in a nation during a given year.
gunboat diplomacy Use of U.S. military forces to police the politics of smaller states.

habeas corpus A writ requiring that a prisoner be brought before a court in order to determine whether his or her imprisonment is legal.
home rule A form of local political autonomy drafted by a city in the form of a "home-rule charter" that, when approved by the state, cannot be changed by the state's legislature.
human rights Primarily economic and social rights.

impeachment The formal charging of a public official with misconduct in office by a competent tribunal; in the case of a president, the charge is brought by the House of Representatives.
implied powers, doctrine of Argument that acts that are consistent with the Constitution are constitutional, because they are implied even though not specifically enumerated. The power of Congress "to make all laws which shall be necessary and proper" for executing its enumerated powers is an example of implied power.
impoundment Presidential refusal to allow an agency to spend funds appropriated by Congress.
incumbent The holder of an office.
independent agency A governmental regulatory commission or governmental corporation that is independent of any regular executive department.
independent regulatory commission A government agency or advisory panel that regulates some commercial activity or sector of the economy and that is independent of any regular executive department.
indirect primary A preliminary election in which voters elect delegates who then meet to pick a candidate to run in a general election.
inflation Continual rise in prices, generally attributed to an increase in the volume of money and credit relative to the amount of available goods.
inherent powers Those powers inherent in the federal government by virtue of its being a state or nation.
initiative A law voted on by the general public after it is proposed by petition.
injunction A writ granted by a court whereby a person or group is required to do or to refrain from doing a specified act.
institutional racism The process by which institutions set the context within which some people are kept poor and powerless by being denied real opportunities for education, good jobs, good housing, and political roles, whether or not people hold racist attitudes.
institutions The bodies of government, such as the Congress and the courts.
integration Bringing together people who have been segregated.

interest group An organized group whose members have common views about certain policies or actions and so undertake activities to influence government officials and policies.
internal colonialism The treatment of a minority group as if it were a colony.
internal representation The way government represents the people within its borders.
internal ruling power Power to govern the people of the United States; representing the government to the people.
Iron Curtain The dividing line between Communist Eastern Europe and non-Communist Western Europe.

Jim Crow laws Legislation designed to discriminate against blacks, especially in the South.
judicial branch The branch of government consisting of the Supreme Court and the other courts.
judicial review The power of the courts to assess the actions of individuals and agencies or the laws of Congress, states, and localities to determine whether or not they are in accord with the Constitution.
justiciable question Any question that can be decided by the courts, the judicial branch of government.

kitchen cabinet An informal group of advisors to the president.

laissez-faire The policy of governmental nonintervention in the economy.
lame duck A president unable to run again and so thought to be less powerful; more generally, an official who has been defeated in a bid for reelection but who must serve until the inauguration of the elected candidate.
law A uniform system of rules to govern or prescribe certain behavior for everyone living within a given area or legal jurisdiction.
legislative branch The branch of government consisting of the Congress.
legislative veto Provision in a bill reserving to Congress (two-house veto) or a congressional committee (committee veto) or to the entire House or Senate (one house veto) the power to veto by majority vote an act by an agency.
legitimacy Authority accepted as legal or right.
lobbyist A representative of a special interest.
logrolling The trading of votes by legislators to secure favorable action on legislation of interest to each one.

majority More than 50 percent of the votes cast.
majority leader The leader of the majority party in a legislative body.
majority opinion Written explanation of the views of court justices voting in the majority on a case.
majority rule Rule by more than 50 percent of the electorate.
majority whip The whip of the majority party. See whip.
mandamus, writ of A writ that orders a government official or court to perform duties required of it by law.

mass media Means of communication, such as TV, radio, and newspapers, that are characterized by mass audiences, standardized communication, and concentrated ownership and control.
melting pot The view that America is a mixture of many different nationalities, which are melted down to produce the American culture and personality.
merit system Civil service system in which jobs are granted on the basis of competitive testing.
military-industrial complex President Eisenhower's term for the alleged alliance between the military and the industries that supply its material needs who combine to influence defense spending for mutual gain.
minority leader The leader of the minority party in a legislative body.
minority whip The whip of the minority party. See whip.
monarchy A form of government headed by a king or a queen.
monetary policy Primarily, decisions about currency supply and how much credit to extend to banks for use in making loans to business and individuals.
multilateral treaty A treaty among three or more nations.
multinational corporation A company whose operations are conducted in various countries, which can influence the economies and politics of the countries within which they operate.
multiparty system A political system with three or more major political parties.

national supremacy, doctrine of Argument that states cannot act in ways that effectively render the Constitution less than the supreme law of the land.
nation-state A form of political organization in which a relatively homogeneous people inhabits a sovereign state.
naturalized citizen An alien who becomes a citizen.
natural law A body of law derived from the nature of man and society.
natural monopoly A monopoly that develops spontaneously because such a system is the most efficient means for providing a specific good or service.
natural rights Rights to which one is entitled by virtue of being a human being.
necessary and proper clause Clause in the Constitution (Article 1, Section 8) giving Congress power "to make all laws which shall be necessary and proper" for executing its enumerated powers.
negative income tax A proposed welfare reform that would pay money to poor families who receive less than a stated minimum annual income.
Nixon Doctrine The doctrine proclaimed by President Nixon after Vietnam that other countries would henceforth have to bear the military burden of their own defense.
nonpartisan election An election in which the candidates do not represent or run as members of political parties.

off-year elections Elections in years in which a presidential election does not occur.
ombudsman An individual whose office serves as a channel through which a citizen can express his or her grievances over the operation of a bureau or the action of a bureaucrat and seek whatever redress is appropriate.
one-house veto See legislative veto.
one man, one vote The principle that one person's vote should be worth as much as another's; specifically, apportionment of seats in a legislature based on equal population segments.
open-housing laws Laws prohibiting discrimination in the sale or rental of housing in order to open opportunities and neighborhoods to minorities and other excluded groups.
open primary A primary in which persons can vote for the candidates of either party regardless of their own party membership.
opinion leader Persons or groups whose opinions on issues and policies are especially valued and who therefore influence the opinions of others.
orderly marketing agreement A voluntary agreement between the United States and an exporting country to limit the number of goods that country ships to the United States.
oversight, congressional The responsibility Congress has for keeping an eye on how well the various parts of the executive branch are fulfilling their responsibilities to carry out the laws and how effectively they are spending their appropriations.

pacifist A person who on principle is opposed to the use of violence because he or she believes violence to be immoral.
parliamentary government A system of government in which the head of government is elected by, and responsible to, the legislature.
participatory democracy A system sought by some in which citizens play increased political roles in deciding the things that affect their lives.
partisanship The holding of attitudes associated with a particular party, or assertion of affiliation with that party.
party See political party.
party identification The tendency of a person to say that he or she belongs to (or identifies with) a particular political party.
party loyalty Voting for the candidates of one's party.
party professionals People who serve a party not only during an election but also between elections.
paternalism A system under which an authority dominates the private lives of individuals by supplying their needs and regulating their conduct on the assumption that such domination is in the best interests of the dominated.
patronage Government jobs given to political supporters.
per curiam decision Literally, "for the court"; an indication that the decision was reached by vote of the court.
perquisites ("perks") Privileges of office (car, staff, etc.) in addition to regular salary or wages.
personal racism Racist beliefs held by an individual. See racism.
petit jury A jury that is selected to decide on the facts at issue in a single case.
platform A declaration of the principles and positions held by a political party or a candidate for office.

plural executive A system under which two or more people would serve as president.

pluralist theory The theory that power is shared among a number of different groups, none strong enough to dominate but each able to protect its own interests with help from others.

plurality The margin of votes by which one candidate leads the next candidate – not necessarily a majority.

plurality rule Rule by the candidate who gets more votes than any other candidate, but not necessarily a majority.

pocket veto An indirect veto of a legislative act by an executive who refuses to sign the act or formally veto it and simply holds it until after the adjournment of the legislature.

policies The rules for action that government develops.

political culture The values held by most citizens that influence their political and social attitudes and behavior.

political machine A well-entrenched organization of leaders and followers that is generally able to control nominations.

political party An organization that runs candidates in an election.

politico An officeholder who is concerned primarily with reelection or personal advancement.

politics Dispute over claims to the authority to decide what some part of reality is or should be.

poll, opinion A survey of a few people designed or intended to represent how a large group thinks on a topic.

poll tax A fee that was to be paid when one registered to vote.

popular votes Votes cast by the people in the November presidential election.

populism A political movement designed to unite the interests of farmers and union members that led to the formation of the People's party in 1891.

positive law Law established by a legislature or other governmental authority.

positive rights Rights to basic human needs.

positive state A term for an activist government intervening in various matters, including sometimes the private lives of citizens, to protect the interests of society as a whole.

power The capacity to decide or act.

precedent Any action or statement that establishes a new approach or pattern and sets an example for the future.

prejudice A predisposition, not based in reason, to react unfavorably to a particular individual or group.

presidential elector An individual selected by a party and elected by the voters of a given state who then casts a vote for president and vice-president in the electoral college.

president pro tempore The presiding officer of the Senate when the vice-president is not present; presiding officer is always a senator of the majority party.

pressure group An organized special-interest group that puts pressure on government institutions in order to get what it wants.

private interest The interest of one or more individuals.

private law A law that deals with a specific matter or individual rather than with general legislative concerns; a law that does not affect the public at large.

private sector All nongovernmental segments of the economy, e.g., business and industry.

procedural due process See due process.

processes The types of politicking such as elections and lobbying by which people and interests attempt to determine what happens.

progressive tax A tax that takes a larger percentage from those with larger resources.

proportional-representation primary A primary in which delegates are apportioned to the candidates according to the percentage of the total vote that they received.

Proposition 13 A referendum provision passed by California voters in the spring of 1978 to set strict limits to the possible increases in local property taxes.

protectionism The policy of setting up high tariff barriers or low import quotas in order to protect domestic industry from foreign competition by limiting quantities of imported goods, thus raising the price of these goods.

pseudo-event Daniel Boorstin's term for events planned or planted so they can be reported; also called "media events."

public affairs The concerns of all the people.

public goods Goods such as national defense and police protection that must be supplied to all the people.

public law A law that deals with general legislative concerns and affects the public at large.

public opinion The collection of preferences about candidates, policies, and party, plus political knowledge and ideology, held by individuals.

pure democracy Direct rule by the people.

quasi-judicial function The power of regulatory agencies to adjudge disputes and render decisions that have the same judicial status as decisions of the courts.

quasi-legislative function The power of regulatory agencies to make rules (administrative laws) for the organizations and activities they regulate.

quasi-official agency Agencies that foster scientific research and charity operations, run museums, and so forth.

quorum The number of members of a body that must be present in order for business to be legally transacted.

racism Belief that a person's race should be used as a criterion to determine how he or she is treated, implying that some races are, or should be, treated better than others.

random sample In polls, a group of people in which each individual within the whole population being surveyed has an equal chance of being selected.

reapportionment Redrawing the boundaries of election districts as populations change.

recall System by which people sign petitions to get a referendum on whether or not to remove an elected official from office.

recession An economic decline or slowdown.

Reconstruction Period after the Civil War during which northern whites imposed their political will on the defeated South.

redistributive policy Policy designed to benefit one group at the expense of another, as when taxes from some are used for welfare payments to others.
referendum A law or resolution voted on by the general public after it is proposed by the legislature or by petition.
registration The process of enrolling formally as a voter prior to an election in order to be eligible to vote in that election.
regression tax A tax that puts the heaviest burden on those least able to pay.
regulatory agency See **independent regulatory commission.**
regulatory policy Policy that sets the conditions under which private activities operate.
representative democracy A system in which decisions are made by officials who are elected at regular intervals by the people and who represent the people in making decisions for them.
representative sample In polling, a group of people that is supposed to represent with considerable accuracy the overall thinking of the entire group from which the sample was chosen.
reprivatization Turning over to private business functions (such as trash collection) now done by government bureaucrats.
republic A form of government in which authority derives ultimately from the people, who may or may not be allowed to exercise it.
republican government A government in which supreme power resides in the people who are entitled to vote and is exercised by elected officers and representatives who are responsible to the people and who govern according to law.
reserved powers Those powers reserved by the Constitution to the states.
revenue sharing Program by which federal government gives funds to state and local governments without specifying the use to which the funds must be put.
reverse discrimination Discrimination in favor of those previously discriminated against in order to overcome the effects of previous discrimination.
roll-call vote In Congress, a vote in which a legislator votes and is recorded for or against a measure after his or her name has been called.
rule of four The Supreme Court's practice of agreeing either to hear oral argument on a case or decide it without oral argument when any four Supreme Court justices agree to review the case.
Rules Committee The House committee that decides which bills passed by committee will be allowed to be voted upon by the entire House, and under what terms.
runoff election An election held when no candidate in a previous election received a required percentage of the total votes cast.

safe seat A House or Senate seat for which there is little competition between the parties because the election of the candidate of one or the other party is virtually assured.
SALT Strategic Arms Limitations Talks between the United States and the Soviet Union.
sampling The process by which a pollster picks small numbers of people whose views should be representative of those who are not polled.
segregation The separation or isolation of a racial or other group by setting up barriers to regular intercourse; de jure segregation is grounded in law, whereas de facto segregation is grounded in custom or practice.
select committee A congressional committee set up temporarily to conduct a special investigation or other business.
senatorial courtesy The unwritten rule that the president should consult with senators of a state before appointing a federal judge in that state and should allow a senator of his own party an absolute veto over the nomination.
seniority system System in Congress whereby first choice of committee positions, etc., goes to the longest-serving member.
separation of powers Allocation of powers among the branches of government at one level.
separatism Desire of a minority of members within a state to gain independence from that state or at least greater control over their own lives – to be separate from the state or its ruling power.
SES See **socioeconomic status.**
sexism The attitudes, beliefs, practices, policies, laws, and behaviors discriminating against men or women on the basis of their gender.
sharing of powers The sharing of responsibilities at the national level (through checks and balances) among branches and among the levels of the federal system.
Snowbelt General term for northern states.
socioeconomic status (SES) The various factors such as occupation, income, and social class that determine one's status in society.
sovereignty Supreme power over a body politic.
Speaker of the House The member of the majority party in the House of Representatives who is selected by the party to preside over sessions of the House.
special interest An interest shared by only a segment of the community.
special public A particular group of people, or those people holding a particular opinion.
split ticket A ballot cast by a voter who chooses candidates from several parties.
spoils system Civil service system by which a political victor replaces present officeholders with his or her own supporters.
standing committees The permanent committees in the Senate and the House.
standing to sue The condition of a person who is entitled to go to court to bring suit.
stare decisis Literally, "let the decision stand"; the principle that precedent should govern legal decisions until a particular precedent is overturned.
states' rights All rights not granted to the federal government by the Constitution nor forbidden by it to the separate states.
statutory law Legislation; law made by statutes.
statutory powers Those powers based on laws, or statutes, passed by Congress.

strict construction Literal reading of the Constitution to determine what the Founding Fathers really said.

subculture A group whose members share beliefs and ideals distinct from those of the larger culture.

subgovernments Members of congressional committees, lobbyists, and heads of bureaucratic agencies who meet informally to decide questions about programs and budgets.

subpoena A court order declaring that something must be done under penalty of punishment.

subsidy A grant of money or special privilege to a person or group to stimulate activity that the recipient would otherwise not be inclined to undertake.

suffrage The right to vote; franchise.

Sunbelt General term for southern states.

sunset laws Laws requiring that an existing program or agency be regularly reviewed for its effectiveness and then terminated or specifically extended based on this review.

sunshine laws Laws requiring that meetings of agencies or government units be open to the public.

sympathy vote A vote cast for an underdog simply because he or she is behind in the polls.

tariff A tax on an imported good that is a percentage of the good's value. Same as "duty."

tax subsidy A special tax break granted to businesses or individuals in efforts to affect their behavior—e.g., interest deductions and investment tax credits.

three-fifths-person compromise The decision by the Constitutional Convention to count slaves as three-fifths persons in apportioning the House of Representatives.

transnationalism Attitude of interest in, and concern about, the status and welfare of others across national boundaries.

treaty An agreement between sovereign states.

trustee role The role of a legislator who believes that he or she is a free agent to vote according to his or her assessment of an issue and not according to the wishes of his or her constituents.

two-house veto See legislative veto.

two-party system A political system with two major parties that tend to dominate any other parties that might arise.

unalienable rights Rights that cannot be lost, renounced, or taken away.

underdog effect The tendency of some voters to support the candidate whom the polls show to be behind.

unicameral legislature A legislature that has only one house. In the United States, only Nebraska has such a legislature.

unitary government Government with all power centered on one level.

U.S. Code The government publication that includes the text of all laws currently in force.

urban homesteading Program by which a family is given a run-down home in an urban area on condition that it renovate it (often with the help of low-interest loans) and live in it for a certain period of time.

vested interests Special interests that are benefiting from the way things are and that seek to preserve the status quo.

veto Power of the president to refuse to sign a bill passed by Congress; it then becomes law only if two-thirds of each house votes in favor of overriding the veto.

victimless crime A crime that hurts no one, other than perhaps its perpetrator.

Virginia Plan The proposal in the Constitutional Convention to apportion both the Senate and House on the basis of population.

voluntary expatriation Renouncing one's citizenship simply by declaring that one no longer wishes to be a citizen.

welfare state A state with a type of government that meets or attempts to meet the various human needs over and above the physical safety of its citizens.

whip The person in a legislative body who, with deputy whips, is responsible for rounding up, or whipping into line, party members when a vote is coming up.

white primary A primary in which only whites could vote.

zero-based budgeting A system that requires each governmental program or agency to justify itself and each aspect of its budget each year.

Index